CHILTON'S

ELECTRONIC COMPONENT LOCATOR MANUAL

Publisher Kerry A. Freeman, S.A.E.
Editor-In-Chief Dean F. Morgantini, S.A.E. □ **Managing Editor** David H. Lee, A.S.E., S.A.E.
Senior Editor Richard J. Rivele, S.A.E. □ **Senior Editor** Nick D'Andrea □ **Senior Editor** Ron Webb
Project Manager Peter M. Conti, Jr. □ **Project Manager** Ken Grabowski, A.S.E., S.A.E.
Project Manager Martin J. Gunther □ **Project Manager** Richard T. Smith
Service Editors Lawrence C. Braun, S.A.E., A.S.C., Robert E. Doughten
Jeff H. Fisher, A.S.E., Jacques Gordon, Michael L. Grady, Ben Greisler, S.A.E.,
Jeffrey M. Hoffman, Steve Horner, Neil Leonard, A.S.E., James R. Marotta,
Robert McAnally, Steven Morgan, Michael W. Parks, John H. Rutter, Don Schnell,
James B. Steele, Larry E. Stiles, Jim Taylor, Anthony Tortorici, A.S.E., S.A.E.
Editorial Consultants Edward K. Shea, S.A.E., Stan Stephenson

Manager of Manufacturing John J. Cantwell
Production Manager W. Calvin Settle, Jr., S.A.E
Assistant Production Manager Andrea Steiger
Mechanical Artists Lisa Gressen, Marsha Park Herman,
Lorraine Martinelli, Kim Tansey
Special Projects Peter Kaprielyan

National Sales Manager Lawrence R. Rufo
Manager, National Account Sales Donald A. Wright
National Manager Sales Administration David H. Flaherty
National Account Sales Coordinator Jacquelyn T. Powers
Regional Sales Managers Herbert Marshall, Larry W. Marshall, Bruce McCorkle

OFFICERS
President Gary R. Ingersoll
Senior Vice President Ronald A. Hoxter

CHILTON BOOK COMPANY
*ONE OF THE **DIVERSIFIED PUBLISHING COMPANIES,***
*A PART OF **CAPITAL CITIES/ABC, INC.***
Manufactured in USA • Chilton Way, Radnor, Pa. 19089
ISBN 0-8019-8280-4 1234567890 1098765432 ISSN 1050-110X

SAFETY NOTICE

Proper service and repair procedures are vital to the safe, reliable operation of all motor vehicles, as well as the personal safety of those performing repairs. This manual outlines procedures for servicing and repairing vehicles using safe, effective methods. The procedures contain many NOTES, CAUTIONS and WARNINGS which should be followed along with standard safety procedures to eliminate the possibility of personal injury or improper service which could damage the vehicle or compromise its safety.

It is important to note that the repair procedures and techniques, tools and parts for servicing motor vehicles, as well as the skill and experience of the individual performing the work vary widely. It is not possible to anticipate all of the conceivable ways or conditions under which vehicles may be serviced, or to provide cautions as to all of the possible hazards that may result. Standard and accepted safety precautions and equipment should be used when handling toxic or flammable fluids, and safety glasses or other protection should be used during cutting, grinding, chiseling, prying, or any other process that can cause material removal or projectiles.

Some procedures require the use of tools specifically designed for a specific purpose. Before substituting another tool or procedure, you must be completely satisfied that neither your personal safety, nor the performance of the vehicle will be endangered.

PART NUMBERS

Part numbers listed in this reference are not recommendations by Chilton for any product by brand name. They are references that can be used with interchange manuals and aftermarket supplier catalogs to locate each brand supplier's discrete part number.

Although information in this manual is based on industry sources and is complete as possible at the time of publication, the possibility exists that some car manufacturers made later changes which could not be included here. While striving for total accuracy, Chilton Book Company cannot assume responsibility for any errors, changes or omissions that may occur in the compilation of this data.

Contents

Component Locator

SECTION 1

CHRYLSER, DODGE AND PLYMOUTH EXCEPT LIGHT TRUCKS AND VANS

Fuses, Circuit Breakers and Flashers

NOTE: In addition to all specified circuit breakers, all vehicles have headlight switches with internal circuit breakers.

ARIES AND RELIANT

The fuse block is located behind a removable access panel, below the steering column. The hazard flasher is plugged into the fuse block and the turn signal flasher is hanging near the block.

Two 30 amp circuit breakers are located in the fuse block. One is for the power window motors. The other is for the power seats and door locks.

SPIRIT, ACCLAIM AND LEBARON LANDAU

The fuse block is located behind the steering column cover, accessible by removing the fuse access panel above the hood latch release lever. The relay and flasher module is located behind an access panel in the glovebox. Included in the module are the hazard and turn signal flashers.

Two 30 amp circuit breakers are located in the fuse block. One is for the power window motors. The other is for the power seats and door locks.

LANCER AND LEBARON GTS

The fuse block is located behind the glove box door, accessible by removing the fuse access panel. The relay and flasher module is located behind the cupholder in the center of the instrument panel. The entire module can be removed by pushing it up and off of of its mounting bracket. Included in the module are the hazard and turn signal flashers.

Two 30 amp circuit breakers are located in the fuse block. One is for the power window motors. The other is for the power seats and door locks.

DYNASTY, NEW YORKER LANDAU NEW YORKER SALON, IMPERIAL AND NEW YORKER 5TH AVENUE

The fuse panel is located behind the glove box door. To remove the panel, pull it out from the bottom and slide the tabs out from the top. Additional fuses are in the Power Distribution Center located near the left side strut tower in the engine compartment.

The relay and flasher module is located behind the cupholder. The entire module can be removed by pushing it up and off of its mounting bracket. Included in the module are the hazard and turn signal flashers.

1989

Two 30 amp circuit breakers are located in the fuse block. One is for the power window motors. The other is for the power seats, door locks, mirrors, load leveller and concealed headlamp doors.

1990–91

A 30 amp circuit breaker for the Load Leveling Air Suspension is located in the fuse block. A second 30 amp circuit breaker for the power windows, seats and door locks is located in the relay panel above the fuse block.

DAYTONA AND LEBARON

The fuse block is located behind a removable access panel to the left of the lower portion of the steering column. In 1991, a power distribution center containing additional fuses was added, located behind the battery.

1989

The hazard flasher is plugged into the fuse block and the turn signal flasher is hanging near the block.

Two 30 amp circuit breakers are located in the fuse block. One is for the power window motors and convertible top. The other is for the power seats and door locks, horns and horn relay, air horn, seat bladder inflators and concealed headlamp doors.

1990

A yellow combination flasher for the turn signals and hazard switch is located under the instrument panel to the right of the steering column, clipped to the A/C distribution duct.

Two 30 amp circuit breakers are located in the fuse block. One is for the power window motors. The other is for the power seats, horn and concealed headlamp doors.

1991

A yellow combination flasher for the turn signals and hazard switch is located under the instrument panel to the right of the steering column, clipped to the A/C distribution duct.

Two 30 amp circuit breakers are located in the fuse block. One is for the power window motors. The other is for the power seats, door locks and horn.

OMNI AND HORIZON

1989

The fuse block, which contains the fuses, circuit breaker and flashers, is located on the left side kick panel, below the left side of the instrument panel.

1990

The fuse block is located on the left side kick panel. The relay bank is located above the fuse block and contains the hazard and turn signal flashers.

SHADOW AND SUNDANCE

The fuse block is located behind the steering column cover, accessible by removing the fuse access panel above the hood latch release lever. The relay and flasher module is located behind an access panel in the glovebox. Included in the module are the hazard and turn signal flashers.

1989

Two 30 amp circuit breakers are located in the fuse block. One is for the power window motors. The other is for the power door locks and passive belt motors and solenoids.

1990

Two 30 amp circuit breakers are located in the fuse block. One is for the power window motors. The other is for the power door locks.

1991

A 30 amp circuit breaker for the power window motors is located in the fuse block.

CHRYSLER TC

The fuse block is located behind a removable access panel to the left of the lower portion of the steering column. The hazard flasher is plugged into the fuse block and the turn signal flasher is hanging near the block.

Two 30 amp circuit breakers are located in the fuse block. One is for the power window motors. The other is for the power seats, door locks, horn and horn relay. A 6 amp circuit breaker for the deck lid release is also located in the fuse block.

GRAN FURY, DIPLOMAT AND FIFTH AVENUE (RWD)

The fuse block is located behind a removable access panel to the left of the lower portion of the steering column. The hazard flasher is plugged into the fuse block and the turn signal flasher is hanging near the block.

Two 30 amp circuit breakers are located in the fuse block. One is for the power window motors and illuminated entry relay. The other is for the power seats and door locks. A 6 amp circuit breaker for the police relay package (where applicable) is also located in the fuse block.

LASER

Circuit breakers, if equipped, are located in the main fuse box, which is located under the left side dash. Other breakers could be located at the relay boxs under the hood.

MONACO

The interior fuse block is located under the left side of the instrument panel. Included in the fuse block are circuit breakers for any combination of the following items: power seats, door locks, sunroof, windows and passive restraint system, and Daytime Running Lights (Canada).

The lamp module, which takes the place of a conventional flasher, is located in the trunk mounted on the right side of the shelf panel.

Fusible Links

EXCEPT LASER, 1991 DAYTONA, LEBARON AND MONACO AND 1990–91 DYNASTY, NEW YORKER AND IMPERIAL

All fusible links are in the form of hypalon-insulation wire, and are either 12, 14, 16, 18 or 20 gauge. All are located in the left front area of the engine compartment in front of the left front wheel housing or shock tower.

1991 DAYTONA, LEBARON AND MONACO AND 1990–91 DYNASTY, NEW YORKER AND IMPERIAL

Fusible links are in the form of replaceable cartridge fuses located at the battery and right side relay box on Laser, or in the underhood Power Distribution Center on 1991 Daytona, LeBaron and Monaco, and 1990–91 Dynasty, New Yorker and Imperial.

Relays, Sensors, Switches, Modules and Computers Locations

OMNI AND HORIZON

- **A/C Clutch Relay** – located on the left side fender shield.
- **A/C Compressor Zener Diode** – is located to the left of the compressor, within the connector.
- **A/C Cycling Switch** – is located on the H-valve.
- **A/C High Pressure Relief Valve** – is located on the filter/drier assembly.
- **A/C Low Pressure Cut-Off Switch** – is located on the H-valve.
- **A/C Thermal Switch** – is located on the H-valve.
- **A/C-Heater Blower Motor Resistor** – is located on the right side plenum.
- **Air Bag Diagnostic Connector** – is located at the right side of the console.
- **Air Bag Sensors** – are located at the right and left side closure panels.
- **Air Bag System Diagnostic Module** – is located in the center console.
- **Auto Shutdown Relay** – is located on the left front inner fender panel.
- **Automatic Idle Speed Motor** – is located on the throttle body assembly.
- **Automatic Idle Speed Solenoid** – is located on the right side inner fender shield.
- **Chime Module** – is located above the glovebox.
- **Coolant Temperature Sending Unit** – is located on the right side of the cylinder head.
- **Coolant Temperature Sensor** – is located on the thermostat housing.
- **Cooling Fan Motor Relay** – is located on the left side fender shield.
- **Daytime Running Lights Module (Canada)** – is located in the upper right side dash panel.

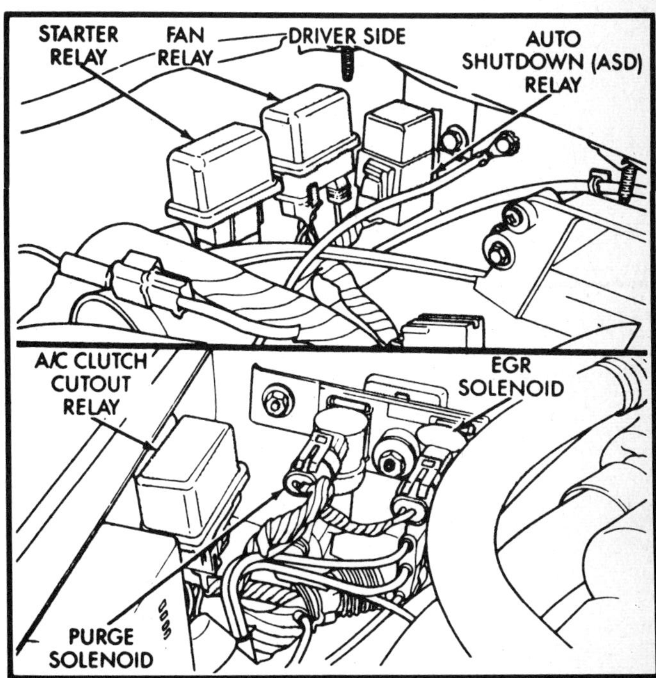

Relay and solenoid identification – 1990 Omni and Horizon

• **Diagnostic Connector**—is located in front of the left front shock tower.

• **Dimmer Switch**—is mounted on the steering column.

• **Distance Sensor**—is located at the rear of the transaxle.

• **EGR Solenoid**—is located on the right side inner fender shield.

• **Engine Oil Pressure Sending Unit**—is located on the left front side of the block.

• **Fuel Pump Relay**—is located in the engine compartment, on the left inner fender panel.

• **Horn Relay**—is located on or near the fuse block.

• **Ignition Time Delay Relay**—is located above the fuse block.

• **Intermittent Wiper Control Module**—is located on the brake pedal support bracket.

• **Manifold Absolute Pressure (MAP) Sensor**—is located on the right side of the dash panel.

• **Oil Pressure Switch**—is located on the lower left side of the cylinder block.

• **Oxygen Sensor**—is located in the exhaust manifold.

• **Purge Solenoid**—is located on the right side inner fender shield.

• **Rear Window Defrost Timer/Relay**—is mounted on the end of the defrost switch.

• **Seatbelt Warning Buzzer**—is located on the fuse block.

• **Single Board Engine Controller (SBEC)**—is located in the engine compartment behind the battery.

• **Single Module Engine Controller (SMEC)**—is located in the engine compartment behind the battery.

• **Starter Relay**—is located on the left front inner fender panel.

• **Throttle Body Temperature Sensor**—is located on the throttle body.

• **Throttle Position Sensor**—is located on top of the throttle body.

• **Time Delay Relay**—is taped the harness near the fuse block.

• **Transaxle Part Throttle Unlock Switch**—is located on left front of the transaxle.

ARIES, RELIANT, LANCER AND LEBARON GTS

• **A/C Compressor Clutch Relay**—is located on the left side inner fender panel.

• **A/C Compressor Zener Diode**—is located to the left of the compressor, within the connector.

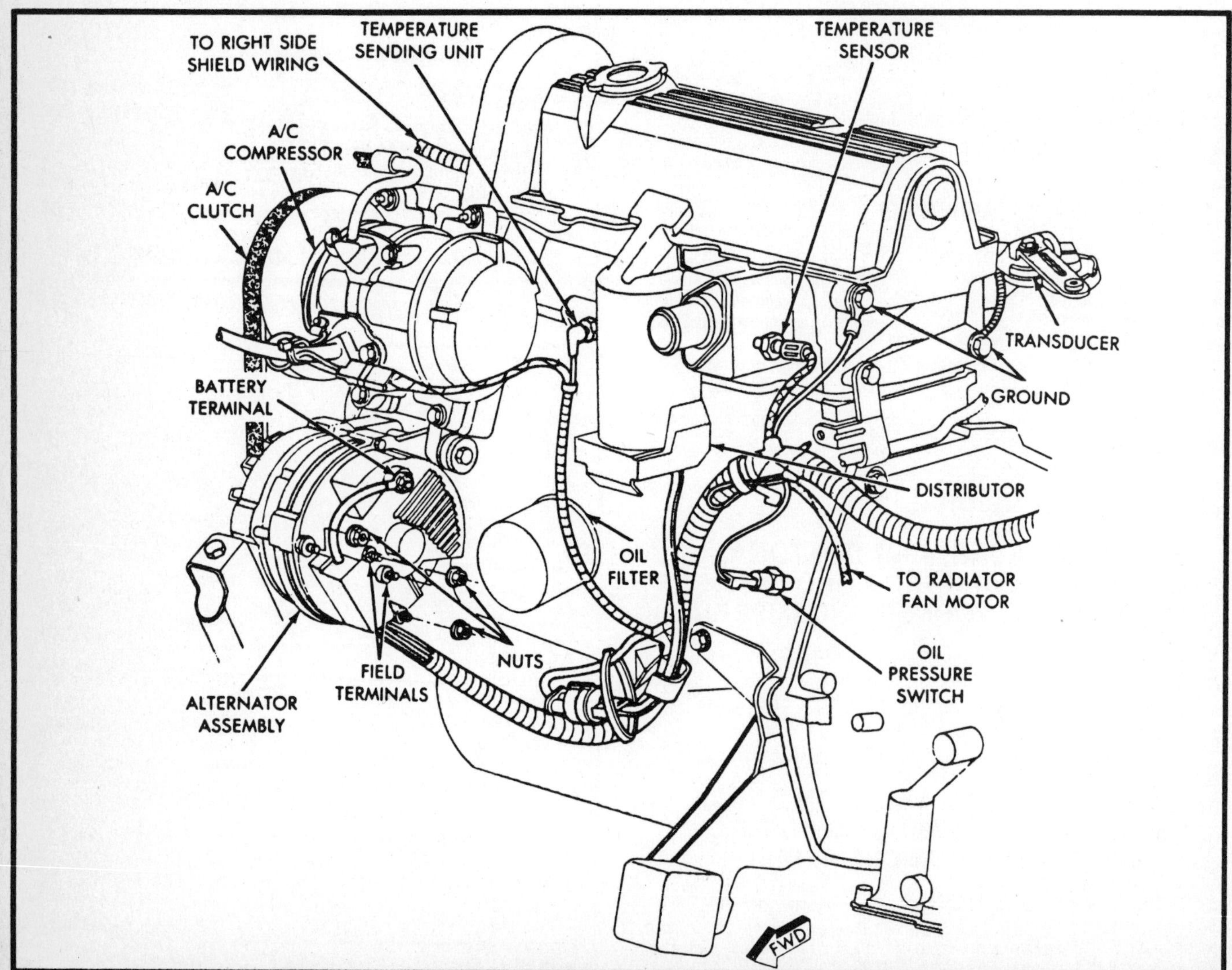

Engine component locations—2.2L and 2.5L engines

• **A/C Fin**—Sensed Cycling Clutch Switch—is located in the evaporator housing.

• **A/C High Pressure Relief Valve**—is located on the filter/drier assembly.

• **A/C Low Pressure Cutoff Switch**—is located on the H—valve.

• **A/C Wide Open Throttle Cut-Out Relay**—is located on the left front inner fender panel.

• **A/C-Heater Blower Motor Resistor**—is located on the right side of the heater box.

• **Air Temperature Sensor**—is located in the center of the intake manifold on turbocharged engines.

• **Ambient Air Temperature Sensor (for overhead console)**—is located on the vertical grille support.

• **Automatic Idle Speed Motor**—is located on the throttle body assembly.

• **Automatic Shutdown Relay**—is located on the left front inner fender panel.

• **Baro Read Solenoid**—is located on the right side inner fender panel.

• **Brake Warning Light Switch**—is located on the combination valve below the master cylinder.

• **Canister Purge Solenoid**—is located next to the MAP sensor.

• **Cargo Lamp Switch**—is located on the release latch inside the liftgate.

• **Coolant Temperature Sending Unit**—is located on the right side of the cylinder head.

• **Coolant Temperature Sensor**—is located on the thermostat housing.

• **Detonation Sensor**—is located on the intake manifold on turbocharged engines.

• **Diagnostic Connector**—is located in the left side of the engine compartment.

• **Dimmer Switch**—is mounted on the steering column.

• **Distance Sensor**—is located on the transaxle assembly.

• **EGR Diagnostic Solenoid (Californa only)**—is located on the right side inner fender panel.

• **EGR Purge Solenoid**—is located on the right side inner fender panel.

• **Fog Lamps Switch Timer**—is located within the switch.

• **Gauge Alert Module**—is mounted on the instrument cluster printed circuit board.

• **Head Lamp Delay Relay**—is located behind the instrument panel next to the chime module.

• **Horn Relay**—is located in the relay/flasher module on Lancer and LeBaron GTS and on the fuse block on Aries and Reliant.

• **Intermittent Wiper Control Module**—is located on the lower left reinforcement.

• **Key-In, Seat Belt, Head Lamp-On Warning Chime or Buzzer**—is located above or behind the glove box.

• **Liftgate Ajar Diode (Aries and Reliant)**—is located in the left rear wheel housing underneath the interior trim panel.

• **Liftgate Ajar Switch**—is located on the liftgate latch.

• **Low Fuel Relay**—is mounted on the instrument cluster printed circuit board.

• **Low Washer Fluid Sensor**—is located in the washer fluid bottle.

• **Manifold Absolute Pressure (MAP) Sensor**—is located on the right side shock tower.

• **Name Brand Speaker Relay**—is located under the radio.

• **Oil Pressure Switch/Sending Unit**—is located on the lower left side of the cylinder block.

• **Oxygen Sensor**—is located in the exhaust manifold.

• **Part Throttle Unlock Switch**—is located on the transaxle assembly.

• **Radiator Fan Relay**—is mounted on the left front shock tower.

• **Radio Filter Choke**—is located under the radio.

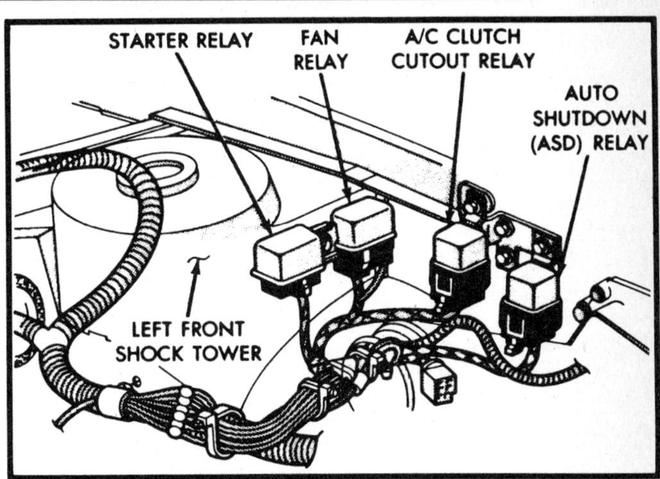

Relay identification—1989 vehicles with turbocharged engine

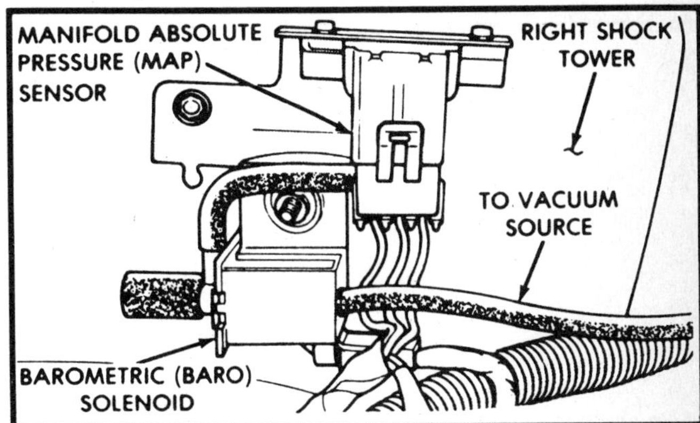

Baro solenoid and MAP sensor—1989 vehicles with turbocharged engine

• **Rear Window Defrost Timer/Relay**—is mounted on the end of the defrost switch.

• **Single Module Engine Controller (SMEC)**—is located in the engine compartment, behind the battery.

• **Speed Control Servo**—is located under the battery tray, in the engine compartment.

• **Starter Relay**—is located on the left front shock tower.

• **Tachometer Drive Module**—is mounted on the instrument cluster printed circuit board.

• **Throttle Position Sensor**—is located on the throttle body assembly.

• **Time Delay Relay**—is located in the fuse block.Trunk Lamp Switch—is located on the base of the trunk lamp.

• **Visor Map Light Switch**—is located within the lamp assembly.

• **Wastegate Solenoid**—is located on the right side inner fender panel.

SHADOW AND SUNDANCE

• **A/C Compressor Clutch Relay**—is located on the left side inner fender panel.

• **A/C Compressor Zener Diode**—is located to the left of the compressor, within the connector.

• **A/C Fin-Sensed Cycling Clutch Switch**—is located in the evaporator housing.

• **A/C High Pressure Cut-Off Switch**—is located on the compressor.

• **A/C High Pressure Relief Valve** – is located on the filter/drier assembly or on the compressor.

• **A/C Low Pressure Cut-Off Switch** – is located on the H-valve.

• **A/C Wide Open Throttle Cut-Out Relay** – is located on the left front inner fender panel.

• **A/C-Heater Blower Motor Resistor** – is located near the air inlet on the plenum.

• **Air Bag Diagnostic Connector** – is located at the right side of the console.

• **Air Bag Sensors** – are located at the right and left side closure panels.

• **Air Bag System Diagnostic Module** – is located in the center console.

• **Air Temperature Sensor** – is located in the center of the intake manifold on turbocharged models.

• **Ambient Air Temperature Sensor (for overhead console)** – is located on the radiator closure panel.

• **Automatic Idle Speed Motor** – is located on the throttle body assembly.

• **Automatic Shutdown Relay** – is located on the left front inner fender panel.

• **Baro Read Solenoid** – is located on the right side inner fender panel.

• **Brake Warning Light Switch** – is located on the combination valve below the master cylinder.

• **Canister Purge Solenoid** – is located next to the MAP sensor.

• **Clutch Interlock Switch** – is located on a bracket to the left of the clutch pedal.

• **Coolant Temperature Sending Unit** – is located on the right side of the cylinder head.

• **Coolant Temperature Sensor** – is located on the thermostat housing.

• **Daytime Running Lights Module (Canada)** – is located in the left front inner fender shield.

• **Detonation Sensor** – is located on the intake manifold on turbocharged engines.

• **Diagnostic Connector** – is located in the left side of the engine compartment.

• **Dimmer Switch** – is mounted on the steering column.

• **Distance Sensor** – is located on the transaxle assembly.

• **EGR Diagnostic Solenoid (California)** – is located on the right side inner fender panel.

• **EGR Purge Solenoid** – is located on the right side inner fender panel.

• **Fog Lamp Relay** – is located above the glovebox.

• **Horn Relay** – is located in the relay/flasher module.

• **Intermittent Wiper Control Module** – is located on the lower left reinforcement.

• **Key-In, Seat Belt, Head Lamp-On Warning Chime or Buzzer** – is located above the glove box.

• **Liftgate Ajar Switch** – is located on the liftgate latch.

• **Liftgate Latch Switch** – is located on the base of the trunk lamp.

• **Low Fuel Relay** – is mounted on the message center printed circuit board.

• **Low Washer Fluid Sensor** – is located in the washer fluid bottle.

• **Manifold Absolute Pressure (MAP) Sensor** – is located on the right side shock tower.

• **Name Brand Speaker Relay** – is located under the radio.

• **Oil Pressure Switch/Sending Unit** – is located on the lower left side of the cylinder block.

• **Oxygen Sensor** – is located in the exhaust manifold.

• **Part Throttle Unlock Switch** – is located on the transaxle assembly.

• **Passive Belt Control Module and Diagnostic Connector (1989)** – are located under the center of the instrument panel, mounted on the forward console brace.

• **Radiator Fan Relay** – is mounted on the left front shock tower.

• **Rear Window Defrost Timer/Relay** – is located within the defroster switch.

• **Single Board Engine Controller (SBEC)** – is located in the engine compartment, behind the battery.

• **Single Module Engine Controller (SMEC)** – is located in the engine compartment, behind the battery.

• **Speed Control Servo** – is located under the battery tray, in the engine compartment.

• **Starter Relay** – is located on the left front shock tower.

• **Throttle Body Temperature Sensor** – is located on the throttle body.

• **Throttle Position Sensor** – is located on the throttle body assembly.

• **Time Delay Relay** – is located in the relay module.VAC Vent Solenoid – is located on the right side inner fender panel.

• **Visor Map Light Switch** – is located within the lamp assembly.

• **Wastegate Solenoid** – is located on the right side inner fender panel.

SPIRIT, ACCLAIM AND LEBARON LANDAU

• **A/C Compressor Clutch Relay** – is located on the left side inner fender panel.

• **A/C Compressor Zener Diode** – is located to the left of the compressor, within the connector.

• **A/C Fin-Sensed Cycling Clutch Switch** – is located in the evaporator housing.

• **A/C High Pressure Cut-Off Switch** – is located on the compressor.

• **A/C High Pressure Relief Valve** – is located on the filter/drier assembly or on the compressor.

• **A/C Low Pressure Cut-Off Switch** – is located on the H-valve.

• **A/C-Heater Blower Motor Resistor** – is located near the air inlet on the plenum.

• **Anti-lock Brake Controller** – is located under the battery tray.

• **Anti-lock Brake Pump Motor Relay** – is located behind the battery, or on the left side inner fender panel, midway between the strut tower and SBEC.

• **Anti-lock Brake System Diagnostic Connector** – is located on the left side tower reinforcement, or behind the fuse access panel.

• **Anti-lock Brake System Relay** – is located behind the battery.

• **Anti-lock Brake Warning Lamp Relay** – is located behind the battery.

• **Anti-lock Brake Wheel Sensors** – are located at each wheel.

• **Air Bag Diagnostic Connector** – is located at the right side of the console.

• **Air Bag Sensors** – are located at the right and left side closure panels.

• **Air Bag System Diagnostic Module** – is located in the center console.

• **Automatic Idle Speed Motor** – is located on the throttle body assembly.

• **Automatic Shutdown Relay** – is located on the left inner fender panel.

• **Baro Read Solenoid** – is located on the right side inner fender panel.

• **Body Computer** – is located in the right side kick panel.

• **Brake Warning Light Switch (without Anti-lock Brakes)** – is located on the combination valve below the master cylinder.

• **Clutch Interlock Switch** – is located on a bracket to the left of the clutch pedal.

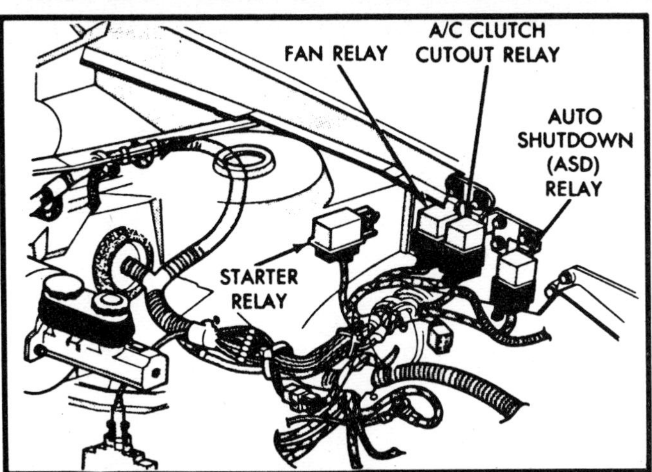

Relay identification—1989–90 vehicles except Omni, Horizon, Dynasty, New Yorker, Imperial and 1989 vehicles with turbocharged engine

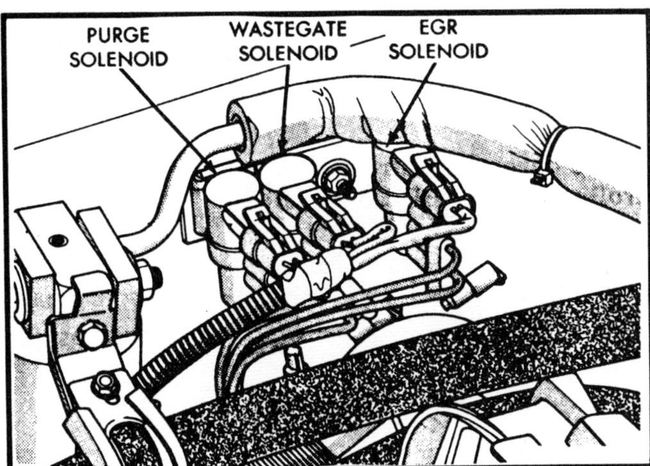

Solenoid identification—1989–90 vehicles except Omni, Horizon and vehicles with Turbo IV engine. Note that vehicles may not be equipped with all 3 solenoids

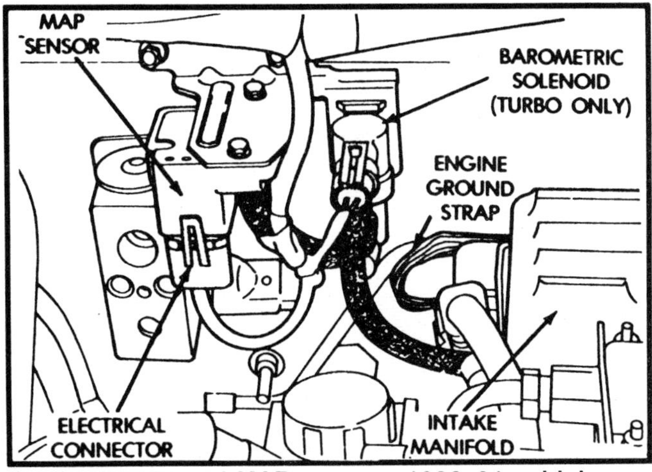

Baro solenoid and MAP sensor—1990–91 vehicles with turbocharged engine

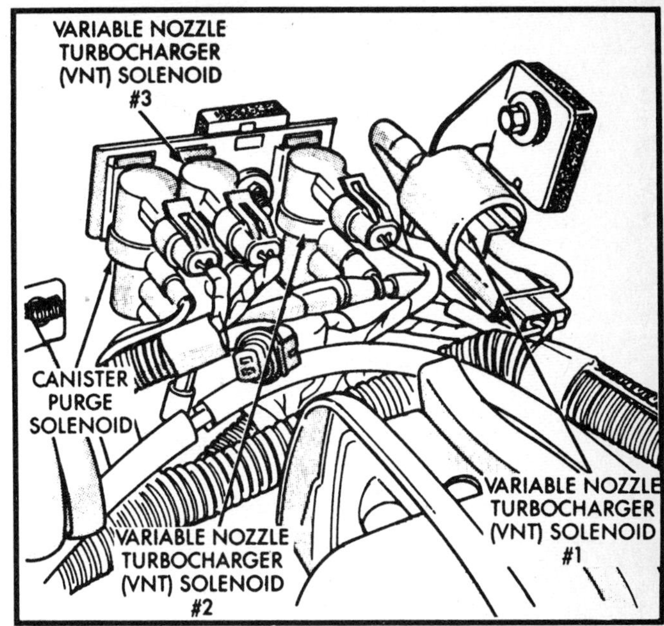

Solenoid identification—Vehicles with Turbo IV engine

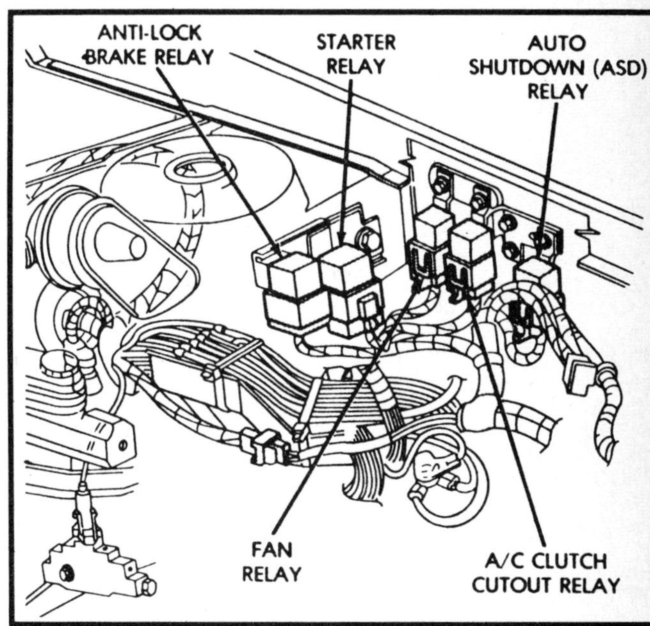

Relay identification—1991 vehicles except Daytona, LeBaron, Dynasty, New Yorker and Imperial. Note that vehicles may not be equipped with all 5 relays, depending on accessories

- **Coolant Temperature Sending Unit**—is located on the right side of the cylinder head on 2.2L and 2.5L engines. The sending unit is located on the thermostat housing on 3.0L engine.
- **Coolant Temperature Sensor**—is located on the thermostat housing on 2.2L and 2.5L engines and on the cylinder head between the thermostat housing and distributor on 3.0L engine.
- **Daytime Running Lights Module (Canada)**—is located in the left front inner fender shield.

• **Detonation Sensor**—is located on the intake manifold on turbocharged engines.
• **Dimmer Switch**—is mounted on the steering column.
• **Distance Sensor (except electronic transaxle)**—is located on the transaxle assembly.
• **EGR Diagnostic Solenoid (California)**—is located on the right side inner fender panel.
• **EGR Purge Solenoid**—is located on the right side inner fender panel.
• **Electronic Transaxle Controller**—is located on the right side inner fender panel.
• **Electronic Transaxle Output Speed and Turbine Speed Sensors**—are located on the front of the transaxle.
• **Electronic Transaxle PRNDL Switch**—is located on the front of the transaxle.
• **Electronic Transaxle Reverse Light Relay**—is located on the right side inner fender panel.
• **Electronic Transaxle Safety Shut-Down Relay**—is located on the right side fender shield.
• **Electronic Transaxle Solenoids and Pressure Switch**—are located on the top front of the transaxle.
• **Engine Diagnostic Connector**—is located in front of the left side shock tower.
• **Fog Lamp Relay**—is located on the right mid reinforcement.
• **Horn Relay**—is located in the relay/flasher module.
• **Intermittent Wiper Control Module**—is located on the lower left reinforcement.
• **Key-In, Seat Belt, Head Lamp-On Warning Chime or Buzzer**—is located above the glove box.
• **Low Fuel Relay**—is mounted on the instrument cluster printed circuit board.
• **Low Washer Fluid Sensor**—is located in the washer fluid bottle.
• **Manifold Absolute Pressure (MAP) Sensor**—is located on the right side shock tower.
• **Name Brand Speaker Relay**—is located on the right side mid-reinforcement.
• **Oil Pressure Switch/Sending Unit**—is located on the lower left side of the cylinder block on 2.2L and 2.5L engines and on the oil filter adaptor on 3.0L engine.
• **Oxygen Sensor**—is located in the (rear) exhaust manifold.
• **Part Throttle Unlock Switch**—is located on the transaxle assembly.
• **Purge Solenoid**—is located on the front of the right side shock tower.
• **Radiator Fan Relay**—is mounted on the left front shock tower.
• **Radio Filter Choke**—is located on the right side mid-reinforcement.
• **Rear Window Defrost Timer/Relay**—is located within the defroster switch.
• **Single Board Engine Controller (SBEC)**—is located in the engine compartment, behind the battery.
• **Single Module Engine Controller (SMEC)**—is located in the engine compartment, behind the battery.
• **Speed Control Servo**—is located under the battery tray, in the engine compartment.
• **Starter Relay**—is located on the left front shock tower.
• **Throttle Body Temperature Sensor**—is located on the throttle body.
• **Throttle Position Sensor**—is located on the throttle body assembly.
• **Time Delay Relay**—is located in the relay module.Visor Map Light Switch—is located within the lamp assembly.
• **Wastegate Solenoid**—is located on the right side inner fender panel.

1989 DAYTONA AND LEBARON

• **A/C Compressor Clutch Relay**—is located on the right side inner fender panel.
• **A/C Compressor Zener Diode**—is located to the left of the compressor, within the connector.
• **A/C Fin-Sensed Cycling Clutch Switch**—is located in the evaporator housing.
• **A/C High Pressure Relief Valve**—is located on the filter/drier assembly.
• **A/C Low Pressure Cut-Off Switch**—is located on the H-valve.
• **A/C-Heater Blower Motor Resistor**—is located behind the glovebox.
• **Air Bag Diagnostic Connector**—is located at the right side of the console.
• **Air Bag Sensors**—are located at the right and left side closure panels.
• **Air Bag System Diagnostic Module**—is located in the center console.
• **Air Horn Compressor**—is located on the right rear radiator yoke.
• **Ambient Air Temperature Sensor (for ATC)**—is located on the upper right rear surface of the A/C unit.
• **Ambient Air Temperature Sensor (for overhead console)**—is located on the left front bumper support.
• **ATC Power Module**—is located in the lower right side of the instrument panel.
• **ATC Vacuum Module**—is located on the A/C unit, behind the glovebox.
• **Automatic Idle Speed Motor**—is located on the throttle body assembly.
• **Automatic Shutdown Relay**—is located on the left front inner fender panel.
• **Baro Read Solenoid**—is located on the right side inner fender panel.
• **Brake Fluid Level Sensor**—is located in the rear of the master cylinder.
• **Brake Pad Wear Indicators**—are part of the pad assemblies.
• **Brake Warning Light Switch**—is located on the combination valve below the master cylinder.
• **Charge Temperature Sensor**—is located in the center of the intake manifold on turbocharged engines.
• **Concealed Headlamp Control Module**—is located on top of the dash panel.
• **Coolant Level Sensor**—is located at the top of the coolant overflow reservoir.
• **Coolant Temperature Sending Unit**—is located on the right side of the cylinder head.
• **Coolant Temperature Sensor**—is located on the thermostat housing.
• **Detonation Sensor**—is located on the intake manifold on turbocharged engines.
• **Diagnostic Connector**—is located in the left side of the engine compartment.
• **Dimmer Switch**—is mounted on the steering column.
• **Distance Sensor**—is located on the transaxle assembly.
• **EGR Diagnostic Solenoid (California)**—is located on the right side inner fender panel.
• **EGR Purge Solenoid**—is located on the right side inner fender panel.
• **Electric Back Light (EBL) and Power Top Switch Lamp Module**—is located in the console.
• **Electric Back Light (EBL) Cut Off Switch**—is located on the left side quarter panel.
• **Electronic Low Fuel Signal Relay**—is plugged into the rear of the visual message center printed circuit board.
• **Fog Lamps Switch Timer**—is located within the switch Headlamp Outage Module—is clipped to the fuse block on LeBaron.

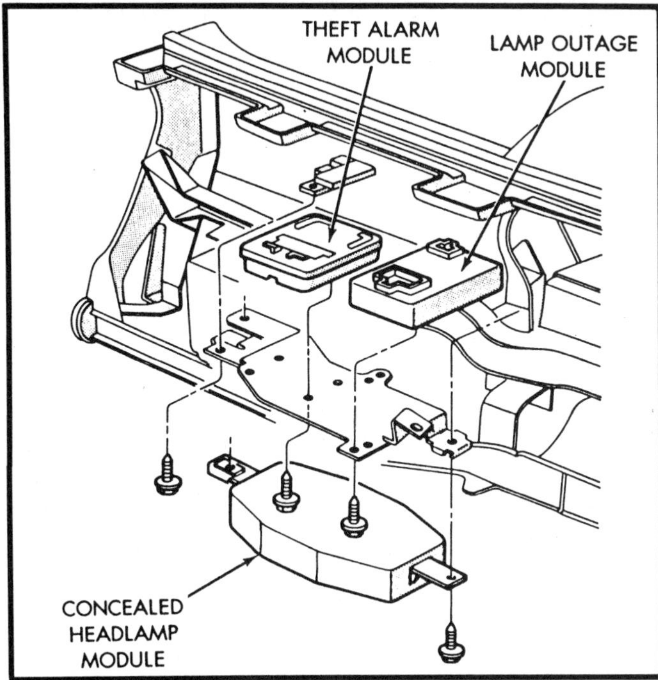

Module identification behind the glovebox – 1989–91 Daytona, LeBaron and TC. Note that in 1990–91, concealed headlamp control was incoroporated into the body computer, but the other 2 modules will still be present

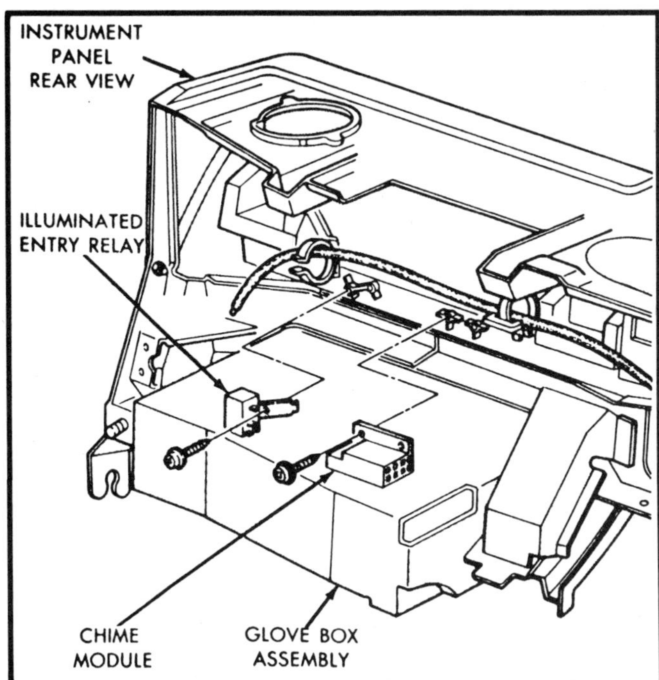

Module and relay identification behind the glove box – 1989 Daytona, LeBaron and TC

- **Heated Rear Window Timer/Relay (convertible)** – is located near the power top motor.
- **Horn Relay** – is located in the relay/flasher module on the fuse block.
- **Illuminated Entry Relay** – is located over the glovebox.
- **Intermittent Wiper Control Unit** – is located on the lower left reinforcement.
- **Key-in, seatbelt, Headlight-on Chime Module with Time Delay or Electronic Voice Alert** – is located above the glove box.
- **Low Washer Fluid Sensor** – is located in the washer fluid bottle.
- **Manifold Absolute Pressure (MAP) Sensor** – is located on the right side shock tower.
- **Oil Pressure Switch/Sending Unit** – is located on the lower left side of the cylinder block.
- **Oxygen Sensor** – is located in the exhaust manifold.
- **Part Throttle Unlock Switch** – is located on the transaxle assembly.
- **Power Antenna and Name Brand Speaker Relay** – is wrapped with foam tape and taped to the harness under the radio.
- **Power Convertible Top Relay** – is located on the power top motor mounting bracket.
- **Radiator Fan Relay** – is mounted on the left front shock tower.
- **Radio Filter Choke** – is located over the radio.
- **Rear Window Defrost Timer/Relay (except convertible)** – is part of the defrost switch.
- **Single Module Engine Controller (SMEC)** – is located in the engine compartment, behind the battery.
- **Speed Control Servo** – is located under the battery tray, in the engine compartment.
- **Starter Relay** – is located on the left front shock tower.
- **Tachometer Module** – is plugged into the rear of the instrument cluster printed circuit board.
- **Throttle Position Sensor** – is located on the throttle body assembly.
- **Time Delay Relay** – is located in the fuse block.
- **Transaxle Pressure Switch** – is located at the left front of the transaxle.
- **Visor Map Light Switch** – is located within the lamp assembly.
- **Wastegate Solenoid** – is located on the right side inner fender panel.

1990 DAYTONA AND LEBARON

- **A/C Clutch Relay** – is located on the right side inner fender panel.
- **A/C Compressor Zener Diode** – is located to the left of the compressor, within the connector.
- **A/C Electronic Cycling Clutch Switch** – is located in the evaporator housing.
- **A/C High Pressure Cut-Off Switch** – is located on the compressor.
- **A/C High Pressure Relief Valve** – is located on the compressor.
- **A/C Low Pressure Cut-Off and Damped Pressure Switches** – is located on the H-valve.
- **A/C-Heater Blower Motor Resistor** – is located on the right side plenum without A/C or behind the glove box if equipped with A/C.
- **Air Bag Diagnostic Connector** – is located at the right side of the console.
- **Air Bag Sensors** – are located at the right and left side closure panels.
- **Air Bag System Diagnostic Module** – is located in the center console.
- **Ambient Temperature Sensor (for the overhead console)** – is located at the center of the radiator enclosure panel.
- **ATC In-Car Ambient Temperature Sensor** – is located in the right rear of the instrument cluster.

• **ATC Power Module** – is located in the lower right side dash panel area.

• **ATC Vacuum Module** – is located on the A/C unit behind the glove box.

• **Auto Shutdown Relay** – is located on the left side inner fender panel.

• **Automatic Idle Speed Motor** – is located on the throttle body assembly.

• **Baro Read Solenoid** – is located on the right side inner fender panel.

• **Body Computer** – is located in the right side kick panel.

• **Both Auto Door Lock Relays** – are located in the relay bank on the left side kick panel.

• **Brake Fluid Level Sensor** – is located in the rear of the master cylinder.Brake Warning Light Switch – is located on the combination valve below the master cylinder.

• **Coolant Temperature Sending Unit** – is located on the right side of the cylinder head on 2.2L and 2.5L engines. The sending unit is located on the thermostat housing on 3.0L engine.

• **Coolant Temperature Sensor** – is located on the thermostat housing on 2.2L and 2.5L engines and on the cylinder head between the thermostat housing and distributor on 3.0L engine.

• **Daytime Running Lights Module (Canada)** – is located in the left front inner fender shield.

• **Detonation Sensor** – is located on the intake manifold on turbocharged engines.

• **Dimmer Switch** – is mounted on the steering column.

• **Diode Package** – is located in the relay bank on the left side kick panel.

• **Distance Sensor (except electronic transaxle)** – is located on the transaxle assembly.

• **EGR Diagnostic Solenoid (California)** – is located on the right side inner fender panel.

• **Electric Back Light (EBL) Cut-Off Switch** – is located in the left inner quarter panel.

• **Electronic Engine Node Module** – is located on the front of the radiator closure panel.

• **Electronic Transaxle Controller** – is located on the right side inner fender panel.

• **Electronic Transaxle Output Speed and Turbine Speed Sensors** – are located on the front of the transaxle.

• **Electronic Transaxle PRNDL Switch** – is located on the front of the transaxle.

• **Electronic Transaxle Reverse Light Relay** – is located on the right side inner fender panel.

• **Electronic Transaxle Safety Shut-Down Relay** – is located on the right side fender shield.

• **Engine, Transmission and Electronic Systems (except restraint and suspension) Diagnostic Connector** – is located in front of the left side shock tower.

• **Fog Lamps Relay** – is located in the relay bank on the left side kick panel.

• **High Beam Relay** – is located in the relay bank on the left side kick panel.

• **Horn Relay** – is located in the relay bank on the left side kick panel.

• **Illuminated Entry Relay** – is located above the glove box.

• **Key-In and Seat Belt Warning Chime** – is integral with the body computer.

• **Lamp Outage Module** – is located above the glove box.

• **Left Front Turn Signal Relay** – is located in the relay bank on the left side kick panel.

• **Left Rear Turn Signal and Stop Lamps Relay** – is located in the relay bank on the left side kick panel.

• **Left Side Cornering Lamp Relay** – is located in the relay bank on the left side kick panel.

• **Low Beam Relay** – is located in the relay bank on the left side kick panel.

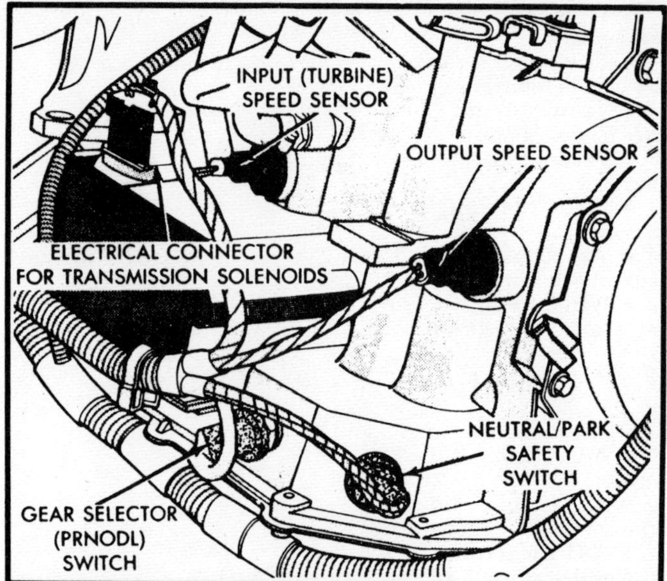

Electronic automatic transaxle sensors and switches identification – 1989–91 vehicles

• **Low Washer Fluid Sensor** – is located in the washer fluid bottle.

• **Manifold Absolute Pressure (MAP) Sensor** – is located on the right side shock tower.

• **Name Brand Speakers and Power Antenna Relay** – is located in the relay bank on the left side kick panel.

• **Oil Pressure Switch/Sending Unit** – is located on the lower left side of the cylinder block on 2.2L and 2.5L engines and on the oil filter adaptor on 3.0L engine.

• **Oxygen Sensor** – is located in the (rear) exhaust manifold.

• **Parking Lamps Relay** – is located in the relay bank on the left side kick panel.

• **Part Throttle Unlock Switch** – is located on the transaxle assembly.

• **Power Top Relay** – is located on the power top motor mounting bracket.

• **Purge Solenoid** – is located on the front of the right side shock tower.

• **Purge Solenoid** – is located on the right side inner fender panel.

• **Radiator Fan Relay** – is located on the left inner fender panel.

• **Radio Choke** – is located above the radio.

• **Rear Window Defrost Timer/Relay** – is located within the defroster switch.

• **Right Front Turn Signal Relay** – is located in the relay bank on the left side kick panel.

• **Right Rear Turn Signal and Stop Lamps Relay** – is located in the relay bank on the left side kick panel.

• **Right Side Cornering Lamp Relay** – is located in the relay bank on the left side kick panel.

• **Single Board Engine Controller (SBEC)** – is located in the engine compartment, behind the battery.

• **Speed Control Servo** – is located under the battery tray, in the engine compartment.

• **Starter Relay** – is located on the left side inner fender panel.

• **Throttle Body Temperature Sensor** – is located on the throttle body.

• **Throttle Position Sensor** – is located on the throttle body assembly.

• **Timer Relay**—is located in the relay bank on the left side kick panel.

• **Transaxle Solenoids and Pressure Switch**—are located on the top front of the transaxle.

• **Vacuum Vent Solenoid**—is located on the right side inner fender panel.

• **Vehicle Theft Alarm Module**—is located above the glove box.

• **Visor Map Light Switch**—is located within the lamp assembly.

• **Wastegate Solenoid**—is located on the front of the right side shock tower.

• **Windshield Washer Relay**—is located in the relay bank on the left side kick panel.

1991 DAYTONA AND LEBARON

1991 Daytona and Lebaron

• **A/C Clutch Relay**—is located in the power distribution center.

• **A/C Compressor Zener Diode**—is located to the left of the compressor, within the connector.

• **A/C Electronic Cycling Clutch Switch**—is located in the evaporator housing.

• **A/C High Pressure Cut-Off Switch**—is located on the compressor.

• **A/C High Pressure Relief Valve**—is located on the compressor.

• **A/C Low Pressure Cut-Off and Damped Pressure Switches**—is located on the H-valve.

• **A/C-Heater Blower Motor Resistor**—is located on the right side plenum without A/C or behind the glove box if equipped with A/C.

• **Air Bag Sensors**—are located at the right and left side closure panels.

• **Air Bag System Diagnostic Module**—is located in the center console.

• **Ambient Temperature Sensor (for the overhead console)**—is located at the center of the radiator enclosure panel.

• **Anti-lock Brake System Controller**—is located below the battery tray.

• **Anti-lock Brake System Diagnostic Connector**—is located behind the fuse access panel, inside Anti-lock Brake Pump Motor Relay—is located behind the battery, or on the left side inner fender panel, midway between the strut tower and SBEC.

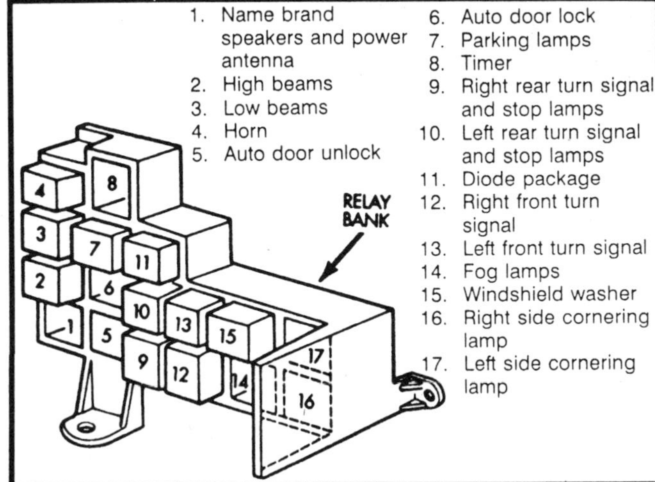

Relay identification—1990-91 Daytona and LeBaron. Vacancies represent relays used with optional equipment

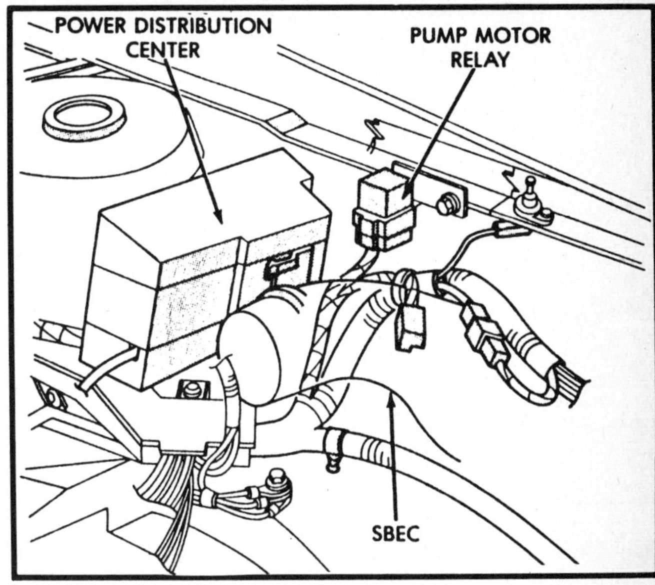

ABS pump motor relay location—1991 Daytona and LeBaron

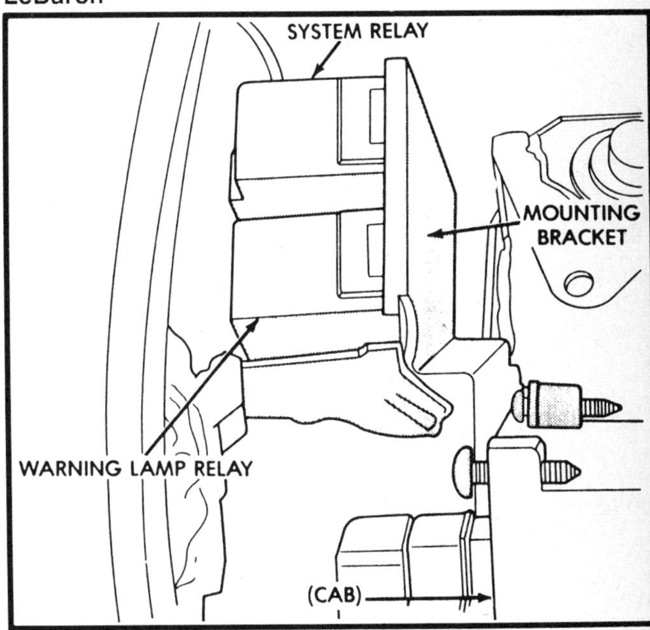

ABS controller and relays—1991 vehicles except Dynasty, New Yorker and Imperial

• **Anti-lock Brake System Relay**—is located behind the battery.

• **Anti-lock Brake Warning Lamp Relay**—is located behind the battery.the passenger compartment.

• **Anti-lock Brake Wheel Sensors**—are located at each wheel.

• **ATC In-Car Ambient Temperature Sensor**—is located in the right rear of the instrument cluster.

• **ATC Power Module**—is located in the lower right side dash panel area.

• **ATC Vacuum Module**—is located on the A/C unit behind the glove box.

• **Auto Shutdown Relay**—is located in the power distribution center.

• **Automatic Idle Speed Motor** – is located on the throttle body assembly.

• **Baro Read Solenoid** – is located on the right side inner fender panel.

• **Body Computer** – is located in the right side kick panel.

• **Both Auto Door Lock Relays** – are located in the relay bank on the left side kick panel.

• **Brake Fluid Level Sensor** – is located in the rear of the master cylinder.Brake Warning Light Switch (without Anti-lock Brake) – is located on the combination valve below the master cylinder.

• **Coolant Temperature Sensor** – is located on the thermostat housing on 2.2L and 2.5L engines and on the cylinder head between the thermostat housing and distributor on 3.0L engine.

• **Daytime Running Lights Module (Canada)** – is located in the left front inner fender shield.

• **Detonation Sensor** – is located on the intake manifold on turbocharged engines.

• **Dimmer Switch** – is mounted on the steering column.

• **Diode Package** – is located in the relay bank on the left side kick panel.

• **Distance Sensor (except electronic transaxle)** – is located on the transaxle assembly.

• **EGR Diagnostic Solenoid (California)** – is located on the right side inner fender panel.

• **Electric Back Light (EBL) Cut-Off Switch** – is located in the left inner quarter panel.

• **Electronic Engine Node Module** – is located on the front of the radiator closure panel.

• **Electronic Transaxle Controller** – is located on the right side inner fender panel.

• **Electronic Transaxle Output Speed and Turbine Speed Sensors** – are located on the front of the transaxle.

• **Electronic Transaxle PRNDL Switch** – is located on the front of the transaxle.

• **Electronic Transaxle Reverse Light Relay** – is located on the right side inner fender panel.

• **Electronic Transaxle Safety Shutdown Relay** – is located in the Power Distribution Center.

• **Engine, Transmission and Electronic Systems (except Anti-lock Brake) Diagnostic Connector** – is located in front of the left side shock tower.

• **Fog Lamps Relay** – is located in the relay bank on the left side kick panel.

• **Headlamp Open/Close Relay No.1** – is located in the power distribution center.

• **Headlamp Open/Close Relay No.2** – is located in the power distribution center.

• **High Beam Relay** – is located in the relay bank on the left side kick panel.

• **Horn Relay** – is located in the relay bank on the left side kick panel.

• **Key-In and Seat Belt Warning Chime** – is integral with the body computer.

• **Lamp Outage Module** – is located above the glove box.

• **Left Front Turn Signal Relay** – is located in the relay bank on the left side kick panel.

• **Left Rear Turn Signal and Stop Lamps Relay** – is located in the relay bank on the left side kick panel.

• **Left Side Cornering Lamp Relay** – is located in the relay bank on the left side kick panel.

• **Low Beam Relay** – is located in the relay bank on the left side kick panel.

• **Low Washer Fluid Sensor** – is located in the washer fluid bottle.

• **Manifold Absolute Pressure (MAP) Sensor** – is located on the right side shock tower.

• **Name Brand Speakers and Power Antenna Relay** – is located in the relay bank on the left side kick panel.

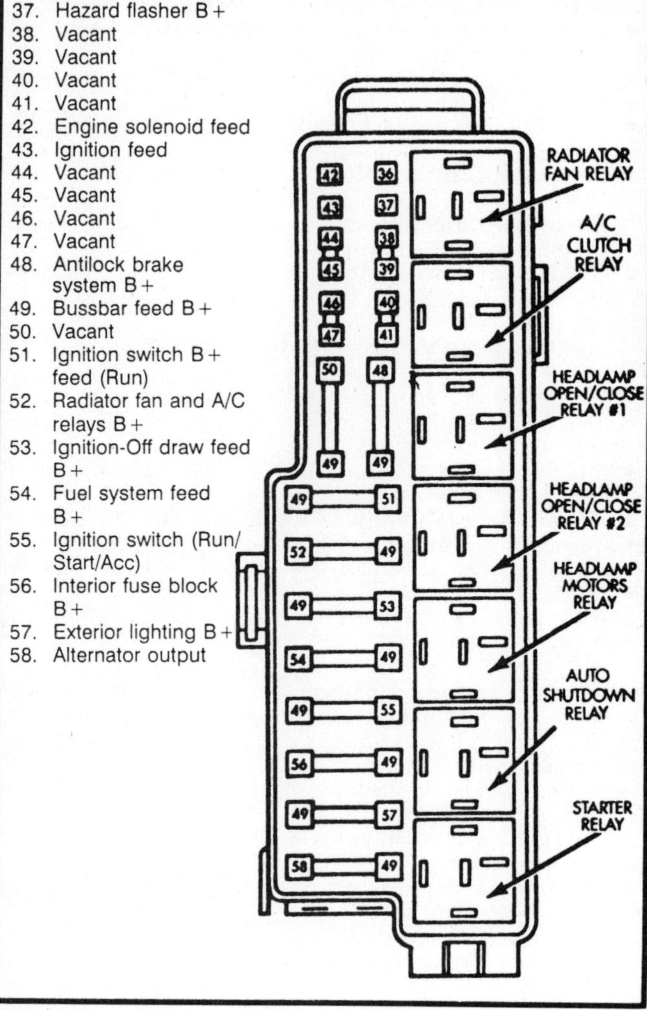

Power Distribution Center – 1991 Daytona and LeBaron

• **Oil Pressure Switch/Sending Unit** – is located on the lower left side of the cylinder block on 2.2L and 2.5L engines and on the oil filter adaptor on 3.0L engine.

• **Oxygen Sensor** – is located in the (rear) exhaust manifold.

• **Parking Lamps Relay** – is located in the relay bank on the left side kick panel.

• **Part Throttle Unlock Switch** – is located on the transaxle assembly.

• **Power Top Relay** – is located on the power top motor mounting bracket.

• **Purge Solenoid** – is located on the front of the right side shock tower.

• **Purge Solenoid** – is located on the right side inner fender panel.

• **Radiator Fan Relay** – is located in the power distribution center.

• **Radio Choke** – is located above the radio.

• **Rear Window Defrost Timer/Relay** – is located within the defroster switch.

• **Right Front Turn Signal Relay** – is located in the relay bank on the left side kick panel.

• **Right Rear Turn Signal and Stop Lamps Relay** – is located in the relay bank on the left side kick panel.

- **Right Side Cornering Lamp Relay**—is located in the relay bank on the left side kick panel.
- **Single Board Engine Controller (SBEC)**—is located in the engine compartment, behind the battery.
- **Speed Control Servo**—is located under the battery tray, in the engine compartment.
- **Starter Relay**—is located in the power distribution center.
- **Temperature Sending Unit**—is located on the right side of the cylinder head on 2.2L and 2.5L engines. The sending unit is located on the thermostat housing on 3.0L engine.
- **Throttle Body Temperature Sensor**—is located on the throttle body.
- **Throttle Position Sensor**—is located on the throttle body assembly.
- **Timer Relay**—is located in the relay bank on the left side kick panel.
- **Transaxle Solenoids and Pressure Switch**—are located on the top front of the transaxle.
- **Vacuum Vent Solenoid**—is located on the right side inner fender panel.
- **Vehicle Theft Alarm Module**—is located above the glove box.
- **Visor Map Light Switch**—is located within the lamp assembly.
- **Wastegate Solenoid**—is located on the front of the right side shock tower.
- **Windshield Washer Relay**—is located in the relay bank on the left side kick panel.

1989 DYNASTY AND NEW YORKER LANDAU

- **A/C Ambient Temperature Switch**—is located on the outboard on the center radiator yoke.
- **A/C Compressor Clutch Relay**—is located on the left side inner fender panel.
- **A/C Compressor Zener Diode**—is located to the left of the compressor, within the connector.
- **A/C Fan Cutout Switch**—is located on the compressor discharge tube.
- **A/C Fin-Sensed Cycling Clutch Switch**—is located in the evaporator housing.
- **A/C High Pressure Cut-Off Switch**—is located on the compressor.
- **A/C High Pressure Relief Valve**—is located on the filter/drier assembly or on the compressor.
- **A/C Low Pressure Cut-Off Switch**—is located on the H-valve.
- **A/C-Heater Blower Motor Resistor**—is located near the air inlet on the plenum.

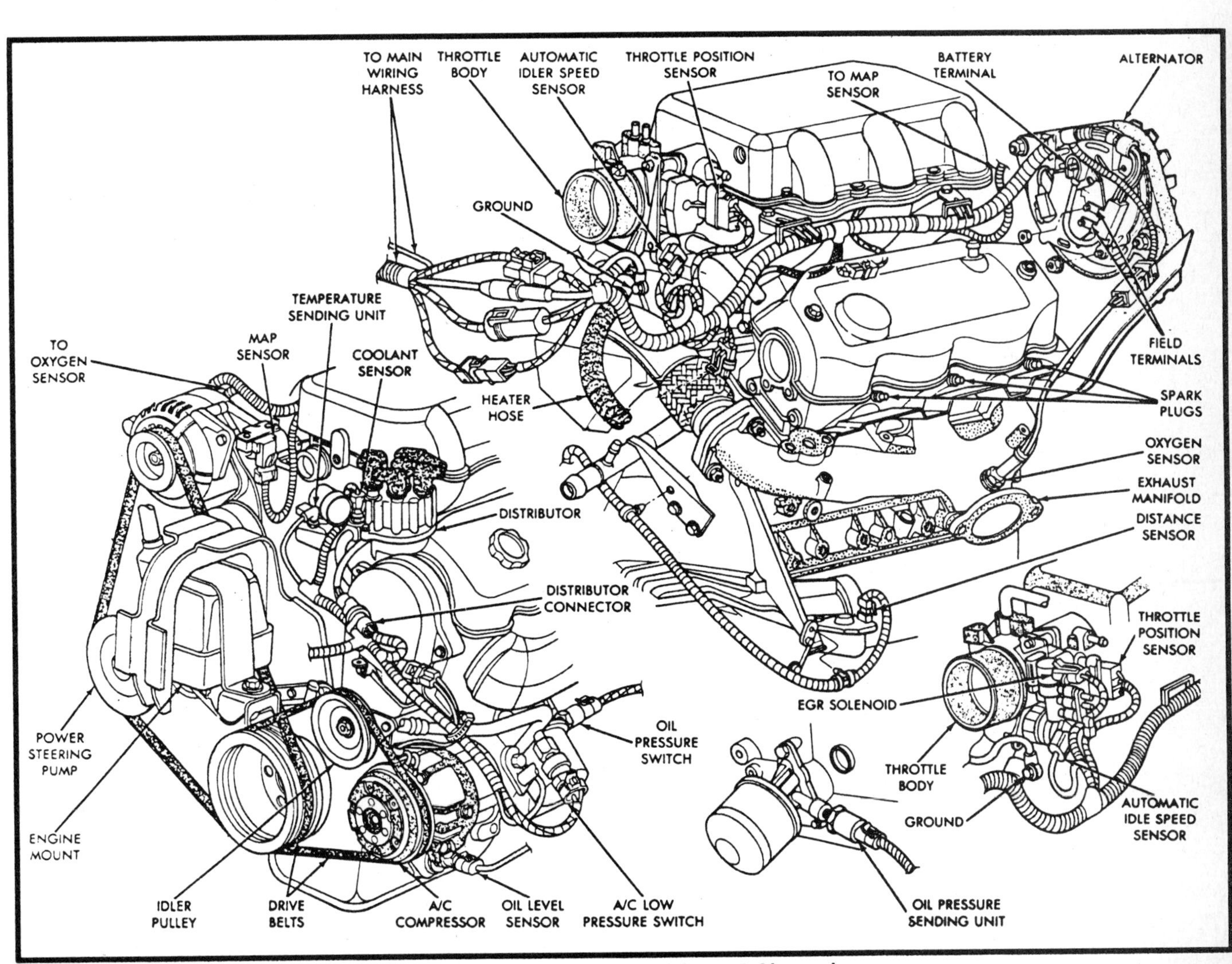

Engine and throttle body mounted switches, sensors and wiring—3.0L engine

• **Anti-lock Brake Controller** – is located in the trunk between the rear seat bulkhead and the rear bulkhead trim panel.
• **Anti-lock Brake Over-Voltage Protection Relay** – is located on the left side inner fender panel, just ahead of the battery.
• **Anti-lock Brake Pump/Motor Relay** – is located on the left side inner fender panel, just ahead of the battery.
• **Anti-lock Brake Wheel Sensors** – are located at each wheel.
• **ATC In-Car Ambient Temperature Sensor** – is located in the right rear of the instrument cluster.
• **ATC Power and Vacuum Module** – is located in the lower right side dash panel area.
• **Automatic Air Load Leveling Suspension Air Exhaust Solenoid** – is located on the compressor, located underbody on the right rear quarter panel.
• **Automatic Air Load Leveling Suspension Compressor Relay** – is located next to the control module in the trunk.
• **Automatic Air Load Leveling Suspension Compressor** – is located underbody, on the right rear quarter panel.
• **Automatic Air Load Leveling Suspension Diagnostic Connectors** – are located near the control module in the trunk.
• **Automatic Air Load Leveling Suspension Module** – is located in the right rear quarter panel inside the trunk.
• **Automatic Idle Speed Motor** – is located on the throttle body assembly.
• **Automatic Shutdown Relay** – is located on the left inner fender panel.
• **Body Computer Functions Diagnostic Connector** – is located to the right of the steering column.
• **Body Computer** – is located in the right side kick panel.
• **Brake Fluid Level Sensor** – is located in the rear of the master cylinder
Brake Pad Wear Sensors – are located on the pads themselves.
• **Brake Warning Light Switch (without Anti-lock Brake)** – is located on the combination valve below the master cylinder.
• **California EGR Solenoid** – is located behind the throttle body.
• **Concealed Headlamp Module** – is located above the glove box.
• **Concealed Headlamp Relays** – are located on the right side fender shield.
• **Coolant Temperature Sensor** – is located on the thermostat housing on 2.5L engine and on the cylinder head between the thermostat housing and distributor on 3.0L engine.
• **Deck Lid Pull Down Unit** – is located at the deck lid striker location.
• **Deck Lid Release Solenoid** – is located at the rear of the deck lid.
• **Dimmer Switch** – is mounted on the steering column.
• **Distance Sensor (except electronic transaxle)** – is located on the transaxle assembly.
• **EGR Diagnostic Solenoid (California)** – is located on the right side inner fender panel.
• **Electric Transaxle Diagnostic Connector** – is located to the right of the steering column.
• **Electronic A/C Cycling Switch** – is located on the right side of the dash panel on vehicles equipped with 2.5L engine.
• **Electronic Transaxle Controller** – is located on the right side inner fender panel.
• **Electronic Transaxle Output Speed and Turbine Speed Sensors** – are located on the front of the transaxle.
• **Electronic Transaxle PRNDL Switch** – is located on the front of the transaxle.
• **Electronic Transaxle Reverse Light Relay** – is located on the right side inner fender panel.
• **Electronic Transaxle Safety Shut-Down Relay** – is located on the right side fender shield.

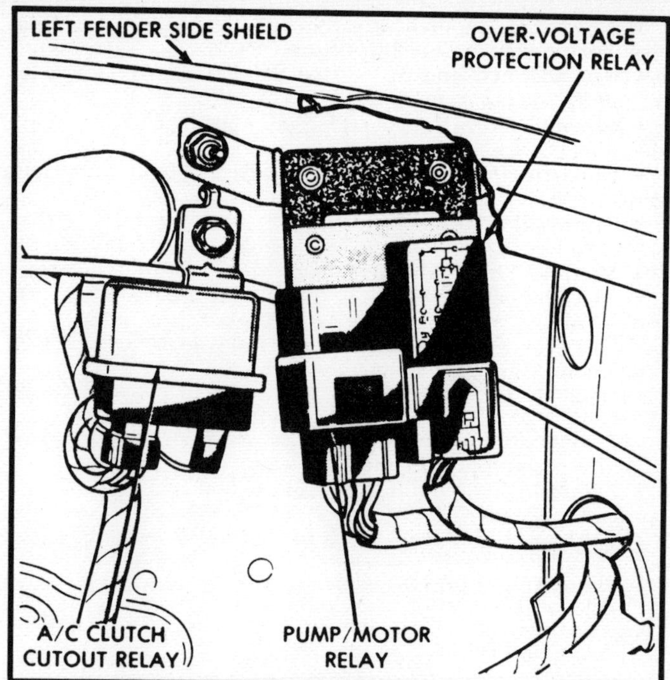

Relay identification – 1989 Dynasty and New Yorker

• **Electronic Transaxle Solenoids and Pressure Switch** – are located on the top front of the transaxle.
• **Engine Diagnostic Connector** – is located in front of the left side shock tower.
• **Horn Relay** – is located in the relay/flasher bank, located on the lower reinforcement.
• **Key-In and Seat Belt Warning Chime** – is part of the body computer.
• **Lamp Outage Module** – is located above the glove box.
• **Low Washer Fluid Sensor** – is located in the washer fluid bottle.
• **Manifold Absolute Pressure (MAP) Sensor** – is located on the right side shock tower on 2.5L engine and forward of the alternator on 3.0L engine.
• **Memory Power Seat Module** – is located under the driver's seat.
• **Oil Pressure Switch/Sending Unit** – is located on the lower left side of the cylinder block on 2.5L engines and on the oil filter adaptor on 3.0L engine.
• **Oxygen Sensor** – is located in the (rear) exhaust manifold.
• **Part Throttle Unlock Switch** – is located on the transaxle assembly.
• **Power Antenna and Name Brand Speaker Relay** – is located in the relay module above the glove box.
• **Power Door Lock Relays** – are located in the relay module behind the glove box.
• **Power Sunroof Electronic Module** – is located under the headliner at the rear of the housing.
• **Purge Solenoid** – is located on the front of the right side shock tower.
• **Radiator Fan Relay** – is mounted on the left front shock tower.
• **Radio Filter Choke** – is located below the radio.
• **Rear Window Defrost Timer/Relay** – is located within the defroster switch.
• **Single Module Engine Controller (SMEC)** – is located in the engine compartment, behind the battery.
• **Speed Control Servo** – is located under the battery tray, in the engine compartment.

• **Starter Relay**—is located on the left front shock tower.

• **Temperature Sending Unit**—is located on the right side of the cylinder head on 2.5L engines. The sending unit is located on the thermostat housing on 3.0L engine.

• **Throttle Body Temperature Sensor**—is located on the throttle body assembly.

• **Throttle Position Sensor**—is located on the throttle body assembly.

• **Time Delay Relay**—is located in the relay module behind the glove box.

• **Vehicle Theft Alarm System Module**—is located behind the glovebox.

• **Vehicle Theft Alarm System Switches**—are located at each key cylinder, door jamb and left front fender.

• **Visor Map Light Switch**—is located within the lamp assembly.

1990–91 DYNASTY, NEW YORKER AND IMPERIAL

• **A/C Ambient Temperature Switch**—is located on the outboard on the center radiator yoke.

• **A/C Clutch Relay**—is located in the power distribution center.

• **A/C Compressor Zener Diode**—is located to the left of the compressor, within the connector.

• **A/C Fan Cutout Switch**—is located on the compressor discharge tube.

• **A/C Fin-Sensed Cycling Clutch Switch**—is located in the evaporator housing.

• **A/C High Pressure Cut-Off Switch**—is located on the compressor.

• **A/C High Pressure Relief Valve**—is located on the filter/drier assembly or on the compressor.

• **A/C Low Pressure Cut-Off Switch**—is located on the H-valve.

• **A/C-Heater Blower Motor Resistor**—is located near the air inlet on the plenum.

• **Air Bag Diagnostic Module**—is located in the console center support bracket.

• **Air Bag Sensors**—are located in the left and right front closure panels.

• **Air Load Leveling Suspension Module**—is located in the right rear quarter panel inside the trunk.

• **Anti-lock Brake Controller**—is located in the trunk between the rear seat bulkhead and the rear bulkhead trim panel in 1990, and under the battery tray in 1991.

• **Anti-lock Brake Diagnostic Connector (1991)**—is located under the instrument panel to the left of the steering column.

• **Anti-lock Brake Pump Motor Cartridge Fuse**—is located in the power distribution center.

• **Anti-lock Brake Pump Motor Relay**—is located in the power distribution center.

• **Anti-lock Brake System Cartridge Fuse**—is located in the power distribution center.

• **Anti-lock Brake System Main Relay**—is located in the power distribution center.

• **Anti-lock Brake Warning Lamp Relay**—is located in the power distribution center.

• **Anti-lock Brake Wheel Sensors**—are located at each wheel.

• **Ambient Temperature (ATC) In-Car Sensor**—is located in the right rear of the instrument cluster.

• **ATC Power and Vacuum Module**—is located in the lower right side dash panel area.

• **Automatic Air Load Leveling Suspension Air Exhaust Solenoid**—is located on the compressor, located underbody on the right rear quarter panel.

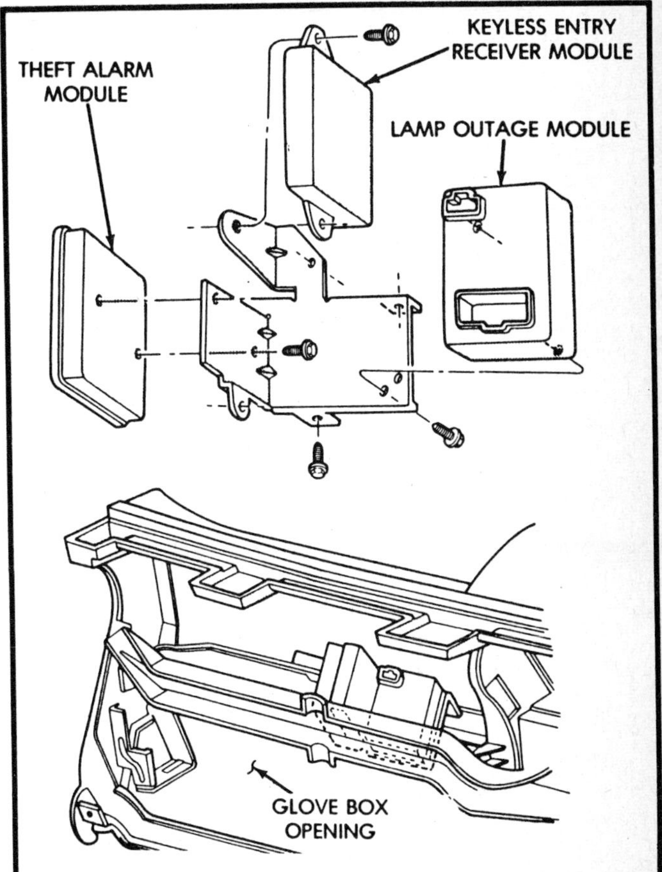

Module identification behind the glovebox—1991 Dynasty, New Yorker and Imperial

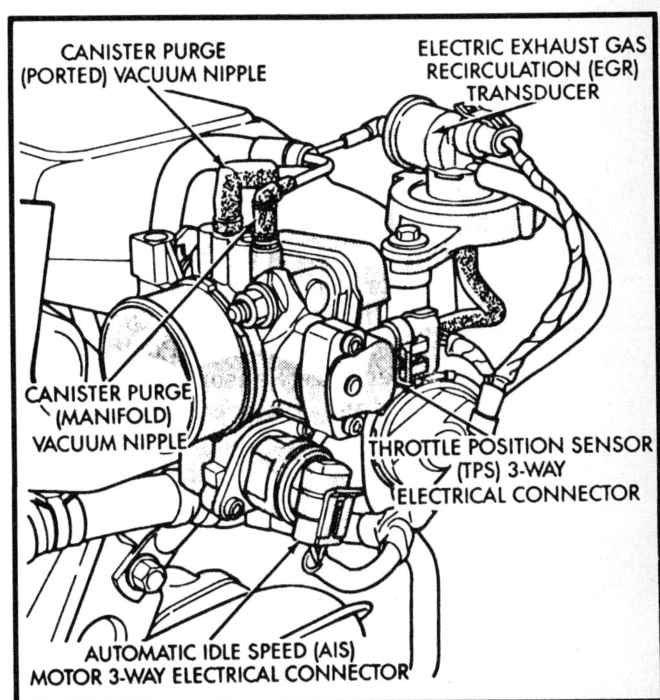

Throttle body and related electrical components—3.3L and 3.8L engines

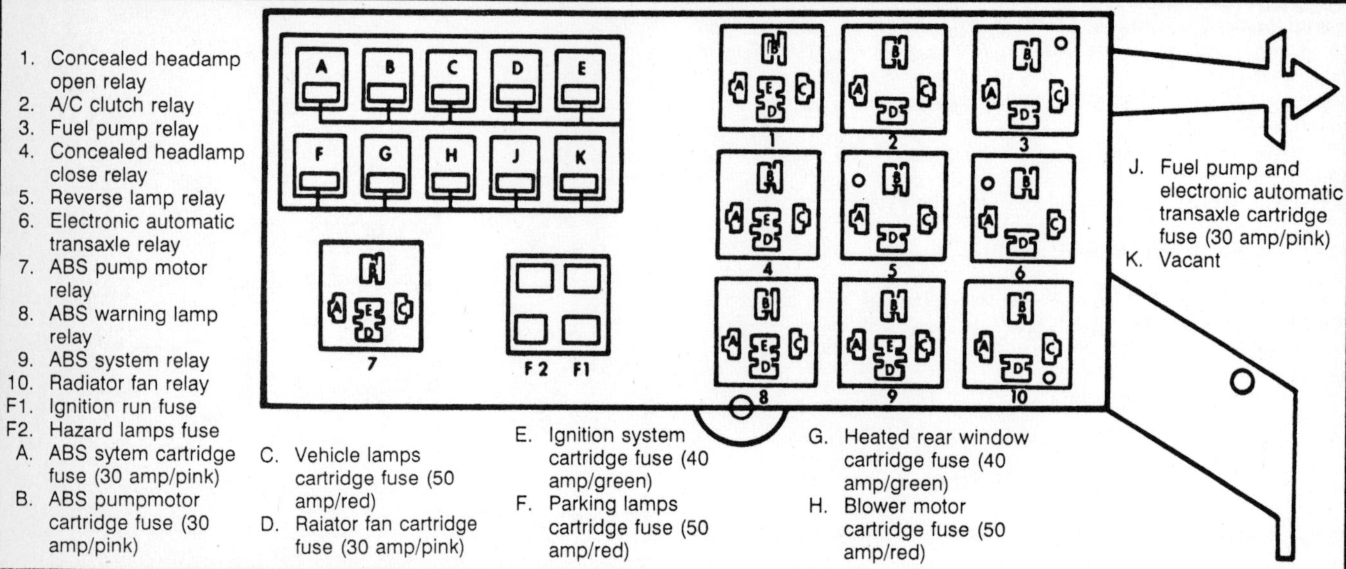

Power Distribution Center—1990–91 Dynasty, New Yorker and Imperial

• **Automatic Air Load Leveling Suspension Compressor Relay**—is located next to the control module in the trunk.

• **Automatic Air Load Leveling Suspension Compressor**—is located underbody, on the right rear quarter panel.

• **Automatic Air Load Leveling Suspension Diagnostic Connectors**—are located near the control module in the trunk.

• **Automatic Air Suspension Air Exhaust Solenoids**—are located on each strut assembly.

• Automatic Air Suspension Compressor Relay—is located next to the control module in the trunk.

• **Automatic Air Suspension Control Module**—is located in the right rear quarter panel inside the trunk.

• **Automatic Air Suspension Height Sensors**—are located in the rear shock and both front strut assemblies.

• **Automatic Day/Night Rear View Mirror Sensors**—are located on the front and rear surfaces of the mirror assembly.

• **Automatic Idle Speed Motor**—is located on the throttle body assembly.

• **Automatic Shutdown Relay**—is located in the power distribution center.

• **Blower Motor Cartridge Fuse**—is located in the power distribution center.

• **Body Computer Functions Diagnostic Connector**—is located to the right of the steering column on C bodies and to the left of the steering column on Y bodies.

• **Body Computer**—is located in the right side kick panel.

• **Brake Fluid Level Sensor**—is located in the rear of the master cylinder

Brake Pad Wear Sensors—are located on the pads themselves.

• **Brake Warning Light Switch (without Anti-lock Brake)**—is located on the combination valve below the master cylinder.

• **California EGR Solenoid**—is located behind the throttle body.

• **Charge Temperature Sensor**—is located on the intake manifold.

• **Concealed Headlamp Closed Relay**—is located in the power distribution center.

• **Concealed Headlamp Module**—is located above the glove box.

• **Concealed Headlamp Open Relay**—is located in the power distribution center.

• **Coolant Temperature Sending Unit**—is located on the right side of the cylinder head on 2.5L engine, on the thermostat housing on 3.0L engine and on the right side of the front head below the thermostat housing on 3.3 and 3.8L engines.

• **Coolant Temperature Sensor**—is located on the thermostat housing on 2.5L engine, on the cylinder head between the thermostat housing and distributor on 3.0L engine and on the top of the head near the thermostat housing on 3.3 and 3.8L engines.

• **Deck Lid Pull Down Unit**—is located at the deck lid striker location.

• **Deck Lid Release Solenoid**—is located at the rear of the deck lid.

• **Dimmer Switch**—is mounted on the steering column.

• **Distance Sensor (except electronic transaxle)**—is located on the transaxle assembly.

• **EGR Diagnostic Solenoid (California)**—is located on the right side inner fender panel.

• **Electronic A/C Cycling Switch**—is located on the right side of the dash panel on vehicles equipped with 2.5L engine.

• **Electronic Transaxle Controller**—is located on the right side inner fender panel.

• **Electronic Transaxle Output Speed and Turbine Speed Sensors**—are located on the front of the transaxle.

• **Electronic Transaxle PRNDL Switch**—is located on the front of the transaxle.

• **Electronic Transaxle Relay**—is located in the power distribution center.

• **Electronic Transaxle Solenoids and Pressure Switch**—are located on the top front of the transaxle.

• **Fuel Pump or Automatic Shutdown Relay**—is located in the power distribution center.

• **Fuel Pump/Electronic Transaxle Cartridge Fuse**—is located in the power distribution center.

• **Hazard Lamps Fuse**—is located in the power distribution center.

• **Heated Rear Window Cartridge Fuse**—is located in the power distribution center.

• **Horn Relay**—is located in the relay/flasher bank, located above the fuse block..

• **Ignition Run Fuse**—is located in the power distribution center.

• **Ignition System Cartridge Fuse** – is located in the power distribution center.

• **Key-In and Seat Belt Warning Chime** – is part of the body computer.

• **Keyless Entry Receiver Module** – is located behind the glovebox.

• **Lamp Outage Module** – is located above the glove box.

• **Low Washer Fluid Sensor** – is located in the washer fluid bottle.

• **Load Leveling Electronic Control Module** – is located behind the right rear quarter panel or in the top of the luggage compartment.

• **Manifold Absolute Pressure (MAP) Sensor** – is located on the right side shock tower on 2.5L engine, forward of the alternator on 3.0L engine and mounted directly to the intake plenum on 3.3L and 3.8L engines.

• **Memory Power Seat Module** – is located under the driver's seat.

• **Oil Pressure Switch/Sending Unit** – is located on the lower left side of the cylinder block on 2.5L engine, on the oil filter adaptor on 3.0L engine and next to the oil filter on 3.3L and 3.8L engines.

• **Oxygen Sensor** – is located in the (rear) exhaust manifold.

• **Park Lamps Cartridge Fuse** – is located in the power distribution center.

• **Part Throttle Unlock Switch** – is located on the transaxle assembly.

• **Power Antenna and Name Brand Speaker Relay** – is located in the relay module above the glove box.

• **Power Door Lock Relays** – are located in the relay module above the glove box.

• **Power Sunroof Electronic Module** – is located under the headliner at the rear of
Powertrain Diagnostic Connector – is located in front of the left side shock tower.

• **Purge Solenoid** – is located on the front of the right side shock tower.

• **Radiator Fan Cartridge Fuse** – is located in the power distribution center.

• **Radiator Fan Relay** – is located in the power distribution center.

• **Radiator Fan Relay** – is mounted on the left front shock tower.

• **Radio Filter Choke** – is located below the radio.

• **Rear Window Defrost Timer/Relay** – is located within the defroster switch.

• **Reverse Lamp Relay** – is located in the power distribution center.

• **Single Board Engine Controller (SBEC)** – is located in the engine compartment, behind the battery.

• **Speed Control Servo** – is located under the battery tray, in the engine compartment.

• **Starter Relay** – is located on the front of the left fender shield.

• **the housing.**

• **Throttle Body Temperature Sensor** – is located on the throttle body assembly.

• **Throttle Position Sensor** – is located on the throttle body assembly.

• **Time and Headlamp Delay Relay** – is located in the relay module above the glove box.

• **Vehicle Lamps Cartridge Fuse** – is located in the power distribution center.

• **Vehicle Theft Alarm System Module** – is located behind the glovebox.

• **Vehicle Theft Alarm System Switches** – are located at each key cylinder, door jamb and left front fender.

• **Visor Map Light Switch** – is located within the lamp assembly.

CHRYSLER TC

• **A/C Clutch Cutout Relay** – is located on the left side inner fender panel.

• **A/C Compressor Clutch Relay** – is located on the left side inner fender panel.

• **A/C Compressor Zener Diode** – is located to the left of the compressor, within the connector.

• **A/C Fin-Sensed Cycling Clutch Switch** – is located in the evaporator housing.

• **A/C High Pressure Cut-Off Switch** – is located on the compressor.

• **A/C High Pressure Relief Valve** – is located on the filter/drier assembly or on the compressor.

• **A/C Low or Differential Pressure Cut-Off Switch** – is located on the H-valve.

• **A/C-Heater Blower Motor Resistor** – is located near the air inlet on the plenum.

• **Anti-lock Brake Auxiliary Relay** – is located on the right side of the engine compartment.

• **Anti-lock Brake Controller** – is located in the right side kick panel.

• **Anti-lock Brake Main Relay** – is located on the right side of the engine compartment.

• **Anti-lock Brake Motor Relay** – is located on the right side of the engine compartment.

• **Anti-lock Brake Wheel Sensors** – are located at each wheel.

• **Air Horn Compressor** – is located on the right rear radiator yoke.

• **Air Temperature Sensor** – is located on the front of the intake manifold.

• **Automatic Idle Speed Motor** – is located on the throttle body assembly.

• **Automatic Shutdown Relay** – is located on the left inner fender panel.

• **Baro Read Solenoid** – is located on the front of the right shock tower.

• **Condenser Fan Switch** – is located on the muffler of the discharge line from the compressor.

• **Coolant Temperature Sending Unit** – is located left front surface on the cylinder head on 2.2L engine. The sending unit is located on the thermostat housing on 3.0L engine.

• **Coolant Temperature Sensor** – is located on the front middle surface of the cylinder head behind the upper radiator hose on 2.2L engine and on the cylinder head between the thermostat housing and distributor on 3.0L engine.

• **Daytime Running Lights Module (Canada)** – is located in the left front inner fender shield.

• **Detonation Sensor** – is located next to the oil filter on 2.2L engine.

• **Dimmer Switch** – is mounted on the steering column.

• **Distance Sensor (except electronic transaxle)** – is located on the transaxle assembly.

• **EGR Solenoid** – is located on the front of the right shock tower.

• **Electronic Transaxle Controller** – is located on the right side inner fender panel.

• **Electronic Transaxle Output Speed and Turbine Speed Sensors** – are located on the front of the transaxle.

• **Electronic Transaxle PRNDL Switch** – is located on the front of the transaxle.

• **Electronic Transaxle Reverse Light Relay** – is located on the right side inner fender panel.

• **Electronic Transaxle Safety Shut-Down Relay** – is located on the right side fender shield.

• **Electronic Transaxle Solenoids and Pressure Switch** – are located on the top front of the transaxle.

• **Engine Diagnostic Connector** – is located in front of the left side shock tower.

• **Horn Relay**—is located on the fuse block.

• **Illuminated Entry Relay**—is located above the glove box.

• **Intermittent Wiper Control Module**—is located on the left side plenum.

• **Key-In, Seat Belt, Head Lamp-On Warning Chime or Buzzer**—is located above the glove box.

• **Knock Sensor**—located in the block below the distributor hold-down clamp on 2.2L engine.Low Washer Fluid Sensor—is located in the washer fluid bottle.

• **Manifold Absolute Pressure (MAP) Sensor**—is located on the right side shock tower.

• **Name Brand Speaker Relay**—is located forward of the console below the radio.

• **Oil Pressure Switch/Sending Unit**—is located on the lower left side of the cylinder block on 2.2L engine and on the oil filter adaptor on 3.0L engine.

• **Oxygen Sensor**—is located in the exhaust manifold.

• **Part Throttle Unlock Switch**—is located on the transaxle assembly.

• **Purge Solenoid**—is located on the front of the right shock tower.

• **Radiator Fan Relay**—is mounted on the left side inner fender panel.

• **Rear Window Defrost Timer/Relay**—is located within the defroster switch.

• **Single Board Engine Controller (SBEC)**—is located in the engine compartment, behind the battery.

• **Single Module Engine Controller (SMEC)**—is located in the engine compartment, behind the battery.

• **Speed Control Servo**—is located under the battery tray, in the engine compartment.

• **Starter Relay**—is located on the left front shock tower.

• **Tachometer Module**—is located on the back of the instrument panel printed circuit board.

• **Throttle Body Temperature Sensor**—is located on the throttle body.

• **Throttle Position Sensor**—is located on the throttle body assembly.

• **Time Delay Relay**—is located in the fuse block.

• **Visor Map Light Switch**—is located within the lamp assembly.

• **Wastegate Solenoid**—is located on the front of the right shock tower.

GRAN FURY, DIPLOMAT, CARAVELLE, NEWPORT AND FIFTH AVENUE (RWD)

• **A/C Ambient Sensor**—is located inside the rear surface of the evaporator assembly.

• **A/C Cycling Switch**—is located on the cycling clutch expansion valve (H-valve).

• **A/C Damped Pressure Cycling Switch**—is located in the A/C refrigerant line.

• **A/C Electronic Servo Motor**—is located in the evaporator heater assembly, above the blend air door shaft.

• **A/C High Pressure Relief Valve**—is located on the filter/drier assembly.

• **A/C In-Car Sensor**—is connected to the aspirator suction nipple and the instrument panel, on the passenger side of the vehicle.

• **A/C Low Pressure Cut-Off Switch**—is located on the cycling clutch expansion valve (H-valve).

• **Accessory Power Relay**—is located on the left side of the brake pedal support bracket.

• **Air Bag Power Module**—is located on the left side of the steering column, underneath the dash panel.

• **All Power Accessories Circuit Breakers**—are located in the fuse block.

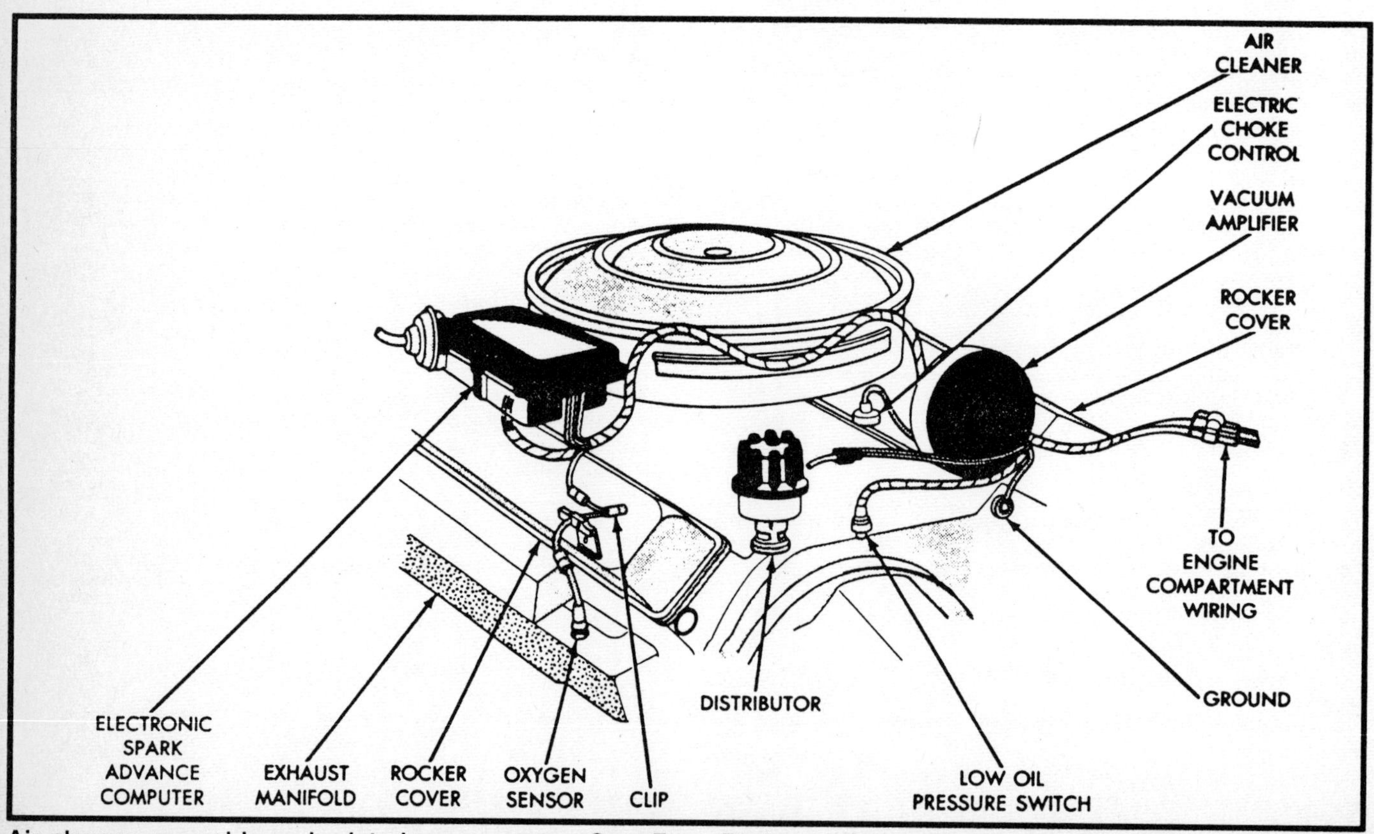

Air cleaner assembly and related components—Gran Fury, Diplomat, Caravelle, Newport and Fifth Avenue (RWD)

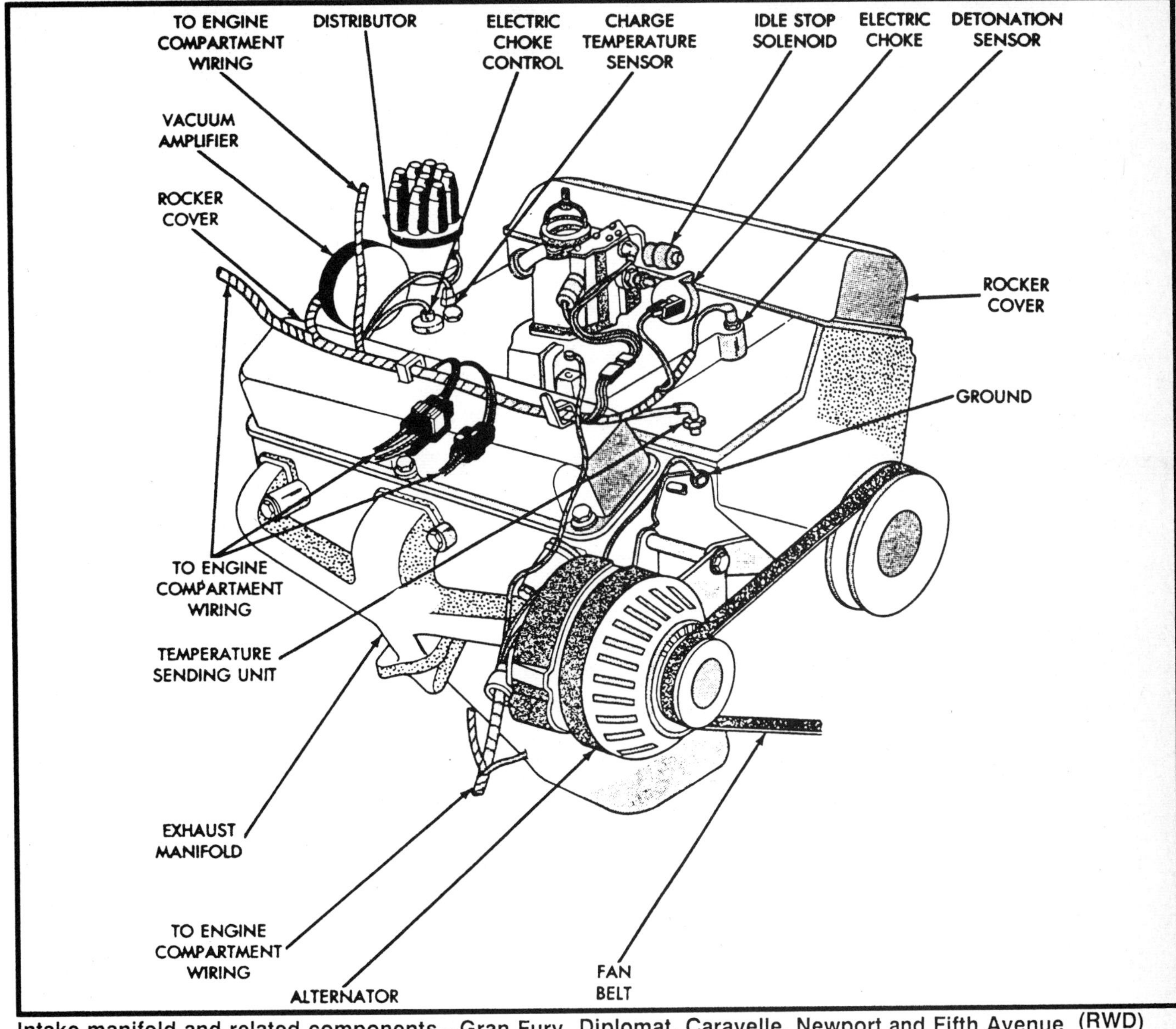

Intake manifold and related components – Gran Fury, Diplomat, Caravelle, Newport and Fifth Avenue (RWD)

- **Ambient Temperature Sensor** – is located under the right side of the dash panel.
- **Brake Warning Light Switch** – is located on the master cylinder.
- **Carburetor Switch** – is located on the lower right side of the carburetor.
- **Charge Temperature Switch** – is located on the intake manifold, in front of the distributor.
- **Chime Module** – is located on the instrument panel left reinforcement bracket.
- **Coolant Temperature Sensor** – is located on the front of the intake manifold.
- **Coolant Vacuum Switch** – is mounted in the thermostat housing.
- **Dimmer Switch** – is mounted on the steering column.
- **Dual Vacuum Solenoid** – is located on the center of the firewall, in the engine compartment, next to the windshield wiper motor.
- **Electric Choke Control** – is located in the intake manifold, on the passenger's side of the vehicle.
- **Horn Relay** – is located in the fuse block, on the left side of instrument panel.
- **Idle Stop Solenoid** – is located on the carburetor.
- **Ignition Ballast Resistor** – is located on the center of the right front inner fender panel.
- **Illuminated Entry Relay** – is located on the lower right side of the brake pedal support brace.
- **Intermittent Wiper Control Module** – is attached to the lower instrument panel reinforcement behind the steering column cover.
- **Low Washer Fluid Sensor** – is located on the washer fluid bottle.
- **Oil Pressure Switch** – is located on the right side of the distributor in the block.
- **Oxygen Feedback Solenoid** – is located in the front of the carburetor.
- **Oxygen Sensor** – is located in the exhaust manifold.
- **Power Antenna and Amplifier Relay** – is taped to the stereo system harness.

• **Power Door Lock Relay**—is located on the lower right kick panel.

• **Rear Window Defrost Relay**—is located on the end of the rear window defrost switch.

• **Seat Belt Warning Buzzer**—is located in the fuse block, on the left side of the instrument panel.

• **Spark Control Computer**—is located on the air cleaner.

• **Speed Control Servo**—is located on the driver's side inner fender panel, in the engine compartment.

• **Starter Relay**—is located in the upper left side of the firewall.

• **Time Delay Relay**—is located in the fuse block, on the left side of the instrument panel.

• **Vacuum Transducer**—is located on the spark control computer.

• **Windshield Washer Low Fluid Level Sensor**—is located on the windshield washer reservoir.

LASER

• **A/C Condenser Fan Relay**—is located in the underhood relay box.

• **A/C Controller**—is located behind the glove compartment.

• **A/C temperature sensors**—are located in the air conditioner housing near the A/C controller.

• **Air Flow Sensor**—is in the air intake stream.

• **Alternator Relay**—is located in the underhood relay box.

• **Automatic Transmission Control Unit**—is located behind the center of the instrument panel.

• **Barometric Pressure Sensor**—is in the air intake stream.

• **Blower High Relay**—is next to the blower motor.

• **Compressor clutch relay**—is located in the underhood relay box.

• **Coolant Temperature Sensor**—is in below the thermostat housing.

• **Crankangle Sensor (1.8L engine)**—is part of the distributor.

• **Crankangle Sensor (2.0L engine)**—is located at the rear of the cylinder head.

• **Cruise Control Diode**—is located in the center of the dash.

• **Cruise Control Module**—is located at the upper left side of the dash.

• **Daylight Running Relay (Canadian Models)**—is located in the underdash relay box.

• **Diagnosis Connector**—is located under the right side dash.

• **Dome Light Relay**—is located behind the left rear quarter panel trim.

• **Door Ajar Diode**—is located at the floor crossmember.

• **Door Lock Control Unit**—is located at the right side kick panel.

• **Door Lock Relay**—is located under the right side dash.

• **EGR Control Solenoid (except turbo)**—is on the firewall near the battery.

• **EGR Control Solenoid (turbocharged)**—is on the firewall on the left side.

• **Engine Control Unit**—is located behind the center of the instrument panel.

• **Fuel Pressure Control Solenoid (turbocharged)**—is on the firewall on the left side.

• **Fuel Pump Check Terminal**—is next to the battery.

• **Hazard Flasher**—is located above the underdash fuse box.

• **Heater Relay**—is located under the left side dash with the fuse box.

• **Ignition Coil Power Transistor**—is located below or near the ignition coil.

• **Ignition Timing Adjustment Terminal**—is next to the battery.

• **Intake Air Temperature Sensor**—is in the air intake stream.

• **Knock Sensor**—is in the middle of the engine on the firewall side.

• **Passing Control Relay**—is located behind left side cowl trim.

• **Pop-up Circuit Diode**—is under the right side of the dash.

• **Pop-up Motor Relay**—is in the underhood relay box.

• **Power Steering Pressure Switch**—is located at the power steering pump.

• **Power Window Relay**—is located in the underhood relay box.

• **Purge Control Solenoid (except turbocharged)**—is on the firewall near the battery.

• **Purge Control Solenoid (turbocharged)**—is on the firewall on the left side.

• **Radio Noise Condenser**—is located next to the battery.

• **Seatbelt Control Unit**—is located at the center column near the seat.

• **Seatbelt Relay**—is located at the center column near the seat.

• **Seatbelt Timer (if equipped)**—is located in the underdash relay box.

• **Starter Relay**—is located in the underdash relay box.

• **TDC Sensor (1.8L engine)**—is part of the distributor.

• **TDC Sensor (2.0L engine)**—is located at the rear of the cylinder head.

• **Theft Alarm Diode**—is under the left side of the dash, next to the fuse panel.

• **Theft Alarm Horn Relay**—is located in the under the center of the dash.

• **Theft Alarm Starter Relay**—is located in the center floor console.

• **Theft Control Alarm**—is located at the right side kick panel.

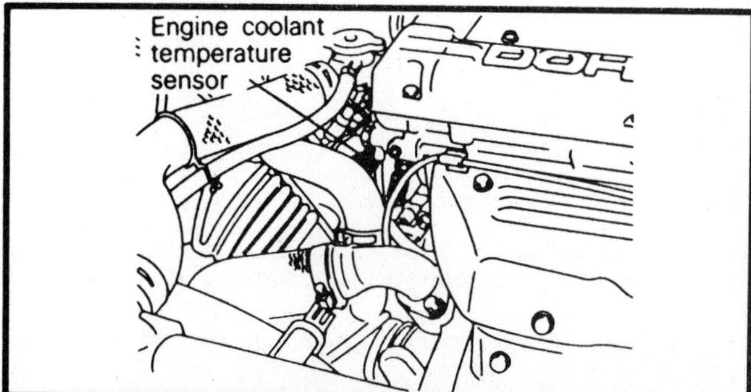

Coolant Temperature sensor—Laser with 2.0L engine

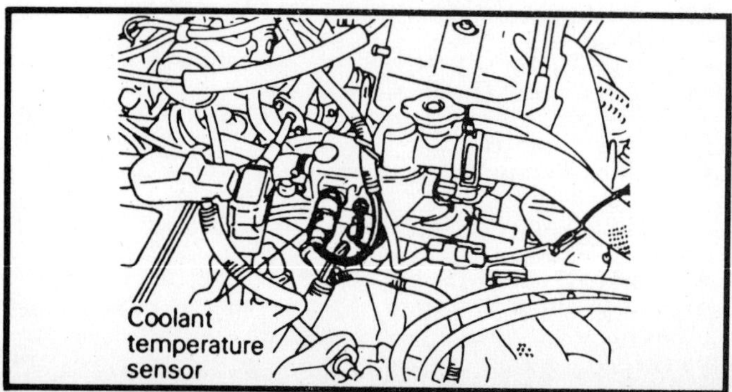

Coolant Temperature sensor—Laser with 1.8L engine

• **Transistor Taillight Relay (if equipped)** – is located under the right side dash.

• **Turn Signal Flasher** – is located above the underdash fuse box.

• **Waste Gate Control Valve** – is next to the air filter assembly.

MONACO

• **A/C Ambient Temperature Sensor** – is located in the front of vehicle, under the bumper on the right side.

• **A/C Clutch Relay (1990–early 91)** – is located in the relay holder, under a plastic cover, on the strut tower.

• **A/C Clutch Relay (late 1991)** – is located in the Power Distribution Center located behind the battery.

• **A/C Electronic Control Module** – is mounted on the right side of the heater housing under the instrument panel.

• **A/C Heater Relays** – are usually mounted on the heater housing under the instrument panel.

• **A/C Low Pressure Cut Off Switch** – is located on the receiver-drier assembly.

• **Antenna Relay** – is located in the relay block, which is located under the center of the instrument panel.

• **Anti-Lock Brakes (ABS) Control Module** – is located on the front of the right side shock tower.

• **Anti-Lock Brakes (ABS) Diagnostic Connector** – is located under the instrument panel to the left of the steering column.

• **Anti-Lock Brakes (ABS) Pump Motor Relay** – is located in the Power Distribution Center located behind the battery.

• **Anti-Lock Brakes (ABS) System Relay** – is located in the Power Distribution Center located behind the battery.

• **Anti-Lock Brakes (ABS) Warning Lamp Relay** – is located in the Power Distribution Center located behind the battery.

• **Automatic Idle Speed Motor** – is locatd on the throttle body assembly.

• **Auto Shutdown Relay (late 1991)** – is located in the Power Distribution Center located behind the battery.

• **B+ Latch Relay** – is located in the relay holder, under a plastic cover, on the strut tower.

• **Charge Temperature Sensor** – is located on the cylinder head, above the bell housing.

• **Chime Module** – is located under the left side of the instrument panel.

• **Coolant Level Sensor** – is located in the coolant reservoir, which is usually located in the engine compartment on the fire wall.

• **Coolant Temperature Sensor** – is located on the rear of the block or may be on the firewall, slightly right of center.

• **Coolant Temperature Sending Unit** – is located on the thermostat housing or on the front right side of the head.

• **Crankshaft Position Sensor** – is mounted on the left front surface of the bell housing.

• **Cruise Control Relay** – is located in the relay block, which is located under the center of the instrument panel.

• **Cruise Control Module (1990)** – is located under the instrument panel, above the hood release handle.

• **Daytime Running Lights Module (Canada)** – is located in the right front area of the engine compartment.

• **Diagnostic Connectors (1990–early 91)** – are located on the right front inner fender panel.

• **Diagnostic Connector (late 1991)** – is located on the left front of the engine compartment near the SBEC.

• **Door Lock Relay** – is located behind or near the passenger's side kick panel or with keyless entry system in the overhead console.

• **EGR Solenoid** – is located on the driver's side inner fender panel in the engine compartment.

• **Electronic Engine Control Unit (1990–early 91)** – is located under the instrument panel on the passenger's side of the vehicle.

• **Electronic Engine Control Unit (late 1991 –)** is located on the left side innner fender battery next to the battery.

• **Engine Fan Relay (1990–early 91)** – is located in the relay holder, under a plastic cover, on the strut tower.

• **Engine Fan Relay (late 1991)** – is located in the power distrubution center, located behind the battery.

• **Engine Speed Sensor** – is located on the left side of the transmission converter housing, behind the rear face of the engine.

• **Fuel Injection Relays** – are located in a relay holder, under the driver's side of the instrument panel.

• **Fuel Level Sensor** – is located on the fuel sending unit, which is located in the fuel tank.

• **Fuel Pump Relay** – is located in the relay holder, under a plastic cover, on the strut tower.

• **Headlamp Module** – is located under the left side of the instrument panel.

• **Headlamp Relays** – are located in the relay block, which is located under the center of the instrument panel.

• **Heater-A/C Control Unit** – is usually attached to the heater housing, which is located under the instrument panel on the passenger's side of the vehicle.

• **Horn Relay** – is located in the relay block, which is located under the center of the instrument panel.

• **Idle Speed Regulator** – is usually located above the left hand cylinder head.

• **Ignition Control Module (ICM)** – is located in the engine compartment, under the ignition coil.

• **Ignition Relay (1990)** – is located in the relay holder, under a plastic cover, on the strut tower.

• **Illuminated Entry Module** – is usually located under the left side of the instrument panel, behind the glove box.

• **Illuminated Entry Relay** – is located in the relay block, located at the center of the instruemnt panel.

• **Interior Temperature Sensor** – is usually located under the center of the instrument panel.

• **Intermittent Wiper Module** – is usually attached to kick panel on the passenger's side of the vehicle or may be behind the glove box.

• **Keyless Entry Receiver** – is located above the windshield.

• **Knock Sensor** – is on the right side of the cylinder block above the motor mount.

• **Lamp Out Module** – is located in the luggage compartment, next to the right rear speaker.

• **Lighting Module** – is located behind the instrument panel, usually near the headlight switch.

• **Manifold Absolute Pressure Sensor (MAP)** – is located on the dash panel, next to the brake booster in the engine compartment.

• **Manifold Air Temperature Sensor (MAT)** – is located on the throttle body adapter, below the throttle body and behind the fitting for the brake booster.

• **Oil Level Sensor** – is located in the bottom of the engine block, near the motor mount on the passenger's side of the vehicle.

• **Oil Pressure Sensor** – is located in the engine block, next to the alternator.

• **Oxygen Sensor (O_2)** – is located in the exhaust pipe, before the catalytic converter.

• **Passive Restraint Diagnostic Connector (1991)** – is located on the left side of the trunk compartment.

• **Passive Restraint Relays** – may be located under either or both front seats.

• **Passive Restraint Module** – is located on the left side of the trunk compartment.

• **Power Deck Lid Release Actuator** – is located in the deck lid near the latch assembly.

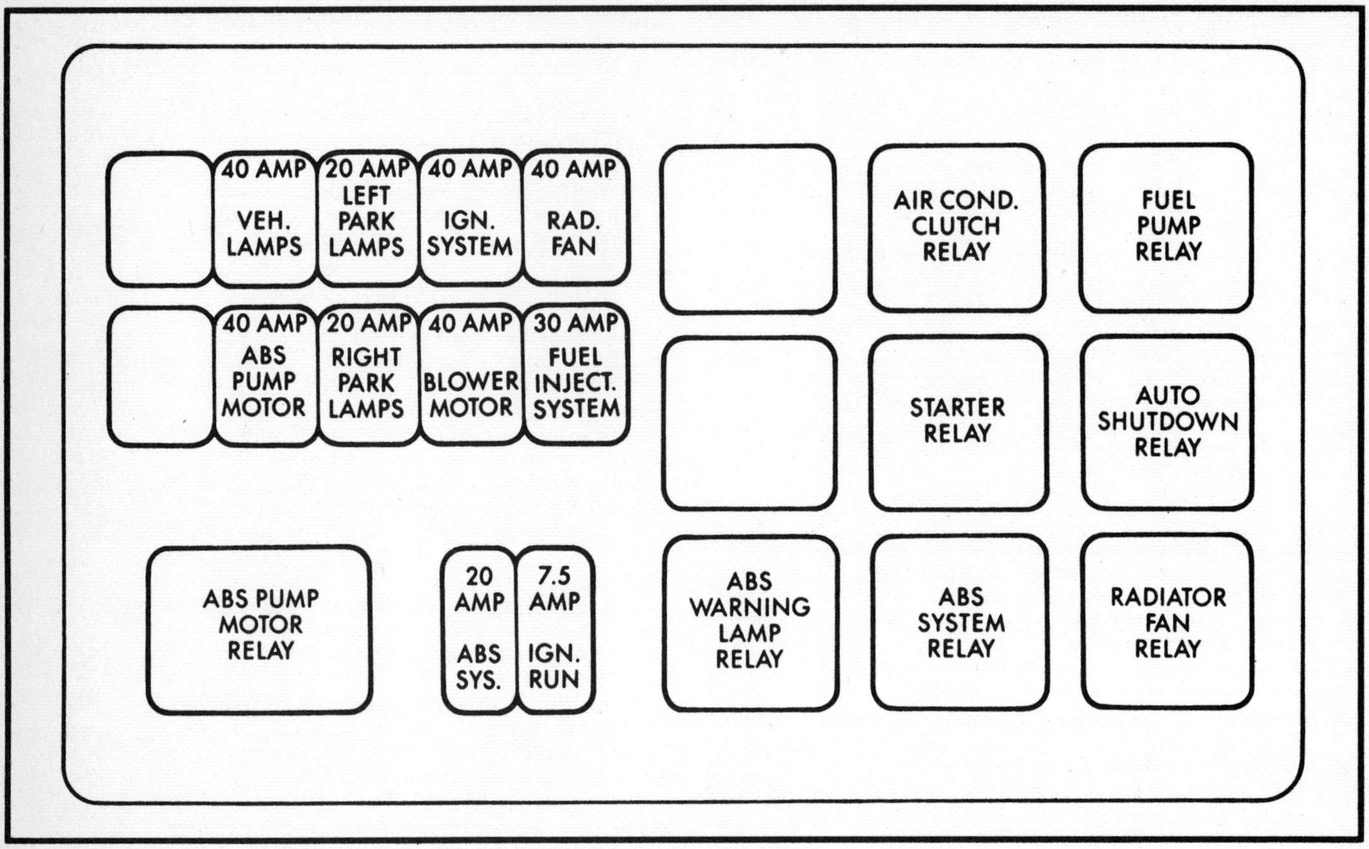

40 AMP
VEH. LAMPS
20 AMP
LEFT PARK LAMPS
40 AMP
IGN. SYSTEM
40 AMP
RAD. FAN
AIR COND. CLUTCH RELAY
FUEL PUMP RELAY
40 AMP
ABS PUMP MOTOR
20 AMP
RIGHT PARK LAMPS
40 AMP
BLOWER MOTOR
30 AMP
FUEL INJECT. SYSTEM
STARTER RELAY
AUTO SHUTDOWN RELAY
ABS PUMP MOTOR RELAY
20 AMP
ABS SYS.
7.5 AMP
IGN. RUN
ABS WARNING LAMP RELAY
ABS SYSTEM RELAY
RADIATOR FAN RELAY

Power Distribution Center component identification—1991 Monaco

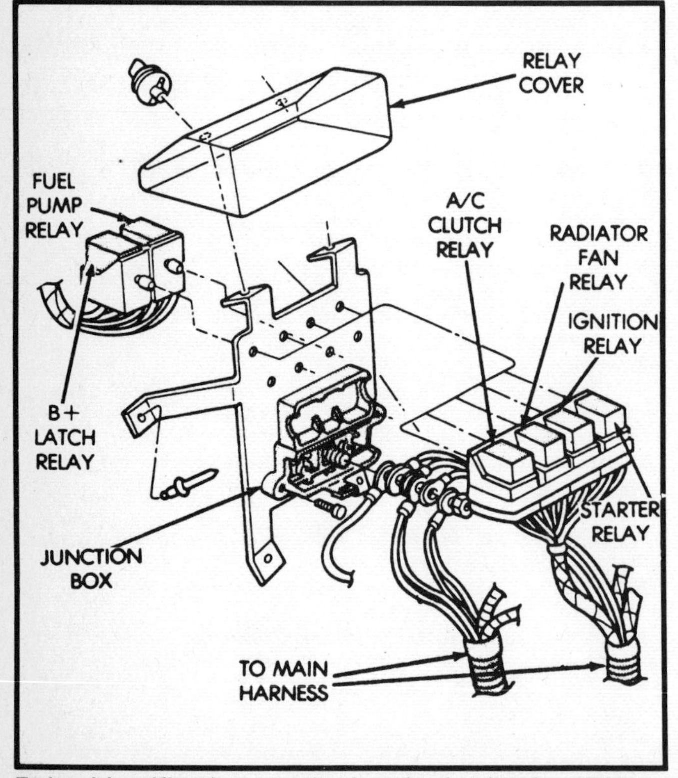

RELAY COVER
FUEL PUMP RELAY
A/C CLUTCH RELAY
RADIATOR FAN RELAY
IGNITION RELAY
B+ LATCH RELAY
STARTER RELAY
JUNCTION BOX
TO MAIN HARNESS

Relay identification—under-hood relay bank—1990–early 91 Monaco

A
K
B
J
C
H
D
G
E
F

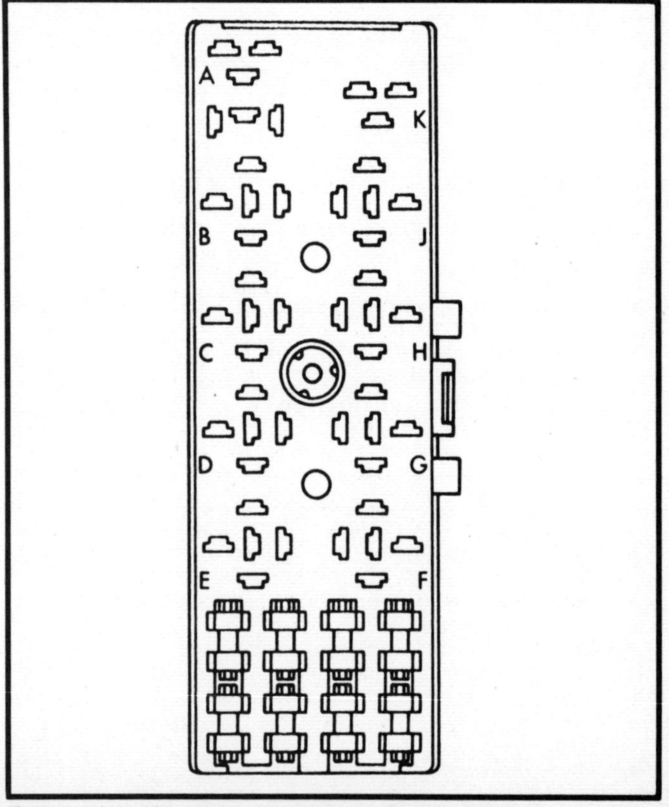

Relay identification—under-dash relay bank

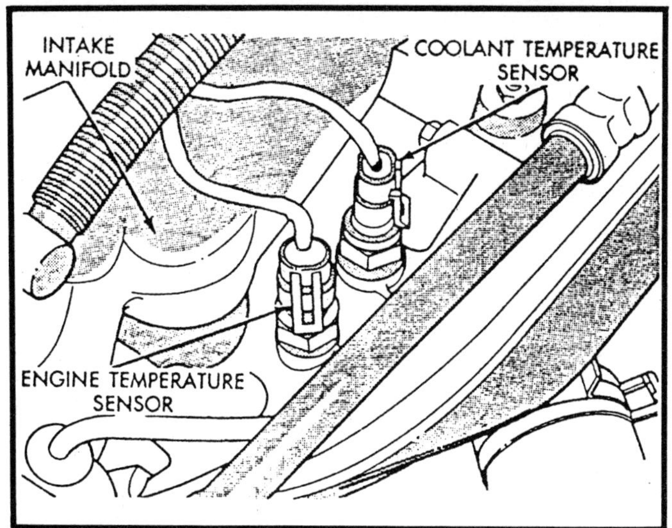

Coolant temperature and engine temperature sensors – 1991 Monaco

- **Power Door Lock Relay** – is located under the left side of the instrument panel.
- **Radio Lamp Relay (1990)** – is located in the relay block, which is located under the center of the instrument panel.
- **Rear Window Defogger Relay** – is located in the relay block, which is located under the center of the instrument panel.
- **Single Board Engine Controller (SBEC)** – is located on the left side inner fender panel, next to the battery.
- **Speed Sensor Module** – is located behind the instrument panel, usually located behind the speedometer.
- **Starter Motor Relay (1990–early 91)** – is located in the relay holder, under a plastic cover, on the strut tower.
- **Starter Motor Relay (late 1991)** – is located in the Power Distribution Center located behind the battery.
- **Stop Lamp/Cruise Cut Off Switch** – is located above the brake pedal on the pedal bracket.
- **Sunroof Relay** – is located on the sunroof motor, under the headliner.
- **Throttle Position Sensor (TPS)** – is attached to the throttle body.
- **Transmission Control Module (AR-4)** – is located in the engine compartment, mounted to the inner fender panel on the passenger's side of the vehicle.
- **Transmission Control Module (ZF-4)** – is located on the left rear portion of the transmission.
- **Trip Computer** – is located behind the instrument panel, next to the radio.
- **Trip Computer Ambient Temperature Sensor** – is located in the front grill, near the headlight on the driver's side of the vehicle.
- **Vehicle Maintenance Module** – is located behind the instrument panel, near the gauges.
- **Washer Fluid Level Sensor** – is located in the washer fluid reservoir, located in the engine compartment.

DODGE AND PLYMOUTH LIGHT TRUCKS AND VANS

Circuit Breakers

DAKOTA

HEADLIGHT SWITCH

There is one circuit breaker located in the headlight switch.

POWER WINDOWS

There is one 30 amp breaker located in fuse cavity No. 3 in the fuse block.

WINDSHIELD WIPER

Both standard and intermittent wipers use one 9 amp breaker located in the wiper switch.

FRONT WHEEL DRIVE

HEADLIGHT SWITCH

There is one circuit breaker located in the headlight switch.

POWER WINDOWS

There is one 30 amp breaker located in fuse cavity No. 3 in the fuse block.

POWER DOOR LOCKS

There is one 30 amp breaker located in fuse cavity No. 8 in the fuse block.

REAR WHEEL DRIVE EXCEPT DAKOTA

HEADLIGHT SWITCH

There is one 20 amp circuit breaker located in the headlight switch.

POWER WINDOWS

This breaker is one of two 30 amp breakers mounted on the steering column support. The other breaker is for the power door locks.

POWER DOOR LOCKS

This breaker is one of two 30 amp breakers mounted on the steering column support. The other breaker is for the power windows.

WINDSHIELD WIPER

Both standard and intermittent wipers use one 9 amp breaker built into the wiper motor.

Fusible Links

In addition to circuit breakers and fuses, some circuits use fusible links to protect the wiring. Like fuses, the fusible links are ONE TIME protection devices that will melt and create an open circuit.

Not all fusible link open circuits can be detected by observation. Always inspect that there is battery voltage passing through the fusible link to verify continuity.

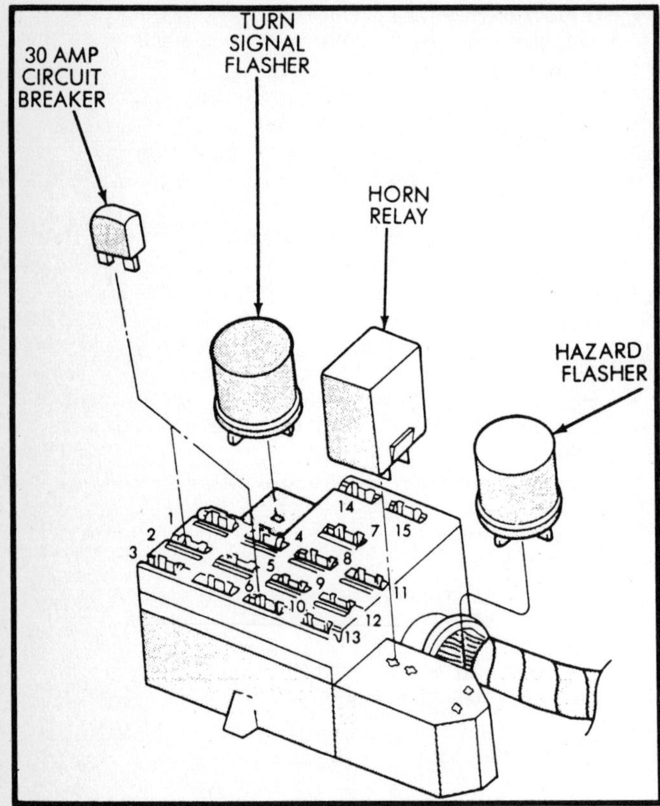

Fuse block—Ramcharger and pickups

NOTE: Do not replace blown fusible links with standard wire. Only fusible wire can be used or damage to the electrical system will occur. Make sure the correct gauge wiring is used.

When a fusible link blows it is very important to find out why it blew. They are placed in vehicle electrical systems for protection

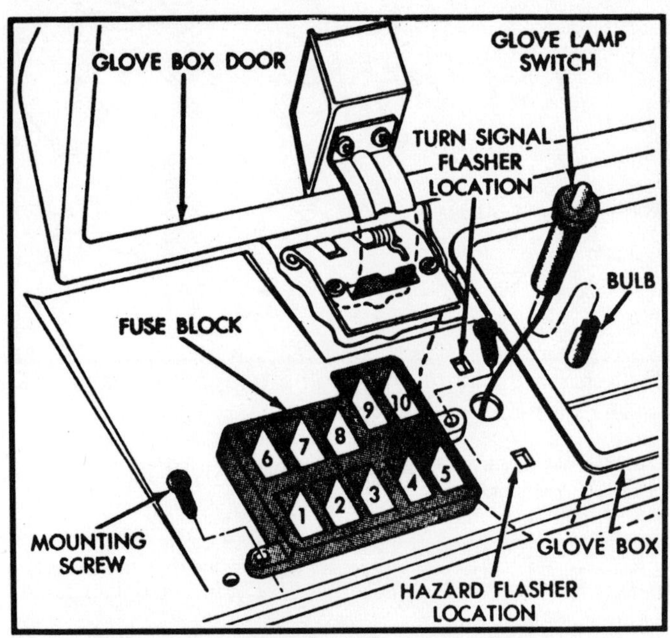

Turn signal and hazard light flashers—Rear wheel drive vans

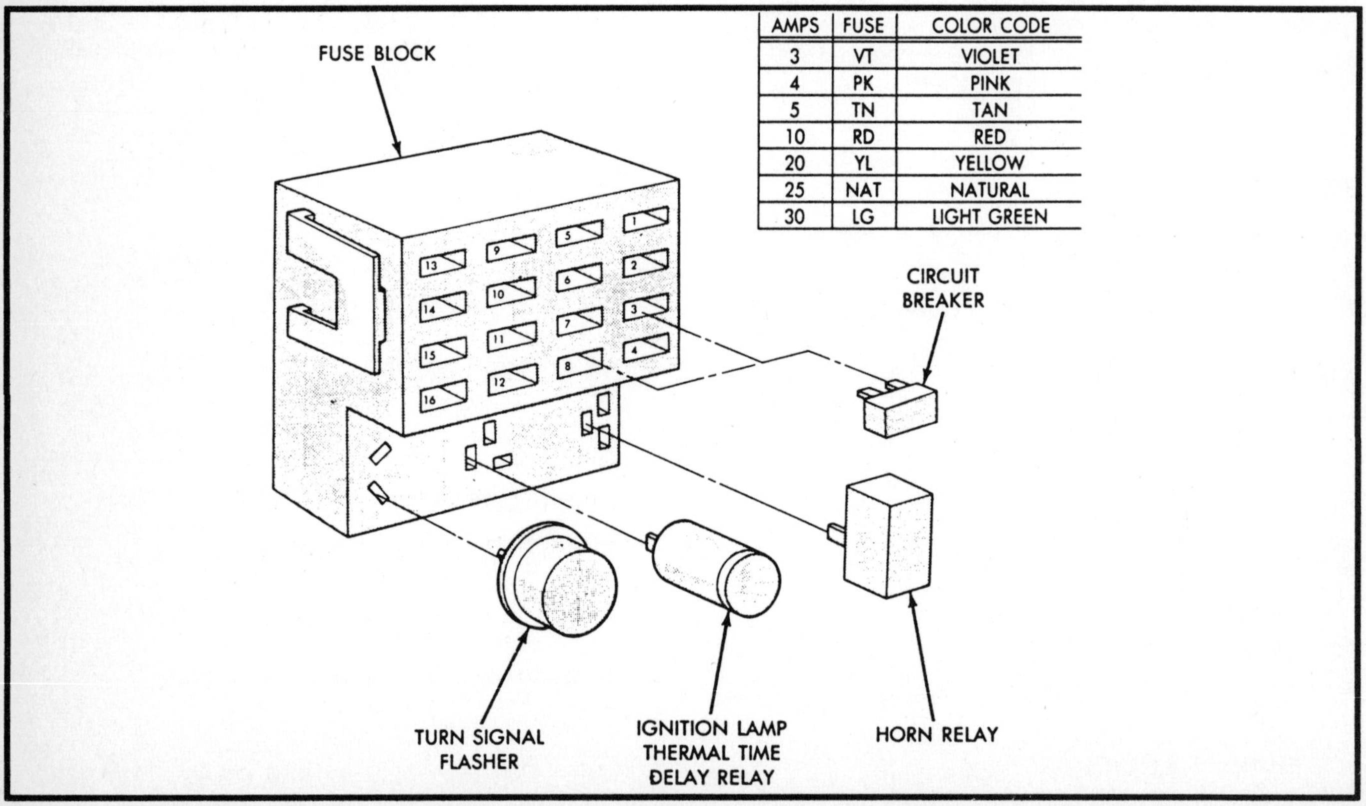

FUSE BLOCK

AMPS	FUSE	COLOR CODE
3	VT	VIOLET
4	PK	PINK
5	TN	TAN
10	RD	RED
20	YL	YELLOW
25	NAT	NATURAL
30	LG	LIGHT GREEN

CIRCUIT BREAKER

TURN SIGNAL FLASHER

IGNITION LAMP THERMAL TIME DELAY RELAY

HORN RELAY

Fuse block—FWD Caravan and Voyager

against dead shorts to ground which can be caused by electrical failure or various wiring failures. Do not just replace the fusible link to correct the problem.

DAKOTA

WHITE 22 GAUGE WIRE

This fusible link is one of several that ties into a main harness splice. It is located at the rear of the battery, on the driver's side front inner fender panel. It feeds fuse No. 1, the 20 amp fuse that powers the hazard flasher.

ORANGE 20 GAUGE WIRE

There are 3 orange fusible links at the main harness splice located at the rear of the battery, on the driver's side shock tower. One feeds fuse No. 14 for the instrument panel electrical components. Another feeds the air conditioning system, if equipped. The third orange wire feeds ignition switch.

GRAY 18 GAUGE WIRE

The are 2 gray fusible links located on the driver's side shock tower. One is a main feed fuse No. 5, the 20 amp fuse for the headlight switch, fuse No. 6, the 10 amp fuse for seatbelt buzzer and brakelights, fuse No. 7, the 15 amp fuse for the horn relay and cigarette lighter, and fuse No. 8, the 20 amp fuse for the power door locks, if equipped. The second gray fusible link connects to the ignition switch.

RED 14 GAUGE WIRE

This fusible link is located on the driver's side shock tower, on vehicles equipped with a 78 amp alternator. It connects to and protects the alternator and charging system. If equipped with a 120 amp alternator the vehicle will use a black 12 gauge wire.

BLACK 12 GAUGE WIRE

This fusible link is located on the driver's side shock tower, on vehicles equipped with a 120 amp alternator. It connects to and protects the alternator and charging system. If equipped with a 78 amp alternator the vehicle will use a red 14 gauge wire.

FRONT WHEEL DRIVE

WHITE 22 GAUGE WIRE

This fusible link is one of several that ties into a main harness splice. It is located at the rear of the battery, on the driver's side front inner fender panel. It feeds fuse No. 1, the 20 amp fuse that powers the hazard flasher.

ORANGE 20 GAUGE WIRE

There are 3 orange fusible links at the main harness splice located at the rear of the battery, on the driver's side shock tower. One feeds fuse No. 14 for the instrument panel electrical components. Another feeds the air conditioning system, if equipped. The third orange wire feeds ignition switch. Note that there could be some variation depending on engine model and if equipped with electronic transaxle.

GRAY 18 GAUGE WIRE

There are 3 gray fusible links located on the driver's side shock tower. One is a main feed to the headlight switch and fuse No. 5, the 20 amp fuse also for the headlight switch, fuse No. 6, the 20 amp fuse for the brakelights, fuse No. 7, the 25 amp fuse for the horn relay and cigarette lighter, and the circuit breaker that plugs into fuse cavity No. 8, the 30 amp breaker fuse for the power seats, power door locks and power mirrors, if equipped. The second gray fusible link connects to the rear defogger and fuse No. 15, the 10 amp fuse protecting a number of courtesy lamps, fuse No. 13 protecting most of the instrument panel indicator lights and fuse No. 14, the 20 amp fuse protecting the liftgate release relay, rear wiper and other circuits. The third gray fusible link goes to the ignition switch.

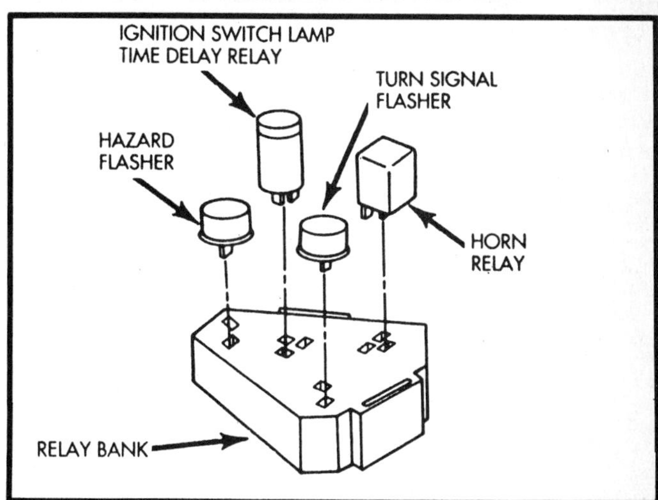

Flasher and relay module—1991 vans

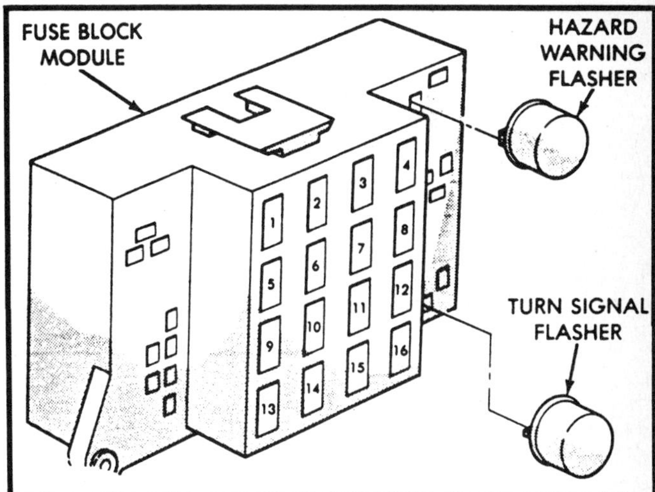

Turn signal and hazard light flashers—Dakota

BLACK 12 GAUGE WIRE

This fusible link is also located on the driver's side shock tower and goes to the alternator.

REAR WHEEL DRIVE EXCEPT DAKOTA

PINK 14 GAUGE WIRE

This fusible link is connected to the battery positive side, is located on the driver's side cowl panel and feeds fuse No. 10, a 20 amp fuse that powers the hazard flasher.

GRAY 18 GAUGE WIRE

There are two gray fusible links, both at the driver's side cowl panel. One feeds the headlamp switch and some other accessories, the other gray fusible link goes to the heated rear window as well as fuse No. 8, the 20 amp fuse that powers the radio and most of the courtesy lamps.

BLACK 12 GAUGE WIRE

This is another of the fusible links at the common connection on the driver's side cowl panel. It is connected to the charging system.

ORANGE 20 GAUGE WIRE

There are two orange fusible links, both at the driver's side cowl panel and both go to the ignition switch.

Relays, Sensors, Switches, Modules and Computers Locations

NOTE: When using this section, some of the components may not be used on a particular vehicle. This is because either the particular component in question was used on an earlier model or later model. This section is being published from the latest information available at the time of publication.

DAKOTA

- **A/C Clutch Relay**—is located on the driver's side fender shield.
- **A/C Low-Pressure Cut-Off Switch**—is located on the H-valve (expansion valve) on the dash panel, right side.
- **A/C Electronic Fin-Sensed Cycling Clutch Switch (Sensor)**—is located in the evaporator housing on the evaporator fins.
- **Air Switching Solenoid (3.9L engine)**—is located at the right rear on top of the engine (blue seal).
- **Anti-lock Brake System**—see Rear Wheel Anti-Lock (RWAL).
- **A/T Neutral Start and Back-Up Switch**—is located on the transmission.
- **Automatic Idle Speed Solenoid (2.5L engine)**—is located on the throttle body.
- **Auto Shutdown Relay (Fuel Pump Relay)**—is located on the left fender side shield on both 2.5L and 3.9L engines.
- **Brake Warning Lamp Switch**—is located on the left front frame rail.
- **Distance Sensor**—is located on the rear of the transmission.
- **Dome and Courtesy Lamp Time Delay Relay**—is located on the fuseblock.

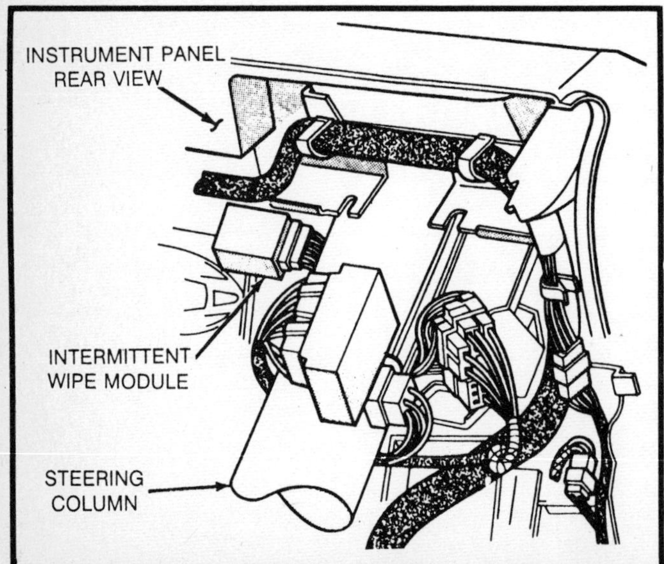

Intermittent wipe module—Dakota

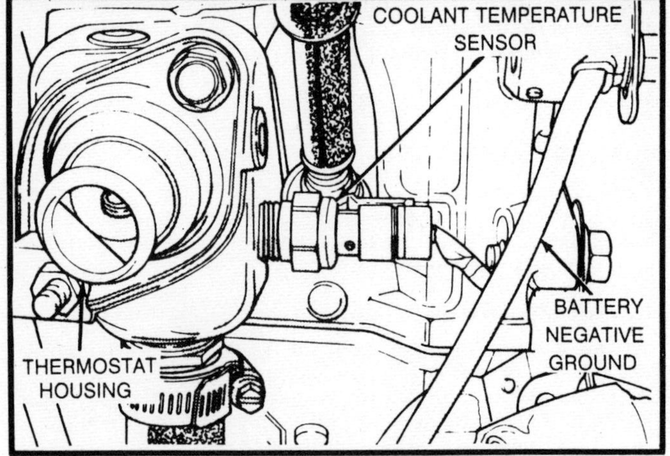

Coolant temperature sensor—Dakota with 2.5L engine

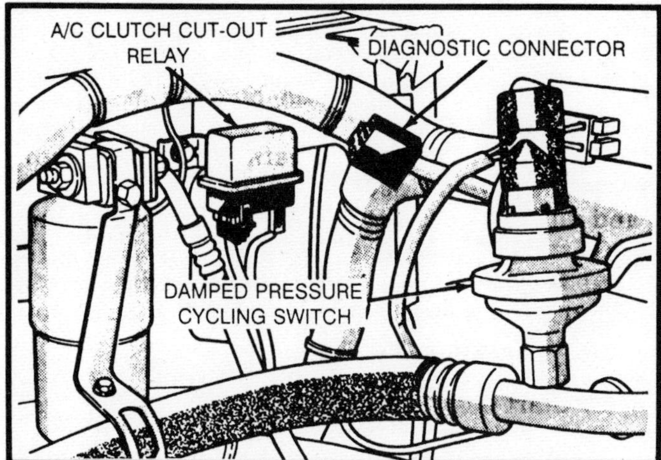

Diagnostic connector location for Chrysler DRBII diagnostic tool—Dakota

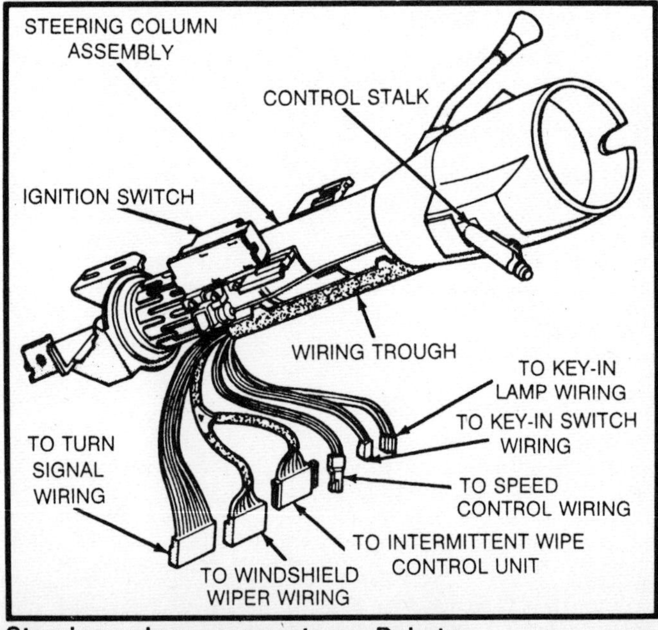

Steering column connectors—Dakota

- **Engine Coolant Sensor (2.5L engine)** – is located at the top left rear of the engine.
- **Engine Coolant Sensor (3.9L engine)** – is located at the top left front of the engine.
- **Exhaust Gas Recirculation Solenoid (2.5L engine)** – is located at the right fender side shield (blue seal).
- **Exhaust Gas Recirculation Solenoid (3.9L engine)** – is located at the right rear on top of the engine (red seal).
- **Four-Speed A/T Overdrive Solenoid and Part Throttle Unlock** – is located on the transmission.
- **Four Wheel Drive Indicator Switch (3.9L engine)** – is located on the right front axle.
- **Fuel Pump (Auto Shutdown) Relay** – is located on the left fender side shield.
- **Fuel Tank Sending Unit With Low Fuel Switch and Pump** – is located in the fuel tank.
- **Hazard Flasher** – is located in the fuseblock on the upper right side.
- **Heated Oxygen Sensor** – is located in the center of the engine exhaust manifold on both 2.5L and 3.9L engines.
- **Heater Blower Motor Resistor** – is located on the right side of the heater plenum.
- **Horn Relay** – is located on the fuseblock, left upper.
- **Ignition Switch** – is located on the steering column.

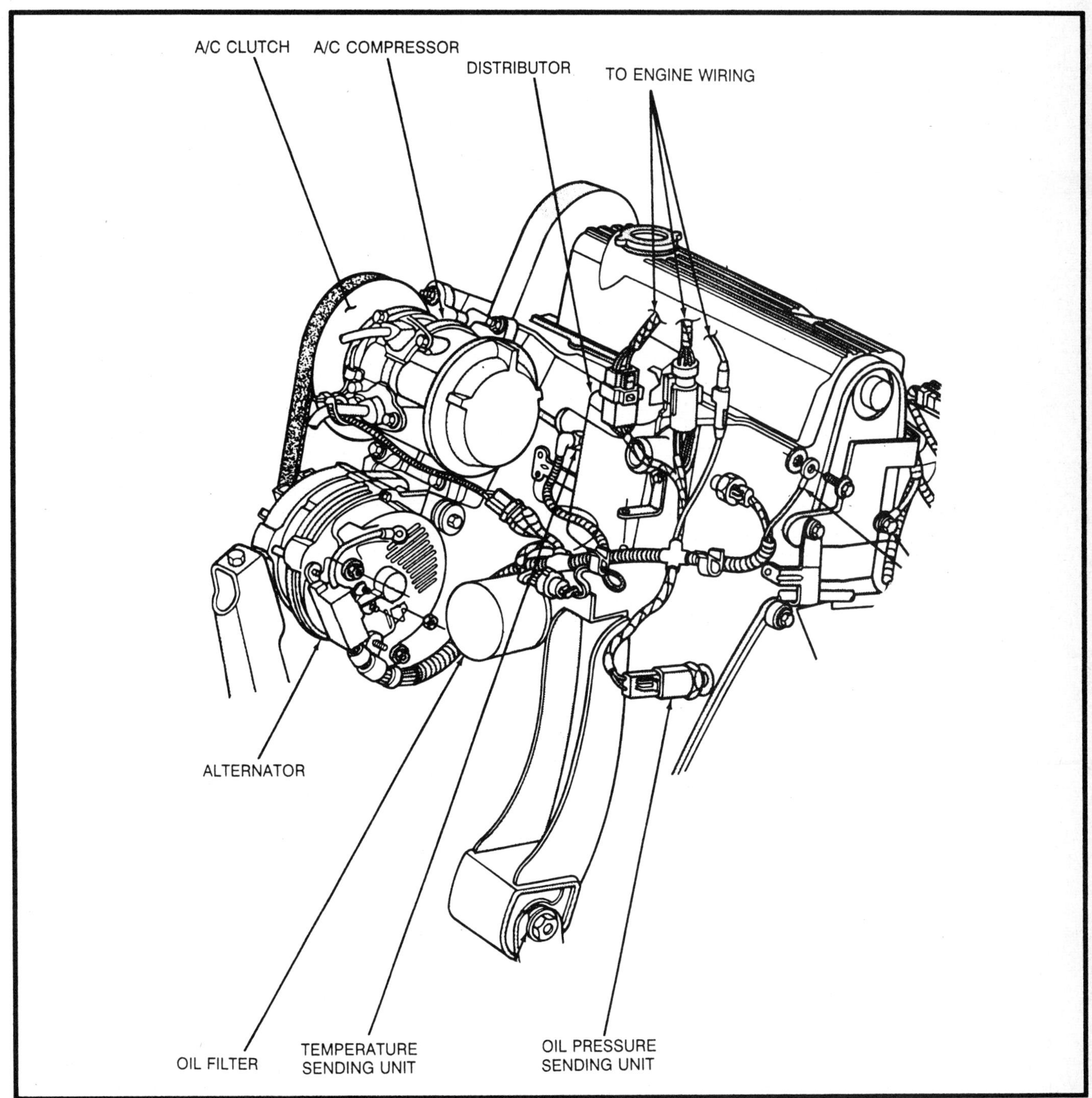

Engine wiring and component identification – Dakota with 2.5L engine

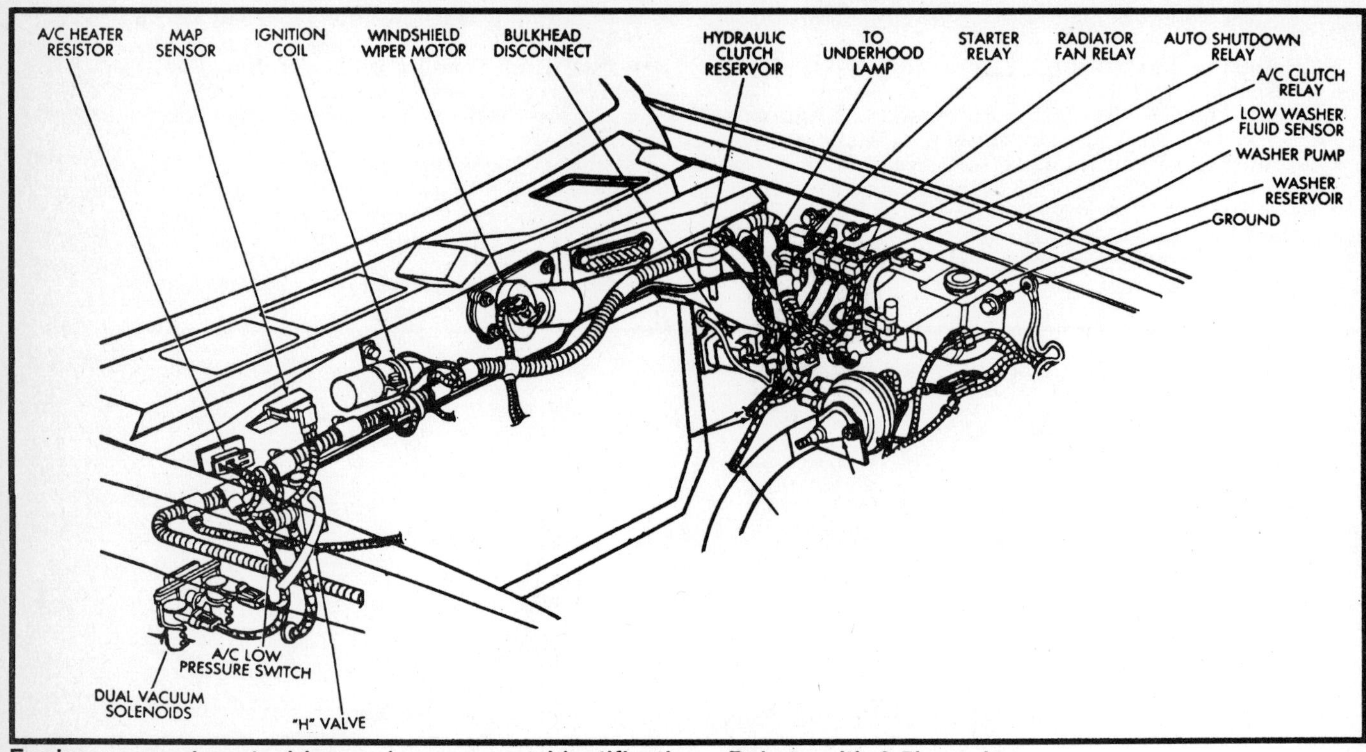

Engine compartment wiring and component identification – Dakota with 2.5L engine

- **Intermittent Wiper Control Unit** – is mounted on a bracket under the steering column.
- **M/T Back-Up Lamp Switch** – is located on the transmission.
- **Manifold Absolute Pressure (MAP) Sensor (2.5L engine)** – is located on the right dash panel.
- **Manifold Absolute Pressure (MAP) Sensor (3.9L engine)** – is located at the top of the throttle body injector.
- **Oil Pressure Switch and Sending Unit (2.5L engine)** – is located on the left side of the engine, rear of the oil filter and motor mount bracket.
- **Oil Pressure Switch and Sending Unit (3.9L engine)** – is located at the top rear of the engine, next to the distributor.
- **Oil Temperature Sending Unit (2.5L engine)** – is located at the left front of the engine.
- **Oil Temperature Sending Unit (3.9L engine)** – is located at the right front of the engine.
- **Oxygen Sensor (Heated)** – is located in the center of the engine exhaust manifold.
- **Parking Brake Switch** – is located on the parking brake.
- **Purge Solenoid (2.5L engine)** – is located at the right fender side shield (red seal).
- **Purge Solenoid (3.9L engine)** – is located at the right rear on top of the engine (green seal).
- **Radiator Fan Relay** – is located on the left fender side shield.
- **Rear Wheel Anti-lock (RWAL) Brake Module** – is located on the right hand side cowl.
- **Rear Wheel Anti-lock (RWAL) Brake Diagnostic Connector** – is located on the left wheelhouse.
- **Rear Wheel Anti-lock (RWAL) Brake Pressure Limiting Valve** – is located on the left frame rail.
- **Reference Ground (2.5L engine)** – is located at the center top rear of the engine.
- **Reference Ground (3.9L engine)** – is located at the center top of the engine.
- **Service Diagnostic Connector** – is located on the lower right side cowl.
- **Single Module Engine Controller (SMEC)** – is located on the right fender side shield.
- **Speed Control Servo** – is located on the left fender shield.
- **Starter Relay** – is located on the left shock housing.
- **Stop Lamp and Speed Control Switch With Speed Control** – is located on the steering column support.
- **Stop Lamp Switch Without Speed Control** – is located on the left of the brake bracket.
- **Throttle Body Temperature Sensor (2.5L engine)** – is located on the throttle body.
- **Throttle Kicker Motor (3.9L engine)** – is located on the throttle body at the left front of the engine.
- **Throttle Position Sensor** – is located on top of the throttle body injector on both 2.5L and 3.9L engines.
- **Transmission Oil Temperature Sender (3.9L engine)** – is located in the cooler line by the radiator.
- **Turn Signal Flasher** – is located in the fuseblock, bottom.
- **Windshield Washer Low Fluid Level Sensor** – is located in the top of the washer reservoir.

FRONT WHEEL DRIVE

- **A/C Ambient Temperature Sensor (3.0L engine)** – is located at the front of the vehicle.
- **A/C Blower Motor** – is located under the instrument panel on the right side.
- **A/C Condenser Fan Motor** – is located at the front of the car, next to the condenser.
- **A/C Condenser Fan Motor Relay** – is located on the left fender side shield.
- **A/C Fan Cut-Out Switch (3.0L engine)** – is located on the left fender side shield.

• **A/C Low Pressure Cut-Out Switch**–is located on the H-Valve on the dash panel right side.

• **Automatic Idle Speed Relay**–is mounted on the throttle body.

• **Automatic Shutdown Relay (2.5L engine)**–is located the left fender side shield.

• **Automatic Transaxle Neutral Start and Back-Up Lamp Switch**–is located on the transaxle.

• **Back-Up Lamp Relay**–is located at the right rear side fender of the engine compartment.

• **Back-Up Lamp Switch, Manual Transaxle**–is located on the transaxle.

• **Brake Warning Lamp Switch**–is located on the left side frame below the master cylinder.

• **Detonation Sensor (2.5L engine)**–is located at the rear of the valve cover on the top of the engine.

• **Diagnostic Connector**–is located on the front of the left shock tower.

• **Distance Sensor**–is located on the rear of transmission.

• **EGR Solenoid (3.0L engine)**–is located on the left fender side shield.

• **Electronic Automatic Transaxle Control Module**–is located on the right fender side shield.

• **Engine Coolant Temperature Sender (2.5L engine)**–is located on the top left of the engine.

• **Engine Coolant Sensor (3.0L engine)**–is located on the top left of the engine.

• **Exhaust Gas Recirculation Diagnostic Solenoid**–is located on the front of the right side shield.

• **Fuel Tank Sending Unit With Low Fuel Switch**–is located on the top of the fuel tank.

• **Fuel Pump (Auto Shutdown) Relay (2.5L engine)**–is located the left fender side shield.

• **Hazard Flasher**–is located on the fuseblock.

• **Headlamp Dimmer Switch**–is located on the steering column.

• **Heater Blower Motor Resistor Block**–is located in the engine compartment plenum-right side.

• **Horn Relay**–is located on the fuseblock.

• **Intermittent Wiper Control Unit**–is bracket mounted under the steering column.

• **Liftgate Release Relay**–is located on the instrument panel below the fuse block.

• **Liftgate Release Solenoid**–is located at the center of the rear liftgate.

• **Liftgate Release Switch**–is located on the instrument panel on the left side.

• **Manifold Absolute Pressure (MAP) Sensor**–is located on the right shock tower.

• **Oil Pressure Switch (3.0L engine)**–is located on the side of the oil filter.

• **Oil Pressure Switch (3.0L engine)**–is located on the left side of the engine.

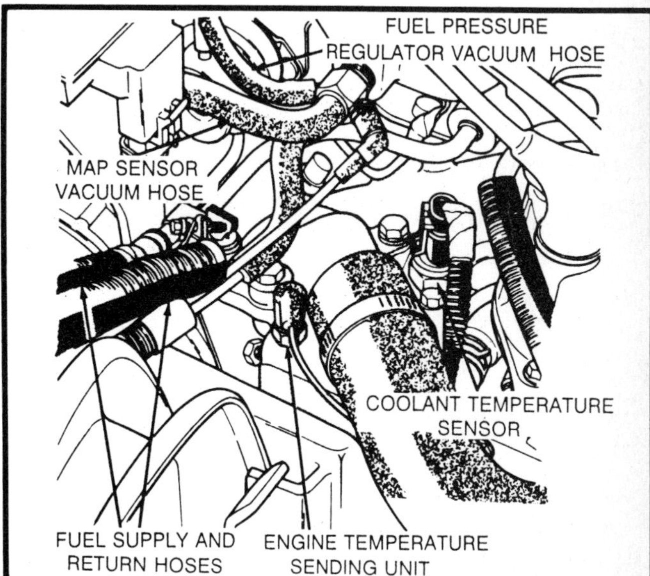

Coolant temperature sensor, 3.0L engine–Caravan and Voyager

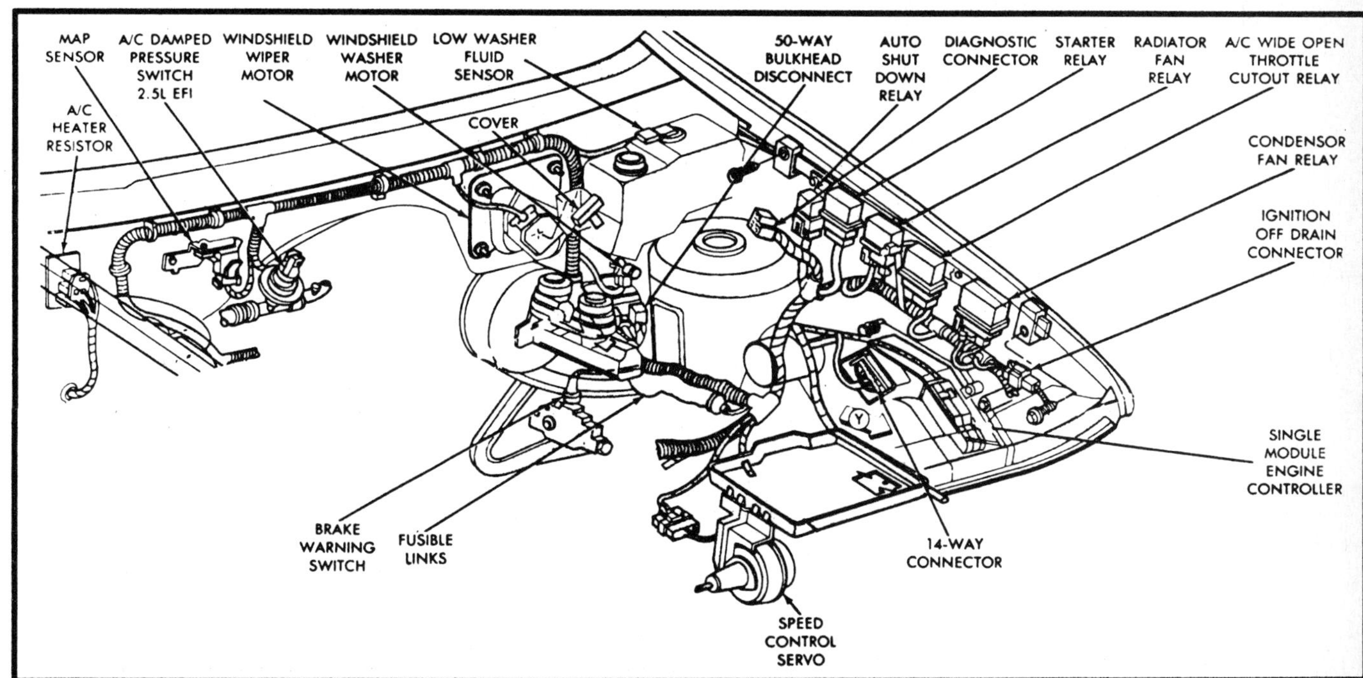

Engine compartment wiring and component identification, 2.5L and 3.0L engines–Caravan and Voyager

- **Output Speed Sensor** – is located on the front of the electronic transaxle.
- **Oxygen Sensor** – is located on the center of the engine exhaust manifold.
- **Parking Brake Switch** – is located on the parking brake assembly.
- **Part Throttle Unlock Switch** – is located on the front left of the transaxle.
- **Purge Solenoid** – is located on the front of the right side shield.
- **Radiator Fan Motor** – is located at the front of the car next to the radiator.
- **Radiator Fan Motor Relay** – is located on the left shock tower.
- **Rear Heater and A/C Assembly (including Switch and Resistor)** – is located behind the driver's seat.
- **Rear Window Defogger Timer** – is built into the mechanical on/off switch
- **Safety Shutdown Mini-Relay for Electronic Transaxle** – is located on the right fender side shield.
- **Single Module Engine Controlled (SMEC)** – is located on the left fender side shield.
- **Speed Control Servo** – is located under the battery tray.
- **Starter Relay** – is located on the left shock housing.
- **Stop Lamp and Speed Control Switch** – is located on the steering column support.
- **Stop Lamp Switch** – is located on the brake support bracket.
- **Temperature Sending Unit** – is located at the front of the engine.
- **Throttle Position Sensor** – is located on the right side of the throttle body.
- **Throttle Body Temperature Sensor** – is located on the throttle body.
- **Turbine Speed Sensor** – is located on the front of the electronic transaxle.
- **Turn Signal Flasher** – is mounted on the fuseblock.
- **Wastegate Solenoid (2.5L Turbocharged engine)** – is located on the front of the right shock tower.
- **Wide Open Throttle Relay** – is located on the left fender side shield.
- **Windshield Washer Low Fluid Level Sensor** – is located at the top of the windshield washer reservoir.
- **Windshield Wiper Intermittent Control Unit** – is located under the instrument panel on the right side of the steering column.

REAR WHEEL DRIVE EXCEPT DAKOTA

- **A/C Cut-Out Relay** – is located on the left side of the dash panel, near the Part Throttle Unlock Relay.
- **A/C Low Pressure Switch** – is located on the right fender side shield.
- **A/C Resistor** – is located in the right side of the plenum.
- **Air Switching Vacuum Solenoid (Blue Seal)** – is located near the right fender panel.
- **Anti-Lock Brake Test Connector** – is clipped to the steering column bracket.
- **Auto Shutdown Relay (Feeds Fuel Pump)** – is located on a bracket below the 50-way bulkhead disconnect fitting.
- **Back-Up Lamp Switch (Manual Transmission)** – is located on the transmission.
- **Brake Warning Switch** – is located on the left side frame panel.
- **Coolant Temperature Sensor** – is next to the thermostat housing on the intake manifold.
- **Distance Sensor** – is located at the rear of the transmission.
- **Emission Maintenance Light** – is reset using the diagnostic connector and the DRB–II tester.
- **EGR Solenoid** – is located near the EGR valve mounting or in the solenoid valve trio-assembly next to the canister purge and air switching solenoids.
- **Flasher and Relay Module (1991)** – is located above the steering column bracket.
- **Fuel Pump (Auto Shutdown) Relay** – is located on a bracket below the 50-way bulkhead disconnect fitting.
- **Fuel Tank Sending Unit and Pump, With EFI Ignition** – is located in fuel tank.
- **Hazard Warning Flasher (except van)** – is located on the right side of the fuse block, near the steering column.
- **Hazard Warning Flasher (van except 1991)** – is located to the right of the glove box.
- **Hazard Warning Flasher (1991 van)** – is mounted in the relay module, near the steering column.
- **Headlamp, Key-In, Seatbelt Combination Buzzer** – is located near the bulkhead connector.
- **Heated Rear Window Defogger Relay** – is located to the right of the steering column.
- **Heater Blower Motor** – is located on the right side dash panel.
- **Heater Resistor** – is located in the right side plenum.
- **Horn and Headlamp Dimmer Switch** – is mounted on the steering column.
- **Horn Relay (vans except 1991)** – is mounted near the bulkhead or near the steering column.
- **Horn Relay (1991 van)** – is mounted in the relay module, near the steering column.
- **Horn Relay (except van)** – is mounted in the fuse box.
- **Ignition Lamp Relay (1991 van)** – is mounted iin the relay module, near the steering column.
- **Intermittent Wiper Control Unit** – is bracket mounted under the steering column.
- **Manifold Absolute Pressure (MAP) Sensor** – is located on the rear of the throttle body.
- **Neutral Safety and Back-Up Lamp Switch** – is located on the transmission.
- **Neutral Safety and Back-Up Lamp Switch** – is located on the transmission.
- **Oil Pressure Sensor** – is located next to the distributor.
- **Overdrive Lockout Solenoid** – is located on the transmission.
- **Oxygen Sensor** – is located in the center of the engine exhaust pipe.
- **Parking Brake Switch** – is located on the parking brake assembly.
- **Part Throttle Unlock Relay** – is located on the left side of the dash panel, used on vehicle with a 3-speed automatic transmission.
- **Part Throttle Unlock Solenoid** – is located at the rear of the transmission, used on vehicle with a 3-speed automatic transmission.
- **Power Door Lock Circuit Breaker** – is mounted on the brake bracket.
- **Power Door Lock Relay** – is mounted on the brake bracket or steering column support.
- **Power Window Circuit Breaker** – is mounted on the brake bracket.
- **Purge Vacuum Solenoid (Green Seal)** – is located near the right fender panel.
- **Rear Heater Relay (Auxiliary)** – is taped to the wiring harness, left of the steering column.
- **Relay and Flasher Module (1991)** – is located above the steering column bracket.
- **Single Module Engine Controller (SMEC)** – is located in the center of the dash panel.
- **Speed Control Servo** – is located on the left top of the radiator yoke.
- **Starter Relay** – is located on the left side of the dash panel.

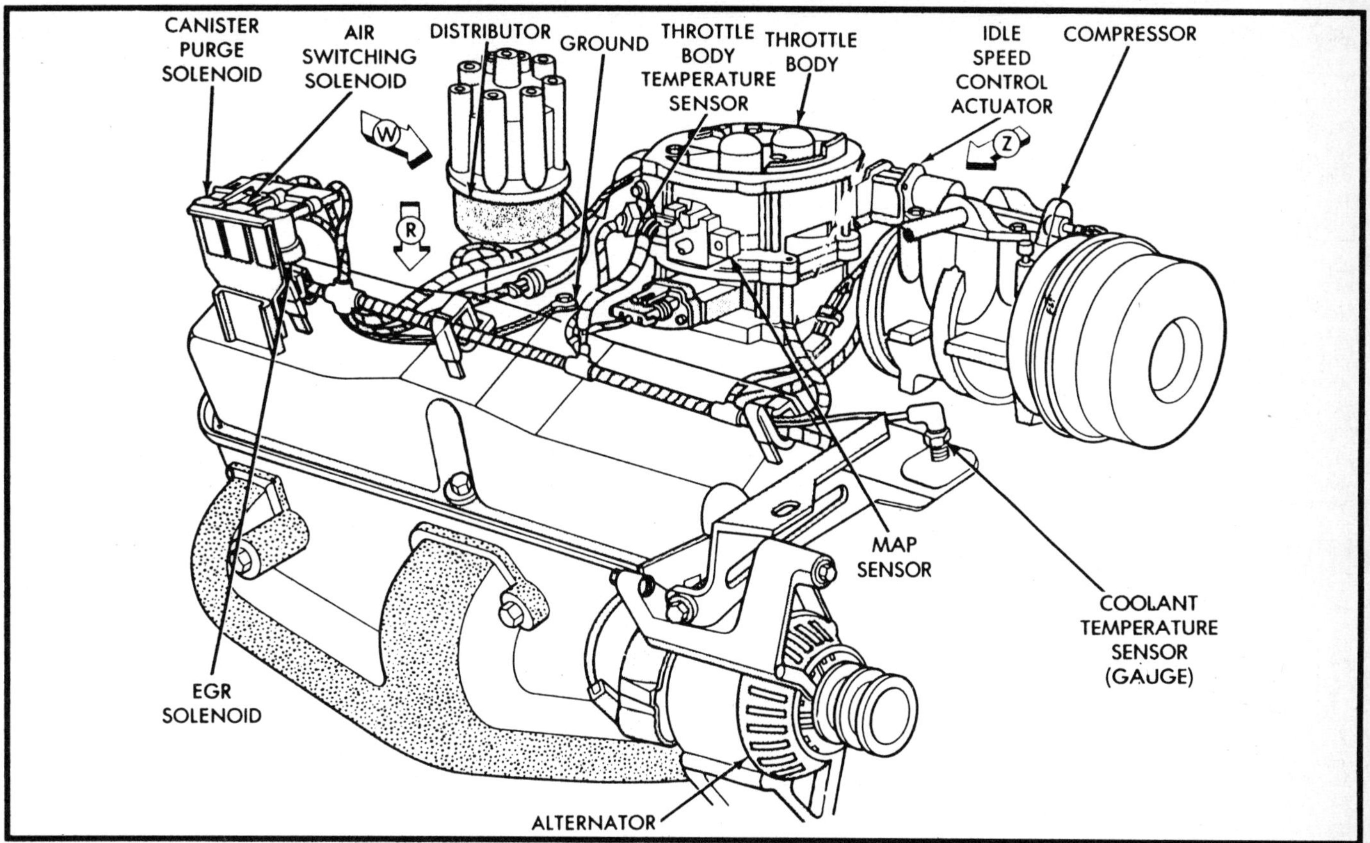

CANISTER PURGE SOLENOID
AIR SWITCHING SOLENOID
DISTRIBUTOR
GROUND
THROTTLE BODY TEMPERATURE SENSOR
THROTTLE BODY
IDLE SPEED CONTROL ACTUATOR
COMPRESSOR
W
R
Z
MAP SENSOR
COOLANT TEMPERATURE SENSOR (GAUGE)
EGR SOLENOID
ALTERNATOR

Engine Component locations—Typical rear wheel drive

WINDSHIELD WIPER MOTOR
A/C CLUTCH RELAY
TO ENGINE WIRING
FUSIBLE LINKS
IGNITION-OFF DRAW CONNECTOR
HEADLAMP GROUND
TO BATTERY
FUEL PUMP RELAY
Z
PART THROTTLE UNLOCK RELAY
STARTER RELAY
R.W.A.L. GROUND

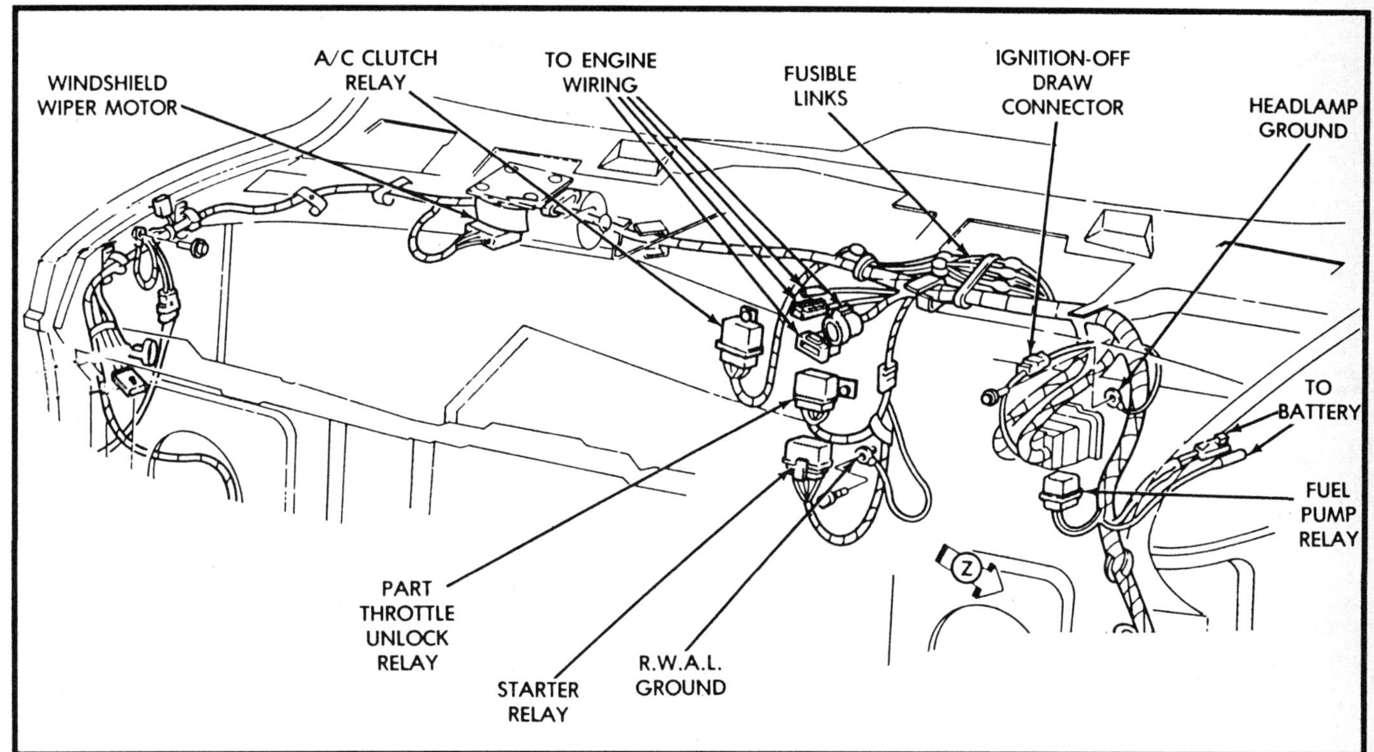

Engine compartment wiring and component identification—1991 Rear wheel drive vans

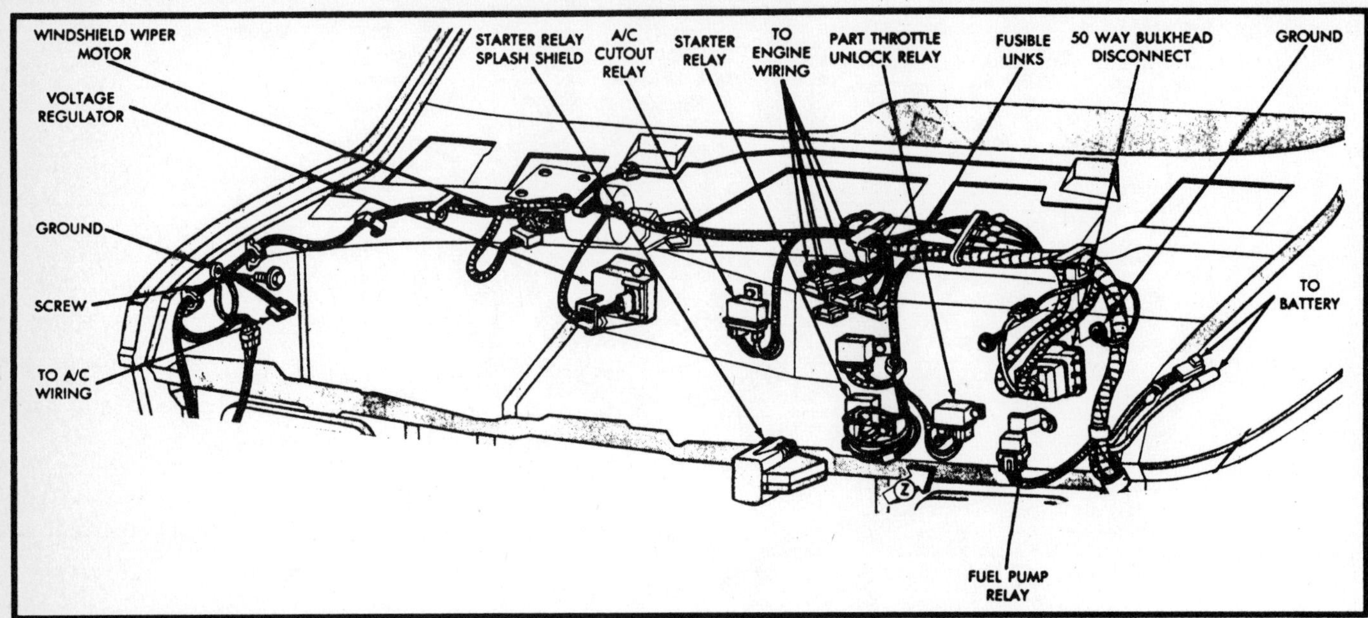

Engine compartment wiring and component identification—1989–90 Rear wheel drive vans

• **Stop Lamp Switch (Without Electronic Speed Control)**—is located on the steering column support.

• **Stop Lamp and Speed Control Switch (With Electronic Speed Control)**—is located on the steering column support.

• **Temperature Sending Unit**—is located at the front of the engine.

• **Throttle Body Temperature Sensor**—is located on the throttle body, 5.2L and 5.9L engines.

• **Throttle Position Sensor**—is located on the top of the throttle body injector.

• **Time Delay Relay (Dome and Courtesy Lights)**—is located on the left cowl side.

• **Turn Signal Flasher (except van)**—is located on the right of the fuse block.

• **Turn Signal Flasher (van except 1991)**—is located next to the fuse box.

• **Turn Signal Flasher (1991 van)**—is mounted in the relay module, near the steering column.

• **Wide Open Throttle Cut-Out Relay**—is located on the left fender side shield.

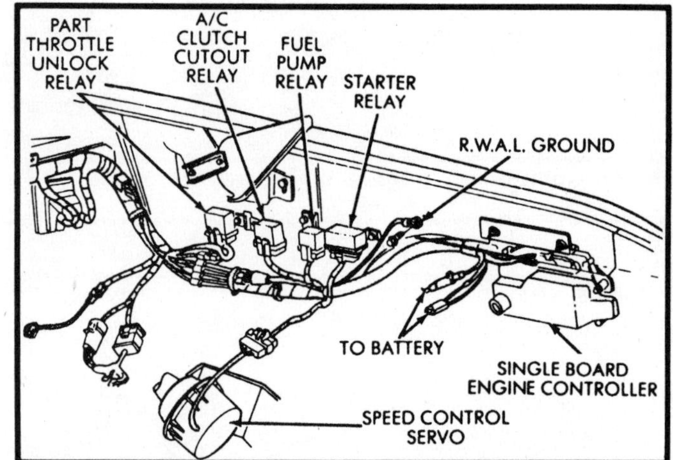

Relay locations—Rear wheel drive pickups and Ramcharger

EAGLE

Fusible Links and Circuit Breakers

PREMIER

HEADLAMPS

There is one 10.5 amp breaker located in the fuse block.

POWER SEAT AND POWER DOOR LOCKS

There is one 30 amp breaker located in the fuse block.

POWER SUNROOF AND INTERMITTENT WIPERS

There is one 30 amp breaker located in the fuse block.

POWER DOOR LOCKS

There is one 30 amp breaker located in the fuse block.

SUMMIT

Fusible links are located in the main relay box, next to the battery.

MPI

The fusible link is in the main relay box at battery—20 amp—blue

HEADLAMPS

The fusible link is in the main relay box at the battery—40 amp—green

RADIATOR FAN MOTOR

The fusible link is in the main relay box at the battery – 30 or 40 amp – pink or green

IGNITION CIRCUIT

The fusible link is in the main relay box at the battery – 40 amp – green

ALTERNATOR CIRCUIT

The fusible link is in the main relay box at the battery – 80 or 100 amp – black or blue

MULTI-PURPOSE FUSE SUPPLY

The fusible link is in the main relay box at the battery – 40 amp – green

POWER WINDOW CIRCUIT

The fusible link is in the main relay box at the battery – 30 amp – pink

DEFOGGER CIRCUIT

The fusible link is in the main relay box at the battery – 30 amp – pink

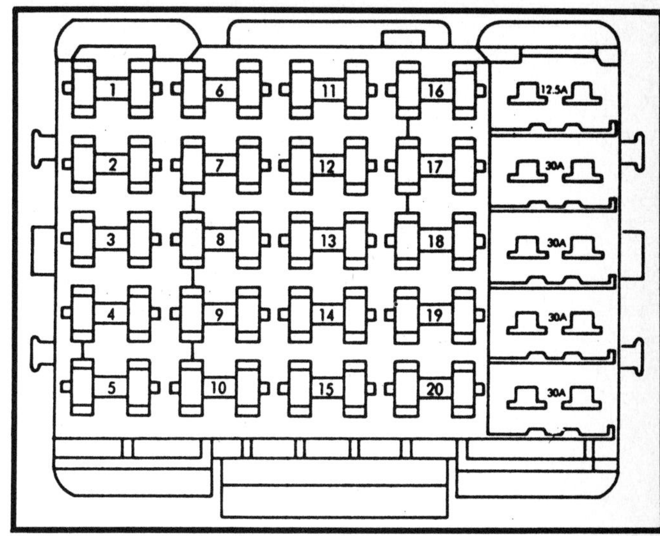

Fuse box – Premier

CAVITY	FUSE/ COLOR	ITEMS FUSED
1		
2	15 AMP BLUE	MIRRORS, CHIME, IOD,VMM, COURTESY LAMPS, TRIP COMPUTER RADIO, DECKLID RELEASE, KEYLESS ENTRY, DOME LAMP, ILL. ENTRY MODULE, UNDERHOOD-GLOVE BOX-TRUNK LAMPS, VDS MODULE
3	5 AMP ORANGE	BACK-UP LAMPS
4	5 AMP ORANGE	VANITY LAMPS
5	20 AMP YELLOW	RADIO, CIGAR LIGHTER, RADIO LAMP
6	5 AMP ORANGE	
7	7.5 AMP VIOLET	AUTOMATIC TRANSMISSION
8	15 AMP BLUE	TRIP COMPUTER, VMM, CHIME SYSTEM ILLUMINATION ENTRY, REAR DEFOGGER RELAY BACK-UP LAMPS, CLOCK, TRANSMISSION COMPUTER (IGNITION)
9	15 AMP BLUE	LAMP CONTROL SYSTEM (IGNITION)
10	10 AMP RED	INSTRUMENT CLUSTER DISPLAYS, HEATER CONTROLS LAMP OUTAGE MODULE, HEATER A/C CONTROLS, PASSIVE RESTRAINT MODULE
11		
12	20 AMP YELLOW	STOP/TURN, HAZARD, PARK, SIDE MARKER AND LICENSE LAMPS (LEFT SIDE)
13	3 AMP VIOLET	INSTRUMENT PANEL ILLUMINATION LCD
14	3 AMP VIOLET	INSTRUMENT PANEL ILLUMINATION, CLOCK, HEATER REAR WINDOW
15	10 AMP RED	INSTRUMENT CLUSTER
16	30 AMP GREEN	REAR DEFOGGER, POWER ANTENNA
17		
18	20 AMP YELLOW	STOP/TURN, PARK, SIDE MARKER AND LICENSE LAMPS (RIGHT SIDE)
19	10 AMP RED	(BATTERY) PASSIVE RESTRAINT SYSTEM
20	20 AMP WHITE	STOP/TURN, HAZARD, PARK, SIDE MARKER AND LICENSE LAMPS (RIGHT SIDE)
21	CIRCUIT BREAKER	HEADLAMPS
22	CIRCUIT BREAKER	POWER SEATS, POWER DOOR LOCKS

Fuse and breaker identification – Premier

Power supply circuit		No.	Rated capacity (A)	Load circuit
Ignition switch	ACC	1	15	Windshield wiper and washer, Rear wiper and washer
	IG1	2	10	Meter and gauges, indicator lights, warning lights, clutch switch <M/T>, seat belt warning timer*
	ACC	3	10	Radio, clock
	IG2	4	10	4 A/T control unit, overdrive switch <4 A/T>, inhibitor switch <4 A/T>, auto-cruise control unit <4 A/T>
	IG1	5	10	Back-up light, inhibitor switch <3 A/T, 4 A/T>, hazard warning light, 3 A/T control unit
	ACC	6	10	Horn, headlight relay, upper beam relay*
		7	15	Cigarette lighter, remote-controlled mirror
Battery		8	10	Dome light, luggage compartment light, clock, radio, MPI control unit, 4 A/T control unit, door-ajar warning light, automatic seat belt control unit, seat belt warning buzzer, key reminder switch
Ignition switch IG2		9	10	Power window relay, defogger relay, defogger timer, defogger switch, heater relay, blower switch, auto compressor control unit, DRL control relay*, DRL control unit*
Battery		10	20	Heater relay
		11	15	Door lock relay, door lock control unit
		12	15	Stop light
Ignition switch IG2		13	–	–

NOTE
*: <Vehicles for Canada>

Under dash fuse identification – Summit

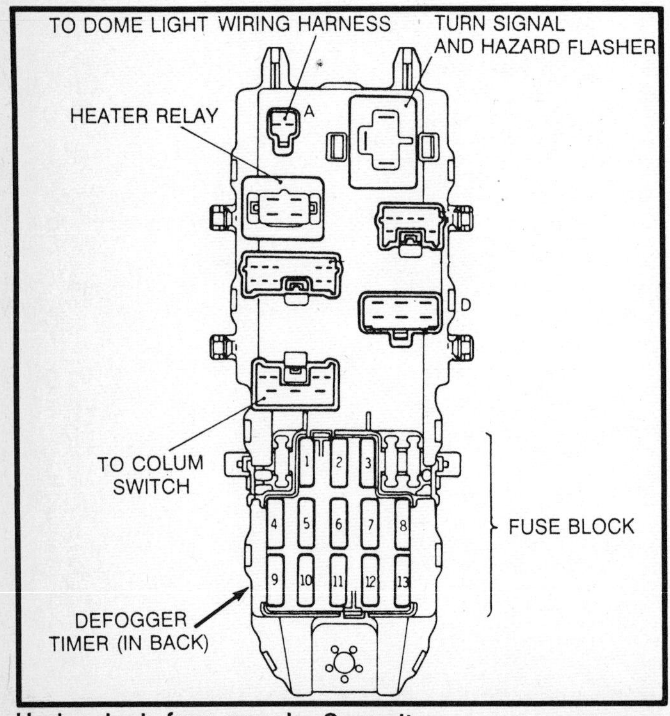

Under dash fuse panel – Summit

1. Alternator relay
2. Radiator fan motor relay
3. Power window relay (or taillamp – Canada)
4. Headlamp relay
5. Alternator circuit – 80 amp or 100 amp (Canada)
6. MPI circuit – 20 amp
7. Headlamp circuit – 40 amp
8. Radiator fan motor – (1.5L engine) 30 amp/(1.6L engine) 40 amp
9. Ignition circuit – 40 amp
10. Hazard warning circuit – 10 amp
11. Multi-purpose fuses – 40 amp
12. Power window circuit – 30 amp
13. Defogger circuit – 30 amp
14. Combination meter – 10 amp
15. Lighting circuit – 15 amp

1 2 3 4
15 GR R
5 6 7 8 9 10
BR R GY W GB
RL
11 12 13 14
WR LR RG YR

Main underhood relay box – Summit

1. Condenser fan motor control relay
2. Condenser fan motor relay
3. A/C compressor relay
4. A/C circuit – 10 amp
5. A/C circuit – 25 amp
6. A/C circuit (1.5L only) – 20 amp

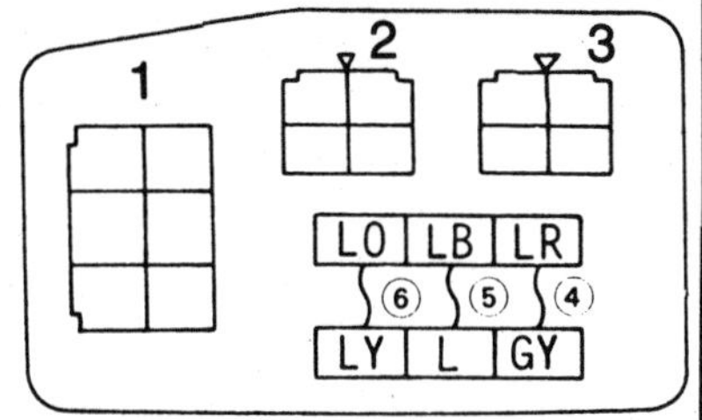

Left side relay box – Summit

TALON

Fusible links are located at the battery and right side relay box. The main fuse box is located under the left side dash. Fuses are also located at the relay boxs under the hood.

MPI

The fusible link is in the main fuse links at battery – 20 amp – blue

RADIATOR FAN MOTOR

The fusible link is in the main fuse links at battery – 30 amp – pink

IGNITION SWITCH CIRCUIT

The fusible link is in the main fuse links at battery – 30 amp – pink

ALTERNATOR

The fusible link is at the underhood relay box – 80 or 100 amp – black or blue

DEFOGGER

The fusible link is at the underhood relay box – 40 amp – green

AUTOMATIC SEATBELTS

The fusible link is at the underhood relay box – 30 amp – pink

POP-UP AND ALTERNATOR CIRCUIT

The fusible link is at the underhood relay box – 30 amp – pink

POWER WINDOWS

The fusible link is at the underhood relay box – 30 amp – pink

MULTI-PURPOSE

The fusible link is at the underhood relay box – 40 amp – green

HEADLAMP

The fusible link is at the underhood relay box – 40 amp – green

Power supply circuit		No.	Rated capacity (A)	Load circuit
Battery		1	10	Automatic seatbelt control unit, key reminder switch, passing control relay, seatbelt warning buzzer, taillight relay, theft-alarm starter relay
Ignition switch	IG2	2	–	–
		3	10	Air conditioner control unit, air conditioner switch, defogger timer, heater relay, power window relay, transistor relay•, daytime running light relay 2•
	ACC	4	10	Radio
		5	15	Cigarette lighter, remote controlled mirror
Battery		6	15	Door lock relay, door lock control unit
Ignition switch	IG2	7	10	4-speed automatic transaxle control unit, auto-cruise control unit <A/T>, combination meter
		8	–	–
	ACC	9	15	Intermittent wiper relay, wiper motor, washer motor
		10	10	Headlight relay, horn, theft-alarm control unit, daytime running light relay 1•
	IG1	11	10	Auto-cruise control unit, auto-cruise control actuator automatic seatbelt control unit, combination meter, theft-alarm control unit, seatbelt timer•
		12	10	Turn-signal and hazard flasher unit
Battery		13	–	–
		14	10	Theft-alarm horn relay
		15	–	–
		16	30	Blower motor
		17	15	Stop light
Ignition switch	IG1	18	10	Back-up light <M/T>, dome light relay
Battery		19	10	4-speed automatic transaxle control unit, dome light, door-ajar warning light, foot light, ignition key illumination light, luggage compartment light, MPI control unit, radio, security light

NOTE
• : <Vehicles for Canada>

Fuse identification – Talon

1. Multi-purpose fusible link – 40 amp
2. Power window fusible link – 30 amp
3. Pop-up/Altenator circuit fusible link – 30 amp
4. Automatic seatbelt fusible link – 30 amp
5. Defogger fusible link – 40 amp
6. Alternator fusible link – 80 or 100 amp
7. Not listed
8. Not listed
9. Headlamp indicator
10. Headlamp fusible link – 40 amp
11. Taillamp circuit – 10 amp
12. Foglamp circuit – 10 amp
13. Hazard lights – 10 amp
14. Taillight relay
15. Foglamp relay
16. Headlamp relay
17. Radiator fan relay
18. Pop-up motor relay
19. Power window relay
20. Alernator relay

Engine compartment right side relay box – Talon

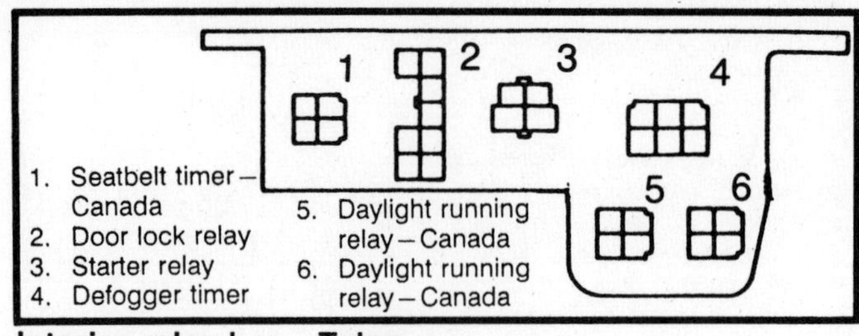

Interior relay box – Talon

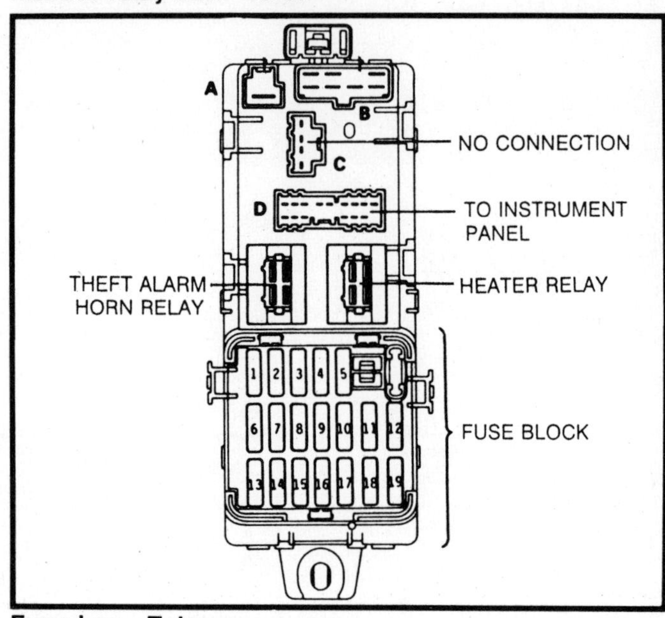

Fuse box – Talon

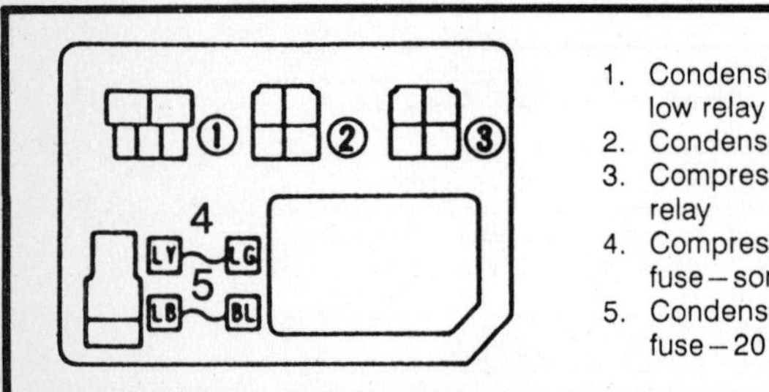

Engine compartment left side relay box – Talon

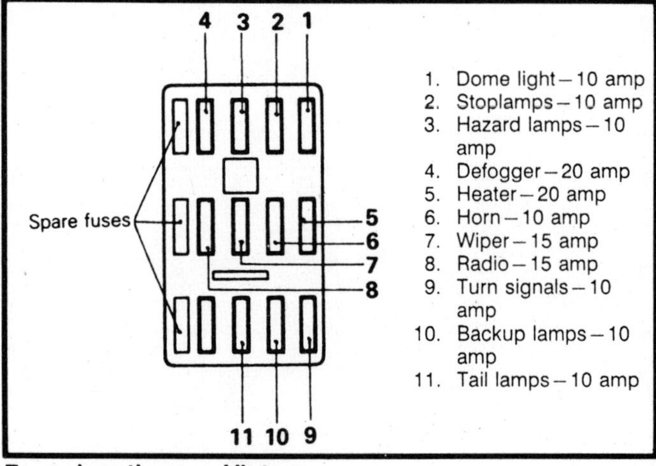

Fuse locations – Vista

VISTA

The Eagle Vista is a Canadian market vehicle. The model design is the same as the Dodge and Plymouth Vista. The main fusible link box is located next to the battery.

MPI

The main fusible link box at battery – 20 amp – blue

DEFOGGER CIRCUIT

The main fusible link box at battery – 30 amp – pink

IGNITION SWITCH CIRCUIT

The main fusible link box at battery – 40 amp – green

ALTERNATOR CIRCUIT

The main fusible link box at battery – 80 amp – black

AUTOMATIC SEAT BELT CIRCUIT

The main fusible link box at battery – 30 amp – pink

Relays, Sensors, Switches, Modules and Computers Locations

NOTE: When using this section, some of the components may not be used on a particular vehicle. This is because either the particular component in question was used on an earlier model or a later model. This section is being published from the latest information available at the time of publication.

1989 PREMIER

4 Cylinder Engine

- **A/C Ambient Temperature Sensor** – is located in the front grill, near the headlight on the passenger's side of the vehicle.
- **A/C Clutch Relay** – is located in the relay holder, under a plastic cover, on the strut tower.
- **A/C Heater Relays** – are usually mounted on the heater housing under the instrument panel.

• **B+ Latch Relay**—is located in the relay holder, under a plastic cover, on the strut tower.

• **Chime Module**—is located under the instrument, above the hood release handle.

• **Coolant Level Sensor**—is located in the coolant reservoir, which is usually located in the engine compartment on the fire wall.

• **Coolant Temperature Sensor**—is located at the front of the cylinder head in the thermostat housing.

• **Cruise Control Module**—is located under the instrument, above the hood release handle.

• **Diagnostic Connectors**—are located on the right front inner fender panel, next to the hevac vacuum reservoir.

• **Door Ajar Sensor**—is located in the door lock mechanism, located inside the door.

• **Door Lock Relay**—is located behind or near the passenger's side kick panel.

• **EGR Solenoid**—is located on the driver's side inner fender panel in the engine compartment.

• **Electronic Control Unit (ECU)**—is located under the instrument panel on the passenger's side of the vehicle.

• **Engine Fan Relay**—is located in the relay holder, under a plastic cover, on the strut tower.

• **Fuel Injection Relays**—are located in a relay holder, under the driver's side of the instrument panel.

• **Fuel Level Sensor**—is located on the fuel sending unit, which is located in the fuel tank.

• **Fuel Pump Relay**—is located in the relay holder, under a plastic cover, on the strut tower.

• **Heater-A/C Control Unit**—is usually attached to the heater housing, which is located under the instrument panel on the passenger's side of the vehicle.

• **Idle Speed Control Motor**—is located on the front side of the throttle body.

• **Ignition Control Module (ICM)**—is located in the engine compartment, under the ignition coil.

• **Ignition Relay**—is located in the relay holder, under a plastic cover, on the strut tower.

• **Illuminated Entry Module**—is usually located under the left side of the instrument panel, behind the glove box.

• **Interior Temperature Sensor**—is usually located under the center of the instrument panel.

• **Intermittent Wiper Module**—is usually attached to kick panel on the passenger's side of the vehicle.

• **Knock Sensor**—is located on the right hand motor mount.

• **Lamp Out Module**—is located in the luggage compartment, next to the rear speaker.

• **Lighting Module**—is located behind the instrument panel, usually near the headlight switch.

• **Manifold Absolute Pressure Sensor (MAP)**—is located on the dash panel, next to the brake booster in the engine compartment.

• **Manifold Air Temperature Sensor (MAT)**—is located in the intake manifold between the number 3 and number 4 runners.

• **Oil Level Sensor**—is located in the bottom of the oil pan.

• **Oil Pressure Sensor**—is located in the engine block, behind the alternator.

• **Oxygen Sensor (O_2)**—is located in the bottom of the exhaust manifold, above the connector for the front exhaust pipe.

• **Rear Window Defogger Relay**—is located in the relay block, which is located under the center of the instrument panel.

• **Speed Sensor**—is located on the left side of the transmission converter housing, behind the rear face of the engine.

• **Speed Sensor Module**—is located behind the instrument panel, usually located behind the speedometer.

• **Starter Motor Relay**—is located in the relay holder, un-

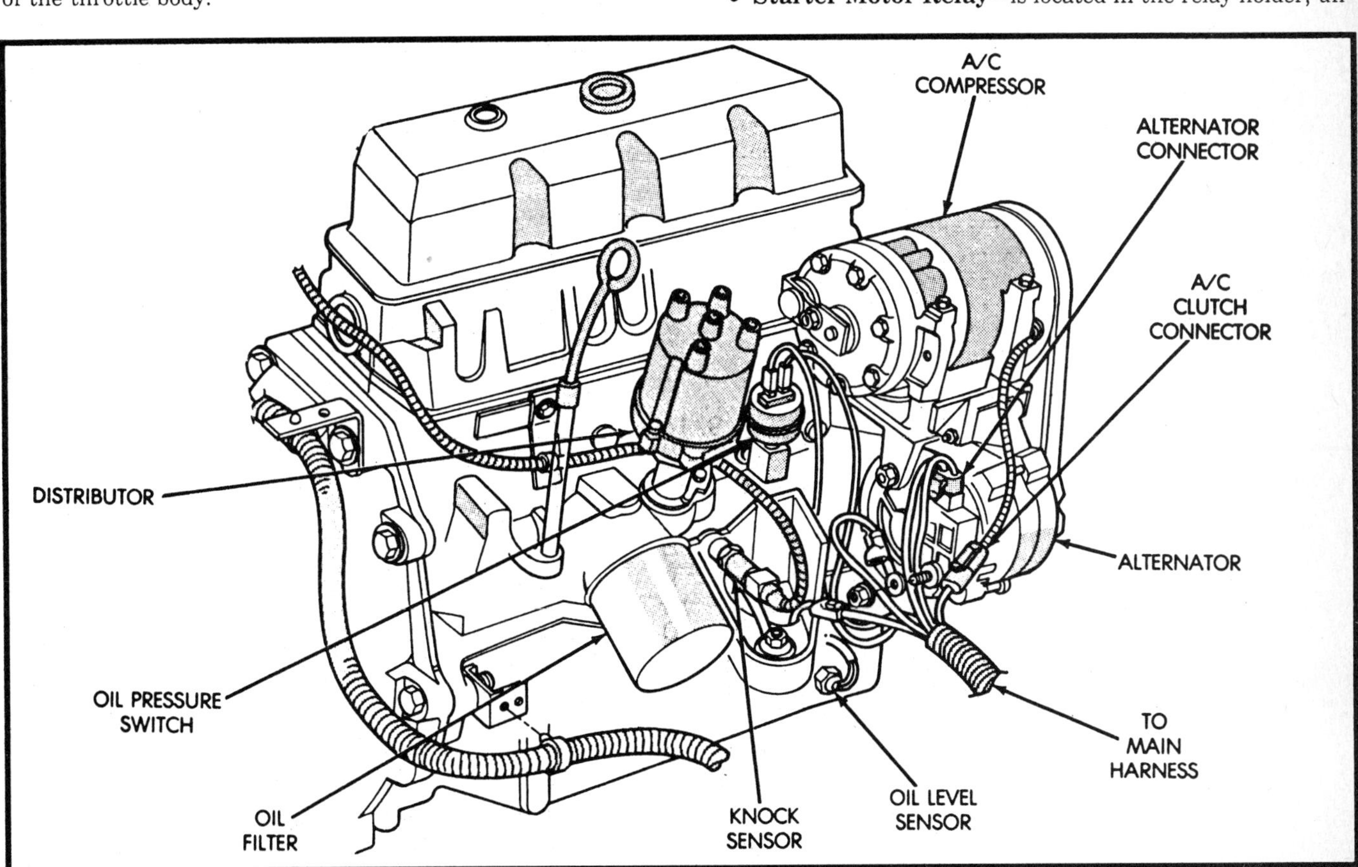

Engine components—2.5L engine Premier

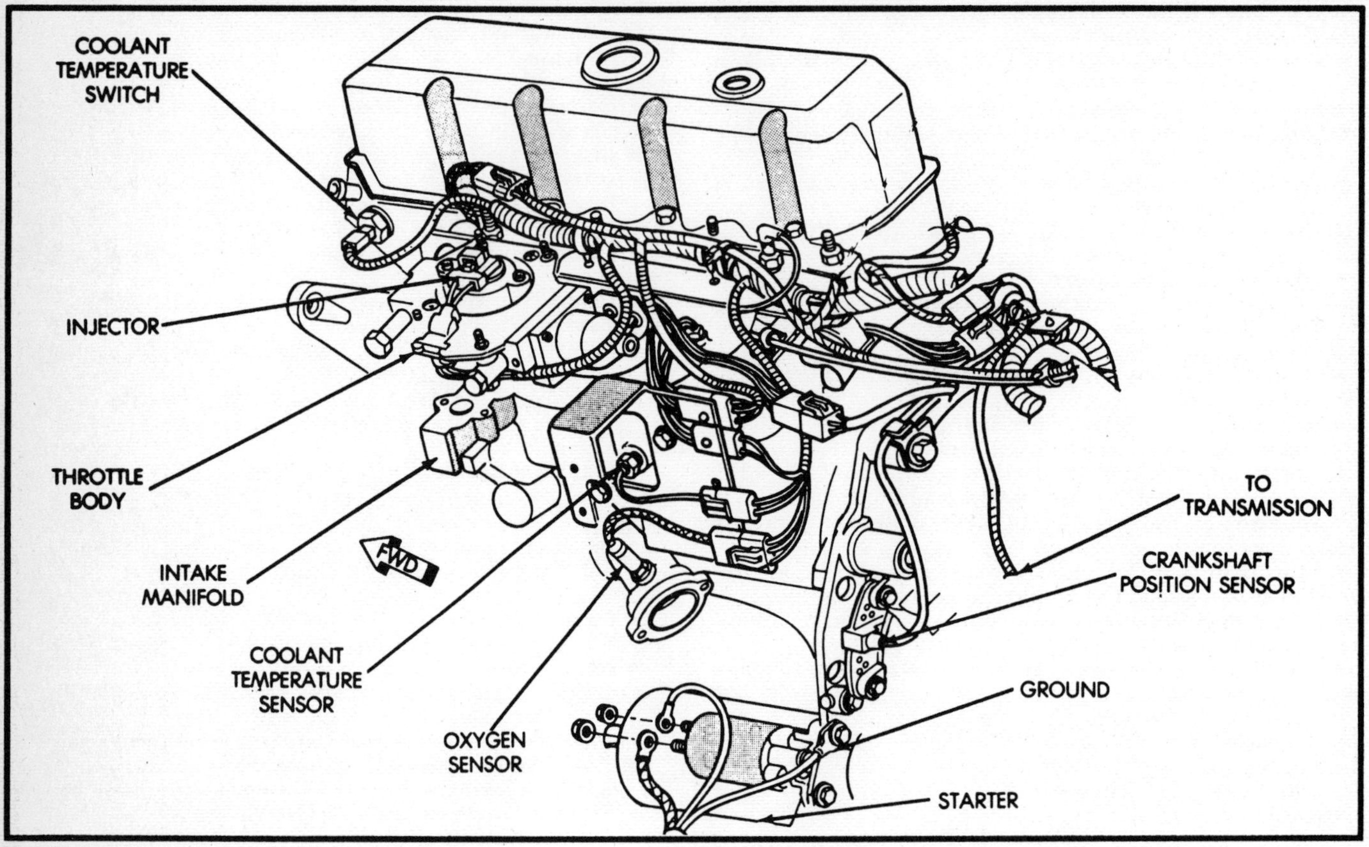

COOLANT TEMPERATURE SWITCH
INJECTOR
THROTTLE BODY
INTAKE MANIFOLD
FWD
COOLANT TEMPERATURE SENSOR
OXYGEN SENSOR
TO TRANSMISSION
CRANKSHAFT POSITION SENSOR
GROUND
STARTER

Engine components – 2.5L engine Premier

der a plastic cover, on the strut tower.

• **Throttle Position Sensor (TPS)** – is located in front of the throttle body.

• **Sunroof Relay** – is located on the sunroof motor.

• **Transmission Control Module (AR-4)** – is located in the engine compartment, mounted to the inner fender panel on the passenger's side of the vehicle.

• **Trip Computer** – is located behind the instrument, usually next to the radio.

• **Trip Computer Ambient Temperature Sensor** – is located in the front grill, near the headlight on the driver's side of the vehicle.

• **Vehicle Maintenance Module** – is located behind the instrument panel, usually near the gauges.

• **Washer Fluid Level Sensor** – is located in the washer fluid reservoir, located in the engine compartment.

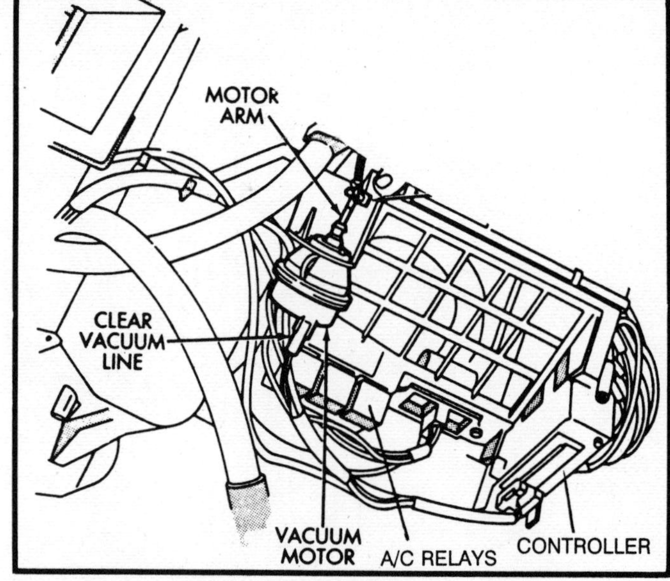

Air conditioning relays and controller – Premier

6 Cylinder Engine

• **A/C Ambient Temperature Sensor** – is located in the front of vehicle, under the bumper on the right side.

• **A/C Clutch Relay** – is located in the relay holder, under a plastic cover, on the strut tower.

• **A/C Heater Relays** – are usually mounted on the heater housing under the instrument panel.

• **Antenna Relay** – is located in the relay block, which is located under the center of the instrument panel at position A.

• **B+ Latch Relay** – is located in the relay holder, under a plastic cover, on the strut tower.

• **Chime Module** – is located under the instrument, above the hood release handle.

• **Coolant Level Sensor** – is located in the coolant reservoir, which is usually located in the engine compartment on the fire wall.

• **Coolant Temperature Sensor** – is located above the water pump in the thermostat housing.

• **Cruise Control Module** – is located under the instrument, above the hood release handle.

• **Diagnostic Connectors** – are located on the right front inner fender panel, next to the hevac vacuum reservoir.

• **Door Ajar Sensor**—is located in the door lock mechanism, located inside the door.

• **Door Lock Relay**—is located behind or near the passenger's side kick panel or with keyless entry system in the overhead console.

• **EGR Solenoid**—is located on the driver's side inner fender panel in the engine compartment.

• **Electronic Control Unit (ECU)**—is located under the instrument panel on the passenger's side of the vehicle.

• **Engine Fan Relay**—is located in the relay holder, under a plastic cover, on the strut tower.

• **Fuel Injection Relays**—are located in a relay holder, under the driver's side of the instrument panel.

• **Fuel Level Sensor**—is located on the fuel sending unit, which is located in the fuel tank.

• **Fuel Pump Relay**—is located in the relay holder, under a plastic cover, on the strut tower.

• **Headlamp Relays**—are located in the relay block, which is located under the center of the instrument panel. Highbeam is at position D and lowbeam at position C.

• **Heater-A/C Control Unit**—is usually attached to the heater housing, which is located under the instrument panel on the passenger's side of the vehicle.

• **Horn Relay**—is located in the relay block, which is located under the center of the instrument panel at position G.

• **Idle Speed Regulator**—is usually located above the left hand cylinder head.

• **Ignition Control Module (ICM)**—is located in the engine compartment, under the ignition coil.

• **Ignition Relay**—is located in the relay holder, under a plastic cover, on the strut tower.

• **Illuminated Entry Module**—is usually located under the left side of the instrument panel, behind the glove box.

• **Interior Temperature Sensor**—is usually located under the center of the instrument panel.

• **Intermittent Wiper Module**—is usually attached to kick panel on the passenger's side of the vehicle.

• **Knock Sensor**—is located on the right side of the cylinder block above the motor mount.

• **Lamp Out Module**—is located in the luggage compartment, next to the rear speaker.

• **Lighting Module**—is located behind the instrument panel, usually near the headlight switch.

• **Manifold Absolute Pressure Sensor (MAP)**—is located on the dash panel, next to the brake booster in the engine compartment.

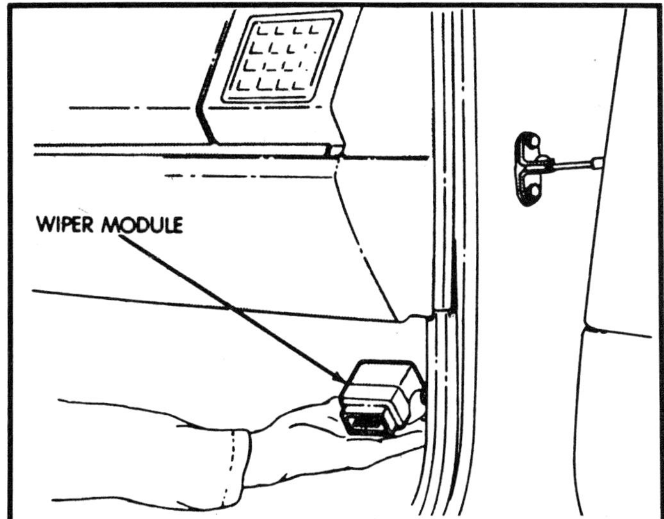

Wiper Module—Premier

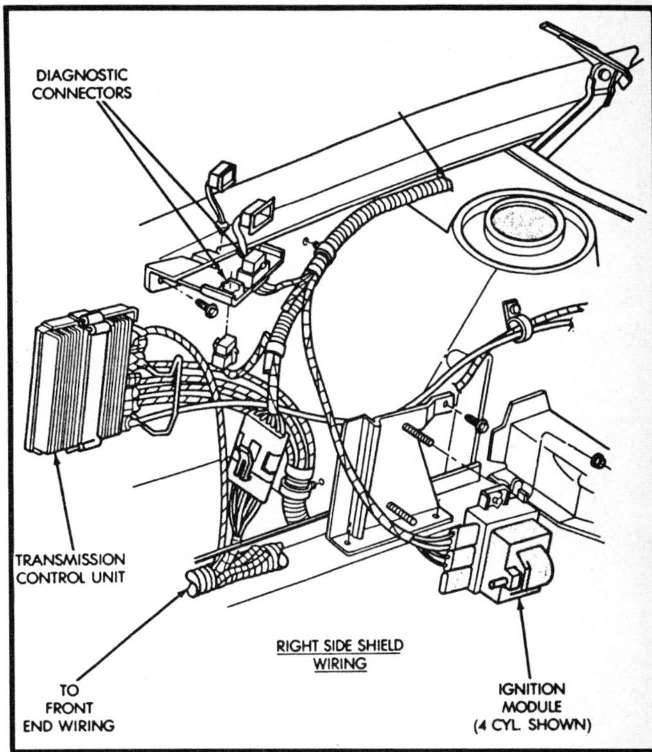

Diagnostic connectors—Premier

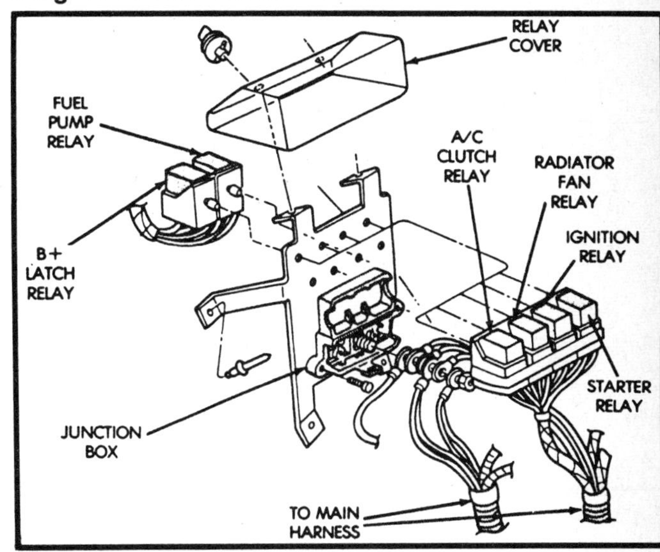

Engine relay identification—Premier

• **Manifold Air Temperature Sensor (MAT)**—is located on the throttle body adapter, below the throttle body and behind the fitting for the brake booster.

• **Oil Level Sensor**—is located in the bottom of the engine block, near the motor mount on the passenger's side of the vehicle.

• **Oil Pressure Sensor**—is located in the engine block, next to the alternator.

• **Oxygen Sensor (O_2)**—is located in the exhaust "Y" pipe, before the catalytic converter.

• **Passive Restraint Relays—are located under the seat on the side that they control.**

• **Passive Restraint Module—is located on the left side of the trunk compartment.**

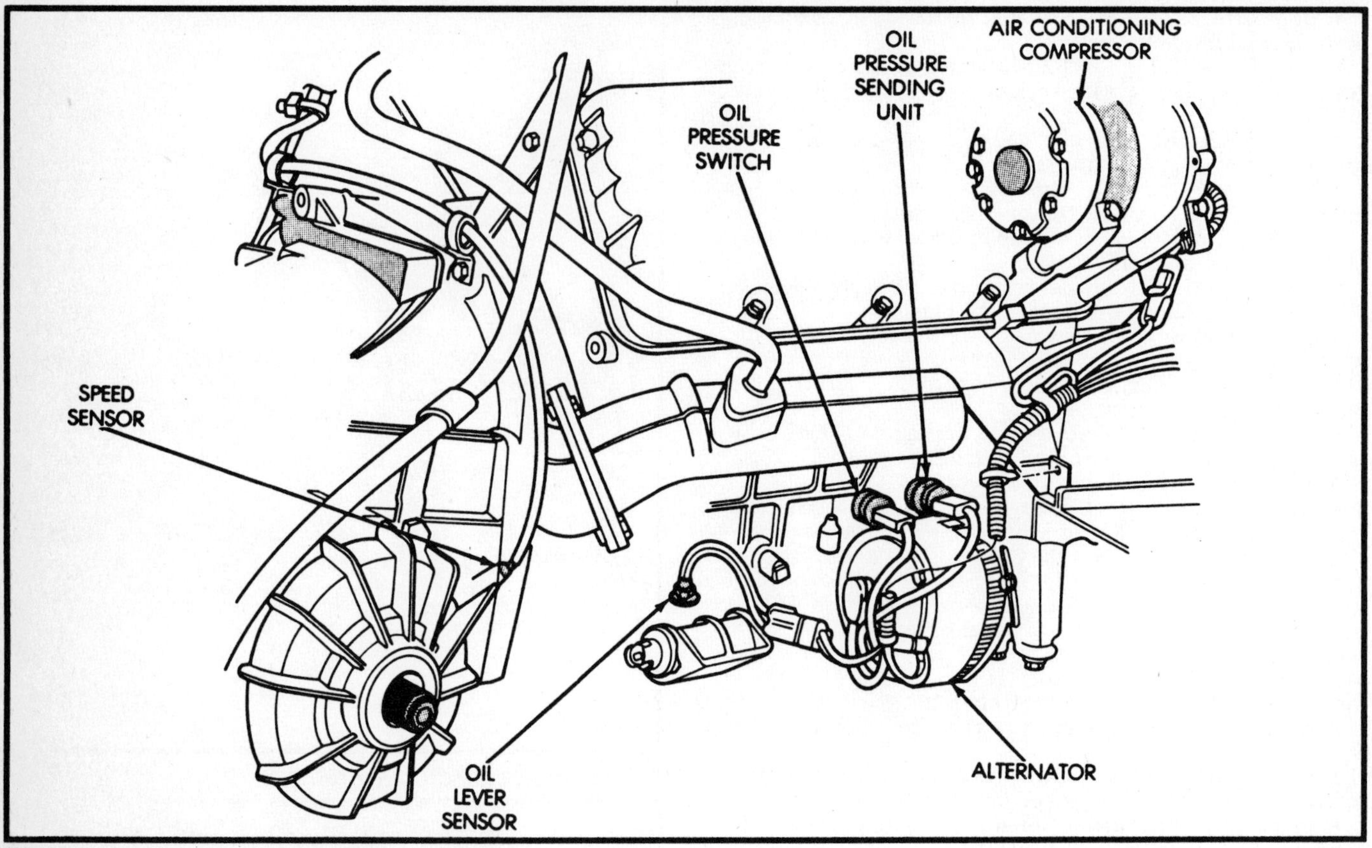

Engine components – 3.0L engine Premier

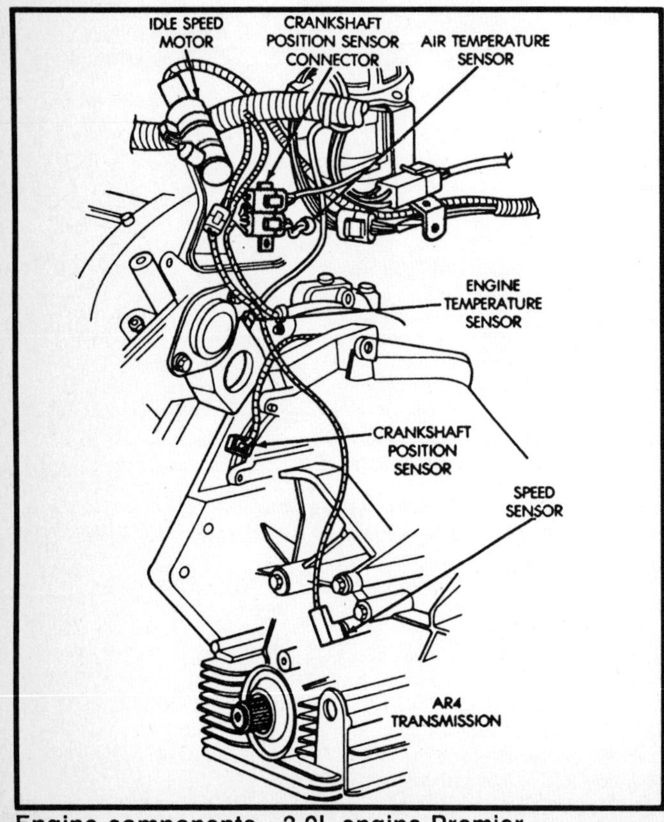

Engine components – 3.0L engine Premier

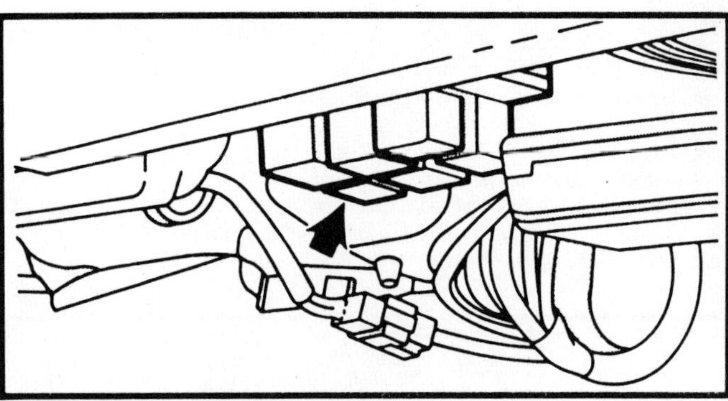

Rear window defogger relay

- **Radio Lamp Relay** – is located in the relay block, which is located under the center of the instrument panel at position H.
- **Rear Window Defogger Relay** – is located in the relay block, which is located under the center of the instrument panel at position B.
- **Engine Speed Sensor** – is located on the left side of the transmission converter housing, behind the rear face of the engine.
- **Speed Sensor Module** – is located behind the instrument panel, usually located behind the speedometer.
- **Starter Motor Relay** – is located in the relay holder, under a plastic cover, on the strut tower.
- **Sunroof Relay** – is located on the sunroof motor, under the headliner.
- **Throttle Position Sensor (TPS)** – is attached to the throttle body.
- **Transmission Control Module (AR-4)** – is located in

1. Air flow and barometric pressure sensor
2. Neutral safety switch
3. Engine coolant temperature (1.5L shown)
4. EGR temperature sensor (California)
5. Ignition timing adjustment terminal
6. Idle speed control servo
7. Throttle position sensor (1.5L)
8. EGR control solenoid
9. Fuel pump check terminal
10. Purge control solenoid
11. Ignition coil power transistor (1.5L shown)
12. Crankangle sensor (1.5L shown)
13. Air conditioner relay
14. Power steering pressure switch
15. Oxygen sensor
16. Injectors

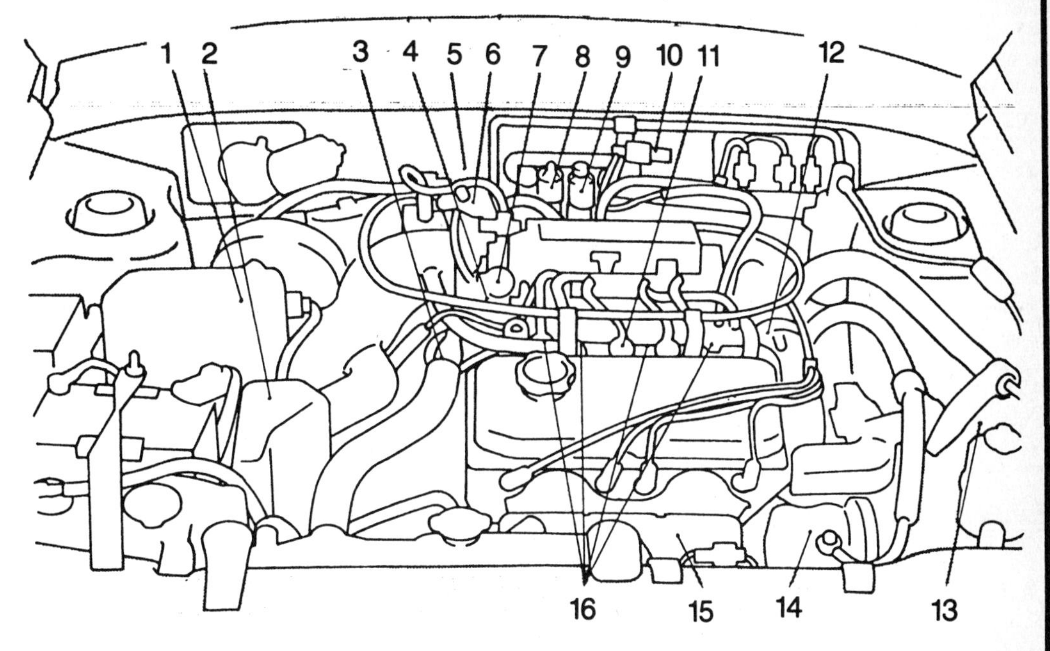

Component locations— Summit

the engine compartment, mounted to the inner fender panel on the passenger's side of the vehicle.

• **Trip Computer**—is located behind the instrument, usually next to the radio.

• **Trip Computer Ambient Temperature Sensor**—is located in the front grill, near the headlight on the driver's side of the vehicle.

• **Vehicle Maintenance Module**—is located behind the instrument panel, usually near the gauges.

• **Washer Fluid Level Sensor**—is located in the washer fluid reservoir, located in the engine compartment.

1990–91 PREMIER

• **A/C Ambient Temperature Sensor**—is located in the front of vehicle, under the bumper on the right side.

• **A/C Clutch Relay (1990–early 91)**—is located in the relay holder, under a plastic cover, on the strut tower.

• **A/C Clutch Relay (late 1991)**—is located in the Power Distribution Center located behind the battery.

• **A/C Electronic Control Module**—is mounted on the right side of the heater housing under the instrument panel.

• **A/C Heater Relays**—are usually mounted on the heater housing under the instrument panel.

• **A/C Low Pressure Cut Off Switch**—is located on the receiver-drier assembly.

• **Antenna Relay**—is located in the relay block, which is located under the center of the instrument panel.

• **Anti-Lock Brakes (ABS) Control Module**—is located on the front of the right side shock tower.

• **Anti-Lock Brakes (ABS) Diagnostic Connector**—is located under the instrument panel to the left of the steering column.

• **Anti-Lock Brakes (ABS) Pump Motor Relay**—is located in the Power Distribution Center located behind the battery.

• **Anti-Lock Brakes (ABS) System Relay**—is located in the Power Distribution Center located behind the battery.

• **Anti-Lock Brakes (ABS) Warning Lamp Relay**—is located in the Power Distribution Center located behind the battery.

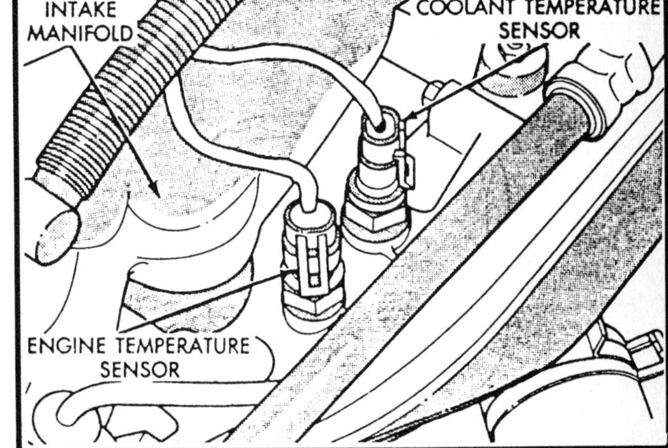

Coolant temperature and engine temperature sensors —1991 Premier

• **Automatic Idle Speed Motor**—is locatd on the throttle body assembly.

• **Auto Shutdown Relay (late 1991)**—is located in the Power Distribution Center located behind the battery.

• **B+ Latch Relay**—is located in the relay holder, under a plastic cover, on the strut tower.

• **Charge Temperature Sensor**—is located on the cylinder head, above the bell housing.

• **Chime Module**—is located under the left side of the instrument panel.

• **Coolant Level Sensor**—is located in the coolant reservoir, which is usually located in the engine compartment on the fire wall.

• **Coolant Temperature Sensor**—is located on the rear of the block or may be on the firewall, slightly right of center.

• **Coolant Temperature Sending Unit**—is located on the thermostat housing or on the front right side of the head.

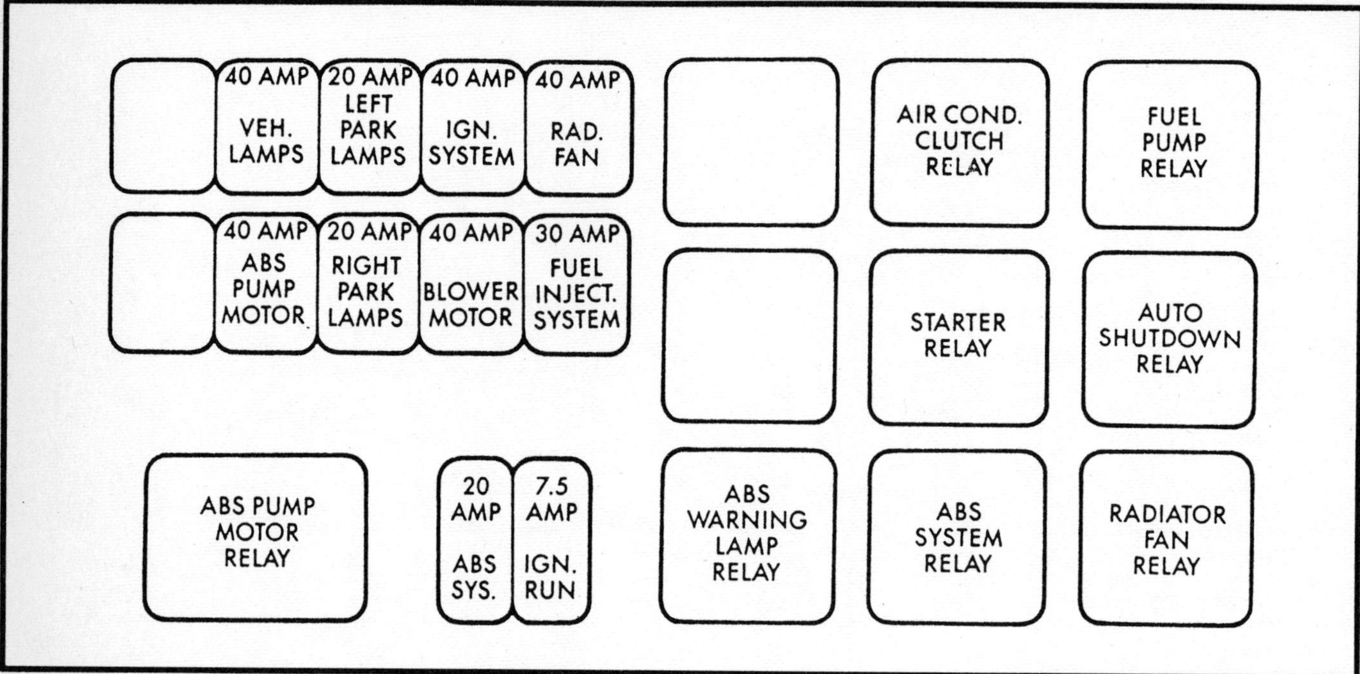

Power Distribution Center component identification—1991

- **Crankshaft Position Sensor**—is mounted on the left front of the bell housing.
- **Cruise Control Relay**—is located in the relay block, which is located under the center of the instrument panel.
- **Cruise Control Module (1990)**—is located under the instrument panel, above the hood release handle.
- **Daytime Running Lights Module (Canada)**—is located in the right front area of the engine compartment.
- **Diagnostic Connectors (1990–early 91)**—are located on the right front inner fender panel.
- **Diagnostic Connector (late 1991)**—is located on the left front of the engine compartment near the SBEC.
- **Door Lock Relay**—is located behind or near the passenger's side kick panel or with keyless entry system in the overhead console.
- **EGR Solenoid**—is located on the driver's side inner fender panel in the engine compartment.
- **Electronic Engine Control Unit (1990–early 91)**—is located under the instrument panel on the passenger's side of the vehicle.
- **Electronic Engine Control Unit (late 1991—)**is located on the left side innner fender battery next to the battery.
- **Engine Fan Relay (1990–early 91)**—is located in the relay holder, under a plastic cover, on the strut tower.
- **Engine Fan Relay (late 1991)**—is located in the Power Distrubution Center located behind the battery.
- **Fuel Injection Relays**—are located in a relay holder, under the driver's side of the instrument panel.
- **Fuel Level Sensor**—is located on the fuel sending unit, which is located in the fuel tank.
- **Fuel Pump Relay**—is located in the relay holder, under a plastic cover, on the strut tower.
- **Headlamp Module**—is located under the left side of the instrument panel.
- **Headlamp Relays**—are located in the relay block, which is located under the center of the instrument panel.
- **Heater-A/C Control Unit**—is usually attached to the heater housing, which is located under the instrument panel on the passenger's side of the vehicle.
- **Horn Relay**—is located in the relay block, which is located under the center of the instrument panel.
- **Idle Speed Regulator**—is usually located above the left hand cylinder head.
- **Ignition Control Module (ICM)**—is located in the engine compartment, under the ignition coil.
- **Ignition Relay (1990)**—is located in the relay holder, under a plastic cover, on the strut tower.
- **Illuminated Entry Module**—is usually located under the left side of the instrument panel, behind the glove box.
- **Illuminated Entry Relay**—is located in the relay block, located at the center of the instruemnt panel.
- **Interior Temperature Sensor**—is usually located under the center of the instrument panel.
- **Intermittent Wiper Module**—is usually attached to kick panel on the passenger's side of the vehicle or may be behind the glove box.
- **Keyless Entry Receiver**—is located above the windshield.
- **Knock Sensor**—is located next to the oil filter on 2.5L engine and on the right side of the cylinder block above the motor mount on 3.0L engine.
- **Lamp Out Module**—is located in the luggage compartment, next to the right rear speaker.
- **Lighting Module**—is located behind the instrument panel, usually near the headlight switch.
- **Manifold Absolute Pressure Sensor (MAP)**—is located on the dash panel, next to the brake booster in the engine compartment.
- **Manifold Air Temperature Sensor (MAT)**—is located on the throttle body adapter, below the throttle body and behind the fitting for the brake booster on 3.0L engine and in the intake manifold between the number 3 and number 4 runners on 2.5L engine.
- **Oil Level Sensor**—is located either in the oil pan or in the bottom of the engine block, near the motor mount on the passenger's side of the vehicle.
- **Oil Pressure Sensor**—is located in the engine block, next to the alternator.
- **Oxygen Sensor (O_2)**—is located in the exhaust pipe, before the catalytic converter.

• **Passive Restraint Diagnostic Connector (1991)** – is located on the left side of the trunk compartment.

• **Passive Restraint Relays** – may be located under either or both front seats.

• **Passive Restraint Module** – is located on the left side of the trunk compartment.

• **Power Deck Lid Release Actuator** – is located in the deck lid near the latch assembly.

• **Power Door Lock Relay** – is located under the left side of the instrument panel.

• **Rear Window Defogger Relay** – is located in the relay block, which is located under the center of the instrument panel.

• **Engine Speed Sensor** – is located on the left side of the transmission converter housing, behind the rear face of the engine.

• **Single Board Engine Controller (SBEC)** – is located on the left side inner fender panel, next to the battery.

• **Speed Sensor Module** – is located behind the instrument panel, usually located behind the speedometer.

• **Starter Motor Relay (1990–early 91)** – is located in the relay holder, under a plastic cover, on the strut tower.

• **Starter Motor Relay (late 1991)** – is located in the Power Distribution Center located behind the battery.

• **Stop Lamp/Cruise Cut Off Switch** – is located above the brake pedal on the pedal bracket.

• **Sunroof Relay** – is located on the sunroof motor, under the headliner.

• **Throttle Position Sensor (TPS)** – is attached to the throttle body.

• **Transmission Control Module (AR-4)** – is located in the engine compartment, mounted to the inner fender panel on the passenger's side of the vehicle.

• **Transmission Control Module (ZF-4)** – is located on the left rear of the transmission.

• **Trip Computer** – is located behind the instrument panel, next to the radio.

• **Trip Computer Ambient Temperature Sensor** – is located in the front grill, near the headlight on the driver's side of the vehicle.

• **Vehicle Maintenance Module** – is located behind the instrument panel, near the gauges.

• **Washer Fluid Level Sensor** – is located in the washer fluid reservoir, located in the engine compartment.

SUMMIT

• **A/T Control Unit** – is located under the middle of the dash, at the console base.

• **A/C Air Temperature Sensors** – are located under the dash in the evaporator housing.

• **A/C Compressor Control Unit** – is located under the dash, above the evaporator.

• **A/C Compressor Relay** – is located in the left underhood relay box.

• **A/C Condensor Fan Control Relay** – is located in the left underhood relay box.

• **A/C Condensor Fan Motor Relay** – is located in the left underhood relay box.

• **Alternator Relay** – is in the right underhood relay box.

• **Crank Angle Sensor (1.5L engine)** – is located in the distributor.

• **Crank Angle Sensor (1.6L engine)** – is located at the end of the cylinder head.

• **Cruise Control Unit** – is located under the left dash, next to the fuse box.

• **Defogger Relay** – is under the left side dash, on the right of the fuse box.

• **Defogger Timer** – is under the left side dash, in the fuse box.

• **Door Lock Control Unit** – is located under the left dash at the kick panel.

• **Door Lock Relay** – is located under the left dash at the kick panel, behind the control unit.

• **EGR Control Solenoid (1.5L engine)** – is located on the firewall.

• **EGR Temperature Sensor (California)** – is located at the base of the EGR valve.

• **EGR Thermal Valve** – is at the front of the engine in a coolant passage.

• **Fuel Pump Check Connector** – is located at the center of the firewall.

• **Hazard Flasher** – is in the left side dash, in the fuse box.

• **Headlamp Highbeam Relay** – is located at the left front fender.

• **Headlamp Relay** – is located in the left underhood relay box.

• **Heater Blower Relay** – is under the left dash, in the under fuse box.

• **MPI Control Relay** – is located under the center console, on the right side.

• **MPI Control Unit** – is located under the dash on the left side, in front of the blower motor.

• **Oxygen Sensor Check Connector (1.6L engine)** – is located under the right side dash, near the blower motor.

• **PCV Valve** – is screwed in the end of the valve cover.

• **Power Steering Pressure Switch** – is located at the power steering pump.

• **Power Transistor** – is mounted next to the ignition coil.

• **Power Window Relay** – is located in the right side underhood relay box. Canadian models may have the relay next to the battery.

• **Radiator Fan Relay** – is located in the right underhood relay box.

• **Running Lamp Controller (Canada)** – is located at the left front fender.

• **Running Lamp Relay (Canada)** – is located at the left front fender.

• **Seatbelt Warning Timer (Canada)** – is located under the top of the dash to the right of the glove compartment.

• **Self-Diagnosis connector** – is located under the left side dash, next to the fuse box.

• **Taillamp Relay (Canada)** – is located in the left underhood relay box.

• **TDC Sensor (1.5L engine)** – is located in the distributor.

• **TDC Sensor (1.6L engine)** – is located at the end of the cylinder head.

• **Turn Signal Flasher** – is in the left side dash, in the fuse box.

• **Vehicle Speed Sensor (Reed Switch)** – is located behind the speedometer in the instrument panel.

TALON

• **A/C Condenser Fan Relay** – is located in the underhood relay box.

• **A/C Controller** – is located behind the glove compartment.

• **A/C temperature sensors** – are located in the air conditioner housing near the A/C controller.

• **Air Flow Sensor** – is in the air intake stream.

• **Alternator Relay** – is located in the underhood relay box.

• **Automatic Transmission Control Unit** – is located behind the center of the instrument panel.

• **Barometric Pressure Sensor** – is in the air intake stream.

• **Blower High Relay** – is next to the blower motor.

• **Compressor clutch relay** – is located in the underhood relay box.

• **Coolant Temperature Sensor**—is in below the thermostat housing.
• **Crankangle Sensor (1.8L engine)**—is part of the distributor.
• **Crankangle Sensor (2.0L engine)**—is located at the rear of the cylinder head.
• **Cruise Control Diode**—is located in the center of the dash.
• **Cruise Control Module**—is located at the upper left side of the dash.
• **Daylight Running Relay (Canadian Models)**—is located in the underdash relay box.
• **Diagnosis Connector**—is located under the right side dash.
• **Dome Light Relay**—is located behind the left rear quarter panel trim.
• **Door Ajar Diode**—is located at the floor crossmember.
• **Door Lock Control Unit**—is located at the right side kick panel.
• **Door Lock Relay**—is located under the right side dash.
• **EGR Control Solenoid (except turbocharged)**—is on the firewall near the battery.
• **EGR Control Solenoid (turbocharged)**—is on the firewall on the left side.
• **Engine Control Unit**—is located behind the center of the instrument panel.
• **Fuel Pressure Control Solenoid (turbocharged)**—is on the firewall on the left side.
• **Fuel Pump Check Terminal**—is next to the battery.
• **Hazard Flasher**—is located above the underdash fuse box.
• **Heater Relay**—is located under the left side dash with the fuse box.
• **Ignition Coil Power Transistor**—is located below or near the ignition coil.
• **Ignition Timing Adjustment Terminal**—is next to the battery.
• **Intake Air Temperature Sensor**—is in the air intake stream.
• **Knock Sensor**—is in the middle of the engine on the firewall side.
• **Passing Control Relay**—is located behind left side cowl trim.
• **Pop-up Circuit Diode**—is under the right side of the dash.
• **Pop-up Motor Relay**—is in the underhood relay box.
• **Power Steering Pressure Switch**—is located at the power steering pump.
• **Power Window Relay**—is located in the underhood relay box.
• **Purge Control Solenoid (except turbocharged)**—is on the firewall near the battery.
• **Purge Control Solenoid (turbocharged)**—is on the firewall on the left side.
• **Radio Noise Condenser**—is located next to the battery.
• **Seatbelt Control Unit**—is located at the center column near the seat.
• **Seatbelt Relay**—is located at the center column near the seat.
• **Seatbelt Timer (if equipped)**—is located in the underdash relay box.
• **Starter Relay**—is located in the underdash relay box.
• **TDC Sensor (1.8L engine)**—is part of the distributor.
• **TDC Sensor (2.0L engine)**—is located at the rear of the cylinder head.
• **Theft Alarm Diode**—is under the left side of the dash, next to the fuse panel.
• **Theft Alarm Horn Relay**—is located in the under the center of the dash.
• **Theft Alarm Starter Relay**—is located in the center floor console.

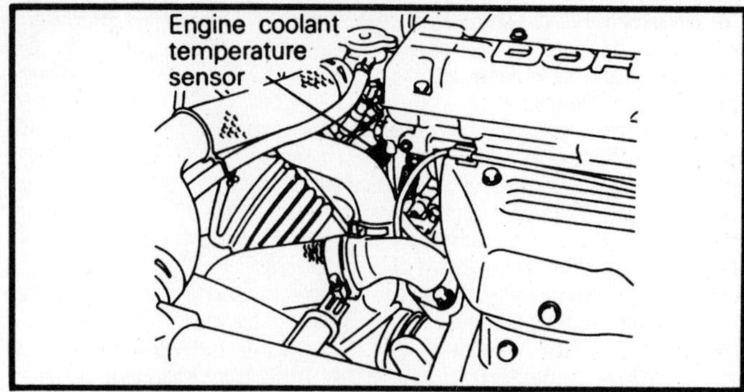

Coolant Temperature sensor—Talon 2.0L engine

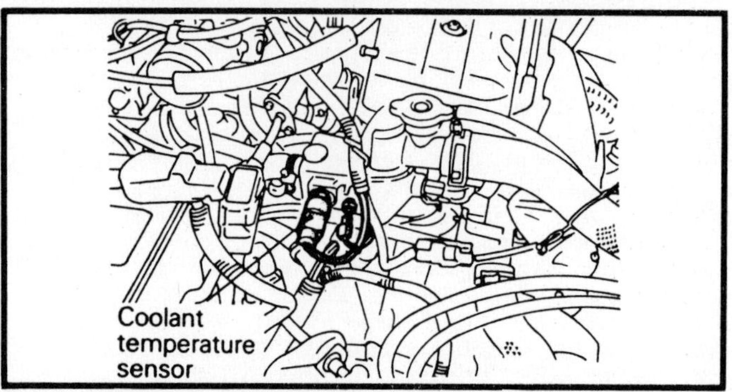

Coolant Temperature sensor—Talon 1.8L engine

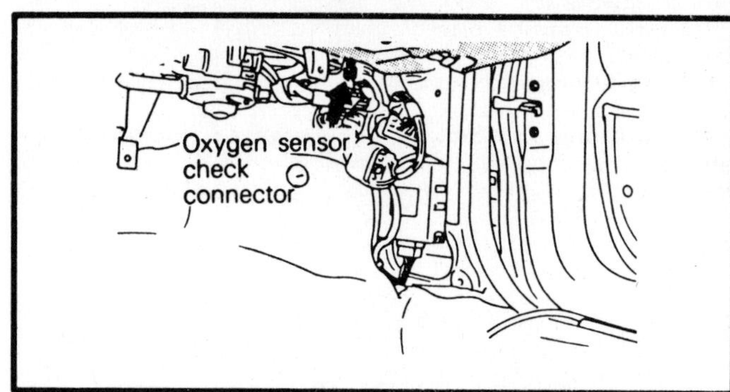

Oxygen Sensor Test Connector— Talon 2.0L

• **Theft Control Alarm**—is located at the right side kick panel.
• **Transistor Taillight Relay (if equipped)**—is located under the right side dash.
• **Turn Signal Flasher**—is located above the underdash fuse box.
• **Waste Gate Control Valve**—is next to the air filter assembly.

VISTA

The Eagle Vista is a Canadian market vehicle. The model design is the same as the Dodge and Plymouth Vista.
• **A/C Compressor Clutch Relay**—is at the center of the left fender.
• **A/C Condenser Fan Relay**—is at the center of the left fender.
• **A/C Control Relay**—is at the center of the left fender.
• **A/C fuses**—are located in the glove compartment and in the harness at the cooling fan.
• **Air Flow Sensor**—is located at the air filter in the intake air stream.

- **Alternator Relay**—is located on the left fender at the fireball.
- **Barometric Pressure Sensor**—is located at the air filter in the intake air stream.
- **Coolant Temperature Sender (gauge)**—is located at the front of the engine and screws in from the front of the engine, just under the thermostat housing.
- **Coolant Temperature Sensor**—is located at the front of the engine and screws down into the manifold.
- **Coolant Thermo Switch**—is located at the front of the engine and screws into the manifold from the firewall side.
- **Crank Angle Sensor**—is in the distributor.
- **Cruise Control Module**—is located at the right rear quarter panel.
- **Daytime Running Relays**—are located on the left fender, near thewasher bottle.
- **Defogger Relay**—is located on the firewall.
- **Defogger Timer**—is located under the dash, near steering column.
- **Engine Control Unit**—is located under the driver's seat.
- **Flasher Unit**—is located under the left dash, in the relay box.
- **Fuel Pump Check Terminal**—is located near the center of the firewall.
- **Ignition Power Transistor**—is next to the ignition coil.
- **Ignition Timing Adjustment Connector**—is located near the center of the firewall, next to the fuel pump check connector.
- **MPI Control Relay**—is located behind the center of the instrument panel at the console.
- **Power Steering Pressure Switch**—is at the power steering pump.
- **Power Window Relay**—is in the main relay box, next to the battery.
- **Purge Control Solenoid**—is located near the center of the firewall.
- **Radiator Fan Motor Relay**—is in the main relay box, next to the battery.
- **Rear Intermittent Wiper Relay**—is located at the right rear quarter panel.
- **Seatbelt Control Unit**—is located at the rear of the center console near the seat.
- **Seatbelt Relay**—is located at the rear of the center console next to the seat it associated with.
- **Seatbelt Timer**—is located under the left side dash.
- **Self-Diagnosis Connector**—is located under the glove compartment.
- **Thermal Switch**—is located at the front of the engine and screws into the manifold from the firewall side.
- **Transmission Control Unit**—is located behind the center of the instrument panel.
- **Vehicle Speed Sensor**—is located behind the instrument panel at the speedometer.

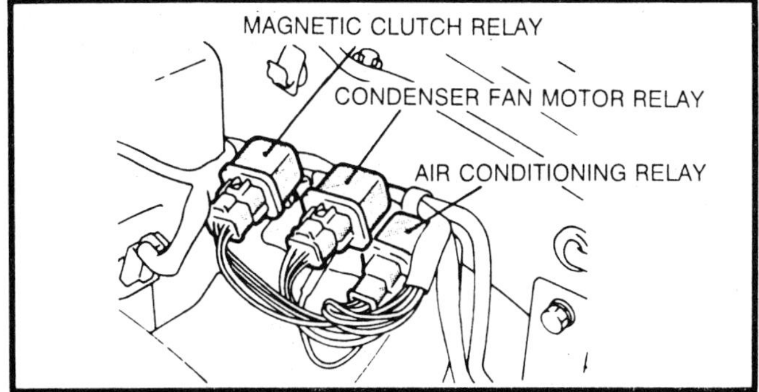

Air conditioning relays—Vista

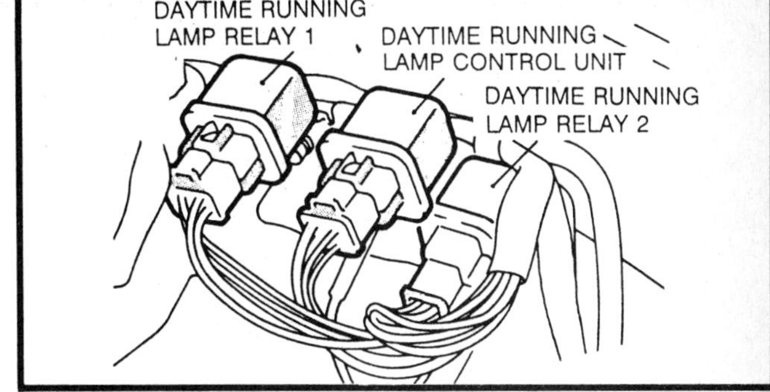

Day light running relays—Vista

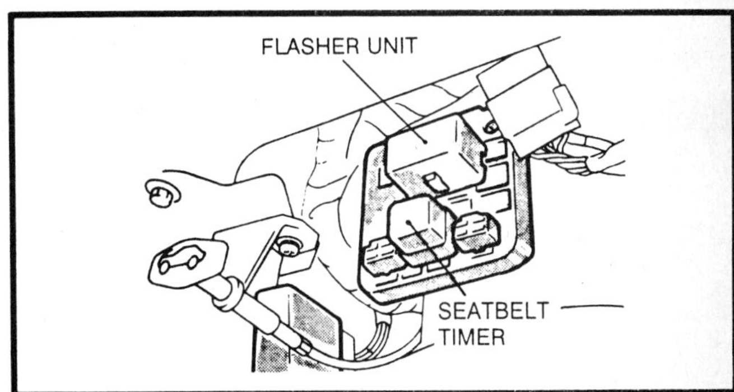

Flasher location—Vista

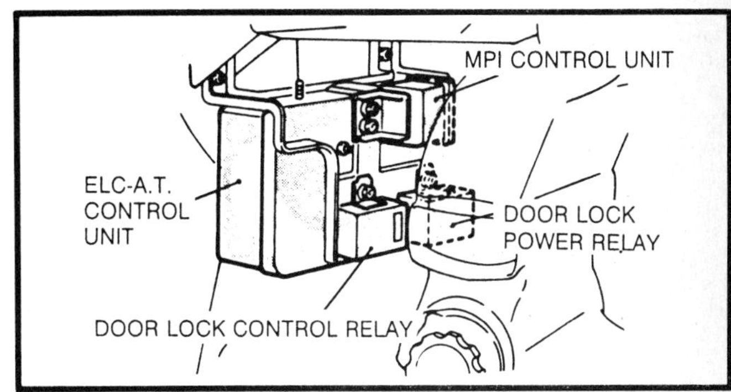

A.T. and MPI controler—Vista

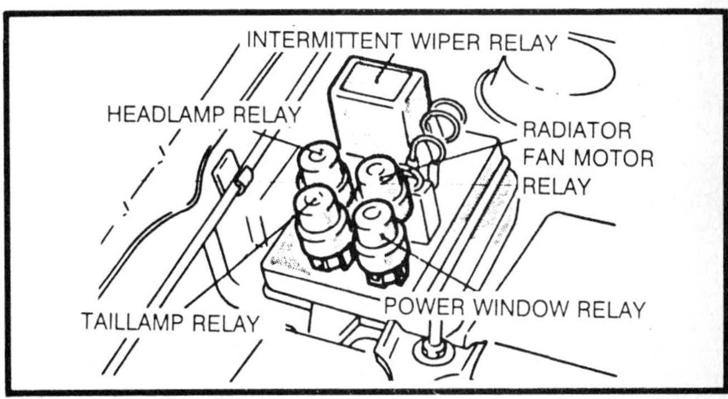

Main relay box

JEEP

Circuit Breaker Locations

Circuit breaker are located in the fuse block for most circuits. Some vehicles may have circuit protection internal with the switch or motor, such as the headlamp switch and wiper motors. The rear wiper motor on most Jeep vehicles has an internal circuit breaker.

WRANGLER

WINDSHIELD WIPER

5.3 amp breaker

KEYLESS ENTRY, DOOR LOCKS, SEAT AND TRAILER PACKAGE

30 amp breaker

COMANCHE AND CHEROKEE

POWER WINDOWS

30 amp breaker

WINDSHIELD WIPER AND WASHER

4.8 amp breaker

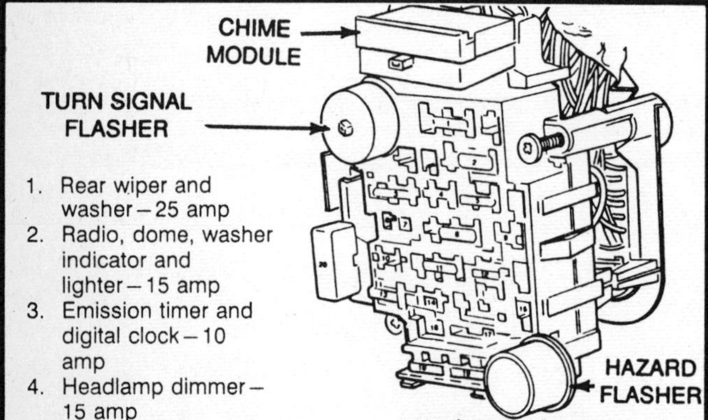

1. Rear wiper and washer—25 amp
2. Radio, dome, washer indicator and lighter—15 amp
3. Emission timer and digital clock—10 amp
4. Headlamp dimmer—15 amp
5. Blower motor—25 amp
6. Keyless entry, door locks, seat and trailer package—30 amp breaker
7. Anti-lock brake pump—2 amp
8. Turn signal flasher and rear defogger—20 amp
9. Courtesy, cargo, dome lamps and clock, entry module and mirrors—10 amp
10. Anti-lock module, pump and fluid level switch—10 amp
11. Headlamp module—11 amp
12. Hazard flasher and stoplamp—12 amp
13. A.T. controls and backup lamps—7.5 amp
14. Radio and power antenna—10 amp
15. Headlamp, dash, clock, radio and parking lamps—10 amp
16. Power windows—30 amp breaker
17. Headlamp, chime and cruise control modules—7.5 amp
18. Rear defogger—25 amp
19. Instrument panel lamps—5 amp
20. Windshield wiper and washer—4.8 amp breaker

Fuse locations—Comanche and Cherokee

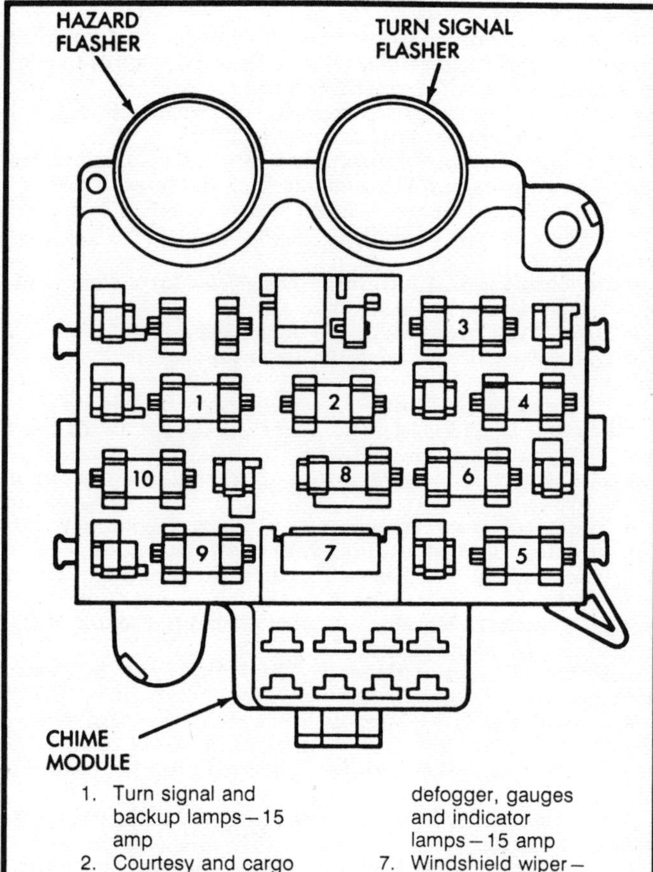

1. Turn signal and backup lamps—15 amp
2. Courtesy and cargo lamps—20 amp
3. Hazard and stop lamps—15 amp
4. Rear defogger—25 amp
5. Blower motor—25 amp
6. Key buzzer, defogger, gauges and indicator lamps—15 amp
7. Windshield wiper—5.3 amp breaker
8. Turn signal and parking lamps—20 amp
9. Instrument panel lamps—5 amp
10. Radio, cruise and lighter—30 amp

Fuse locations—Wrangler

GRAND WAGONEER

POWER WINDOWS AND MIRROR

30 amp breaker

POWER SEATS AND LOCKS

30 amp breaker

WINDSHIELD WIPER

5.5 amp breaker

Relays, Sensors, Switches, Modules and Computers Locations

NOTE: When using this section, some of the components may not be used on a particular vehicle. This is because either the particular component in question was used on an earlier model or a later model. This section is being published from the latest information available at the time of publication.

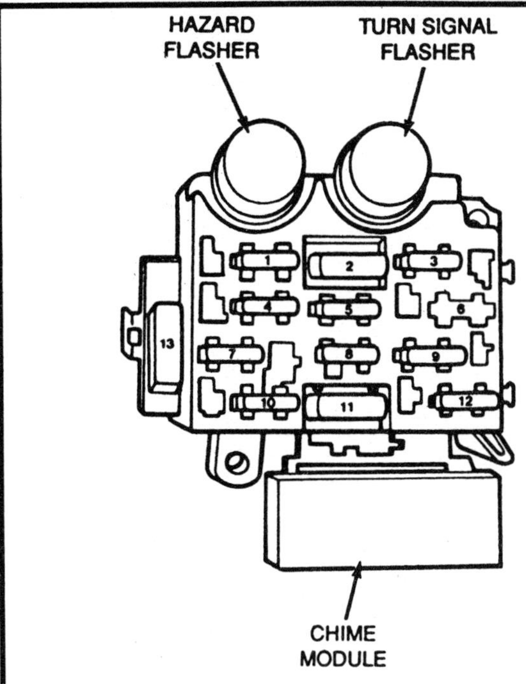

1. Rear wiper—20 amp
2. Power windows and mirror—30 amp breaker
3. Stop lamps, hazard lamps and cruise control—20 amp
4. Turn signal and backup lamps—15 amp
5. Dome, courtesy, underhood, and entry lamps
6. Not used
7. ACC. Radio light and lighter
8. Parking, tail, instrument lamps and chime module—20 amp
9. Ignition On lamps, including defogger and compass—3 amp
10. ACC lamps, instrument panel—3 amp
11. Power seats and locks—30 amp breaker
12. A/C control module—25 amp
13. Windshield wiper—5.5 amp breaker

Fuse locations—Grand Wagoneer

- **4WD Command Trac Switch**—is located next to the battery.
- **4WD Indicator Switch (Grand Wagoneer)**—is mounted at the transfer case.
- **4WD Vacuum Switch**—is located under the hood at the right of the firewall.
- **A/C Blower Motor Resistors**—is located in or on heater/evaporator blower housing.
- **A/C Blower Relay**—is located under the dash.
- **A/C Compressor Relay**—is located on the right side inner fender panel.
- **A/C Diode**—is located in or near the connector at the compressor.
- **A/C ECM (Grand Wagoneer)**—is located under the dash, just above the accelerator pedal.
- **A/C Pressure Switch**—is on the receiver drier, accumulator or in line at the right fender.
- **Air Control Solenoids**—are located at the valve cover toward the rear of the engine.
- **Air Temperature (MAT) Sensor (Grand Wagoneer)**—is located in the air cleaner housing.
- **Altitude Jumper wire (FBC)**—is a 2 terminal connector located behind the dash panel in back of the radio.
- **Antenna Relay**—is behind the passenger side kick panel.
- **Anti-lock brake (Modulator power) Relay**—is located on the front of the right fender well.
- **Anti-lock brake (Yellow indicator) Relay**—is located on the right fender well.
- **Anti-lock Brake ECU**—is located under the rear seat cushion or behind left quarter panel.
- **Anti-lock Brake Pump Relay**—is part of the pump motor harness and is located on the passenger side of the engine compartment.
- **B+ Latch Relay**—is located on the right side inner fender panel or on the Wrangler it may be located at the right side of the battery.
- **Canister Purge Solenoid**—is mounted at the base of the battery holddown.
- **Chime Module**—is located at the fuse box.
- **Console Temperature Sensor**—is located behind the left headlamp.
- **Coolant Temperature Sensor (FBC)**—is located in front of the carburetor.
- **Coolant Temperature Sensor (MPI)**—is installed in the engine water jacket on the left side of the engine.
- **Coolant Temperature Sensor (TBI)**—is installed in the intake manifold coolant jacket.
- **Coolant Temperature Switch (FBC)**—is located at the rear of the cylinder head.
- **Cooling Fan Relay (if equipped)**—is located on the left fender. This relay may be used on 6 cylinder vehicles.
- **Cooling Fan Switch (if equipped)**—is located on in the radiator. This switch may be used on 6 cylinder vehicles.
- **Crankshaft Position Sensor (CPS)**—is attached to the flywheel housing.
- **Cruise Control Module (except Wrangler)**—is under the dash on right side or on the Grand Wagoneer at the transmission tunnel.
- **Cruise Control Module (Wrangler)**—is under the dash below the fuse box.
- **Defogger Diode (Grand Wagoneer)**—is in the harness under the left side of the dash.
- **Defogger Relay (except Wrangler)**—is under the dash, to the right of the steering column.
- **Defogger Relay (Wrangler)**—is under the dash at left kick panel.
- **Defogger Timer (Grand Wagoneer)**—is in the rear tailgate.
- **Diagnostic Connector (FBC)**—is located next to the battery or next to relays on the right fender.
- **Diagnostic Connector**—is located next to the battery or next to relays on the right fender.
- **Downstream Solenoid (FBC)**—is located on a bracket mounted to the rear of the cylinder head.
- **ECU Starter Relay**—is mounted next to the battery hold down bracket, in the relay block or at the rear of the right fender.
- **EGR Valve Solenoid (MPI)**—is mounted on the left inner fender near the fuel pump ballast resistor.
- **EGR Valve Solenoid-MJ,XJ models with TBI**—is mounted at the right shock tower.
- **EGR Valve Solenoid-YJ models with TBI**—is mounted at the base of the battery holddown.
- **Electronic Control Unit (ECU)**—is located underneath the instrument panel between the steering column and the heater housing.
- **Electronic Control Unit (FBC)**—see MCU.
- **Electronic Transmission ECU**—is located under the dash near the accelerator pedal.
- **Emission Maintenance Timer (except Wrangler)**—is mounted under the dash column to the right of the steering column.

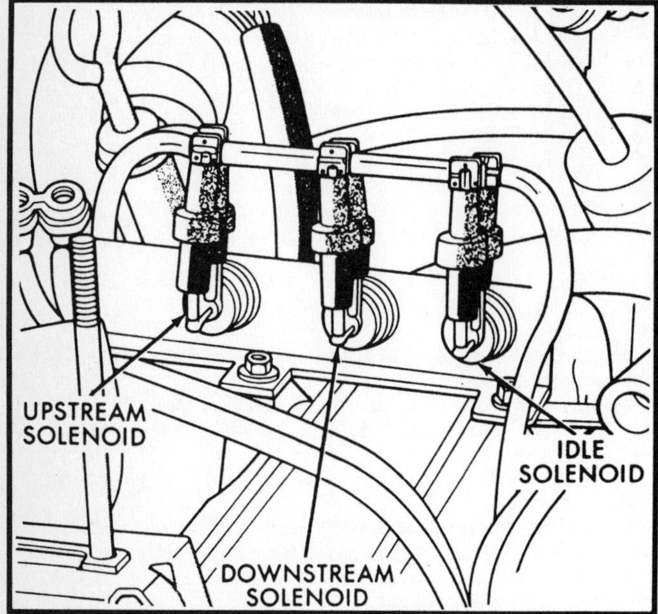

Air Control Solenoids—4.2L engine

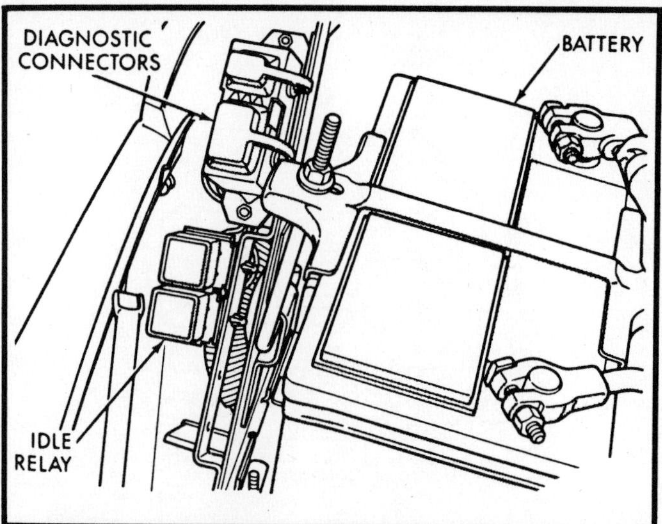

Idle Relay—4.2L engine

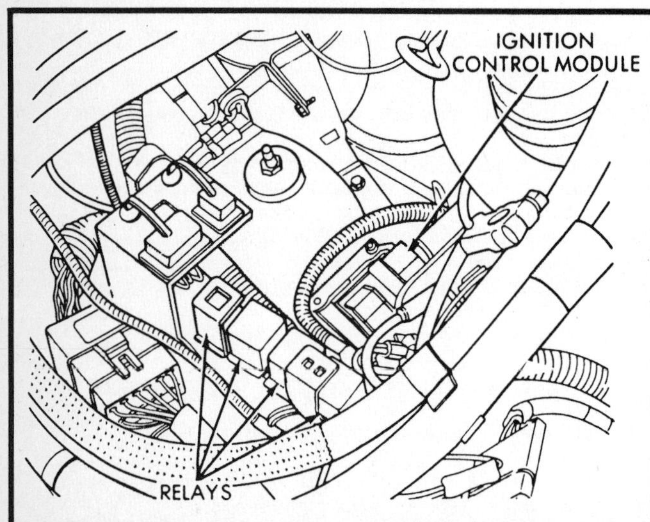

Fuel pump, B+ latch, A/C compressor relays—2.5L engine with TBI

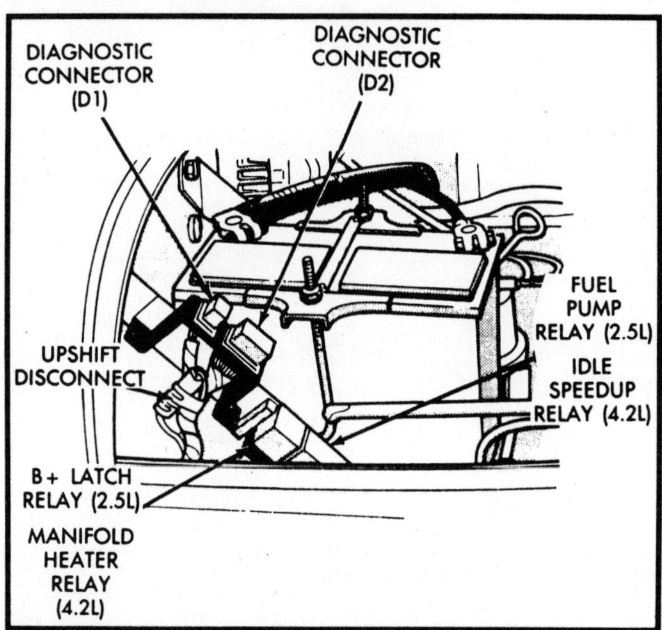

Diagnostic Connectors and fuel pump relay—Wrangler

- **Emission Maintenance Timer (Wrangler)**—is mounted under the dash column to the right of the accelerator pedal.
- **Engine Speed Sensor**—See crankshaft position sensor.
- **Fan Control Relay**—is located on the right fender well.
- **Fog Light Relay**—Behind left headlamp or at front left fender.
- **Fuel Pump Relay**—is located on the front of the right strut tower.
- **Fuel Pump Resistor (MPI)**—is located on the left front fender panel
- **Hazard Flasher**—is located at the fuse box.
- **Hazard Flasher**—is located at the fuse box.
- **Headlamp Sentinel Module**—is attached to the inner instrument panel next to the headlamp switch.
- **Horn Relay**—is located near the fuse box.
- **Idle Relay (FBC)**—is located next to the battery.
- **Idle Solenoid (FBC)**—is located on a bracket mounted to the rear of the cylinder head.
- **Ignition Coil**—is located on the right side inner fender panel.
- **Ignition Control Module (2.5L engine, except Wrangler)**—is on the right shock tower area.
- **Ignition Control Module (2.5L engine, Wrangler)**—is left of the battery on the firewall area.
- **Ignition Control Module (4.0L engine)**—is mounted to the ignition coil assembly.
- **Ignition Control Module (4.2L engine)**—is located at the bottom of the radiator overflow bottle.
- **Ignition Control Module (5.9L engine)**—is mounted to the left wheel well.
- **Ignition Control Module**—is located on the right side inner fender panel.
- **Intake Manifold Heater Switch (FBC)**—Is located in the intake manifold water jacket.
- **Key Less Entry Module**—is located overhead, between the visors or in the console.

• **Knock Sensor (FBC)**—is located in the intake manifold.

• **Knock Sensor (MPI)**—is located below the coolant temperature sensor, slightly to the right. Accessible from below.

• **Low Fuel Module (Grand Wagoneer)**—is behind the dash with the gauges.

• **Maintenance Reminder Module**—is under dash near steering column.

• **Manifold Absolute Pressure (MAP) Sensor**—is mounted under the hood on the dash panel.

• **Manifold Air Temperature (MAT) Sensor (except Grand Wagoneer)**—is installed in the intake manifold with the sensor element extending into the air stream.

• **Manifold Heater Relay (if equipped)**—is next to the battery, on 6 cylinder vehicles.

• **MCU (Mirco Computer Assembly)**—is located in the passenger compartment.

• **Oil Pressure Sending Unit**—is on the right side of the engine.

• **Oxygen Heater Relay (MPI)**—is located on the right inner fender panel.

• **PCV Solenoid Valve**—is mounted in the PCV hose between the PCV valve and intake manifold or carburetor base.

• **Power Door Lock Relay (except Grand Wagoneer)**—is under dash, behind the kick panel.

• **Power Door Lock Relay (Grand Wagoneer)**—is under right side of the dash.

• **Radio Light Relay**—is behind the glovebox.

• **Rollover and Pressure Relief Valve**—is mounted in the fuel tank.

• **Speed Sensor (except Wrangler)**—is located behind the instrument panel.

• **Speed Sensor (Wrangler)**—is located above the front driveshaft and is in-line with the speedometer cable.

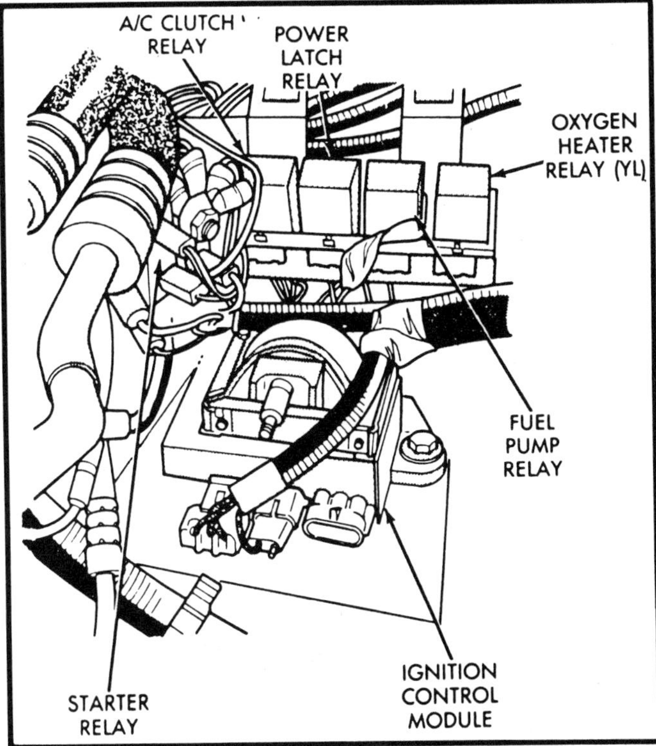

Relay identification—Cherokee and Comanche

• **Thermal Time Switch (FBC)**—is located inside the air cleaner.

• **Throttle Position Sensor**—is mounted on the throttle body and connected to the throttle shaft.

• **Towing Light Relays**—are located in the left rear quarter panel.

• **Turn Signal Flasher**—is located at the fuse box.

• **Upstream Solenoid (FBC)**—is located on a bracket mounted to the rear of the cylinder head.

• **Vacuum Switches (FBC)**—are located together in a bracket attached to the center of the firewall under the hood.

• **Wiper Delay Module**—is located under the left side of the instrument panel.

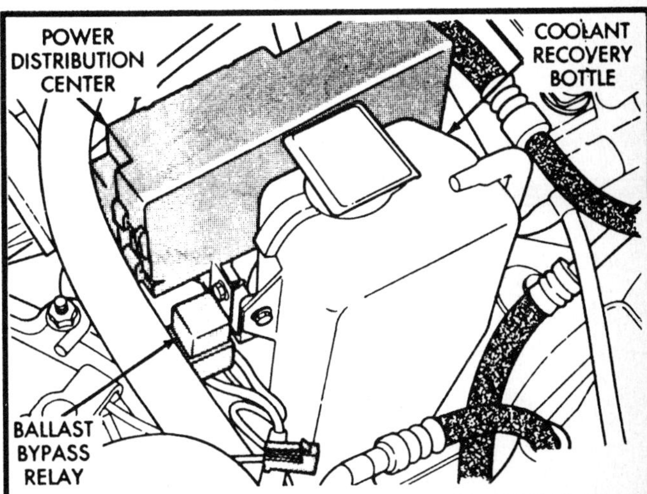

Ballast Bypass (fuel pump control) Relay

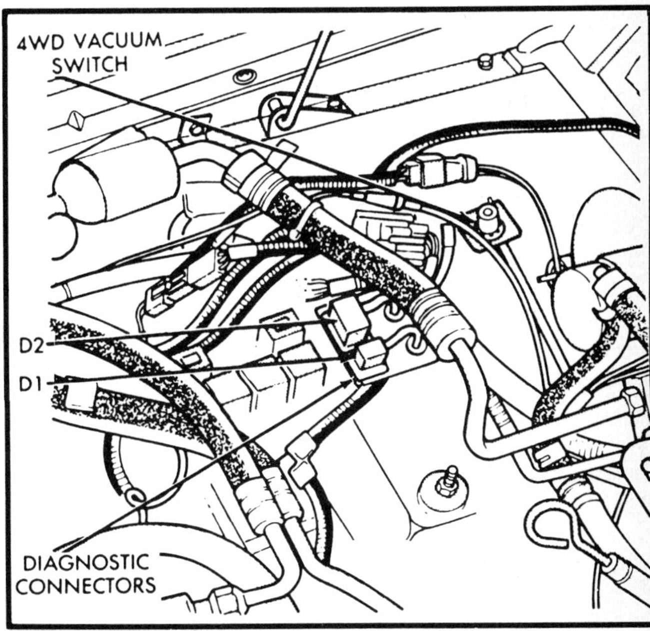

Diagnostic Connectors and 4WD switch—Cherokee and Comanche

FORD MOTOR COMPANY EXCEPT LIGHT TRUCK AND VAN

Circuit Breakers

CONTINENTAL

WINDSHIELD WIPER/WASHER AND GOVERNOR

The circuit breaker is located at the bottom center of the fuseblock; fuse position 2

COUGAR AND THUNDERBIRD

POWER WINDOW, MOONROOF, LUGGAGE COMPARTMENT RELEASE

The 20 amp circuit breaker labeled POWER WDO is located in the fuseblock below the instrument panel.

POWER SEATS, POWER DOOR LOCKS, LUMBAR SEATS, FUEL FILLER DOOR

The 20 amp circuit breaker labeled SEAT/LOCK is located in the fuseblock below the instrument panel.

CIGAR LIGHTER, FLASH-TO-PASS

The 20 amp circuit breaker labeled CIGAR LTR is located in the fuseblock below the instrument panel

WINDSHIELD WIPER/WASHER

The 8.5 amp circuit breaker is labeled WIPERS is located in the fuseblock below the instrument panel.

CROWN VICTORIA AND GRAND MARQUIS

INTERVAL WIPER/WASHER

The 8.25 amp circuit breaker is located in the lower center of the fusebox.

REAR LIGHTERS, TAILGATE WINDOW KEY SWITCH, DOOR LOCKS, POWER SEATS

The 30 amp circuit breaker is located in the left center of the fusebox, position 12.

POWER WINDOWS

The 20 amp circuit breaker is located in the right center of the fusebox, near the flasher, in position 14.

ESCORT

HEADLIGHTS AND HIGH BEAM INDICATOR

The 22 amp circuit breaker is incorporated into the headlamp switch.

WINDSHIELD WIPER AND REAR WINDOW

The 8.25 amp circuit breaker is located in the fuse block.

LIFTGATE/HATCHBACK

The 4.5 amp circuit breaker is located on the back of the instrument panel, to the right of the steering column.

COOLING FAN MOTOR

The 12 amp circuit breaker is located in the fuse block.

FESTIVA

No circuit breakers are used.

MARK VII

WINDSHIELD WIPER/WASHER AND GOVERNOR

The 6 amp circuit breaker is located at the bottom center of the fuse panel, position 2.

CIGAR LIGHTERS AND HORN

The 20 amp circuit breaker is located at the left center of the fuse panel, position 13.

POWER WINDOWS, MOONROOF, HEADLAMPS AND AUTOMATIC HEADLAMP DIMMER

The 20 amp breaker is located in the upper center of the fusebox, position 14.

IN-LINE CIRCUIT BREAKER

The in-line breaker is located on the left fender apron, near the starter relay.

MUSTANG

INTERVAL WIPERS

The 8.25 amp circuit breaker is located in the upper center of the fusebox, position 2.

POWER WINDOWS

The 20 amp circuit breaker is located near the hazard flasher in the fusebox, position 14. Additionally, a 20 amp in-line circuit breaker is connected to the starter relay.

LUMBAR SEATS

The 20 amp in-line circuit breaker is connected to the starter relay.

CONVERTIBLE TOP

The 25 amp in-line circuit breaker is located behind the instrument panel, near the left side of the instrument cluster.

PROBE

REAR WINDOW DEFROSTER

The circuit breaker is located in the joint box above the fuse block. It is the plug-in type with a manual reset button.

TAURUS AND SABLE

WINDSHIELD WIPER/WASHER AND GOVERNOR

The circuit breaker is located at the bottom center of the fuseblock; fuse position 2.

CIGAR LIGHTER AND HORN

The circuit breaker is located at the left center of the fuseblock; fuse position 12.

POWER WINDOWS, POWER LOCKS, POWER SEATS, KEYLESS ENTRY, LIFTGATE RELEASE

The circuit breaker is located upper center of fuseblock; fuse position 14.

TEMPO AND TOPAZ

POWER SEATS, POWER WINDOWS, POWER LOCKS AND LUMBAR SEAT

The 20 amp circuit breaker located in the fuse panel.

WINDSHIELD WIPER CIRCUIT AND REAR WINDOW CIRCUIT BREAKER

The 8.25 amp circuit breaker located in the fuse panel.

ALTERNATOR VOLTAGE SENSING CIRCUIT

The 18 amp circuit breaker in the engine compartment wiring harness near the starter motor relay.

OXYGEN SENSOR, ALL WHEEL DRIVE RELAYS, A/C FAN CONTROLLER, FAN TESTER AND ALL WHEEL DRIVE SWITCH

The 20 amp circuit breaker is located in the engine compartment near the starter motor relay.

PASSIVE RESTRAINT MODULE

The 20 amp circuit breaker located in the engine compartment near the starter motor relay.

TRACER

BLOWER MOTOR

The circuit breaker is located in the joint box above the fuse block. It is the plug in type with a manual reset button.

TOWN CAR

WIPER/WASHER, WINDSHIELD WIPER MODULE

The 8.25 amp circuit breaker is located in the lower center of the fuseblock, position 2.

TRUNK LID RELEASE SWITCH

The 20 amp circuit breaker is located in the left center of the fuse box, position 12.

Fusible Links

CONTINENTAL

Air Suspension Motor—within power distribution box mounted in engine compartment.
Air Suspension Module—within power distribution box mounted in engine compartment.
Anti-lock Module—within power distribution box mounted in engine compartment.
Anti-lock Motor—within power distribution box mounted in engine compartment.
Rear Window Defrost—within power distribution box mounted in engine compartment.
Ignition Coil/TFI—within power distribution box mounted in engine compartment.
Electronic Engine Control—within power distribution box mounted in engine compartment.
Fuse Panel/AC Clutch—within power distribution box mounted in engine compartment.
Headlamp—within power distribution box mounted in engine compartment.
Fuse Panel—within power distribution box mounted in engine compartment.
Power Lock and Window—within power distribution box mounted in engine compartment.
Cooling Fan Motor—within power distribution box mounted in engine compartment.
Ignition Switch/Blower Motor—within power distribution box mounted in engine compartment.
Fuse Link A—located at starter relay on left fender apron.
Fuse Link B—located left side of engine compartment, near starter relay.
Fuse Link C—between right front fender and apron, at alternator output control relay.

COUGAR AND THUNDERBIRD

Rear Window Defroster—40 amp fusible link is located in the power distribution box in the engine compartment.
ABS Hydraulic Pump Motor—40 amp fusible link is located in the power distribution box in the engine compartment.
Stop Lamps, Cigar Lighter, Seat/Locks, Fuses, Radio, Anti-Theft—30 amp fusible link is located in the power distribution box in the engine compartment.
Courtesy Lamps, Headlamps—60 amp fusible link is located in the power distribution box in the engine compartment.
Passive Restraints—40 amp fusible link is located in the power distribution box in the engine compartment.
Ignition Coil, EEC Relay, Sensors—30 amp fusible link is located in the power distribution box in the engine compartment.
Fuel Pump—30 amp fusible link is located in the power distribution box in the engine compartment.
Programmed Ride Control—30 amp fusible link is located in the power distribution box in the engine compartment.
Ignition Switch—80 amp fusible link is located in the power distribution box in the engine compartment.
Anti-Lock Brake System—30 amp fusible link is located in the power distribution box in the engine compartment.
Horn, Hazard Flasher, Turn Signal—20 amp fusible link is located in the power distribution box in the engine compartment.
Radio, Vehicle Maintenance Monitor, Electronic Instrument Cluster—5 amp fusible link is located in the power distribution box in the engine compartment.

CROWN VICTORIA AND GRAND MARQUIS

Fusible Links A, AA, E, F, G, H, L, T, U, Y, and Z— are located at the starter relay on the right fender apron.
Fusible Links B and C— are located on the front of the left fender apron.
Fusible Links M, N, and Q—are located on the left front fender apron.
Fusible Link R—is located in the left front of the engine compartment.
Fusible Link W—is connected to the alternator output control relay.

ESCORT

Fusible links service the vehicle's charging and power distribution system. They are located on the left rear of the engine compartment on the left fender apron forward of the shock tower.

FESTIVA

The fusible links protect all the lighting, PTC heater (carbureted), EFI (fuel injection), ignition system, starter system, charging system, windshield wiper system, A/C and heater, cooling fan system, emission control system, rear defroster, clock and audio systems. The links are located in a junction block just above the main fuse panel on the left strut tower within the engine compartment.

MARK VII

Fusible Links A, B, C, D, E, F, H, K, and L—are located on the left front fender apron at the starter relay.
Fusible Link G—is located on the left front fender apron.
Fusible Link M—is located on the right front fender apron, near the wiring sub-harness to the VIP test connectors.
Fusible Link N—is located on the right fender apron at the base of the shock tower.

MUSTANG

Fusible Links A, B, C, D, E, F, G and H—are located at the starter relay.
Fusible Link J—is located near the wire harness to the Heated Exhaust Gas Oxygen Sensor.
Fusible Link N—is located behind the left shock tower.

PROBE

No fusible links are used.

TAURUS AND SABLE

Fuse Link A, B, C, D, E, F, G, K, P, R, T, U and V—left side of engine compartment at starter relay.
Fuse Link H—left side of engine compartment, left side of radiator.
Fuse Link J—Center front of engine compartment, near integrated control module.
Fuse Link N—right front of engine compartment, taped to headlamp junction harness.
Fuse Link S—left side front of engine compartment.

TEMPO AND TOPAZ

Electric Rear Window Defroster and Fuel Filler Door—is located in the wiring harness assembly near the starter motor relay (18 gauge wire).
Headlamp Feed—is located in the engine compartment on the starter motor relay (16 gauge wire).
Ignition Feed—is located near the starter motor relay (16 gauge wire).
Alternator Output—is located in the charging circuit near the starter motor relay (14 gauge wire).
Fan, A/C Clutch and A/C Controller—is located in the wiring assembly on the starter motor relay (20 gauge wire).
EEC Relay, EEC Module and Fuel Pump Relay Fusible Link—is located in the wiring assembly on the starter motor relay (20 gauge wire).
Cooling Fan Relay Fusible Link—is located in the wiring assembly on the starter motor relay (16 gauge wire).
Air Bag Module Fusible Link—is located in the engine compartment near the starter motor relay (20 gauge wire).

TRACER

No fusible links are used.

TOWN CAR

Fusible Links D and E—are located at the right front of the engine compartment, near the engine compartment fusebox.

Relays, Sensors, Switches, Modules and Computers Locations

NOTE: When using this section, some of the components may not be used on a particular vehicle. This is because the particular component in question was used on an earlier model or a later model. If a component is not found in this section, check other vehicles with the same engine or component, as that engine or component may have been introduced earlier on different models. This section is being published from the latest information available at the time of this publication.

CONTINENTAL

- **A/C clutch Cycling Pressure Switch**—is located at the right rear of engine compartment on accumulator.
- **A/C Compressor Clutch Solenoid**—is located at the right front of engine.
- **Air Bag Diagnostic Module**—is behind left instrument panel, above fuse panel.
- **Air Charge Temperature (ACT) Sensor**—is located at the top right side of engine.
- **Air Spring Vent Solenoid**—is located at the top of applicable shock absorber (Left front, left rear, etc.)

Air Suspension Compressor Motor and Vent Solenoid—is located at the right front of engine compartment.

- **Air Suspension Compressor Relay**—is located at the right side of engine compartment at firewall.
- **Air Suspension Electronic Control Module**—is attached to left hinge support in trunk.
- **Air Suspension Electronic Control Module**—is attached to left trunk lid hinge support.
- **Air Suspension Switch**—is located at the left side of trunk.
- **Air Bag Crash Sensors**—see specific location: center, left/right, rear.
- **Air Bag Diagnostic Module**—is behind left side dash, above fuse panel.
- **Alarm Relay**—is located at the rear of car, under left side of package tray.
- **Alternator Output Control Relay**—is between right front fender and apron, located on frame rail.
- **Ambient Temperature Sensor (1989)**—is below left side of front bumper.
- **Ambient Temperature Sensor (except 1989)**—is located at the left side of radiator support.
- **Anti-Theft Controller Module**—is located at the rear of car, below center of package tray.
- **Anti-Theft Diode**—is in harness behind left kick panel at cowl. Diode is located 6 in. (150mm) from courtesy lamp switch.
- **Anti-Theft Disarm Switches**—is inside respective doors at keylock assemblies.
- **Anti-Theft In Line Fuses**—is in wiring harness at rear of car below left side of package shelf.
- **Anti-Theft Inverter Relay**—is under left side of package tray.
- **Anti-Lock Brake System Diode**—is taped within harness, center rear of engine compartment.
- **Anti-Lock Brake Test Connector**—is located at the right front of trunk, below package shelf.
- **Anti-Lock Electronic Control Module**—is located at the right front of trunk, under package tray.
- **Anti-Lock Hydraulic Pump Motor Relay**—is located at the right side of firewall in engine compartment.
- **Anti-Lock Power Relay**—is located at the right side of firewall in engine compartment.
- **Anti-Lock Solenoid Control Valve Body**—is located at the left rear of engine compartment, near brake master cylinder.
- **Anti-theft Controller Module**—is below center of package tray.
- **Anti-theft Starter Interrupt Relay**—is behind center of instrument panel.
- **Autolamp Relay**—is behind center of instrument panel.
- **Autolamp/Autodimmer Control**—is behind left side of instrument panel.
- **AXOD Speed Sensor and Torque Converter Solenoid**—is located at the left rear of transaxle.
- **Backup/Neutral Switch**—is located at the top left of transaxle.
- **Blower Motor Speed Controller**—is behind center of instrument panel.

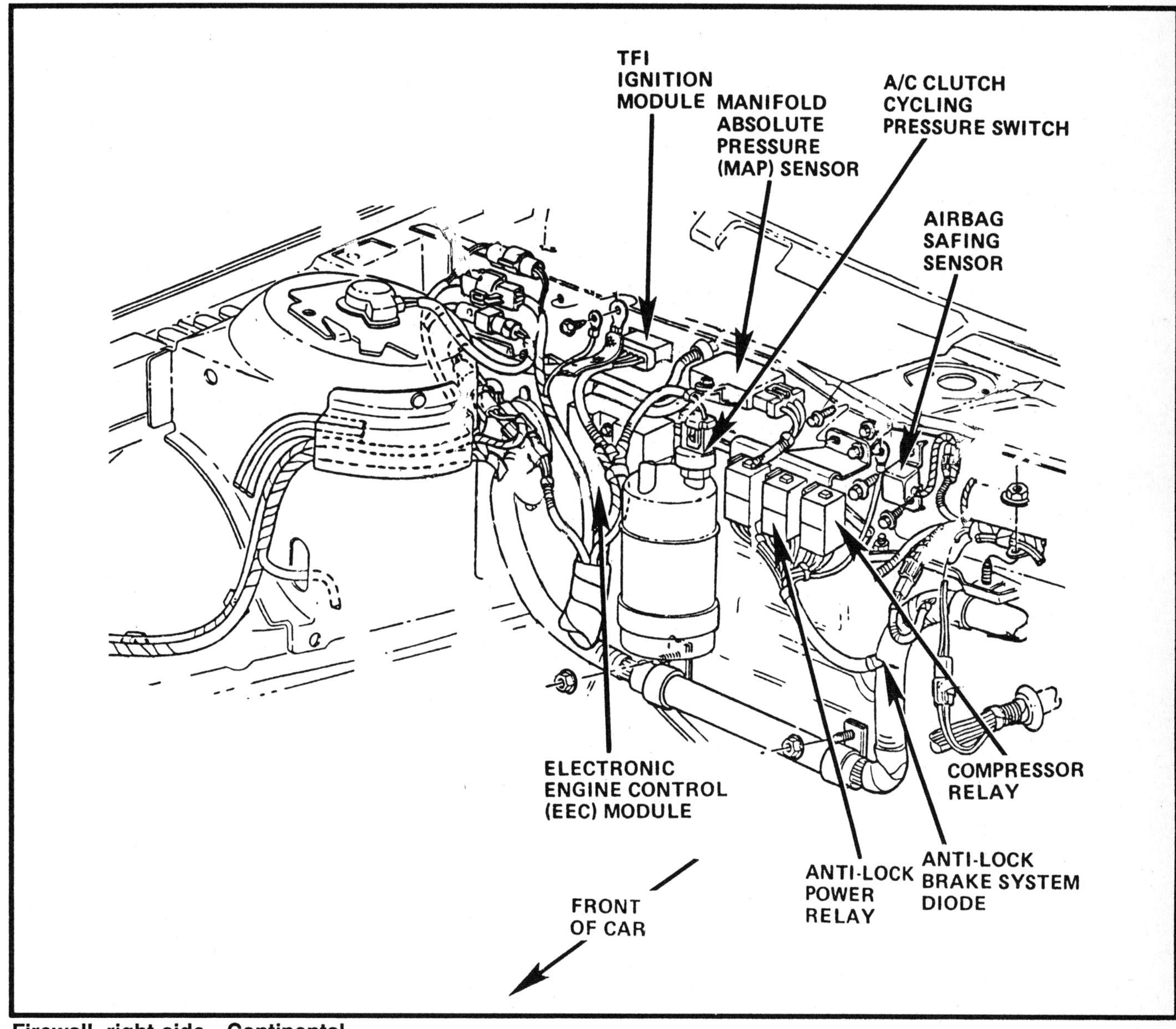

Firewall, right side—Continental

• **Brake Fluid Level Sensor**—is located on brake master cylinder.

• **Brake Lamp Switch**—is located on brake pedal support bracket.

• **Brake Pressure Switch**—is located at the left side of engine compartment below brake master cylinder.

• **Canister Purge Solenoid**—is located at the left front of engine compartment.

• **Center Line Forward Crash Sensor**—is located at the center front of vehicle.

• **Coolant Temperature Sensor**—is located at the left side top of engine, mounted vertically.

• **Cracked Windshield Sense Resistor**—is located at the right side of firewall, below heated windshield.

• **Dual Brake Warning Switch**—is on anti-lock brake control assembly.

• **EGR Vacuum Regulator Solenoid**—is located at the left side of engine, above transaxle.

• **Electric Fuel Pump**—is in fuel tank.

• **Electronic Control Assembly (ECA)**—is located at the right side of firewall in engine compartment.

• **Electronic Flasher**—is behind left side instrument panel, on fuse panel.

• **Engine Coolant Temperature Sensor**—is located at the left side top of engine, mounted vertically.

• **Flasher**—is behind left side of instrument panel, on fuse panel.

• **Fuel Filler Door Release Solenoid**—is behind right rear wheel house.

• **Fuel Gauge Sender**—is in fuel tank.

• **Fuse Panel**—is under left side dashboard.

• **Hard Shock Relay**—is located at the left front of trunk, below package shelf.

• **Headlight Relay**—is located behind left side of instrument panel.

• **Heated Exhaust Gas Oxygen Sensor (HEGO) #1**—is at the lower right front of engine, in exhaust pipe.

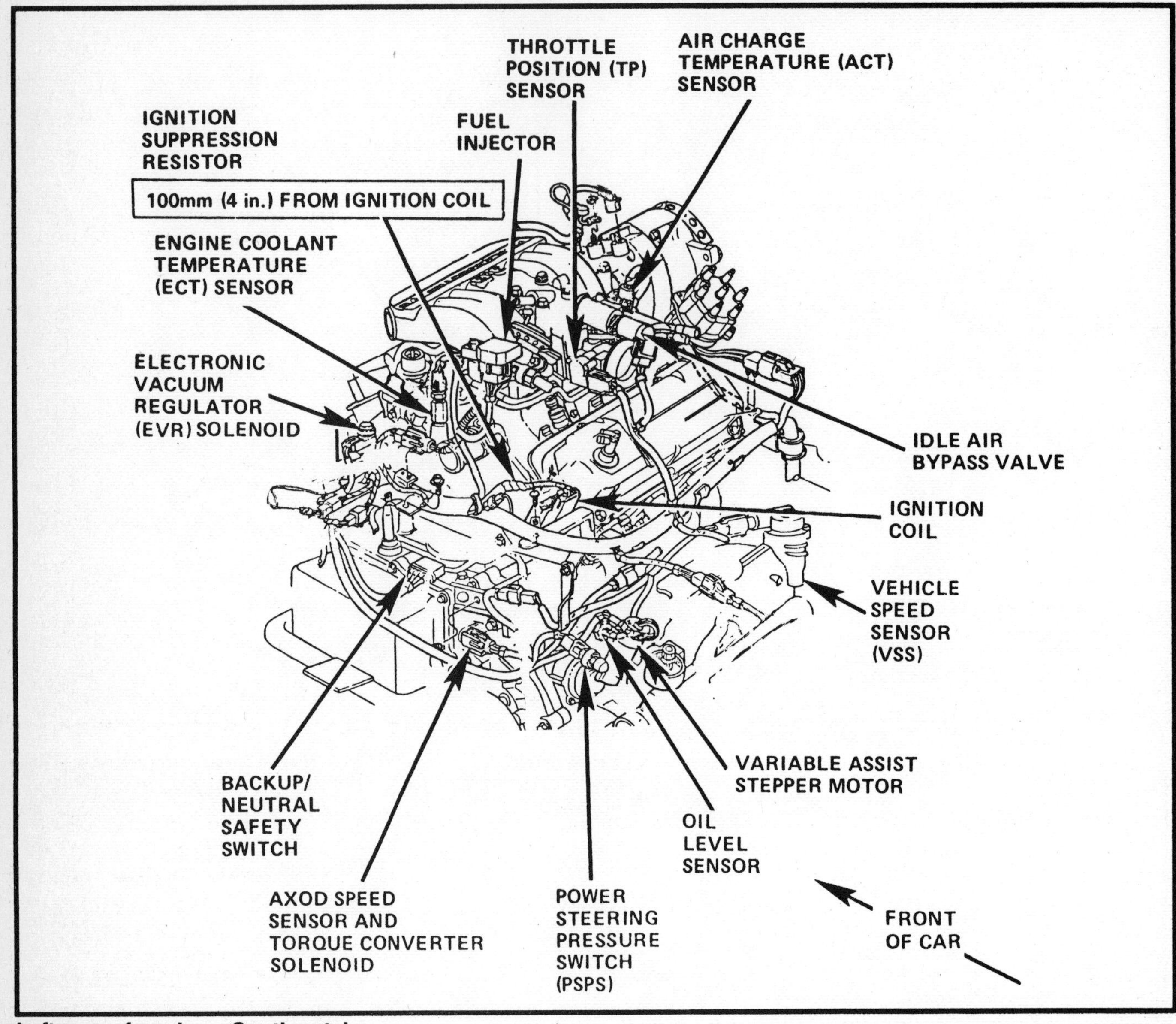

Left rear of engine—Continental

- **Heated Exhaust Gas Oxygen Sensor (HEGO) #2**—is at the left rear of engine.
- **Heated Windshield Control Module**—is located behind left instrument panel.
- **Heated Windshield Control Module**—is located behind left side instrument panel.
- **Heated Windshield Test Connector**—is left rear of engine compartment.
- **Height Sensor, Left Front**—is attached to left front lower control arm.
- **Height Sensor, Rear**—is attached to right side of rear axle.
- **Height Sensor, Right Front**—is attached to left front lower control arm.
- **Hi-Lo Beam Photocell Amplifier**—is mounted on rear view mirror.
- **Hi-Lo Beam Relay**—is behind left side of instrument panel.
- **Horn Relay**—is behind center of instrument panel.
- **Horns, High and Low Pitch**—is under left front of vehicle.
- **Ignition Coil**—is at the left rear of engine, next to valve cover.
- **Ignition Key Warning Switch**—is within steering column.
- **Ignition Resistor**—is taped within harness, 4 in. (100mm) from ignition coil.
- **Ignition Suppression Resistor**—is at the left rear of engine, near ignition coil.
- **In Car Temperature Sensor**—is behind right side of instrument panel, above glove box.
- **Inertia Switch (1989)**—is at the inboard side of left trunk lid hinge support.
- **Inertia Switch (except 1989)**—is on the left rear quarter panel

Integrated Controller Module—is on the left front of engine compartment.

- **Integrated Controller Module**—is on the left front of engine compartment.

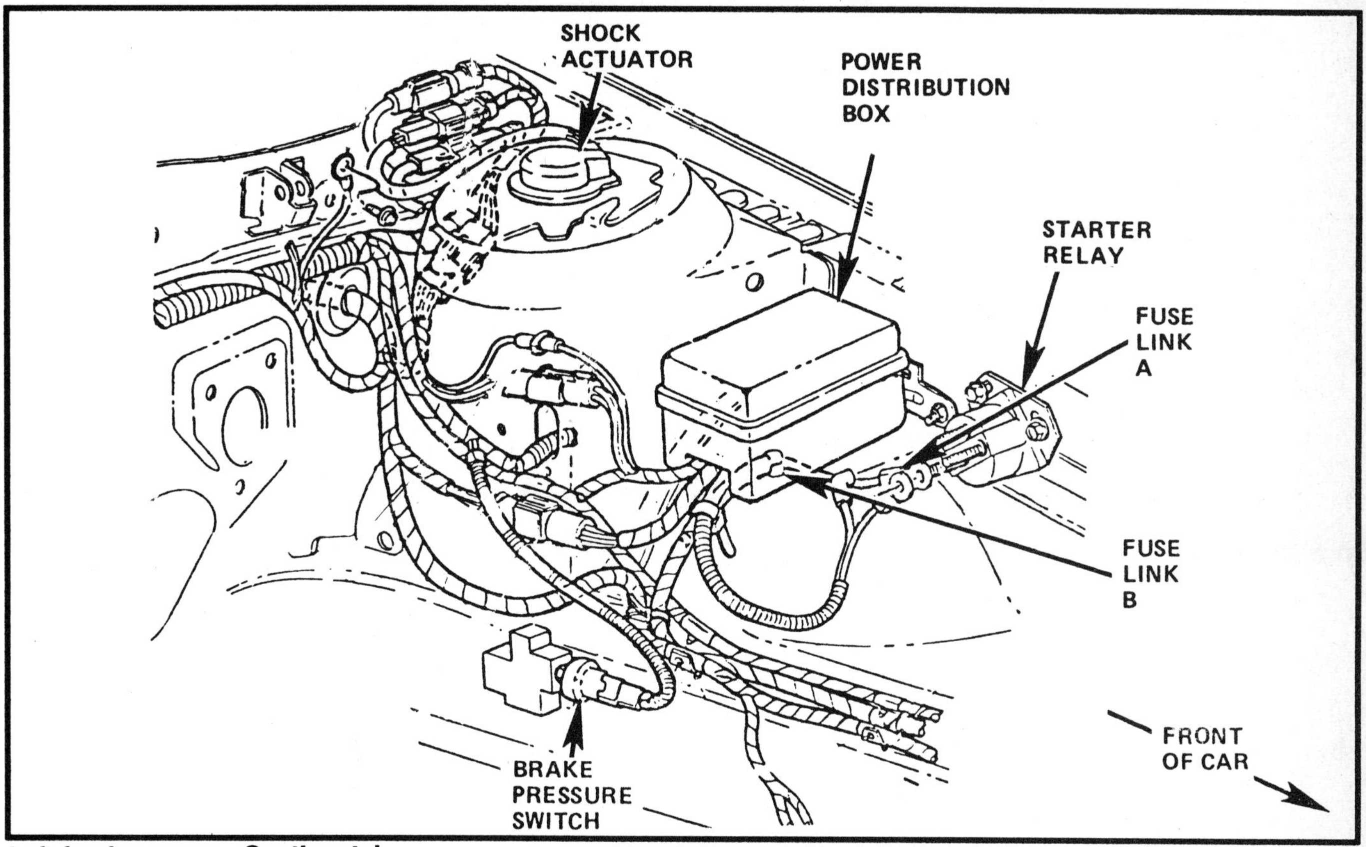

Left fender apron—Continental

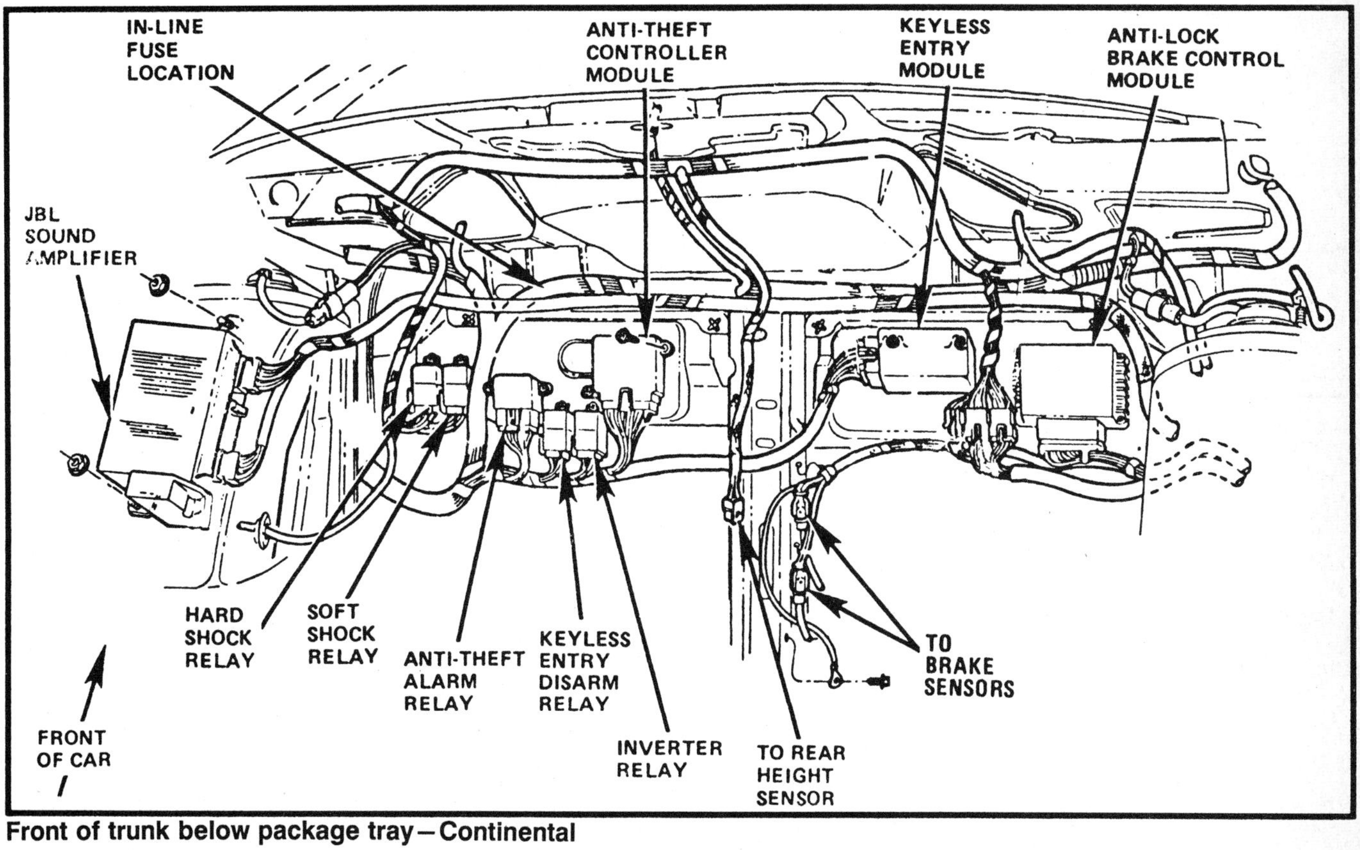

Front of trunk below package tray—Continental

- **Interior Lamp Relay**—is behind right side of instrument panel.
- **Keyless Entry Module**—is under rear package tray, center front of trunk.
- **Lamp Out Warning Module**—is behind left instrument panel, near fuse panel.
- **LCD Dimming Relay**—is behind center of instrument panel.
- **Left Forward Crash Sensor**—is inside left fender apron.
- **Left Front Height Sensor**—is attached to left front lower control arm.
- **Left Seat Belt Switch**—is in driver's seat belt buckle.
- **Left Seat Memory Module**—is under left front seat.
- **Light Sensor/Amplifier (1989)**—is in left top of instrument panel.
- **Manifold Absolute Pressure (MAP) Sensor**—is at the center rear of engine compartment, on firewall.
- **Message Center**—is at the center of instrument panel.
- **Neutral Safety Switch**—is at the top left of transaxle.
- **Oil Level Sensor**—is at the lower left rear of engine.
- **Oil Pressure Switch Resistor**—is at the left side of engine, near oil pressure switch.
- **Oil Pressure Switch**—is on the lower right front of engine.
- **Parking Brake Switch**—is on parking brake lever.
- **PFE Sensor**—is on the left side of engine.
- **Power Distribution Box**—is mounted on left fender apron.
- **Power Steering Pressure Switch (PSPS)**—is on the left rear of engine compartment.
- **Power Steering Variable Assist Module**—is behind left side of instrument panel.
- **Pulse Width Dimming Module**—is behind right side instrument panel, near left side of glove box.
- **Radio Interference Capacitor**—is on the left inner fender panel, above voltage regulator.
- **Rear Defogger Relay and Timer**—is inside defogger switch housing.
- **Rear Height Sensor**—is attached to right side of rear axle.
- **Rear Sensor**—is at the left rear of engine compartment, near firewall.
- **Right Forward Crash Sensor**—is inside right fender apron.
- **Right Front Height Sensor**—is attached to right front lower control arm.
- **Seat Memory Module**—is under left front seat.
- **Self Test Input Connector**—is at the right rear of engine compartment.
- **Shock Actuator**—is near the top of respective shock absorber.
- **Shorting Plug**—is on the right side of engine compartment.
- **Soft Shock Relay**—is at the left front of trunk, below package shelf.
- **Speed Control Servo**—is on the left front strut tower.
- **Star Test Connector**—is at the left side of trunk.
- **Starter Relay**—is on the left fender apron.
- **Steering Rate Sensor**—is inside steering column.
- **Stop Lamp Switch**—is on brake pedal support bracket.
- **Sun Load Sensor**—is at the right side top of instrument panel.
- **TFI Ignition Module**—is attached to firewall in engine compartment, behind center of instrument panel.
- **Throttle Air Bypass Valve Solenoid**—is at the top center of engine.
- **Throttle Position Sensor**—is attached to left side of throttle body.
- **Torque Converter Solenoid**—is at the left rear of transaxle.
- **Trunk Lid Ajar Switch**—is at the rear of trunk.
- **Trunk Lid Lamp Switch**—is on the underside of trunk lid, near trunk lid lamp.
- **Trunk Lid Pull Down Module**—is on the right side of trunk, on hinge.
- **Trunk Lid Pull Down Switch**—is within trunk lid latch assembly.
- **Trunk Lid Release Solenoid**—is on the underside of the trunk lid.
- **Trunk Lid Solenoid Relay**—is at the right front of trunk on hinge.
- **Trunk Lock Removal Switch**—is on the underside of trunk lid.
- **Variable Assist Power Steering Module**—is behind left side of instrument panel.
- **Variable Assist Power Steering Test Connector**—is at the left rear of engine compartment.
- **Variable Assist Stepper Motor**—is at the left rear of engine compartment.
- **Vehicle Speed Sensor**—lower right rear of engine.
- **VIP Self Test Connector**—is on the right rear of engine compartment.
- **Voltage Regulator**—is on left inner fender panel.
- **Warning Chime Module**—is behind center of instrument panel.
- **Washer Fluid Level Switch**—is on front of washer fluid reservoir.
- **Window Safety Relay**—is behind center of instrument panel.
- **Wiper/Washer Interval Governor**—is behind center of instrument panel.

COUGAR AND THUNDERBIRD

- **A/C Clutch Cycling Pressure Switch**—is located at the right firewall, on the accumulator.
- **A/C Clutch Diode (3.8L supercharged engine)**—is taped to the engine wiring harness, 5 inches from A/C clutch coil.
- **A/C Clutch Diode (3.8L engine)**—is taped to the engine wiring harness, 3 inches from A/C clutch coil.
- **A/C Cutout Relay**—is located on the right firewall on the relay bracket.
- **ABS**—see Anti-Lock.
- **Air Charge Temperature Sensor**—is located at the top rear of the engine.
- **Anti-Lock Brake Control Module**—is located in trunk, below center of rear package tray.
- **Anti-Lock Diode**—is located below center of rear package tray, 5 inches from anti-lock brake control module.
- **Anti-Lock Power Relay**—is located on the relay bracket on the right firewall.
- **Anti-Lock pressure Switch**—is located in the brake control unit, left rear of engine compartment.
- **Anti-Lock Solenoid Control Valve Body**—is contained within the brake control unit, left rear of engine compartment.
- **Anti-Lock Test Connector**—is located in the right side of the trunk, behind the wheelwell.
- **Anti-Theft Diode**—is located in the window regulator harness, 11 inches from keyless entry module.
- **Anti-Theft Inline Fuse**—is located in left rear of trunk, behind wheelwell within window regulator harness.
- **Anti-Theft Module**—is located in the left rear of the trunk at the rear of the wheelwell.
- **Anti-Theft Module**—is located in the left rear of the trunk, behind the wheelwell.
- **Auto Lamp Dual Coil Relay**—is located behind the center of the instrument panel, to the left of the glove box.
- **Auto Shock Test Connector**—is located at the right rear of the engine, near the shock tower.
- **Autolamp Light Sensor**—is attached to the top underside of the instrument panel.

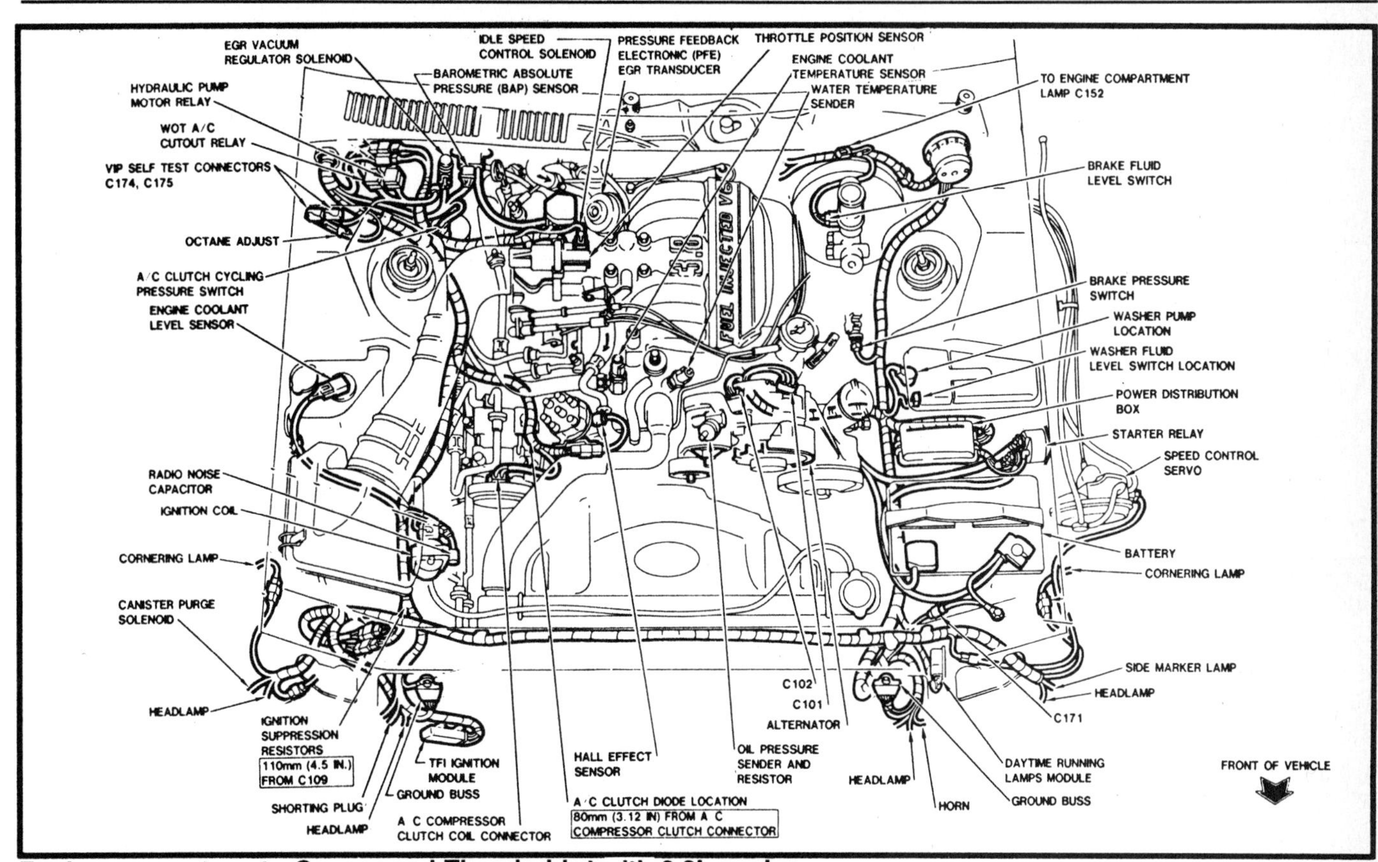

Engine compartment – Cougar and Thunderbird with 3.8L engine

ANTI-LOCK POWER RELAY
EGR VACUUM REGULATOR SOLENOID
BAROMETRIC ABSOLUTE PRESSURE (BAP) SENSOR
BRAKE FLUID LEVEL SWITCH
HYDRAULIC PUMP MOTOR
C166
AIR CHARGE TEMPERATURE SENSOR
C152
G108
SOLENOID CONTROL VALVE
C168
C176
HYDRAULIC PUMP MOTOR RELAY
WOT A/C CUTOUT RELAY
VIP SELF-TEST CONNECTOR C174, C175
C185
C188
ANTI-LOCK PRESSURE SWITCH
LEFT FRONT SHOCK ACTUATOR
OCTANE ADJUST
MAIN HYDRAULIC VALVE
A/C CLUTCH CYCLING PRESSURE SWITCH
RIGHT FRONT SHOCK ACTUATOR
BRAKE PRESSURE SWITCH
WASHER FLUID LEVEL SWITCH
WASHER PUMP
C100
ENGINE COOLANT LEVEL SENSOR
MASS AIR FLOW SENSOR
STARTER RELAY
SPEED CONTROL SERVO
C169
DISTRIBUTORLESS IGNITION SYSTEM MODULE
POWER DISTRIBUTION BOX
CORNERING LAMP
POWER STEERING ACTUATOR
BATTERY
INTEGRATED RELAY CONTROL MODULE
CORNERING LAMP
C170
CANISTER PURGE SOLENOID
OIL PRESSURE SENDER
COOLANT FAN MOTOR
SIDE MARKER LAMP
HEADLAMP
IGNITION COIL
HEADLAMP
CAM SHAFT SENSOR
C128
GROUND BUSS
C139
TACHOMETER TEST CONNECTOR
RADIO NOISE CAPACITOR
DAYTIME RUNNING LAMPS MODULE
HEADLAMP
A/C CLUTCH DIODE
130mm (5.1 IN.) FROM A/C CLUTCH COIL
A/C COMPRESSOR CLUTCH COIL CONNECTOR
GROUND BUSS
HORN
HEADLAMP
FRONT OF VEHICLE

Engine compartment – Cougar and Thunderbird with 3.8L supercharged engine

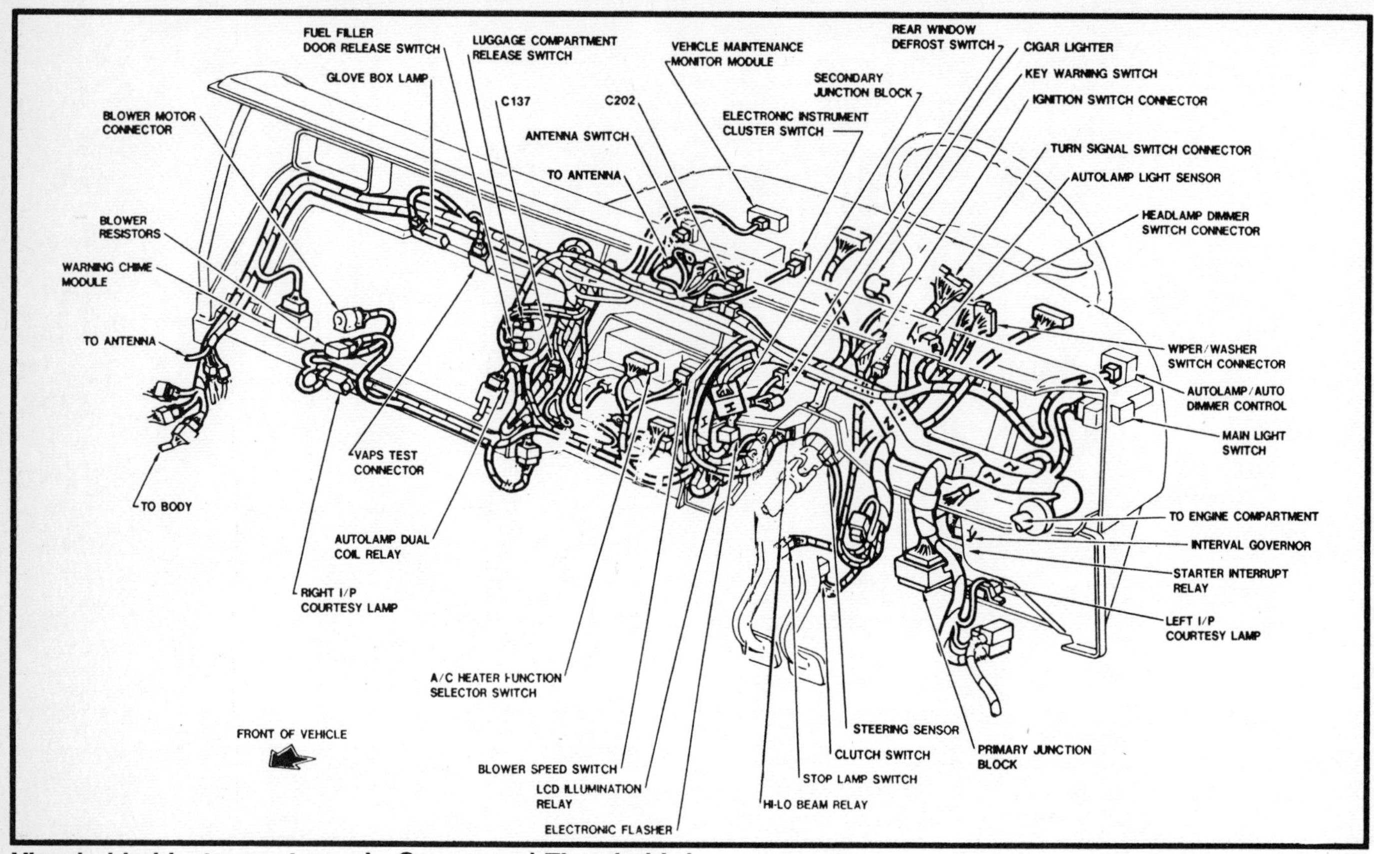

View behind instrument panel—Cougar and Thunderbird

- **Automatic Shock Control Module**—is located under the center of the rear package tray in the trunk.
- **Automatic Shock Control Module**—is located under the center of the rear package tray.
- **Backup/Neutral Safety Switch**—is located on the left side of a manual transmission or at the left rear of an automatic transmission.
- **Barometric Absolute Pressure (BAP) Sensor**—is located on the right side of the firewall in the engine compartment.
- **Blower Motor Resistors**—are located in the heater plenum behind the right instrument panel.
- **Brake Lamp Switch**—is located below instrument panel, on top of brake pedal support.
- **Brake Pressure Switch**—is located in the brake line, below the master cylinder.
- **Camshaft Sensor**—is located on the top front of the engine.
- **Canister Purge Solenoid**—is located at lower right front of engine compartment.
- **Clutch Switch**—is located on the top of the clutch pedal, under the instrument cluster.
- **Crankshaft Sensor**—is located on the top front of the engine.
- **Daytime Running Lamps (DRL) Module (Canadian Vehicles)**—is located at the left front of the engine compartment on the radiator support.
- **Distributorless Ignition System (DIS) Module**—is located on the top right side of the engine.
- **Door Ajar Diodes**—are locate in the window regulator harness, 9 inches from passive restraint module.
- **Door Ajar Switches**—are located in respective door latch assemblies.
- **EEC Module**—is located behind right kick panel in passenger compartment.
- **EEC Power Relay**—is located inside the power distribution box.
- **EGR Vacuum Regulator Solenoid**—is located on the right side of the firewall in the engine compartment.
- **Electronic Engine Control (EEC) Module**—is located behind right kick panel in passenger compartment.
- **Electronic Engine Control (EEC) Power Relay**—is located inside the power distribution box.
- **Electronic Flasher**—is located to the right of the steering column, behind the instrument panel.
- **Engine Coolant Level Sensor**—is located on top of the coolant reservoir at the right fender apron.
- **Flasher**—is located to the right of the steering column, behind the instrument panel.
- **Front Limit Switch (Passive Restraints)**—are located in the top of each A-pillar.
- **Fuel Pump Diode**—is located on top of fuel tank, near the fuel pump.
- **Fuel Pump Relay**—is located In the left side of the trunk, behind the wheelwell.
- **Fuel Pump**—is located in the fuel tank.
- **Fusebox**—is located under the left side instrument panel.
- **Hall Effect Sensor**—is located within the distributor.
- **Hard Ride Relay**—is located under the rear package tray.
- **Heated Exhaust Gas Oxygen (HEGO) Sensors (I or II)**—are located in the respective exhaust manifolds (right or left).
- **High Beam Relay**—is located behind left side of instrument panel to the right of steering column.
- **High/Low Beam Relay**—is located behind left side of instrument panel to the right of steering column.

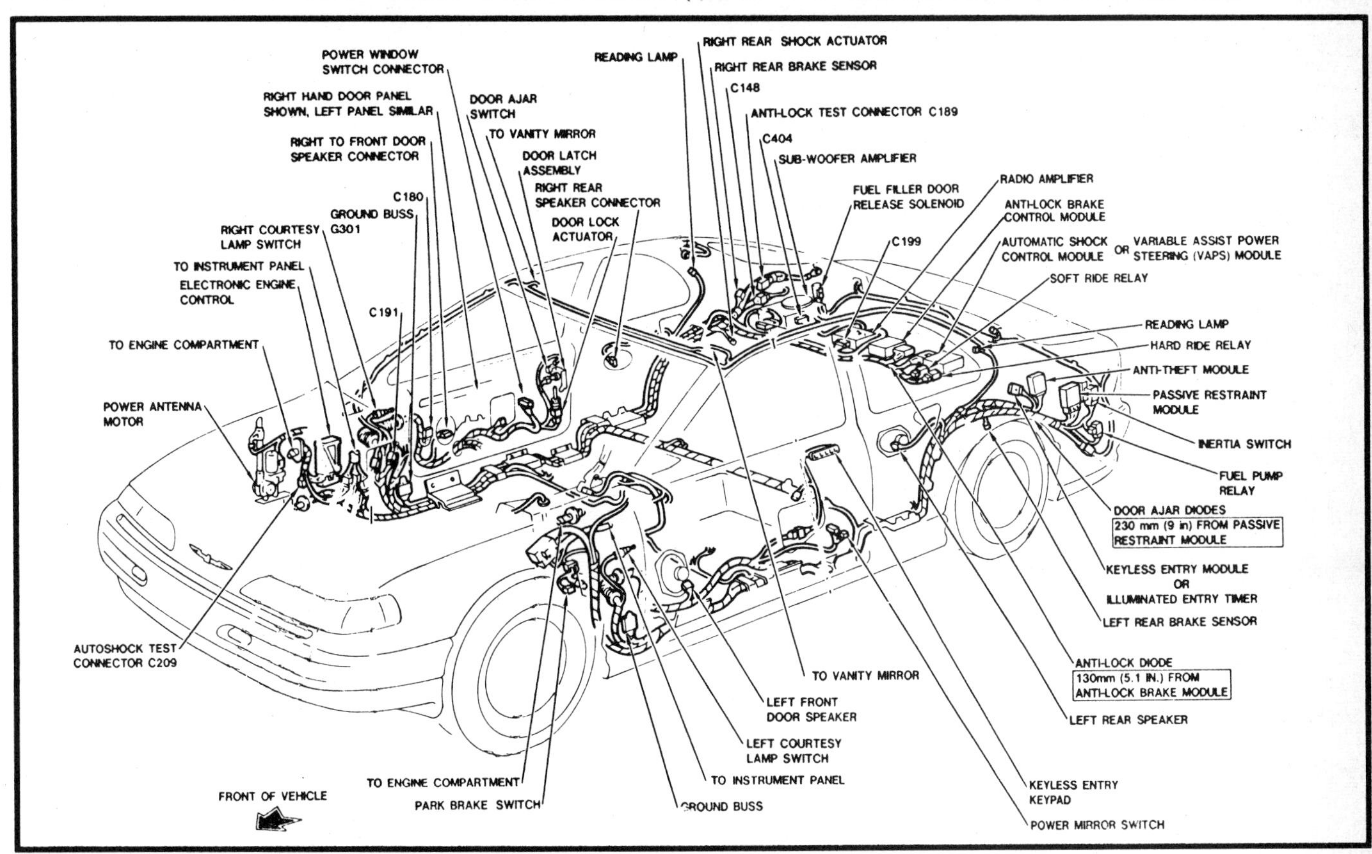

Overall body view—Cougar and Thunderbird

- **Hydraulic Pump Motor Relay**—is located on the relay bracket on the right firewall.
- **Hydraulic Pump Motor**—integrated with hydraulic control unit, on left firewall.
- **Idle Speed Control Solenoid**—is located on the top center of the engine.
- **Ignition Coil (3.8L supercharged engine)**—is located on the front right side of the engine.
- **Ignition Coil (3.8L engine)**—is located on the frame rail, lower right of engine compartment.
- **Ignition Suppression Resistors**—are taped into the engine wiring harness, 4½ inches from connector near integrated relay control module.
- **Illuminated Entry Timer**—is located in the left rear of the trunk, behind the wheelwell.
- **Illuminated Entry Timer**—is located in the left rear of the trunk, behind the wheelwell.
- **Inertia Switch**—is located in the trunk, behind the left wheelwell.
- **Integral Alternator Regulator (IAR)**—is located on the rear of the alternator.
- **Integrated Relay Control Module**—is located in the right front of the engine compartment.
- **Interval Governor**—is located below the left instrument panel to the left of the steering column.
- **Key Warning Switch**—is located within the ignition switch on the steering column.
- **Keyless Entry Module**—is located in the left rear trunk area, behind the wheelwell.
- **LCD Illumination Relay**—is located near the steering column behind the left side instrument panel.
- **Neutral Safety Switch**—is located on the left side of a manual transmission or at the left rear of an automatic transmission.
- **Oil Pressure Sender**—is located at the left front of the engine, near the water pump.
- **Passive Restraint Module**—is located in the left rear of the trunk, behind the wheelwell.
- **Passive Restraint Module**—is located in the left rear of the trunk, behind the wheelwell.
- **Passive Restraint Module**—is located in the left rear trunk area, behind the wheelwell.
- **PFE Transducer**—is located at the upper center of the rear of the engine.
- **Power Distribution Box**—is located in the engine compartment on left fender apron near the battery.
- **Power Steering Actuator**—is located on the lower left side of the engine.
- **Pressure Feedback Electronic (PFE) EGR Transducer**—is located at the upper center of the rear of the engine.
- **Primary Junction Box**—is located under the left side instrument panel.
- **Radio Noise Capacitor**—is located below the right fender apron.
- **Rear Defrost Relay**—is located within the rear defroster switch.
- **Rear Defrost Timer**—is located within the rear defroster switch.
- **Rear Limit Switches (Passive Restraints)**—are located in the bottom of each B-pillar.
- **Seat Belt Switch**—is located in the driver's seat belt buckle.
- **Secondary Junction Block**—is located behind left side of instrument panel, to the right of the steering column.
- **Shock Actuators**—are located at the top of each shock absorber.
- **Shorting Plug**—is located at the right side of the engine, near the TFI ignition module.

• **Soft Ride Relay**—is located in the trunk under the rear package tray.

• **Speed Control Servo**—is located in the left front of the engine compartment, behind the fender.

• **Spool Switch**—is located in the seat belt retracting assembly, mounted to the seat track.

• **Starter Interrupt Relay**—is located behind the left side instrument panel.

• **Starter Relay**—is located on the left fender apron.

• **Steering Sensor**—is located under the left side of instrument panel on the steering column.

• **Stop Lamp Switch**—is located below instrument panel, on top of brake pedal support.

• **TFI Ignition Module**—is located in the lower right front of the engine compartment.

• **Throttle Position Sensor**—is located on the top center of the engine.

• **Top Gear Switch**—is located on the left side of the manual transmission.

• **Trunk Lid Release Solenoid**—is located in the rear of the trunk lid.

• **Variable Assist Power Steering (VAPS) Module**—is located below the center of the rear package tray.

• **Vehicle Maintenance Monitor Module**—is located in the center of the instrument panel.

• **Vehicle Speed Sensor**—is at the left rear side of transmission.

• **Warning Chime Module**—is located behind the right instrument panel, below the glovebox.

• **Washer Fluid Level Switch**—is located in the bottom of the washer fluid reservoir on the left of the engine compartment.

• **Water Temperature Sender**—is located on the top left front of the engine.

• **Water Temperature Switch**—is located at the lower left front of the engine.

• **Wide Open Throttle A/C Cutout Relay**—is located on the right firewall on the relay bracket.

• **Wiper/Washer Interval Governor**—is located below the left instrument panel to the left of the steering column.

• **WOT Relay**—is located on the right firewall on the relay bracket.

CROWN VICTORIA AND GRAND MARQUIS

• **A/C Clutch Cycling Pressure Switch**—is located on accumulator/dryer.

• **A/C Clutch Diode**—is located at right front of engine, in small harness to compressor clutch.

• **Air Bag Diagnostic Module**—is located behind left instrument panel.

• **Air Bag Redundant Power Supply**—is located behind left side of instrument panel, near harness to brake lamp switch.

• **Air Bag Safing Sensor**—is located on left side of engine compartment.

• **Alternator Output Control Relay**—is located at right front of engine compartment.

• **Ambient Temperature Sensor**—is mounted on front center of radiator support.

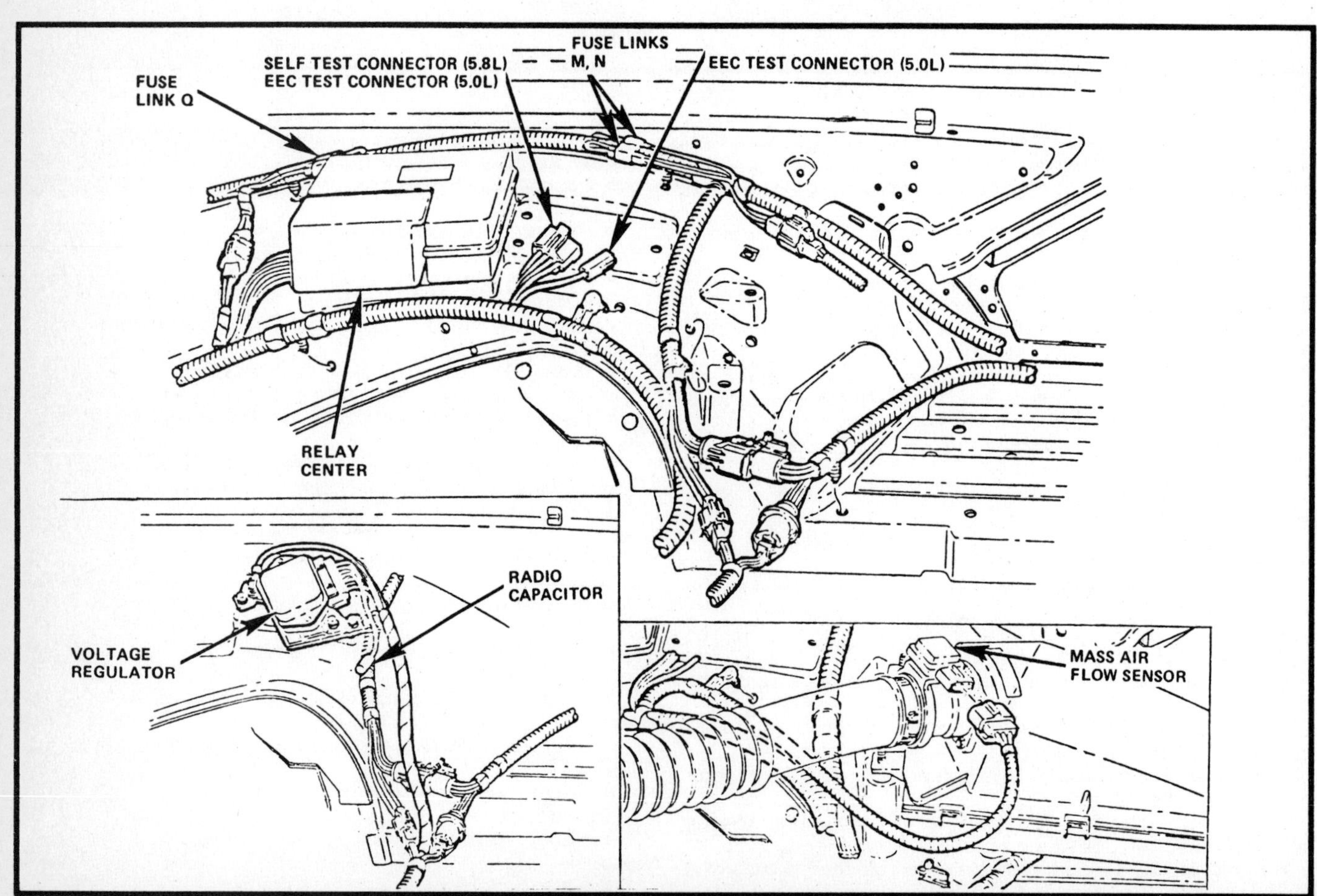

Left Fender Apron—Crown Victoria and Grand Marquis with 5.0L engine

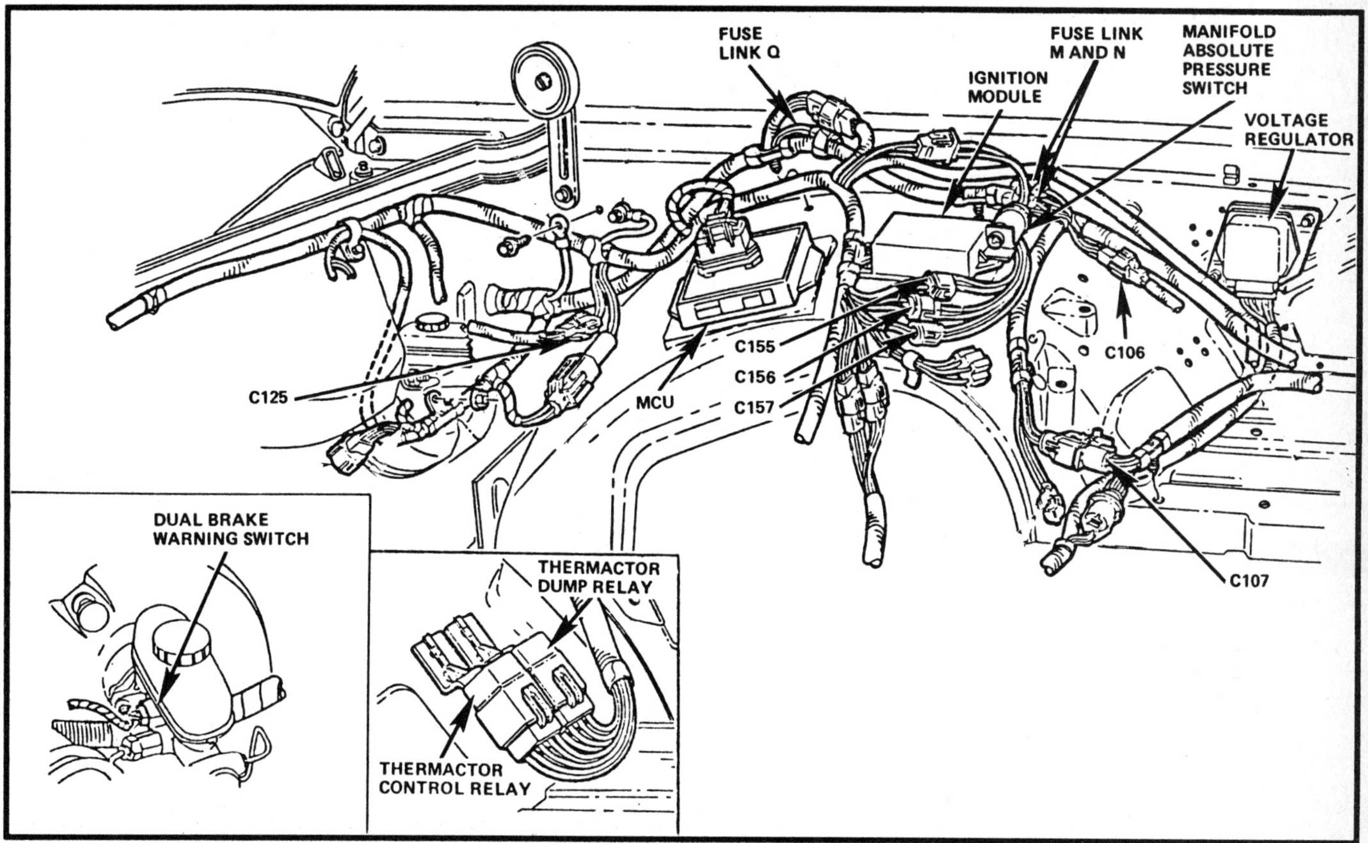

Left Fender Apron—Crown Victoria and Grand Marquis with 5.8L engine

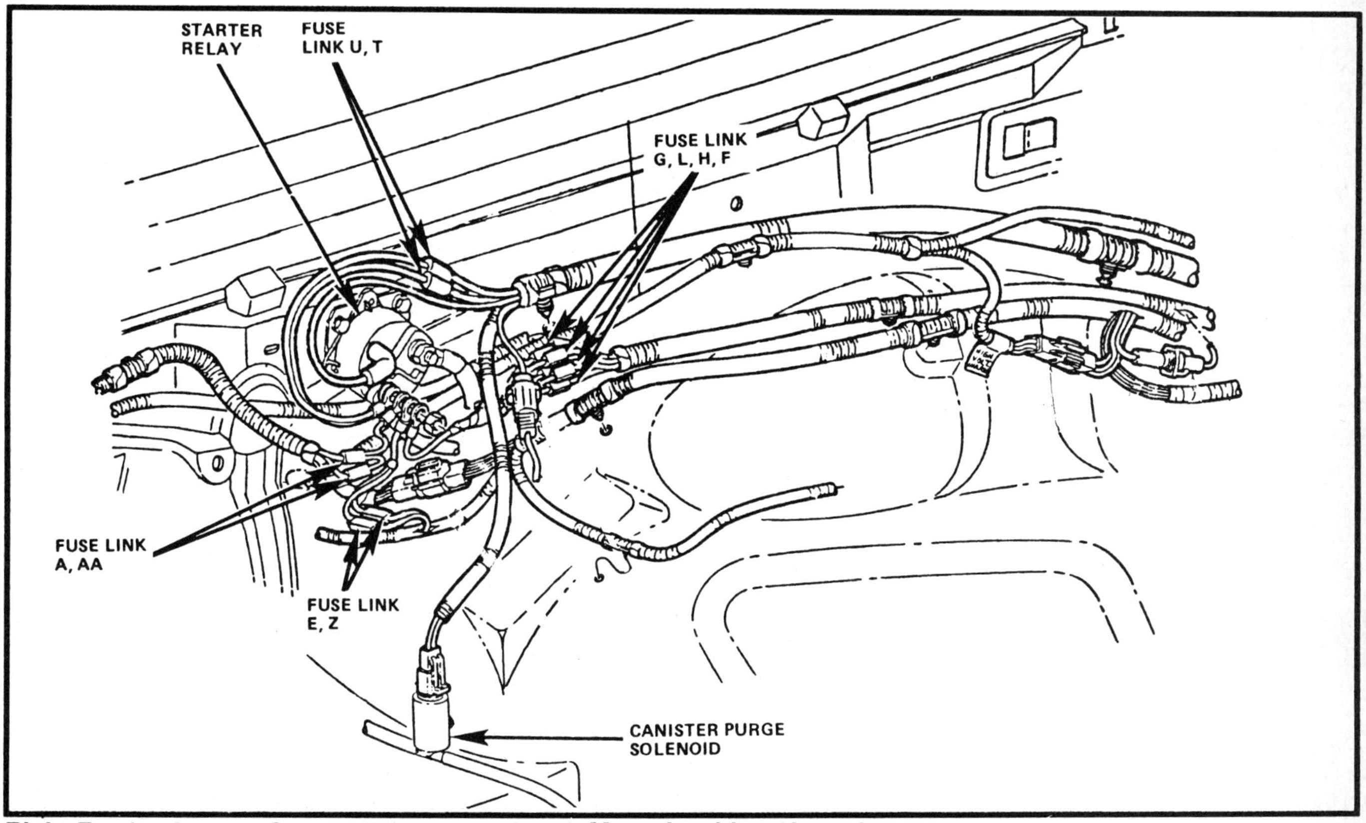

Right Fender Apron—Crown Victoria and Grand Marquis with 5.0L engine

EGR
VENT
SOLENOID
COOLANT
TEMPERATURE
SWITCH
IGNITION
COIL
EGR
VALVE
POSITION
SENSOR
A/C
CLUTCH
DIODE
INTEGRAL
ALTERNATOR
REGULATOR
A/C CLUTCH
FIELD COIL
TFI
IGNITION
MODULE
IGNITION
RESISTOR
ALTERNATOR
FRONT
OF CAR
OIL
PRESSURE
SWITCH

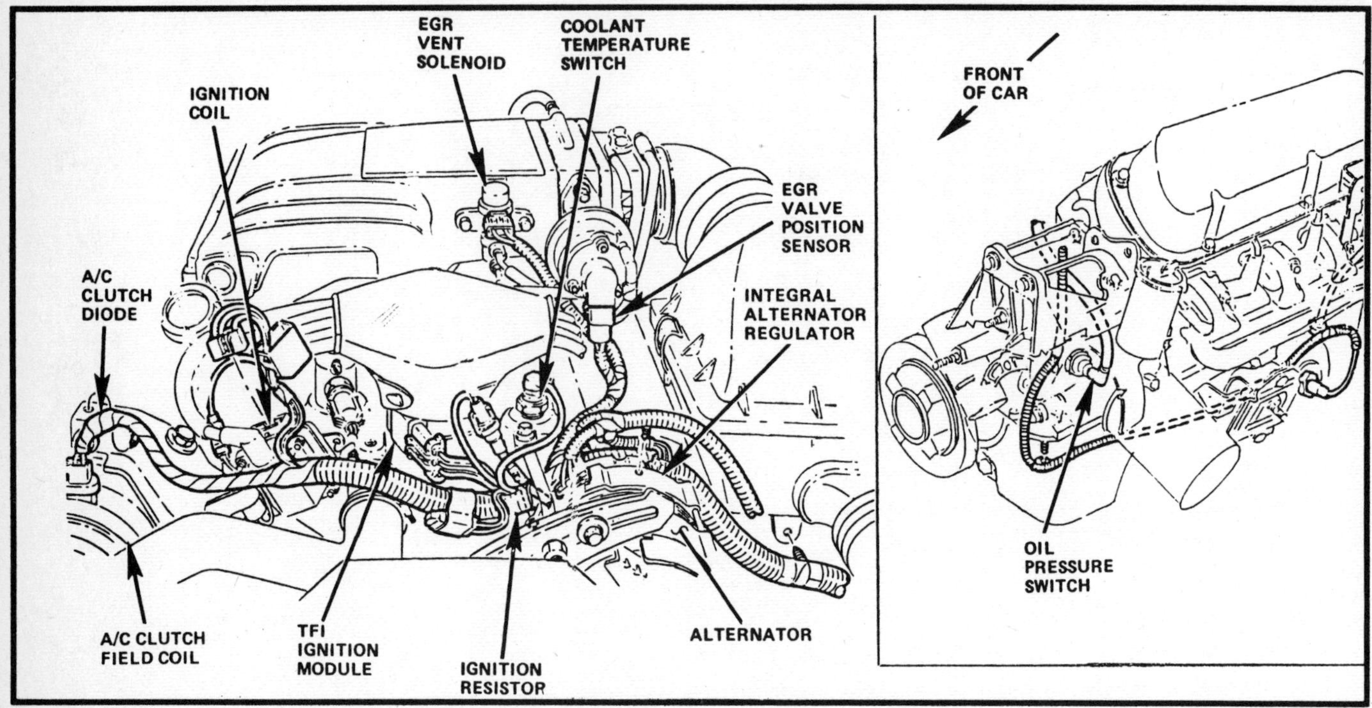

Front of 5.0L engine—Crown Victoria and Grand Marquis

CARBURETOR
ACTUATOR
STEPPER MOTOR
CARBURETOR FLOAT
BOWL VENT SOLENOID
CHOKE
HEATER
MID-ENGINE
TEMPERATURE
SWITCH
IGNITION
COIL
CANISTER
PURGE
SOLENOID
COOLANT
HI/LO
SWITCH

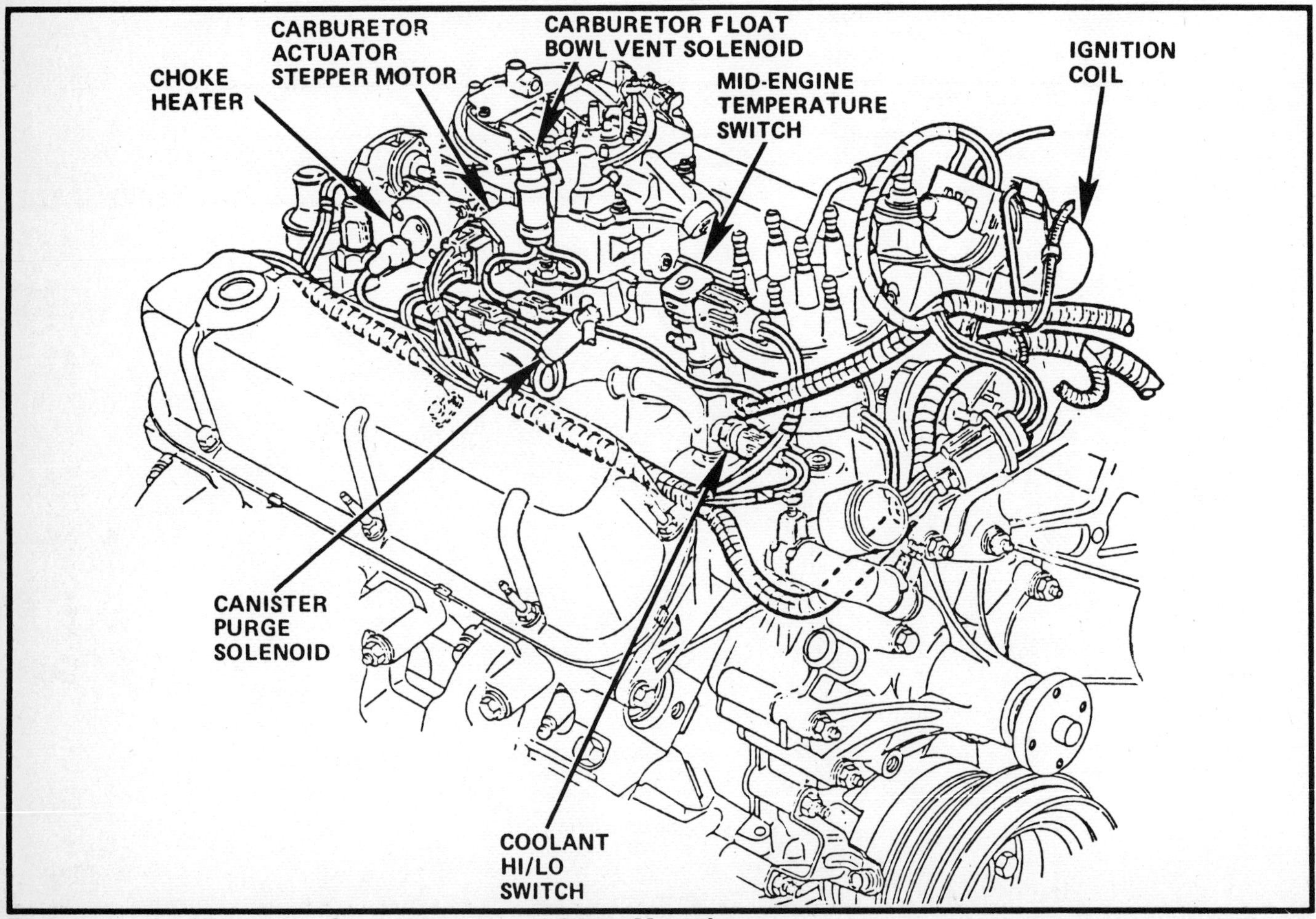

Right side of 5.8L engine—Crown Victoria and Grand Marquis

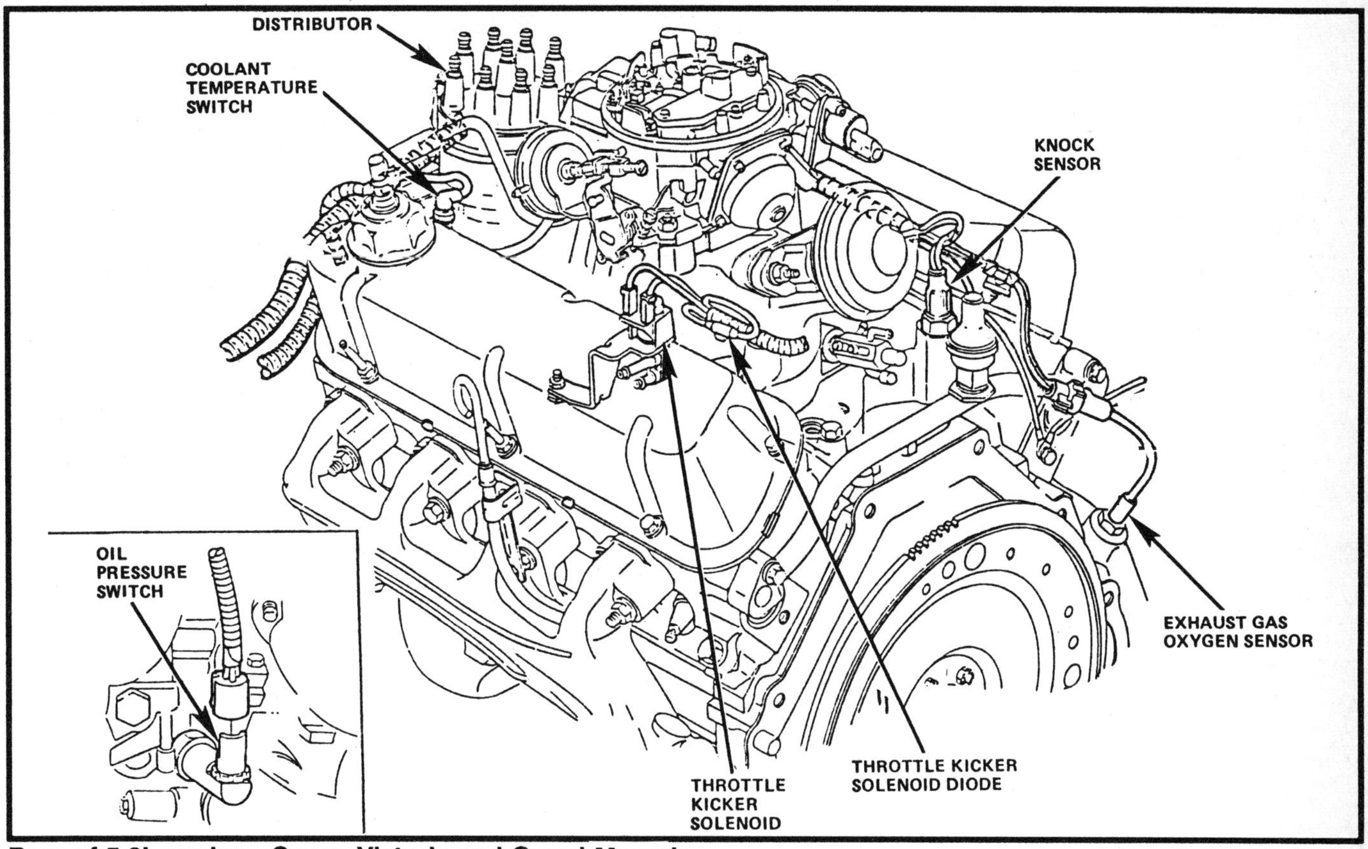

DISTRIBUTOR
COOLANT TEMPERATURE SWITCH
KNOCK SENSOR
OIL PRESSURE SWITCH
EXHAUST GAS OXYGEN SENSOR
THROTTLE KICKER SOLENOID DIODE
THROTTLE KICKER SOLENOID

Rear of 5.8L engine—Crown Victoria and Grand Marquis

THROTTLE KICKER CONTROL RELAY
HORN RELAY
TAB DIODE
STARTER RELAY
FUSE LINKS A, AA
FUSE LINK E, Z
THERMACTOR AIR DIVERTER SOLENOID
THERMACTOR AIR BYPASS SOLENOID
BLOWER MOTOR
BLOWER RESISTOR ASSEMBLY

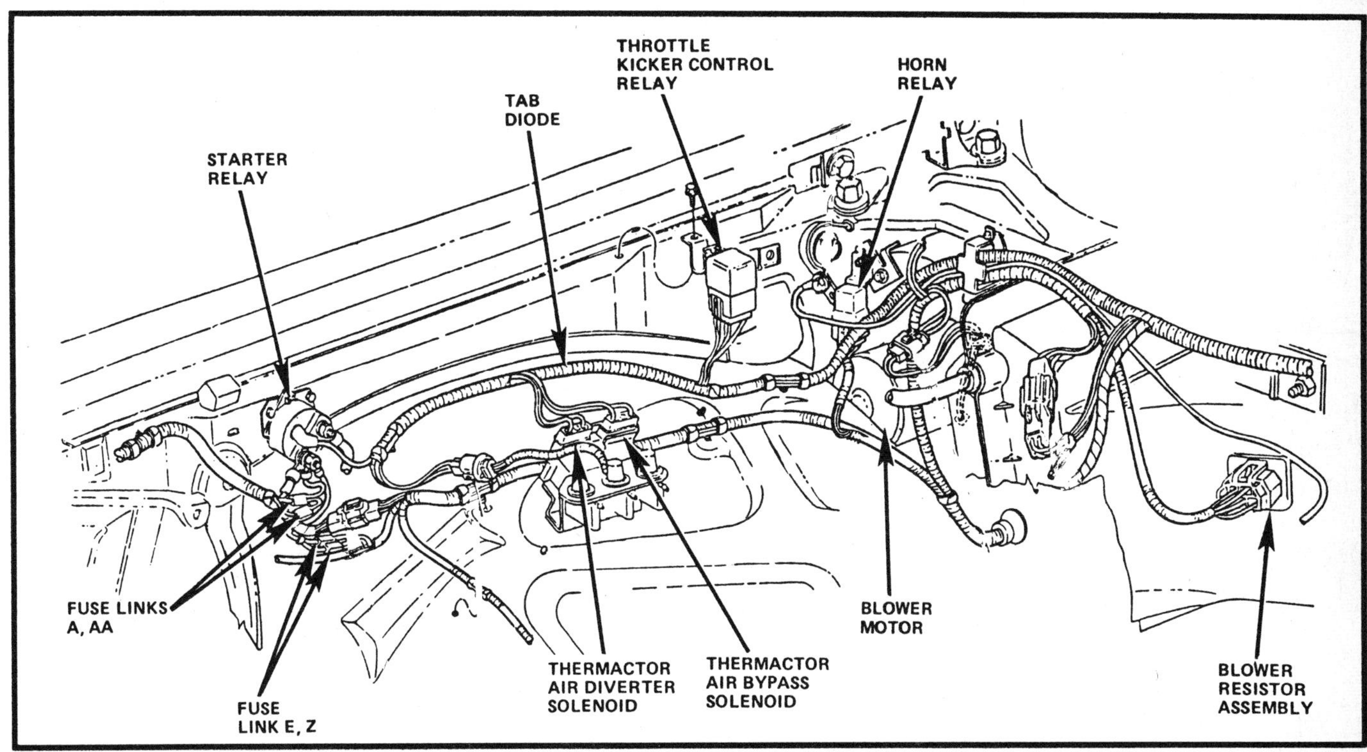

Right fender apron—Crown Victoria and Grand Marquis with 5.8L engine

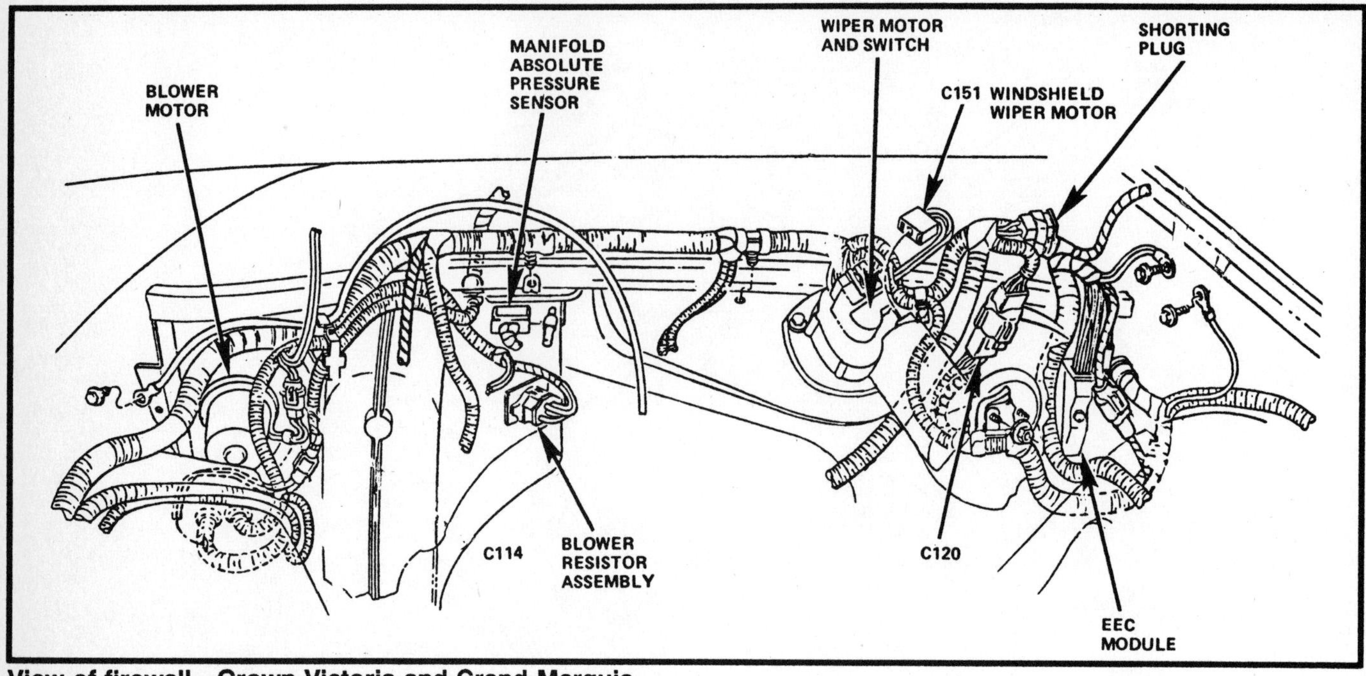

View of firewall—Crown Victoria and Grand Marquis

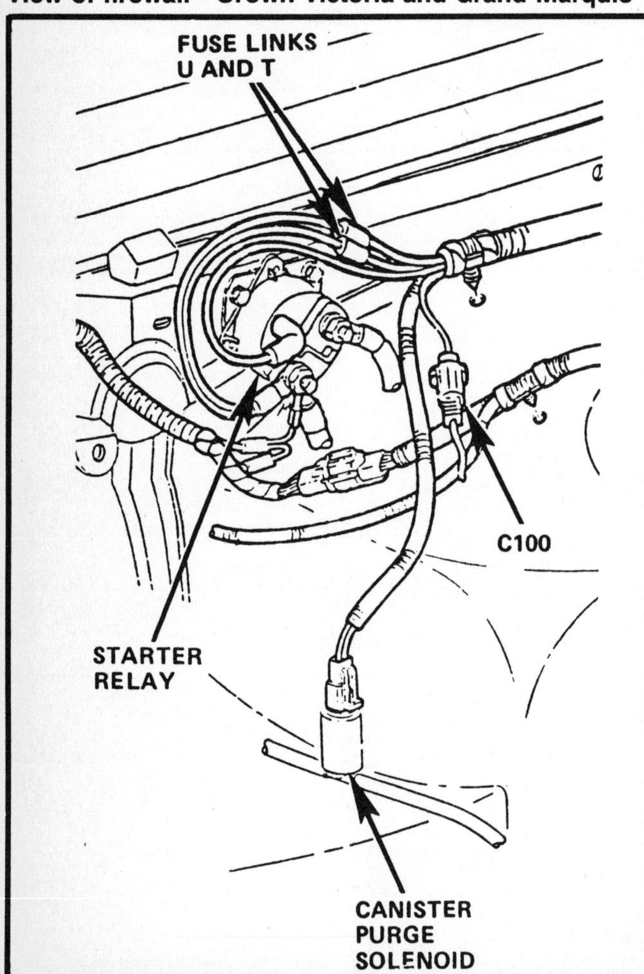

Right fender apron—Crown Victoria and Grand Marquis with 5.0L engine

- **Autolamp Relay**—is located under the instrument panel on the right of the steering column.
- **Backup Switch**—is located on the left side of the transmission.
- **Blower Motor Resistor Assembly**—is located at the right rear of the engine compartment.
- **Canister Purge Solenoid (5.0L engine)**—is located on the front of the right fender apron.
- **Canister Purge Solenoid (5.8L engine)**—is located above the front of the right valve cover.
- **Carburetor Float Bowl Vent Solenoid**—is located on the right side of the carburetor.
- **Center Line Forward Crash Sensor**—is located on the center of the grille opening panel.
- **Compressor Relay**—is located on the left fender apron.
- **Compressor/Vent Solenoid**—is located on the left fender apron in front of the wheelwell.
- **Coolant High/Low Switch**—is located on the top right front of the engine.
- **Coolant Temperature Sensor**—is located at the top left side of the engine.
- **Coolant Temperature Switch**—is located at the top left front of the engine, near the valve cover.
- **Cracked Windshield Sense Resistor**—is located in the right front engine compartment.
- **Daytime Running Lamps (DRL) Module (Canadian vehicles)**—is located behind the center of the instrument panel.
- **Daytime Running Lamps (DRL) Resistor (Canadian vehicles)**—is located on the left front fender apron.
- **Dual Brake Warning Switch**—is located on the left firewall, within the brake master cylinder.
- **EEC Module**—is located on the left side of the firewall.
- **EEC Test Connectors**—are located on the left fender apron, near the harness to the ignition module.
- **EGR Valve Position Sensor**—is located at the top left of the engine.
- **EGR Vent solenoid**—is located at the top left side of the engine, near TFI ignition module.
- **Electric Fuel Pump (Sedan)**—is located on top of the fuel tank.

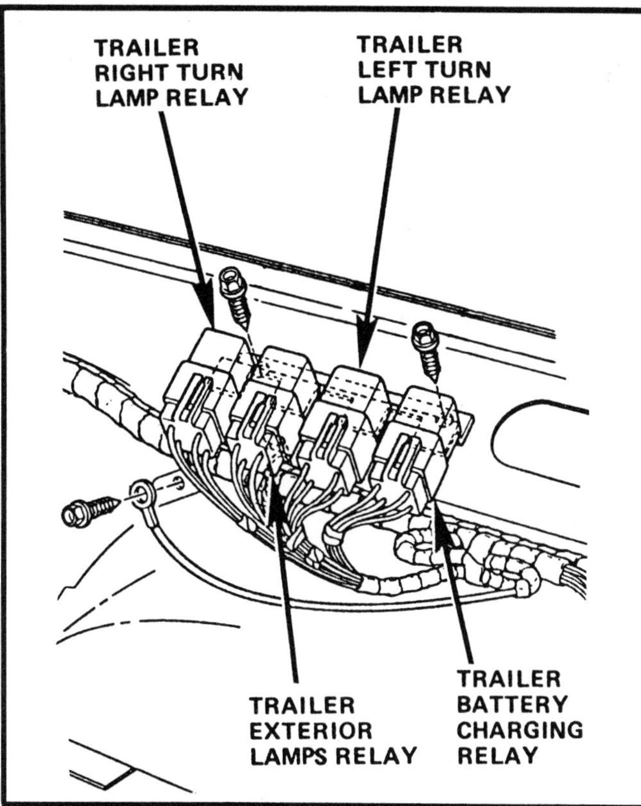

Left rear of wagon—Crown Victoria and Grand Marquis

- **Electric Fuel Pump (Wagon)**—is located at the rear of the fuel tank.
- **Electronic Engine Control (EEC) Module**—is located on the left side of the firewall.
- **Electronic Engine Control (EEC) Test Connectors C118 and C119**—are located on the left fender apron, near the harness to the ignition module.
- **Engine Coolant Temperature Sensor**—is located at the top left side of the engine.
- **Exhaust Gas Oxygen Sensor**—is located in the right exhaust manifold.
- **Fuel Gauge Sender**—is located under rear of car at the fuel tank.
- **Fuel Pump Prime Connector**—is located at the left side of the engine compartment.
- **Hazard Flasher**—is located at the rear of the fuse panel.
- **Heated Exhaust Gas Oxygen (HEGO) Sensors**—are located in the respective exhaust manifolds.
- **Heated Windshield Control Module**—is located behind the right side of the instrument panel.
- **Height Sensor**—is located under the floor to the left of the fuel sensor.
- **Horn Relay**—is attached to the blower motor.
- **Idle Air Bypass Valve**—is located on the upper left side of the engine, above the valve cover.
- **Ignition Key Warning Switch**—is located behind the left side of the instrument panel.
- **Ignition Module**—is located on top of left front wheelwell.
- **Ignition Resistor**—is taped into wiring harness, near the alternator.
- **Illuminated Entry Timer**—is located behind the right side of instrument panel.
- **Impact Inertia Switch**—is attached to the left rear wheelwell.
- **In Car Temperature Sensor**—is located behind the center of the instrument panel.
- **Integrated Regulator**—is located at the rear of the alternator.
- **Interval Wiper/Washer Control**—is located behind the left instrument panel, near the air bag diagnostic module.
- **Knock Sensor**—is located at the top rear of the engine.
- **LCD Dimming Relay**—is located on the left side of the instrument panel to the right of the steering column.
- **Left Forward Crash Sensor**—is located in the left front fender apron.
- **Level Control Module (Sedan)**—is located behind the right wheelwell in the trunk.
- **Level Control Module (Wagon)**—is located at the left rear tailgate pillar.
- **Level Control Module Test Connector**—is located on the right of the trunk, behind the wheelwell near the harness to the Level Control Module.
- **Light Sensor/Amplifier**—is located at the center of the instrument panel near the harness to the clock.
- **Manifold Absolute Pressure (MAP) Sensor (5.0L engine)**—is located at the center of the firewall, above the blower resistor assembly.
- **Manifold Absolute Pressure (MAP) Sensor (5.8L engine)**—is located on top of the left front wheel well.
- **Manifold Charge Temperature Sensor**—is located on upper left side of engine, near wiring harness to injector No. 5.
- **MAP Sensor (5.0L engine)**—is located at the center of the firewall, above the blower resistor assembly.
- **MAP Sensor (5.8L engine)**—is located on top of the left front wheel well.
- **Mass Air Flow Sensor**—is located on the left front fender apron.
- **MCU**—is located on top of the left front wheelwell.
- **Mid Engine Temperature Switch**—is located on the top right front of the engine.
- **Neutral Safety Switch**—is located on the left center side of the transmission.
- **Oil Diode**—is located at the upper rear of the left wheelwell.
- **Oil Pressure Switch**—is located at the lower left front of the engine.
- **Police Power Relay**—is located behind the glove box.
- **Radio Noise Capacitor (5.0L engine)**—is located next to the ignition coil.
- **Radio Noise Capacitor (5.8L engine)**—is located near to the ignition coil.
- **Relay Center**—is located above the left front wheel well, near harness to speed control servo.
- **Reverse Switch**—is located on the left side of the transmission.
- **Right Forward Crash Sensor**—is located in right front fender apron.
- **Seat Belt Switch**—is located in driver's seat belt buckle.
- **Self Test Connector C118**—is located on the left fender apron, near harness to ignition module.
- **Shorting Plug**—is located on the firewall, near the wiper motor.
- **Speed Control Amplifier**—is located behind the instrument panel to the left of the steering column.
- **Speed Control Servo**—is located at the left rear of the engine compartment.
- **Tailgate Switch**—is located in the right tailgate doorjamb assembly.
- **TFI Ignition Module**—is located on the top front of the engine.
- **Thermactor Air Bypass Solenoid (5.0L engine)**—is located at the center rear of the engine.

• **Thermactor Air Bypass Solenoid (5.8L engine)**—is located on top of the right front wheelwell.
• **Thermactor Air Diverter Solenoid (5.0L engine)**—is located at the center rear of the engine.
• **Thermactor Air Diverter Solenoid (5.0L engine)**—is located on top of the right front wheelwell.
• **Thermactor Control Fuse**—is located at the left rear of the engine compartment behind the wheelwell.
• **Thermactor Control Relay**—is located on the front of the left fender apron.
• **Thermactor Dump Relay**—is located on the front of the left fender apron.
• **Thermactor Dump Timer**—is located on the EEC module bracket.
• **Thermal Blower Lockout Switch**—is located on the top right rear of the engine.
• **Throttle Kicker Control Relay**—is located on the right side of the engine compartment above the wheelwell.
• **Throttle Kicker Solenoid Diode**—is located in the harness to the throttle kicker solenoid.
• **Throttle Kicker Solenoid**—is located at the upper left rear of the engine, near the valve cover.
• **Throttle Position Sensor**—is located at the upper left side of the engine, near the harness to injector No. 6.
• **Trailer Battery Charging Relay (Sedan)**—is located near the right rear wheel well.
• **Trailer Battery Charging Relay (Wagon)**—is located above the left rear wheel well.
• **Trailer Exterior Lamps Relay (Sedan)**—is located near the right rear wheel well.
• **Trailer Exterior Lamps Relay (Wagon)**—is located above the left rear wheel well.
• **Trailer Left Turn Lamp Relay (Sedan)**—is located near the right rear wheel well.
• **Trailer Left Turn Lamp Relay (Wagon)**—is located above the left rear wheel well.
• **Trailer Right Turn Lamp Relay (Sedan)**—is located near the right rear wheel well.
• **Trailer Right Turn Lamp Relay (Wagon)**—is located above the left rear wheel well.
• **Trunk Release Solenoid**—is located within the latch assembly.
• **Turn Signal Flasher**—is located on the fuse panel below the left instrument panel.
• **Vehicle Speed Sensor**—is located on the left side of the transmission.
• **Voltage Regulator**—is mounted on the top of the left wheelwell.
• **Warning Chime Module**—is located below the center of the instrument panel.
• **Washer Low Fluid Switch**—is located in the washer fluid reservoir at the left front of the engine compartment.
• **Window Safety Relay**—is located behind the glovebox.

ESCORT

• **A/C Clutch Pressure Switch**—is located on top of the accumulator/drier assembly.
• **A/C Controller**—is located behind the right side of the instrument panel above the glove box.
• **Air Charge Temperature Sensor (CFI)**—is located on the top right rear side of the engine.
• **Air Flow Meter (EFI)**—is located on the left side of the engine compartment near the starter relay.
• **Back-Up/Neutral Safety switch**—is located on the right side of the transaxle case.
• **Barometric Absolute Pressure sensor (EFI)**—is located on the right shock tower.
• **Blower Motor Resistor**—is located behind the right side of the instrument panel in the heater and duct assembly.
• **Canister Purge Solenoid**—is located on the left side of the engine above the transaxle.
• **Clutch Interrupt Switch**—is located behind the left side of the instrument panel on top of the clutch pedal support.
• **Coolant Temperature Sender**—is located left rear side of the engine.
• **Cooling Fan Relay**—is located on the left front corner of the engine compartment near the left headlamp.
• **Cooling Fan Temperature Switch**—is located on the upper left side of the engine near the distributor.
• **Cooling Fan Test Connector C116**—is located left rear side of the engine compartment.
• **Cooling Fan Test Connector C117**—is located left rear side of the engine compartment.
• **Dual Brake Warning Switch**—is located on the brake master cylinder.
• **EGR Vacuum Regulator (CFI)**—is located on the left rear side of the engine behind the shock tower.
• **Electronic Engine Control (EEC) Module**—is located behind the left side of the instrument panel.
• **Electronic Engine Control (EEC) Power Relay**—is located behind the left side of the instrument panel.
• **Engine Coolant Temperature Sensor**—is located on the left rear side of the engine.
• **Front Limit Switches**—are located in the front roof pillars.
• **Fuel Pump**—is located inside the fuel tank.
• **Fuel Pump Relay**—is located behind the left side of the instrument panel.
• **Fusible Links**—are located on the left rear of the engine compartment on the left fender apron forward of the shock tower.
• **Hazard Flasher**—is located behind the left side of the instrument panel.
• **Horn Relay**—is located behind the left side of the instrument panel on the right side of the steering column.
• **Idle Air By-Pass valve (EFI)**—is located on the top left side of the engine.
• **Idle Speed Control Motor (CFI)**—is located on the upper right rear of the engine.
• **Inertia Switch (Sedan)**—is located on the left side of the cargo area.
• **Inertia Switch (Wagon)**—is located on the left rear corner of the cargo area behind the left stoplamp.
• **Manifold Air Pressure Sensor (CFI)**—is located on the right shock tower.

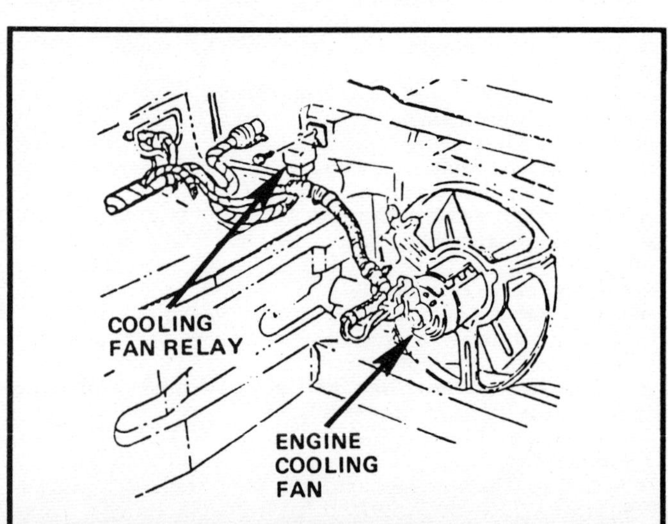

Cooling fan relay location 1989–90 Escort

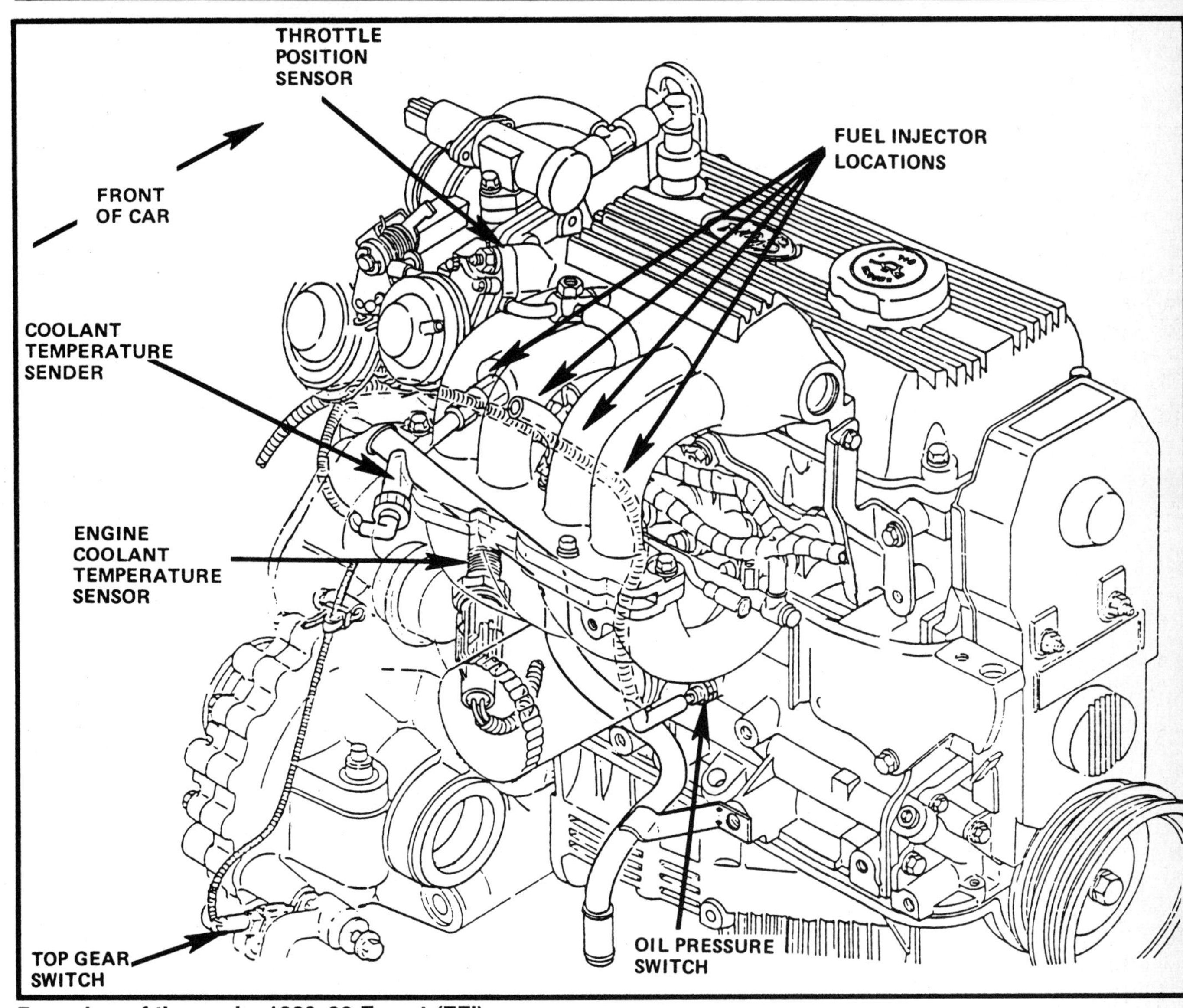

Rear view of the engine1989–90 Escort (EFI)

• **Oil Pressure Switch**—is located to the rear of the engine near the oil filter.

• **Oxygen Sensor**—is located in the exhaust manifold at the front of the engine.

• **Passive Restraint Module**—is located behind the left side of the instrument panel on the right side of the steering column.

• **Pressure Feedback Electronic EGR Transducer (CFI)**—is located on the upper left rear side of the engine.

• **Rear Limit Switches and Motors (3 door)**—are located on the left side of the cargo area.

• **Rear Limit Switches and Motors (5 door and wagon)**—are located inside the respective rear quarter on the front of the wheel well.

• **Shift Indicator Dimmer Relay**—is located behind the right side of the instrument panel.

• **Speed Control Amplifier**—is located on the left side of the instrument panel under the steering column.

• **Speed Control Servo**—is located on the left side of the engine compartment near the shock tower.

• **Starter Relay**—is located on the left hand fender apron forward of the shock tower.

• **Stoplamp Switch**—is located behind the instrument panel on top of the brake pedal support.

• **TFI Ignition Module**—is located on the left side of the engine behind the distributor.

• **Throttle Position Sensor**—is located on the top left rear side of the engine.

• **Turn Signal Flasher**—is in the fuse box, located behind the left side of the instrument panel.

• **Vacuum Dump Valve**—behind the instrument panel on top of the brake pedal support.

• **Vehicle Speed Sensor**—is located on the left rear side of the transaxle.

• **VIP Test Connector**—is located on the right side of the engine compartment.

• **Warning Chime Module**—behind the right side of the instrument panel on the left side of the glove box.

C219
BAROMETRIC ABSOLUTE
PRESSURE (BAP) SENSOR
VIP TEST
CONNECTORS

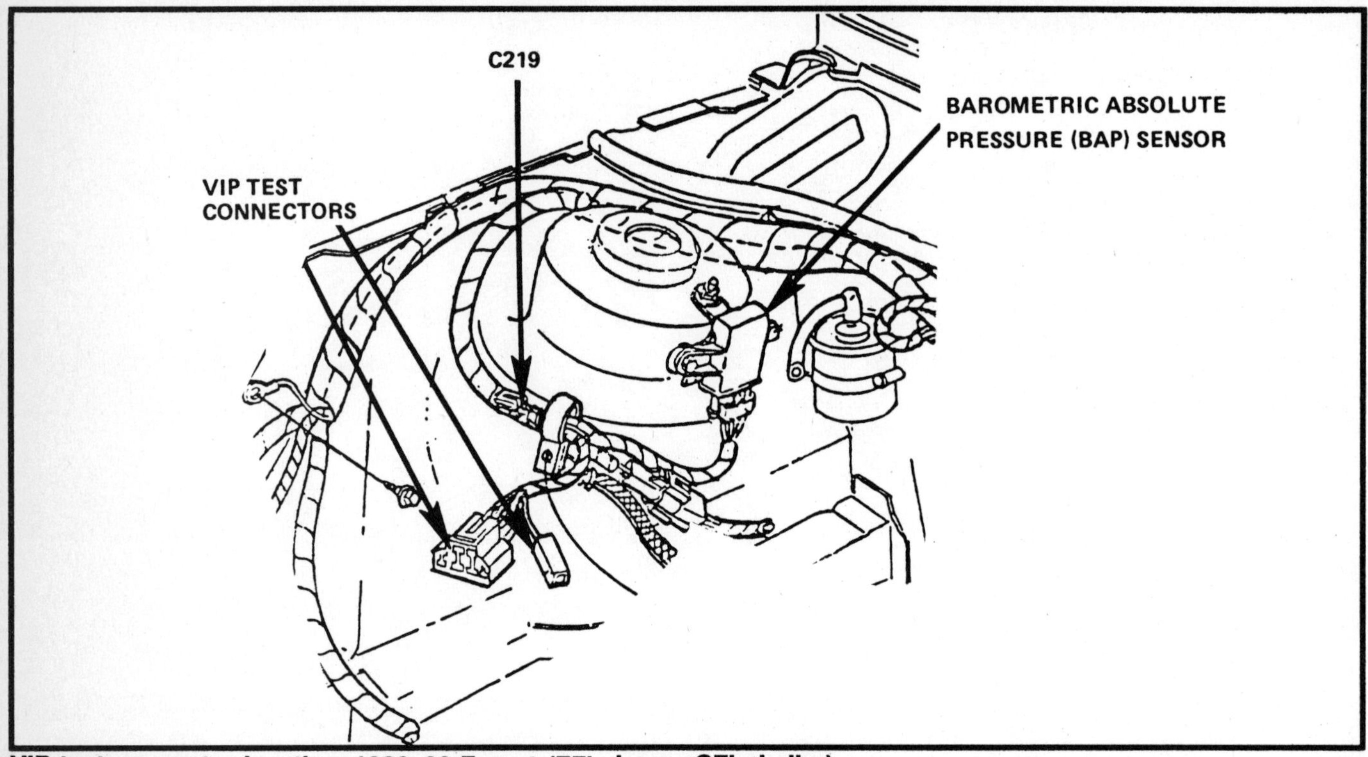

VIP test connector locations1989–90 Escort (EFI shown, CFI similar)

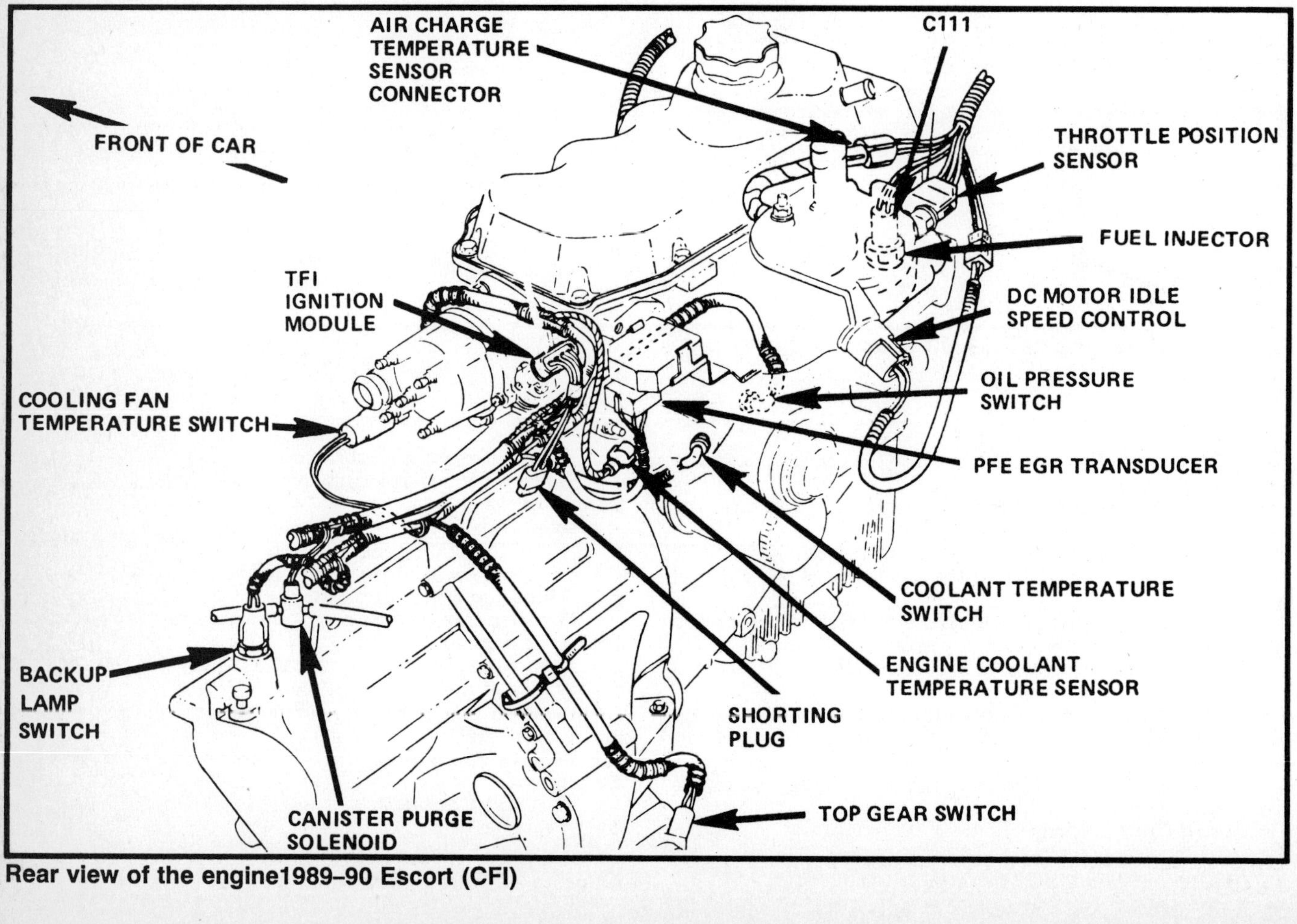

AIR CHARGE
TEMPERATURE
SENSOR
CONNECTOR
C111
FRONT OF CAR
THROTTLE POSITION
SENSOR
FUEL INJECTOR
TFI
IGNITION
MODULE
DC MOTOR IDLE
SPEED CONTROL
OIL PRESSURE
SWITCH
COOLING FAN
TEMPERATURE SWITCH
PFE EGR TRANSDUCER
COOLANT TEMPERATURE
SWITCH
ENGINE COOLANT
TEMPERATURE SENSOR
BACKUP
LAMP
SWITCH
SHORTING
PLUG
CANISTER PURGE
SOLENOID
TOP GEAR SWITCH

Rear view of the engine1989–90 Escort (CFI)

FESTIVA

Carbureted Engine

• **A/C Control Module**—is located under the right side of the instrument panel, on the evaporator housing, below the glove box.

• **A/C Fuse**—this is an in line fuse, which is located behind the instrument panel, to the left of the heater duct assembly.

• **A/C Low Pressure Switch**—is located in the refrigerant line, between the receiver/dryer and the evaporator, near the right engine mount and strut tower.

• **A/C Relays**—these three relays are located in the left front corner of the engine compartment, near the battery.

• **A/C Thermostat**—is located under the right side of the instrument panel, near the evaporator housing, below the glove box.

• **Air Control Valve**—is located on the outside of the air cleaner assembly.

• **Anti-Afterburn Valve**—is located on the engine near the air cleaner assembly.

• **Barometric Pressure Switch**—is located on the firewall in the engine compartment, or under the left hand side of the instrument panel.

• **Boost Sensor**—is located on the left hand side of the firewall, if so equipped.

• **Bowl Vent Solenoid Valve**—is located on the carburetor.

• **Brake Low Fluid Warning Sensor**—is located on the master cylinder.

• **Clutch Interrupt Switch**—is located at the top of the clutch pedal cluster.

• **EFE Heater Grid**—is located under the base of the carburetor.

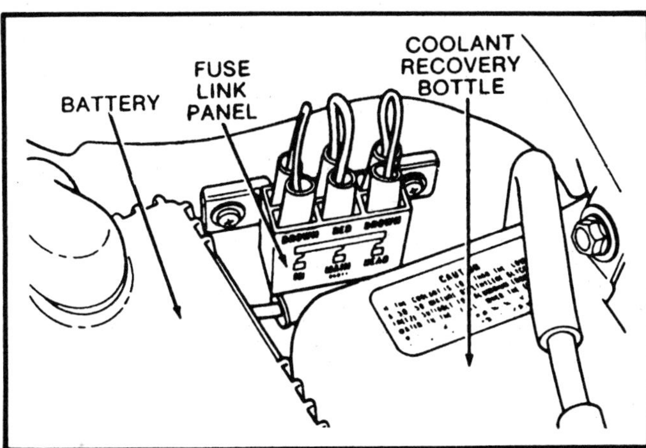

Fusible link locations—Festiva

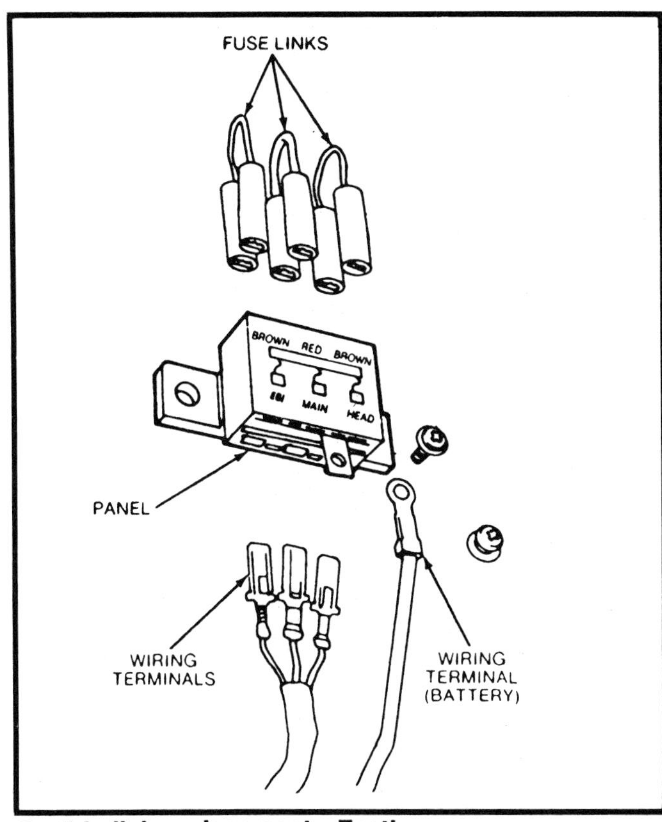

Fusible link replacement—Festiva

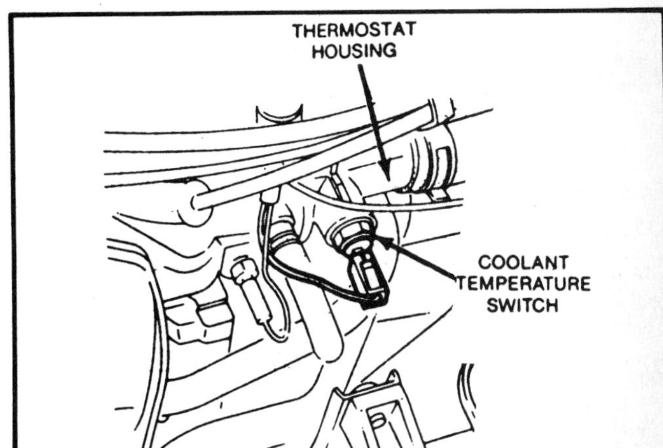

Coolant temperature switch location—Festiva

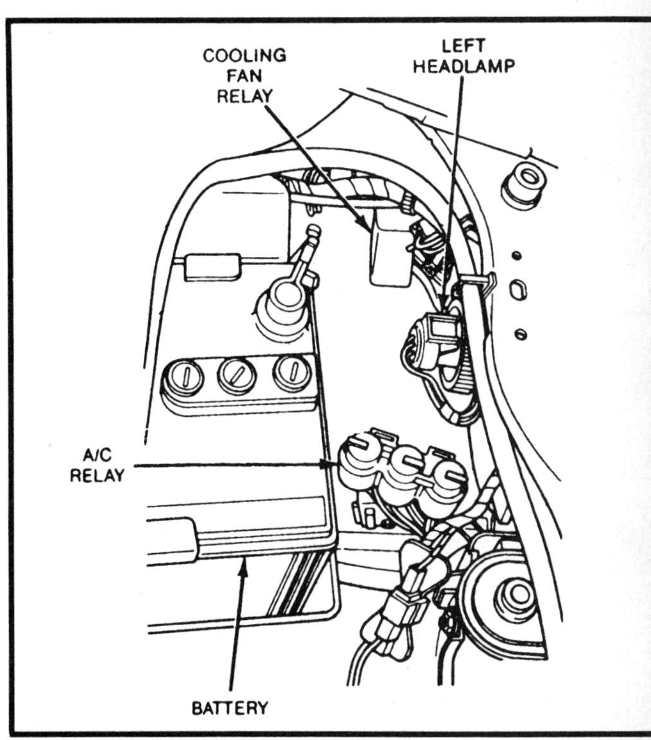

Cooling fan relay location—Festiva

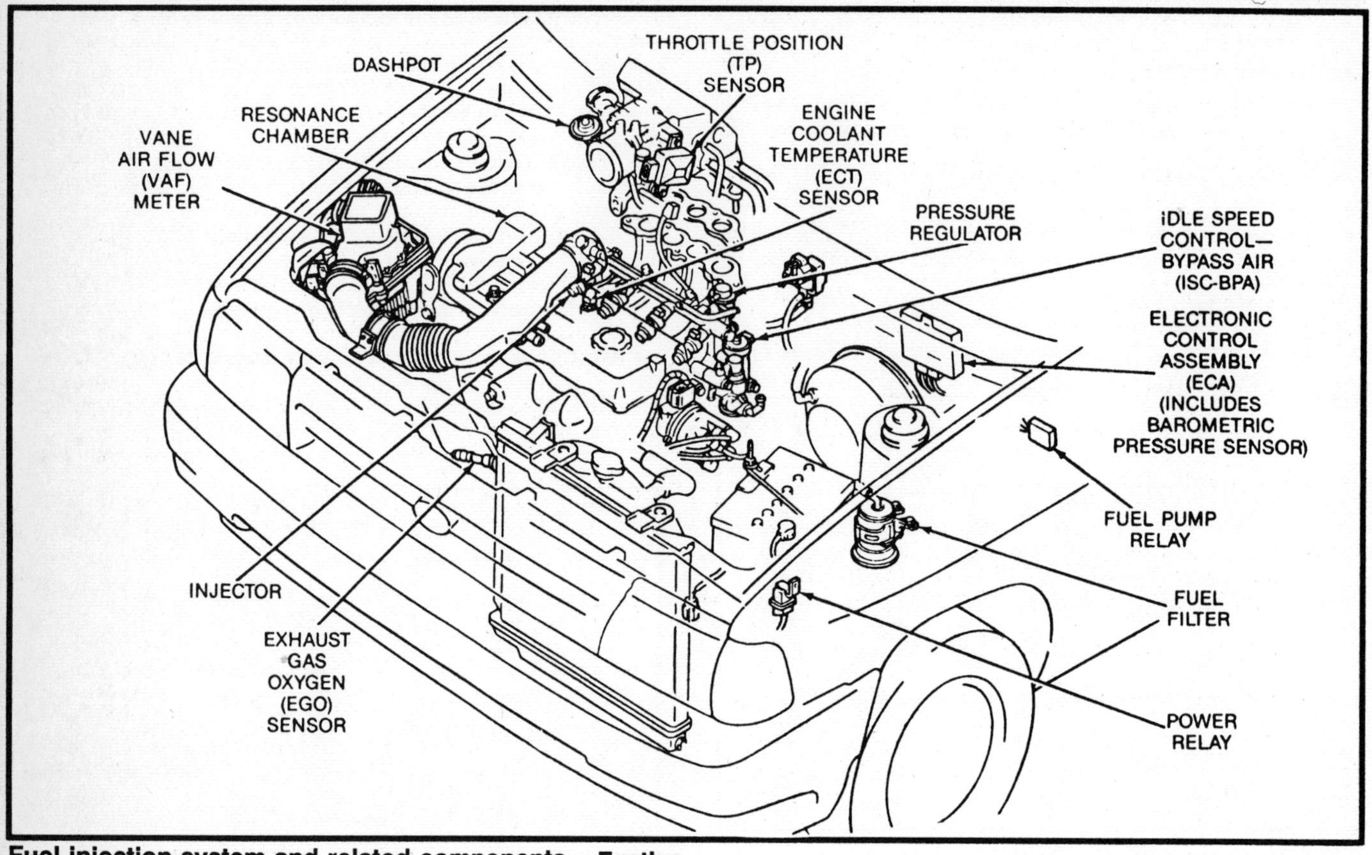

Fuel injection system and related components – Festiva

• **EFE Heater Relay** – is located with two other relays and the key warning buzzer in the upper left hand corner of the passenger compartment, under the instrument panel.

• **EGR Modulation Valve** – is located near the EGR valve.

• **EGR Position Sensor** – is located on the EGR valve, which is located on the intake manifold.

• **EGR Solenoid Valve (No. 1)** – is located on the right hand side of the firewall.

• **EGR Solenoid Valve (No. 2)** – is located on the left hand side of the firewall.

• **Electronic Control Assembly** – is located under the left hand side of the instrument panel, or behind the left hand side kick panel.

• **Engine Coolant Temperature Sensor** – is located on the top of the engine block.

• **Engine Coolant Temperature Switch** – is located in the thermostat housing.

• **Engine Cooling Fan Relay** – is located in the left front corner of the engine compartment, between the battery and the headlight. The relay is behind a protective boot and secured to the inner fender panel.

• **Fuel Filter** – is located next to the fuel pump.

• **Fuel Pump** – is located on the cylinder head assembly.

• **Fuel Vapor Canister** – is located next to left hand side shock tower.

• **Hazard/Turn Signal Relay** – is located with two other relays and the key warning buzzer in the upper left hand corner of the passenger compartment, under the instrument panel.

• **Horn Relay** – is located with two other relays and the key warning buzzer in the upper left hand corner of the passenger compartment, under the instrument panel.

• **Idle Switch** – is located on the carburetor assembly.

• **Interval Governor/Windshield Wiper** – is incorporated in the wiper switch which is located next the combination switch on the steering column.

• **Key Warning Buzzer** – is located with three relays on a bracket in the upper left hand corner of the passenger compartment, under the instrument panel.

• **Manifold Absolute Pressure (MAP) Sensor** – is located on the left hand side of the firewall.

• **Neutral Switch** – is located on the transaxle.

• **Oxygen Sensor** – is located in the exhaust manifold.

• **Purge Canister Valve (No. 2)** – is located on the left hand side of the firewall.

• **Purge Control Valve (No. 1)** – is located on the fuel vapor canister.

• **Radiator Temperature Switch** – is located in the bottom of the radiator.

• **Self-Test Diagnostic Connectors** – are located on the left hand side of the firewall, next to the MAP sensor.

• **Slow Fuel Cut Solenoid Valve** – is located on the carburetor assembly.

• **Speed Servo Diaphragm** – is located next to the carburetor assembly.

• **Three-Way Solenoid Valves** – are located on the left hand side of the firewall, next to the MAP sensor.

• **Vacuum Switch** – is located on the right hand side of the firewall.

• **Vacuum Switching Valve** – is located on or near the left hand side shock tower.

• **Water Thermo Valves** – are located on the top of the engine block.

Fuel Injected Engine

• **A/C Low Pressure Switch** – is located in the refrigerant line, between the receiver/dryer and the evaporator, near the right engine mount and strut tower.

- **A/C Relays**—these three relays are located in the left front corner of the engine compartment, near the battery.
- **Blower Motor Resistor**—is located on the right side of the dash near the blower motor.
- **Canister Purge Solenoid**—is located at the rear of the engine compartment on the right side of the wiper motor.
- **Clutch Interlock Switch**—is mounted on the cowl panel.
- **Condenser Fan Relay**—is located in the front of the three relays that are located in the left front corner of the engine compartment, near the battery.
- **Crankshaft Position Sensor**—is located inside the distributor assembly.
- **Electronic Control Assembly**—is located under the left hand side of the instrument panel, or behind the left hand side kick panel.
- **Engine Coolant Sensor**—is located near the No. 1 injector.
- **Engine Cooling Fan Relay**—is located on the inner left fender panel next to the left headlight. The relay is behind a protective boot.
- **Engine Cooling Fan Temperature Switch**—is located near the thermostat housing.
- **Fuel Pump Inertia Switch**—is located in the left rear quarter panel.
- **Fuse Panel**—is located under the dash to the left of the steering column.
- **Hazard Flasher Module**—is located under the dash behind the ECA.
- **Headlamp Relay**—is located on the left inner fender panel behind the left headlamp.
- **Horn Relay**—is located behind the left corner of the instrument panel.
- **Ignition Module**—is mounted over the left strut tower.
- **Kickdown Solenoid Valve**—is located on the lower right front corner of the transaxle.
- **Kickdown Switch**—is mounted to the accelerator pedal.
- **Main Relay**—is attached to the left front corner of the side wall.
- **Neutral Gear Switch**—is located on the right rear side of the transaxle.
- **Oil Pressure Switch**—is located in the engine block.
- **Oxygen Sensor**—is located in the exhaust manifold.
- **Parking Lamp Relay**—is located on the right front corner of the engine compartment on the inner fender panel.
- **Passive Restraint Module**—is located under the driver's seat.
- **Power steering Switch**—is attached to the power steering pump.
- **RPM Test Connector**—is located on the left rear side of the engine compartment next to the ignition module.
- **Throttle Position Sensor**—is located on the left side of the throttle body.
- **Wide Open Throttle A/C Cut-Off Relay**—is located in the middle of the three relays that are located in the left front corner of the engine compartment, near the battery.

MARK VII

- **A/C Clutch Cycling Pressure Switch**—is located on the right firewall, near the fender apron.
- **A/C Clutch Diode**—is located on the top left front of the engine, under the A/C compressor clutch.
- **A/C WOT Cutout Relay**—is located on the left fender apron, near the shock tower.
- **ABS**—See Anti-Lock Brakes.

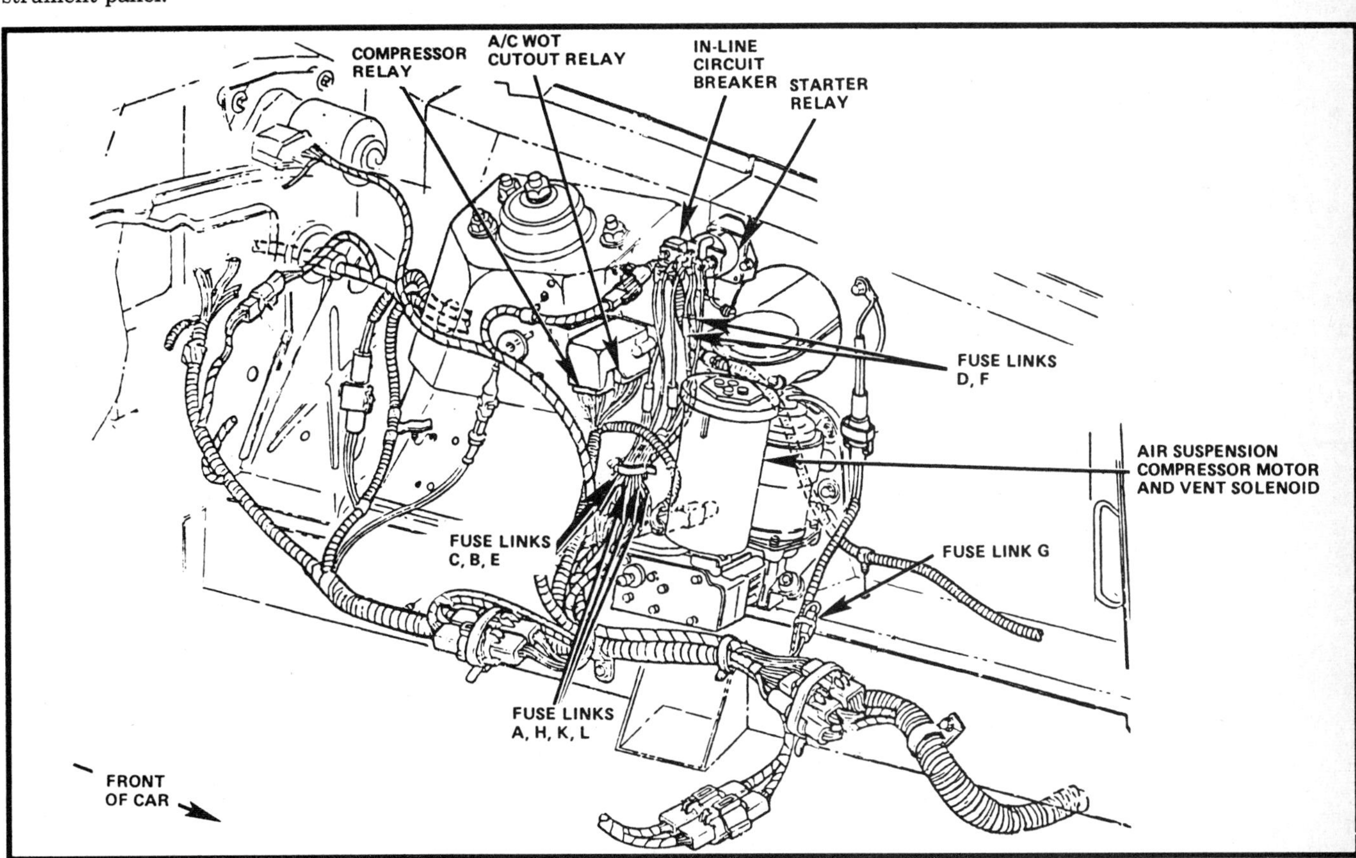

Left fender apron—Mark VII

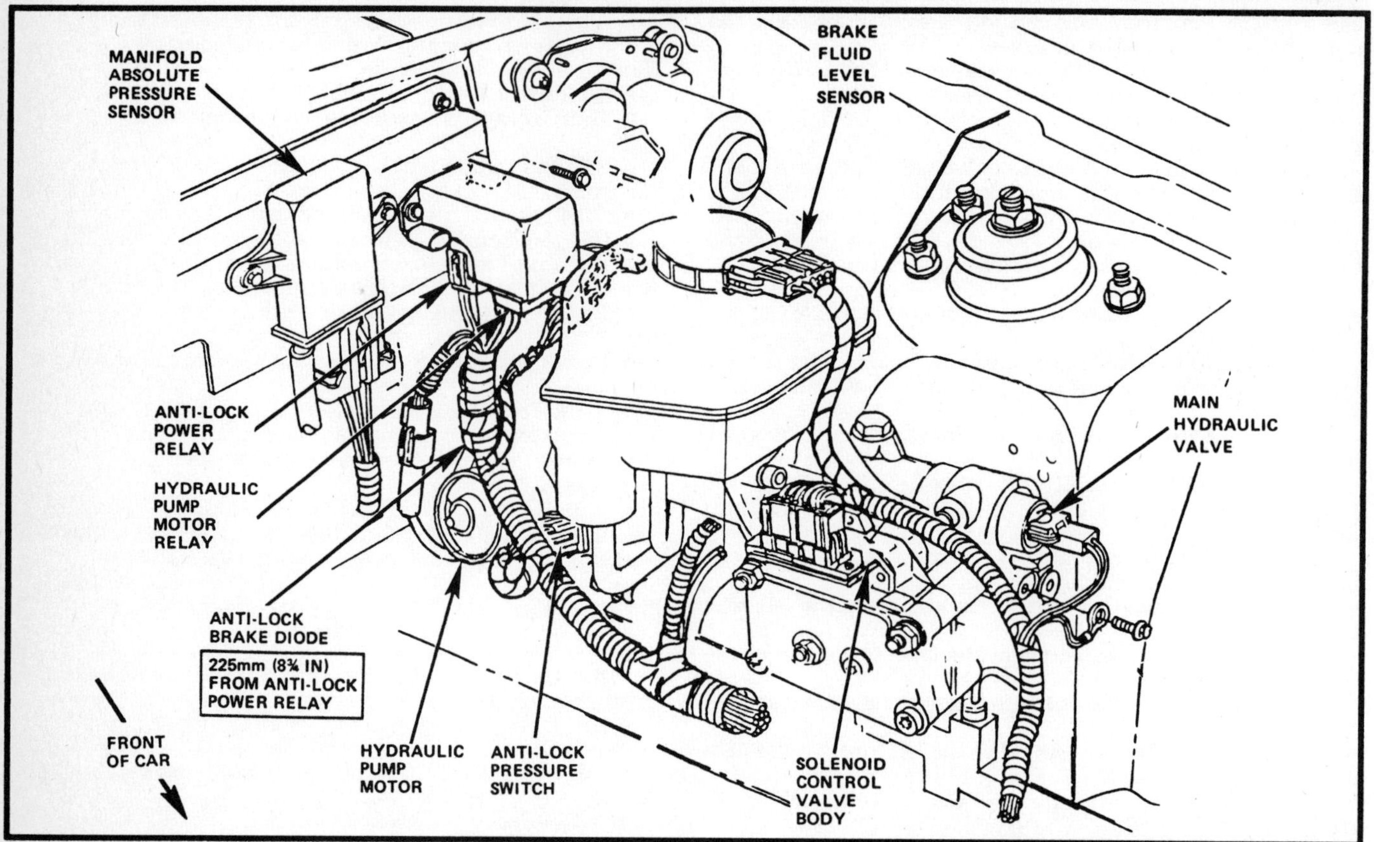

Left fender apron (continued) and left firewall—Mark VII

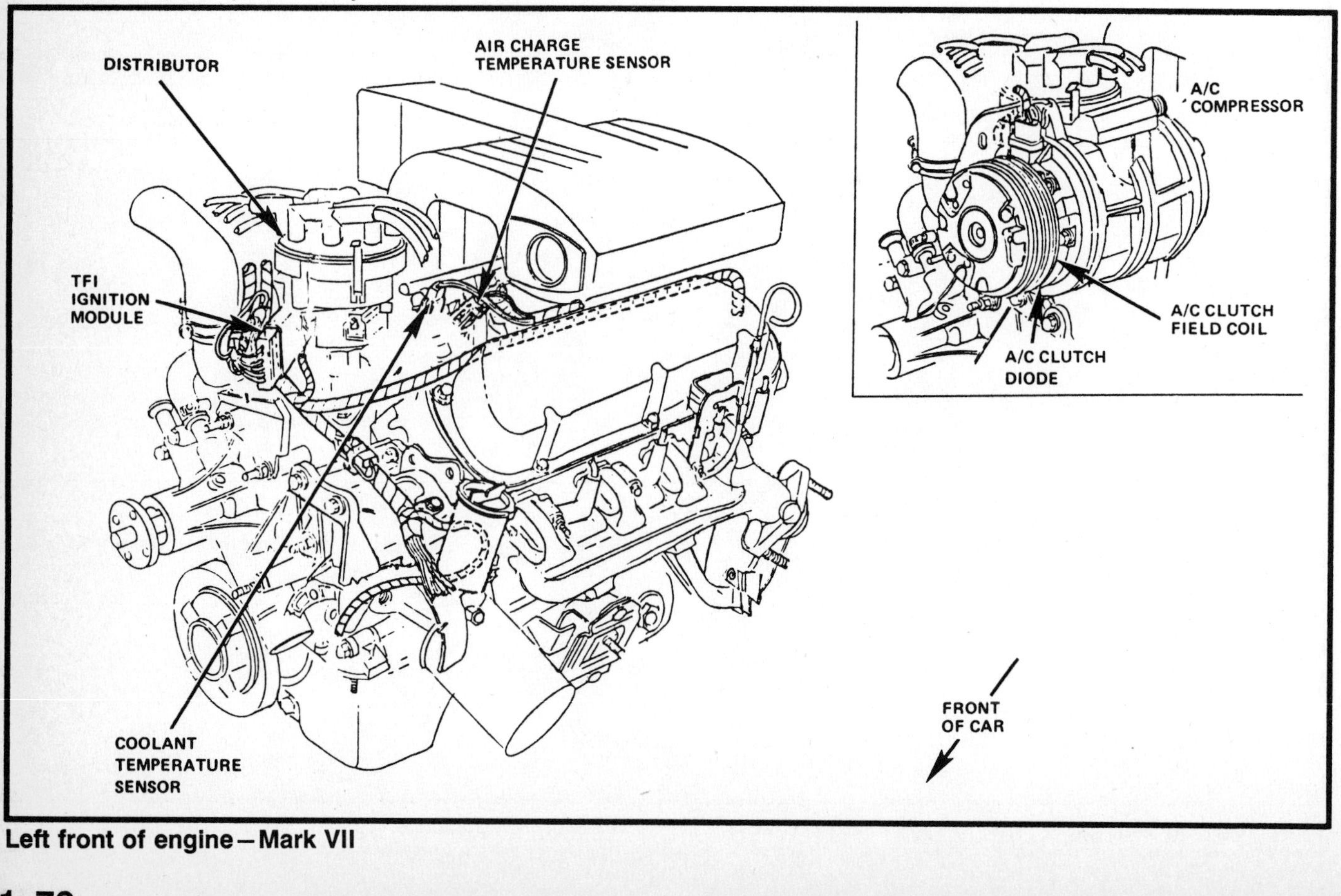

Left front of engine—Mark VII

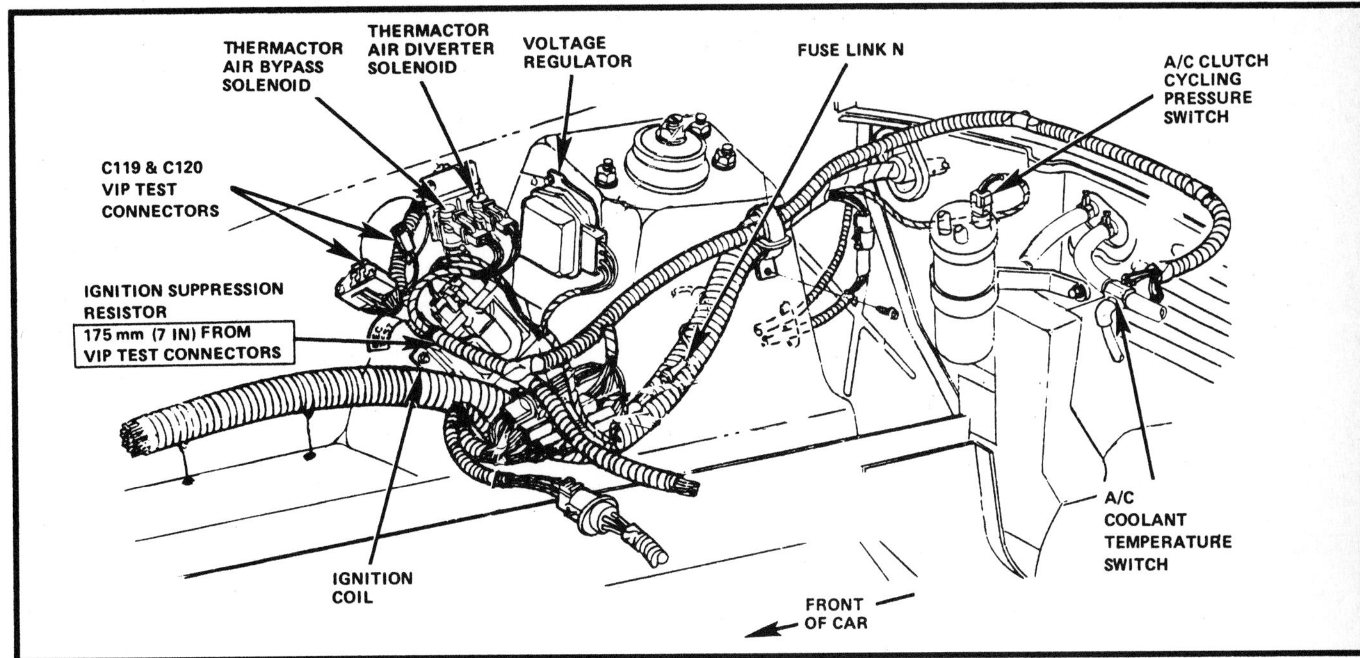

Right fender apron—Mark VII

• **Air Bag Backup Power Supply**—is located behind the right side of instrument panel, near wiring sub—harness to glove box lamp.

• **Air Bag Diagnostic Module**—is located behind center of instrument panel, near radio wiring harness.

• **Air Charge Temperature Sensor**—is located on top left side of engine near distributor.

• **Air Spring Solenoids**—are located at the top of each air spring.

• **Air Suspension Compressor Motor and Vent Solenoid**—is located on the left fender apron, near the starter relay.

• **Air Suspension Electronic Control Module**—is located in the trunk, attached to the left hinge support.

• **Air Suspension Test Connector**—is located under the rear package tray, attached to left hinge support.

• **Ambient Temperature Sensor**—is located on the radiator grille brace.

• **Anti-Lock Brake Control Module**—is located under the rear package tray, near the center of the vehicle.

• **Anti-Lock Brake Diode**—is located at left rear of engine compartment, near the hydraulic pump motor.

• **Anti-Lock Brake Power Relay**—is located on the firewall, behind the brake master cylinder.

• **Anti-Lock Brake Pressure Switch**—is located on the left fender apron, near the power booster assembly.

• **Anti-Lock Brake Test Connector**—is located under the rear package tray, near anti-lock brake control module.

• **Anti-Theft Alarm Relay**—is located under the right side of the rear package tray.

• **Anti-Theft Controller Module**—is located under the right side of the rear package tray.

• **Anti-Theft Horn Relay**—is located under the rear package tray, near the wiring to the left rear radio speaker.

• **Anti-Theft In Line Fuse A**—is located under the rear package tray, near the right rear radio speaker.

• **Anti-Theft In Line Fuse B**—is located under the rear package tray, near the right rear radio speaker.

• **Anti-Theft Inverter Relay**—is located under right side of rear package tray.

• **Anti-Theft Starter Interrupt Relay**—is located under the left instrument panel, near the ground buss bracket.

• **Autolamp Relay**—is located behind the instrument panel, to the left of the defrost actuator.

• **Automatic Temperature Control (ATC) Coolant Temperature Switch**—is located on the right side of the firewall.

• **Automatic Temperature Control (ATC) Feedback Isolation Relay**—is located behind right side of instrument panel, near rear of glove box.

• **Automatic Temperature Control (ATC) Module**—is located at the right side of the instrument panel, to right of defrost actuator.

• **Backup/Neutral Safety Switch**—is located on the left side of the transmission.

• **Blower Motor Speed Controller**—is located behind the right side of instrument panel.

• **Brake Fluid Level Sensor**—is located within the brake master cylinder.

• **Canister Purge Solenoid**—is located on top of the engine at the right front, near distributor.

• **Center Line Forward Crash Sensor**—is located above the center of the radiator.

• **Compressor Relay**—is located on the left fender apron near the shock tower.

• **Coolant Temperature Sender**—is located on top of the engine, left side.

• **Coolant Temperature Sensor**—is located on top of the engine, left side.Courtesy Lamp Diode—is located at the bottom of the left kick panel.

• **Daytime Running Lamps (DRL) Module (Canadian vehicles)**—is located at the front of the left fender apron.

• **Driver's Seat Belt Switch**—is located within the left front seat belt buckle.

• **EEC**—See Electronic Engine Control.

• **EGR Valve Position Sensor**—is located behind the throttle body at the top right rear of the engine.

• **EGR Vent Solenoid**—is located on the rear of the right fender apron.

• **Electric Fuel Pump**—is located within the fuel tank.

• **Electronic Engine Control Module**—is located behind the right kick panel.

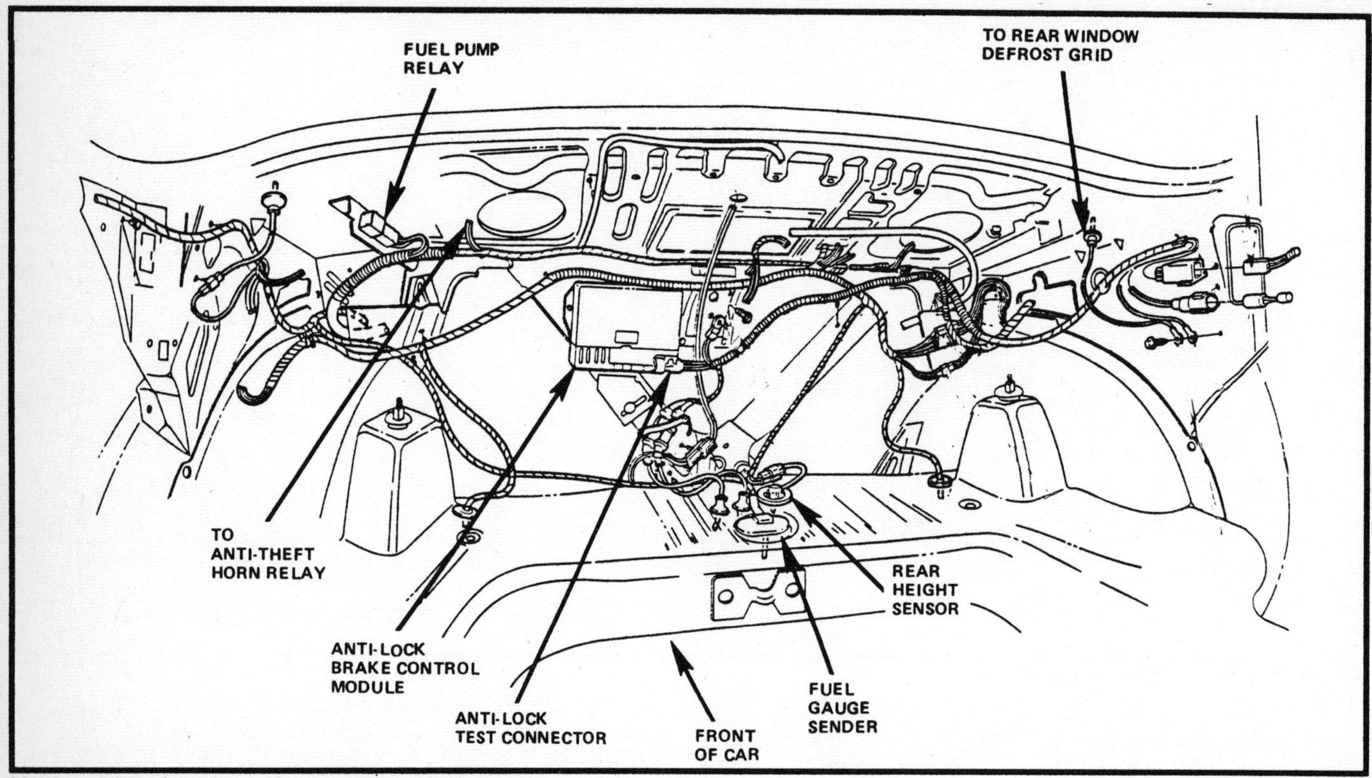

Underside of rear package tray—Mark VII

- **Electronic Engine Control Power Relay**—is located on the right fender apron.
- **Engine Coolant Temperature Sensor**—is located at the top right of the engine, near the distributor.
- **Forward Crash Sensors (Left/Right)**—are located above the left and right headlamp.
- **Front Height Sensors (Left and Right)**—are attached front lower control arms.
- **Fuel Gauge Sender**—is located on the fuel tank.
- **Fuel Pump Relay**—is located in the trunk, outboard of left trunk lid hinge support.
- **Hazard/Turn Signal Flasher**—is located behind lower left corner of fuse panel.
- **Heated Exhaust Gas Oxygen (HEGO) Sensors**—are located in the exhaust manifolds.
- **High/Low Beam Photocell Amplifier**—is located on the rear view mirror.
- **High/Low Beam Relay**—is located on the right fender apron, near the right front height sensor.
- **Hydraulic Pump Motor Relay**—is located on the firewall, behind brake master cylinder.
- **Ignition Suppression Resistor**—is located on the right fender apron, near ignition coil.
- **In Car Temperature Sensor**—is located behind the top center of the instrument panel.
- **In Line Fuse**—a 10 amp fuse is located under the right of the package tray, near the anti-theft module.
- **Inertia Switch**—is located at the inboard side of the left trunk lid hinge support.
- **Instrument Illumination Module**—is located behind the right instrument panel, near the rear of the glove box.
- **Interval Washer/Wiper Module**—is located behind the left side of the instrument panel.
- **Keyless Entry Module**—is located under the rear package tray.
- **Keyless/Anti-Theft Disarm Relay**—is located under the right side of the rear package tray.
- **Lamp Out Warning Module**—is located behind the instrument panel, near the steering column.
- **Light/Sensor Amplifier**—is located on the left side of the instrument panel, above the fuse panel.
- **Low Oil Level Relay**—is located on the right side of the instrument panel, behind the glove box.
- **Low Oil Level Sender Switch**—is located in the left side of oil pan.
- **Neutral Safety Switch**—is located on the left side of the transmission.
- **Oil Pressure Switch**—is located on the lower left side of the engine.
- **Outside (Ambient) Temperature Sensor**—is located behind the center of the radiator grille.
- **Overhead Indicator Module**—is located in the ceiling, near the harness to the moonroof switch.
- **Pulse Width Dimming Module**—is located behind the left instrument panel, near the wiring sub—harness to the fuse panel.
- **Rear Defrost Control Module**—is located behind the right side of the instrument panel.
- **Rear Defrost Relay and Timer**—contained within rear defrost control module, behind the right side of the instrument panel.
- **Rear Height Sensor**—is located in the center rear of trunk floor.
- **Shorting Plug**—is located on front of engine, near harness to TFI ignition module.
- **Starter Relay**—is located on the left fender apron.
- **TFI Ignition Module**—is attached to the distributor.
- **Thermactor Air Bypass Solenoid**—is located on the right fender apron.
- **Thermactor Air Diverter Solenoid**—is located on the right fender apron.
- **Throttle Position Sensor**—is located at the right rear of the engine, attached to the right side of the throttle body.

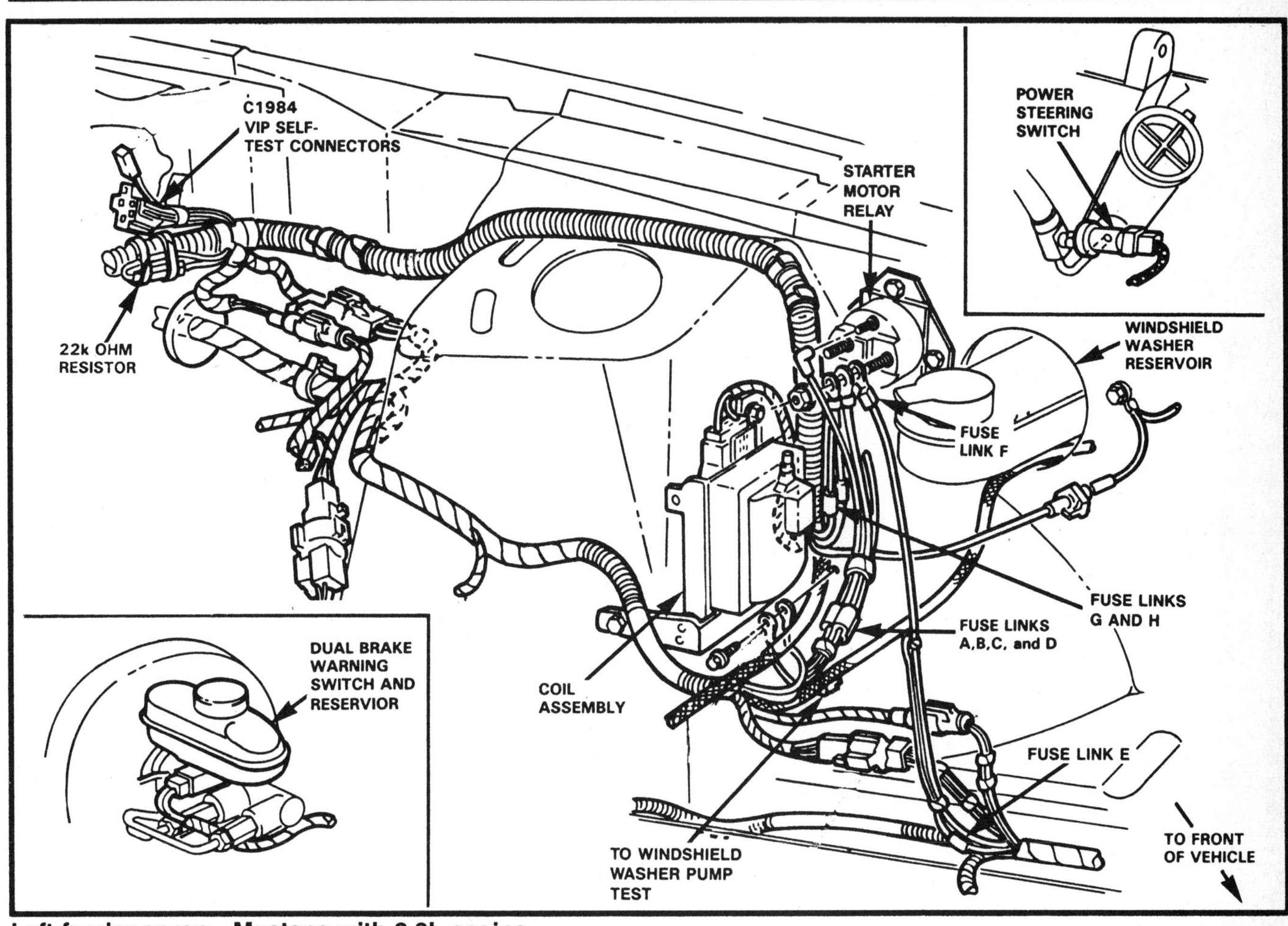

Left fender apron – Mustang with 2.3L engine

- **Trip Minder** – is located under the center of the instrument panel, near harness to blower motor.
- **Turn Signal/Hazard Flasher** – is located behind lower left corner of fuse panel.
- **Vehicle Speed Sensor (VSS)** – is located on the left rear of the transmission.
- **VIP Test Connectors C119 and C120** – are located on the right fender apron, forward of the shock tower.
- **Warning Chime Module** – is located behind the center of the instrument panel.
- **Washer Fluid Level Sensor** – is located on the rear of the washer fluid reservoir, on the left of the engine compartment.
- **Washer/Wiper Interval Module** – is located behind the left side of the instrument panel.
- **WOT A/C Cutout Relay** – is located on the left fender apron, near the shock tower.

MUSTANG

- **A/C Clutch Cycling Pressure Switch** – is located on top of the A/C suction accumulator.
- **A/C Clutch Diode (2.3L engine)** – is located on the right side of the engine compartment.
- **A/C Clutch Diode (5.0L engine)** – is located at the left side of the engine compartment, near the A/C compressor.
- **A/C Compressor Cut Out Relay (1989)** – is located on the left side of the engine compartment.
- **A/C Compressor Cut Out Relay (except 1989)** – is located on the right fender apron.
- **A/C Cooling Fan Controller (2.3L engine)** – is attached to the left instrument panel support.
- **Air Bag Backup Power Supply** – is located behind the right instrument panel, above the glove box.
- **Air Bag Diagnostic Module** – is located behind the center of the instrument panel.
- **Air Charge Temperature Sensor** – is located on the intake manifold.
- **Automatic Transmission Solenoid** – is located on the left side of the automatic transmission.
- **Backup/Neutral Safety Switch** – is located in the transmission assembly.
- **Barometric Absolute Pressure (BAP) Sensor** – is located at the center of the firewall.
- **Barometric Pressure Sensor (5.0L engine)** – is located on the left firewall.
- **Blower Resistors** – is located under the right side of the instrument panel near the blower motor.
- **Brake Lamp Switch** – is located on top of the brake pedal support.
- **Canister Purge Solenoid** – is located on the left side of the engine.
- **Center Line Crash Sensor** – is located at the top center of the radiator support.
- **Clutch Safety Switch** – is located above the clutch pedal.
- **converter Clutch Override Solenoid** – is located on the left side of the transmission.
- **Convertible Top Raise/Lower Relays** – are located in the luggage compartment, behind the rear seat.

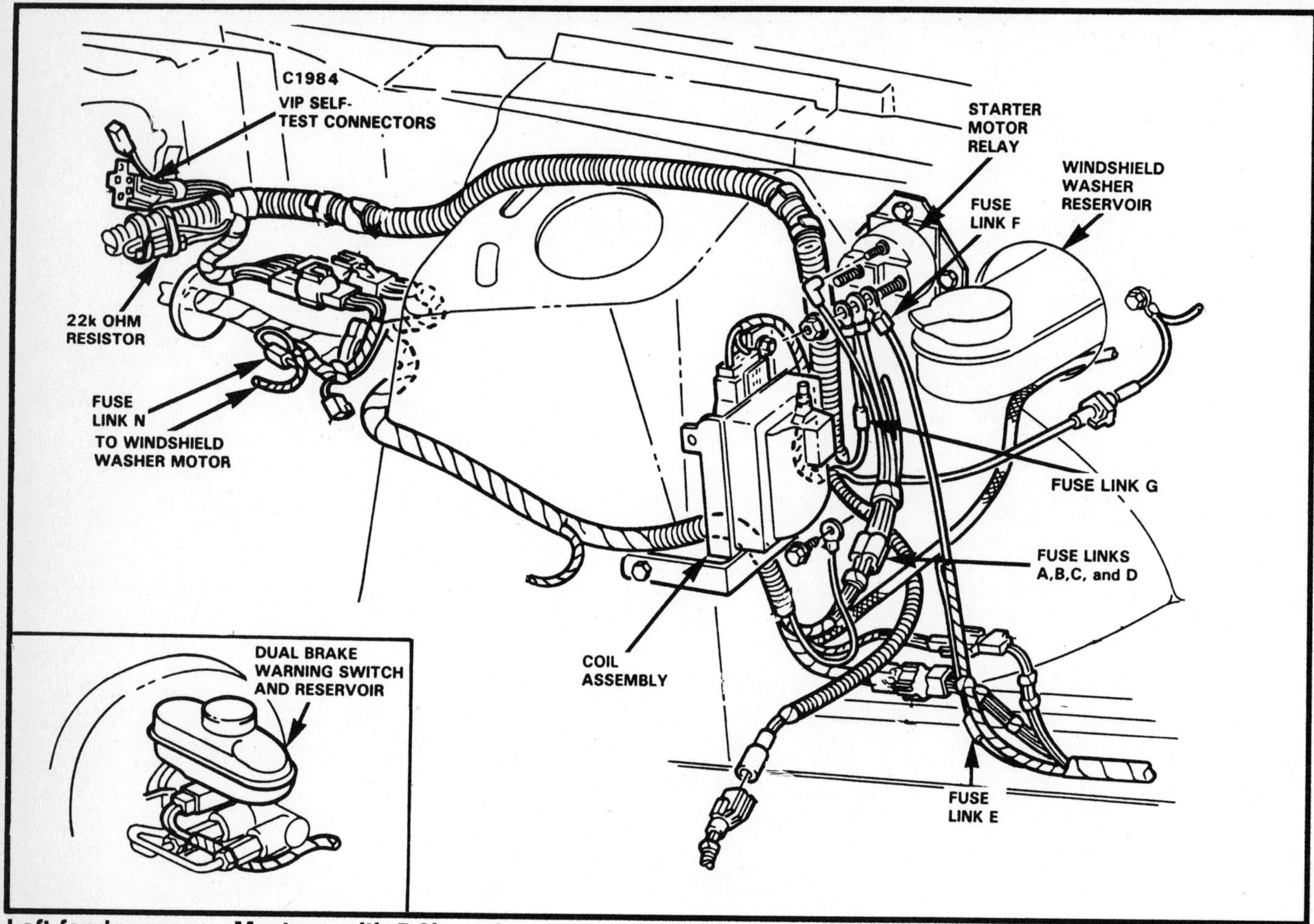

Left fender apron—Mustang with 5.0L engine

- **Coolant Temperature Sender**—is located at the left rear of the engine.
- **Coolant Temperature Sensor**—is located on top of the engine.
- **Daytime Running Lamps (DRL) Module (Canadian vehicles)**—is located inside the front of the left fender.
- **Defroster Control Relay/Timer**—is located on the left side of the instrument panel, near the fuse panel.
- **Dual Brake Warning Switch**—is located on the left fender apron.
- **EEC**—See Electronic Engine Control.
- **EGR Vacuum Regulator Solenoid**—is located on the right fender apron.
- **EGR Valve Position Sensor**—is located at the top right of the engine.
- **EGR Vent Solenoid**—is located on the right fender apron.
- **Electronic Engine Control (EEC) Module**—is located behind the right kick panel.
- **Electronic Engine Control (EEC) Power Relay**—is located on the EEC Module bracket behind the right kick panel.
- **Engine Coolant Temperature Sensor**—is located on top of the engine.
- **Engine Indicator Diode**—is located behind the left instrument panel, taped into the main harness.
- **Forward Crash Sensors**—are located within each front fender.
- **Fuel Filler Door Release Solenoid**—is located under the right tail lamp assembly.
- **Fuel Pump Diode**—is located under the rear of the car, behind the fuel tank.
- **Fuel Pump Relay**—is located under the driver's seat.
- **Fuel Pump**—is located in the fuel tank.
- **Hazard Flasher**—is located in the fuse panel.
- **Heated Exhaust Gas Oxygen (HEGO) Sensors**—are located at the rear of the exhaust manifolds.
- **Horn Relay**—is located behind the instrument panel, near the instrument cluster.
- **Ignition Coil**—is located near the front of the left shock tower.
- **Ignition Supression Resistor**—is located at the left rear of the engine compartment, taped into the engine harness.
- **Inertia Switch**—is located on the left side of the spare tire well.
- **Knock Sensor (2.3L engine)**—is located in the lower intake manifold.
- **LCD Illumination Relay**—is located behind center of the instrument panel.
- **Liftgate/Decklid Release Solenoid**—is located within the latch assembly.
- **Low Coolant Level Switch (1989)**—is located in the radiator.
- **Low Coolant Level Switch (except 1989)**—is located in the coolant reservoir.
- **Low Oil Level Relay**—is located on the left instrument panel brace.
- **Low Oil Level Switch**—is located in the oil pan at the rear of the engine.

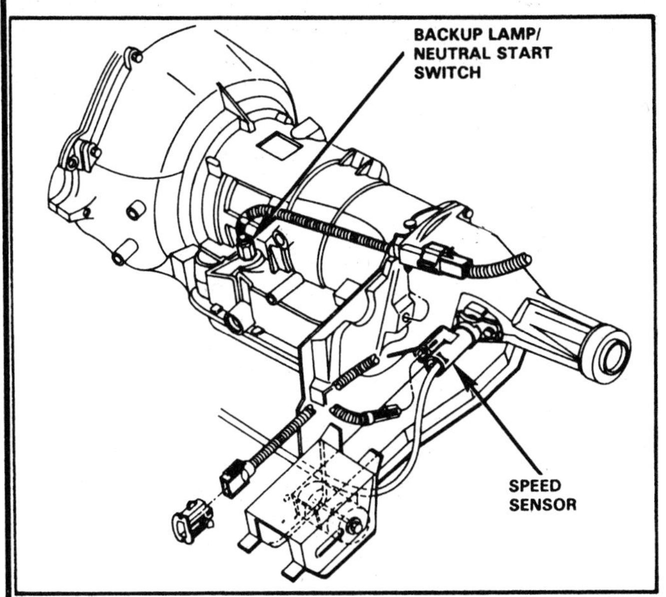

Transmission Wiring 5.0L AOD Trans.

BACKUP LAMP/
NEUTRAL START
SWITCH

CONVERTER
CLUTCH
OVERRIDE
SOLENOID

SPEED
SENSOR

Transmission Wiring 2.3L A4LD Trans.

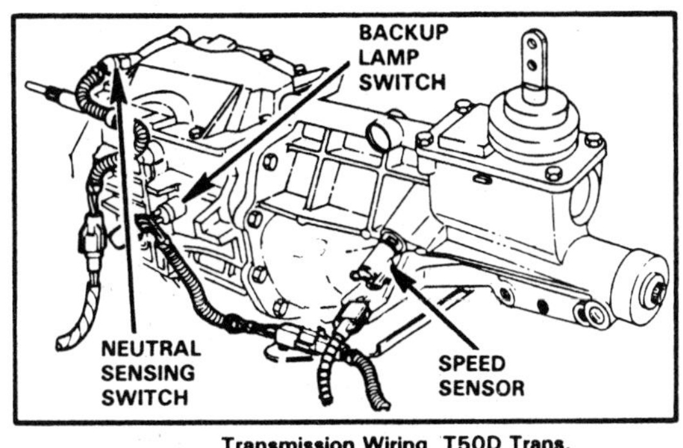

Transmission Wiring T50D Trans.

Transmission electrical components—Mustang

- **Low Oil Warning Relay**—is located behind the left side of the instrument panel.
- **Manifold Absolute Pressure (MAP) Sensor (2.3L engine)**—is located on the right front fender apron.
- **MAP Sensor (2.3L engine)**—is located on the right front fender apron.
- **Mass Airflow Sensor (5.0L engine)**—is located on the air inlet above the intake manifold.
- **Neutral Drive Switch**—is located on the left side of the transmission.
- **Neutral Safety Switch**—is located in the transmission assembly.
- **Neutral Sensing Switch**—is located on the clutch pedal.
- **Oil Pressure Sender (2.3L engine)**—is located at the left rear of the engine.
- **Oil Pressure Sender (5.0L engine)**—is located at the left front of the engine.
- **Power Steering Pressure Switch**—is located at the lower left side of the engine compartment.
- **Power Steering Pressure Switch**—is located on the steering gear.
- **Power Window Safety Relay**—is located behind the left kick panel.
- **Rear Crash Sensor**—is located inside the front of the left rear quarter panel.
- **Rear Defrost Control Relay/Timer**—is located on the left side of the instrument panel, near the fuse panel.
- **Reverse Switch**—is located in the transmission assembly.
- **Seatbelt Switch**—is located in the driver's seatbelt buckle.
- **Speed Control Amplifier**—is located behind the left kick panel.
- **Speed Control Servo**—is located on the left door pillar, under the fender.
- **Speed Sensor**—is located on the transmission.
- **Starter Relay**—is located at the left front fender.
- **Stoplamp Switch**—is located on top of the brake pedal support.
- **TFI Ignition Module (except 1989 5.0L engine)**—is located at the center front of the engine.
- **TFI Ignition Module (1989 5.0L engine)**—is located on the side of the distributor.
- **Thermactor Air Bypass and Diverter Solenoids**—are located on the right front fender apron.
- **Throttle Position Sensor (2.3L engine)**—is located on the top center of the engine.
- **Turn Signal Flasher**—is located behind the instrument panel below the instrument cluster.
- **Vehicle Speed Sensor**—is located on the transmission.
- **VIP Self Test Connectors**—are located on the left fender apron.
- **Warning Chime Module**—is located behind the center of the instrument panel.

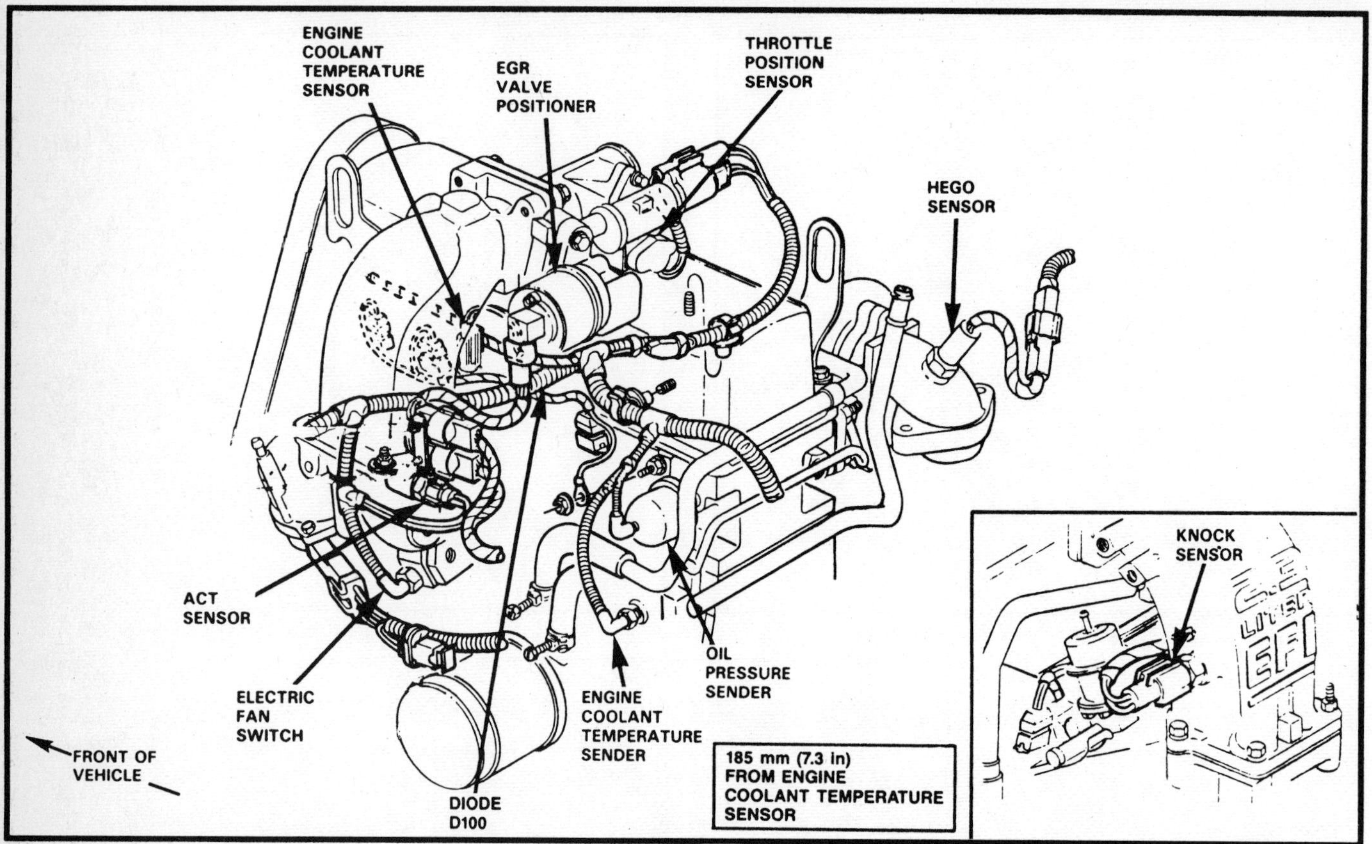

Engine electrical components – Mustang with 2.3L engine

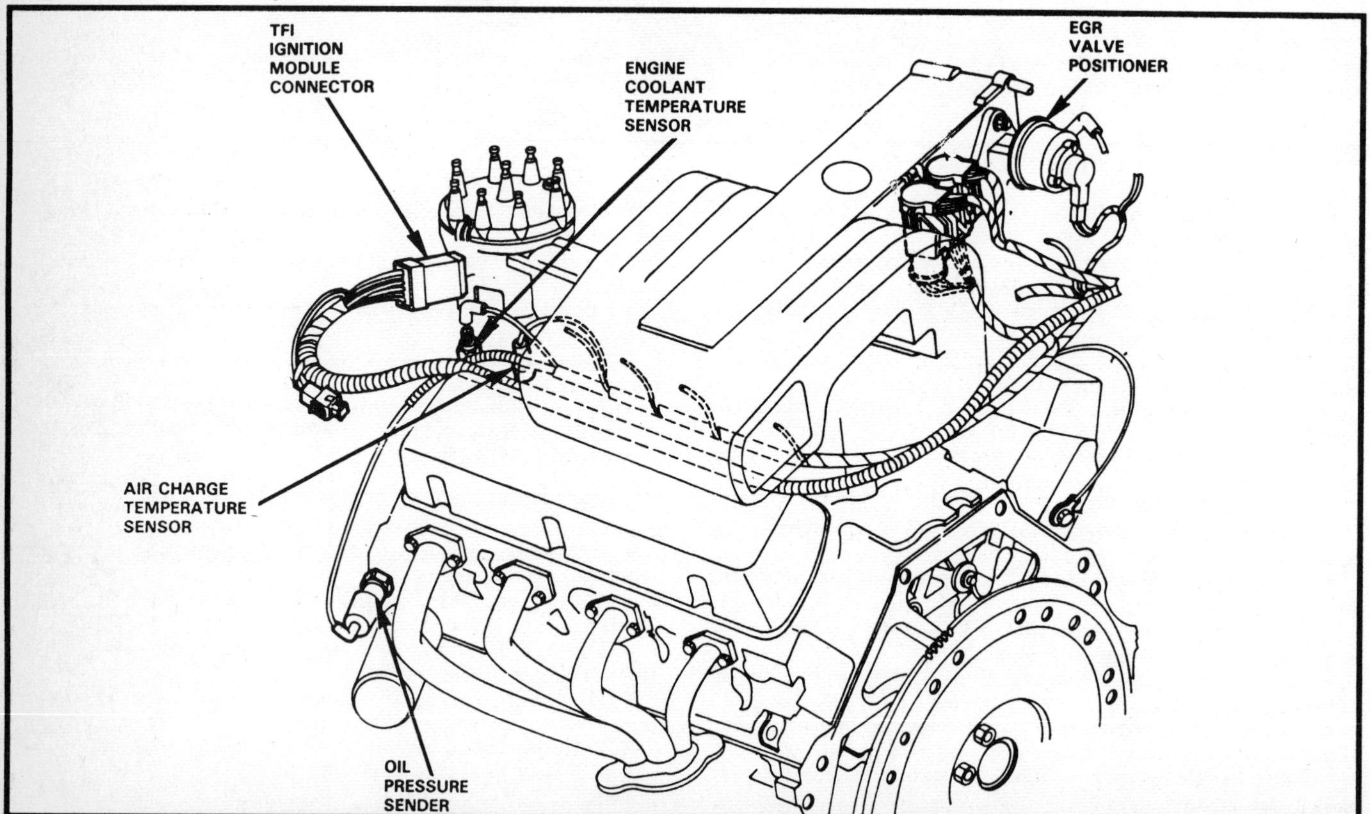

Left rear view of 5.0L engine – Mustang

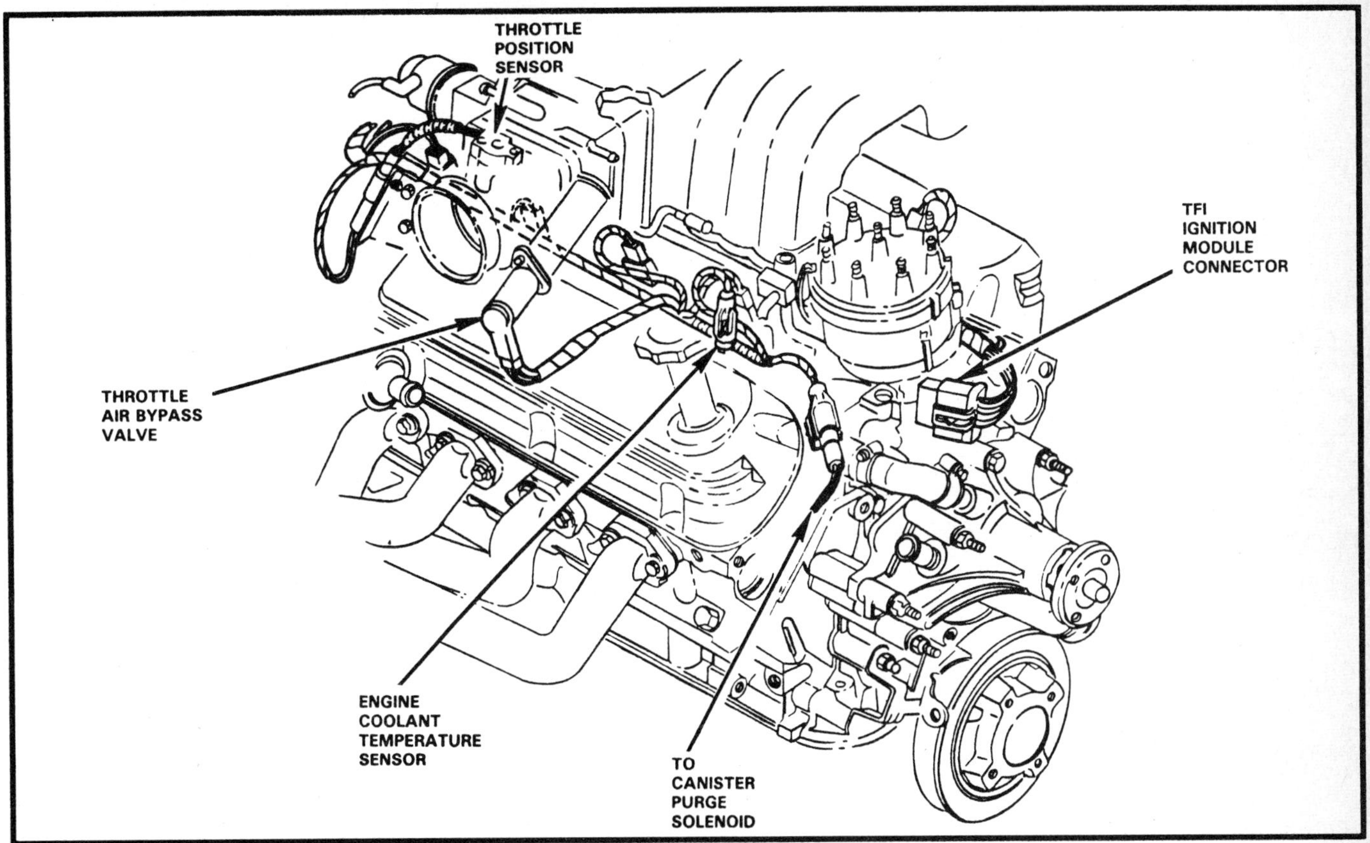

Right front view of 5.0L engine—Mustang

• **Windshield Washer Pump Test Connector**—is located on the left side of the engine compartment.Wiper/Washer Interval Governor—is located under the left side of the instrument panel, attached to the brace.

• **WOT Compressor Cut Out Relay (1989)**—is located on the left side of the engine compartment.

• **WOT Compressor Cut Out Relay (except 1989)**—is located on the right fender apron.

PROBE

• **4EAT Control Module**—is located in the dash to the left of the steering column.

• **A/C Relay (3.0L engine)**—is located to the left of the blower motor.

• **Anti-Lock Brake Actuator Assembly**—is located at the master cylinder.

• **Anti-Lock Brake Control Module**—is located under the left front seat.

• **Anti-Lock Brake Relay**—is located near the master cylinder.

• **Air Charge Temperature Sensor (3.0L engine)**—is located to the rear of the injectors.

• **Blower Motor Relay**—is located forward of the battery.

• **Blower Motor Resistor**—is located near the blower motor.

• **Blower Motor**—is located in the heater case.

• **By-Pass Air Control Valve (2.2L engine)**—is located on the rear of the distributor to the left of the fuel injectors.

• **Canister Purge Solenoid**—is located in the center of the engine compartment near the bulkhead.

• **Clutch Interlock Switch**—is located in the dash to the right of the steering column.

• **Condenser Fan Relay**—is located on the right front side of the condenser.

• **Coolant Level Sensor**—is located at the top of the radiator.

• **Cooling Fan Relay No. 1 (4EAT automatic transaxle only)**—is located in the engine compartment relay box.

• **Cooling Fan Relay No. 2**—is located in the engine compartment relay box.

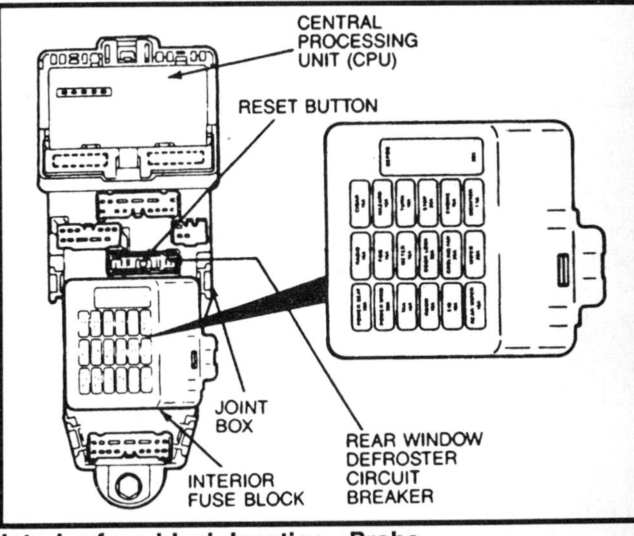

Interior fuse block location—Probe

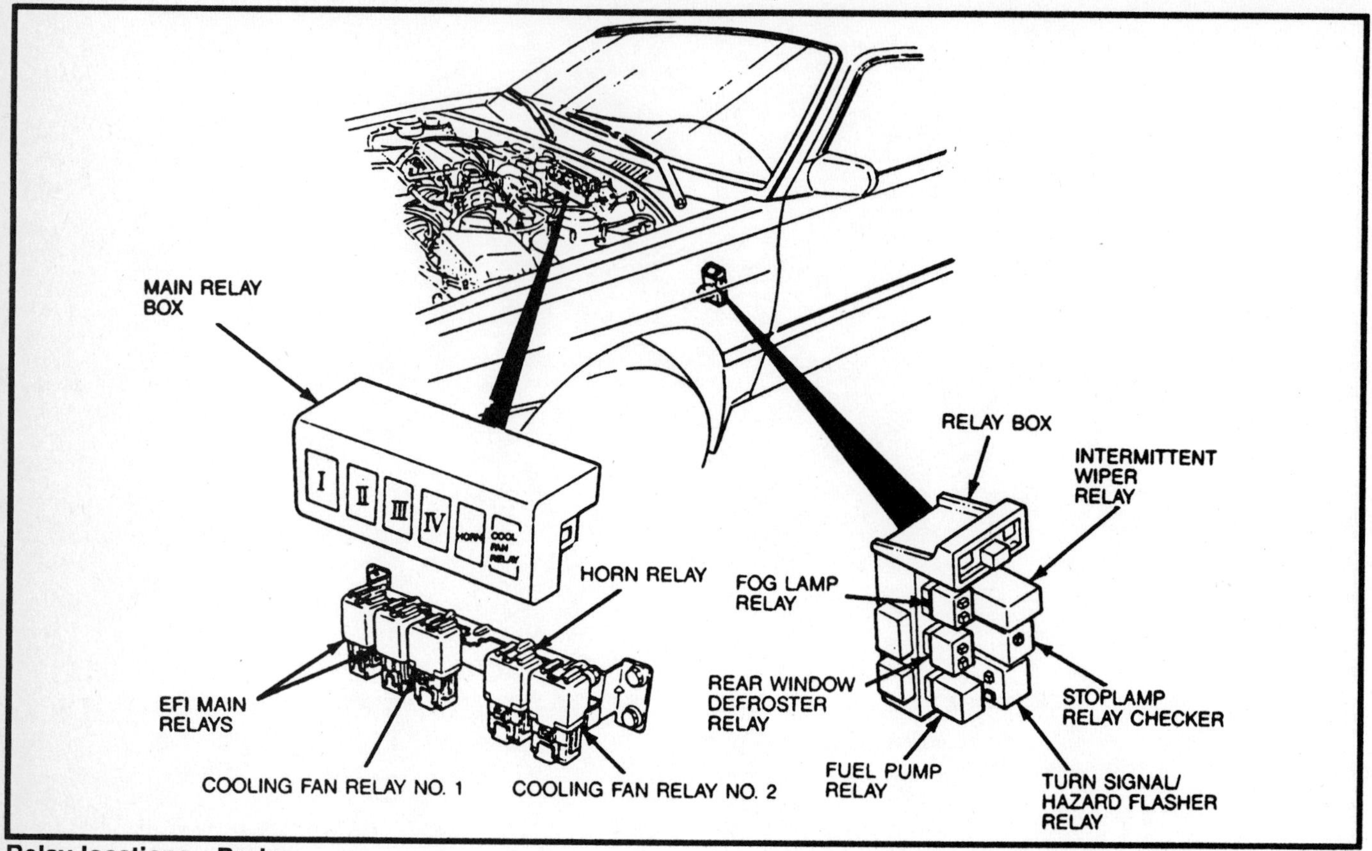

Relay locations—Probe

- **Crankshaft Position Sensor (2.2L turbocharged engine)**—is located inside the distributor.
- **Daytime Running Lamp (DRL) Control Module (Canada)**—is located in the dash to the left of the steering column.
- **EFI Main Relays**—are located in the engine compartment relay box.
- **EGR Solenoid Valve (2.2L engine)**—is located to the rear of the injectors near the bulkhead.
- **EGR Valve Position Sensor (2.2L engine—California)**—is located on the EGR valve slightly above the alternator.
- **Electronic Control Assembly (2.2L engine)** —is located in the bottom center of the dash.
- **Electronic Engine Control unit (3.0L engine)**—is located in the bottom center of the dash.
- **Engine Coolant Temperature Sensor (2.2L engine)**—is located in the center of the engine compartment.
- **Engine Coolant Temperature Sensor (3.0L engine)**—is located in the center of the engine compartment to the left of the injectors.
- **EVR Solenoid Valve (3.0L engine—California)**—is located on the right rear side of the engine compartment.
- **Fog Lamp Relay**—is located in the relay box under the dash.
- **Fuel Pump Inertia Switch**—is located in the liftgate area under the left trim panel.
- **Fuel Pump Relay**—is located in the relay box under the dash.
- **Headlamp Relay**—is located forward of the washer reservoir.
- **Heater Control Module**—is located behind the center of the dash.
- **Horn Relay**—is located in the engine compartment relay box.
- **Idle Speed Control solenoid (3.0L engine)**—is located to the rear of the distributor and to the of the injectors.
- **Ignition Module (2.2L engine)**—is located on the left rear side of the engine compartment.
- **Integral Relay Control Module (3.0L engine)**—is located in the rear center of the engine compartment.
- **Interior Fuse Panel**—is located just above the left side kick panel.
- **Interior Relay Box**—is mounted to the bulkhead on the left side of the instrument panel under the dash.
- **Intermittent Wiper Relay**—is located in the relay box under the dash.
- **Knock Control Module (2.2L turbocharged engine)**—is located on the right side of the relay box to the rear of the turbocharger.
- **Knock Sensor (2.2L turbocharged engine)**—is located above the alternator, or to the side of the oil filter.
- **Main Fuse Block**—is located on the left side of the engine compartment near the battery.
- **Main Relay Box**—is located on the upper left side of the bulkhead in the engine compartment.
- **MAP Sensor (3.0L engine)**—is located to the right of the engine compartment relay box.
- **Neutral Safety Switch**—is located on the transaxle.
- **Oil Level Module (3.0L engine)**—is located above the ECA.
- **Oil Level Sensor**—is located in the oil pan.
- **Oil Pressure Sender**—is located in the left rear side of the engine block.
- **Oxygen Sensor**—is located in the exhaust manifold.
- **Passive Restraint Control Module**—is located behind the left inside rear quarter trim panel.
- **PFE EGR (3.0L engine—California)**—is located to the rear of the injectors.

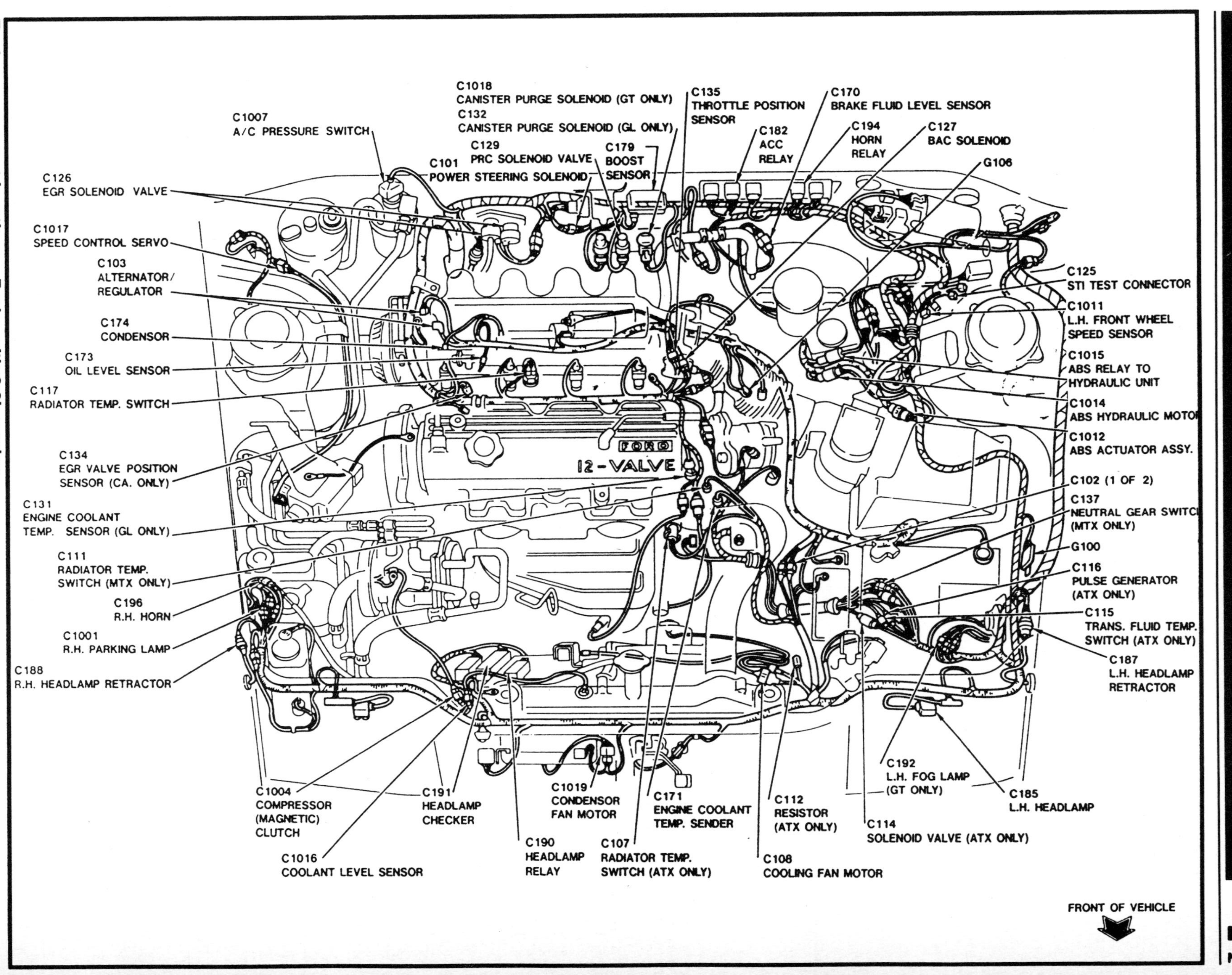

Engine component locations—Probe with 2.2L engine

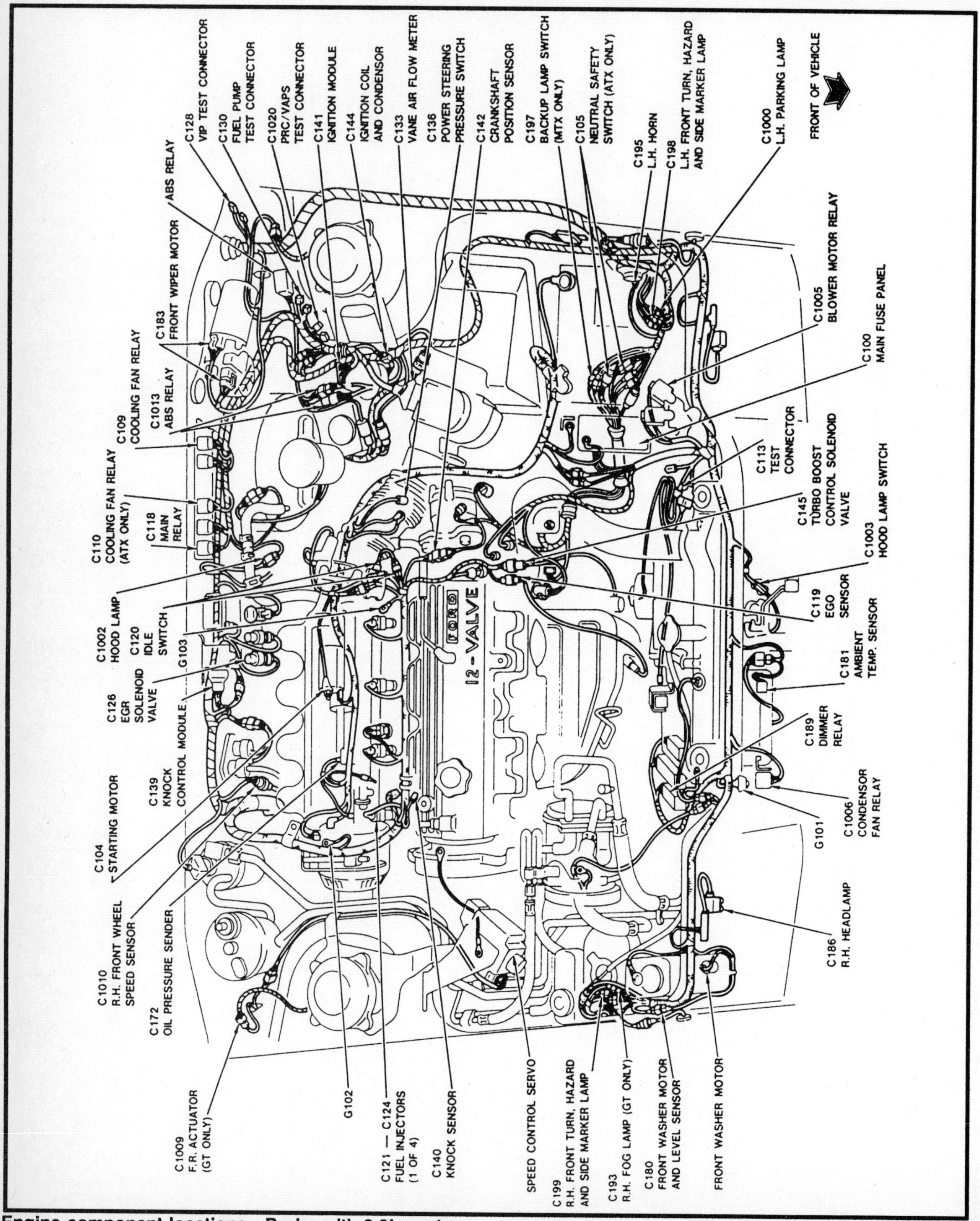

C128 VIP TEST CONNECTOR
C130 FUEL PUMP TEST CONNECTOR
C1020 PRC/VAPS TEST CONNECTOR
C141 IGNITION MODULE
C144 IGNITION COIL AND CONDENSOR
C133 VANE AIR FLOW METER
C136 POWER STEERING PRESSURE SWITCH
C142 CRANKSHAFT POSITION SENSOR
C197 BACKUP LAMP SWITCH (MTX ONLY)
C105 NEUTRAL SAFETY SWITCH (ATX ONLY)
C195 L.H. HORN
C198 L.H. FRONT TURN, HAZARD AND SIDE MARKER LAMP
C1000 L.H. PARKING LAMP
FRONT OF VEHICLE
ABS RELAY
C183 FRONT WIPER MOTOR
COOLING FAN RELAY
C1013 ABS RELAY
C109 COOLING FAN RELAY
C1005 BLOWER MOTOR RELAY
C100 MAIN FUSE PANEL
C110 COOLING FAN RELAY (ATX ONLY)
C118 MAIN RELAY
C113 TEST CONNECTOR
C145 TURBO BOOST CONTROL SOLENOID VALVE
C1003 HOOD LAMP SWITCH
C1002 HOOD LAMP
C120 IDLE SWITCH
G103
FORD
12-VALVE
C119 EGO SENSOR
C126 EGR SOLENOID VALVE
C181 AMBIENT TEMP. SENSOR
C139 KNOCK CONTROL MODULE
C189 DIMMER RELAY
C104 STARTING MOTOR
G101
C1006 CONDENSOR FAN RELAY
C1010 R.H. FRONT WHEEL SPEED SENSOR
C172 OIL PRESSURE SENDER
C186 R.H. HEADLAMP
C1009 F.R. ACTUATOR (GT ONLY)
G102
C121 — C124 FUEL INJECTORS (1 OF 4)
C140 KNOCK SENSOR
SPEED CONTROL SERVO
C199 R.H. FRONT TURN, HAZARD AND SIDE MARKER LAMP
C193 R.H. FOG LAMP (GT ONLY)
C180 FRONT WASHER MOTOR AND LEVEL SENSOR
FRONT WASHER MOTOR

Engine component locations – Probe with 2.2L engine

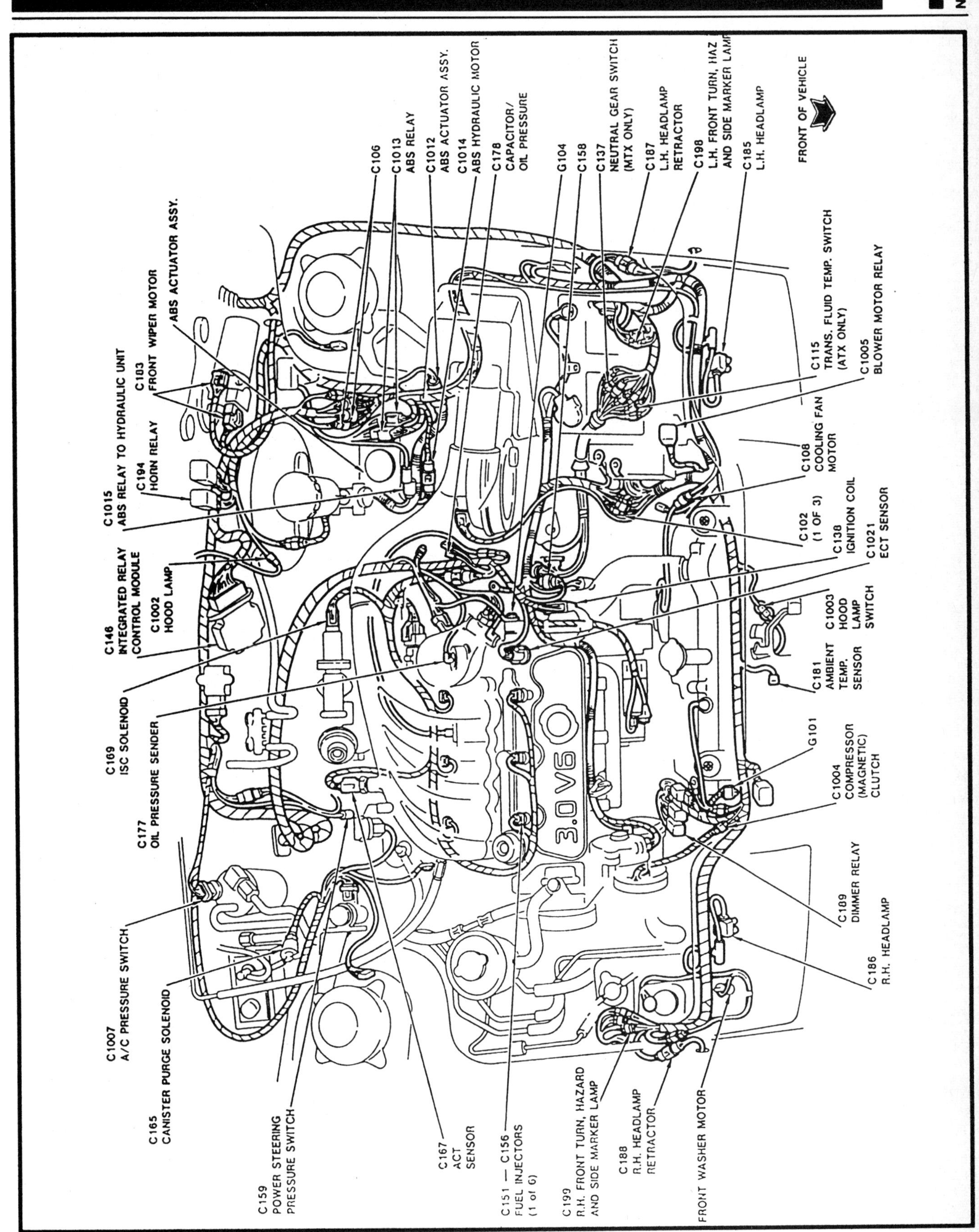

Engine component locations—Probe with 3.OL engine

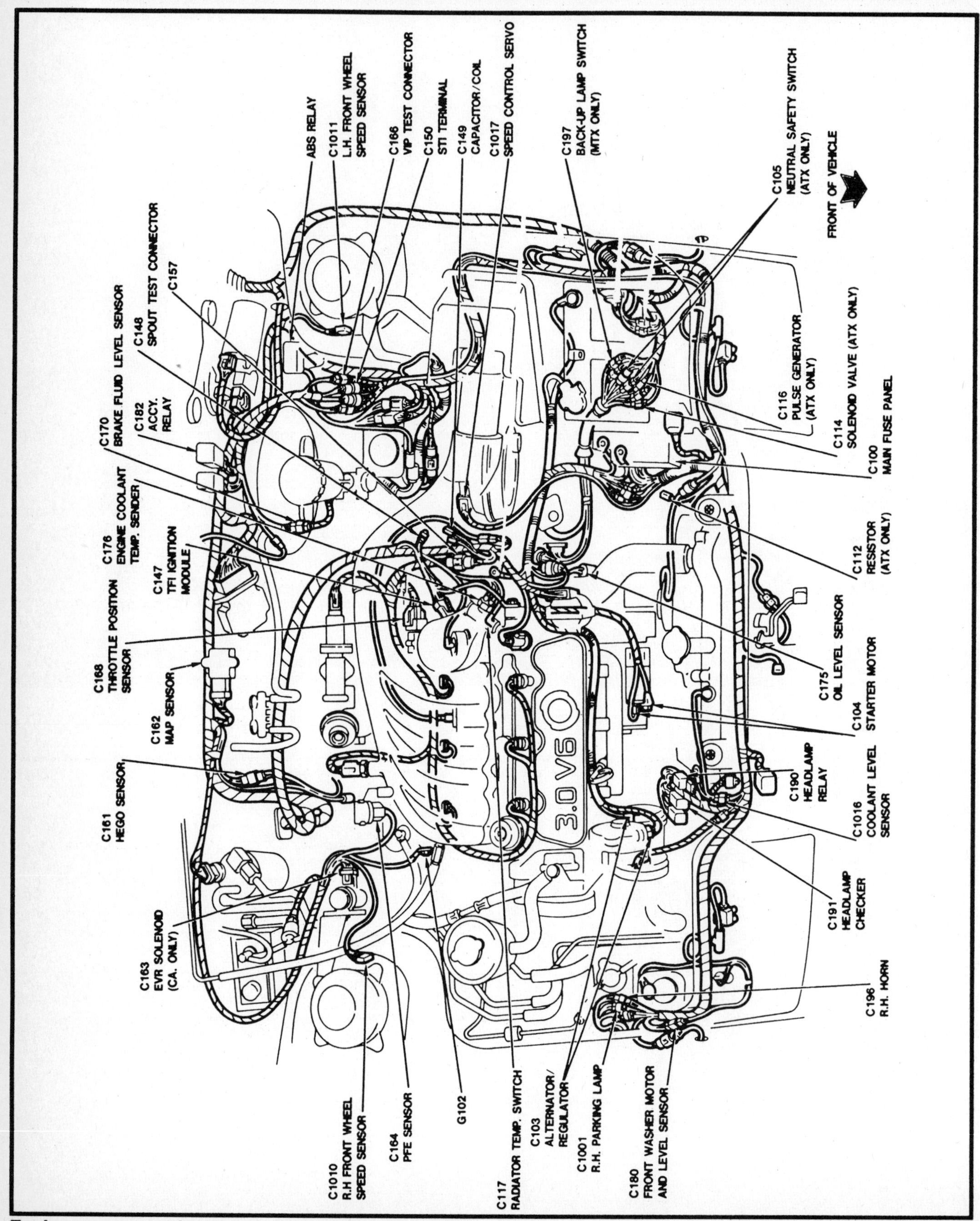

Engine component locations—Probe with 3.OL engine

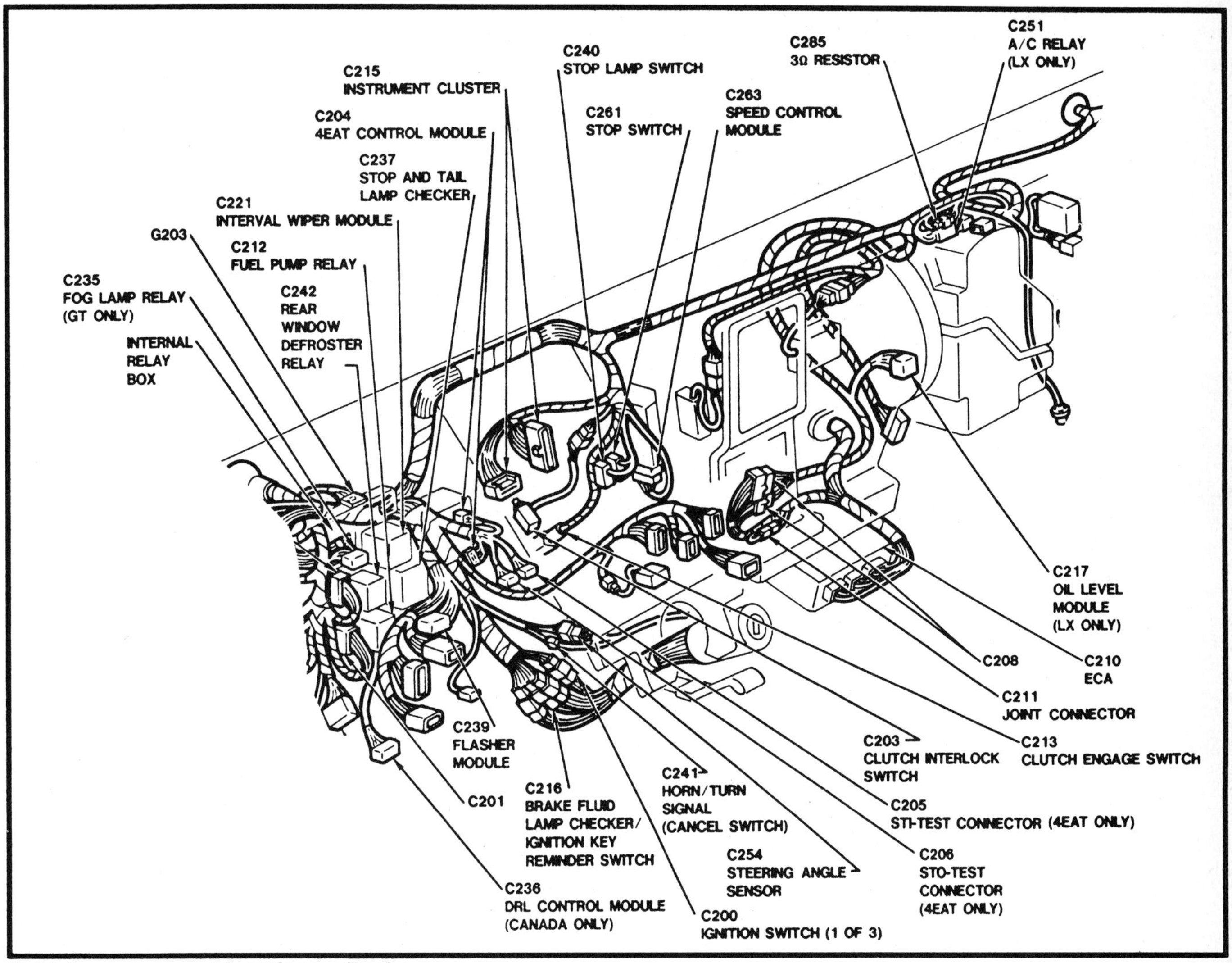

C215
INSTRUMENT CLUSTER
C240
STOP LAMP SWITCH
C285
3Ω RESISTOR
C251
A/C RELAY
(LX ONLY)
C204
4EAT CONTROL MODULE
C261
STOP SWITCH
C263
SPEED CONTROL
MODULE
C237
STOP AND TAIL
LAMP CHECKER
C221
INTERVAL WIPER MODULE
G203
C212
FUEL PUMP RELAY
C235
FOG LAMP RELAY
(GT ONLY)
C242
REAR
WINDOW
DEFROSTER
RELAY
INTERNAL
RELAY
BOX
C217
OIL LEVEL
MODULE
(LX ONLY)
C208
C210
ECA
C211
JOINT CONNECTOR
C239
FLASHER
MODULE
C203
CLUTCH INTERLOCK
SWITCH
C213
CLUTCH ENGAGE SWITCH
C241
HORN/TURN
SIGNAL
(CANCEL SWITCH)
C201
C216
BRAKE FLUID
LAMP CHECKER/
IGNITION KEY
REMINDER SWITCH
C205
STI-TEST CONNECTOR (4EAT ONLY)
C254
STEERING ANGLE
SENSOR
C206
STO-TEST
CONNECTOR
(4EAT ONLY)
C236
DRL CONTROL MODULE
(CANADA ONLY)
C200
IGNITION SWITCH (1 OF 3)

Vehicle component locations—Probe

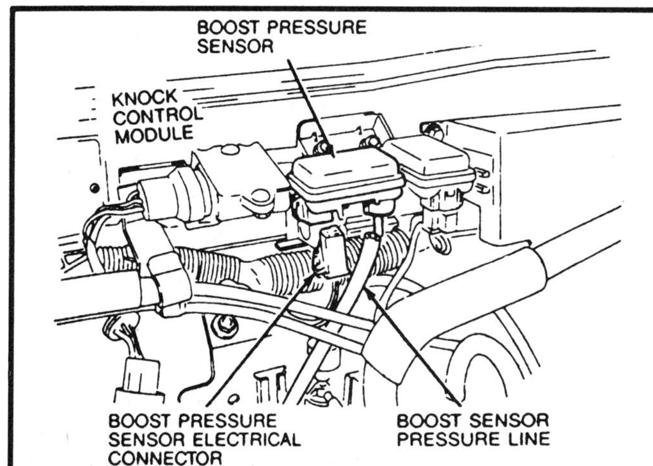

BOOST PRESSURE
SENSOR
KNOCK
CONTROL
MODULE
BOOST PRESSURE
SENSOR ELECTRICAL
CONNECTOR
BOOST SENSOR
PRESSURE LINE

Boost pressure sensor location—Probe with 2.2L turbocharged engine

- **Power Door Lock Relay**—is located behind the left interior rear quarter trim panel.
- **Power Steering Control Module**—is located under the left front seat.
- **Power Steering Pressure Switch (2.2L engine)**—is located on the left rear side of the engine compartment.
- **Power Steering Pressure Switch (3.0L engine)**—is located on the left rear side of the engine compartment.
- **Pressure Regulator Control solenoid valve (2.2L engine)**—is located in the center of the engine compartment near the bulkhead.
- **Programmed Ride Control Actuators (Front and Rear)**—are located at the top of the struts.
- **Programmed Ride Control Module**—is located under the passenger seat.
- **Radiator Temperature Switch**—is located on the intake manifold.
- **Rear Defroster Relay**—is located in the relay box under the dash.
- **Refrigerant Pressure Switch**—is located on the right rear side of the alternator.
- **Shift Lock Control Module**—is located in the shifter housing at the center of the console.

• **Spout Connector (3.0L engine)**—is located on the left rear side of the engine compartment.
• **Steering Angle Sensor**—is located at the steering column behind the steering wheel.
• **STI Terminal (3.0L engine)**—is located on the left rear side of the engine compartment.
• **Stop/Tail Light Checker Relay**—is located in the relay box under the dash.
• **TFI Module (3.0L engine)**—is located on the right front side of the engine compartment to the left of the injectors.
• **TFI Module**—is located on the right front side of the engine compartment.
• **Turbo Boost Control Solenoid Valve (2.2L turbocharged engine)**—is located in front of the distributor.
• **Turn Signal/Hazard Flasher Relay**—is located in the relay box under the dash.

TAURUS AND SABLE

• **A/C Clutch Cycling Pressure Switch (except SHO engine)**—is at right the rear of engine compartment mounted on A/C accumulator.
• **A/C Clutch Cycling Pressure Switch (SHO engine)**—is at the right front of engine, mounted on A/C accumulator.
• **Air Bag Backup Power Supply**—is behind right instrument panel, right side of glove box.
• **Air Bag Diagnostic Module**—is behind center of instrument panel.
• **Air Bag Rear Sensor**—is inside left kick panel.
• **Air Charge Temperature Sensor (2.5L engine)**—is on the left rear of intake manifold.
• **Air Charge Temperature Sensor (3.0L engine)**—is on the top of engine.
• **Air Charge Temperature Sensor (SHO engine)**—is on the left side of engine, in air cleaner.
• **Alternator Output Control Relay**—is between right front inner fender and fender splash shield.
• **Ambient Temperature Sensor**—is at the left front of engine compartment on left side of radiator.
• **Anti-Lock Brake Control Module (except SHO engine)**—is at right fender apron.
• **Anti-Lock Brake Control Module (SHO engine)**—is at the lower left front of engine compartment.
• **Anti-Lock Brake Diode**—is on the left rear corner of engine compartment, taped to wiring harness
anti-Lock Motor Relay—is on the lower left front of engine compartment.
• **Anti-Lock Power Relay**—is at the left rear corner of engine compartment.
• **Anti-Lock Test Connector**—is at the left rear corner of engine compartment.
• **Autolamp Dual Coil Relay**—is behind center of instrument panel, mounted on brace.
• **AXOD Speed Sensor and Torque Converter Solenoid**—is at the lower left rear of engine.
• **Barometric Absolute Pressure (BAP) Sensor**—is on the right side of firewall.
• **Blower Motor Resistors**—is behind right side of instrument panel, inside heater plenum.
• **Brake Fluid Level Sensor**—is at the lower left front of engine compartment.
• **Brake Lamp Switch**—is behind left side instrument panel, on pedal support.
• **Cam Sensor**—is on the right side of engine.
• **Canister Purge Solenoid (2.5L, 3.0L and 3.8L engine)**—is on the left front side of engine.

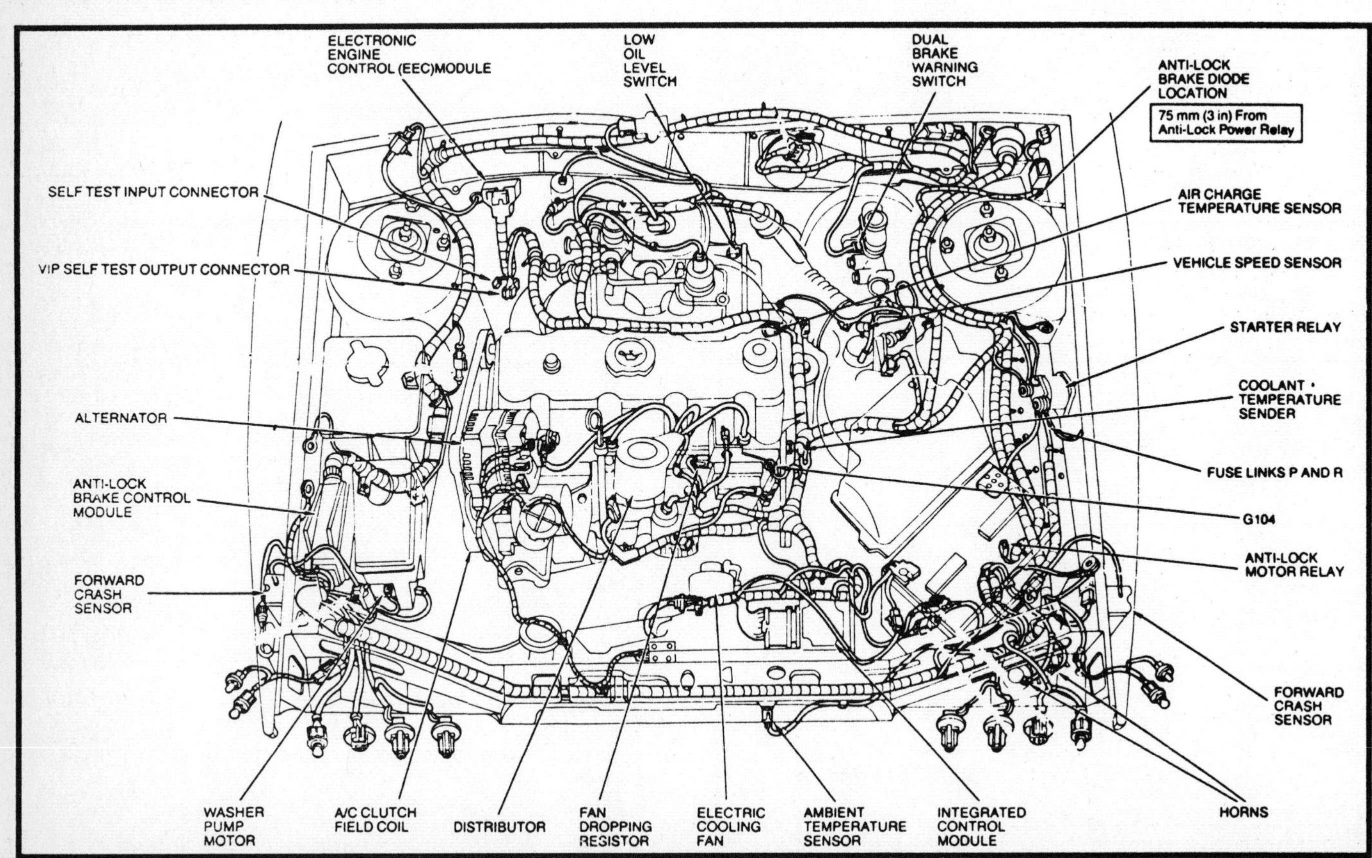

Component locations—Taurus and Sable with 2.5L engine

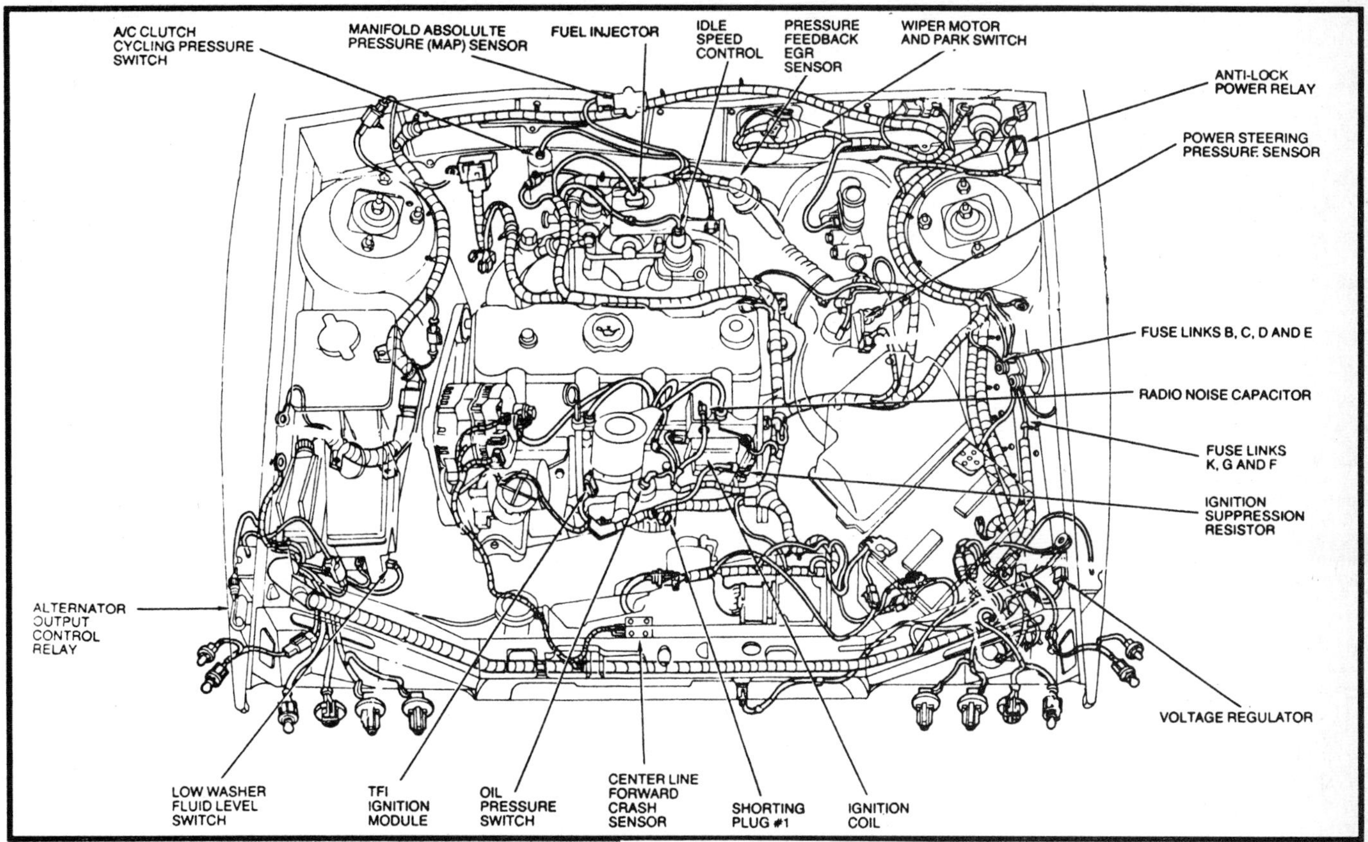

Component locations—Taurus and Sable with 2.5L engine (continued)

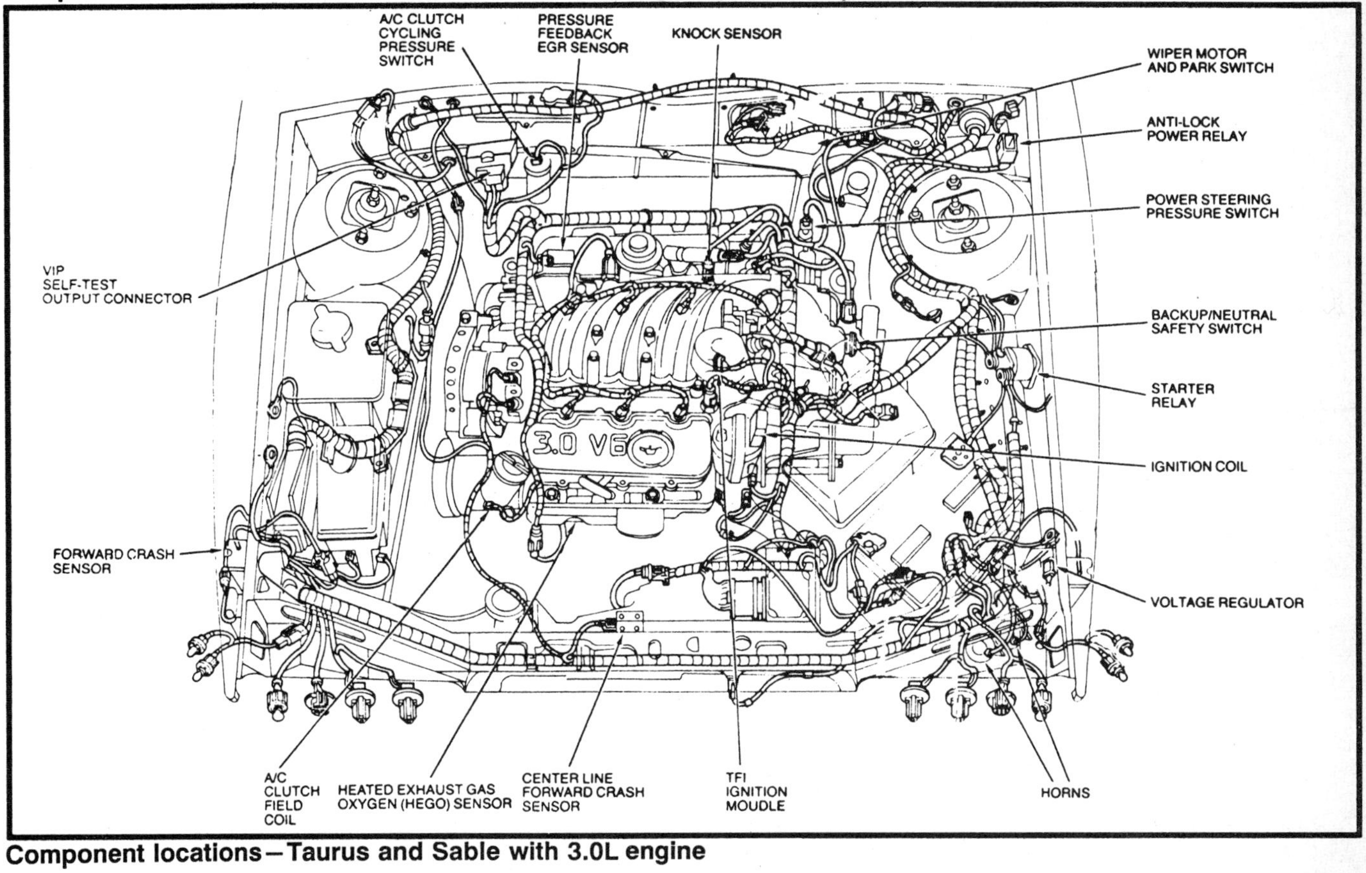

Component locations—Taurus and Sable with 3.0L engine

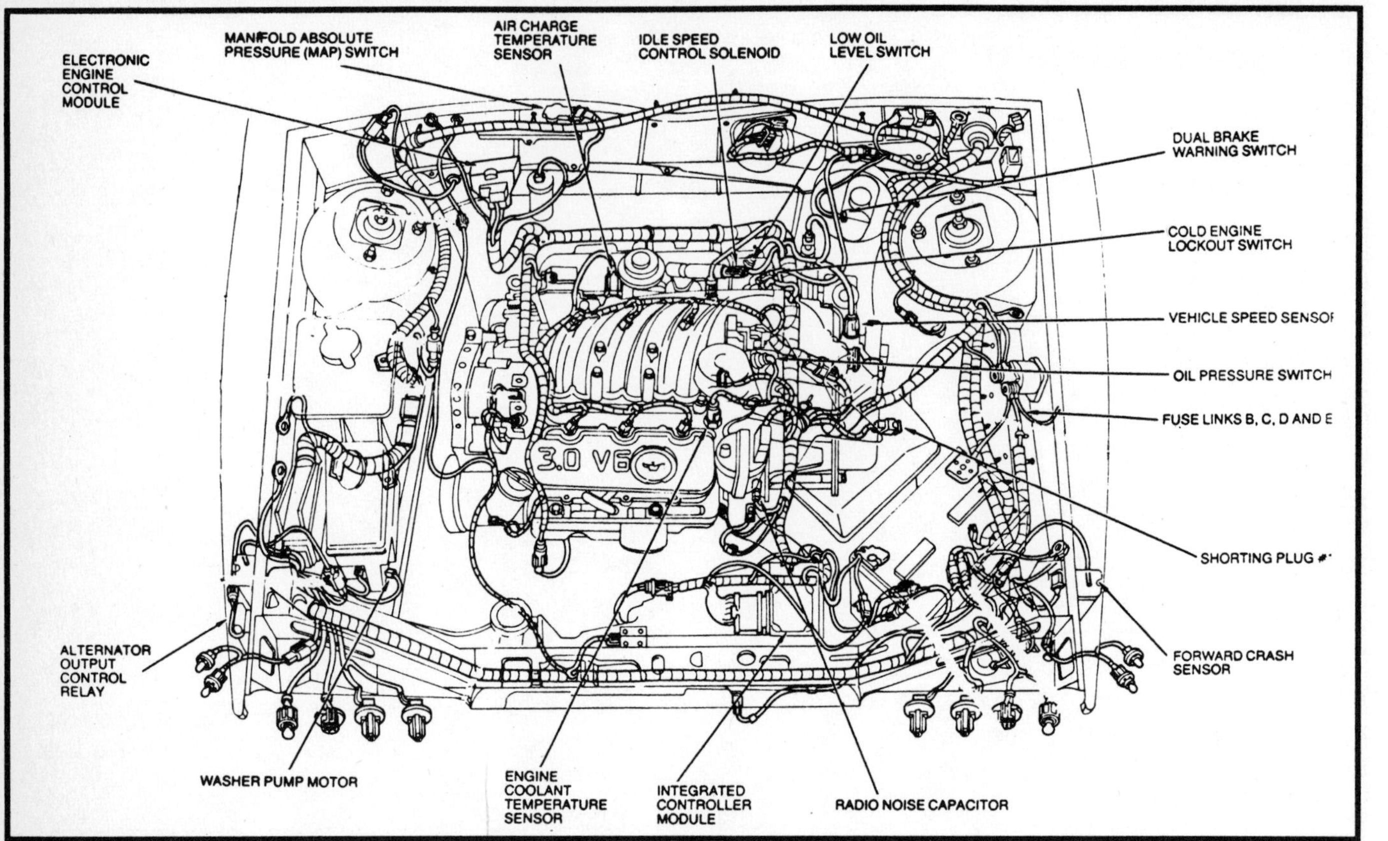

Component locations—Taurus and Sable with 3.0L engine (continued)

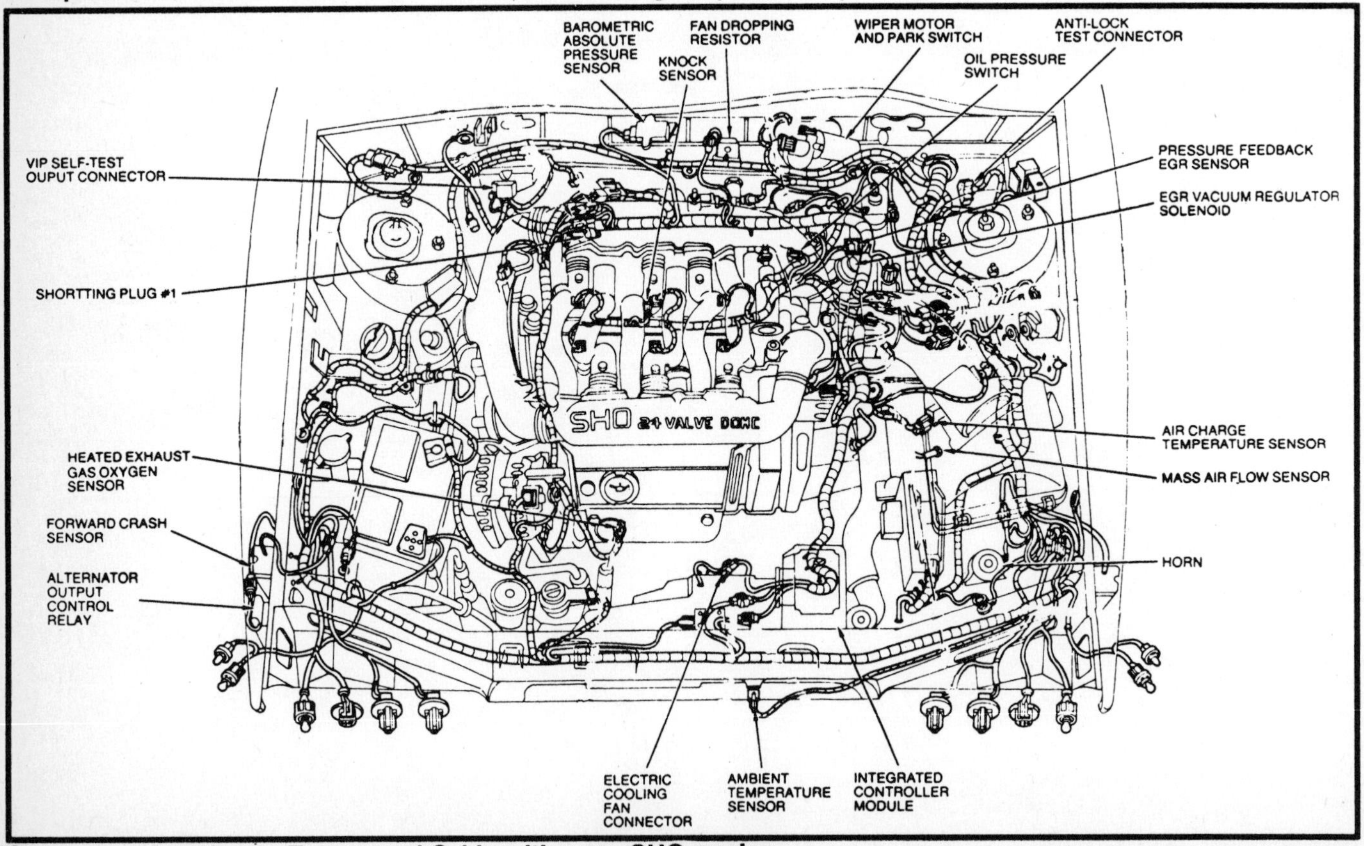

Component locations—Taurus and Sable with 3.0L SHO engine

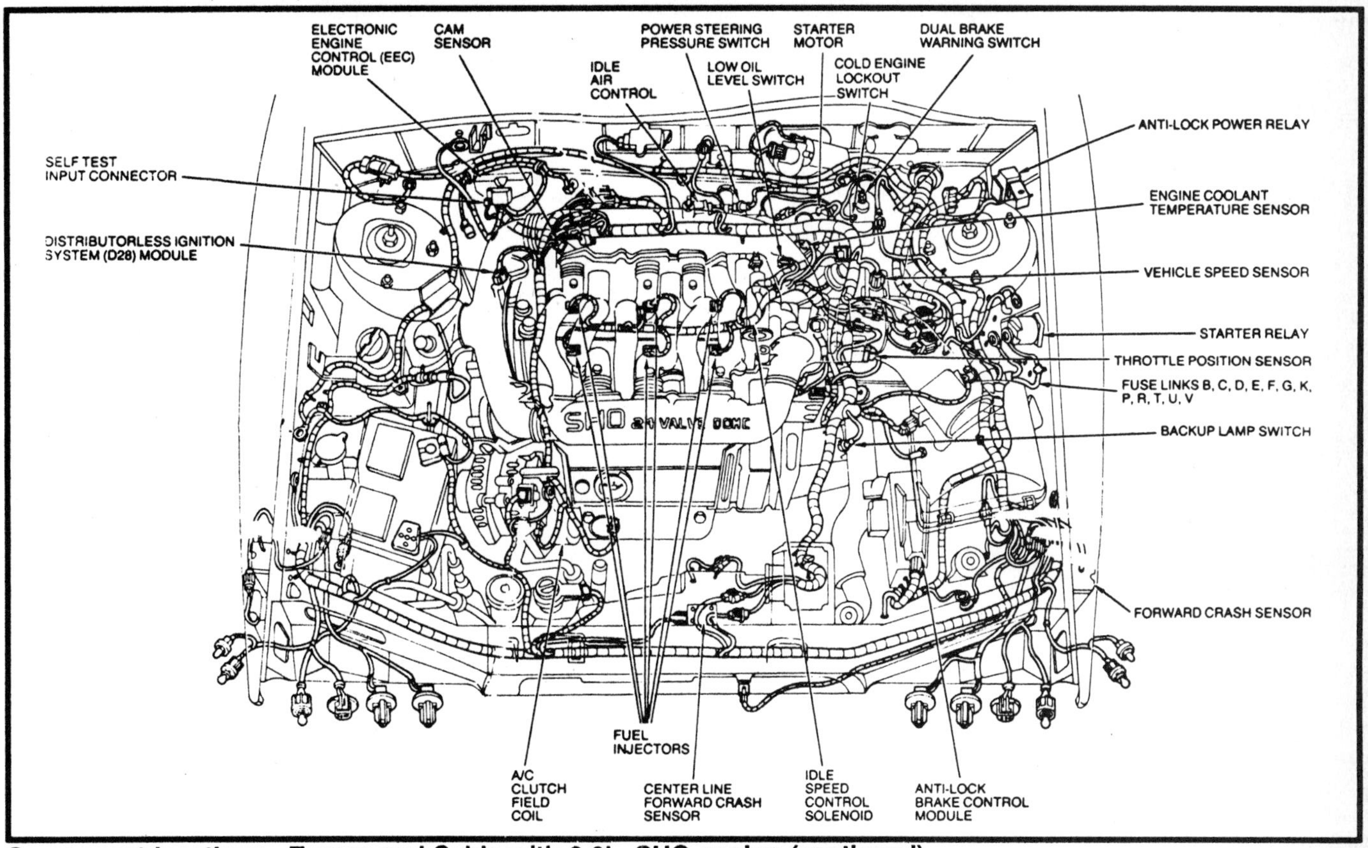
ELECTRONIC ENGINE CONTROL (EEC) MODULE
CAM SENSOR
POWER STEERING PRESSURE SWITCH
STARTER MOTOR
DUAL BRAKE WARNING SWITCH
IDLE AIR CONTROL
LOW OIL LEVEL SWITCH
COLD ENGINE LOCKOUT SWITCH
ANTI-LOCK POWER RELAY
SELF TEST INPUT CONNECTOR
ENGINE COOLANT TEMPERATURE SENSOR
DISTRIBUTORLESS IGNITION SYSTEM (D28) MODULE
VEHICLE SPEED SENSOR
STARTER RELAY
THROTTLE POSITION SENSOR
FUSE LINKS B, C, D, E, F, G, K, P, R, T, U, V
BACKUP LAMP SWITCH
SHO 24 VALVE DOHC
FORWARD CRASH SENSOR
FUEL INJECTORS
A/C CLUTCH FIELD COIL
CENTER LINE FORWARD CRASH SENSOR
IDLE SPEED CONTROL SOLENOID
ANTI-LOCK BRAKE CONTROL MODULE

Component locations—Taurus and Sable with 3.0L SHO engine (continued)

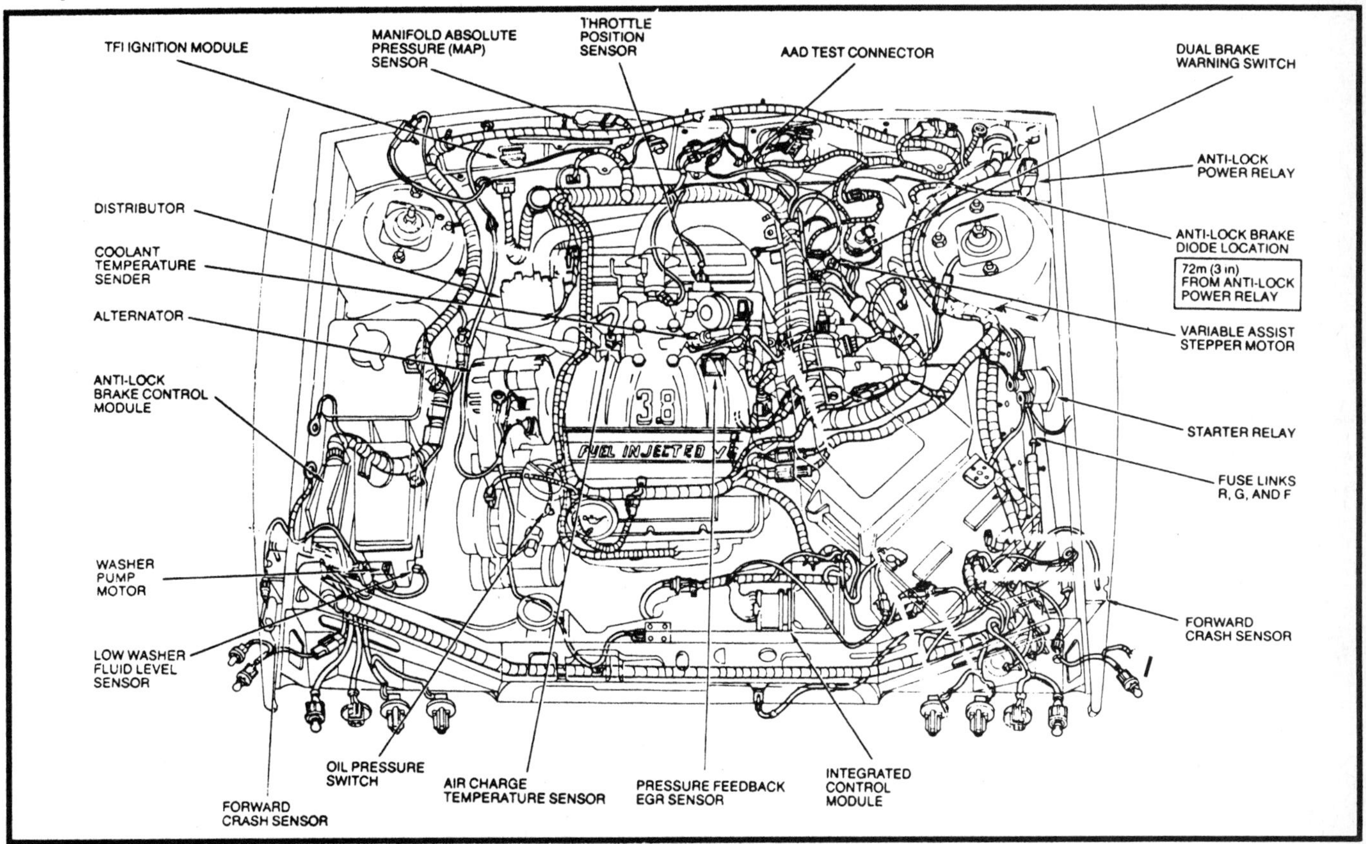
TFI IGNITION MODULE
MANIFOLD ABSOLUTE PRESSURE (MAP) SENSOR
THROTTLE POSITION SENSOR
AAD TEST CONNECTOR
DUAL BRAKE WARNING SWITCH
ANTI-LOCK POWER RELAY
DISTRIBUTOR
ANTI-LOCK BRAKE DIODE LOCATION
72m (3 in) FROM ANTI-LOCK POWER RELAY
COOLANT TEMPERATURE SENDER
ALTERNATOR
VARIABLE ASSIST STEPPER MOTOR
ANTI-LOCK BRAKE CONTROL MODULE
3.8
FUEL INJECTED V6
STARTER RELAY
FUSE LINKS R, G, AND F
WASHER PUMP MOTOR
FORWARD CRASH SENSOR
LOW WASHER FLUID LEVEL SENSOR
OIL PRESSURE SWITCH
AIR CHARGE TEMPERATURE SENSOR
PRESSURE FEEDBACK EGR SENSOR
INTEGRATED CONTROL MODULE
FORWARD CRASH SENSOR

Component locations—Taurus and Sable with 3.8L engine

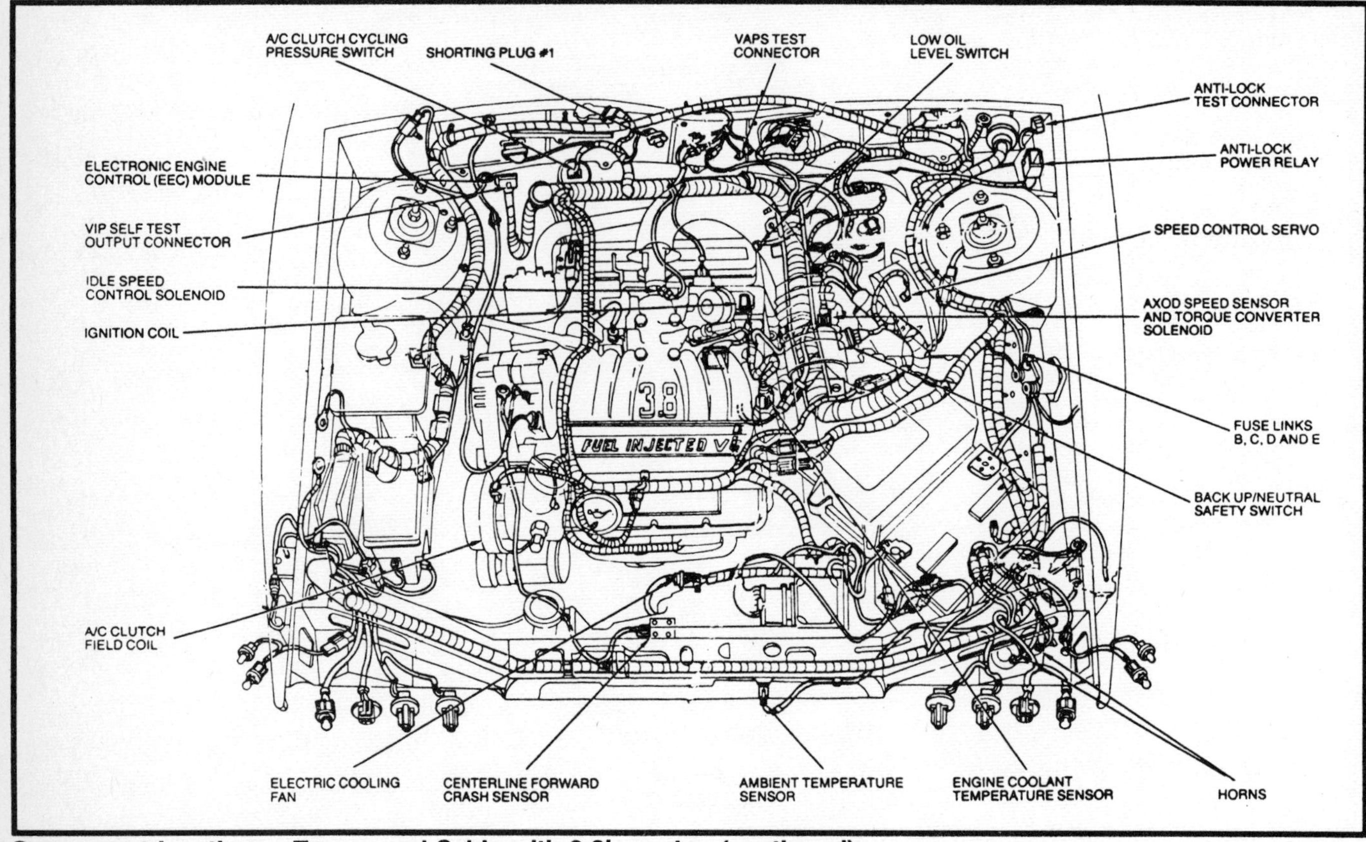

Component locations—Taurus and Sable with 3.8L engine (continued)

• **Canister Purge Solenoid (2.5L, 3.0L and 3.8L engine)**—is on the left front side of engine.

• **Canister Purge Solenoid (SHO engine)**—is at the left side of radiator support.

• **Center Line Forward Crash Sensor**—is at the top center of radiator support.

• **Clutch Interrupt Switch**—is on clutch pedal support, behind left instrument panel.

• **Cold Engine Lockout Switch**—is at the top left rear of engine.

• **Cracked Windshield Sense Resistor**—is on the right front of engine compartment, at alternator output control relay.

• **Crank Position Sensor**—is at the lower right rear of engine.

• **Daytime Running Lamps (DRL) Module (Canadian vehicles)**—is at the lower left front of engine compartment.

• **Diagnostic Warning Module**—is behind right instrument panel, above glove box.

• **Distributorless Ignition System (DIS) Module**—is on the right side of engine.

• **Door Ajar Switches**—is at door handle assembly within respective doors.

• **Driver's Seat Belt Switch**—is within left front seat belt assembly.

• **Dual Brake Warning Switch**—is at the left rear of engine compartment, within brake master cylinder.

• **EGR Vacuum Regulator Solenoid (2.5L and 3.0L engine)**—is at the right side of engine compartment at shock tower.

• **EGR Vacuum Regulator Solenoid (2.5L and 3.0L engine)**—is at the right side of engine compartment at shock tower.

• **EGR Vacuum Regulator Solenoid (SHO engine)**—is at the left rear of engine compartment.

• **Electronic Automatic Temperature Control (EATC) Module**—is behind center of instrument panel.

• **Electronic Engine Control (EEC) Module**—is in the engine compartment, right side of firewall.

• **Engine Coolant Temperature Sensor (2.5L engine)**—is at the left rear of engine, below manifolds.

• **Engine Coolant Temperature Sensor (3.0L, 3.8L and SHO engine)**—is at the top left side of engine.

• **Fan Dropping Resistor (2.5L and 3.0L engine)**—is at the left front of engine.

• **Fan Dropping Resistor (SHO engine)**—is at the center of firewall.

• **Fog Light Relay**—is behind center of instrument panel, mounted on brace. Fog Light Fuse—is behind left side of instrument panel, near fuse panel.

• **Forward Crash Sensors**—is inside lower front of each front fender.

• **Fuel Pump**—is inside fuel tank.

• **Fuel Sender**—is inside fuel tank.

• **Fuse Panel**—is behind left lower instrument panel
Heated Exhaust Gas Oxygen (HEGO) Sensor #1 (2.5L engine)—is at the center rear of engine in exhaust manifold.

• **Heated Exhaust Gas Oxygen (HEGO) Sensor #1 (3.0L engine)**—is at the lower right front of engine in exhaust manifold.

• **Heated Exhaust Gas Oxygen (HEGO) Sensor #1 (3.8L engine)**—is at the center rear of engine in exhaust manifold.

• **Heated Exhaust Gas Oxygen (HEGO) Sensor #1 (SHO engine)**—is at the lower left rear of engine in exhaust manifold.

• **Heated Exhaust Gas Oxygen (HEGO) Sensor #2 (3.8L engine)**—lower right front of engine in exhaust manifold.

• **Heated Exhaust Gas Oxygen (HEGO) Sensor #2 (SHO engine)**—is at the lower right front of engine in exhaust manifold.

• **Heated Windshield Control Module**—is at the right side of steering column, behind instrument panel.

• **Heated Windshield Control Module**—is at the right side of steering column, behind instrument panel
Heated Windshield Test Connector—is at the left rear of engine compartment.

• **Horn Relay**—is behind center of instrument panel, mounted on brace.

• **Idle Air Control**—is at the top rear of engine.

• **Idle Speed Control (2.5L engine)**—is at the top rear of engine.

• **Ignition Suppressor Resistor (2.5L engine)**—is on the left front of engine, near ignition coil.

• **Ignition Suppressor Resistor (3.0L and 3.8L engine)**—is on the left side of engine, near ignition coil.

• **Illuminated Entry Module (Sedan)**—is behind rear seat, under left side of package tray.

• **Illuminated Entry Module (Wagon)**—is inside center of left rear quarter panel.

• **In Car Temperature Sensor**—is behind top right side of instrument panel.

• **Inertia Switch (Sedan)**—is inside front of left rear quarter panel.

• **Inertia Switch (Wagon)**—is inside center of rear quarter panel.

• **Integrated Control Module**—is at the front of engine compartment, on radiator support.

• **Interval Wiper/Washer Module**—is behind center of instrument panel, mounted on brace.

• **Key Warning Switch**—is contained within ignition switch.

• **Keyless Entry Module (Sedan)**—is behind rear seat, under left side of package tray.

• **Keyless Entry Module (Wagon)**—is inside center of left rear quarter panel.

• **Knock Sensor (except SHO engine)**—is at the center rear of engine.

• **Knock Sensor (SHO engine)**—is at the lower left front of engine on air cleaner assembly.

• **LCD Dimming Relay**—is behind center of instrument panel, mounted on brace.

• **Liftgate Ajar Switch**—is at the lower center of liftgate, part of latch assembly.

• **Liftgate Mercury Switch**—is inside top of liftgate.

• **Liftgate Release Relay**—is at the right rear corner of cargo area.

• **Liftgate Release Solenoid**—is in the bottom of liftgate.

• **Light Sensor/Amplifier**—is attached to underside of right side instrument panel.

• **Low Oil Level Relay**—is behind center of instrument panel, mounted on brace.

• **Low Oil Level Relay**—is behind center of instrument panel, mounted on brace.

• **Low Oil Level Switch (2.5L engine)**—is at the lower right rear of engine.

• **Low Oil Level Switch (3.0L, 3.8L and SHO engine)**—is at the lower center rear of engine.

• **Low Washer Fluid Level Switch**—is at the right front of engine compartment, within washer fluid reservoir.

• **Luggage Compartment Mercury Switch**—is at the left front corner of trunk lid, near hinge.

• **Manifold Absolute Pressure (MAP) Sensor**—is at the right side of firewall.

• **MAP Sensor**—is on the right side of firewall.

• **Mass Air Flow Sensor**—is on the top left side of engine on air cleaner assembly.

• **Moonroof Relay**—is behind right side of instrument panel.

• **Neutral Safety Switch**—is at the left side of engine, on top of transaxle.

• **Oil Pressure Switch (2.5L engine)**—is at the center front of engine, near oil filter.

• **Oil Pressure Switch (3.0L engine)**—is on the left side of engine.

• **Oil Pressure Switch (3.8L engine)**—is on the lower right side of engine.

• **Oil Pressure Switch (SHO engine)**—is at the lower left rear of engine.

• **Pedal Position Switch**—is behind left side of instrument panel, on brake pedal support.

• **Police Accessory Circuit Breaker**—is at the left side of engine compartment, near starter relay.

• **Police Accessory Relay**—is behind center of instrument panel.

• **Power Steering Pressure Switch**—is at the lower left rear of engine.

• **Pressure Feedback EGR Sensor (2.5L engine)**—is at the left rear of engine.

• **Pressure Feedback EGR Sensor (3.0L engine)**—is at the top right side of engine.

• **Pressure Feedback EGR Sensor (3.8L and SHO engine)**—is at the top left side of engine.

• **Radiator Coolant Sensor**—is at the right front of engine compartment.

• **Radio Noise Capacitor (2.5L and 3.0L engine)**—is at the left front of engine, near ignition coil.

• **Radio Noise Capacitor (3.8L engine)**—is at the left rear of engine, near ignition coil.

• **Radio Noise Capacitor (SHO engine)**—is at the top of engine, at left front.

• **Rear Courtesy Lamp Diode**—is at the top left corner of cargo compartment within rear lamp harness.

• **Rear Defogger Relay and Timer**—is inside defogger switch housing.

• **Reverse Switch**—is on the left side of engine, on top of transaxle.

• **Self Test Input Connector**—is on the right rear of engine compartment, near EEC module.

• **Shorting Plug #1 (2.5L engine)**—is at the center front of engine.

• **Shorting Plug #1 (3.0L engine)**—is at the left side of engine.

• **Shorting Plug #1 (3.8L engine)**—is at the right rear of engine compartment.

• **Shorting Plug #1 (SHO engine)**—is at the right rear side of engine.

• **Shorting Plug #2 (SHO engine)**—is at the center front of engine compartment.

• **Solenoid Control Valve Body**—is at the lower left front of engine compartment.

• **Speed Control Servo**—is on the left side of engine compartment, on shock tower.

• **Starter Relay**—is on the left front fender apron, in front of shock tower.

• **Stop Lamp Switch**—is behind left side instrument panel, on pedal support.

• **Sunload Sensor**—is behind top left side of instrument panel.

• **TFI Ignition Module (2.5L engine)**—is at the center front of engine.

• **TFI Ignition Module (3.0L engine)**—is at the top left side of engine, connected to distributor assembly.

• **TFI Ignition Module (3.8L engine)**—is on the right side of firewall.

• **Throttle Position Sensor (2.5L engine)**—is at the rear center of engine, on right side of injection assembly.

• **Throttle Position Sensor (3.0L engine)**—is on the top left side of engine.

• **Throttle Position Sensor (3.8L engine)**—is on the top

center of engine.

• **Throttle Position Sensor (SHO engine)**–is on the top left side of engine compartment.

• **Trunk Release Solenoid**–is at the right rear of trunk lid, part of trunk latch assembly.

• **Variable Assist Power Steering (VAPS) Module**–is at the right side of steering column, behind instrument panel.

• **Variable Assist Power Steering (VAPS) Test Connector**–is at the left rear of engine compartment.

• **Variable Assist Stepper Motor**–is at the lower left rear of engine.

• **Vehicle Speed Sensor (2.5L engine)**–is on the left rear of transaxle.

• **Vehicle Speed Sensor (3.0L, 3.8L engine)**–is at the center rear of engine.

• **Vehicle Speed Sensor (SHO engine)**–is at the lower left rear of engine or mounted on transaxle.

• **VIP Self Test Output Connector**–is at the right rear of engine compartment, near EEC module.

• **Voltage Regulator**–is on the left front fender apron.

• **Warning Chime Module**–is behind lower left instrument panel.

• **Window Safety Relay**–is behind right kick panel.

TEMPO AND TOPAZ

• **2WD Vacuum Solenoid**–is located on the left side of the engine compartment.

• **4WD Vacuum Solenoid**–is located on the left side of the engine compartment.

• **A/C Cooling Fan Controller**–is located behind the right side of the instrument panel.

• **Air Bag Diagnostic Module and Back-Up Power Supply**–are located behind the left side of the instrument panel next to the fuse panel. The steering column covers must be remove to gain access.

• **Air Charge Temperature Sensor**–is located in the intake manifold on the right side of the engine.

• **All Wheel Drive relays 1 and 2**–are located behind the right side of the instrument panel.

• **Back-Up Lamp Switch**–is located on the lower left side of the manual transaxle case.

• **Back-Up Lamp/Neutral Safety Switch**–is located on the rear side of the automatic transaxle case.

• **Blower Motor Resistor**–is located in the heater housing near the blower motor.

• **Canister Purge Solenoid**–is located on the left side of the engine on top of the transaxle.

• **Clutch Cycling Pressure switch**–is located on the accumulator.

• **Clutch Interrupt Switch**–is located on the clutch pedal support.

• **Coolant Temperature Sender**–is located in the cylinder head on the left side of the engine.

• **Cooling Fan Relay**–is located left front side of the engine compartment.

• **Cooling Fan Temperature Switch**–is located on the upper left side of the engine near the ignition coil.

• **Cooling Fan Test Connector (C102)**–is located in front of the left strut tower.

• **Cooling Fan Test Connector (C103)**–is located in front of the left strut tower.

• **ECA Power Relay**–is located behind the right side of the instrument panel.

• **EGR Vacuum Regulator**–is mounted on the left strut tower.

• **EGR Valve Positions Sensor**–is located on the front center of the dash.

• **Electronic Control Assembly (ECA)**–is located behind the left side of the instrument panel.

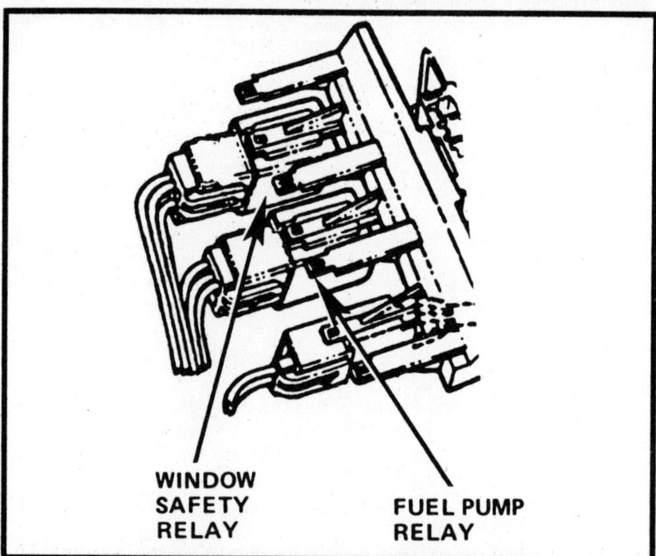

Fuel pump and window safety relay locations–Tempo and Topaz

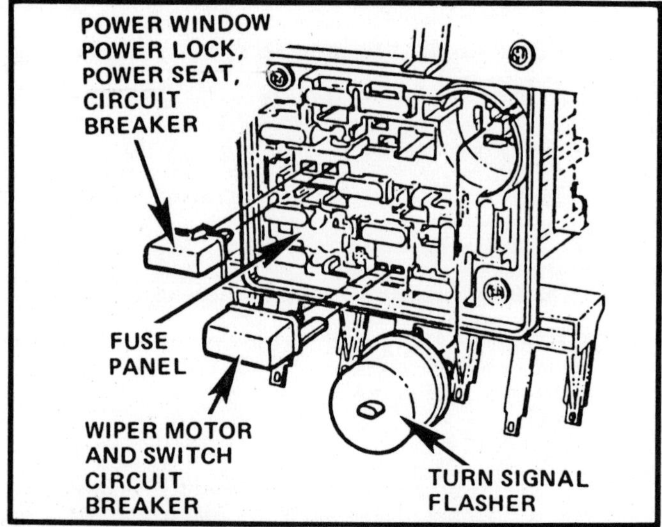

Fuse panel location–Tempo and Topaz

• **Engine Coolant Temperature Sensor**–is located on the top left side of the engine.

• **Front Center Crash Sensor**–is located on the radiator support.

• **Fuse Panel**–is located behind the left bottom of the instrument panel.

• **Hazard Flasher**–The hazard flasher unit is located behind the fuse panel.

• **Horn Relay**–is located behind the left side of the instrument panel above the fuse panel.

• **Idle Control Solenoid**–is located on the top left rear side of the engine.

• **Ignition Suppressor Resistor**–is located in the engine harness at the left rear side of the engine compartment.

• **Illuminated Entry Timer**–is located under the center of the rear package tray.

• **Inertia Switch**–is located in the trunk on the left hinge support.

• **Left Front Crash Sensor**–is located on the left fender apron under the left inner fender splash shield. The splash shield must be removed to gain access to sensor.

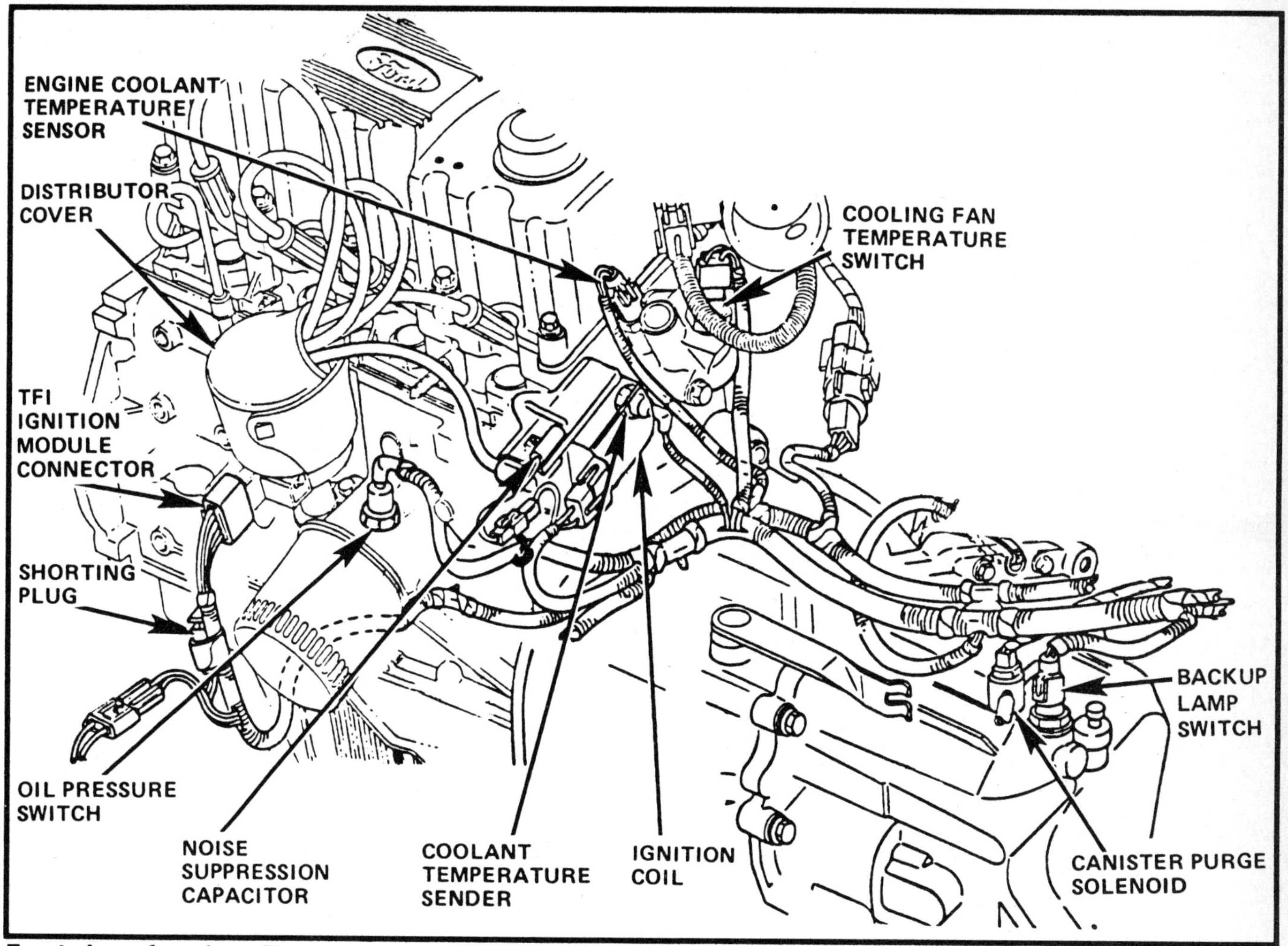

ENGINE COOLANT TEMPERATURE SENSOR
DISTRIBUTOR COVER
TFI IGNITION MODULE CONNECTOR
SHORTING PLUG
OIL PRESSURE SWITCH
NOISE SUPPRESSION CAPACITOR
COOLANT TEMPERATURE SENDER
IGNITION COIL
COOLING FAN TEMPERATURE SWITCH
BACKUP LAMP SWITCH
CANISTER PURGE SOLENOID

Front view of engine—Tempo and Topaz with 2.3L EFI engine

- **Manifold Air Pressure (MAP) sensor**—is mounted on the right strut tower.
- **Oil Pressure Switch**—is located at the oil filter on the lower front side of the engine.
- **Oxygen Sensor**—is located in the exhaust manifold.
- **Passive Restraint Module**—is located behind the right side of the instrument panel above the glove box.
- **Power Steering Pressure Switch**—is located in the power steering hoses on the top right side of the engine.
- **Rear Crash Sensor**—is located at the cowl in the passenger compartment.
- **Rear Window Defroster Relay**—is located behind the left side of the instrument panel to the right of the steering column.
- **Right Front Crash Sensor**—is located on the right fender apron under the right inner fender splash shield. The splash shield must be removed to gain access to sensor.
- **Shift Indicator Dimmer Relay**—is located behind the left side of the instrument panel.
- **Speed Control Amplifier**—is located behind the left side of the instrument panel next to the fuse panel.
- **Speed Control Diode**—is located behind the left side of the instrument panel near the fuse panel approximately 5 in. from the speed control amplifier.
- **Speed Control Servo**—is located on the right side of the engine compartment.

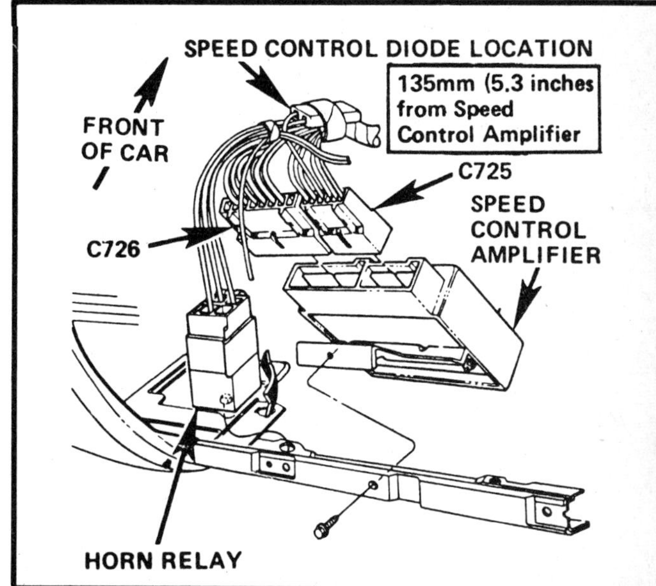

SPEED CONTROL DIODE LOCATION
135mm (5.3 inches from Speed Control Amplifier
FRONT OF CAR
C725
SPEED CONTROL AMPLIFIER
C726
HORN RELAY

Speed control diode, speed control amplifier and horn relay locations—Tempo and Topaz

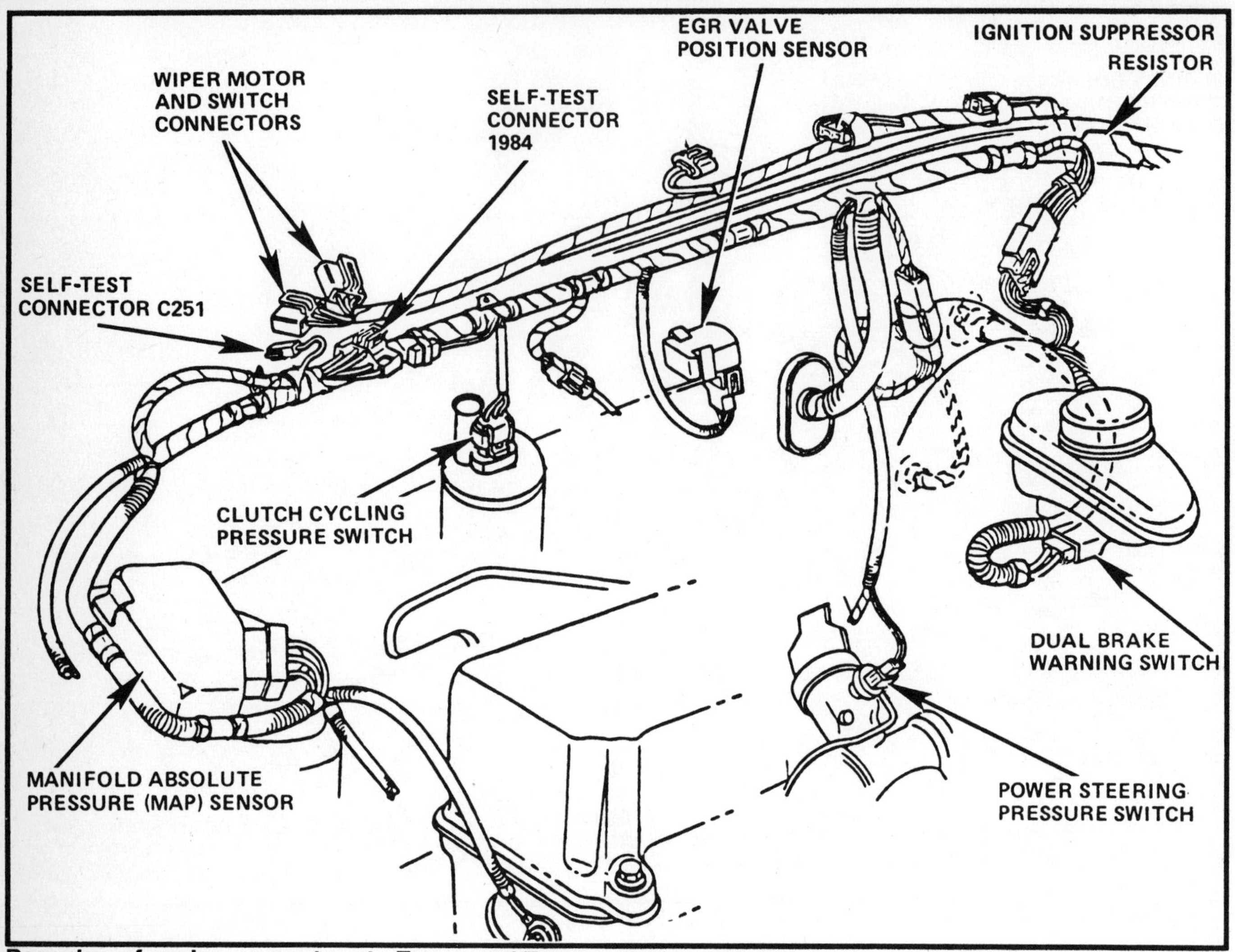

Rear view of engine compartment—Tempo and Topaz with 2.3L EFI engine.

- **Speed Sensor**—is located left rear side of the transaxle.
- **Start/Ignition Diode**—is taped to the wiring harness in front of the left strut tower.
- **Starter Relay**—is located on the left fender apron in front of the strut tower.
- **TFI Ignition Module**—is connected to the right side of the distributor.
- **Throttle Position Sensor**—is located on the top left side of the engine.
- **Turn Signal Flasher**—is located in the front of the fuse panel.
- **Vacuum Dump Valve**—is located at the top of the brake pedal support above the stop lamp switch.
- **VIP Self-Test Connector (1984)**—is located near the wiper motor on the right side of the dash.
- **VIP Self-Test Connector (C251)**—is located near the wiper motor on the right side of the dash.
- **Warning Chime Module**—is located behind the left side of the instrument panel to the right of the steering column.
- **Window Safety Relay**—is located behind the left side of the instrument panel above the fuse panel.

TRACER

- **A/C Control Module**—is located under the instrument panel, on or near the evaporator housing.
- **A/C Cut-Out Relay**—is located in front of the left front shock tower in the engine compartment.
- **A/C Fuse**—this is an in line fuse, which is located behind the instrument panel, to the left of the heater duct assembly.
- **A/C Heater Blower Motor Resistors**—is located on top of the evaporator housing which is located under the instrument panel.
- **A/C Low Pressure Switch**—is installed on the liquid line beneath the high side gauge port between the evaporator and the receiver dryer.
- **A/C Relay (No. 1)**—is located on the left front shock tower in the engine compartment.
- **A/C Relay (No. 2)**—is located on the left front shock tower in the engine compartment.
- **A/C Relay (No. 3)**—is located on the left front shock tower in the engine compartment.
- **A/C Solenoid Valve**—is located next to the battery tray in the engine compartment.
- **A/C Thermistor**—is located under the instrument panel, on or near the evaporator housing.
- **Air By-Pass Valve**—is located on the fuel rail assembly next to the throttle body.
- **Anti-Afterburn Valve**—is located next to the air cleaner assembly.
- **Back-Up/Neutral Safety Switch**—is located on the transaxle.

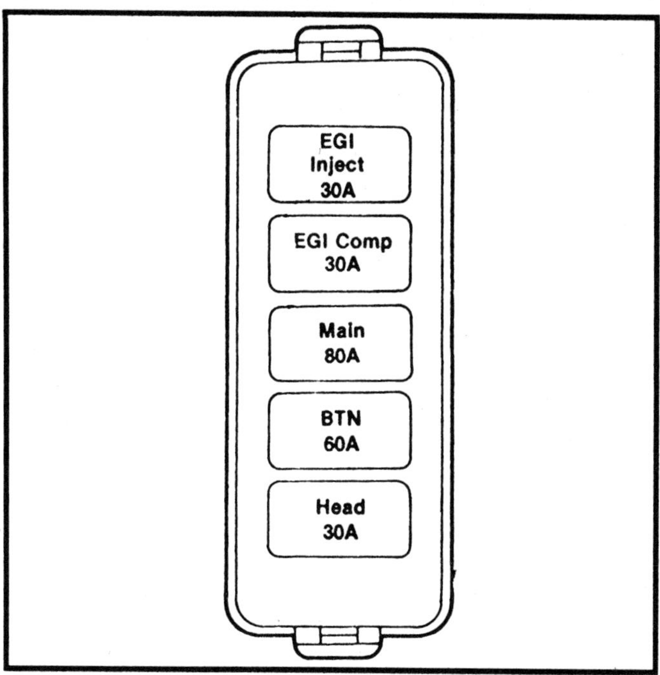

Main fuse panel location—1989–90 Tracer

- **Barometric Pressure Sensor**—is located on the center of the firewall.
- **Bowl Vent Solenoid (Canadian with carburetor)**—is located on the carburetor assembly.
- **Brake Low Fluid Warning Sensor**—is located on the master cylinder.
- **Clutch Interrupt Switch**—is located at the top of the clutch pedal cluster.
- **Coolant Temperature Sensor**—is located in the intake manifold or the thermostat housing.
- **Coolant Temperature Switch**—is located in the intake manifold, near the carburetor, if equipped.
- **Cooling Fan Relay**—is located in the left front side of the engine compartment, next to the coolant recovery bottle.
- **Cooling Fan Thermostatic Switch**—is located in the thermostat housing.
- **Door Buzzer Relay**—is located in the electrical equipment panel, located above the fuse block.
- **EGR Modulation Valve (Canadian with carburetor)**—is located near the EGR valve.
- **Electric Fuel Pump**—is located in the fuel tank.
- **Electronic Control Assembly**—is located under the center of the instrument panel.
- **Engine Coolant Temperature Sensor**—is located in, or near the bottom of the radiator.
- **Fuel Filter**—is located on the center of the firewall.
- **Fuel Pump Relay**—is mounted under the center of the instrument panel.
- **Fuel Vapor Canister**—is located next to left hand side shock tower.
- **Hazard Flasher**—The hazard flasher/turn signal unit is located above the fuse block under the left side of the instrument panel.
- **Horn Relay**—is located in the left front side of the engine compartment, next to the coolant recovery bottle.
- **Idle Speed Control Solenoid Valve**—is located on the intake plenum, if so equipped.
- **Idle Switch (Canadian with carburetor)**—is located on the carburetor assembly.
- **Idle-Up Control Module**—is located behind a cover panel in the console area under the instrument panel.

Fuse	Affect These Items
Head 30A (Main)	Headlight
BTN 60A (Main)	Stop lights, horn, power door lock, turn and hazard flasher lights, sliding sunroof, interior and stop light. Luggage compartment light Courtesy lights (R.H.) (L.H.) Door lock cylinder light Auto clock, seat belt warning Logical mode control
Main 80A (Main)	Charging system Remote control mirror Audio system Cigarette lighter Air conditioner Heater control system Cooling fan system Headlight cleaner Front wiper and washer Rear wiper and washer Reverse lights Cruise control system Meter and warning lights Kick down (A/T) Emission and fuel control system Rear window defroster Power window Ignition system (EGI & carburetor)
PTC 30A (MAIN)	P.T.C. Heater
EGI COMP. 30A (MAIN)	Idle-up control
EGI INJ. 30A (MAIN)	Emission and fuel injection

Main fuse circuits—1989–90 Tracer

- **Idle-Up Solenoid**—is located on the left hand side of the firewall.
- **Inertia Switch (Sedan)**—is mounted on the left rear side of the spare tire well, in the luggage compartment.
- **Inertia Switch (Wagon)**—is located behind the axle jack access panel of the right rear quarter panel, in the luggage compartment.
- **Oxygen Sensor**—is located in the exhaust manifold.
- **PTC Heater Grid**—is located under the base of the carburetor.
- **PTC Heater Relay**—is located under in the engine compartment on the inner fender apron, next to the coolant recovery reservoir.
- **Purge Canister Valve (No. 2)**—is located on the fuel vapor canister.
- **Purge Control Valve (No. 1)**—is located on the fuel vapor canister.
- **RPM Control Module (Canadian with carburetor)**—

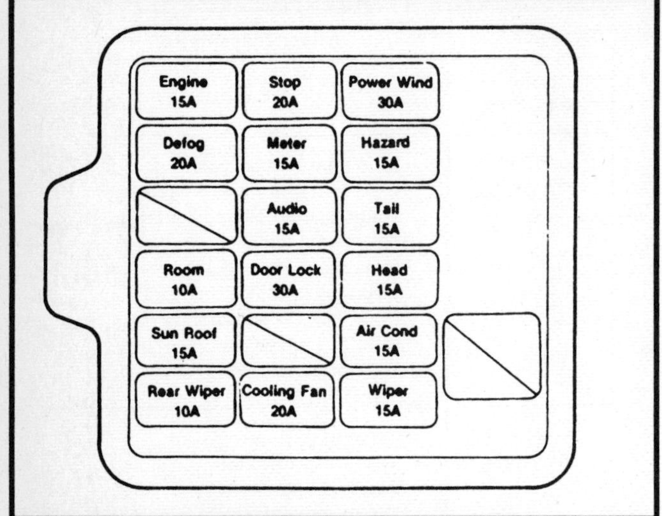

Interior fuse panel location—1989–90 Tracer

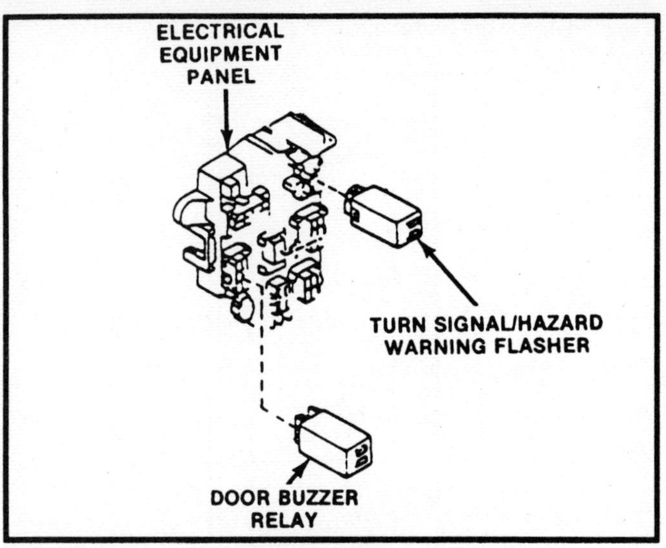

Hazard flasher/turn signal—1989–90 Tracer

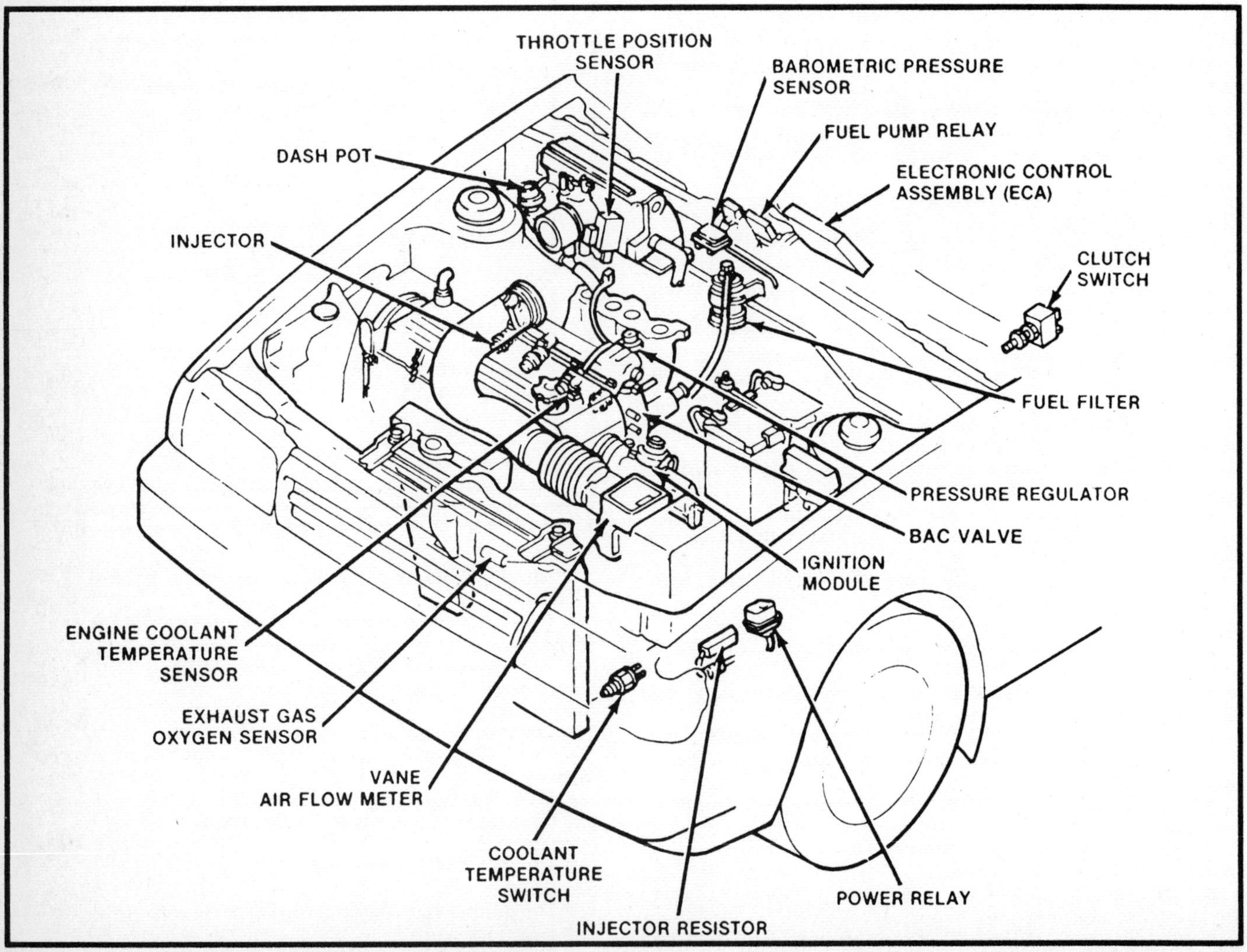

Fuel injection system components—Tracer

is located under the center of the instrument panel, near the accelerator pedal.

• **Self-Test Diagnostic Connectors**—are behind the left hand side shock tower next to the firewall.

• **Slow Fuel Cut Solenoid Valve (Canadian with carburetor)**—is located on the carburetor assembly.

• **Speed Control Servo**—is located on the left front shock tower.

• **Speed Control Unit**—is located behind the left front kick panel.

• **Speed Sensor**—is located on behind the speedometer in the instrument cluster.

• **Throttle Kickdown Switch**—is located at the top of the throttle pedal bracket.

• **Throttle Position Sensor**—is located on or near the throttle body assembly.

• **Transaxle Vacuum Diaphragm**—is located on the side of the transaxle assembly.

• **Turn Signal/Hazard Relay**—is located in the electrical equipment panel, located above the fuse block.

• **Vane Air Flow Meter**—is located in between the air cleaner and throttle body assembly.

• **Vane Air Temperature Sensor**—is located in between the air cleaner and throttle body assembly.

• **Water Temperature Switch (Canadian with carburetor)**—is located in the intake manifold, behind the carburetor. This one is used for the PTC heater.

• **Water Temperature Switches (Canadian with carburetor)**—are located in the front of the intake manifold.

• **Water Thermo Valve (Canadian with carburetor)**—is located in the front of the intake manifold.

TOWN CAR

• **A/C Clutch Cycling Pressure Switch**—is located at the right rear of the engine compartment on the accumulator.

• **A/C Clutch Diode**—is located above the front of the A/C compressor, taped in the engine harness.

• **A/C Cut Out Relay**—is located on the left fender apron, under the relay cover.

• **ABS**—see Anti-Lock.

• **Air Bag Diagnostic Module**—is located behind the left side of the instrument panel.

• **Air Bag Redundant Power Supply**—is located behind the left side of the instrument panel.

• **Air Bag Safing Sensor**—is located behind the left side instrument panel, at the left side kick panel.

• **Air Charge Temperature Sensor**—is located on the top left side of the engine, forward of the throttle body.

• **Air Suspension Capacitor**—is located in the right side of the trunk, near the air suspension module.

• **Air Suspension Switch**—is located on the right side of the trunk.

• **Air Suspension Test Connector C408**—is located on the right side of the trunk, near the air suspension control module.

• **Air Suspension/EVO Module**—is located in the right side of the trunk.

• **Alternator Output Control Relay**—is located on the right side of the engine compartment.

• **Ambient Temperature Sensor**—is located at the left front of the engine.

• **Anti-Lock Brake Diode**—is located at the right front cor-

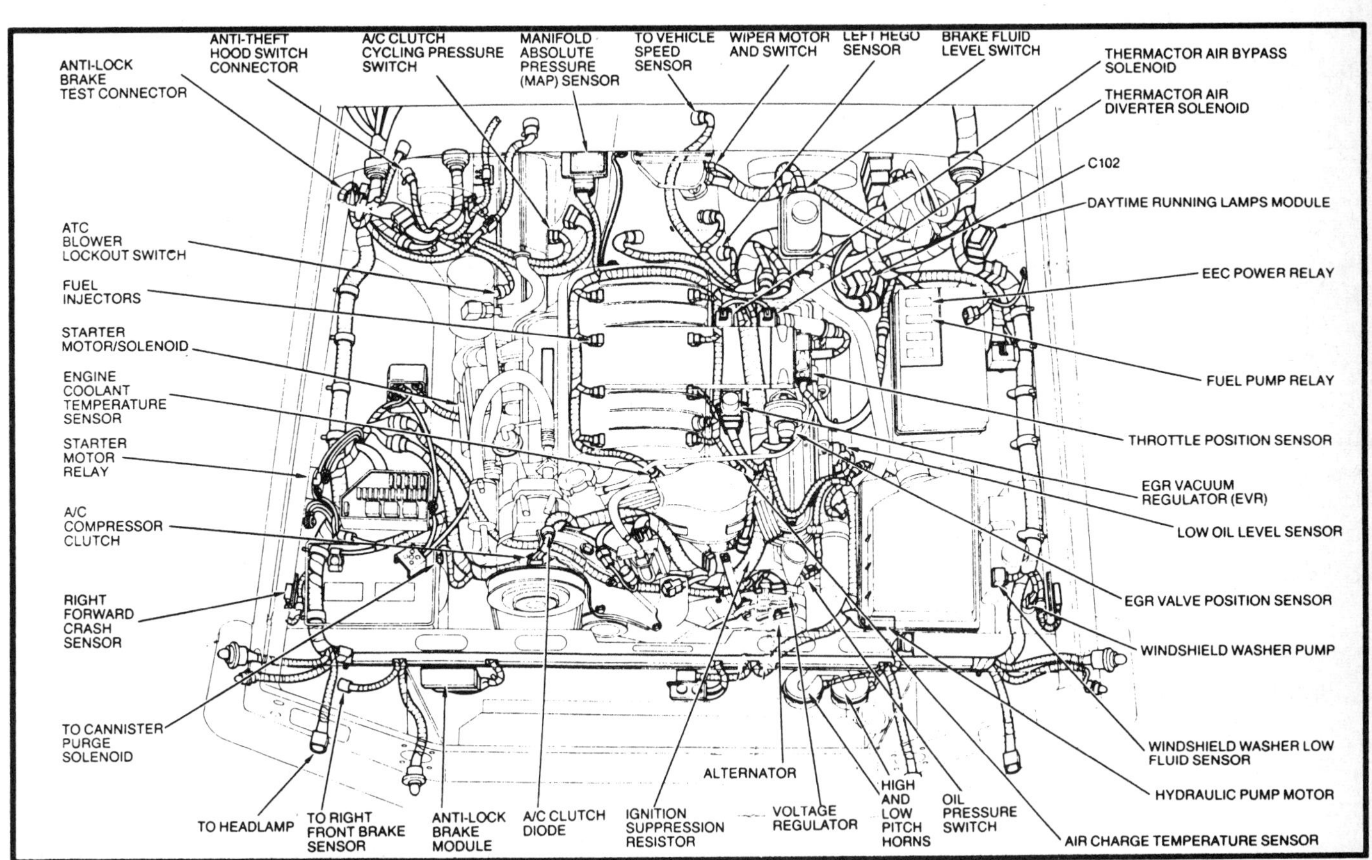

Engine compartment—Town Car with 5.0L engine

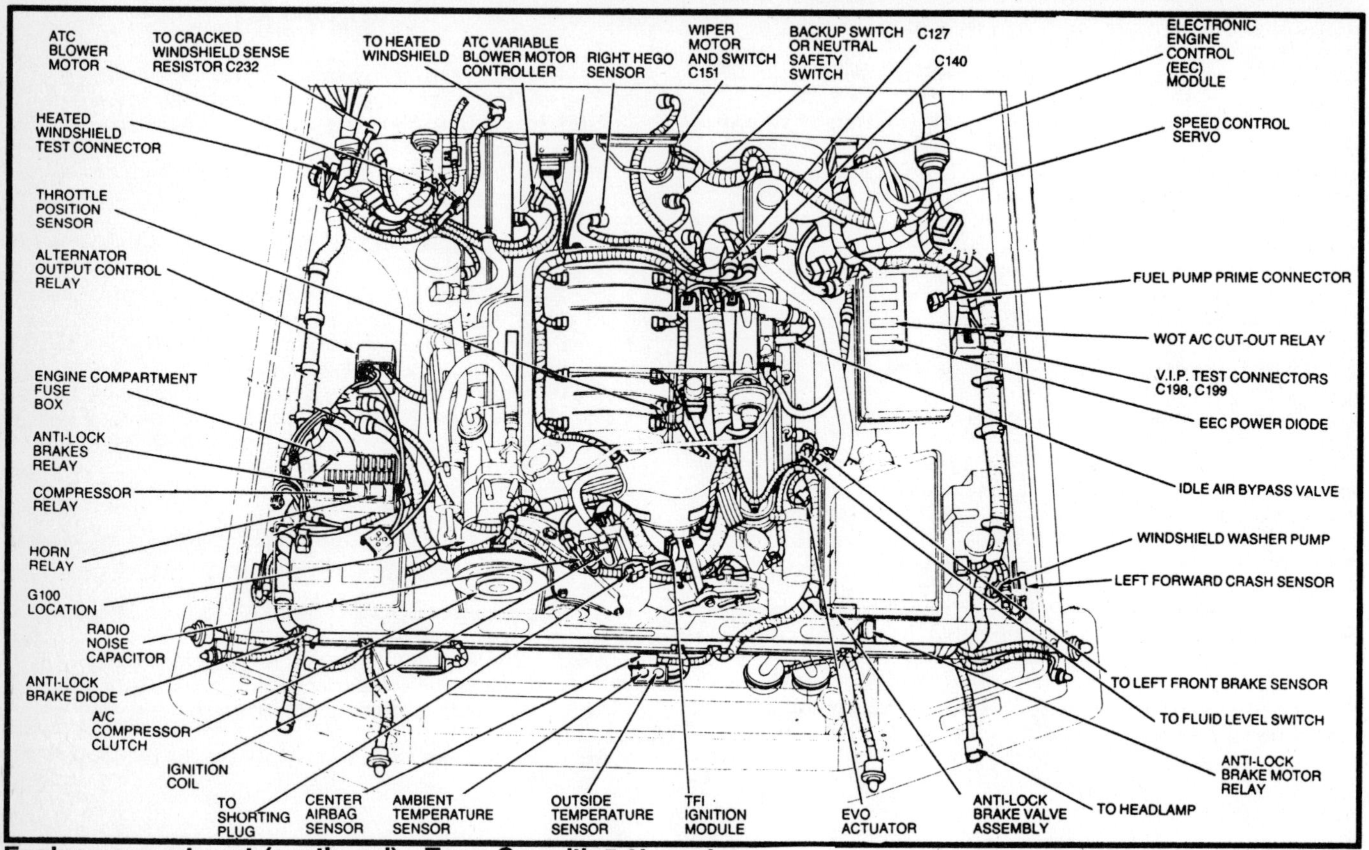

ATC BLOWER MOTOR
TO CRACKED WINDSHIELD SENSE RESISTOR C232
TO HEATED WINDSHIELD
ATC VARIABLE BLOWER MOTOR CONTROLLER
RIGHT HEGO SENSOR
WIPER MOTOR AND SWITCH C151
BACKUP SWITCH OR NEUTRAL SAFETY SWITCH
C127
C140
ELECTRONIC ENGINE CONTROL (EEC) MODULE
HEATED WINDSHIELD TEST CONNECTOR
SPEED CONTROL SERVO
THROTTLE POSITION SENSOR
ALTERNATOR OUTPUT CONTROL RELAY
FUEL PUMP PRIME CONNECTOR
WOT A/C CUT-OUT RELAY
ENGINE COMPARTMENT FUSE BOX
V.I.P. TEST CONNECTORS C198, C199
EEC POWER DIODE
ANTI-LOCK BRAKES RELAY
COMPRESSOR RELAY
IDLE AIR BYPASS VALVE
WINDSHIELD WASHER PUMP
HORN RELAY
LEFT FORWARD CRASH SENSOR
G100 LOCATION
RADIO NOISE CAPACITOR
ANTI-LOCK BRAKE DIODE
TO LEFT FRONT BRAKE SENSOR
A/C COMPRESSOR CLUTCH
TO FLUID LEVEL SWITCH
IGNITION COIL
ANTI-LOCK BRAKE MOTOR RELAY
TO SHORTING PLUG
CENTER AIRBAG SENSOR
AMBIENT TEMPERATURE SENSOR
OUTSIDE TEMPERATURE SENSOR
TFI IGNITION MODULE
EVO ACTUATOR
ANTI-LOCK BRAKE VALVE ASSEMBLY
TO HEADLAMP

Engine compartment (continued)—Town Car with 5.0L engine

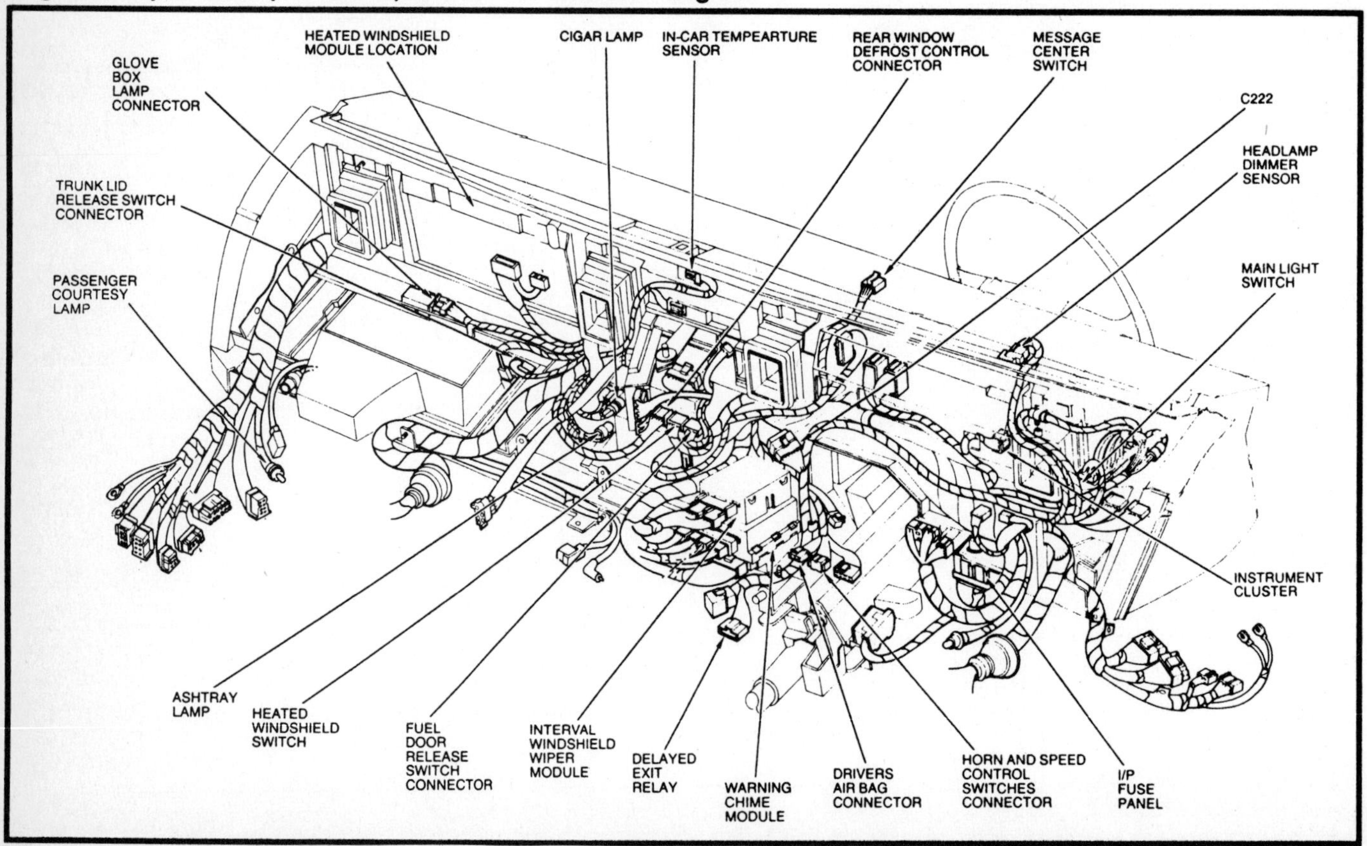

GLOVE BOX LAMP CONNECTOR
HEATED WINDSHIELD MODULE LOCATION
CIGAR LAMP
IN-CAR TEMPEARTURE SENSOR
REAR WINDOW DEFROST CONTROL CONNECTOR
MESSAGE CENTER SWITCH
C222
HEADLAMP DIMMER SENSOR
TRUNK LID RELEASE SWITCH CONNECTOR
PASSENGER COURTESY LAMP
MAIN LIGHT SWITCH
INSTRUMENT CLUSTER
ASHTRAY LAMP
HEATED WINDSHIELD SWITCH
FUEL DOOR RELEASE SWITCH CONNECTOR
INTERVAL WINDSHIELD WIPER MODULE
DELAYED EXIT RELAY
WARNING CHIME MODULE
DRIVERS AIR BAG CONNECTOR
HORN AND SPEED CONTROL SWITCHES CONNECTOR
I/P FUSE PANEL

View behind dash—Town Car

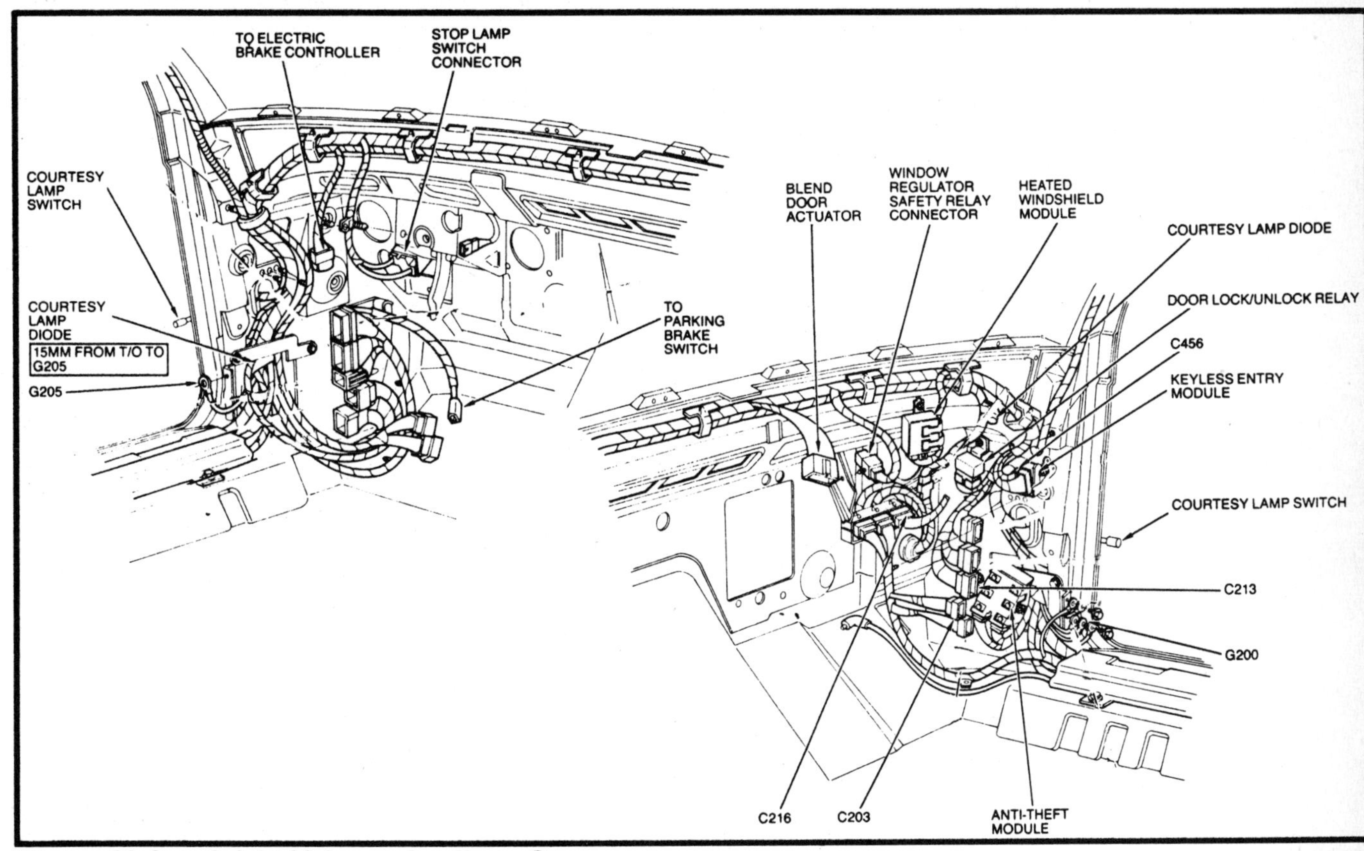

Views of left and right kick panels—Town Car

ner of the engine compartment within the harness near the right park/turn signal lamp.

• **Anti-Lock Brake Module**—is located in the right front engine compartment.

• **Anti-Lock Brake Motor Relay**—is located in the left front of the engine compartment.

• **Anti-Lock Brake Relay**—is located in the engine compartment fuse box at the right front of engine compartment.

• **Anti-Lock Brake Switch**—is located behind the left side instrument panel.

• **Anti-Lock Brake Test Connector**—is located on the right wheelwell.

• **Anti-Theft Hood Switch**—is located on the right side of the engine compartment.

• **anti-Theft Module**—is located behind right side of the instrument panel at the kick panel.

• **Automatic Temperature Control (ATC) Lockout Switch**—is located on the right side of the firewall.

• **Automatic Temperature Control (ATC) Variable Blower Motor Controller**—is located behind the right side of the instrument panel, attached to the blower plenum.

• **Backup Switch**—is located at the lower left side of the transmission case.

• **Barometric Absolute Pressure (BAP) Sensor**—is located at the right center of the firewall.

• **Brake Fluid Level Switch**—is located at the left rear corner of the engine compartment.

• **Brake Lamp Switch**—is located on top of the brake pedal bracket.

• **Canister Purge Solenoid**—is located on the right side of the engine compartment.

• **Center Air Bag Sensor**—is located at the front center of the engine compartment.

• **Compressor Cut Out Relay**—is located on the left fender apron, under the relay cover.

• **Compressor Relay**—is located in the engine compartment fuse box at the right front of engine compartment.

• **Coolant Temperature Sender**—is located at the top of the engine, on left side of distributor.

• **Coolant Temperature Sensor**—is located at the top of the engine, on right side of distributor.

• **Courtesy Lamp Diode**—is located at left front kick panel, taped to main body harness.

• **Cracked Windshield Sense Resistor**—is located at the rear of the right fender apron.

• **Day/Night Sensor/Amplifier**—is located behind left side of instrument panel.

• **Daytime Running Lamps (DRL) Module (Canadian vehicles)**—is located in the left rear of the engine compartment.

• **Delayed Exit Relay**—is located behind the left side of the instrument panel.

• **Door Ajar Switches**—are located within the respective door at the latch assembly.

• **Door Lock/Unlock Relay**—is located behind right side kick panel.

• **EEC**—See Electronic Engine Control

EGR Vacuum Regulator (EVR)—is located on the right side of the engine.

• **EGR Valve Position Sensor**—is located on top of the engine, to the rear of the throttle body.

• **Electric Brake Controller**—is located behind the left side of the instrument panel.

• **Electric Fuel Pump**—is located within the fuel tank.

• **Electronic Engine Control (EEC) Module**—is located behind the left side of the instrument panel.

• **Electronic Engine Control (EEC) Power Diode**—is located at left fender apron, under relay cover.

• **Electronic Engine Control (EEC) Power Relay**—is located at left fender apron, under relay cover.

• **Engine Compartment Fuse Box**—is located at the right front of engine compartment, behind the battery.

• **Engine Coolant Temperature Sender**—is located at the top of the engine, on left side of distributor.

• **Engine Coolant Temperature Sensor**—is located at the top of the engine, on right side of distributor.

• **EVO Actuator**—is located on the left side of the engine compartment.

• **Fuel Door Release Solenoid**—is located on the left side of the trunk.

• **Fuel Gauge Sender**—is located within the fuel tank.

• **Fuel Pump Relay**—is located at the left fender apron, under the relay cover.

• **Fuse Panel**—is located under the left side instrument panel.

• **Hazard Flasher**—is located behind the fuse panel.

• **Headlamp Dimmer Sensor**—is located in the center of the upper windshield header, near the rear view mirror.

• **Heated Windshield Module**—is located behind the right kick panel.

• **Height Sensor**—is located under trunk floor to the left of fuel gauge sender.

• **High/Low Beam Relay**—is located behind the left side of the instrument panel.

• **Horn Relay**—is located in the engine compartment fuse box at the right front of engine compartment.

• **Ignition Suppression Resistor**—is located at the top left front of the engine, taped into engine wiring harness.

• **In Car Temperature Sensor**—is located behind the top center of the instrument panel.

• **Inertia Switch**—is located in the trunk, attached to the left wheelwell.

• **Interior Fuse Panel**—is located under the left side instrument panel.

• **Interval Windshield Wiper Module**—is located behind the center of the instrument panel below the radio.

• **Keyless Entry Module**—is located behind right kick panel.

• **Left Forward Crash Sensor**—is located inside left front fender.

• **Linear Height Sensor**—is located under trunk floor to the left of fuel gauge sender.

• **Low Oil Level Sensor**—is located on the left side of the oil pan.

• **Manifold Absolute Pressure (MAP) Sensor**—is located on the right center of the firewall.

• **MAP Sensor**—is located on the right center of the firewall.

• **Mass Air Flow Sensor**—is located at the left side of the engine.

• **Memory Seat Module**—is located under the driver's seat.

• **Message Center Switch Module**—is located under the left instrument panel, attached to the center brace.

• **Neutral Safety Switch**—is located on the left side of the transmission.

• **Oil Pressure Switch**—is located above the oil filter at lower left of engine.

• **Outside Temperature Sensor**—is located at the center front of the engine compartment.

• **Radio Noise Capacitor**—is located on the top front of the engine.

• **Rear Air Spring Solenoids**—are integral with the respective air spring.

• **Reverse Switch**—is located at the lower left side of the transmission case.

• **Right Forward Crash Sensor**—is located inside right front fender.

• **Shorting Plug**—is located on the top right side of the engine, behind the alternator.

• **Starter Relay**—is located on the right front fender apron.

• **Steering Wheel Rotation Sensor**—is located inside the top of the steering column.

• **Stop Lamp Switch**—is located on top of the brake pedal bracket.

• **TFI Ignition Module**—is mounted on the side of the distributor.

• **Thermactor Air Bypass Solenoid**—is located on the top center of the engine.

• **Thermactor Air Diverter Solenoid**—is located on the top center of the engine.

• **Trailer Battery Charging Relay**—is located on left rear wheelwell in the trunk.

• **Trailer Exterior Lamp Relay**—is located on left rear wheelwell in the trunk.

• **Trailer Left Turn Lamp Relay**—is located on left rear wheelwell in the trunk.

• **Trailer Right Turn Lamp Relay**—is located on left rear wheelwell in the trunk.

• **Trunk Lid Release Solenoid**—is located in the center rear of the trunk lid.

• **Turn Signal Flasher**—is located on the fuse panel under the left instrument panel.

• **Vehicle Speed Sensor**—is located on the left rear side of the transmission.

• **VIP Test Connectors C198 and C199**—are located on the left front fender apron.

• **Voltage Regulator**—is located on the alternator.

• **Warning Chime Module**—is located behind the center of the instrument panel, below the radio.

• **Warning Lamps Module**—is located behind left side of instrument panel, near the instrument cluster.

• **Window Regulator Safety Relay**—is located behind right kick panel.

• **Windshield Washer Low Fluid Sensor**—is located in the washer reservoir, left front fender apron.

• **WOT A/C Cut Out Relay**—is located on the left fender apron, under the relay cover.

FORD MOTOR COMPANY LIGHT TRUCK AND VAN

Circuit Breakers

Circuit breakers open when a circuit overload exceeds their rated amperage. Once open, the cycling type used for the windshield wipers and headlights will automatically reset after a certain length of time. If the overload which caused them to open is still present in the circuit, they will continue to open and reset until the overload is cleared. The non-cycling type used for power windows and power door locks, will stay open once it has been tripped until the overload is removed.

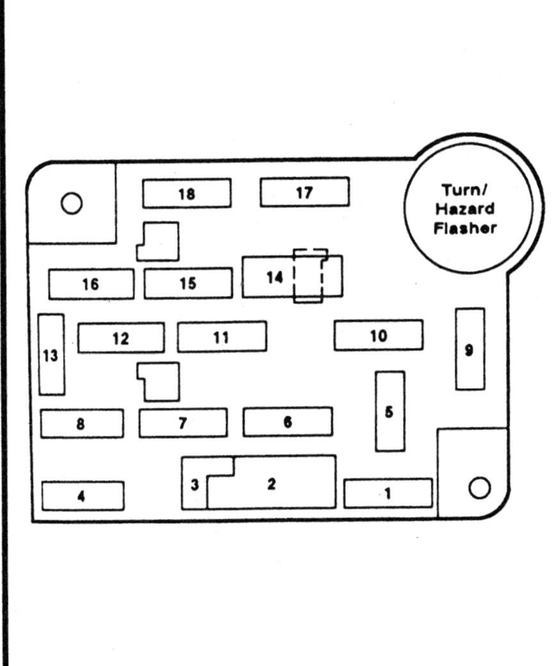

Fuse Position	Amps	Circuits Protected
1	15	Turn/Stop/Hazard Lamps
2	6 c.b.	Windshield Wiper/Washer
3	—	(Not Used)
4	15	Exterior Lamps, Interior Lamps
5	15	Turn/Stop/Hazard Lamps, Electronic Engine Control
6	20	Speed Control, Illuminated Entry, Warning Chime
7	20	Rear Anti-lock Brakes
8	15	Interior Lamps
9	30	A/C-Heater
10	20	Multi-function Switch
11	15	Radio
12	20	Rear Cigar Lighter, Power Lumbar Seats
13	5	Instrument and Control Illumination
14	20 c.b.	Power Windows
15	15	Electronic 4 Wheel Drive
16	20	Horns, Front Cigar Lighter
17	10	Electronic Instrument Cluster
18	10	Warning Chime, Instrument Cluster

NOTE: Power Door Locks are protected by a 30 amp in-line fuse.

Fuse panel—typical Aerostar

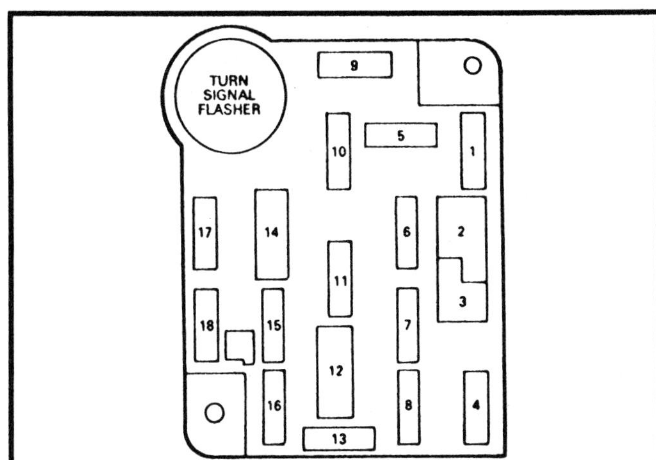

Fuse panel—typical Fuse block

AEROSTAR

POWER DISTRIBUTION

The circuit breaker is located behind the left side of the instrument panel.

POWER WINDOWS

The 20 amp circuit breaker is located in the fuse block.

WINDSHIELD WIPER WASHER

The 6 amp circuit breaker is located in the fuse block.

E-SERIES VANS

WINDSHIELD WIPER AND WASHER

The 7.5 amp circuit breaker is located in the fuse block.

POWER DOOR LOCKS

The 20 amp circuit breaker is located in the fuse block.

RANGER AND BRONCO II

LIFTGATE WIPER/WASHER

The Inline circuit breaker, (used in Bronco II only) is located behind the right side of the instrument panel.

WINDSHIELD WIPERS

The 6 amp circuit breaker is located in the fuse block.

MULTI-FUNCTION SWITCH, LIGHTER AND POWER LUMBAR SEATS

The 20 amp circuit breaker is located in the fuse block.

POWER WINDOWS

The 20 amp circuit breaker is located in the fuse block.

BRONCO AND F-SERIES LIGHT TRUCKS

POWER DOOR LOCK, ALL WHEEL DRIVE, POWER TAILGATE WINDOW

The 30 Amp Circuit Breaker is located in the fuse block.

POWER WINDOWS

The 30 amp circuit breaker is located in the fuse block.

Fuse Position	Amps	Circuits Protected
1	15	Radio, Dome/Cargo Lamps
2	6 c.b.	Windshield Wipers
4	15	Stop/Hazard Lamps
5	15	Turn Lamps, Backup Lamps, Brake Fluid Level Sensor, Rear Window Defrost
6	15	Rear Wiper/Washer
7	10	A/C Compressor Control
8	20	Horn
9	30	A/C - Heater Blower
10	15	Lamps on Warning, Park/License Lamps, Engine Compartment Lamp
11	15	Radio, Electric Shift Control, Speed Control
12	20 c.b.	Multi-Function Switch, Cigar Lighter, Power Lumbar Seats
13	10	Instrument Illumination
14	20 c.b.	Power Windows
15	20	Rear Anti-Lock Brakes
16	15	Radio Amplifier
17	15	Electric Shift Control, Key Seatbelt, Lamps on Warning, Low Oil Level Relay, Instrument Cluster
18	10	Heated EGO

Fuse assignment—Ranger and Bronco II

Fuse Position	Amps	Circuits Protected
1	15	Stop/Hazard Lamp, Speed Control
2	7.5 c.b.	Windshield Wiper/Washer, Interval Wiper/Washer
3	—	(Not Used)
4	15	Instrument Panel Illumination, Running Lamps, Radio/Clock Illumination, Heater And A/C Control Illumination
5	15	Turn Signal, Backup Lamps, Dual Battery Relay Coil, Daytime Running Lamps
6	20	Speed Control, Customer Convenience Plug (located above fuse panel-Hot in RUN or ACCY)
7	—	(Not Used)
8	15	Dome Lamp, Map Lamp, Radio Memory, Power Door Lock Relays, Cargo Lamp
9	15	A/C Heater Blower Motor Relay Coil, A/C Clutch, Overdrive Cancel
10	20	Cigar Lighter
11	15	Radio and Clock, Premium Sound
12	20 c.b.	Power Door Locks
13	5	Instrument Panel Illumination Lamps
14	20	Power Windows
15	—	(Not Used)
16	15	Horn, Speed Control, Daytime Running Lamps
17	20	Anti-lock Brakes
18	15	Instrument Panel Warning Lamps, Warning Chime, Fuel Pump

Fuse assignment—typical E-Series

Fuse Position	Amps	Circuits Protected
1	15	Stop and Hazard Lamps, Anti-lock Brakes, Speed Control
2	—	(Not Used)
3	—	(Not Used)
4	15	Exterior Illumination, Instrument Illumination, Radio Clock Illumination
5	15	Turn Lamps, Daytime Running Lamps, Overdrive Switch, Backup Lamps, HEGO Sensor and rear Window Defrost (Bronco Only)
6	15	Speed Control and All Wheel Drive (Bronco Only)
7	—	(Not Used)
8	15	Dome Lamp, Map Lamp, Radio Memory, Cargo Lamps
9	30	A/C-Heater Blower Motor Relay Coil, A/C Clutch
10	5	Instrument Illumination
11	15	Radio and Clock
12	30 c.b.	Power Door Lock, All Wheel Drive, Power Tailgate Window (Bronco Only)
13	—	(Not Used)
14	30 c.b.	Power Windows
15	10	Fuel Tank Selector (Diesel Only)
16	30	Horn, Cigar Lighter and Speed Control
17	20	Anti-lock Brakes
18	15	Instrument Cluster Gauges and Indicators, Warning Chime, Diesel Warning Indicators and IMS/EVL Module

Fuse assignment—typical F-Series

Fusible Links

The fusible links are circuit protection devices incorporated into the wiring harness for some electrical equipment. These fusible links, like fuses, open when the amperage through them is to excessive. Never replace fusible link wire with standard wire, always use wire with hypalon insulation and make sure it is the same gauge as the original wire.

AEROSTAR

Fuse Link A—located on the left fender apron.
Fuse Link B—located on the left fender apron.
Fuse Link C—located on the left fender apron, at the starter relay.
Fuse Link D—located on the left fender apron, at the starter relay.
Fuse Link E—located on the left fender apron, at the starter relay.
Fuse Link F—located on the left fender apron, at the starter relay.
Fuse Link G—located at the right rear of the engine compartment, taped to the engine harness.
Fuse Link H—located at the right rear of the engine compartment.

Fuse Link J—located on the left fender apron, at the starter relay.
Fuse Link K—located on the left fender apron, at the starter relay.
In-line Fuse—located at the left side of the instrument panel.

E-SERIES

Fuse Link A—located on the lower left corner of the firewall, near the auxiliary blower relay.
Fuse Link B—located on the right fender apron, near the starter motor relay.
Fuse Link C—located at the auxiliary battery relay.
Fuse Link D—located on the firewall, left the the dual brake warning switch.
Fuse Link E—located on the firewall, left of the dual brake warning switch.
Fuse Link F—located on the right fender apron, at the starter relay.
Fuse Link G—located right front corner of the engine compartment, near the blower motor relay.
Fuse Link H—located on the right fender apron, by the starter relay.
Fuse Link L—located on the right fender apron, by the starter relay.
Fuse Link M—located on the right fender apron, by the starter relay.
Fuse Link R—located on the right fender apron, near the starter relay.
Fuse Link S—located in the center front of the firewall.
Fuse Link W—located in the center front of the firewall.

BRONCO AND F-SERIES

Fuse Link A—located on the front right fender apron, in the engine control harness.
Fuse Link B—located on the front right fender apron, in the engine control harness.
Fuse Link C—located on the front right fender apron, in the engine control harness.
Fuse Link F—located on the front right fender apron, in the engine control harness.
Fuse Link G—located on the front right fender apron, in the engine control harness.
Fuse Link J—located on the front right fender apron, at the starter relay.
Fuse Link L—located on the front right fender apron, in the engine control harness.
Fuse Link M—located on the front right fender apron, in the engine control harness.
Fuse Link N—located on the front right fender apron, in the engine control harness.
Fuse Link P—located on the front right fender apron, in the engine control harness.
Fuse Link W—located on the front right fender apron, in the engine control harness.
Fuse Link X—located at the rear of the right fender apron, in the engine control harness.
Fuse Link Y—located at the rear of the right fender apron, in the engine control harness.

Relays, Sensors, Switches, Modules and Computers Locations

NOTE: When using this section, some of the components may not be used on a particular vehicle. This is because the particular component in question was used on an earlier model or a later model. If a component is not found in this section, check other vehicles with the same engine or component, as that engine or component may have been introduced earlier on different models. This section is being published from the latest information available at the time of this publication.

AEROSTAR

- **Air Charge Temperature Sensor**—is located at the front left side of the engine.
- **A/C Clutch Diode (4.0L engine)**—is located on the top left side of the engine, at the air conditioning compressor clutch.
- **A/C Pressure Cycling Switch**—is located on the top of the accumulator, near the blower motor.
- **Amplifier**—is located on the left side of the instrument panel, under the steering column.
- **Anti-lock Brake (RABS)**—see Rear Anti-lock Brake (RABS).
- **Auxiliary Heater Power Relay**—is located on the left fender apron.
- **Back-up/Neutral Safety switch**—is located on the center left side of the automatic transmission.
- **Backup Lamp Switch**—is located on the left side of the manual transmission.
- **Barometric Absolute Pressure Sensor**—is located on the center of the firewall.
- **Blower Motor Resistors**—are located above the blower motor.
- **Canister Purge Solenoid**—is located on the top of the engine, below the intake.
- **Chime Module**—is located behind the left side of the instrument panel.
- **Coolant Temperature Sender**—is located on the front right side of the engine.
- **Courtesy Lamp Relay**—is located at the left rear corner of the cargo area.
- **Day/Night Illumination Relay**—is located behind the left side of the instrument panel, near the low oil level relay.
- **Daytime Running Lamps (DRL) Module**—is located left on the fender apron.
- **Differential Speed Sensor**—is located on top of the differential housing.
- **Door Lock/Unlock Control Relay**—is located in the right cowl area.
- **Dual Brake Warning Switch**—is located at the left rear of the engine compartment, near the dual brake master cylinder.
- **EDIS Module**—is located on the right front of the fender apron.
- **EEC Power Relay**—is located on the fender apron.
- **Electronic 4WD Module**—is located below the left front seat.
- **Electronic Engine Control Module (EEC)**—is located at the left rear corner of the engine compartment.
- **Engine Coolant Temperature Sensor**—is located at the left side of the engine.
- **Front Axle Speed Sensor**—is located on the front axle.
- **Fuel Pump Relay**—is located on the left fender apron.
- **Graphic Equalizer**—is located on the lower center of the instrument panel.
- **Hazard Flasher**—is located behind the left side of the instrument panel on the fuse block.
- **Horn Relay**—is located at the lower left on the instrument panel, near low oil relay.
- **Ignition Suppression Resistor**—is located at the left rear of the engine compartment, taped to the engine harness.
- **Illuminated Entry Timer**—is located behind the left B–pillar.
- **Inertia Switch**—is located behind the right side of the instrument panel, near the cowl panel.
- **Key Warning Switch**—is located at the top of the instrument column.

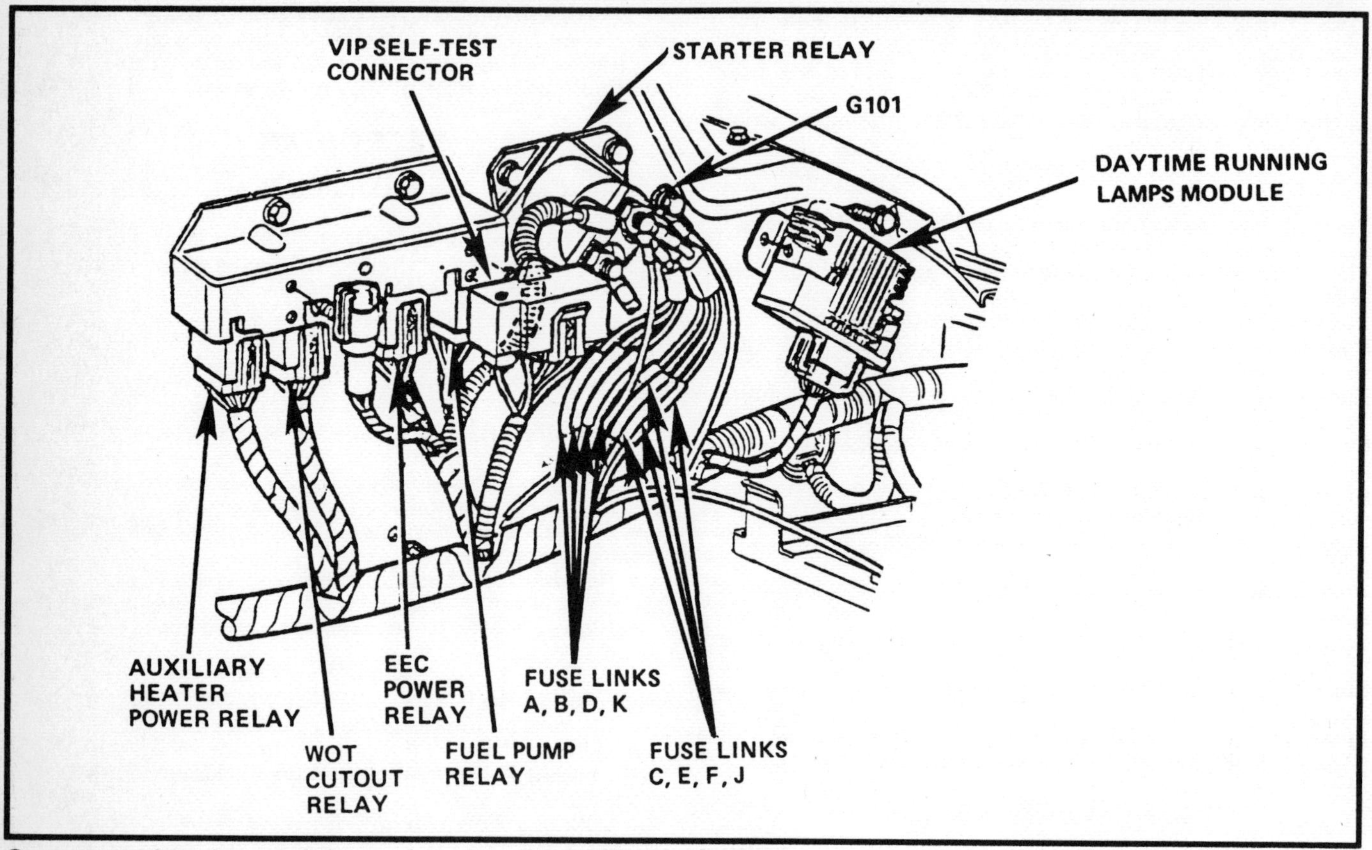

Component locations, left front of engine compartment—Areostar

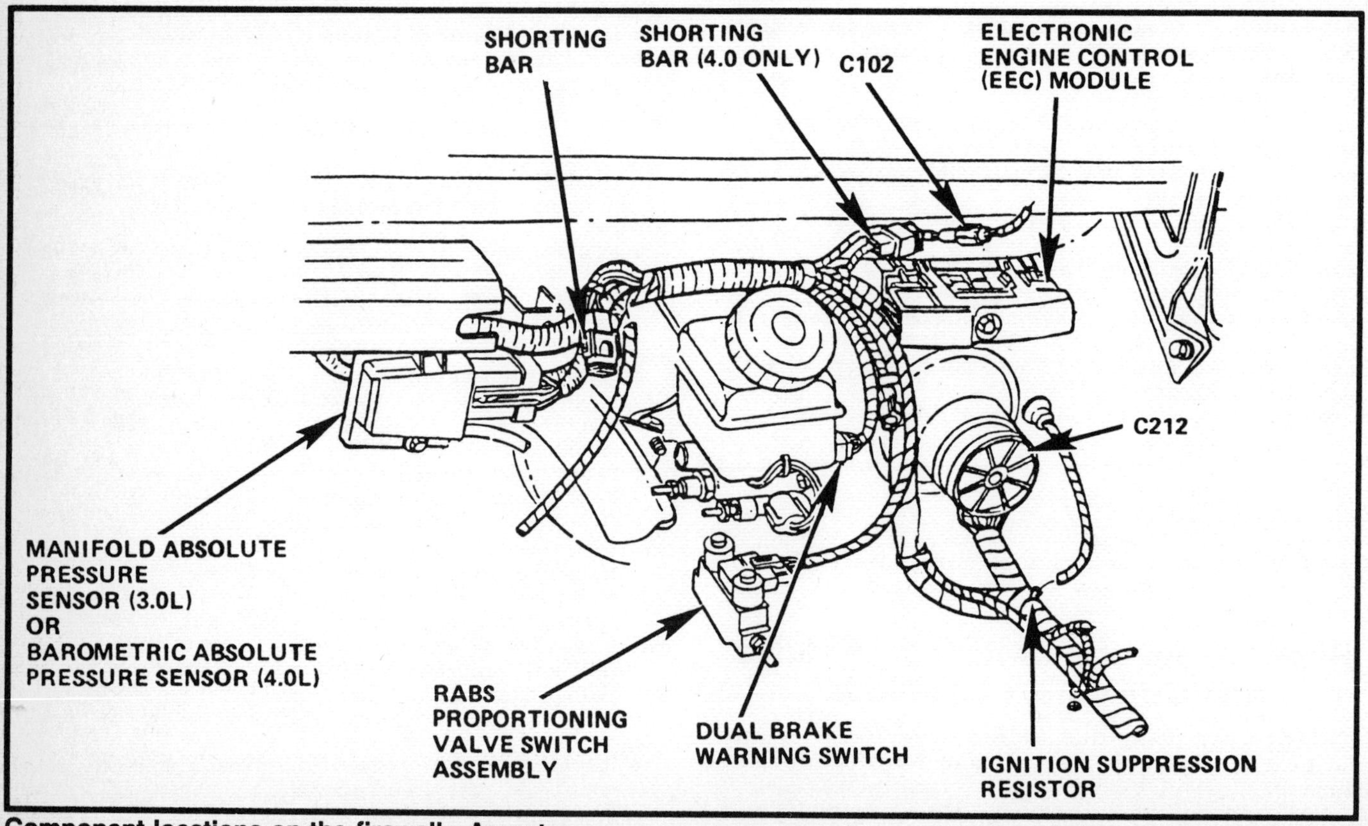

Component locations on the firewall—Aerostar

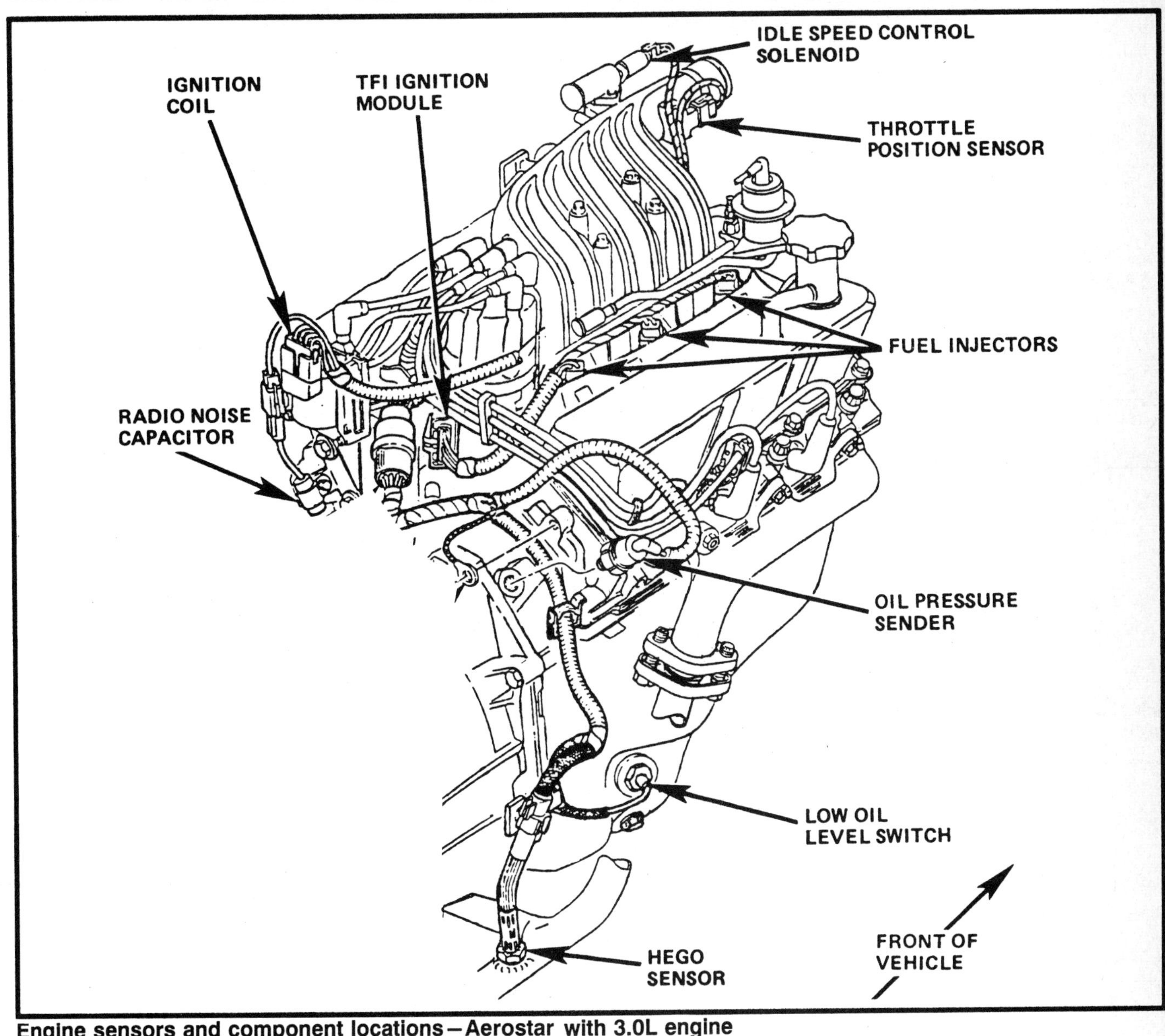

Engine sensors and component locations—Aerostar with 3.0L engine

- **Low Oil Level Relay**—is located on the left side behind the instrument panel, near the horn relay.
- **Low Oil Level Switch**—is located right side of the engine, on the oil pan.
- **Low Washer Fluid Level Switch**—is located at the left front of the engine compartment, in the washer fluid reservoir.
- **Manifold Absolute Pressure Sensor**—is located at the center of the firewall.
- **Mass Air Flow Sensor**—is located at the right front of the engine compartment.
- **Oil Pressure Switch**—is located at the top right rear of the engine.
- **Oxygen (HEGO) Sensor**—is located at the lower right side of the engine, on the exhaust manifold.
- **Park Brake Switch**—is located on the brake support.
- **Park Diode/Resistor**—is located behind the left side of the instrument panel.
- **RABS Proportioning Valve Switch Assembly**—is located at the left rear of the engine compartment.
- **Radio Noise Capacitor (3.0L engine)**—is located at the left rear of the engine.
- **Radio Noise Capacitor (4.0L engine)**—is located at the right rear of the engine.
- **Rear Anti-lock Brake Module (RABS)**—is located at the left side of the instrument panel, mounted to the instrument anti-shake brace.
- **Rear Axle Speed Sensor**—mounted on the rear axle.
- **Speed Control Amplifier**—is located under the left side of the instrument panel.
- **Starter Relay**—is located on the left front fender apron.
- **Stoplight Switch**—is located behind the left side of the instrument panel, on the brake pedal support.
- **TFI Module**—is located center of the engine, near the distributor.
- **Throttle Position Sensor**—is located at the top front of the engine.
- **Trip Computer Module**—is located behind the left side of the instrument panel.

• **WOT Air Conditioning Cutout Relay** – is located on the fender apron, near the auxiliary air relay.

E-SERIES VANS

• **A/C Clutch Pressure Switch** – is located on the right side of the firewall, near the blower motor.
• **A/C Compressor Clutch Diode** – taped inside harness, near the conditioning clutch connector.
• **Air Charge Temperature Sensor (5.0L, 5.8L and 7.5L engines)** – is located at the top of the engine, in lower intake manifold runner No. 6.
• **Anti-lock Brake Module** – is located on the left side of the firewall.
• **Anti-Lock Brake Test Connector C416** – is located on the right fender apron, near the EEC power relay.
• **Anti-Lock Brake Test Connector C417** – is located behind the left side of the instrument panel, near the fuse panel.
• **Auxiliary Battery Relay** – is located on the left fender apron, near the low beam headlamp.
• **Auxiliary Blower Relay** – is located in the left rear corner of the engine compartment.
• **Auxiliary Blower Resistors** – is located in the auxiliary blower motor plenum, on the left side of the engine compartment.
• **Auxiliary Heater/Blower Motor Resistor** – is located on the right side of the firewall, near the blower motor.
• **Backup/Neutral Safety switch** – is located in the center left side of the transmission.
• **Blower Motor Relay** – is located in the right front corner of the engine compartment.
• **Canister Purge Solenoid** – is located on the right side of the engine, connected to the throttle body.
• **Cold Idle Solenoid** – is located center on top of the engine.
• **Cold Timing Advance Solenoid** – is located on the top right side of the engine.
• **Coolant temperature Sender (4.9L engine)** – is located a the top rear of the engine.
• **Coolant temperature Sender (5.0L and 5.8L engines)** – is located on the lower left front of the engine.
• **Coolant temperature Sender (7.3L engine)** – is located in the front, on the right side of the front cover near the center of the engine.

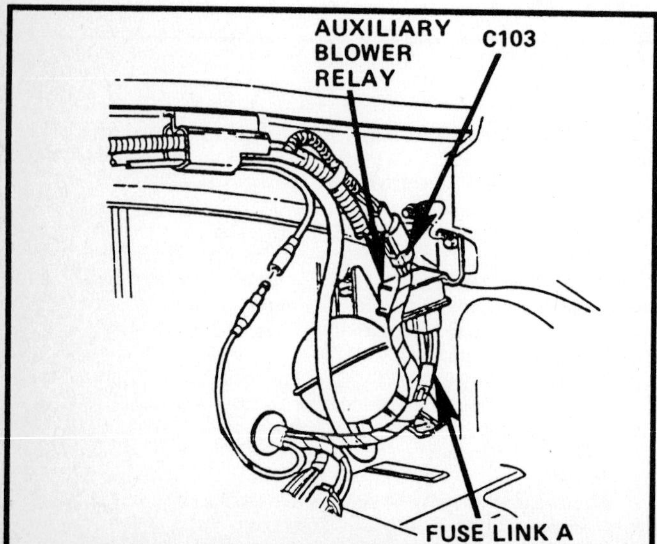

Auxiliary blower relay – E-Series

• **Coolant temperature Sender (7.5L engine)** – is located on top of the engine, near the distributor.
• **Daytime Running Lamps (DRL) Module** – is located on the left fender apron, near the windshield washer pump motor.

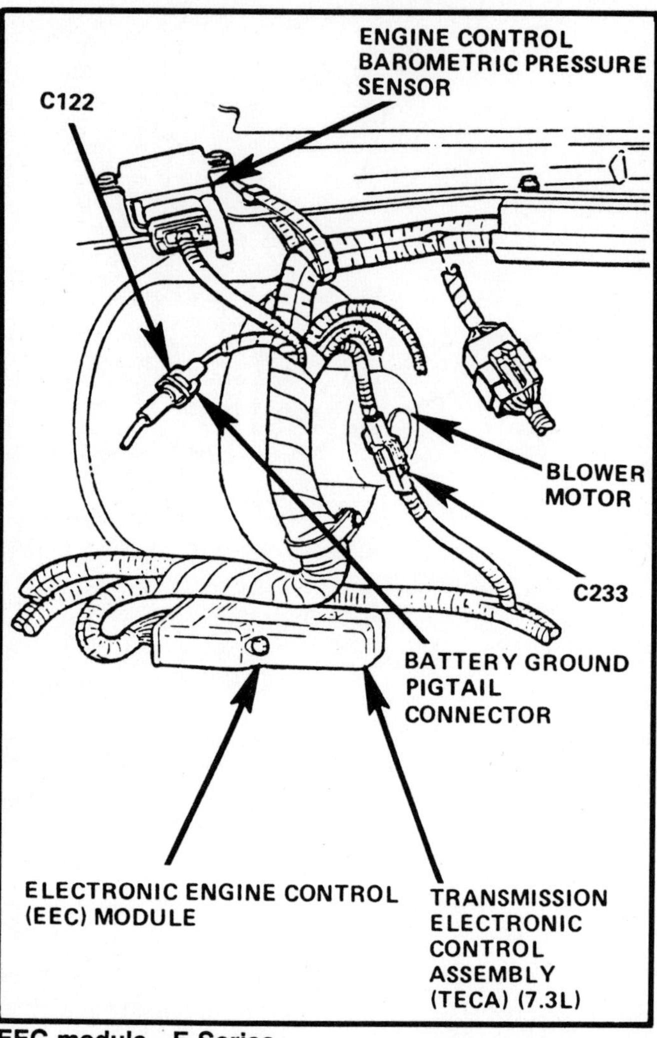

EEC module – E-Series

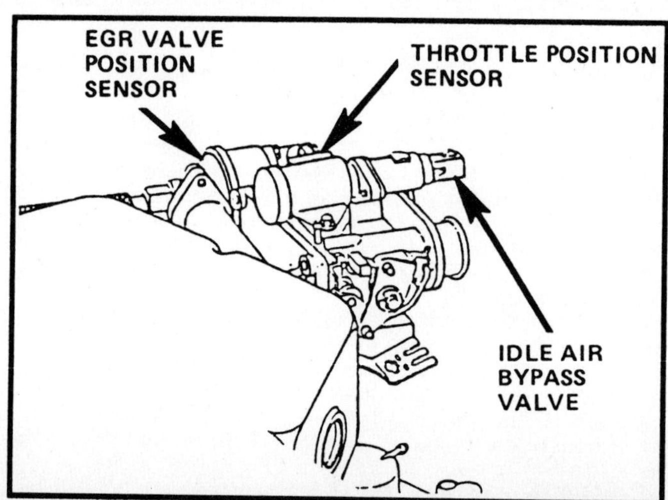

Intake area components – E-Series with 4.9L engine

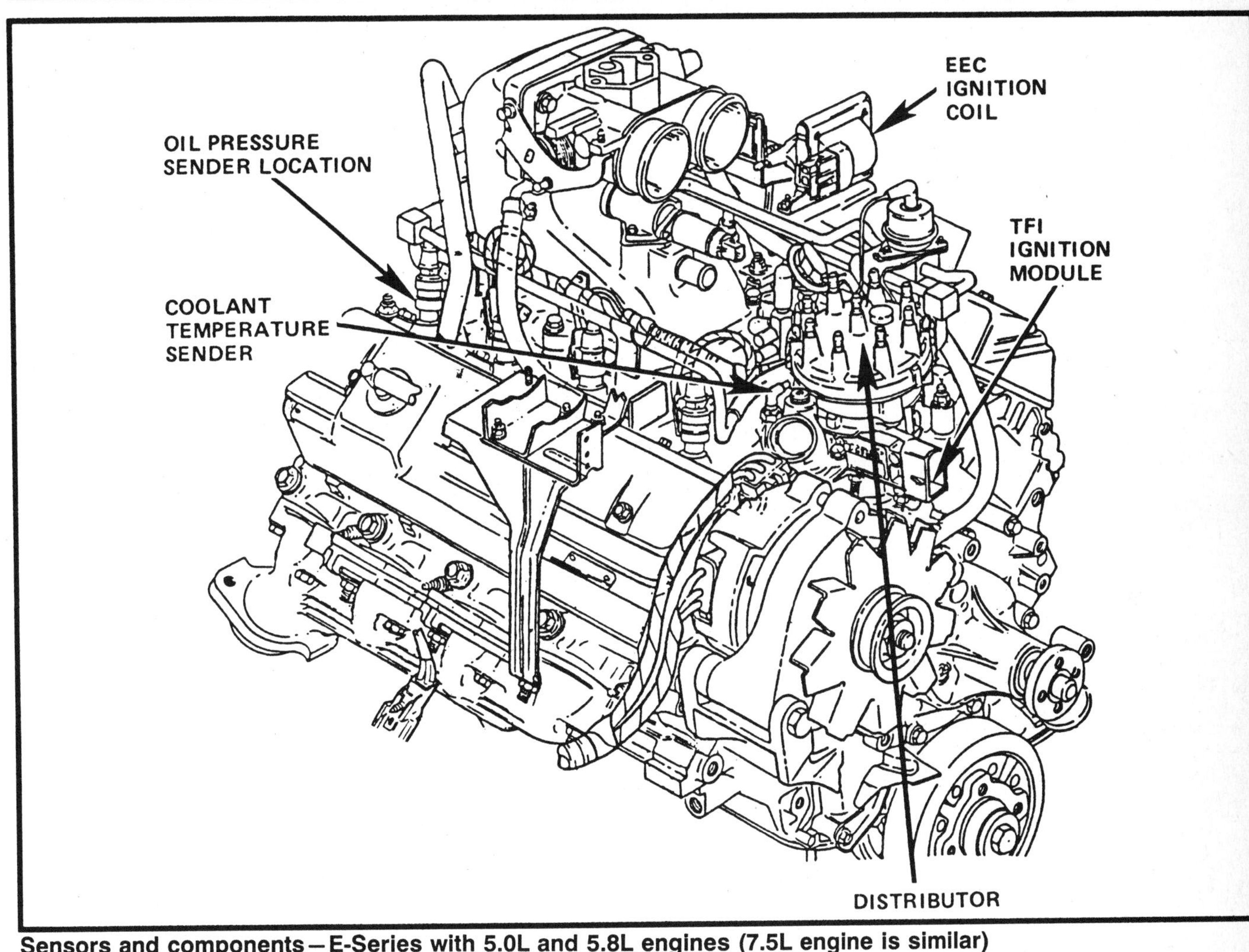

Sensors and components – E-Series with 5.0L and 5.8L engines (7.5L engine is similar)

• **Diesel Warning Lamp Module** – is located behind the left side of the instrument panel.

• **Door Lock/Unlock Control Relay** – is located behind the left side of the instrument panel, above the fuse panel.

• **Dual Brake Warning Diode/Resistor Assembly** – is located behind the left side of the instrument panel.

• **EEC Power Relay** – is located on left fender apron, near the battery.

• **EGR Solenoid (5.0L, 5.8L and 7.5L engines)** – is located on the top right side of the engine, on the coil support bracket.

• **EGR Valve Position Sensor (4.9L engine)** – is located on top of the EGR valve, near the throttle body.

• **EGR Valve Position Sensor (5.0L, 5.8L and 7.5L engines)** – is located on the left front of the engine, on the EGR valve.

• **Electronic Engine Control (EEC) Module (5.0L engine)** – is located on the right side of the fender apron, under blower motor.

• **Electronic Engine Control (EEC) Module (5.8L engine)** – is located on the right side of the fender apron, under blower motor.

• **Electronic Engine Control (EEC) Module (7.5L engine)** – is located on the right side of the fender apron, under blower motor.

• **Emission Warning Indicator** – is located on the left side of the instrument panel, near the main light switch.

• **Engine Control Barometric Pressure Sensor** – is located on the right corner of the firewall, above the blower motor.

• **Engine Coolant Temperature Sensor** – is located on the top front of the engine, on the heater outlet elbow.

• **Engine Temperature Switch** – is located on the front left side of the engine.

• **Front Blower Switch** – is located in the center of the instrument panel.

• **Fuel Injection Pump Lever Sensor** – is located on top of the engine, on the left side of the injector pump.

• **Fuel Pump Relay** – is located on the right fender apron, near the battery.

• **Fuel Shut-off Solenoid** – is located on top of the engine.

• **Fuse panel** – is located behind the left side of the instrument panel, next to the left cowl panel.

• **Glow panel Plug Controller** – is located top center, rear of the engine.

• **Hazard Flasher** – is located behind the left side of the instrument panel, on the fuse panel.

• **Heated Exhaust Gas Oxygen (HEGO) Sensor** – is located at the lower right side of the engine, mounted on the exhaust pipe.

• **Horn Relay** – is located behind the left side of instrument panel, attached to the bottom of the steering column.

• **Ignition Suppression Resistor (7.5L engine)** – is located behind the wiring protection cover between the master

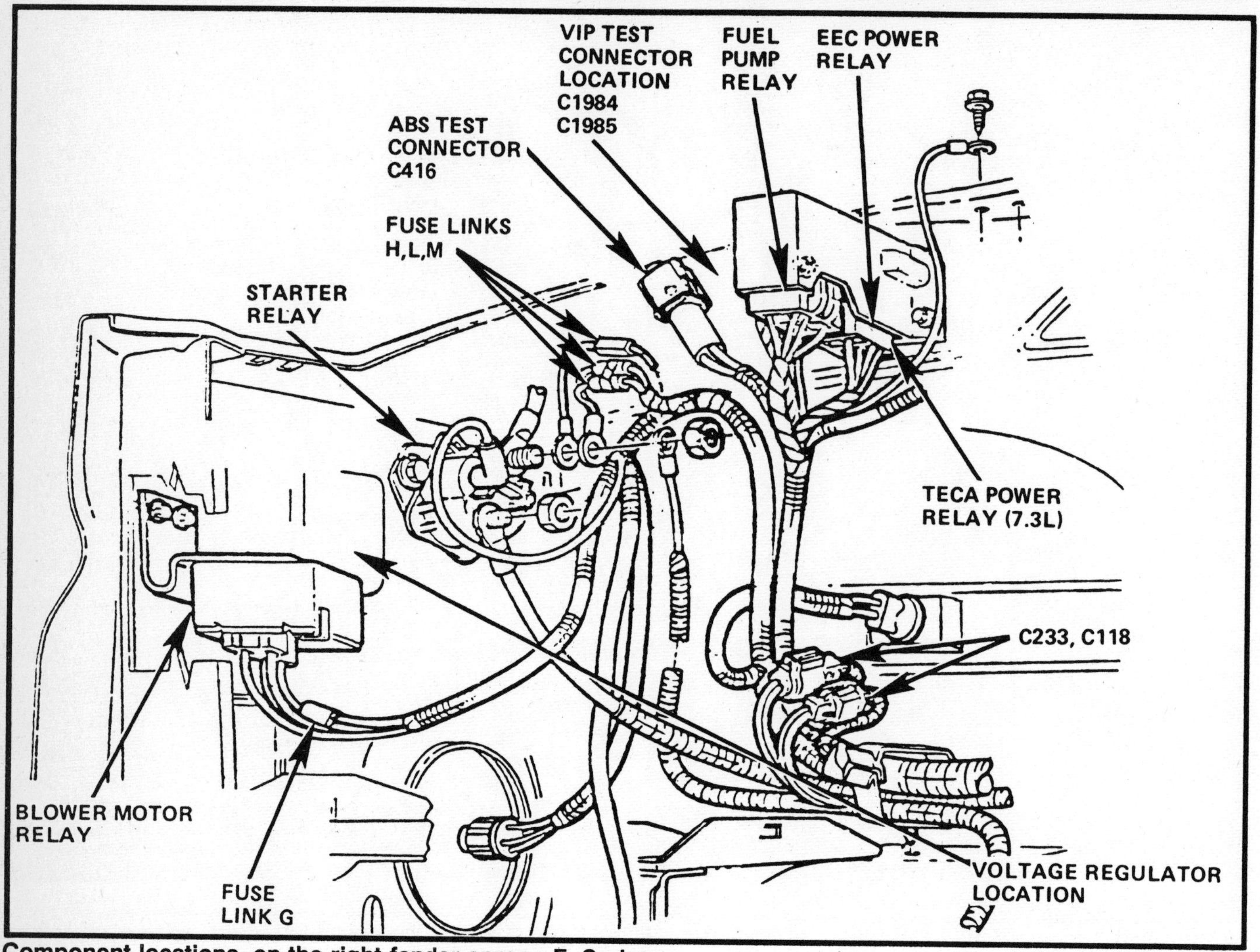

VIP TEST
CONNECTOR
LOCATION
C1984
C1985
FUEL
PUMP
RELAY
EEC POWER
RELAY
ABS TEST
CONNECTOR
C416
FUSE LINKS
H,L,M
STARTER
RELAY
TECA POWER
RELAY (7.3L)
C233, C118
BLOWER MOTOR
RELAY
FUSE
LINK G
VOLTAGE REGULATOR
LOCATION

Component locations, on the right fender apron – E- Series

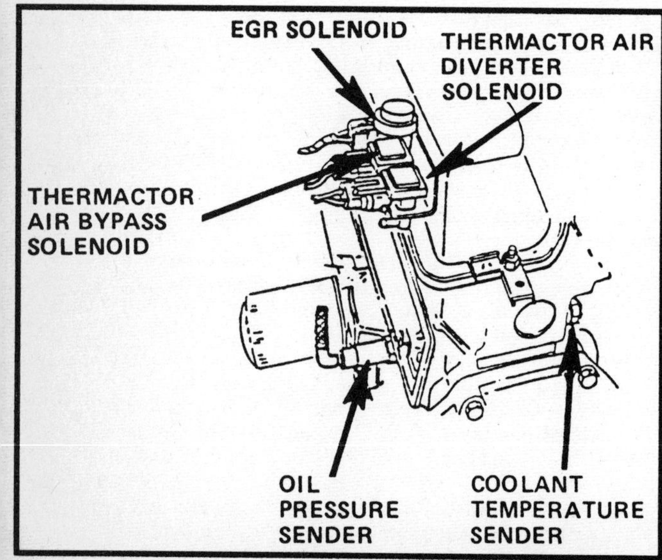

EGR SOLENOID
THERMACTOR AIR
DIVERTER
SOLENOID
THERMACTOR
AIR BYPASS
SOLENOID
OIL
PRESSURE
SENDER
COOLANT
TEMPERATURE
SENDER

Component locations – E-Series with 4.9L engine

cylinder and the center of the engine compartment.

- **Knock Sensor (4.9L engine)** – is located on the lower left side of the engine.
- **Knock Sensor (5.0L, 5.8L and 7.5L engines)** – is located on the lower left side of the intake manifold.
- **Low Vacuum Warning Switch** – is located on the left fender apron, below the washer bottle.
- **Manual Lever Position Sensor** – is located on the left side of the transmission.
- **Oil Pressure sender (4.9L engine)** – is located on the lower left rear side of the engine.
- **Oil Pressure Sender (5.0L, 5.8L and 7.5L engines)** – is located at the top center of the engine.
- **Oil Pressure Sender (7.3L engine)** – is located at the top center of the engine.
- **Overheat Indicator Diode** – is located behind the left side of the instrument panel.
- **Power Steering Pressure Switch** – is located on the lower left fender, near the gear box.
- **Speed Control Amplifier** – is located behind the left side of the instrument panel, on the steering column brace.
- **Shorting Connector** – is located on right side of engine compartment, near fender apron.
- **Tachometer Sensor (except 7.3L engine)** – is located center front of the engine, near throttle position sensor.

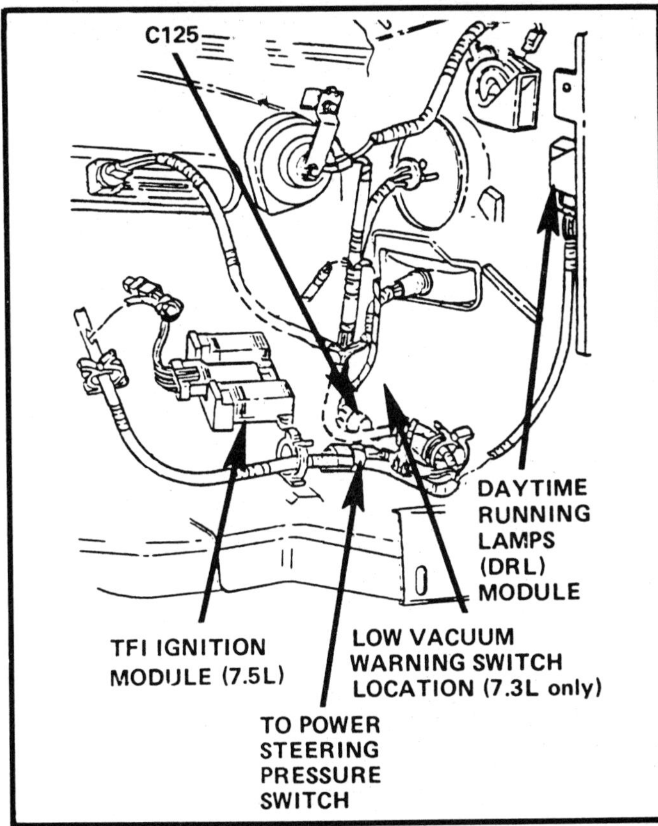

Component locations, on the left front fender – E-Series

- **Tachometer Sensor (7.3L engine)** – is located at the top center front of the engine, on the front cover plate, near the fuel injection pump lever sensor.
- **TECA Power Relay** – is located on the right side of the firewall.
- **TFI Ignition Module (4.9L engine)** – is located side of the engine, at the base of the distributor.
- **TFI Ignition Module (5.0L and 5.8L engines)** – is located at the top front of the engine, on the distributor.
- **TFI Ignition Module (7.5L engine)** – is located on the left fender apron.
- **Throttle Position Sensor (4.9L engine)** – is located at the top of the engine, left side of the throttle body.
- **Throttle Position Sensor (5.0L and 5.8L engine)** – is located on top of the engine, on the throttle body.
- **Throttle Position Sensor (7.5L engine)** – is located on the top right side of the engine.
- **Trailer Exterior Lamps Relay** – is located at the left rear of the vehicle, below left tail lamp.
- **Turn Signal Flasher** – is located behind side of instrument panel, on fuse panel.
- **Vehicle Speed Sensor** – is located on the rear left side of the transmission.
- **VIP Test Connector C1984** – is located inside the right front fender.
- **VIP Test Connector C1985** – is located inside the right front fender.
- **Warning Chime Module** – is located behind the left side of the fuse panel bracket.

BRONCO AND F-SERIES LIGHT TRUCKS

- **A/C Resistor Diode** – is located on the left fender apron, near the relay assembly.
- **Air Charge Temperature Sensor (4.9L engine)** – is located at the top front center of the engine, near the intake runner No. 6.
- **Air Charge Temperature Sensor (5.0L and 5.8L engines)** – is located at the top front center of the engine, near intake runner No. 1.
- **Air Charge Temperature Sensor (7.5L engines)** – is located at the top front center of the engine

Anti-Lock Brake Rear Axle Sensor – is located on the differential.

- **Back-up Lamp Switch** – is located on the right rear of the transmission.
- **Blower Resistors** – is located on the heater housing assembly, near the blower motor.
- **Canister Purge Solenoid (4.9L engine)** – is located on top of the engine.
- **Canister Purge Solenoid (5.8L engine)** – is located on the right side of the engine, near the throttle body.
- **Canister Purge Solenoid (7.5L engine)** – is located on the right side of the engine.
- **Cargo Lamp Diode (Bronco)** – is located at the rear left side of the cargo area.
- **Cargo Lamp Diode (F-Series)** – is located in the interior lamp feed harness, near the cargo lamp, on the rear of the cab.
- **Charge Indicator Lamp Relay** – is located on the right fender apron, near the starter relay.
- **Clutch Interlock Switch Jumper** – is located on the clutch pedal support.
- **Clutch Interlock Switch** – is located on the clutch pedal support.
- **Cold Idle Solenoid** – is located at the top center front of the engine.
- **Cold Timing Advance Solenoid** – is located at the top left side of the engine.
- **Coolant Temperature Sender (4.9L engine)** – is located front of the engine, in the thermostat housing.
- **Coolant Temperature Sender (5.0L, 5.8L and 7.3L engines)** – is located on the left side of the engine.
- **Daytime Running Lamps (DRL) Module** – is located in the left front of the engine compartment, near the horns.
- **Diesel/Warning Lamp Module** – is located behind the left side of the instrument panel.
- **Dual Brake Warning Diode/Resistor Assembly** – is located in the main harness, near the anti-lock brake module.
- **EEC Power Relay** – is located on the left fender apron, on the relay assembly.
- **EGR Control Solenoid (4.9L engine)** – is located on the left side of the engine, on the rear rocker cover bracket.
- **EGR Control Solenoid (5.0L and 5.8L engines)** – is located on the left rear side of the engine, on the coil support bracket.
- **EGR Vacuum Regulator (EVR) Solenoid** – is located at the left rear of the engine.
- **EGR Valve Position Sensor (4.9L engine)** – is located on the left side of the engine.
- **EGR Valve Position Sensor (5.0L and 5.8L engines)** – is located at the front right side of the engine, on the EGR valve.
- **EGR Valve Position Sensor (7.5L engine)** – is located on the left rear of the engine.
- **Electronic Brake Control Unit** – is located behind the left cowl.
- **Electronic Shift Control Module** – is located behind the right cowl panel.
- **Electronic Transfer Case Assembly** – is located on the right side of the undercarriage, near the transmission.
- **Engine Coolant Temperature Sensor** – is located at the front of the engine, on the thermostat housing.
- **Engine RPM Sensor (with E4OD transmission)** – is located at the left front of the engine.

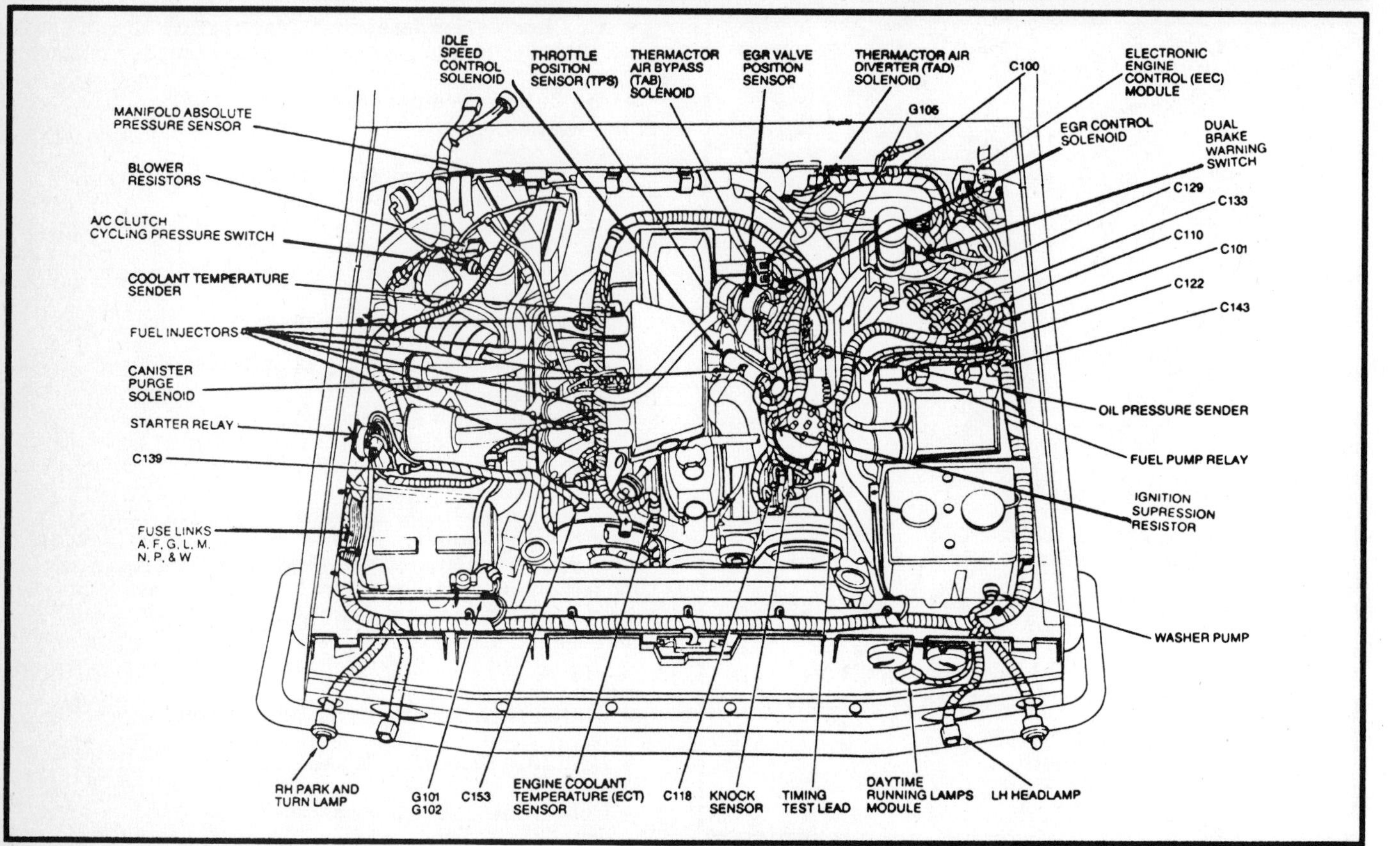

IDLE SPEED CONTROL SOLENOID
THROTTLE POSITION SENSOR (TPS)
THERMACTOR AIR BYPASS (TAB) SOLENOID
EGR VALVE POSITION SENSOR
THERMACTOR AIR DIVERTER (TAD) SOLENOID
C100
ELECTRONIC ENGINE CONTROL (EEC) MODULE
G106
MANIFOLD ABSOLUTE PRESSURE SENSOR
EGR CONTROL SOLENOID
DUAL BRAKE WARNING SWITCH
BLOWER RESISTORS
C129
C133
A/C CLUTCH CYCLING PRESSURE SWITCH
C110
C101
COOLANT TEMPERATURE SENDER
C122
C143
FUEL INJECTORS
CANISTER PURGE SOLENOID
OIL PRESSURE SENDER
STARTER RELAY
C139
FUEL PUMP RELAY
IGNITION SUPRESSION RESISTOR
FUSE LINKS A, F, G, L, M, N, P, & W
WASHER PUMP
RH PARK AND TURN LAMP
G101 G102
C153
ENGINE COOLANT TEMPERATURE (ECT) SENSOR
C118
KNOCK SENSOR
TIMING TEST LEAD
DAYTIME RUNNING LAMPS MODULE
LH HEADLAMP

Engine sensors and component locations – F-Series with 4.9L engine

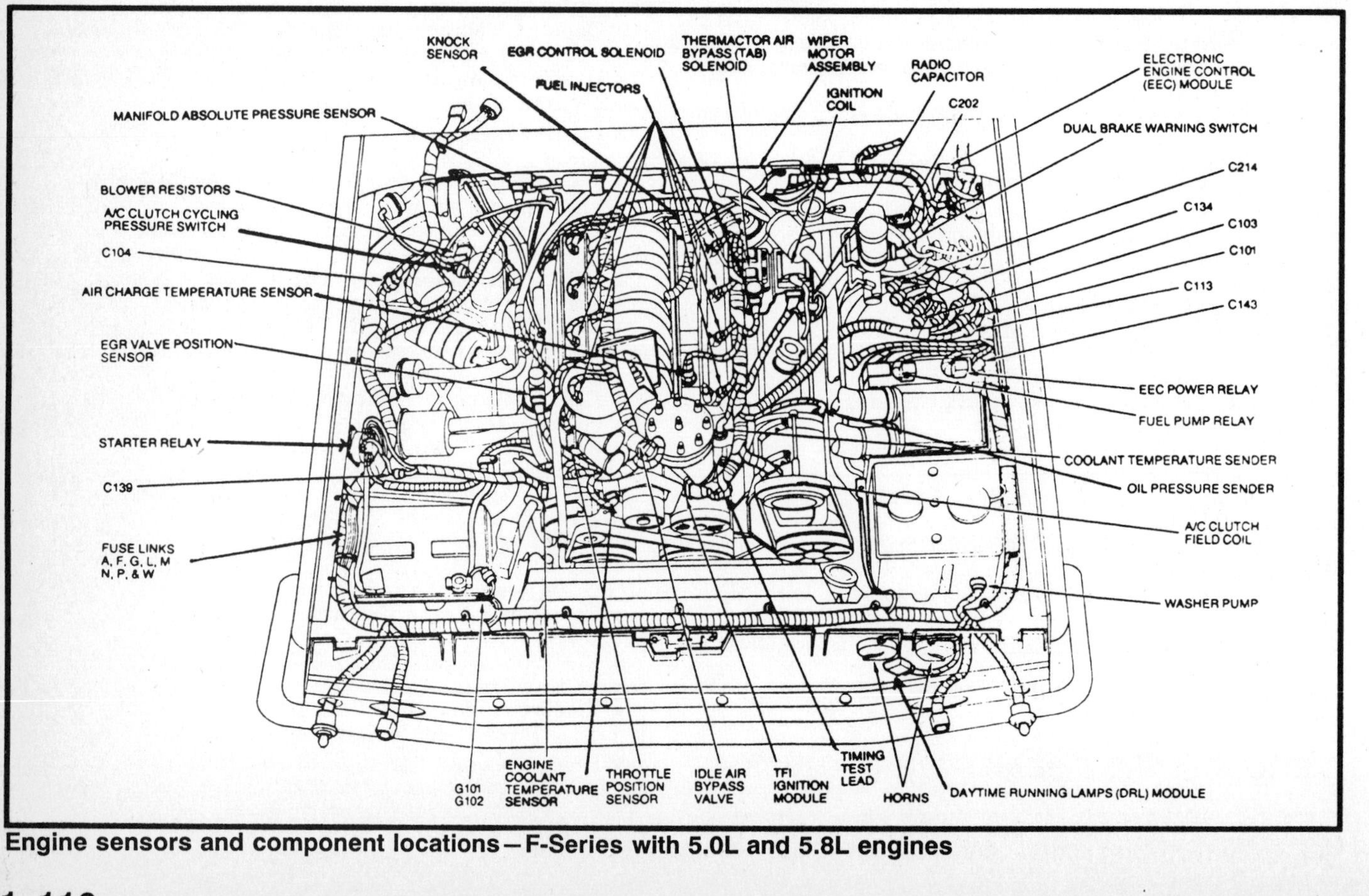

KNOCK SENSOR
EGR CONTROL SOLENOID
THERMACTOR AIR BYPASS (TAB) SOLENOID
WIPER MOTOR ASSEMBLY
RADIO CAPACITOR
ELECTRONIC ENGINE CONTROL (EEC) MODULE
FUEL INJECTORS
IGNITION COIL
C202
MANIFOLD ABSOLUTE PRESSURE SENSOR
DUAL BRAKE WARNING SWITCH
C214
BLOWER RESISTORS
C134
A/C CLUTCH CYCLING PRESSURE SWITCH
C103
C104
C101
C113
AIR CHARGE TEMPERATURE SENSOR
C143
EGR VALVE POSITION SENSOR
EEC POWER RELAY
FUEL PUMP RELAY
STARTER RELAY
COOLANT TEMPERATURE SENDER
C139
OIL PRESSURE SENDER
A/C CLUTCH FIELD COIL
FUSE LINKS A, F, G, L, M N, P, & W
WASHER PUMP
G101 G102
ENGINE COOLANT TEMPERATURE SENSOR
THROTTLE POSITION SENSOR
IDLE AIR BYPASS VALVE
TFI IGNITION MODULE
TIMING TEST LEAD
HORNS
DAYTIME RUNNING LAMPS (DRL) MODULE

Engine sensors and component locations – F-Series with 5.0L and 5.8L engines

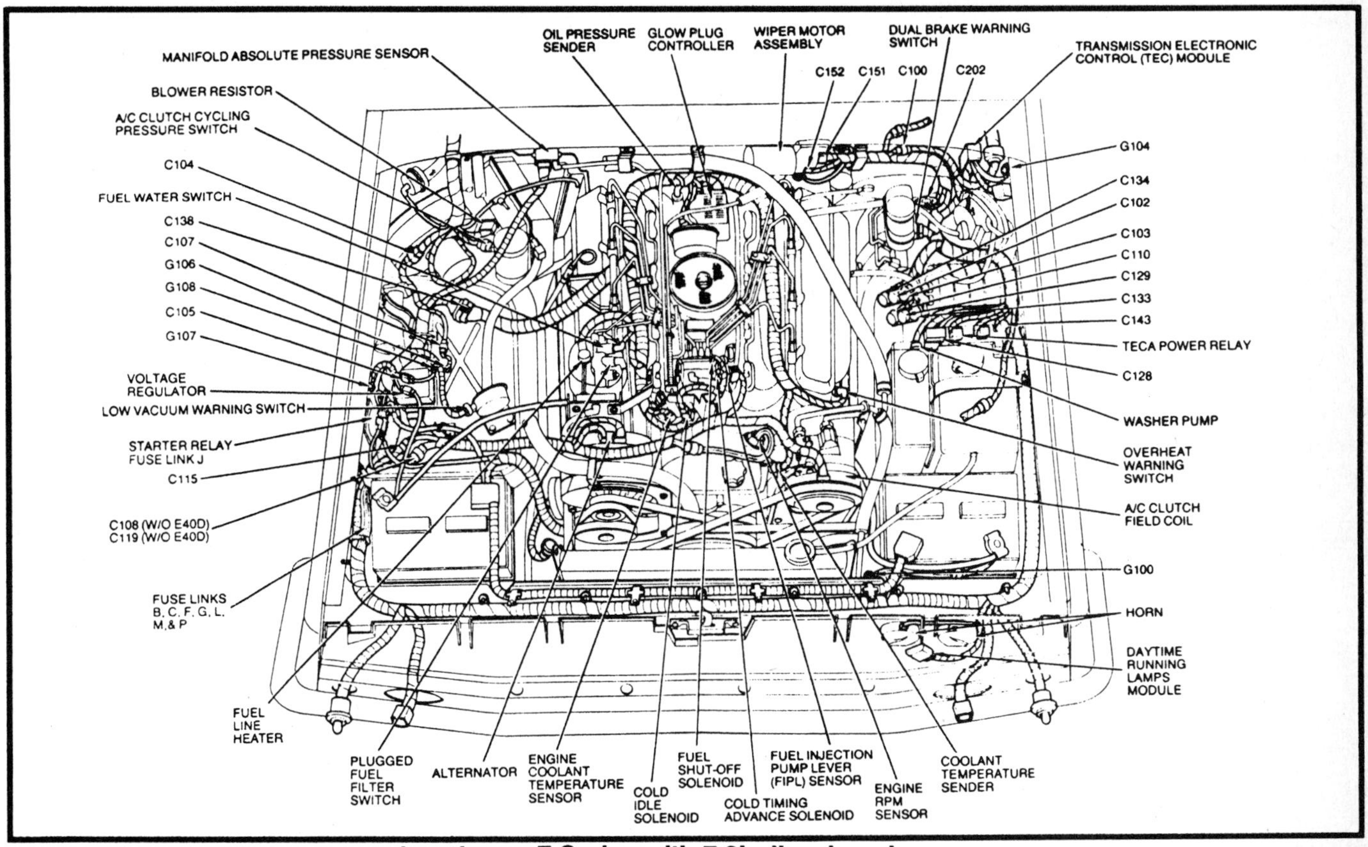

MANIFOLD ABSOLUTE PRESSURE SENSOR
OIL PRESSURE SENDER
GLOW PLUG CONTROLLER
WIPER MOTOR ASSEMBLY
DUAL BRAKE WARNING SWITCH
TRANSMISSION ELECTRONIC CONTROL (TEC) MODULE
C152
C151
C100
C202
BLOWER RESISTOR
A/C CLUTCH CYCLING PRESSURE SWITCH
C104
FUEL WATER SWITCH
C138
C107
G106
G108
C105
G107
VOLTAGE REGULATOR
LOW VACUUM WARNING SWITCH
STARTER RELAY
FUSE LINK J
C115
C108 (W/O E40D)
C119 (W/O E40D)
FUSE LINKS B, C, F, G, L, M, & P
FUEL LINE HEATER
G104
C134
C102
C103
C110
C129
C133
C143
TECA POWER RELAY
C128
WASHER PUMP
OVERHEAT WARNING SWITCH
A/C CLUTCH FIELD COIL
G100
HORN
DAYTIME RUNNING LAMPS MODULE
PLUGGED FUEL FILTER SWITCH
ALTERNATOR
ENGINE COOLANT TEMPERATURE SENSOR
COLD IDLE SOLENOID
FUEL SHUT-OFF SOLENOID
COLD TIMING ADVANCE SOLENOID
FUEL INJECTION PUMP LEVER (FIPL) SENSOR
ENGINE RPM SENSOR
COOLANT TEMPERATURE SENDER

Engine sensors and component locations—F-Series with 7.3L diesel engine

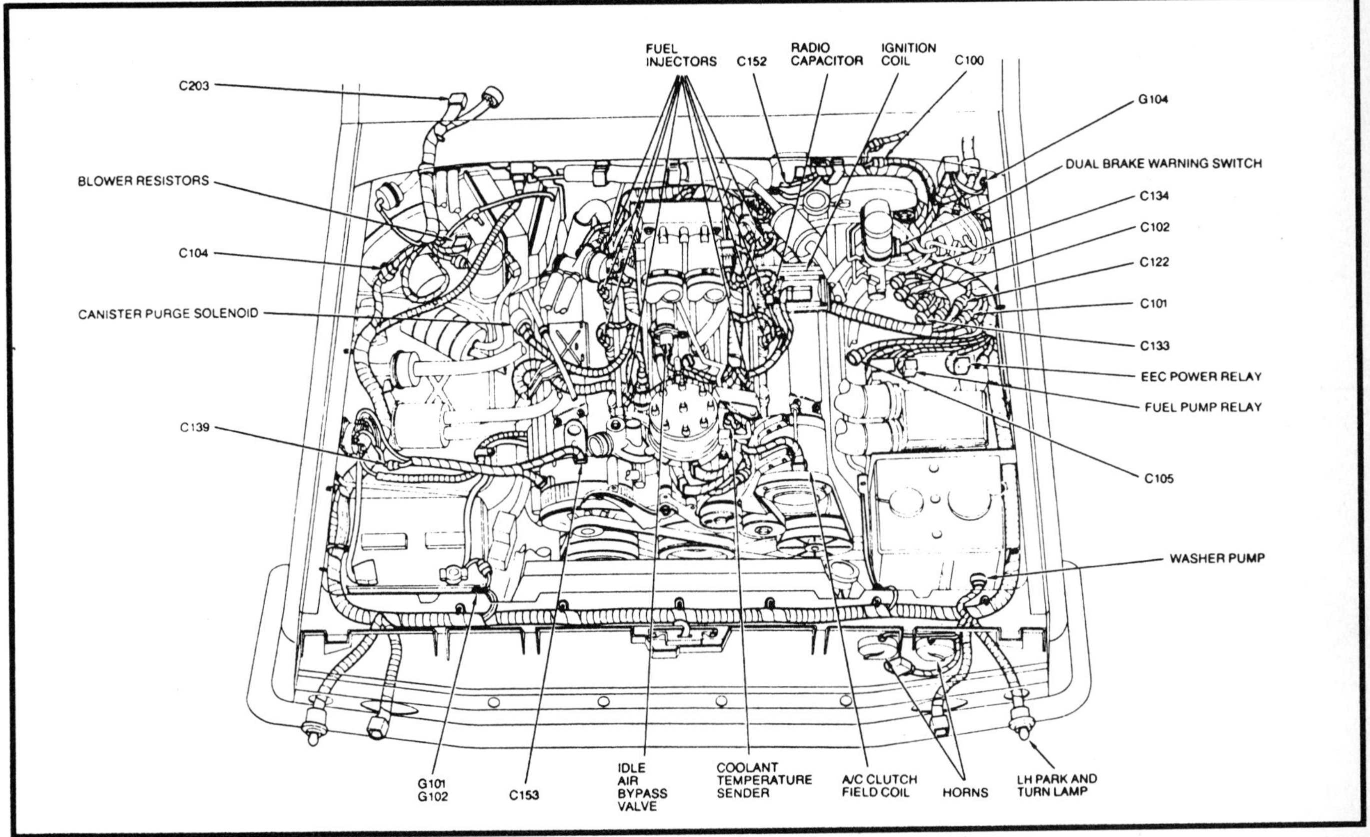

FUEL INJECTORS
C152
RADIO CAPACITOR
IGNITION COIL
C100
C203
G104
BLOWER RESISTORS
DUAL BRAKE WARNING SWITCH
C134
C104
C102
C122
CANISTER PURGE SOLENOID
C101
C133
EEC POWER RELAY
FUEL PUMP RELAY
C139
C105
WASHER PUMP
G101
G102
C153
IDLE AIR BYPASS VALVE
COOLANT TEMPERATURE SENDER
A/C CLUTCH FIELD COIL
HORNS
LH PARK AND TURN LAMP

Engine sensors and component locations—F-Series with 7.5L engine

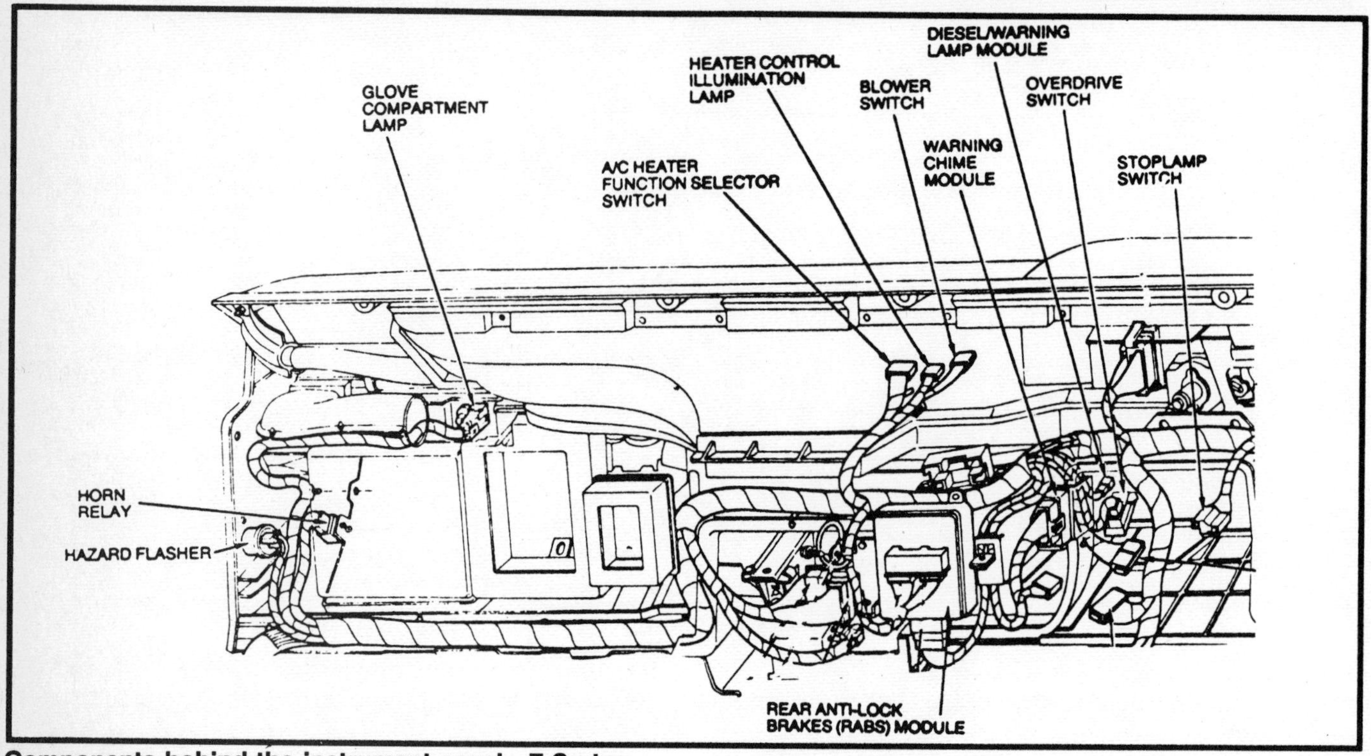

Components behind the instrument panel – F-Series

- **Engine RPM Sensor (without E4OD transmission)** – is located at the top front of the engine.
- **Engine Temperature Switch** – is located on front left side of the engine.
- **Fuel Injection Pump Lever (FIPL) Sensor** – is located on the left side of the engine.
- **Fuel Line Heater** – is located on the right front side of the engine, near the fuel filter.
- **Fuel Pump Relay** – is located on the left fender apron.
- **Fuel Tank Selector Switch** – is located on the left side of the main frame, rear of the cab.
- **Fuel Water Switch** – is located on the front right side of the engine, near the fuel filter.
- **Fuse Panel** – is located behind the left side of the instrument panel.
- **Glow Plug Controller** – is located at the top center rear of the engine.
- **Hazard Flasher** – is located behind the right side of the instrument panel.
- **Heated Exhaust Gas Oxygen (HEGO) Sensor** – is located in the exhaust pipe, in front of the catalyst.
- **Horn Relay Jumper** – is located behind the right side of the instrument panel, near the hazard flasher.
- **Horn Relay** – is located behind the right side of the instrument panel, near the hazard flasher.
- **Idle Air Bypass Valve (5.0L and 5.8L engines)** – is located at the center front of the engine, on the throttle body.
- **Idle Air Bypass Valve (7.5L engine)** – is located at the top center of the engine.
- **Idle Speed Control Solenoid** – is located at the left side of the engine.
- **Ignition Suppression Resistor** – is located at the left side of the engine, taped in the harness.
- **Inertia Switch** – is located behind the left cowl panel.
- **Knock Sensor** – is located left side of the engine near the ignition coil.
- **Low Vacuum Warning Switch** – is located on the right fender apron.
- **Manifold Absolute Pressure Sensor** – is located on the right side of the fire wall.
- **Manual Lever Position Sensor** – is located on the left side of the transmission.
- **Oil Pressure Switch (4.9L engine)** – is located on the left side of the engine.
- **Oil Pressure Switch (5.0L and 5.8L engines)** – is located on the left side of the engine, near the oil filter.
- **Oil Pressure Switch (7.3L engine)** – is located at the top rear of the engine.
- **Oil Pressure Switch (7.5L engine)** – is located on the top right rear of the engine.
- **Over Heat Warning Switch** – is located at the left front of the engine.
- **Plugged Fuel Filter Switch** – is located in the fuel filter housing.
- **Power Steering Pressure Switch** – is located on the left fender apron.
- **RABS Test Connector C143** – is located on the fender apron, near the EEC power relay.
- **Rear Anti-lock Valve Assembly** – is located on the frame, near the transmission.
- **Speed Control Amplifier** – is located behind the center of the instrument panel, near the radio.
- **Speed Control Servo** – is located left rear of the engine compartment, near the master cylinder.
- **Starter Relay** – is located on the lower right side of the engine.
- **Stop Lamp Switch** – is located on the brake pedal support.
- **TECA Power Relay** – is located on the front of the left fender apron.
- **TFI ignition Module (4.9L engine)** – is located on the left side of the engine, on the distributor.
- **TFI ignition Module (5.0L and 5.8L engines)** – is located on front of the engine, below the distributor.
- **TFI ignition Module (7.5L engine)** – is located at the left rear of the engine compartment.

- **Thermactor Air Bypass Solenoid (4.9L engine)**—is located left side of the engine, on the rear rocker cover bracket.
- **Thermactor Air Bypass Solenoid (5.0L and 5.8L engines)**—is located at the left rear side of the engine, on the coil support bracket.
- **Thermactor Air Bypass Solenoid (7.5L engine)**—is located at the left rear of the engine.
- **Thermactor Air Diverter Solenoid (4.9L engine)**—is located on the left side of the engine.
- **Thermactor Air Diverter Solenoid (5.0L and 5.8L engines)**—is located left rear side of the engine, on the coil support bracket.
- **Throttle Position Sensor (4.9L engine)**—is located on the left side of the engine, on the throttle body shaft.
- **Throttle Position Sensor (5.0L and 5.8L engines)**—is located at the lower right front of the engine, on the throttle body shaft.
- **Timing Test Lead (4.9L, 5.0L and 5.8L engines)**—is located at the left side of the engine.
- **Timing Test Lead (7.5L engine)**—is located rear of the left fender apron.
- **Trailer Marker Lamps Relay**—is located on the left fender apron.
- **Transmission Electronic Control Assembly (TECA)**—is located on the left side of the firewall, below the master cylinder.
- **Turn Signal Flasher**—is located behind the left side of the instrument panel.
- **Vehicle Speed Sensor**—is located on the left rear side of the automatic transmission.
- **Warning Chime Module**—is located behind the center of the instrument panel.

RANGER AND BRONCO II

- **A/C Compressor Clutch Diode**—taped to the harness, near the compressor clutch solenoid.
- **A/C WOT Cutout Relay**—is located at the right fender apron, under power distribution box.
- **Air Charge Temperature Sensor (2.3L engine)**—is located at the top left side of the engine.
- **Air Charge Temperature Sensor (2.9L engine)**—is located at the top right side of the engine.
- **Air Charge Temperature Sensor (4.0L engine)**—is located at the top left side of the engine.
- **Back-up Light Switch (Mazda transmission)**—is located on the right side of the transmission.
- **Back-up Light Switch (Mitsubishi transmission)**—is located on the right side of the transmission.
- **Back-up/Neutral Safety Switch**—is located on the left side of the transmission.
- **Barometric Manifold Absolute Pressure (BMAP) Sensor**—is located at the top side of firewall.
- **Blower Resistors**—is located at the right rear of the engine compartment, near the blower motor.
- **Brake Fluid Level Sensor**—is located at the left rear of the engine compartment, on the brake fluid reservoir.
- **Brake Warning Diode/Resistor Assembly**—is located on the left side of the engine compartment, taped in the harness.
- **Canister Purge Solenoid**—is located in the left front of the engine compartment.
- **Clutch Triple Function Switch**—is located at the top of the clutch pedal, below the left side the instrument panel.
- **Coolant Temperature Sender (2.3L engine)**—is located at the left rear side of the engine.
- **Coolant Temperature Sender (2.9L engine)**—is located at the top front of the engine.
- **Coolant Temperature Sender (4.0L engine)**—is located at the top front of the engine.
- **Courtesy Lamp Diode (Ranger)**—is located at the top of the B–pillar, taped on harness, near the dome lamp.
- **Courtesy Lamp Diode (Super Cab)**—is located at the rear of the cab roof, near the cargo lamp.
- **Daytime Running Lamps (DRL) Module**—is located at the top left side of the radiator support.
- **DIS Ignition Module (2.3L engine)**—is located on the left side of the engine.

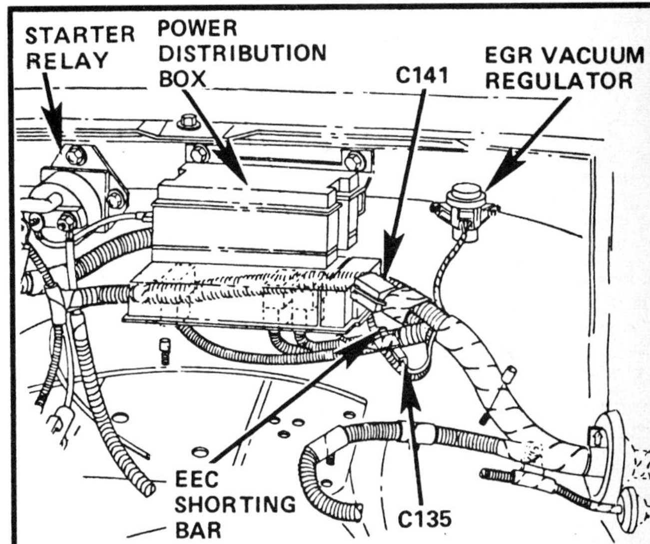

Right fender component locations—2.3L engine

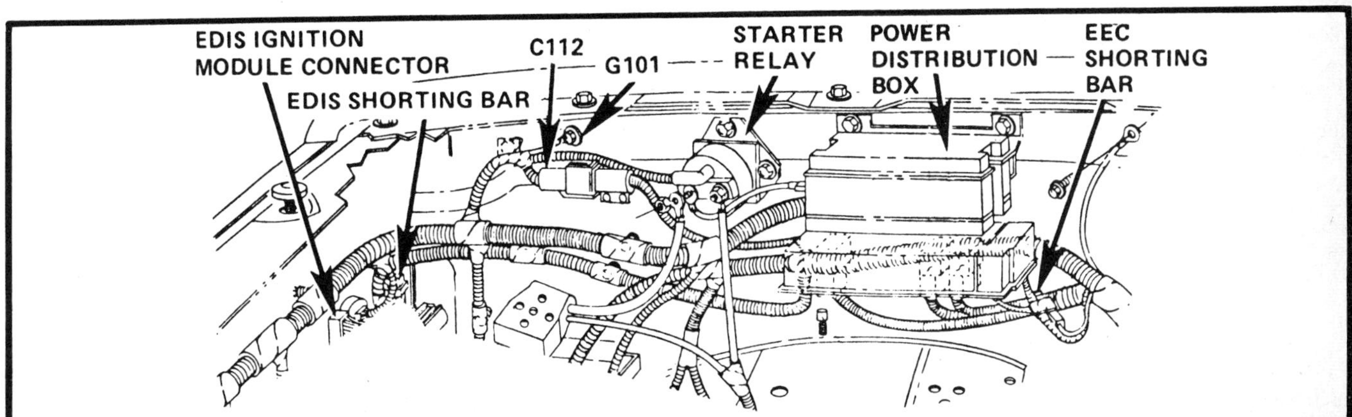

View of the right fender apron, component locations—4.0L engine

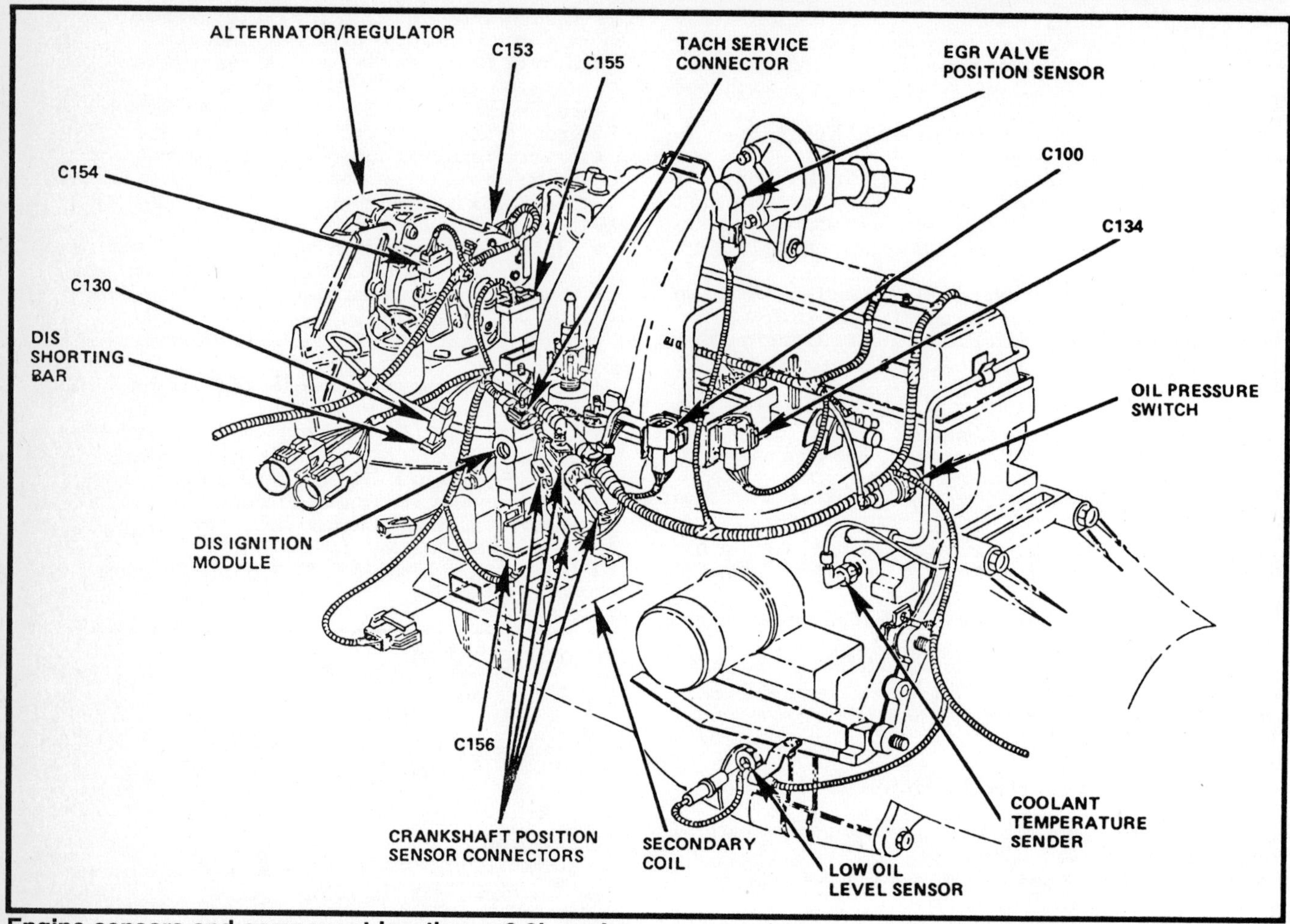

Engine sensors and component locations—2.3L engine

- **EDIS Ignition Module (4.0L engine)**—is located on the right side of the battery, mounted on the radiator support.
- **EEC Power Relay**—is located at the right fender apron, under the power distribution box.
- **EGR Vacuum Regulator Solenoid**—is located on the rear of the right fender apron.
- **EGR Valve Position Sensor**—is located at the top left side of the engine.
- **Electric Shift Control (EEC) Module (2.3L engine)**—is located behind the right cowl panel.
- **Electric Shift Control (EEC) Module (2.9L engine)**—is located behind the right cowl panel.
- **Electric Shift Control (EEC) Module (4.0L engine)**—is located behind the right cowl panel.
- **Electric Shift Control Module (Bronco)**—Between left B-pillar, in front of the left rear wheel well.
- **Engine Coolant Temperature Sensor (2.3L engine)**—is located at the lower left side of the engine.
- **Engine Coolant Temperature Sensor (2.9L engine)**—is located at top front of the engine.
- **Engine Coolant Temperature Sensor (4.0L engine)**—is located at top front of the engine.
- **Fuse Panel**—is located behind the left side of the instrument panel.
- **Hazard Flasher**—is located at the rear of the fuse panel, below the turn signal flasher.
- **Heated Exhaust Gas Oxygen (HEGO) Sensor**—is located at the right rear of the engine compartment, on the exhaust manifold.
- **Horn Relay**—is located behind the lower left side of the instrument panel, to the right of the steering column.
- **Idle Speed Control Solenoid (2.3L engine)**—is located at the top right side of the engine.
- **Idle Speed Control Solenoid (4.0L engine)**—is located at the top left side of the engine.
- **Ignition Key Warning Switch**—is located at the top of the steering column.
- **Ignition Suppression Resistor**—is located in the engine control sensor harness, on the left side of the engine compartment.
- **In-line Circuit Breaker**—is located behind the right side of the instrument panel.
- **Inertia Switch**—is located below the right side of the instrument panel.
- **Low Oil Level Relay (2.3L engine)**—is located behind the lower right side of the instrument panel.
- **Low Oil Level Sensor (2.3L engine)**—is located at the lower left rear of the engine.
- **Low Oil Level Sensor (2.9L and 4.0L engines)**—is located at the lower left rear of the engine.
- **Power Distribution Box**—is located on right fender apron.
- **Power Steering Pressure Switch**—is located on the left side of the engine compartment.
- **RABS Test Connector C124**—is located the top of the left fender apron.
- **RABS Test Connector C212**—is located below the left side the instrument panel, near the park brake.

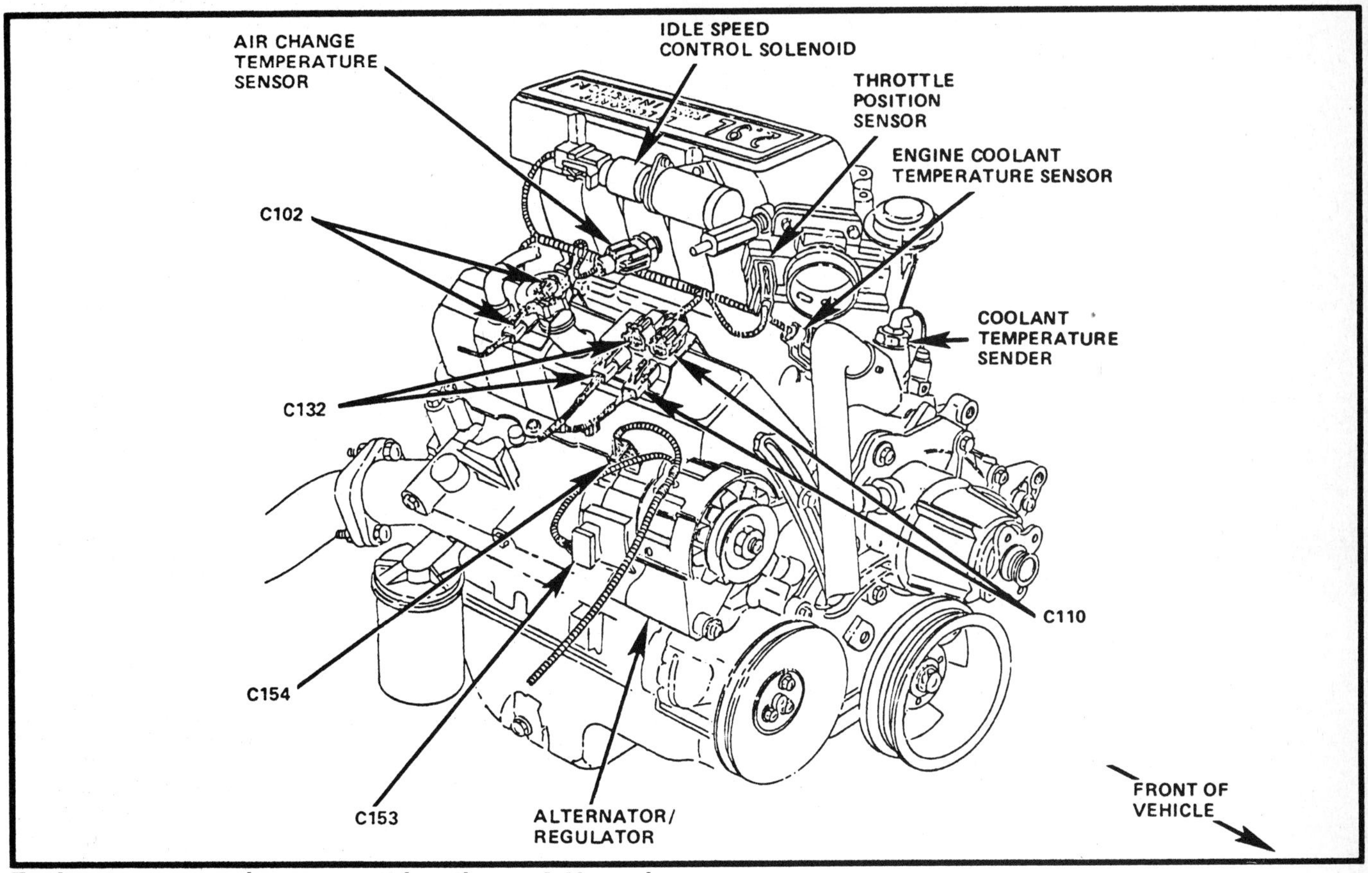

Engine sensors and component locations—2.9L engine

• **Rear Anti-lock Brake Module**—is located behind the center of the instrument panel, on the left side of the ashtray assembly.

• **Rear Axle Sensor**—is located on top of the differential case.

• **Self Test Connector C125**—is located at the right fender apron, rear the power distribution box.

• **Starter Relay**—is located on the right fender apron, near the battery.

• **Shorting Bar**—is located at left front of engine.

• **Tach Service Connector**—is located on the left side of the engine, near the EDIS ignition module.

• **TFI Ignition Module**—is located at the rear of the engine, on the distributor.

• **Throttle Position Sensor (2.3L engine)**—is located at the top right side of the engine.

• **Throttle Position Sensor (2.9L engine)**—is located at the top right front of the engine.

• **Throttle Position Sensor (4.0L engine)**—is located at the left side of the engine.

• **Turn Signal Flasher**—is located behind the left side of the instrument panel, on the fuse panel.

• **Variable Speed Sensor (VSS) 2WD**—is located at the lower right front of the engine.

• **Variable Speed Sensor (VSS) 4WD**—is located at the top of the transfer case.

• **Windshield Wiper Module**—is located behind the center of the instrument panel, left side of the ashtray.

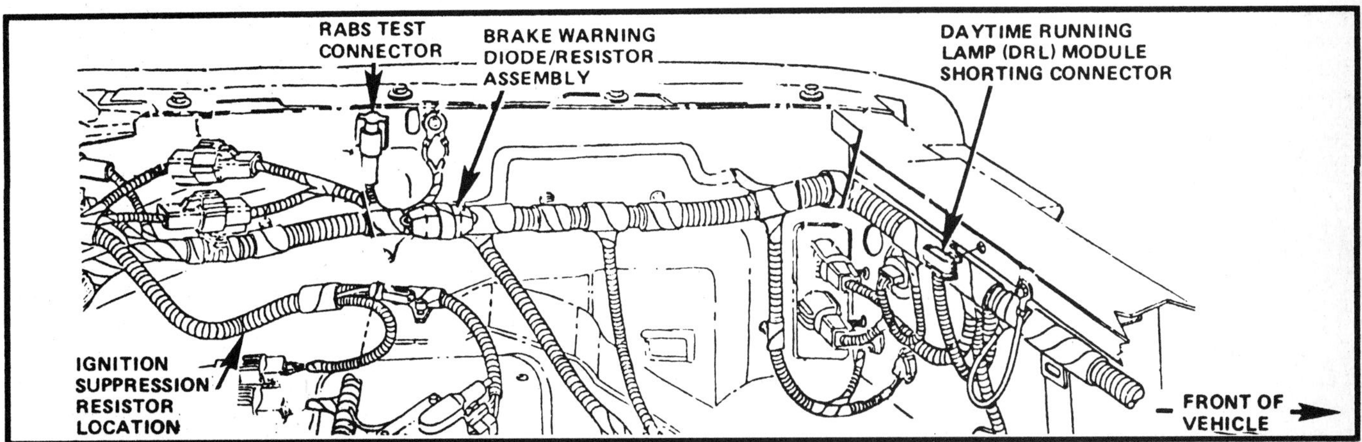

Left fender apron—typical 1990

BUICK

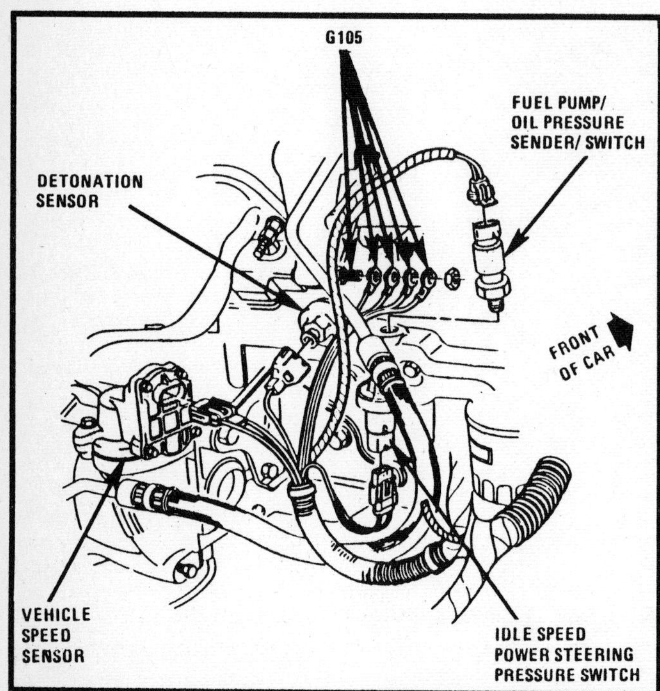

Oil pressure switch location—Century with 3.3L VIN N engine

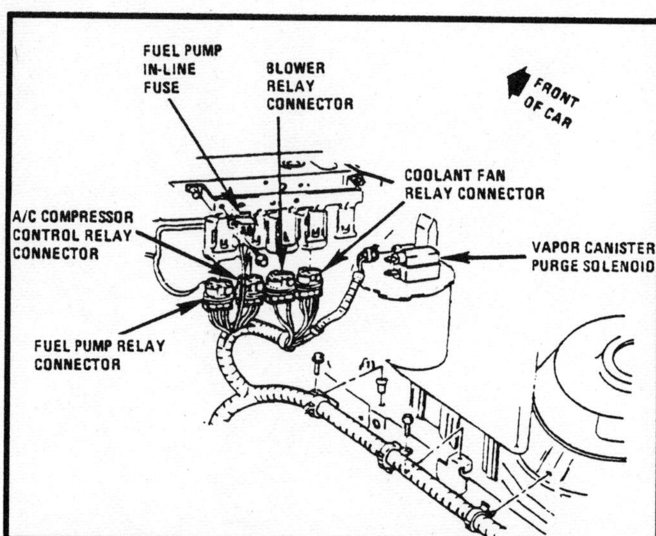

Relay locations—Century with 3.3L VIN N engine

Circuit Breakers

ALL MODELS

HEADLIGHTS

This circuit breaker is incorporated in the headlight switch.

NOTE: On all models, except the Riviera and Reatta there is a thermo circuit breaker incorporated in the headlight switch assembly to protect the headlight circuits. The Riviera models, use a circuit breaker which is located in the fuse block.

WINDSHIELD WIPERS

This circuit breaker is incorporated in the windshield wiper motor.

POWER ACCESSORIES

Circuit breakers for power accessories are located in the fuse block, convenience center and/or relay centers. They protect the following circuits; rear window defogger, power windows, power seats and power door locks, alarm systems, keyless entry, sunroofs, etc. if equipped.

Fusible Links

All models are equipped with fusible links which attach to the lower ends of main feed wires and connect at the battery or starter solenoid. The fusible links are like fuses because they are both a 1 time circuit protection device. All fusible links are four wire gauge sizes smaller than the circuit in which they are intended to protect. When the circuit has an overload the fusible link will melt and create an open in that circuit thus cutting of the power to the overloaded circuit.

Not all fusible link open circuits can be detected by observation. Always inspect that there is battery voltage passing through the fusible link to verify continuity.

The same wire size fusible link must be used when replacing a blown fusible link. Fusible links are available with two types of insulation; Hypalon and Silicone. Service fusible links made with Hypalon insulation, must be replaced with the same Hypalon insulated wire. Fusible links with Silicone insulation can use either insulation.

NOTE: Never make a fusible link longer than 9 in. (228mm) for it will not provide sufficient overload protection.

To replace a damaged fusible link, cut it off beyond the splice. Replace with a repair link. When connecting the repair link, strip the wire and use staking type pliers to crimp the splice securely in two places.

Fusible Links are located at the battery junction block, starter solenoid, alternator and the battery. On some models there are fusible links located at the EST distributor to protect the computer command control system. Some of the other important circuits that may be protected with a fusible link are, the electronic control module (ECM), fuse block, charging systems, fuel injectors, A/C systems, heater blower motors, headlights and other computers and sensors through out the vehicle. Never replace fusible link wire with standard wire, always use wire with hypalon insulation and make sure it is the same gauge as the original wire.

Relay, Sensors And Computer Locations

NOTE: When using this section, some of the components may not be used on a particular vehicle. This is because the particular component in question was used on an earlier model or a later model. If a component is not found in this section, check other vehicles of the same body line, as that component may have been introduced earlier on different models. This section is being published from the latest information available at the time of this publication.

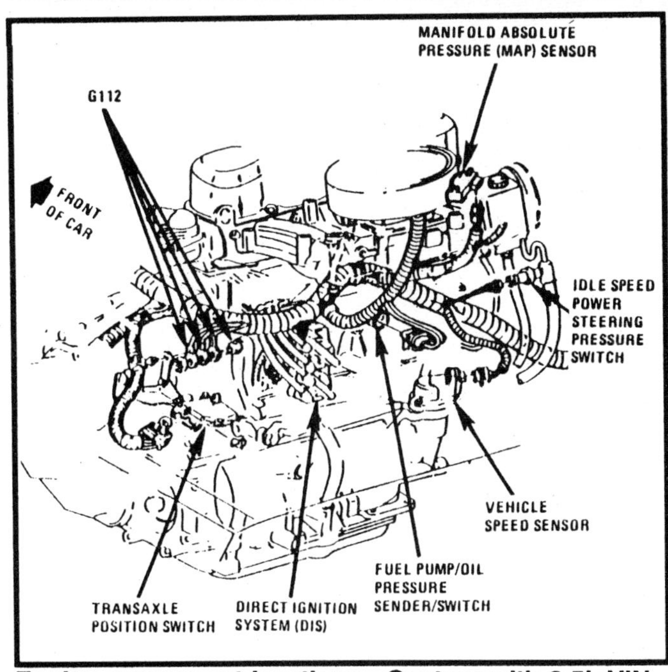

Engine component locations—Century with 2.5L VIN R engine

CENTURY

- **A/C Compressor Control Relay**—is located on the right hand front corner of the engine compartment.
- **A/C Defrost Vacuum Motor**—is located behind the instrument panel, on top of the plenum.
- **A/C Diode (VIN N)**—is at the right front of the engine, below the air conditioning compressor.
- **A/C Diode (VIN R)**—is in the connector or below the alternator.
- **A/C Diode (VIN W)**—is located in the A/C compressor clutch connector.
- **A/C Heater Vacuum Motor**—is located behind the instrument panel, on the right hand side of the plenum.
- **A/C High Pressure Cutoff Switch**—is in the rear of the air conditioning compressor.
- **A/C Low Pressure Cutoff Switch**—is in the rear of the air conditioning compressor.
- **A/C Pressure Cycling Switch**—is located on the firewall near the accumulator.
- **Antenna Relay (1989)**—is located under the instrument panel, behind the glove box.
- **Antenna Relay (except 1989)**—is located in the front fender, on the rail assembly.
- **Assembly Line Diagnostic Link (ALDL) Connector**—is located in the center of the instrument panel, underneath the steering column.
- **Audio Alarm Module**—is located under the left side of the instrument panel, in the convenience center.

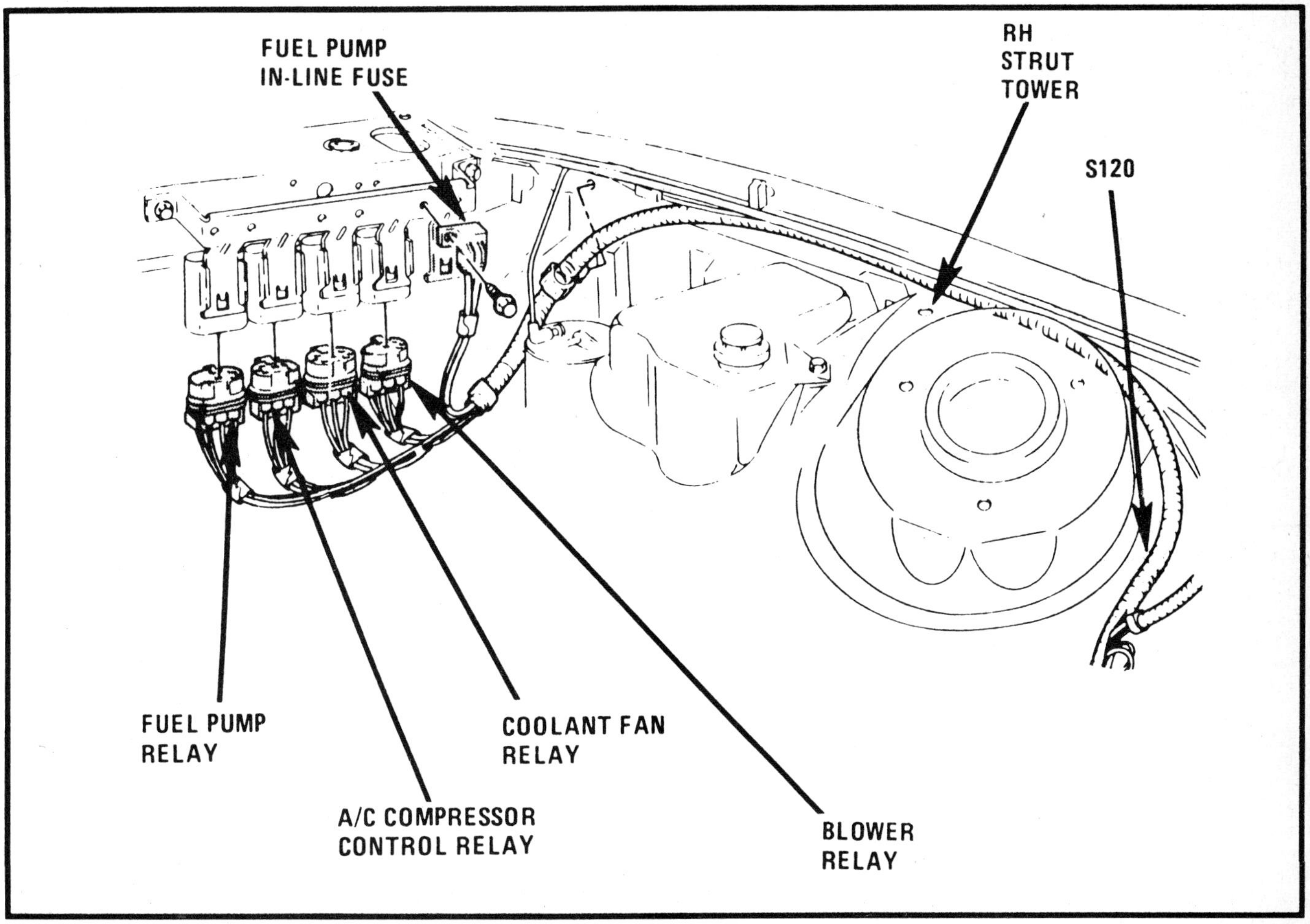

FUEL PUMP IN-LINE FUSE
RH STRUT TOWER
S120
FUEL PUMP RELAY
COOLANT FAN RELAY
A/C COMPRESSOR CONTROL RELAY
BLOWER RELAY

Relay locations—Century with 2.5L VIN R engine

• **Automatic Transaxle Selector Switch**—is located on the top left hand side of the transaxle.

• **Battery Junction Block**—is located at the right front of the engine compartment, at the relay bracket.

• **Blower Relay**—is located on the relay bracket, at the right front of the engine compartment.

• **Blower Resistors**—is located in the module on the right hand side of the firewall.

• **Brake Pressure Switch**—is located on the left side of the master cylinder.

• **Buzzer Module**—is located in the convenience center.

• **Chime Module (alarm module)**—is in the convenience center.

• **Computer Controlled Coil Ignition (CCCI) Module (VIN N)**—is located at the lower right front of the engine.

• **Convenience Center**—is located behind the instrument panel, to the left of the steering column.

• **Coolant Fan Pressure Switch (VIN W)**—is located on the right hand front of the engine, to the left of the compressor.

• **Coolant Fan Relay (VIN N)**—is located in the right hand front of the engine compartment on a bracket.

• **Coolant Fan Relay (VIN R)**—is located in front of the left front shock tower.

• **Coolant Fan Relay (VIN W)**—is located in the right hand front of the engine compartment on a bracket.

• **Coolant Temperature Fan Switch (VIN R)**—is located on the top left side of the engine, to the left of the valve cover.

• **Coolant Temperature Sensor (VIN N)**—is at the top right side of the engine, below the alternator.

• **Coolant Temperature Sensor (VIN R)**—is located on the left hand side of the engine, below the coolant outlet.

• **Coolant Temperature Sensor (VIN W)**—is located on the top of the engine, to the left of the throttle body.

• **Coolant Temperature Switch (VIN R)**—is located on the left hand side of the engine, near the coolant outlet.

• **Coolant Temperature Switch (VIN W)**—is located on the left rear of the engine, to the left of the valve cover.

• **Crankshaft Sensor (VIN N)**—is located at the right side of the engine, behind the air conditioning compressor.

• **Crankshaft Sensor (VIN W)**—is located on the rear of the engine, below the exhaust manifold.

• **Cruise Control Check Valve (VIN R)**—is located above the blower module on the center of the firewall.

• **Cruise Control Check Valve (VIN W)**—is located behind the engine, on the center of the firewall.

• **Cruise Control Module**—is located above the accelerator pedal, under the instrument panel.

• **Cruise Control Servo**—is located in front of the left front shock tower, on the fender apron.

• **Daytime Running Lights (DRL) Module**—is behind the center of the instrument panel, near the turn signal flasher.

• **Detonation (Knock) Sensor (VIN N)**—is located at the lower right side of the engine.

• **Detonation (Knock) Sensor (VIN W)**—is located on the right hand rear of the engine, below the exhaust manifold.

• **Diode Assembly**—is mounted at the center of the engine compartment, above the air conditioning module.

• **Door Lock Relay Assembly (1989)**—is located under the instrument panel, to the right of the glove box.

• **Door Lock Relay Assembly (except 1989)**—is located under the instrument panel, on right shroud.

• **EGR Solenoid Valve**—is located on a bracket, above the left side of the valve cover, if so equipped.

• **Electronic Control Module (ECM)**—is located under the right side of the instrument panel, behind the glove box.

• **Electronic Control Module (VIN R)**—is located under the right side of the instrument panel, to the right of the glove box.

• **Electronic Level Control Height Sensor**—is located on the frame under the rear of the vehicle.

• **Electronic Level Control Relay**—is located on the frame behind the left rear wheel well.

• **Fuel Pump In-Line Fuse (VIN N)**—is located in the right hand front of the engine compartment on the relay bracket.

• **Fuel Pump In-Line Fuse (VIN R)**—is located in the right hand front of the engine compartment on the relay bracket, if equipped.

• **Fuel Pump In-Line Fuse (VIN W)**—is located in the right hand front of the engine compartment on a bracket.

• **Fuel Pump Prime Connector (VIN N)**—is at the left rear of the engine compartment, near the C100 connector.

• **Fuel Pump Prime Connector (VIN R)**—is clipped to the EFI harness ahead of the transaxle.

• **Fuel Pump Prime Connector (VIN W)**—is located near the grommet on the left hand side of the firewall.

• **Fuel Pump Relay (VIN N)**—is at the right front of the engine compartment, on the relay bracket.

• **Fuel Pump Relay (VIN R)**—is located in the relay bracket on the right side of the firewall.

• **Fuel Pump Relay (VIN W)**—is located in the right hand front of the engine compartment on a bracket.

• **Fuel Pump/Oil Pressure Sender (VIN R)**—is at the rear of the engine, to the right of the direct ignition system.

• **Fuel Pump/Oil Pressure Switch (VIN N)**—is at the lower right rear of the engine.

• **Fusible Links**—are located at the battery junction block, starter solenoid and the battery.

• **Hazard Flasher/Relay**—is located in the convenience center.

• **Heater Water Valve Vacuum Motor**—is located behind the center of the engine.

• **High Speed Coolant Fan Relay**—is located on the left front side of the engine, if so equipped.

• **Horn Relay**—is located under the instrument panel, in the convenience center.

• **Idle Air Control Motor (VIN N)**—is on the top left of the engine, behind the throttle body.

• **Idle Air Control Stepper Motor**—is located behind the left side of the throttle body assembly.

• **Idle Air Control Valve (VIN W)**—is located on the top of the engine, in front of the throttle body.

• **Idle Speed Power Steering Pressure Switch (VIN N)**—is located at the lower right rear of the engine, in the power steering hydraulic line.

• **Low Coolant Module**—is located behind the instrument panel, to the left of the steering column.

• **Low Coolant Probe**—is located in the right rear side of the radiator.

• **Low Speed Coolant Fan Relay**—is located near the battery, on the left side of the radiator shroud, if so equipped.

• **Manifold Air Pressure Sensor (VIN R)**—is located on the top of the engine, on the right side of the air cleaner assembly.

• **Manifold Air Pressure Sensor (VIN W)**—is located behind the right front shock tower, near the firewall.

• **Manifold Air Temperature Sensor (VIN R)**—is located on the rear of the engine, in the intake manifold.

• **Mass Air Flow (MAF) Sensor (VIN N)**—is at the top left of the engine, above the throttle body.

• **Mass Air Flow In-Line Fuse (VIN W)**—is located on a bracket on the left front shock tower.

• **Mass Air Flow Relay (VIN W)**—is located on a bracket on the left front shock tower.

• **Mass Air Flow Sensor (VIN W)**—is located on the left hand side of the engine, in the air intake duct.

• **Oil Pressure Switch (VIN R)**—is located on the rear of the engine, below the exhaust manifold.

• **Oil Pressure Switch (VIN W)**—is located on the left front of the engine, below the direct ignition system.

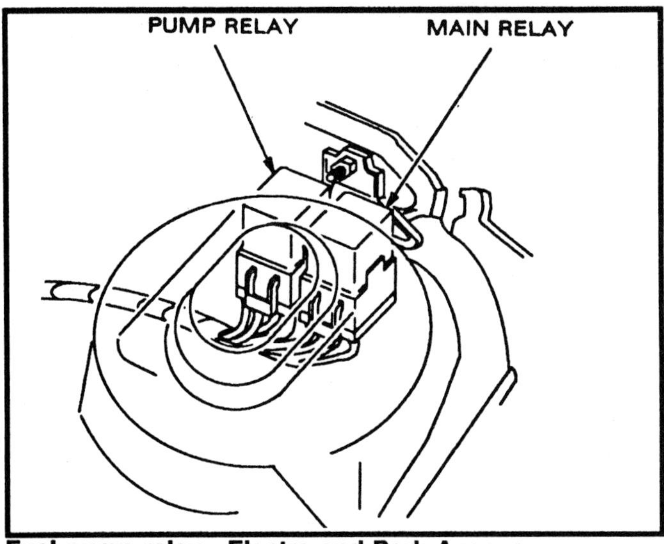

Fuel pump relay—Electra and Park Avenue

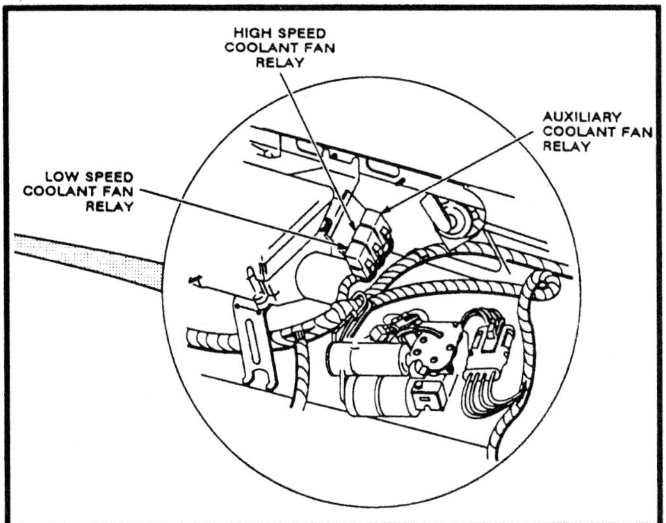

Coolant fan relay—Electra and Park Avenue

• **Oxygen Sensor (except VIN R)**—is located in the rear of the engine, in the base of the exhaust manifold. This location may vary in the exhaust manifold.

• **Oxygen Sensor (VIN R)**—is located in the front of the engine, in the bottom of the exhaust manifold.

• **Passive Restraint Control Module**—is located on the right shroud.

• **Photoresistor**—is mounted at the top center of the dash, above the radio.

• **Position EGR Solenoid**—is located on the top rear of the engine.

• **Power Steering Cutout Switch**—is located on the bottom of the steering rack.

• **Power Steering Pressure Switch (VIN R)**—is located at the right rear side of the engine.

• **Purge Solenoid Valve**—is located in the right hand front side of the engine compartment, on the canister.

• **Rear Wiper Relay**—is located in the top center of the tailgate, if so equipped.

• **Recirculating/Outside Air Vacuum Motor**—is located behind the instrument panel in the right side of the plenum.

• **Release Relay**—is behind the right side of the instrument panel, above the fuse box.

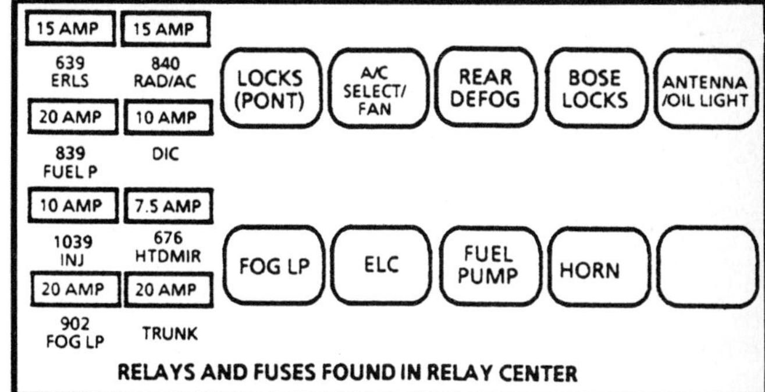

Fuses and Relays in Relay Center—Electra, Park Avenue and LeSabre

• **Remote Dimmer Module**—is located behind the left side of the instrument panel, near the shroud.

• **Remote Keyless Entry (RKE) Module**—is at the center of the luggage compartment, near the wheelhouse.

• **Remote Power Headlight Unit**—is located behind the instrument panel, to the left of the steering column.

• **Seat Belt In-Line Fuse**—is behind the right side of the instrument panel, near the fuse box.

• **Seat Capacitor A**—is located under the left front seat, in the harness. The capacitor is connected between the main power to switches and ground.

• **Seat Capacitors**—are under the respective front seat in the connector harness.

• **Sentinel Amplifier**—is located under the center of the instrument panel, behind the ashtray.

• **Sentinel Photocell**—is located on the top left side of the instrument panel, in the end of the defrost grill.

• **Starter Interrupt Relay**—is taped to the instrument panel harness, above the right side ashtray, if so equipped.

• **Steering and Electronics Module**—is at the underside of the steering column.

• **Tailgate Release Relay**—is located above the fuse block, under the right hand side of the instrument panel.

• **Tailgate Release Solenoid**—is located in the lower center of the tailgate.

• **Theft Deterrent Controller**—is located under the instrument panel, below the headlight switch, if so equipped.

• **Theft Deterrent Relay**—is strapped to the controller, under the instrument panel, if so equipped.

• **Throttle Position Sensor (except VIN R)**—is located on the top of the engine, on the front of the throttle body.

• **Throttle Position Sensor (VIN N)**—is on the front of the throttle body.

• **Throttle Position Sensor (VIN R)**—is located on the right hand front of the engine, in the right hand front of the throttle body.

• **Translator Module**—is at the underside of the steering column.

• **Turn Signal Flasher**—is located on a bracket above the accelerator pedal.

• **Vacuum Release Valve**—is located on the brake pedal support, under the instrument panel.

• **Vapor Canister Purge Solenoid**—is located at the front right corner of the engine compartment, on or near the canister.

• **Vehicle Speed Sensor Buffer**—is located under the left side of the instrument panel, behind the instrument cluster.

• **Vehicle Speed Sensor**—is connected to the rear center of the instrument cluster.

• **Water Heater Valve**—is located behind the center of the engine.

• **Wiper/Washer Motor Module**—is located on the left side of the firewall.

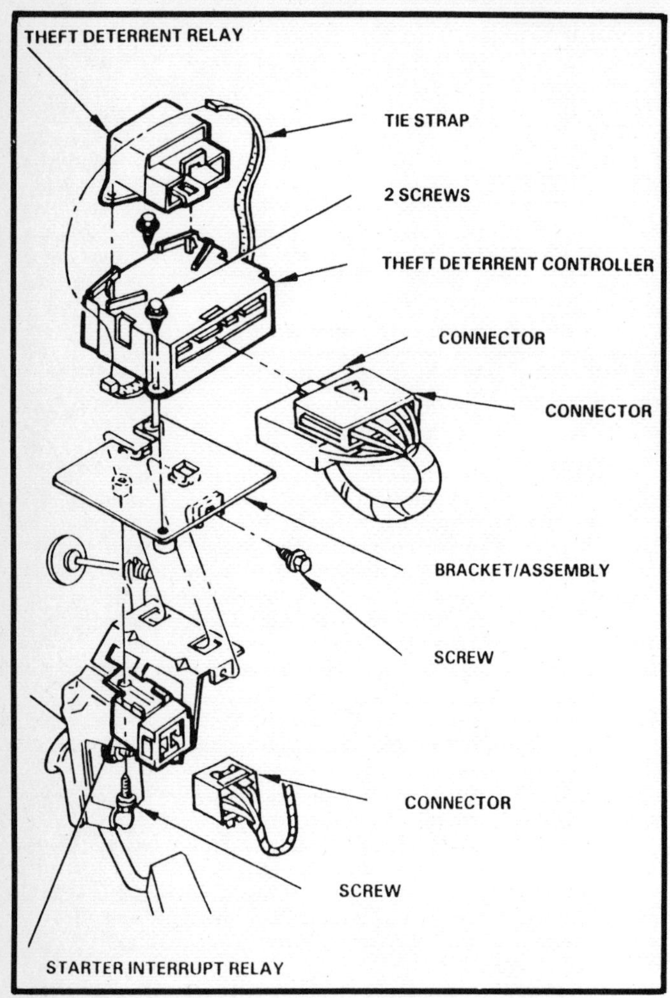

Theft deterrent components – Electra and Park Avenue

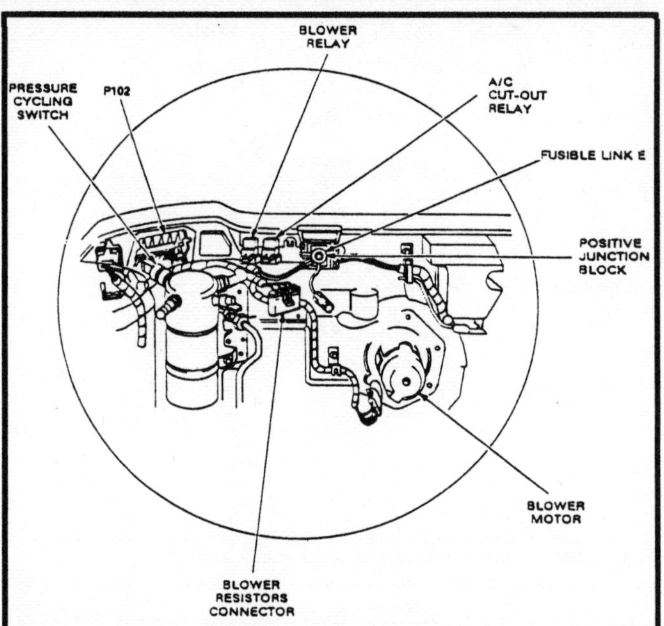

Heater and air conditioning components – Electra and Park Avenue

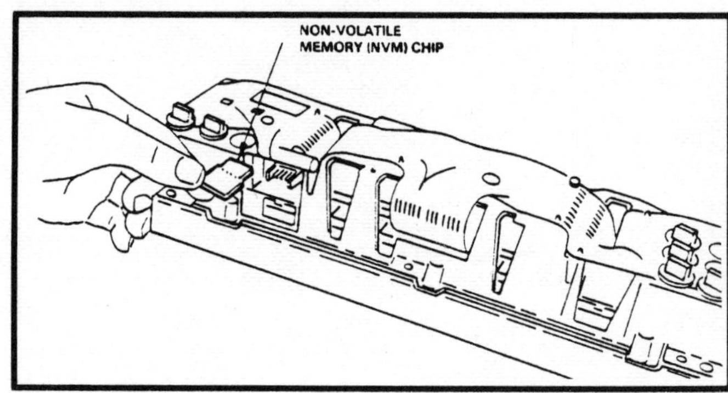

Non-Volatile memory chip – Electra and Park Avenue

ELECTRA AND PARK AVENUE

- **A/C Air Inlet Door Vacuum Motor** – is located behind the instrument panel, on the left hand side of the plenum.
- **A/C Ambient Sensor** – is located behind the radiator grill on the shroud support.
- **A/C Aspirator** – is located in the right hand side of the instrument panel, above the glove box.
- **A/C Compressor Clutch Diode** – is located in the connector at the rear of the compressor.
- **A/C Compressor Control Relay** – is located on the firewall.
- **A/C Compressor High Pressure Cutout Switch** – is located in the left hand end of the compressor.
- **A/C Compressor Low Pressure Cutout Switch** – is located near the right hand side shock tower, in the engine compartment.
- **A/C Constant Run Relay** – is located on the right side of the firewall in the engine compartment.
- **A/C Dual Pressure Switch** – is located in the pressure line, located in the right hand corner of the engine compartment.
- **A/C Heater Blower Control Module** – is located above the A/C module on the right side of the firewall in the engine compartment.
- **A/C Heater Blower Relay** – is located on the right side of the firewall in the engine compartment, above the A/C module.
- **A/C Heater Relay** – is located on the right side of the firewall in the engine compartment, if so equipped.
- **A/C Heater Resistors** – are located on the right side of the firewall in the engine compartment, in the top of the plenum.
- **A/C In-Car Sensor** – is located in the right hand side of the instrument panel, above the glove box.
- **A/C Mode Door Vacuum Motor** – is located behind the instrument panel, on the left hand side of the plenum.
- **A/C Vacuum Delay Porous Plug** – is located in the orange vacuum line, near the door motor.
- **Amplifier Relay** – is located under the right side of the dash panel, near the connector C201 or in the relay center.
- **Anti-Lock Brake Diode** – is located under the left hand side of the instrument panel.
- **Anti-Lock Brake Main Relay Fuse** – is located behind the left hand side shock tower on the firewall.
- **Anti-Lock Brake Main Relay** – is located behind the left hand side shock tower on the firewall.
- **Anti-Lock Brake Main Valve** – is located in the on the brake master cylinder.
- **Anti-Lock Brake Pressure Switch** – is located in the on the brake master cylinder.

• **Anti-Lock Brake Pump Fuse** – is located behind the left hand side shock tower on the firewall.

• **Anti-Lock Brake Pump Motor** – is located in the on the brake master cylinder.

• **Anti-Lock Brake Tooth Sensor Ring** – is located on the inner side of the wheels.

• **Anti-Lock Brake Valve Block** – is located in the on the brake master cylinder.

• **Anti-Lock Brake Wheel Speed Sensors** – is located on the respective brake assembly at each wheel.

• **Assembly Line Diagnostic Link (ALDL) Connector** – is located under the left side of the dash panel, to the right of the steering column.

• **Automatic Door Lock Controller** – is located behind the right side of the dash, on connector C201.

• **Automatic Door Lock Diode** – is located behind the right side of the dash panel, in the connector near C201.

• **Blower Relay** – is located above the A/C module on the firewall.

• **Brake Fluid Level Sensor** – is located in the on the brake master cylinder.

• **Brake Warning System Diode** – is located in the instrument panel wiring harness under the right side of the dash panel, to the right of the plenum, if so equipped.

• **Camshaft Sensor** – is located on the right side of the engine, above the crank pulley.

• **Canister Purge Solenoid** – is located on the canister in the left hand front corner of the engine compartment.

• **Cellular Mobile Phone Transceiver** – is located on the left hand rear side of the trunk.

• **Computer Controlled Coil Ignition (CCCI) Module** – is located on the rear of the engine, on top of the valve cover. The ignition module is at the base of the coil assembly.

• **Coolant Fan Switch** – is located on the top right hand side of the engine and to the left of the alternator.

• **Coolant Temperature Sensor** – is located on the top right hand side of the engine, to the left of the alternator.

• **Cooling Fan Diode** – is taped to the harness in the left hand front corner of the engine compartment, below the coolant relays.

• **Crankshaft Sensor** – is located on the right hand side of the engine, near the crank pulley.

• **Cruise Control Brake/Switch** – is located above the brake pedal on the brake pedal support bracket.

• **Cruise Control Module** – is located above the accelerator pedal.

• **Cruise Control Servo** – is located on the left hand side of the engine, above the transaxle cover.

• **CTS** – See Coolant Temperature Sensor.

• **Decoder Module** – is located under the right side of the instrument panel.

• **Defogger Relay** – is located under the center of the dash panel, below the A/C control head.

• **Defroster Vacuum Motor** – is located under the instrument panel, to the left hand side of the plenum.

• **Detonation Sensor** – is located on the top left hand side of the engine, near the air intake duct.

• **Electronic Brake Control Module (ECM)** – is located behind the left hand side of the instrument panel.

• **Electronic Climate Control Programmer (EEC)** – is located under the right side of the dash panel, on the right side of the plenum.

• **Electronic Control Module (ECM)** – is located behind the right side of the instrument panel.

• **Electronic Level Control Compressor** – is located in the engine compartment, in front of the left wheelwell.

• **Electronic Level Control Diode** – is located in the instrument panel wiring harness, behind the radio.

• **Electronic Level Control Height Sensor** – is located on the frame, above the right hand rear lower suspension arm.

• **Electronic Level Control Relay** – is located on a bracket to the left of the level control compressor.

• **Electronic Level Control Test Connector** – is tape to the hose, neat the ELC compressor.

• **Electronic Spark Control Module (ESC)** – is located on the center of the firewall in the engine compartment.

• **Electronic Tune Radio Diode** – is located in the instrument panel wiring harness, behind the radio.

• **Electronic Vacuum Regulator Valve** – is located on the top of the engine, in front of the rear valve cover.

• **Fiber Optic Light Source** – are located one in each door, if so equipped.

• **Fuel Door Release Solenoid** – is located in the trunk, above the left hand wheel well.

• **Fuel Pump Fuse** – is located behind the shock tower on the left hand side of the firewall.

• **Fuel Pump Prime Connector** – is located in the engine compartment, near the right hand fender apron.

• **Fuel Pump Relay** – is located behind the shock tower on the left hand side of the firewall.

• **Gear Selector Switch** – is located on the left hand side of the transaxle.

• **Hazard Flasher Relay** – is located behind the instrument panel, on the right side of the steering column brace.

• **Headlight Washer Relay** – is located on the fluid reservoir on the front of the right front shock tower, if so equipped.

• **Heavy Duty Coolant Fan Relay** – is located on the left hand side of the engine compartment on the fender apron.

• **High Mount Stop Light Relays** – are located on the left rear wheelwell inside the trunk, if so equipped.

• **High Speed Coolant Fan Relay** – is located on the left hand side of the engine compartment on the fender apron.

• **Horn Relay** – is located under the left side of the dash panel, to the left of the steering column.

• **Idle Air Control Valve** – is located on the top of the engine, near the intake air duct.

• **Illuminated Entry Timer** – is located behind the right side of the dash, behind the glove compartment.

• **Instrument Panel Inverter** – is located behind the right hand side of the instrument panel trim, above the glove box.

• **Key Pad Module** – is located in the driver's door, near the door lock motor.

• **Keyless Entry Diode** – is located behind the right side of the dash panel, near connector C201.

• **Keyless Entry Module (1989)** – is located in the trunk, above the rear wheel well.

• **Keyless Entry Module (except 1989)** – is located above the glove compartment.

• **Low Brake Vacuum Relay** – is located behind the right side of the dash near connector C201, if so equipped.

• **Low Speed Coolant Fan Relay** – is located on the fender apron in the left hand side of the engine compartment.

• **Manifold Air Temperature (MAT) Sensor** – is located on the left hand side of the engine, in the air intake duct.

• **Mass Air Flow (MAF) Sensor** – is located on the left side of the engine, in the air intake duct.

• **MAT Sensor** – See Manifold Air Temperature Sensor.

• **Memory Disable Relay** – is located behind the right side of the dash near connector C201, if so equipped.

• **Multi-Function Chime Module** – is located behind the right side of the dash trim, above the glove box.

• **Non-Volatile Memory (NVM) Chip** – is located in the instrument cluster assembly.

• **Oil Light Relay** – is located on the right side of the firewall in the engine compartment.

• **Oil Pressure Switch** – is located on the lower right side of the engine.

• **Oxygen Sensor** – is located in the rear of the engine, in the base of the exhaust manifold.

• **Power Antenna Relay**—is located in the right side of the trunk, near the antenna motor.

• **Power Door Lock Relay (1989)**—is located behind the right side of the dash panel, on the top right side of connector C201.

• **Power Door Relay Assembly (except 1989)**—is located behind the right side of the dash panel, to the right of connector C201.

• **Power Door Unlock Relay (1989)**—is located behind the right side of the dash panel, to the right of connector C201.

• **Power Seat Diode**—is located in the connector at the front of each seat, if so equipped.

• **Power Seat Memory Module**—is under the left side of the driver's seat.

• **Power Seat Recliner Capacitor**—is located in the connector at the front of each seat, if so equipped.

• **Power Seat Relay**—is located on the lower seat rail under the seat, if so equipped.

• **Power Steering Cutout Switch**—is located in the steering gear assembly.

• **Power Window Circuit Breaker**—is located in the fuse block.

• **Recirculating/Outside Air Vacuum Motor**—is located behind the instrument panel in the left side of the plenum.

• **Select Switch Relay**—is located behind the right side of the dash panel, on the bottom of connector C201, if so equipped.

• **Sentinel Amplifier (1989)**—is located under the center of the instrument panel, to the right of the steering column.

• **Sentinel Control**—is located under the left hand side of the instrument panel, near the light switch.

• **Sentinel Photocell**—is located on the top left side of the instrument panel, in the end of the speaker grill.

• **Sentinel/Daytime Running Lights Module (except 1989)**—is located under the center of the instrument panel, to the right of the steering column.

• **Starter Interrupt Relay (1989)**—is located on a bracket under the left side of the dash panel, to the left of the steering column.

• **Starter Interrupt Relay (except 1989)**—is located on a bracket under the theft controller.

• **Sunroof Limit Switch**—is located in the left hand side of the windshield header.

• **Sunroof Module**—is located in the left hand front roof rail, near pillar A.

• **TCC Brake Switch**—is located above the brake pedal on the brake pedal support.

• **Theft Deterrent Controller**—is located under the left side of the dash panel, to the left of the steering column.

• **Theft Deterrent Diode**—is taped to the instrument panel wiring harness under the right side of the dash panel, in a connector near the right hand shroud.

• **Theft Deterrent Relay (1989)**—is located behind a bracket under the left side of the instrument panel.

• **Theft Deterrent Relay (except 1989)**—is located on the theft controller.

• **Throttle Position Sensor**—is located on the left hand side of the engine, near the throttle body.

• **Timer/Flasher Module**—is located behind the left hand side of the instrument panel, near the grommet.

• **Torque Converter Clutch Controller**—is located on the right side of the firewall in the engine compartment, if so equipped.

• **TPS**—See Throttle Position Sensor.

• **Trunk Lid Tamper Switch**—is located on the under side of the trunk lid.

• **Trunk Pull-Down In-Line Fuse**—is located near the latch at the center of the trunk lid.

• **Trunk Pull-Down Unit**—is located near the latch at the center of the trunk lid.

• **Trunk Release Solenoid**—is located on the under side of the trunk lid, near the latch.

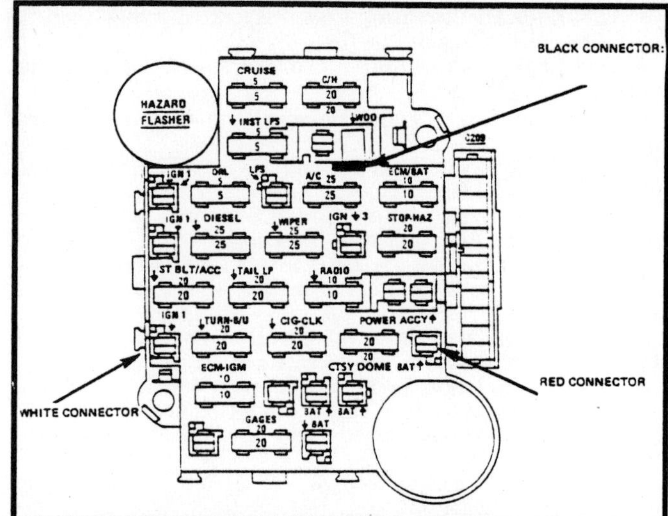

Fuse box identification—Estate Wagon

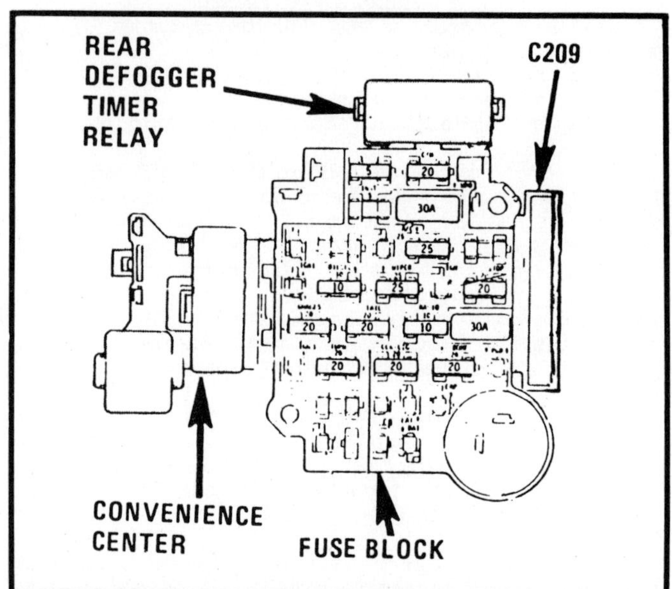

Defogger and convenience center location—Estate Wagon

• **Turn Signal Flasher**—is located under the instrument panel, on the left side of the steering column brace.

• **Vacuum Release Valve**—is located on the brake pedal support, under the instrument panel.

• **Vehicle Speed Sensor Buffer**—is located under the right side of the dash panel, on the right side of the plenum.

• **Vehicle Speed Sensor**—is located at the rear of the engine, on the right hand side of the transaxle.

• **Wiper/Washer Fluid Level Switch**—is located on the washer reservoir.

• **Wiper/Washer Motor Module**—is located on the left side of the firewall.

ESTATE WAGON

• **A/C Actuator Air Inlet Valve**—is located under the instrument panel, on the right hand side of the A/C plenum.

• **A/C Actuator Defrost Valve**—is located under the instrument panel, on the right hand side of the A/C plenum.

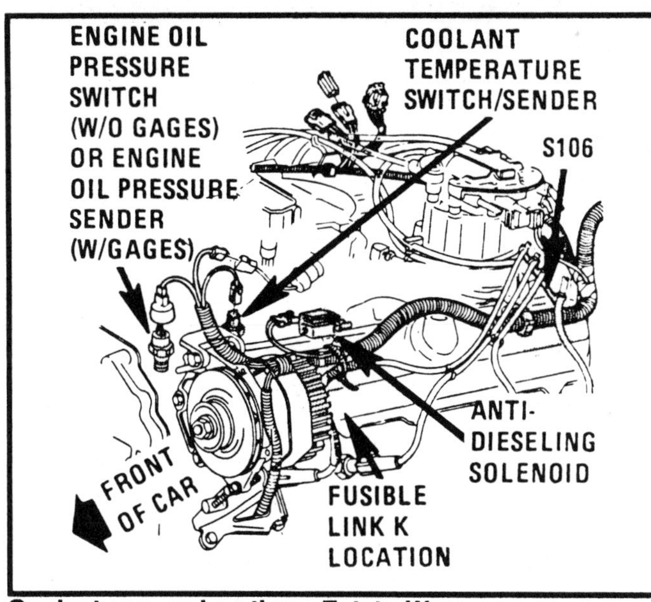

Coolant sensor location—Estate Wagon

- **A/C Actuator Lower Diverter Valve**—is located under the instrument panel, on the right hand side of the A/C plenum.
- **A/C Actuator Upper Diverter Valve**—is located under the instrument panel, on the right hand side of the A/C plenum.
- **A/C Ambient Temperature Sensor**—is located in the right hand air inlet, below the screen.
- **A/C Clutch and Blower Control Module**—is located on the blower module.
- **A/C Compressor Clutch Diode**—is taped inside the A/C compressor clutch connector.
- **A/C Compressor Cutout Relay**—is located on the right hand side of the firewall.
- **A/C Defroster Vacuum Motor**—is located under the instrument panel, on the lower edge of the A/C plenum.
- **A/C Heater Blower Relay**—is located on the right side of the firewall in the engine compartment, near the blower motor.
- **A/C Heater Blower Resistors**—are located on the right side of the firewall in the engine compartment, beside the blower motor.
- **A/C Heater Water Valve Vacuum Motor**—is located behind the rear of the engine, on the heater/water valve.
- **A/C In-Car Sensor**—is located in the upper instrument panel trim, to the left of the right hand speaker.
- **A/C Lower Mode Vacuum Motor**—is located under the instrument panel, on the left side of the A/C plenum.
- **A/C Pressure Cycling Switch**—is located on the right side of firewall in the engine compartment, on the accumulator.
- **A/C Recirculating/Outside Air Vacuum Motor**—is located behind the instrument panel and is a part of the A/C plenum.
- **A/C Upper Mode Vacuum Motor**—is located under the instrument panel, on the left side of the A/C plenum.
- **AIR Diverter Valve**—is located on the rear of the air pump.
- **AIR Select Switching Valve**—is located on the behind the air pump.
- **Alternator Diode**—is located in the engine wiring harness, near the distributor.
- **Anti-Dieseling Solenoid**—is located in the engine harness, in front of the left hand side of the engine on the valve cover.
- **Automatic Door Lock Controller**—is attached to the upper right hand shroud.
- **Barometric Pressure Sensor**—is located below the right hand side of the instrument panel and the kick panel.
- **Brake Pressure Switch**—is located below the master cylinder on the firewall.
- **CB Transceiver**—is located behind the instrument panel, above the radio.
- **Convenience Center**—is located on the left hand side of the fuse block.
- **Coolant Temperature Sensor**—is located on the top front of the engine on the manifold.
- **Coolant Temperature Switch**—is located on the top left hand front of the engine on the manifold.
- **Cruise Control Brake/Switch**—is located above the brake pedal on the brake pedal support bracket.
- **Cruise Control Module**—is located under the instrument panel, to the left of the steering column.
- **Cruise Control Servo**—is located on the left hand front side of the engine.
- **Daytime Running Lights (DRL) Module**—is located behind the instrument panel, on the right side of the steering column.
- **Defogger Timer Relay**—is on the top of the fuse box.
- **Diagnostic Dwell Meter Connector (VIN Y)**—is taped to the engine harness, near the carburetor.
- **Dropping Resistor (DRL)**—is located behind the instrument panel, on the right side of the steering column.
- **Electronic Control Module (ECM)**—is located below the right side of the instrument panel, at the shroud.
- **Electronic Level Control Compressor**—is located in the engine compartment, in front of the left hand wheel well.
- **Electronic Level Control Diode**—is located in the instrument panel wiring harness, behind the radio, if so equipped.
- **Electronic Level Control Height Sensor**—is located under the left hand rear of the vehicle.
- **Electronic Level Control Relay**—is located on the left hand front fender, near or behind the battery.
- **Electronic Level Control Test Connector**—is tape to the hose, next the ELC compressor, if so equipped.
- **Fiber Optic Light Source**—is taped to the wiring harness, above the radio.
- **Fuse Box**—is behind the left side of the instrument panel, near the shroud.
- **Gear Selector Switch**—is located on the lower part of the steering column.
- **Hazard Flasher/Relay**—is located in the fuse block.
- **Heater/Water Valve**—is located behind the rear of the engine in the top of the engine block.
- **Horn Relay**—is located in the convenience center.
- **Ignition Switch**—is located at the base of the steering column.
- **Illuminated Entry Timer**—is behind the left side of the instrument panel, on the left side of the steering column.
- **Illuminated Entry Timer**—is located on the upper left hand shroud, behind the right hand side of the instrument panel, on the instrument panel support.
- **Light Driver Module**—is taped to the wiring harness, above the glove box.
- **Low Coolant Probe**—is in the right rear of the radiator.
- **Multi-Function Chime Module**—is located behind the left side of the instrument panel, to the right of the steering column.
- **Oil Pressure Sender**—is located on the top right side of the engine.
- **Oil Pressure Switch**—is located on the top right side of the engine.
- **Oxygen Sensor**—is located in the rear of the engine, in the top right hand rear of the exhaust manifold.
- **Power Antenna Relay**—is located behind the right hand side of the instrument panel.
- **Power Door Lock Relay Assembly**—is located in the upper right hand shroud near the lower access hole.

• **Power Master Brake Relay**—is located below the master cylinder, which is located on the firewall.

• **Power Seat Recliner Motor**—is located under the inner side of the seat.

• **Power Seat Relay**—is located under the seats.

• **Sentinel Amplifier**—is located under the right hand side of the instrument panel, on the instrument panel support.

• **Sentinel Photocell**—is located on the top left side of the instrument panel, in the end of the speaker grill.

• **Tailgate Ajar Switch**—is located inside the lower right hand corner of the tailgate assembly.

• **Tailgate Block Out Switch**—is located in the upper right hand corner of the tailgate.

• **Tailgate Lock Relay Assembly**—is located in the upper right hand shroud near the lower access hole.

• **Throttle Position Sensor**—is located in front of the carburetor, or throttle body.

• **Timer Module**—is behind the left side of the instrument panel, on the right side of the steering column.

• **Triple Solenoid Assembly**—is located on the rear of the left hand valve cover.

• **Turn Signal Flasher**—is located in the fuse box.

• **Twilight Sentinel Amplifier**—is behind the instrument panel, on the panel support bracket.

• **Twilight Sentinel Control**—is on the left side of the instrument panel, near the headlight switch.

• **Twilight Sentinel Photocell**—is on the top left side of the instrument panel.

• **Vacuum Release Valve**—is located on the brake pedal support, under the instrument panel.

• **Vehicle Speed Sensor Buffer**—is located under the left side of the instrument panel, to the right of the light switch.

• **Vehicle Speed Sensor**—is located at the top of the right hand the right hand front wheel well.

• **Wiper/Washer Fluid Level Switch**—is located on the washer reservoir.

• **Wiper/Washer Pulse Timer Relay**—is incorporated into the wiper/washer assembly.

• **Wiper/Washer Ratchet Release Solenoid Diode**—is taped to the inside of the wiper/washer connector.

• **Wiper/Washer Relay Diode**—is taped to the inside of the wiper/washer connector.

LE SABRE

• **A/C Ambient Temperature Sensor**—is located in the front of the vehicle, in front of the radiator.

• **A/C Aspirator**—is located behind the right hand side of the instrument panel.

• **A/C Blower Control Module**—is located on the front of the firewall, in the center of the A/C plenum.

• **A/C Blower Relay**—is located in the engine compartment at the center of the firewall, near the blower motor.

• **A/C Blower Resistors**—is located on the right side of the firewall, on the A/C module (plenum).

• **A/C Compressor Clutch Diode**—is taped to the inside compressor connector on the front of the compressor.

• **A/C Compressor Control Relay**—is located in the engine compartment at the center of the firewall, on a bracket.

• **A/C Coolant Fan Pressure Switch**—is located on the A/C line in the right hand front of the engine compartment.

• **A/C Defrost Valve Vacuum Actuator**—is located under the center of the instrument panel, on the left hand side of the A/C plenum.

• **A/C High Pressure Cutout Switch**—is located on the left end of the A/C compressor.

• **A/C In-Car Sensor**—is located near the glove box, under the right hand side of the instrument panel.

• **A/C In-Car Temperature Sensor**—is located at the top of the dash, near the speaker grille and photocell sensor.

• **A/C Mode Valve Vacuum Actuator**—is located under the center of the instrument panel, on the left hand side of the A/C plenum.

• **A/C Outside Air Valve Vacuum Actuator**—is located under the center of the instrument panel, on the left hand side of the A/C plenum.

• **A/C Pressure Cycling Switch**—is located on the right hand rear of the engine compartment, on the A/C line.

• **A/C Select Relay**—is located in the relay center, at position 'D'.

• **A/C Vacuum Delay Porous Plug**—is located under the instrument panel, in the orange vacuum line, on the left side of the A/C plenum.

• **A/C Vacuum Line Connector**—is located under the instrument panel, near the A/C-heater control assembly.

• **A/C-Heater Blower Resistors**—is located in the engine compartment on the center of the firewall, near the A/C module.

• **Anti-Lock Brake Controller In-Line Fuse**—is located behind the strut tower, in the left hand rear corner of the engine compartment.

• **Anti-Lock Brake Controller**—is located under the left hand side of the instrument panel, near the parking brake.

• **Anti-Lock Brake Diode**—is located behind the instrument panel, to the left of the steering column.

• **Anti-Lock Brake Main Relay**—is located behind the strut tower, in the left hand rear corner of the engine compartment.

• **Anti-Lock Brake Main Valve**—is located on the master cylinder, in the left hand front corner of the engine compartment.

• **Anti-Lock Brake Pump In-Line Fuse**—is located behind the strut tower, in the left hand front corner of the engine compartment.

• **Anti-Lock Brake Pump Relay**—is located behind the strut tower, in the left hand front corner of the engine compartment.

• **Anti-Lock Brake Valve Block**—is located below the master cylinder, in the left hand front corner of the engine compartment.

• **Anti-Lock Brake Wheel Speed Sensor**—is located in each wheel spindle.

• **Assembly Line Data Link Connector**—is located under the left side of the instrument panel, to the left of the steering panel.

• **Audio Alarm Module**—is located behind the right side of the instrument panel, above the glove box, if equipped.

• **Auxiliary Coolant Fan Relay**—is located on a bracket, coolant fan relay bracket.in the left front of the engine compartment, in front of the strut tower.

• **Brake Fluid Level Sensor**—is located on the left hand side of the engine compartment, in the front of the brake fluid reservoir.

• **Brake Fluid Level Switch**—is located on the left hand side of the firewall, in the brake fluid reservoir.

• **Brake Pressure Sensor**—is located on the left hand side of the engine compartment, below the master cylinder.

• **Camshaft Sensor**—is located on the lower right hand side of the engine, above the lower pulley.

• **Cellular Mobile Telephone Transceiver Assembly**—is located in the trunk compartment.

• **Chime Module**—is located behind the right hand side of the instrument panel.

• **Computer Controlled Coil Ignition Module (VIN C)**—is located on top right front of the engine.

• **Coolant Fan Diode**—is taped in the engine harness, behind the left hand fender well.

• **Coolant Fan Relay**—is located on a bracket, in the left hand front of the engine compartment, in front of the strut tower.

• **Coolant Temperature Sensor (VIN C)**—is located on the top left hand side of the engine.

• **Coolant Temperature Switch**—is located on the top right hand side of the engine, to the left of the alternator.
• **Crankshaft Sensor**—is located on the lower right hand side of the engine, above the lower pulley.
• **Cruise Control Brake/Switch**—is located above the brake pedal on the brake pedal support bracket.
• **Cruise Control Module**—is located under the left side of the instrument panel, above the accelerator pedal.
• **Cruise Control Servo**—is located at the left hand side of the engine, above the transaxle.
• **Cruise Control Vacuum Release Valve**—is located above the brake pedal on the brake pedal support bracket.
• **CTS**—See Coolant Temperature Sensor.
• **Decoder Module**—is located under the right side of the instrument panel.
• **Defogger Capacitor**—is located behind the rear seat, near the right hand rear quarter pillar.
• **Defogger Time Relay**—is located in the relay center.
• **Delco-Bose Music System In-Line Fuse**—is located near the right hand kick panel, under the instrument panel.
• **Delco-Music System Relay**—is located in the relay center.
• **Detonation (Knock) Sensor**—is located on the lower right side of the engine.
• **EGR Module (VIN C)**—is located on the top center of the engine.
• **Electronic Climate Control Programmer**—is located behind the right side of the instrument panel, to the left of the glove box.
• **Electronic Control Module (ECM) Resistor (VIN C)**—is located in the engine harness, behind the right hand side of the instrument panel, if so equipped.
• **Electronic Control Module (ECM)**—is located behind the right side of the instrument panel.
• **Electronic Level Control Compressor**—is located behind the headlights, in the left hand side of the engine compartment.
• **Electronic Level Control Height Sensor**—is located on the frame, above the rear crossmember.
• **Electronic Level Control Relay**—is located in the relay center, at position 'K'.
• **Electronic Level Control Test Connector**—is located in the engine compartment, near the ELC compressor.
• **Electronic Spark Control (ESC) Module**—is located on a relay bracket on the center of the firewall, in the engine compartment.
• **Electronic Vacuum Regulator Valve Module**—is located at the top center of the rear valve cover.
• **Fog Light Relay**—is located in the relay center, at position 'F'.
• **Fuel Door Release Solenoid**—is located in the left hand side of the trunk, above the wheel well, if so equipped.
• **Fuel Pump Prime Connector**—is taped to the wire harness, on the lower right hand side of the engine compartment, near the right wheelwell.
• **Fuel Pump Relay**—is located in the relay center.
• **Gear Selector Switch**—is located on the left hand side of the transaxle.
• **Hazard Relay**—is located on the right side of the steering column brace, behind the instrument panel.
• **Headlight Dimmer Switch**—is located on the left hand side of the steering column.
• **Heavy Duty Coolant Fan Relay**—is located on a bracket, in the left front of the engine compartment, in front of the strut tower.
• **High Speed Coolant Fan Relay**—is located on a bracket, in the left front of the engine compartment.
• **Horn Relay**—is located in the relay center, at position 'J'.
• **Idle Air Control Valve**—is located on the top left hand side of he engine.
• **Ignition Key Warning Switch**—is located in the top of the steering column, below the turn/hazard switch.
• **Ignition Switch**—is located behind the instrument panel, on the center of the steering column.
• **Keyless Entry Diode**—is behind the left side of the instrument panel, in the harness near the theft deterrent relay.
• **Low Coolant Sensor Assembly**—is located in the radiator, if so equipped.
• **Low Speed Coolant Fan Relay**—is located on a bracket, in the left front of the engine compartment, if so equipped.
• **Manifold Air Temperature (MAT) Sensor**—is located on the air intake duct, near the left side of the engine.
• **MAP Sensor**—See Manifold Absolute Pressure (MAP) Sensor.
• **Mass Airflow (MAF) Sensor**—is located in the air induction duct work, near the left of the engine.
• **MAT Sensor**—See Manifold Air Temperature Sensor.
• **Negative Junction Block**—is located ahead of the strut, on the right hand side of the engine compartment.
• **Oil Light Relay**—is located in the relay center.
• **Oil Pressure Sensor/Switch**—is located on the lower right hand rear of the engine.
• **Oxygen Sensor**—is located on the exhaust manifold.
• **Positive Junction Block**—is located on a bracket, on the right wheelwell.
• **Power Antenna Relay**—is located below the antenna mast, in the right side of the trunk compartment.
• **Power Door Lock Relay Assembly**—is located on the shroud, behind the right side of the instrument panel.
• **Power Steering Pressure Switch**—is located on the left hand rear of the engine, in the power steering line.
• **Relay Center**—is located under the right hand side of the instrument panel.
• **Seatbelt Lap Retractor Solenoids**—are located in the lower rear portion of the front doors.
• **Seatbelt Retractor Module**—is located at the right hand kick panel, under the instrument panel.
• **Seatbelt Retractor Module**—is located at the right hand kick panel, under the instrument panel.
• **Seatbelt Retractor Switches**—are located in the center rear of the front doors, at the latch assembly.
• **Seatbelt Shoulder Retractor Solenoids**—are located in the lower rear portion of the front doors.
• **Seatbelt Switch**—is part of the driver's seatbelt assembly.
• **Seatbelt Timer Module**—are located in the center of the front doors, if so equipped.
• **Sunroof Relay**—is located at the top center of the windshield header.
• **Theft Deterrent Controller**—is above the accelerator pedal.
• **Theft Deterrent Controller**—is located behind the left hand side of the instrument panel, above the accelerator.
• **Theft Deterrent Diode**—is located behind the left hand side of the instrument panel, taped to the harness.
• **Theft Deterrent Diode**—is taped in the harness behind the left side of the instrument panel.
• **Theft Deterrent Relay**—is above the accelerator pedal.
• **Theft Deterrent Relay**—is located behind the left hand side of the instrument panel, above the accelerator.
• **Throttle Position Sensor**—is located on the throttle body.
• **Torque Converter Clutch Brake Switch**—is located on the brake pedal support, under the instrument panel.
• **TPS**—See Throttle Position Sensor.
• **Transaxle Position Switch**—is located on the left hand rear of the engine, on top of the transaxle.
• **Trunk Lid Pull**—Down Unit—is located in the rear of the trunk at the striker plate, if so equipped.
• **Trunk Lid Release Solenoid**—is located on the underside of trunk lid, near the latch, if so equipped.

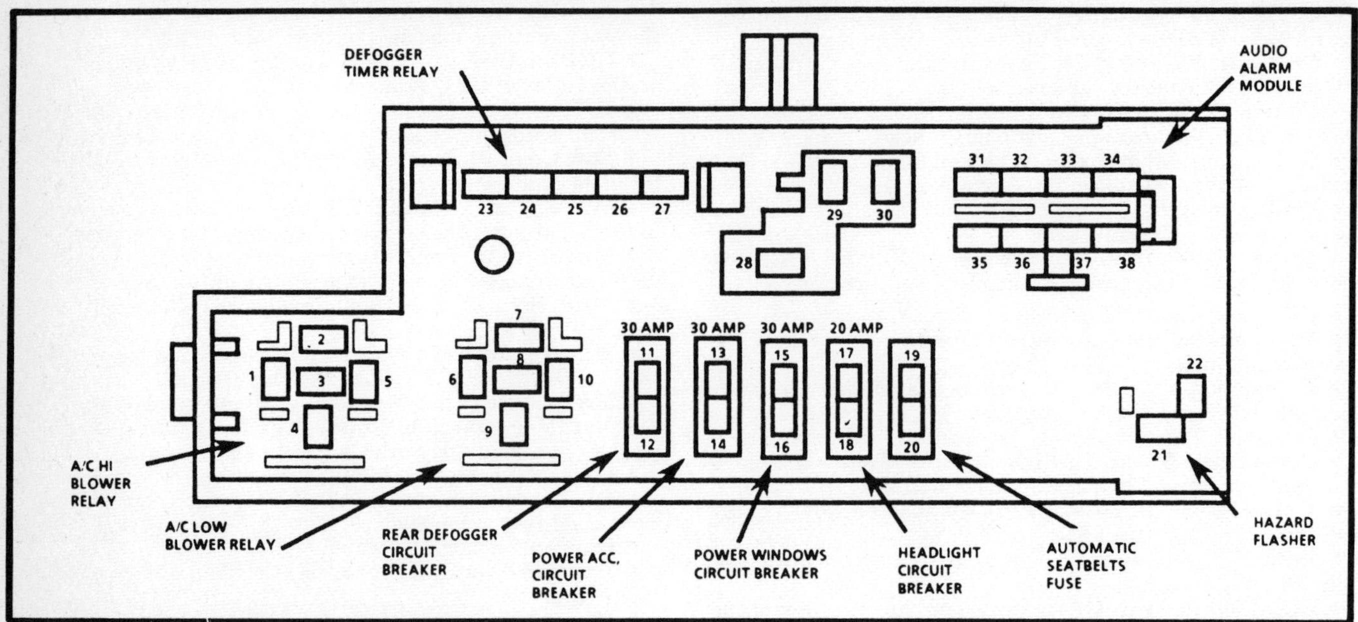

Component center identification – Regal

• **Turn Signal Relay** – is located at the left of the steering column, behind the instrument panel.

• **Vapor Canister Purge Solenoid** – is located in the left hand front corner of the engine compartment.

• **Vehicle Speed Sensor Buffer** – is located behind the right hand side of the instrument panel, on the right hand side of the A/C plenum.

• **Vehicle Speed Sensor** – is located on the right hand side of the transaxle.

• **Washer Motor Module** – is located on the right hand side the engine compartment, at the bottom of the washer reservoir.

• **Washer Pump Motor Diode** – is located in the washer motor connector.

• **Window Circuit Breaker** – is located at the top right corner of the fuse block.

• **Wiper Motor Module** – is located on the left hand corner of the firewall in the engine compartment.

• **Wiper Motor Relay Diode** – is located in the wiper motor connector, the relay is incorporated into the wiper module.

• **Wiper/Washer Fluid Level Sensor** – is located in the washer fluid reservoir.

REGAL

• **A/C Air Temperature Valve Motor** – is located behind the instrument panel, in the right hand side of the plenum.

• **A/C Bi-Level Valve Vacuum Actuator** – is located behind the instrument panel, on the right hand side of the A/C plenum.

• **A/C Compressor Clutch Diode** – is taped to the inside compressor connector on the front of the compressor.

• **A/C Defroster Vacuum Motor** – is located under the instrument panel, on the right side of the A/C plenum.

• **A/C Heater Blower Resistors** – are located on the right front of the firewall, on the plenum.

• **A/C Heater Water Valve Vacuum Motor** – is located behind the rear of the engine, under the heater hoses.

• **A/C Heater/Defrost Bi-Directional Vacuum Actuator** – is located under the instrument panel, on the right side of the A/C plenum.

• **A/C High Pressure Switch** – on the back of the compressor.

• **A/C In-Car Sensor** – is located in the upper instrument panel trim, in the right hand speaker grill assembly.

• **A/C Intermediate Pressure Switch** – is located in the left hand front of the engine compartment, on the accumulator.

• **A/C Low Pressure Switch** – is located behind the A/C compressor.

• **A/C Pressure Transducer** – is on the front right of the engine compartment, in the refrigerant line.

• **A/C Recirculating Door Vacuum Actuator** – is located behind the right side of the instrument panel, on the right hand side of the A/C plenum.

• **A/C Solenoid Box** – is located under the right side of the instrument panel, on the right hand side of the A/C plenum above the blower motor.

• **A/C Upper Mode Vacuum Motor** – is located under the instrument panel, on the right hand front side of the A/C plenum.

• **A/C Vacuum Solenoid Programmer** – is located under the right hand side of the instrument panel.

• **A/C Valve Vacuum Actuator** – is located behind the instrument panel, on the plenum.

• **A/C Vent Valve Vacuum Actuator** – is located under the right side of the instrument panel, on the right hand side of the A/C plenum.

• **Accumulator (ABS) Pressure Switch** – is on the right side of the master cylinder.

• **Antenna Motor** – is behind the right rear wheelhousing.

• **Antenna Relay** – is behind the right rear wheelhousing.

• **Anti-Lock Brake Controller** – is located below the right hand front seat.

• **Anti-Lock Brake Power Center** – is located on the radiator support, above the right hand headlight.

• **Antilock Brake Diode** – is behind the right side of the instrument panel.

• **Antilock Brake Power Center** – is located at the front left of the engine compartment, in front of the strut.

• **Assembly Line Diagnostic (ALDL) Connector** – is located on the bottom of the instrument panel, to the right of the steering column.

• **Brake Fluid Level Switch** – is located on the left side of the firewall, on the brake master cylinder.

• **Brake Pressure Switch** – is located on the lower left hand rear of the engine compartment on the frame rail.

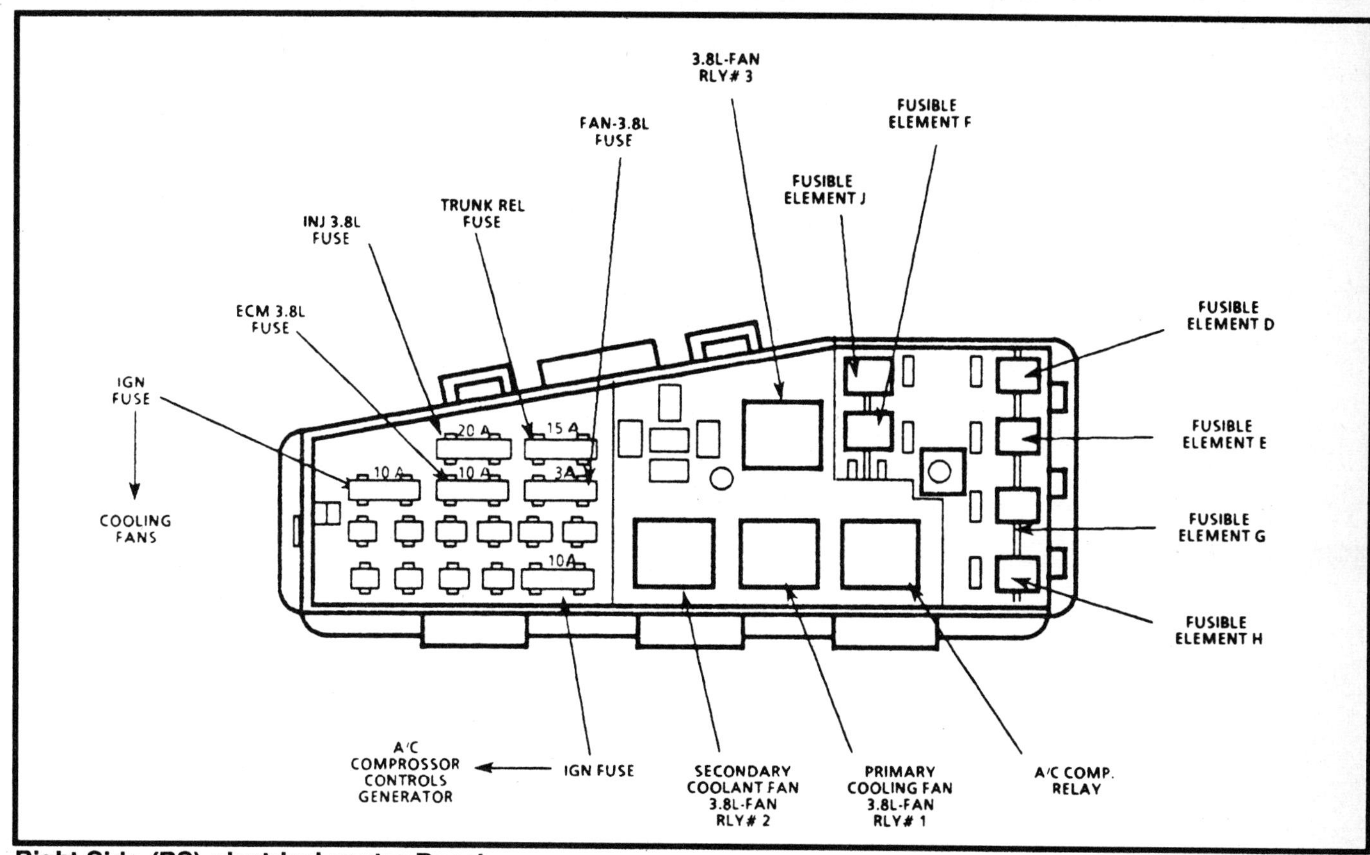

Right Side (RS) electrical center-Regal

- **Canister Purge Solenoid**—is located in the front of the engine compartment, behind the headlights.
- **Cellular Phone Transceiver**—is located in the left hand front of the trunk.
- **Chime Module**—is plugged into the component center.
- **Circuit Breakers**—are located in the component center or the fuse box.
- **Component Center**—is located behind the right hand side of the instrument panel, behind the instrument panel compartment.
- **Computer Controlled Coil Ignition (CCCI) Module (VIN L)**—is located at the right front of the engine.
- **Computer Controlled Coil Ignition Module (except VIN L)**—is located on the rear of the engine, above the intake manifold.
- **Convenience Center**—See Component Center.
- **Coolant Fan Delay Relay**—is located above the wheel well, on the left hand rear side of the engine compartment, if equipped.
- **Coolant Fan Relay (1989 Heavy Duty)**—is located in the engine compartment, behind the right hand side of the radiator.
- **Coolant Fan Relay (except 1989 Heavy Duty)**—is located in the engine compartment, in the right side electrical center.
- **Coolant Fan Relay No. 3 (3.8L engine)**—is located in the engine compartment, in the right side electrical center.
- **Coolant Level and Corrosivity Sensor**—is located behind the top of right hand side of the radiator.
- **Coolant Temperature Sensor**—is located at the top of the engine, below the coolant outlet.
- **Crankshaft Sensor (except VIN L)**—is located at the right hand front of the engine, below the direct ignition system.
- **Crankshaft Sensor (VIN L)**—is located at the right hand front of the engine.
- **Cruise Control Brake/Switch**—is located above the brake pedal on the brake pedal support bracket.
- **Cruise Control Check Valve**—is located in the vacuum line ahead of the strut tower.
- **Cruise Control Module**—is located under the left side of the instrument panel, on the left side of the brake pedal support.
- **Cruise Control Servo**—is located in the left hand front side of the engine compartment, on the inner fender well.
- **Cruise Control Vacuum Release Valve**—is located on the top of the brake pedal assembly.
- **Cruise Control Vacuum Tank**—is located in the left hand front wheel well, behind the headlight.
- **Daytime Running Light Module**—is behind the left side of the instrument panel to the left of the steering column.
- **Defogger Relay**—is plugged into the component center.
- **Detonation (Knock) Sensor**—is located on the right rear of the engine, below the exhaust manifold.
- **Diode (Headlamp) Assembly**—is to the left of the steering column.
- **EGR/RVB/ILC Solenoid Assembly**—is located above the valve cover on the left hand rear of the engine.
- **Electrical Center (left side)**—is located in the engine compartment near the left strut tower.
- **Electrical Center (right side)**—is located in the engine compartment near the right strut tower.
- **Electronic Control Module (ECM) Fuse**—is located in the left side electrical center.
- **Electronic Control Module (ECM)**—is located in the engine compartment, on the front of the right hand strut tower.
- **Electronic Spark Control Module (ESC)**—is located on the bracket at the top of the right front fender well.

- **Forward Lamp Electrical Center**—is located in the right hand front portion of the engine compartment.
- **Fuel Pump Prime Connector**—is taped to the wire harness, below the left side electrical center.
- **Fuel Pump Relay**—is located in the left side electrical center.
- **Fuel Pump/Oil Pressure Switch**—is located on the lower right hand front side of the engine, to the left of the oil filter.
- **Fuse Box**—is on the right side of the instrument panel, in the instrument panel compartment.
- **Fusible Elements**—are located at the electrical centers and at the alternator.
- **Hazard Flasher/Relay**—is located in the component center.
- **Heater Blower Relays**—are located in the component center.
- **High Speed Coolant Fan Relay**—is located above the wheel well, on the left hand rear side of the engine compartment.
- **Horn Relay**—is located in the forward light electrical center.
- **Idle Air Control Valve**—is located on the top of the engine, at the bottom of the throttle body.
- **Ignition Switch**—is located behind the instrument panel, on the center of the steering column.
- **Inline Resistor (VIN L)**—is located on the right side of the engine compartment.
- **Inverter**—is located in the trunk behind the center of the rear seat.
- **Keyless Entry Module**—is on the left front of the luggage compartment.
- **Left Hand Lap Retractor Solenoid**—is located in the door harness, inside of the bottom of the middle of the door.
- **Left Hand Seatbelt Shoulder Retractor Solenoid**—is located in the door harness, inside of the bottom left hand rear door.
- **Left Side Electrical Center**—is located in the engine compartment, on the left hand strut tower.
- **Low Speed Coolant Fan Relay**—is located above the wheel well, on the left hand rear side of the engine compartment.
- **MAF Sensor**—See Mass Air Flow Sensor.
- **Manifold Absolute Pressure (MAP) Sensor**—is behind the top side of the engine, on the air intake.
- **Manifold Absolute Temperature (MAT) Sensor**—is located on the air cleaner duct, near the right hand strut tower.
- **MAP Sensor**—See Manifold Absolute Pressure Sensor.
- **Mass Air Flow (MAF) Sensor (VIN L)**—is on the top left side of the engine.
- **MAT Sensor**—See Manifold Absolute Temperature.
- **Oil Pressure/Fuel Pump Switch**—is located on the lower right hand front side of the engine, to the left of the oil filter.
- **Park/Turn Relay**—is located in the forward lamp electrical center.
- **Passive Restraint Control Module**—is located behind the right hand side of the instrument panel.
- **Photoresistor**—is on the top left side of the instrument panel, near the speaker.
- **Power Antenna Relay**—is located behind the right hand side of the instrument panel, to the right of the glove box.
- **Power Door Lock Relay**—is at the right shroud above the access hole.
- **Power Master Brake Relay**—is located on the firewall, below the master cylinder. Power Steering Pressure Switch—is located on the steering gear assembly, near the input shaft.
- **Primary Coolant Fan Relay**—is located in the engine compartment, in the right side electrical center.
- **Radio Capacitor**—is located in the lower left hand corner of the fuse block.
- **Right Hand Lap Retractor Solenoid**—is located in the door harness, inside of the bottom of the middle of the door.
- **Right Hand Seatbelt Shoulder Retractor Solenoid**—is located in the door harness, inside of the bottom right hand rear door.
- **Right Side Electrical Center**—is located in the engine compartment, on the right hand strut tower.
- **Seatbelt Switch**—is located in the right hand half of the driver's seatbelt.
- **Seatbelt Timer Module**—is behind the right side of the instrument panel.
- **Secondary Coolant Fan Relay**—is located in the engine compartment, in the right side electrical center.
- **Starter Interrupt Relay**—is taped to the instrument panel harness, near the fuse block.
- **Sunroof Control Module**—is at the top center of the windshield header.
- **Theft Deterrent Controller**—is located under the left side of the dash panel, near the kick panel.
- **Theft Deterrent Diode**—is located behind the left side instrument panel, in connector C857.
- **Theft Deterrent Relay**—is located behind the instrument panel to the left of the steering column.
- **Throttle Position Sensor**—is located at the front of the throttle body.
- **Torque Converter Clutch Relay Solenoid**—is located in the automatic transaxle.
- **Transaxle Position Switch**—is located on the transaxle, below the brake master cylinder.
- **Trunk Lock Tamper Switch**—is located on the under side of the trunk lid, at the lid lock center.
- **Trunk Release Solenoid**—is located on the under side of the trunk lid, at the lid lock center.
- **Turbo Boost Gauge Sensor**—is located on the right front inner fender above the wheel well.
- **Turbo Boost Indicator Switch**—is located on the right front fender, above the wheel well.
- **Turn Signal Flasher**—is located under the instrument panel, on the right side of the steering column.
- **Twilight Sentinel Amplifier**—is located under the instrument panel, near the radio.
- **Twilight Sentinel Photocell**—is located at the top center of the instrument panel.
- **Vapor Canister Purge Solenoid (except VIN L)**—is located in the right hand front of the engine compartment, on the canister.
- **Vapor Canister Purge Solenoid (VIN L)**—is located on the top left rear of the engine, on the intake plenum.
- **Vehicle Speed Sensor Buffer**—is located under the instrument panel, to the left of the radio.
- **Vehicle Speed Sensor**—is located behind the right hand rear of the engine on the transaxle.
- **Wiper/Washer Motor Module**—is located on the upper left corner of the firewall in the engine compartment.

RIVIERA AND REATTA

- **A/C Air Inlet Door Vacuum Motor**—is located behind the instrument panel, on the right side of the A/C plenum.
- **A/C Ambient Sensor**—is located on the center front of the vehicle, on the radiator bracket.
- **A/C Aspirator**—is located behind the right hand side of the instrument panel.
- **A/C Bi-Directional Mode Door Vacuum Motor**—is located behind the instrument panel, on the A/C plenum.
- **A/C Compressor Clutch Diode**—is taped to the inside compressor connector on the front of the compressor.
- **A/C Compressor Relay**—is located in the underhood relay center, at position 'J'.
- **A/C Defrost Door Vacuum Motor**—is located behind the instrument panel, on the A/C plenum.
- **A/C High Side Temperature Sensor**—is located on the A/C line, in the center of the firewall.

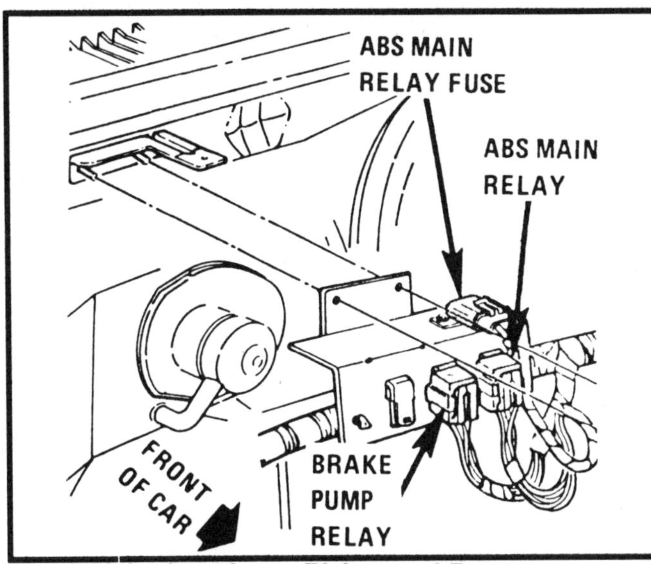

Anti-lock brake relays—Riviera and Reatta

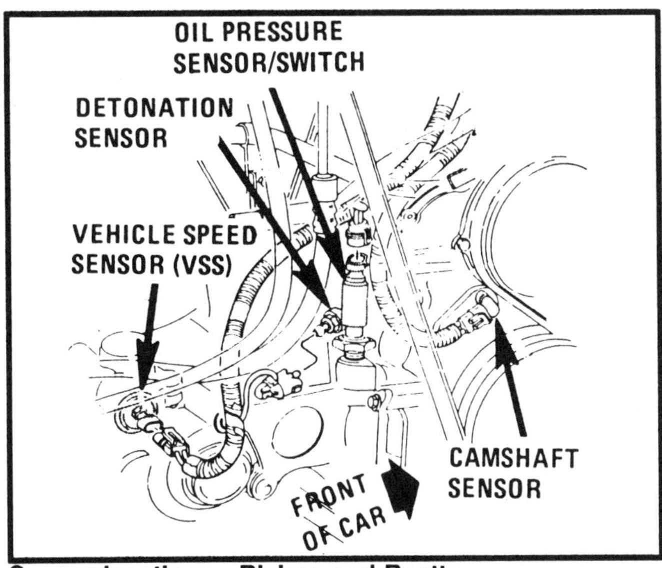

Sensor locations—Riviera and Reatta

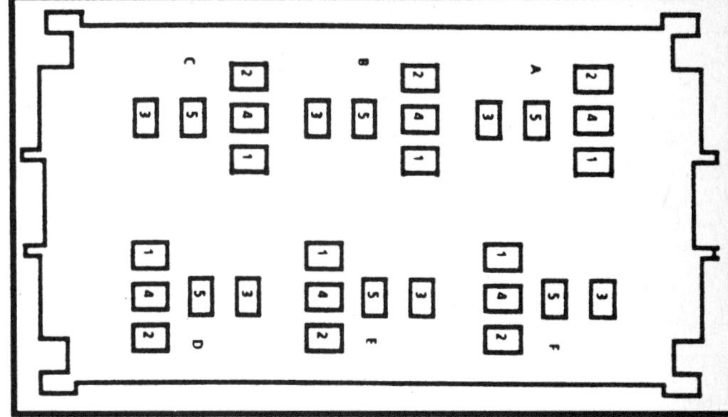
Mirco-Relay identification—Riviera and Reatta

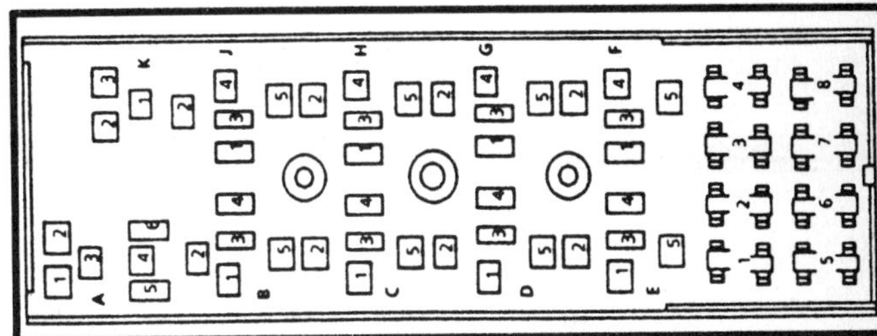
Underhood and interior relay center identification—Riviera and Reatta

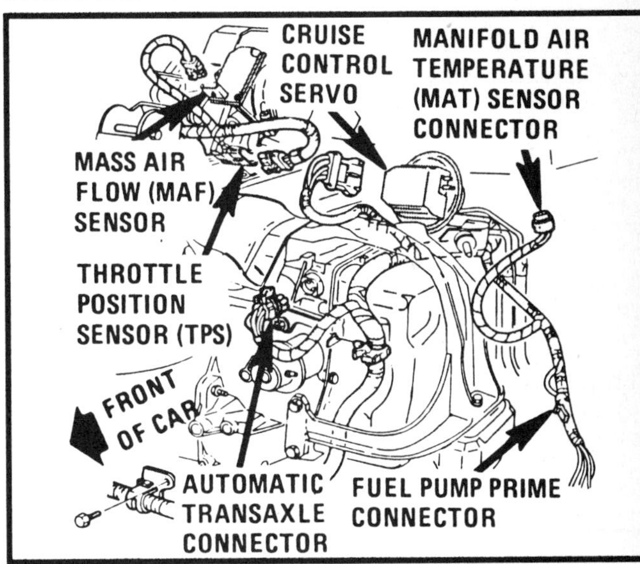

Fuel pump prime connector and sensors—Riviera and Reatta

- **A/C In-Car Sensor**—is located behind the right side of the instrument panel.
- **A/C Low Pressure Switch**—is located on the A/C line, in the center of the firewall.
- **A/C Low Side Temperature Sensor**—is located on the A/C line, in the center of the firewall.
- **A/C Lower Mode Door Vacuum Actuator**—is located behind the instrument panel, on the A/C plenum.
- **A/C Outside Air Valve Vacuum Actuator**—is located behind the instrument panel, on the A/C plenum.
- **A/C Pressure Switch**—is located on the left hand front of the engine compartment, on the A/C line.
- **A/C Upper Mode Door Vacuum Actuator**—is located behind the instrument panel, on the A/C plenum.
- **Ambient Sensor**—is incorporated into the automatic day/night mirror.
- **Amplifier Relay**—is located at the bottom right side of the passenger compartment, near the rear of the right front door sill.
- **Anti-Lock Brake Controller Fuse**—is located behind the instrument panel, to the right of the steering column.
- **Anti-Lock Brake Diode**—is located behind the instrument panel, to the left of the steering column.
- **Anti-Lock Brake Electronic Control Module**—is located in the left side of the trunk on the rear wheelhouse.
- **Anti-Lock Brake Main Relay Fuse**—is located on the center of the firewall.
- **Anti-Lock Brake Main Relay**—is located on the center of the firewall.
- **Anti-Lock Brake Pump Fuse**—is located on the center of the firewall.
- **Anti-Lock Brake Pump Relay Fuse**—is located on the center of the firewall.
- **Anti-Lock Brake Pump Relay**—is located on the center of the firewall.

• **Anti-Lock Brake Wheel Speed Sensor**—is located in each wheel spindle.

• **Assembly Line Diagnostic Link (ALDL) Connector**—is located under the instrument panel, near to the parking brake.

• **Automatic Door Lock Module**—is located in the passenger compartment, below the right hand front seal, behind the instrument panel to the right of the steering column on the 1988–89 models.

• **Body Computer Module (BCM)**—is located behind the right side of the instrument panel, behind the glove box.

• **Bow Power Relay (Reatta except 1989)**—is located in the mirco relay center, at position 'F'.

• **Bow Pulldown Motor Relay**—is below the tonneau cover, on the right sheerwall.

• **Brake Switch Capacitor 1**—is located behind the instrument panel, at the top of the brake pedal support, on the brake switch connector.

• **Brake Switch Capacitor 2**—is in the dash wiring harness, to the right of the steering wheel.

• **Brake Switch**—is located behind the instrument panel, at the top of the brake pedal support.

• **Camshaft Sensor**—is located on lower right hand side of the engine, above the lower pulley.

• **Canister Purge Solenoid**—is located in the left hand front corner of the engine compartment.

• **Cathode Ray Tube Controller (CRTC)**—is located behind the front console.

• **Central Power Supply (early 1989)**—is located behind the left side of the instrument panel, above the brake pedal.

• **Central Power Supply (except 1989)**—is located below the center of the instrument panel, a at the front of the console.

• **Chime Module (1989)**—is located behind the right side of the instrument panel, above the glove box.

• **Chime Module (except 1989)**—is located behind the left side of the instrument panel, above parking brake.

• **Computer Controlled Coil Ignition (CCCI) Module**—is located on the right hand top of the rear valve cover.

• **Console Accessory Switch Module**—is located in the front console.

• **Console Electro Luminescent Inverter**—is located below the rear of the front console.

• **Coolant Temperature Sensor**—is located on front of engine behind alternator or under the throttle body.

• **Coolant Temperature Switch**—is located on front of engine behind alternator.

• **Cooling Fan Pusher Relay**—is located in the underhood relay center, at position 'D'.

• **Cooling Pusher Fan High Speed Relay**—is located in the underhood relay center, at position 'C'.

• **Cooling Pusher Fan Low Speed Relay**—is located in the underhood relay center, at position 'G'.

• **Courtesy Lamps Relay (except 1989)**—is located in the mirco relay center, at position 'B'.

• **Courtesy Light Relay (1989)**—is located in the interior relay center at position 'C'.

• **Crankshaft Sensor**—is located at the right hand front of the engine, below the direct ignition system. Sensor is between the lower pulley and the A/C compressor.

• **Cruise Control Check Valve**—is located on the left hand rear side of the engine. Cruise Control Servo—is located on the left hand side of the engine compartment, above the transaxle.

• **Daytime Running Light (DRL) Relay (Riviera)**—is located in the underhood relay center at position 'E'.

• **Daytime Running Light (DRL) Resistor**—is located on the left front of the engine compartment, near the underhood relay center.

• **Defogger Relay (1989)**—is located in the interior relay center at position 'D'.

• **Defogger Relay (1990-91)**—is located in the mirco relay center at position 'E'.

• **Defogger Relay (Riviera)**—is located in the interior relay center, at position 'D'.

• **Delco Bose Music System Diode**—is located at the music system relay.

• **Delco Bose Music System Relay**—is located below the right hand seat.

• **Delco Bose Relays (Riviera except 1989)**—are located in the mirco relay center at position 'D' and 'F'.

• **Detonation (Knock) Sensor**—is located on top left hand side of the engine, behind the main pulley or above the right drive axle.

• **Door Lock Relay**—is located on the left hand shroud, on the conduit.

• **EGR Solenoid Assembly (VIN C)**—is located on the top rear of the engine.

• **Electronic Climate Control Power Module**—is located in the center of the firewall, maybe combined with the climate programmer.

• **Electronic Climate Control Programmer**—is located under the right side of the instrument panel, on the right side of the plenum next to the ECU.

• **Electronic Compass Module**—is located under the right side of the instrument panel.

• **Electronic Control Module (ECM)**—is located behind the instrument panel on or behind the right (kick panel) shroud in 1989 or to the left of the heater and A/C programmer module after 1989.

• **Electronic Level Control Compressor**—is located underneath the car, on top of the right hand side crossmember.

• **Electronic Level Control Height Sensor**—is attached to left side of the rear crossmember.

• **Electronic Level Control Relay (1989)**—is located in the interior relay center, at position 'K'.

• **Electronic Level Control Relay (Riviera, except 1989)**—is located in the mirco relay center, at position 'A'.

• **Fog Lamp Relay (Reatta)**—is located in the interior relay center, at position 'B'.

• **Fuel Door Release Solenoid**—is located in the left hand side of the trunk, above the wheel well.

• **Fuel Pump Prime Connector**—is taped to the wire harness, on the lower left hand front of the engine compartment or maybe just to the left of the cruise control servo.

• **Fuel Pump Relay (1989)**—is located on the right hand side of the engine compartment.

• **Fuel Pump Relay (except 1989)**—is located in the interior relay center at position 'C'.

• **Fusible Links**—are located mainly at the power junction block. Other location can include battery and alternator, dependent on options.

• **Gear Selector Switch**—is located at the left hand rear of the engine, on top of the transaxle.

• **Glove Box Release Solenoid**—is located behind the right hand side of the instrument panel, above the glove box.

• **Graphics Control Center**—is located in the center of the dash.

• **Hazard Flasher**—is mounted on the right side of the steering column.

• **Headlight Door Diode (1989)**—is at the right front of the console, forward of the interior relay center.

• **Headlight Door Module**—is at the left front corner of the engine compartment below the underhood relay center.

• **Headlight Door Motors (Reatta)**—are located behind the headlights.

• **Headlight Sensor**—is incorporated into the automatic day/night mirror.

• **High Beam Relay (Riviera)**—is located in the interior relay center, at position 'B'.

• **High/Low Beam Relay (Reatta)**—is located in the interior relay center, at position 'E' and 'B'.

• **Horn Relay**—is located in the underhood relay center, position 'B'.

• **HVAC Programmer**—is located behind the instrument panel, on the right side of the A/C module.

• **Idle Air Control Motor (VIN C)**—is located on the top right hand side of the engine, at the rear of the throttle body.

• **Ignition Key Warning Switch**—is located at the base of the steering column.

• **Ignition Switch**—is located in the top of the steering column.

• **In-Line Fuse A**—is located behind the left hand side of the instrument panel, to the left of the steering column.

• **Instrument Panel Electro Luminescent Inverter**—is located behind the instrument panel, to the left of the cluster.

• **Interior Relay Center**—is located behind the center of the instrument panel, front of the console.

• **Isolated Ground Junction Block**—is located in the right hand front of the engine compartment, next to the power junction box.

• **Keyless Entry Module (Reatta Convertible)**—is located below the cover, along the center of the rear shelf.

• **Keyless Entry Module (Reatta Coupe)**—is located behind the left rear door sill.

• **Keyless Entry Module (Riviera)**—is located under the rear package shelf in the trunk, if so equipped.

• **Lamp Monitor Module**—is located behind the left hand side of the instrument panel, near the parking brake.

• **Left Hand Door Electro Luminescent Inverter**—is located in the left hand door.

• **Left Hand Door Lock Fiber Optic Light**—is located near the lower rear portion of the left hand door.

• **Low Beam Relay (Riviera)**—is located in the interior relay center, at position 'E'.

• **Low Brake Fluid Switch**—is located on the master cylinder.

• **Manifold Air Temperature (MAT) Sensor**—is located on the air intake assembly, near the left of the engine.

• **Mass Airflow (MAF) Sensor**—is located on the throttle body.

• **Memory Acknowledge Module**—is located in the left hand door.

• **Mirco Relay Center (Reatta)**—is located at the right side of the trunk, on the rear wheelwell.

• **Mirco Relay Center (Rivera)**—is located at the front center of the trunk, below the rear shelf.

• **Mute Module**—is located in the console.

• **Oil Level Sensor**—is located at the lower front of the engine, near the starter.

• **Oil Pressure Sensor/Switch**—is located on the lower right hand rear of the engine.

• **Oxygen Sensor**—is located on rear of the exhaust manifold.

• **Park/Turn Light Relays (Reatta)**—are located in the underhood relay center. The left side relay is at position 'E' the right side is at position 'F'.

• **Pass Key Decoder Module**—is located behind the left side of the instrument panel, to the left of the steering column support.

• **Power Antenna Relay**—is located in the ιrunk, in the rear of the right hand wheel well.

• **Power Junction Block**—is located in the right hand front of the engine compartment, on the inner fender panel.

• **Power Steering Cutout Switch**—is located on the steering rack.

• **Radio Diode**—is located at the radio receiver.

• **Radio Receiver**—is located in the console.

• **Retained Accessory Power Relay**—is located in the interior relay center, at positions 'H' and 'J'.

• **Right Hand Door Electro Luminescent Inverter**—is located in the right hand door.

• **Right Hand Door Lock Fiber Optic Light**—is located near the lower rear portion of the right hand door.

• **Seat (Left Hand) Memory Diagnostic Connector**—is located under driver's seat.

• **Seat (Left Hand) Memory Module**—is located under driver's seat.

• **Seat Lumbar/Thigh Compressor**—is located in each front seat.

• **Seat Recliner Motor**—is located in each front seat.

• **Seatbelt Switch**—is located in the driver's right hand seatbelt.

• **Starter Enable Relay**—is behind the left side of the instrument panel, on the left of the steering column bracket.

• **Starter Interrupt Relay**—is located behind the instrument panel, to the left of the steering column.

• **Stop/Turn Trailer Relays**—are located in trunk, near the right and wheel well.

• **Sunload Sensor**—is located behind the center of the instrument panel.

• **Sunroof Limit Switch**—is located in the roof, near the front of the sunroof.

• **Sunroof Relays**—is at the center of the header harness, near the sunroof actuator assembly.

• **Sunroof Switch**—is located in the right hand side of the windshield pillar.

• **Sunroof Timer Module**—is located in the right hand side of the windshield pillar.

• **Target Lamp**—is located in the mobile phone harness, in console.

• **Theft Deterrent Control Module**—is located behind the instrument panel, to the left of the steering column.

• **Theft Deterrent Diode**—is taped to the instrument panel wiring harness connector, below the chime module.

• **Theft Deterrent In-Line Fuse**—is located behind the instrument panel, to the left of the steering column.

• **Theft Deterrent Relay**—is located behind the instrument panel, to the left of the steering column.

• **Throttle Position Sensor**—is located on top of the engine, near the throttle body.

• **Tonnuau Release Relay**—is located below the cover on the right sheerwall.

• **TPS Test Connector**—is taped to the wiring harness at the left front side of the engine compartment.

• **Transaxle Position Switch**—is located on the left hand rear of the engine, on top of the transaxle.

• **Transceiver**—is located in the trunk.

• **Trunk Lid Pull**—Down Unit—is located in the rear of the trunk at the striker plate.

• **Trunk Lid Release Relay (Reatta)**—is located on the right side of the trunk compartment.

• **Trunk Lid Release Solenoid (Reatta)**—is located in the rear of the trunk compartment lid.

• **Trunk Lid Tamper Switch**—is incorporated in the trunk lock assembly.

• **Trunk Release Relay (Reatta)**—is located in the mirco relay center, at position 'A'.

• **Trunk/Tonneau Ajar Relay**—is below the tonneau cover, on the right sheerwall.

• **Turn Signal Alert Module**—is located under the instrument panel, on the left side of the steering column, in front of the theft control module.

• **Turn Signal Flasher**—is mounted on the right side of the steering column.

• **Turn Signal Relay (Reatta except 1989)**—is located in the mirco relay center, the right is at position 'C' and the left is at position 'D'.

• **Turn/Hazard Module (1989)**—is located under the instrument panel, on the left side of the steering column.

• **Twilight Crank Diode**—is located behind the left side of the instrument panel, to the left of the steering column.

• **Twilight Crank Relay**—is located behind the left side of the instrument panel, to the left of the steering column.

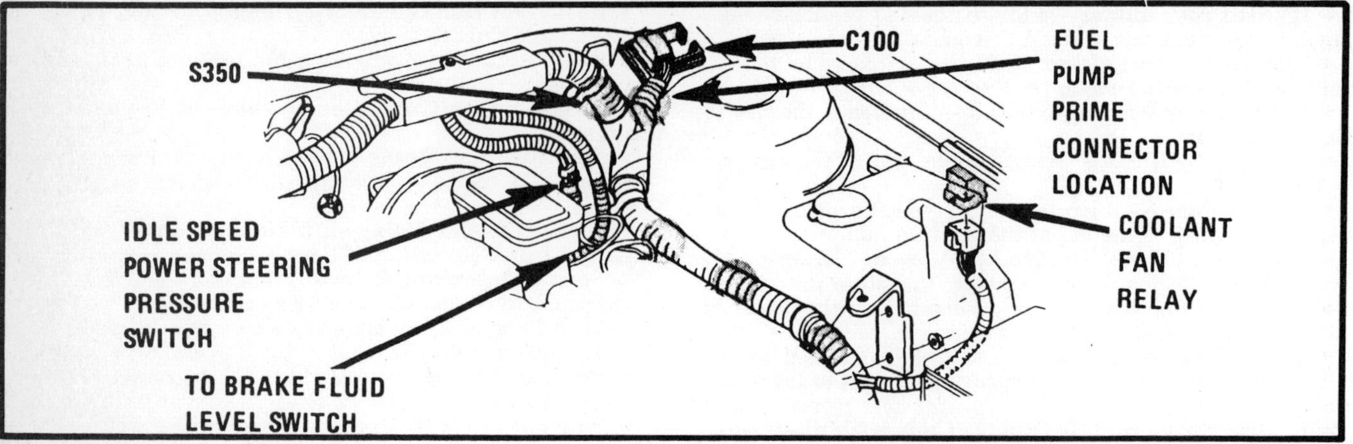

Idle speed switch—Skyhawk

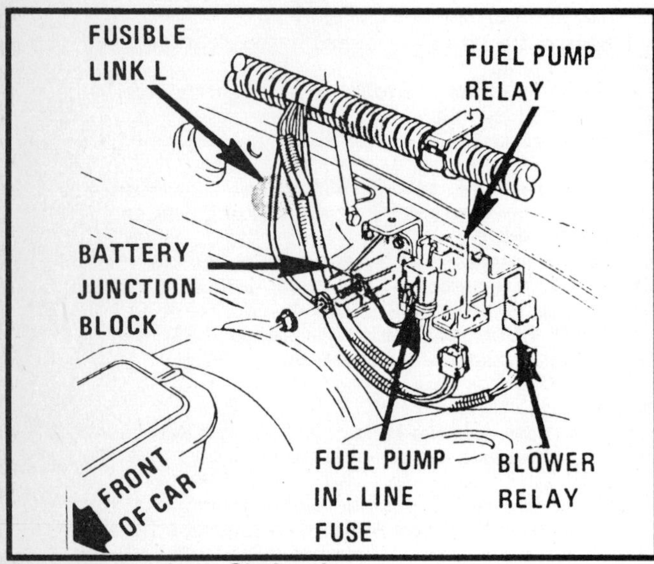

Fuel pump relay—Skyhawk

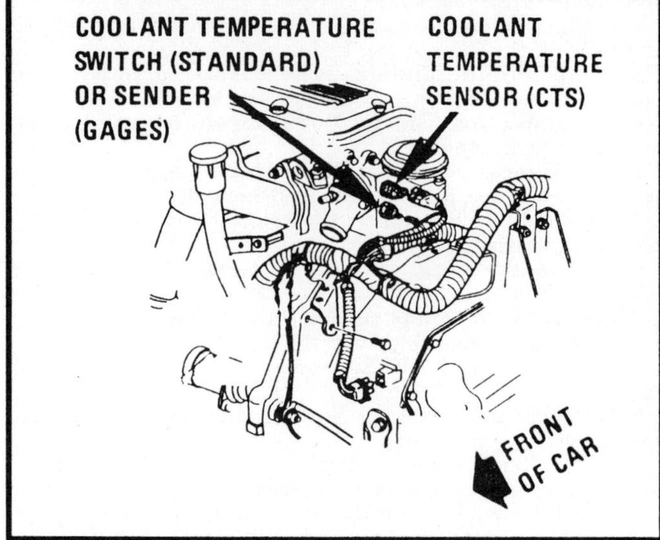

Coolant temperature sensor—Skyhawk

- **Twilight Headlight Relay**—is located in the interior relay center, at position 'G'.
- **Twilight Park Light Relay**—is located in the interior relay center, at position 'F'.
- **Twilight Photocell**—is located on top of instrument panel, above the radio.
- **Underhood Relay Center (1989)**—is located on the inner left front fender panel, behind the headlights.
- **Underhood Relay Center (except 1989)**—is located at the left front of the engine compartment, behind the windshield washer reservoir.
- **Vacuum Delay Porous Plug**—is located in the orange vacuum line, near the vacuum motor.
- **Vacuum Release Valve**—is located behind the instrument panel, at the top of the brake pedal support.
- **Vacuum Tank**—is located in the left hand side of the engine compartment, on the frame.
- **Vehicle Access Code (VAC) Connector (Reatta)**—is at the left side of the trunk on the top of the left rear wheelhousing.
- **Vehicle Access Code (VAC) Connector (Riviera)**—is under the rear shelf, below the keyless entry module.
- **Vehicle Speed Sensor**—is located behind the engine, on the top right hand side of the transaxle.
- **Wiper/Washer Capacitor**—is located in the dash harness, behind the left side of the instrument panel.
- **Wiper/Washer Fluid Level Switch**—is located on the washer reservoir.

SKYHAWK

- **A/C Compressor Clutch Diode**—is taped to the inside compressor connector on the front of the compressor.
- **A/C Compressor Control Relay**—is located behind the right front shock tower.
- **A/C Heat Vacuum Motor**—is located under the instrument panel, on the right side of the A/C plenum.
- **A/C Heater Blower Relay (VIN 1)**—is located on the left hand side of the firewall, near the master cylinder.
- **A/C Heater Blower Resistors**—are located on the front center of the firewall, in the A/C heater module.
- **A/C High Pressure Cutout Switch (VIN 1)**—is located on the right hand front side of the engine.
- **A/C In-Car Temperature Sensor**—is located on the right side of the dash, above the glove box, if so equipped.
- **A/C Low Pressure Cutout Switch**—is located on the compressor.
- **A/C Pressure Cycling Switch**—is located behind the right hand side shock tower.
- **A/C Recirculating/Outside Air Vacuum Motor**—is located behind the instrument panel on the top right hand side of the A/C module.

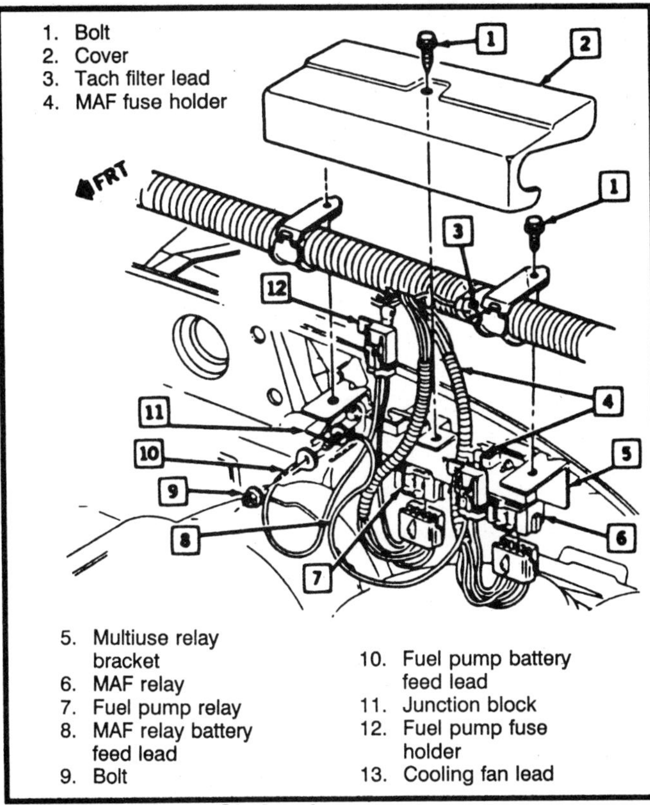

Relay locations – Skyhawk

• **A/C-Heater/Defrost Vacuum Motor** – is located under the instrument panel, on the right side of the A/C plenum.

• **Assembly Line Diagnostic Link (ALDL)** – is located behind the instrument panel, on the right side of the fuse block housing.

• **Blocking Diode** – is located in the instrument panel harness, near the bulkhead connector.

• **Brake Pressure Switch (VIN 1)** – is located on the left hand side of the brake fluid reservoir.

• **Canister Purge Solenoid** – is located on the vapor canister, behind the headlights.

• **Clutch Start Switch** – is located above the clutch pedal, in the passengers compartment.

• **Convenience Center** – is located behind the left side of the instrument panel, at the kick panel.

• **Coolant Fan Relay (VIN 1)** – on the left front fender in front of the shock tower.

• **Coolant Fan Resistor Relay** – is located on the left hand side of the firewall, near the master cylinder.

• **Coolant Temperature Sender (VIN 1)** – is located on the left side of the engine, near the coolant outlet.

• **Coolant Temperature Sensor (VIN 1)** – is located on the left side of the engine under the water outlet.

• **Cruise Control Brake/Switch** – is located above the brake pedal on the brake pedal support bracket.

• **Cruise Control Check Valve** – is located in the engine compartment, on the "T" branch of the servo vacuum hose.

• **Cruise Control Module** – is located behind the instrument panel, to the right of the steering column.

• **Cruise Control Servo** – is located on the left hand strut tower in the engine compartment.

• **Cruise Control Vacuum Tank** – is located in the left hand front of the engine compartment, below the battery.

• **Defogger Time Relay** – is located behind the left side of the dash panel, if so equipped.

• **Direct Ignition System (DIS)** – is located on the rear of the engine, below the intake manifold.

• **EGR Control Solenoid** – is located behind the right hand shock tower in the engine compartment.

• **Electronic Control Module (ECM)** – is located behind the glove box.

• **Electronic Fuel Injection Ambient Sensor** – is located on the engine cowl above the washer reservoir, if so equipped.

• **Electronic Speed Sensor** – is located on the top right side of the transaxle.

• **Electronic Vacuum Regulator Valve** – is located on the left rear of the engine, behind the intake air duct.

• **Engine Metal Temperature Sensor (VIN 1)** – is located below the front of the right side of the valve cover.

• **Fog Lamp Relay** – is located behind the center of the instrument panel, below the radio.

Fuel Control Fuse – is located on the upper left hand side of the firewall.

• **Fuel Pump In-Line Fuse** – is located on the firewall, behind the brake booster, if so equipped.

• **Fuel Pump Prime Connection (VIN 1)** – is located behind the left hand side shock tower in the engine compartment.

• **Fuel Pump Relay (VIN 1)** – is located on the left hand side of the engine, in front of the firewall under the relay bracket cover.

• **Fuel Pump/Oil Pressure Switch** – is located on the rear of the engine, below the manifold.

• **Gear Selector Switch** – is located at the rear left hand side of the engine, on top of the transaxle.

• **Hatch/Tailgate/Trunk Release Relay** – is taped to the wire harness, located behind the right side of the radio, if so equipped.

• **Hazard Flasher** – is located in the convenience center.

• **Headlight Door Module** – is located in the left hand rear corner of the engine compartment.

• **Headlight Door Motors** – are located behind the headlights.

• **High Beam Cutout Relay** – is located behind the left side of the instrument panel, above the fuse block, if so equipped.

• **Horn Relay** – is located on the convenience center.

• **Idle Air Control Valve (VIN 1)** – is located on the top of the engine, at the bottom of the throttle body.

• **Idle Speed Power Steering Pressure Switch** – is located at the left rear of the engine, near the brake booster.

Ignition Switch – is located on the right hand side of the steering column.

• **Junction Block** – is located on the front of the dash, near the hood assist rod.

• **Knock Sensor** – is located on the right side of the starter below the starter.

• **Low Coolant Module** – is located behind the instrument panel, to the right of the fuse block.

• **Low Coolant Probe** – is located on the front of the vehicle, on the right front side of the radiator.

• **Lumbar Control Pump Motor Relay** – is located underneath the front seat, if so equipped.

• **Manifold Absolute Pressure Sensor (VIN 1)** – is located on the firewall, near the wiper motor.

• **Manifold Air Temperature Sensor (VIN 1)** – is located on top of the engine, on the throttle body.

• **Mass Airflow Sensor** – is located on the top of the left side of the engine, behind the air cleaner.

• **Oil Pressure Switch (VIN 1)** – is located on the rear of the engine, below the manifold.

• **Outside Air Temperature Sensor** – is located in the engine compartment, behind the right side of the grill, if so equipped.

• **Oxygen Sensor** – is located in the exhaust manifold.

• **Power Antenna Relay** – is located behind the instrument panel, below the right side of the radio.

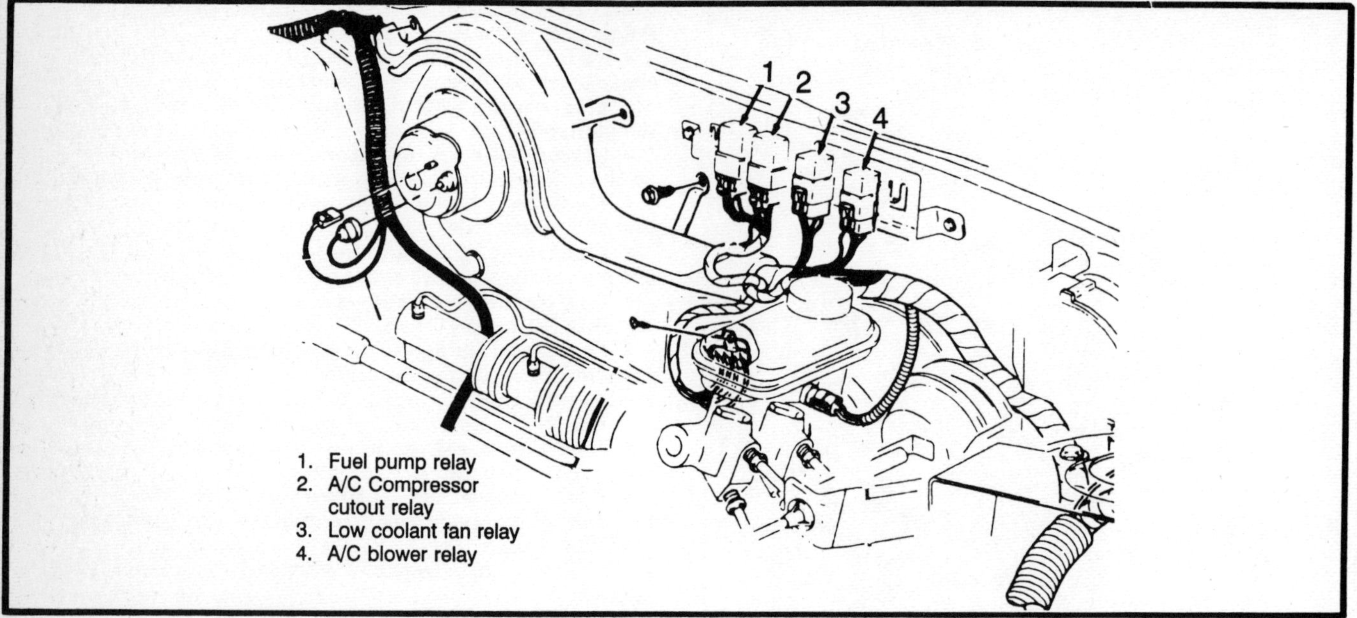

Relay locations – Skylark

- **Power Door Lock Relay** – is located behind the instrument panel, above steering column.
- **Power Steering Switch** – is located on the left hand side of the firewall, near the master cylinder.
- **Power Unit Dimmer** – is located behind the instrument panel, to the left of the steering column, if so equipped.
- **Power Window Circuit Breaker** – is located in the fuse block.
- **Release Relay** – is taped to the instrument panel harness, behind the radio or glove box.
- **Release Solenoid (Hatchback)** – is located below the right hand side of the hatchback window.
- **Release Solenoid (Sedan)** – is located near the rear compartment lock mechanism.
- **Seat Belt Retractor Solenoids** – are located next to the seats at the base of the door pillars.
- **Spark Adjust (VIN 1)** – is located behind the instrument panel, near the ECM.
- **Starter Solenoid (VIN 1)** – is located on the lower front of the engine.
- **Tachometer Filter** – is located on the left hand side of the firewall, on a relay bracket.
- **Tail Gate Ajar Switch** – is located on the lower portion of the tailgate.
- **Throttle Position Sensor** – is located on the throttle body.
- **Torque Converter Clutch Relay (TCC)** – is located on the transmission cowling.
- **Turbo Release Relay** – is located on the transaxle cowling.
- **Turn Signal Flasher** – is located under the instrument panel, on the left side of the steering column bracket.
- **Twilight Sentinel Amplifier** – is located behind the instrument panel, to the left of the steering column, if so equipped.
- **Twilight Sentinel Photocell** – is located on the dash panel, on the right side of the defrost vent, if so equipped.
- **Vehicle Speed Sensor Buffer** – is located behind the instrument cluster, below the speed sensor.

Vehicle Speed Sensor – is located behind the instrument panel, the right of the steering column, if so equipped.

- **Wiper/Washer Motor Module** – is located on the top center of the firewall in the engine compartment.

SKYLARK

- **A/C Compressor Clutch Diode** – in the air conditioning compressor clutch connector.
- **A/C Compressor Refrigerant Pressure Sensor** – at the right front of engine compartment.
- **A/C Control Relay** – at the front center of dash, on relay bracket.
- **A/C Dual Pressure Switch** – is located on the right hand front side of the engine compartment on the A/C line.
- **A/C Heater Blower Resistors** – are located on the blower assembly, on the right hand front side of the firewall.
- **A/C Heater Vacuum Motor** – is located under the center of the instrument panel.
- **A/C Heater Vacuum Tank** – is located under the center of the instrument panel.
- **A/C Heater/Defrost Vacuum Motor** – is located under the center of the instrument panel.
- **A/C High Pressure Cut** – Out Switch (VIN U) – is located on the compressor.
- **A/C High Pressure Cut** – Out Switch – lower right front of engine, on the left end of the air conditioning compressor.
- **A/C High Speed Blower Relay (VIN D)** – is located on the relay bracket at the center of the firewall.
- **A/C High Speed Blower Relay (except VIN D)** – is located on the relay bracket at the right hand side of the firewall, or same location as VIN D.
- **A/C High Speed Coolant Fan Relay** – is located on the relay bracket on the center of the firewall.
- **A/C Low Pressure Cut** – Out Switch (VIN U) – is located on the compressor.
- **A/C Low Pressure Cut** – Out Switch – lower right front of engine, on the left end of the air conditioning compressor.
- **A/C Low Speed Coolant Fan Relay** – is located on the relay bracket on the center of the firewall.
- **A/C Recirculating/Outside Air Vacuum Motor** – is located behind the center of the instrument panel.
- **A/C Temperature Door Motor** – is located behind the instrument panel, above the A/C control head.
- **Antenna Relay** – at the right rear corner of the luggage compartment.
- **Assembly Line Diagnostic (ALDL) Link** – is located behind the instrument panel, to the right of the steering column.

• **Audio/Buzzer Alarm Module**—is located on the fuse block or above the glove box.

• **Automatic Door Lock Controller**—is located behind the right kick panel, at the top, if so equipped.

• **Blower Resistor Assembly**—at the right side of dash, on the blower assembly.

• **Brake Fluid Level Switch**—at the left side of the brake fluid reservoir.

• **Clutch Start Switch**—is located above the clutch pedal.

• **Computer Controlled Coil Ignition (CCCI) Module**—at the top right front of engine.

• **Convenience Center**—behind the left side of instrument panel.

• **Coolant Fan Relay**—at the front center of dash, on the relay bracket.

• **Coolant Temperature Sensor (VIN D)**—is located on the left hand rear side of the engine, behind the coolant outlet.

• **Coolant Temperature Sensor (VIN N)**—at the right side of engine, below the generator.

• **Coolant Temperature Sensor (VIN U)**—is located on the top left hand side of the engine.

• **Cooling Fan In-Line Fuse**—is located on the left front shock tower, if so equipped.

• **Cooling Fan Relay**—is located on the relay bracket at the center of the firewall in the engine compartment.

• **Crankshaft Position Sensor (VIN N)**—at the lower right side of engine, behind crankshaft pulley.

• **Cruise Control Brake/Switch**—is located above the brake pedal on the brake pedal support bracket.

• **Cruise Control Check Valve (VIN D)**—is located in the right hand side of the engine compartment.

• **Cruise Control Check Valve (VIN N and U)**—at the center of dash.

• **Cruise Control Check Valve (VIN U)**—maybe located in the left hand side of the engine compartment, near the cruise control servo.

• **Cruise Control Module**—is located under the left side of the instrument panel, above the accelerator pedal.

• **Cruise Control Release Valve**—on the brake pedal support.

• **Cruise Control Servo**—is located on the left hand strut tower in the engine compartment.

• **Daytime Running Lights (DRL) Module**—at the left front corner of the engine compartment.

• **Detonation Sensor (VIN N)**—at the lower right rear of engine, near the air conditioning hose.

• **Direct Ignition System (DIS)**—at left rear of the engine.

• **Door Lock Relay**—behind the right side of the instrument panel.

• **Engine Control Module (ECM)**—behind the right side of the instrument panel, near the instrument panel compartment.

• **Fuel Pump In-Line Fuse**—is located on the left front shock tower, if so equipped.

• **Fuel Pump Prime Connector**—at the left front of dash, tapped to wiring harness.

• **Fuel Pump Relay**—at the front center of dash, on the relay bracket.

• **Fuel Pump Relay (early 1989)**—maybe located on the right hand end of the relay bracket at the center of the firewall in the engine compartment.

• **Fuel Pump/Oil Pressure Switch (VIN D)**—at the top left side of engine.

• **Fuel Pump/Oil Pressure Switch (VIN U)**—at the left rear of engine, to the right side of the direct ignition system.

• **Fuse Block**—behind the left side of the instrument panel, to the left of the steering column.

• **Hazard Flasher**—is located in the convenience center.

• **High Blower Relay**—at the front center of dash, on the relay bracket.

• **Horn Relay**—is located in the convenience center.

• **Idle Air Control Motor**—at the top left rear of the throttle body.

• **Idle Air Control Valve (VIN D)**—is located on the right hand side of the throttle body.

• **Idle Air Control Valve (VIN U)**—is located at the base of the throttle body.

• **Idle Speed Power Steering Pressure Switch (VIN D)**—is located on the left hand rear of the engine, ahead of the coolant outlet.

• **Idle Speed Power Steering Pressure Switch (VIN N)**—at lower left front of dash, on left side of the brake booster.

• **Ignition Switch**—is located on the lower right hand side of the steering column.

• **Integrated Direct Ignition (IDI) System**—is located in the left hand rear side of the engine.

• **Interior Capacitor**—is located in the front light harness, behind the left hand front lights panel.

• **Manifold Absolute Pressure (MAP) Sensor (VIN D)**—at the front center of engine compartment, on the radiator support.

• **Manifold Absolute Pressure (MAP) Sensor (VIN U)**—at the right rear of the engine, on the air cleaner.

• **Manifold Air Temperature (MAT) Sensor (VIN D)**—at the lower left front of engine compartment, on the air cleaner.

• **Manifold Air Temperature (MAT) Sensor (VIN U)**—at the right side of throttle body, on the intake manifold.

• **Mass Air Flow (MAF) Senor**—at the left front of engine, in air intake duct.

• **Oil Pressure Relay**—is located behind the right hand side of the instrument panel.

• **Oil Pressure Sender/Switch (VIN D)** —is located at the top left hand rear of the engine.

• **Oil Pressure Sender/Switch (VIN U)**—is located at the lower right hand rear of the engine, to the right of the direct ignition module.

• **Oxygen Sensor (VIN D and N)**—at the rear of the engine, in the exhaust manifold.

• **Oxygen Sensor (VIN U)**—at the front of the engine, in the exhaust manifold.

• **Parking Brake Switch (with console)**—in the console, at the base of the parking brake.

• **Parking Brake Switch (without console)**—at the left side shroud.

• **Power Accessories Circuit Breaker**—is located in the fuse block.

• **Power Antenna Capacitor**—is located in the front light harness, behind the left hand front lights panel.

• **Power Antenna Relay**—is located in the right hand corner of the trunk.

• **Power Door Lock Relay**—is located near the base of the right hand side shroud.

• **Power Steering Switch**—is located on the left hand side of the firewall, near the master cylinder.

• **Power Window Circuit Breaker**—is located in the fuse block.

• **Radio Amplifier Power Relay**—is located in the console ahead of the gear selector.

• **Remote Dimmer Module (interior lights)**—behind the instrument panel, to the right of steering column bracket.

• **Seat Belt Retractor Module**—is located under the left hand side of the instrument panel, near the kick panel.

• **Seat Belt Retractor Solenoid**—is located in the lower center of each door.

• **Seat Belt Retractor Switches**—are located in the base of each door pillar.

• **Seat Belt Switch**—is part of the driver's seatbelt assembly.

• **Starter Solenoid**—is located on the lower front of the engine.

• **Surge Tank Low Coolant Switch**—at the right front of the engine compartment, in the coolant reservoir.

• **Throttle Position Sensor (VIN D)**—at the top of the engine, on the left side of the throttle body.

• **Throttle Position Sensor (VIN M and U)**—at the top of the engine, on the right side of the throttle body.

• **Transaxle Position Switch (VIN D)**—is located on the left hand rear of the engine, on top of the transaxle.

• **Transaxle Position Switch**—at the top left rear of the transaxle.

• **Trunk Release Solenoid**—is located underside of the trunk lid.

• **Turn Signal Flasher**—is located under the instrument panel, on the right side of the steering column bracket.

• **Vapor Canister Purge Solenoid**—at the right front of the engine compartment.

• **Vehicle Speed Sensor (VIN D)**—is located on the left hand rear of the engine.

• **Vehicle Speed Sensor (VIN U)**—is located on the right hand rear of the engine, with automatic transmission.

• **Vehicle Speed Sensor (VIN U**—is located on the rear of the engine, below the direct ignition system module, with manual transmission.

• **Vehicle Speed Sensor Buffer**—is located behind the right hand side of the instrument panel.

• **Wiper Pulse Module**—is located behind the left side of the instrument panel.

• **Wiper/Washer Fluid Level Switch**—is located on the washer reservoir.

• **Wiper/Washer Motor Module**—is located on the left hand side of the firewall in the engine compartment.

CADILLAC

Circuit Breakers

ALLANTE

RETAINED ACCESSORY POWER

There is one 30 amp circuit breaker located in the fuse block.

POWER SEATS AND DOOR LOCKS

There is one 30 amp circuit breaker located in the fuse block, protects the power seat and door lock circuits.

IGNITION AND POWER DOOR SWITCHES

There is one 30 amp circuit breaker located in the fuse block, protects the ignition and power door switch circuits.

DEFOGGER AND POWER TOP PULL DOWN

There is one 30 amp circuit breaker located in the fuse block, protects the defogger and convertible top circuits.

WINDSHIELD WIPER

This circuit breaker is integral with the headlight switch.

POWER WINDOWS

On each power window motor there is a self resetting circuit breaker.

POWER ACCESSORIES

Circuit breakers for power accessories are located in the fuse block, convenience center and/or relay centers. They protect the following circuits; rear window defogger, power windows, power seats and power door locks, alarm systems, keyless entry, sunroofs, etc. if equipped.

BROUGHAM

HEADLIGHTS—TWILIGHT SENTINEL

This 16.5 amp circuit breaker is integral with the headlight wiper switch.

TRUNK LID PULL DOWN

There is one 20 amp in-line fuse located behind the right hand fabric rear end panel, next to the pull down unit, which is inside the trunk.

THEFT DETERRENT

There is a 20 amp in-line fuse used for the lights and a 25 amp in-line fuse used for the horn, which is located on a bracket above the steering column.

WINDSHIELD WIPER

This circuit breaker is integral with the headlight switch.

POWER WINDOWS

On each power window motor there is a self resetting circuit breaker.

POWER ACCESSORIES

Circuit breakers for power accessories are located in the fuse block, convenience center and/or relay centers. They protect the following circuits; rear window defogger, power windows, power seats and power door locks, alarm systems, keyless entry, sunroofs, etc. if equipped.

DEVILLE AND FLEETWOOD

HEADLIGHTS—TWILIGHT SENTINEL

This 16.5 amp circuit breaker is integral with the headlight wiper switch.

TRUNK LID PULL DOWN

There is one 20 amp in-line fuse located behind the right hand fabric rear end panel, next to the pull down unit, which is inside the trunk.

THEFT DETERRENT

There is a 20 amp in-line fuse used for the lights and a 25 amp in-line fuse used for the horn, which is located on a bracket above the steering column.

HEATED MIRROR

There is one 7.5 amp in-line fuse about 6 inches from the right hand junction block in-line with the wiring harness.

POWER WINDOWS

There is one 30 amp circuit breaker located in the fuse block, protects the power window circuits.

HORN

There is one 30 amp circuit breaker located in the fuse block, protects the horn circuits.

WINDSHIELD WIPER

This circuit breaker is integral with the headlight switch.

POWER WINDOWS

On each power window motor there is a self resetting circuit breaker.

POWER ACCESSORIES

Circuit breakers for power accessories are located in the fuse block, convenience center and/or relay centers. They protect the following circuits; rear window defogger, power windows, power seats and power door locks, alarm systems, keyless entry, sunroofs, etc. if equipped.

ELDORADO

DELAYED ACCESSORY BREAKER

There is one 30 amp circuit breaker located in the fuse block.

POWER SEATS

There is one 30 amp circuit breaker located in the fuse block, protects the power seats circuits.

HORN AND DEFOGGER

There is one 30 amp circuit breaker located in the fuse block, protects the defogger and convertible top circuits.

LO-BEAM

There is one 10 amp circuit breaker located in the fuse block, protects the Lo-Beam circuits.

HI-BEAM

There is one 10 amp circuit breaker located in the fuse block, protects the Hi-Beam circuits.

WINDSHIELD WIPER

This circuit breaker is integral with the headlight switch.

HEADLIGHTS – TWILIGHT SENTINEL

This circuit breaker is integral with the headlight switch.

POWER WINDOWS

On each power window motor there is a self resetting circuit breaker.

POWER ACCESSORIES

Circuit breakers for power accessories are located in the fuse block, convenience center and/or relay centers. They protect the following circuits; rear window defogger, power windows, power seats and power door locks, alarm systems, keyless entry, sunroofs, etc. if equipped.

SEVILLE

DELAYED ACCESSORY BREAKER

There is one 30 amp circuit breaker located in the fuse block.

POWER SEATS

There is one 30 amp circuit breaker located in the fuse block, protects the power seats circuits.

HORN AND DEFOGGER

There is one 30 amp circuit breaker located in the fuse block, protects the defogger and convertible top circuits.

LO-BEAM

There is one 10 amp circuit breaker located in the fuse block, protects the Lo-Beam circuits.

HI-BEAM

There is one 10 amp circuit breaker located in the fuse block, protects the Hi-Beam circuits.

WINDSHIELD WIPER

This circuit breaker is integral with the headlight switch.

HEADLIGHTS – TWILIGHT SENTINEL

This circuit breaker is integral with the headlight switch.

POWER WINDOWS

On each power window motor there is a self resetting circuit breaker.

POWER ACCESSORIES

Circuit breakers for power accessories are located in the fuse block, convenience center and/or relay centers. They protect the following circuits; rear window defogger, power windows, power seats and power door locks, alarm systems, keyless entry, sunroofs, etc. if equipped.

Fusible Links

Most fusible links are located at the battery junction block. Other locations, depending on options, include battery, starter solenoid and alternator. The fusible link wire gauge size is marked on the insulation and each link is four sizes smaller than the cable it is designed to protect. The same wire with special hypalon insulation must be used when replacing a fusible link.

Relay, Sensors And Computer Locations

NOTE: When using this section, some of the components may not be used on a particular vehicle. This is because the particular component in question was used on an earlier model or a later model. If a component is not found in this section, check other vehicles of the same body line, as that component may have been introduced earlier on different models. This section is being published from the latest information available at the time of this publication.

ALLANTE

- **A/C Aspirator** – is located behind the right hand side of the instrument panel, above the instrument panel compartment.
- **A/C Compressor Clutch Relay** – is located on the right hand front fender panel, in the engine compartment.
- **A/C Compressor Cutoff Relay** – is located on the right hand front fender panel, in the engine compartment.
- **A/C Heater Programmer** – is located behind the right hand side of the instrument panel, on right hand side of the plenum.
- **A/C Heater/Defrost Valve Vacuum Actuator** – is located under the instrument panel, on the end of the A/C plenum.
- **A/C High Side Temperature Sensor** – is located on the right hand front side of the engine compartment on the A/C line.
- **A/C In-Car Temperature Sensor** – is located below the center of the instrument panel, ahead of the console.
- **A/C Low Pressure Switch** – is located on the right hand front side of the engine compartment, on the rear of the accumulator.
- **A/C Low Side Temperature Sensor** – is located on the right hand front side of the firewall in the engine compartment, above the blower motor.
- **A/C Outside Air Valve Vacuum Actuator** – is located under the instrument panel, on the end of the A/C plenum.
- **A/C up-Down Valve Actuator** – is located under the instrument panel, on the end of the A/C plenum.
- **A/C Vacuum Delay Porous Plug** – is located under the instrument panel, on the end of the A/C plenum.
- **Air Bag** – See Supplemental Inflatable Restraint (SIR) System.
- **Air Diverter Valve** – is located on the left hand front side of the engine.
- **Air Select/Switching Valve** – is located on the left hand front side of the engine.

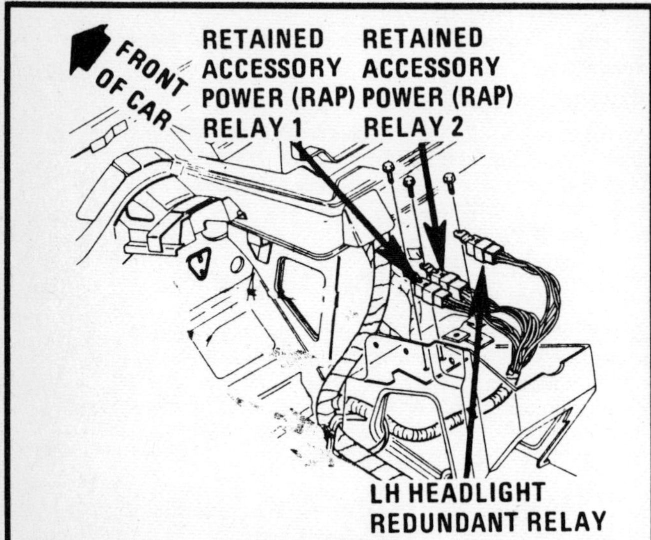

Retained power relays—Allante

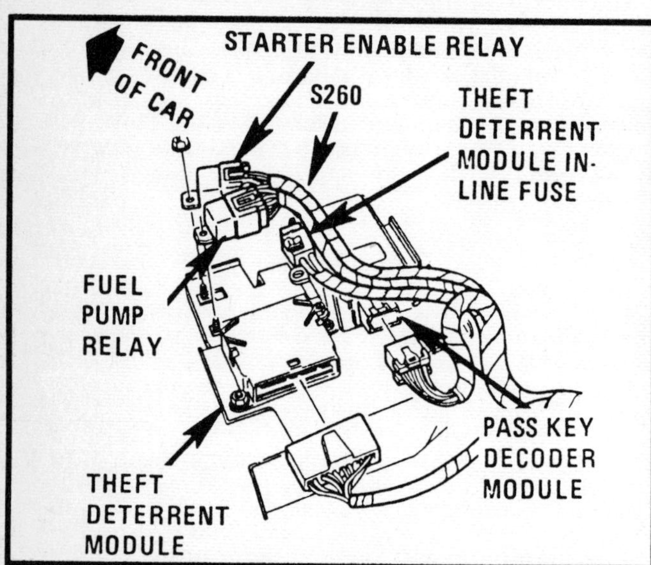

Theft deterrent components—Allante

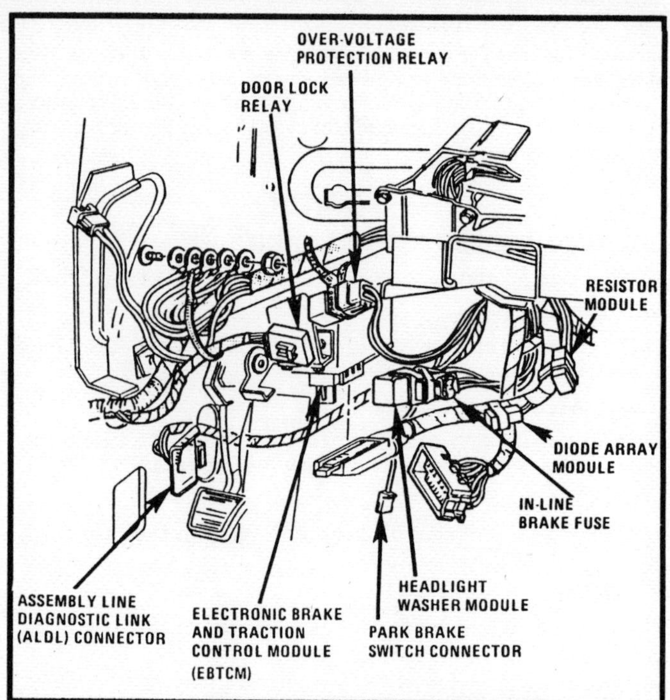

Components under left instrument panel—Allante

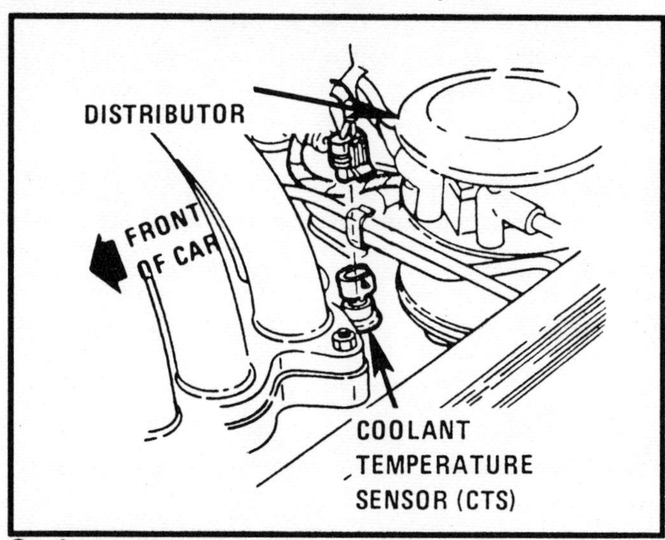

Coolant temperature sensor—Allante

- **Assembly Line Diagnostic Link (ALDL) Connector**—is located under the instrument panel, to the left of the parking brake.
- **Battery Temperature Sensor**—is part of the positive battery cable.
- **Body Computer Module**—is located behind the center of the instrument panel.
- **Brake Fluid Level Sensor**—is located on the top of the brake fluid reservoir.
- **Brake Pump Relay**—is located on the right hand front fender panel, in the engine compartment.
- **Canister Purge Solenoid**—is located in the right hand front corner of the engine compartment, on top of the canister.
- **Cellular Telephone Transceiver In-Line Fuse**—is located behind the left hand seat, behind the access panel.
- **Cellular Telephone Transceiver**—is located behind the left hand seat, behind the access panel.
- **Central Power Supply**—is located under the left hand side of the instrument panel to the right side of the steering column.
- **Chime Module**—is located behind the right hand side of the instrument panel, above the instrument panel compartment.
- **Climate Control/Driver Information Center**—is located in the center of the instrument panel, ahead of the console.
- **Coolant Fan Choke**—is located under the headlight, under the right hand front of the vehicle.
- **Coolant Fan Control Module**—is located under the headlight, under the right hand front of the vehicle.
- **Coolant Fan Diode**—is located in the forward lights harness, in the right hand front of the engine compartment.
- **Coolant Fan Relay**—is located on the radiator support, in the right hand front of the engine compartment.
- **Coolant Temperature Sensor**—is located on the left hand top side of the engine, to the right of the distributor.

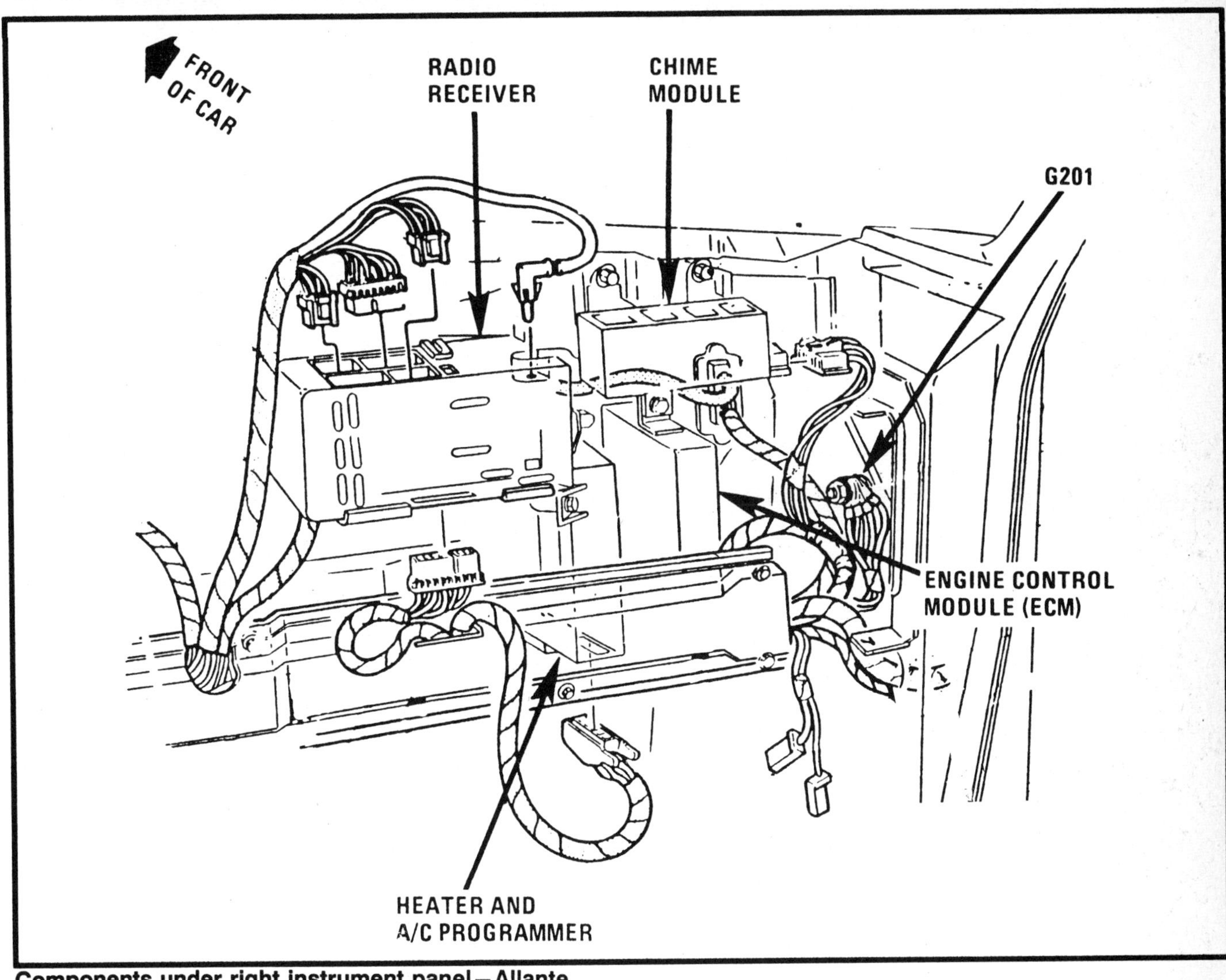

Components under right instrument panel—Allante

• **Cruise Control Check Valve**—is located in the engine compartment, on the right hand side of the firewall, in the vacuum line.

• **Cruise Control Servo**—is located on the right hand top of the engine, behind the alternator.

• **Cruise Control Vacuum Release Valve**—is located above the brake pedal on the brake pedal support bracket.

• **Cruise Control Vacuum Tank**—is located in the right hand front fender, behind the wheel.

• **Defogger Relay**—is located in the right hand side of the trunk, behind the wheelhouse.

• **Delco-Bose Music System Diode**—is located in the main harness, right hand side of the trunk.

• **Delco-Bose Music System Speaker Relay**—is located in the right hand side of the trunk, behind the wheel house.

• **Diode Array Module**—is located behind the left hand side of instrument panel, near the steering column.

• **Electronic Brake Control Module (ECM)**—is located behind the left hand side of the instrument panel, to the left of the steering column.

• **Electronic Control Module (ECM)**—is located behind the right hand side of the instrument panel near the shroud (kick panel).

• **Electronic Vacuum Regulator Valve**—is located at the right hand rear side of the engine, above the exhaust manifold.

• **Engine Metal Temperature Switch**—is located on the left hand rear side of the engine, near the exhaust manifold.

• **Express Window Down Module**—is under the arm rest plate on the door that it controls.

• **Fan Control Module**—is located under the right headlight.

• **Fuel Door Release Solenoid**—is located below the left seat, below the speaker.

• **Fuel Pump Prime Connector (1989)**—is located near the right hand side strut tower, in the engine compartment.

• **Fuel Pump Prime Connector (except 1989)**—is located near the right rear of the engine, taped to the engine wiring harness near the dash grommet.

• **Fuel Pump Relay**—is located behind the right hand side of the instrument panel, behind the radio.

• **Fuse Box**—is in the center console, under the ashtray.

• **Hard Top/Soft Top Close Relay (except 1989)**—is located behind the left seat, behind the access panel on the relay bracket.

• **Hard Top/Soft Top Left Relay (except 1989)**—is located behind the left seat, below the access panel on the relay bracket.

• **Hard Top/Soft Top Left Timer Relay (except 1989)**—is located behind the left seat, behind the access panel taped to the harness.

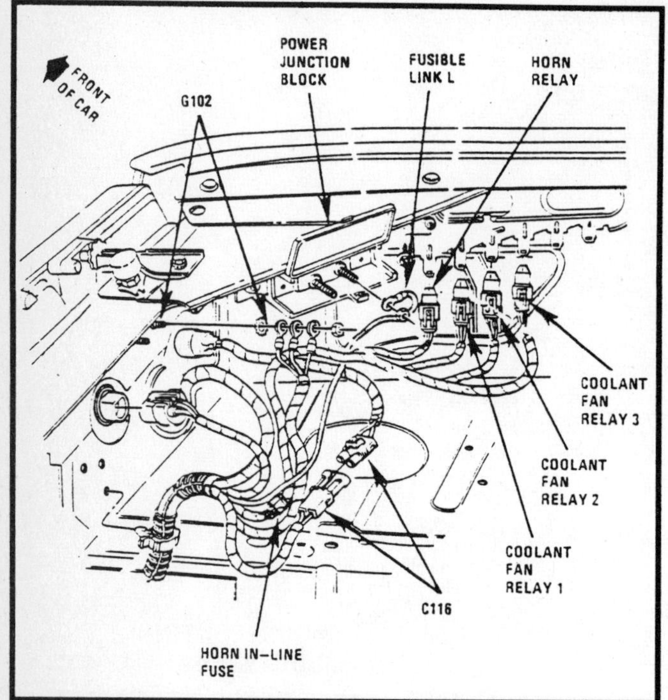

Relay locations—1990 Allante

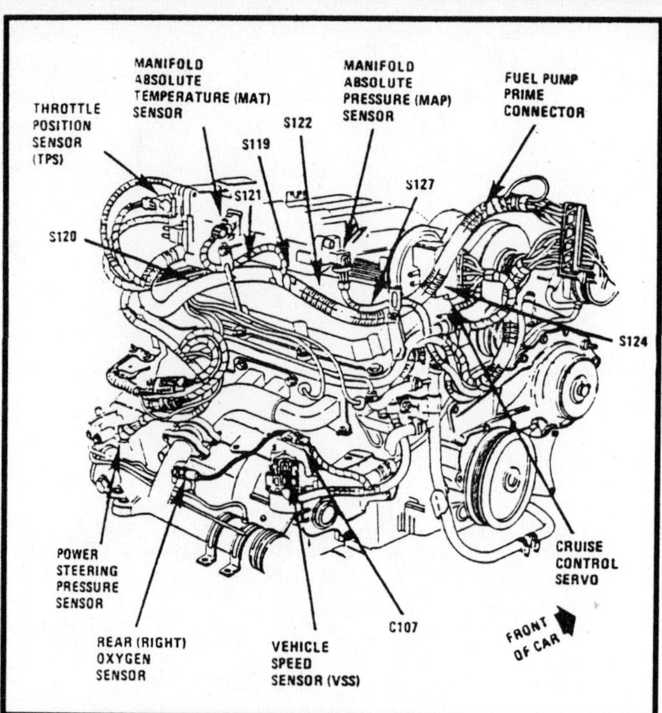

Engine sensor locations—Allante

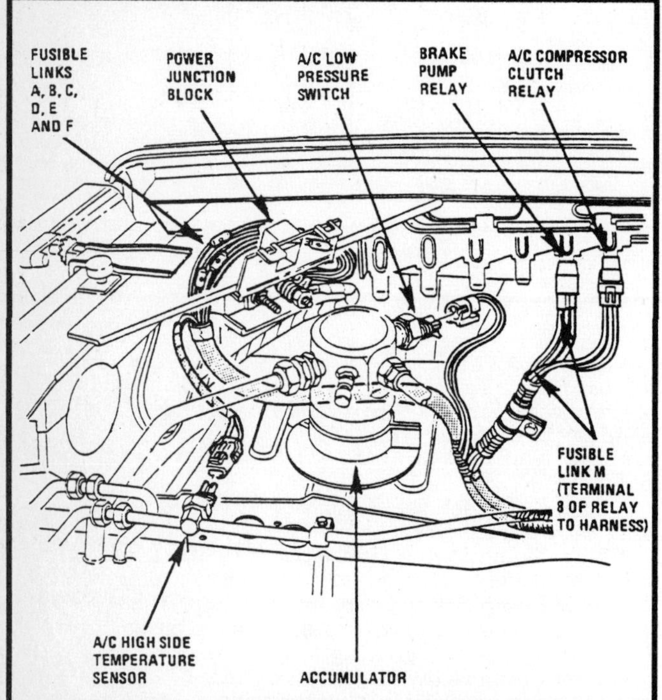

Air conditioning relay locations—Allante

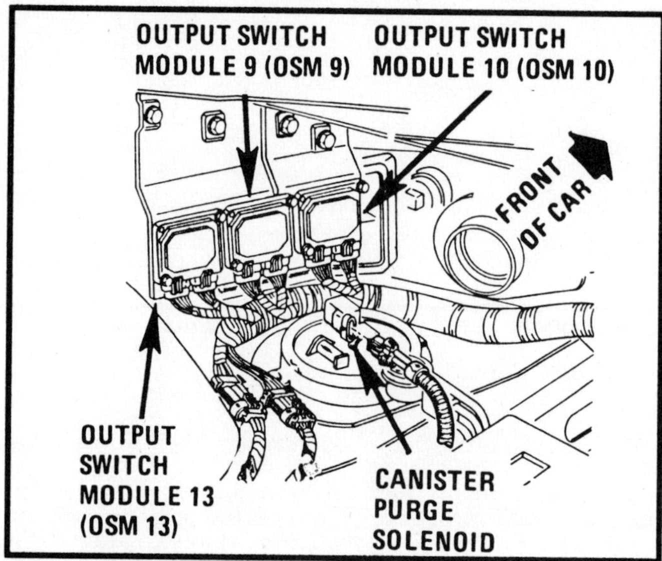

Output switch modules—Allante

• **Hard Top/Soft Top Open Relay (except 1989)**—is located behind the left seat, behind the access panel on the relay bracket.

• **Hard Top/Soft Top Pull Down Unit (1989)**—is located behind the seats, below the center of the soft top.

• **Hard Top/Soft Top Right Relay (except 1989)**—is located behind the left seat, behind the access panel on the relay bracket.

• **Hard Top/Soft Top Right Timer Relay (except 1989)**—is located behind the left seat, behind the access panel taped to the harness.

• **Hard Top/Soft Top Switch Diode 1 (except 1989)**—is located behind the left seat, behind the access panel, in the harness 10 in. from the switch.

• **Hard Top/Soft Top Switch Diode 2 (except 1989)**—is located behind the left seat, behind the access panel, in the harness 10 in. from the switch.

• **Headlight Washer Module**—is located behind the left hand side of the instrument panel, on the support bracket.

• **Headlight Washer Pump**—is located in the left hand side of the engine compartment, on the washer reservoir.

• **Horn In-Line Fuse** – is located on the right hand front of the engine compartment, near the horn relay.

• **Horn Relay** – is located on the right hand front fender panel, in the engine compartment.

• **Hydraulic Modulator** – is located on the left hand front of the firewall.

• **Idle Speed Control Assembly** – is located at the top left of the engine, in front of the throttle body.

• **Ignition Key Warning Switch** – is located in the upper portion of the steering column.

• **Ignition Switch** – is located on the left hand side of the steering column.

• **In-Line Brake Fuse** – is located under the instrument panel to the left side of the steering column.

• **Isolated Ground Junction Block** – is located behind the right hand seat, behind the access panel.

• **Isolated Power Junction Block** – is located behind the right hand seat, behind the access panel.

• **Left Hand Headlight Redundant Relay** – is located in the left hand side of the engine compartment, on the radiator support.

• **Left Hand Taillight Redundant Relay** – is located in the right hand side of the trunk, behind the wheel house.

• **Low Coolant Level Module** – is located behind the instrument panel, to the left of the steering column.

• **Low Coolant Switch** – is located in the right hand front side of the radiator.

• **Manifold Absolute Pressure (MAP) Sensor** – is located on the top of the engine, on the right hand side of the intake plenum.

• **Manifold Air Temperature (MAT) Sensor** – is located on the left hand top of the engine, in the rear of the intake plenum.

• **Maxi Fuse Panel** – is located behind the right rear seat, behind the access panel, under the speaker.

• **Memory Seat Relay** – is on the seat module, under the seat that it controls.

• **Mercury Switch** – is located on the underside of the trunk lid.

• **Oil Pressure Sensor** – is located on the left hand top of the engine, to the left of the distributor.

• **Oil Pressure Switch** – is located on the left hand top of the engine, above the transaxle.

• **Output Switch Module No. 2** – is located on the left hand rear of the trunk, on the base of the end panel.

• **Output Switch Module No. 3** – is located on the left hand rear of the trunk, on the base of the end panel.

• **Output Switch Module No. 4** – is located on the right hand side of the trunk, above the rear wheelhouse.

• **Output Switch Module No. 5** – is located on the right hand side of the trunk, above the rear wheelhouse.

• **Output Switch Module No. 6** – is located on the right hand rear of the trunk, on the base of the end panel.

• **Output Switch Module No. 7** – is located on the right hand rear of the trunk, on the base of the end panel.

• **Output Switch Module No. 8** – is located under the left hand front of the vehicle, under the headlight.

• **Output Switch Module No. 9** – is located under the left hand front of the vehicle, under the headlight.

• **Output Switch Module No. 10** – is located under the left hand front of the vehicle, under the headlight.

• **Outside Air Temperature Sensor** – is located in front of the radiator, below the hood latch.

• **Over Voltage Protection Relay** – is located under the instrument panel to the left side of the steering column.

• **Oxygen (Left) Sensor** – is located in the front of the engine at the base of the exhaust manifold.

• **Oxygen (Right) Sensor** – is located in the rear of the engine at the base of the exhaust manifold.

• **PASS Key Decoder Module** – is located behind the right side of the instrument panel, behind the radio receiver.Power Antenna Relay – is located in the right hand rear corner of the trunk, on or near the antenna assembly.

• **Power Door Lock Relay** – is located behind the left hand side of the instrument panel, on the instrument brace or above the parking brake.

• **Power Junction Block** – is located in the right hand corner of the engine compartment.

• **Power Module In-Line (30 amp) Fuse** – is located in the main harness, behind the right hand seat, behind the access panel.

• **Power Module** – is located in the rear of the engine compartment, on the firewall.

• **Power Steering Pressure Sensor** – is located on the left hand rear of the engine, on the steering rack.

• **Power Steering Switch** – is located on the left hand rear of the engine, on the steering rack.

• **Radio Diode** – is in the main harness, in the right rear corner of the trunk near the wheelhousing.

• **Radio Mute Module** – is located in the center console.

• **Radio Receiver** – is located behind the right hand side of the instrument panel, behind the instrument panel compartment.

• **Radio RF Signal Splitter** – is at the right rear corner of the trunk.

• **Rear Fuse Panel** – is located in the right hand rear of the trunk, behind the wheelhouse.

• **Retained Accessory Power Relay No. 1** – is located behind the right hand side of the instrument panel, above the heater and A/C plenum.

• **Retained Accessory Power Relay No. 2** – is located behind the right hand side of the instrument panel, above the heater and A/C plenum.

• **Right Front Signal Splitter** – is located in the right hand rear of the corner of the trunk.

• **SIR Diagnostic/Energy Reserve Module** – is located behind the left side of the instrument panel, on the bracket above the brake pedal.

• **SIR Dual Sensor** – is behind the right side of the instrument panel, below the cowl.

• **SIR Forward Sensor** – is in front of the radiator, on the right side of the hood latch.

• **SIR Resistor Module** – is behind the left side of the instrument panel, taped to the EBTCM branch of the main harness.

• **Soft Top Position Switch** – is located behind the lower left hand seat, near the lower left hand hinge assembly.

• **Speed Dependent Damping (SDD) Controller** – is located behind the left seat, behind the access panel.

• **Starter Enable Relay (except 1989)** – is located behind the right hand side of the instrument panel, behind the radio receiver.

• **Starter Interrupt Relay (1989)** – is located behind the right hand side of the instrument panel, above the heater and A/C plenum.

• **Starter Solenoid** – is located on the lower left hand front of the engine.

• **Sunload Sensor** – is located on the center of the instrument panel, below the defrost grille.

• **Theft Deterrent Controller In-Line Fuse** – is located behind the right hand side of the instrument panel, above the heater and A/C plenum.

• **Theft Deterrent Controller** – is located behind the right hand side of the instrument panel, above the heater and A/C plenum.

• **Throttle Position Sensor** – is located on the rear of the throttle body.

• **TPS Test Point Connector** – is located near the right hand side strut tower in the engine compartment.

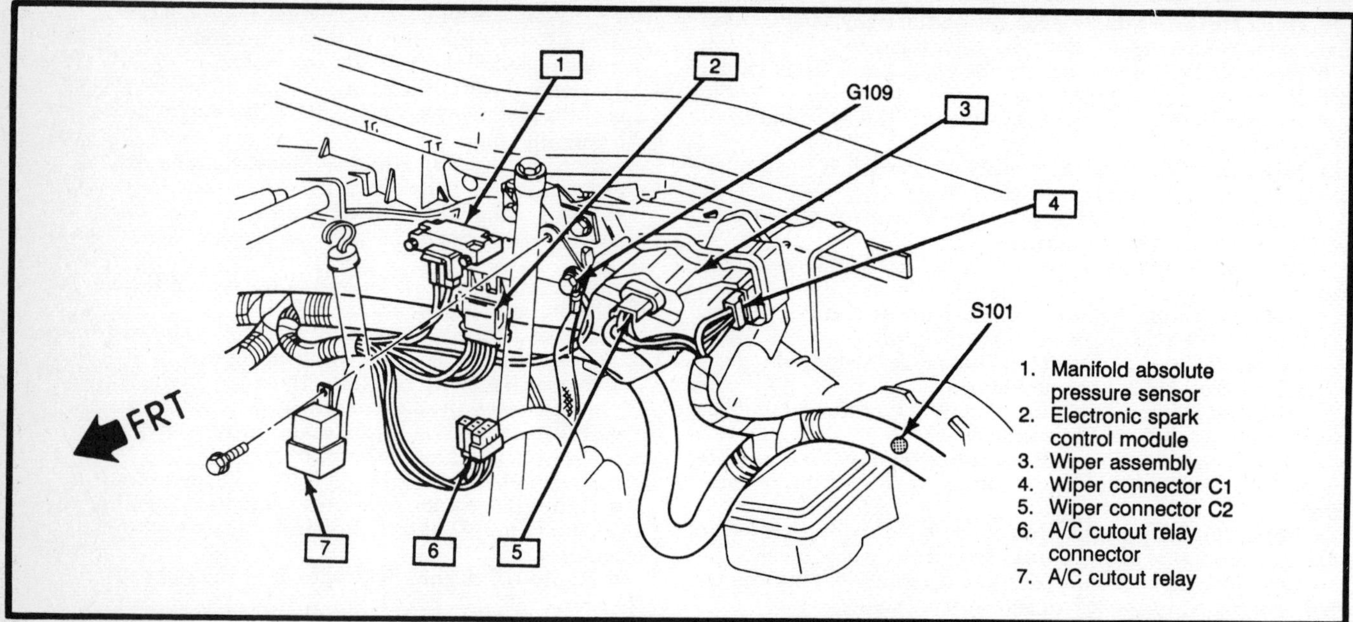

Air conditioning relay locations – Brougham

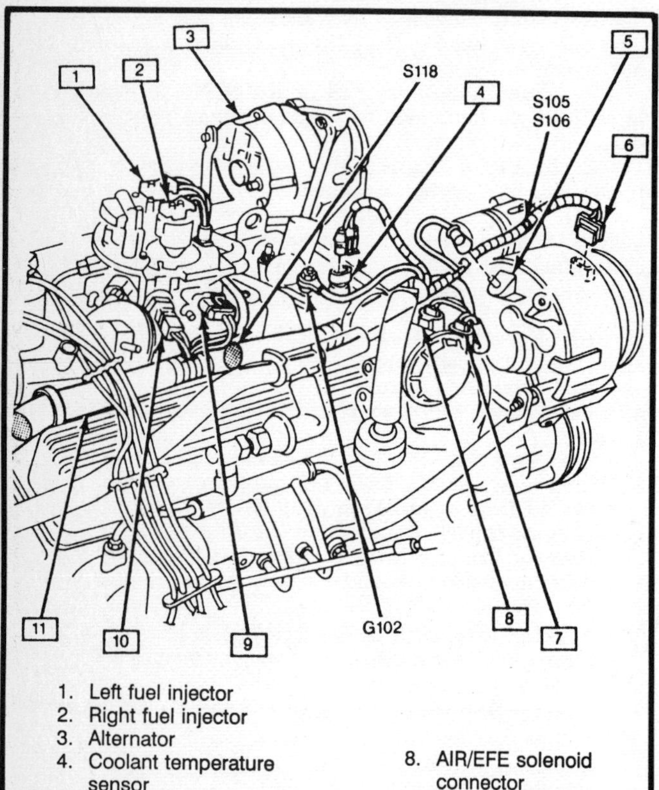

Engine sensor locations – Brougham

- **Transaxle Position Switch** – is located on the lower left hand rear of the engine, mounted on the transaxle.
- **Transaxle Temperature Sensor** – is located on the left hand side of the engine.
- **Trunk Lid Pull** – Down Unit – is located on the center of the trunk, mounted on the end panel.
- **Trunk Lid Release Solenoid** – is located on the rear of the trunk, on the under side of the trunk lid.
- **Trunk Light Switch** – is located on the underside of the trunk lid.
- **Twilight Sentinel Photocell** – is located behind the center of the instrument panel, below the defrost vent.
- **Vehicle Speed Sensor** – is located on the right hand rear side of the engine, mounted on the transaxle.
- **Viscous Converter Clutch (VCC) Brake Switch** – is located behind the left hand side of the instrument panel, on the brake pedal support.
- **Wheel Speed Sensors** – is located at each wheel, behind the dust shield.
- **Wiper/Washer Fluid Switch** – is located on the top of the washer fluid reservoir.
- **Wiper/Washer Motor Capacitor** – is located on the left hand side of the firewall, in the connector.
- **Wiper/Washer Motor Module** – is located on the left hand side of the firewall, behind the strut tower in the engine compartment.

BROUGHAM

- **A/C Air Inlet Valve Vacuum Actuator** – is located under the center of the instrument panel, near the ECC programmer.
- **A/C Ambient Temperature Sensor** – is located behind the glove box.
- **A/C Compressor Clutch Diode** – is located in the connector at the rear of the compressor.
- **A/C Compressor Cycling Switch** – is mounted on top of the evaporator assembly.
- **A/C Cutout Relay** – is located on the right hand rear of the engine on the valve cover.
- **A/C Heater/Defroster Valve Vacuum Actuator** – is taped below the A/C module, next to the dash panel.
- **A/C In-Car Temperature Sensor** – is located in the top of the instrument panel, to the left hand side of the glove box.
- **A/C Low Pressure Switch** – is located in the rear head of the A/C compressor.

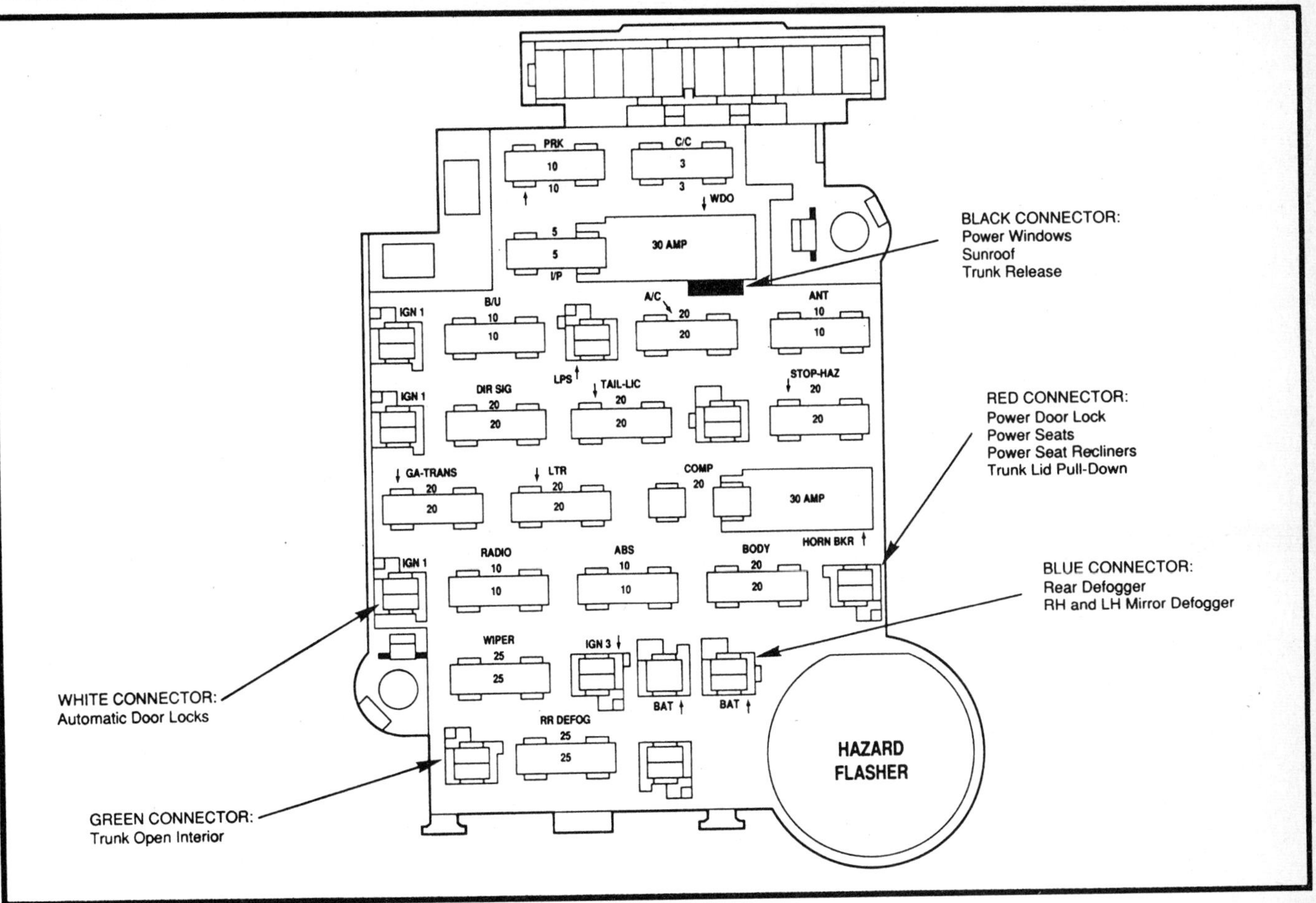

BLACK CONNECTOR:
Power Windows
Sunroof
Trunk Release

RED CONNECTOR:
Power Door Lock
Power Seats
Power Seat Recliners
Trunk Lid Pull-Down

BLUE CONNECTOR:
Rear Defogger
RH and LH Mirror Defogger

WHITE CONNECTOR:
Automatic Door Locks

GREEN CONNECTOR:
Trunk Open Interior

HAZARD FLASHER

Fuse box identification—1990 Brougham

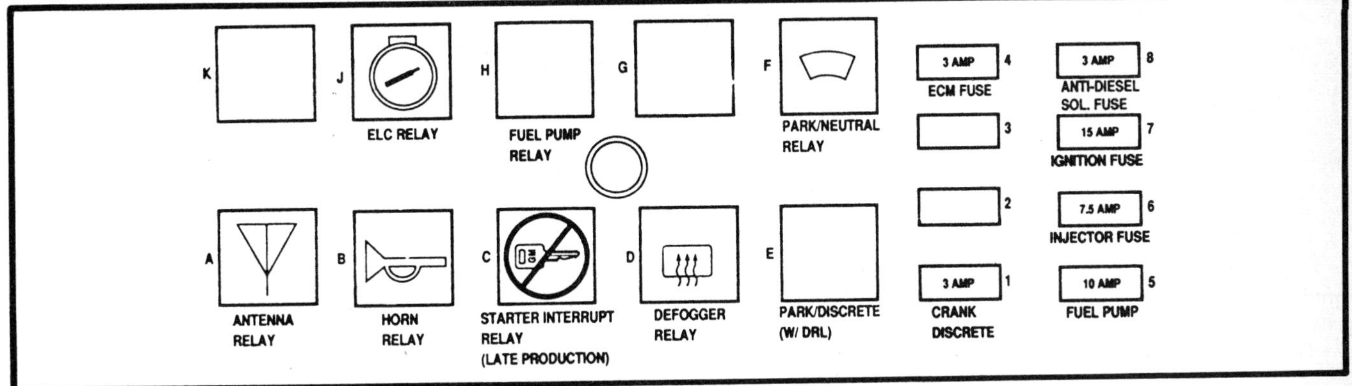

Accessory relay center identification—Brougham

- **A/C Mode Valve Vacuum Actuator**—are located on the left hand side of the A/C module, next to the dash panel.
- **A/C Vacuum Delay Porous Plug**—is located in the organ hose near the ECC programmer.
- **Accessory Relay Panel**—is located behind the instrument panel, to the left of the steering column.
- **Accessory Relay Panel**—is next to the fuse box.
- **AIR Control Solenoid (VIN 7)**—is located at the upper right side of the engine, above the valve cover.
- **AIR Control Valve (VIN 7)**—is located at the upper right side of the engine, above the valve cover.
- **AIR Diverter Valve (VIN Y)**—is located on the upper right hand front side of the engine.
- **AIR Select/Switching Valve (VIN Y)**—is located on the upper right hand front side of the engine.
- **Alternator Diode**—is taped to the wiring harness at the left front of the firewall.
- **Anti-Dieseling Solenoid (VIN Y)**—is located on the left hand side of the engine on the valve cover.
- **Assembly Line Diagnostic Link (ALDL) Connector**—is located at the bottom center of the dash panel.

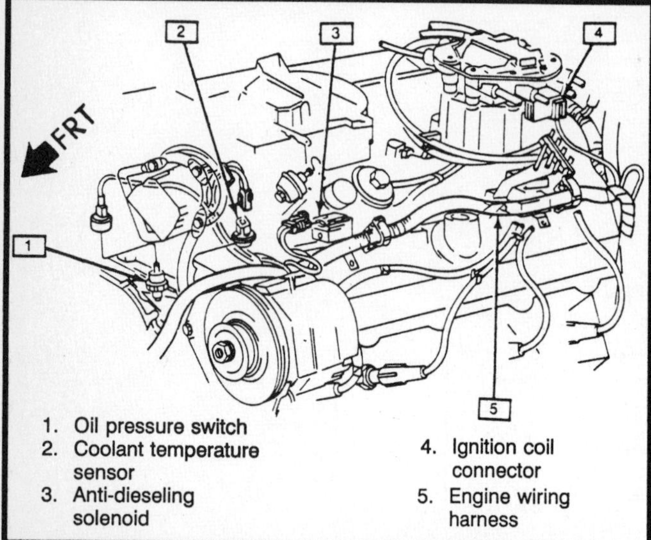

Engine sensor locations—Brougham with 5.0L VIN Y engine

• **Audio Alarm Module**—is located behind the instrument panel, to the left of the radio.

• **Automatic Door Lock Controller (early 1989)**—is located behind the right side of the dash, near the glove box.

• **Automatic Door Lock Controller (except 1989)**—is located at the upper right shroud.

• **Automatic Door Lock Diode**—is located behind the right side of the dash panel, if so equipped.

• **Brake Pressure Switch**—is located on the frame, to the left of the left hand exhaust manifold.

• **Canister Purge Solenoid (VIN 7)**—is located at the left front corner of the engine compartment.

• **Canister Purge Solenoid (VIN Y)**—is located in the right hand front corner of the engine compartment, on top of the canister.

• **CHECK ENGINE Light Driver Module (VIN Y)**—is located behind the center of the instrument panel.

• **Chime Module**—is behind the left instrument panel, on the left of the radio control head.

• **Coolant Temperature Sensor (VIN 7)**—is located at the front center of the intake manifold.

• **Coolant Temperature Sensor (VIN Y)**—is located on the left hand top side of the engine.

• **Coolant Temperature Switch (VIN Y)**—is located on the left hand front side of the engine.

• **Cruise Control Module**—is located behind the instrument panel, to the left of the radio.

• **Cruise Control Servo**—is located on the left hand side of the engine.

• **Cruise Control Vacuum Release Valve**—is located above the brake pedal on the brake pedal support bracket.

• **Defogger In-Line Fuse**—is located under the left side of the dash, near the fuse block.

• **Defogger Relay**—is located in the accessory relay panel.

• **Detonation (Knock) Sensor (VIN 7)**—is located at the lower right side of the engine, near the starter solenoid.

• **Diagnostic Dwell Meter Connector (VIN Y)**—is taped to the ECM harness at the front of the engine, behind the valve cover.

• **Diode Module (VIN Y)**—is located behind the center of the instrument cover, taped to the harness.

• **Diode Module**—is located above the fuse box.

• **Door Lock Relay (except 1989)**—is located at the lower right side of shroud.

• **ECC Programmer**—is behind the glove compartment.

• **Electronic Brake Control Module (EBCM)**—is under the right side of instrument panel, under the glove compartment.

• **Electronic Climate Control Programmer (ECC)**—is located under the right side of the dash panel, to the left of the glove box.

• **Electronic Control Module (ECM)**—is located behind the right side of the dash panel, near the glove box.

• **Electronic Control Power Module (ECC)**—is located behind the right side of the dash panel, mounted on top of the evaporator housing.

• **Electronic Level Control (ELC) Test Connector**—is in the ELC wiring harness, to the left of the brake booster.

• **Electronic Level Control Compressor**—is located near the left hand front wheel.

• **Electronic Level Control Diode**—is located in the instrument panel wiring harness, behind the radio, if so equipped.

• **Electronic Level Control Height Sensor**—is attached to rear crossmember.

• **Electronic Level Control Relay**—is located in the accessory relay panel.

• **Electronic Level Control Test Connector**—is located to the left of the brake booster.

• **Electronic Spark Control (ESC) Module (VIN 7)**—is located above the right rear of the engine.

• **Electronic Spark Control Module (ESC)**—is located on the right side of the firewall in the engine compartment.

• **Exhaust Gas Recirculation Solenoid (VIN 7)**—is located at the rear of the engine above the left valve cover.

• **Fuel Pump Prime Connector (VIN 7)**—is located on the right side of the engine compartment, near the blower motor.

• **Fuel Pump/Oil Pressure Switch (VIN 7)**—is located at the lower left rear of the engine.

• **Fuse Box**—is behind the instrument panel, to the left of the steering column.

• **Fusible Link**—most fusible links are located at the junction block near the battery. Other link locates may include the starter solenoid and alternator.

• **Gear Selector Switch**—is located on the upper base of the steering column.

• **Hazard Flasher**—is located in the fuse block.

• **Heater Water Valve**—is located on the right hand side of the engine.

• **Horn Relay**—is located in the accessory relay panel.

• **Ignition Key Warning Switch**—is located in the upper portion of the steering column, above the ignition keyhole.

• **Ignition Switch**—is located at the base of the steering column.

• **ILC/EGR/RVB Solenoid Assembly (VIN Y)**—is located in the left hand rear side of the engine, near the valve cover.

• **Illuminated Entry Timer**—is located behind the instrument panel, to the left of the steering column.

• **Lock Enable Relay (except 1989)**—is taped to the door lock controller.

• **Manifold Absolute Pressure (MAP) Sensor**—is located on the bulkhead, behind the distributor.

• **Manifold Air Temperature (MAT) Sensor (VIN 7)**—is in the bottom of the air cleaner.

• **Manifold Vacuum Sensor (VIN Y)**—is located on the right hand side of engine compartment.

• **Mixture Control Solenoid (VIN Y)**—is located on the carburetor.

• **Oil Pressure Switch (VIN Y)**—is located on the left hand top side of the engine.

• **Opera Lamp Inverter**—is located behind the left hand rear wheel well.

• **Outside Air Temperature Sensor**—is located in the rear of the radiator grille.

• **Over Voltage Protection (OVP) Relay**—is under the right side of instrument panel, under the glove compartment.
• **Oxygen Sensor**—is located in the rear of the engine at the base of the exhaust manifold.
• **Park/Neutral Reverse Relay**—is located forward of the instrument panel harness under the steering column.
• **Passive Restraint Module**—is at the center of the instrument panel, below the ashtray.
• **Power Antenna Relay**—is located in the accessory relay panel.
• **Power Door Lock Enable Relay**—is taped to the assembly line data link.
• **Power Door Lock Relay**—is located at the lower right hand shroud.
• **Radio Receiver**—is behind the instrument panel to the left of the radio control head.
• **Seatbelt Chime**—is located behind the instrument panel, to the left of the radio.
• **Seatbelt Switch**—is part of the driver's seatbelt assembly.
• **Sentinel Amplifier**—is located behind the left side of the instrument panel, below the light switch.
• **Sentinel Photocell**—is located on the corner of the left side speaker grille.
• **Starter Interrupt Relay (1989)**—is located above the lower base of the steering column.
• **Starter Interrupt Relay (1990-91)**—is located in the accessory relay panel.
• **Starter Interrupt Relay (early 1990)**—is located above the lower base of the steering column.
• **Starter Solenoid**—is located on the lower left hand front of the engine.
• **Sun Roof Actuator Assembly**—is located in the windshield header above the right seat.
• **Sunroof Actuator Assembly**—is at the center of the windshield header.
• **Sunroof Relay**—is attached to or part of the sunroof actuator assembly.
• **Tachometer Test Connector (VIN 7)**—is at the top rear of the distributor.
• **Theft Deterrent Controller**—is located under the left side of the dash panel, mounted on the brake pedal support.
• **Theft Deterrent Diode (A)**—is located forward of the instrument panel, to the left of the brake pedal support or in the controller module.
• **Theft Deterrent Relay**—is strapped to the theft deterrent controller.
• **Throttle Position Sensor**—is located on the top center of the engine.
• **Trunk Lid Tamper Switch**—is located in the rear center of the trunk lid.
• **Trunk Pull**—Down In-Line Fuse—is located in the rear of the trunk, near the pull down unit.
• **Trunk Pull**—Down Unit—is located in the center rear of the trunk.
• **Trunk Release Solenoid**—is located in the rear center of the trunk lid.
• **Trunk Release Switch**—is located in the glove box.
• **Turn Signal Flasher**—is located under the instrument panel, on the right side of the steering column bracket.
• **Vehicle Speed Sensor (early 1989)**—maybe mounted on the back of the speedometer.
• **Vehicle Speed Sensor (except 1989)**—is mounted on the back of the transmission.
• **Vehicle Speed Sensor Buffer (VIN 7)**—is behind the glove compartment.
• **Vehicle Speed Sensor Buffer (VIN Y)**—is located under the dash panel, to the left of the radio.
• **Wiper/Washer Fluid Level Switch**—is located on the top of the washer fluid reservoir.

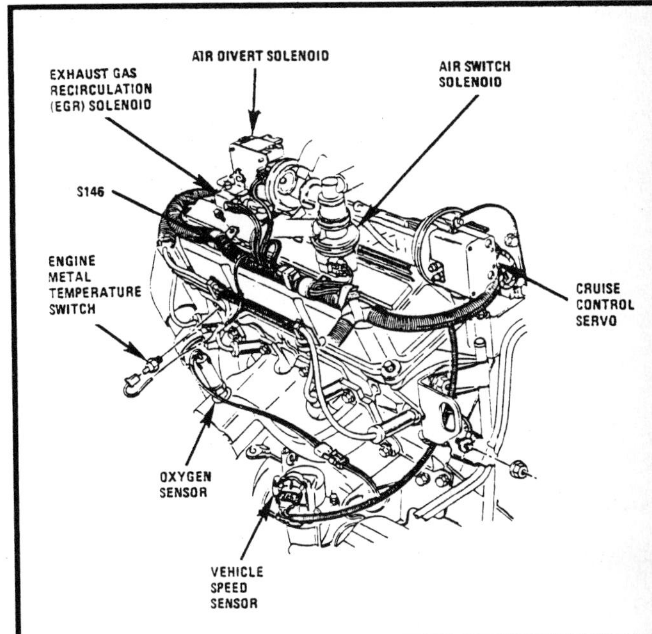

Engine sensor locations—Deville and Fleetwood

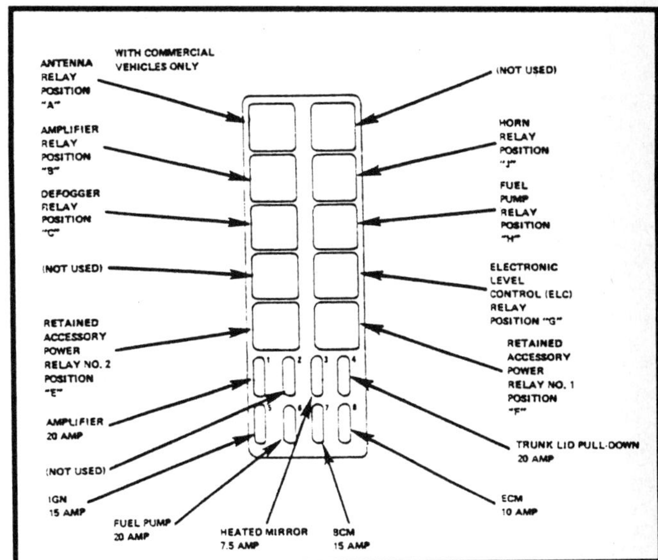

Relay center identification—1990 Deville

DEVILLE AND FLEETWOOD

• **A/C Air Inlet Valve Vacuum Motor**—is located under the center of the instrument panel.
• **A/C Compressor Clutch Diode**—is located in the connector at the rear of the compressor.
• **A/C Compressor Cutout Switch**—is located on top of the accelerator bracket, if so equipped.
• **A/C Heater/Defroster Valve Vacuum Motor**—is located behind the center of the instrument panel.
• **A/C Heater/Water Valve Vacuum Motor**—is located behind the engine on the center of the firewall.
• **A/C High Side Temperature Sensor**—is located on the right hand front side of the engine compartment, near the right strut tower.

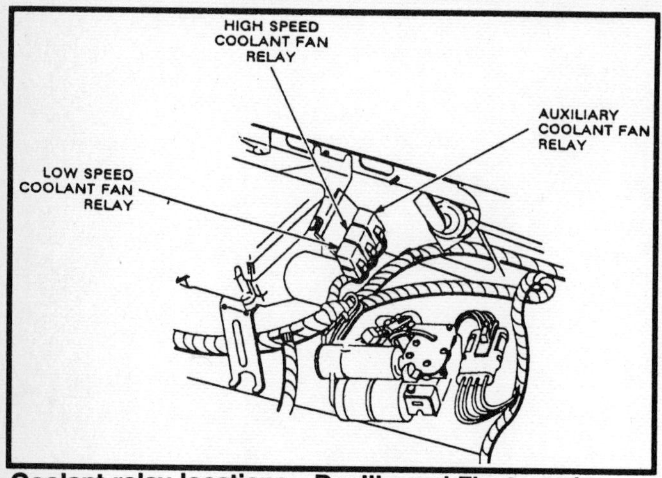

Coolant relay locations—Deville and Fleetwood

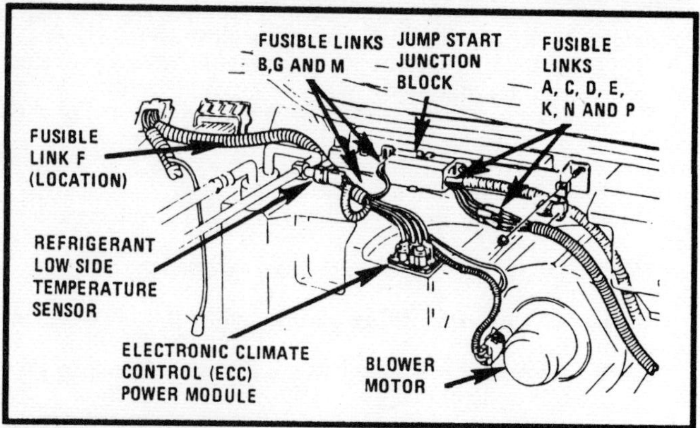

Fusible links locations—Deville and Fleetwood

• **A/C In-Car Temperature Sensor**—is located in the top right hand side of the instrument panel.

• **A/C Low Pressure Switch**—is located on the A/C accumulator, near the right hand fender.

• **A/C Low Side Temperature Sensor**—is located on the right hand front side of the firewall, in the engine compartment.

• **A/C Mode Valve Vacuum Actuator**—is located under the center of the instrument panel.

• **A/C Outside Air Temperature Sensor**—is located in the center of the radiator grille.

• **A/C Vacuum Delay Porous Plug**—is located behind the center of the instrument panel, in the orange hose, near the inlet valve motor.

• **Air Bag**—See Supplemental Inflatable Restraint (SIR) System.

• **AIR Diverter Valve**—is located on the upper right hand rear of the engine, above the valve cover.

• **AIR Switch Solenoid**—is located on the upper right hand rear of the engine, above the valve cover.

• **Ambient Sensor**—is incorporated into the automatic day/night mirror.

• **Amplifier Relay**—is in the relay center at position B.

• **Anti-lock Brake Controller Fuse**—is located on the left hand side of the firewall, to the right of the wiper motor.

• **Anti-lock Brake Diode**—is located behind the right hand side of the instrument panel, in the connector, near the dash grommet.

• **Anti-lock Brake Electronic Control Module**—is located behind the left hand side of the instrument panel, near the left hand shroud.

• **Anti-lock Brake Fluid Level Switch**—is located on the master cylinder assembly.

• **Anti-lock Brake Hydraulic Pump Motor Fuse**—is located on the left hand side of the firewall, to the right of the wiper motor.

• **Anti-lock Brake Hydraulic Pump Motor Relay**—is located on the left hand side of the firewall, to the right of the wiper motor.

• **Anti-lock Brake Main Relay**—is located on the left hand side of the firewall, to the right of the wiper motor.

• **Anti-lock Brake Solenoid Valve**—is located on the bottom left side of the master cylinder assembly.

• **Anti-lock Brake Speed Sensors**—are located on the brake assembly, on each wheel.

• **Anti-lock Brake Valve Block Connector**—is located on the brake hydraulic unit.

• **Assembly Line Diagnostic Link (ALDL) Connector**—is located on the bottom center of the instrument panel.

• **Astro Roof Control Module**—is located along the right roof rail, above the right front door.

• **Automatic Door Lock Controller**—is located behind the right side of the dash, to the left of the relay center.

• **Automatic Door Lock Diode**—is located behind the right side of the dash panel.

• **Back—Up Switch**—is located on the top of the transaxle.

• **Body Computer Module (BCM)**—is located behind the right hand side of the instrument panel, behind the glove box.

• **Brake Booster Low Vacuum Switch**—is located in the left side of the power brake booster, if equipped.

• **Brake Fluid Level Switch**—is located on the master cylinder assembly.

• **Brake Pressure Switch**—is located on the master cylinder assembly, if so equipped.

• **Calibration Timer Module**—is located behind the right hand side of the instrument panel, near the top left side of the glove box.

• **Canister Purge Solenoid**—is located in the right hand front corner of the engine compartment, on or near the canister.

• **CB Amplifier**—is located under the right side of the instrument panel, near the right hand shroud.

• **Console In-Line Fuse**—is below the center console.

• **Coolant Temperature Sensor**—is located on the top center of the engine, behind the distributor.

• **Cooling Fan Control Filter Assembly**—is located in the left hand front of the engine compartment, behind the headlights.

• **Cooling Fan Control High Speed Relay**—is located on the left side of the engine compartment, on the relay bracket.

• **Cooling Fan Control Low Speed Relay**—is located on the left side of the engine compartment, on the relay bracket.

• **Cooling Fan Control Module**—is located in the left hand front of the engine compartment, behind the headlights.

• **Cooling Fan Diode**—is taped to the harness, near the electronic control level compressor.

• **Cruise Control Servo**—is located on the front of the engine, near the left hand end of the cylinder head.

• **Cruise Control Vacuum Release Valve**—is located above the brake pedal on the brake pedal support bracket.

• **Cruise Control Vacuum Solenoid**—is located on the front of the engine, near the left hand end of the cylinder head.

• **Cruise/Viscous Converter Clutch Brake Switch**—is located above the brake pedal on the brake pedal support bracket.

• **CTS**—See Coolant Temperature Sensor.

• **Defogger Relay**—is in the relay center at position C.

• **Demand Hi Beam Relay**—is taped to the harness, near the light switch.

• **Dimming Sentinel Amplifier**—is located in the center of the windshield header, as part of the courtesy lamp assembly.

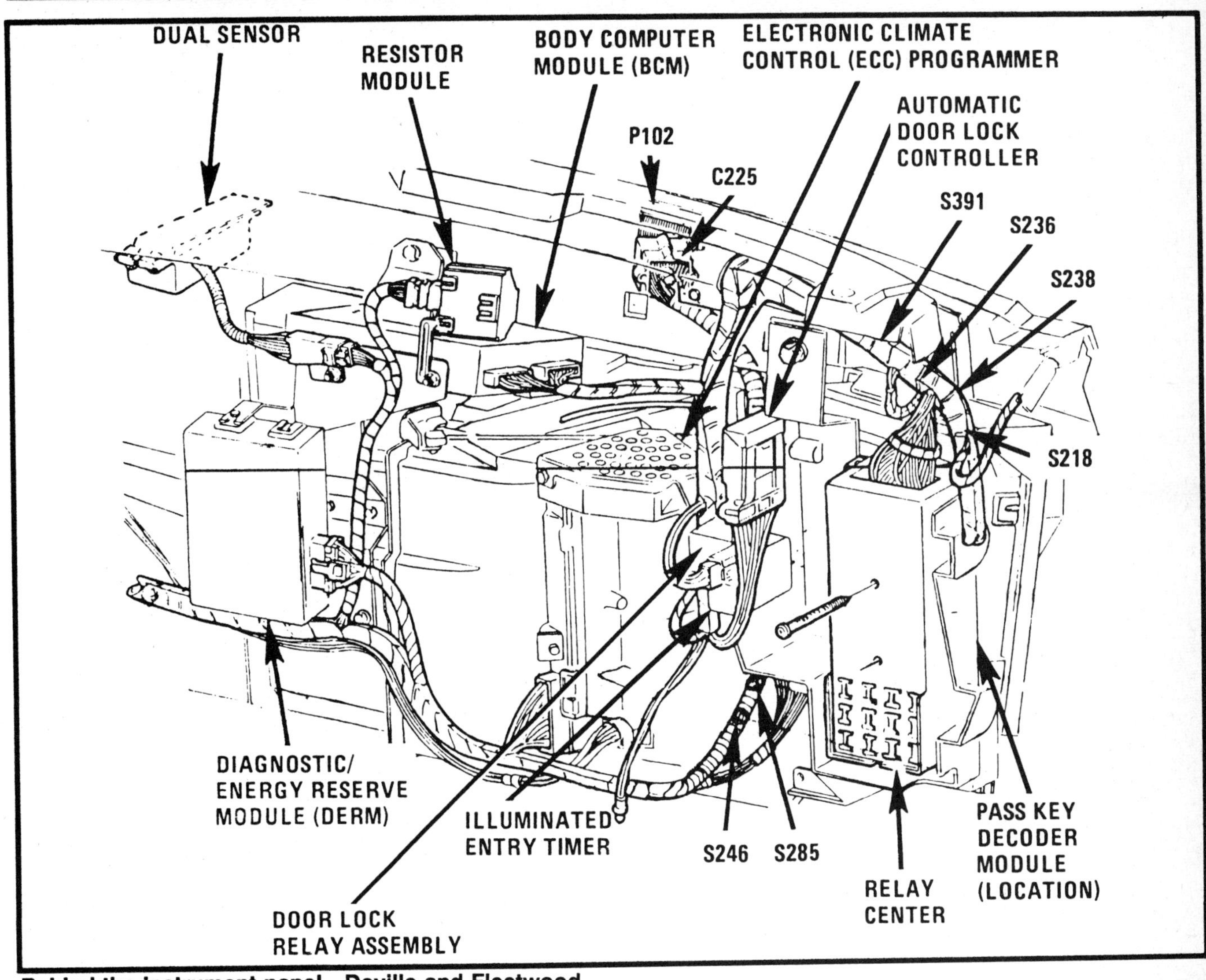

Behind the instrument panel—Deville and Fleetwood

- **Dimming Sentinel Power Relay**—is located under the left side of the instrument panel, to the left of the steering column.
- **Direction Relay**—is under the center console.
- **Early Fuel Evaporation (EFE) Heater**—is located under the throttle body.
- **Early Fuel Evaporation (EFE) Relay**—is located in the relay center.
- **EGR Solenoid**—is located on the top left rear of the engine or in the center of the intake manifold.
- **Electric Vacuum Pump**—is located below the battery in the left hand front fender apron.
- **Electronic Climate Control (ECC) Programmer**—is located in the engine compartment, on the center of the firewall.
- **Electronic Control Module (ECM)**—is located behind the right side of the instrument panel, near the shroud.
- **Electronic Control Power (ECC) Module**—is located on the center of the firewall, in the engine compartment.
- **Electronic Level Control (ELC) Compressor**—is located on the left hand side of the engine compartment.
- **Electronic Level Control Height Sensor**—is located on the right hand wheel well, to the left of the coil spring.
- **Electronic Level Control Relay**—is in the relay center at position G.
- **Electronic Level Control Test Connector**—is located near the top of the electronic level control compressor.
- **Engine Metal Temperature Switch**—is located on the left hand rear side of the engine, at the exhaust manifold.
- **Express Down Window Module**—is in the lower front the left door.
- **Factory Priming Input Connector**—is located on the top left hand side of the engine, taped to the engine harness.
- **Fog Light Relay**—is located on the left hand side of the firewall.
- **Fuel Door Release Solenoid**—is located in the trunk at the fuel tank door.
- **Fuel Pump Prime Connector**—is located on the left side of the engine compartment, taped to the composite harness.
- **Fuel Pump Relay**—is in the relay center at position H.
- **Hazard Relay**—is located in the right hand side of the steering column support.
- **Headlight Sensor**—is incorporated into the automatic day/night mirror.
- **Heated Windshield Control Module**—is located behind the left side of the instrument panel, to the right of the steering column.
- **Heated Windshield Power Module**—is located at the

right front of the engine compartment, behind the right headlamp assembly.

- **Horn Relay**—is located in the relay center at position J.
- **Idle Speed Control**—is located on the right front side of the throttle body.
- **Ignition Key Warning Switch**—is located in the upper portion of the steering column.
- **Ignition Switch**—is located on the center of the steering column.
- **Illuminated Entry Timer**—is located behind the instrument panel, on the relay bracket.
- **Jump Start Junction Block**—is located on the left hand front inner fender, in front of the wheel well.
- **Manifold Absolute Pressure (MAP) Sensor**—is located on the center of the firewall, above the blower motor.
- **Manifold Air Temperature (MAT) Sensor**—is located on the top right center of the engine.
- **Oil Pressure Switch**—is located on the left hand top of the engine, near the distributor.
- **Opera Lamp Inverter**—is located in the trunk on the right hand rear wheel well.
- **Oxygen Sensor**—is located in the rear of the engine at the base of the exhaust manifold.
- **Passive Restraint Timer Module**—is located behind the right side of the instrument panel, to the left of the relay center.
- **Pneumatic Seat Control Module**—is located under the respective seat.
- **Power Antenna Relay (1989)**—is located behind the right side of the dash panel, below the connector C201.
- **Power Antenna Relay (except 1989)**—is located on the right side of the trunk, behind the wheelhousing. Commercial vehicles have the relay in the relay center at position A.
- **Power Door Lock Relay Assembly**—is located behind the right side of the dash panel, on the top right side of connector C201.
- **Power Door Main Unlatch Relay (Limo)**—is near the base of the right hand shroud, under the instrument panel.
- **Power Rear Window Relay Assembly**—is located near the base of each B—pillar.
- **Power Seat Diode**—is located in the connector at the front of each seat.
- **Power Seat Memory Module**—is under the left side of the driver's seat.
- **Power Seat Recliner Capacitor**—is located in the connector at the front of each seat.
- **Power Steering Switch**—is located on the rear of the engine, on the steering box.
- **Power Window Diode**—is located in the left hand door harness, below the window switch connector.
- **Radio Amplifier**—is located under the right side of the instrument panel, near the right hand shroud.
- **Radio Mute Module**—is located behind the center of the instrument panel.
- **Radio Splitter**—is located under the right side of the instrument panel, below the glove box.
- **Radio Transceiver**—is located in the left hand rear corner of the trunk.
- **Relay Center**—is located behind the instrument panel, below the glove box.
- **Retained Accessory Power Relay No. 1**—is in the relay center at position F.
- **Retained Accessory Power Relay No. 2**—is in the relay center at position E.
- **Seat Latch Relay**—is located under the center console.
- **Seat Memory Module**—is under the right side of the left seat.
- **Seat Recliner Capacitor**—is located below each front seat, across the motor terminals.
- **Seatbelt Switch**—is part of the driver's seatbelt assembly.
- **SIR Diagnostic/Energy Reserve Module (DERM)**—is behind the right side of the instrument panel, below the BCM.
- **SIR Dual Sensor**—is behind the instrument panel to the left of the glove compartment.
- **SIR Forward Discriminating Sensor**—is at the center of the engine compartment, at the radiator.
- **SIR Resistor Module**—is behind the right side of the instrument panel, below the BCM.
- **Starter Interrupt Relay**—is located on a bracket under the left side of the dash panel, to the left of the steering column.
- **Starter Solenoid**—is located on the lower left hand side of the engine.
- **Starting and Charging System Factory Test Connector**—is located behind the alternator.
- **Sunroof Limit Switch**—is located in the windshield header above the left hand visor.
- **Sunroof Timer Module**—is located in the windshield header above the left hand visor.
- **Theft Deterrent Controller**—is located under the left side of the dash panel, to the left of the steering column or above the accelerator pedal.
- **Theft Deterrent Diode**—Taped to the instrument panel wiring harness under the right side of the dash panel.
- **Theft Deterrent In-Line Fuses**—are located under the left side of the dash panel, next to the steering column.
- **Theft Deterrent Relay**—is located behind a bracket under the left side of the instrument panel, near the controller.
- **Throttle Position Sensor**—is located on the rear of the throttle body.
- **TPS Test Point Connector**—is located on the firewall, taped to the wiring harness in the engine compartment.
- **TPS**—See Throttle Position Sensor.
- **Trunk Pull**—Down In-Line Fuse—near the latch at the center of the trunk lid.
- **Trunk Pull**—Down Unit—is located near the latch at the center of the trunk lid.
- **Trunk Release Solenoid**—is located in the rear center of the trunk lid.
- **Turn Signal Relay**—is located in the left hand side of the steering column trim panel.
- **Twilight Sentinel Amplifier**—is located under the left side of the dash panel, to the right of the light switch.
- **Twilight Sentinel Photocell**—is located on the top left side of the dash panel, in the corner of the left hand speaker grille.
- **Vacuum Pump Relay**—is located in the relay center.
- **Vehicle Speed Sensor Buffer**—is located under the right side of the dash panel, on the right side of the relay center.
- **Vehicle Speed Sensor**—is located on the right hand rear side of the engine, mounted on the transaxle.
- **Wiper/Washer Fluid Level Switch**—is located on the top of the washer fluid reservoir.
- **Wiper/Washer Module**—is located on the left hand side of the firewall.

ELDORADO AND SEVILLE

- **A/C Air Inlet Valve Vacuum Motor**—is located under the center of the instrument, to the left side of the A/C module.
- **A/C Aspirator**—is located in the center of the instrument panel, to the left of the glove box.
- **A/C Compressor Clutch Diode**—is located in the connector at the rear of the compressor.
- **A/C Compressor Clutch Relay**—is located in the underhood relay center, at position 'K'.
- **A/C Defrost Valve Vacuum Motor**—is located under the center of the instrument, to the left side of the A/C module.
- **A/C Heater Programmer**—is located behind the right hand side of the instrument panel, on the right side of the A/C module.

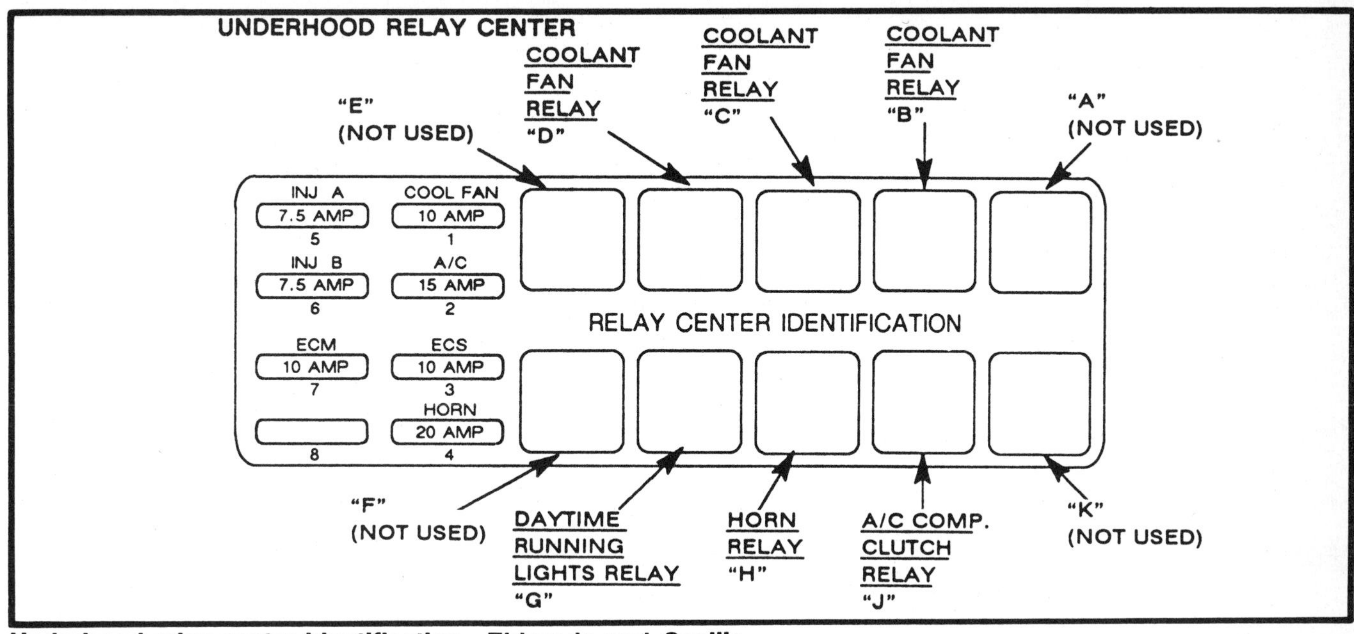

Underhood relay center identification—Eldorado and Seville

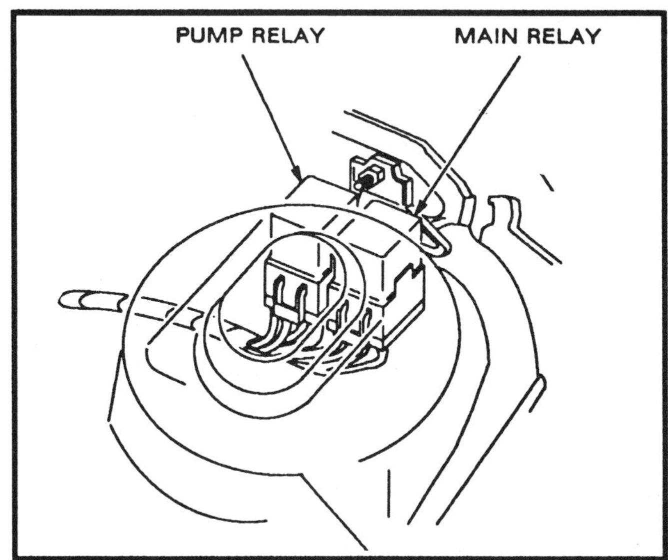

Fuel pump relay—Deville and Fleetwood

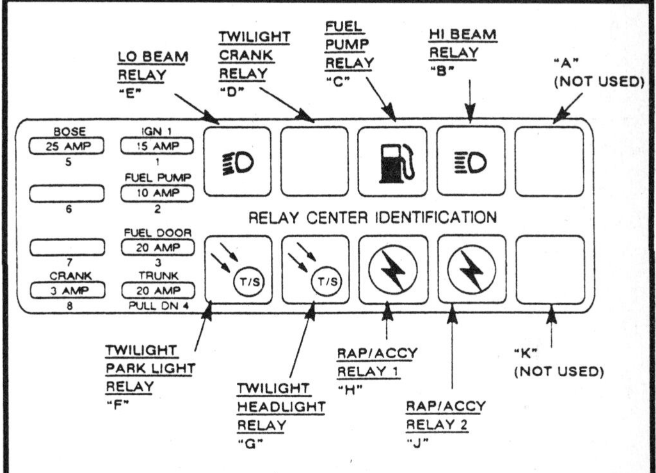

Interior relay center identification—Eldorado and Seville

• **A/C Heater Resistors**—are located on the right side of the firewall in the engine compartment, in the top of the plenum, if so equipped.

• **A/C Heater/Water Valve Vacuum Motor**—is located behind the engine on the center of the firewall.

• **A/C High Side Temperature Sensor**—is located on the center of the firewall on the A/C line, to the right of the blower motor.

• **A/C In-Car Temperature Sensor**—is located in the center of the instrument panel, to the left of the glove box.

• **A/C Low Side Temperature Switch**—is located on the right hand front side of the firewall on the A/C line.

• **A/C Outside Air Temperature Sensor**—is located in the left hand corner of the radiator grille.

• **A/C Sunload Sensor**—is located in the top center of the instrument panel, to the left of the glove box.

• **A/C up-Down Valve Vacuum Motor**—is located under the center of the instrument, to the left side of the A/C module.

• **A/C Vacuum Delay Porous Plug**—is located behind the center of the instrument panel, in the orange vacuum hose.

• **AIR Divert Solenoid (VIN 3 and 5)**—is located at the top of the engine over the rear of the valve cover.

• **Air Diverter Valve**—is located on the top of the engine, over the rear valve cover.

• **AIR Switch Solenoid (VIN 3 and 5)**—is located at the right top of the engine over the valve cover.

• **AIR Switch Solenoid**—is located on the top of the engine, over the rear valve cover.

• **Alternator Disable Connector**—is taped to the engine harness, behind the generator.

• **Alternator Disable Connector**—is taped to the wiring harness, behind the alternator.

• **Ambient Sensor**—is incorporated into the automatic day/night mirror.

• **Amplifier Relay**—is located at the right side of the passenger compartment, near the rear of the right front door sill.

• **Anti-lock Brake Control Fuse (5 amp)**—is located under the instrument panel, to the right of the steering column.

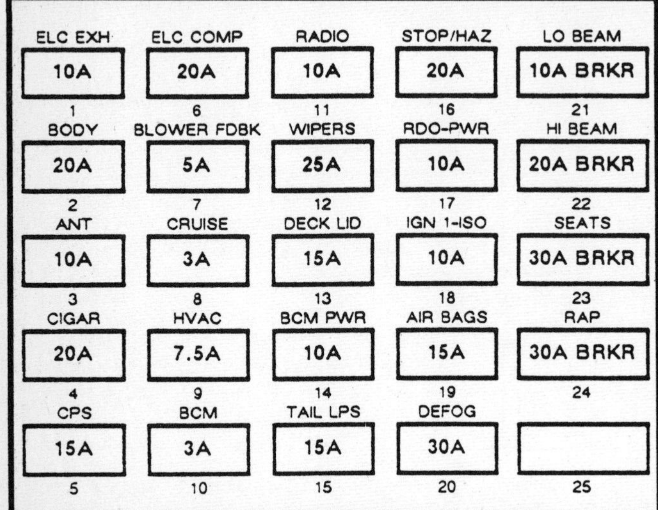

Fuse box identification – Eldorado and Seville

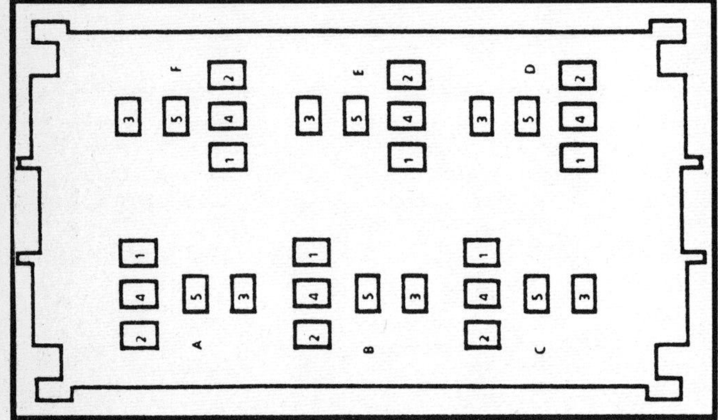

Mirco relay center identification – Eldorado and Seville

- **Anti-lock Brake Diode** – is in the trunk, on the left rear wheelhousing, above the EBCM.
- **Anti-lock Brake Electronic Control Module (ECBM)** – is located in the luggage compartment, on the left hand wheel house.
- **Anti-lock Brake Main Relay Fuse (30 amp)** – is located on the center of the firewall, on the relay bracket.
- **Anti-lock Brake Main Relay** – is located on the center of the firewall, on the relay bracket.
- **Anti-lock Brake Pump Fuse (5 amp)** – is located on the center of the firewall, on the relay bracket.
- **Anti-lock Brake Pump Fuse (30 amp)** – is located on the center of the firewall, on the relay bracket.
- **Anti-lock Brake Pump Relay (30 amp)** – is located on the center of the firewall, on the relay bracket.
- **Anti-lock Brake Wheel Sensors** – are located in each wheel spindle.
- **Assembly Line Diagnostic Link Connector** – is located under the left side of the instrument panel, to the right of the parking brake.
- **Astro Roof Actuator Assembly** – is located in the windshield header.
- **Automatic Door Lock Module** – is located behind the instrument panel, to the right of the steering column.
- **Automatic Transaxle Temperature Sensor** – is located under the left hand side of the transaxle.
- **Body Computer Module** – is located behind the right hand side of the instrument panel, behind the glove box.

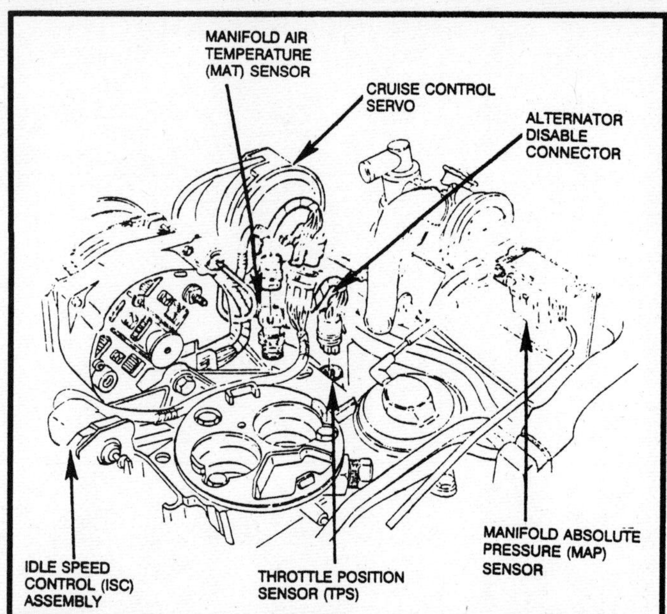

Engine component locations – 1990 Eldorado and Seville

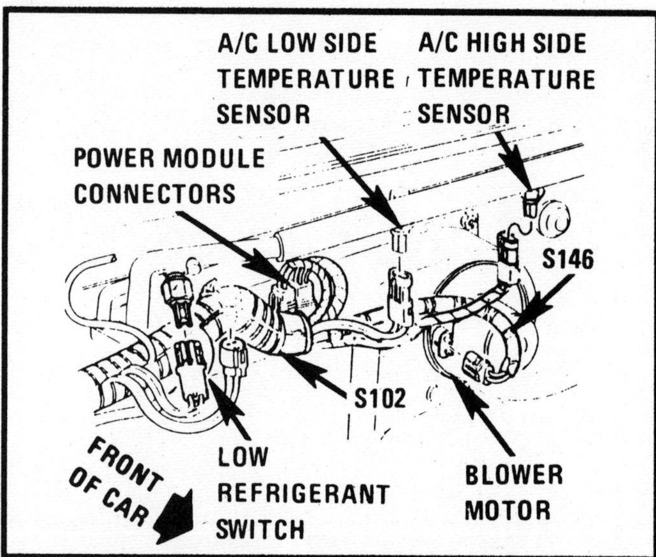

Air conditioning component locations – 1990 Eldorado and Seville

- **Canister Purge Solenoid (VIN 3 and 5)** – is located at the left front of the engine compartment, below the underhood relay center.
- **Canister Purge Solenoid** – is located in the left hand front corner of the engine compartment, on top of the canister, under the relay center.
- **Cellular Mobile Telephone Fuse (10 amp)** – is located in the interior relay center.
- **Central Power Supply (1989)** – is located behind the left hand side of the instrument panel, to the right of the steering column.
- **Central Power Supply (except 1989)** – is located behind the center of the instrument panel, below the radio.
- **Chime Module Diode** – is taped to the harness, behind the right hand side of the instrument panel.

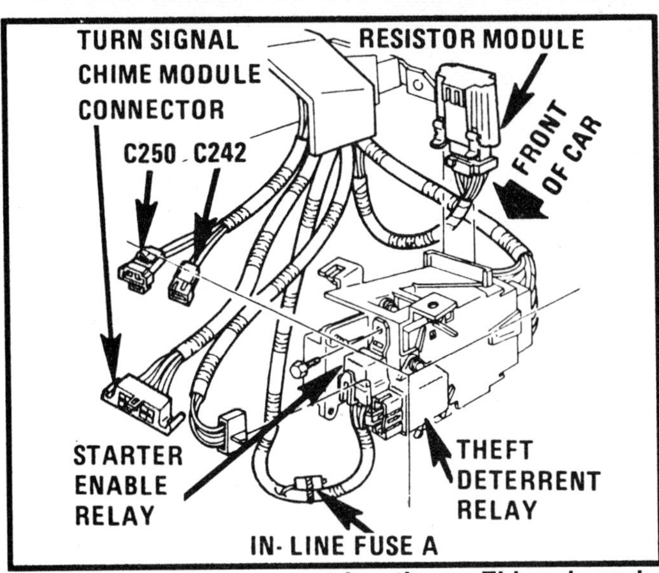

Theft deterrent component locations – Eldorado and Seville

• **Chime Module** – is located behind the right hand side of the instrument panel, near the shroud.

• **Climate Control Driver Information Center (CCDIC)** – is behind the left side of the instrument panel, to the right of the steering column.

• **Coolant Fan Control Module** – is located in the right hand front of the engine compartment, in front of the radiator.

• **Coolant Fan Diode** – is located in the engine harness, in the left hand front of the engine.

• **Coolant Fan Puller** – is located behind the radiator, in the front of the engine compartment.

• **Coolant Fan Pusher** – is located in front of the radiator, in the front of the engine compartment.

• **Coolant Fan Relay** – is located in the underhood relay center, at position 'C'. The 1990-91 vehicles have additional coolant relays at positions 'B' and 'D'.

• **Coolant Temperature Sensor (VIN 3 and 5)** – is located at the top left side of the engine, behind the distributor.

• **Coolant Temperature Sensor** – is located on the top left side of the engine, near the distributor.

• **Courtesy Light Relay (except 1989)** – is located in the mirco relay center, at position 'B'.

• **Courtesy Lights Relay** – is located behind the center of the instrument panel, to the left of the interior relay center.

• **Cruise Control Servo** – is located on the right hand front of the engine, near the generator.

• **Cruise Control Vacuum Release Valve** – is located above the brake pedal on the brake pedal support bracket.

• **Daytime Running Lights Relay** – is located in the underhood relay center, at position 'G'.

• **Defogger Relay (except 1989)** – is located in the mirco relay center, at position 'E'.

• **Delco Bose Relays (except 1989)** – are located in the mirco relay center, at position 'D' and 'F'.

• **Delco-Bose Music System Amplifier Relay Diode** – is located on the cross – body harness, at the right hand front door sill.

• **Delco-Bose Music System Amplifier Relay** – is located on the right hand side of the passenger compartment, near the rear of the front door sill.

• **EGR Solenoid** – is located on the top right hand side of the engine, behind the generator.

• **Electronic Climate Control Power Module** – is located on the center front of the dash, in the plenum.

• **Electronic Control Module (ECM)** – is located behind the right side of the dash panel, near the glove box.

• **Electronic Level Control Compressor** – is located below the vehicle, near the right rear wheel well.

• **Electronic Level Control Height Sensor** – is located below the vehicle, near the right rear wheel well.

• **Electronic Level Control Relay (1989)** – is located in the interior relay center, at position 'K'.

• **Electronic Level Control Relay (except 1989)** – is located in the mirco relay center, at position 'A'.

• **Electronic Level Control Test Connector** – is located near the top of the electronic level control compressor, if so equipped.

• **Engine Metal Temperature Switch** – is located on the rear of the engine, in the left hand side of the cylinder head.

• **Exhaust Gas Recirculation Solenoid (VIN 3 and 5)** – is located at the top left of the engine, over the valve cover.

• **Factory Priming Input Connector (VIN 3 and 5)** – is located at the left front corner of the engine compartment, taped to the harness.

Fiber Optic Light Source – are located one in each door.

• **Fuel Door Release Solenoid** – is located in the trunk at the fuel tank door.

• **Fuel Pump Relay** – is located in the interior relay center, at position 'C'.

• **Fuel Tank Fuse (3 amp)** – is located in the interior relay panel.

• **Headlight Sensor** – is incorporated into the automatic day/night mirror.

• **Headlights On Resistor** – is part of the flex circuit, located behind the left hand side of the instrument panel.

• **Hi Beam Relay** – is located in the interior relay center, at position 'B'.

• **Horn Relay (1989)** – is located in the underhood relay center, at position 'B'.

• **Horn Relay (except 1989)** – is located in the underhood relay center, at position 'H'.

• **Idle Speed Control Motor (VIN 3 and 5)** – is located on the top right of the engine, next to the throttle body.

• **Idle Speed Control Motor** – is located on the right front side of the throttle body.

• **Ignition Key Warning Switch** – is located in the upper portion of the steering column.

• **Ignition Switch** – is located on the top of the steering column.

• **Interior Relay Center** – is located behind the right hand side of the instrument panel, below the glove box.

• **ISO Ground Junction Block** – is located on the right hand side of the engine compartment.

• **ISO In-Line Fuse (A)** – is taped to the dash harness, to the left of the steering column.

• **ISO Power Junction Block** – is located on the right hand front fender, behind the battery.

• **Left Hand Trailer Relay** – is located in the right hand rear corner of the trunk.

• **Low Beam Relay** – is located in the interior relay center, at position 'E'.

• **Manifold Absolute Pressure (MAP) Sensor (VIN 3 and 5)** – is on the top left side of the engine, above the rear valve cover.

• **Manifold Absolute Pressure (MAP) Sensor** – is located on the top right hand side of the engine, above the rear valve cover.

• **Manifold Air Temperature (MAT) Sensor (VIN 3 and 5)** – is on the top right side of the engine, behind the alternator.

• **Mirco Relay Center** – is at the center front of the trunk compartment, below the rear shelf.

• **Oil Pressure Switch (VIN 3 and 5)** – is on the left side of the engine, near the oil filter.

• **Oil Pressure Switch**—is located on the left hand side of the engine, below the air intake.

• **Oxygen Sensor Front (VIN 3 and 5)**—is on the left front of the engine, below the exhaust manifold.

• **Oxygen Sensor Rear (VIN 3 and 5)**—is on the left rear of the engine, below the exhaust manifold.

• **Oxygen Sensor**—is located in the exhaust manifold.

• **PASS Key Decoder Module**—is behind the left side of the instrument panel, to the left of the steering wheel, on the side of the theft deterrent module.

• **Power Antenna Relay**—is located on the right hand side of the trunk compartment, on or near the antenna assembly.

• **Power Antenna Transceiver**—is located on the left hand side of the trunk compartment.

• **Power Door Relay**—is located on the left hand shroud, on the conduit.

• **Power Seat Air Pump Assembly**—is located under the center of the rear seat.

• **Power Seat Control Module**—is located under the center of the rear seat.

• **Power Seat Lumbar Compressor Capacitor**—is located in each front lumbar compressor connector.

• **Power Seat Lumbar Compressor**—is located in each front seat.

• **Power Seat Recliner Capacitor**—is located in the recliner motor connector.

• **Power Seat Solenoid/Valve Assembly**—is located under each front seat.

• **Power Steering Cutout Switch (VIN 3)**—is located on the left rear of the engine, on the steering rack.

• **Power Steering Cutout Switch (VIN 5)**—is located on the left rear of the engine, behind the transaxle.

• **Power Steering Cutout Switch**—is located on the left hand rear of the engine compartment, behind the transaxle.

• **Power Window Capacitors (Front)**—are located inside the window motor jumper connectors.

• **Power Window Capacitors (Rear)**—are located inside the window motor jumper connectors.

• **Radio Filter**—is located in the left hand front side of the engine compartment, below the underhood relay center.

• **Radio Mute Module**—is located below the rear of the console.

• **Rear Defogger Relay (1989)**—is located in the interior relay center, at position 'D'.

• **Retained Accessory Power In-Line Circuit Breaker**—is taped to the dash harness, behind the right hand side of the instrument panel.

• **Retained Accessory Power No. 1 Relay**—is located in the interior relay panel, at position 'H'.

• **Retained Accessory Power No. 2 Relay**—is located in the interior relay panel, at position 'J'.

• **Right Hand Trailer Relay**—is located in the right hand rear corner of the trunk.

• **Seat Control Module**—is located below the center console.

• **Seatbelt Switch**—is part of the driver's seatbelt assembly.

• **Starter Interrupt Relay**—is located under the left hand side of the instrument panel, near the center of the steering column.

• **Starter Solenoid**—is located on the lower left hand side of the engine.

• **Stop Light Switch Capacitor**—is located in the stop light switch.

• **Stoplamp Switch Capacitor**—is in the stoplamp switch connector.

• **Theft Deterrent Diodes**—is taped to the wiring harness behind the right hand side of the instrument panel.

• **Theft Deterrent In-Line Fuse (A)**—is located to the left of the steering column, taped to the dash harness.

• **Theft Deterrent Module**—is located under the left side of the dash, near the top of the shroud.

• **Theft Deterrent Relay**—is located under the left side of the instrument panel, on or near the theft deterrent controller.

• **Throttle Position Sensor**—is located on the top right side of the engine, on the throttle body.

• **TPS Test Point Connector**—is taped to the wiring harness behind the throttle body, in the engine compartment.

• **Transaxle Position Switch**—is located on the top left side of the transaxle.

• **Trunk Lid Tamper Switch**—is located near the latch at the center of the trunk lid.

• **Trunk Pull**—Down In-Line Fuse—is located in the interior relay center.

• **Trunk Pull**—Down Unit—is located near the latch at the center of the trunk lid.

• **Trunk Release Solenoid**—is located near the latch at the center of the trunk lid.

• **Turn Signal Alert Module**—is located behind the left hand side of the instrument panel, above the parking brake.

• **Turn Signal/Hazard Module**—is located in the center of the console, under the radio.

• **Twilight Crank Diode**—is taped in the harness, located under the right side of the instrument panel.

• **Twilight Crank Relay (except 1989)**—is located in the interior relay center, at position 'D'.

• **Twilight HeadLight Relay**—is located in the interior relay center, at position 'G'.

• **Twilight Park Light Relay**—is located in the interior relay center, at position 'F'.

• **Twilight Sentinel Photocell**—is located on the top center of the instrument panel, to the left of the glove box.

• **Underhood Relay Center**—is located on the left hand front side of the engine compartment, behind the headlights.

• **Vacuum Pump**—is located at the bottom of the right front inner fender panel, in front of the wheelwell.

• **VATS System**—See PASS Key System.

• **Vehicle Speed Sensor Buffer**—is located under the left side of the dash panel, near the steering column, is so equipped.

• **Vehicle Speed Sensor**—is located on the right side of the transaxle.

• **Wiper/Washer Capacitor**—is taped in the harness, located under the left side of the instrument panel.

• **Wiper/Washer Fluid Level Switch**—is located on the top of the washer fluid reservoir.

• **Wiper/Washer Module**—is located on the left hand side of the firewall.

CHEVROLET

Circuit Breakers

BERETTA AND CORSICA

HEADLIGHTS

There is a circuit breaker incorporated in the headlight switch to protect the headlight circuit.

WINDSHIELD WIPER

This circuit breaker is integral with the windshield wiper motor, to prevent the motor from an overloading condition, such as heavy snow.

POWER WINDOWS

This 35 amp circuit breaker is located in the fuse block, and protects the power window circuit.

POWER ACCESSORIES

This 35 amp circuit breaker is located in the fuse block and protects the circuits for the power door locks and rear window defogger.

CAMARO

HEADLIGHTS

There is a circuit breaker incorporated in the headlight switch to protect the headlight circuit.

WINDSHIELD WIPER

This circuit breaker is integral with the windshield wiper motor, to prevent the motor from an overloading condition, such as heavy snow.

POWER ACCESSORIES

Circuit breakers for power accessories are located in the fuse block, convenience center and/or relay centers. They protect the following circuits; rear window defogger, power windows, power seats and power door locks, alarm systems, keyless entry, sunroofs, etc. if equipped.

CAPRICE

HEADLIGHTS

There is a circuit breaker incorporated in the headlight switch to protect the headlight circuit.

WINDSHIELD WIPER

This circuit breaker is integral with the windshield wiper motor, to prevent the motor from an overloading condition, such as heavy snow.

POWER ACCESSORIES

Circuit breakers for power accessories are located in the fuse block, convenience center and/or relay centers. They protect the following circuits; rear window defogger, power windows, power seats and power door locks, alarm systems, keyless entry, sunroofs, etc. if equipped.

CAVALIER

HEADLIGHTS

There is a circuit breaker incorporated in the headlight switch to protect the headlight circuit.

WINDSHIELD WIPER

This circuit breaker is integral with the windshield wiper motor, to prevent the motor from an overloading condition, such as heavy snow.

POWER WINDOWS

This 35 amp circuit breaker is located in the fuse block, and protects the power window circuit.

POWER ACCESSORIES

This 35 amp circuit breaker is located in the fuse block and protects the circuits for the power door locks, power seats and rear window defogger.

CELEBRITY

HEADLIGHTS

There is a circuit breaker incorporated in the headlight switch to protect the headlight circuit.

WINDSHIELD WIPER

This circuit breaker is integral with the windshield wiper motor, to prevent the motor from an overloading condition, such as heavy snow.

POWER ACCESSORIES

This 30 amp circuit breaker is located in the fuse block and protects the circuits for the rear window defogger, power door locks, power seats and rear wiper/washer.

POWER WINDOWS

This 30 amp circuit breaker is located in the fuse block, and protects the circuits for the power windows, rear window wiper/washer (Wagon), power tailgate release and trunk release (with manual transaxle).

CORVETTE

HEADLIGHTS

There is a circuit breaker incorporated in the headlight switch to protect the headlight circuit.

WINDSHIELD WIPER

This circuit breaker is integral with the windshield wiper motor, to prevent the motor from an overloading condition, such as heavy snow.

POWER ACCESSORIES

Circuit breakers for power accessories are located in the fuse block, convenience center and/or relay centers. They protect the following circuits; rear window defogger, power windows, power seats and power door locks, alarm systems, keyless entry, sunroofs, etc. if equipped.

POWER WINDOWS

This 30 amp circuit breaker is located in the fuse block, and protects the power window circuit.

Fusible Links

In addition to circuit breakers and fuses, some circuits use fusible links to protect the wiring. Like fuses, the fusible links are 1 time protection devices that will melt and create an open circuit.

Not all fusible link open circuits can be detected by observation. Always inspect that there is battery voltage passing through the fusible link to verify continuity.

Each fusible link is four wire gauge sizes smaller than the cable it is designed to protect. The same wire size fusible link must be used when replacing a blown fusible link. Fusible links are available with two types of insulation; Hypalon and Silicone. Service fusible links made with Hypalon insulation, must be replaced with the same Hypalon insulated wire. Fusible links with Silicone insulation can use either insulation.

NOTE: Never make a fusible link longer than 9 in. (228mm) for it will not provide sufficient overload protection.

To replace a damaged fusible link, cut it off beyond the splice. Replace with a repair link. When connecting the repair link, strip the wire and use staking type pliers to crimp the splice securely in two places.

The fusible links are used on all models and are usually located in the engine compartment. Except for the 1991 Caprice, most fusible links are located at the starter solenoid. The 1991 Caprice has most fusible links at the battery junction block. But other locations include the junction block at the right front of the engine compartment, next to the battery and near the alternator. Most models that are equipped with Electronic Spark Timing use a fusible link at the electronic spark timing distributor.

Relay, Sensors And Computer Locations

NOTE: When using this section, some of the components may not be used on a particular vehicle. This is because the particular component in question was used on an earlier model or a later model. If a component is not found in this section, check other vehicles of the same body line, as that component may have been introduced earlier on different models. This section is being published from the latest information available at the time of this publication.

BERETTA AND CORSICA

- **A/C Compressor Clutch Diode**—is taped to the inside compressor connector on the front of the compressor.
- **A/C Compressor Control Relay**—is located on the center of the firewall, on the relay bracket.
- **A/C Heater Valve Vacuum Actuator**—is located under the right hand side of the instrument panel, on the right hand side of the A/C plenum.
- **A/C Heater/Defrost Valve Vacuum Actuator**—is located under the right hand side of the instrument panel, on the right hand side of the A/C plenum.
- **A/C Outside Air Valve Vacuum Actuator**—is located under the right hand side of the instrument panel, on the right hand side of the A/C plenum.
- **A/C Temperature Valve Motor**—is located under the center of the instrument panel, near the A/C-heater control assembly.
- **A/C Vacuum Line Connector**—is located under the center of the instrument panel, to the right of the A/C-heater control assembly.
- **A/C-Heater Blower Relay**—is located on the center of the firewall, on the relay bracket.
- **A/C-Heater Blower Resistors**—are located in the engine compartment, on the front left side of the blower module.
- **A/C-High Pressure Cutout Switch**—is located on the A/C refrigerant line, in the right hand front corner of the engine compartment.
- **A/C-Low Pressure Cutout Switch (VIN 1 and G)**—is located at the right front of the engine at the left end of the A/C compressor.
- **A/C-Low Pressure Cutout Switch (VIN A)**—is at the right front of the engine, near the alternator.
- **A/C-Low Pressure Cutout Switch (W)**—is located on the A/C compressor.
- **Assembly Line Diagnostic Link Connector**—is located under the left side of the instrument panel, to the left of the steering column.
- **Back**—Up Switch—is located on the left hand side of the transaxle.
- **Battery Junction Block**—is located on the center of the firewall, on the relay bracket.
- **Brake Fluid Level Switch**—is located on the left hand side of the brake fluid reservoir.
- **Brake Release Relay**—is below the left side of the instrument panel, on the left shroud.
- **Canister Purge Solenoid**—is located in the right hand front corner of the engine compartment, on top of the canister.
- **Clutch Start Switch**—is located behind the clutch pedal, below the clutch pedal support.
- **Convenience Center**—is located under the left hand side of the instrument panel, to the left of the steering column.
- **Convertible Top Relays**—are in the left side of the luggage compartment.
- **Coolant Fan Pressure Switch**—is located in the right hand front corner of the engine compartment, on the refrigerant line.
- **Coolant Fan Relay**—is located on the center of the firewall, on the relay bracket.
- **Coolant Module**—is located behind the instrument panel, above the left side of the steering column or taped to the instrument panel wiring harness.
- **Coolant Sensor**—is located in the engine compartment, on the right hand front side of the radiator.
- **Coolant Temperature Sensor (VIN 1 and G)**—is located on the top left side of the engine, on the coolant outlet.
- **Coolant Temperature Sensor (VIN W)**—is located on the top left hand side of the engine.
- **Coolant Temperature Switch (VIN 1 and G)**—is located on the left side of the engine, on the coolant outlet.
- **Coolant Temperature Switch (VIN A)**—is located at the left rear of the engine.
- **Coolant Temperature Switch (VIN W)**—is located on the left side of the engine, above the exhaust manifold.
- **Crank Position Sensor (VIN W)**—is located on the rear of the engine, below the right hand side of the exhaust manifold.
- **Cruise Control Check Valve**—is located in the center rear of the engine, near the relay bracket.
- **Cruise Control Clutch Switch**—is located above the clutch pedal on the clutch pedal support bracket.
- **Cruise Control Module**—is located behind the the right hand side of the instrument panel, above the instrument panel compartment.
- **Cruise Control Servo**—is located in front of the left hand front side strut tower, in the engine compartment.
- **Cruise Control Vacuum Release Valve**—is located above the brake pedal on the brake pedal support bracket.
- **Cruise Control Vacuum Tank**—is located in the left hand front of the engine compartment, below the battery.
- **Daytime Running Lamps Circuit Breaker**—is located behind the right instrument panel, taped to the wiring harness, near the fuse box.
- **Daytime Running Lamps Module**—is located behind the right instrument panel, at the shroud.
- **Defogger Time Relay**—is located behind the left side of the instrument panel, to the right of the steering column.
- **Detonation (Knock) Sensor (VIN W)**—is located on the right hand rear of the engine, below the exhaust manifold.
- **Digital Cluster Switch Module**—is located behind the left instrument panel.
- **Direct Ignition System (VIN 1)**—is located on the rear of the engine, below the intake manifold.
- **Direct Ignition System (VIN W)**—is located on the front of the engine, below the intake manifold.
- **EGR Electronic Vacuum Regulator (VIN W)**—is located on the top left hand rear of the engine, near the throttle body.

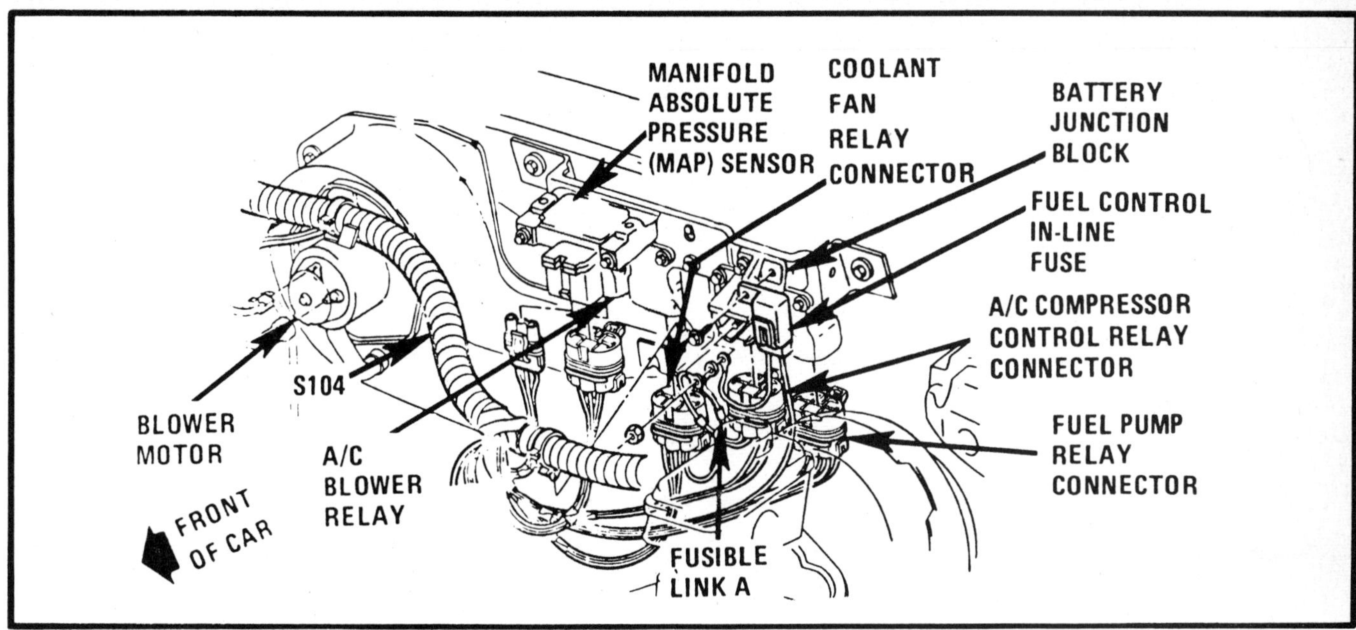

Relay locations – Beretta and Corsica

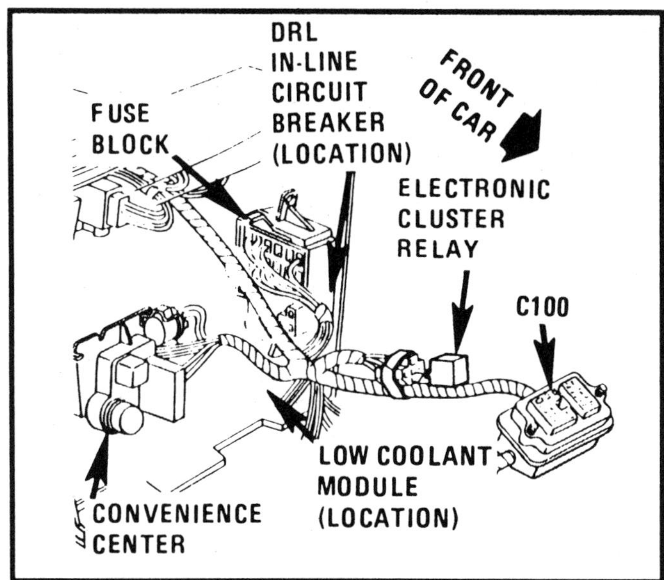

Convenience center locations – Beretta and Corsica

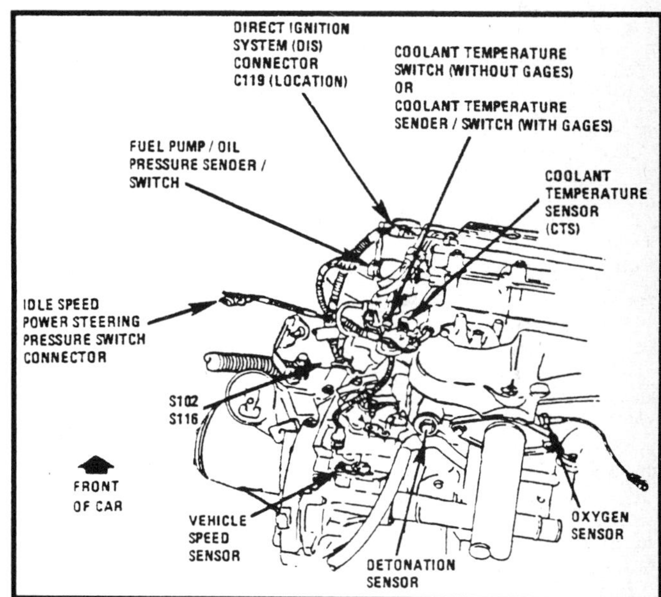

Sensor locations – Beretta and Corsica with 2.3L VIN A engine

• **Electronic Cluster Relay** – is located behind the left hand side of the instrument panel, taped to the instrument panel harness.

• **Electronic Control Module (ECM)** – is located behind the right side of the instrument panel, near the shroud.

• **Engine Metal Temperature Switch (VIN 1)** – is located on the front of the cylinder head, on the right side of the engine, if so equipped.

• **Fog Lamp Relay** – is at the left front of the engine compartment, on the radiator support bracket.

• **Fuel Control In-Line Fuse** – is located on the center of the firewall, on the relay bracket.

• **Fuel Prime Connector** – is located near the strut tower, in the left hand rear corner of the engine compartment.

• **Fuel Pump Relay** – is located on the center of the firewall, on the relay bracket.

• **Fuel Pump/Oil Pressure Sender/Switch (VIN 1)** – is located on the center of the engine, below the direct ignition system.

• **Fuel Pump/Oil Pressure Sender/Switch (VIN A)** – is located on the left side of the engine, near the direct ignition system.

• **Fuel Pump/Oil Pressure Sender/Switch (VIN W)** – is located on the right hand side of the engine, below the water pump.

• **Fuse Box** – is behind the left side of the instrument panel, near the shroud.

• **Fusible Links** – most fusible links are located at the starter solenoid. Some fusible links are at the junction block at the rear of the engine compartment or at the alternator.

• **Hazard Flasher** – is located on the convenience center.

• **Headlamp Diode Assembly** – is at the to right of the instrument panel.

• **Horn Relay**—is located on the convenience center.
• **Idle Air Control Valve (VIN 1)**—is located on the right front side of the throttle body.
• **Idle Air Control Valve (VIN T)**—is located on the top left hand side of the engine, above the valve cover.
• **Idle Air Control Valve (VIN W)**—is located on the top left hand side of the engine, on the throttle body.
• **Idle Speed Power Steering Pressure Switch (except VIN A)**—is located on the left hand front of the firewall, below the brake reservoir.
• **Idle Speed Power Steering Pressure Switch (VIN A)**—is located at the top left side of the engine.
• **Ignition Key Warning Switch**—is located in the steering column, near the key cylinder.
• **Ignition Switch**—is located on the right hand side of the steering column.
• **Instrument Panel Switch Module (Digital Cluster)**—is located behind the left hand side of the instrument panel.
• **Interior Lights Switch Module**—is behind the left side of the instrument panel.
• **Low Coolant Module**—is located behind the instrument panel, above the left side of the steering column or taped to the instrument panel wiring harness.
• **Low Coolant Sensor**—is located in the engine compartment, on the right hand front side of the radiator.
• **Luggage Compartment Release Relay**—is located below the left side of the instrument panel, on the left shroud.
• **Luggage Compartment Release Solenoid (Coupe)**—is located in the center rear of the luggage compartment.
• **Luggage Compartment Release Solenoid (Sedan)**—is located in the rear of the luggage compartment lid.
• **Manifold Absolute Pressure (MAP) Sensor**—is located on the center of the firewall, on the relay bracket.
• **Manifold Air Temperature (MAT) Sensor (VIN 1 and G)**—is located on the throttle body, at the top rear of the engine.
• **Manifold Air Temperature Sensor (VIN W)**—is located on the top left hand front on the engine on the air cleaner assembly.
• **Mass Air Flow Sensor (VIN W)**—is located on the top left hand front on the engine on the air cleaner assembly.
• **Mass Airflow In-Line Fuse**—is located on the relay bracket on the firewall, if so equipped.
• **Mass Airflow Relay**—is located on the relay bracket on the firewall, if so equipped.
• **Outside Air Temperature Sensor**—is located in the engine compartment, on the front of the radiator, near the hood latch.
• **Oxygen Sensor**—is located in the exhaust manifold.
• **Power Door Lock Relay Assembly**—is located behind the instrument panel, near the left hand shroud.
• **Remote Dimmer**—is located behind the instrument panel, to the left of the steering column.
• **Seatbelt Lap Retractor Release Solenoid**—is located in each front door, in the lower center of the door.
• **Seatbelt Retractor Release Solenoid Timer**—is located below the left hand side of the instrument panel, on the upper left hand shroud.
• **Seatbelt Shoulder Retractor Release Solenoid**—is located in each front door, at the rear of the doors.
• **Seatbelt Switch**—is part of the driver's seatbelt assembly.
• **Starter Solenoid**—is located on the lower left hand side of the engine.
• **Throttle Position Sensor**—is located on the top rear side of the engine, on the throttle body.
• **TPS Test Point Connector**—is taped to the wiring harness behind the throttle body, in the engine compartment.
• **Transaxle Position Switch**—is located on the top left side of the transaxle.
• **Turn Signal Flasher**—is located on the left hand side of the steering column.

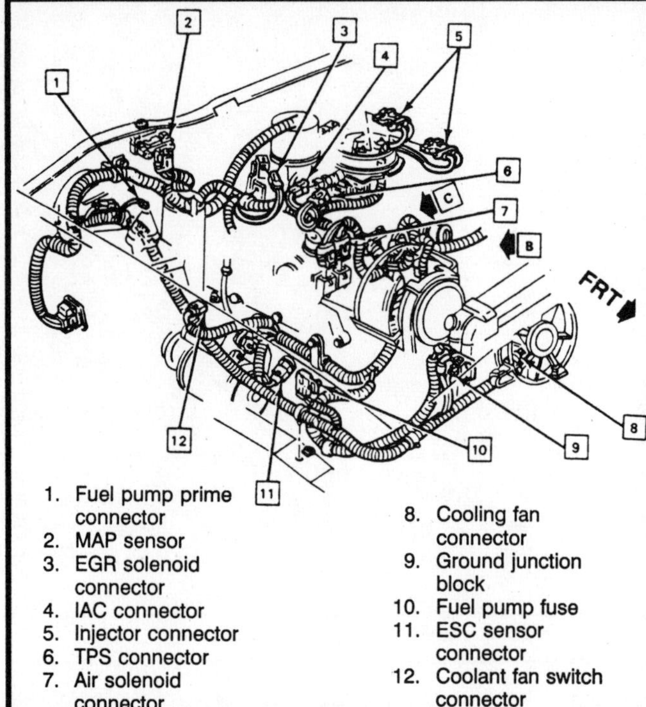

Component locations—Camaro

• **Vehicle Speed Sensor**—is located on the right side of the transaxle, with automatic transmission.
• **Vehicle Speed Sensor**—is located on the left side of the transaxle, with manual transmission.
• **Wiper/Washer Motor Module**—is located on the left hand side of the firewall in the engine compartment.

CAMARO

• **A/C Blower Resistors**—are located near the blower motor on the A/C module, on the A/C plenum housing.
• **A/C Blower Speed High Speed Relay**—is located near the blower module on the A/C module.
• **A/C Compressor Diode**—is taped to the inside of the compressor clutch connector.
• **A/C Compressor Relay**—is located on the left side engine firewall.
• **A/C Cooling Fan Pressure Switch**—is on the right side of the engine compartment, on the A/C line.
• **A/C Heater/Defrost Vacuum Motor**—is located under the right hand side of the instrument panel, on the left hand side of the A/C plenum.
• **A/C Lower Mode Vacuum Motor**—is located under the right hand side of the instrument panel, on the lower left hand side of the A/C plenum.
• **A/C Pressure Cycling Switch**—is located on the accumulator/drier.
• **A/C Recirculating/Outside Air Vacuum Motor**—is located under the instrument panel, on the rear of the air intake assembly.
• **A/C Upper Mode Vacuum Motor**—is located under the right hand side of the instrument panel, on the left hand side of the A/C plenum.
• **A/C Vacuum Tank**—is located on the front left hand side of the firewall, if equipped.
• **Air Diverter Valve**—is located on the right hand front of the engine.

• **Air Select Valve (VIN S)**—is located on the right hand valve cover.

• **Air Select Valve**—is located on the right hand front of the engine.

• **Alternator Diode (Isolation)**—is located in the wiring harness, near the fuse block.

• **Assembly Line Diagnostic Link**—is located under the left hand side of the instrument panel.

• **Audio Alarm Assembly**—is located in the convenience center.

• **Back**—Up Switch—is located on the left hand side of the transaxle.

• **Brake Pressure Switch**—is located on the left hand side of the brake fluid reservoir.

• **Burn Off Relay**—is located in the left hand rear corner of the engine compartment, on a relay bracket.

• **Canister Purge Solenoid Valve (VIN T)**—is on the right front of the engine compartment.

• **Canister Purge Solenoid**—is located in the left hand front corner of the engine compartment, on top of the canister.

• **Clutch Start Switch**—is located behind the clutch pedal, below the clutch pedal support.

• **Cold Start Injector**—is located on the top rear of the engine.

• **Cold Start Switch**—is located on the top front of the engine.

• **Convenience Center**—is located under the left hand side of the instrument panel, to the right of the steering column.

• **Coolant Fan (A/C) Pressure Switch**—is located in the lower right hand front corner of the engine compartment, on the refrigerant line.

• **Coolant Fan Relay (VIN F and 8)**—is located on the right hand rear side of the radiator.

• **Coolant Fan Relay (VIN S)**—is located on the left hand front side of the Coolant Fan Sensor (VIN T)—is located on the top of the engine, under the intake plenum.

• **Coolant Fan Switch (except VIN S)**—is located in the lower right hand side of the engine.

• **Coolant Fan Switch (VIN S)**—is located on the top right hand rear side of the engine.

• **Coolant Temperature Sensor (VIN F and 8)**—is located on the top right hand side of the engine.

• **Coolant Temperature Sensor (VIN S)**—is located on the top left hand front side of the engine.

• **Coolant Temperature Switch (VIN S)**—is located on the top left hand front side of the engine.

• **Coolant Temperature Switch**—is located on the left hand side of the engine, below the valve cover.

• **Cruise Control Module**—is located behind the right hand center side of the instrument panel.

• **Cruise Control Servo**—is located in the left hand front corner of the engine compartment.

• **Cruise Control Vacuum Tank**—is located in the left hand front corner of the engine compartment.

• **Daytime Running Light Module**—is behind the left instrument panel, near the fuse box.

• **Defogger Timer/Relay**—is behind the right side of the instrument panel.

• **EGR Vacuum Sensor Diagnostic Connector (VIN F)**—is on the top of the engine, in the vacuum line to the EGR valve.

• **Electronic Control Module (ECM)**—is located behind the right side of the instrument panel.

• **Electronic Spark Control Module**—is located on the left side of the engine firewall.

• **Electronic Vacuum Regulator**—is on the top right hand rear section of the engine.

• **Fog Light Relay (1989)**—is located in the upper left hand front corner of the engine compartment.

• **Fog Light Relay (1990)**—is located at the rear corner of the engine compartment.

• **Fog Light Relay (1991)**—is located at rear of the engine compartment or behind the instrument panel near the fuse box.

• **Fuel Pump In-Line Fuse**—is located on the right front wheelhousing, if so equipped.

• **Fuel Pump Prime Connector (except E)**—is left front of cowl, near the relay bracket.

• **Fuel Pump Relay (VIN F and 8)**—is located on the left hand front side of the firewall, on the relay bracket.

• **Fuel Pump Relay (VIN S)**—is located in the left hand rear corner of the engine compartment.

• **Fuel Pump Switch**—is located on the top rear corner of the engine.

• **Fuel Pump/Oil Pressure Sender Switch (Except VIN E)**—is on the lower left side of the engine.

• **Fuel Pump/Oil Pressure Sender Switch (VIN E)**—is on the rear lower left side of the engine.

• **Fuel Pump/Oil Pressure Sender/Switch**—is located on the top center rear of the engine.

• **Fuse Box**—is behind the left side of the instrument panel.

• **Fusible Links**—most fusible links are located at the starter solenoid. But other locations include the junction block at the right front of the engine compartment, next to the battery and near the alternator.

• **Gear Selector Switch**—is located in the console at the gear selector.

• **Hatch Contact Assembly**—is located in the rear of the vehicle, top center of the end panel, in the cargo compartment.

• **Hatch Pull Down Unit**—is located in the center of the end panel, in the cargo compartment.

• **Hatch Release Relay**—is located under the front part of the console.

• **Hatch Release Solenoid**—is located in the center of the end panel, in the cargo compartment.

• **Hazard Flasher/Relay**—is located on the convenience center.

• **Heater Blower Resistors**—are located on the near blower motor.

• **Heavy Duty Coolant Fan Relay (VIN F and 8)**—is located in the right hand rear corner of the engine compartment.

• **Heavy Duty Coolant Fan Switch (VIN F and 8)**—is located in the right hand rear corner of the engine.

• **Hood Louver Solenoid**—is located on the left side of the hood louver assembly. Horn Relay—is located in the convenience center.

• **Idle Air Control Stepper Motor**—is located on the top of the engine, near the throttle body.

• **Ignition In-Line Fuse (No. 1)**—is located at the right hand front of the firewall.

• **Ignition In-Line Fuse (No. 2)**—is located at the battery.

• **Ignition In-Line Fuse (No. 3)**—is located on the right hand inner fender panel, near the battery.

• **Ignition In-Line Fuse (No. 4)**—is located on the right hand inner fender panel, near the battery.

• **Ignition Key Warning Switch**—is located in the steering column, near the key cylinder.

• **Ignition Switch**—is located at the base of the steering column.

• **Isolation Relay**—is located behind the right headlight.

• **Junction Block**—is located on the right side of the radiator support bracket.

• **Knock Sensor (VIN T)**—is on the lower right side of the engine.

• **Knock Sensor**—is located on the lower right side of the engine, near the starter solenoid.

• **Light Monitor Module**—is located on the upper left side of the dash panel, above the clutch pedal.

• **Low Blower Relay**—is located on the right side of the firewall, near the blower motor.

• **Manifold Absolute Pressure (MAP) Sensor** – is located on the air cleaner assembly or at the rear center of the engine compartment.

• **Manifold Vacuum Switch** – is located on the firewall, to the left of the vacuum tank.

• **MAP Sensor** – See Manifold Absolute Pressure (MAP) Sensor.

• **Mass Air Flow Relay (VIN F and 8)** – is located on the relay bracket, in the left hand rear corner of the engine compartment.

• **Mass Air Flow Relay (VIN S)** – is located on the right side of the radiator support bracket.

• **Mass Air Flow Sensor (VIN F and 8)** – is located on the top of the engine, on the air intake duct.

• **Mass Air Flow Sensor (VIN S)** – is located on the air intake duct, located before the throttle body.

• **Mass Air Flow Sensor In-Line Fuse (5.0L EFI)** – is located behind the battery, near the positive battery cable.

• **Mass Air Flow Sensor In-Line Fuse (V6)** – is located in the right front corner of the engine compartment.

• **Mass Air Temperature Sensor (VIN F and 8)** – is located on top rear of the engine, on the air intake shroud.

• **Oil Pressure Switch (VIN S)** – is located on the lower left hand side of the engine.

• **Oil Pressure Switch** – is located on the top rear center of the engine.

• **Oxygen Sensor** – is located in the exhaust manifold/ Pass Key Decoder Module – is located behind the right side of the instrument panel.

• **Power Accessories Circuit Breaker** – is located in the fuse block.

• **Power Antenna Relay** – is located behind the right side of the instrument panel, near the ECM.

• **Power Door Lock Relay Assembly** – is located behind the left kick panel in the lower opening.

• **Power Steering Switch** – is at the left front of the engine compartment.

• **Power Steering Switch** – is located on the left hand front of the engine compartment.

• **Power Window/Rear Wiper Circuit Breaker** – is located in the fuse block.

• **Radio Amplifier Relay** – is located behind the right hand side of the instrument panel.

• **Radio Capacitor** – is located on the right hand side of the firewall, near the blower motor.

• **Rear Defogger Timer/Relay** – is located below the right side of the instrument panel, near the ECM.

• **Redundant Coolant Fan Switch (5.0L EFI)** – is located on the engine, near the distributor.

• **Resistance Wire** – is located under the left side of the instrument panel, near the ignition switch.

• **Road Rally Assembly** – is located behind the right hand side of the instrument panel, below the glove box.

• **Seat Belt Warning Buzzer** – is located in the convenience center, if so equipped.

• **Seatbelt Switch** – is part of the driver's seatbelt assembly.

• **SIR DERM** – is behind the right side of the instrument panel.SIR Resistor Module – is behind the left side of the instrument panel.

• **Starter Enable Relay** – is located below the left side of the instrument panel, on the kick panel.

• **Starter Solenoid** – is located on the lower right hand side of the engine.

• **Tachometer Filter** – is located on the top rear of the engine, near the distributor.

• **Throttle Position Sensor** – is located on the top front section of the engine.

• **Transaxle Converter Clutch (TCC) Solenoid** – is located in the transaxle assembly.

• **Turn Signal Flasher (1989)** – is located on the right hand side of the steering column.

• **Turn Signal Flasher (except 1989)** – is located behind the left instrument panel, clipped to the fuse block.

• **Vehicle Speed Sensor Buffer** – is behind the left side of the instrument panel.

• **Vehicle Speed Sensor Buffer** – is taped to the dashboard wiring harness, near the bulkhead connector.

• **Vehicle Speed Sensor** – is located on the printed circuit at the rear of the speedometer on most models. On tuned and multiport injection it is located on the left side of the transmission below the shifter.

• **Wide Open Throttle Relay** – is located in the left rear corner of the engine compartment.

• **Wiper/Washer Fluid Level Switch** – is located on the washer reservoir, in the engine compartment.

• **Wiper/Washer Motor Module** – is located on the upper left side of the engine firewall.

1989–90 CAPRICE

• **A/C Blower Relay** – is located in the engine compartment at the right side of the firewall, near the blower motor.

• **A/C Blower Resistors** – is located in the engine compartment on the right side of the firewall near the blower motor.

• **A/C Blower/Clutch Control Module** – is located on the top of the blower housing, if so equipped.

• **A/C Compressor Clutch Diode** – is taped to the inside compressor connector on the front of the compressor.

• **A/C Cutout Relay** – is located on the front of the dash, on the A/C Heater module.

• **A/C Defrost Vacuum Motor** – is located under the right hand side of the instrument panel, on the top of the A/C plenum.

• **A/C Heater Vacuum Motor** – is located under the right hand side of the instrument panel, on the left hand side of the A/C plenum.

• **A/C Pressure Cycling Switch** – is located on the accumulator/drier.

• **A/C Programmer (Tempmatic)** – is located behind the right side of the instrument panel, if so equipped.

• **A/C Recirculating/Outside Air Vacuum Motor** – is located under the instrμment panel, on the right hand end of the plenum.

• **A/C Vacuum Tank** – is located on the front left hand side of the firewall, if equipped.

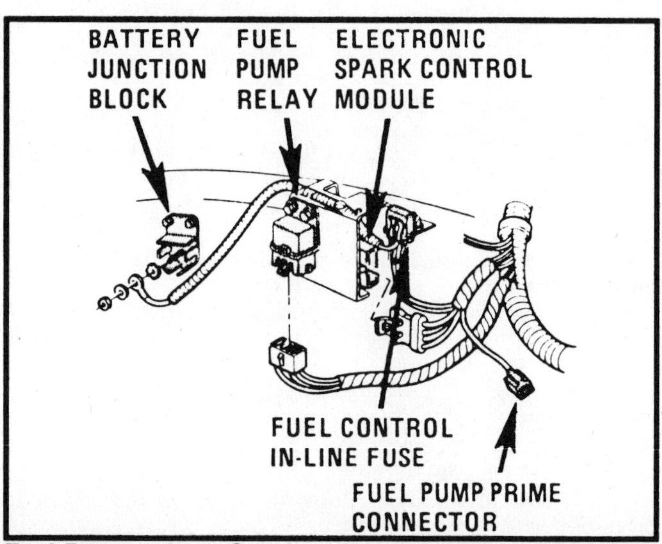

Fuel Pump relay – Caprice with 4.3L VIN Z and 5.0L VIN E engine

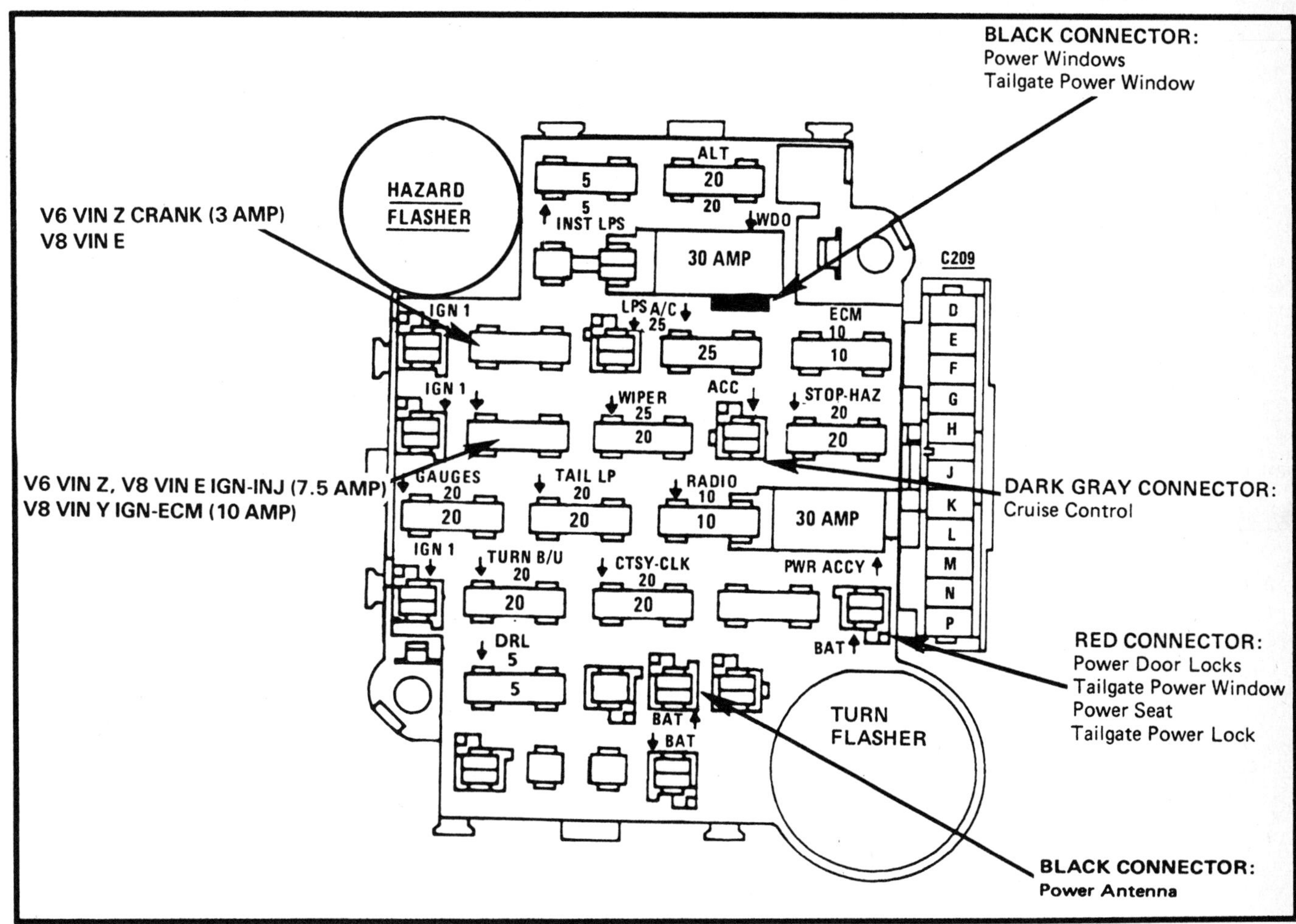

Fuse box identification—Caprice wagon

- **AIR Diverter Valve**—is located on the right hand front of the engine, behind the air pump.
- **AIR Select Valve**—is located on the right hand front of the engine, behind the air pump.
- **Alternator Diode**—is taped to the instrument panel harness, near the fuse block, if so equipped.
- **Ambient Light Sensor**—is located behind the center of the instrument panel.
- **Anti-Dieseling Solenoid (VIN Y)**—is located on the top left hand front of the engine, on the valve cover.
- **Assembly Line Data Link Connector**—is located under the left side of the dash panel, near the steering panel.
- **Audio Alarm Module**—is located in the convenience center.
- **Back**—Up Switch—is incorporated in the gear select switch.
- **Battery Junction Block**—is located on the right inner fender panel, behind the battery.
- **Brake Fluid Level Switch**—is located on the left hand side of the brake fluid reservoir.
- **Canister Purge Solenoid (VIN E and Z)**—is located in the left hand front corner of the engine compartment, on top of the canister.
- **Canister Purge Solenoid (VIN Y)**—is located in the right hand front corner of the engine compartment, on top of the canister.
- **CB Transceiver**—is located under the center of the instrument panel, above the radio, if so equipped.
- **Convenience Center**—is located under the left hand side of the instrument panel, near the shroud.
- **Coolant Temperature Sender/Switch (VIN E and Z)**—is located on the top left hand front of the engine, below the valve cover.
- **Coolant Temperature Sender/Switch (VIN Y)**—is located on the left front side of the engine, to the right of the valve cover.
- **Coolant Temperature Sensor (VIN E and Z)**—is located on the front of the engine near the coolant outlet.
- **Coolant Temperature Sensor (VIN Y)**—is located on the left front side of the engine, to the right of the valve cover.
- **Cruise Control Check Valve**—is located at the top of the engine.
- **Cruise Control Module**—is located under the left side of the dash, to the left of the steering column.
- **Cruise Control Servo (VIN E and Z)**—is located in the left hand front corner of the engine compartment, on the wheelhouse.
- **Cruise Control Servo (VIN Y)**—is located at the left front side of the engine.
- **Cruise Control Vacuum Release Valve**—is located above the brake pedal on the brake pedal support bracket.
- **Cruise Control Vacuum Tank (VIN Y)**—is located in the left hand front corner of the engine compartment, on the wheel house.
- **Cruise Control Vacuum Tank (VIN Z)**—is located in

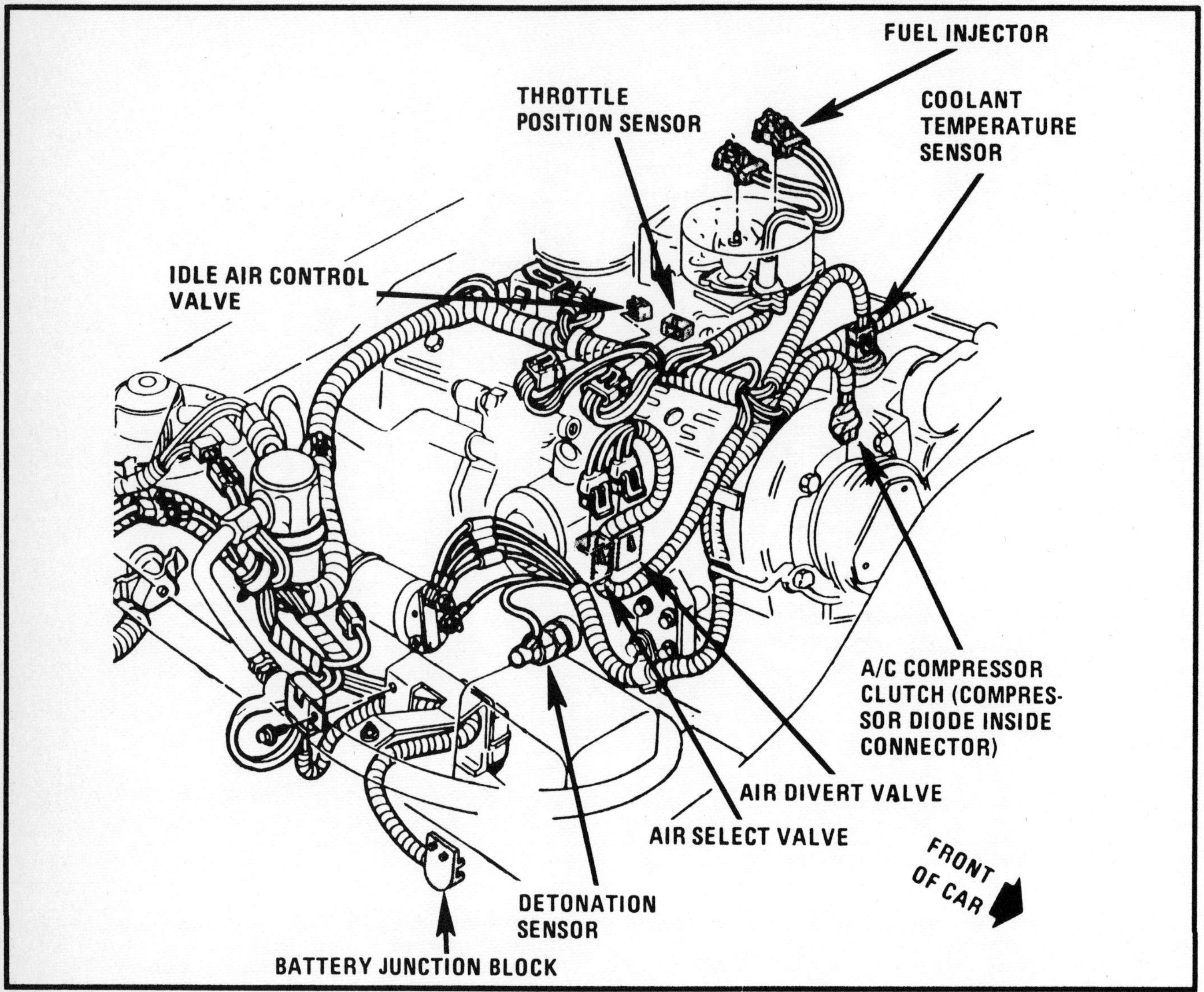

FUEL INJECTOR
THROTTLE POSITION SENSOR
COOLANT TEMPERATURE SENSOR
IDLE AIR CONTROL VALVE
A/C COMPRESSOR CLUTCH (COMPRESSOR DIODE INSIDE CONNECTOR)
AIR DIVERT VALVE
AIR SELECT VALVE
FRONT OF CAR
DETONATION SENSOR
BATTERY JUNCTION BLOCK

Sensor locations—Caprice with 5.0L VIN E engine

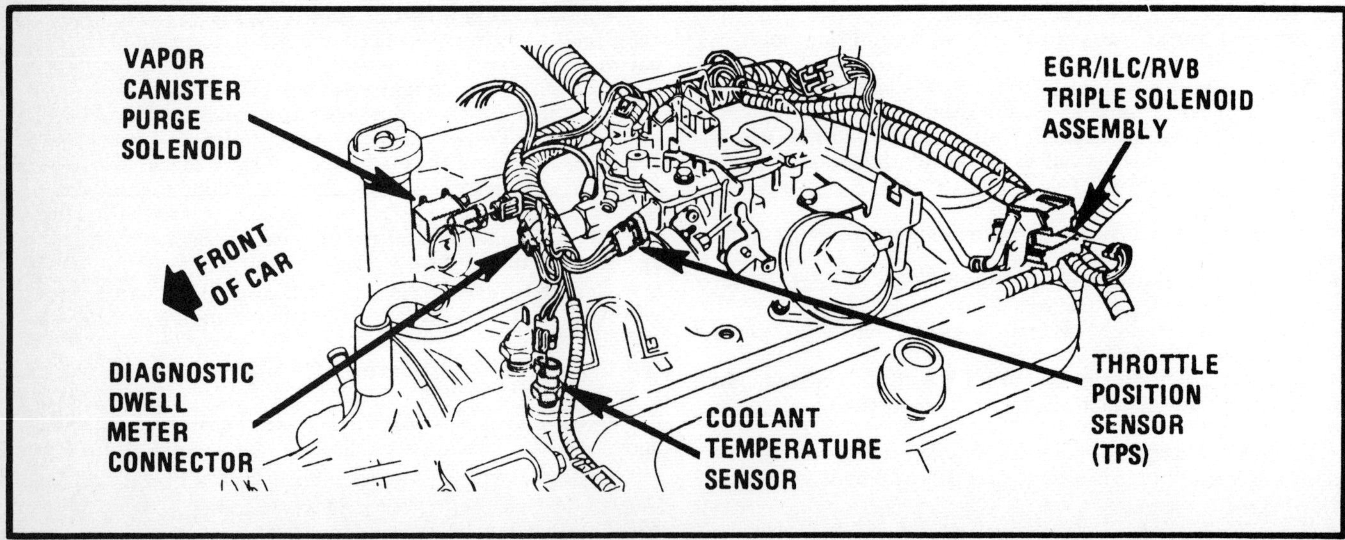

VAPOR CANISTER PURGE SOLENOID
EGR/ILC/RVB TRIPLE SOLENOID ASSEMBLY
FRONT OF CAR
DIAGNOSTIC DWELL METER CONNECTOR
COOLANT TEMPERATURE SENSOR
THROTTLE POSITION SENSOR (TPS)

Sensor locations—Caprice wagon with 5.0L VIN Y engine

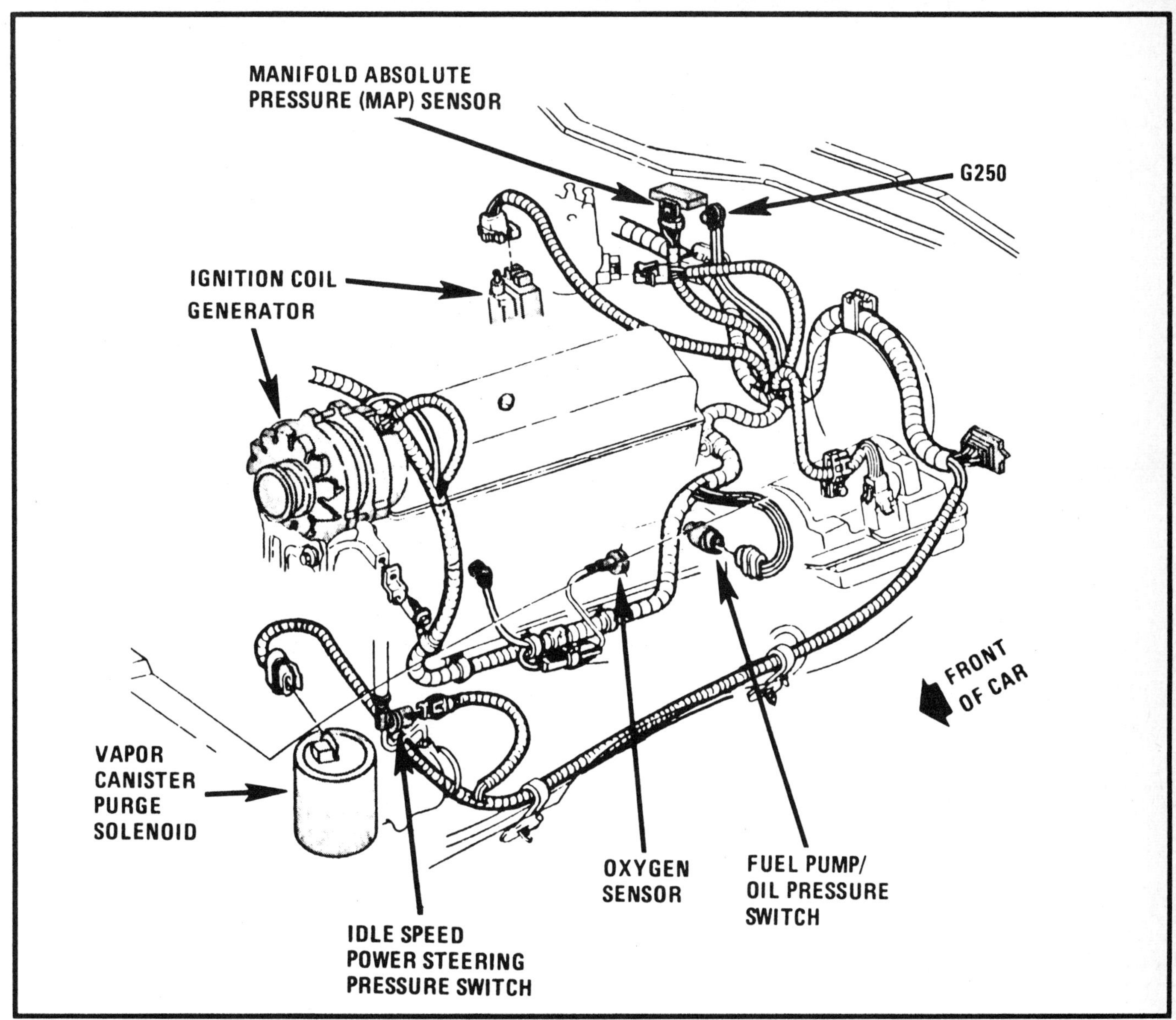

Sensor locations—Caprice with 5.0L VIN E and 4.3L VIN Z engine

the left hand front corner of the engine compartment, on cruise control equiped vehicles.

- **Daytime Running Lights (DRL) Module**—is located behind the instrument panel, on the right side of the steering column.
- **Defogger Time Relay**—is located on the top of the fuse block.
- **Detonation (Knock) Sensor (VIN E)**—is located at the lower right front side of the engine, near the starter.
- **Detonation (Knock) Sensor (VIN Y)**—is located at the lower left hand front side of the engine.
- **Detonation (Knock) Sensor (VIN Z)**—is located at the lower left rear side of the engine.
- **Diagnostic Dwell Meter Connector (VIN Y)**—is taped the wiring harness in front of the throttle body.
- **Dropping Resistor (DRL)**—is located behind the instrument panel, on the right side of the steering column.
- **EGR Diagnostic Connector (VIN Z)**—is located at the top of the engine, at the rear of the left valve cover.
- **EGR/ILC/RVB Triple Solenoid Assembly (VIN Y)**—is on the top left hand rear of the engine, on the valve cover.
- **Electronic Control Module (ECM)**—is located behind the right kick panel.
- **Electronic Spark Control (ESC) Module**—is located on the right hand inner fender panel, in the engine compartment.
- **Electronic Vacuum Regulator (VIN Z)**—is on the top right hand rear section of the engine.
- **Engine Oil Pressure Sender/Switch (VIN Z)**—is located on the top center rear of the engine.
- **Fuel Control In-Line Fuse**—is located on the right inner fender panel, if so equipped.
- **Fuel Pump In-Line Fuse**—is located on the right front wheelwell.
- **Fuel Pump Prime Connector (VIN E and Z)**—is located near the wheel well, taped to the harness.
- **Fuel Pump Relay**—is located on the upper right inner fender panel.

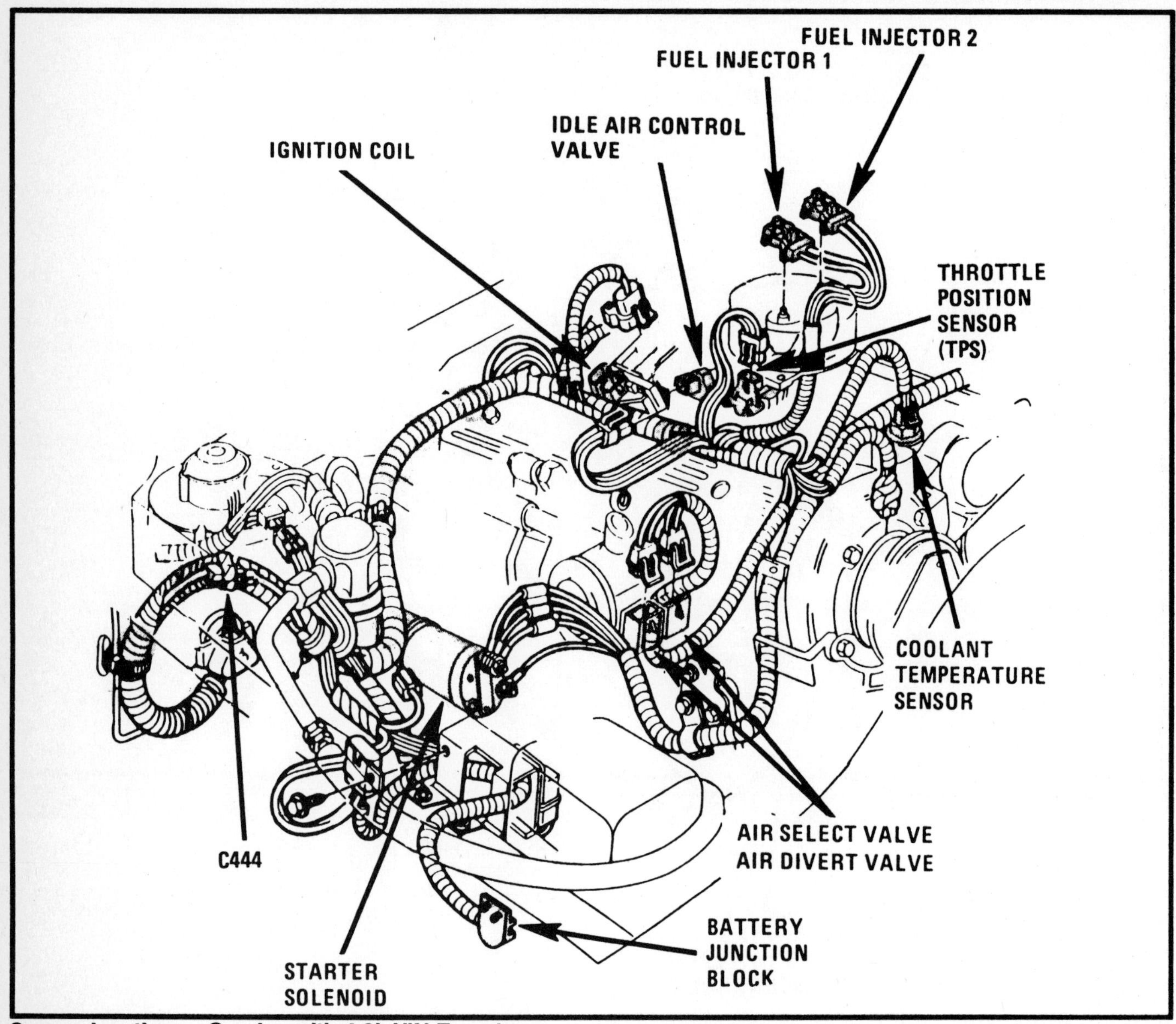

Sensor locations—Caprice with 4.3L VIN Z engine

• **Fuel Pump/Oil Pressure Sender/Switch**—is located on the top center rear of the engine.

• **Gear Selector Switch**—is located on the lower part of the steering column.

• **Hazard Relay**—is located in the fuse block.

• **Heater Blower Resistors**—are located near the blower motor.

• **Heater Water Valve Vacuum Motor**—are located on the rear of the engine in the heater hose.

• **Heater Water Valve**—are located on the rear of the engine in the heater hose.

• **Horn Relay**—is located in the convenience center.

• **Idle Air Control Stepper Motor**—is located on the top of the engine, on the right side of the throttle body.

• **Ignition Key Warning Switch**—is located in the steering column, near the key cylinder.

• **Ignition Switch**—is located at the base of the steering column.

• **Manifold Absolute Pressure (MAP) Sensor (VIN E and Z)**—is located on the center of the firewall, in the engine compartment.

• **Manifold Absolute Pressure (MAP) Sensor (VIN Y)**—is located on the right hand inner fender well.

• **Manifold Air Temperature (MAT) Sensor (VIN E and Z)**—is located inside the air cleaner, near the distributor.

• **Multi-Function Chime Module**—is located in the convenience center.

• **Oil Pressure Sender/Switch**—is located on the top left hand front of the engine, near the valve cover.

• **Oxygen Sensor**—is located on the exhaust manifold.

• **Power Antenna Relay**—is located on the bracket under the instrument panel, to the left of the instrument panel compartment.

• **Power Door Lock Relay Assembly**—is located behind the bottom right kick panel.

• **Power Master Brake Cylinder Relay**—is located in the connector at the brake reservoir pump motor.

• **Power Master Cylinder Brake In-Line Fuse**—is locat-

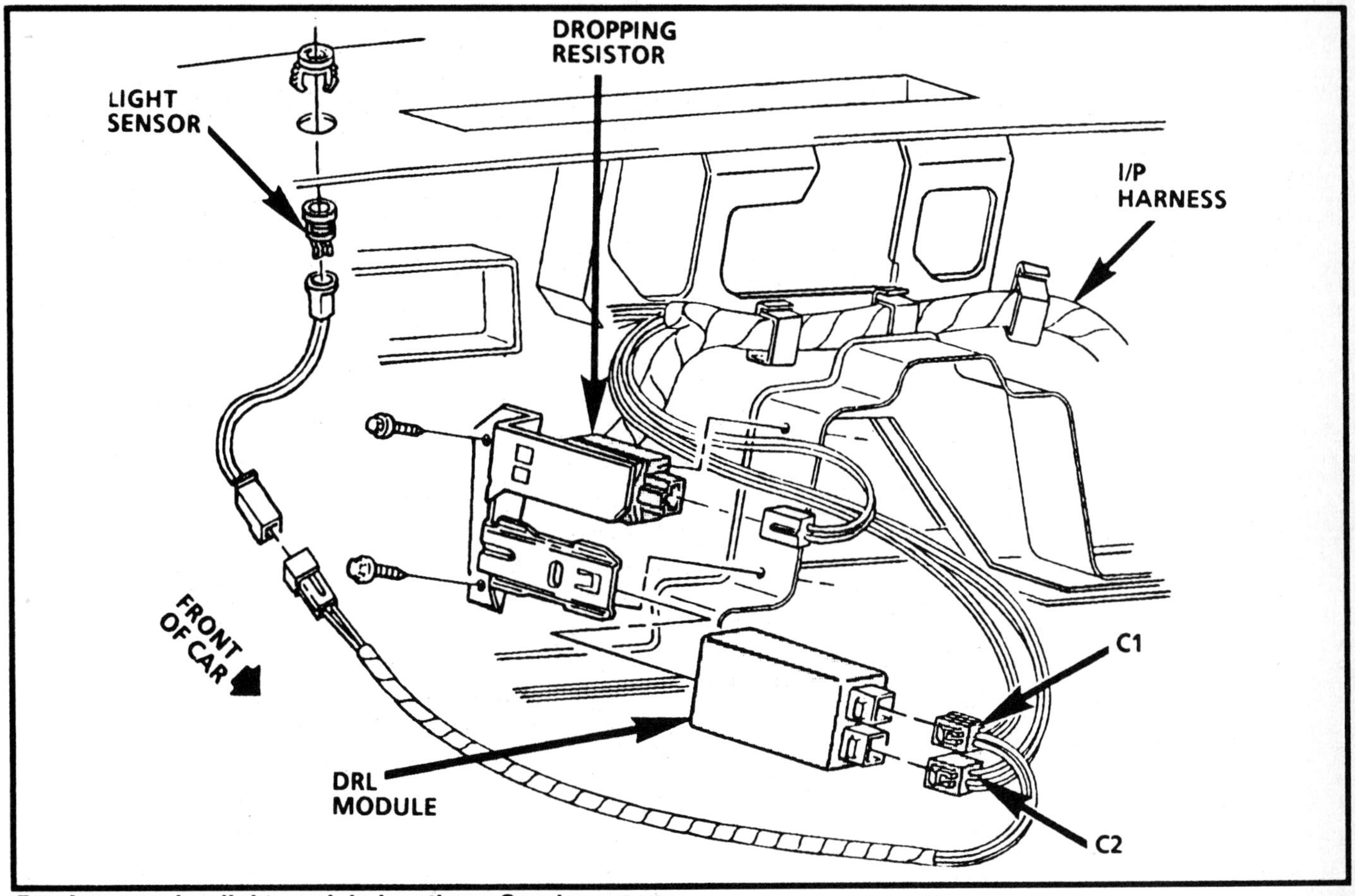

Daytime running light module location—Caprice wagon

ed under the left side of the dash panel, in the connector near the fuse block.

- **Power Steering Pressure Switch**—is located on the left hand front of the engine compartment, near the steering box.
- **Resistance Wire**—is located on the rear of the instrument panel dimmer switch.
- **Seatbelt Switch**—is part of the driver's seatbelt assembly.
- **Starter Solenoid (VIN E and Z)**—is located on the lower right rear of the engine.
- **Starter Solenoid (VIN Y)**—is located on the lower left hand side of the engine.
- **Tailgate Ajar Switch**—is located inside the lower right hand corner of the tailgate assembly.
- **Tailgate Block**—Out Switch—is located inside the upper right hand corner of the tailgate assembly.
- **Tailgate Key Switch**—is located inside the upper right hand center of the tailgate assembly.
- **Throttle Position Sensor**—is located on the carburetor or throttle body.
- **Timer Module**—is behind the left side of the instrument panel, on the right side of the steering column.Trailer Relays—are located on the lower right corner of the fuse block, if so equipped.
- **Trunk Release Solenoid**—is located in the rear center of the trunk lid.
- **Turn Signal Relay**—is located in the fuse block.
- **Twilight Sentinel Amplifier**—is located behind the center of the instrument panel.
- **Twilight Sentinel Photocell**—is located behind the center of the instrument panel.
- **Vacuum Sensor (VIN Z)**—is located on the center front engine firewall.
- **Vehicle Speed Sensor Buffer**—is taped to the instrument panel wiring under the left side of the instrument panel.
- **Vehicle Speed Sensor**—is located behind the left hand side of the instrument panel, taped to the harness.
- **Washer Pump Motor Diode**—is located in the washer motor connector.
- **Wiper Motor Relay Diode**—is located near the wiper/washer assembly in connector.
- **Wiper/Washer Relay**—is incorporated into the wiper/washer assembly.
- **CHECK ENGINE Light Driver (VIN Y)**—is taped to the instrument panel harness, in the right of the instrument panel compartment, above the glove box.

1991 CAPRICE

- **A/C Compressor Relay**—is at the right rear of the engine compartment, attached to the multi-use relay bracket.
- **A/C Diode**—is located at the compressor, in the wiring harness.
- **A/C Pressure Cycling Switch**—is on the accumulator.
- **ABS Hydraulic Modulator**—is on the left side of the engine compartment, just to the left of the alternator.
- **Air Control Solenoid**—is on the right side of the engine, behind the A/C compressor.
- **Antenna Relay**—is under the left instrument panel, to the left of the convenience center.
- **Audio Alarm Module**—is in the convenience center.

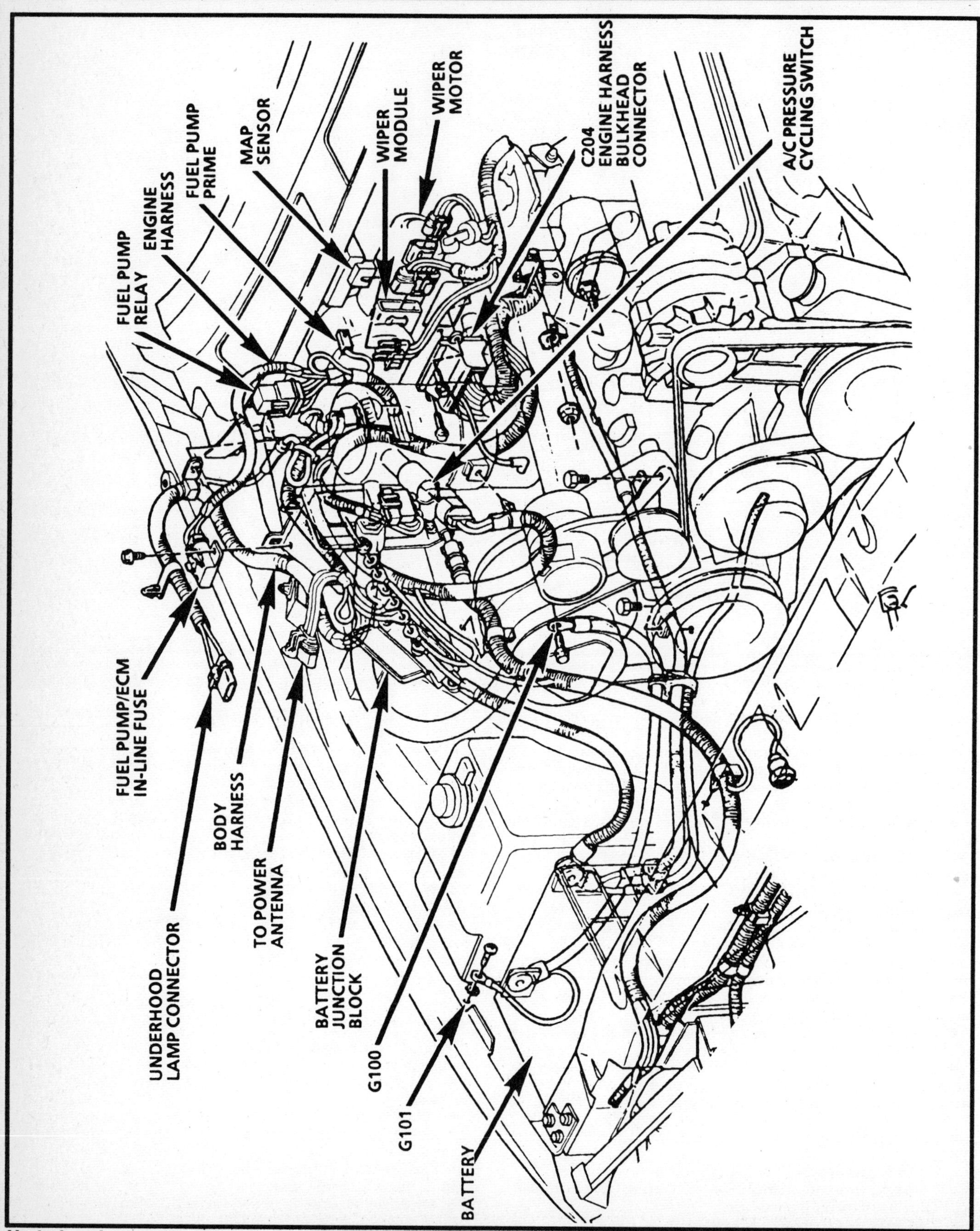

Underhood component locations – 1991 Caprice sedan

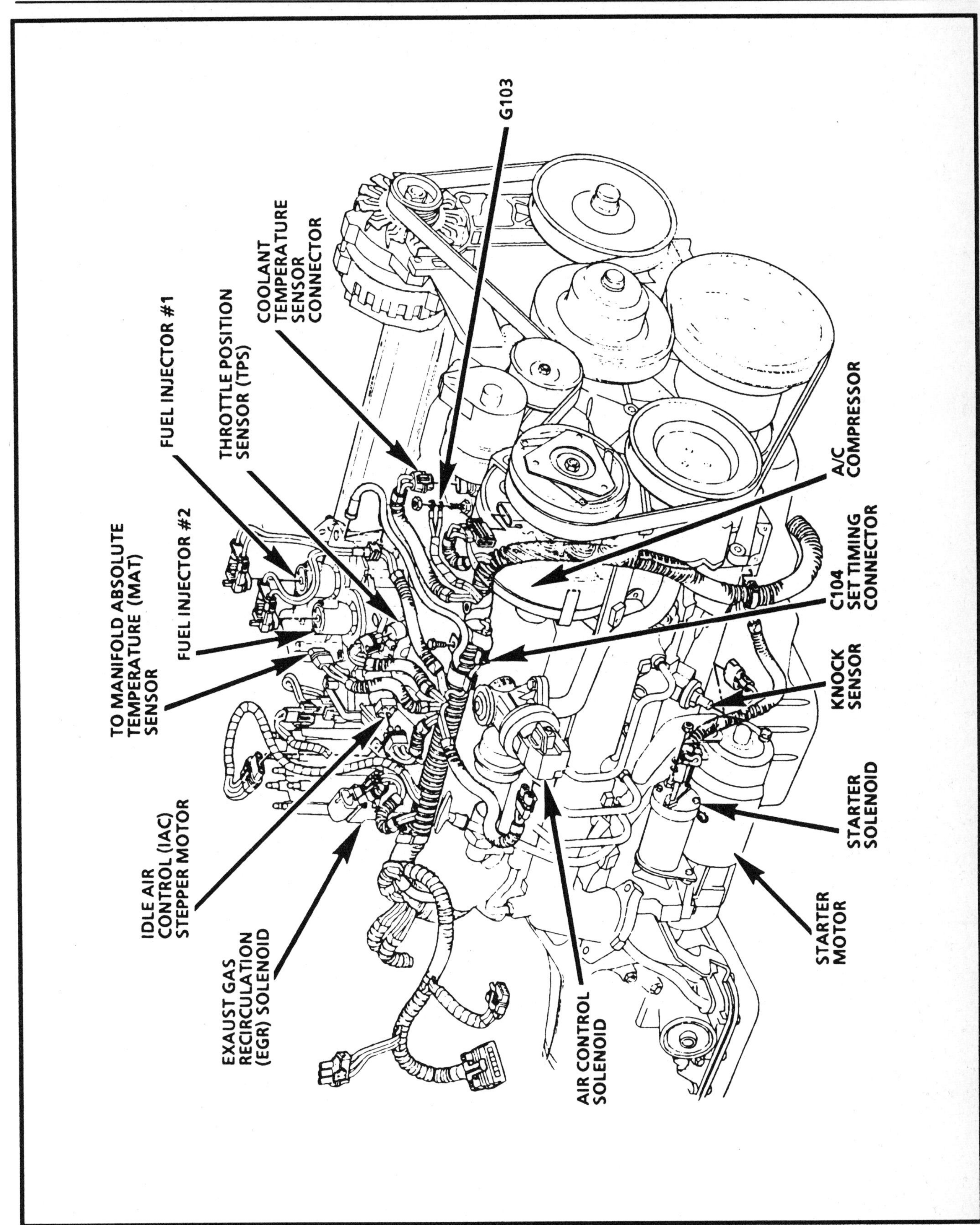

Engine sensor locations—1991 Caprice sedan

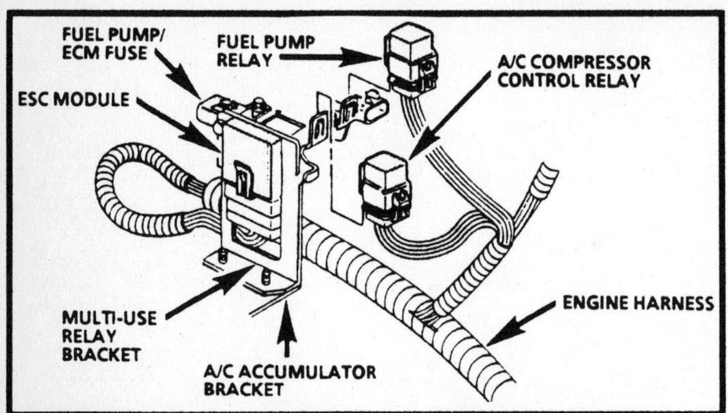

Fuse pump relay and fuse—1991 Caprice sedan

- **Battery Junction Block**—is in the engine compartment mounted to the right wheelhousing.
- **Blower Resistors**—are located under the left instrument panel at the heater duct.
- **Convenience Center**—is under the left side of the instrument panel, just left of the steering column.
- **Coolant Module**—is Low Coolant Temperature Module.
- **Coolant Probe**—is in right rear of the radiator.
- **Coolant Temperature Sensor**—is next to the thermostat housing.
- **Coolant Temperature Switch/Sender**—is on the front left side of the engine, below the manifold.
- **Cruise Control Module**—is attached to the left front wheelhousing.
- **Daylight Running Module**—is above the base of the steering column.
- **Door Lock Relay**—is at the base of the left A—pillar, behind the kick panel.
- **ECM Inline Fuse**—is attached to the multi-use relay bracket, at the rear of the engine compartment.
- **ECM**—See Electronic Control Module

EGR solenoid—See Exhaust Gas Recirculation solenoid.

- **Electronic Brake Control Module (EBCM)**—is inside the luggage compartment on the left wheelhousing.
- **Electronic Control Module (ECM)**—is attached to the base of the right A—pillar.
- **Electronic Spark Control**—is attached to the multi-use relay bracket at the right rear of the engine compartment.
- **ESC Module**—See Electronic Spark Control.
- **Exhaust Gas Recirculation Solenoid**—is located to the right of the distributor.
- **Fuel Pump Fuse**—is attached to the multi-use relay bracket, at the rear of the engine compartment.
- **Fuel Pump Relay**—is attached to the multi-use relay bracket, at the rear of the engine compartment.
- **Fuse Box**—is on the left A—pillar, accessible with door open.
- **Fusible links**—are located at the battery junction block.
- **Hazard Signal Flasher**—is in the convenience center, on the left side of the instrument panel.
- **HEI Module**—See High Energy Ignition Module

High Blower Relay—is located under the right instrument panel to the right of the blower motor.

- **High Blower Relay**—is under the right instrument panel, on the right side of the blower motor.
- **High Energy Ignition Module**—is inside the distributor.
- **Horn Relay**—is in the convenience center.
- **Idle Air Control (IAC) Stepper Motor**—is attached to the throttle body.
- **Keyless Entry Module**—is in the front luggage compartment attached to the rear shelf.
- **Keyless Programming Connector**—is at the left rear of the luggage compartment.
- **Knock Sensor**—is on the right side of the engine, just in front of the starter.
- **Low Coolant Probe**—is in right rear of the radiator.
- **Low Coolant Temperature Module**—is clipped to the bottom of the carrier under the instrument panel.
- **Low Oil Module**—is clipped to the bottom of the carrier under the instrument panel.
- **Manifold Absolute Pressure (MAP) Sensor**—is at the rear of the engine compartment, above the windshield wiper motor module.
- **Manifold Air Temperature (MAT) Sensor**—is attached to the right side of the air cleaner.
- **MAP Sensor**—See Manifold Absolute Pressure (MAP) Sensor.
- **MAT Sensor**—See Manifold Air Temperature (MAT) Sensor.
- **Oil Level Sensor**—is on the left side of the engine, forward of the bell housing near the drain plug.
- **Oil Module**—is Low Coolant Temperature Module.
- **Overvoltage Protection (OVP) Relay**—is inside the luggage compartment attached to the support on the left wheelhousing.
- **Oxygen Sensor**—is located in the exhaust manifold.
- **Photocell Light Sensor**—is on top of the instrument panel, mounted to the defrost grill.
- **Power Steering Pressure Switch**—is located at the power steering pump.
- **Seatbelt Switch**—is part of the right side seatbelt.
- **SIR Arming Sensor**—is behind the left side of the instrument panel, to the right of the steering wheel.
- **SIR DERM**—is above the convenience center under the instrument panel on the left.
- **SIR Resistor Module**—is on the left side of the instrument panel above the parking brake.
- **Timing Adjustment Connector**—breaks out of the wiring harness just behind the air conditioning compressor.
- **Torque Converter Clutch Cruise Control Release Switch**—is behind the left instrument panel on the right of the convenience center.
- **Transmission Position Switch**—is at the steering column.
- **Turn Signal Flasher**—is in the convenience center, on the left side of the instrument panel.
- **Twilight Sentinel Module**—is located above the steering column.
- **Vehicle Speed Sensor Buffer**—is under the left side instrument panel, at the top of the convenience center.
- **Vehicle Speed Sensor**—is at the left rear of the transmission, near the driveshaft.
- **Windshield Wiper Motor Module**—is on the right rear of the engine compartment below the MAP sensor.

CAVALIER

- **A/C and Heater Check Valve**—is located behind the center of the instrument panel, on the right side of the A/C plenum.
- **A/C Compressor Clutch Diode**—is taped inside the A/C compressor clutch connector.
- **A/C Compressor Control Relay**—is located behind the right front shock tower.
- **A/C Heat Valve Vacuum Actuator**—is located under the instrument panel, on the right side of the A/C plenum.
- **A/C Heater Blower Resistors**—are located on the front left side of the A/C plenum.
- **A/C Heater/Defrost Valve Vacuum Actuator**—is located behind the center of the instrument panel, on the lower right side of the A/C plenum.
- **A/C High Pressure Cutout Switch**—is located on the left hand side of the engine compartment, in front of the A/C compressor.

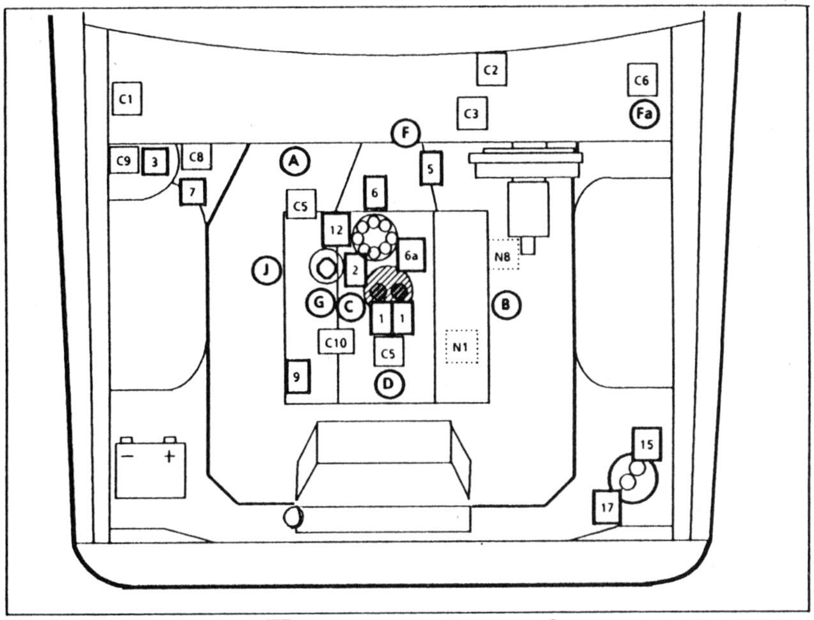

COMPUTER HARNESS
C1 Electronic Control Module (ECM)
C2 ALDL diagnostic connector
C3 "SERVICE ENGINE SOON" light
C5 ECM harness grounds
C6 Fuse panel
C8 Fuel pump "test" connector
C9 Fuel pump/ECM fuse
C10 Set timing connector

NOT ECM CONNECTED
N1 Positive Crankcase Ventilation (PCV)
N8 Oil pressure switch

CONTROLLED DEVICES
1 Fuel injector
2 Idle Air Control (IAC) motor
3 Fuel pump relay
5 Torque Converter Clutch (TCC) connector
6 EST distributor
6a Remote ignition coil
7 Electronic Spark Control (ESC) module
9 AIR Electric Diverter (EDV) valve solenoid
12 EGR solenoid
15 Fuel vapor canister solenoid
17 Fuel vapor canister

Exhaust Gas Recirculation valve

INFORMATION SENSORS
A Manifold Absolute Pressure (MAP) sensor
B Oxygen (O_2) sensor
C Throttle Position Sensor (TPS)
D Coolant Temperature Sensor (CTS)
F Vehicle Speed Sensor (VSS)
Fa Vehicle Speed Sensor (VSS) buffer
G IAT (in air cleaner)
J ESC knock

5.0L and 5.7L engine component component locations—1991 Caprice sedan

- **A/C Low Pressure Cutout Switch**—is located on the right hand side of the engine, on the A/C compressor.
- **A/C Outside Air Valve Vacuum Actuator**—is located under the instrument panel, on the right side of the A/C plenum.
- **A/C Vacuum Line Connector**—is located under the instrument panel, behind the left hand side of the glove box.
- **A/C Vacuum Solenoid**—is located behind the center of the instrument panel, on the A/C plenum, if so equipped.
- **A/C Vacuum Tank**—is located behind the center of the instrument panel, on the right side of the A/C plenum, if equipped.
- **Assembly Line Diagnostic Link (ALDL)**—is located behind the instrument panel, on the right side of the fuse block.
- **Audio Alarm Module**—is located in the convenience center.
- **Back**—Up Switch (4 speed)—is located in the console, at the base of the gear selector.
- **Back**—Up Switch (5 speed)—is located on the left hand side of the transaxle.
- **Battery Junction Block**—is located on the left hand side of the firewall, near the relay bracket.
- **Blower Relay**—is located on the left hand side of the firewall, on the relay bracket.
- **Canister Purge Solenoid**—is located in the right hand front corner of the engine compartment, on top of the canister.
- **Clutch Start Switch**—is located behind the clutch pedal, below the clutch pedal support.
- **Convenience Center**—is located under the left hand side of the instrument panel, to the left of the steering column. Near the fuse block.

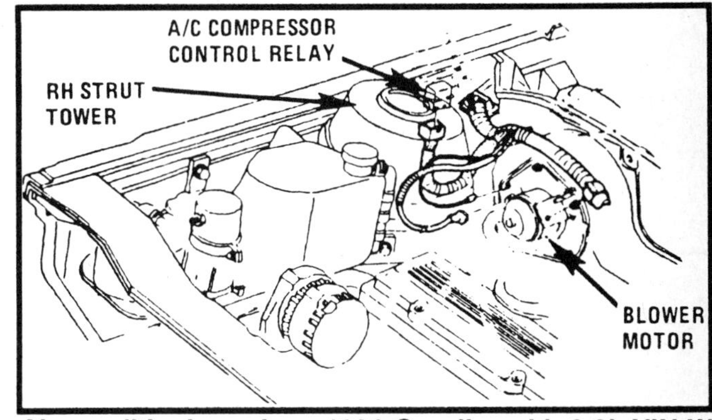

Air conditioning relay—1991 Cavalier with 2.8L VIN W engine

- **Convertible Roof Hydraulic Power Assembly**—is located in the trunk, behind the center of the rear seat.
- **Convertible Roof Relay**—is located at the left front of the luggage compartment.
- **Coolant Fan Pressure Switch**—is located in the lower right hand front corner of the engine compartment, on the refrigerant line.

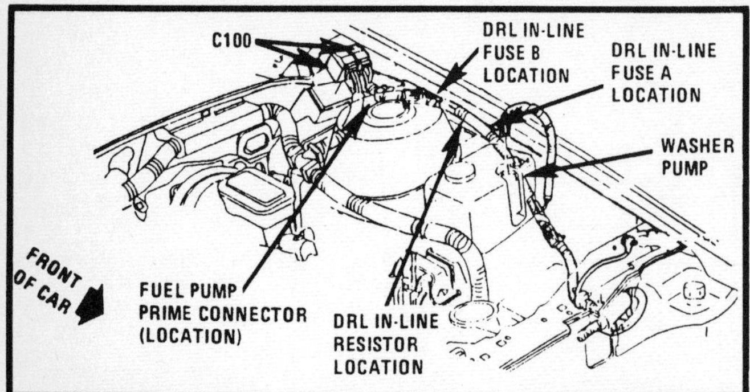

Fuel pump prime connector—1991 Cavalier with 2.8L VIN W engine

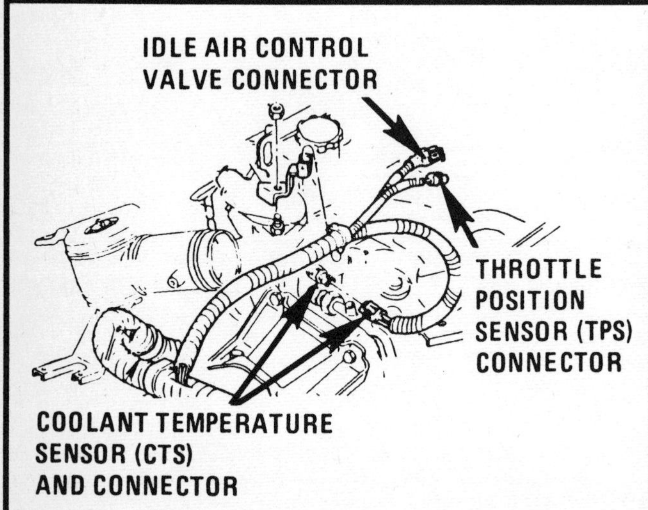

Throttle sensor test connector—1991 Cavalier with 3.1L VIN T engine

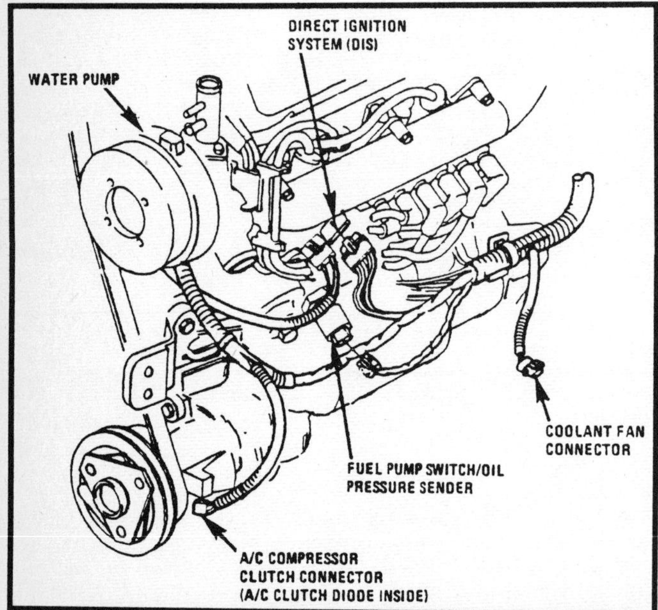

Fuel pump switch—1991 Cavalier with 3.1L VIN T engine

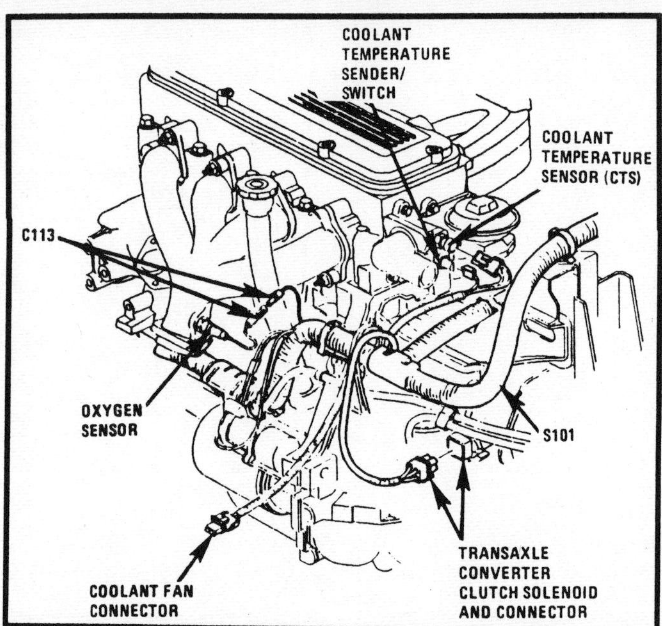

Coolant temperature switch—1991 Cavalier with 2.2L VIN G engine

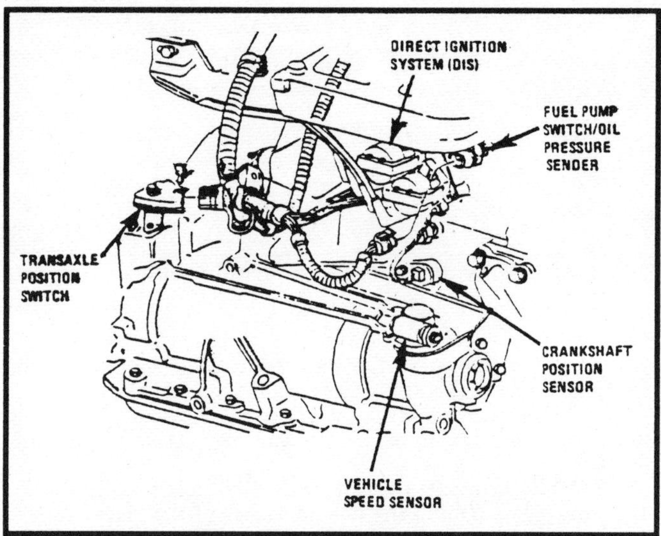

Fuel pump switch—1991 Cavalier VIN G engine

- **Coolant Fan Relay (1989)**—on the left front fender in front of the shock tower.
- **Coolant Fan Relay (except 1989)**—on the front left of the engine compartment, behind the battery.
- **Coolant Temperature Sender/Switch (VIN 1)**—is located on the left side of the engine, near the coolant outlet.
- **Coolant Temperature Sender/Switch (VIN G)**—is located on the left side of the engine, behind the coolant outlet.
- **Coolant Temperature Sender/Switch (VIN T)**—is located on the left side of the engine, above the exhaust manifold.
- **Coolant Temperature Sender/Switch (VIN W)**—is located on the left side of the engine, above the exhaust manifold.
- **Coolant Temperature Sensor (VIN 1)**—is located on the left side of the engine under the water outlet.
- **Coolant Temperature Sensor (VIN G and T)**—is located on the left side of the engine behind the water outlet.
- **Coolant Temperature Sensor (VIN W)**—is located on the right hand front side of the engine on the water outlet.

• **Crankshaft Sensor (VIN 1)** – is located on the right hand rear of the engine, above the transaxle.

• **Crankshaft Sensor (VIN T)** – is located on the right rear of the engine, below the exhaust.

• **Crankshaft Sensor (VIN W)** – is located on the center rear of the engine, above the transaxle.

• **Cruise Control Check Valve** – is located on the center rear of the engine.

• **Cruise Control Clutch Release Valve** – is located above the on the clutch pedal support bracket.

• **Cruise Control Module (1989 Cavalier/CS)** – is located behind the right side of the dash panel, above the glove box.

• **Cruise Control Module (1989 R/S and Z24)** – is located behind the left hand side of the instrument panel, near the base of the left hand shroud.

• **Cruise Control Module (except 1989)** – is located behind the left side of the instrument panel, near the top of the shroud.

• **Cruise Control Servo** – is located on the front of the left hand shock tower in the engine compartment.

• **Cruise Control Vacuum Release Valve** – is located above the brake pedal on the brake pedal support bracket.

• **Cruise Control Vacuum Tank** – is located in the left hand front corner of the engine compartment, on the fender panel.

• **Daytime Running Lights (DRL) Module** – is located at the left front corner of the engine compartment.

• **Defogger Time Relay** – is part of the control assembly.

• **Detonation (Knock) Sensor** – is located on the right hand rear side of the engine, below the exhaust manifold.

• **Digital Exhaust Gas Recirculation (DEGR) Assembly (VIN T)** – is located at the left rear of the engine, behind the throttle body.

• **Direct Ignition System (VIN 1)** – is located on the front of the engine, below the intake manifold.

• **Direct Ignition System (VIN W)** – is located on the front of the engine, below the exhaust manifold.

• **DRL In-Line Resistor** – is on the left side of the engine, near the strut tower.

• **Electronic Control Module (ECM)** – is located behind the glove box, under the right hand side of the instrument panel.

• **Electronic EGR Vacuum Regulator Valve (VIN W)** – is on the left hand rear of the engine, behind the air intake duct.

• **Engine Metal Temperature Switch** – is located on the right hand front side of the engine, on the front cylinder head.

• **Fog Lamp Relays** – are taped to the instrument panel harness, near the fog lamp switch, or above the fuse box.

• **Fuel Pump In-Line Fuse** – is located on the left hand side of the firewall, on the relay bracket.

• **Fuel Pump Prime Connector** – is located in the left hand rear side of the engine compartment, near connector C100.

• **Fuel Pump Relay** – is located on the left hand side of the firewall, on the relay bracket.

• **Fuel Pump Switch (VIN 1)** – is located on the center rear of the engine, below the direct ignition system.

• **Fuel Pump Switch (VIN W)** – is located on the rear of the engine, below the intake manifold.

• **Fuel Pump/Oil Pressure Switch (VIN G)** – is located on the rear of the engine, below the intake manifold.

• **Fuel Pump/Oil Pressure Switch (VIN T)** – is located on the right front of the engine, above the oil filter.

• **Fuse Box** – is under the left side of the instrument panel.

• **Hatch/Tailgate/Trunk Release Relay** – is taped to the wire harness, located behind the right side of the radio.

• **Hazard Relay** – is located on the convenience center.

• **Horn Relay** – is located on the convenience center.

• **Idle Air Control Stepper Motor (VIN 1)** – is located on the top of the engine, on the right side of the throttle body.

• **Idle Air Control Stepper Motor (VIN W)** – is located on the top of the engine, on the left side of the throttle body.

• **Idle Air Control Valve (VIN G)** – is located on the top of the engine, on the right front of the throttle body.

• **Idle Air Control Valve (VIN T)** – is located at the left side of the engine, on the throttle body.

• **Idle Speed Power Steering Pressure Switch** – is located on the left hand side of the firewall, above the brake master cylinder.

• **Ignition In-Line Fuse** – is located on the left hand side of the firewall, near the relay bracket.

• **Ignition Key Warning Switch** – is located in the steering column, near the key cylinder.

• **Ignition Switch** – is located on the top right hand side of the steering column.

• **Left Hand Seatbelt Retractor Solenoid** – is located beside the left hand front seat, at the base of the B – pillar.

• **Low Coolant Module** – is located behind the instrument panel, to the right side of the steering column.

• **Low Coolant Probe** – is located in the engine compartment, on the right front side of the radiator.

• **Low Coolant Switch** – is located on the right side of the engine compartment, in the surge tank.

• **Manifold Absolute Pressure (MAP) Sensor (VIN G and T)** – is located on the left of the blower motor.

• **Manifold Air Temperature (MAT) Sensor (VIN 1)** – is located on the rear of the engine, above the throttle body.

• **Manifold Air Temperature (MAT) Sensor (VIN G)** – is located on the left rear of the engine, in the air cleaner.

• **Manifold Air Temperature (MAT) Sensor (VIN T)** – is located on the left front of the engine compartment, on the right side of the air cleaner.

• **Mass Airflow (MAF) Sensor (VIN W)** – is located on the top of the left side of the engine, on the air intake duct.

• **Mass Airflow Relay (VIN W)** – is located on the left hand side of the firewall, on the relay bracket.

• **Mass Airflow Sensor In-Line Fuse (VIN W)** – is located on the left hand side of the firewall.

• **Oil Pressure Switch (VIN 1)** – is located on the right hand rear of the engine, below the intake manifold.

• **Oil Pressure Switch (VIN W)** – is located on the right hand rear of the engine, near the oil filter.

• **Outside Air Temperature Sensor** – is located in the engine compartment, in the right hand front of the radiator.

• **Oxygen Sensor** – is located in the exhaust manifold.

• **Power Accessories/Convertible Top Circuit Breaker** – is located in the fuse block.

• **Power Antenna Relay** – is located behind the instrument panel, below the right side of the radio, if so equipped.

• **Power Door Lock Relay** – is located on the upper right side of the steering column support.

• **Power Window Circuit Breaker** – is located in the fuse block.

• **Release Relay** – is located behind the center of the instrument panel, taped to the wiring harness. The 1991 vehicle does not use a relay.

• **Release Solenoid (Hatchback)** – is located in the lower rear portion of the hatchback.

• **Release Solenoid (Sedan/Coupe)** – is located near the rear compartment lock mechanism.

• **Release Solenoid (Station Wagon)** – is located below the right hand side of the tailgate window.

• **Remote Dimmer Module** – is located behind the instrument panel, on the left side of the steering column bracket.

• **Rheostat Power Unit Dimmer** – is located under the left hand side of the instrument panel, to the left of the steering column.

• **Right Hand Seatbelt Retractor Solenoid** – is located beside the right hand front seat, at the base of the B – pillar.

• **Seatbelt Switch** – is part of the driver's seatbelt assembly.

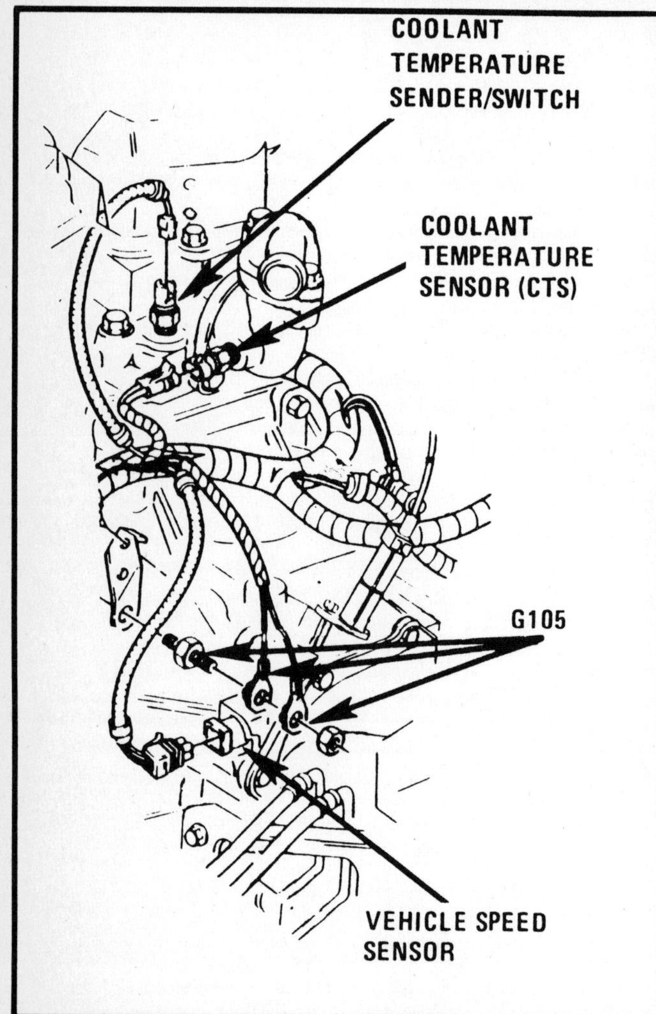

Coolant temperature switch—Celebrity with 2.5L VIN R engine

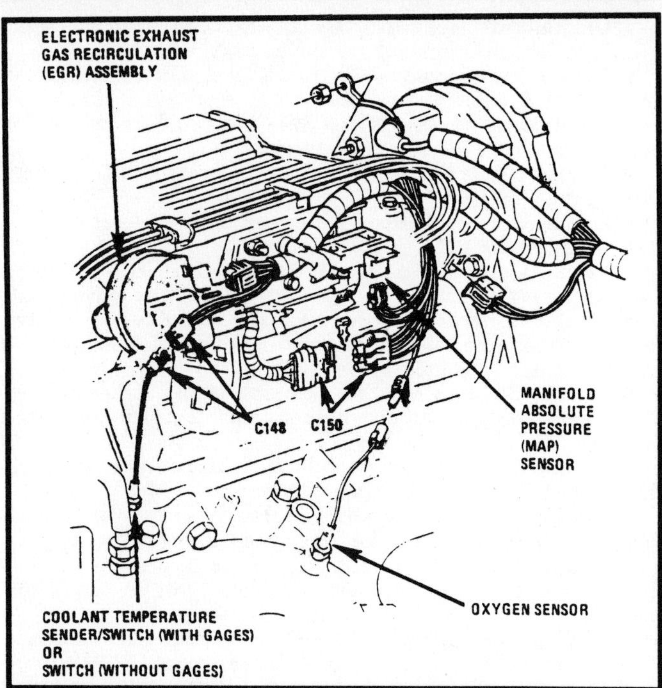

Coolant temperature switch—Celebrity with 2.8L VIN W engine

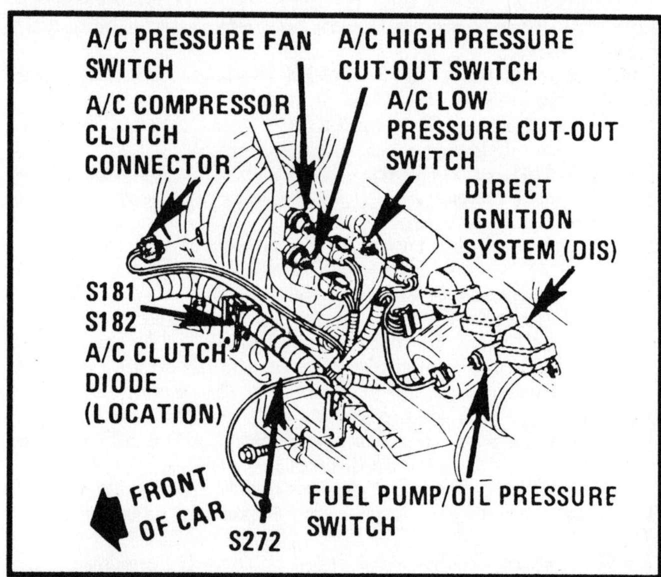

Air conditioning components—Celebrity with 2.8L VIN W engine

- **Starter Solenoid**—is located on the lower left hand front side of the engine.
- **Tachometer Filter**—is located at the left rear of the engine compartment, near the cooling fan relay.
- **Tailgate Ajar Switch**—is located inside the lower center portion of the tailgate assembly.
- **Throttle Position Sensor**—is located on the throttle body.
- **Timing Test Connector (VIN 1)**—is located behind the right hand side of the instrument panel, taped to the wire leading to connector C207.
- **Torque Converter Clutch Relay (TCC)**—is located on the transmission cowling, if so equipped.
- **Transaxle Position Switch**—is located on the left hand side of the transaxle.
- **Turn Signal Flasher**—is located on the side of the steering column bracket.
- **Vehicle Speed Sensor**—is located on the right side of the transaxle.
- **Wiper/Washer Motor Module**—is located on the upper left side of the engine firewall.

CELEBRITY

- **A/C Blower Relay**—is located on the right side of the firewall, on the A/C module (plenum).
- **A/C Blower Resistors**—is located on the right side of the firewall, on the A/C module (plenum).
- **A/C Compressor Clutch Diode**—is taped to the inside compressor connector on the front of the compressor.
- **A/C Coolant Fan Pressure Switch (VIN W)**—is located on the right hand front of the engine, near the left end of the compressor.
- **A/C Defrost Vacuum Actuator**—is located under the center of the instrument panel, on the top of the A/C plenum.
- **A/C Fan Pressure Switch (VIN T)**—is located at the right front of the engine, in the air conditioner line.
- **A/C Heater Vacuum Actuator Bi-Directional**—is lo-

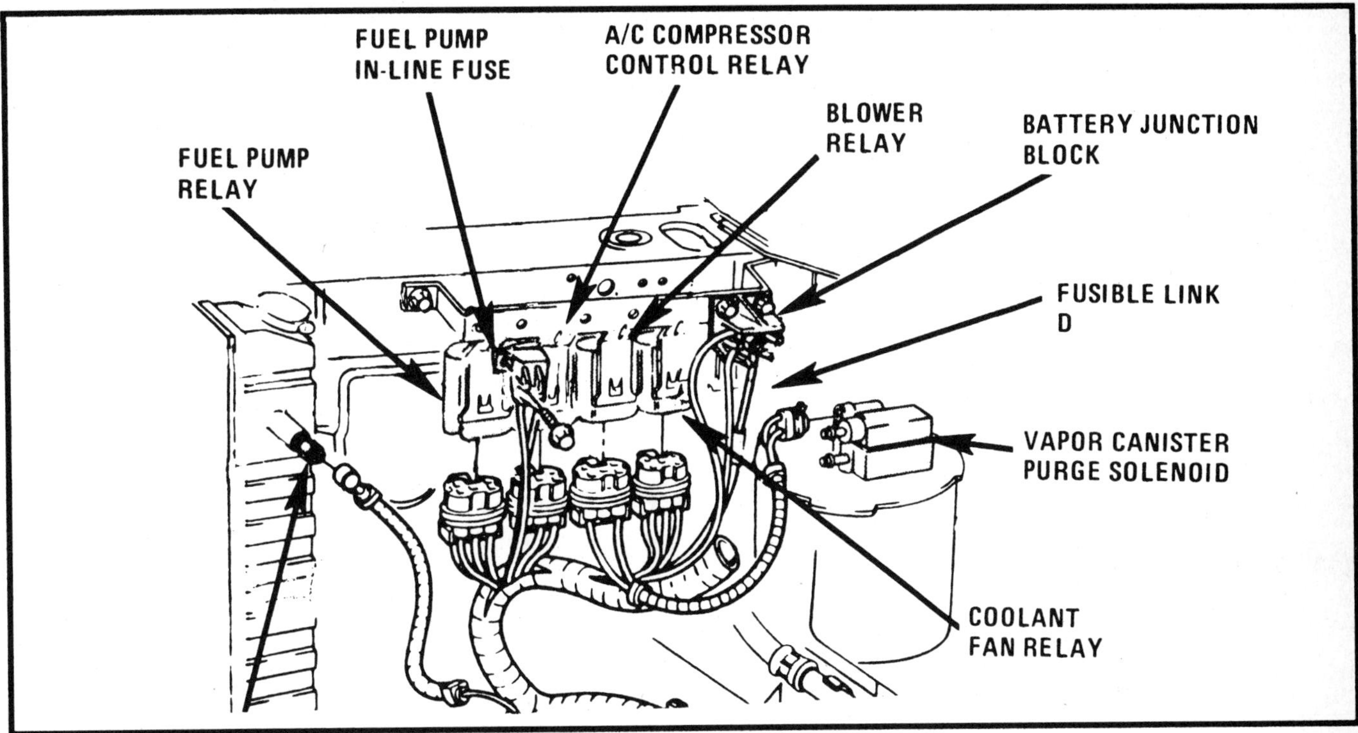

Relay locations—Celebrity with 2.8L VIN W engine

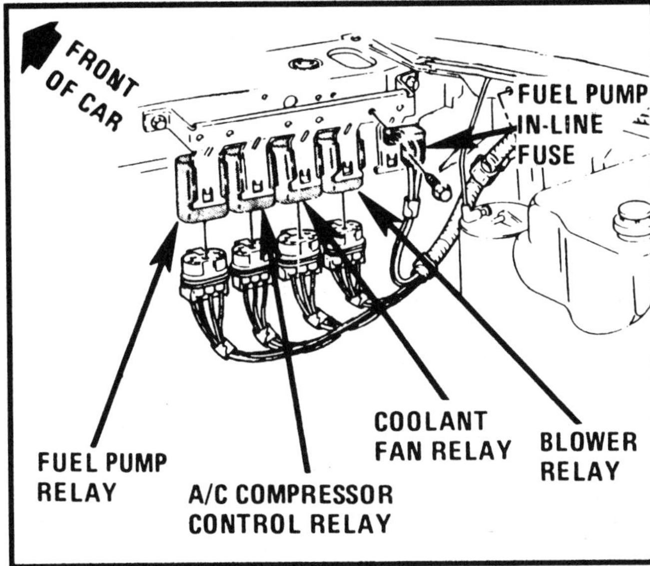

Relay locations—Celebrity with 2.5L VIN R engine

cated under the center of the instrument panel, on the right side of the A/C plenum.

- **A/C High Pressure Cutout Switch**—is located on the left side of the compressor.
- **A/C Low Pressure Cutout Switch**—is located on the A/C compressor.
- **A/C Recirculation/Outside Air Vacuum Actuator**—is located under the center of the instrument panel, on the right side of the A/C plenum.
- **A/C Vacuum Tank**—is located in the center of the firewall, above the A/C and heater module, if equipped.
- **Air Diverter Valve (VIN W)**—is located on the right hand rear of the engine, in front of the AIR pump.
- **Assembly Line Diagnostic Link (ALDL) Connector**—is located on the bottom of the instrument panel, to the left of the steering column.
- **Audio Alarm Module**—is located in the convenience center.
- **Back**—Up Switch—is located on the left hand side of the transaxle.
- **Battery Junction Block**—is located at the right front of the engine compartment, at the relay bracket.
- **Brake Pressure Switch**—is located on the left hand side of the brake fluid reservoir.
- **Canister Purge Solenoid (VIN T)**—is located at the right rear of the engine compartment, on the canister.
- **Canister Purge Solenoid (VIN W)**—is located in the right hand front corner of the engine compartment, on top of the canister.
- **Clutch Start Switch**—is located behind the clutch pedal, below the clutch pedal support.
- **Control Module**—is located behind the instrument panel, to the right of the steering column.
- **Convenience Center**—is located behind the left side of the instrument panel, to the left of the steering column.
- **Coolant Fan Relay (VIN R)**—is located on the left front wheel well on the bracket.
- **Coolant Fan Relay (VIN W)**—is located in the engine compartment, behind the right hand headlights.
- **Coolant Temperature Sensor (VIN R)**—is located on the top left hand side of the engine, below the coolant outlet.
- **Coolant Temperature Sensor (VIN T)**—is located at the top left side of the engine.
- **Coolant Temperature Sensor (VIN W)**—is located on the top left hand side of the engine, below the throttle body.
- **Crank Position Sensor (VIN W)**—is located on the rear of the engine, below the exhaust manifold.
- **Crankshaft Position Sensor (VIN T)**—is located at the lower right rear of the engine.
- **Cruise Control Check Valve**—is located at the right hand rear of the engine compartment.

• **Cruise Control Servo**—is located in the left hand front corner of the engine compartment, on the wheelhouse.

• **Cruise Control Vacuum Release Valve**—is located above the brake pedal on the brake pedal support bracket.

• **Cruise Control Vacuum Tank**—is located in the right hand front corner of the engine compartment.

• **Daytime Running Lights (DRL) Module**—is located behind the right side of the instrument panel, below the right front speaker.

• **Defogger Timer Relay**—is located behind the instrument panel, under the instrument cluster.

• **Detonation (Knock) Sensor (VIN W)**—is located right hand rear of the engine, below the exhaust manifold.

• **Detonation (Knock) Sensor (VIN T)**—is located at the lower right rear of the engine, above the speed sensor.

• **Digital Exhaust Gas Recirculation (DER) Assembly (VIN T)**—is at the top rear of the engine, above the coolant temperature sender.

• **Diode Assembly**—is mounted at the center of the engine compartment, above the air conditioning module.

• **Direct Ignition System (VIN R)**—is located on the front of the engine, below the intake manifold.

• **Direct Ignition System (VIN T)**—is at the lower front of the engine above the oil filter.

• **Direct Ignition System (VIN W)**—is located on the front of the engine, above the oil filter.

• **Electronic Control Module (ECM)**—is located behind the right side of the instrument panel.

• **Fuel Pump In-Line Fuse (except VIN T)**—same as VIN T or may be located in the engine compartment, behind the right hand headlights.

• **Fuel Pump In-Line Fuse (VIN T)**—is at the front of the engine compartment, on the relay bracket.

• **Fuel Pump Prime Connector (VIN R)**—is taped to the engine harness, below the coolant outlet.

• **Fuel Pump Prime Connector (VIN T)**—is at the left rear of the engine compartment, near the C100 connector.

• **Fuel Pump Prime Connector (VIN W)**—is taped to the engine harness, near connector C100.

• **Fuel Pump Relay (VIN R)**—is located on the right hand side of the firewall, on the relay bracket.

• **Fuel Pump Relay (VIN T)**—is on the relay bracket at the right front of the engine compartment.

• **Fuel Pump Relay (VIN W)**—is located in the engine compartment, behind the right hand headlights.

• **Fuel Pump/Oil Pressure Sender (VIN T)**—is at the lower front of the engine, above the oil filter.

• **Fuel Pump/Oil Pressure Switch (VIN R)**—is located at the rear of the engine, below the throttle body.

• **Fuel Pump/Oil Pressure Switch (VIN W)**—is located on the left hand side of the engine, below the intake duct.

• **Fusible Links**—are located at the battery junction block, starter solenoid and the battery.

• **Hazard Flasher**—is located in the convenience center.

• **Headlight Dimmer Switch**—is located behind the left hand side of the instrument panel, on the steering column.

• **Heater Blower Resistors**—is located on the right side of the firewall, near the blower motor.

• **Horn Relay**—is located on the convenience center.

• **Idle Air Control Motor (VIN T)**—is on the top left side of the engine.

• **Idle Air Control Stepper Motor (VIN R)**—is located on the top of the engine, on the rear of the throttle body.

• **Idle Air Control Valve (VIN W)**—is located on the top of the engine, on the front of the throttle body.

• **Idle Speed Power Steering Pressure Switch (VIN R)**—is located on the right hand rear side of the engine, in the power steering hydraulic line.

• **Idle Speed Power Steering Pressure Switch (VIN T)**—is on the lower right rear of the engine compartment, on the power steering line.

• **Idle Speed Power Steering Pressure Switch (VIN W)**—is located on the steering rack, ahead of the frame crossmember.

• **Ignition Key Warning Switch**—is located on the steering column, below the turn/hazard switch.

• **Ignition Switch**—is located it the middle of the steering column.

• **Junction Block No. 1**—is located in the left hand side of the engine compartment, on front of the strut tower.

• **Junction Block No. 2**—is located in the engine compartment, behind the right hand headlights.

• **Low Coolant Module**—is located behind the right hand side of the instrument panel.

• **Low Coolant Probe**—is located in the engine compartment, on the right front side of the radiator.

• **Manifold Absolute Pressure (MAP) Sensor (VIN R)**—is located on the air cleaner assembly.

• **Manifold Absolute Pressure (MAP) Sensor (VIN T)**—is at the top right end of the engine, behind the alternator.

• **Manifold Absolute Pressure (MAP) Sensor (VIN W)**—is located on the upper right hand front of the firewall, behind the strut tower.

• **Manifold Air Temperature (MAT) Sensor (VIN R)**—is located on the rear of the engine, above the throttle body.

• **Manifold Air Temperature (MAT) Sensor (VIN T)**—is at the top of the engine on the air cleaner.

• **Mass Air Flow Sensor In-Line Fuse (VIN W)**—is located in the engine compartment, on the front of the left shock tower.

• **Mass Airflow (MAF) Sensor (VIN W)**—is located on the air cleaner, forward of the left hand strut tower.

• **Mass Airflow Relay (VIN W)**—is located in the engine compartment, on the front of the left shock tower.

• **Oil Pressure Switch (VIN R)**—is located on the right hand rear of the engine, below the throttle body.

• **Oil Pressure Switch (VIN W)**—is located on the front of the engine, above the oil filter.

• **Oxygen Sensor**—is located in the exhaust manifold.

• **Position EGR Solenoid (VIN W)**—is located on the top left hand rear of the engine, above the valve cover.

• **Power Accessories Circuit Breaker**—is located in the fuse block.

• **Power Antenna Relay**—is located behind the instrument panel on the rear of the glove box, if so equipped.

• **Power Door Lock Relay**—is located on the right shroud, above the center access hole.

• **Power Window Circuit Breaker**—is located in the fuse block.

• **Rear Wiper Module**—is located in the top center of the tailgate.

• **Seatbelt Switch**—is part of the driver's seatbelt assembly.

• **Starter Solenoid**—is located on the lower front portion of the engine.

• **Tailgate Ajar Switch**—is located inside the lower center portion of the tailgate assembly.

• **Tailgate Lock Switch**—is located in the middle center of the tailgate assembly.

• **Tailgate Release Relay**—is located behind the left hand side of the instrument panel, taped to the instrument panel harness.

• **Tailgate Release Solenoid**—is located in the center of the tailgate assembly, behind the panel.

• **Throttle Position Sensor (VIN T)**—is at the top left rear of the engine, near the throttle body.

• **Throttle Position Sensor (except VIN T)**—is located on the throttle body.

• **Transaxle Position Switch**—is located on the left hand side of the transaxle.

• **Trunk Release Relay**—is located behind the left hand

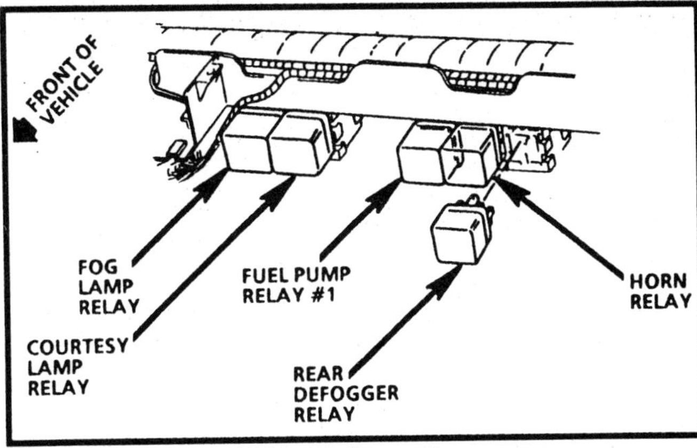

Relay locations – 1990–91 Corvette

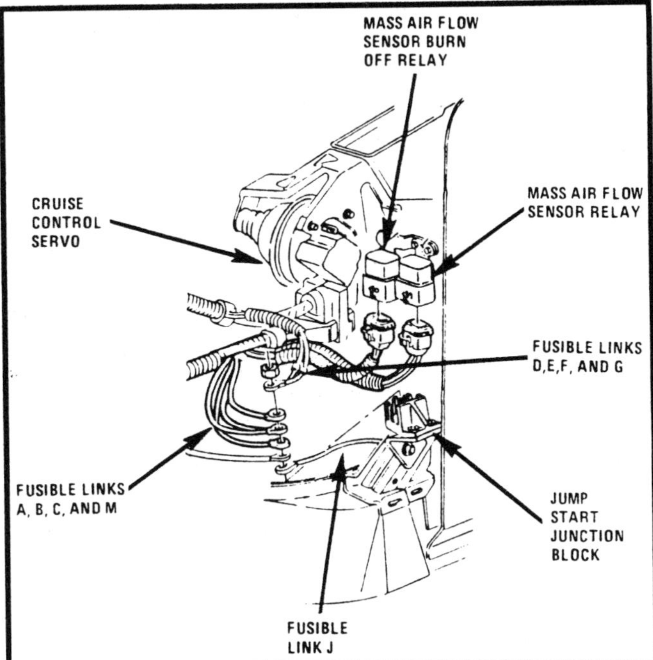

Relay locations – 1989 Corvette

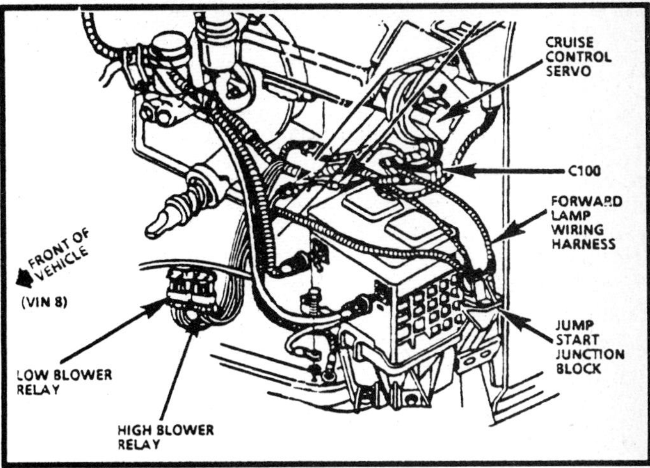

Fan Relay locations – 1989 Corvette

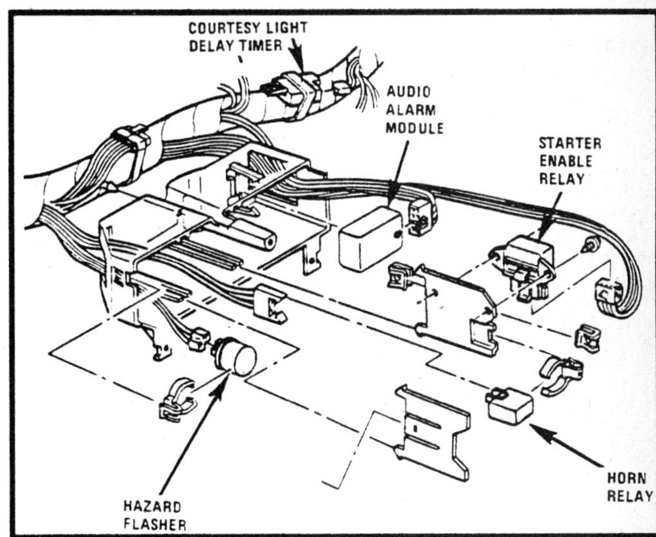

Starter enable relay – 1989 Corvette

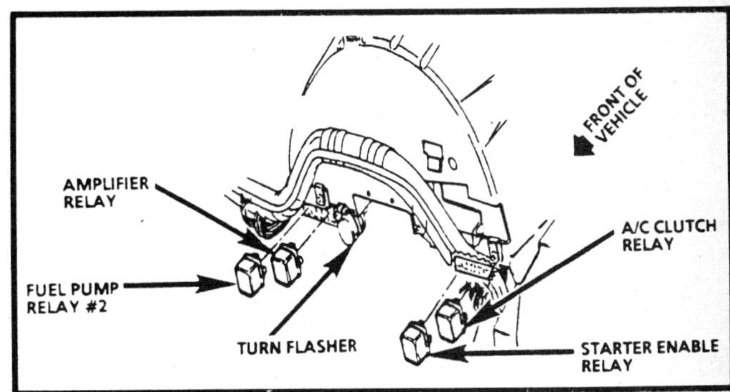

Starter enable relay – 1990–91 Corvette

side of the instrument panel, taped to the instrument panel harness.

- **Trunk Release Solenoid** – is located in the center of the trunk lid.
- **Turn Signal Flasher** – is located on the right hand side of the steering column.
- **Vehicle Speed Sensor** – is on the right rear of the engine, on the transaxle.
- **Wiper/Washer Motor Module** – is located on the upper left side of the engine firewall.

CORVETTE

- **A/C Air Mix Valve Actuator** – behind the right side of instrument panel, on the heater/air conditioning plenum.

A/C Clutch Diode – in the air conditioning compressor clutch connector.

- **A/C Coolant Fan Switch** – at the rear of engine compartment, on the air conditioning line.
- **A/C Defrost Valve Vacuum Actuator** – behind the right side of instrument panel, on the heater/air conditioning plenum.
- **A/C Front Mode Valve Vacuum Actuator** – behind the right side of instrument panel, on the heater/air conditioning plenum.
- **A/C High Pressure Cut** – Out Switch – at the rear of engine compartment, on the air conditioning line.
- **A/C In-Car Sensor** – is located behind the right side air conditioner outlet.
- **A/C Outside Air Valve Vacuum Actuator** – behind the right side of instrument panel.

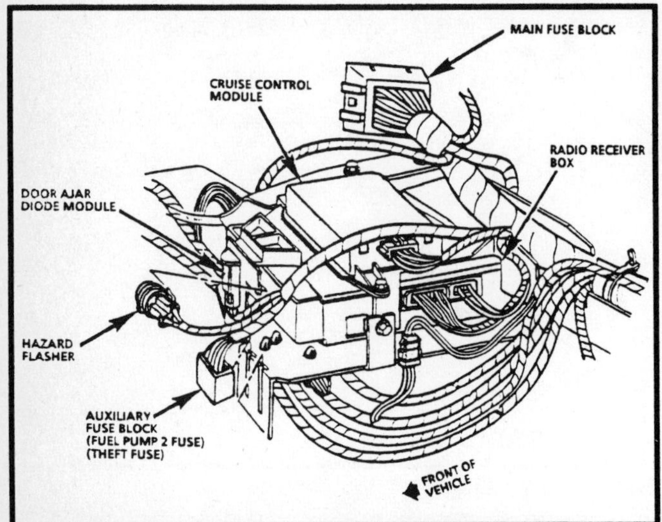

Cruise control module—1990–91 Corvette

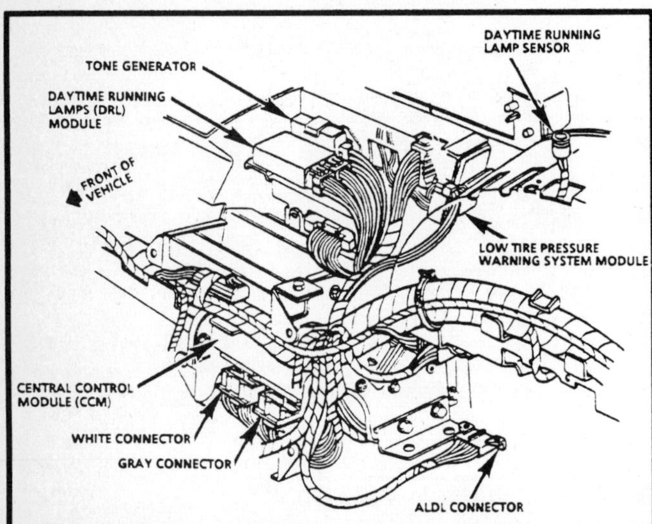

Low tire pressure module—1990–91 Corvette

- **A/C Pressure Cycling Switch**—at the top of evaporator housing, on air conditioning line.
- **A/C Rear Mode Valve Vacuum Actuator**—behind the right side of instrument panel, on the heater/air conditioning plenum.
- **A/C Temperature Control, In Car Sensor (Convertible)**—in the center of cargo compartment lid.
- **A/C Temperature Control, In Car Sensor (Coupe)**—above the left side seat, on the center lock pillar.
- **A/C Underhood Fuse**—at the right rear of engine compartment, near blower motor.
- **Air Divert Valve**—at the front of engine, above the water pump.
- **Air Select/Switching Valve**—front of engine, above the water pump.
- **Airbag Module**—See Supplemental Inflatable Restraint Module.
- **Ambient Light Sensor**—is at the top of the instrument panel.
- **Ambient Temperature Override Switch**—is located behind the instrument panel, on the rear of connector C100, if equipped.
- **Amplifier Relay**—is located behind the center of the instrument panel, to the right of the radio.
- **Antenna Motor**—at the left rear of the cargo compartment, near side marker.
- **Antenna Relay (Convertible)**—at the left rear of cargo compartment, above wheelhouse.
- **Antenna Relay (Coupe)**—at the left rear of cargo compartment, on the end panel.
- **Antenna Relay Capacitor No. 1**—inside the antenna relay connector.
- **Antenna Relay Capacitor No. 2**—taped to the front body harness, near antenna relay.
- **Anti-Lock Brake Diode**—is located under the left hand side of the cargo compartment, behind the driver's seat.
- **Anti-Lock Brake Wheel Sensors**—are located on each wheel spindle.
- **Antilock Brake System (ABS) Control Module**—underneath the left side of cargo compartment, behind the drive's seat.
- **Assembly Line Diagnostic Link (ALDL) Connector**—below the left side of instrument panel.
- **Audio Alarm Module**—behind the center of instrument panel, in the multi-use center.
- **Auxiliary Coolant Fan Relay**—at the front of engine compartment, to the left of radiator support.
- **Auxiliary Fuse Block**—behind the center of instrument panel, on multi-use center.
- **Back Up Lights Switch**—under the vehicle, on the left side of transmission.
- **Blower Control Module**—at the front of dash, left side of evaporator housing.
- **Blower Relay**—at the right front of dash, above the blower motor.
- **Blower Resistors**—at the front of dash, on left side of evaporator housing.
- **Bow Release Relay**—at the right front of cargo compartment.
- **Brake Fluid Level Switch**—at the left front of dash, on the brake master cylinder.
- **Brake Switch Capacitor 1 (ABS)**—taped to the instrument panel harness, near the brake switch connector.
- **Brake Switch Capacitor 2**—at the left side of instrument panel, in brake switch connector.
- **Brake Switch**—at the top of brake pedal bracket.
- **Central Control Module**—is behind the middle of the instrument panel.
- **Clutch Start Switch**—behind the instrument panel, at the top of clutch pedal bracket.
- **Computer Aided Gear Selector Solenoid**—under the vehicle, on the left side of transmission.
- **Coolant Fan Relay**—at the front of engine compartment, on the left side of radiator shroud.
- **Coolant Fan Temperature Switch**—at the left side of engine, behind the generator.
- **Coolant Temperature Sender**—at the right side of engine, near the starter solenoid.
- **Coolant Temperature Sensor**—at the front of engine, below the throttle body.
- **Courtesy Lamp Relay**—is at the bottom of the right side of the instrument panel.
- **Courtesy Light Delay Timer**—behind the right side on instrument panel, near the multi-use center.
- **Cruise Control Check Valve**—at right rear of engine, near the distributor.
- **Cruise Control Clutch Switch**—behind the instrument panel, at top of the clutch pedal bracket.
- **Cruise Control Servo**—at the left rear of engine compartment, near the battery.
- **CTS**—See Coolant Temperature Sensor.
- **Daytime Running Light (DRL) Module**—is at the top

right side of the instrument panel, near the driver information center.

- **Deck Lid Release Relay**—is at the right front of the cargo compartment, above the wheelhousing.
- **Defogger Relay**—behind the center of instrument panel, on the heater/air conditioning programmer.
- **Detonation (Knock) Sensor**—at the right side of engine, ahead of the starter.
- **Diode Module**—at the rear of the cargo compartment, to the right of fuel filter.
- **Door Arm Switch**—in each door.
- **Door Lock Cylinder Switch**—in each door.
- **Door Lock Motor**—at the lower rear area of each door.
- **Electronic Control Module 1989 (ECM)**—behind the right side of instrument panel.
- **Electronic Control Module except 1989 (ECM)**—behind the left rear of the engine compartment.
- **Electronic Spark Timing (EST) Distributor**—at the top rear of engine.
- **Electronic Spark Timing (EST) Module**—at the right front of dash, on the right side of the evaporator housing.
- **Exhaust Gas Recirculation (EGR) Diagnostic Switch**—at the right rear of engine, near the distributor.
- **Exhaust Gas Recirculation (EGR) Solenoid**—at the top left front of engine, near the front of valve cover.
- **Fog Lamp Relay**—is on the bottom right side of the instrument panel.
- **Fuel Pump Relay (1989)**—at the left front of dash, to the right of the brake master cylinder.
- **Fuel Pump Relay (1990)**—below the right side of instrument panel, left of the glove compartment.
- **Fuse Block**—behind the right side of instrument panel.
- **Gear Selector Relay**—at the left rear of engine compartment, near the battery.
- **Hatch Ajar Switch**—at the rear of cargo compartment, on the end panel.
- **Hatch Release Relay**—is at the right of the cargo compartment, on the end panel.
- **Hazard Flasher (1989)**—behind the center of instrument panel, in the multi-use center.
- **Hazard Flasher (except 1989)**— is behind the right side of the instrument panel, near the radio receiver box.
- **Headlight Control Unit**—at the lower left front of engine compartment.
- **Headlight Dimmer Switch**—behind the instrument panel, at the left center of steering column.
- **Heater A/C Programmer**—behind left side of instrument panel, to the right of steering column.
- **Horn Relay (1989)**—behind the center of instrument panel, in multi-use center.
- **Horn Relay (except 1989)**—behind the lower right side of the instrument panel.
- **Idle Air Control Motor**—at the front of engine, below the throttle body.
- **Ignition Key Warning Switch**—at the top of steering column, below the turn/hazard switch assembly.
- **Incandescent Power Driver**—is behind the left side of the instrument panel, left of the instrument cluster.
- **Jump Start Junction Block**—at the left rear of engine compartment, behind the battery.
- **Lateral Acceleration Switch**—below the console, near the shift control lever.
- **Left Bow Release Solenoid**—at the left side of cargo compartment, above the wheelhouse.
- **Left Front Low Tire Pressure Indicator Sensor**—on the left front wheel.
- **Left Front Shock Absorber Actuator**—on top of the left front shock absorber.
- **Left Front Wheel Speed Sensor**—on the left front wheel spindle.
- **Left Headlight Door Motor Assembly**—at the left front of vehicle.
- **Left Rear Low Tire Pressure Indicator Sensor**—on the left rear wheel.
- **Left Rear Shock Absorber Actuator**—on top of the left rear shock absorber.
- **Left Rear Wheel Speed Sensor**—on the left rear wheel spindle.
- **Left Window Motor Capacitor**—taped to the console harness, near the left power window switch.
- **Low Coolant Module**—behind the instrument panel, near the fuse block.
- **Low Coolant Sensor**—at the right front of engine compartment, on the radiator.
- **Low Tire Pressure Indicator Module**—behind the right side of instrument panel.
- **Manifold Absolute Pressure (MAP) Sensor**—is at the rear of the plenum.
- **Manifold Absolute Temperature (MAT) Sensor**—at the right rear of engine.
- **Manifold Air Temperature (MAT) Sensor**—is located at the rear of the engine, under the plenum.
- **MAP Sensor**—See Manifold Absolute Pressure (MAP) Sensor.
- **Mass Air Flow (MAF) Sensor (1989)**—at the front of engine, ahead of the throttle body.
- **Mass Air Flow (MAF) Sensor Burn Off Relay (1989)**—at the left rear of engine compartment, behind the battery.
- **Mass Air Flow (MAF) Sensor Relay**—at the left rear of engine compartment, behind the battery.
- **MAT Sensor**—See Manifold Air Temperature Sensor.
- **Modulator Valve**—underneath the left side of cargo compartment, behind the drive's seat.
- **Module Relay (ABS)**—underneath the left side of cargo compartment, behind the drive's seat.
- **Multi-Function Lever**—at the top left of steering column.
- **Oil Pressure Switch/Sender**—at top left rear of engine.
- **Oil Temperature Sensor**—at the lower left rear of engine, above the oil filter.
- **Oil Temperature Sensor**—is at the top rear of the engine, above the oil filter.
- **Overdrive Enable Switch**—underneath the console, near the shift control lever.
- **Oxygen Sensor**—at the left side of engine, in the exhaust downpipe.
- **Parking Brake Switch**—at the left door sill, on the parking brake assembly.
- **Pass Key Decoder Module**—behind the right side of instrument panel, near the fuse block.
- **Primary Coolant Fan Relay**—at the front of engine compartment, to the left of radiator support.
- **Right Bow Release Solenoid**—at the right side of cargo compartment, near side marker.
- **Right Front Low Tire Pressure Indicator Sensor**—on the right front wheel.
- **Right Front Shock Absorber Actuator**—on top of the right front shock absorber.
- **Right Front Wheel Speed Sensor**—on the right front wheel spindle.
- **Right Headlight Door Motor Assembly**—at the right front of vehicle.
- **Right Rear Low Tire Pressure Indicator Sensor**—on the right rear wheel.
- **Right Rear Shock Absorber Actuator**—on top of the right rear shock absorber.
- **Right Rear Wheel Speed Sensor**—on the right rear wheel spindle.

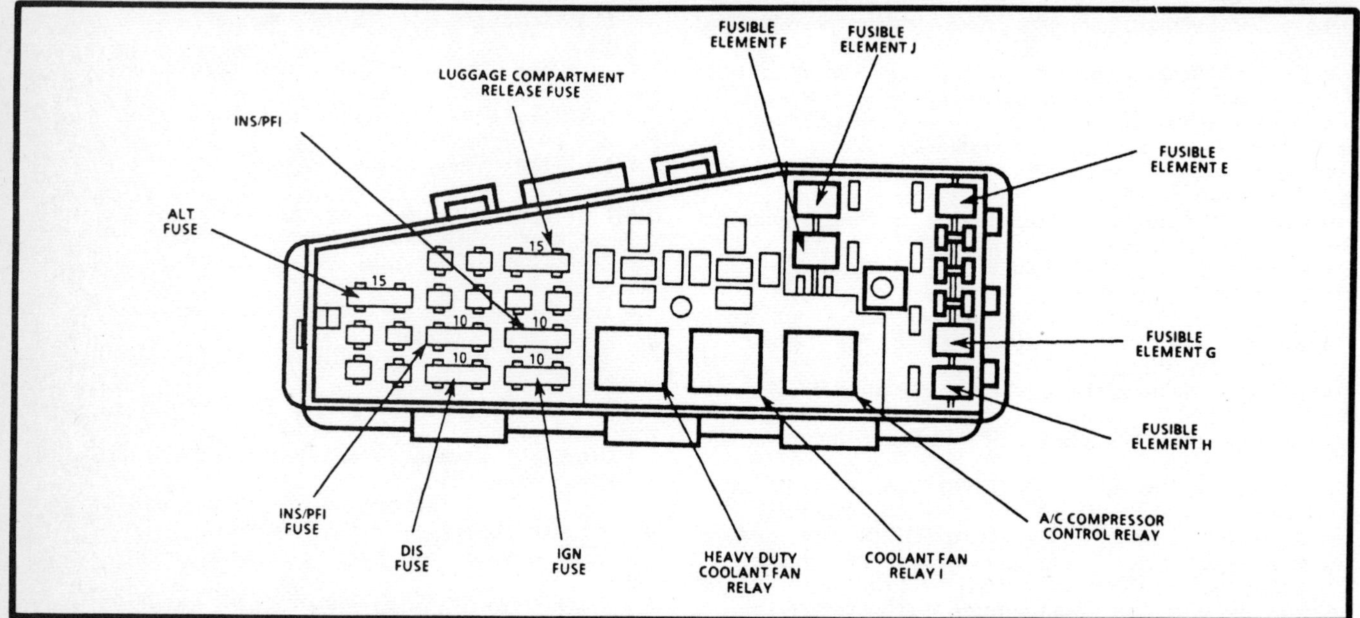

Right Side (RS) electrical center—Lumina

- **Right Window Motor Capacitor**—taped to the console harness, near the right power window switch.
- **Safety Belt Switch**—part of the driver's safety belt buckle assembly.
- **Seat Motor Assembly**—below each front seat.
- **Secondary Coolant Fan Relay**—at the front of engine compartment, to the left of radiator support.
- **Selective Ride Control (SRC) Module**—is under the rear cargo deck lid.
- **Shift Relay**—is at the right rear corner of the engine compartment, above the battery.
- **SIR Module**—See Supplemental Inflatable Restraint Module.
- **Starter Enable Relay**—behind the center of instrument panel, on the multi-use center or to the left of the steering column.
- **Sun Load Sensor**—is at the top center of the defroster grille.
- **Supplemental Inflatable Restraint (SIR) Module**—is in the middle of the instrument panel and below the central control module.
- **Tachometer Filter**—at the top rear center of engine.
- **Theft Deterrent Controller**—behind the right side of instrument panel, near the fuse block.
- **Theft Deterrent Module**—See Central Control Module.
- **Throttle Position Switch**—at the front of engine, on the right side of throttle body.
- **Tone Generator**—is located behind the left side of the instrument panel, near the driver information center.
- **Torque Convertor Clutch (TCC)/Cruise Brake Switch**—at the top of brake pedal bracket.
- **TPS**—See Throttle Position Sensor.
- **Transmission Position Switch**—in the console, at the base of the shift control lever.
- **Turn Flasher**—behind the right side of instrument panel, near the fuse block.
- **Vapor Canister Purge Solenoid**—at the left front of engine compartment, below the headlight.
- **Vehicle Speed Sensor (VSS)**—at the left rear of transmission tailshaft housing.
- **Washer Pump Motor**—at the right rear of engine compartment, below the washer fluid reservoir.

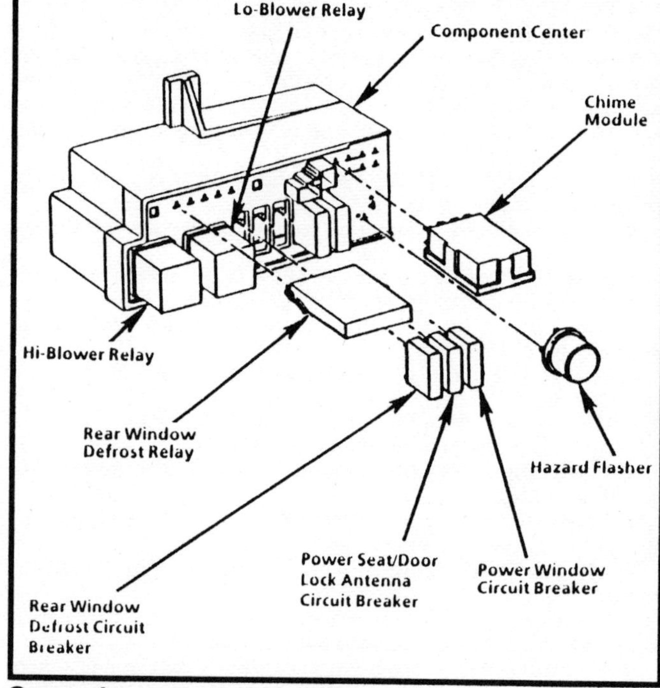

Convenience center—Lumina

- **Wiper Motor Module Capacitor**—at the left front of dash, taped to the wiper motor harness.
- **Wiper Motor Module**—at the left front of dash.

LUMINA

- **A/C Air Temperature Valve Motor**—is located behind the instrument panel, in the right hand side of the plenum.
- **A/C Bi-Level Valve Vacuum Actuator**—is located behind the instrument panel, on the right hand side of the A/C plenum.

• **A/C Compressor Clutch Diode**–is taped to the inside compressor connector on the front of the compressor.

• **A/C High Pressure Switch**–on the back of the compressor.

• **A/C In-Car Sensor**–is located in the upper instrument panel trim, in the right hand speaker grill assembly.

• **A/C Pressure Transducer**–is on the front right of the engine compartment, in the refrigerant line.

• **A/C-Defroster Vacuum Motor**–is located under the instrument panel, on the right side of the A/C plenum.

• **A/C-Heater Blower Resistors**–are located on the at the blower motor near the plenum.

• **A/C-Heater Water Valve Vacuum Motor**–is located behind the rear of the engine, under the heater hoses.

• **A/C-Heater/Defrost Bi-Directional Vacuum Actuator**–is located under the instrument panel, on the right side of the A/C plenum.

• **A/C-Intermediate Pressure Switch**–is located in the left hand front of the engine compartment, on the accumulator.

• **A/C-Low Pressure Switch**–is located behind the A/C compressor.

• **A/C-Recirculating Door Vacuum Actuator**–is located behind the right side of the instrument panel, on the right hand side of the A/C plenum.

• **A/C-Solenoid Box**–is located under the right side of the instrument panel, on the right hand side of the A/C plenum above the blower motor.

• **A/C-Upper Mode Vacuum Motor**–is located under the instrument panel, on the right hand front side of the A/C plenum.

• **A/C-Valve Vacuum Actuator**–is located behind the instrument panel, on the plenum.

• **A/C-Vent Valve Vacuum Actuator**–is located under the right side of the instrument panel, on the right hand side of the A/C plenum.

• **Accumulator (ABS) Pressure Switch**–is on the right side of the master cylinder.

• **Antenna Motor**–is behind the right rear wheelhousing.

• **Antenna Relay**–is behind the right rear wheelhousing.

• **Anti-Lock Brake Controller**–is located below the right hand front seat.

• **Anti-Lock Brake Power Center**–is located on the radiator support, above the right hand headlight.

• **Antilock Brake Diode**–is behind the right side of the instrument panel.

• **Antilock Brake Power Center**–is located at the front left of the engine compartment, in front of the strut.

• **Assembly Line Diagnostic Connector**–is located on the bottom of the instrument panel, to the right of the steering column.

• **Brake Fluid Level Switch**–is located on the left side of the firewall, on the brake master cylinder.

• **Brake Pressure Switch**–is located on the lower left hand rear of the engine compartment on the frame rail.

• **Canister Purge Solenoid**–is located in the front of the engine compartment, behind the headlights.

• **Cellular Phone Transceiver**–is located in the left hand front of the trunk.

• **Chime Module**–is plugged into the component center.

• **Circuit Breakers**–are located in the component center or the fuse box.

• **Component Center**–is located behind the right hand side of the instrument panel, behind the instrument panel compartment.

• **Computer Controlled Coil Ignition (CCCI) Module**–is located on the rear of the engine, above the intake manifold.

• **Convenience Center**–See Component Center.

• **Coolant Fan Relay**–is located in the engine compartment, in the right side electrical center.

• **Coolant Level and Corrosivity Sensor**–is located behind the top of right hand side of the radiator.

• **Coolant Temperature Sensor**–is located at the top of the engine, below the coolant outlet.

• **Crankshaft Sensor (VIN T)**–is located at the right rear of the engine.

• **Cruise Control Brake/Switch**–is located above the brake pedal on the brake pedal support bracket.

• **Cruise Control Check Valve**–is located in the vacuum line ahead of the strut tower.

• **Cruise Control Module**–is located under the left side of the instrument panel, on the left side of the brake pedal support.

• **Cruise Control Servo**–is located in the left hand front side of the engine compartment, on the inner fender well.

• **Cruise Control Vacuum Release Valve**–is located on the top of the brake pedal assembly.

• **Cruise Control Vacuum Tank**–is located in the left hand front wheel well, behind the headlight.

• **Daytime Running Light Module**–is behind the left side of the instrument panel to the left of the steering column.

• **Defogger Relay**–is plugged into the component center.

• **Detonation (Knock) Sensor**–is located on the right rear of the engine, below the exhaust manifold.

• **Diode (Headlamp) Assembly**–is to the left of the steering column.

• **Direct Ignition System (VIN R)**–is located at the left rear of the engine, below the intake manifold.

• **Direct Ignition System (VIN T)**–is located at the left front of the engine, above the starter.

• **EGR/RVB/ILC Solenoid Assembly**–is located above the valve cover on the left hand rear of the engine.

• **Electrical Center (left side)**–is located in the engine compartment near the left strut tower.

• **Electrical Center (right side)**–is located in the engine compartment near the right strut tower.

• **Electronic Control Module (ECM) Fuse**–is located in the left side electrical center.

• **Electronic Control Module (ECM)**–is located in the engine compartment, on the front of the right hand strut tower.

• **Electronic Spark Control Module (ESC)**–is located on the bracket at the top of the right front fender well.

• **Fuel Pump Prime Connector**–is taped to the wire harness, below the left side electrical center.

• **Fuel Pump Relay**–is located in the left side electrical center.

• **Fuel Pump/Oil Pressure Switch (VIN R)**–is located on the right rear of the engine.

• **Fuel Pump/Oil Pressure Switch (VIN T)**–is located on the lower right hand front side of the engine, above the oil filter.

• **Fuse Box**–is on the right side of the instrument panel, in the instrument panel compartment.

• **Fusible Elements**–are located at the electrical centers and at the alternator.

• **Hazard Flasher Relay**–is located in the component center.

• **Heater Blower Relays**–are located in the component center.Horn Relay–is located on the right front side of the engine compartment.

• **Idle Air Control Valve (VIN R)**–is located on the top of the engine, at the front of the throttle body.

• **Idle Air Control Valve (VIN T)**–is located on the top of the engine, at the bottom of the throttle body.

• **Ignition Switch**–is located behind the instrument panel, on the center of the steering column.

• **Inverter**–is located in the trunk behind the center of the rear seat.

• **Keyless Entry Module**–is on the left front of the luggage compartment.

• **Left Hand Lap Retractor Solenoid**–is located in the door harness, inside of the bottom of the middle of the door.

• **Left Hand Seatbelt Shoulder Retractor Solenoid**–is located in the door harness, inside of the bottom left hand rear door.

- **Left Side Electrical Center**—is located in the engine compartment, on the left hand strut tower.
- **Low Speed Coolant Fan Relay**—is located above the wheel well, on the left hand rear side of the engine compartment.
- **MAF Sensor**—See Mass Air Flow Sensor.
- **Manifold Absolute Pressure (MAP) Sensor**—is behind the top side of the engine, on the air intake.
- **Manifold Absolute Temperature (MAT) Sensor**—is located on the air cleaner duct, near the right hand strut tower.
- **MAP Sensor**—See Manifold Absolute Pressure Sensor.
- **MAT Sensor**—See Manifold Absolute Temperature.
- **Oil Pressure/Fuel Pump Switch (VIN R)**—is located on the right rear of the engine.
- **Oil Pressure/Fuel Pump Switch (VIN T)**—is located on the lower right hand front side of the engine, above the oil filter.
- **Passive Restraint Control Module**—is located behind the right hand side of the instrument panel.
- **Photoresistor**—is on the top left side of the instrument panel, near the speaker.
- **Power Antenna Relay**—is located behind the right hand side of the instrument panel, to the right of the glove box.
- **Power Door Lock Relay**—is at the right shroud above the access hole.
- **Power Master Brake Relay**—is located on the firewall, below the master cylinder. Power Steering Pressure Switch—is located on the steering gear assembly, near the input shaft.
- **Primary Coolant Fan Relay**—is located in the engine compartment, in the right side electrical center.
- **Radio Capacitor**—is located in the lower left hand corner of the fuse block.
- **Right Hand Lap Retractor Solenoid**—is located in the door harness, inside of the bottom of the middle of the door.
- **Right Hand Seatbelt Shoulder Retractor Solenoid**—is located in the door harness, inside of the bottom right hand rear door.
- **Right Side Electrical Center**—is located in the engine compartment, on the right hand strut tower.
- **Seatbelt Switch**—is located in the right hand half of the driver's seatbelt.
- **Seatbelt Timer Module**—is behind the right side of the instrument panel.
- **Secondary Coolant Fan Relay**—is located in the engine compartment, in the right side electrical center.
- **Starter Interrupt Relay**—is taped to the instrument panel harness, near the fuse block.
- **Sunroof Control Module**—is at the top center of the windshield header.
- **Sunroof Control Module**—is at the top center of the windshield.
- **Theft Deterrent Controller**—is located under the left side of the dash panel, near the kick panel.
- **Theft Deterrent Diode**—is located behind the left side instrument panel, in connector C857.
- **Theft Deterrent Relay**—is located behind the instrument panel to the left of the steering column.
- **Throttle Position Sensor**—is located at the front of the throttle body.
- **Torque Converter Clutch Relay Solenoid**—is located in the automatic transaxle.
- **Transaxle Position Switch**—is located on the transaxle, below the brake master cylinder.
- **Trunk Lock Tamper Switch**—is located on the under side of the trunk lid, at the lid lock center.
- **Trunk Release Solenoid**—is located on the under side of the trunk lid, at the lid lock center.
- **Turbo Boost Gauge Sensor**—is located on the right front inner fender above the wheel well.
- **Turbo Boost Indicator Switch**—is located on the right front fender, above the wheel well.
- **Turn Signal Flasher**—is located under the instrument panel, on the right side of the steering column.
- **Twilight Sentinel Amplifier**—is located under the instrument panel, near the radio.
- **Twilight Sentinel Photocell**—is located at the top center of the instrument panel.
- **Vapor Canister Purge Solenoid**—is located in the right hand front of the engine compartment, on the canister.
- **Vehicle Speed Sensor Buffer**—is located under the instrument panel, to the left of the radio.
- **Vehicle Speed Sensor**—is located behind the right hand rear of the engine on the transaxle.
- **Wiper/Washer Motor Module**—is located on the upper left corner of the firewall in the engine compartment.

OLDSMOBILE

Circuit Breakers

ALL MODELS

HEADLIGHTS

This circuit breaker is incorporated in the headlight switch.

WINDSHIELD WIPERS

This circuit breaker is incorporated in the windshield wiper motor.

POWER ACCESSORIES

Circuit breakers for power accessories are located in the front of the fuse block, convenience centers and relay centers. They protect the following circuits; rear window defogger, power windows, power seats and power door locks, alarm systems, sunroofs, etc. if equipped.

Fusible Links

In addition to circuit breakers and fuses, some circuits use fusible links to protect the wiring. Like fuses, the fusible links are 1 time protection devices that will melt and create an open circuit.

Not all fusible link open circuits can be detected by observation. Always inspect that there is battery voltage passing through the fusible link to verify continuity.

Each fusible link is four wire gauge sizes smaller than the cable it is designed to protect. The same wire size fusible link must be used when replacing a blown fusible link. Fusible links are available with two types of insulation; Hypalon and Silicone. Service fusible links made with Hypalon insulation, must be replaced with the same Hypalon insulated wire. Fusible links with Silicone insulation can use either insulation.

NOTE: Never make a fusible link longer than 9 in. (228mm) for it will not provide sufficient overload protection.

To replace a damaged fusible link, cut it off beyond the splice. Replace with a repair link. When connecting the repair link, strip the wire and use staking type pliers to crimp the splice securely in two places.

CALAIS AND CIERA

These models use fusible links attached to the starter solenoid and battery junction block to protect the charging and the lighting circuits. These fusible links are also used to protect the electronic control module and another to protect the electronic fuel injection.

CUTLASS AND DELTA 88

The Delta 88 and Cutlass models use 2 fusible links attached to the starter solenoid to protect the charging and the lighting circuits. One fusible link for the charging system, is located behind the alternator. Other links are located at the power junction block or at the component they protect.

CUSTOM CRUISER

The Custom Cruiser uses fusible links attached to the starter solenoid and battery junction block. Other fusible links maybe located at the alternator or at the component they protect. Fusible links are also used to protect the electronic control module and another to protect the electronic fuel injection, if equipped.

TORONDO AND TROFEO

The fusible links are located mainly at the power junction block. Other location can include battery and alternator, dependent on options.

NINETY-EIGHT REGENCY

Use fusible links attached to the starter solenoid to protect the charging and the lighting circuits. A fusible link for the charging system is located behind the alternator. There is a fusible link used for charging system which is located between the alternator and the jump start junction block. There is also a fusible link located behind the battery used for ignition system. Others are located at the power junction block or at the component they protect.

In-Line Fuses

Many vehicles use in-line fuses located near the fuse block or the protected component. The fuel pump relay, theft deterrent system and power seat assembly are some of the locations that may use in-line fuses.

Relay, Sensors And Computer Locations

NOTE: When using this section, some of the components may not be used on a particular vehicle. This is because the particular component in question was used on an earlier model or a later model. If a component is not found in this section, check other vehicles of the same body line, as that component may have been introduced earlier on different models. This section is being published from the latest information available at the time of this publication.

CALAIS

• **A/C Clutch Diode**—in the air conditioning compressor clutch connector.
A/C Compressor Refrigerant Temperature Sensor—at the right front of engine compartment.
• **A/C Control Relay**—at the front center of dash, on relay bracket.

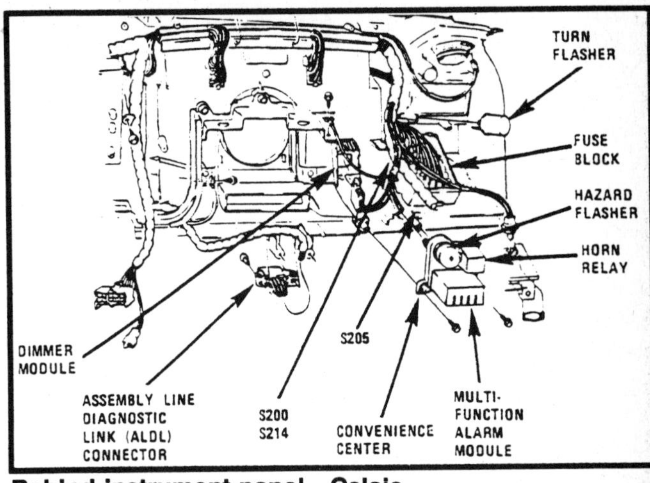

Behind instrument panel—Calais

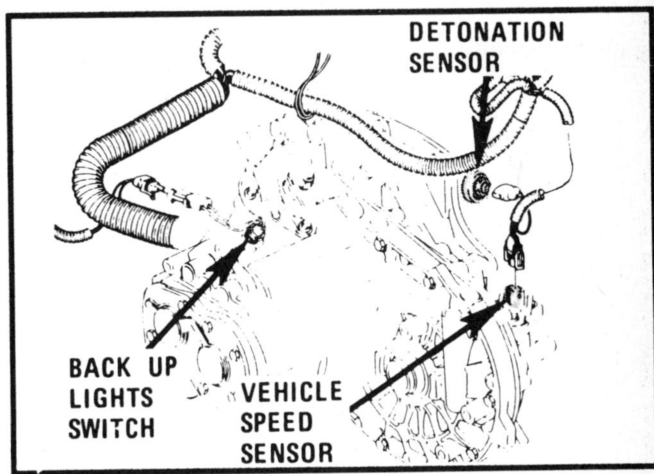

Detonation (knock) sensor location—Calais with 2.3L VIN A engine

• **A/C Coolant Fan Dual Pressure Switch (1989 VIN D)**—is located on the right hand front of the engine compartment, to the right of the radiator, if equipped.
• **A/C Cut**—Out Relay—is located on the relay bracket at the center of the firewall in the engine compartment.
• **A/C Defrost Valve Vacuum Actuator**—is located under the center of the instrument panel.
• **A/C Heater Valve Vacuum Actuator**—is located under the center of the instrument panel.
• **A/C High Pressure Cutout Switch**—is located on the left end of the compressor.
• **A/C Low Pressure Cutout Switch**—is located on the left end of the compressor.
• **A/C Outside Air Valve Vacuum Actuator**—is located under the center of the instrument panel.
• **A/C Vacuum Tank (VIN D)**—is located in the lower right hand front of corner of the engine compartment.
• **Antenna Relay**—behind the right side of the instrument panel, below the speaker.
• **Assembly Line Diagnostic Link (ALDL) Connector**—under the left side of the instrument panel, below the steering column.
• **Audio Alarm Module**—at the left side of the steering column, on the convenience center.
• **Back**—Up Switch—is located on the left hand end of the transaxle.

• **Blower Resistors**—are located on the right hand side of the firewall, in the blower module.

• **Brake Cruise Release Valve**—on the brake pedal support.

• **Brake Fluid Level Switch**—is located on the left hand side of the firewall, in the brake fluid reservoir.

• **Clutch Start Switch**—is located above the clutch pedal, in the passengers compartment.

• **Computer Controlled Coil Ignition (CCCI) Module**—at the top right front of engine.

• **Convenience Center**—behind the instrument panel, to the left of the steering column.

• **Coolant Fan Relay**—at the front center of dash, on the relay bracket.

• **Coolant Temperature Sensor (VIN A and D)**—at the left rear of engine, behind the coolant outlet.

• **Coolant Temperature Sensor (VIN N)**—at the right side of engine, below the alternator.

• **Coolant Temperature Sensor (VIN U)**—top left side of engine, near the coolant outlet.

• **Crankshaft Position Sensor (VIN A)**—at the front center of engine, above the oil filter.

• **Crankshaft Position Sensor (VIN D)**—is located on the center front of the engine, above the oil filter.

• **Crankshaft Position Sensor (VIN N)**—at the lower right side of engine, near the air conditioning compressor.

• **Cruise Control Brake/Switch**—is located above the brake pedal on the brake pedal support bracket.

• **Cruise Control Check Valve (VIN A and D)**—at the right front of the engine compartment.

• **Cruise Control Check Valve (VIN D)**—is located in the right hand side of the engine compartment.

• **Cruise Control Check Valve (VIN N and U)**—at the center of dash.

• **Cruise Control Clutch Switch**—is located above the clutch pedal on the clutch pedal support bracket.

• **Cruise Control Module**—under the left side of the instrument panel, near shroud.

• **Cruise Control Servo**—is located near the left hand strut tower in the engine compartment.

• **Cruise Control Vacuum Tank**—is located in the lower left hand front of the engine compartment.

• **Detonation Sensor (VIN A and D)**—at the top left rear of engine.

• **Detonation Sensor (VIN N)**—at the lower right rear of engine, near the air conditioning hose.

• **Dimmer Module**—is located behind the left hand side of the instrument panel, to the left of the steering column.

• **Direct Ignition System (DIS)**—at the rear of the engine, above the transaxle.

• **Door Lock Relay Assembly**—behind the right side of the instrument panel, on the right side shroud.

• **Driver Information Center (DIC) Lights Monitor Module**—is located below the center of the dash panel, in front of the console, if so equipped.

• **Electronic Control Module (ECM)**—is located behind the right side of the instrument panel, near the instrument panel compartment.

• **Fog Light Relay**—at the inner left side fender panel, front of the strut tower.

• **Fuel Pump Prime Connector**—left rear of engine compartment.

• **Fuel Pump Relay**—at center rear of the engine compartment, on the relay bracket.

• **Fuel Pump/Oil Pressure Switch (VIN A and D)**—at the top left rear of engine.

• **Fuel Pump/Oil Pressure Switch (VIN N)**—at the lower right rear of engine, behind the water pump.

• **Fuel Pump/Oil Pressure Switch (VIN U)**—at the lower rear of engine, above the transaxle.

• **Fuse Block**—behind the left side of the instrument panel, to the left of the steering column.

• **Fusible Link Junction Block**—is located in the left hand front side of the engine compartment, below the washer fluid reservoir.

• **Hazard Flasher**—is located in the convenience center.

• **Headlight Dimmer Switch**—is located behind the instrument panel, to the left of the steering column.

• **High Blower Relay**—is located on the relay bracket on the center of the firewall in the engine compartment.

• **High Speed Coolant Fan Relay**—is located on the relay bracket on the center of the firewall in the engine compartment.

• **Horn Relay**—is located in the convenience center.

• **Idle Air Control Motor (VIN N)**—at top of engine, left rear of the throttle body.

• **Idle Air Control Valve (VIN U)**—at top of engine, left rear of the throttle body.

• **Idle Air Control Valve (VIN A and D)**—at top of engine, right side of the throttle body.

• **Idle Speed Power Steering Pressure Switch (except VIN D)**—at lower left front of dash, on left side of the brake booster.

• **Idle Speed Power Steering Pressure Switch (VIN D)**—is located on the left hand side of the engine, in front of the coolant outlet.

• **Ignition Key Warning Switch**—is located on the top of the steering column.

• **Ignition Switch**—is located behind the instrument panel, on the lower right hand side of the steering column.

• **Integrated Direct Ignition (IDI) System (VIN D)**—is located on the top left hand rear side of the engine.

• **Keyless Entry Module**—is located on the left side of the luggage compartment, above the wheelhousing.

• **Knock (Detonation) Sensor (VIN A and D)**—is located at the lower left hand rear of the engine.

• **Low Coolant Module**—is located under the right hand side of the instrument panel.

• **Low Coolant Probe**—is located in the upper right hand side of the radiator.

• **Luggage Compartment Lid Release Solenoid**—at the center underside of the luggage compartment lid.

• **Manifold Absolute Pressure (MAP) Sensor (VIN A and D)**—at the front center of engine compartment, above intake manifold.

• **Manifold Air Temperature (MAT) Sensor (VIN A and D)**—at the top left front of engine compartment, in the intake manifold.

• **Manifold Air Temperature (MAT) Sensor (VIN U)**—at the right side of throttle body, on the intake manifold.

• **MAP Sensor**—See Manifold Absolute Pressure (MAP) Sensor.

• **Mass Air Flow (MAF) Sensor (VIN N)**—at the top of engine, at the left side of the throttle body.

• **MAT Sensor**—See Manifold Air Temperature Sensor.

• **Oxygen Sensor**—at the rear of the engine, in the exhaust manifold.

• **Power Accessories Circuit Breaker**—is located in the fuse block or the convenience center.

• **Power Antenna Relay**—is located behind the right side of the instrument panel, below the speaker.

• **Power Door Lock Relay Assembly**—is located behind the right side of the instrument panel, on the upper right hand shroud.

• **Power Window Circuit Breaker**—is located in the fuse block.

• **Power Window Module**—at front center of the driver's door.

• **Rear Defogger Timer Relay**—behind the right side of the instrument panel, below speaker.

• **Safety Belt Lap Retractor Solenoid**—in the rear area of each front door.

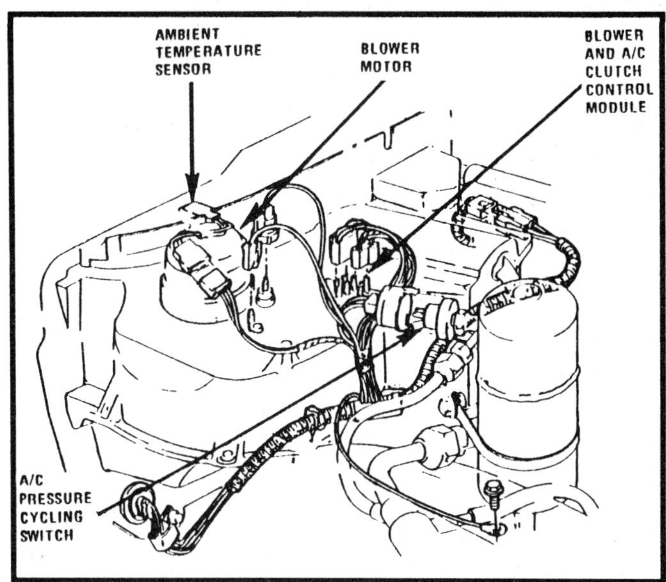

Air conditioning components—Custom Cruiser

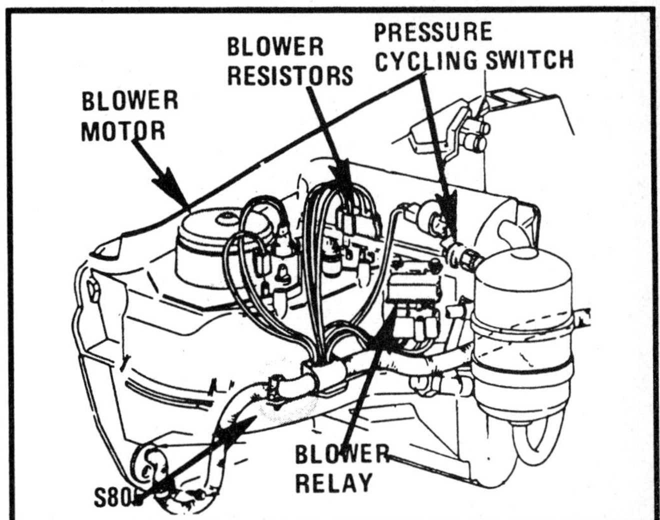

Blower relay—Custom Cruiser

- **Safety Belt Retractor Switch**—in the rear area of each front door, on latch assembly.
- **Safety Belt Shoulder Retractor Solenoid**—in the bottom center of each front door.
- **Safety Belt Switch**—in the drive's seatbelt buckle assemble.
- **Seat Belt Indicator Driver Module**—is located behind the left hand side of the instrument panel, near the grommet.
- **Seat Belt Lap Retractor Solenoid**—are located in the rear of each front door.
- **Seat Belt Retractor Switches**—are located in the rear of each front door, on the latch assembly.
- **Seat Belt Shoulder Retractor Solenoid**—is located in the rear of each front door.
- **Seat Belt Switch**—is part of the driver's seatbelt assembly.
- **Starter Solenoid**—is located on the lower hand front of the engine.
- **Surge Tank Low Coolant Switch**—at the right front corner of engine compartment.
- **Tachometer Filter**—at the left side of the engine compartment, near the battery.
- **Throttle Position Sensor (VIN A, D and N)**—at the top of the engine, on the left side of the throttle body.
- **Throttle Position Sensor (VIN U)**—at the top of the engine, on the right side of the throttle body.
- **TPS Sensor**—See Throttle Position Sensor.
- **Transaxle Position Switch**—at the top left rear of the transaxle.
- **Turn Signal Flasher**—is located under the left hand side of the instrument panel, above the fuse block.
- **Vapor Canister Purge Solenoid**—is located on the vapor canister, in the right hand front of the engine compartment.
- **Vehicle Speed Sensor (Automatic Transaxle)**—at the rear of engine, on the right end of the transaxle.
- **Vehicle Speed Sensor (Manual Transaxle)**—at the left rear of engine, on the top of the transaxle.
- **Wiper/Washer Motor Module**—is located in the left front of the firewall, to the left of the brake booster.

CUSTOM CRUISER

- **A/C Actuator Air Inlet Valve**—is located under the instrument panel, on the right hand side of the A/C plenum.

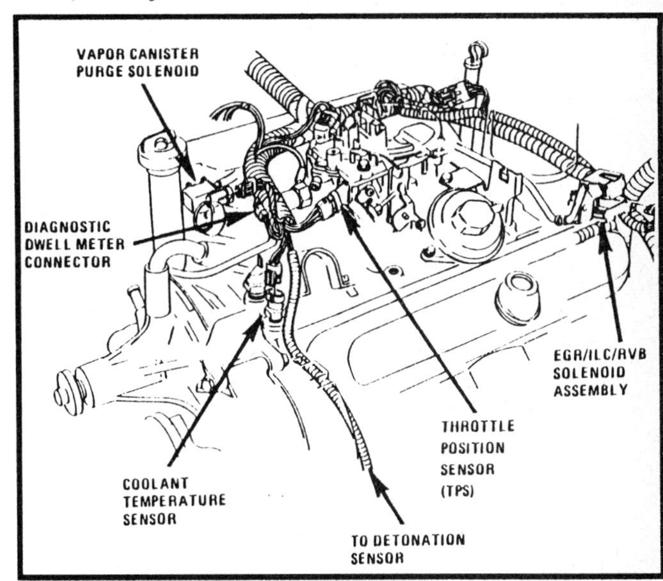

Engine sensors—Custom Cruiser

- **A/C Actuator Defrost Valve**—is located under the instrument panel, on the right hand side of the A/C plenum.
- **A/C Actuator Lower Diverter Valve**—is located under the instrument panel, on the right hand side of the A/C plenum.
- **A/C Actuator Upper Diverter Valve**—is located under the instrument panel, on the right hand side of the A/C plenum.
- **A/C Ambient Temperature Sensor**—is located in the right hand air inlet, below the screen.
- **A/C Clutch and Blower Control Module**—is located on the blower module.
- **A/C Compressor Clutch Diode**—is taped inside the A/C compressor clutch connector.
- **A/C Compressor Cutout Relay**—is located on the right hand side of the firewall.
- **A/C Defroster Vacuum Motor**—is located under the instrument panel, on the lower edge of the A/C plenum.
- **A/C Heater Blower Relay**—is located on the right side of the firewall in the engine compartment, near the blower motor.
- **A/C Heater Blower Resistors**—are located on the right side of the firewall in the engine compartment, beside the blower motor.

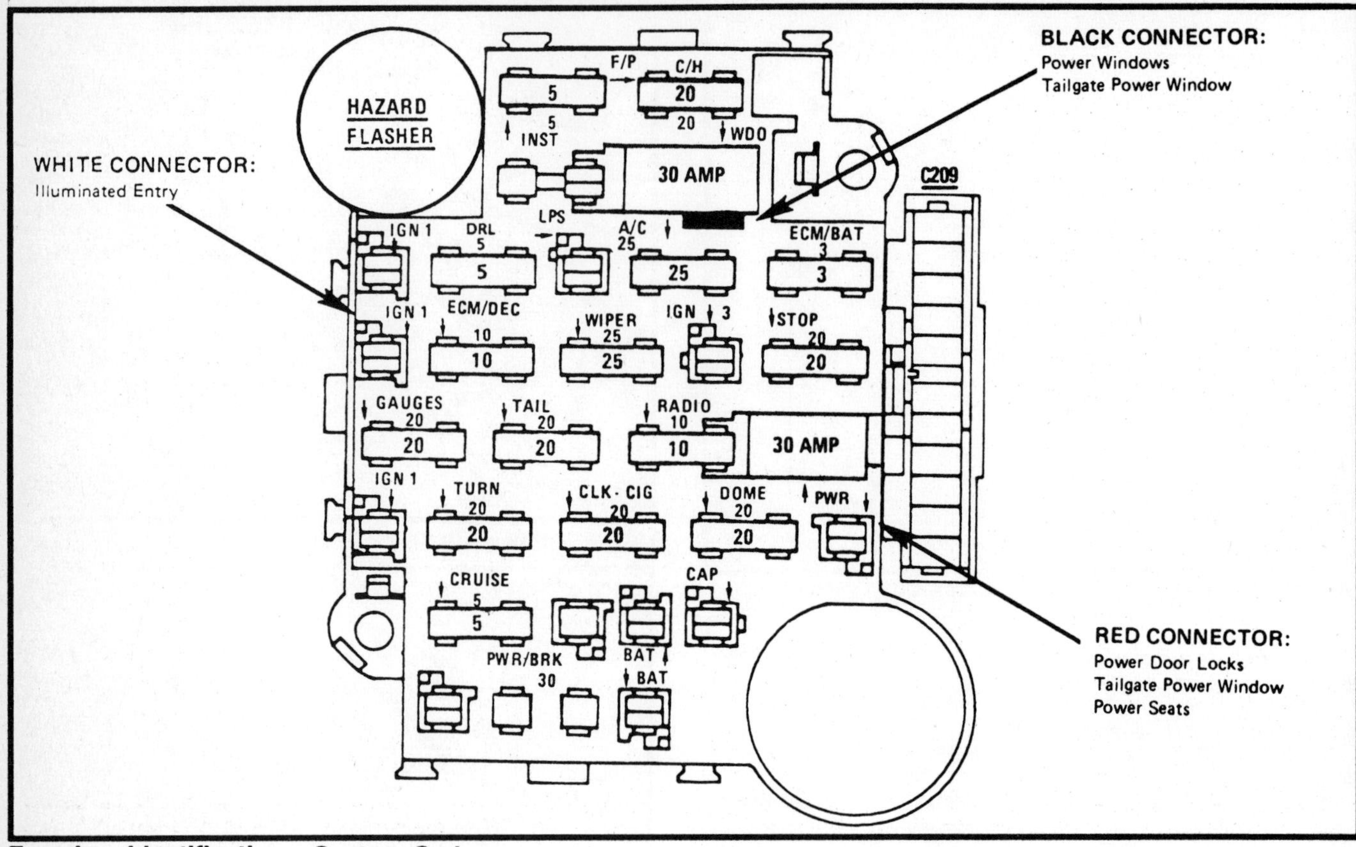

Fuse box identification – Custom Cruiser

• **A/C Heater Water Valve Vacuum Motor** – is located behind the rear of the engine, on the heater/water valve.

• **A/C In-Car Sensor** – is located in the upper instrument panel trim, to the left of the right hand speaker.

• **A/C Lower Mode Vacuum Motor** – is located under the instrument panel, on the left side of the A/C plenum.

• **A/C Pressure Cycling Switch** – is located on the right side of firewall in the engine compartment, on the accumulator.

• **A/C Recirculating/Outside Air Vacuum Motor** – is located behind the instrument panel and is a part of the A/C plenum.

• **A/C Upper Mode Vacuum Motor** – is located under the instrument panel, on the left side of the A/C plenum.

• **AIR Diverter Valve** – is located on the rear of the air pump.

• **AIR Select Switching Valve** – is located on the behind the air pump.

• **Alternator Diode** – is located in the engine wiring harness, near the distributor.

• **Anti-Dieseling Solenoid** – is located in the engine harness, in front of the left hand side of the engine on the valve cover.

• **Automatic Door Lock Controller** – is attached to the upper right hand shroud.

• **Barometric Pressure Sensor** – is located below the right hand side of the instrument panel and the kick panel.

• **Brake Pressure Switch** – is located below the master cylinder on the firewall.

• **CB Transceiver** – is located behind the instrument panel, above the radio.

• **Convenience Center** – is located on the left hand side of the fuse block.

• **Coolant Temperature Sensor** – is located on the top front of the engine on the manifold.

• **Coolant Temperature Switch** – is located on the top left hand front of the engine on the manifold.

• **Cruise Control Brake/Switch** – is located above the brake pedal on the brake pedal support bracket.

• **Cruise Control Module** – is located under the instrument panel, to the left of the steering column.

• **Cruise Control Servo** – is located on the left hand front side of the engine.

• **Daytime Running Lights (DRL) Module** – is located behind the instrument panel, on the right side of the steering column.

• **Defogger Timer Relay** – is on the top of the fuse box.

• **Diagnostic Dwell Meter Connector (VIN Y)** – is taped to the engine harness, near the carburetor.

• **Dropping Resistor (DRL)** – is located behind the instrument panel, on the right side of the steering column.

• **Electronic Control Module (ECM)** – is located below the right side of the instrument panel, at the shroud.

• **Electronic Level Control Compressor** – is located in the engine compartment, in front of the left hand wheel well.

• **Electronic Level Control Diode** – is located in the instrument panel wiring harness, behind the radio, if so equipped.

• **Electronic Level Control Height Sensor** – is located under the left hand rear of the vehicle.

• **Electronic Level Control Relay** – is located on the left hand front fender, near or behind the battery.

• **Electronic Level Control Test Connector** – is tape to the hose, next the ELC compressor, if so equipped.

• **Fiber Optic Light Source** – is taped to the wiring harness, above the radio.

• **Fuse Box**—is behind the left side of the instrument panel, near the shroud.
• **Gear Selector Switch**—is located on the lower part of the steering column.
• **Hazard Flasher/Relay**—is located in the fuse block.
• **Heater/Water Valve**—is located behind the rear of the engine in the top of the engine block.
• **Ignition Switch**—is located at the base of the steering column.
• **Illuminated Entry Timer (early 1989)**—is behind the left side of the instrument panel, on the left side of the steering column.
• **Illuminated Entry Timer (except 1989)**—is located on the upper left hand shroud, behind the right hand side of the instrument panel, on the instrument panel support.
• **Light Driver Module**—is taped to the wiring harness, above the glove box.
• **Low Coolant Probe**—is in the right rear of the radiator.
• **Multi-Function Chime Module**—is located behind the left side of the instrument panel, to the right of the steering column.
• **Oil Pressure Sender**—is located on the top right side of the engine.
• **Oil Pressure Switch**—is located on the top right side of the engine.
• **Oxygen Sensor**—is located in the rear of the engine, in the top right hand rear of the exhaust manifold.
• **Power Antenna Relay**—is located behind the right side of the instrument panel, below the glove compartment.
• **Power Door Lock Relay Assembly**—is located in the upper right hand shroud near the lower access hole.
• **Power Master Brake Relay**—is located below the master cylinder, which is located on the firewall.
• **Power Seat Recliner Motor**—is located under the inner side of the seat.
• **Power Seat Relay**—is located under the seats.
• **Sentinel Amplifier**—is located under the right hand side of the instrument panel, on the instrument panel support.
• **Sentinel Photocell**—is located on the top left side of the instrument panel, in the end of the speaker grill.
• **Tailgate Ajar Switch**—is located inside the lower right hand corner of the tailgate assembly.
• **Tailgate Block Out Switch**—is located in the upper right hand corner of the tailgate.
• **Tailgate Lock Relay Assembly**—is located in the upper right hand shroud near the lower access hole.
• **Throttle Position Sensor**—is located in front of the carburetor, or throttle body.
• **Timer Module**—is behind the left side of the instrument panel, on the left side of the steering column.
• **Triple Solenoid Assembly**—is located on the rear of the left hand valve cover.
• **Turn Signal Flasher**—is located at the base of the steering column, behind the instrument panel.
• **Twilight Sentinel Amplifier**—is behind the instrument panel, on the panel support bracket.
• **Twilight Sentinel Control**—is on the left side of the instrument panel, near the headlight switch.
• **Twilight Sentinel Photocell**—is on the top left side of the instrument panel.
• **Vacuum Release Valve**—is located on the brake pedal support, under the instrument panel.
• **Vehicle Speed Sensor Buffer**—is located under the left side of the instrument panel, to the right of the light switch.
• **Vehicle Speed Sensor**—is located at the top of the right hand the right hand front wheel well.
• **Wiper/Washer Fluid Level Switch**—is located on the washer reservoir.
• **Wiper/Washer Pulse Timer Relay**—is incorporated into the wiper/washer assembly.

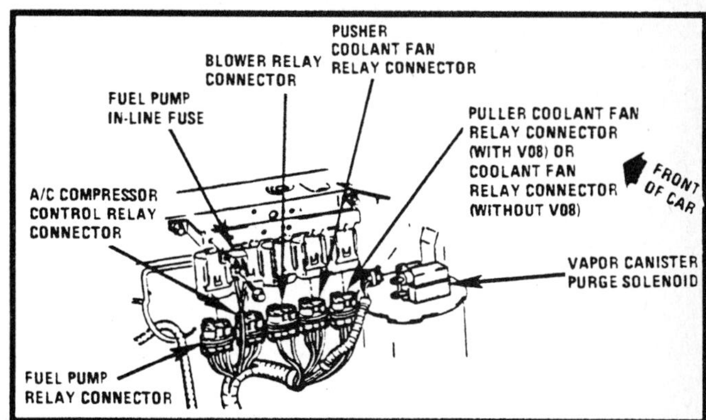

Relay locations—Ciera and Cutlass Cruiser with 3.3L VIN N engine

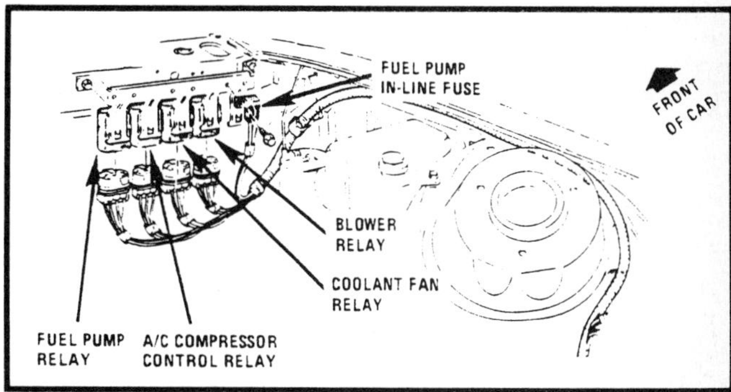

Relay locations—Ciera and Cutlass Cruiser with 2.5L VIN R engine

• **Wiper/Washer Ratchet Release Solenoid Diode**—is taped to the inside of the wiper/washer connector.
• **Wiper/Washer Relay Diode**—is taped to the inside of the wiper/washer connector.

CIERA AND CUTLASS CRUISER

• **A/C Blower Relay**—is located on the right hand side of the firewall, on the heater and A/C module.
• **A/C Blower Resistors**—is located on the right hand side of the firewall, on the heater and A/C module.
• **A/C Compressor Clutch Diode (VIN N)**—is inside the wiring harness at the lower right front of the engine, near the air conditioning compressor.
• **A/C Compressor Clutch Diode (VIN R)**—is inside the wiring harness at the lower right front of the engine.
• **A/C Compressor Clutch Diode (VIN W)**—is taped inside the A/C compressor clutch connector.
• **A/C Compressor Control Relay (VIN N)**—is located on the right hand corner of the engine compartment, on a bracket.
• **A/C Compressor Control Relay (VIN R early)**—is located on the right hand corner of the engine compartment, behind the strut tower.
• **A/C Compressor Control Relay (VIN R)**—is located on the right hand corner of the engine compartment, on a bracket.
• **A/C Compressor Control Relay (VIN W)**—is located on the right hand corner of the engine compartment, on a bracket.
• **A/C Defrost Valve Vacuum Actuator**—is located under the center of the instrument panel, behind the A/C heater control head.
• **A/C Dual Pressure Switch**—is located in the right front corner of the engine compartment, on the A/C line.
• **A/C Heater Valve Vacuum Actuator**—is located under

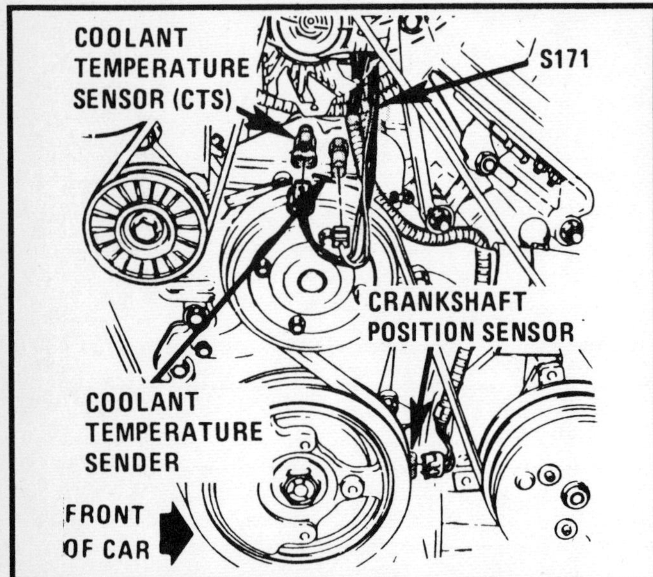

Coolant temperature sensor—Ciera and Cutlass Cruiser with 3.3L VIN N engine

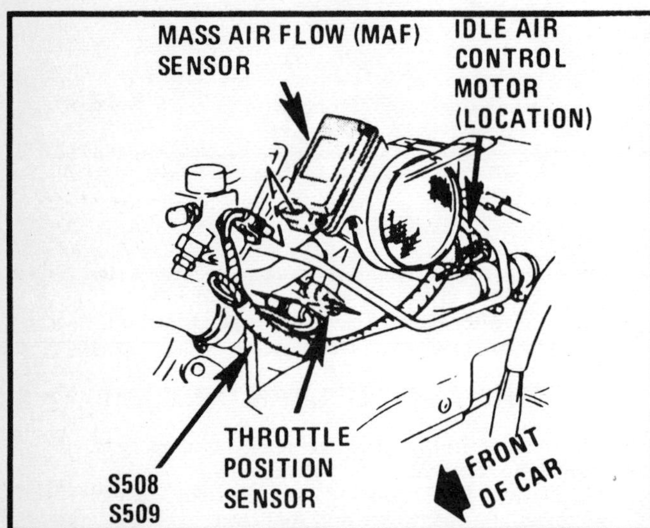

MAF sensor—Ciera and Cutlass Cruiser with 3.3L VIN N engine

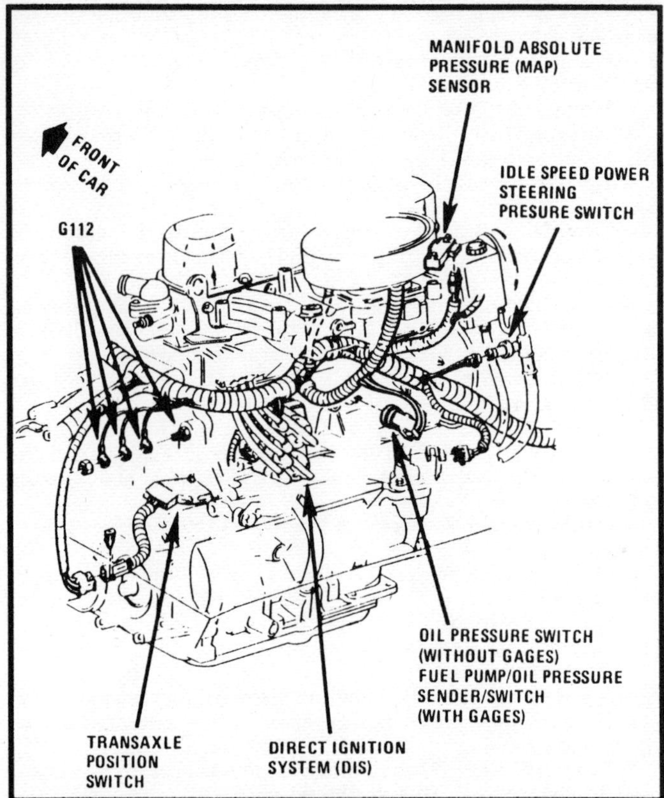

Oil pressure switch location—Ciera and Cutlass Cruiser with 2.5L VIN R engine

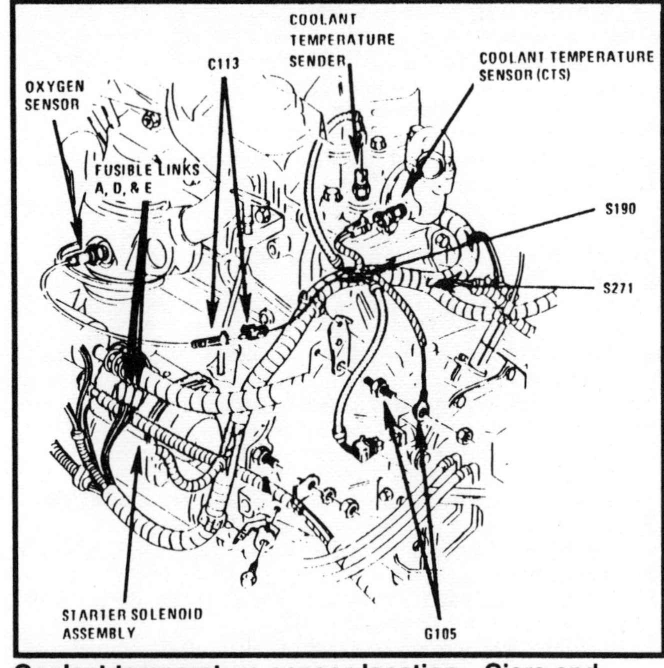

Coolant temperature sensor location—Ciera and Cutlass Cruiser with 2.5L VIN R engine

the center of the instrument panel, on the right side of the A/C plenum.

• **A/C High Pressure Cutout Switch (VIN R and W)**—is located near the A/C compressor, on the A/C line.

• **A/C High Pressure Switch**—is located near the A/C compressor, on the A/C line.

• **A/C Low Pressure Switch**—on most vehicles is located on the left side of the compressor, or can be near the A/C compressor, on the A/C line.

• **A/C Outside Air Valve Vacuum Actuator**—is located under the center of the instrument panel, on the right side of the A/C plenum.

• **A/C Pressure Cycling Switch**—is located on the accumulator/drier, on the right hand side of the firewall.

• **A/C Vacuum Tank**—is located in the center of the firewall, above the blower motor, if equipped.

• **Assembly Line Diagnostic Link (ALDL) Connector**—is located on the bottom of the instrument panel, near the steering column.

• **Audio Alarm Module**—is located in the convenience center.

• **Battery Junction Block No. 1**—is located in the left hand side of the engine compartment, on front of the strut tower.

• **Battery Junction Block No. 2**—is located in the right hand side of the engine compartment, on a bracket.

• **Battery Junction Block**—is located at the right front of the engine compartment, at the relay bracket.

• **Brake Fluid Level Switch**—is located on the left hand side of the firewall, to the left of the brake fluid reservoir.

• **Canister Purge Solenoid (VIN N)**—is at the right front corner of the engine compartment, on or near the canister.

• **Cigarette Lighter In-line Fuse**—is behind the right side of the instrument panel, near the fuse box.

• **Computer Controlled Coil Ignition (CCCI) Module (VIN N)**—is located at the lower right front of the engine.

• **Convenience Center**—is located behind the right hand side of the instrument panel, near the shroud.

• **Coolant Fan A/C Pressure Switch**—is located in the right front corner of the engine compartment, on the A/C line.

• **Coolant Fan Delay Relay**—is located on the left hand front strut tower, in the engine compartment.

• **Coolant Fan In-Line Fuse**—is located in the engine compartment in front of the left front shock tower, if so equipped.

• **Coolant Fan Relay (VIN R)**—is located on the left hand front strut tower, in the engine compartment.

• **Coolant Fan Relay (VIN W)**—is located on a bracket in the right hand side compartment.

• **Coolant Fan Relay Diode**—is located in the engine/SFI wiring harness, near the brake master cylinder.

• **Coolant Fan Switch**—is located on the top right hand side of the engine.

• **Coolant Temperature Sender/Switch (VIN R)**—is located on the top left hand side of the engine.

• **Coolant Temperature Sender/Switch (VIN W)**—is located on the top left hand rear corner of the engine.

• **Coolant Temperature Sensor (VIN N)**—is at the top right side of the engine, below the alternator.

• **Coolant Temperature Sensor (VIN R)**—is located on the top left hand side of the engine.

• **Coolant Temperature Sensor (VIN W)**—is located on the top left hand rear corner of the engine.

• **Crankshaft Sensor (VIN N)**—is located at the right side of the engine, behind the air conditioning compressor.

• **Crankshaft Sensor (VIN W)**—is located on the rear of the engine, below the exhaust manifold.

• **Cruise Control Check Valve**—is located on the center front of the firewall, in the engine compartment.

• **Cruise Control Module**—is located behind the instrument panel, above the accelerator pedal.

• **Cruise Control Servo**—is located in the left hand front corner of the engine compartment, on the strut tower.

• **Cruise Control Vacuum Release Valve**—is located above the brake pedal on the brake pedal support bracket.

• **Cruise Control Vacuum Tank**—is located in the lower right hand front corner of the engine compartment.

• **Cruise Control/Brake Switch**—is located above the brake pedal on the brake pedal support bracket.

• **Daytime Running Light (DRL) Module**—is behind the instrument panel, below the speaker.

• **Defogger Timer Relay**—is located behind the instrument panel, under the instrument cluster, incorporated with the rear defogger control.

• **Detention (Knock) Sensor (VIN N)**—is located at the lower right side of the engine.

• **Detention (Knock) Sensor (VIN W)**—is located right hand rear of the engine, below the exhaust manifold.

• **Diode Assembly**—is mounted at the center of the engine compartment, above the air conditioning module.

• **Direct Ignition System (VIN R)**—is located on the front of the engine, below the intake manifold.

• **Direct Ignition System (VIN W)**—is located on the front of the engine, below the exhaust manifold.

• **EGR Solenoid Valve (VIN W)**—is located on the top rear of the engine on the valve cover.

• **Electronic Control Module (ECM)**—is located behind the right side of the instrument panel.

• **Electronic Vacuum Regulator Valve (VIN W)**—is located on the top rear of the engine on the valve cover.

• **Engine Oil Pressure Sender/Switch (VIN R)**—is located on the right hand rear of the engine, to the right of the DIS.

• **Engine Oil Pressure Sender/Switch (VIN W)**—is located on the right hand front of the engine, above the oil filter.

• **Fog Light Relay**—is behind the instrument panel, near the left shroud, or on the right hand side of the steering column.

• **Fuel Pump In-Line Fuse (VIN N)**—is at the right front of the engine compartment, on the relay bracket.

• **Fuel Pump In-Line Fuse**—is located on a bracket in the right hand side compartment.

• **Fuel Pump Prime Connector (VIN N)**—is at the left rear of the engine compartment, near the C100 connector.

• **Fuel Pump Prime Connector (VIN R and W)**—is taped to the engine harness on the left hand side of the firewall, behind the strut tower.

• **Fuel Pump Relay (VIN N)**—is at the right front of the engine compartment, on the relay bracket.

• **Fuel Pump Relay (VIN R)**—is located on the right hand rear side of the engine compartment, behind the strut tower.

• **Fuel Pump Relay (VIN W)**—is located on a bracket in the right hand front side of the engine compartment.

• **Fuel Pump/Oil Pressure Switch (VIN N)**—is at the lower right rear of the engine.

• **Fuel Pump/Oil Pressure Switch (VIN W)**—is located on the top left hand side of the engine.

• **Fusible Links**—are located at the battery junction block, starter solenoid and the battery.

• **Hazard Flasher**—is located in the convenience center.

• **Headlight Dimmer Switch**—is located behind the left hand side of the instrument panel, on the steering column.

• **Heater Blower Resistors**—is located on the right hand side of the firewall, on the heater and A/C module.

• **Horn Relay**—is located on the convenience center.

• **Idle Air Control Motor (VIN N)**—is on the top left of the engine, behind the throttle body.

• **Idle Air Control Motor (VIN W)**—is located on the top of the engine, on the front of the throttle body.

• **Idle Air Control Valve (VIN R)**—is located on the top of the engine, on the rear of the throttle body.

• **Idle Speed Power Steering Pressure Switch (VIN N)**—is located at the lower right rear of the engine, in the power steering hydraulic line.

• **Idle Speed Power Steering Pressure Switch (VIN R)**—is located on the right hand rear side of the engine, below the intake manifold, usually in the power steering hydraulic line.

• **Idle Speed Power Steering Pressure Switch (VIN W)**—is below the rear of the engine, located on the steering rack, ahead of the frame crossmember.

• **Ignition Key Warning Switch**—is located on the steering column, below the turn/hazard switch.

• **Ignition Switch**—is located on the lower portion of the steering column.

• **Low Coolant Module**—is located behind the right hand side of the instrument panel.

• **Low Coolant Sensor**—is located in the engine compartment, on the right hand rear side of the radiator.

• **Luggage Compartment Lid Release Solenoid**—is located in the center of the luggage compartment lid, near the lock.

• **Manifold Absolute Pressure (MAP) Sensor (VIN R)**—is located on the air cleaner assembly.

• **Manifold Absolute Pressure (MAP) Sensor (VIN W)**—is located on the upper right hand front of the firewall, behind the strut tower.
• **Manifold Air Temperature (MAT) Sensor (VIN R)**—is located on the top right rear of the engine, in the intake manifold.
• **Mass Air Flow (MAF) Sensor (VIN N)**—is at the top left of the engine, in the air duct.
• **Mass Air Flow Sensor In-Line Fuse**—is located in the engine compartment, on the front of the left strut tower.
• **Mass Airflow (MAF) Sensor (VIN W)**—is located on the air intake duct, on the left hand side of engine.
• **Mass Airflow Relay (VIN W)**—is located in the engine compartment, on the front of the left shock tower.
• **Oxygen Sensor**—is located in the exhaust manifold.
• **Park/Marker License Relay**—is located behind the left hand side of the instrument panel, taped to the harness.
• **Passive Restraint Control Module**—is at the right front shroud.
• **Power Accessories Circuit Breaker**—is located in the fuse block.
• **Power Antenna Relay (1989)**—is located behind the instrument panel near the rear of the glove box.
• **Power Antenna Relay (except 1989)**—is located in the right front fender, at the bass of the antenna.
• **Power Door Lock Relay**—is located on the right shroud, to the right of the glove box.
• **Power Window Circuit Breaker**—is located in the fuse block.
• **Puller (Front) Coolant Fan Relay**—is located in the engine compartment, on the front of the left strut tower.
• **Puller (Rear) Coolant Fan Relay**—is located on a relay bracket on the right hand side of the firewall.
• **Rear Wiper Auto/Park Module**—is located in the top center of the tailgate.
• **Rear Wiper Motor Module**—is located in the top center of the tailgate.
• **Seatbelt Switch**—is part of the driver's seatbelt assembly.
• **Starter Solenoid**—is located on the lower front portion of the engine.
• **Sunroof Actuator Assembly**—is at the center line of the roof.
• **Sunroof Relay**—is attached to the actuator assembly.
• **Tailgate Ajar Switch**—is located inside the lower center portion of the tailgate assembly.
• **Tailgate Lock Switch**—is located in the middle center of the tailgate assembly.
• **Tailgate Release Relay**—is located behind the left hand side of the instrument panel, taped to the instrument panel harness.
• **Tailgate Release Solenoid**—is located in the center of the tailgate assembly, behind the panel.
• **Throttle Position Sensor**—is located on the throttle body.
• **Transaxle Position Switch**—is located on the left hand side of the transaxle.
• **Turn Signal Flasher**—is located on the right hand side of the steering column.
• **Vehicle Speed Sensor**—is located on the rear of the instrument cluster.
• **Wiper/Washer Motor Module**—is located on the upper left side of the engine firewall.

CUTLASS SUPREME

• **A/C Air Temperature Valve Motor**—is located under the instrument panel, on the right hand side of the plenum.
• **A/C and Heater Control Interface Module**—is located in the steering column.

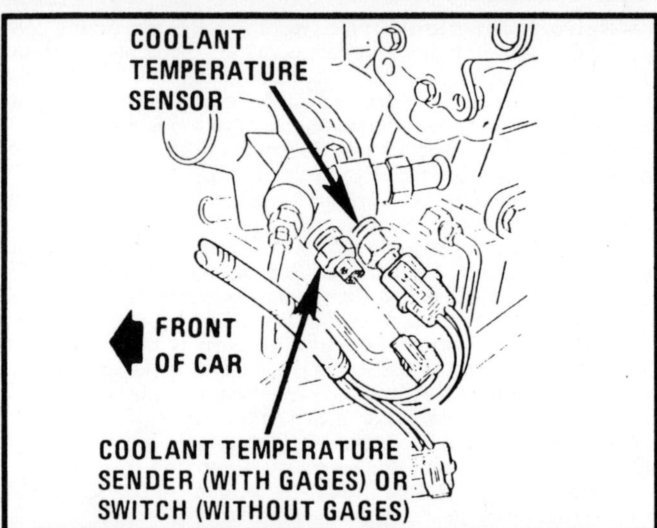

Coolant temperature sensor—Cutlass Supreme with 2.3L VIN D engine

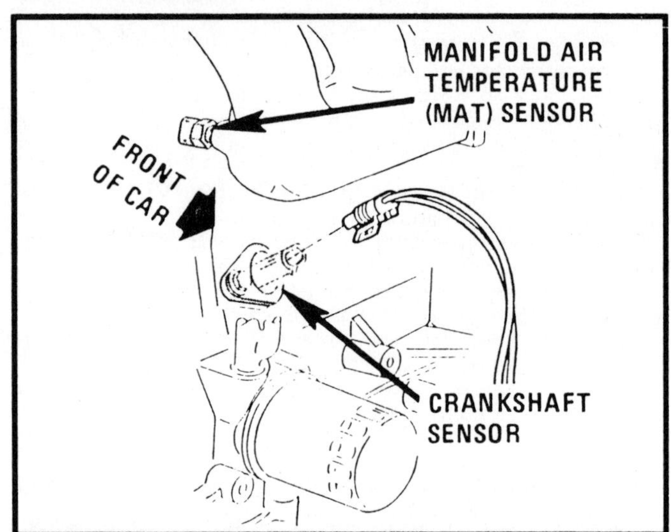

Crankshaft position sensor—Cutlass Supreme with 2.3L VIN D engine

• **A/C Bi-Level Valve Vacuum Actuator**—is located under the instrument panel, on the right hand side of the plenum.
• **A/C Compressor Clutch Diode**—is taped to the inside compressor connector on the front of the compressor or near the connector in the wiring harness.
• **A/C Compressor Control Relay**—is located in the right side electrical center.
• **A/C Heater/Defroster Bi-Directional Valve Vacuum Actuator**—is located under the instrument panel, on the right hand side of the plenum.
• **A/C High Blower Relay**—is located in the component center.
• **A/C Intermediate Pressure Switch (VIN W)**—is located on the accumulator/drier, in the left hand side of the engine compartment.
• **A/C Low Blower Relay**—is located in the component center.
• **A/C Pressure Cycling Switch**—is located on the accumulator/drier.
• **A/C Pressure Transducer**—is on the top left side of the engine.

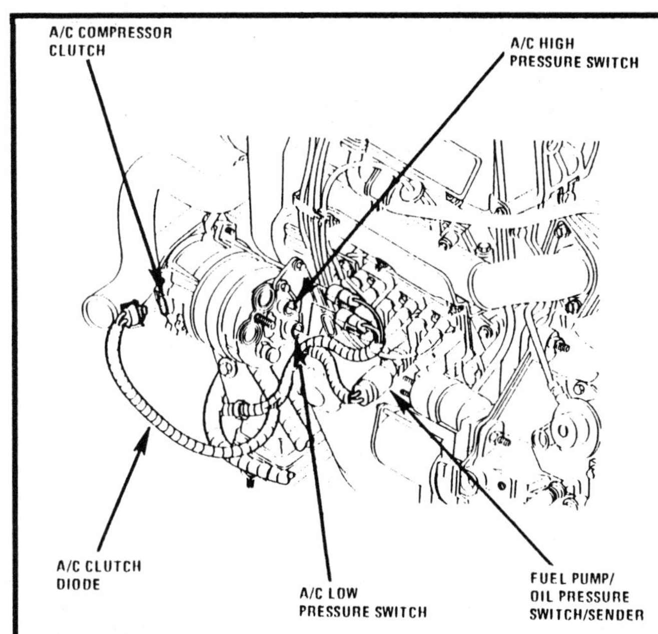

Fuel pump/oil pressure switch—Cutlass Supreme with 3.1L VIN T engine

- **A/C Recirculating Valve Vacuum Actuator**—is located under the instrument panel, on the right hand end of the plenum.
- **A/C Solenoid Box**—is located under the instrument panel, on the right hand end of the plenum.
- **A/C Vent Valve Vacuum Actuator**—is located under A/C-Blower Resistors—is located in the engine compartment on the right side of the firewall near the blower motor.
- **A/C-High Pressure Cutout Switch**—is located on the left end of the compressor.
- **A/C-Low Pressure Cutout Switch**—is located on the left end of the compressor.
- **Air Control Valve (VIN D)**—is on the top left side of the engine.
- **Anti-lock Brake Control**—is under the right front seat.
- **Antenna Motor**—is behind the right rear wheelhousing.
- **Antenna Relay**—is located behind the right hand rear wheel well, in the fender.
- **Antilock Brake Power Center**—is located at the left side of the engine compartment, on the inner fender.
- **Assembly Line Data Link Connector**—is located under the left hand side of the instrument panel, to the right of steering column.
- **Back**—Up Switch—is located on the transaxle column.
- **Battery Junction Block**—is located on the right inner fender panel, behind the battery.
- **Brake Fluid Level Switch**—is located on the left hand side of the brake fluid reservoir.
- **Brake Pressure Switch**—is located on the left hand side of the brake fluid reservoir.
- **Canister Purge Solenoid (VIN A and D)**—is located at the top front of the engine.
- **Canister Purge Solenoid (VIN W and T)**—is located in the right hand front corner of the engine compartment, on the canister.
- **Chime Module**—is located in the component center.
- **Component Center**—is located behind the right hand side of the instrument panel, on the right side of the plenum.
- **Component Center**—is located under the right hand side of the instrument panel, behind the glove box.
- **Convenience Center (early 1989)**—is located under the left hand side of the instrument panel, near the headlight switch,.
- **Convenience Center**—See Component Center.
- **Coolant Fan Relay (VIN W and T)**—is located in the right side electrical center.
- **Coolant Fan Relays (VIN D)**—are located in the right side electrical center.
- **Coolant Level and Corrosivity (VIN W)**—is located on the top right hand rear of the radiator.
- **Coolant Temperature Sender/Switch (VIN W)**—is located on the left hand side of the engine, below the coolant outlet.
- **Coolant Temperature Sensor (VIN W)**—is located on the left hand side of the engine, below the coolant outlet.
- **Coolant Temperature Switch (VIN A and D)**—is located on the left side of the engine, near the coolant outlet.
- **Crankshaft Sensor (VIN A and D)**—is located on the lower front of the engine, near the oil filter.
- **Crankshaft Sensor (VIN T)**—is located on the on the right hand front of the engine, above the oil filter.
- **Crankshaft Sensor (VIN W)**—is located on the on the right hand front of the engine, below the direct ignition system.
- **Cruise Control Brake/Switch**—is located above the brake pedal on the brake pedal support bracket.
- **Cruise Control Check Valve**—is located in the vacuum line, in front of the left hand strut tower.
- **Cruise Control Clutch Switch**—is located above the clutch pedal, on the clutch pedal support.
- **Cruise Control Module**—is located above the brake pedal on the brake pedal support bracket.
- **Cruise Control Servo**—is located in front of the left hand strut tower, in the engine compartment.
- **Cruise Control Vacuum Release Valve**—is located above the brake pedal on the brake pedal support bracket.
- **Cruise Control Vacuum Tank**—is located in the left hand front corner of the engine compartment.
- **Daytime Running Light Module**—is behind the left side of the instrument panel to the left of the steering column, near the courtesy lamp.
- **Defogger Time Relay**—is located in the component center.
- **Detonation (Knock) Sensor (VIN D)**—is located on the lower left rear of the engine.
- **Detonation (Knock) Sensor (VIN W and T)**—is located on the right rear of the right hand rear of the engine, below the exhaust manifold.
- **Digital Exhaust Gas Recirculation (DEGR) Assembly (VIN T)**—is at the top rear of the engine.
- **Diode (Headlamp) Assembly**—is to the left of the steering column, near the courtesy lamp.
- **Direct Ignition System (VIN W)**—is located on the on the right hand front of the engine, below the exhaust manifold.
- **Electronic Control Module (ECM) Fuse**—is located in the right electrical center.
- **Electronic Control Module (ECM)**—is located on the right hand strut tower, in the engine compartment.
- **Electronic Vacuum Regulator Valve (VIN W)**—is on the top right hand rear section of the engine.
- **Engine Oil Pressure Sender/Switch (VIN W)**—is located on the right hand front of the engine, above the oil filter.
- **Engine Oil Pressure Sender/Switch (except VIN W)**—See Fuel Pump/Oil Pressure switch.
- **Exhaust Gas Recirculation Solenoid (VIN D)**—is located at the left rear of the engine on the exhaust manifold.
- **Fog Light Relay**—is located in the forward light electrical center.
- **Forward Light Electrical Center**—is located on the right hand front of the engine compartment.
- **Fuel Pump Prime Connector**—is taped to the wiring harness, below the left side electrical center.

• **Fuel Pump Relay**—is located in the left side electrical center.

• **Fuel Pump/Oil Pressure Switch (VIN D)**—is located on the left side of the engine above the coolant outlet.

• **Fuel Pump/Oil Pressure Switch (VIN W and T)**—is located on the lower right hand front side of the engine, near the oil filter.

• **Gear Selector Switch**—is located on the lower part of the steering column.

• **Hazard Flasher/Relay**—is in the component center.

• **Headlight Dimmer Switch**—is located behind the instrument panel, on the left hand side of the steering column.

• **Heater Blower Resistors**—are located on the right hand front firewall, on the heater module.

• **Heater Water Valve**—is located on the rear of the engine in the heater hose.

• **Horn Relay (with fog lights)**—is located in the forward light electrical center.

• **Horn Relay (without fog lights)**—is at the right front of corner of the engine compartment.

• **Idle Air Control Motor (VIN W)**—is located on the top of the engine, on the throttle body.

• **Ignition Key Warning Switch**—is located on the top of the steering column.

• **Ignition Switch**—is located at the lower right hand side of the steering column.

• **Inside Temperature Sensor**—is behind the right side of the instrument panel.

• **Integrated Direct Ignition System (IDIS)**—is on the top left side of the engine.

• **Keyless Entry Module**—is located at the top rear shelf, near the right rear speaker.

• **Left Side Electrical Center**—is located on the left hand strut tower, in the engine compartment.

• **Lumbar Seat Air Pump Motor**—is located under the driver's seat.

• **Lumbar Seat Air Pump Valve Assemblies**—is located under the right and left front seats.

• **Lumbar Seat Control Module**—is located under the driver's seat.

• **Manifold Absolute Pressure (MAP) Sensor (VIN A and D)**—is located at the top front of the engine.

• **Manifold Absolute Pressure (MAP) Sensor (VIN W and T)**—is located on the on the air intake plenum, top of the engine.

• **Manifold Air Temperature (MAT) Sensor (VIN A and D)**—is located on lower front of the engine.

• **Manifold Air Temperature (MAT) Sensor (VIN W and T)**—is located on the on the air intake plenum, near the right hand strut tower.

• **MAP Sensor**—See Manifold Absolute Pressure Sensor.

• **Mass Air Flow (MAF) Sensor (VIN W)**—is located on the on the air intake plenum, near the right hand strut tower.

• **MAT Sensor**—See Manifold Absolute Temperature.

• **Oil Pressure/Fuel Pump Switch (VIN D)**—is located on the left side of the engine above the coolant outlet.

• **Oil Pressure/Fuel Pump Switch (VIN W and T)**—is located on the lower right hand front side of the engine, near the oil filter.

• **Outside Temperature Sensor**—is located behind the front bumper.

• **Oxygen Sensor**—is located in the exhaust manifold.

• **Photoresistor**—is on the top left side of the instrument panel, near the speaker.

• **Power Accessory Circuit (30 amp) Breaker**—is located in the component center.

• **Power Antenna Relay**—is located behind the right hand rear wheel well, in the fender.

• **Power Door Lock Relay**—is at the right shroud above the access hole. On 1989 vehicles it may be located in the component center.

• **Power Seat Control Module**—is under the seat, if equipped.

• **Power Steering Pressure Switch (VIN W)**—is located on the steering gear assembly, near the input shaft.

• **Power Window Circuit (30 amp) Breaker**—is located in the component center.

• **Primary Coolant Fan Relay (VIN D)**—is located in the right side electrical Secondary Coolant Fan Relay (VIN D)—is located in the right side electrical center.

• **Radio Control Interface Module**—is located in the steering column.

• **Radio Control Interface Module**—is located in the steering column.

• **Right Side Electrical Center**—is located on the right hand strut tower, in the engine compartment.

• **Seat Belt Lap Retractor Solenoid**—are located in the rear of each front door.

• **Seat Belt Passive Restraint Control Module**—is located behind the right hand side of the instrument panel.

• **Seat Belt Retractor Switches**—are located in the rear of each front door, on the latch assembly.

• **Seat Belt Shoulder Retractor Solenoids**—are located in the rear of each front door.

• **Seatbelt Switch**—is part of the driver's seatbelt assembly.

• **Secondary Coolant Fan Relay**—is in the right side electrical center

Sun Roof/Window Circuit (30 amp) Breaker—is located in the fuse block.

• **Sunroof Control Module**—is located at the top center of the windshield header.

• **Switch and Electronics Control Interface Module**—is located in the steering column.

• **the instrument panel, on the right hand side of the plenum.**

• **Third and Fourth Gear Switches**—are located in the middle of the left side of the transmission.

• **Throttle Position Sensor**—is located on side of the throttle body.

• **Torque Converter Clutch Solenoid**—is located in the middle of the left side of the transmission.

• **Transaxle Position Switch**—is located on the transaxle.

• **Trunk Release Solenoid**—is located in the rear center of the trunk lid.

• **Turn Signal Relay**—is located under the instrument panel, to the right of the steering column.

• **Vehicle Speed Sensor Buffer**—is taped to the instrument panel wiring under the left hand side of the instrument cluster.

• **Vehicle Speed Sensor**—is located at the side of the transaxle.

• **Wiper/Washer Motor Module**—is located on the upper left side of the engine firewall.

DELTA 88 AND NINETY-EIGHT

• **A/C Ambient Temperature Sensor (Tempmatic)**—is located behind the center of the instrument panel.

• **A/C Blower OFF Relay**—is located in the relay center, at position 'D'.

• **A/C Blower Relay**—is located in the engine compartment at the center of the firewall, near the blower motor.

• **A/C Compressor Clutch Diode**—is taped to the inside compressor connector on the front of the compressor.

• **A/C Compressor Relay (Tempmatic)**—is taped to the A/C control harness, behind the center of the instrument panel.

• **A/C Coolant Fan Pressure Switch**—is located at the right rear of the radiator, in the front of the engine compartment.

• **A/C Cut**—Out Relay—is located on a relay bracket, in the rear of the engine compartment.

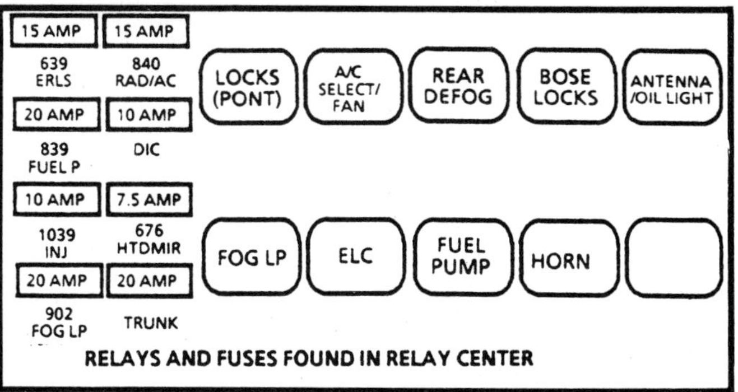

Relay center identifications—Delta 88 and Ninety-Eight

• **A/C Defrost Valve Vacuum Actuator**—is located under the center of the instrument panel, on the left hand side of the A/C plenum.

• **A/C Dual Pressure Switch**—is located on a the A/C line, in the right hand front of the engine compartment.

• **A/C High Pressure Cut**—Out Switch—is located on the left end of the A/C compressor.

• **A/C In-Car Sensor (Tempmatic)**—is located behind the trim panel, under the right hand side of the instrument panel.

• **A/C Mode Valve Vacuum Actuator**—is located under the center of the instrument panel, on the left hand side of the A/C plenum.

• **A/C Outside Air Valve Vacuum Actuator**—is located under the center of the instrument panel, on the left hand side of the A/C plenum.

• **A/C Pressure Cycling Switch**—is located on the right hand rear of the engine compartment, on the A/C line.

• **A/C Programmer (Tempmatic)**—is located behind the right side of the instrument panel.

• **A/C Slave Valve Vacuum Actuator**—is located under the center of the instrument panel, on the right hand side of the A/C plenum.

• **A/C Vacuum Delay Porous Plug**—is located under the instrument panel, in the orange vacuum line, on the left side of the A/C plenum.

• **A/C Vacuum Line Connector**—is located under the instrument panel, near the A/C-heater control assembly.

• **A/C-Heater Blower Resistors**—is located in the engine compartment on the center of the firewall, near the A/C module.

• **Airbag**—See Inflatable Restraint (IR) System.

• **Alarm Module**—is located behind the right hand side of the instrument panel, above the glove box.

• **Anti-Lock Brake Diode**—is located behind the instrument panel, to the left of the steering column.

• **Anti-Lock Brake Electronic Control Module**—is located under the left hand side of the instrument panel, near the parking brake.

• **Anti-Lock Brake Main Relay In-Line Fuse**—is located behind the strut tower, in the left hand front corner of the engine compartment.

• **Anti-Lock Brake Main Relay**—is located behind the strut tower, in the left hand front corner of the engine compartment.

• **Anti-Lock Brake Main Valve**—is located on the master cylinder, in the left hand front corner of the engine compartment.

• **Anti-Lock Brake Pump In-Line Fuse**—is located behind the strut tower, in the left hand front corner of the engine compartment.

• **Anti-Lock Brake Pump Relay**—is located behind the strut tower, in the left hand front corner of the engine compartment.

• **Anti-Lock Brake Valve Block**—is located below the master cylinder, in the left hand front corner of the engine compartment.

• **Anti-Lock Brake Wheel Speed Sensor**—is located in each wheel spindle.

• **Arming Switch**—is located under the right hand seat.

• **Assembly Line Data Link Connector**—is located under the left side of the instrument panel, to the left of the steering panel.

• **Automatic Door Lock Controller**—is located on a relay bracket, behind the right side of the instrument panel.

• **Automatic Door Lock Diode**—is located behind the left kick panel, near the lower access hole, if so equipped.

• **Auxiliary Coolant Fan Relay**—is located on a bracket, in the left hand front of the engine compartment.

• **Brake Fluid Level Sensor**—is located on the left hand side of the engine compartment, in the front of the brake fluid reservoir.

• **Brake Fluid Level Switch**—is located on the left hand side of the firewall, in the brake fluid reservoir.

• **Brake Pressure Sensor**—is located on the left hand side of the engine compartment, below the master cylinder.

• **Brake Timer Module**—is located behind the left hand side of the instrument panel, above the parking brake.

• **Camshaft Sensor**—is located on the right hand side of the engine, above the lower pulley.

• **CB Mute Module**—is located behind the center of the instrument panel, to the right of the steering column.

• **CB Signal Splitter**—is located behind the center of the instrument panel, to the right of the steering column.

• **CB Transceiver Assembly**—is located behind the center of the instrument panel, to the right of the steering column.

• **Chime Module**—is located behind the center of the instrument panel, to the left of the ashtray.

• **Computer Controlled Coil Ignition Module (VIN C)**—is located on top right front of the engine, near the alternator.

• **Coolant Fan (High and Low) Relays**—are located on a bracket, in the left hand front of the engine compartment.

• **Coolant Fan Diode**—is taped in the engine harness, behind the right hand side of the instrument panel.

• **Coolant Temperature Sensor**—is located on the top left hand side of the engine.

• **Coolant Temperature Switch**—is located on the top right hand side of the engine, to the left of the alternator.

• **Crankshaft Sensor**—is located on the right hand side of the engine, above the lower pulley.

• **Cruise Control Brake/Switch**—is located above the brake pedal on the brake pedal support bracket.

• **Cruise Control Module**—is located under the left side of the instrument panel, to the left of the steering column.

• **Cruise Control Servo**—is located at the left hand side of the engine, above the transaxle.

• **Cruise Control Vacuum Release Valve**—is located above the brake pedal on the brake pedal support bracket.

• **CTS**—See Coolant Temperature Sensor.

• **Defogger Capacitor**—is located behind the rear seat, near the right hand rear quarter pillar.

• **Defogger Time Relay**—is located in the relay center, at position 'C'.

• **Detonation (Knock) Sensor**—is located on the lower right hand side of the engine.

• **Driver Inflator Module**—is located in the steering wheel hub.

• **Driver Information Center Module**—is located behind the right side of the instrument panel.

• **EGR Module (VIN C)**—is located on the top center of the engine.

• **Electronic Control Module (ECM) Resistor (VIN C)**—is located in the engine harness, behind the right hand side of the instrument panel.

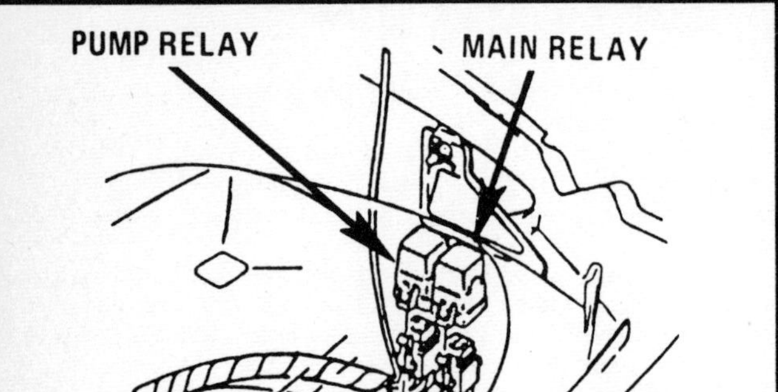

Pump relay—Delta 88 and Ninety-Eight

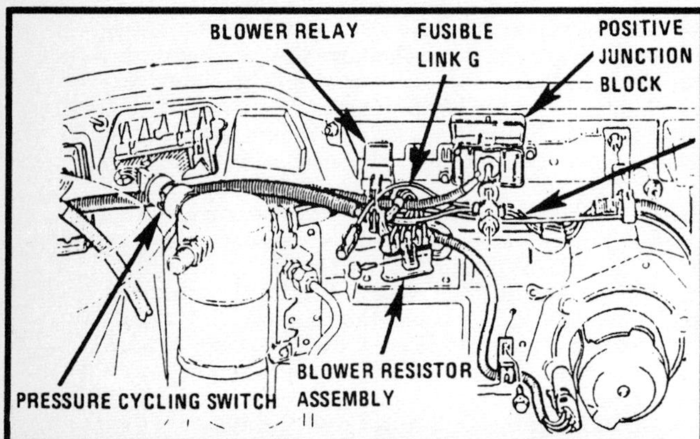

Junction block location—Delta 88 and Ninety-Eight

- **Electronic Control Module (ECM)**—is located behind the right kick panel.
- **Electronic Level Control Compressor**—is located behind the headlights, in the left hand side of the engine compartment.
- **Electronic Level Control Height Sensor**—is located on the frame, above the right hand rear lower suspension arm.
- **Electronic Level Control Relay**—is located in the relay center, at position 'K'.
- **Electronic Level Control Test Connector**—is located in the engine compartment, near the ELC compressor.
- **Fog Light Relay**—is located in the relay center, at position 'F'.
- **Forward Sensor**—is located in the front of the vehicle, in front of the radiator.
- **Fuel Door Release Solenoid**—is located in the left hand side of the trunk, above the wheel well.
- **Fuel Pump Prime Connector**—is taped to the wire harness, on the lower right hand side of the engine compartment.
- **Fuel Pump Relay**—is located in the relay center, at position 'H''.
- **Fuel Pump Relays**—are located at the left rear of the engine compartment and in the relay center.
- **Hazard Relay**—is located on the right side of the steering column brace, behind the instrument panel.
- **Head/Park Light Switch Fiber Optic**—is located behind the left hand side of instrument panel, near the head/park light switch.
- **Headlight Dimmer Switch**—is located on the left hand side of the steering column.
- **High Speed Coolant Fan Relay**—is located on a bracket, in the left hand front of the engine compartment.
- **Horn Relay**—is located in the relay center, at position 'J'.
- **Idle Air Control Valve**—is located on the top left hand side of the engine.
- **Idle Speed Power Steering Pressure Switch**—is located on the steering rack, below the left hand rear of the engine.
- **Ignition Key Warning Switch**—is located in the top of the steering column, below the turn/hazard switch.
- **Ignition Switch**—is located behind the instrument panel, on the lower right hand side of the steering column.
- **Illuminated Entry Timer**—is located on a relay bracket, behind the right hand side of the instrument panel.
- **Inflatable Restraint (IR) System Module**—is under the right front seat.
- **Inflatable Restraint System Test Connector**—is located at the bottom of the steering column.
- **Inflatable Restraint System Voltage Converter**—is located under the right hand front seat.
- **IR Energy Reserve Module**—is located under the right hand seat.
- **IR Passenger Compartment Sensor/Diagnostic Module**—is located under the right hand front seat.
- **IR System Arming Sensor**—is under the right front seat.
- **IR System Energy Reserve**—is under the right front seat.
- **IR System Forward Sensor**—is in front of the radiator.IR System Module—is under the right front seat.
- **IR System Passenger Compartment Sensor**—is under the right front seat.
- **Keyless Entry Diode**—is behind the left side of the instrument panel, in the harness near the theft deterrent relay.
- **Left Hand Horn Capacitor**—is located in the horn jumper harness, in the left hand front corner of the engine compartment.
- **Low Coolant Sensor Assembly**—is located in the radiator.
- **Low Speed Coolant Fan Relay**—is located on a bracket, in the left hand front of the engine compartment.
- **Lumbar Seat Air Pump Assembly**—is located in the center console.
- **Lumbar Seat Control Module**—is located in the center console.
- **Lumbar Seat Solenoid/Valve Assembly**—are located below each seat.
- **MAF**—See Manifold Air Flow Sensor.
- **Main Relay**—is located at the left rear of the engine compartment.
- **Manifold Air Temperature (MAT) Sensor**—is located on the air cleaner canister, near the left side of the engine.
- **Mass Airflow (MAF) Sensor**—is located in the air induction duct work, near the left of the engine.
- **MAT Sensor**—See Manifold Air Temperature Sensor.
- **Negative Junction Block**—is located ahead of the strut, on the right hand side of the engine compartment.
- **Oil Pressure Sensor/Switch**—is located on the lower right hand side of the engine, below the water pump.
- **Outside Temperature Sensor**—is located on the front of the vehicle, on the right hand center brace.
- **Oxygen Sensor**—is located on the exhaust manifold.
- **Photocell Sensor**—is mounted at the speaker grille.
- **Positive Junction Block**—is located on a bracket, on the center of the firewall, in the engine compartment.
- **Power Antenna Relay (Touring Sedan)**—is located below the antenna mast, in the right side of the trunk compartment.
- **Power Antenna Relay**—is located in the relay center, at position 'A'.
- **Power Door Lock Relay Assembly**—is located on a relay bracket, behind the right side of the instrument panel.

- **Power Seat Module**–is located under the left hand front seat.
- **PRNDL Decoder Module**–is located to the left of the steering column, under the instrument panel.
- **Radio Amplifier Relay**–is located in the relay center, at position 'B'.
- **Relay Center**–is located under the right hand side of the instrument panel.
- **Right Hand Horn Capacitor**–is located in the horn jumper harness, in the right hand front corner of the engine compartment.
- **Seatbelt Indicator Driver Module**–is located at the right hand kick panel, under the instrument panel.
- **Seatbelt Lap Retractor Solenoids**–are located in the lower rear portion of the front doors.
- **Seatbelt Retractor Switches**–are located in the center rear of the front doors, at the latch assembly.
- **Seatbelt Shoulder Retractor Solenoids**–are located in the lower rear portion of the front doors.
- **Seatbelt Switch**–is part of the driver's seatbelt assembly.
- **Seatbelt Timer Module**–are located in the center of the front doors.
- **Starter Solenoid**–is located on the lower hand front of the engine.
- **Steering Column Coil Assembly**–is located in the underside of the steering wheel.
- **Sunroof Limit Switch**–is located in the roof, near the top of the left hand windshield pillar.
- **Sunroof Module**–is located in the roof, above the left hand front door.
- **Sunroof Relay**–is located at the top center of the windshield header.
- **Theft Deterrent Controller**–is above the accelerator pedal.
- **Theft Deterrent Diode**–is taped in the harness behind the left side of the instrument panel.
- **Theft Deterrent Relay**–is above the accelerator pedal.
- **Throttle Position Sensor**–is located on the left hand side of the throttle body.
- **Torque Converter Clutch Brake Switch**–is located on the brake pedal support, under the instrument panel.
- **TPS**–See Throttle Position Sensor.
- **Transaxle Position Switch**–is located on the left hand rear of the engine, on top of the transaxle.
- **Trunk Lid Pull**–Down Unit–is located in the rear of the trunk at the striker plate.
- **Trunk Lid Release Solenoid**–is located on the underside of trunk lid, near the latch.
- **Turn Signal Relay**–is located at the left of the steering column, behind the instrument panel.
- **Twilight Sentinel Amplifier**–is located on a bracket behind the right side of the instrument panel.
- **Twilight Sentinel Photocell**–is located in the right hand side of the right hand defrost grille.
- **Vapor Canister Purge Solenoid**–is located in the left hand front corner of the engine compartment.
- **Vehicle Speed Sensor Buffer**–is located behind the right hand side of the instrument panel, on the right hand side of the plenum.
- **Vehicle Speed Sensor**–is located on the right hand side of the transaxle.
- **Voice/Alarm Module**–is located behind the right hand side of the instrument panel, above the glove box.
- **Washer Pump Motor Diode**–is located in the washer motor connector.
- **Window and Sunroof Circuit Breaker**–is located at the top right corner of the fuse block.
- **Window Down Express Module**–is located in the door.

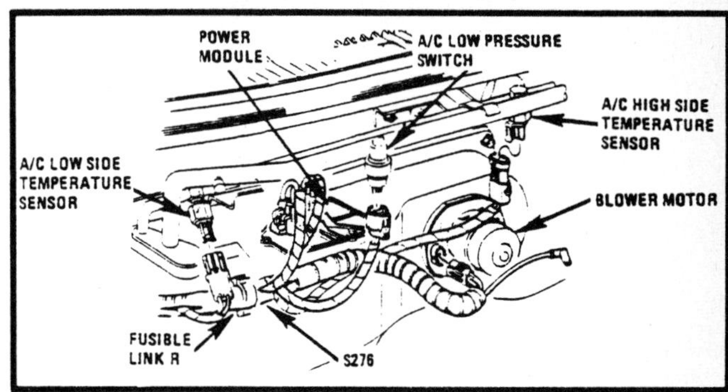

Air conditioning lower pressure switch–Toronado and Trofeo

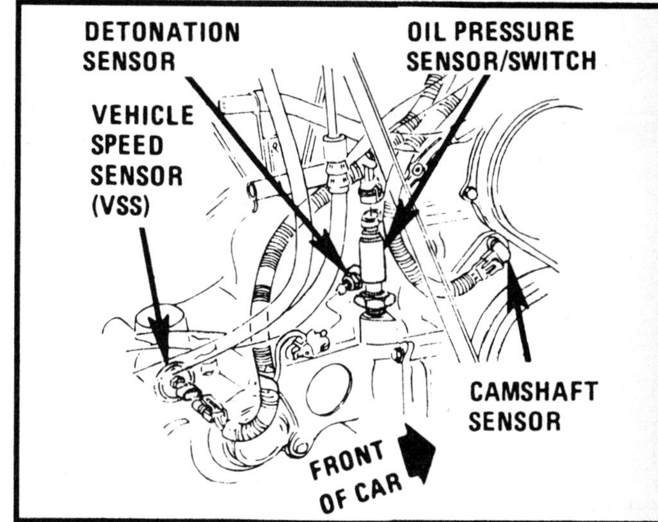

Engine sensors–Toronado and Trofeo

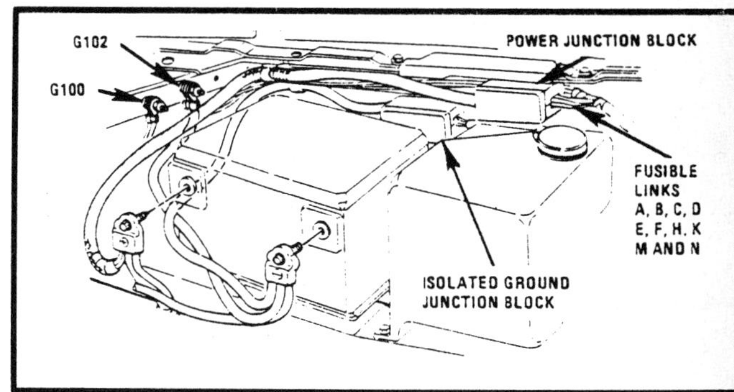

Power junction blocks–Toronado and Trofeo

- **Wiper Motor Relay Diode**–is located in the wiper motor connector, the relay is incorporated into the wiper module.
- **Wiper/Washer Fluid Level Sensor**–is located in the washer fluid reservoir.
- **Wiper/Washer Motor Module**–is located on the upper left corner of the firewall in the engine compartment.

TORONADO AND TROFEO

- **A/C Aspirator**–is located behind the right hand side of the instrument panel, on top of the A/C plenum.

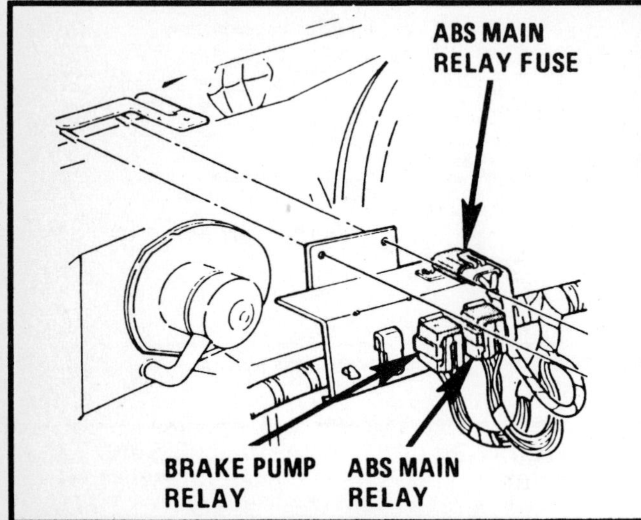

Anti-lock brake relay—Toronado and Trofeo

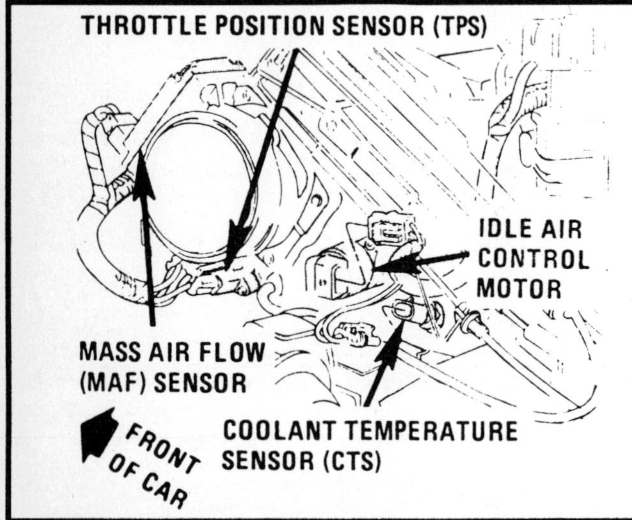

MAF sensor—Toronado and Trofeo

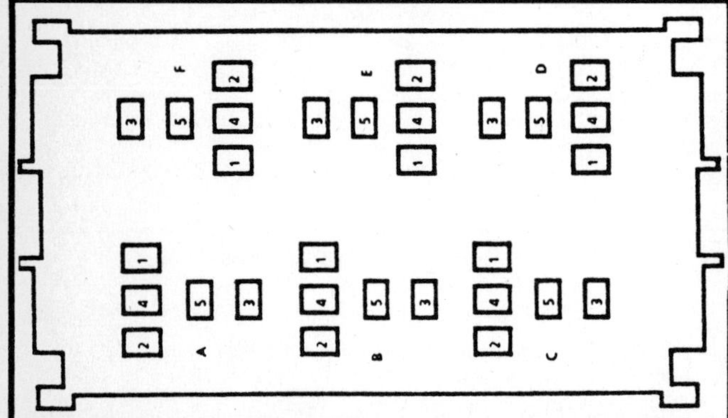

Mirco relay identification—1990–91 Toronado and Trofeo

• **A/C Blower Relay**—is located near the blower motor.

• **A/C Compressor Clutch Diode**—is located on the A/C clutch connector.

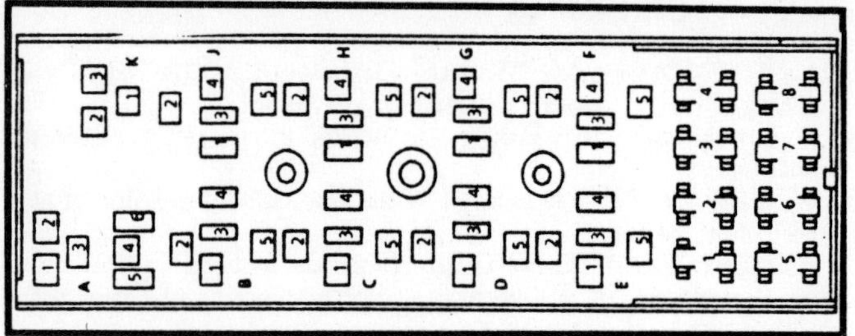

FUSE POSITION	FUSE FUNCTION
1	A/C Compressor Clutch
2	Headlight Doors
3	Not Used
4	Not Used
5	Coolant Fans
6	Fog Lights
7	Phone Battery
8	Not Used

Underhood and interior relay center identification—Toronado and Trofeo

• **A/C Compressor Clutch Relay**—is located in the underhood relay center, at position 'J'.

• **A/C Heater Blower Resistors**—is located on the top left side of the blower assembly.

• **A/C Heater Programmer**—is located behind the instrument panel, on the right hand side of the A/C plenum.

• **A/C High Pressure Coolant Fan Switch**—is located on the A/C line, in the left hand front of the engine compartment.

• **A/C High Side Temperature Sensor**—is located on the A/C line, in the center of the firewall.

• **A/C In-Car Sensor**—is located behind the right side of the instrument panel, near the glove box.

• **A/C Low Pressure Switch**—is located on the A/C line, in the center of the firewall.

• **A/C Low Side Temperature Sensor**—is located on the A/C line, in the center of the firewall.

• **A/C Lower Mode Door Vacuum Actuator**—is located behind the instrument panel, on the A/C plenum.

• **A/C Outside Air Valve Vacuum Actuator**—is located behind the instrument panel, on the A/C plenum.

• **A/C Outside Temperature Sensor**—is located in front of the radiator, in the engine compartment.

• **A/C Power Module**—is located on the center of the firewall, in the heater and A/C Heater module.

• **A/C Upper Mode Door Vacuum Actuator**—is located behind the instrument panel, on the A/C plenum.

• **A/C Vacuum Delay Porous Plug**—is located behind the instrument panel, in the orange vacuum line.

• **Air Bag**—See Supplemental Inflatable Restraint (SIR) System.

• **Antenna Relay (1989)**—is located in the interior relay center, at position 'A'.

• **Antenna Relay (except 1989)**—may be located next to the antenna or in the relay center.

• **Anti-Lock Brake Controller Fuse**—is located behind the instrument panel, to the right of the steering column.

• **Anti-Lock Brake Diode**—is located behind the instrument panel, to the left of the steering column (on the right of the steering column on column shift models).

• **Anti-Lock Brake Electronic Control Module**—is located on the left hand rear wheelhouse, in the luggage compartment.

• **Anti-Lock Brake Main Relay Fuse**—is located on the center of the firewall.

• **Anti-Lock Brake Main Relay**—is located on the center of the firewall.

• **Anti-Lock Brake Pump Fuse**—is located on the center of the firewall.

• **Anti-Lock Brake Pump Relay Fuse**—is located on the center of the firewall.

• **Anti-Lock Brake Pump Relay**—is located on the center of the firewall.

• **Anti-Lock Brake Wheel Speed Sensor**—is located in each wheel spindle.

• **Assembly Line Diagnostic Link (ALDL) Connector**—is located under the instrument panel, near to the parking brake.

• **Automatic Door Lock Module**—is behind the top left side of the instrument panel, to the right of the steering column.

• **Backup Lamps Relay (1989)**—is located in the interior relay center, at position 'H'.

• **Body Computer Module (BCM)**—is located behind the right side of the instrument panel, behind the glove box.

• **Brake Fluid Level Switch**—is located on the left side of the brake fluid reservoir.

• **Brake Switch Capacitor No. 1**—is located behind the left hand side of the instrument panel, in the brake switch connector.

• **Brake Switch Capacitor No. 2**—is located in the instrument panel harness, to the right of the steering column.

• **Brake Switch**—is located above the brake pedal on the brake pedal support bracket.

• **Camshaft Sensor**—is located on lower right hand side of the engine, below the water pump.

• **Cellular Telephone Transceiver**—is located in the left hand front of the luggage compartment.

• **Central Power Supply**—is located behind the left side of the instrument panel, above the brake pedal.

• **Chime Module**—is located under the instrument panel, near to the parking brake.

• **Computer Controlled Coil Ignition Module**—is located on the front of the engine on the valve cover.

• **Coolant Fan High Relay (except 1989)**—is located in the underhood relay center, at position 'D'.

• **Coolant Puller Fan High Relay (1989)**—is located in the underhood relay center, at position 'C'.

• **Coolant Puller Fan Low Relay**—is located in the underhood relay center, at position 'G'. .

• **Coolant Puller Fan Relay (1989)**—is located in the underhood relay center, at position 'D'.

• **Coolant Puller Fan Relay (except 1989)**—is located in the underhood relay center, at position 'C'.

• **Coolant Temperature Sensor**—is located on right hand side of engine, behind alternator or under the throttle body.

• **Coolant Temperature Switch**—is located on right hand side of engine, behind alternator.

• **Courtesy Lamp Relay (1989)**—is located in the interior relay center, at position 'C'.

• **Courtesy Light Relay (except 1989)**—is located in the mirco relay center 2, at position 'B'.

• **Crankshaft Sensor**—is located at the right hand front of the engine, ahead of the lower pulley.

• **Cruise Control Brake Switch**—is located above the brake pedal on the brake pedal support bracket.

• **Cruise Control Check Valve**—is located on the left hand rear side of the engine. Cruise Control Servo—is located on the left hand side of the engine compartment, above the transaxle.

• **Cruise Control Vacuum Release Valve**—is located above the brake pedal on the brake pedal support bracket.

• **Cruise Control Vacuum Tank**—is located in the left hand side of the engine compartment, on the frame.

• **Defogger Relay (1989)**—is located in the interior relay center, at position 'D'.

• **Defogger Relay (except 1989)**—is located in the mirco relay center 2, at position 'E'.

• **Delco Bose Music System Diode**—is located in the crossbar harness, near the right hand door sill.

• **Delco Bose Relays (except 1989)**—are located in the mirco relay center 2, at position 'D' and 'F'.

• **Detonation (Knock) Sensor**—is located at the lower right side of the engine, above the drive axle.

• **Electronic Control Module (ECM)**—is located behind the right kick panel.

• **Electronic Level Control (ELC) Compressor**—is located underneath the vehicle, on the support assembly.

• **Electronic Level Control (1989)**—is located in the interior relay center, at position 'K'.

• **Electronic Level Control Height Sensor**—is attached to lower suspension arm, underneath the left hand rear vehicle.

• **Electronic Level Control Relay (except 1989)**—is located in the mirco relay center 2, at position 'A'.

• **Electronic Level Control Relay**—is located in the underhood relay center, at position 'K'.

• **Electronic Spark Control Unit**—is located on the center of the firewall.

• **Electronic Vacuum Regulator Valve Module**—is located at the top center of the rear valve cover.

• **Exhaust Gas Recirculation Solenoid Assembly**—is at the rear of the engine, above the left valve cover.

• **Fog Light Relay**—is located in the underhood relay center, at position 'F'.

• **Fuel Door Release Solenoid**—is located in the left hand side of the trunk, above the wheel well.

• **Fuel Pump Prime Connector**—is taped to the wire harness, on the lower left hand front of the engine compartment. May be located near the cruise control servo.

• **Fuel Pump Relay (1989)**—is located in the rear of the engine compartment, to the left of the blower motor.

• **Fuel Pump Relay (except 1989)**—is located in the mirco relay center 1, at position 'A'.

• **Fusible Links**—are located mainly at the power junction block. Other location can include battery and alternator, dependent on options.

• **Hazard Flasher**—is located under the instrument panel, on the right hand side of the steering column.

• **Headlight Doors Module**—is located underhood behind the left headlights.

• **Headlight Doors Relay (1989)**—is located in the underhood relay center, at position 'A'.

• **Hi Beam Inhibit Relay**—is located in the underhood relay center, at position 'H'.

• **Horn Relay**—is located in the underhood relay center, position 'B'.

• **Idle Air Control Motor**—is located on the left hand side of the engine, on the rear of the throttle body.

• **Idle Speed Power Steering Pressure Switch**—is located on the steering rack, in the left hand rear corner of the engine compartment.

• **Ignition Key Warning Switch**—is located at the top of the steering column.

• **Ignition Switch**—is located in the top of the steering column.

• **Interior Relay Center**—is located behind the right side of the instrument panel, behind the glove box. After 1989 this relay center is called mirco relay center No. 1.

• **Isolated Ground Junction Block**—is located in the right hand front of the engine compartment, above the battery.

• **Luggage Compartment Lid Pull**—Down Unit—is located in the rear of the trunk at the striker plate.

• **Luggage Compartment Lid Release Solenoid**—is located in the rear of the trunk at the striker plate.

• **Luggage Compartment Lid Tamper Switch**—is incorporated into the luggage compartment lock switch.

• **Lumbar Seat Air Pump Assembly**—is located in the center console.

• **Lumbar Seat Control Module**—is located in the center console.

• **Lumbar Seat Left Hand Seat Solenoid Valve Assembly**—is located under the left hand front seat.

• **Lumbar Seat Right Hand Seat Solenoid Valve Assembly**—is located under the right hand front seat.

• **Manifold Air Temperature (MAT) Sensor**—is located on the air intake assembly, near the left of the engine.

• **Mass Airflow (MAF) Sensor**—is located in the air induction duct work, near the left of the engine.

• **Mirco Relay Center 1 (except 1989)**—is located behind the glove compartment. In 1989 relay center was called the interior relay center.

• **Mirco Relay Center 2**—is located in the front of the luggage compartment, below the rear shelf.

• **Oil Pressure Sensor/Switch**—is located on the right hand side of the engine, behind the water pump.

• **Oxygen Sensor**—is located at the right rear of the exhaust manifold.

• **PASS Key Decoder Module**—is to the left of the steering column.

• **Power Accessories Circuit Breaker**—is located in the fuse block.

• **Power Door Lock Relay**—is located on the conduit, on the left hand shroud (kick panel).

• **Power Junction Block**—is located in the right hand front of the engine compartment, above the battery.

• **Power Window Capacitors**—are located inside the connectors, in the center front of the door.

• **Power Window Circuit Breaker**—is located in the fuse block.

• **Puller Coolant Fan**—is located behind the radiator, in the left hand front of the engine compartment.

• **Pusher Coolant Fan**—is located in front of the radiator, in the left hand front of the engine compartment.

• **Radio Mute Module**—is located in the console, ahead of the console compartment.

• **Seat Control Module**—is in the center console, near the seat air pump assembly.

• **Seatbelt Switch**—is located in the driver's right hand seatbelt.

• **SIR Dual Sensor**—is located behind the right side of the instrument panel, to the left of the glove compartment.

• **SIR Energy Reserve Module**—is located behind the instrument panel, to the right of the steering wheel.

• **SIR Forward Sensor**—is located at the center front of the engine compartment.

• **SIR Resistor Module**—is located behind the left side of the instrument panel, above the parking brake.

• **Starter Interrupt Relay**—is located to the left of the steering column.

• **Starter Solenoid**—is located on the lower left hand front of the engine.

• **Sun Load Sensor**—is located in the top center of the instrument panel.

• **Sunroof Limit Switch**—is located in the left hand side of the windshield header, near the roof rail.

• **Sunroof Relay**—is in the center of the windshield header.

• **Sunroof Timer Module**—is located in the left hand side of the windshield header, near the roof rail.

• **Theft Deterrent Diode**—is located in the instrument panel harness above the fuse block, if so equipped.

• **Theft Deterrent Exterior Lights Relay**—is located behind the left hand side of the instrument panel, above the steering column.

• **Theft Deterrent Horn Relay**—is located behind the left hand side of the instrument panel, above the steering column.

• **Theft Deterrent In-Line Fuse**—is located behind the left hand side of the instrument panel, to the left of the steering column.

• **Theft Deterrent Module**—is located behind the left hand side of the instrument panel, to the left of the steering column.

• **Theft Deterrent Relay**—is located behind the left hand side of the instrument panel, to the left of the steering column.

• **Throttle Position Sensor**—is located on the left front side of the throttle body.

• **Trailer Adapter Connector**—is located in the right hand rear of the luggage compartment.

• **Transaxle Position Switch**—is located on the left hand rear of the engine, on top of the transaxle.

• **Turn Signal Alarm**—is located under the instrument panel, behind the left switch assembly.

• **Turn Signal Flasher**—is located under the instrument panel, on the right hand side of the steering column.

• **Twilight Crank Sentinel Headlamps Relay (except 1989)**—is located in the mirco relay center 1, at position 'D'.

• **Twilight Sentinel Crank Relay (1989)**—is located in the interior relay center, at position 'J'.

• **Twilight Sentinel Headlamps Relay(except 1989)**—is located in the mirco relay center 1, at position 'C'.

• **Twilight Sentinel Headlights Relay (1989)**—is located in the interior relay center, at position 'G'.

• **Twilight Sentinel Park Light Relay(except 1989)**—is located in the mirco relay center 1, at position 'B'.

• **Twilight Sentinel Park Lights Relay (1989)**—is located in the interior relay center, at position 'F'.

• **Twilight Sentinel Photocell**—is located on the top of the instrument panel, above the radio.

• **Underhood Relay Center**—is located on the inner left front fender panel, behind the left hand headlights.

• **Vapor Canister Purge Solenoid**—is located in the left hand front corner of the engine compartment, behind the headlights.

• **Vehicle Speed Buffer**—is located on the left side of the instrument cluster, if so equipped.

• **Vehicle Speed Sensor**—is located on the right hand side of the transaxle.

• **Voice/Chime Module**—is located under the instrument panel, near to the parking brake.

• **Washer Fluid Level Switch**—is located on the washer fluid reservoir.

• **Wiper Motor Relay Diode**—is located in the wiper motor connector.

• **Wiper/Washer Capacitor**—is located in the dash harness, behind the left side of the instrument panel.

• **Wiper/Washer Motor Module**—is located on the left hand side of the firewall, behind the strut tower.

PONTIAC

Circuit Breakers

ALL MODELS

HEADLIGHTS

This circuit breaker is incorporated in the headlight switch.

WINDSHIELD WIPERS

This circuit breaker is incorporated in the windshield wiper motor.

POWER REMOTE MIRRORS

This circuit breaker is located in the fuse box or may incorporated into the power mirror motors on some vehicles.

POWER WINDOWS

This circuit breaker may be incorporated with the power window motors.

POWER ACCESSORIES

Circuit breakers for power accessories are located in the fuse block, convenience center and/or relay centers. They protect the following circuits; rear window defogger, power windows, power seats and power door locks, alarm systems, keyless entry, sunroofs, etc. if equipped.

Fusible Links

ALL MODELS

In addition to circuit breakers and fuses, some circuits use fusible links to protect the wiring. Like fuses, the fusible links are 1 time protection devices that will melt and create an open circuit.

Not all fusible link open circuits can be detected by observation. Always inspect that there is battery voltage passing through the fusible link to verify continuity.

Each fusible link is four wire gauge sizes smaller than the cable it is designed to protect. The same wire size fusible link must be used when replacing a blown fusible link. Fusible links are available with two types of insulation; Hypalon and Silicone. Service fusible links made with Hypalon insulation, must be replaced with the same Hypalon insulated wire. Fusible links with Silicone insulation can use either insulation.

NOTE: Never make a fusible link longer than 9 in. (228mm) for it will not provide sufficient overload protection.

To replace a damaged fusible link, cut it off beyond the splice. Replace with a repair link. When connecting the repair link, strip the wire and use staking type pliers to crimp the splice securely in two places.

Some of the most important circuits to be protected with fusible links are the Electronic Control Module (ECM), A/C-Heater blower motors, fuel injection systems, fuse blocks, headlights and the charging system. On most models there are two fusible links located at the starter solenoid, which are used to protect the charging and lighting circuits. There may be a fusible link used at each headlight door to protect the headlight system on the Firebird. There is one fusible link located near the battery positive terminal, which is used for the protection of the electronic control module on the Firebird.

There is a fusible link located at the electronic spark timing distributor for the early fuel evaporation heater relay, if equipped on the 6000 and 6000 STE. There is a fusible link at the starter for the cooling fan on 6000 and 6000 STE.

The Lemans has it's fusible links at the starter solenoid and on the left side of the engine compartment in front of the strut tower. The 6000 and 6000 STE fusible links are located at the battery junction block, starter solenoid and the battery.

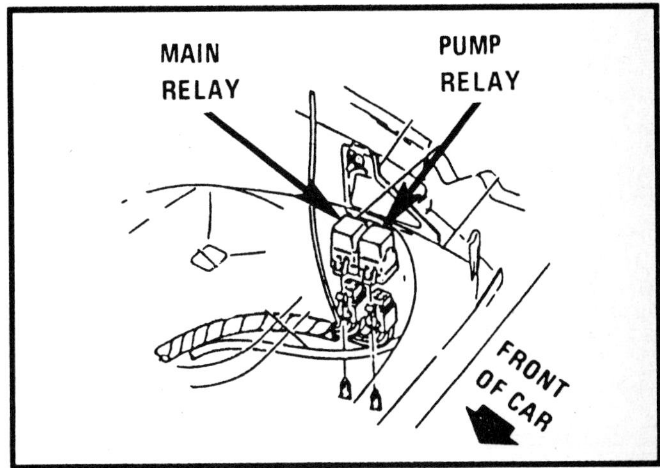

Main relay—Bonneville

Most Pontiacs have the fusible links at the starter solenoid. But other locations include the junction block at the right front of the engine compartment, next to the battery and near the alternator.

Relay, Sensors And Computer Locations

NOTE: When using this section, some of the components may not be used on a particular vehicle. This is because the particular component in question was used on an earlier model or a later model. If a component is not found in this section, check other vehicles of the same body line, as that component may have been introduced earlier on different models. This section is being published from the latest information available at the time of this publication.

BONNEVILLE

- **A/C Ambient Temperature Sensor**—is located in the front of the vehicle, in front of the radiator.
- **A/C Aspirator**—is located behind the right hand side of the instrument panel.
- **A/C Blower Control Module**—is located on the front of the firewall, in the center of the A/C plenum.
- **A/C Blower Relay**—is located in the engine compartment at the center of the firewall, on a relay bracket.
- **A/C Blower Resistors**—is located on the right side of the firewall, on the A/C module (plenum).
- **A/C Compressor Clutch Diode**—is taped to the inside compressor connector on the front of the compressor.
- **A/C Compressor Control Relay**—is located in the engine compartment at the center of the firewall, on a bracket.
- **A/C Coolant Fan Pressure Switch**—is located on the A/C line in the right hand front of the engine compartment.
- **A/C Cut**—Out Relay—is located in the engine compartment at the right side of the firewall, on a bracket.
- **A/C Defrost Valve Vacuum Actuator**—is located under the center of the instrument panel, on the left hand side of the A/C plenum.

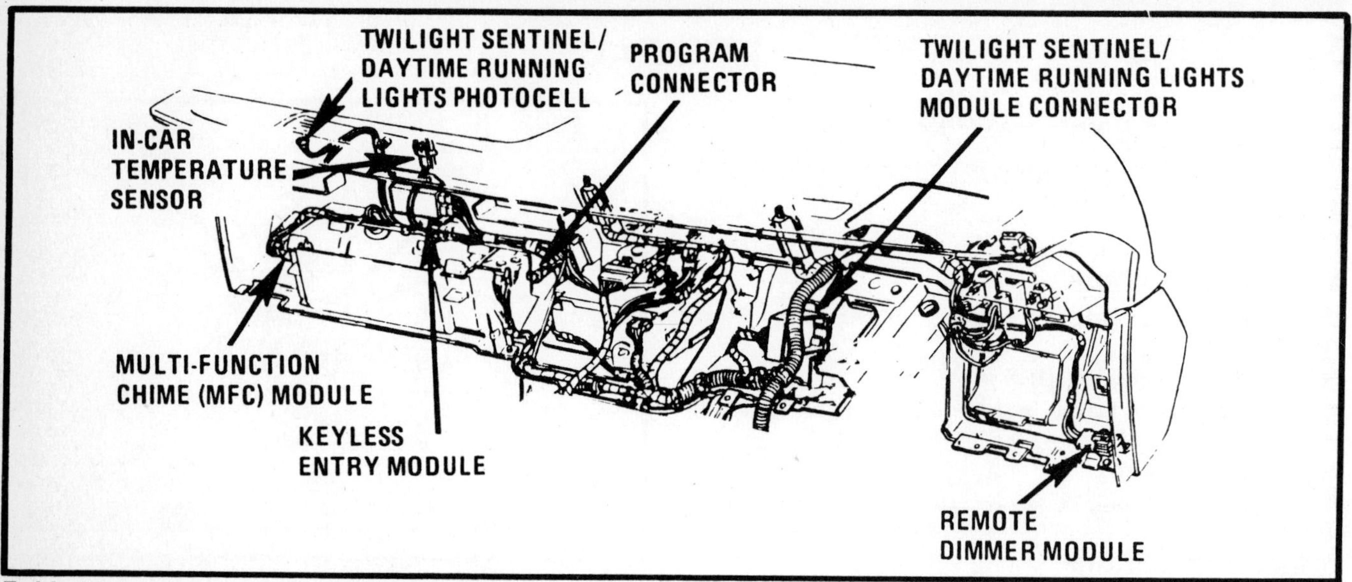

Behind instrument panel—1990 Bonneville

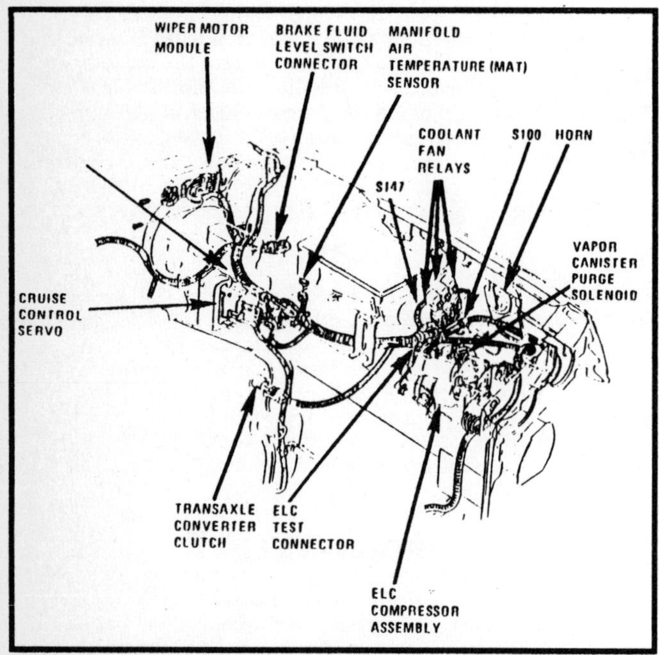

Underhood components—1990 Bonneville

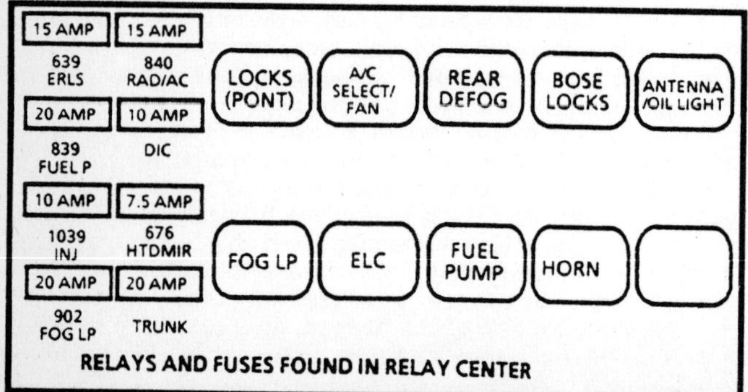

Relay center identification—Bonneville

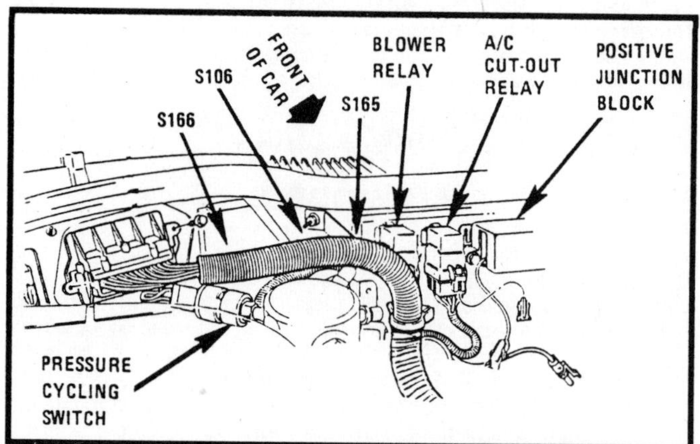

Blower and Air conditioning relays—Bonneville

- **A/C Heater/Water Valve Vacuum Actuator**—is located under the center of the instrument panel, on the right hand side of the A/C plenum.
- **A/C High Pressure Cut**—Out Switch—is located on the left end of the A/C compressor.
- **A/C In-Car Sensor**—is located near the glove box, under the right hand side of the instrument panel.
- **A/C Mode Valve Vacuum Actuator**—is located under the center of the instrument panel, on the left hand side of the A/C plenum.
- **A/C Outside Air Valve Vacuum Actuator**—is located under the center of the instrument panel, on the left hand side of the A/C plenum.
- **A/C Pressure Switch**—is located on the right hand rear of the engine compartment, on the A/C line.
- **A/C Select Relay**—is located in the relay center, at position 'D'.
- **A/C Slave Valve Vacuum Actuator**—is located under the right hand side of the instrument panel, on the right hand side of the A/C plenum.
- **A/C Vacuum Delay Porous Plug**—is located under the instrument panel, in the orange vacuum line, on the left side of the A/C plenum.
- **A/C Vacuum Line Connector**—is located under the instrument panel, near the A/C-heater control assembly.

• **A/C-Heater Blower Resistors**—is located in the engine compartment on the center of the firewall, near the A/C module.

• **Anti-Lock Brake Controller In-Line Fuse**—is located behind the strut tower, in the left hand rear corner of the engine compartment.

• **Anti-Lock Brake Controller**—is located under the left hand side of the instrument panel, near the parking brake.

• **Anti-Lock Brake Diode**—is located behind the instrument panel, taped to the brake controller lead.

• **Anti-Lock Brake Main Relay Fuse**—is located behind the strut tower, in the left hand rear corner of the engine compartment.

• **Anti-Lock Brake Main Relay**—is located behind the strut tower, in the left hand rear corner of the engine compartment.

• **Anti-Lock Brake Main Valve**—is located on the master cylinder, in the left hand front corner of the engine compartment.

• **Anti-Lock Brake Pump Fuse**—is located behind the strut tower, in the left hand front corner of the engine compartment.

• **Anti-Lock Brake Pump Relay**—is located behind the strut tower, in the left hand front corner of the engine compartment.

• **Anti-Lock Brake Tooth Sensor Ring**—is located in each wheel spindle.

• **Anti-Lock Brake Valve Block**—is located below the master cylinder, in the left hand front corner of the engine compartment.

• **Anti-Lock Brake Wheel Speed Sensor**—is located in each wheel spindle.

• **Assembly Line Data Link Connector**—is located under the left side of the instrument panel, to the left of the steering panel.

• **Audio Alarm Module**—is located behind the right hand side of the instrument panel, above the glove box.

• **Auxiliary Coolant Fan Relay**—is located on a bracket, in the left hand front of the engine compartment, in front of the strut tower.

• **Brake Fluid Level Sensor**—is located on the left hand side of the engine compartment, in the front of the brake fluid reservoir.

• **Brake Fluid Level Switch**—is located on the left hand side of the firewall, in the brake fluid reservoir.

• **Brake Pressure Sensor**—is located on the left hand side of the engine compartment, below the master cylinder.

• **Camshaft Sensor**—is located on the lower right hand side of the engine, above the lower pulley.

• **Cellular Mobile Telephone Transceiver Assembly**—is located in the trunk compartment, if so equipped.

• **Chime Module**—is located behind the right hand side of the instrument panel, if so equipped.

• **Computer Controlled Coil Ignition Module (VIN C)**—is located on top right front of the engine, near the alternator.

• **Coolant Fan Diode**—is taped in the engine harness, behind the right hand side of the instrument panel.

• **Coolant Fan Relays (High and Low)**—are located on a bracket, in the left hand front of the engine compartment, to the right of the coolant fan assembly.

• **Coolant Fan Resistors**—are located at the cooling fan.

• **Coolant Temperature Sensor (VIN C)**—is located on the top left hand side of the engine.

• **Coolant Temperature Switch**—is located on the top right hand side of the engine, behind the alternator.

• **Crankshaft Sensor**—is located on the lower right hand side of the engine, behind the A/C compressor.

• **Cruise Control Brake/Switch**—is located above the brake pedal on the brake pedal support bracket.

• **Cruise Control Module**—is located under the left side of the instrument panel, to the left of the steering column.

• **Cruise Control Servo**—is located at the left hand side of the engine compartment, below the brake hydraulic unit.

• **Cruise Control Vacuum Release Valve**—is located above the brake pedal on the brake pedal support bracket.

• **Defogger Capacitor**—is located behind the rear seat, near the right hand rear quarter pillar.

• **Defogger Time Relay**—is located in the relay center.

• **Delco-Bose Music System In-Line Fuse**—is located near the right hand kick panel, under the instrument panel.

• **Delco**—Bose Music System Relay—is located near the right hand kick panel, under the instrument panel, or in the relay center.

• **Detonation (Knock) Sensor (VIN C)**—is located on the lower right hand side of the engine.

• **Driver Information Center Module**—is located behind the right side of the instrument panel, above the plenum.

• **EGR Module (VIN C)**—is located on the top center of the engine.

• **Electronic Climate Control Programmer**—is located behind the right side of the instrument panel, to the left of the glove box.

• **Electronic Compass Module (ECM)**—is located in front of the luggage compartment, underside of the package shelf.

• **Electronic Control Module (ECM) Resistor (VIN C)**—is located in the engine harness, behind the right hand side of the instrument panel, if so equipped.

• **Electronic Control Module (ECM)**—is located behind the right side of the instrument panel.

• **Electronic Level Control Compressor**—is located behind the headlights, in the left hand side of the engine compartment.

• **Electronic Level Control Height Sensor**—is located on the rear lower A frame.

• **Electronic Level Control Inflator Solenoid Valve**—is located in the right hand front of the luggage compartment.

• **Electronic Level Control Inflator Switch**—is located in the right hand front of the luggage compartment.

• **Electronic Level Control Inflator Timer Relay**—is located in the right hand front of the luggage compartment.

• **Electronic Level Control Relay**—is located in the relay center, at position 'K'.

• **Electronic Level Control Test Connector**—is located in the engine compartment, near the ELC compressor.

• **Electronic Spark Control (ESC) Module**—is located on a relay bracket on the center of the firewall, in the engine compartment.

• **Electronic Vacuum Regulator Valve Module**—is located at the top center of the rear valve cover.

• **Fog Light Relay**—is located in the relay center, at position 'F'.

• **Fuel Door Lock Relay Assembly**—is located behind the right hand side of the instrument panel, on the left of the relay center.

• **Fuel Door Release Solenoid**—is located in the left hand side of the trunk, above the wheel well, if so equipped.

• **Fuel Pump Prime Connector**—is taped to the wire harness, on the lower right hand side of the engine compartment, near the right hand wheelwell, near the battery.

• **Fuel Pump Relays**—are located at the left rear of the engine compartment and in the relay center.

• **Gear Selector Switch**—is located on the left hand side of the transaxle.

• **Hazard Relay**—is located on the right side of the steering column brace, behind the instrument panel.

• **Headlight Dimmer Switch**—is located on the left hand side of the steering column.

• **Headlight Washer Timer Module**—is located behind the right hand side of instrument panel, to the left of the relay center.

• **Heavy Duty Coolant Fan Relay**—See High Speed Coolant Fan Relay.

- **High Speed Coolant Fan Relay**—is located on a bracket, in the left hand front of the engine compartment.
- **Horn Relay**—is located in the relay center.
- **Idle Air Control Valve**—is located on the top left hand side of the engine.
- **Idle Speed Power Steering Pressure Switch**—is located on the left hand rear of the engine, in the power steering unit.
- **Ignition Key Warning Switch**—is located in the top of the steering column, below the turn/hazard switch.
- **Ignition Switch**—is located behind the instrument panel, on the center of the steering column.
- **Illuminated Entry Timer**—is located behind the right hand side of the instrument panel, on the left of the relay center.
- **Keyless Entry Diode**—is behind the left side of the instrument panel, in the harness near the theft deterrent relay.
- **Keyless Entry Module**—is located behind the right side of the instrument panel, above the instrument panel compartment.
- **Lights Monitor Module**—is located behind the right hand side of instrument panel, near the kick panel.
- **Low Coolant Sensor Assembly**—is located in the radiator, if so equipped.
- **Low Speed Coolant Fan Relay**—is located on a bracket, in the left hand front of the engine compartment.
- **Luggage Compartment Ajar Switch**—is located on a the underside of the luggage compartment lid, near the latch.
- **Luggage Compartment Lid Pull**—Down Unit—is located in the rear of the trunk at the striker plate, if so equipped.
- **Luggage Compartment Release Solenoid**—is located on the underside of trunk lid, near the latch, if so equipped.
- **Luggage Compartment Release Switch**—is located behind the glove box.
- **Lumbar Seat Air Pump Assembly**—is located under the right hand front seat.
- **Lumbar Seat Control Module**—is located under the right hand front seat.
- **Lumbar Seat Solenoid/Valve Assembly**—is located under the each of the front seats.
- **MAF**—See Manifold Air Flow Sensor.
- **CTS**—See Coolant Temperature Sensor.
- **Main Relay**—is located at the left rear of the engine compartment.
- **Manifold Air Temperature (MAT) Sensor**—is located on the air intake duct, below the air filter assembly.
- **Mass Airflow (MAF) Sensor**—is located in the air induction duct work, near the left of the engine.
- **MAT Sensor**—See Manifold Air Temperature Sensor.
- **Negative Junction Block**—is located ahead of the strut, on the right hand side of the engine compartment.
- **Oil Light Relay**—is located in the relay center.
- **Oil Pressure Sensor/Switch**—is located on the lower right hand rear of the engine.
- **Oxygen Sensor**—is located on the exhaust manifold.
- **Photocell Sensor**—is mounted at the speaker grille.
- **Positive Junction Block**—is located on a bracket, on the right hand side of the firewall.
- **Power Antenna Relay**—is located below the antenna mast, in the right side of the trunk compartment.
- **Power Door Lock Relay**—is located in the relay center, at position 'B'.
- **Power Door Lock Relay Assembly (early 1989)**—is located behind the right hand side of the instrument panel, on the left of the relay center.
- **Power Door Un-Lock Relay**—is located in the relay center, at position 'E'.
- **Relay Center**—is located under the right hand side of the instrument panel.
- **Remote Dimmer Module**—is located under the left hand side of the instrument panel, at the kick panel.
- **Seatbelt Lap Retractor Solenoids**—are located in the lower rear portion of the front doors.
- **Seatbelt Retractor Module**—is located at the right hand kick panel, under the instrument panel.
- **Seatbelt Retractor Switches**—are located in the center rear of the front doors, at the latch assembly.
- **Seatbelt Shoulder Retractor Solenoids**—are located in the lower rear portion of the front doors.
- **Seatbelt Switch**—is part of the driver's seatbelt assembly.
- **Seatbelt Time Delay Module**—are located in the center of the front doors, if so equipped.
- **Starter Interrupt Relay**—is located under the left hand side of the instrument panel, above the accelerator pedal.
- **Starter Solenoid**—is located on the lower front of the engine.
- **Sun Roof Limit Switch**—is located in the roof above the left hand 'A' pillar.
- **Sunroof Relay**—is located at the top center of the windshield header.
- **Theft Deterrent Controller**—is located behind the left hand side of the instrument panel, above the accelerator.
- **Theft Deterrent Diode**—is located behind the left hand side of the instrument panel, taped to the harness.
- **Theft Deterrent Relay**—is located behind the left hand side of the instrument panel, above the accelerator.
- **Throttle Position Sensor**—is located on the left hand side of the throttle body.
- **Torque Converter Clutch Brake Switch**—is located on the brake pedal support, under the instrument panel.
- **TPS**—See Throttle Position Sensor.
- **Transaxle Position Switch**—is located on the left hand rear of the engine, on top of the transaxle.
- **Turn Signal Relay**—is located at the left of the steering column, behind the instrument panel.
- **Twilight Sentinel Amplifier**—is mounted on the right hand side of the steering column bracket.
- **Twilight Sentinel Photocell**—is mounted on the top right hand side of the instrument panel.
- **Vapor Canister Purge Solenoid**—is located in the left hand front corner of the engine compartment.
- **Vehicle Speed Sensor Buffer**—is located behind the right hand side of the instrument panel, on the right hand side of the A/C plenum.
- **Vehicle Speed Sensor**—is located on the right hand side of the transaxle.
- **Washer Motor Module**—is located on the right hand side of the engine compartment, at the bottom of the washer reservoir.
- **Washer Pump Motor Diode**—is located in the washer motor connector.
- **Window Circuit Breaker**—is located at the top right corner of the fuse block.
- **Window Down Express Module**—is located in the door.
- **Wiper Motor Module**—is located on the left hand corner of the firewall in the engine compartment.
- **Wiper Motor Relay Diode**—is located in the wiper motor connector, the relay is incorporated into the wiper module.
- **Wiper/Washer Fluid Level Sensor**—is located in the washer fluid reservoir.

FIREBIRD

- **A/C Blower High Speed Relay**—is located near the blower motor on the A/C module.
- **A/C Blower Resistors**—are located near the blower motor on the A/C module.
- **A/C Compressor Diode**—is taped to the inside of the compressor clutch connector or wiring harness.
- **A/C Compressor Relay**—is located on the left side engine firewall, on the relay bracket.

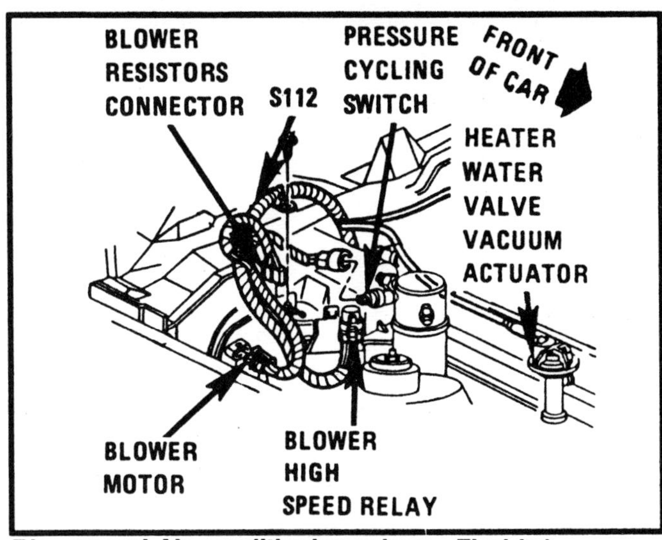

Blower and Air conditioning relays – Firebird

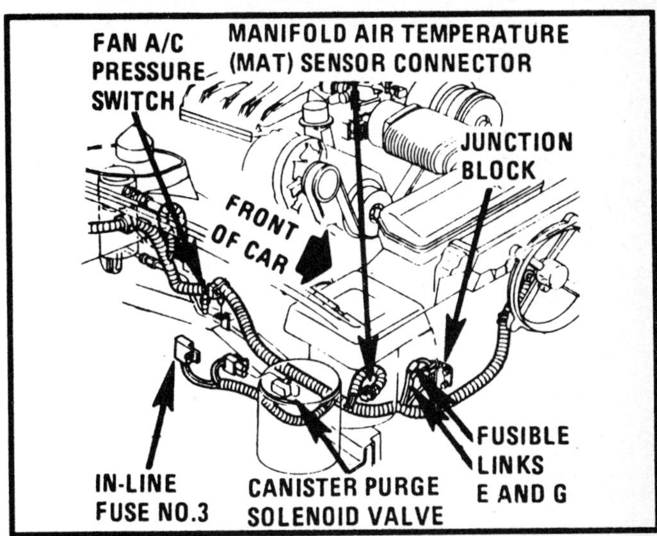

Fusible links – Firebird with 3.1L VIN T engine

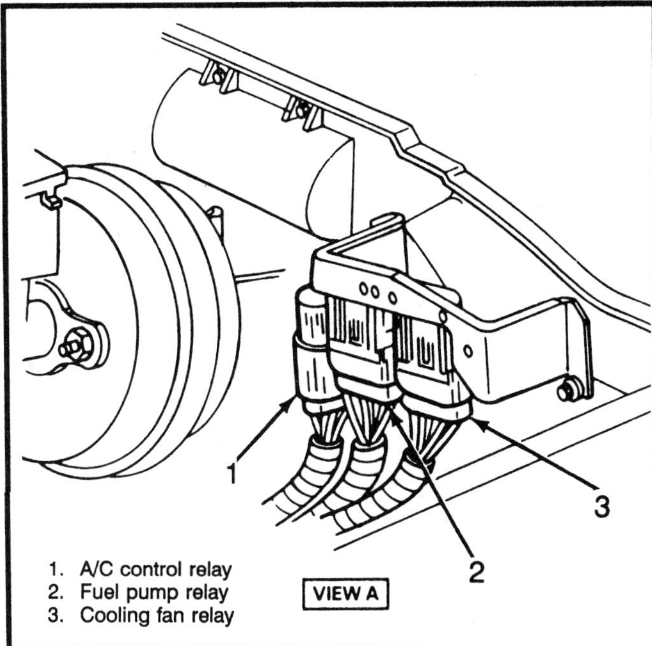

Relays – Firebird

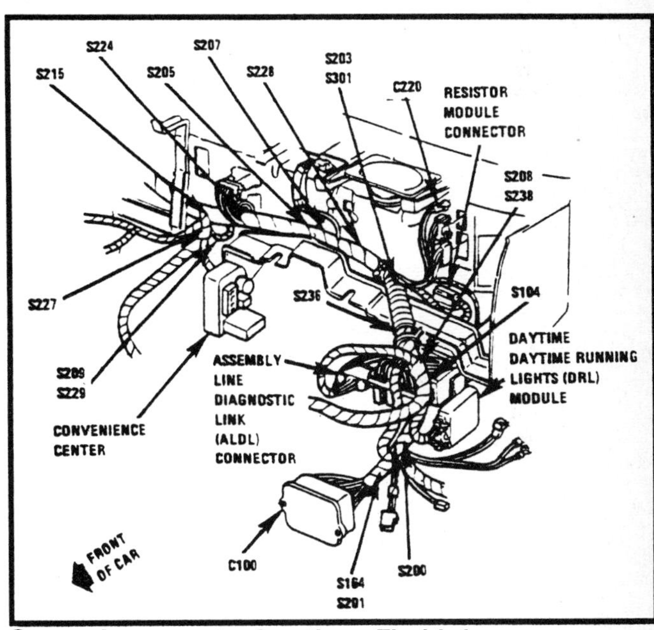

Convenience center location – Firebird

- **A/C Cooling Fan Pressure Switch** – is on the right side of the engine compartment, on the A/C line.
- **A/C Heater/Defrost Vacuum Motor** – is located under the right hand side of the instrument panel, on the left hand side of the A/C plenum.
- **A/C High Pressure Switch** – is located behind the A/C compressor.
- **A/C Lower Mode Vacuum Motor** – is located under the right hand side of the instrument panel, on the lower left hand side of the A/C plenum.
- **A/C Pressure Cycling Switch** – is located on the accumulator/drier.
- **A/C Recirculating/Outside Air Vacuum Motor** – is located under the instrument panel, on the rear of the air intake assembly.
- **A/C Upper Mode Vacuum Motor** – is located under the right hand side of the instrument panel, on the left hand side of the A/C plenum.
- **A/C Vacuum Tank** – is located on the front left hand side of the firewall, if equipped.
- **Air Diverter Valve** – is located on the right hand front of the engine.
- **Air Select Valve (VIN S)** – is located on the right hand valve cover.
- **Air Select Valve** – is located on the right hand front of the engine.
- **Alternator Diode (Isolation)** – is located in the wiring harness, near the fuse block.
- **Assembly Line Diagnostic Link** – is located under the left hand side of the instrument panel, to the right of the steering column.
- **Audio Alarm Assembly** – is located in the convenience center.
- **Auxiliary Coolant Fan Relay (VIN H)** – is located in the right hand front corner of the engine compartment.
- **Auxiliary Coolant Fan Switch (VIN H)** – is located on the lower right hand rear of the engine.

• **Auxiliary Coolant Fan Switch** – is on the lower right side of the engine.

• **Auxiliary Cooling Fan Relay** – is at the left front of the dash on the relay bracket.

• **Back** – Up Switch – is located on the left hand side of the transaxle.

• **Barometric Pressure Sensor (VIN H)** – is located on the top right side of the engine firewall.

• **Brake Fluid Level Sensor** – is located on the left hand side of the brake fluid reservoir.

• **Brake Pressure Switch** – is located on the left hand side of the brake fluid reservoir.

• **Brake Release Relay** – is taped to the harness, behind the right hand side of the instrument panel.

• **Burn Off Relay** – is located in the left hand rear corner of the engine compartment, on a relay bracket.

• **Canister Purge Solenoid Valve (VIN T)** – is on the right front of the engine compartment.

• **Canister Purge Solenoid** – is located in the left hand front corner of the engine compartment, on top of the canister.

• **Clutch Start Switch** – is located behind the clutch pedal, below the clutch pedal support.

• **Cold Start Injector** – is located on the top rear of the engine.

• **Cold Start Switch** – is located on the top front of the engine.

• **Convenience Center** – is located under the left hand side of the instrument panel, to the right of the steering column.

• **Coolant Fan Pressure Switch** – is located in the lower right hand front corner of the engine compartment, on the refrigerant line.

• **Coolant Fan Relay (VIN E and S)** – is located on the left hand front side of the firewall, on the relay bracket.

• **Coolant Fan Relay (VIN F and 8)** – is located on the right hand rear side of the radiator.

• **Coolant Fan Sensor (VIN T)** – is located on the top of the engine, under the intake plenum.

• **Coolant Fan Switch (except VIN S)** – is located in the lower right hand side of the engine.

• **Coolant Fan Switch (VIN S)** – is located on the top right hand rear side of the engine.

• **Coolant Temperature Sensor (VIN E and S)** – is located on the top left hand front side of the engine.

• **Coolant Temperature Sensor (VIN F and 8)** – is located on the top right hand side of the engine.

• **Coolant Temperature Switch (VIN S)** – is located on the top left hand front side of the engine.

• **Coolant Temperature Switch** – is located on the left hand side of the engine, below the valve cover.

• **Cruise Control Module** – is located behind the right hand center side of the instrument panel.

• **Cruise Control Servo** – is located in the left hand front corner of the engine compartment.

• **Cruise Control Vacuum Tank** – is located in the left hand front corner of the engine compartment.

• **Daytime Running Light Module** – is behind the left instrument panel, near the fuse box.

• **Defogger Timer/Relay** – is behind the right side of the instrument panel.

• **Diagnostic Dwell Meter Connector (VIN H)** – is taped next to the ECM harness, behind the right wheel well.

• **Driver Information Center Module** – is located under the right side of the instrument panel, above the plenum, if so equipped.

• **EGR Solenoid** – is on the top right hand rear of the engine.

• **EGR Vacuum Sensor Diagnostic Connector (VIN F)** – is on the top of the engine, in the vacuum line to the EGR valve.

• **Electronic Control Module (ECM)** – is located behind the right side of the instrument panel.

• **Electronic Spark Control Module** – is located on the left side of the engine firewall.

• **Electronic Vacuum Regulator** – is on the top right hand rear section of the engine.

• **Fog Light Relay** – is located in the upper left hand front fender or the left rear corner of the engine compartment. The 1991 vehicle have the relay behind the instrument panel near the fuse box.

• **Fuel Pump In-Line Fuse** – is located on the right front wheelwell, if so equipped.

• **Fuel Pump Prime Connector (except E)** – is left front of cowl, near the relay bracket.

• **Fuel Pump Relay** – is located in the left hand rear corner of the engine compartment, on the relay bracket.

• **Fuel Pump Switch** – is located on the lower left hand side of the engine.

• **Fuel Pump/Oil Pressure Sender Switch (Except VIN E)** – is on the lower left side of the engine.

• **Fuel Pump/Oil Pressure Sender Switch (VIN E)** – is on the lower rear left side of the engine.

• **Fuel Pump/Oil Pressure Sender/Switch** – is located on the top center rear of the engine.

• **Fuse Box** – is behind the left side of the instrument panel.

• **Fusible Links** – most fusible links are located at the starter solenoid. But other locations include the junction block at the right front of the engine compartment, next to the battery and near the alternator.

• **Gear Selector Switch** – is located in the console at the gear selector.

• **Hatch Contact Assembly** – is located in the rear of the vehicle, top center of the end panel, in the cargo compartment.

• **Hatch Pull Down Unit** – is located in the center of the end panel, in the cargo compartment.

• **Hatch Release Relay (1989)** – is located under the front part of the console.

• **Hatch Release Relay (except 1989)** – is located behind the right side of the instrument panel.

• **Hatch Release Solenoid** – is located in the center of the end panel, in the cargo compartment.

• **Hazard Relay** – is located on the convenience center.

• **Headlight Dimmer Switch** – is located on the left hand side of the steering column.

• **Headlight Door Module** – is located on the left hand side of the firewall, next to the wiper motor.

• **Heater Blower Resistors** – are located on the near blower motor.

• **Heavy Duty Coolant Fan Relay (VIN F and 8)** – is located in the right hand rear corner of the engine compartment.

• **Heavy Duty Coolant Fan Relay (VIN H)** – is located in the right hand rear corner of the engine compartment.

• **Heavy Duty Coolant Fan Switch (VIN F and 8)** – is located in the right hand rear corner of the engine.

• **Heavy Duty Coolant Fan Switch (VIN H)** – is located in the right hand rear corner of the engine compartment.

• **Hood Louver Solenoid** – is located on the left side of the hood louver assembly.

• **Horn Relay** – is located in the convenience center.

• **Idle Air Control Stepper Motor** – is located on the top of the engine, near the throttle body.

• **Ignition In-Line Fuse (No. 1)** – is located at the right hand front of the firewall.

• **Ignition In-Line Fuse (No. 2)** – is located at the battery.

• **Ignition In-Line Fuse (No. 3)** – is located on the right hand inner fender panel, near the battery.

• **Ignition In-Line Fuse (No. 4)** – is located on the right hand inner fender panel, near the battery.

• **Ignition Key Warning Switch** – is located in the steering column, near the key cylinder.

• **Ignition Switch** – is located at the top of the steering column.

• **Isolation Relay** – is located behind the right headlight.

• **Junction Block**—is located on the right side of the radiator support bracket.
• **Knock Sensor (VIN T)**—is on the lower right side of the engine.
• **Knock Sensor**—is located on the lower right side of the engine, near the starter solenoid.
• **Light Monitor Module**—is located behind the left side of the instrument panel, at the base of the steering column.
• **Low Blower Relay**—is located on the right side of the firewall, near the blower motor.
• **Lumbar Seat Air Pump Assembly**—is located under the right and left front seats.
• **Lumbar Seat Air Pump Motor Relay**—is located under the left hand front seat.
• **Lumbar Seat Air Pump Motor**—is located under the left hand front seat.
• **Manifold Absolute Pressure (MAP) Sensor**—is located on the air cleaner or at the rear center of the engine compartment.
• **Manifold Air Temperature (MAT) Sensor (except E)**—is located on the front of the air cleaner assembly.
• **Manifold Air Temperature Sensor (VIN E)**—is located on the top right hand rear of the engine.
• **Manifold Vacuum Switch**—is located on the firewall, to the left of the vacuum tank.
• **MAP Sensor**—See Manifold Absolute Pressure (MAP) Mass Air Flow Relay (VIN F and 8)—is located on the relay bracket, in the left hand rear corner of the engine compartment.
• **Mass Air Flow Relay (VIN S)**—is located on the right side of the radiator support bracket.
• **Mass Air Flow Sensor (VIN F and 8)**—is located on the top of the engine, on the air intake duct.
• **Mass Air Flow Sensor (VIN S)**—is located on the air intake duct, located before the throttle body.
• **Mass Air Flow Sensor In-Line Fuse**—is located in the right front corner of the engine compartment.
• **Mass Air Temperature Sensor (VIN F and 8)**—is located on top rear of the engine, on the air intake shroud.
• **MAT Sensor**—See Manifold Air Temperature (MAT) Sensor.
• **Oil Pressure Switch (VIN S)**—is located on the lower left hand side of the engine.
• **Oil Pressure Switch**—is located on the top rear center of the engine.
• **Oxygen Sensor**—is located in the exhaust manifold/ Power Accessories Circuit Breaker—is located in the fuse block.
• **Power Antenna Relay**—is located behind the right side of the instrument panel, near the ECM.
• **Power Door Lock Relay Assembly**—is located behind the left kick panel in the lower opening.
• **Power Steering Switch**—is at the left front of the engine compartment.
• **Power Steering Switch**—is located on the left hand front of the engine compartment.
• **Power Window/Rear Wiper Circuit Breaker**—is located in the fuse block.
• **Radio Capacitor**—is located on the right hand side of the firewall, near the blower motor.
• **Radio Sub**—Woofer Amplifier—is located under the right hand center of the instrument panel, to the right of the center air vent.
• **Rear Defogger Timer/Relay**—is located below the right side of the instrument panel, near the ECM.
• **Redundant Coolant Fan Switch (5.0L EFI)**—is located on the engine, near the distributor.
• **Remote Dimmer Module**—is located under the left hand side of the instrument panel, at the right side of the steering column.
• **Resistance Wire**—is located under the left side of the instrument panel, near the ignition switch.
• **Road Rally Assembly**—is located behind the right hand side of the instrument panel, below the glove box.
• **Seat Belt Warning Buzzer**—is located in the convenience center, if so equipped.
• **Seatbelt Switch**—is part of the driver's seatbelt assembly.
• **SIR DERM**—is behind the right side of the instrument panel.
• **SIR Resistor Module**—is behind the left side of the instrument panel.
• **Starter Enable Relay**—is located below the left side of the instrument panel, on the kick panel.
• **Starter Enable Relay**—is located on the left side of the steering column, under the instrument panel.
• **Starter Solenoid**—is located on the lower right hand side of the engine.
• **Tachometer Filter**—is located on the top rear of the engine, near the distributor.
• **Throttle Kicker Relay (VIN H)**—is located on the right hand side of the radiator bracket, in the front of the engine compartment.
• **Throttle Position Sensor**—is located on the top front section of the engine.
• **Transaxle Converter Clutch (TCC) Solenoid**—is located in the transaxle assembly.
• **Turn Signal Flasher**—is located on the right hand side of the steering column.
• **Vacuum Sensor (VIN H)**—is located on the upper left side of the engine firewall.
• **VATS Decoder Module**—is located under the left hand side of the instrument panel, above the steering column.
• **Vehicle Speed Sensor Buffer**—is behind the left side of the instrument panel.
• **Vehicle Speed Sensor Buffer**—is taped to the dashboard wiring harness, near the bulkhead connector.
• **Vehicle Speed Sensor**—is located on the printed circuit at the rear of the speedometer.
• **Vehicle Speed Sensor**—is located on the printed circuit at the rear of the speedometer on most models. On tuned and multiport injection it is located on the left side of the transmission below the shifter.
• **Wide Open Throttle Relay**—is located in the left rear corner of the engine compartment.
• **Wiper/Washer Fluid Level Switch**—is located on the washer reservoir, in the engine compartment.
• **Wiper/Washer Motor Module**—is located on the upper left side of the engine firewall.

GRAND AM

• **A/C Compressor Clutch Diode**—is located in the connector at the compressor clutch.
• **A/C Compressor Control Relay**—is located on the relay bracket at the center of the firewall in the engine compartment.
• **A/C Cooling Fan Relay**—is located on the relay bracket at the center of the firewall in the engine compartment.
• **A/C Cut**—Out Relay—is located on the relay bracket at the center of the firewall in the engine compartment.
• **A/C Defrost Valve Vacuum Actuator**—is located under the center of the instrument panel.
• **A/C Dual Pressure Switch**—is located on A/C line, on the right hand front of the radiator.
• **A/C Heater Blower Motor Relay**—is located on the right side of the firewall in the engine compartment, to the left of the blower motor.
• **A/C Heater Valve Vacuum Actuator**—is located under the center of the instrument panel.
• **A/C High Pressure Cutout Switch**—is located on the left end of the compressor.
• **A/C Low Pressure Cutout Switch**—is located on the left end of the compressor.

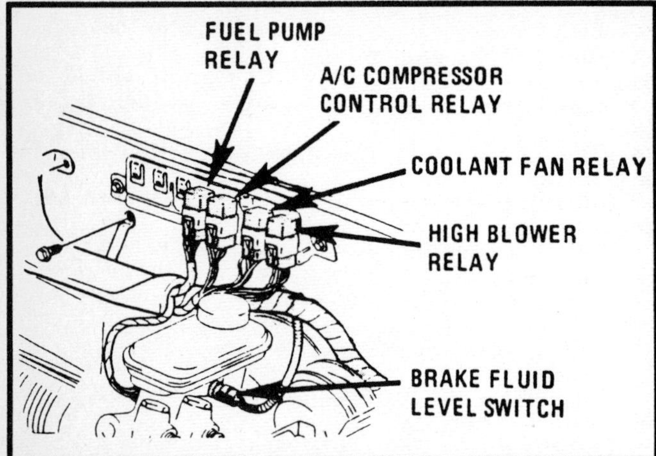

Relay locations—Grand AM

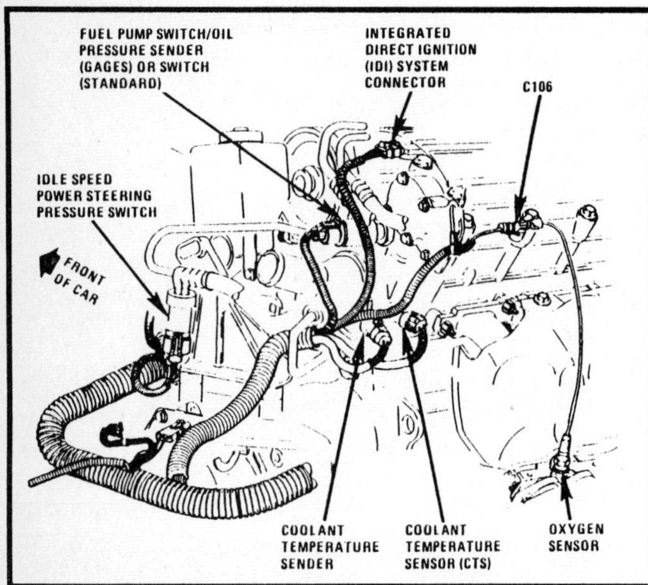

Coolant temperature locations—Grand AM

- **A/C Outside Air Valve Vacuum Actuator**—is located under the center of the instrument panel.
- **A/C Pressure Cycling Switch (VIN M)**—is located on the right hand front of the firewall.
- **A/C Vacuum Tank**—is located behind the center of the instrument panel, on vehicle without cruise control.
- **Assembly Line Diagnostic (ALDL) Link**—is located behind the left hand side of the instrument panel, to the left of the steering column.
- **Audio Alarm Module**—is located on the fuse block or above the glove box.
- **Audio Amplifier**—is located behind the center of the instrument panel.
- **Back**—Up Switch (M/T)—is located on the left hand end of the transaxle.
- **Blower Resistors**—are located on the right hand side of the firewall, in the blower module.
- **Brake Fluid Level Switch**—is located on the left hand side of the firewall, in the brake fluid reservoir.
- **Canister Purge Solenoid**—is located on the vapor canister, in the right hand front of the engine compartment.
- **Clutch Start Switch**—is located above the clutch pedal, on the clutch pedal support.
- **Coolant Temperature Sender/Switch (VIN M)**—is located at the top left hand side of the engine, near the distributor.
- **Coolant Temperature Sender/Switch (VIN U)**—is located at the top left hand side of the engine.
- **Coolant Temperature Sensor (VIN A and D)**—is located at the top left rear of the engine, near the coolant outlet.
- **Coolant Temperature Sensor (VIN M)**—at the top right front engine.
- **Coolant Temperature Sensor (VIN M)**—is located at the top right hand front of the engine.
- **Coolant Temperature Sensor (VIN U)**—is located at the top left hand front of the engine.
- **Cooling Fan Relay**—is located is located on the relay bracket at the center of the firewall in the engine compartment.
- **Crankshaft Position Sensor (VIN A and D)**—at the front center of engine, above the oil filter.
- **Cruise Control Brake/Switch**—is located above the brake pedal on the brake pedal support bracket.
- **Cruise Control Check Valve (VIN A and D)**—at the right front of the engine compartment.
- **Cruise Control Check Valve (VIN M)**—is located in the center of the firewall, near the intake manifold.
- **Cruise Control Check Valve (VIN U)**—is located in the lower left hand rear corner of the engine compartment.
- **Cruise Control Clutch/Switch**—is located above the clutch pedal on the clutch pedal support bracket.
- **Cruise Control Module**—is attached under the rear of the left side of the dash panel, near the shroud.
- **Cruise Control Servo**—is located near the left hand strut tower in the engine compartment.
- **Cruise Control Vacuum Tank**—is located in the lower left hand front corner of the engine compartment.
- **CTS**—See Coolant Temperature Sensor.
- **Daytime Running Light (DRL) Module**—is located at the left front of the engine compartment.
- **Defogger Timer Relay**—is located behind the left side of the instrument panel, near the fuse block.
- **Detonation (Knock) Sensor (VIN A, D and U)**—is located at the lower rear of the engine.
- **Direct Ignition System (DIS)**—is located at the left hand rear of the engine.
- **Driver Information Center (DIC) Display Module**—is located in the center of the dash, below the radio.
- **Driver Information Center Lights Monitor Module**—is located behind the center of the dash panel, near the radio.
- **EGR Electronic Vacuum Regulator Valve (EVRV)**—at the top rear of engine.
- **Electronic Control Module (ECM)**—is located behind the right side kick panel.
- **Electronic Vacuum Regulator Valve (VIN M)**—is located on the top rear of the engine.
- **Exhaust Gas Recirculating (EGR) Valve**—at the top center of engine.
- **Fog Light Relay**—is located on the left front inner fender panel, in front of the shock tower.
- **Fuel Pump Prime Connector (A, D and U)**—is located on the left rear of the engine compartment, taped to the wiring harness.
- **Fuel Pump Prime Connector (VIN M)**—is located on the left hand side of the engine compartment, near the transaxle.
- **Fuel Pump Relay**—is located on the relay bracket at the center of the firewall in the engine compartment.
- **Fuel Pump/Oil Pressure Switch (VIN A and D)**—is located on the top left side of the engine.
- **Fuel Pump/Oil Pressure Switch (VIN U)**—at the lower rear of engine, above the transaxle.

- **Gear Selector Switch**—is located on the top of the left hand of the transaxle.
- **Hazard Flasher**—is located behind the center of the instrument panel, near the radio.
- **Headlight Dimmer Switch**—is located behind the instrument panel, to the left of the steering column.
- **High Blower Relay**—is located on the relay bracket on the center of the firewall in the engine compartment.
- **High Speed Coolant Fan Relay**—is located on the relay bracket on the center of the firewall in the engine compartment.
- **Horn Relay**—is taped to the instrument panel wiring harness, behind the instrument panel near the fuse block.
- **Idle Air Control Valve (VIN M and L)**—is located on the left hand side of the engine, on the left hand side of the throttle body.
- **Idle Air Control Valve (VIN U)**—is located on the top of the engine, on the left hand rear of the throttle body.
- **Ignition Key Warning Switch**—is located on the top of the steering column.
- **Ignition Switch**—is located behind the lower right side of the steering column.
- **Illumination Control Relay**—is located behind the center of the instrument panel, near the radio.
- **Integrated Direct Ignition (IDI) System**—is on the top left of the engine.
- **Light Monitor Module**—behind center of instrument panel, near the radio.
- **Low Coolant Module**—is located under the right hand side of the instrument panel, if so equipped.
- **Low Coolant Probe**—is located on the radiator, if equipped.
- **Low Coolant Switch**—is located on the right side of the engine compartment, in the surge tank.
- **Low Speed Coolant Fan Relay**—is located on the relay bracket on the center of the firewall in the engine compartment.
- **Lumbar Seat Air Pump Motor Relay**—is located under the driver's seat.
- **Lumbar Seat Air Pump Motor**—is located under the driver's seat.
- **Lumbar Seat Air Pump Valve Assemblies**—is located under the right and left front seats.
- **Manifold Absolute Pressure Sensor (VIN A and D)**—is located at the center front of the engine.
- **Manifold Absolute Pressure Sensor (VIN M)**—is located on the top of the engine, ahead of the air intake plenum.
- **Manifold Absolute Pressure (MAP) Sensor (VIN U)**—is located on the rear of the engine, on the air cleaner assembly.
- **Manifold Air Temperature Sensor (VIN A and D)**—is located on the left front of the engine, in the air intake manifold.
- **Manifold Air Temperature Sensor (VIN M)**—is located on the top of the engine, ahead of the air intake plenum.
- **Manifold Air Temperature Sensor (VIN U)**—is located on the top of the engine, near the throttle body.
- **MAP Sensor**—See Manifold Absolute Pressure Sensor.
- **MAT Sensor**—See Manifold Air Temperature Sensor.
- **Oil Pressure Switch/Sender (VIN A and D)**—is located on the top left side of the engine.
- **Oil Pressure Switch/Sender (VIN M)**—is located on the lower right hand rear of the engine.
- **Oil Pressure Switch/Sender (VIN U)**—is located on the left hand rear of the engine.
- **Oxygen Sensor (VIN M and U)**—at the front of the engine, in the exhaust manifold.
- **Oxygen Sensor (VIN A and D)**—is located in the exhaust manifold, location may vary.
- **Power Accessories Circuit Breaker**—is located in the fuse block.
- **Power Antenna Relay**—is located behind the right side of the instrument panel, near the glove box.
- **Power Door Lock Relay Assembly**—is located behind the right side kick panel.
- **Power Steering Idle Speed Switch (VIN A and D)**—is located on the lower left side of the engine, near the coolant outlet.
- **Power Steering Pressure Switch (except A and D)**—is located on the lower left side of the firewall, to the left of the brake booster.
- **Power Window Circuit Breaker**—is located in the fuse block.
- **Remote Dimmer Module**—is located behind the instrument panel, to the right of the steering column.
- **Seat Belt Indicator Driver Module**—is located behind the left hand side of the instrument panel, near the fuse block.
- **Seat Belt Lap Retractor Solenoid**—are located in the rear of each front door.
- **Seat Belt Retractor Switches**—are located in the rear of each front door, on the latch assembly.
- **Seat Belt Shoulder Retractor Solenoids**—are located in the rear of each front door.
- **Seat Belt Switch**—is part of the driver's seatbelt assembly.
- **Starter Solenoid (except VIN M)**—is located on the lower left hand front of the engine.
- **Starter Solenoid (VIN M)**—is located on the lower rear of the engine.
- **Tachometer Filter**—is located in the left hand front of the engine compartment, behind the battery.
- **Throttle Position Sensor**—is located on the throttle body.
- **Trunk Ajar Switch**—is located on the rear of the trunk lid.
- **Trunk Release Solenoid**—is located on the center of the trunk lid.
- **Turn Signal Flasher**—is located under the left hand side of the instrument panel, to the left of the steering column.
- **Turn/Stop Relays**—are located in the left hand side of trunk.
- **Vehicle Speed Sensor (ATX)**—is located at the rear of the engine, on the right end of the transaxle.
- **Vehicle Speed Sensor (MTX)**—is located at the rear of the engine, on the top of the transaxle.
- **Vehicle Speed Sensor Buffer**—is located behind the left side of the instrument panel, near the fuse block.
- **Washer Fluid Level Switch**—is located on the left front inner fender panel, in front of the strut tower.
- **Waste Gate Solenoid (VIN M)**—is located on the right side of the throttle body.
- **Waste Gate Solenoid (VIN M)**—at the top of engine, near throttle body.
- **Wiper/Washer Motor Module**—is located on the left side of the firewall.

GRAND PRIX

- **A/C Air Temperature Valve Motor**—is located under the instrument panel, on the right hand side of the plenum.
- **A/C Bi-Level Valve Vacuum Actuator**—is located under the instrument panel, on the right hand side of the plenum.
- **A/C Compressor Clutch Diode**—is taped to the inside compressor connector on the front of the compressor or near the connector in the wiring harness.
- **A/C Compressor Control Relay**—is located in the right side electrical center.
- **A/C Heater/Defroster Bi-Directional Valve Vacuum Actuator**—is located under the instrument panel, on the right hand side of the plenum.
- **A/C High Blower Relay**—is located in the component center.
- **A/C Intermediate Pressure Switch (VIN W)**—is located on the accumulator/drier, in the left hand side of the engine compartment.

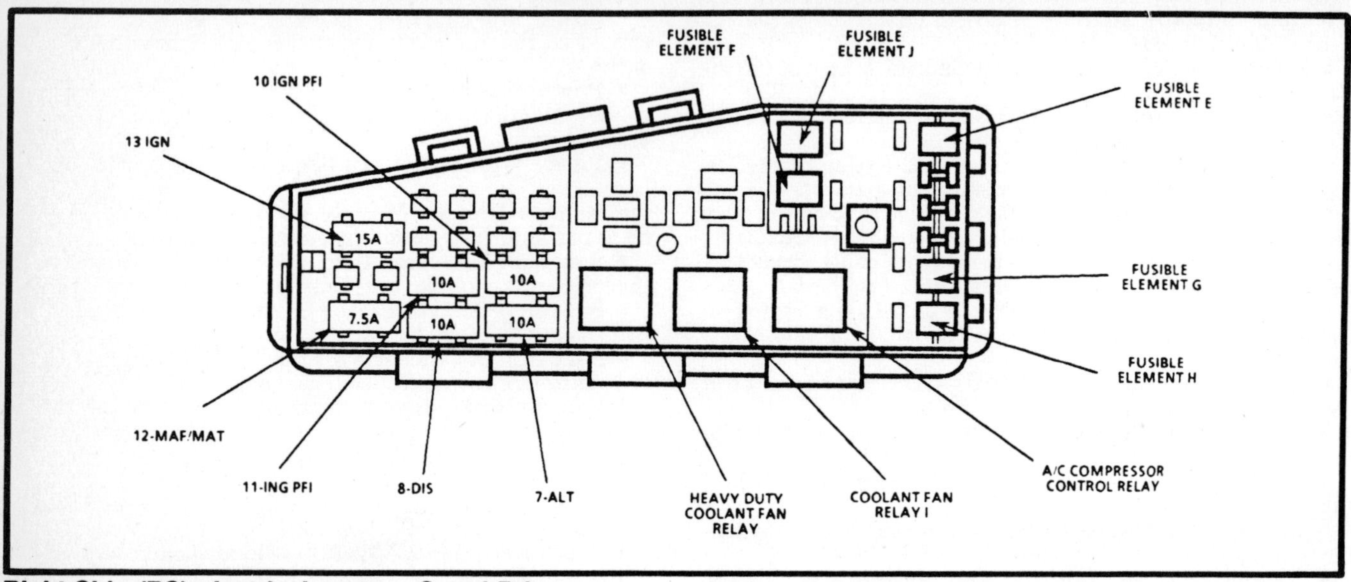

Right Side (RS) electrical center—Grand Prix

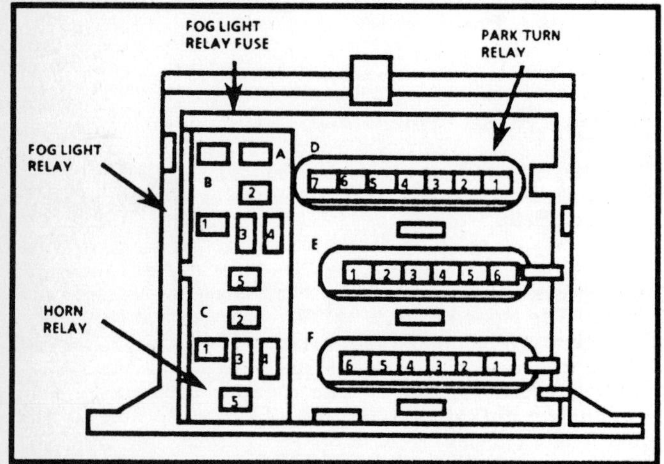

Forward light electrical center—Grand Prix

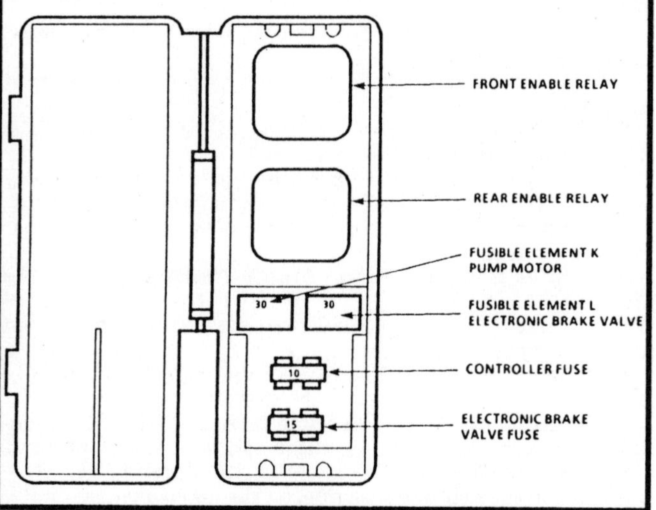

Anti-lock brake power center—Grand Prix

- **A/C Low Blower Relay**—is located in the component center.
- **A/C Pressure Cycling Switch**—is located on the accumulator/drier.
- **A/C Pressure Transducer**—is on the top left side of the engine.
- **A/C Recirculating Valve Vacuum Actuator**—is located under the instrument panel, on the right hand end of the plenum.
- **A/C Solenoid Box**—is located under the instrument panel, on the right hand end of the plenum.
- **A/C Vent Valve Vacuum Actuator**—is located under A/C-Blower Resistors—is located in the engine compartment on the right side of the firewall near the blower motor.
- **A/C-High Pressure Cutout Switch**—is located on the left end of the compressor.
- **A/C-Low Pressure Cutout Switch**—is located on the left end of the compressor.
- **Air Control Valve (VIN D)**—is on the top left side of the engine.
- **Air Diverter Valve**—is located on the right hand front of the engine, in front of the valve cover, near the air pump.
- **Air Select Valve**—is located on the right hand front of the engine, in front of the valve cover, near the air pump.
- **Antilock Brake Control**—is under the right front seat.
- **Antenna Motor**—is behind the right rear wheelhousing.
- **Antenna Relay**—is behind the right rear wheelhousing.
- **Antilock Brake Power Center**—is located at the front left of the engine compartment.
- **Assembly Line Data Link (ALDL) Connector**—is located under the left hand side of the instrument panel, to the right of steering column.
- **Back**—Up Switch—is located on the transaxle column.
- **Battery Junction Block**—is located on the right inner fender panel, behind the battery.
- **Brake Fluid Level Switch**—is located on the left hand side of the brake fluid reservoir.
- **Brake Pressure Switch**—is located on the left hand side of the brake fluid reservoir.
- **Canister Purge Solenoid (VIN D)**—is located at the top front of the engine.
- **Canister Purge Solenoid (VIN W and T)**—is located in

the right hand front corner of the engine compartment, on the canister.

- **Chime Module**—is located in the component center.
- **Clutch Start Switch**—is located above the clutch pedal, on the clutch pedal support.
- **Component Center**—is located under the right hand side of the instrument panel, behind the glove box.
- **Convenience Center**—See Component Center.
- **Coolant Fan Relay (VIN W and T)**—is located in the right side electrical center.
- **Coolant Fan Relays (VIN D)**—are located in the right side electrical center.
- **Coolant Level and Corrosivity (VIN W)**—is located on the top right hand rear of the radiator.
- **Coolant Temperature Sender/Switch (VIN W)**—is located on the left hand side of the engine, below the coolant outlet.
- **Coolant Temperature Sensor (VIN W)**—is located on the left hand side of the engine, below the coolant outlet.
- **Coolant Temperature Switch (VIN A and D)**—is located on the left side of the engine, near the coolant outlet.
- **Crankshaft Sensor (VIN D)**—is located on the lower front of the engine, near the oil filter.
- **Crankshaft Sensor (VIN T)**—is located on the on the right hand front of the engine, above the oil filter.
- **Crankshaft Sensor (VIN W)**—is located on the on the right hand front of the engine, below the direct ignition system.
- **Cruise Control Brake/Switch**—is located above the brake pedal on the brake pedal support bracket.
- **Cruise Control Check Valve**—is located in the vacuum line, in front of the left hand strut tower.
- **Cruise Control Module**—is located above the brake pedal on the brake pedal support bracket.
- **Cruise Control Servo**—is located in front of the left hand strut tower, in the engine compartment.
- **Cruise Control Vacuum Release Valve**—is located above the brake pedal on the brake pedal support bracket.
- **Cruise Control Vacuum Tank**—is located in the left hand front corner of the engine compartment.
- **Daytime Running Light Module**—is behind the left side of the instrument panel to the left of the steering column, near the courtesy lamp.
- **Defogger Time Relay**—is located in the component center.
- **Detonation (Knock) Sensor (VIN D)**—is located on the lower left rear of the engine.
- **Detonation (Knock) Sensor (VIN W and T)**—is located on the right rear of the right hand rear of the engine, below the exhaust manifold.
- **Diode (Headlamp) Assembly**—is to the left of the steering column, near the courtesy lamp.
- **Direct Ignition System (VIN W)**—is located on the on the right hand front of the engine, below the exhaust manifold.
- **Electronic Control Module (ECM) Fuse**—is located in the right electrical center.
- **Electronic Control Module (ECM)**—is located on the right hand strut tower, in the engine compartment.
- **Electronic Vacuum Regulator Valve (VIN W)**—is on the top right hand rear section of the engine.
- **Engine Oil Pressure Sender/Switch (except W)**—is located on the top center rear of the engine This location can vary.
- **Engine Oil Pressure Sender/Switch (VIN W)**—is located on the right hand front of the engine, above the oil filter.
- **Exhaust Gas Recirculation Solenoid (VIN D)**—is located at the left rear of the engine on the exhaust manifold.
- **Fog Light Relay**—is located in the forward light electrical center.
- **Forward Light Electrical Center**—is located on the right hand front of the engine compartment.
- **Fuel Pump Prime Connector**—is taped to the wiring harness, below the left side electrical center.
- **Fuel Pump Relay**—is located in the left side electrical center.
- **Fuel Pump/Oil Pressure Switch (VIN D)**—is located on the left side of the engine above the coolant outlet.
- **Fuel Pump/Oil Pressure Switch (VIN W and T)**—is located on the lower right hand front side of the engine, near the oil filter.
- **Gear Selector Switch**—is located on the lower part of the steering column.
- **Hazard Flasher/Relay**—is in the component center.
- **Headlight Dimmer Switch**—is located behind the instrument panel, on the left hand side of the steering column.
- **Heater Blower Resistors**—are located on the right hand front firewall, on the heater module.
- **Heater Water Valve**—is located on the rear of the engine in the heater hose.
- **Horn Relay**—is located in the forward light electrical center.
- **Idle Air Control Motor**—is located on the top of the engine, on or near the throttle body.
- **Ignition Key Warning Switch**—is located on the top of the steering column.
- **Ignition Switch**—is located at the lower right hand side of the steering column.
- **Integrated Direct Ignition System (IDIS)**—is on the top left side of the engine.
- **Keyless Entry Module**—is located at the right rear of the luggage compartment on the rear window panel.
- **Left Side Electrical Center**—is located on the left hand strut tower, in the engine compartment.
- **Lumbar Seat Air Pump Motor**—is located under the driver's seat.
- **Lumbar Seat Air Pump Valve Assemblies**—is located under the right and left front seats.
- **Lumbar Seat Control Module**—is located under the driver's seat.
- **Manifold Absolute Pressure (MAP) Sensor (VIN D)**—is located at the top front of the engine.
- **Manifold Absolute Pressure (MAP) Sensor (VIN W and T)**—is located on the on the air intake plenum, top of the engine.
- **Manifold Air Temperature (MAT) Sensor (VIN D)**—is located on lower front of the engine.
- **Manifold Air Temperature (MAT) Sensor (VIN W and T)**—is located on the on the air intake plenum, near the right hand strut tower.
- **MAP Sensor**—See Manifold Absolute Pressure Sensor.
- **Mass Air Flow (MAF) Sensor (VIN W)**—is located on the on the air intake plenum, near the right hand strut tower.
- **MAT Sensor**—See Manifold Absolute Temperature.
- **Oil Pressure/Fuel Pump Switch (VIN D)**—is located on the left side of the engine above the coolant outlet.
- **Oil Pressure/Fuel Pump Switch (VIN W and T)**—is located on the lower right hand front side of the engine, near the oil filter.
- **Oxygen Sensor**—is located in the exhaust manifold.
- **Photoresistor**—is on the top left side of the instrument panel, near the speaker.
- **Power Accessory Circuit (30 amp) Breaker**—is located in the component center.
- **Power Antenna Relay**—is located behind the right hand rear wheel well, in the fender.
- **Power Door Lock Relay**—is at the right shroud above the access hole. On 1989 vehicles it may be located in the component center.
- **Power Seat Control Module**—is under the seat, if equipped.

• **Power Steering Pressure Switch (VIN W)** – is located on the steering gear assembly, near the input shaft.

• **Power Window Circuit (30 amp) Breaker** – is located in the component center.

• **Primary Coolant Fan Relay (VIN D)** – is located in the right side electrical Secondary Coolant Fan Relay (VIN D) – is located in the right side electrical center.

• **Radio Control Interface Module** – is located in the steering column.

• **Right Side Electrical Center** – is located on the right hand strut tower, in the engine compartment.

• **Seat Belt Lap Retractor Solenoid** – are located in the rear of each front door.

• **Seat Belt Passive Restraint Control Module** – is located behind the right hand side of the instrument panel.

• **Seat Belt Retractor Switches** – are located in the rear of each front door, on the latch assembly.

• **Seat Belt Shoulder Retractor Solenoids** – are located in the rear of each front door.

• **Seatbelt Switch** – is part of the driver's seatbelt assembly.

• **Secondary Coolant Fan Relay** – is in the right side electrical center.

• **Sun Roof/Window Circuit (30 amp) Breaker** – is located in the fuse block.

• **Sunroof Control Module** – is located at the top center of the windshield header.

• **Switch and Electronics Control Interface Module** – is located in the steering column.

• **the instrument panel, on the right hand side of the plenum.**

• **Third and Fourth Gear Switches** – are located in the middle of the left side of the transmission.

• **Throttle Position Sensor** – is located on side of the throttle body.

• **Torque Converter Clutch Solenoid** – is located in the middle of the left side of the transmission.

• **Transaxle Position Switch** – is located on the transaxle.

• **Trunk Release Solenoid** – is located in the rear center of the trunk lid.

• **Turn Signal Relay** – is located under the instrument panel, to the right of the steering column.

• **Vehicle Speed Sensor Buffer** – is taped to the instrument panel wiring under the left hand side of the instrument cluster.

• **Vehicle Speed Sensor** – is located at the side of the transaxle.

• **Wiper/Washer Motor Module** – is located on the upper left side of the engine firewall.

LEMANS

• **A/C Blower Motor and A/C Control Relay** – is located in the relay block attached to the fuse block.

• **A/C Blower Resistors** – are located on the right hand front of the firewall.

• **A/C Compressor Clutch Diode** – is taped to the inside compressor connector on the front of the compressor.

• **A/C Compressor Control Relay** – is located in the relay block attached to the fuse block.

• **A/C Defroster Valve Vacuum Actuator** – is located under the instrument panel, on the right hand side of the plenum.

• **A/C Heater Bi-Directional Valve Vacuum Actuator** – is located under the instrument panel, on the right hand side of the plenum.

• **A/C High Pressure Cut** – Out Switch – is located on the left end of the A/C compressor.

• **A/C High Pressure Switch** – is located on the left end of the A/C compressor.

• **A/C Low Pressure Cut** – Out Switch – is located on A/C line, in the lower right hand front corner of the engine compartment.

• **A/C Outside Air Valve Vacuum Actuator** – is located under the instrument panel, on the right hand side of the plenum.

• **Assembly Line Data Link Connector** – is located under the right hand side of the instrument panel, on top of the ECM, on the right hand shroud.

• **Back** – Up Light Switch – is located on the top rear of the transaxle.

• **Brake Fluid Level Switch** – is located on the left hand side of the brake fluid reservoir.

• **Brake Switch** – is located above the brake pedal on the brake pedal support bracket.

• **Charge Relay** – is behind the left side of the instrument panel, left of the fuse box.

• **Clutch Switch** – is located above the clutch pedal on the clutch pedal support bracket.

• **Coolant Fan Relay** – is located in the relay block attached to the fuse block.

• **Coolant Fan Resistor** – is located near the battery, in the left hand side of the instrument panel.

• **Coolant Temperature Sender/Switch** – is located on the top right hand rear of the engine, by the alternator.

• **Coolant Temperature Sensor (VIN 6)** – is located on the top of engine below the throttle body.

• **Coolant Temperature Sensor (VIN K)** – is at the front left side of the engine below the distributor.

• **Daytime Running Lights Relay** – is behind the center of the instrument panel.

• **Defogger Relay** – is located in the relay block attached to the fuse block.

• **Electronic Control Module (ECM)** – is located behind the right kick panel.

• **Engine Temperature Switch** – is located on the lower front of the engine.

• **Fog Light Relay** – is located in the relay block attached to the fuse block.

• **Fuel Pump Relay** – is located in the relay block attached to the fuse block.

• **Fuse block** – is located behind the left side of the instrument panel.

• **Fusible Links** – are located at the starter solenoid and on the left side of the engine compartment in front of the strut tower.

• **Hazard Flasher Relay** – is located in the relay block attached to the fuse block.

• **Idle Air Control Valve** – is located at the top of the engine on the right side of the throttle body.

• **Ignition Switch** – is located at the lower right hand side of the steering column. Passive Restraint Control Module – is behind the right side of the instrument panel.

• **Manifold Absolute Pressure Sensor** – is located on the center of the firewall.

• **Oil Pressure/Fuel Pump Switch** – is located on the lower right hand rear of the engine.

• **Oxygen Sensor** – is located on the exhaust manifold.

• **Seatbelt Switch** – is part of the driver's seatbelt assembly.

• **Throttle Position Sensor** – is located on the left hand side of the throttle body. Vehicle Speed Buffer – is on the clutch pedal support.

• **Torque Converter Clutch Solenoid** – is located in the middle of the left side of the transmission.

• **Transaxle Position Switch** – is located on the transaxle.

• **Turn Signal Relay** – is located under the instrument panel, to the right of the steering column, if so equipped. Newer models use the hazard flasher for both functions.

• **Vehicle Speed Sensor** – is located on the rear of the transaxle.

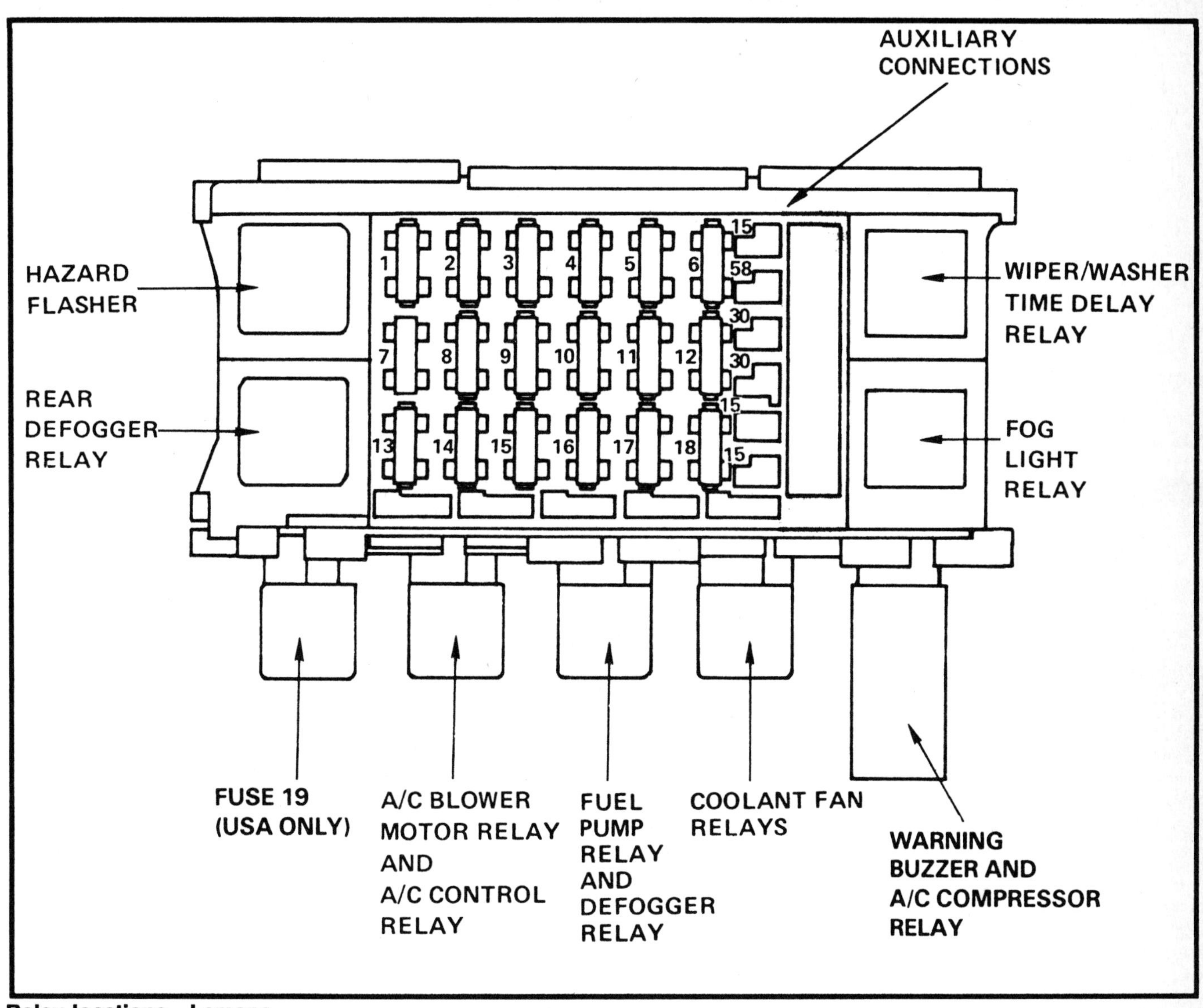

Relay locations—Lemans

• **Warning Buzzer**—is located in the relay block attached to the fuse block.

• **Wiper/Washer Time Delay Relay**—is located in the relay block attached to the fuse block.

SAFARI

• **A/C Blower Relay**—is located in the engine compartment at the right side of the firewall, near the A/C module.

• **A/C Blower Resistors**—is located in the engine compartment on the right side of the firewall near the blower motor.

• **A/C Compressor Clutch Diode**—is taped to the inside compressor connector on the front of the compressor.

• **A/C Cutout Relay**—is located on the front of the firewall, on the A/C Heater module.

• **A/C Defrost Vacuum Motor**—is located under the right hand side of the instrument panel, on the top of the A/C plenum.

• **A/C Heater Vacuum Motor**—is located under the right hand side of the instrument panel, on the left hand side of the A/C plenum.

• **A/C Pressure Cycling Switch**—is located on the accumulator/drier.

• **A/C Recirculating/Outside Air Vacuum Motor**—is located under the instrument panel, on the right hand end of the plenum.

• **A/C Vacuum Tank**—is located on the front left hand side of the firewall, on vehicles without cruise control.

• **Air Diverter Valve**—is located on the right hand front of the engine, behind the air pump..

• **Air Select Valve**—is located on the right hand front of the engine, behind the air pump.

• **Alternator Diode**—is taped to the instrument panel harness, near the fuse block.

• **Anti-Dieseling Solenoid**—is located on the top left hand front of the engine, on the valve cover.

• **Assembly Line Data Link Connector**—is located under the left side of the instrument panel, to the left of the steering column.

• **Audio Alarm Module**—is located in the convenience center, if so equipped.

• **Battery Junction Block**—is located on the right inner fender panel, behind the battery.

• **Brake Fluid Level Switch**—is located on the left hand side of the brake fluid reservoir.

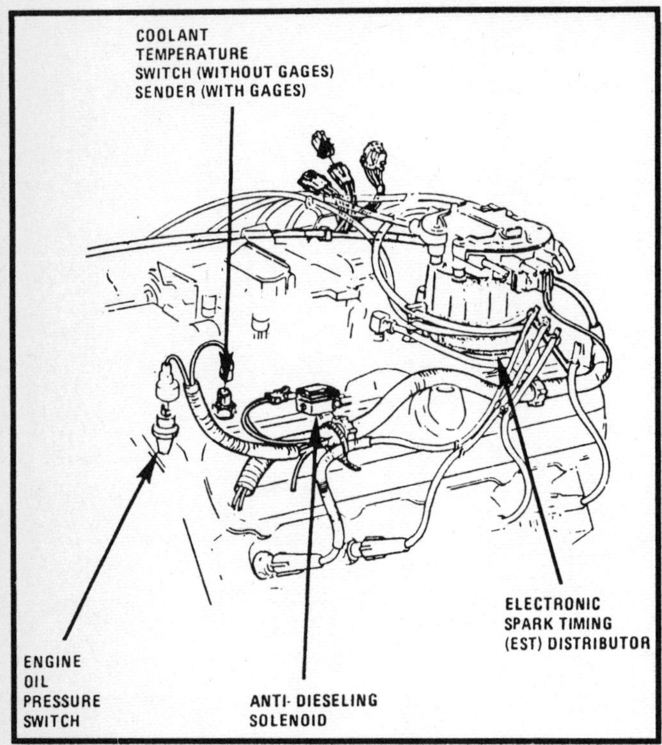

Coolant temperature sensor—Safari

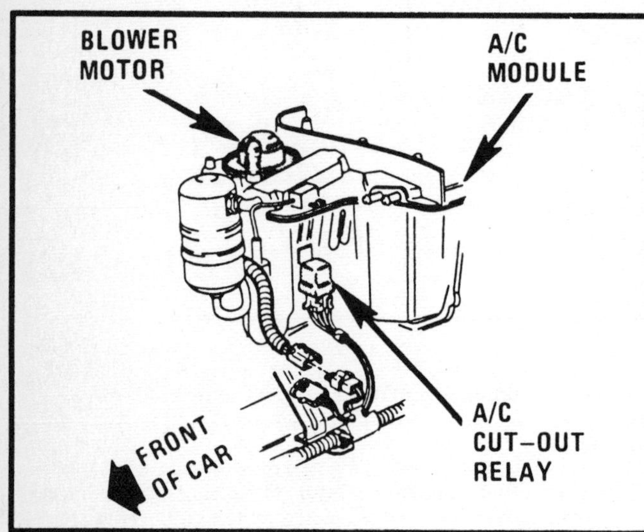

Air condition cutout relay—Safari

- **Brake Fluid Level Switch**—is located on the left hand side of the firewall, on the frame.
- **Brake Switch**—is located above the brake pedal on the brake pedal support bracket.
- **Canister Purge Solenoid**—is located in the right hand front corner of the engine compartment, on top of the canister.
- **CB Transceiver**—is located under the center of the instrument panel, above the radio, if so equipped.
- **CHECK ENGINE Light Driver**—is taped to the instrument panel harness, in the right of the instrument panel compartment, above the glove box.

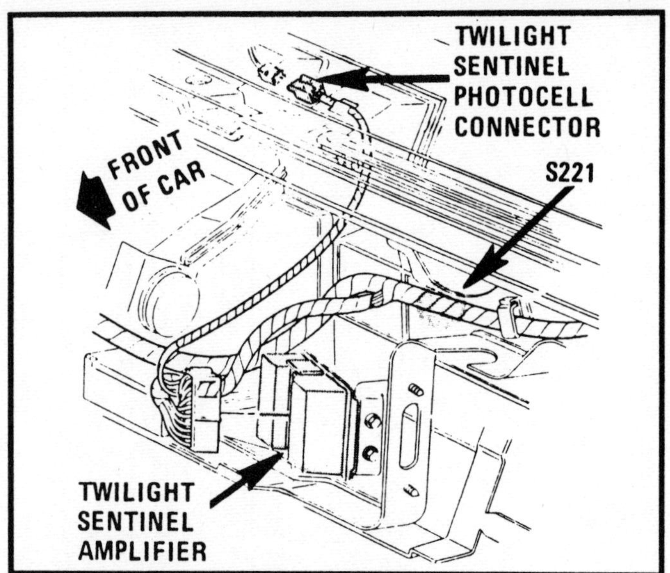

Sentinel amplifier location—Safari

- **Convenience Center**—is located under the left hand side of the instrument panel, on the left side of the fuse block.
- **Coolant Temperature Sender/Switch**—is located on the left front side of the engine, to the right of the valve cover.
- **Coolant Temperature Sensor**—is located on the top front center of the engine, near the water pump.
- **Cruise Control Brake/Switch**—is located above the brake pedal on the brake pedal support bracket.
- **Cruise Control Check Valve**—is located at the top of the engine.
- **Cruise Control Module**—is located under the left side of the dash, to the left of the steering column.
- **Cruise Control Servo**—is located at the top front side of the engine, in the engine compartment.
- **Cruise Control Vacuum Release Valve**—is located above the brake pedal on the brake pedal support bracket.
- **Cruise Control Vacuum Tank**—is located in the left hand front corner of the engine compartment, on the wheel house.
- **Defogger Time Relay**—is located on the top of the fuse block.
- **Detonation (Knock) Sensor**—is located at the lower left hand front of the engine.
- **Diagnostic Dwell Meter Connector**—is taped the ECM wiring harness, in the center front of the engine.
- **EGR/ILC/RVB Triple Solenoid Assembly**—is on the top left hand rear of the engine, on the valve cover.
- **Electronic Control Module (ECM)**—is located behind the right kick panel.
- **Electronic Spark Control (ESC) Module**—is located on the right hand inner fender panel, in the engine compartment.
- **Gear Selector Switch**—is located on the lower part of the steering column.
- **Hazard Relay**—is located in the fuse block.
- **Headlight Dimmer Switch**—is located on the left hand side of the steering column.
- **Heater Blower Resistors**—are located on the right hand side of the firewall, in the heater plenum.
- **Heater Water Valve Vacuum Motor**—are located on the rear of the engine in the heater hose.
- **Heater Water Valve**—are located on the rear of the engine in the heater hose.
- **Horn Relay**—is located in the convenience center.

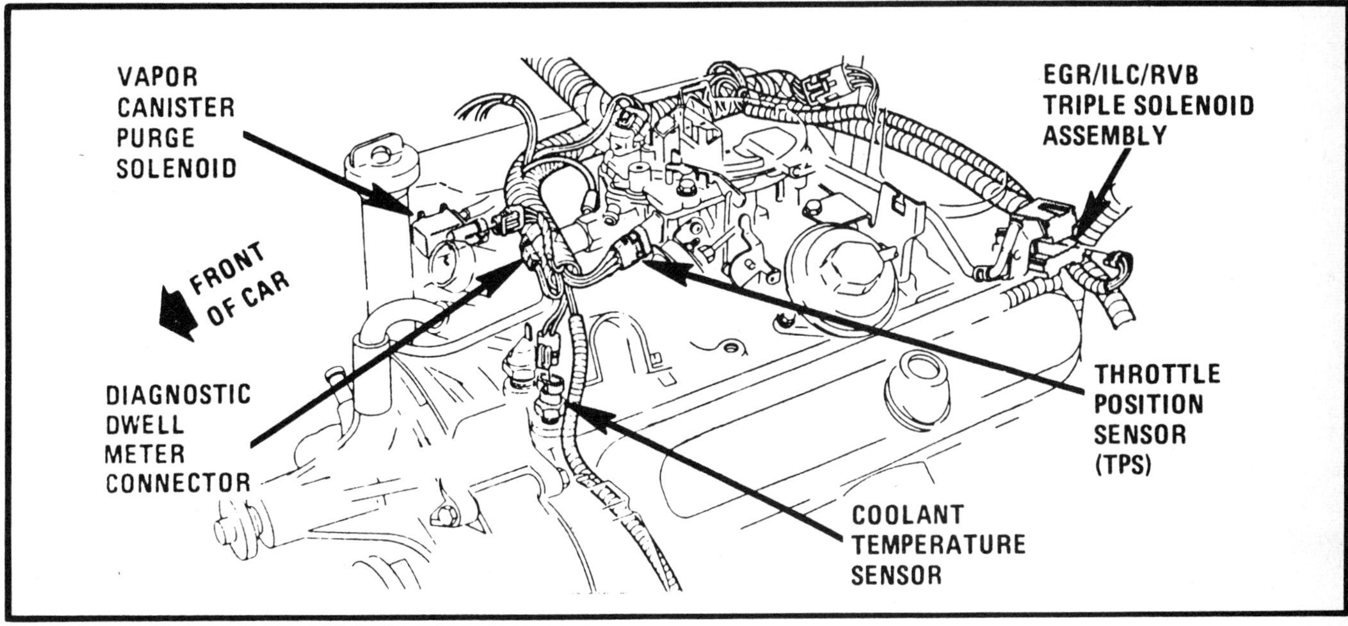

Engine sensor locations—Safari

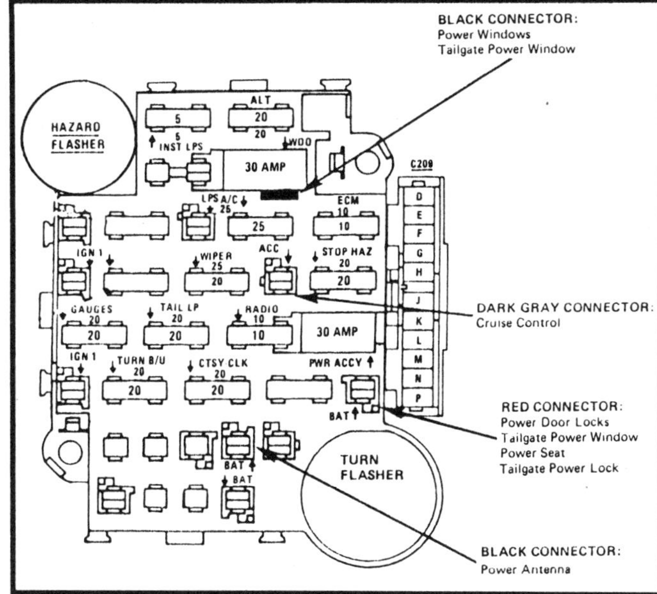

Fuse box identification—Safari

- **Ignition Key Warning Switch**—is located in the steering column, near the key cylinder.
- **Ignition Switch**—is located at the base of the steering column.
- **Manifold Absolute Pressure Sensor**—is located on the right hand inner fender well.
- **Multi-Function Chime Module**—is located in the convenience center or in the instrument panel harness, under the left side of the instrument panel.
- **Oil Pressure Sender/Switch**—is located on the top left hand front of the engine, near the valve cover.
- **Oxygen Sensor**—is located on the exhaust manifold.
- **Power Antenna Relay**—is located on the bracket under the instrument panel, to the left of the glove box.
- **Power Door Lock Relay Assembly**—is located behind the bottom right kick panel.
- **Seatbelt Switch**—is part of the driver's seatbelt assembly.
- **Starter Solenoid**—is located on the lower left hand side of the engine.
- **Tailgate Ajar Switch**—is located inside the lower right hand corner of the tailgate assembly.
- **Tailgate Block**—Out Switch—is located inside the upper right hand corner of the tailgate assembly.
- **Tailgate Key Switch**—is located inside the upper right hand center of the tailgate assembly.
- **Throttle Position Sensor**—is located on the carburetor or throttle body.
- **Trailer Auxiliary Connector**—is located in the left hand rear corner of the cargo compartment.
- **Trailer Connector**—is located in the rear of the vehicle, below the tailgate.
- **Trailer Relays**—are located on the lower right corner of the fuse block, if so equipped.
- **Turn Signal Relay**—is located in the fuse block.
- **Twilight Sentinel Amplifier**—is behind the instrument panel, on the panel support bracket.Twilight Sentinel Control—is on the left side of the instrument panel, near the headlight switch.
- **Twilight Sentinel Photocell**—is on the top left side of the instrument panel.
- **Vehicle Speed Sensor Buffer**—is taped to the instrument panel wiring under the left side of the instrument panel, to the left of the steering column.
- **Vehicle Speed Sensor**—is located behind the left hand side of the instrument panel, behind the speedometer.
- **Washer Pump Motor Diode**—is located in the washer motor connector.
- **Wiper Motor Relay Diode**—is located near the wiper/washer assembly in connector C2.
- **Wiper/Washer Relay**—is incorporated into the wiper/washer assembly.

SUNBIRD

- **A/C Blower Relay**—is located on the rear of the right hand strut tower, in the engine compartment.
- **A/C Compressor Clutch Diode**—is taped inside the A/C compressor clutch connector.

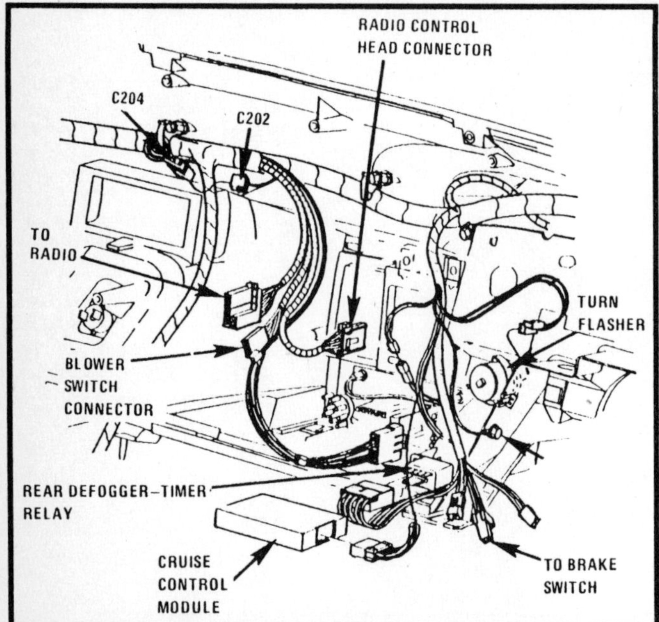

Behind the instrument panel – 1991 Sunbird

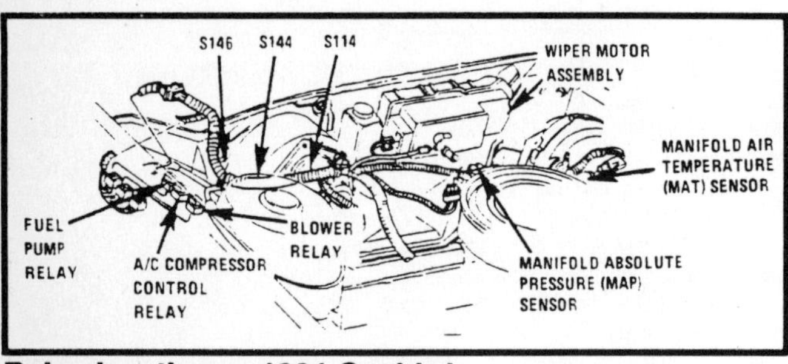

Relay locations – 1991 Sunbird

- **A/C Compressor Control Relay** – is located behind the right front shock tower, in the engine compartment.
- **A/C Defrost Vacuum Motor** – is located under the instrument panel, on the right side of the A/C plenum.
- **A/C Heat Vacuum Motor** – is located under the instrument panel, on the right side of the A/C plenum.
- **A/C Heater Blower Resistors (1991)** – are located at the center of the engine compartment, to the left of the blower motor.
- **A/C Heater Blower Resistors** – are located on the front left side of the plenum, on the firewall.
- **A/C High Pressure Cutout Switch** – is located on the left hand side of the A/C compressor.
- **A/C Low Pressure Cutout Switch** – is located on the left hand side of the A/C compressor.
- **A/C Pressure Cycling Switch** – is located behind the right front shock tower, in the engine compartment, usually on the accumulator/drier.
- **A/C Recirculating/Outside Air Vacuum Motor** – is located under the instrument panel, above the right hand footwell.
- **A/C Vacuum Line Connector** – is located under the instrument panel, behind the right hand side of the glove box.
- **A/C Vacuum Tank** – is located on the left hand front fender, in the engine compartment.
- **Assembly Line Diagnostic Link (ALDL)** – is located behind the instrument panel, on the right side of the fuse block.
- **Audio Alarm Module** – is located in the convenience center.
- **Back** – Up Switch – is located on the top of the transaxle.
- **Blocking Diode** – is located in the instrument panel harness, near the fuse block.
- **Brake Pressure Switch** – is located on the lower left side of the brake fluid reservoir.
- **Brake Switch** – is located on the brake pedal support bracket.
- **Clutch Switch** – is located on the clutch pedal support bracket.
- **Convenience Center** – is located under the left hand side of the instrument panel, near the kick panel.
- **Convertible Roof Relay** – is located at the left front of the luggage compartment.
- **Coolant Fan Relay** – is located on the left hand side of the firewall, in the engine compartment.
- **Coolant Fan Resistor Relay** – is located on the left hand side of the firewall, in the engine compartment.
- **Coolant Temperature Sender/Switch** – is located on the left hand side of the engine, under the distributor.
- **Coolant Temperature Sensor (VIN K)** – is located on the right front side of the engine on the coolant outlet.
- **Coolant Temperature Sensor (VIN M)** – is located on the right hand front of the engine on the coolant outlet.
- **Crankshaft Position Sensor (VIN T)** – is located at the top of the transaxle.
- **Cruise Control Brake Release Valve** – is located on the brake pedal support bracket.
- **Cruise Control Check Valve** – is located on the lower left hand rear of the engine compartment.
- **Cruise Control Module** – is located behind the instrument panel, below the steering column.
- **Cruise Control Servo** – is located on the front of the left hand shock tower in the engine compartment.
- **Cruise Control Vacuum Tank** – is located in the left hand front corner of the engine compartment, on the fender panel.
- **Cruise Control/Brake Switch** – is located on the brake pedal support bracket.
- **Daytime Running Lights (DRL)** – is located at the left front corner of the engine compartment.
- **Defogger Time Relay** – is located behind the left side of the instrument panel, on the instrument panel brace.
- **Detonation (Knock) Sensor (VIN T)** – is located on the lower right rear of the engine, below the starter solenoid.
- **Digital Exhaust Gas Recirculation (DEGR) Assembly (VIN T)** – is located at the left rear of the engine, above the starter solenoid.
- **DRL In-Line Resistor** – is on the left side of the engine, near the strut tower.
- **Electronic Control Module (ECM)** – is located behind the right hand side of the instrument panel, behind the glove box.
- **Electronic EGR Vacuum Regulator Valve (VIN M)** – is located on the top of the engine.
- **Fog Lamp Relay** – is located in the left hand front corner of the engine compartment, near the battery.
- **Fuel Pump In-Line Fuse** – is located on the firewall, behind the brake booster, if so equipped.
- **Fuel Pump Prime Connector** – is located at the left rear side of the engine compartment.
- **Fuel Pump Relay** – is located on the rear of the right hand shock tower, in the engine compartment.
- **Fuel Pump/Oil Pressure Switch** – is located at the lower right rear of the engine, near the oil filter.
- **Gear Select Switch** – is located on the left hand side of the transaxle.
- **Hatch Release Relay** – is taped to the wire harness, located behind the right side of the radio.
- **Hazard Relay** – is located on the convenience center.

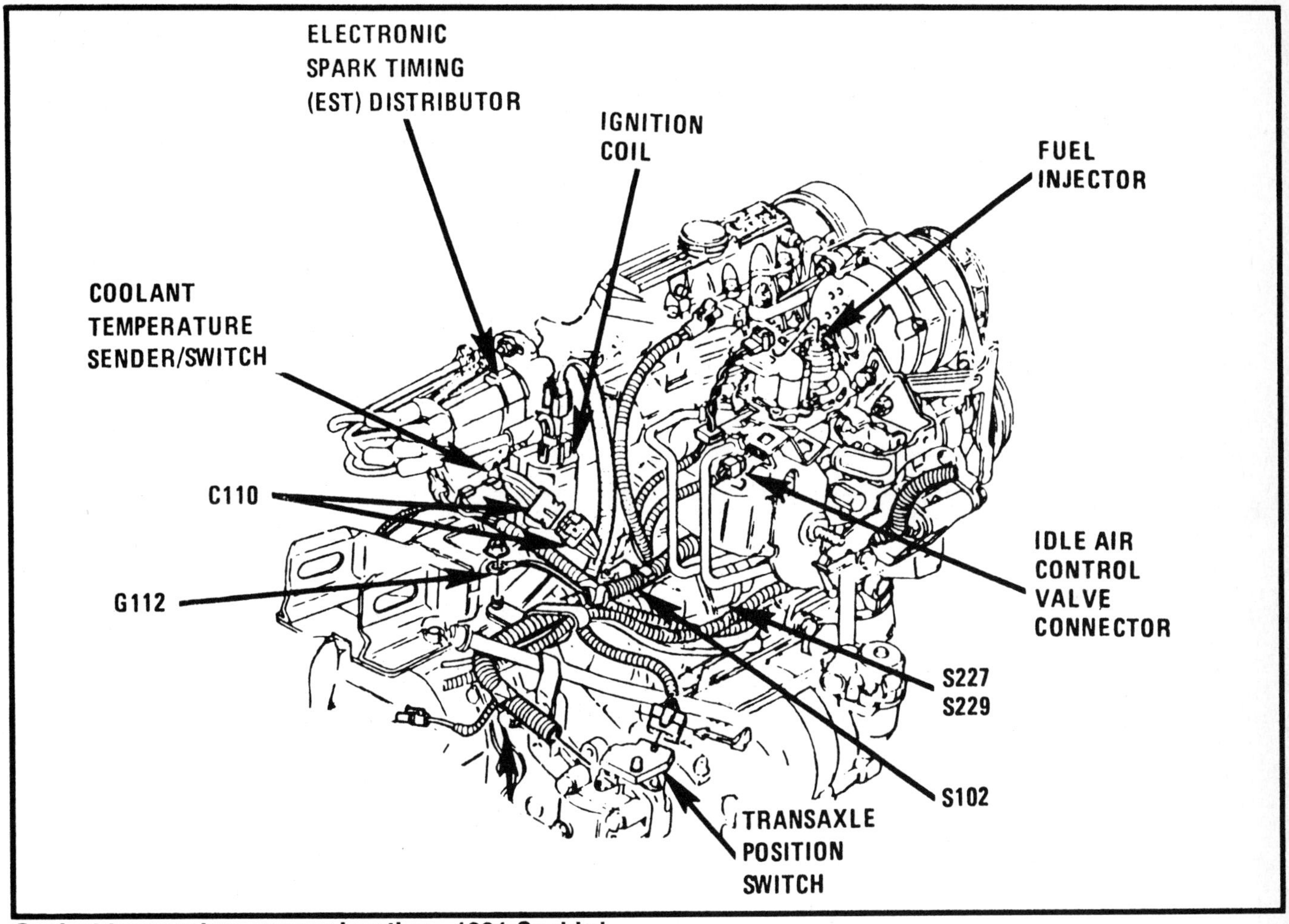

ELECTRONIC SPARK TIMING (EST) DISTRIBUTOR
IGNITION COIL
FUEL INJECTOR
COOLANT TEMPERATURE SENDER/SWITCH
C110
G112
IDLE AIR CONTROL VALVE CONNECTOR
S227
S229
S102
TRANSAXLE POSITION SWITCH

Coolant temperature sensor location—1991 Sunbird

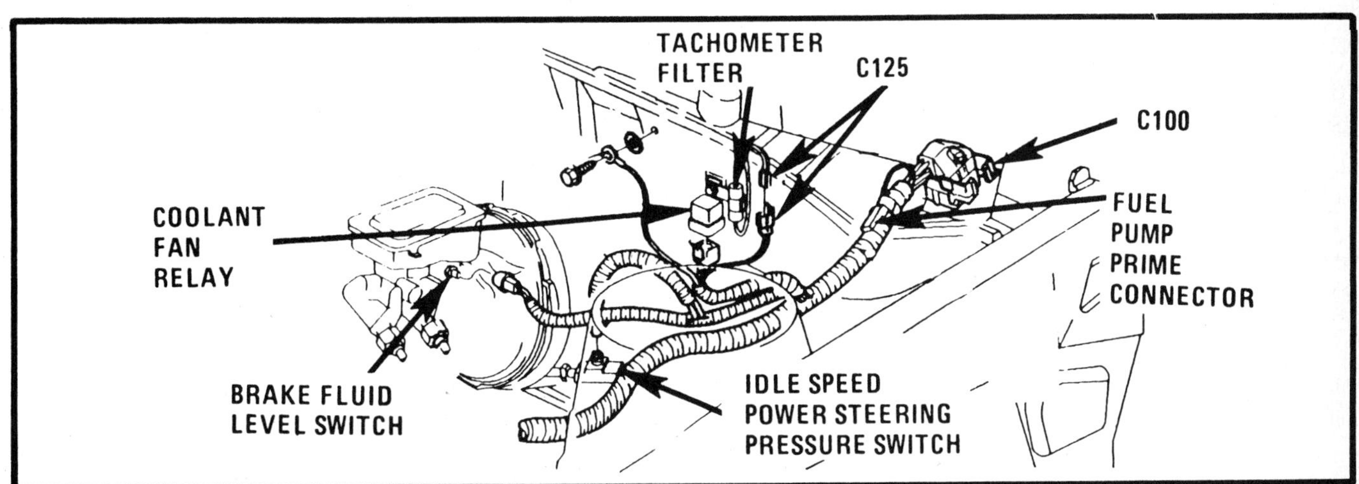

Fuel pump prime connector location—1991 Sunbird

- **Headlight Dimmer Switch**—is located on the middle of the left hand side of the steering column.
- **Headlight Door Controller**—is located on the left hand front strut tower, in the engine compartment.
- **Horn Relay**—is located on the convenience center.
- **Idle Air Control Valve (VIN K)**—is located on the top of the engine, on the left side of the throttle body.
- **Idle Air Control Valve (VIN M)**—is located on the top of the engine, on the right side of the throttle body.
- **Idle Air Control Valve (VIN T)**—is located on the top of the engine, on the upper right side of the throttle body.
- **Idle Speed Steering Pressure Switch**—is located at the left rear of the engine compartment, on the lower left side of the brake booster.

• **Ignition Key Warning Switch** – is located in the steering column, near the key cylinder.

• **Ignition Switch** – is located on the top right hand side of the steering column.

• **Knock Sensor (VIN M)** – is located on the right side of the starter below the starter.

• **Lumbar Seat Air Pump Motor** – is located under the driver's seat.

• **Lumbar Seat Air Pump Motor/Relay** – is located under the driver's seat.

• **Lumbar Seat Air Pump Valve Assemblies** – is located under the right and left front seats.

• **Manifold Absolute Pressure (MAP) Sensor (VIN K)** – is located on the top of the engine, on the rear of the air cleaner.

• **Manifold Absolute Pressure (MAP) Sensor (VIN M)** – is located on the top of the engine, behind the alternator.

• **Manifold Absolute Pressure (MAP) Sensor (VIN T)** – at the rear of the engine compartment on the firewall.

• **Manifold Air Temperature (MAT) Sensor (VIN K)** – is located on the top of the engine, on the air cleaner.

• **Manifold Air Temperature (MAT) Sensor (VIN M)** – is located on the top of the engine, under the intake plenum.

• **Manifold Air Temperature (MAT) Sensor (VIN T)** – is located at the rear of the engine, on the manifold.

• **Oil Pressure Sender/Switch** – is located on the lower right hand rear of the engine, near the oil filter.

• **Oxygen Sensor** – is located in the exhaust manifold.

• **Power Accessories Circuit Breaker** – is located in the fuse block.

• **Power Door Lock Relay** – is located behind the left hand side of the instrument panel, above the steering column.

• **Power Steering Pressure Switch** – is located on the left hand side of the firewall, above the brake master cylinder.

• **Power Window Circuit Breaker** – is located in the fuse block.

• **Release Solenoid (Hatchback)** – is located in the lower rear of the hatchback lid.

• **Release Solenoid (Sedan/Coupe)** – is located near the rear compartment, lock mechanism.

• **Release Solenoid (Station Wagon)** – is located below the right hand side of the tailgate window.

• **Remote Dimmer Module** – is located behind the instrument panel, on the left side of the steering column bracket.

• **Seat Belt Retractor Solenoid** – is located near the base of each B–pillar.

• **Seatbelt Switch** – is part of the driver's seatbelt assembly.

• **Starter Solenoid** – is located on the lower left hand front side of the engine.

• **Tachometer Filter** – is located at the left rear of the engine compartment, near the cooling fan relay.

• **Tachometer Filter** – is located on the left hand front of the dash, near the coolant fan relay.

• **Tailgate Ajar Switch** – is located inside the lower center portion of the tailgate assembly.

• **Throttle Position Sensor (VIN K)** – is located on the top rear of the engine, on the rear of the throttle body.

• **Throttle Position Sensor (VIN M)** – is located on the top rear of the engine, on the right side of the throttle body.

• **Turn Signal Flasher** – is located on the right hand side of the steering column bracket.

• **Vehicle Speed Sensor** – is located on the right hand side of the transaxle.

• **Waste Gate Solenoid** – is located on the top center of the engine, on the rear cylinder head.

• **Wiper/Washer Motor Module** – is located on the center of the engine firewall.

6000 AND 6000 STE

• **A/C Bi-Level Heater Vacuum Actuator (STE)** – is located under the center of the instrument panel, on the right side of the A/C plenum.

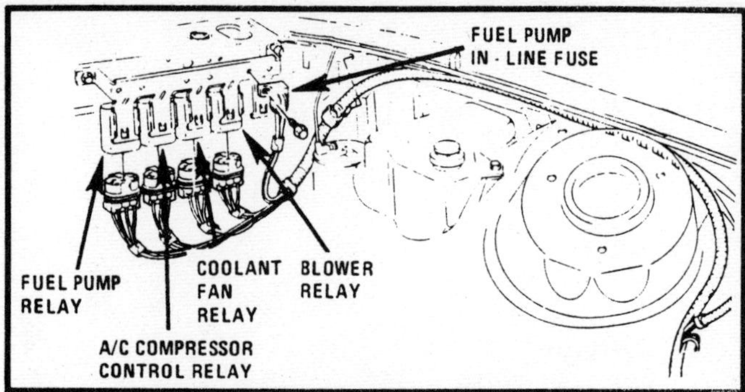

Relay locations – 6000 with 2.5L VIN R engine

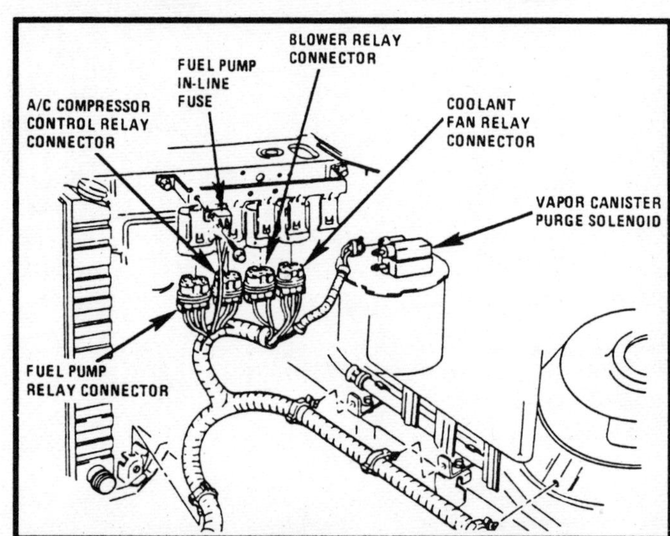

Relay locations – 6000 with 3.1L VIN T engine

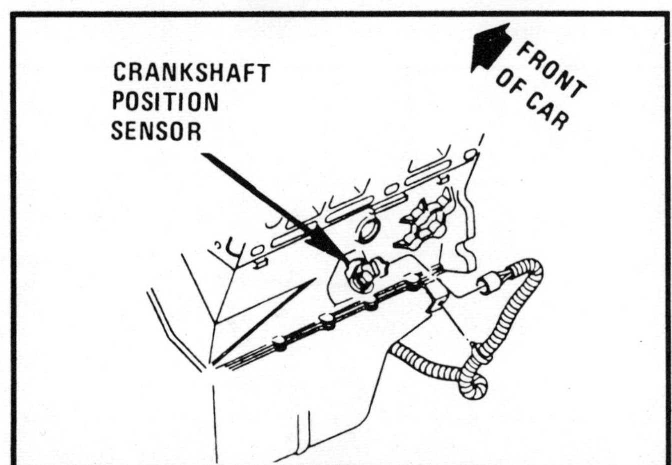

Crank position sensor – 6000 with 3.1L VIN T engine

• **A/C Blower Relay** – is located on the right side of the firewall, on the A/C module (plenum).

• **A/C Blower Resistors** – is located on the right side of the firewall, on the A/C module (plenum).

• **A/C Compressor Clutch Diode** – is taped to the inside compressor connector on the front of the compressor.

• **A/C Compressor Control Relay (VIN R)** – is located on the right hand side of the firewall, on a relay bracket.

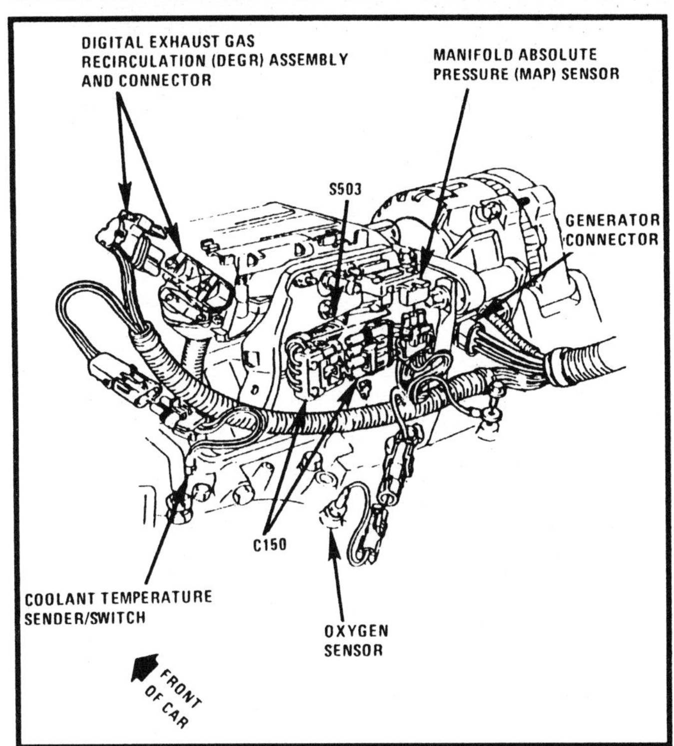

Coolant temperature sensor—6000 with 3.1L VIN T engine

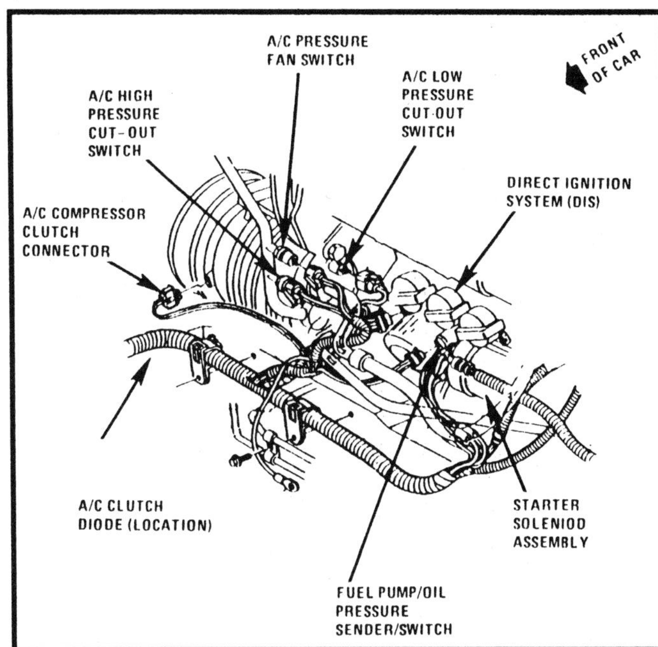

Air conditioning components—6000 with 3.1L VIN T engine

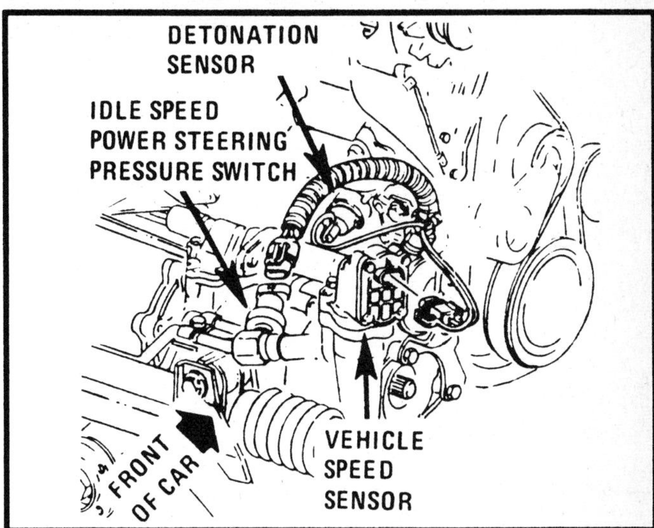

Detonation (knock) sensor—6000 with 3.1L VIN T engine

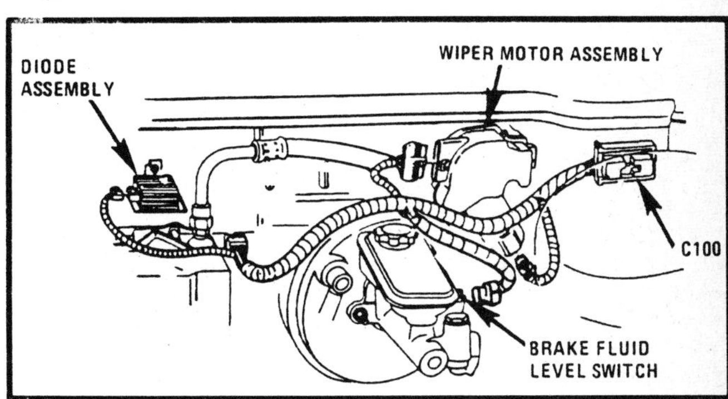

Diode assembly—6000

• **A/C Compressor Control Relay (VIN T)**—is located on the right front corner of the engine compartment, on the relay bracket.

• **A/C Compressor Control Relay (VIN W)**—is located on the right hand front corner of the engine compartment.

• **A/C Coolant Fan Pressure Switch (VIN W)**—is located on the right hand front of the engine, in the A/C line near the left end of the compressor.

• **A/C Defrost Vacuum Actuator**—is located under the center of the instrument panel, on the top of the A/C plenum.

• **A/C Fan Pressure Switch (VIN T)**—is located at the right front of the engine, in the air conditioner line.

• **A/C Heater Vacuum Actuator**—is located under the center of the instrument panel, on the right side of the A/C plenum.

• **A/C High Blower Relay (STE)**—is located on the right hand side of the firewall, near the blower motor.

• **A/C High Pressure Cutout Switch (VIN R)**—is located on the rear of the compressor.

• **A/C High Pressure Cutout Switch (VIN W)**—is located on the A/C line, right hand front of the engine.

• **A/C Low Blower Relay (STE)**—is located on the center of the firewall, to the left of the blower motor.

• **A/C Low Pressure Cutout Switch (VIN R)**—is located on the rear of the A/C compressor.

• **A/C Low Pressure Cutout Switch (VIN W)**—is located on the A/C line, right hand front of the engine.

• **A/C Recirculation/Outside Air Vacuum Actuator**—is located under the center of the instrument panel, on the right side of the A/C plenum.

• **A/C Temperature Door Mode (STE)**—is located under the center of the instrument panel, on the top of the A/C plenum.

• **A/C Vacuum Solenoid Module (STE)**—is located behind the glove box.

• **A/C Vacuum Tank (STE)**—is located on the right hand inner fender.

• **A/C Vacuum Tank**—is located in the center of the firewall, above the A/C and heater module, on vehicles without cruise control.

• **Air Diverter Valve (VIN W)**—is located on the top right hand rear of the engine, in front of the AIR pump.

• **Anti-Lock Brake Diode**—is taped to the instrument panel wiring harness, behind the right side of the instrument panel.

• **Anti-Lock Brake Electronic Control Module**—is located under the right hand side of the instrument panel.

• **Anti-Lock Brake Fluid Level Sensor**—is located near the left hand strut tower, in the engine compartment.

• **Anti-Lock Brake Main Relay**—is located on the right hand side of the firewall, on a relay bracket.

• **Anti-Lock Brake Main Relay Fuse**—is located on the right hand side of the firewall, on a relay bracket.

• **Anti-Lock Brake Main Valve**—is located on the master cylinder, in the engine compartment.

• **Anti-Lock Brake Pressure Switch**—is located near the left hand strut tower, in the engine compartment.

• **Anti-Lock Brake Pump Fuse**—is located behind the strut tower, in the left hand front corner of the engine compartment, on a relay bracket.

• **Anti-Lock Brake Pump Motor**—is located in the left hand front corner of the engine compartment.

• **Anti-Lock Brake Pump Relay**—is located on the front of the strut tower, in the left hand front corner of the engine compartment.

• **Anti-Lock Brake Valve Block**—is located on the strut tower, in the left hand front corner of the engine compartment.

• **Anti-Lock Brake Wheel Speed Sensor**—is located in each wheel spindle.

• **Assembly Line Diagnostic Link**—is located on the bottom of the instrument panel, to the right of the steering column.

• **Audio Alarm Module**—is located in the convenience center.

• **Back**—Up Light Switch—is located on the left hand side of the transaxle.

• **Battery Junction Block No. 1**—is located in the left hand side of the engine compartment, on front of the strut tower.

• **Battery Junction Block No. 2**—is located in the right hand front of the engine compartment.

• **Battery Junction Block**—is located at the right front of the engine compartment, at the relay bracket.

• **Brake Pressure Switch**—is located on the left hand side of the brake fluid reservoir.

• **Brake Switch**—is located behind the brake pedal, below the brake pedal support.

• **Canister Purge Solenoid (VIN W)**—is located in the right hand front corner of the engine compartment, on top of the canister.

• **Clutch Start Switch**—is located behind the clutch pedal, below the clutch pedal support.

• **Convenience Center (1989)**—is located behind the right side of the instrument panel, to the left of the ECM.

• **Convenience Center (except 1989)**—is located behind the right side of the instrument panel, near the fuse box.

• **Coolant Fan Relay (VIN R)**—is located on the left front strut tower on the bracket.

• **Coolant Fan Relay (VIN W)**—is located in the engine compartment, behind the right hand headlights.

• **Coolant Temperature Sender/Switch (VIN R)**—is located on the top of the engine, below the left hand side valve cover.

• **Coolant Temperature Sender/Switch (VIN W)**—is located on the left hand rear of the engine, below the valve cover.

• **Coolant Temperature Sensor (VIN R)**—is located on the top left hand side of the engine, below the coolant outlet.

• **Coolant Temperature Sensor (VIN T)**—is located at the top left side of the engine.

• **Coolant Temperature Sensor (VIN W)**—is located on the top left hand side of the engine, below the throttle body.

• **Crank Position Sensor (VIN W)**—is located on the lower rear of the engine, below the exhaust manifold.

• **Crankshaft Position Sensor (VIN T)**—is located at the lower right rear of the engine.

• **Cruise Control Check Valve**—is located in the vacuum line, at the rear of the engine compartment.

• **Cruise Control Module**—is located behind the instrument panel, to the right of the steering column, above the accelerator pedal.

• **Cruise Control Servo**—is located in the left hand front corner of the engine compartment, on the wheelhouse.

• **Cruise Control Vacuum Release Valve**—is located above the brake pedal on the brake pedal support bracket.

• **Cruise Control Vacuum Tank**—is located in the right hand front corner of the engine compartment.

• **Daytime Running Lights (DRL) Module**—is behind the center of the instrument panel, near the turn signal flasher.

• **Defogger Timer Relay**—is located behind the instrument panel, under the instrument cluster.

• **Detonation (Knock) Sensor (VIN T)**—is located at the lower right rear of the engine, above the speed sensor.

• **Digital Exhaust Gas Recirculation (DER) Assembly (VIN T)**—is at the top rear of the engine, above the coolant temperature sender.

• **Diode Assembly**—is mounted at the center of the engine compartment, above the air conditioning module.

• **Direct Ignition System (VIN R)**—is located on the top left hand rear of the engine.

• **Direct Ignition System (VIN T)**—is at the lower front of the engine above the oil filter.

• **Direct Ignition System (VIN W)**—is located on the front of the engine, above the oil filter.

• **Driver Information Center**—is located behind the right hand side of the instrument panel.

• **EGR Position Solenoid (VIN W)**—is located on the top left hand rear of the engine compartment.

• **Electronic Control Module (ECM)**—is located behind the right side of the instrument panel.

• **Electronic Level Control Compressor**—is located on the behind the left hand rear wheel, above the shield.

• **Electronic Level Control Compressor Relay**—is located on the behind the left hand rear wheel, above the shield.

• **Electronic Level Control Compressor**—is located on the rear frame, to the left of the spare tire wheel well.

• **Electronic Level Control Height Sensor (Sedan)**—is located on the rear frame, above the right hand rear lower suspension arm.

• **Electronic Level Control Height Sensor (Station Wagon)**—is located on the rear frame, in front of the fuel tank.

• **Electronic Level Control Height Sensor**—is located below the vehicle, near the right hand rear wheel.

• **Electronic Level Control Inflator Solenoid Valve**—is located in the left hand rear of the trunk, behind the wheel well.

• **Electronic Level Control Inflator Switch**—is located in the end panel, near the trunk lock mechanism.

• **Electronic Level Control Inflator Timer Relay**—is located in the left hand rear of the trunk, behind the wheel well.

• **Electronic Level Control Relay (Sedan)**—is located in luggage compartment, behind the left hand wheel well.

• **Electronic Level Control Relay (Station Wagon)**—is located in left hand side of the cargo compartment.

• **Electronic Level Control Relay**—is located in the left hand rear of the trunk, behind the wheel well.

• **Electronic Level Control Test Connector**—is located in the engine compartment, near the ELC compressor.

● **Fog Light Relay**—is taped to the instrument panel harness, to the right of the steering column.

● **Fuel Pump In-Line Fuse (VIN T)**—is at the front of the engine compartment, on the relay bracket.

● **Fuel Pump Prime Connector (STE)**—is located in the right hand corner of the engine compartment.

● **Fuel Pump Prime Connector (VIN R)**—is taped to the engine harness, in front of the transaxle.

● **Fuel Pump Prime Connector (VIN T)**—is at the left rear of the engine compartment, near the C100 connector.

● **Fuel Pump Prime Connector (VIN W)**—is taped to the engine harness,in the left hand rear of the engine compartment, near connector C100.

● **Fuel Pump Relay (VIN R)**—is located on the right hand side of the firewall, on the relay bracket.

● **Fuel Pump Relay (VIN T)**—is on the relay bracket at the right front of the engine compartment.

● **Fuel Pump Relay (VIN W)**—is located in the right hand corner of the engine compartment.

● **Fuel Pump/Oil Pressure Sender (VIN T)**—is at the lower front of the engine, above the oil filter.

● **Fuel Pump/Oil Pressure Switch (VIN R)**—is located on the rear of the engine, to the right of the DIS system.

● **Fuel Pump/Oil Pressure Switch (VIN W)**—is located on the top left hand rear of the engine.

● **Fusible Links**—are located at the battery junction block, starter solenoid and the battery.

● **Hazard Flasher**—is located in the convenience center.

● **Headlight Dimmer Switch**—is located behind the left hand side of the instrument panel, on the steering column.

● **Heater Blower Resistors**—is located on the right side of the firewall, near the blower motor.

● **Horn Relay**—is located on the convenience center.

● **Idle Air Control Motor (VIN T)**—is on the top left side of the engine.

● **Idle Air Control Stepper Motor (VIN R)**—is located on the top of the engine, on the left hand rear of the throttle body.

● **Idle Air Control Valve (VIN W)**—is located on the top left hand side of the engine, on the front of the throttle body.

● **Idle Speed Power Steering Pressure Switch (VIN R)**—is located on the right hand rear side of the engine, in the power steering hydraulic line.

● **Idle Speed Power Steering Pressure Switch (VIN T)**—is on the lower right rear of the engine compartment, on the power steering line.

● **Idle Speed Power Steering Pressure Switch (VIN W)**—is located on the steering rack, in the lower right hand rear of the engine compartment.

● **Ignition Key Warning Switch**—is located on the steering column, below the turn/hazard switch.

● **Ignition Switch (STE)**—is located behind the left hand side of the instrument panel, to the right of the steering column.

● **Ignition Switch**—is located it the middle of the steering column.

● **Detention (Knock) Sensor (VIN W)**—is located on the lower rear of the engine, below the exhaust manifold.

● **Low Coolant Module**—is located behind the left hand side of the instrument panel.

● **Low Coolant Sensor**—is located in the engine compartment, on the right front side of the radiator.

● **Lumbar Seat Air Pump Assembly**—is located in the center console.

● **Lumbar Seat Control Module**—is located in the center console.

● **Lumbar Seat Solenoid/Valve Assembly**—are located below each seat.

● **Manifold Absolute Pressure (MAP) Sensor (VIN T)**—is at the top right end of the engine, behind the alternator.

● **Manifold Absolute Pressure (MAP) Sensor (VIN R)**—is located on the right hand side of the air cleaner assembly.

● **Manifold Absolute Pressure (MAP) Sensor (VIN W)**—is located on the upper right hand front of the firewall, behind the strut tower.

● **Manifold Air Temperature (MAT) Sensor (VIN T)**—is at the top of the engine on the air cleaner.

● **Manifold Air Temperature (MAT) Sensor (VIN R)**—is located on the top right and rear of the engine, on the intake manifold.

● **Mass Air Flow Sensor In-Line Fuse (VIN W)**—is located in the engine compartment, on the front of the left shock tower.

● **Mass Airflow Relay (VIN W)**—is located in the engine compartment, on the front of the left shock tower.

● **Mass Airflow (MAF) Sensor (VIN W)**—is located on the air intake, on the top left hand side of the engine.

● **Oil Pressure Switch (VIN R)**—is located on the right hand rear of the engine, to the right of the distributor.

● **Oil Pressure Switch (VIN W)**—is located on the front of the engine, above the oil filter.

● **Oxygen Sensor**—is located in the exhaust manifold.

● **Passive Restraint Control Module**—is at the right shroud, above the center access hole.

● **Photoresistor**—is mounted at the top center of the instrument panel.

● **Power Accessories Circuit Breaker**—is located in the fuse block.

● **Power Antenna Relay**—is located in the right hand front corner of the trunk.

● **Power Door Lock Relay**—is located on the right shroud, above the center access hole.

● **Power Seat Module**—is located under the left hand front seat.

● **Power Window Circuit Breaker**—is located in the fuse block.

● **Rear Wiper Module**—is located in the top center of the tailgate.

● **Release Relay**—is located behind the right side of the instrument panel, near the instrument panel compartment.

● **Seat Belt In-Line Fuse**—is behind the right side of the instrument panel, near the convenience center.

● **Seat Capacitor A**—is located under the left front seat, in the harness. Connected between the main power to switches and ground.

● **Seat Capacitors**—are under the respective front seat in the connector harness, across the motor wires.

● **Seatbelt Switch**—is part of the driver's seatbelt assembly.

● **Starter Solenoid**—is located on the lower left hand front portion of the engine.

● **Steering and Electronics Module**—is at the underside of the steering column.

● **Tailgate Ajar Switch**—is located inside the lower center portion of the tailgate assembly.

● **Tailgate Lock Switch**—is located in the middle center of the tailgate assembly.

● **Tailgate Release Relay**—is located behind the right hand side of the instrument panel, near the fuse block.

● **Tailgate Release Solenoid**—is located in the center of the tailgate assembly, behind the panel.

● **Throttle Position Sensor (VIN T)**—is at the top left rear of the engine.

● **Throttle Position Sensor (except VIN T)**—is located on the throttle body.

● **Transaxle Position Switch**—is located on the left hand side of the transaxle.

● **Translator Module**—is at the underside of the steering column.

● **Trunk Release Relay**—is located behind the right hand side of the instrument panel, near the fuse block, if so equipped.

● **Trunk Release Solenoid**—is located in the center of the trunk lid.

- **Turn Signal Flasher**—is located on the right hand side of the steering column, above the ALDL connector.
- **Canister Purge Solenoid (VIN T)**—is located at the right rear of the engine compartment, on the canister.
- **Vehicle Speed Sensor**—is on the right rear of the engine, on the transaxle.
- **Washer Fluid Level Switch**—is located in the washer fluid reservoir.
- **Washer Motor Module**—is located on the upper left side of the engine compartment, in the washer reservoir.
- **Wiper Motor Module**—is located on the upper left side of the engine firewall.

LIGHT TRUCKS, VANS AND APVS

General Motors Corporation Light Truck Body Codes

Body Code	Chevrolet	GMC
C	Pickup 2WD	Sierra Pickup 2WD
G	Sportvan Chevyvan	Rally Van Vandura Van
K	Pickup 4WD	Sierra Pickup 4WD
L	Astro Van 4WD	Safari 4WD
M	Astro Van 2WD	Safari 2WD
R	Suburban 2WD Crew Cab 2WD	Suburban 2WD Crew Cab 2WD
S	S-10 Blazer 2WD S-10 Pickup 2WD	S-15 Jimmy 2WD S-15 Pickup 2WD
T	S-10 Blazer 4WD S-10 Pickup 4WD	S-15 Jimmy 4WD S-15 Pickup 4WD
V	Blazer (Full Size) Suburban 4WD Crew Cab 4WD	Jimmy (Full Size) Suburban 4WD Crew Cab 4WD

C—Body pickups are 2WD and include C1500, C2500 and C3500 trucks.
K—Body pickups are 4WD and include K1500, K2500 and K3500 trucks.

CIRCUIT BREAKERS

Device or Circuit Protected	Models	Amps.	Location
Headlamp and parking lamp circuit	RV-P-G	15	Lamp switch
Tailgate window motor, side window motor	RV	30	Dash (forward side)
Power door locks, rear defogger and tailgate power window key switch	RV	30	Fuse Panel
Power windows	G	30	Fuse Panel
Power door locks	G	30	Fuse Panel
Rear A/C (C69 overhead)	G	35	Dash (forward side)

Circuit Breakers

C/K SERIES PICKUP TRUCK

All circuit breakers are located in the convenience center or the fuse box.

G SERIES—VANS

All circuit breakers are located in the convenience center or the fuse box.

ASTRO AND SAFARI VANS

All circuit breakers are located in the convenience center or the fuse box.

BLAZER, JIMMY, CREWCAB AND SUBURBAN

Most circuit breakers are located in the fuse box. The headlamp circuit breaker is part of the headlamp switch assembly. Some breakers may be locatdd at the forward side of the dash.

S SERIES—BLAZER, JIMMY AND PICKUP

All circuit breakers are located in the convenience center or the fuse box.

SILHOUETTE, TRANS SPORT AND LUMINA APV

All circuit breakers are located in the convenience center or the fuse box.

Fusible Links

C/K SERIES PICKUP TRUCK

The fusible links are located on the junction block. The junction block is on the right side of the cowl. The junction block and relays probably have a protective cover over them.

G SERIES—VANS

The fusible links are located at the starter solenoid, battery, junction block and the alternator. The exact location, component and amperage vary dependent on vehicle year and option packages. On vans equipped with an auxiliary battery, there are also a fusible link between the secondary battery and the auxiliary junction block/relay assembly.

ASTRO AND SAFARI VANS

The fusible links are located at the starter solenoid or the battery junction block. and the alternator. The exact amperage will vary dependent on vehicle year and option packages.

BLAZER, JIMMY, CREWCAB AND SUBURBAN

All models are equipped with fusible links which attach to the lower ends of main feed wires and connect at the battery, starter solenoid or the junction blocks through out the vehicle. The fusible link wire gauge size is marked on the insulation and each link is four sizes smaller than the cable it is designed to protect. The same wire with special hypalon insulation must be used when replacing a fusible link.

S SERIES—BLAZER, JIMMY AND PICKUP

The fusible links are located at the starter solenoid, battery and the alternator. The exact location, component and amperage vary dependent on vehicle year and option packages.

SILHOUETTE, TRANS SPORT AND LUMINA APV

Most of the fusible links are located at the starter solenoid. Dependent on vehicle year and option packages fusible links may be located at the battery, junction block or the alternator.

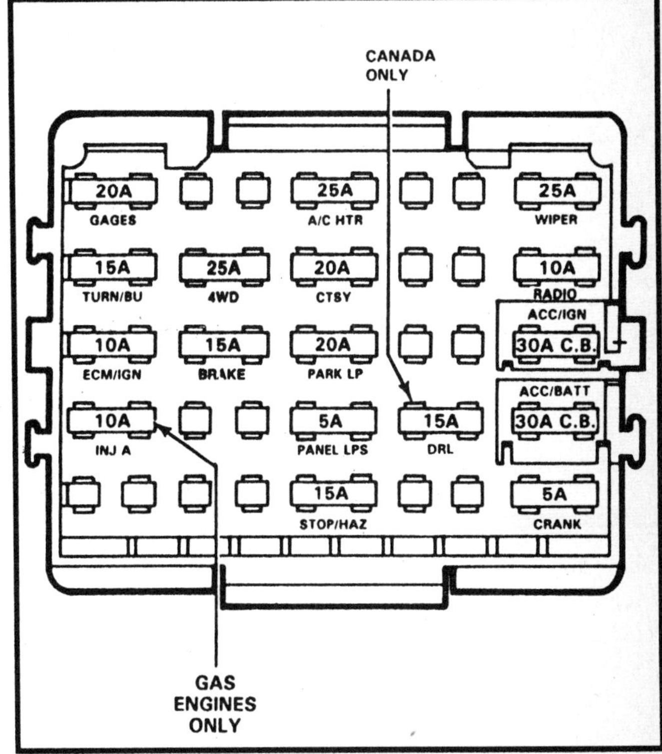

Fuse block identification—Blazer/Jimmy, Crewcab and Suburban

Relay, Sensors And Computer Locations

NOTE: When using this section, some of the components may not be used on a particular vehicle. This is because the particular component in question was used on an earlier model or a later model. This section is being published from the latest information available at the time of this publication.

C/K, R/V AND G SERIES BLAZER, JIMMY, CREWCAB, PICKUP, SUBURBAN, AND VANS

- **A/C Pressure Cycling Switch**—is on the top rear of the accumulator.
- **Air Devert Module (7.4L engine)**—is at the rear of the engine.
- **Auxiliary Fan Relay (Van)**—is located next to the fuel pump relay.
- **Audio Headlamp Alarm**—plugs in below the fuse box.
- **Auxiliary Fan Switch**—is located in the side of the engine above the starter.
- **Blower Relay**—is located at the blower motor housing.
- **Blower Resistor**—is on the blower motor housing.
- **Coolant Temperature Sensor**—is located at the center front of the engine.
- **Coolant Temperature Cutout Switch (Van)**—is at the thermostat housing.
- **Coolant Fan Temperature Switch (Van)**—is in the right cylinder head.
- **Convenience Center**—is located behind a pull cover in the dash to the left of the steering column, when equipped.
- **Cruise Control Module (except Van)**—is located to the right of the steering column.
- **Cruise Control Module (Van)**—is mounted at the parking brake assembly.
- **Door Lock Relay (except Van)**—is located on the brake pedal bracket.
- **Door Lock Relay (Van)**—is located under the top left side of the dash.
- **Electronic Control Module (except Van)**—is located under the right side dash, behind the glove box.
- **Electronic Control Module (Van)**—is located under the driver's seat.
- **Engine Check Lamp Relay (7.4L engine)**—is at the rear of the engine.
- **Fuel Module (C/K and G)**—is located with the electronic control module.
- **Fuel Module (R/V)**—is located at the brake pedal bracket.
- **Fuel Pump Relay (C/K)**—is located at the right rear of the engine, maybe protected by a cover.
- **Fuel Pump Relay (C/K, R/V 7.4L engine)**—is located at the right rear of the engine.
- **Fuel Pump Relay (R/V 5.7L engine)**—is located at the right rear of the engine.
- **Fuel Pump Relay (Van)**—is located on the right near the radiator.
- **Fuel Pump Test Connector (C/K)**—is located near the fuse panel.
- **Fuel Pump Test Connector (C/K, R/V 7.4L engine)**—is located at the right rear of the engine.
- **Fuel Pump Test Connector (R/V 5.7L engine)**—is located at the right rear of the engine, next to the fuel pump relay.
- **Fuel Pump Test Connector (Van)**—is located on the right near the radiator.
- **Fuel Pump Oil Pressure Switch (except Van)**—is left side of engine near or under the exhaust.
- **Fuel Pump Oil Pressure Switch (Van)**—is left side of engine near power steering or near the distributor.
- **Manifold Absolute Pressure (MAP) sensor**—is mounted on or next to the air cleaner.

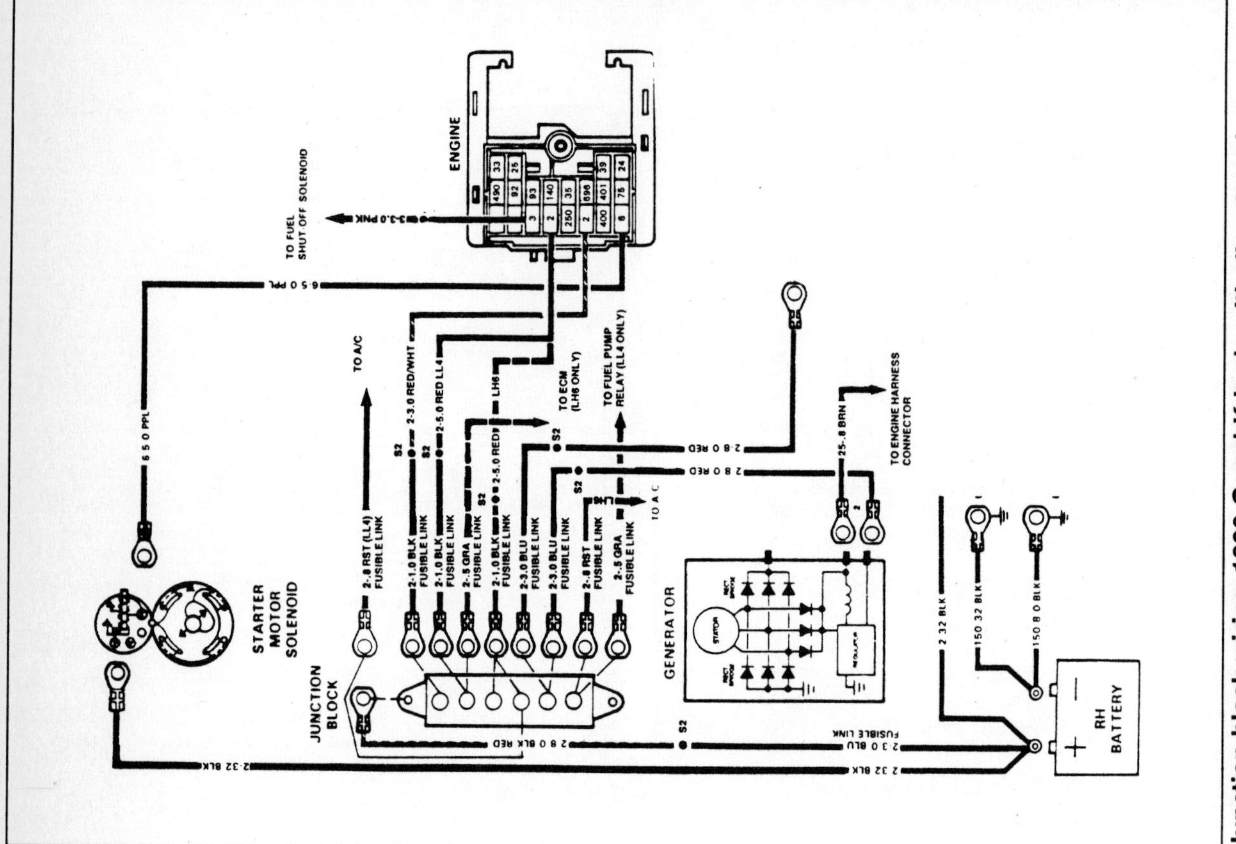

Junction block wiring–1990 C and K-body with diesel engine

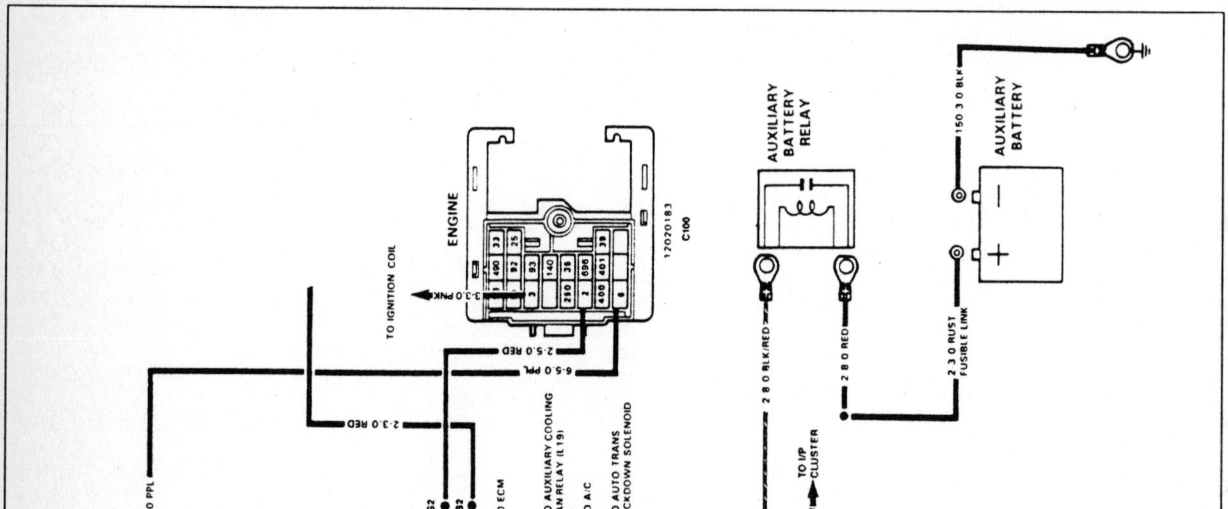

Junction block wiring–1990 C and K-body with gasoline engine

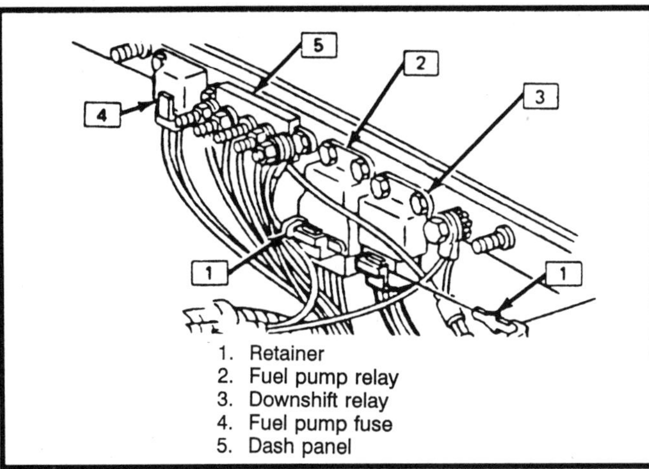

1. Retainer
2. Fuel pump relay
3. Downshift relay
4. Fuel pump fuse
5. Dash panel

Junction block and relay locations – C and K-body pickups

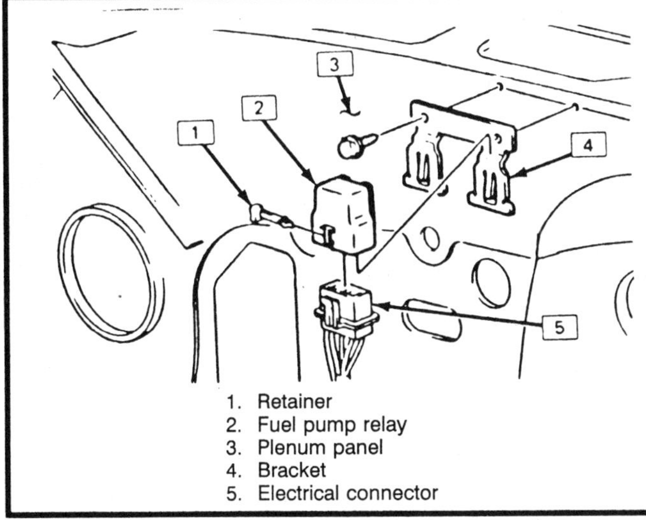

1. Retainer
2. Fuel pump relay
3. Plenum panel
4. Bracket
5. Electrical connector

Junction block and relay locations – Blazer/Jimmy, Crewcab and Suburban

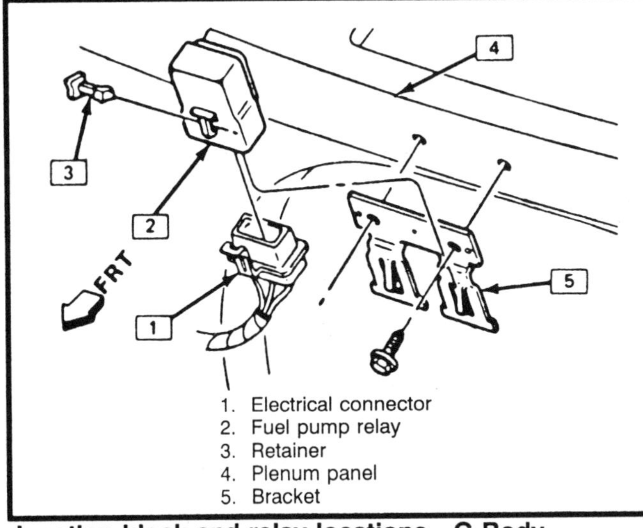

1. Electrical connector
2. Fuel pump relay
3. Retainer
4. Plenum panel
5. Bracket

Junction block and relay locations – G-Body

- **MAP Sensor** – see Manifold Absolute Pressure sensor.
- **Oil Pressure Switch (2.5L engine)** – is located on the left side of the engine under the exhaust manifold.
- **Oil Pressure Switch (4.3L engine)** – is located at the left rear of the engine, near the distributor.
- **Parking Brake Switch** – is under the left side of the instrument panel, on top of the parking brake assembly.
- **Throttle Position Sensor** – is located at the throttle body.
- **Trailer Connector** – is at the right rear of the vehicle.
- **Transmission Converter Clutch (TCC) Solenoid** – is mounted on the left side of the transmission.
- **Transmission Position Switch** – is located on the steering column.
- **Turn Signal Flasher** – is located behind the left side of the instrument panel, near the hood release cable.
- **Vehicle Speed Sensor (Electronic Cluster)** – is on the rear of the transmission.
- **Vehicle Speed Sensor (Standard Cluster)** – is on the rear of the instrument panel next to the speedometer.
- **Washer Pump** – is above the left fenderwell, next to the solvent bottle.

S SERIES – BLAZER/JIMMY AND PICKUP

- **A/C Compressor Diode** – is inside the compressor connector.
- **A/C Cutout Relay** – is above the left fender apron.
- **A/C Low Charge Switch** – is in the rear of the compressor.
- **A/C Pressure cycling switch** – is on the top rear of the accumulator.
- **Air Deverter Valve (2.8L engine)** – is located on the lower right front of the engine.
- **Assembly Line Diagnostic Link (ALDL)** – is located below the instrument panel to the right of the steering column.
- **Audio Alarm Module** – is connected to the convenience center.
- **Blower Resistor** – is on the blower motor housing.
- **Convenience Center** – is located below the left side of the instrument panel, to the left of the steering.
- **Coolant Temperature Sensor (2.5L engine)** – is at the right front of the engine, on the thermostat housing.
- **Coolant Temperature Sensor (2.8L/4.3L engine)** – is at the left upper front of the engine.
- **Cruise Control Module** – is located behind the instrument panel on the left.
- **Elapsed Timer Module** – is mounted near the electronic control module.
- **Electronic Control Module (2.5L engine)** – is located behind the right side of the instrument panel.
- **Electronic Spark Control (ESC) Module** – is at the center of the firewall.
- **Electronic Spark Timing (EST) Distributor (2.5L engine)** – is beneath the intake manifold.
- **Electronic Spark Timing (EST) Distributor (2.8L engine)** – is at the top rear of the engine.
- **Electronic Vacuum Regulator Valve (2.8L engine)** – is at the rear of the throttle body.
- **Fuel Pump Prime Connector (2.5L engine)** – is located at the center of the firewall.
- **Fuel Pump Prime Connector (2.8L – 1989)** – is located next to the fuel pump relay on the on the left fender apron.
- **Fuel Pump Prime Connector (2.8L except 1989)** – is located next to ECU.
- **Fuel Pump Prime Connector (4.3L – 1989)** – is located next to the fuel pump relay on the on the left fender apron.
- **Fuel Pump Prime Connector (4.3L except 1989)** – is located next to the ESC module on the center of the firewall.

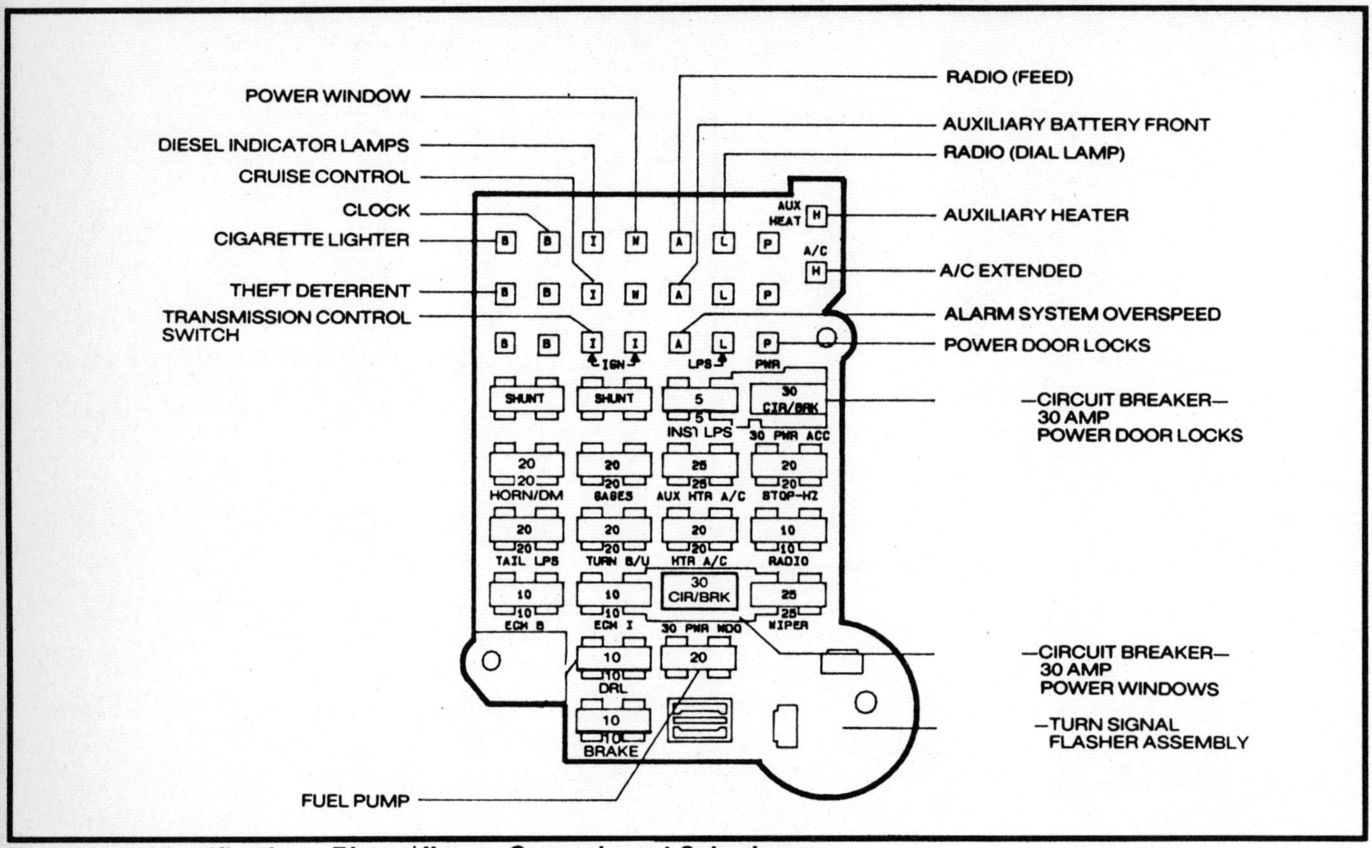

RADIO (FEED)
POWER WINDOW
AUXILIARY BATTERY FRONT
RADIO (DIAL LAMP)
DIESEL INDICATOR LAMPS
CRUISE CONTROL
CLOCK
CIGARETTE LIGHTER
AUXILIARY HEATER
A/C EXTENDED
THEFT DETERRENT
TRANSMISSION CONTROL SWITCH
ALARM SYSTEM OVERSPEED
POWER DOOR LOCKS
—CIRCUIT BREAKER— 30 AMP POWER DOOR LOCKS
SHUNT
5 INST LPS
30 CIR/BRK 30 PWR ACC
20 HORN/DM
20 GAGES
25 AUX HTR A/C
20 STOP-HZ
20 TAIL LPS
20 TURN B/U
20 HTR A/C
10 RADIO
10 ECM B
10 ECM I
30 CIR/BRK 30 PWR WDO
25 WIPER
10 DRL
20
10 BRAKE
—CIRCUIT BREAKER— 30 AMP POWER WINDOWS
—TURN SIGNAL FLASHER ASSEMBLY
FUEL PUMP

Fuse block identification – Blazer/Jimmy, Crewcab and Suburban

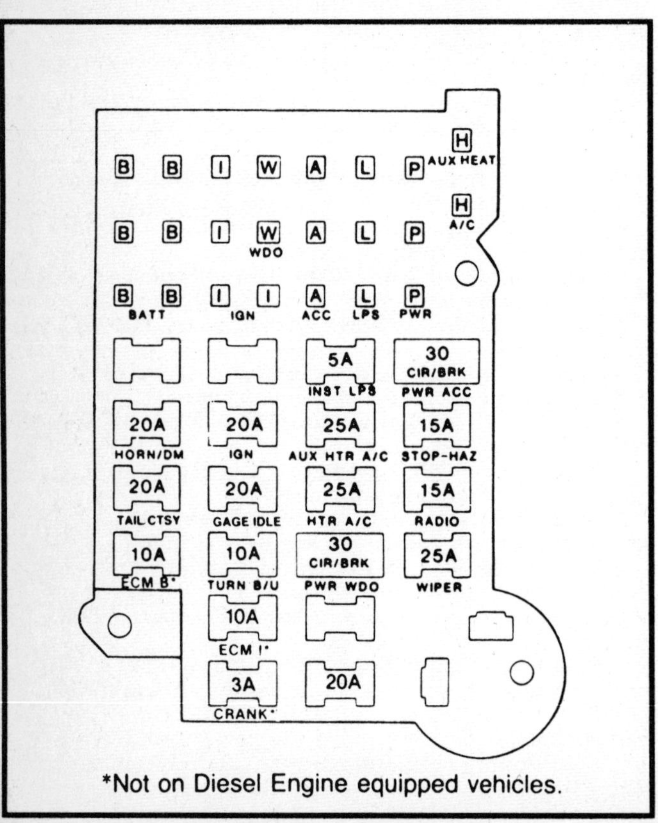

AUX HEAT
A/C
WDO
BATT
IGN
ACC
LPS
PWR
30 CIR/BRK
5A INST LPS
PWR ACC
20A HORN/DM
20A IGN
25A AUX HTR A/C
15A STOP-HAZ
20A TAIL CTSY
20A GAGE IDLE
25A HTR A/C
15A RADIO
10A ECM B*
10A TURN B/U
30 CIR/BRK PWR WDO
25A WIPER
10A ECM I*
3A CRANK*
20A
*Not on Diesel Engine equipped vehicles.

Fuse block identification – G-body vans

- **Junction Block (C/K)** – is at the right front of the cowl, behind the cover.
- **Fuse Box** – is located left side of the instrument panel by the kick panel.
- **Hazard Flasher (except Van)** – under the left instrument panel, above the convenience center.
- **Hazard Flasher (Van)** – under the left instrument panel, near radio adapter and below headlamp switch.
- **MAP Sensor** – see Manifold Absolute Pressure sensor.
- **Oil Pressure Switch (7.4L engine)** – is located at the left front of the engine.
- **Oil Pressure Switch (except 7.4L engine)** – is located to the left of the distributor.
- **Rear Defogger Relay** – is located at the fuel box.
- **Transmission Downshift Relay** – is located next to the fuel pump relay.
- **Turn Signal Flasher** – is located at the fuse box.
- **Vehicle Speed Sensor** – is located behind the instrument panel at the speedometer.

ASTRO AND SAFARI VANS

- **Assembly Line Diagnostic Link (ALDL)** – is located below the instrument panel to the left, at the convenience center.
- **Audio Alarm Module** – is on the left side of the instrument panel, left of the steering or plugged into the convenience center.
- **Back-Up Lamp Switch** – is located on the left rear of the transmission.
- **Battery Junction Block** – is located at the bulkhead connector.

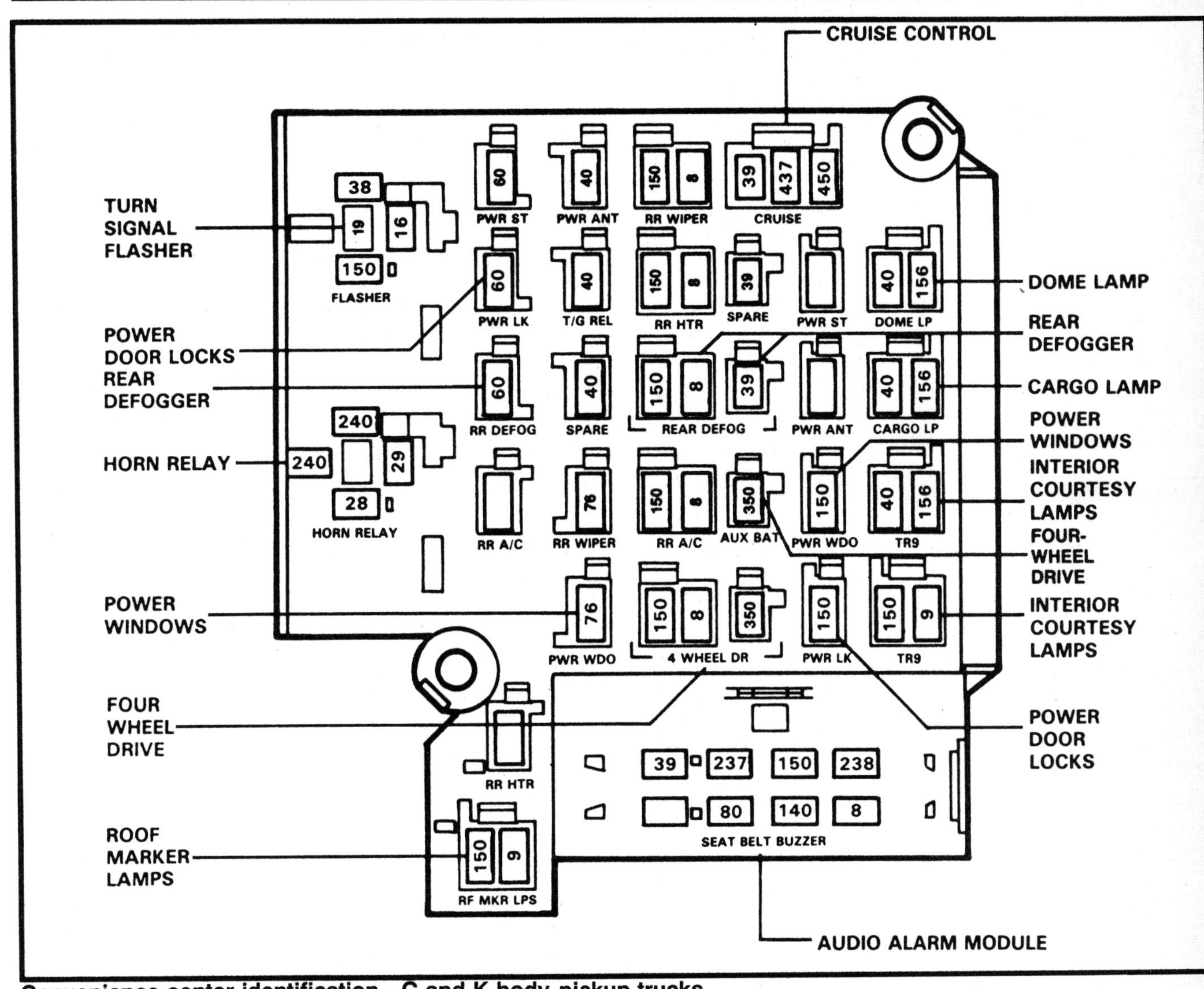

Convenience center identification—C and K-body pickup trucks

• **Blower Resistors**—are located on the blower motor housing.

• **Brake Pressure Switch**—is mounted on the master cylinder.

• **Convenience Center**—is located behind the left side of the instrument panel, left of the steering column.

• **Coolant Temperature Sensor (2.5L engine)**—is at the left front of the engine, on the coolant outlet.

• **Coolant Temperature Sensor (4.3L engine)**—is at the lower side of the left cylinder head.

• **Coolant Temperature Sensor/Switch (2.5L engine)**—is at the rear of the cylinder head.

• **Coolant Temperature Switch (4.3L engine)**—is at the left side of the engine, above the exhaust manifold.

• **Cruise Control Module (Electronic Cluster)**—is located on the left, near the brake booster.

• **Cruise Control Module (Standard Cluster)**—is located on the left side of the instrument panel on the rear of the dash.

• **Cruise Control Servo**—is mounted to the intake manifold.

• **Door Lock Control Module**—is located behind the right side of the instrument panel at the top of the cowl.

• **Door Lock Relay Assembly**—is located behind the right side of the instrument panel at the top of the cowl.

• **EGR Valve Solenoid**—is on the intake manifold in front of the throttle body.

• **Electronic Control Unit**—is located behind the right cowl panel.

• **Electronic Spark Control Module (4.3L engine)**—is located on the right side of the engine above the valve cover.

• **Electronic Spark Timing (EST) Distributor (2.5L engine)**—is beneath the intake manifold.

• **Fuel Pump Relay**—is located on the right side of the engine compartment.

• **Fuse box**—is located under the instrument panel next to the steering column.

• **Hazard Flasher**—is located behind the left side of the instrument panel, at the convenience center.

• **High Beam Cutout Relay**—is at the convenience center.

• **High Blower Relay**—is on the right side near the blower housing.

• **Horn Relay**—is connected to the convenience center.

• **Knock Sensor (4.3L engine)**—is located at the left rear of the engine under the exhaust manifold.

• **Manifold Absolute Pressure (MAP) sensor**—is mounted to the air cleaner.

'G' SERIES RPO:LB4 ENGINE CODE:Z 4.3L V6

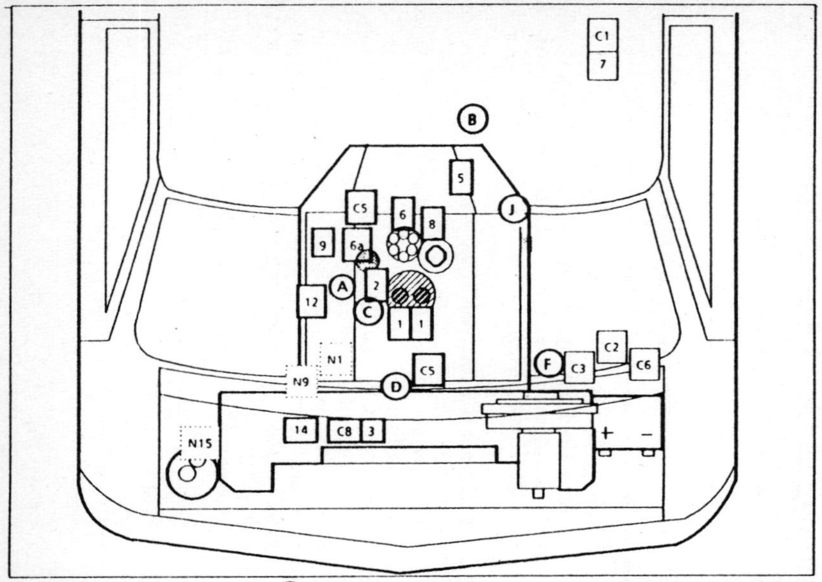

COMPUTER COMMAND CONTROL

- C1 Electronic Control Module (E.C.M.)
- C2 ALDL diagnostic connector
- C3 "SERVICE ENGINE SOON" light
- C5 ECM harness ground
- C6 Fuse panel
- C8 Fuel pump test connector

ECM INFORMATION SENSORS

- A Manifold Absolute Pressure (M.A.P.)
- B Exhaust oxygen
- C Throttle position (T.P.S.)
- D Coolant temperature
- F Vehicle speed (V.S.S.)
- J Electronic Spark Control Knock (E.S.C.)

EMISSION COMPONENTS (NOT ECM CONTROLLED)

- N1 Crankcase vent valve (PCV)
- N9 Air Pump
- N15 Fuel Vapor Canister

ECM CONTROLLED COMPONENTS

- 1 Fuel injector
- 2 Idle air control
- 3 Fuel pump relay
- 5 Transmission Converter Clutch Connector
- 6 Electronic Spark Timing Distributor (E.S.T.)
- 6a Remote ignition coil
- 7 Electronic Spark Control module (E.S.C.)
- 8 Oil pressure switch
- 9 Electric Air Control solenoid (E.A.C.)
- 12 Exhaust Gas Recirculation Vacuum Solenoid
- 14 Transmission downshift relay (THM-400 only)

Component locations—G-body with 4.3L engine

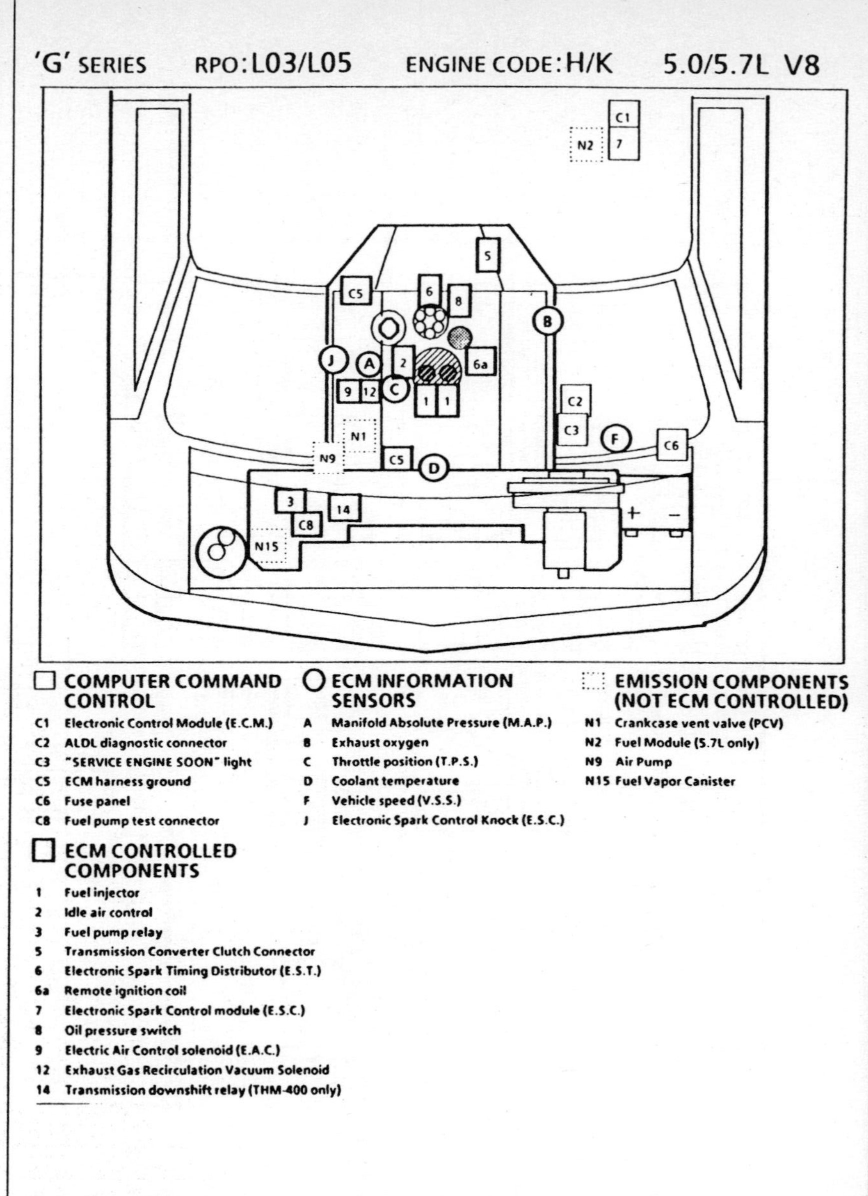

'G' SERIES RPO:L03/L05 ENGINE CODE:H/K 5.0/5.7L V8

COMPUTER COMMAND CONTROL

- C1 Electronic Control Module (E.C.M.)
- C2 ALDL diagnostic connector
- C3 "SERVICE ENGINE SOON" light
- C5 ECM harness ground
- C6 Fuse panel
- C8 Fuel pump test connector

ECM INFORMATION SENSORS

- A Manifold Absolute Pressure (M.A.P.)
- B Exhaust oxygen
- C Throttle position (T.P.S.)
- D Coolant temperature
- F Vehicle speed (V.S.S.)
- J Electronic Spark Control Knock (E.S.C.)

EMISSION COMPONENTS (NOT ECM CONTROLLED)

- N1 Crankcase vent valve (PCV)
- N2 Fuel Module (5.7L only)
- N9 Air Pump
- N15 Fuel Vapor Canister

ECM CONTROLLED COMPONENTS

- 1 Fuel injector
- 2 Idle air control
- 3 Fuel pump relay
- 5 Transmission Converter Clutch Connector
- 6 Electronic Spark Timing Distributor (E.S.T.)
- 6a Remote ignition coil
- 7 Electronic Spark Control module (E.S.C.)
- 8 Oil pressure switch
- 9 Electric Air Control solenoid (E.A.C.)
- 12 Exhaust Gas Recirculation Vacuum Solenoid
- 14 Transmission downshift relay (THM-400 only)

Component locations—G-body with 5.0L and 5.7L engine

'G' SERIES RPO: L19 ENGINE CODE: N 7.4L V8

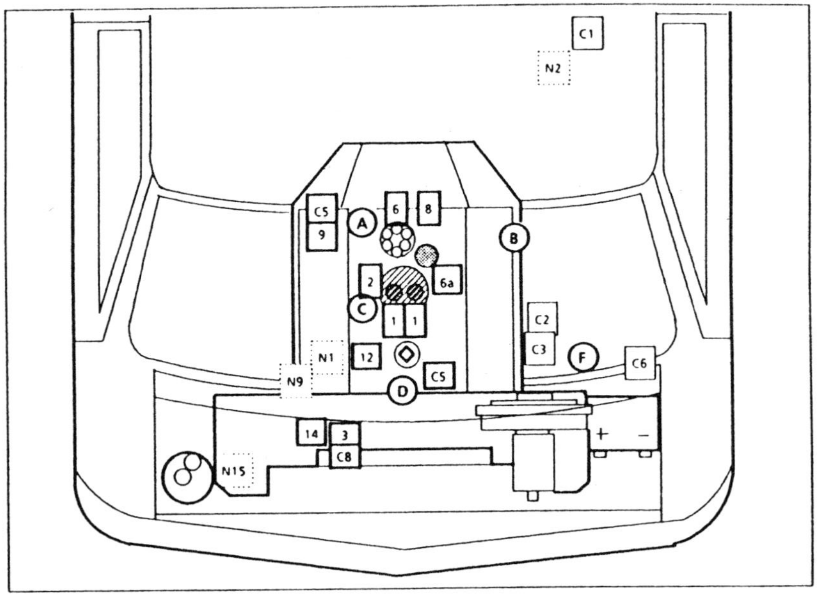

☐ COMPUTER COMMAND CONTROL
- C1 Electronic Control Module (E.C.M.)
- C2 ALDL diagnostic connector
- C3 "SERVICE ENGINE SOON" light
- C5 ECM harness ground
- C6 Fuse panel
- C8 Fuel pump test connector

☐ ECM CONTROLLED COMPONENTS
- 1 Fuel injector
- 2 Idle air control
- 3 Fuel pump relay
- 6 Electronic Spark Timing Distributor (E.S.T.)
- 6a Remote ignition coil
- 8 Oil pressure switch
- 9 Electric Air Control solenoid (E.A.C.)
- 12 Exhaust Gas Recirculation Vacuum Solenoid
- 14 Transmission downshift relay (THM-400 only)

◯ ECM INFORMATION SENSORS
- A Manifold Absolute Pressure (M.A.P.)
- B Exhaust oxygen
- C Throttle position (T.P.S.)
- D Coolant temperature
- F Vehicle speed (V.S.S.)

⬚ EMISSION COMPONENTS (NOT ECM CONTROLLED)
- N1 Crankcase vent valve (PCV)
- N2 Fuel Module
- N9 Air Pump
- N15 Fuel Vapor Canister

Component locations – G-body with 7.4L engine

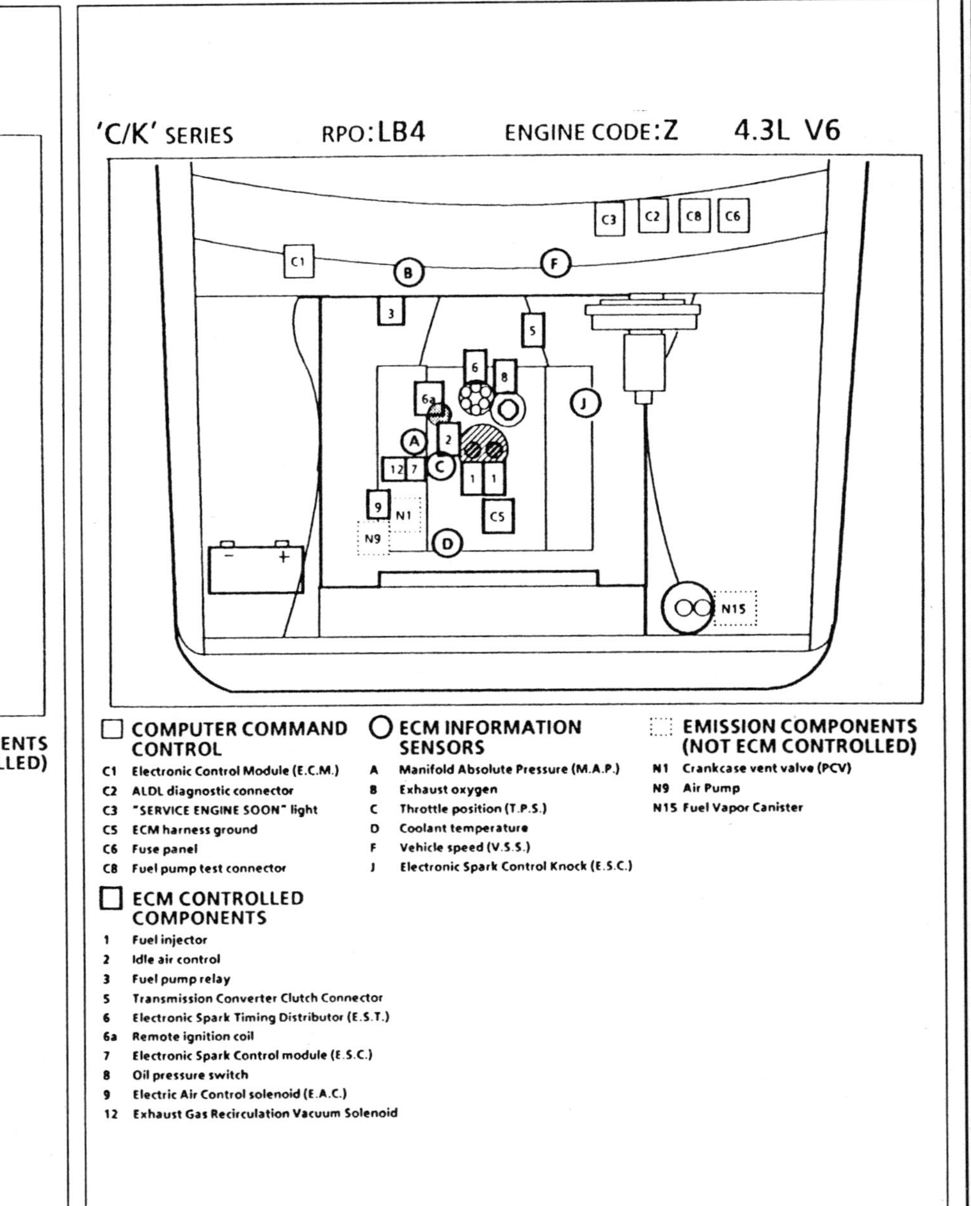

☐ COMPUTER COMMAND CONTROL
- C1 Electronic Control Module (E.C.M.)
- C2 ALDL diagnostic connector
- C3 "SERVICE ENGINE SOON" light
- C5 ECM harness ground
- C6 Fuse panel
- C8 Fuel pump test connector

☐ ECM CONTROLLED COMPONENTS
- 1 Fuel injector
- 2 Idle air control
- 3 Fuel pump relay
- 5 Transmission Converter Clutch Connector
- 6 Electronic Spark Timing Distributor (E.S.T.)
- 6a Remote ignition coil
- 7 Electronic Spark Control module (E.S.C.)
- 8 Oil pressure switch
- 9 Electric Air Control solenoid (E.A.C.)
- 12 Exhaust Gas Recirculation Vacuum Solenoid

◯ ECM INFORMATION SENSORS
- A Manifold Absolute Pressure (M.A.P.)
- B Exhaust oxygen
- C Throttle position (T.P.S.)
- D Coolant temperature
- F Vehicle speed (V.S.S.)
- J Electronic Spark Control Knock (E.S.C.)

⬚ EMISSION COMPONENTS (NOT ECM CONTROLLED)
- N1 Crankcase vent valve (PCV)
- N9 Air Pump
- N15 Fuel Vapor Canister

Component locations – C and K-body with 4.3L engine

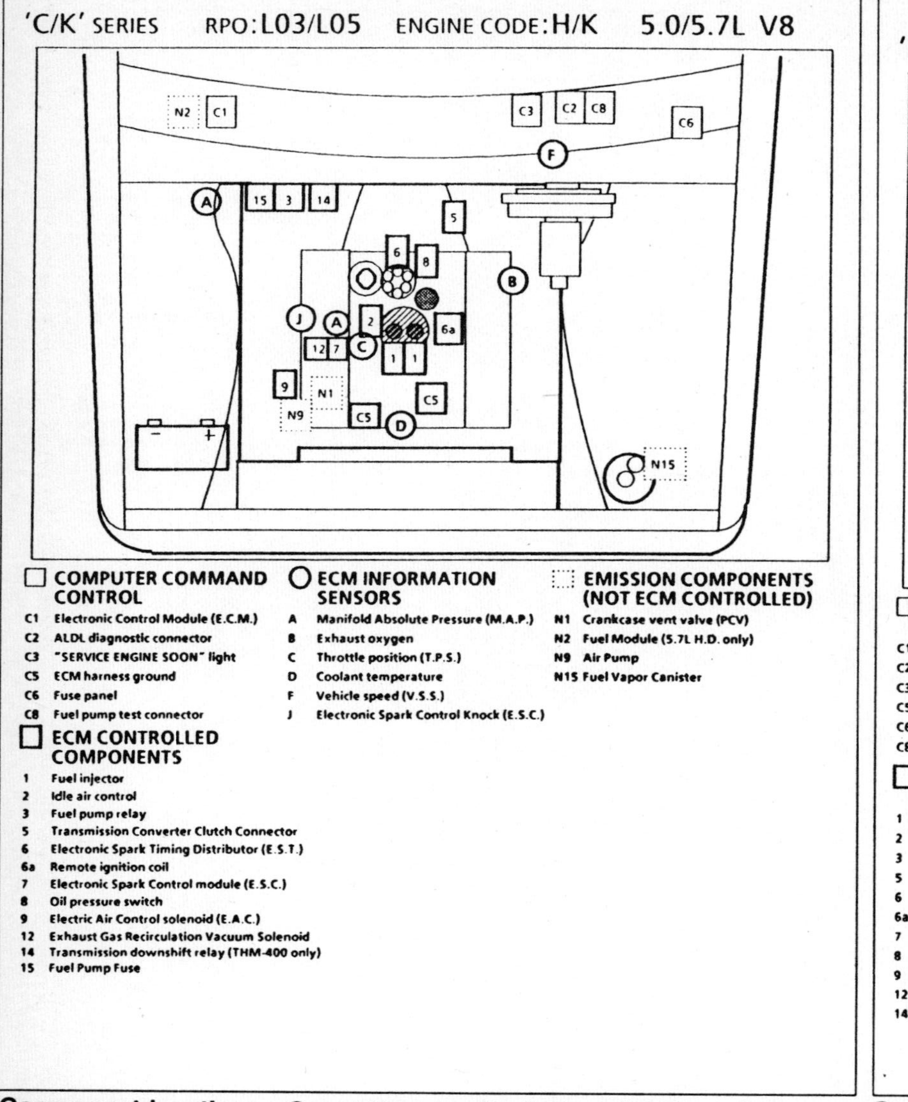

Component locations—C and K-body with 5.0L and 5.7L engine

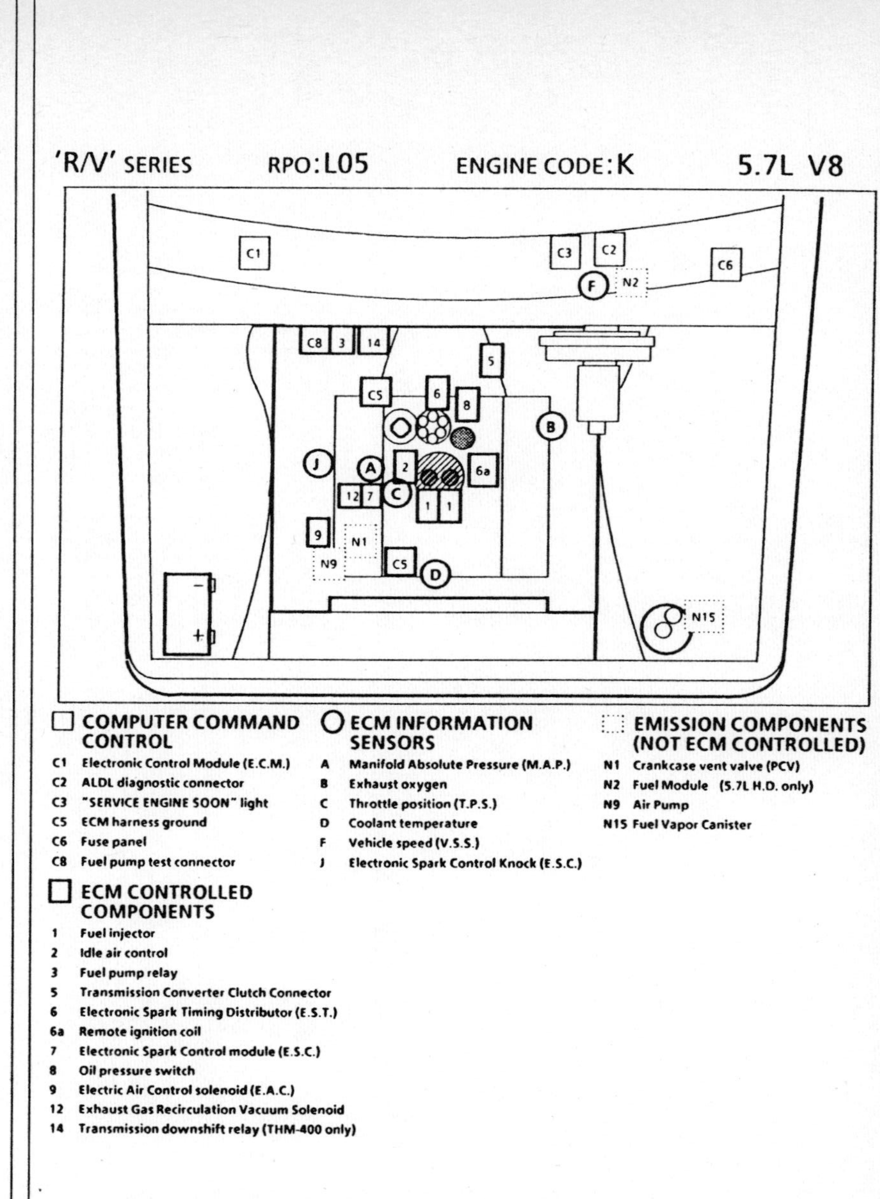

Component locations—Blazer/Jimmy, Crewcab and Suburban with 5.7L engine

'G' SERIES RPO: L19 ENGINE CODE: N 7.4L V8

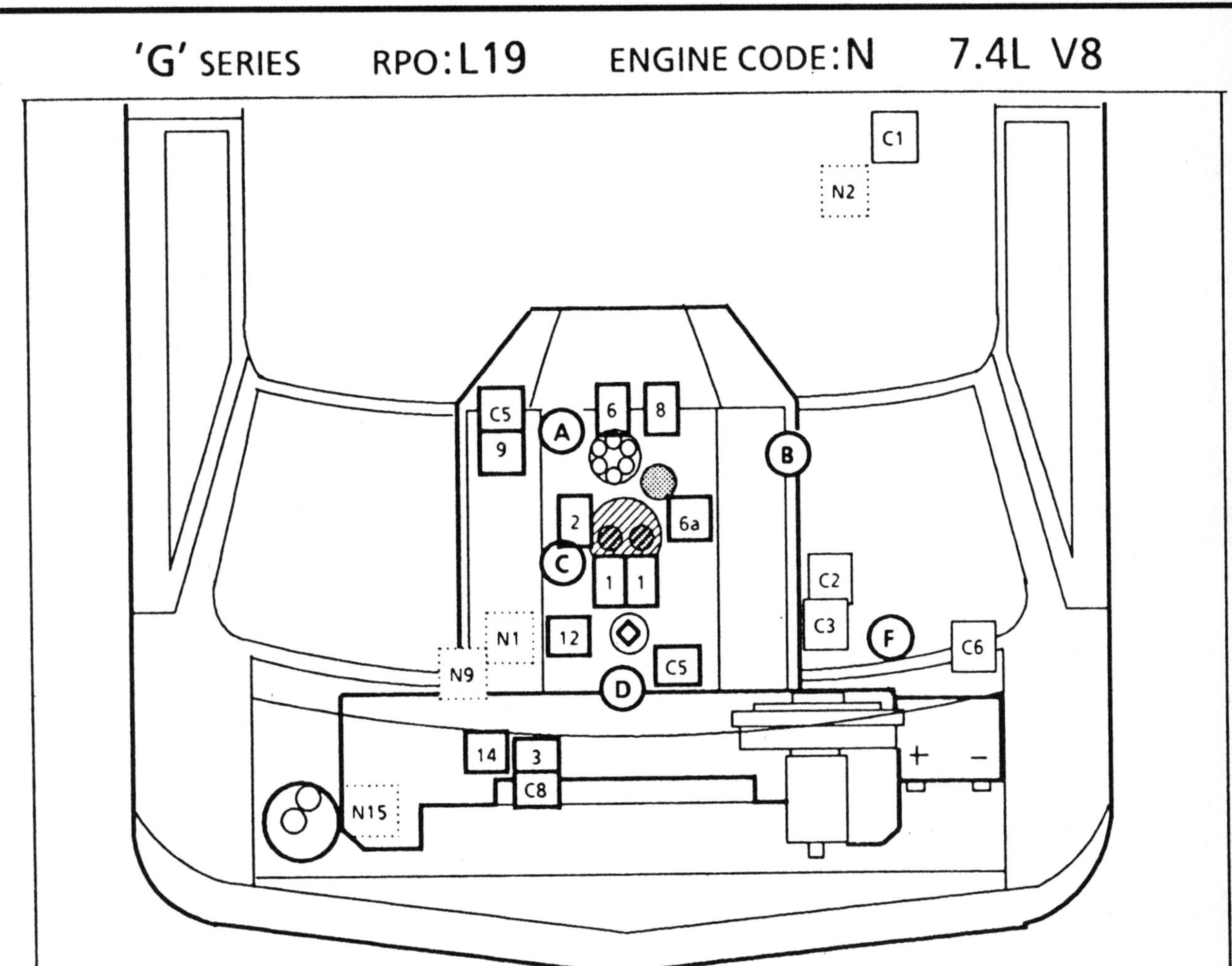

COMPUTER COMMAND CONTROL

- C1 Electronic Control Module (E.C.M.)
- C2 ALDL diagnostic connector
- C3 "SERVICE ENGINE SOON" light
- C5 ECM harness ground
- C6 Fuse panel
- C8 Fuel pump test connector

ECM CONTROLLED COMPONENTS

- 1 Fuel injector
- 2 Idle air control
- 3 Fuel pump relay
- 6 Electronic Spark Timing Distributor (E.S.T.)
- 6a Remote ignition coil
- 8 Oil pressure switch
- 9 Electric Air Control solenoid (E.A.C.)
- 12 Exhaust Gas Recirculation Vacuum Solenoid
- 14 Transmission downshift relay (THM-400 only)

ECM INFORMATION SENSORS

- A Manifold Absolute Pressure (M.A.P.)
- B Exhaust oxygen
- C Throttle position (T.P.S.)
- D Coolant temperature
- F Vehicle speed (V.S.S.)

EMISSION COMPONENTS (NOT ECM CONTROLLED)

- N1 Crankcase vent valve (PCV)
- N2 Fuel Module
- N9 Air Pump
- N15 Fuel Vapor Canister

Component locations – 7.4L engine

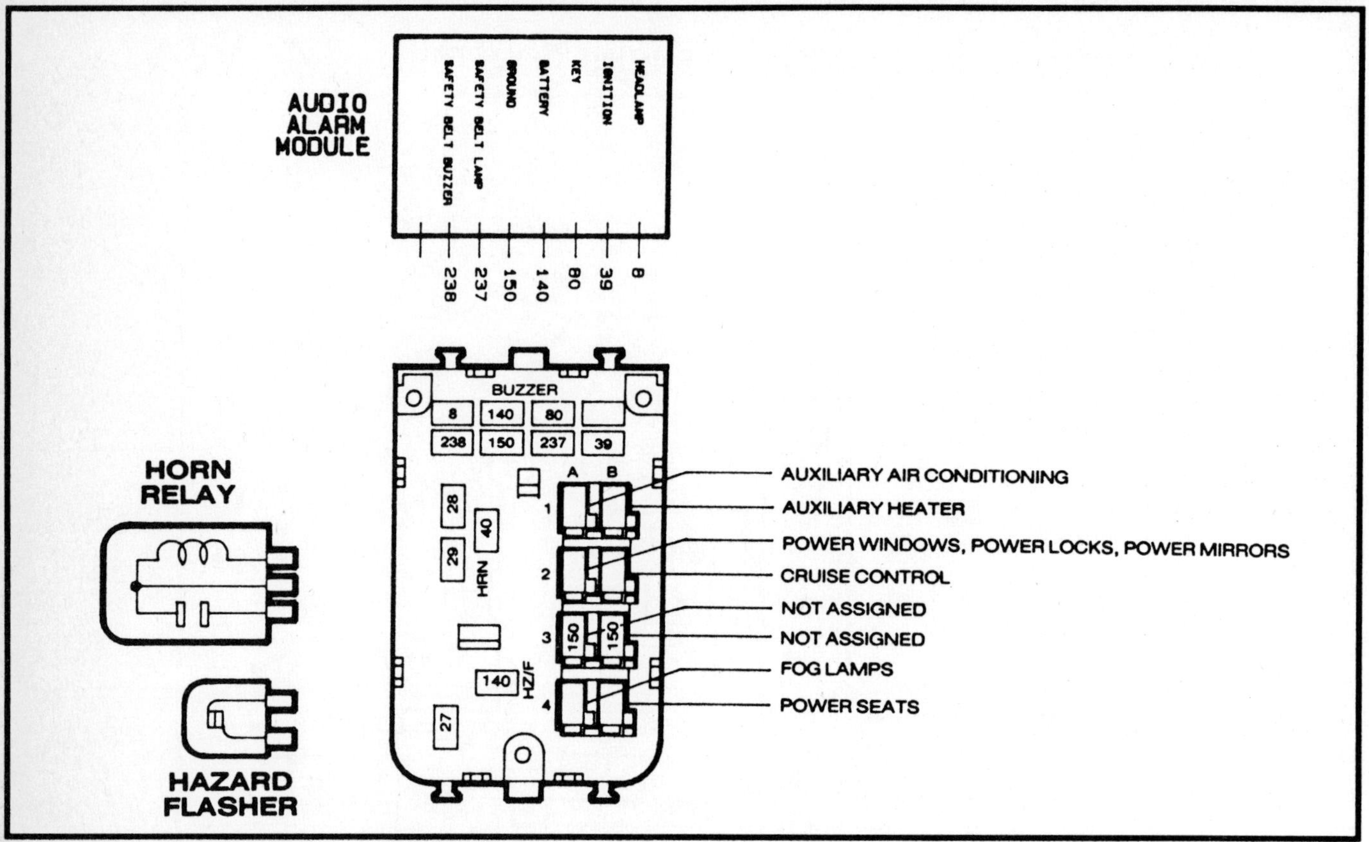

Convenience Center—Astro and Safari Vans

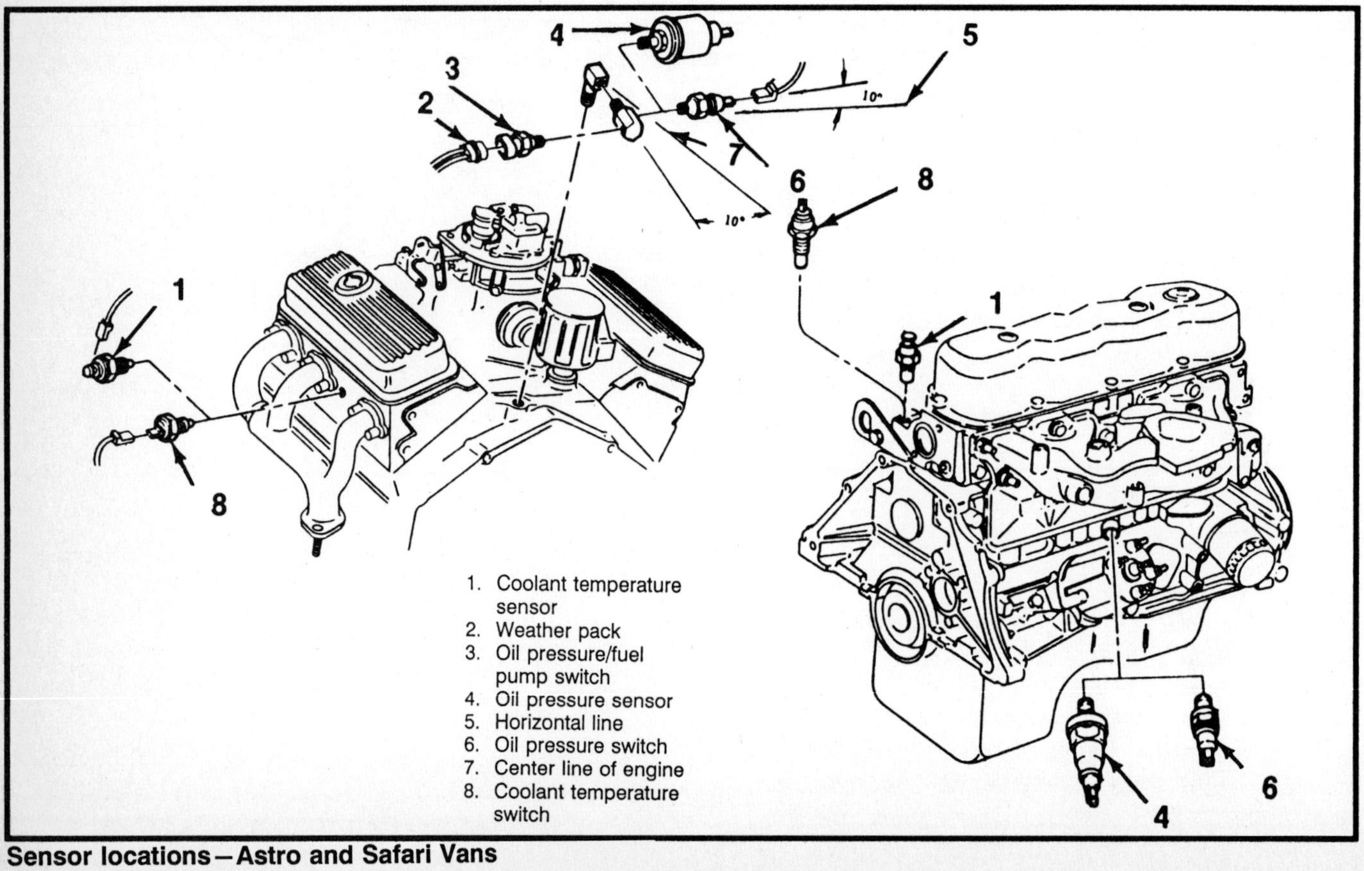

Sensor locations—Astro and Safari Vans

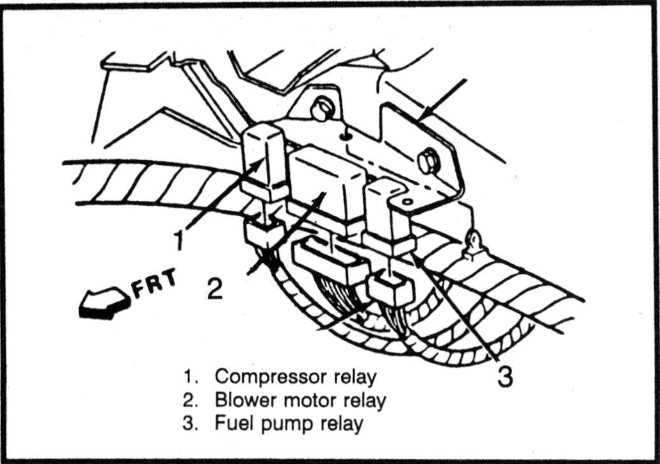

Relay identification—Astro and Safari Vans

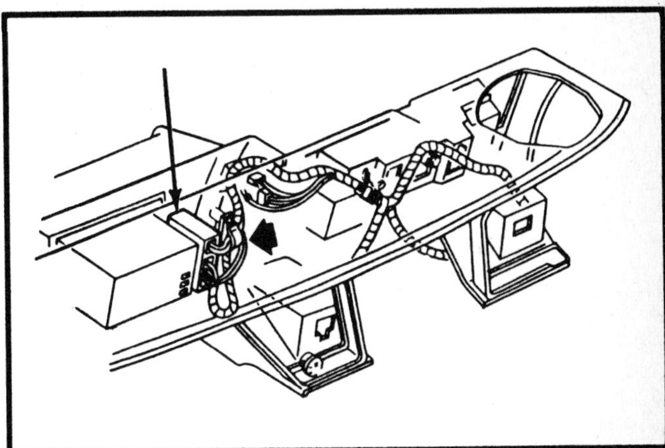

Digital Radio Adapter Controller—Astro and Safari Vans

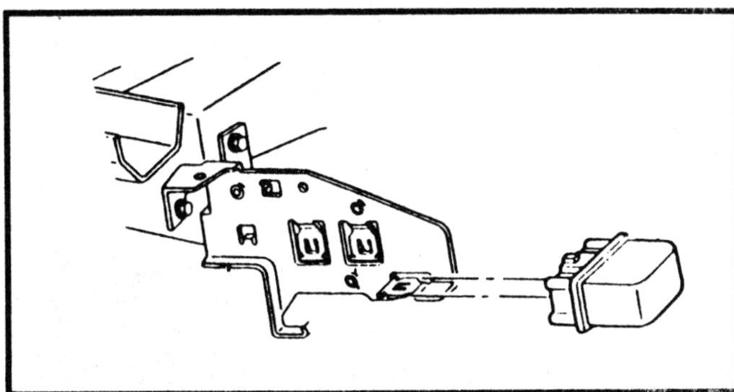

Blower motor relay—Astro and Safari Vans

- **Fuel Pump Relay (except 1991—4.3L engine)**—is on the left front fender apron.
- **Fuel Pump Relay (1991—4.3L engine)**—is on the left side of power brake.
- **Fuse Box**—is behind the left side of the instrument panel.
- **Hazard Flasher**—is behind the left side of the instrument panel at the convenience center.
- **High Blower Relay**—is at the right side of the dash near the blower housing.
- **Idle Air Control Stepper Motor (2.8L/4.3L engine)**—is at the left rear of the throttle body.
- **Knock Sensor (2.8L/4.3L engine)**—is located at the left rear of the engine at the rear of the cylinder head.
- **Manifold Absolute Pressure (MAP) sensor**—is mounted to the air cleaner.
- **MAP Sensor**—see Manifold Absolute Pressure sensor.
- **Oil Pressure Relay**—is above the left front wheel left side of the engine.
- **Oil Pressure Sensor (2.5L/2.8L engine)**—is at the oil filter attachment.
- **Oil Pressure Sensor (4.3L engine)**—is at the top rear of the filter attachment.
- **Oil Pressure Switch (2.5L engine)**—is located on the right side of the engine under the manifold.
- **Oil Pressure Switch (2.8L engine)**—is located on the lower left side of the engine.
- **Oil Pressure Switch (4.3L engine)**—is located to the left of the distributor.
- **Parking Brake Switch**—is behind the left side of the instrument panel, above the kick panel.
- **Rear Window Defogger Timer/Relay**—On models that may not incorporate the timer with the switch, the timer/relay is on the brake pedal support bracket.

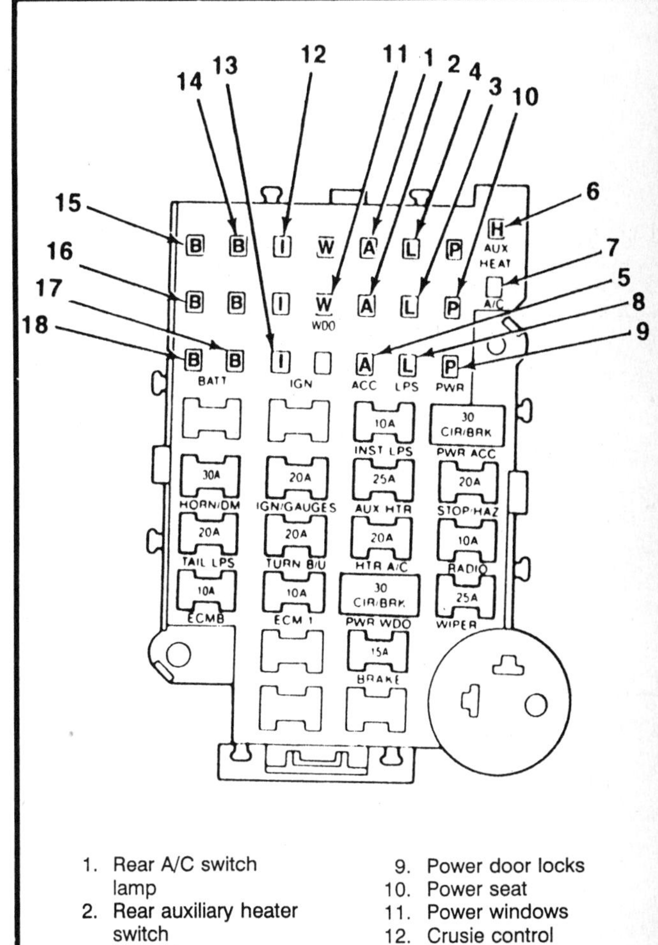

Fuse block identification—Astro and Safari Vans

'M' SERIES RPO:LN8 ENGINE CODE:E 2.5L L4

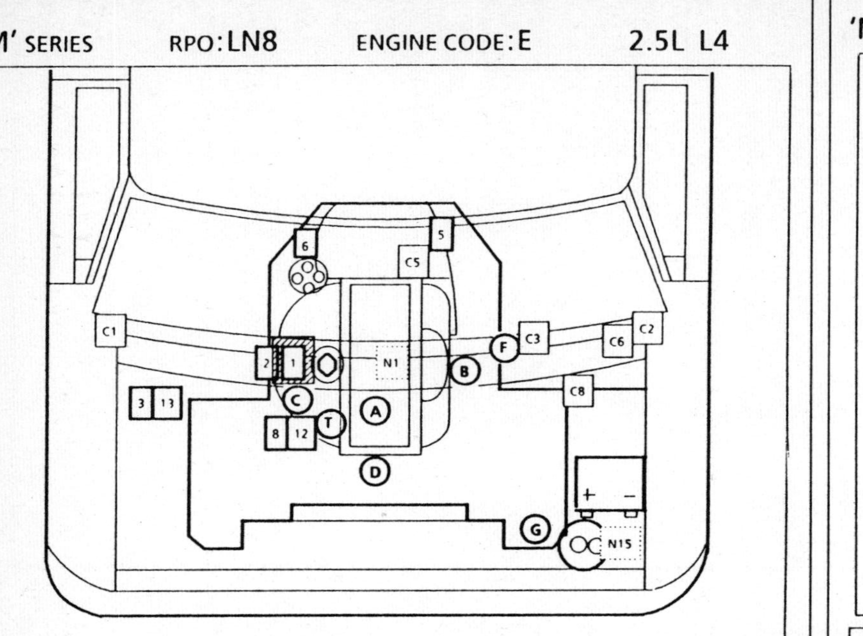

☐ COMPUTER COMMAND CONTROL

- C1 Electronic Control Module (E.C.M.)
- C2 ALDL diagnostic connector
- C3 "SERVICE ENGINE SOON" light
- C5 ECM harness ground
- C6 Fuse panel
- C8 Fuel pump test connector

○ ECM INFORMATION SENSORS

- A Manifold pressure (M.A.P.)
- B Exhaust oxygen
- C Throttle position (T.P.S.)
- D Coolant temperature
- F Vehicle speed (V.S.S.)
- G Power Steering Pressure
- T Manifold Air Temperature (M.A.T.)

⬚ EMISSION COMPONENTS (NOT ECM CONTROLLED)

- N1 Crankcase vent (PCV) valve
- N15 Fuel vapor canister

☐ ECM CONTROLLED COMPONENTS

- 1 Fuel injector
- 2 Idle air control
- 3 Fuel pump relay
- 5 Transmission Converter Clutch Connector
- 6 Electronic Spark Timing Distributor (E.S.T.)
- 8 Oil pressure switch
- 12 Exhaust Gas Recirculation Vacuum Solenoid
- 13 A/C relay

Component locations—Astro and Safari Vans with 2.5L engine

'M' SERIES RPO:LB4 ENGINE CODE:Z 4.3L V6

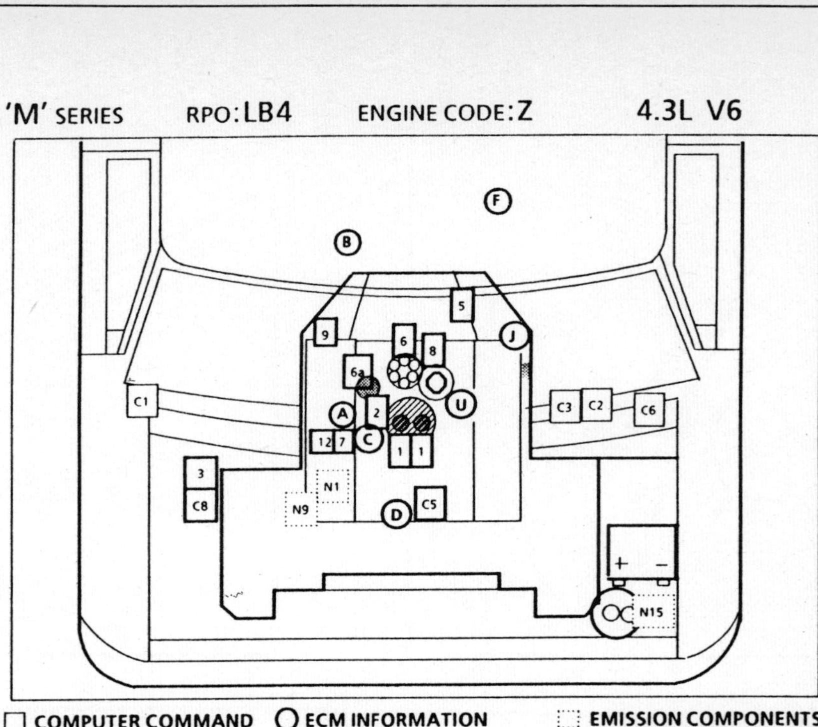

☐ COMPUTER COMMAND CONTROL

- C1 Electronic Control Module (E.C.M.)
- C2 ALDL diagnostic connector
- C3 "SERVICE ENGINE SOON" light
- C5 ECM harness ground
- C6 Fuse panel
- C8 Fuel pump test connector

○ ECM INFORMATION SENSORS

- A Manifold Absolute Pressure (M.A.P.)
- B Exhaust oxygen
- C Throttle position (T.P.S.)
- D Coolant temperature
- F Vehicle speed (V.S.S.)
- J Electronic Spark Control Knock (E.S.C.)

⬚ EMISSION COMPONENTS (NOT ECM CONTROLLED)

- N1 Crankcase vent valve (PCV)
- N9 Air Pump
- N15 Fuel Vapor Canister

☐ ECM CONTROLLED COMPONENTS

- 1 Fuel injector
- 2 Idle air control
- 3 Fuel pump relay
- 5 Transmission Converter Clutch Connector
- 6 Electronic Spark Timing Distributor (E.S.T.)
- 6a Remote ignition coil
- 7 Electronic Spark Control module (E.S.C.)
- 8 Oil pressure switch
- 9 Electric Air Control solenoid (E.A.C.)
- 12 Exhaust Gas Recirculation Vacuum Solenoid

Component locations—Astro and Safari Vans with 4.3L engine

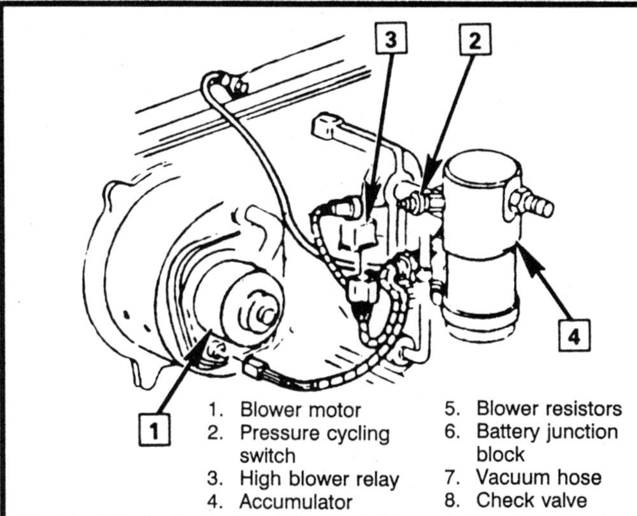

Blower Relay location—S Series

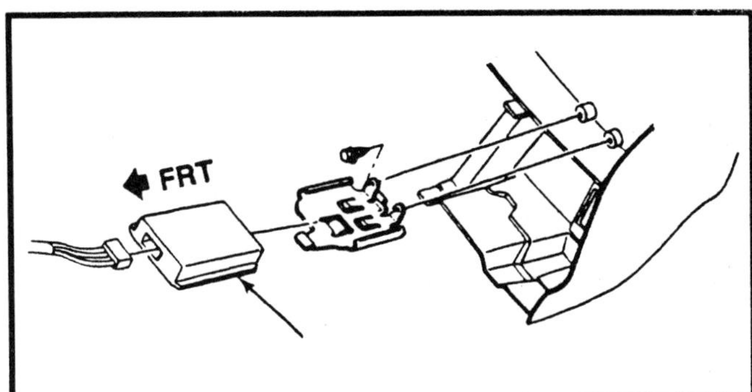

Cruse control module—S Series

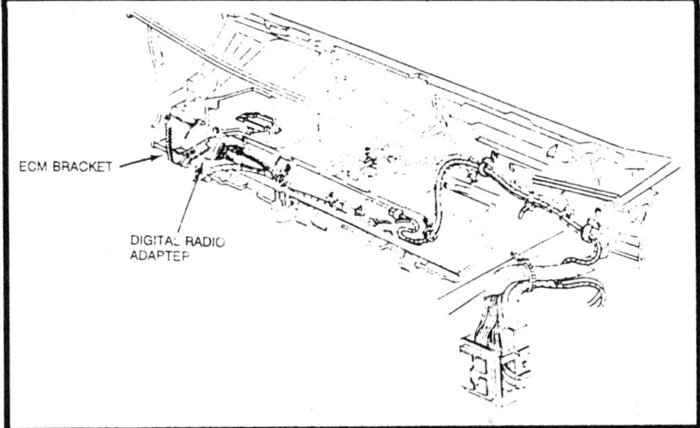

Digital radio controller—S Series

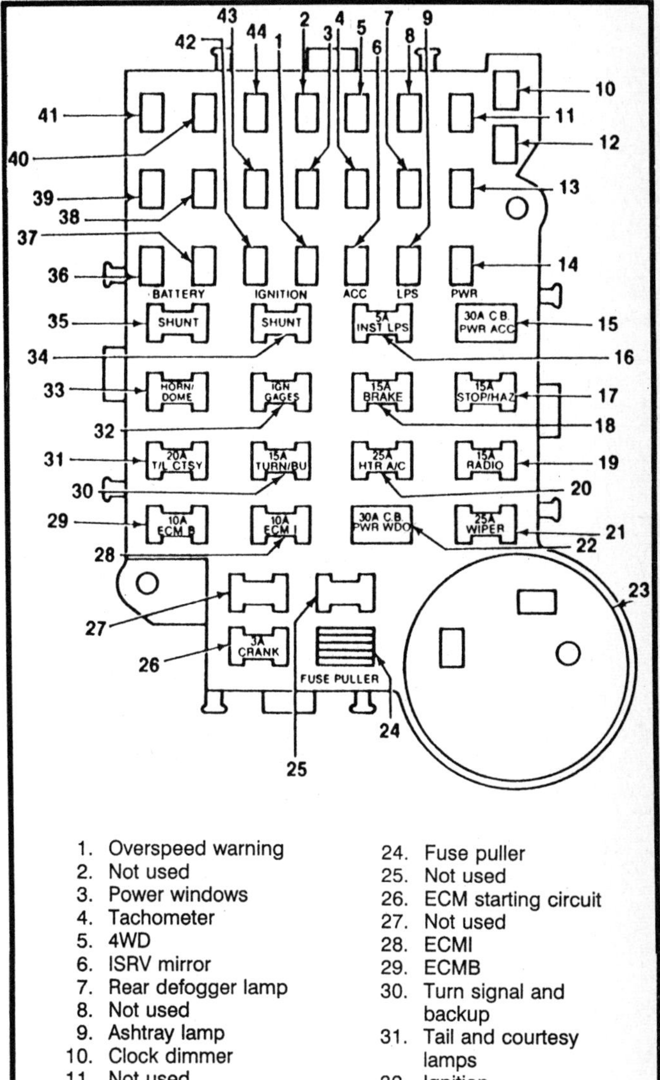

1. Overspeed warning
2. Not used
3. Power windows
4. Tachometer
5. 4WD
6. ISRV mirror
7. Rear defogger lamp
8. Not used
9. Ashtray lamp
10. Clock dimmer
11. Not used
12. Not used
13. Rear defogger
14. Power door locks
15. Power accessories—30 amp breaker
16. Instrumentation lamps
17. Stop and hazard
18. RWAL
19. Radio
20. Heater and A/C
21. Wiper
22. Power windows—30 amp breaker
23. Turn signal flasher
24. Fuse puller
25. Not used
26. ECM starting circuit
27. Not used
28. ECMI
29. ECMB
30. Turn signal and backup
31. Tail and courtesy lamps
32. Ignition
33. Horn and dome
34. Shunt
35. Shunt
36. Dome lamp
37. Headlamp system
38. Courtesy lamp system
39. INstrument panel compartment lamp
40. Lift gate release
41. Clock
42. Rear defogger timer
43. Automatic transmission
44. Cruise control

Fuse block identification—S Series

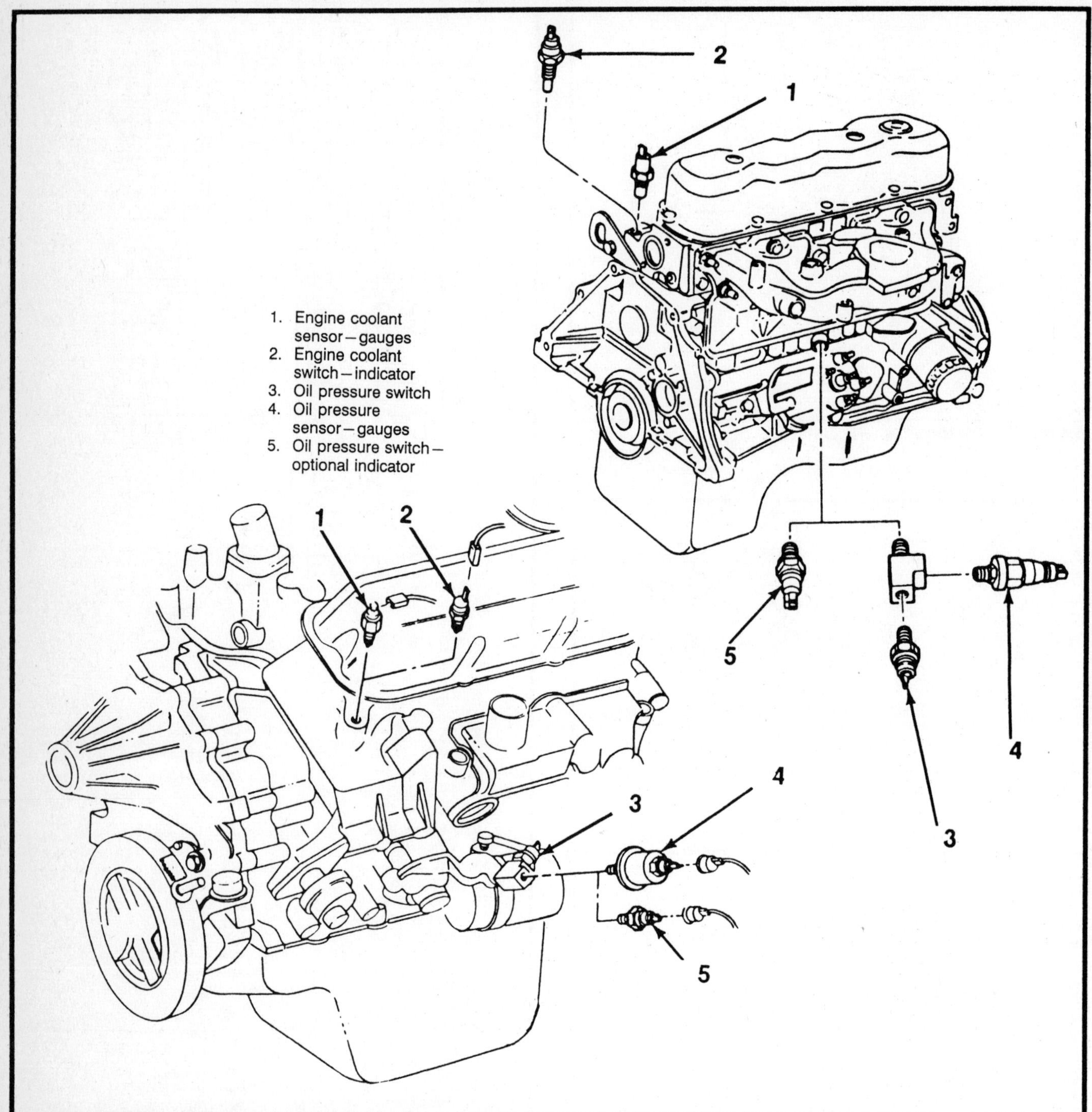

Sensor locations—S Series with 2.5L and 2.8L engine

• **Rear Window Release Relay**—is located behind the left side of the instrument panel.

• **Rear Window Release Solenoid**—is located in the center of the tailgate.

• **Speed Sensor**—is located behind the instrument panel at the speedometer.

• **Steering Pressure Switch (2.5L engine)**—is located at the front of the left fender apron.

• **TACH Signal Filter**—is below the wiper motor.

• **Timing Adjustment Connector**—is a single tan wire with a black tracer, that breaks out of the wiring harness under the right dash just below the heater assembly.

• **Throttle Position Sensor**—is located at the throttle body.

• **Trailer Connector**—is at the right rear of the vehicle.

• **Transmission Converter Clutch (TCC) Solenoid**—is mounted on the left side of the transmission.

• **Transmission Position Switch**—is located on the steering column.

• **Turn Signal Flasher**—is in the fuse box.

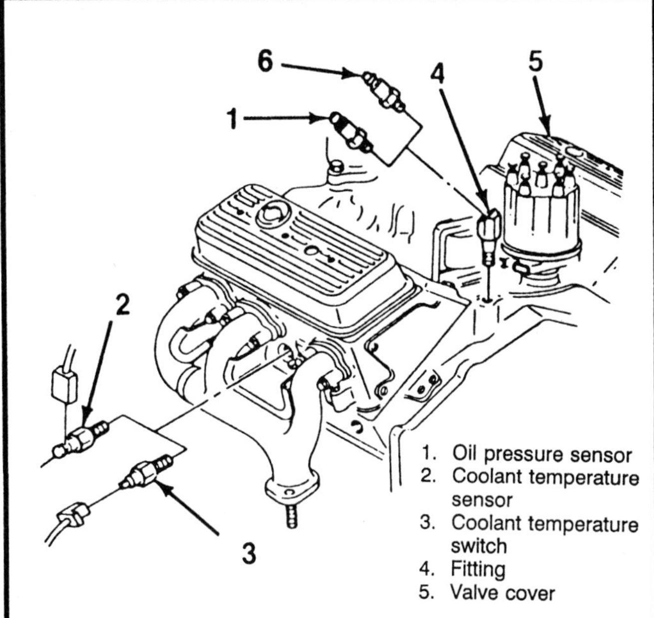

Sensor locations—S Series with 4.3L engine

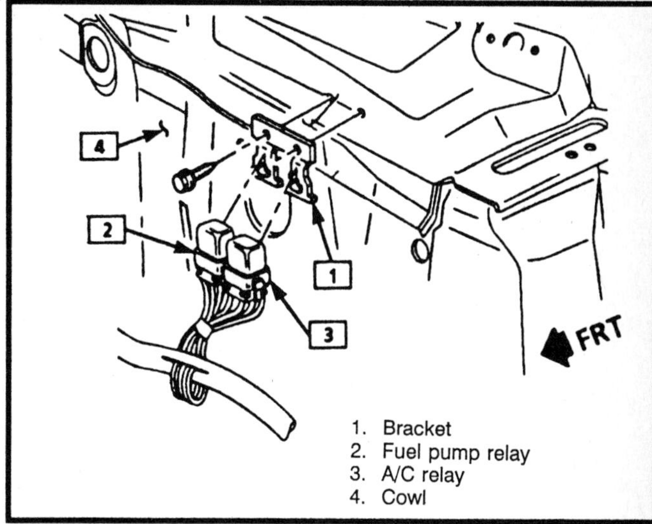

Relay locations—S Series with 4.3L engine

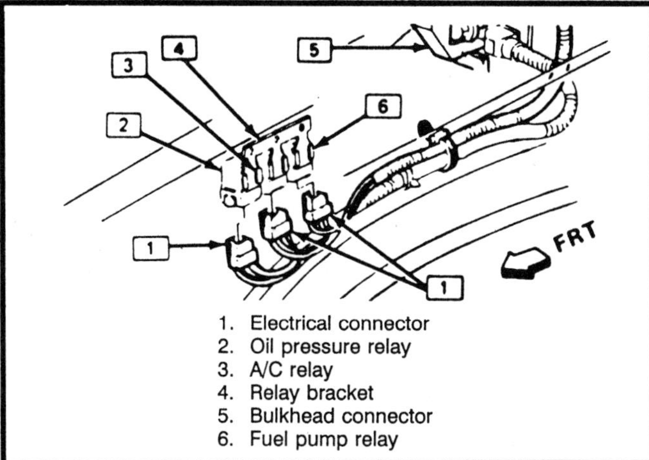

Relay locations—S Series with 2.5L and 2.8L engine

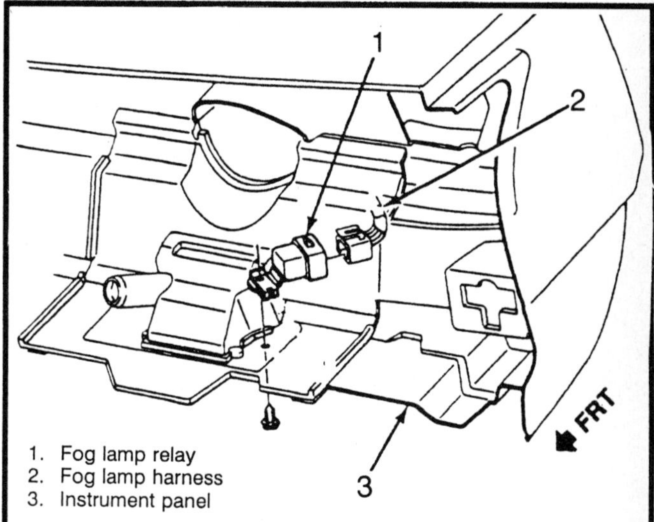

Fog lamp relay locations—S Series

• **Vehicle Speed Sensor Buffer**—is located behind the left side of the instrument panel on the wiring harness.

• **Washer Pump**—is above the left fender well, next to the solvent bottle.

SILHOUETTE, TRANS SPORT AND LUMINA APV

• **A/C Clutch Diode**—is taped in the engine harness next to the compressor connector.

• **A/C Compressor Relay**—is located on the behind the right headlamp capsule.

• **A/C High Pressure Switch**—is located in the back of the compressor.

• **A/C Low Pressure Switch**—is located in the back of the compressor.

• **A/C Pressure Switch**—is located below the accumulator.

• **Assembly Line Diagnostic Link (ALDL)**—is located below the instrument panel to the left of the steering column.

• **Audio Alarm Module**—is connected to the convenience center.

• **Auxiliary Blower Motor**—is located a the base of the left B—pillar.

• **Auxiliary Blower Resistor**—is below the heater and the A/C module assembly, mounted to the floor duct outlet.

• **Blower High Speed Relay**—is in the engine compartment, mounted to the heater and A/C control module assembly.

• **Blower low speed relay**—is connected to the convenience center.

• **Blower Resistor**—is in the engine compartment mounted to the heater and A/C control module assembly.

• **Brake Fluid Level Switch**—is on the left side of the brake fluid reservoir.

• **Convenience Center**—is located below the right side of the instrument panel.

• **Coolant Temperature Sensor**—is in front of the distributor.

• **Cooling Fan Relay**—is located behind the right headlamp capsule.

• **Courtesy Lamp Diode**—is taped in the harness near the top of the left B—pillar.

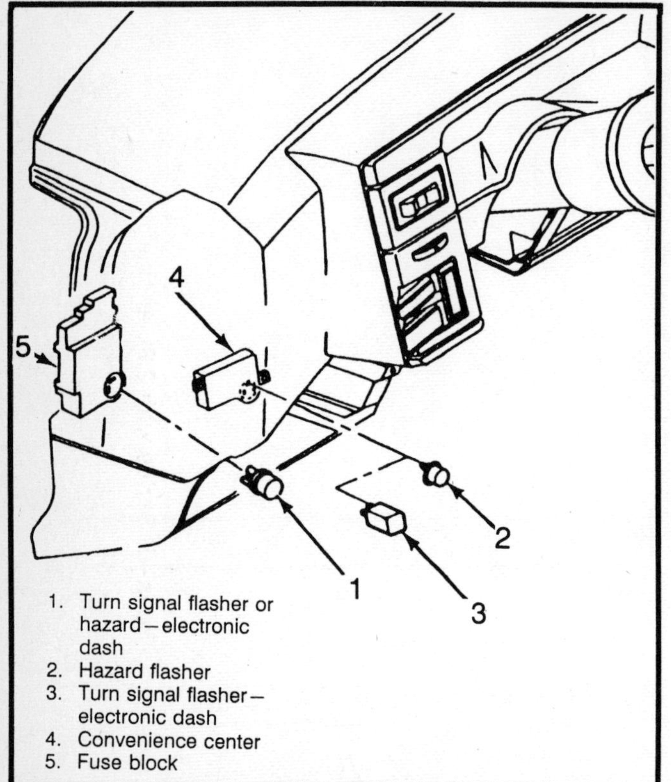

Under instrument panel components – S Series

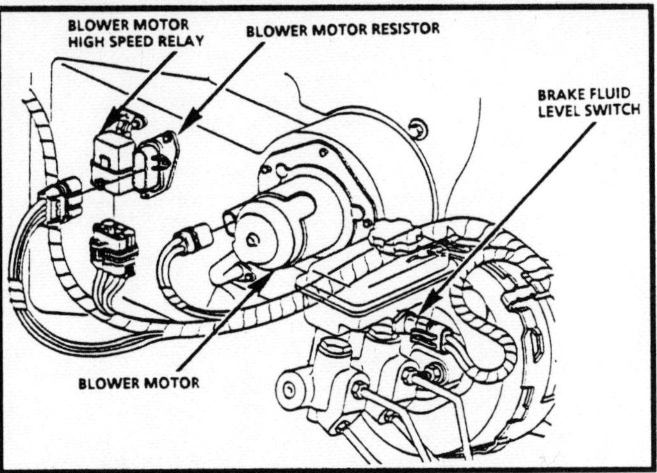

Blower motor relay locations – Silhouette, Trans Sport and Lumina APV

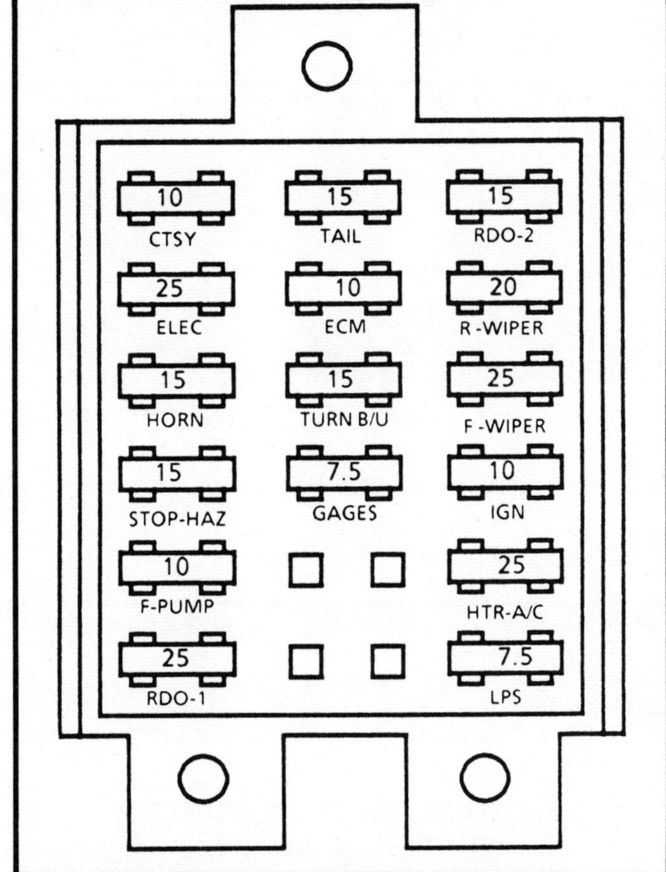

Fuse box identification – Silhouette, Trans Sport and Lumina APV

• **Cruise Control Module** – is located behind the instrument panel to the left of the steering column.

• **Cruise Control Servo** – is in the engine compartment, mounted to the left wheel housing.

• **Defroster Valve Vacuum Actuator** – is mounted to the left side of the heater module assembly.

• **Door Lock Relay** – is located on the left A – pillar behind the kick panel.

• **EGR Electronic Vacuum Regulator Valve (EVRV)** – is located on the right of the engine above the water pump.

• **Electronic Control Module (ECM)** – is located below the right side of the instrument panel, behind the convenience center.

• **Electronic Level Control (ELC) Inflator Timer Relay** – is located behind the left rear wheel housing.

• **Electronic Level Control (ELC) Relay** – is behind the left rear wheel housing with the ELC timer.

• **Electronic Level Control Height Sensor** – is mounted to the center of the rear crossmember.

• **Electronic Spark Control (ESC) Module** – behind the instrument panel, behind the convenience center
Electronic Spark Timing (EST) Distributor – is at the left rear of the engine.

• **Fuel Level Sender** – is located at the fuel tank.

• **Fuel Pump Prime Connector** – is located in the wiring harness, behind the battery.

• **Fuel Pump Relay** – is located behind the right headlamp capsule.

• **Hazard Flasher** – is connected to the convenience center.

• **Heater Defroster Bi** – Directional Vacuum Actuator – is mounted to the left upper heater module assembly.

• **Horn Relay** – is connected to the convenience center.

• **Idle Air Control (IAC) Motor** – is mounted to the side of the throttle body.

• **Ignition Coil** – is located at the left rear side of the engine.

• **Knock Sensor** – is located right side of the engine, near the oxygen. It is connect to the harness as the vehicle speed sensor.

• **Manifold Absolute Pressure (MAP) sensor** – is mounted to the air cleaner.

• **MAP Sensor** – see Manifold Absolute Pressure sensor.

• **Oil Pressure Sender/Fuel Pump Switch** – is located next to the oil filter.

'S' SERIES RPO:LN8 ENGINE CODE:E 2.5L L4

□ COMPUTER COMMAND CONTROL
- C1 Electronic Control Module (E.C.M.)
- C2 ALDL diagnostic connector
- C3 "SERVICE ENGINE SOON" light
- C5 ECM harness ground
- C6 Fuse panel
- C8 Fuel pump test connector

□ ECM CONTROLLED COMPONENTS
- 1 Fuel injector
- 2 Idle air control
- 3 Fuel Pump relay
- 5 Transmission Converter Clutch Connector
- 6 Electronic Spark Timing Distributor (E.S.T.)
- 8 Oil Pressure Switch
- 12 Exhaust Gas Recirculation Vacuum Solenoid
- 13 A/C relay

○ ECM INFORMATION SENSORS
- A Manifold pressure (M.A.P.)
- B Exhaust oxygen
- C Throttle position (T.P.S.)
- D Coolant temperature
- F Vehicle speed (V.S.S.)
- G Power Steering Pressure
- T Manifold Air Temperature (M.A.T.)

⬚ EMISSION COMPONENTS (NOT ECM CONTROLLED)
- N1 Crankcase vent valve (PCV)
- N15 Fuel Vapor Canister

Component locations—S Series with 2.5L engine

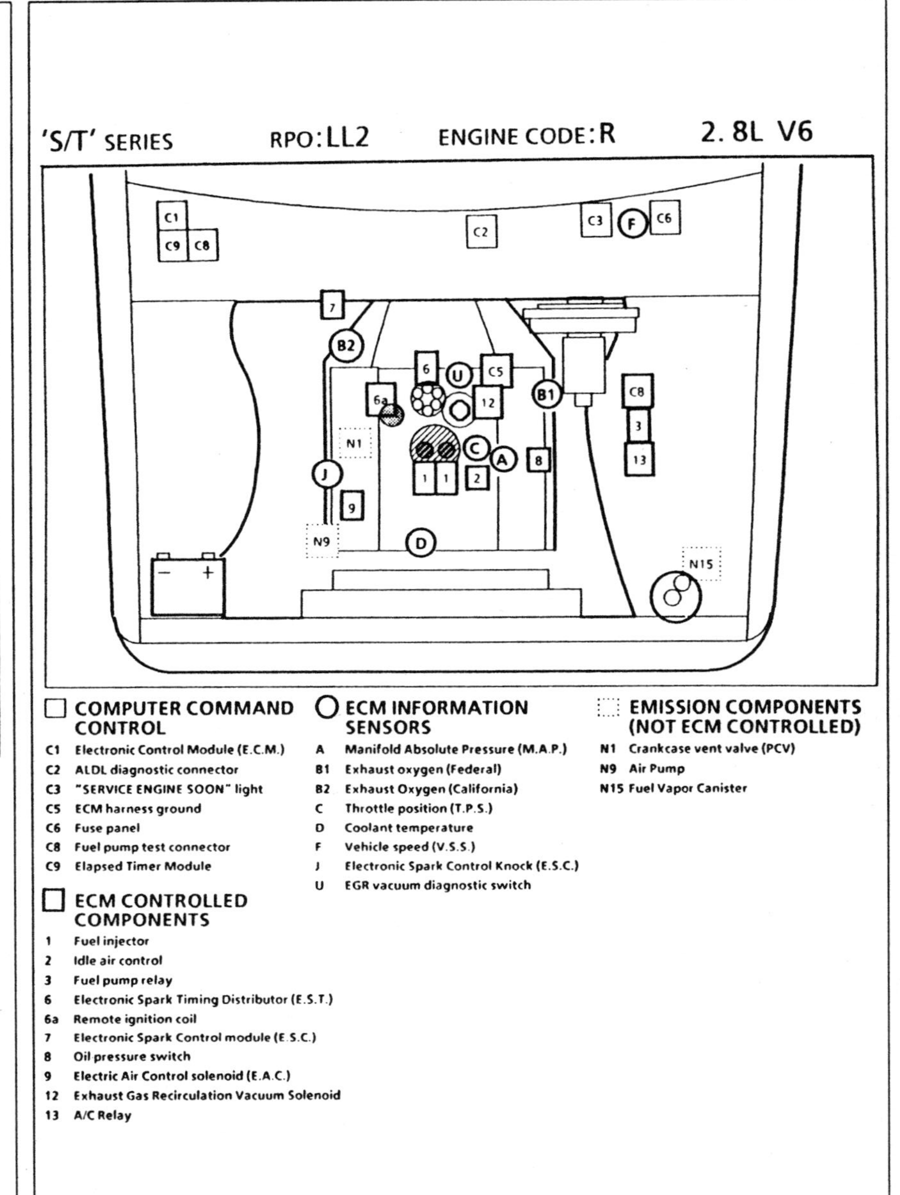

□ COMPUTER COMMAND CONTROL
- C1 Electronic Control Module (E.C.M.)
- C2 ALDL diagnostic connector
- C3 "SERVICE ENGINE SOON" light
- C5 ECM harness ground
- C6 Fuse panel
- C8 Fuel pump test connector
- C9 Elapsed Timer Module

□ ECM CONTROLLED COMPONENTS
- 1 Fuel injector
- 2 Idle air control
- 3 Fuel pump relay
- 6 Electronic Spark Timing Distributor (E.S.T.)
- 6a Remote ignition coil
- 7 Electronic Spark Control module (E.S.C.)
- 8 Oil pressure switch
- 9 Electric Air Control solenoid (E.A.C.)
- 12 Exhaust Gas Recirculation Vacuum Solenoid
- 13 A/C Relay

○ ECM INFORMATION SENSORS
- A Manifold Absolute Pressure (M.A.P.)
- B1 Exhaust oxygen (Federal)
- B2 Exhaust Oxygen (California)
- C Throttle position (T.P.S.)
- D Coolant temperature
- F Vehicle speed (V.S.S.)
- J Electronic Spark Control Knock (E.S.C.)
- U EGR vacuum diagnostic switch

⬚ EMISSION COMPONENTS (NOT ECM CONTROLLED)
- N1 Crankcase vent valve (PCV)
- N9 Air Pump
- N15 Fuel Vapor Canister

Component locations—S Series with 2.8L engine

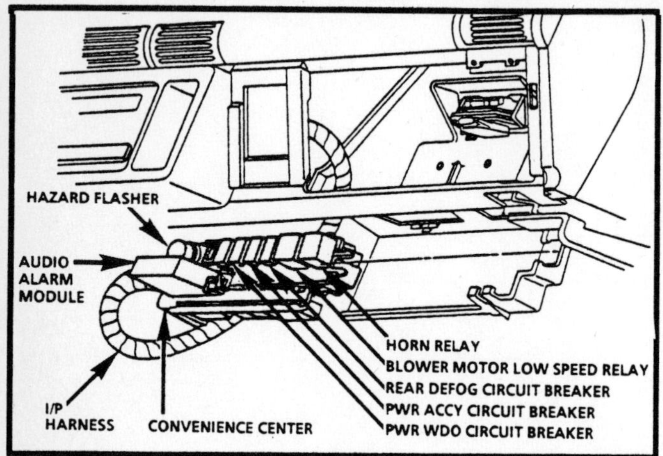

Convenience center and circuit breakers – Silhouette, Trans Sport and Lumina APV

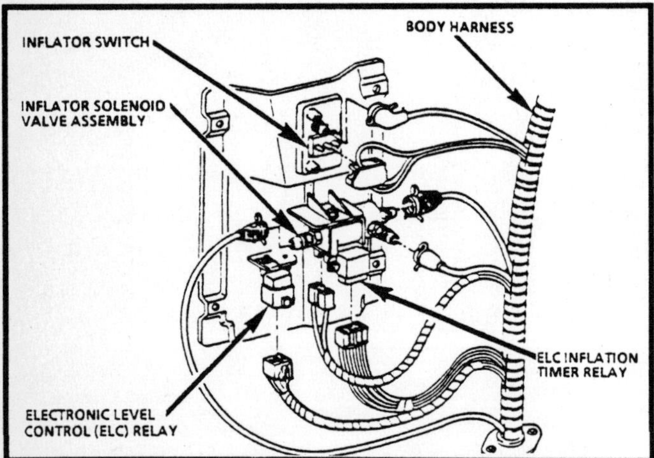

Electronic lever control relay – Silhouette, Trans Sport and Lumina APV

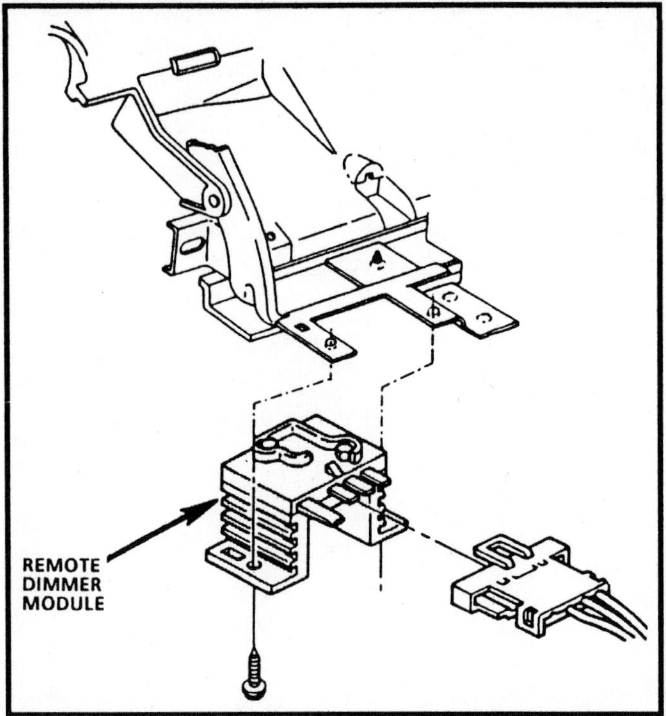

Remote dimmer module – Silhouette, Trans Sport and Lumina APV

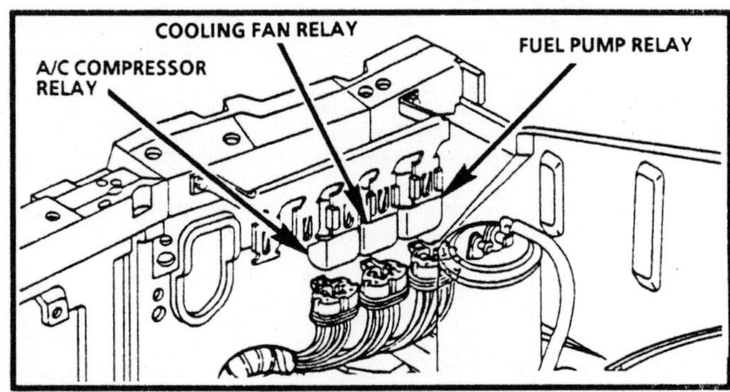

Relay locations – Silhouette, Trans Sport and Lumina APV

- **Panel Valve Vacuum Actuator** – is mounted to the right side of the heater module assembly.
- **Parking Brake Switch** – is located on the lower left A–pillar, it is part of the parking brake assembly.
- **PWR ACCY Circuit Breaker** – is connect to the convenience center.
- **Rear Window Defogger Circuit Breaker** – is connect to the convenience center.
- **Rear Window Defogger Relay** – is connected to the convenience center.
- **Rear Window Washer Motor** – is mounted to the solvent container.
- **Rear Window Wiper Module** – is in the lift gate.
- **RECIR Valve Vacuum Actuator** – is mounted to the left side of the heater module assembly.
- **Remote Dimmer Module** – is located behind the instrument panel to the left of the steering column.
- **Resistor for System Isolation** – is located between the radio and connector C215.
- **Solenoid Box** – is mounted below the instrument panel to the right of the heater module.
- **Starter Solenoid** – is part of the starter.
- **TACH Signal Filter** – is at the left rear of the engine, next to the coil.
- **Temperature Door Actuator** – is located on the top right of the heater and A/C module assembly.
- **Temperature Door Actuator** – is mounted to the top right side of the heater module.
- **Throttle Position Sensor** – is mounted to the throttle body.
- **Timing Adjustment Connector** – in the engine compartment, above the right wheel housing.
- **Transaxle Converter Clutch (TCC) Solenoid** – is mounted to the front of the transaxle.
- **Transaxle gear position switch** – is located on top of the transaxle.
- **Turn Signal Flasher** – is located behind the instrument panel to the left of the steering column, above the parking brake.
- **Vehicle Speed Sensor (VVS)** – is mounted to the top of the transaxle.
- **Vehicle Speed Sensor Buffer** – is located behind the instrument panel above the convenience center.
- **Windshield Wiper Module** – is located next to the engine on the right wheel well.

'S/T' SERIES RPO:LB4 ENGINE CODE:Z 4.3L V6

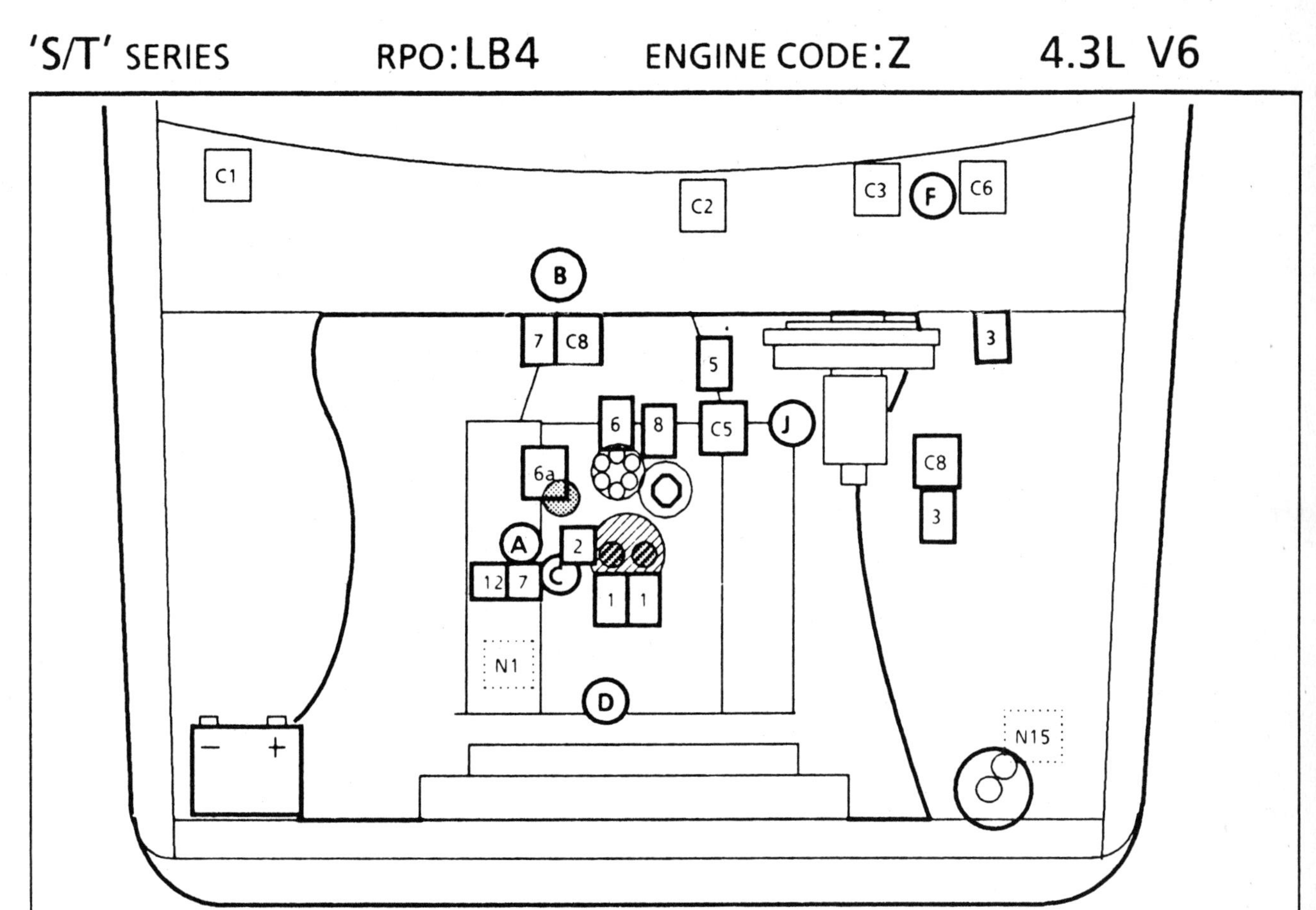

COMPUTER COMMAND CONTROL

- C1 Electronic Control Module (E.C.M.)
- C2 ALDL diagnostic connector
- C3 "SERVICE ENGINE SOON" light
- C5 ECM harness ground
- C6 Fuse panel
- C8 Fuel pump test connector

ECM INFORMATION SENSORS

- A Manifold Absolute Pressure (M.A.P.)
- B Exhaust oxygen
- C Throttle position (T.P.S.)
- D Coolant temperature
- F Vehicle speed (V.S.S.)
- J Electronic Spark Control Knock (E.S.C.)

EMISSION COMPONENTS (NOT ECM CONTROLLED)

- N1 Crankcase vent valve (PCV)
- N15 Fuel Vapor Canister

ECM CONTROLLED COMPONENTS

- 1 Fuel injector
- 2 Idle air control
- 3 Fuel pump relay
- 5 Transmission Converter Clutch Connector
- 6 Electronic Spark Timing Distributor (E.S.T.)
- 6a Remote ignition coil
- 7 Electronic Spark Control module (E.S.C.)
- 8 Oil pressure switch
- 12 Exhaust Gas Recirculation Vacuum Solenoid

Component locations—S Series with 4.3L engine

"U" **APV** RPO:LG6 VIN D 3.1L V6 TBI

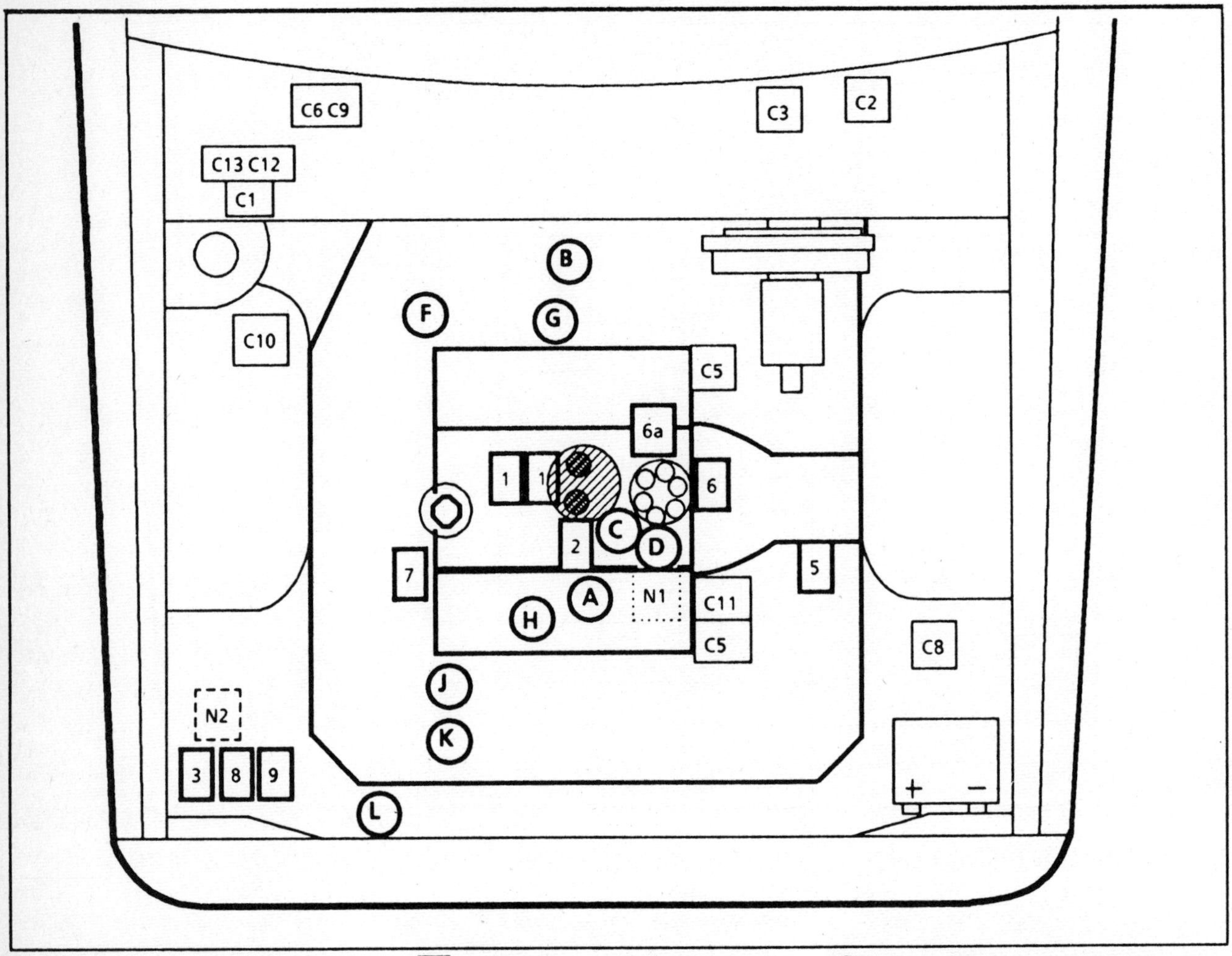

COMPUTER HARNESS

- C1 Electronic Control Module
- C2 ALDL diagnostic connector
- C3 "SERVICE ENGINE SOON" light
- C5 ECM harness grounds
- C6 Fuse panel
- C8 Fuel pump test connector
- C9 Fuel pump fuse & ECM power
- C10 Set timing connector
- C11 Engine Grounds
- C12 Electronic Spark Control Module
- C13 Vehicle Speed Buffer

NOT ECM CONNECTED

- N1 Crankcase vent valve (PCV)
- N2 Fuel Vapor Canister

CONTROLLED DEVICES

- 1 Fuel injectors
- 2 Idle Air Control (IAC) motor
- 3 Fuel pump relay
- 5 Torque Converter Clutch (TCC) connector
- 6 EST distributor
- 6a Remote ignition coil
- 7 Electronic Vacuum Regulator Valve (EVRV) EGR
- 8 Cooling fan relay
- 9 A/C fan relay (if applicable)

Exhaust Gas Recirculation valve

INFORMATION SENSORS

- A Manifold Absolute Pressure (MAP) (attached to air cleaner)
- B Exhaust oxygen
- C Throttle Position Sensor (TPS)
- D Coolant temperature
- F Vehicle Speed Sensor (VSS)
- G Knock Sensor
- H Oil Pressure Fuel Pump Switch
- J A/C low pressure switch
- K A/C high pressure switch
- L Intermediate pressure A/C fan switch

Component locations—Silhouette, Trans Sport and Lumina APV

Component Locator

ACURA

Circuit Breakers

INTEGRA

1989

Fuses may be found in the dash fuse box; located under the left side of the dashboard next to the tilt lever, or the under hood fuse box, which is located under a cover at the right rear of the engine compartment.

The fuse for the hazard lights is located under a cover, attached to the positive battery cable.

1990–91

Fuses breakers are found in the dash fuse box; located below the left side of the dashboard behind the kick panel, or in the main fuse box; located at the right rear corner of the engine compartment, on the shock tower.

LEGEND

Fuses breakers may be found in the dash fuse box; located under the dashboard behind the left kick panel, or in the under-hood relay box; located on the left side of the engine compartment.

NSX

Fuses breakers for this vehicle may be found at 3 different locations. In the main fuse box; located in the left front corner of the engine compartment, in the dash fuse box; located under the left side of the dash in the kick panel, or in the relay box; located in the right rear corner of the front storage compartment.

Fusible Links

Fusible links for the Integra are located in the underhood/main fuse box, located on either the right side of the engine compartment on 1990–91, or at the center rear of the engine compartment on 1989.

Fusible links for the Legend (Coupe and Sedan) are located in the underhood relay box, located on the left side of the engine compartment.

Fusible links for the NSX are located in the main fuse box; located in the left front corner of the engine compartment, or in the relay box; located in the right rear corner of the front storage compartment.

Fusible links in these vehicles are not of the typical wire type construction. They more closely resemble a larger version of the ATZ blade type fuse.

Relays, Sensors, Modules and Computer Locations

1989 INTEGRA

- **A/C Compressor Clutch Relay**—is located at the right front the of engine compartment, above the coolant reservoir.
- **A/C Condenser Fan Relay**—is located at the right front of the engine compartment, above the coolant reservoir.
- **A/C Dual Pressure Switch**—is located at the left front of the engine compartment, behind turn signal light.
- **A/C Thermostat**—is located at the right side of the dash, on evaporator.
- **Atmospheric Pressure Sensor**—is located under the left side of the dash, left of heater assembly.
- **Backup Light Switch**—is located at the lower right front of the transmission.
- **Blower Motor**—is located under the right side of dash, at the kick panel.
- **Blower Relay**—is located under the right side of the dash, under the headlight retractor control.
- **Blower Resistors**—are located under the right side of dash, on top of blower assembly.
- **Brake Fluid Level Switch**—is located at the left rear corner of the engine compartment, inside the fluid reservoir.

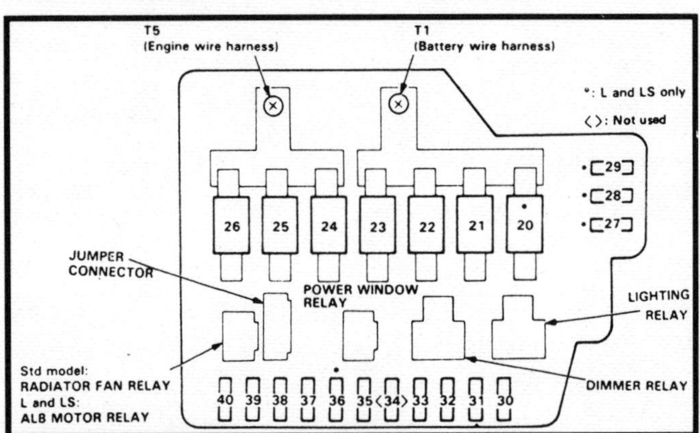

Under hood relay box—Legend

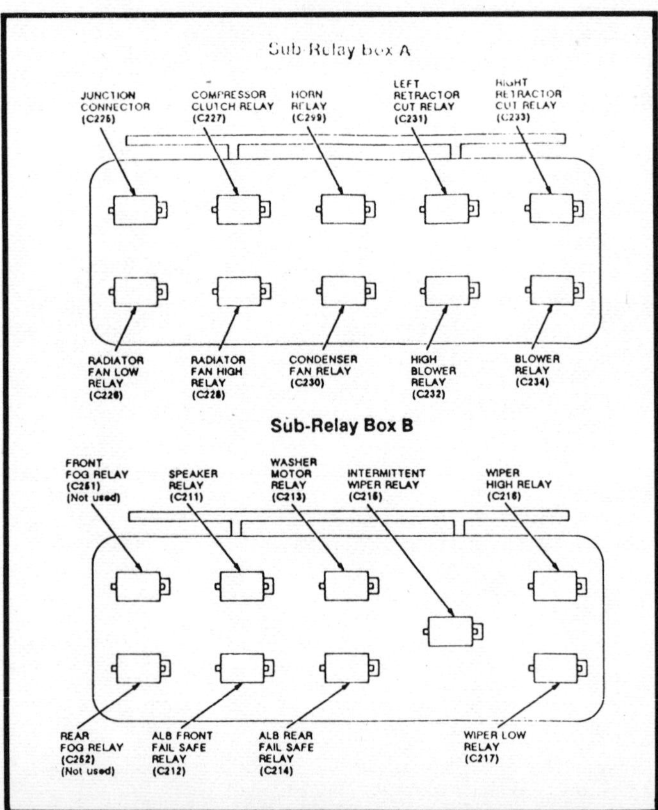

Sub-relay boxes—1991 NSX

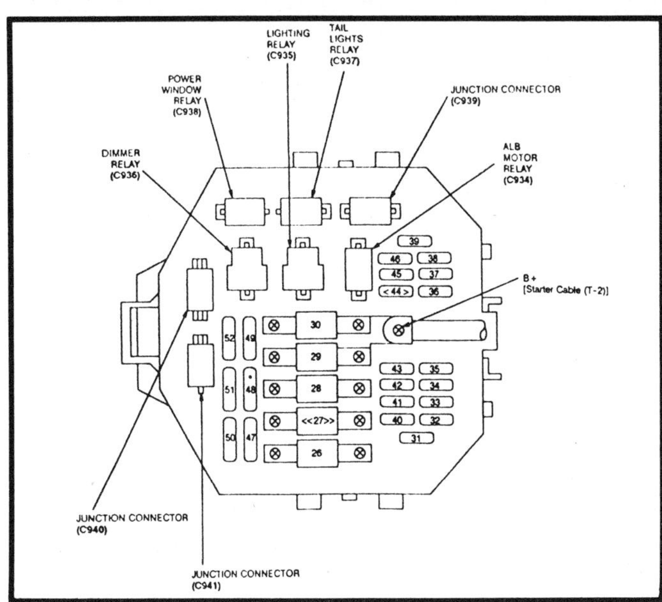

Relay box—1991 NSX

• **Brake Light switch**—is located under the left side of dash, left of the steering column.

• **Clutch Switch**—is located under the left side of dash, left of the steering column.

• **Coolant Temperature Sender**—is located at the right side of engine, next to the coolant temperature sensor.

• **Coolant Temperature Sensor**—is located at the right side of engine.

• **Cooling Fan Thermostat**—is located at the right front of the engine compartment, behind the radiator.

• **Cruise Control Unit**—is located under the left side of the dash, at the kick panel.

• **Cruise Control Actuator**—is located at the left front fender panel.

• **Cylinder Sensor**—is located at the right front of the engine, under the ignition wiring.

• **Dash Fuse Box**—is located under the left side of the dash, near the tilt lever.

• **EFI Main Relay**—is located behind left side of the dash.

• **Electronic Air Control Valve**—is located at the top rear of the engine.

• **Emissions Control Unit**—is located under the right front seat.

• **Fuel Injector Resistors**—are located at the left rear corner of engine compartment, on the cowl.

• **Hatch Light Switch**—is located at the center of the hatch, behind the end panel.

• **Headlight Retractor Control Unit**—is located under right side of the dash, behind the kick panel.

• **Heater Function Control Motor**—is located under left side of the dash, left of the heater assembly.

• **Heater Recirculation Control Motor**—is located under the right side of dash, at the kick panel.

• **Idle Up Solenoid Valve**—is located at the center rear of the engine compartment, on the cowl panel.

• **Ignition Key Switch**—is located at the left side of the dash below the steering column, under a cover.

• **Ignition Switch**—is located at the left side of the dash below the steering column, under a cover.

• **Ignition Timing Adjusting Connector**—is located at the center rear of the engine compartment.

• **Intake Air Temperature Sensor**—is located at the top center of the engine.

• **Integrated Control Unit**—is located behind the left side of the dash, next to the power window relay.

• **Lights On Warning Chime**—is located under the left side of the dash, at the kick panel.

• **Manifold Absolute Pressure Sensor**—is located at the top center of the engine.

• **Neutral Safety Switch**—is located under the console, below the gear selector.

• **Oxygen Sensor**—is located at the right front of the engine.

• **Parking Brake Switch**—is located at the rear of the console.

• **Power Door Lock Control Unit**—is located under the left front seat.

• **Power Window Control Unit**—is located inside the left front door.

• **Power Window Relay**—is located behind the left side of the dash, next to the integrated control unit.

• **Purge Cut-Off Solenoid Valve**—is located at the center rear of the engine compartment.

• **Radiator Fan Relay**—is located at the right front of the engine compartment, above the coolant reservoir.

• **Radio Noise Condenser**—is located at the right rear of the engine compartment, on the distributor.

• **Rear Window Defogger Relay**—is located under right side of the dash, at the kick panel.

• **Resonator Control Solenoid Valve**—is located at the center rear of the engine compartment.

• **Retractor Motor (left)**—is located at the left front inner panel.

• **Retractor Relay (left)**—is located under the left side of the dash, at the kick panel.

• **Retractor Motor (right)**—is located at the right front inner fender panel.

• **Retractor Relay (right)**—is located under left side of the dash, at the kick panel.

• **Seat Belt Switch**—is located inside the seat belt receiver.

• **Shift Position Console Switch**—is located under the console, below the gear selector.

• **Throttle Angle Sensor**—is located at the top rear of the engine.

• **Turn Signal/Hazard Relay**—is located in the dash fuse box.

• **Under Hood Fuse Box**—is located at the right rear of the engine compartment.

• **Wiper Timer Relay**—is located in the dash fuse box.

1990–91 INTEGRA

• **A/C Compressor Relay**—is located at the left front of the engine compartment, near the radiator.

• **A/C Pressure Switch**—is located at the left front of the engine compartment, on the bottom of the A/C line.

• **A/C Thermo Switch**—is located below the center of the dash, right of the heater assembly.

• **Air Intake Temperature Sensor**—is located at the left rear of the engine compartment, on the intake manifold.

• **ALB Control Unit (hatchback)**—is located at the right of the rear seat, behind the quarter panel trim.

• **ALB Fail Safe Relay (rear and front)**—are located at the right front side of the engine compartment.

• **ALB Fail Safe Relay (front)**—is located at the right side of engine compartment, on the relay bracket.

• **ALB Modulator Solenoid Unit**—is located at the right rear of the engine compartment, under the master cylinder.

• **ALB Motor Relay**—is located at the right front side of the engine compartment.

• **ALB Motor**—is located at the front right side of the engine compartment, under the battery.

• **ALB Pressure Switch**—is located at the right front side of the engine compartment, under the battery.
• **ALB Speed Sensors**—are located behind the wheels.
• **ALB Test Connector**—is located on the floor, under the left front seat.
• **Anti-lock Brake System (ABS)**—see Anti-lock Brakes (ALB).
• **Anti-lock Brake Test Connector**—is located at the left side of the floor, below the carpet.
• **Anti-lock Brakes**—see ALB
• **Automatic Seat Belt Control Unit**—is located behind the right side of the dash, at the kick panel.
• **Automatic Seat Belt Motor (left)**—is located left of the rear seat, behind the trim panel.
• **Automatic Seat Belt Motor (right)**—is located right of the rear seat, behind the trim panel.
• **Automatic Transmission Control Unit**—is located behind the left side of the dash.
• **Automatic Transmission Speed Pulser**—is located at the right rear of the engine compartment.
• **Back Up Lights Switch**—is located at the lower right front of the transmission.
• **Brake Fluid Level Switch**—is located at the left rear of the engine compartment, in the brake fluid reservoir.
• **Brake Fluid Level Switch**—is located below the master cylinder reservoir cap.
• **Brake Switch**—is located behind the left side of the dash, on the brake pedal support.
• **Chime Module**—is located at the center of the dash, behind the front console.
• **Chime Module**—is located behind the center of the dash.
• **Cigarette Lighter Relay**—is located behind the center of the dash.
• **Clutch Interlock Switch**—is located behind the left side of the dash.
• **Clutch Switch**—is located behind the left side of the dash, on the clutch pedal support.
• **Condenser Fan Motor**—is located at the left front of the engine compartment, behind the radiator.
• **Condenser Fan Relay**—is located at the left front of the engine compartment, near the radiator.
• **Coolant Temperature Gauge Sensor**—is located the right side of the engine, next to the coolant temperature sensor.
• **Coolant Temperature Switch**—is located at the lower left rear of the engine, near the oil filter.
• **Cooling Fan Relay**—is located at the right front of the engine compartment, near the radiator.
• **Cooling Fan Timer Unit**—is located behind the center of the dash.
• **Cruise Control Actuator**—is located at the left side of the engine compartment, in front of the shock tower.
• **Cruise Control Unit**—is located behind the left side of the dash, above the kick panel.
• **Dash Fuse Box**—is located below the left side of the dash, at kick the panel.
• **Daytime Running Lights Relay**—is located behind right side of the dash, at the kick panel.
• **Defogger Grid Radio Noise Condenser**—is located below left side of dash, behind the kick panel.
• **EGR Control Solenoid Valve**—is located at the right rear of the engine compartment.
• **EGR Valve Lift Solenoid**—is located at the right side of the engine.
• **Electronic Air Control Valve**—is located at the center rear of the engine, behind the throttle body.
• **Fan Timer Relay**—is located below the center of the dash, right of the heater assembly.
• **Fog Light Relay**—is located behind the left side of dash, at the kick panel.
• **Fresh/Recirculate Motor**—is located behind right side of the dash.
• **Front End Switch**—is located in the right front windshield pillar, behind the trim panel.
• **Fuel Injection**—see Program Fuel Injection (PGM-FI).
• **Fuel Injector Resistors**—are located at the left rear corner of the engine compartment.
• **Fuel Tank Unit**—is located below the center of the rear seat, inside the fuel tank.
• **Hazard Relay/Turn Signal**—is located behind the left side of the dash.
• **Heater Control Function Motor**—is located below the left side of the dash, right of the steering column.
• **Heater Function Control Motor**—is located behind the center of dash, on the left side of heater assembly.
• **Idle Control Solenoid Valve**—is located at the right side of the engine compartment.
• **Ignition Switch**—is located at the right side of the steering column, behind the steering column covers.
• **Ignition Timing Adjusting Connector**—is located below the right side of the dash.
• **Key Interlock Solenoid**—is located at the right side of the steering column.
• **Key Interlock Switch**—is located at the right side of the steering column, on the ignition switch.
• **Lock-Up Control Solenoid**—is located at the right front of the engine.
• **Main Fuse Box**—is located at the right rear corner of the engine compartment, on the shock tower.
• **Manifold Absolute Temperature Sensor**—is located at the center rear of the engine compartment.
• **Oil Pressure Switch**—is located below the vehicle, at the left rear of the engine.
• **Oil Temperature Switch**—is located below the vehicle, at the left rear of the engine.
• **Oxygen Sensor**—is located at the center front of the engine.
• **Parking Brake Switch**—is located below the rear of the console.
• **PGM-FI Electronic Control Unit**—is located on the right front floor, below the carpet.
• **PGM-FI Main Relay**—is located behind the left side of the dash.
• **Power Antenna Motor (Hatchback)**—is located at the left side of the cargo area, behind the quarter trim panel.
• **Power Door Lock Control Unit**—is located behind the left side of the dash.
• **Power Steering Switch**—is located at the left rear of the engine compartment, on the intake manifold.
• **Power Window Motor**—is located at the front of the door, behind the door trim panel.
• **Pressure Regulator Cut-Off Solenoid Valve**—is located at the left rear of the engine compartment.
• **Purge Gas Cut-Off Solenoid Valve**—is located at the left rear of the engine compartment.
• **Radiator Fan Relay**—is located at the right front of the engine compartment.
• **Radio Noise Condenser**—is located at the right side of the engine, near the distributor.
• **rear ALB Fail Safe Relay**—is located at the right side of the engine compartment, on the relay bracket.
• **Rear Window Defogger Relay**—is located at the left kick panel.
• **Shift Control Solenoid**—is located at the right front of the engine.
• **Shift Lock Solenoid**—is located below the front of the console.
• **Shift Position Console Switch**—is located below the center console, below the gear selector lever.
• **Shift Position Console Switch**—is located below the front of the console.
• **Shoulder Anchor Switch**—is located at the top of the right center pillar.

• **Shoulder Seat Belt Retractor (front)**—is located at the right side of the left front seat.

• **Starter Relay**—is located behind center of the dash.

• **Sunroof Relay**—is located behind the left side of the dash, at the kick panel.

• **Throttle Angle Sensor**—is located at the center rear of the engine.

• **Trailer Connector (hatchback)**—is located at the left rear corner of the cargo area, behind the trim panel.

• **Trailer Connector (sedan)**—is located at the left rear of the trunk, behind the rear trim panel.

• **Turn Signal/Hazard Relay**—is located behind the left side of the dash.

LEGEND

• **A/C Compressor Clutch Relay**—is located at the right front of the engine compartment, near the washer fluid bottle.

• **A/C Condenser Fan Relay**—is located at the left side of the engine compartment.

• **A/C Condenser Fan Resistor**—is located below the center front of the engine, behind a trim panel.

• **A/C Condenser Fan Timer Relay**—is located at the right front of the engine compartment, near the washer fluid bottle.

• **A/C Pressure Switch**—is located at the right front of the engine compartment.

• **Air Bags**—see Supplemental Restraint System (SRS) Air Suction Control Solenoid Valve—is located at the left rear of the engine compartment.

• **ALB Control Unit**—is located at the left rear passenger compartment, behind the rear seat.

• **ALB Fail Safe Relay (front and rear)**—is located at the left front of the engine compartment, near the battery.

• **ALB Modulator Solenoid Unit**—is located at the left side of the engine compartment.

• **ALB Motor Relay**—is located in the under hood relay box, on the left side of the engine compartment.

• **ALB Motor**—is located at the left front of the engine compartment, under the air intake.

• **ALB Pressure Switch**—is located at the lower left front of the engine compartment, under the battery tray.

• **ALB Speed Sensors**—are located on the wheel hub assemblies.

• **ALB Test Connector**—is located on the right side of the floor.

• **Ambient Temperature Sensor**—is located below the center of the front bumper.

• **Amplifier Relay/Fuse Block**—is located behind the left side of the dash.

• **Anti-lock Brake System**—see Anti-Lock Brakes (ALB).

• **Automatic Transmission Control Unit**—is located on the right side of the floor.

• **Blower Motor**—is located is located behind the right side of the dash.

• **Blower Relay**—is located behind the right side of the dash.

• **Brake Level Fluid Switch**—is located at the left rear of the engine compartment, in the master cylinder reservoir.

• **Brake Light Sensor (left)**—is located at the left rear of the trunk, behind the trim panel.

• **Brake Light Sensor (right)**—is located at the right rear of the trunk, behind the trim panel.

• **Brake Switch**—is located behind the left side of the dash.

• **Bypass Control Solenoid Valve**—is located at the left rear of the engine compartment.

• **Clutch Interlock Switch**—is located below the left side of the dash.

• **Clutch Switch**—is located below the left side of the dash.

• **Combination Switch**—is located on the left side of the steering wheel.

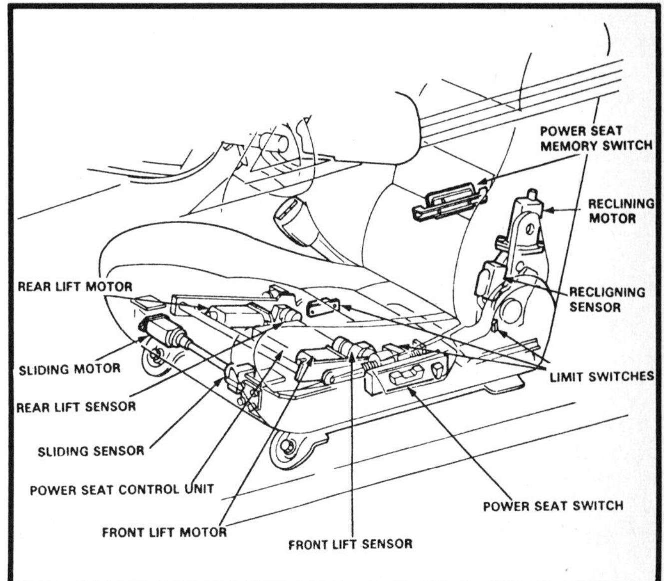

Power seat components—Legend

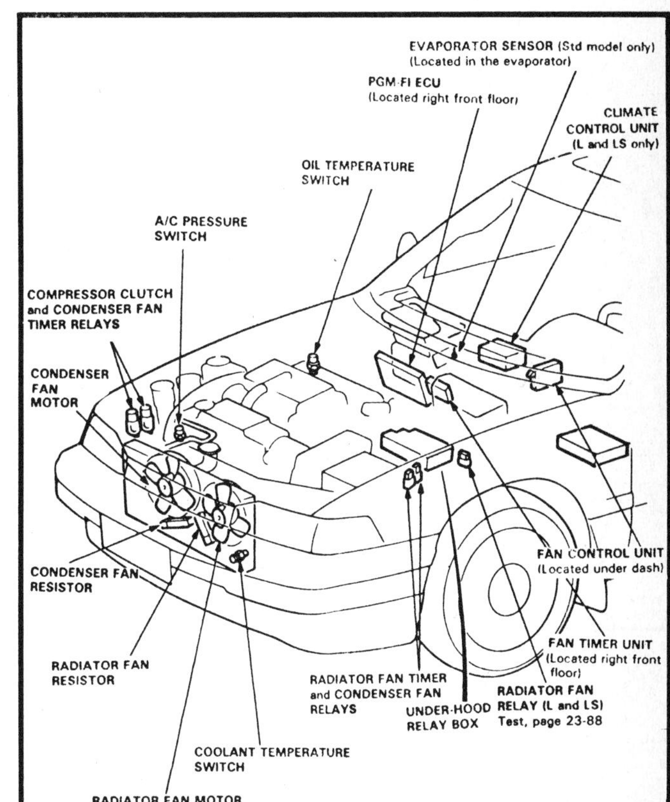

Cooling components—Legend

• **Coolant Fluid Level Switch**—is located at the right front of the engine compartment.

• **Coolant Temperature Gauge Sensor**—is located at the left front of the engine.

• **Coolant Temperature Sensor**—is located at the left front of the engine, near the air intake assembly.

• **Crankshaft Sensor**—is located at the right front of the engine compartment, behind a cover plate.

• **Cruise Control Actuator**—is located at the right front of the engine compartment.

• **Cruise Control Unit**—is located behind the left side of the dashboard, near the dash junction box.

• **Dash Relay Box**—is located behind the left side of the dash.

• **Dimmer Control Amplifier**—is located behind the left side of the dash.

• **Dimmer Relay**—is located in the under hood relay box, on the left side of the engine compartment.

• **EGR Solenoid Control Valve**—is located at the left rear of the engine compartment.

• **EGR Valve Lift Sensor**—is located at the left front of the engine.

• **Electronic Control Unit**—is located below the right front floor.

• **Electronic Idle Control Valve**—is located at the top left side of the engine.

• **Emission Control Box**—is located at the left rear of the engine compartment.

• **Evaporator Sensor**—is located behind the right side of the dash.

• **Fan Timer Unit**—is located below the right front floor.

• **Fresh/Recirculation Motor**—is located behind the right side of the dash.

• **Fuel Injection**—see Program Fuel Injection (PGM-FI).

• **Fuel Injector Connectors**—are located at the left front of the engine.

• **Fuel Injector Resistors**—are located at the right rear of the engine compartment.

• **Fuse Block/Amplifier Relay**—is located behind the left side of the dash.

• **High Speed Blower Relay**—is located behind the right side of the dash.

• **Ignition Timing Adjuster**—is located at the left rear of the engine compartment.

• **In-Car Temperature Sensor**—is located on the under side of the console.

• **Information Center Control Unit**—is located behind the right side of the dash.

• **Intake Air Temperature Sensor**—is located at the left front of the engine.

• **Integrated Control Unit**—is located behind the left side of the dash.

• **Lift Limit Switch (front)**—is located under the drivers seat.

• **Lift Limit Switch (rear)**—is located under the drivers seat.

• **Lift Memory Sensor (front)**—is located under the drivers seat.

• **Lift Memory Sensor (rear)**—is located under the drivers seat.

• **Lift Motor (front seat)**—is located under the drivers seat.

• **Lift Motor (rear seat)**—is located under the drivers seat.

• **Lighting Relay**—is located in the under hood relay box, on the left side of the engine compartment.

• **Lock-Up Control Solenoid Valve**—is located at the left front of the engine, near the battery.

• **Manifold Absolute Pressure Sensor**—is located at the left rear of the engine compartment.

• **Mode Door Selector Motor**—is located behind the left side of the dash.

• **Neutral Safety Switch**—is located below the center of the console.

• **Noise Suppressor (left)**—is located under the drivers seat.

• **Noise Suppressor (right)**—is located under the front passenger seat.

• **Oil Level Switch**—is located at the lower right front of the engine.

• **Oil Pressure Switch**—is located at the lower right side of the engine.

• **Oil Temperature Sensor**—is located at the top right side of the engine.

• **Oxygen Sensor (front)**—is located at the front of the engine.

• **Oxygen Sensor (rear)**—is located at the right rear of the engine compartment.

• **Parking Brake Switch**—is located at the center of the floor, at the front of the parking brake lever mounting plate.

• **Power Door Lock Control Unit**—is located behind the left side of the dash.

• **Power Seat Control Unit**—is located under the drivers seat.

• **Power Steering Idle Boost Switch**—is located behind the center rear of the engine.

• **Power Transistor**—is located behind the right side of the dash.

• **Power Window Control Unit**—is located at the front of the drivers door.

• **Power Window Relay**—is located in the under hood relay box, on the left side of the engine compartment.

• **Pressure Regulator Cut-Off Solenoid Valve**—is located at the left rear of the engine compartment.

• **Radiator Fan Control Unit**—is located behind the center of the dash.

• **Radiator Fan Relay**—is located at the left side of the engine compartment, in the under hood relay box.

• **Radiator Fan Resistor**—is located below the center front of the engine, behind a trim panel.

• **Radiator Fan Temperature Sensor**—is located below the left front of the engine, behind a trim panel.

• **Radiator Fan Timer Relay Diode**—is located behind the left side of the dash, taped in the harness.

• **Radiator Fan Timer Relay**—is located at the left side of the engine compartment.

• **Radio Noise Condenser**—is located at the left rear of the engine compartment.

• **Resonator Control Solenoid Valve**—is located behind the left side of the front bumper.

• **Seat Belt Presenter Motor Assembly (left)**—is located under the drivers seat.

• **Seat Belt Presenter Motor Assembly (right)**—is located under the front passenger seat.

• **Security Control Unit**—is located at the right front of the trunk, behind the trim panel.

• **Shift Control Solenoid Valve**—is located at the left front of the engine compartment.

• **Shift Lock Solenoid**—is located under the center console.

• **Shift Position Console Switch**—is located below the center of the console.

• **Sliding Limit Switch (left seat)**—is located under the drivers seat.

• **Sliding Limit Switch (right seat)**—is located under the front passenger seat.

• **Sliding Memory Sensor**—is located under the drivers seat.

• **Sliding Motor (Passenger)**—is located under the front passenger seat.

• **Sliding Motor**—is located under the drivers seat.

• **SRS Junction Box**—is located under the left side of the dashboard.

• **SRS Sensor (left front)**—is located inside the left front fender.

• **SRS Sensor (right front)**—is located inside the right front fender.

• **SRS Unit**—is located below the front of the console.

• **Sunlight Sensor**—is located at the top left side of the dash, near the VIN plate.

• **Throttle Angle Sensor**—is located at the top left side of the engine.
• **Trailer Connector**—is located at the left rear of the trunk, behind the trim panel.
• **Under Hood Relay Box**—is located at the left side of the engine compartment.
• **Washer Fluid Level Sensor**—is located at the right front of the vehicle, behind the bumper cover.
• **Washer Motor**—is located at the right front of the vehicle, behind the bumper cover.
• **Winter Position Switch**—is located behind the dashboard lower panel.
• **Wiper Control Unit**—is located behind the dashboard lower panel.

NSX

• **A/C Compressor Clutch Relay**—is located in sub relay box A, at the rear of the front compartment.
• **A/C Pressure Switches**—are located at the left rear of the front compartment.
• **Accelerator Pedal Sensor**—is located at the upper left side of the engine.
• **Air Mixture Control Motor**—is located at the left side of the passenger footwell.
• **ALB Control Unit**—is located behind the right side of the dash.
• **ALB Fail Safe Relay (front)**—is located in sub relay box B, at the rear of the front compartment.
• **ALB Fail Safe Relay (rear)**—is located in sub relay box B, at the rear of the front compartment.
• **ALB Modulator Solenoid Unit**—is located at the left side of the front compartment.
• **ALB Motor Relay**—is located in the relay box, at the rear of the front compartment.
• **ALB Motor**—is located at the left side of the front compartment.
• **Ambient Temperature Sensor**—is located at the front of the vehicle, in the grill.
• **Anti-lock Brake System (ABS)**—see anti-lock Brakes (ALB).
• **Back Up Lights Switch**—is located at the upper left side of the engine.
• **Blower Relay (High)**—is located in sub relay box A, at the rear of the front compartment.
• **Blower Relay**—is located in sub relay box A, at the rear of the front compartment.
• **Brake Fluid Level Switch**—is located at the left rear of the front compartment, in the master cylinder reservoir.
• **Brake Light Switch**—is located above the brake pedal.
• **Cancel Switches**—are located at the base of the combination switches, on the steering column.
• **Cigarette Lighter Relay**—is located below the front of the console.
• **Clutch Interlock Switch**—is located at the left side of the driver footwell.
• **Clutch Switch**—is located at the left side of the driver footwell.
• **Coolant Temperature Sender**—is located at the lower left side of the engine.
• **Coolant Temperature Sensor**—is located at the lower left side of the engine.
• **Cooling Fan Control Unit**—is located at the center of the rear bulkhead.
• **Cruise Control Actuator**—is located at the left side of the front compartment.
• **Cruise Control Unit**—is located behind the right side of the dash.
• **Dimmer Control Amplifier**—is located at the left side of the bulkhead.
• **Dimmer Relay**—is located in the relay box, at the rear of the front compartment.
• **Door Key Cylinder Switch**—is located inside the door.
• **EGR Lift Valve Sensor**—is located at the top left side of the engine.
• **Electronic Air Control Valve**—is located at the top left side of the engine.
• **Emission Control Box**—is located at the left rear of the engine compartment.
• **Engine Compartment Fan Relay**—is located at the right side of the engine compartment.
• **Fan Coolant Temperature Sensor**—is located at the upper left side of the engine.
• **Fuel Injection**—see Program Fuel Injection (PGM-FI).
• **Fuel Injector Resistors**—are located at the right side of the engine compartment.
• **Fuel Pump Relay**—is located at the left side of the bulkhead.
• **Fuel Pump Resistor**—is located at the right front of the engine compartment.
• **Fuel Tank Unit**—is located at the left side of the rear bulkhead.
• **Head Light Retractor Brake/Drive Relay (right and left)**—is located at the right rear of the front compartment.
• **Head Light Retractor Control Relay (left)**—is located in sub relay box A, at the rear of the front compartment.
• **Head Light Retractor Control Relay (right)**—is located in sub relay box A, at the rear of the front compartment.
• **Heater Core Temperature Sensor**—is located at the right side of the driver footwell.
• **Hood Switch**—is located at the front of the front compartment.
• **Horn Relay**—is located in sub relay box A, at the rear of the front compartment.
• **Ignition Key Switch**—is located under the right side of the steering column, on the ignition switch.
• **Ignition Service Connector**—is located at the right side of the engine compartment.
• **Ignition Switch**—is located under the right side of the steering column.
• **In Car Temperature Sensor**—is located at the front of the console.
• **Intake Air Temperature Sensor**—is located at the top left side of the engine.
• **Integrated Control Unit**—is located in front of the dash fuse box.
• **Jump Start Terminal**—is located in the main fuse box, in the left front corner of the engine compartment.
• **Left Dash Sensor**—is located at the left side of the driver footwell.
• **Lighting Relay**—is located in the relay box, at the rear of the front compartment.
• **Lights On Chime Relay**—is located below the left side of the dash.
• **Mode Door Selector Motor**—is located at the left side of the passenger footwell.
• **Parking Brake Switch**—is located below the rear of the console.
• **PGM-FI Electronic Control Unit**—is located at the right side of the rear bulkhead.
• **Power Amplifier Relay**—is located in sub relay box B, at the rear of the front compartment.
• **Power Door Lock Control Unit**—is located behind the right side of the dash.
• **Power Seat Slide Motor**—is located under the left side seat.
Power Window Relay—is located in the relay box, at the rear of the front compartment.
• **Radiator Fan Resistor**—is located on the radiator fan shroud.

- **Rear Window Defogger Relay**—is locates located under the right side seat.
- **Power Transistor**—is located at the rear of the front compartment, above the blower motor.
- **Power Window Control Unit**—is located inside the drivers door.
- **Relay Box**—is located at the right rear of the front compartment.
- **Retractable Headlights Control Unit**—is located at the center of the rear bulkhead.
- **Right Dash Sensor**—is located behind the right kick panel.
- **Security Control Unit**—is located behind the right side of the dash.
- **Security Indicator**—is located at the top rear of the driver door.
- **Spool Valve Solenoid (front)**—is located at the lower left side of the engine.
- **Starter Relay**—is located behind the right side of the dash.
- **Steering Angle Sensor**—is located in the steering column, behind the combination switches.
- **Sunlight Sensor**—is located behind the left center of the dash.
- **Taillight Relay**—is located in the relay box, at the rear of the front compartment.
- **TCS/Fail Safe Relay**—is located at the left side of the bulkhead.
- **Throttle Actuator**—is located at the top left side of the engine.
- **Throttle Angle Sensor**—is located at the top left side of the engine.
- **Traction Control Unit**—is located at the left side of the bulkhead.
- **Trunk Release Solenoid**—is located at the left side of the trunk.
- **Turn Signal Hazard Lights Relay Assembly**—is located left of the steering column under the dash.
- **Valve Timing Pressure Switch (front)**—is located at the lower left side of the engine.
- **Valve Timing Pressure Switch (rear)**—is located at the left rear of the engine compartment.
- **Vent Motor**—is located at the left side of the passenger footwell.
- **Washer Motor**—is located at the front of the front compartment.
- **Washer Relay**—is located in sub relay box B, at the rear of the front compartment.
- **Wiper Relays (high, intermittent and low)**—are located in sub relay box B, at the rear of the front compartment.

CHRYSLER IMPORTS

Circuit Breakers

Fuses are located in the multi purpose fuse box. The fuse box is located under the left side of the dash. Fuses are also located in the sub-fusible link box, under the right side of the dash and at the left front of the engine compartment.

Fusible Links

Fusible links are located at the main fusible link box next to the battery and at the sub fusible link box near the shock tower.

Relays, Sensors, Modules and Computer Locations

COLT

- **A/C Air Temperature Sensors**—are located under the dash in the evaporator housing.
- **A/C Compressor Control Unit**—is located under the dash, above the evaporator.
- **A/C Compressor Relay**—is located in the left underhood relay box.
- **A/C Condensor Fan Control Relay**—is located in the left underhood relay box.
- **A/C Condensor Fan Motor Relay**—is located in the left underhood relay box.
- **Alternator Relay**—is in the right underhood relay box.
- **Crank Angle Sensor**—is located in the distributor.
- **Cruise Control Unit**—is located under the left dash, next to the fuse box.
- **Defogger Relay**—is under the left side dash, on the right of the fuse box.
- **Defogger Timer**—is under the left side dash, in the fuse box.
- **Door Lock Control Unit**—is located under the left dash at the kick panel.
- **Door Lock Relay**—is located under the left dash at the kick panel, behind the control unit.
- **EGR Control Solenoid**—is located on the firewall.
- **EGR Temperature Sensor (California)**—is located at the base of the EGR valve.
- **EGR Thermal Valve**—is at the front of the engine in a coolant passage.
- **Fuel Pump Check Connector**—is located at the center of the firewall.
- **Hazard Flasher**—is in the left side dash, in the fuse box.
- **Headlamp Highbeam Relay**—is located at the left front fender.
- **Headlamp Relay**—is located in the left underhood relay box.
- **Heater Blower Relay**—is under the left dash, in the under fuse box.
- **MPI Control Relay**—is located under the center console, on the right side.
- **MPI Control Unit**—is located under the dash on the left side, in front of the blower motor.
- **Oxygen Sensor Check Connector**—is located under the right side dash, near the blower motor.
- **PCV Valve**—is screwed in the end of the valve cover.
- **Power Steering Pressure Switch**—is located at the power steering pump.
- **Power Transistor**—is mounted next to the ignition coil.
- **Power Window Relay**—is located in the right side underhood relay box. Canadian models may have the relay next to the battery.
- **Radiator Fan Relay**—is located in the right underhood relay box.
- **Running Lamp Controller (Canada)**—is located at the left front fender.

• **Running Lamp Relay (Canada)**—is located at the left front fender.
• **Seatbelt Warning Timer (Canada)**—is located under the top of the dash to the right of the glove compartment.
• **Self-Diagnosis connector**—is located under the left side dash, next to the fuse box.
• **Taillamp Relay (Canada)**—is located in the left underhood relay box.
• **TDC Sensor**—is located in the distributor.
• **Transmission Control Unit**—is located under the middle of the dash, at the console base.
• **Turn Signal Flasher**—is in the left side dash, in the fuse box.
• **Vehicle Speed Sensor (Reed Switch)**—is located behind the speedometer in the instrument panel.

COLT VISTA

• **A/C Compressor Clutch Relay**—is at the center of the left fender.
• **A/C Condenser Fan Relay**—is at the center of the left fender.
• **A/C Control Relay**—is at the center of the left fender.
• **A/C Fuses**—are located in the glove compartment and in the harness at the cooling fan.
• **Air Flow Sensor**—is located at the air filter in the intake air stream.
• **Alternator Relay**—is located on the left fender at the firewall.
• **Barometric Pressure Sensor**—is located at the air filter in the intake air stream.
• **Coolant Temperature Sender (gauge)**—is located at the front of the engine and screws in from the front of the engine, just under the thermostat housing.
• **Coolant Temperature Sensor**—is located at the front of the engine and screws down into the manifold.
• **Coolant Thermo Switch**—is located at the front of the engine and screws into the manifold from the firewall side.
• **Crank Angle Sensor**—is in the distributor.
• **Cruise Control Module**—is located at the rear of the vehicle in the right side quarter panel.
• **Daytime Running Relays**—are located on the left fender, near the washer bottle.
• **Defogger Relay**—is located on the firewall.
• **Defogger Timer**—is located under the dash, near steering column.
• **Engine Control Unit**—is located under the driver's seat.
• **Flasher Unit**—is located under the left dash, in the relay box.
• **Fuel Pump Check Terminal**—is located near the center of the firewall.
• **Ignition Power Transistor**—is next to the ignition coil.
• **Ignition Timing Adjustment Connector**—is located near the center of the firewall, next to the fuel pump check connector.
• **MPI Control Relay**—is located behind the center of the instrument panel at the console.
• **Power Steering Pressure Switch**—is at the power steering pump.
• **Power Window Relay**—is in the main relay box, next to the battery.
• **Purge Control Solenoid**—is located near the center of the firewall.
• **Radiator Fan Motor Relay**—is in the main relay box, next to the battery.
• **Rear Intermittent Wiper Relay**—is located at the right rear quarter panel.
• **Seatbelt Control Unit**—is located at the rear of the center console near the seat.
• **Seatbelt Relay**—is located at the rear of the center console next to the seat it associated with.
• **Seatbelt Timer**—is located under the left side dash.
• **Self-Diagnosis Connector**—is located under the glove compartment.
• **Thermal Switch**—is located at the front of the engine and screws into the manifold from the firewall side.
• **Transmission Control Unit**—is located behind the center of the instrument panel.
• **Vehicle Speed Sensor**—is located behind the instrument panel at the speedometer.

CONQUEST

• **A/C Compressor Clutch Relay**—is located on the relay block on the left front inner fender panel.
• **A/C Dual Pressure Switch**—is located in the A/C line next to the receiver.
• **A/C Heater Blower Motor Relay**—is located on the blower motor housing.
• **A/C-Heater Blower Motor Resistor**—is located on the blower motor housing.
• **A/C Power Relay**—is located on the evaporator housing.
• **A/C Pressure Switch (W/Intercooler)**—is located on the A/C line next to the receiver.
• **A/C Thermister**—is located on the A/C evaporator housing.
• **Airflow Sensor**—is located inside the air cleaner housing.
• **Automatic A/C Control Unit**—is located behind the automatic A/C panel.
• **Automatic A/C Evaporator Temperature Sensor**—is located on the A/C evaporator fins.
• **Automatic A/C In-Car Photo Sensor**—is located on the instrument panel.
• **Automatic A/C In-Car Temperature Sensor**—is located on the right lower outlet vent.
• **Automatic A/C In-Car Temperature Sensor**—is located on the rear part of roll bar trim.
• **Automatic A/C Power Transistor**—is located on the blower unit air outlet.
• **Automatic A/C Temperature Controller**—is located on the evaporator housing.
• **Automatic A/C Vacuum Solenoid Valves**—is located on the A/C evaporator housing.
• **Automatic Seat Belt Control Unit**—is located in the center console, in the passenger's compartment.
• **Automatic transmission Diode**—is located above the left hand side kick panel.
• **Back-Up Light Switch**—is located on the right side of the transmission.
• **Brake/Stoplight Switch**—is located above the brake pedal.
• **Blower Motor High Speed Relay**—is located under the right hand side of the instrument panel.
• **Blower Motor Relay**—is located under the left hand side of the instrument panel, to the right of the steering column.
• **Blower Motor Starter Cut-Out Relay**—is located under the right hand side of the instrument panel.
• **Chassis Diode**—is located below the left side of the instrument panel.
• **Condenser Fan Relay**—is located on the left hand inner fender panel in the engine compartment.
• **Coolant Temperature Sensor**—is located in the front of the intake manifold.
• **Cooling Fan Relays**—are located on the right front corner of the engine compartment.
• **Detonation (Knock) Sensor**—is located on the right front of the engine.
• **Diagnostic Connector**—is located under the right side of the instrument panel.
• **Downshift Solenoid**—is located on the side of the transmission.

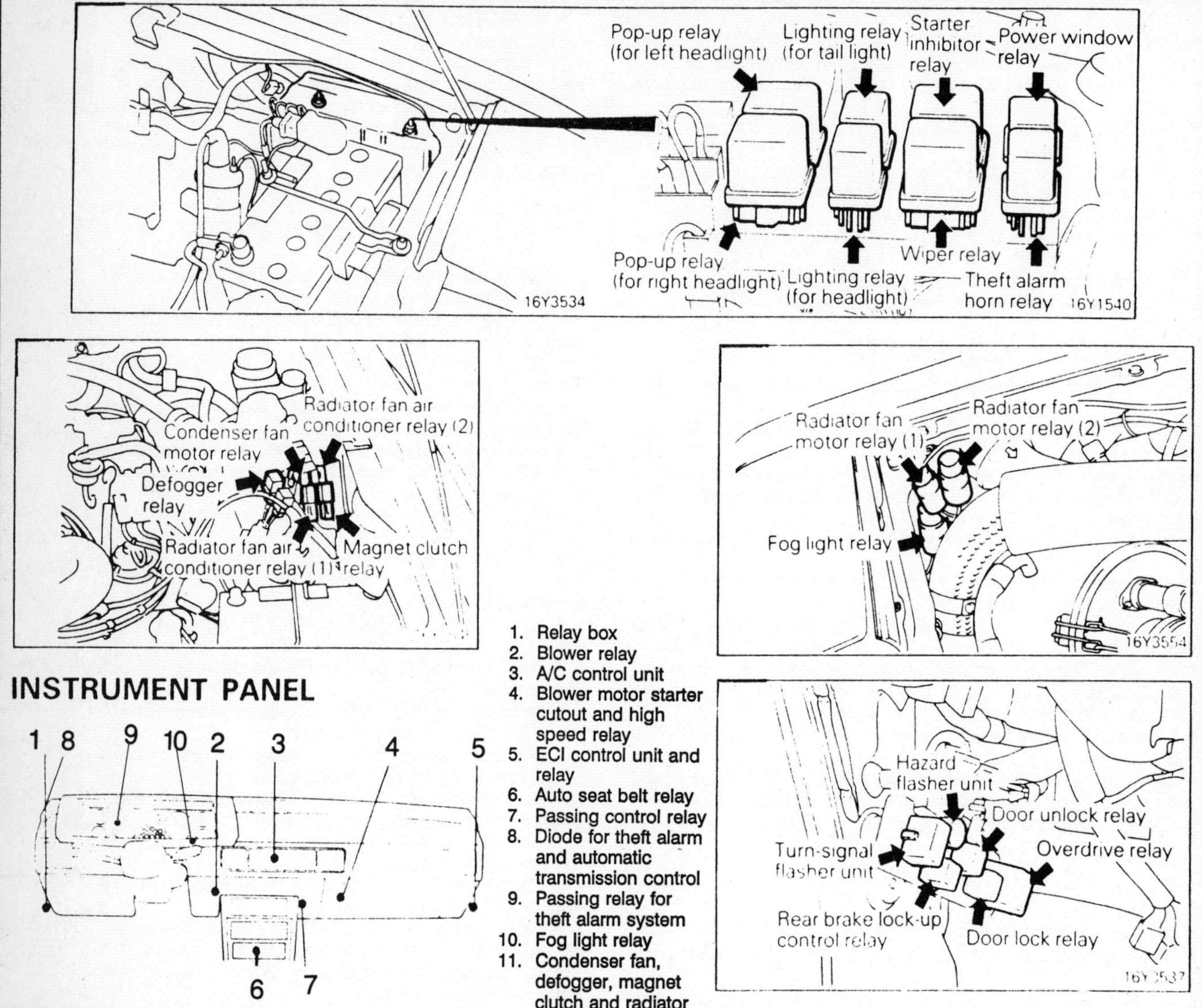

Instrument panel components—Conquest

- **ECI Control Relay**—is located behind the right hand side kick panel.
- **ECI Control Unit**—is located behind the right hand side kick panel.
- **ECI & Oxygen Sensor Test Connector**—is located near the right shock tower.
- **ECU Control Relay**—is located above the ECU on the right side kick panel.
- **EGR Control Solenoid**—is located on the left inner fender.
- **Electric Controlled Injection (ECI) Resistors**—are located on the right headlight support.
- **Electric Controlled Injection (ECI) Diodes**—one is located behind the right hand side kick panel, one is located under the left of the instrument panel.
- **Electronic Control Unit (ECU)**—is located on the right hand side kick panel.
- **Electronic Time & Alarm Control System (ETACS) Unit**—is located under the driver's seat.
- **Engine Spark Control (ESC) Ignitor**—is located on the left inner fender panel.
- **Engine Speed Sensor**—is located on the back of the speedometer.
- **Fog Light Diodes**—one is located behind the instrument panel, one is located on the center of the instrument panel to the right of the console.
- **Fog Light Relay**—is located near the right headlight door.
- **Foot Area Temperature Sensor**—is located under the right hand side of the instrument panel.
- **Fuel Gauge Sending Unit**—is located in the top of the fuel tank.
- **Fuel Pump**—is located in the top of the fuel tank.
- **Fuel Pump Test Connector**—is located near the right shock tower.
- **"G" Sensor**—is located on the rear floor crossmember.
- **Hazard Flasher**—is located under the left hand side instrument panel.

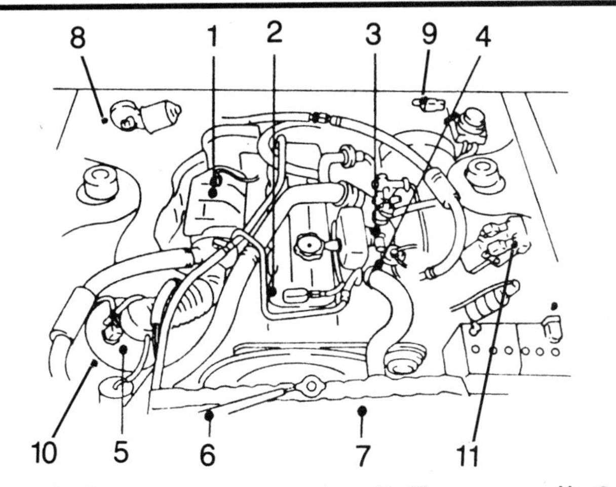

1. Oxygen sensor
2. Detonation sensor
3. Throttle position sensor
4. Coolant temperature sensor
5. Air flow sensor
6. Thermo sensor No. 1
7. Thermo sensor No. 2
8. Diode for theft alarm and automatic transmission
9. Diode for theft alarm
10. Diode for fog light
11. Diode for rear brake lockup control unit

Engine compartment—Conquest

- **Headlight Lighting Relay**—is located on the front relay panel.
- **Ignition Timing Adjusting Terminal**—is located near the right shock tower.
- **Inhibitor Switch**—is located on the right side of the transmission.
- **Instrument Panel Lighting Control**—is located on the A/C evaporator housing.
- **Interior Temperature Sensor**—is located on the front center of the roof headliner.
- **Left Headlight Pop-Up Relay**—is located on the front relay panel.
- **Intake Air Temperature Sensor**—is located inside the air cleaner.
- **Manifold Pressure Sensor**—is located on the left corner of the engine compartment.
- **Oil Pressure Sender**—is located on the side of the engine near the oil filter.
- **Oil Pressure Switch**—is located on the front of the engine block.
- **Overdrive Relay**—is located under the left side of the instrument panel.
- **Parking Brake Switch**—is located at the base of the parking brake lever.
- **Passing Control Relay**—is located under the right side of the instrument panel near radio.
- **Passing Control Relay (w/Theft Alarm System)**—is located on the left hand side of the firewall.
- **Pop-Up Relay**—is located on the left hand front corner of the engine compartment.
- **Power Antenna Relay**—is located in the front of the left hand side rear taillight.
- **Power Door Lock Relay**—is located under the left hand side of the instrument panel.
- **Power Door Un-Lock Relay**—is located under the left hand side of the instrument panel.
- **Power Window Relay**—is located on the front relay panel, in the left hand front corner of the engine compartment.
- **Pulse Generator**—is located on the transmission extension housing.
- **Radiator A/C Fan Relay**—is located on the front relay panel, in the left hand inner fender panel in the engine compartment.
- **Radiator Fan Relay**—is located on the right hand front corner of the engine compartment.
- **Rear Brake Lock-Up Control Modulator**—is located on the right rear corner of the engine compartment.
- **Rear Brake Lock-Up Control Relay**—is located under the left hand side of the instrument panel.
- **Rear Brake Lock-Up Control Unit**—is located under the right hand rear luggage compartment panel.
- **Rear Brake Lock-Up Diode**—is located above the left hand side kick panel.
- **Rear Brake Lock-Up Resistor**—is located above the left hand side kick panel.
- **Rear Brake Lock-Up Solenoid Valve**—is located on the rear brake lock-up modulator.
- **Rear Defroster Relay**—is located on the left hand front corner in the engine compartment.
- **Rear Defroster Relay**—is located on the front relay panel.
- **Relay Panels**—are located on the left hand side kick panel and the front of the engine compartment.
- **Right Headlight Pop-Up Relay**—is located on the front relay panel.
- **Self Test Connector**—is located in the top center of the glove box.
- **Speed Control Unit**—is located behind the trim panel on the rear of the luggage compartment.
- **Speed Control Vacuum Pump Relay**—is located on the right rear of the engine compartment.
- **Speed Control Vacuum Switch**—is located on the right rear corner of the engine compartment.
- **Starter Inhibitor Relay**—is located on the left hand front corner in the engine compartment.
- **TAC Unit**—is located on the top of the driver's front door pillar.
- **Taillight Lighting Relay**—is located on the front relay panel.
- **Thermo Sensor 1**—is located on the front of the radiator support.
- **Thermo Sensor 2**—is located on the bottom of the radiator.
- **Throttle Position Sensor**—is located on the throttle body assembly.
- **Turn Signal Flasher**—is located under the left hand side of the instrument panel.
- **Vacuum Pump Relay**—is located on the right hand rear corner of the engine compartment.
- **Wiper Power Relay**—is located on the front relay panel, on the left front inner fender panel.
- **Wiper Low & High Relay**—is located on the front relay panel, on the left front inner fender panel.

CHRYSLER IMPORT TRUCKS

Circuit Breakers

Fuses are located under the left side of the dash.

Fusible Links

Main and sub-fusible link boxes are located at the left side of the engine compartment, on the fender.

Relays, Sensors, Modules and Computer Locations

1989 RAM 50

- **4WD Indicator Switch**—is located on the transmission.
- **A/C Electric Clutch Cycling Switch**—is located in the refrigerant cooling lines near the reciever drier.
- **A/C Hi/Low Switch**—is located near the condenser.
- **Air Control Valve**—is located on the air cleaner.
- **Auto Choke Relay**—is located at the device box on the left front fender in the engine compartment.
- **Auto Choke Relay**—is located at the left fender in the engine compartment.
- **Automatic Free-Wheeling Hub Control Unit**—is located at the left side kick panel.
- **Automatic Free-Wheeling Hub Indicator Control Unit**—is located at the right side kick panel.
- **Automatic Transmission Diode**—is located under the left side of the dash to the left of the steering column.
- **Backup Light Switch (manual transmission)**—is located at the transmission.
- **Blower Motor Resistor**—is located under the right side of the dash.
- **Bowl Vent Valve**—is located at the side of the carburetor.
- **Brake Fluid Level Switch**—is located at the master cylinder.
- **Buzzer**—is located under the left side of the dash.
- **Coolant Temperature Sensor**—is located at the right side of the engine on the intake manifold.
- **Coolant Temperature Switch (automatic transmission)**—is located at the left side of the engine.
- **Device Box**—is located at the left side of the engine compartment on the fender.
- **EGR Valve**—is located at the front of the engine on the intake manifold.
- **Engine Speed Sensor**—is located at the right rear of the engine compartment.
- **Feedback Carburetor Electronic Control Unit**—is located under the right side of the dash near the blower motor.
- **Feedback Solenoid Valve**—is located at the carburetor.
- **Fuse Block**—is located under the left side of the dash.
- **Hazard/Turn Signal**—is located under the left side of the dash.
- **High Altitude Compensator**—is located at the device box.
- **Inhibitor switch (automatic transmission)**—is located at the transmission.
- **Intermittent Wiper Relay**—is located inside the steering column.
- **Main Fusible link**—is located at the battery.
- **Mixture Control Valve**—is located in the carburetor.
- **Oil pressure Sender (2.6L engine)**—is located at the right side of the engine.
- **Oil Pressure Switch (2.0L engine)**—is located at the right side of the engine.
- **Overdrive Relay**—is located under the left side of the dash.
- **Overdrive Switch**—is located at the gear selector lever.
- **Oxygen Sensor**—is located at the exhaust manifold.
- **PCV valve**—is located at the front of the rocker arm cover.
- **Pulse Generator**—is located at the transmission.
- **Purge Control Valve**—is located at the firewall.
- **Reed Valve**—is located at the rear of the engine near the firewall.
- **Seat Belt Timer Relay**—is located under the left side of the dash.
- **Secondary Air Control Solenoid Valve**—is located in the device box.
- **Thermo Valve**—is located on the intake manifold at the front of the engine.
- **Throttle Opener Control Solenoid Valve**—is located next to the device box on the left fender.
- **Throttle Position Sensor**—is located on the carburetor.
- **Turn Signal/Hazard Relay**—is located under the left side of the dash.
- **Vacuum Switch**—is located in the device box.
- **Vehicle Speed Sensor (reed switch)**—is located at the speedometer.

1990–91 RAM 50

- **4WD Indicator Switch**—is located on the transmission.
- **A/C Compressor Relay**—is located at the left rear of the engine compartment.
- **A/C Low Pressure Switch**—is located at the right front of the engine compartment.
- **Air Flow Sensor**—is located in the air cleaner on the right side of the engine compartment.
- **Automatic Transmission Indicator Diode**—is located under the left side of the dash near the fuse box.
- **Backup Light Switch (manual transmission)**—is located on the transmission.
- **Coolant Temperature Sensor**—is located at the intake manifold.
- **Crankshaft Angle Sensor**—is located at the distributor.
- **Cruise Control Unit**—is located at the left rear of the passenger compartment.
- **Cruise Control Vacuum Pump Relay**—is located at the right rear of the engine compartment.
- **Cruise Control Vacuum Pump**—is located on the right side of the firewall.
- **Daytime Running Light Relay (Canada)**—is located on the left side of the engine compartment.
- **Daytime Running Lights Diode**—is located under the left side of the dash near the fuse box.
- **EGR Control Solenoid Valve**—is located on the left side of the engine.
- **EGR Temperature Sensor**—is located at the EGR valve.
- **EGR Valve**—is mounted to the left side of the engine.
- **Engine Control Relay**—is located at the right side kick panel.
- **Engine Control Unit**—is located at the left side of the dash near the glove box.
- **Fuel Pump Check Terminal**—is located at the right rear of the engine compartment.
- **Fuse Box**—is located under the left side of the dash.
- **Hazard/Turn Signal Relay**—is located in the relay box.
- **Idle Position Switch**—is located at the throttle body.

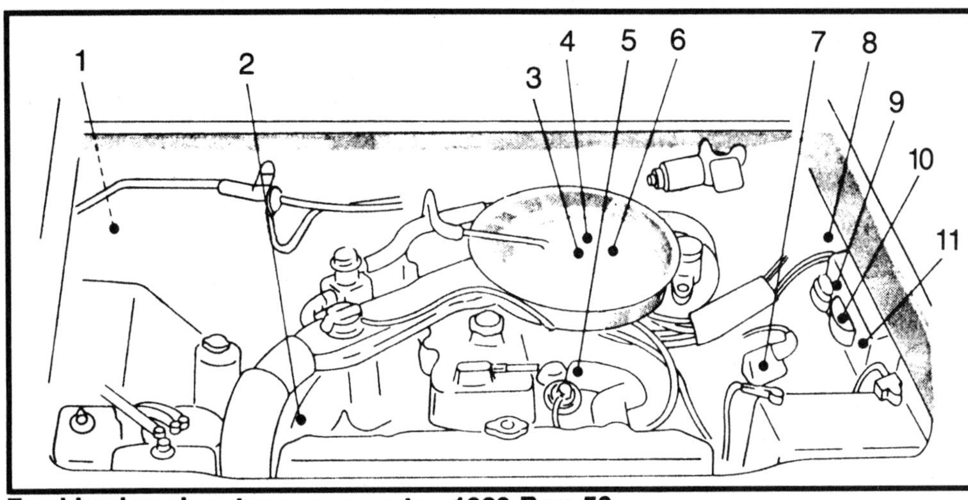

1. Engine control unit
2. Oxygen sensor
3. Feedback solenoid valve
4. Slow cut solenoid
5. Coolant temperature sensor
6. Throttle position sensor
7. Engine speed sensor
8. Throttle opener control solenoid valve
9. Secondary air control solenoid valve
10. Throttle position sensor
11. Electric choke relay

Feed back carburetor components—1989 Ram 50

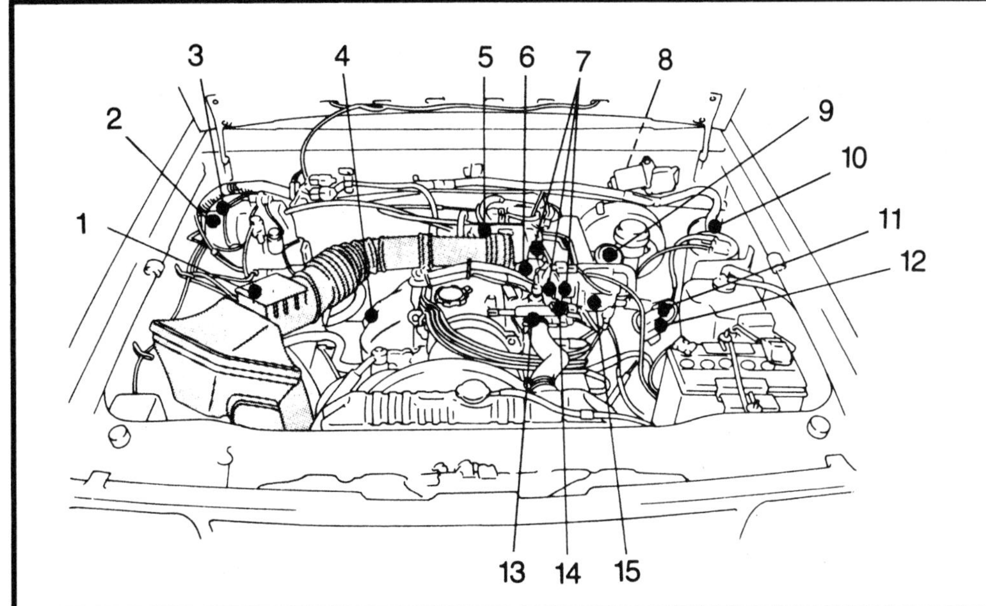

1. Air flow sensor
2. Ignition timing adjustment terminal
3. Fuel pump check terminal
4. Oxygen sensor
5. Idle speed control servo
6. Throttle position sensor
7. Injector
8. Inhibitor switch
9. EGR temperature sensor
10. A/C compressor power relay
11. Purge control solenoid valve
12. EGR control solenoid valve
13. Coolant temperature sensor
14. Ignition coil power transistor
15. Crankshaft angle/ TDC sensor

Fuel Injection component location—1990–91 Ram 50

• **Idle Speed Control Servo**—is located at the throttle body.

• **Ignition Check Terminal**—is located at the right rear of the engine compartment.

• **Ignition Timing Adjuster**—is located at the right rear of the engine compartment.

• **Inhibitor Switch (automatic transmission)**—is located at the gear selector lever.

• **Main Fusible Link**—is located at the battery.

• **Motor Position Sensor**—is located at the throttle body.

• **Noise Filter**—is located on the right side of the firewall.

• **Over Drive Relay**—is located in the relay box.

• **Oxygen Sensor Check Terminal**—is located at the right rear of the engine compartment.

• **Oxygen Sensor**—is located in the exhaust.

• **PCV Valve**—is located at the front of the rocker arm cover.

• **Power Transistor**—is located at the ignition coil.

• **Power Window Relay**—is located in the relay box.

• **Pulse Generator**—is located on the transmission.

• **Purge Control Solenoid Valve**—is located at the left side of the engine compartment.

• **Resistor With Diode**—is located at the battery.

• **Seat Belt Warning Timer**—is located in the relay box.

• **Self Diagnosis Terminal**—is located at the fuse box.

• **Sub-Fusible Link**—is located at the left rear of the engine compartment.

• **TDC Sensor**—is located in the distributor.

• **Throttle Position Sensor**—is located at the throttle body.

• **Transmission Oil Temperature Sensor (4WD/automatic transmission)**—is located at the transmission.

• **Turn Signal/Hazard Relay**—is located in the relay box.

• **Vacuum Switch**—is located is located at the right rear of the engine compartment.

• **Vehicle Speed Sensor (reed switch)**—is located at the speedometer.

DAIHATSU

Circuit Breakers

The main and sub fuse boxes on Rocky models are located under the left side of the dash. The main and sub fuse boxes on Charade are located undeer the steering column.

Fusible Links

The fusible link box is located next to the battery on all models.

Relays, Sensors, Modules and Computer Locations

CHARADE

• **A/C Acceleration Cut Switch**—is located at the accelerator pedal.
• **A/C Amplifier**—is located under the dash at the blower motor.
• **A/C Cut Amplifier**—is located under the dash above the blower motor.
• **A/C Dual Pressure Switch**— is located under the dash on the heater box.
• **Auxiliary Air Valve**—is located inside the throttle body.
• **Belt Control ECU**—is located under the left side of the dash.
• **Bimetal Vacuum Sensing Valve**—is located next to the distributor.
• **Circuit Opening Relay**—is located under the dash near the left kick panel.
• **Coolant Temperature Sensor**—is located near the distributor.
• **Cruise Control ECU**—is located under the left side of the dash.
• **Distributor Vacuum Switching Valve**—is located at the rear of the throttle body near the firewall.
• **Door Lock Control Relay**—is located under the dash near the defogger switch.
• **EGR Vacuum Switching Valve**—is located at the rear of the throttle body near the firewall.
• **EGR Valve Modulator**—is located above the distributor on the left side of the engine.
• **EGR Valve**—is located above the distributor on the left side of the engine.
• **Electronic Control Unit**—is located above the glove box in the right side of the dash.
• **Electronic Fuel Injection (EFI) Test Connector**—is located in front of the master cylinder.
• **Fan Relay**—is located in the relay box.
• **Fuel Pump Relay**—is located in the relay box.
• **Fuse block**—is located under the left side of the dash, near the steering column.
• **Headlight Relay**—is located under the left side of the dash.
• **Horn Relay**—is located under the left side of the dash.
• **Idle Speed Control Vacuum Switching Valve**—is located at the front of the throttle body near the EGR valve.
• **Idle Up Vacuum Sensing Valve**—is located at the right side of the engine compartment.
• **Injector Relay**—is located in the relay box.
• **Intake Air Temperature Sensor**—is located inside the throttle body.
• **Key Warning Buzzer**—is located under the left side of the dash.

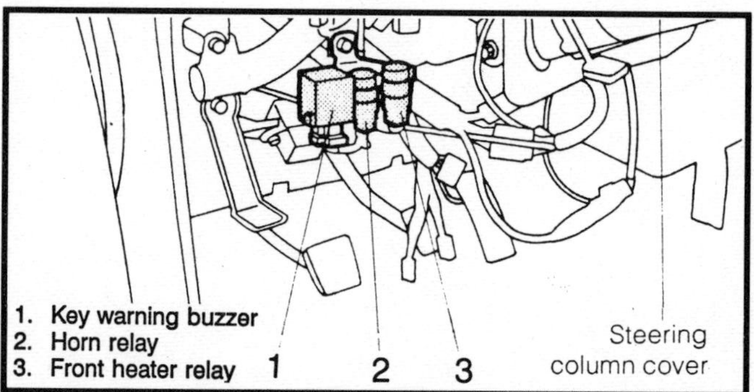

Under dash components—Rocky

• **Main Relay**—is located in the relay box next to the battery.
• **Neutral Start Switch**—is located on the transmission.
• **Oxygen Sensor**—is located in the exhaust manifold.
• **Pressure Sensor Vacuum Sensing Valve**—is located next to the pressure sensor.
• **Pressure Sensor**—is located in a box on the firewall.
• **Relay Box**—is located next to the battery.
• **Shift Lock Controller**—is located under the left side of the dash.
• **Spark Advance Vacuum Switching Valve (manual transmission)**—is located at the front of the engine near the exhaust manifold.
• **Start Injector Time Switch**—is located under the distributor.
• **Starter Relay**—is located under the left side of the dash.
• **Sub-Fuse Block**—is located in the fuse block.
• **Throttle Position Sensor**—is located at the throttle body.
• **Turn Signal Flasher**—is located in the fuse block.
• **Vehicle Speed Sensor**—is located on the side of the transmission.
• **Wiper Relay**—is located in the fuse block.

ROCKY

• **A/C Acceleration Cut Amplifier**—is located above the glove box.
• **A/C Amplifier**—is located above the glove box.
• **A/C Condenser Fan Relay**—is located at the left front of the engine compartment.
• **Back-Up Light Switch**—is located at the top of the transmission near the bell housing.
• **Bi-Metal Vacuum Switching Valve**—is located behind the distributor.
• **Brake Level Warning Switch**—is located inside the master cylinder.
• **Coolant Temperature Sensor**—is located under the distributor.
• **EGR Modulator**—is located next to the EGR valve.
• **EGR Vacuum Switching Valve**—is located between the throttle body and the EGR modulator.
• **Electronic Control Unit (ECU)**—is located in the right side kick panel.
• **Emissions Timer Switch**—is located in the odometer assembly.
• **Exhaust Gas Recirculation (EGR) Valve**—is located on the distributor side of the engine.
• **Fusible link box**—is located is located at the right front of the engine compartment.

• **Headlight Cleaner Relay**—is located under the right side of the dash, at the kick panel.
• **Headlight Relay**—is located at the right front of the engine compartment.
• **Heater Relay (Front)**—is located to the left of the steering column under the dash.
• **Heater Relay (Rear)**—is located under the left side of the dash, at the kick panel.
• **Horn Relay**—is located to the left of the steering column under the dash.
• **Idle Speed Control Vacuum Switching Valve**—is located near the EGR vacuum switching valve.
• **Intake Air Temperature Sensor**—is located inside the throttle body.
• **Intermittent Wiper Relay**—is located under the center of the dash, near the heater control panel.
• **Key Reminder Buzzer**—is located to the left of the steering column under the dash.
• **Lamp Control Relay**—is located under the dash above and to the left of the steering column.
• **Light Control Relay**—is located behind the instrument cluster.
• **Oil Pressure Switch**—is located near the oil filter.
• **Oxygen Sensor**—is located in the exhaust manifold or downpipe.
• **Pressure Sensor Vacuum Switching Valve**—is located on the firewall at the rear of the engine compartment.
• **Pressure Sensor**—is located on the firewall at the rear of the engine compartment.
• **Relay Box**—is located at the right front of the engine compartment.
• **Starter Relay**—is located under the left side of the dash, at the kick panel.
• **Throttle Position Sensor**—is located inside the throttle body.
• **Throttle Positioner**—is located on the throttle body.
• **Transfer Position Detect Switch**—is located at the top of the transmission near the shifter.

GEO

Circuit Breakers

METRO

This vehicle does not incorporate circuit breakers.

PRIZM

This vehicle incorporates three 30 amp circuit breakers. A 30 amp circuit breaker for the A/C heater blower motor, which is located in junction block 1, behind passenger's side kick panel. Two 30 amp circuit breakers, one for the rear window defogger and rear window defogger indicator light, which is located in junction block 2, behind the driver's side kick panel and one for the power windows and door locks, which is located in junction block 2, behind driver's side kick panel.

SPECTRUM

This vehicles does not incorporate circuit breakers.

STORM

This vehicle incorporates circuit breakers which are located in fuse block, on the passenger's side, behind the kick panel. These circuit breakers are usually used to protect the power accessories circuits from overheating.

TRACKER

This vehicle does not incorporate circuit breakers.

Fusible Links

Fusible links on Spectrum can be found near the battery. On Metro and Storm, they are located inside the fuse/relay box. On Tracker and Prizm, they are located inside the engine compartment, in the fusible link box.

Relays, Sensors, Modules and Computer Locations

METRO

• **A/C Accelerator Cut-Off Switch (manual transmission)**—is mounted above accelerator lever.
• **A/C Clutch Relay**—is located in fusible link box.
• **A/C Condenser Fan Relay**—is located in fusible link box.
• **A/C Controller**—is located below right side of instrument panel.
• **A/C Coolant Temperature Sensor**—is located in right engine compartment, in intake manifold.
• **A/C Coolant Temperature Switch (1991)**—is located right rear of engine, above alternator.
• **A/C Dual Pressure Switch**—is located in right engine compartment, near strut tower.
• **A/C Switch**—is located center of instrument panel, below the radio.
• **A/C Vacuum Switching Valve (1991)**—is mounted to the bulkhead, right of the ignition coil.
• **Air Bag**—see Supplement Inflatable Restraint (SIR).
• **Assembly Line Data Link (ALDL, 1991 Convertible)**—is located below left side of instrument panel.
• **Automatic Transaxle Control Module**—is located under instrument panel, right of steering column.
• **Automatic Transaxle Diagnostic Connector (1991)**—is located below instrument panel, right of steering column.
• **Back-Up Switch (manual transaxle)**—is located near engine harness, above transaxle.
• **Blower Speed Selector Switch**—is located on center of instrument panel, below radio.
• **Brake Fluid Level Switch**—is located on brake fluid reservoir.
• **Combination Switch**—is located on left side of steering column.
• **Clutch Start Switch (manual transaxle)**—is located in center of engine compartment, above transaxle.
• **Coolant Temperature Sensor**—is located left side of engine, under the air filter housing.

- **Diagnostic Connector**—is located below the instrument panel, right of steering column.
- **Diagnostic Energy Reserve Module (DERM, 1991 Convertible)**—is located behind the instrument panel, right of steering column.
- **Diagnostic Lamp**—is located below the instrument panel, right of steering column.
- **Diagnostic Switch (1989–90)**—is located below instrument panel, right of steering column.
- **Dimmer Switch**—is located in combination switch.
- **Diode Cluster (1991 manual transaxle)**—is located behind the instrument panel, left of the steering column.
- **Door Latch Switch (left)**—is located in left front door latch.
- **Door Latch Switch (right)**—is located in right door latch.
- **Door Switch (left)**—is located left door frame.
- **Duty Check Coupler**—is located left rear of engine compartment, in front of resistor.
- **Engine Control Module (ECM)**—is located under instrument panel, left of steering column
- **EPI Main Fuse**—is located in left engine compartment, in fusible link box.
- **Electronic Port Injection (EPI) Main Relay**—is located in fusible link box.
- **Exhaust Gas Recirculation Vacuum Switching Valve (EGR VSV)**—is located in engine compartment, forward of valve cover.
- **Fan Thermostat Switch (1991)**—is located in on the thermostat housing.
- **Front Lap Belt Retractor Solenoid (left)**—is located in front left door.
- **Front Lap Belt Retractor Solenoid (right)**—is located in right front door.
- **Front Shoulder Belt Retractor Solenoid (left)**—is located in left front door.
- **Front Shoulder Belt Retractor Solenoid (right)**—is located in right front door.
- **Front Wiper/Washer Switch**—is located on right side of instrument panel cluster shroud.
- **Fuel Pump Relay**—is located in left engine compartment, in fusible link box.
- **Fuse and Relay Box (1991)**—is located left side of engine compartment, behind battery.
- **Fusible Link Box**—is located in left engine compartment, behind battery.
- **Gear Selector Switch (automatic transaxle)**—is located in center of engine compartment, top of transaxle.
- **Horn Relay (1989–90)**—is located in left engine compartment, on fusible link box.
- **Horn Relay (1991)**—is located on the left side of the engine compartment, on the fuse/relay box.
- **Idle Speed Controller Solenoid Valve**—is located left side of engine, under air filter housing.
- **Ignition Key Warning Switch**—is located right side of steering column.
- **Junction Block**—is located behind left side of instrument panel.
- **Manifold Absolute Pressure (MAP) Sensor**—is located right rear side of engine, on bulkhead.
- **Manifold Air Temperature (MAT) Sensor**—is located left side of engine, attached to the air filter housing.
- **Neutral Safety Switch (automatic transaxle)**—Is located in the center of engine compartment, above transaxle.
- **Oil Pressure Switch**—is located in front of engine, behind the right A/C condenser fan.
- **Oxygen Sensor**—is located front of engine, behind A/C condenser fan.
- **Parking Brake Switch**—is located in passenger compartment, behind gear selector.
- **Radiator Fan Switch**—is located upper rear of engine, near distributor.
- **Rear Defogger Switch**—is located on right side of instrument panel cluster shroud.
- **Rear Wiper/Washer Switch**—is located on instrument panel, right of steering column.
- **Safety Belt Controller**—is located under instrument panel, left of steering column.
- **Safety Belt Diode (1991)**—is located behind right instrument panel, near grommet.
- **Safety Belt Switch (left)**—is located in left safety belt buckle.
- **Shift Lever Switch (automatic transaxle)**—is located in center of engine compartment, above transaxle.
- **Shift Lock Solenoid (automatic transaxle)**—is located next to base of shift selector.
- **Shift Solenoid (automatic transaxle)**—is located on top of transaxle.
- **SIR Arming Sensor (1991 Convertible)**—is located behind the right side of the instrument panel.
- **SIR Forward Discriminating Sensor (1991 Convertible)**—is located in front of engine compartment, behind the A/C condenser fan.
- **SIR Fuse Box (1991 Convertible)**—is located below instrument panel, attached to the junction block.
- **SIR Inflator Module (1991 Convertible)**—is located in the steering column.
- **SIR Passenger Compartment Discriminating Sensor (1991 Convertible)**—is located behind the instrument panel, right of the steering column.
- **SIR Resistor Module (1991 Convertible)**—is located behind the right side of the instrument panel.
- **Stoplamp Switch**—is located on top of brake pedal.
- **Throttle Position Sensor (1989–90)**—is located on throttle body.
- **Throttle Position Sensor (1991)**—is located right rear of engine, above alternator.
- **Turn Switch**—is located in combination switch.
- **Vehicle Speed Sensor (1989–90)**—is located on top of transaxle.
- **Vehicle Speed Sensor (1991)**—is located behind the center of the instrument panel cluster.
- **Warning Alarm Module**—is located under lower instrument panel, left of steering column.

PRIZM

- **A/C Clutch Relay**—is located to the left of the battery, in junction block 5.
- **A/C Cutout Switch**Is located in the engine compartment, left of the right hand strut tower, near the bulkhead.
- **A/C Compressor Temperature Switch (1991)**—is located on the top of the A/C compressor.
- **A/C Diode**—is located on the right side of the instrument panel, behind the glove box.
- **A/C Dual Pressure Switch**—is located on the right side of the engine compartment, near the right strut tower.
- **A/C Fan Relay 2**—is located left of the battery, in junction block 5.
- **A/C Coolant Temperature Cutout Switch (1991)**—is located on the Lower right side of the radiator.
- **A/C Idle-Up Vacuum Switching Valve (1991, Except GSi)**—is located in the right rear of the engine compartment.
- **A/C Idle-Up Vacuum Switching Valve (1991 GSi)**—is located in the left rear of the engine compartment.
- **A/C Pressure Switch**—is located on the right side of the engine compartment, near the right strut tower.
- **A/C Switch**—is located in the center of the instrument panel, above the radio.
- **Audio Alarm Module**—is located behind the lower left hand shroud, connected to junction block 1.

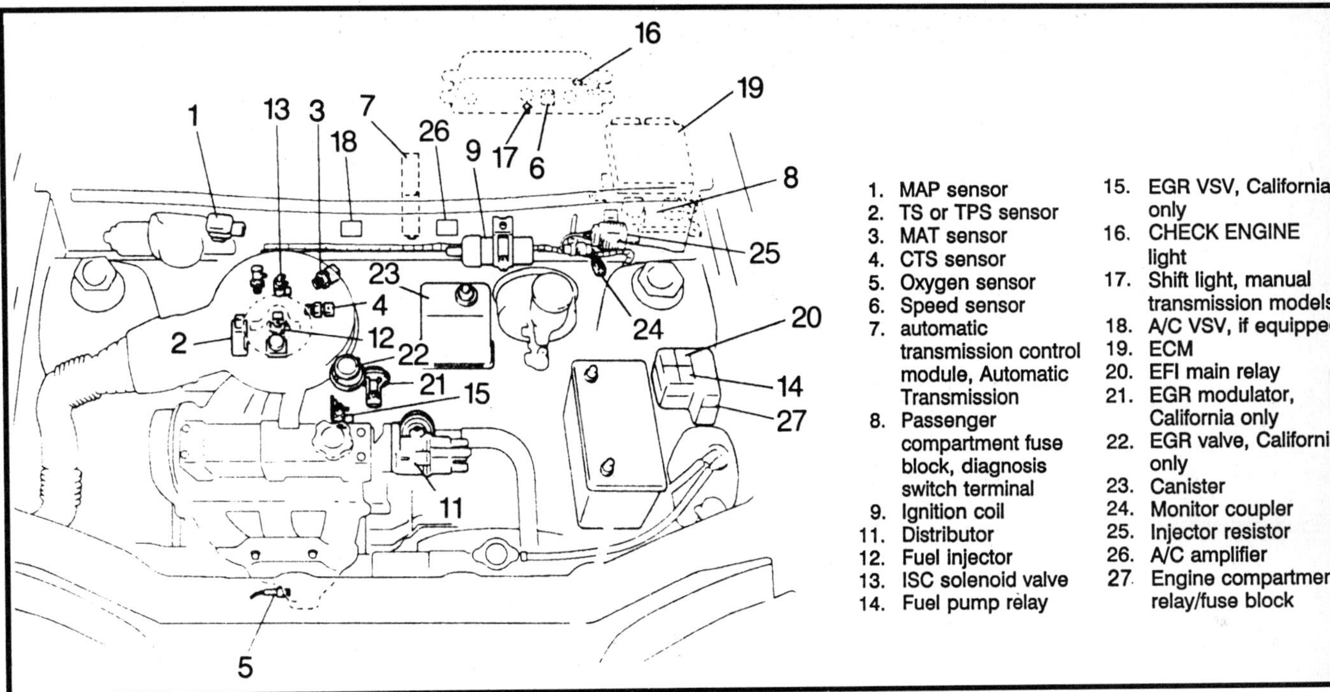

Engine compartment components location—Metro

• **Automatic Transaxle Control Module (1991)**—is located on front of gear selector console.

• **Back-Up Lamp Switch**—is located on the left hand side of the engine compartment, on the top of the transmission.

• **Belt Buckle Switch (left)**—is located in the left belt buckle latch.

• **Blower Control Switch**—is located under the center of the instrument panel.

• **Blower Resistor**—is located under the instrument panel, behind the glove box.

• **Blower Switch**—is located in the center of the instrument panel.

• **Brake Fluid Level Warning Switch**—is located inside the engine compartment, in the brake fluid reservoir.

• **Brake Warning Switch**—is located in the engine compartment, left of the vacuum booster.

• **Circuit Opening Relay (1989–90)**—is located on the ECM.

• **Circuit Opening Relay (1991)**—is located behind the center of the instrument panel, below the radio.

• **Clutch Switch**—is located under the left side of the instrument panel.

• **Cold Start Injector Timer**—is located on the engine, below the distributor.

• **Coolant Fan Temperature Switch**—is located on the coolant outlet below the distributor.

• **Coolant Temperature Sensor (CTS)**—is located on the engine, below and behind the distributor (green connector).

• **Coolant Temperature Switch (1991)**—is located in left front of the engine compartment.

• **Cruise Control Clutch Release Switch (1991)**—is located under the left side of the instrument panel.

• **Cruise Control Diode (1991)**—is located behind the lower right shroud.

• **Cruise Control Module**—is located behind the lower right kick panel.

• **Cruise Control Switch**—is located under the instrument panel, left of the steering column.

• **Cruise Control Vacuum Switch**—is located in the engine compartment, in front of the right strut tower.

• **Cruise/Stoplamp Switch**—is located behind the instrument panel on the brake pedal support.

• **Diagnostic Connector**—is located in the engine compartment, in front of the left strut tower.

• **Door Lock Relay**—is located behind instrument panel, left of steering column.

• **Electronic Control Module (ECM)**—is located in the center of the instrument panel, behind the radio.

• **ECM-IG Fuse**—is located on the left hand shroud, attached to junction block 1.

• **Electronic Controlled Transmission (ECT) Select Switch (1991 GSi Automatic Transaxle)**—is located in floor console, at base of gear selector lever.

• **Electronic Fuel Injection (EFI) Main Relay**—is located above the left hand front wheel well, in junction block 2.

• **Engine Control Module (ECM, 1991)**—is located in front of console, under the heater case.

• **Engine Main Relay**—is located above the left front wheel wheel, in junction block 2.

• **Exhaust Gas Recirculation (EGR) Temperature Sensor (1991 California)**—is located on the right rear of engine, near bulkhead.

• **Exhaust Gas Recirculation (EGR) Vacuum Switching Valve (1991 California)**—is located in rear engine compartment, near bulkhead.

• **Exhaust Oxygen Sensor**—is located in the tail pipe, near the exhaust manifold.

• **Fan Idle-Up Diode (1991 GSi)**—is located behind the left shroud.

• **Flasher Relay**—is located behind the left kick panel.

• **Front Door Jamb Switch (right)**—is located forward of the right front door frame.

• **Front Door Jamb Switch (left)**—is located on the left front door support.

• **Fuel Pressure Regulator Vacuum Switching Valve (1991)**—is located in the left rear engine compartment, mounted on mass airflow sensor.

• **Fuse Block**—is located at junction block 1, lower left shroud.

• **Fusible Link Box**—is located on the battery positive cable.

• **Hazard Switch**—is located on the instrument panel, right of the gauge cluster.

• **Headlamp Relay**—is located above the left hand front wheel well, in junction block 2.

• **Heater Circuit Breaker**—is located behind the right hand shroud, in junction Block 4.

• **Heater Control Switch**—is located in the center of the instrument panel, above the radio.

• **Heater Relay**—is located behind the right hand shroud, in junction block 4.

• **Horn Relay**—is located above the left handfront wheel well, in junction block 2.

• **Horn Switch**—is located on the steering wheel center pad.

• **Idle-Up Diode**—is located behind the left side of the instrument panel, near the shroud.

• **Idle-Up Vacuum Switching Valve (1991)**—is located on right rear of engine.

• **Ignition Key Warning Switch**—is located in the steering column, in the lock cylinder.

• **Ignition Switch**—is located on the upper right hand side of the steering column.

• **Intake Air Temperature (IAT) Sensor**—is located in the left rear of engine compartment.

• **Junction Block 1**—is located behind the left shroud.

• **Junction Block 2**—is located above the left front wheel well, in the engine compartment.

• **Junction Block 3**—is located behind the instrument panel support brace, above the steering column.

• **Junction Block 4**—is located behind the the right shroud.

• **Junction Block 5**—is located in the engine compartment, left of the battery.

• **Junction Connector**—is located behind the instrument panel, left of the steering column.

• **Knock Sensor (1991)**—is mounted on the rear of engine.

• **Manifold Absolute Pressure (MAP) Sensor**—is located in center of bulkhead, behind the intake plenum.

• **Manifold Air Temperature (MAT) Sensor**—is located in the rear of the air cleaner.

• **Mass Airflow Sensor (1991 GSi)**—is located in left side of the engine compartment, near junction block 2.

• **Neutral Safety Switch**—is located on the lower front side of the transaxle.

• **Neutral Start Switch**—is located on the left side of the engine compartment, top of the transaxle.

• **Oxygen Sensor**—is located in front of engine, in exhaust manifold.

• **Oxygen Sensor (1991 GSI, California)**—is located under vehicle, near catalytic converter.

• **Oil Pressure Sending Unit**—is located in front of engine, above and to the left of the oil filter.

• **Oil Pressure Switch (1991)**—is located in the right front of the engine.

• **Parking Brake Switch**—is located on the floor.

• **Power Window Circuit Breaker**—is located behind the left kick panel, near junction block 1.

• **Power Window Master Switch**—is located in the left front door.

• **Power Window Relay (1989–90)**—is located behind the right shroud, in junction block 4.

• **Power Window Relay (1991)**—is located behind left kick panel, near junction block 1.

• **Radiator Fan Relay 1**—is located above left front wheel well, in junction block 2.

• **Refrigerant Pressure Switch (1991)**—is located on the right side of engine compartment, near the right strut tower.

• **Retractor Switch (1991)**is located under the floor console, in front of left belt retractor.

• **Revolution Detecting Sensor (1991 GSi)**—is mounted on rear of the A/C compressor.

• **Seatbelt Switch**—is located in the left seatbelt buckle.

• **Shift Lock Control Module (1991)**—is located under the floor console, in front of parking brake.

• **Shift Lock Solenoid (1991)**—is located under floor console, in front of Parking brake.

• **Stoplamp Switch**—is located behind the instrument panel, on the brake pedal support.

• **Sunroof Switch**— is located on center front of the roof headliner.

• **Tail-Lamp Relay**—is located behind the left shroud, in junction box 1.

• **Throttle Positioner Sensor**—is mounted on the rear throttle assembly.

• **Transaxle Control Switch (1991 GSi)**—is located on top of gear selector lever.

• **Turn Signal Flasher**—is located in the upper left kick panel.

• **Vehicle Speed Sensor**—is mounted inside the speedometer head, in instrument panel cluster.

• **Washer Change Valve (1991)**—is located in engine compartment, behind the right strut tower.

• **Windshield Washer Diode**—is located behind the instrument panel, left of the steering column.

• **Windshield Wiper Cruise Control Engage Switch (1991)**—is located in the right side of the steering column.

SPECTRUM

• **A/C Cycling Switch**—is located behind the A/C compressor, on front grille support.

• **A/C Dual Pressure Switch**—is mounted on the top of the A/C condenser, in the engine compartment.

• **A/C Relay**—is located under the left side of the instrument panel.

• **A/C Resistor**—is located on the A/C evaporator housing.

• **A/C Thermo Switch**—is located on the A/C evaporator housing.

• **Air Inlet Temperature Sensor**—is located on the bottom of the air cleaner assembly.

• **Altitude Sensing Switch**—is located on the front of the carburetor.

• **Assembly Line Diagnostic Link**—is located under the right side of the dash panel, near the kick panel.

• **Back-Up Switch (manual transaxle)**—is located on the top of the transaxle.

• **Clutch/Start Switch (manual transaxle)**—is located on the top of the clutch pedal bracket.

• **Check Engine Lamp**—is located on the instrument cluster.

• **Choke Relay**—is located on the right side of the firewall, in the engine compartment.

• **Coolant Temperature Sensor**—is located on the intake manifold.

• **Coolant Temperature Switch (CTS)**—is located on the engine block, behind the A/C compressor.

• **Cooling Fan Relay**—is located on the left front inner fender panel, in front of the battery.

• **Cruise Control Brake Switch**—is located on the top of the brake pedal bracket.

• **Cruise Control Clutch Switch (manual transaxle)**—is located on the top of the clutch pedal bracket.

• **Cruise Control Module**—is located under the instrument panel on the drivers side, on the steering column support bracket.

• **Cruise Control Servo**—is located on the left rear side of the engine compartment.

• **Diode Box**—is located under the right side of the dash panel, near the kick panel.

• **Early Fuel Evaporation (EFE) Relay**—is located on the right side of the fire wall, in the engine compartment.

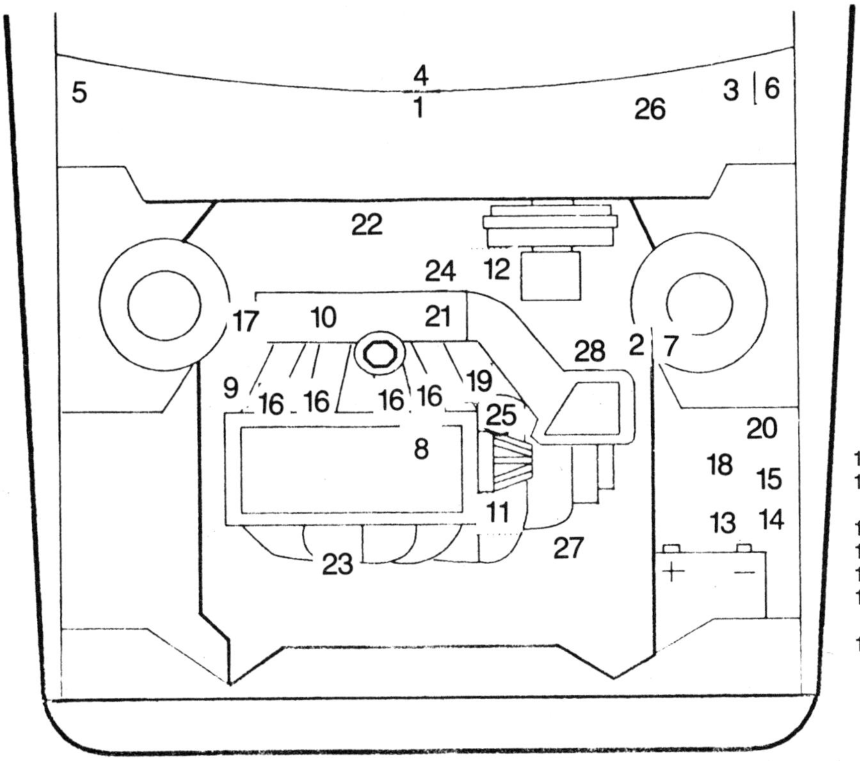

1. Electronic Control Module (ECM)
2. Check connector
3. CHECK ENGINE light
4. Circuit opening relay
5. ECM harness grounds
6. Fuse panel
7. Fuel pump test connector
8. PCV valve
9. Fuel pressure regulator valve
10. Cold start injector
11. Cold start injector valve switch
12. Fuel vapor canister
13. A/C fan relay No. 1
14. A/C fan relay No. 2
15. A/C compressor relay
16. Fuel injectors
17. Idle vacuum switching valve (VSV)
18. EFI main relay
19. EGR vacuum switching valve (VSV)—California models
20. Cooling fan relay
21. Throttle body
22. Manifold absolute pressure (MAP) sensor
23. Oxygen sensor
24. Throttle switch (TS)
25. Coolant temperature sensor (CTS)
26. Vehicle speed sensor (VSS)
27. Park/neutral switch
28. Manifold air temperature (MAT sensor)

Engine compartment components location—1989–90 Prizm

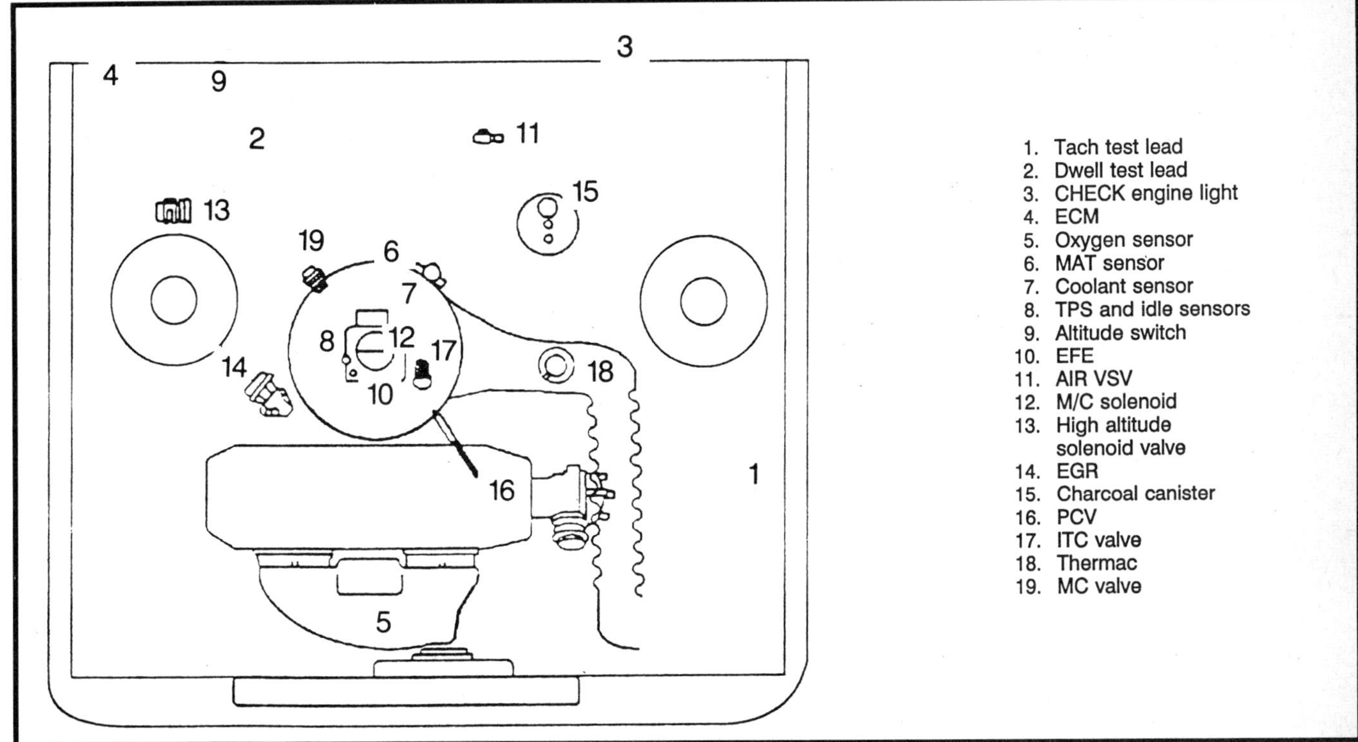

1. Tach test lead
2. Dwell test lead
3. CHECK engine light
4. ECM
5. Oxygen sensor
6. MAT sensor
7. Coolant sensor
8. TPS and idle sensors
9. Altitude switch
10. EFE
11. AIR VSV
12. M/C solenoid
13. High altitude solenoid valve
14. EGR
15. Charcoal canister
16. PCV
17. ITC valve
18. Thermac
19. MC valve

Engine compartment components location— Spectrum

- **Electronic Control Module (ECM)**—is located under the right side of the dash panel, behind the kick panel.
- **Fast Idle Control Diaphragm (FICD) Relay**—is located on the right side of the firewall, in the engine compartment.
- **Front Harness Diodes**—are located under the left hand side of the instrument panel.
- **High Altitude Solenoid Valve**—is located in the right rear of the engine compartment.
- **Ignition Main Relay**—is located behind the left hand side of the instrument panel.
- **Inhibit Switch (automatic transaxle)**—is located on the right rear side of the transaxle.
- **Key Warning Buzzer**—is located near the center of the dash, to the right of the instrument panel.
- **Kick-Down Solenoid (automatic transaxle)**—is located in the left side of the engine compartment.
- **Noise Filter**—is located on the right front shock tower.
- **Oil Pressure Switch**—is located on the lower right rear section of the engine.
- **Oxygen Sensor**—is located in the exhaust manifold.
- **Power Steering Pressure Switch**—is located on the power steering hydraulic pressure line.
- **Rear Window Defogger Relay**—is located behind the left hand side od the instrument panel.
- **Restart Relay**—is located under the left side of the instrument panel, near the kick panel.
- **Seatbelt Timer**—is located on the back of the instrument panel cluster.
- **Stop Light Relay**—is located in the rear trunk panel.
- **Throttle Positioner Switch**—is located on the side of the carburetor.
- **Transaxle Gear Switches**—are located on the top rear side of the transaxle.
- **Turn Signal/Hazard Flasher Relay**—is located behind the left hand side of the instrument panel.
- **Upshift Relay**—is located under the left side of the instrument panel, near the left kick panel.
- **Vehicle Speed Sensor**—is located on the side of the transaxle.
- **Windshield/Wiper Delay Relay**—is located behind the left hand side of the instrument panel.

STORM

- **A/C Cut Control Unit**—is mounted of top of evaporator housing.
- **A/C Switch**—is located in center of instrument panel.
- **Air Bag**—see Supplement Inflatable Restraint (SIR).
- **Assembly Line Diagnostic Link (ALDL)**—is located behind the right side kick panel.
- **Arming Sensor**—is located behind center of instrument panel.
- **Back-Up Lamp Switch**—is located on top center of transaxle.
- **Brake Fluid Switch**—is mounted on brake fluid reservoir.
- **Clutch Interrupt Switch**—is located above clutch pedal.
- **Clutch Start Switch**—is located above clutch pedal.
- **Combination Switch**—is located on left side of steering column.
- **Coolant Fan Check Connector**—is located right rear of engine compartment.
- **Coolant Temperature Sensor**—is located on thermostat housing.
- **Diagnostic Connector**—right lower kick panel.
- **Diagnostic Energy Reserve Module (DERM)**—is located under center console.
- **Door Switch (left)**—is located in left door jam.
- **Door Switch (right)**—is located in right door jam.
- **Economy Switch**—is located in center of console.
- **EGR Vacuum Switching Valve**—is located in rear of engine compartment.
- **Electronic Thermo Switch**—is located on top of the evaporator housing.
- **Engine Control Module (ECM)**—is located behind the left kick panel.
- **Fan Switch**—is located behind center of instrument panel.
- **Flasher Unit**—is located behind lower left instrument panel.
- **Fog Lamp Switch**—is located on instrument panel, left of steering column.
- **Forward Sensor**—is located in engine compartment behind grille.
- **Fuse Block**—is located behind left kick panel.
- **Fuse and Relay Box**—is located in left engine compartment.
- **Idle Air Control Valve**—is located front of common chamber.
- **Ignition Switch**—is located on the right steering column.
- **Inhibitor Switch**—is located on top center of transaxle.
- **Intake Air Vacuum Switching Valve**—is located rear of engine compartment.
- **Intermittent Relay**—is located behind lower left of instrument panel.
- **Junction Connector**—is located behind center of instrument panel.
- **Manifold Absolute Pressure (MAP) Sensor**—is located center of bulkhead.
- **Manifold Air Temperature (MAT) Sensor**—is located on air cleaner box.
- **Mission Switch**—is located on transaxle.
- **Oil Pressure Switch**—is located right rear corner of engine.
- **Parking Brake Switch**—is located on parking brake.
- **Park/Neutral Switch**—is located on top center of transaxle.
- **Power Steering Pressure Switch**—is located on power steering pump.
- **Oxygen Sensor**—is located in engine compartment, on exhaust manifold.
- **Rear Defogger Relay**—is located behind left side of instrument panel, in junction block.
- **Reed Switch**—is located behind speedometer.
- **Relay Box**—in right side of engine compartment.
- **Safety Belt Switch**—is located on base of driver's safety belt buckle.
- **SIR Arming Sensor**—is located behind center of instrument panel
- **SIR Module**—is located behind steering wheel.
- **SIR Passenger Compartment Sensor**—is located under console asembly.
- **Speedometer Reed Switch**—is located behind speedometer.
- **Stop Lamp Switch**—is located above the brake pedal.
- **Thermo Switch**—is located on lower left side of radiator.
- **Throttle Position Sensor**—is located on common chamber of engine.
- **Upshift Indicator Relay**—is located behind the right kick panel.
- **Vehicle Speed Sensor**—is located on rear of transaxle.
- **Windshield Wiper/Washer Switch**—is located on instrument panel, right of cluster.

TRACKER

- **A/C Clutch Relay**—is located inside the right fender, near the fusible link box.
- **A/C Condenser Fan Motor Relay**—is located inside right fender, near fusible link box.

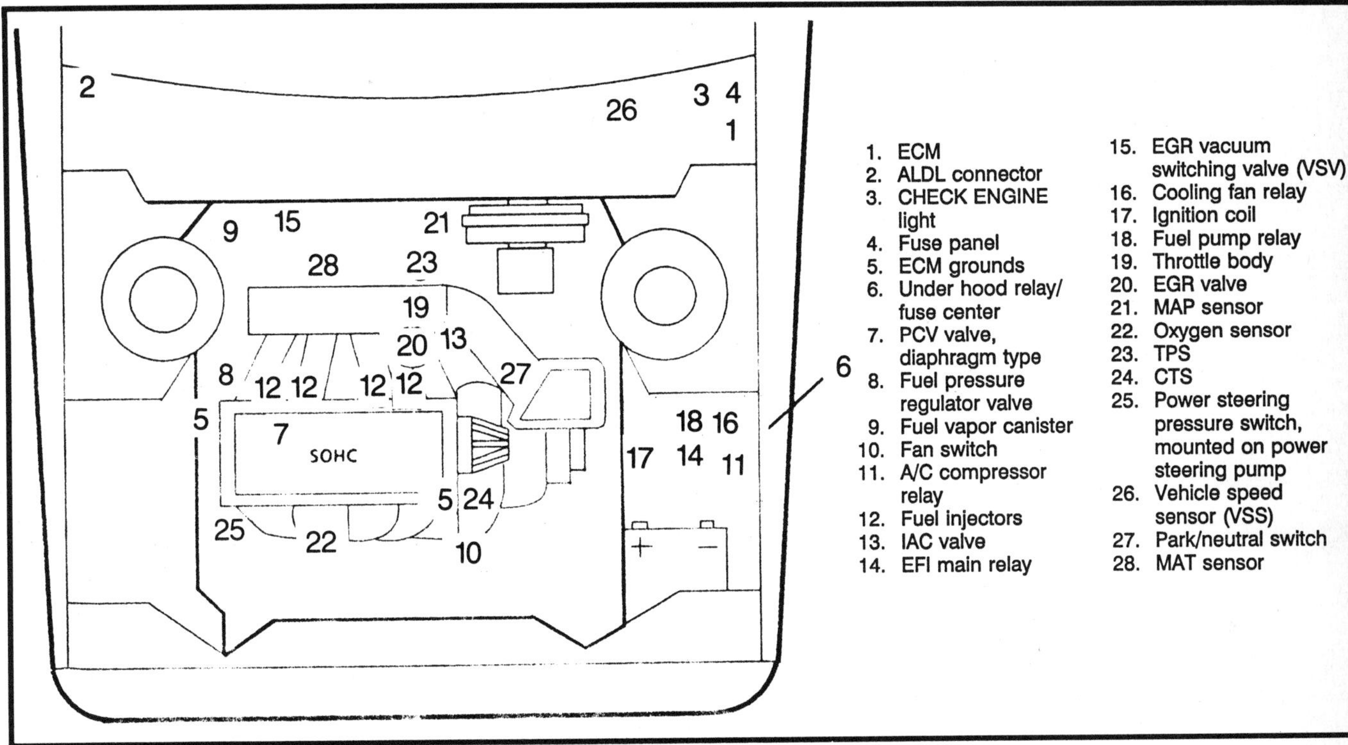

Engine compartment components location—Storm

- **A/C Coolant Temperature Sensor**—is located on intake plenum, behind upper radiator hose.
- **A/C Dual Pressure Switch**—is located on the right side of the radiator, on receiver/dryer.
- **A/C Fuse Holder (1991)**—is located in right engine compartment, attached to A/C clutch relay.
- **A/C Switch**—is located in the center of the instrument panel, above radio.
- **Back-Up Switch**—is mounted on top of the transfer case.
- **Belt Buckle Switch**—is located on the driver's side seat belt buckle.
- **Blower Speed Selector Switch (1991)**—is located center of instrument panel, above radio.
- **Brake Fluid Level Switch**—is located in left rear of engine compartment, on the brake fluid reservoir.
- **Cancel Switch (Except California)**—is located below steering column, behind the access panel.
- **Canister Purge Vacuum Switching Valve (1991)**—is located on right side of engine compartment, near strut tower.
- **Check Engine Cancel Switch (1991)**—is located below steering column, behind the access panel.
- **Clutch Start Switch**—is located under left side of instrument panel, above the clutch pedal.
- **Combination Switch**—is located on the left side of the steering column.
- **Condenser Fan Motor Relay**—is located inside the right fender , near the fusible link box.
- **Control Relay**—is located under the left side of the instrument panel, left of the steering column.
- **Coolant Temperature Sensor**—is located on the right side of engine, behind coolant hose.
- **Daytime Running Lamp Controller**—is located behind instrument panel, left of steering column.
- **Diagnostic Terminals**—is located under the left side of the instrument panel, in the fuse box.
- **Diode Cluster**—is located on main harness, in combination switch branch.
- **Door Switch (left)**—is located at bottom right corner of door frame.
- **Door Switch (right)**—is located in bottom right corner of door frame.
- **Dual Pressure Switch**—is located on the right side of the radiator, on receiver/dryer.
- **Duty Check Coupler (1991)**—is located in the right side of the engine compartment, near the fusible link box.
- **Engine Control Module (ECM)**—is located under the left side of the instrument panel, left of steering column.
- **Exhaust Gas Recirculation (EGR) Temperature Sensor (California)**—is located on engine, left of throttle body.
- **Exhaust Gas Recirculation Vacuum Switching Valve (EGR VSV)**—is located in engine compartment, ahead of valve cover, blue connector.
- **Fifth Gear Switch (manual transmission)**—is located on left side of the transmission.
- **Four Wheel Drive Indicator Switch**—is located on top of the transfer case.
- **Fuel Pump Relay (1991)**—is located under the left side of the instrument panel, mounted to the ECM.
- **Fuse Block**—is located under left side of instrument panel, left of steering column.
- **Fusible Link Box**—is located in engine compartment, on right inner fender.
- **Horn Relay (1989–90)**—is located under the left side of the instrument panel, left of steering column.
- **Horn Relay (1991)**—is located under the instrument panel, mounted to the ECM.
- **Idle Air Control Solenoid**—is located on the right side of throttle body.
- **Idle Speed Control Solenoid Valve (1991)**—is located on the right side of the throttle body.
- **Idle-Up Vacuum Switching Valve (VSV)**—is located in engine compartment, ahead of valve cover, brown connector.
- **Ignition Switch**—is located on the right side of steering column.

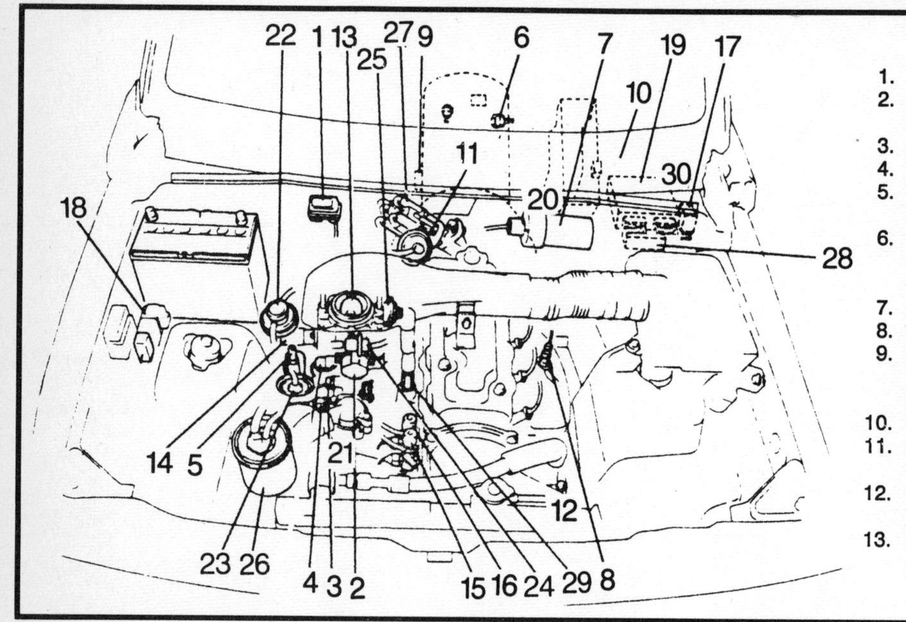

1. MAP sensor
2. Throttle position sensor
3. MAT sensor
4. CTS
5. REGTS, California only
6. 5th gear switch, manual transmission models
7. Ignition coil
8. Oxygen sensor
9. Shift switch, automatic transmission models
10. Cancel switch
11. Crank angle sensor, in distributor
12. Power steering pressure switch
13. Fuel injector
14. Idle speed control valve
15. Throttle opener VSV
16. EGR VSV
17. Fuel pump relay
18. TCC relay, automatic transmission models
19. ECM
20. Igniter assembly
21. Canister purge VSV
22. EGR modulator
23. EGR valve
24. Fuel pressure regulator
25. Throttle opener
26. Fuel vapor canister
27. Distributor
28. Fuse box
29. PCV
30. Main relay
31. Pressure sensor

Engine compartment components location—Tracker

- **Jumper Connector (1991)**—is located under the left side, near the ECM.
- **Key Switch**—is located on the right side of the steering column.
- **Main Relay (1991)**—is located under left side of instrument panel, mounted to ECM.
- **Manifold Air Temperature (MAT) Sensor**—is located below the throttle body, in intake plenum.
- **Manifold Absolute Pressure (MAP) Sensor**—is located behind the engine, on bulkhead.
- **Oil Pressure Switch**—is located on the left side of engine compartment, above oil filter.
- **Oxygen Sensor**—is located on left side of engine, in exhaust manifold.
- **Parking Brake Switch**—is located in front passenger's compartment, between seats.
- **Positive Temperature Coefficient (PTC) Relay (automatic transmission)**—is mounted on the fusible link box.
- **Power Steering Pressure Switch**—is located in the power steering pump.
- **Pressure Limit Valve (1991)**—is located left rear of the engine compartment, near the strut tower.
- **Rear Defogger Switch**—is located in the instrument panel, left of the steering column.
- **Rear Wheel Anti-Lock (RWAL) Brake Controller (1991)**—is located under left instrument panel, near the fuse block.
- **Rear Wheel Anti-Lock (RWAL) Brake Diagnostic Connector (1991)**—is located under left instrument panel, near fuse block.
- **Rear Wheel Anti-Lock (RWAL) Brake Relay (1991)**—is located under the left of the instrument panel, mounted to the ECM.
- **Rear Wheel Anti-Lock (RWAL) Brake Speed Sensor (1991)**—is located in the differential housing.
- **Rear Wiper/Washer Switch**—is located in the instrument panel, right of the steering column.
- **Stoplamp Relay (Right, 1991)**—is located behind the left Rear Trim Panel, above wheel well.
- **Seat Belt Switch**—is located on floor of passenger compartment, in seat belt latch.

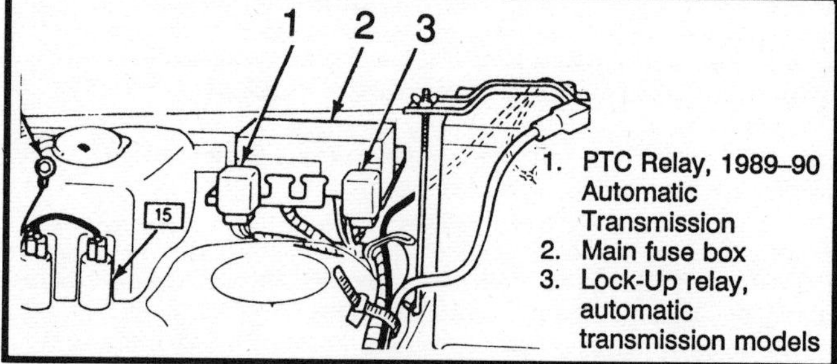

Right inner fender component locations—Tracker

- **Seat Belt Relay**—is located above the left rear wheel well, behind the passenger compartment.
- **Shift Lock Diode (automatic transission)**—is located behind the instrument panel, left of the steering column.
- **Shift Lock Relay (automatic transmission)**—Is located under left side of instrument panel, above brake pedal.
- **Shift Lock Solenoid**—is located under shift selector.
- **Shift Switch (automatic transmission)**—is located on the right side of transmission.
- **Stoplamp Relay (Left, 1991)**—is located behind the left rear trim panel, above the wheel well.
- **Stoplamp Switch**—is located under left side of the instrument panel, above the brake pedal.
- **Throttle Position Sensor**—is located on throttle boby.
- **Torque Converter Clutch Lock-Up Relay (automatic transmission)**—in engine compartment, on right inner fender.
- **Torque Converter Clutch Lock-Up Solenoid (automatic transmission)** —is located on right side of transmission.
- **Turn Relay (1989–90)**—is located behind instrument panel, above the fuse block.
- **Turn Relay (1991)**—is located under left side of instrument panel, mounted to the ECM.
- **Turnlamp Relays (1991)**—are located behind left rear trim panel above wheel well.
- **Warning Buzzer Module**—is located in the instrument panel, left of the steering column.

HONDA

Circuit Breakers

Fuses are found in the fuse box; located below the left side of the dashboard, or in the relay box; located at the right rear corner of the engine compartment.

Fusible Links

Fusible links for Honda are located in the relay box; located at the right rear corner of the engine compartment.

Relays, Sensors, Modules and Computer Locations

1989 ACCORD

- **A/C Compressor Clutch Relay**—is located on the front left corner of the engine compartment.
- **A/C Delay Control Unit**—is located under the right side of the instrument panel, on the left side of the blower motor housing.
- **A/C Diode**—is located on the front left corner of the engine compartment.
- **A/C Heater Blower Motor**—is located behind the glove box, on the bottom of the blower motor housing.
- **A/C Idle Boost Solenoid Valve**—is located on the carburetor.
- **A/C Idle-Up Solenoid Valve**—is located on the rear center of the engine compartment.
- **A/C Low Pressure Switch**—is located on the front left side of the engine compartment.
- **A/C Thermostat**—is located behind the center console, on the evaporator core housing.
- **Air Suction Control Solenoid Valve**—is located in the carburetor emission control box.
- **Anti-Afterburn Control Solenoid Valve**—is located on the carburetor.
- **Automatic transmission Idle Control Solenoid Valve**—is located in the emission control box.
- **Atmospheric Pressure Sensor**—is located under the right side of the instrument panel.
- **Back-Up Light Switch (manual transaxle)**—is located on the clutch housing, toward the front of the car.
- **Brake Fluid Level Sensor**—is located in the brake master cylinder reservoir cap.
- **Brake Light Failure Sensor**—is attached to the taillight assembly.
- **Brake Light Switch**—is located on the bracket above the brake pedal.
- **Cold Advance Solenoid Valve**—is located in the emission control box.
- **Condenser Fan Motor**—is located on the front left side of engine compartment, behind radiator.
- **Condenser Fan Relay**—is located in the relay box.
- **Constant Vacuum Control Valve**—is located in emission control box.
- **Coolant Temperature Sending Unit**—is located in the thermostat housing.
- **Coolant Temperature Sensor**—is located on top of the engine.
- **Cooling Fan Diode**—is located on the left front corner of the engine compartment.
- **Cooling Fan Motor**—is located on the front right side of the engine compartment, behind the radiator.

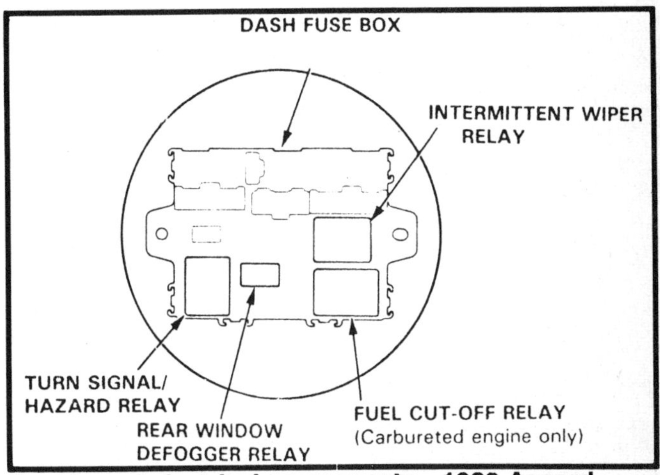

Dashboard electrical components—1989 Accord

- **Cooling Fan Relay**—is located in the relay box.
- **Cooling Fan Thermoswitch**—is located on the bottom right corner of radiator, below the cooling fan.
- **Cooling Fan Temperature Switch**—is located on the bottom right corner of radiator, below the cooling fan.
- **Cooling Fan Timer Control Unit**—is located under the front right seat.
- **Crank Angle Sensor**—is located on the distributor end of the engine.
- **Cranking Leak Solenoid Valve**—is located in the carburetor emission control box.
- **Cruise Control Actuator**—is located on the left side of the engine compartment.
- **Cruise Control Clutch Switch (manual transaxle)**—is located on the bracket above the clutch pedal.
- **Cruise Control Unit**—is located under the left side of instrument panel above the fuse box.
- **Dashlight Brightness Control Unit**—is attached to the instrument panel lower panel.
- **EFE Heater (carbureted)**—is located inside of the carburetor.
- **EFE Heater Control Unit (carbureted)**—is located under the driver's seat.
- **EFE Heater Relay**—is located on the rear right side of engine compartment.
- **Resistor**—is located on the left fender apron.
- **EGR Control Solenoid Valve**—is located in the emission control box.
- **Emission Control Box**—is located on the right side of the firewall.
- **Fast Idle Control Solenoid Valve**—is located in the emission control box.
- **Feedback Control Solenoid Valve**—is located on the carburetor.
- **Fuel Cut-Off Relay (carbureted)**—is located on the back side of the fuse box.
- **Fuel Gauge Sending Unit**—is located in the fuel tank under the right access cover.
- **Fuel Injection**—see Program Fuel Injection (PGM-FI).
- **Fuel Pump Motor**—is located in the fuel tank under the left access cover.
- **Fuse Box**—is located behind the left side of instrument panel.
- **Headlight Retractor Motor**—is located behind the headlight.

• **Headlight Retractor Relays**—are located on the front left side of the engine compartment.
• **Idle Boost Solenoid Valve**—is located in the carburetor emission box.
• **Idle Control Solenoid Valve**—is located on the rear left corner of the engine compartment.
• **Intake Air Temperature Sensor**—is located in the air cleaner housing, near the snorkel.
• **Integrated Control Unit**—is located in the center console under the heater.
• **Intermittent Windshield Wiper Relay**—is located on the back side of fuse box.
• **Lights-On Chime**—is located on the instrument panel lower panel.
• **Main Relay**—is located on the left kick panel near the fuse box.
• **MAP Sensor**—is located in the emission control box.
• **Neutral Start Switch (automatic transaxle)**—is located at the base of the shift lever.
• **Oxygen Sensor (carbureted)**—is located on the left center of the engine compartment, on the exhaust manifold.
• **Oxygen Sensor (fuel injected)**—is located on the center of the engine compartment, on the exhaust manifold.
• **Oil Pressure Sending Unit**—is located on the cylinder block, above the oil filter.
• **Oil Pressure Switch**—is located on the top of engine above the oil filter.
• **Parking Brake Switch**—is located at the base of the parking brake lever.
• **PGM-FI ECU**—is located under the driver's seat.
• **Power Antenna Motor**—is located under the left side of instrument panel, above the fuse box.
• **Power Door Lock Control Unit**—is located under the front right seat.
• **Power Window Control Unit**—is located within the driver's door.
• **Power Window Relay**—is located in the relay box.
• **Radiator Fan Relay**—is located in the relay box.
• **Rear Window Defogger Relay**—is located on the back side of fuse box.
• **Rear Window Wiper Motor**—is located on the center of liftgate.
• **Relay Box**—is located on the right side of engine compartment, near battery.
• **Retractor Headlight Control Unit**—is located on the left kick panel, left of the fuse box.
• **Seat Belt Switch**—is located at the base of the driver's seat belt buckle.
• **Shift Lever Position Switch**—is located attached to the shift lever.
• **Slow Mixture Cut-Off Solenoid Valve**—is located on the carburetor.
• **Solenoid Valve Control Unit (Carbureted)**—is located under the driver's seat.
• **Sunroof Relays**—are located under the front right seat.
• **Thermosensor**—is located in the cylinder head, near the thermostat housing.
• **Throttle Angle Sensor**—is located on the rear center of the engine compartment.
• **Turn Signal/Hazard Relay**—is located on the back side of the fuse box.
• **Vacuum Holding Solenoid Valve**—is located in the carburetor emission control box.
• **Vacuum Switches (3)**—are located in the carburetor emission control box.
• **Washer Pumps (2)**—are located behind the left side of the bumper, under washer reservoir.
• **Windshield Wiper Motor**—is located on the left rear corner of the engine compartment, on firewall.

1990–91 ACCORD

• **A/C Compressor Clutch Relay**—is located at the left front of the engine compartment.
• **A/C Condenser Fan Relay**—is located at the left front of the engine compartment.

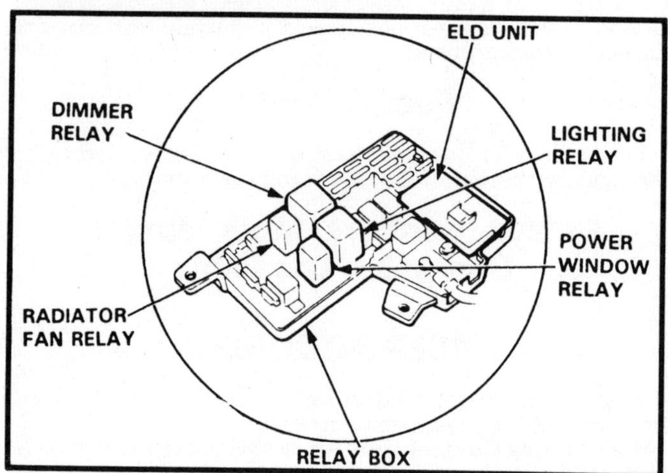

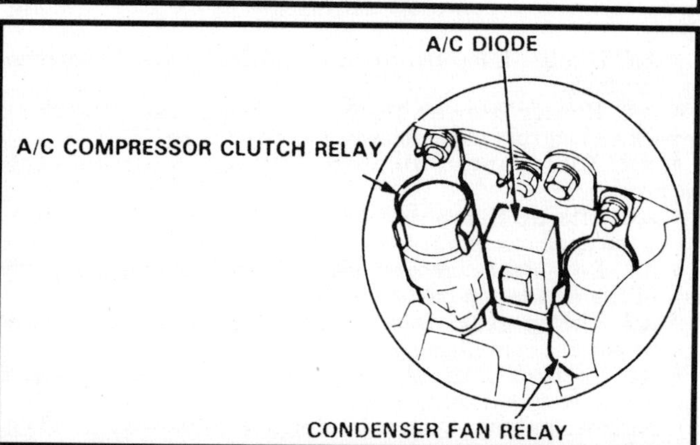

Relays and control unit locations—1990–91 Accord

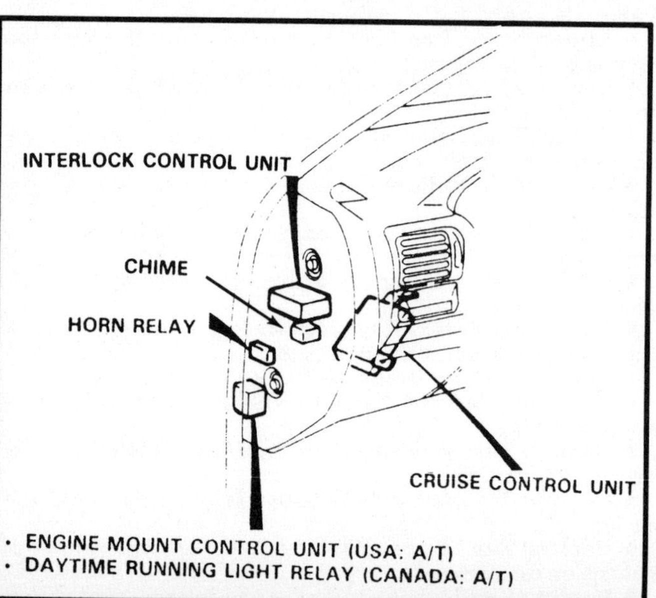

Dashboard relays and control units—1990–91 Accord

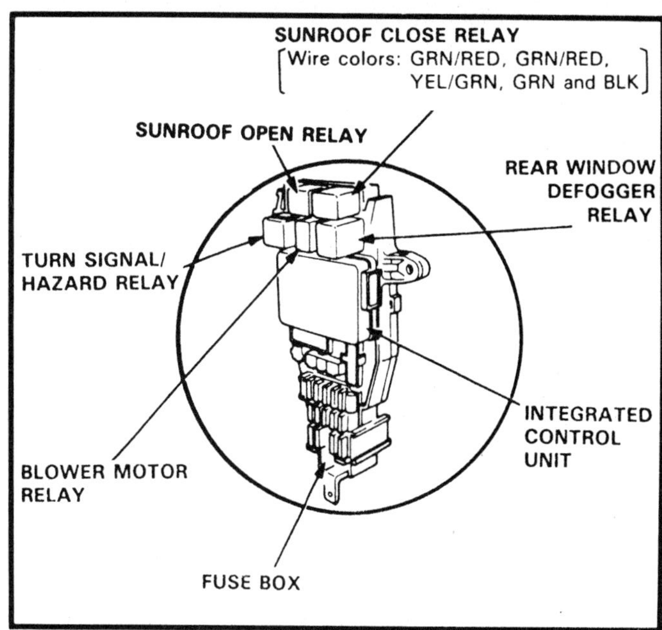

Dashboard relays and control units—1990–91 Accord

• **A/C Diode**—is located at the left front of the engine compartment.

• **A/C Dual Pressure Switch**—is located at the left front of the engine compartment, next to the condenser.

• **A/C Thermostat**—is located at the top of the evaporator core.

• **Air Bags**—see Supplemental Restraint System (SRS).

• **Air Boost Valve**—is located next to the master cylinder at the left rear of the engine compartment.

• **ALB Control Unit**—is located —is located at the front right of the trunk, attached to the body brace.

• **ALB Fail Safe Relay**—is located at the bottom of the ALB control unit.

• **ALB Fuses**—are located in the ALB fuse box.

• **ALB Modulator Solenoid Unit**—is located at the right rear of the engine compartment.

• **ALB Motor Relay**—is located in the anti-Lock brake fuse box.

• **ALB Pressure Switch**—is located at the right front of the vehicle, near the pump motor.

• **ALB Speed Sensors**—are located at each axle shaft.

• **ALB Fuse Box**—is located on the right side of the engine compartment.

• **Anti-Lock Brake System**—see Anti-Lock Brakes (ALB).

• **Automatic Seat Belt Front Position Switch**—is located at the windshield pillar, behind the trim cover.

• **Automatic Shoulder Seat Belt Control Unit**—is located under the passengers seat.

• **Automatic Transmission Control Unit**—is located on the right front floor or under the right side of the dash, near the right side foot well.

• **Back-up Light Switch**—is located in the transaxle case near the starter motor.

• **Blower Motor Relay**—is located in the under dash fuse box.

• **Brake Fluid Level Switch**—is located inside the master fluid reservoir, at the left rear side of the engine compartment.

• **Brake Light Failure Sensor**—is located behind the taillight maintenance lid at the rear of the trunk.

• **Brake Light Switch**—is located at the brake pedal mounting bracket.

• **Bypass Control Diaphragm**—is located next to the air boost valve at the right rear of the engine compartment.

• **Bypass Control Solenoid Valve**—is located on the alternator side of the engine, below the valve cover.

• **Chime**—is located under the left side of the dash.

• **Cigarette Lighter Relay**—is located under the left side of the dash.

• **Clutch Interlock Switch**—is located under the left side of the dash, on the clutch pedal bracket.

• **Clutch Switch**—is located at the clutch pedal mounting bracket.

• **Condenser Fan Relay**—is located at the left front of the engine compartment.

• **Console Switch (automatic transaxle)**—is located at the base of the automatic transmission shift control lever.

• **Constant Vacuum Control (CVC) Valve**—is located inside the PGM-FI control box.

• **Coolant Temperature (TW) Switch**—is located at the top of the engine on the exhaust side or at the distributor side of the engine, near the radiator hose.

• **Coolant Temperature Sender**—is located on the distributor side of the engine, mounted in the cylinder head.

• **Cooling Fan Timer Relay**—is located under the left side of the dash, at the firewall.

• **Cowl Sensor**—is located inside the SRS control unit.

• **Crank Angle Sensor**—is located inside the distributor housing, at the right side of the engine.

• **Cruise Control Switch**—is located at the steering wheel.

• **Cruise Control Unit**—is located under the dash, to the left of the steering column.

• **Cylinder Sensor**—is located inside the distributor housing, at the right side of the engine.

• **Daytime Running Light Relay**—is located under the left side of the dash, near the kick panel.

• **Dimmer Relay**—is located in the relay box.

• **Door Mirror Switch**—is located at the left front door.

• **Door Switch**—is located in the center of the rear door jamb.

• **EGR Control Solenoid Valve**—is located inside the PGM-FI control box.

• **Electric Load Detector Unit**—is located in the right rear corner of the engine compartment.

• **Electronic Air Control Valve (EAVC)**—is located behind the engine at the center of the firewall.

• **Engine Mount Control Unit**—is located under the left or right side of the dash, near the kick panel.

• **Exhaust Gas Recirculation (EGR) Valve**—is located at the top of the engine on the valve cover.

• **Fast Idle Valve**—is located at the center of the firewall next to the EAVC.

• **Fuel Injection**—see Program Fuel Injection (PGM-FI).

• **Fuel Sender Unit**—is located at the top of the fuel tank.

• **Function Control Motor**—is located at the left side of the heater assembly under the dash.

• **Horn Relay**—is located under the left side of the dash, near the kick panel.

• **Ignition Switch**—is located under the dash, mounted to the left of the steering column.

• **Injector Resistor**—is located at the left rear of the engine compartment.

• **Intake Air Temperature (TA) Sensor**—is located on the alternator side of the engine, next to the master cylinder.

• **Intake Control Solenoid Valve**—is located at the right front of the engine compartment, behind the air intake tubes.

• **Integrated Control Unit**—is located inside the dash fuse box, at the left kick panel.

• **Interlock Control Unit**—is located under the left side of the dash.

• **Intermittent Wiper Relay**—is located under the relay box.

• **Key Interlock Solenoid**—is located in the steering lock assembly.
• **Key Interlock Switch**—is located in the steering lock assembly.
• **Key Off Timer Circuit**—is located inside the integrated control unit, at the left kick panel.
• **Lap Seat Belt Switch**—is located at the shoulder seat belt retractor.
• **Latch Switch**—is located inside the door latch at the rear of the door.
• **Lighting Relay**—is located in the relay box.
• **Lock-Up Control Solenoid Valve**—is located at the top of the transmission, under the distributor.
• **Manifold Absolute Pressure (MAP) Sensor**—is located inside the PGM-FI control box.
• **NC Speed Sensor**—is located under the distributor.
• **NM Speed Sensor**—is located at the right front of the engine compartment, next to and below the battery.
• **Oil Pressure Switch**—is located below the oil filter on the exhaust manifold side of the engine.
• **Oxygen Sensor**—is located at the exhaust manifold/exhaust down pipe junction or just ahead of the catalytic converter.
• **Parking Brake Switch**—is located at the base of the parking brake lever, under the console.
• **Performance/Economy Switch**—is located inside the automatic transmission control lever.
• **PGM-FI Control Box**—is located at the right rear of the engine compartment.
• **PGM-FI Electronic Control Unit**—is located at the right front floor.
• **PGM-FI Main Relay**—is located under the left side of the dash.
• **Power Door Lock Control Unit**—is located inside the left front door, behind the door panel.
• **Power Door/Tailgate Lock Control Unit**—is located in the left front door.
• **Power Window Master Switch**—is located at the left front door.
• **Power Window Relay**—is located in the relay box.
• **Purge Cut-Off Solenoid Valve**—is located inside the PGM-FI control box.
• **Radiator Fan Relay**—is located in the relay box.
• **Rear Lock Position Switch**—is located at the rear of the automatic seat belt track.
• **Rear Window Defogger Circuit**—is located inside the integrated control unit, at the left kick panel.
• **Rear Window Defogger Relay**—is located in the under dash fuse box.
• **Relay Box**—is located inside the electric load detector unit, at the right rear corner of the engine compartment.
• **Seat Belt Switch**—is located inside the seat belt receiver.
• **Seat Heater Main Relay**—is located under the center of the dash.
• **Seat Heater Relay (left)**—is located under the left seat.
• **Seat Heater Relay (right)**—is located under the right seat.
• **Seat Heater Relay**—is located under the right side of the dash, at the kick panel.
• **Service Check Connector**—is located under the dash, at the right kick panel.
• **Shift Control Solenoid Valve**—is located at the front center of the engine compartment.
• **Shift Lock Solenoid**—is located under the console.
• **Shift Position Console Switch**—is located at the front of the shifter mounting bracket.
• **Shoulder Buckle Motor**—is located at the bottom of the door frame.
• **Shoulder Seat Belt Retractor**—is located on the inside of the seat, next to the console.
• **Side Marker Flasher Circuit**—is located inside the integrated control unit.
• **Speed Sensor**—is located under the coolant thermostat housing.
• **SRS Control Unit**—is located under the center of the dash, at the front of the console.
• **SRS Dash Sensors**—are located under the dash at the left and right sides.
• **Starter Relay**—is located under the left side of the dash.
• **Sun Roof Open Relay**—is located at the dash fuse box.
• **Sunroof Close Relay**—is located in the under dash fuse box.
• **Tailgate Lock Actuator**—is located at the lower portion of the tailgate.
• **Throttle Angle Sensor**—is located on the throttle body at the center rear of the engine compartment.

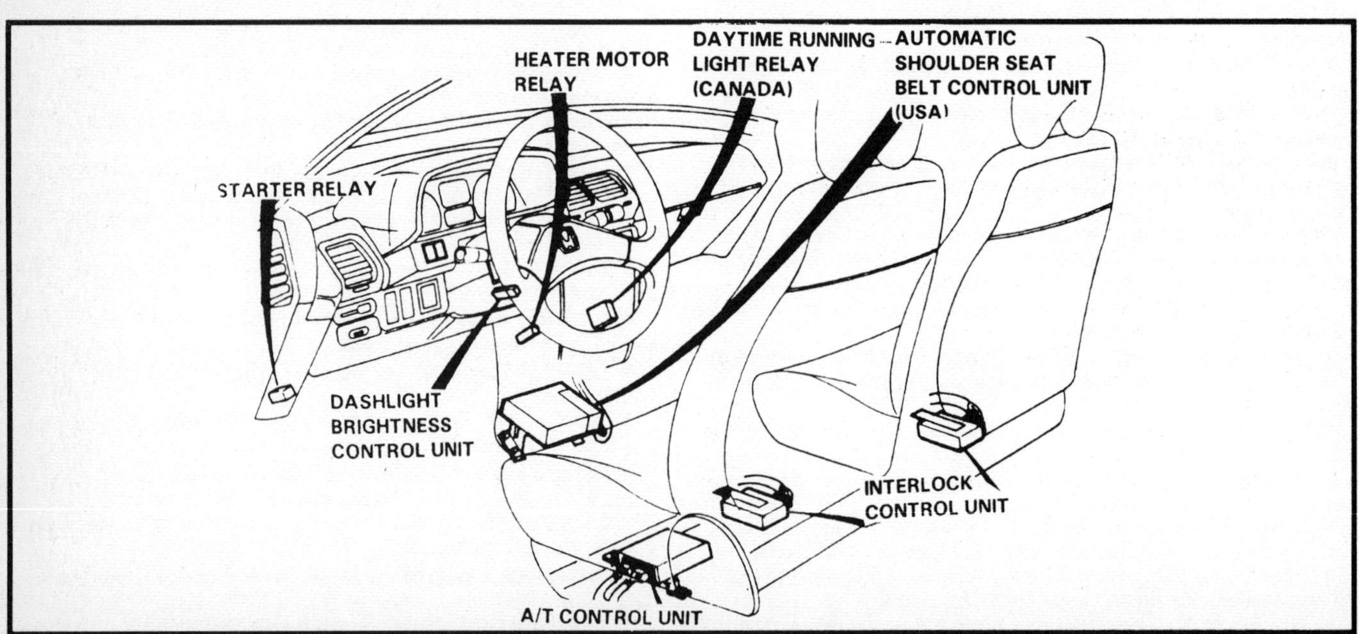

Dashboard and floor components—Civic and CRX

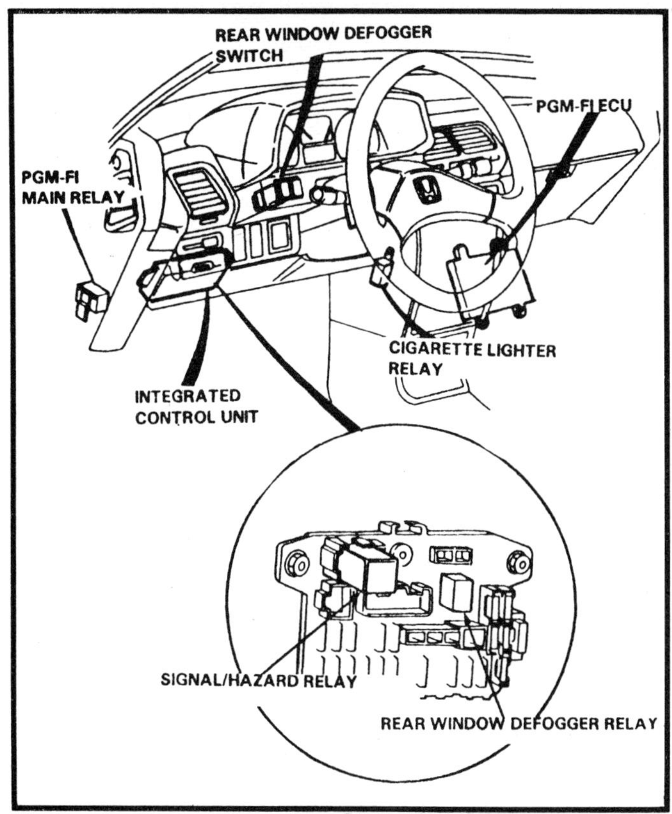

Under dash components—Civic and CRX

- **Top Dead Center (TDC) Sensor**—is located inside the distributor housing, at the right side of the engine.
- **Trunk Latch Switch**—is located in the lower tailgate, under a trim panel.
- **Turn Signal Hazard Relay**—is located in the under dash fuse box.
- **Under Dash Fuse Box**—is located at the left kick panel.

CIVIC AND CRX

- **A/C Clutch Relay**—is located on the right front corner of the engine compartment.
- **A/C Condenser Fan Relay**—is located on the right front corner of the engine compartment.
- **A/C Dual Pressure Switch**—is located at the right front of the engine compartment, on the receiver pipe.
- **A/C Idle Boost Solenoid (Si)**—is located on the firewall near the hood latch.
- **A/C Thermostat**—is located on the bottom side of the heater core housing.
- **A/C-Heater Blower Motor**—is located under the right side of the instrument panel.
- **Air Intake Temperature Sensor**—is located in the manifold runner at the distributor air intake duct.
- **Atmospheric Pressure Sensor**—is located at the right side kick panel.
- **Automatic Seat Belt Control Unit**—is located under the center of the dash.
- **Automatic Seat Belt Retractor (solenoid sensor switch and solenoid)**—is located at the rear of the door, behind the door panel.
- **Back-Up Light Switch**—is located on the transaxle housing near the speedometer holder.
- **Block Thermosensor**—is located on the side of engine block, near oil the filter.

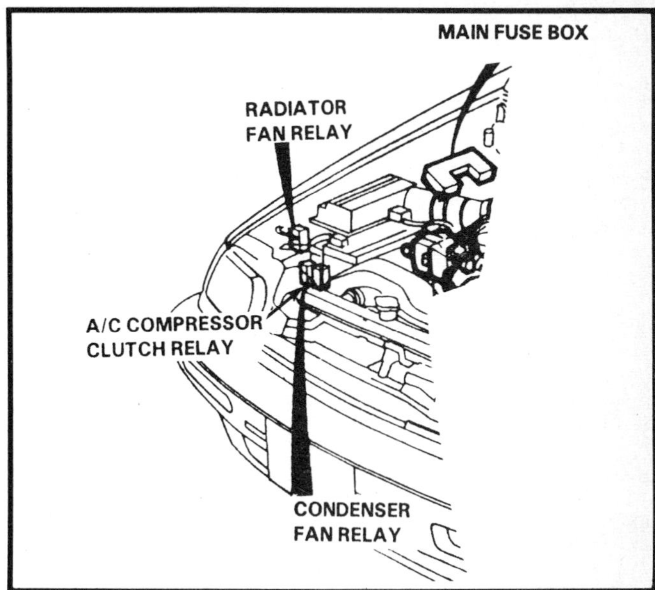

Engine compartment components—Civic and CRX

- **Brake Check Relay (CRX/Si)**—is located under the left side of the instrument panel.
- **Brake Check Relay (Except CRX/Si)**—is located under the left side of the instrument panel.
- **Brake Fluid Level Switch**—is located in the brake fluid reservoir cap.
- **Brake/Stoplight Switch**—is located above the brake pedal on bracket.
- **Cigarette Lighter Relay**—is located under the center of the dash, on the console bracket.
- **Clutch Switch**—is located on the clutch pedal bracket.
- **Console Switch**—is located under the shift lever in the console.
- **Constant Vacuum Control (CVC) Valve**—is located inside the PGM-FI control box.
- **Coolant Temperature (TW) Sensor**—is located on the distributor side of the engine.
- **Cooling Fan Thermosensor**—is located at the distributor side of the engine.
- **Crank Angle Sensor**—is located in the distributor assembly.
- **Cruise Control Unit**—is located under the center of the dash.
- **Dash Fuse Box**—is located under the left side of the instrument panel.
- **Dashlight Brightness Control Unit**—is located under the dash to the right of the steering column.
- **Dashpot Diaphragm**—is located near the throttle cable at the rear of the engine compartment.
- **Daytime Running Light Relay**—is located under the center of the dash.
- **Door Latch Switch**—is located on the rear door jamb.
- **Electric Load Detect Unit**—is located in the main fuse block.
- **Electronic Air Control Valve (EACV)**—is located on the alternator side of the intake manifold.
- **Electronic Control Unit**—is located at the passenger side floor.
- **Exhaust Gas Recirculation (EGR) Control Solenoid Valve**—is located inside the PGM-FI control box.
- **Fast Idle Control Solenoid Valve**—is located at the center rear of the engine compartment.
- **Front Wiper Motor**—is located at the right rear of the engine compartment.

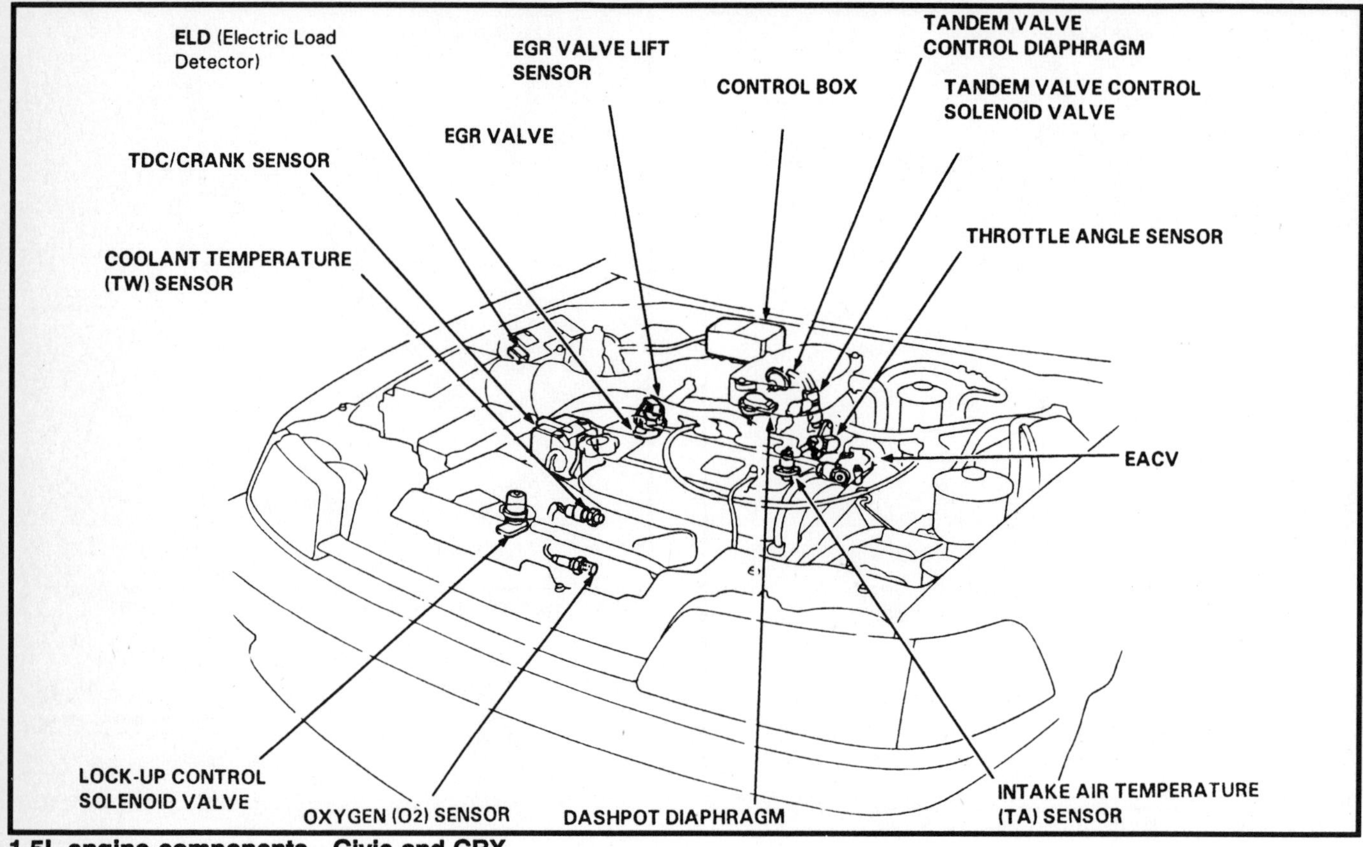

1.5L engine components – Civic and CRX

- **Fuel Gauge Sending Unit** – is located at the front of the fuel tank.
- **Fuel Pump** – is located at the left side of fuel tank (right rear on wagon).
- **Function Control Motor** – is located on the left side of the blower housing.
- **Ignition Key Switch** – is located under the key cylinder on the steering column.
- **Injector Resistor** – is located at the left rear of the engine compartment.
- **Integrated Control Unit** – is located in the dash fuse box.
- **Interlock Control Unit** – is located under the left front seat.
- **Intermittent Wiper Relay** – is located in the integrated control unit at the left kick panel.
- **Lock-Up Control Valve Solenoid** – is located on top of the transaxle.
- **Main Fuse Box** – is located at the right rear of the engine compartment.
- **Main Relay** – is located under the left side of instrument panel.
- **Manifold Absolute Pressure (MAP) Sensor** – is located inside the PGM-FI control box.
- **Noise Filter** – is located on the left side of the condenser fan.
- **Oil Pressure Switch** – is located above the oil filter.
- **Oxygen Sensor** – is located in the exhaust manifold.
- **Parking Brake Switch** – is located under the rear of parking brake lever.
- **PGM-FI Control Box** – is located at the right of the engine compartment.
- **PGM-FI Relay** – is located on the left hand side kick panel, near the hood opener.
- **Power Door Lock Control Unit** – is located in the middle of the driver's side door.
- **Power Window Relay** – is located in the dash fuse box.
- **Purge Cut-Off Solenoid Valve** – is located at the rear of the engine compartment, next to the MAP sensor or in the PGM-FI control box.
- **Radiator Fan Relay** – is located on the right front corner of the engine compartment.
- **Rear Defogger Relay** – is located in the dash fuse box, under the left side of the instrument panel.
- **Rear Wiper Motor** – is located behind the trim panel in the liftgate.
- **Seat Belt Beeper/Reminder** – is located at the front center of the headliner or the center of the gauge cluster.
- **Seat Belt Switch** – is located at the seat belt receptor, next to the console.
- **Shift Position Console Switch** – is located at the base of the floor shifter under the console.
- **Side Marker Flasher Circuit** – is located in the integrated control unit.
- **Starter Relay** – is located at the left kick panel.
- **Sunroof Relay** – is located in the dash fuse box.
- **Tandem Valve Control Diaphragm** – is located behind the the throttle body at the rear of the engine compartment.
- **Tandem Valve Control Solenoid** – is located behind the the throttle body at the rear of the engine compartment.
- **Throttle Angle Sensor** – is located on the alternator side of the throttle body.
- **Turn Signal/Hazard Relay** – is located in the dash fuse box.
- **Two Way Valve** – is located at the left side of the fuel tank.

PRELUDE

- **A/C Compressor Clutch Relays**—are located on the right front corner of the engine compartment, near the battery.
- **A/C Compressor Control Unit**—is located under the right hand side of the dash, near the kick panel.
- **A/C Dual Pressure Switch**—is located in the high pressure line near the A/C receiver-drier.
- **A/C Heater Blower Motor Relay**—is located below the right side of the dash.
- **A/C Heater Blower Motor**—is located under the right side of dash.
- **A/C Thermostatic Switch**—is located on the evaporator housing.

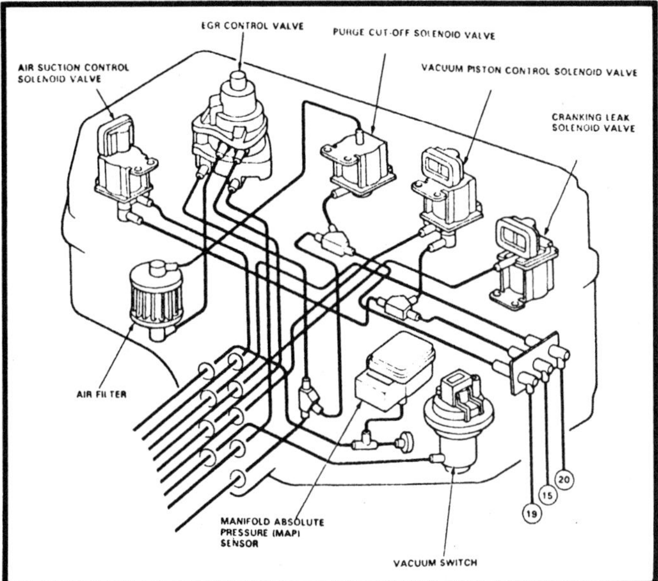

Control Box (carbureted)—Prelude

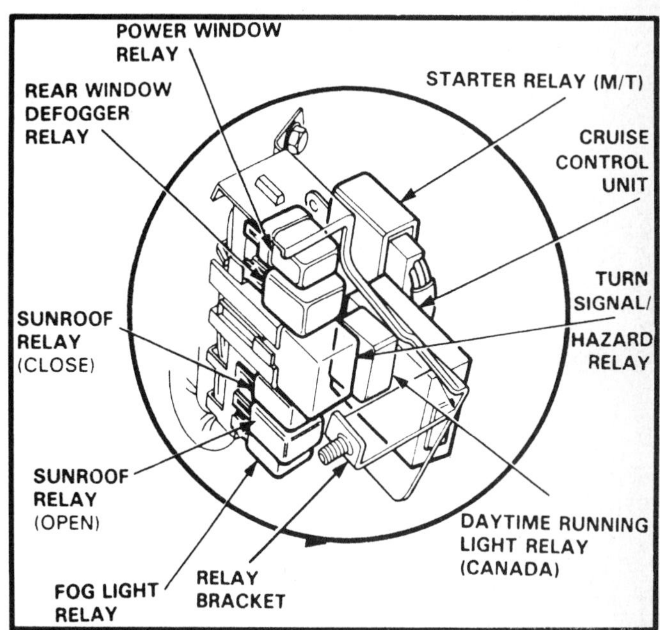

Under dash components—Prelude

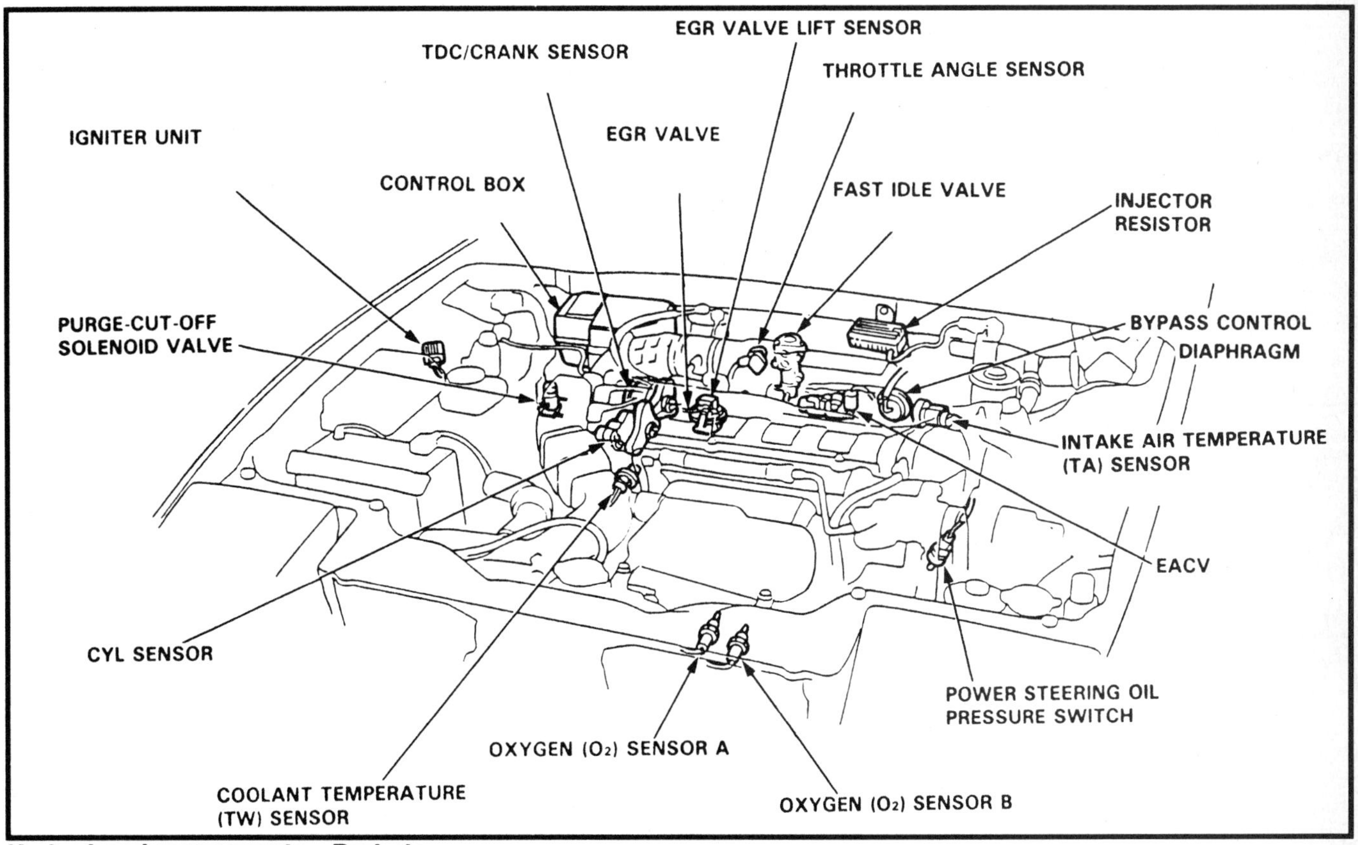

EGR VALVE LIFT SENSOR
TDC/CRANK SENSOR
THROTTLE ANGLE SENSOR
IGNITER UNIT
EGR VALVE
CONTROL BOX
FAST IDLE VALVE
INJECTOR RESISTOR
PURGE-CUT-OFF SOLENOID VALVE
BYPASS CONTROL DIAPHRAGM
INTAKE AIR TEMPERATURE (TA) SENSOR
EACV
CYL SENSOR
POWER STEERING OIL PRESSURE SWITCH
OXYGEN (O_2) SENSOR A
COOLANT TEMPERATURE (TW) SENSOR
OXYGEN (O_2) SENSOR B

Under hood components—Prelude

- **Air Bleed Valves (A and B)**—are located under the air cleaner assembly.
- **Air Leak Solenoid Valve**—is located in the air cleaner assembly.
- **Air Suction Control Solenoid Valve**—is located inside the control box at the left rear of the engine compartment.
- **Air Suction Valve**—is located on the carburetor side of the engine near the valve cover.
- **Air Vent Cut-Off Solenoid Valve**—is located under the air cleaner assembly.
- **ALB Control Unit**—is located under the center of the dash in front of the console, next to the radio panel bracket.
- **ALB Fail Safe Relay (left and right)**—is located in the under hood relay box.
- **ALB Motor Relay (w/4WS)**—is located on the power antenna motor.
- **ALB Motor Relay (except 4WS)**—is located in the under hood relay box.
- **Anti-Lock Brake System**—See Anti-Lock Brakes (ALB).
- **Automatic Seat Belt Control Unit**—is located in the integrated control unit.
- **Automatic Transmission Control Unit**—is located under the center of the dash in front of the console, next to the radio panel bracket.
- **Auxiliary Slow Fuel Cut-Off Solenoid**—is located on the side of the carburetor.
- **Back-Up Light Switch (manual transaxle)**—is located on the side of transaxle near the speedometer holder.
- **Brake Fluid Level Sensor**—is located in the brake master cylinder.
- **Brake/Stoplight Switch**—is located on the brake pedal bracket.
- **Bypass Control Diaphragm**—is located under the injector resistor.
- **Bypass Control Valve Solenoid**—is located inside the control box at the left rear of the engine compartment.
- **Clutch Switch**—is located at the clutch pedal mounting bracket.
- **Condenser Fan Motor**—is located on the back left side of the radiator.
- **Condenser Fan Relay**—is located in the underhood relay box.
- **Constant Vacuum Control (CVC) Valve**—is located inside the control box at the left rear of the engine compartment.
- **Control Box**—is located at the right rear of the engine compartment.
- **Coolant Temperature Sensor**—is located on the exhaust manifold side of the engine near the fresh air duct or at the bottom of the radiator.
- **Coolant Thermosensor**—is located below the coolant temperature sensor.
- **Cooling Fan Thermosensor**—is located on the bottom right corner of the radiator.
- **Cranking Leak Solenoid Valve**—is located inside the control box at the left rear of the engine compartment.
- **Cruise Control Relay**—is located in the fuse box under the left side of the dash.
- **Cylinder Sensor**—is located attached to the distributor side of the engine.
- **Dash Light Brightness Control**—is located under the dash near the steering column.
- **Daytime Running Light Relay**—is located in the fuse box under the left side of the dash.
- **Dimmer Relay**—is located in the underhood relay box.
- **Door Switch**—is located at the rear door frame.
- **EGR Control Solenoid**—is located inside the control box at the left rear of the engine compartment.
- **EGR Control Valve**—is located inside the control box at the left rear of the engine compartment.
- **EGR Valve Lift Sensor**—is located at the top of the engine, next to the distributor.
- **Electronic Air Control Valve (EVAC)**—is located at the rear of the engine compartment, next to the intake air temperature sensor.
- **Electronic Control Unit (ECU)**—is located at the passenger side floor under the carpet.
- **Entry Light Timer Circuit**—is located in the integrated control unit.
- **Exhaust Gas Recirculation (EGR) Valve**—is located at the top of the engine, behind the valve cover.
- **Fast Idle Solenoid**—is located in the throttle body.
- **Fog Light Relay**—is located in the fuse box under the left side of the dash.
- **Fuel Cut-Off Relay**—is located in the fuse box under the left side of the dash.
- **Fuel Gauge Sending Unit**—is located in the top rear of the fuel tank.
- **Fuel Injection**—see Program Fuel Injection (PGM-FI).
- **Fuse Box**—is located under the left side of the dash.
- **Headlight Retract Control Unit**—is located on the left kick panel.
- **Headlight Retract Relays (2)**—are located in the left front corner of engine compartment.
- **Headlight Warning Chime**—is located on the left kick panel.
- **Idle Boost Solenoid Valve**—is located next to the control box on the firewall.
- **Ignition Timing Adjuster**—is located at the right rear of the engine compartment.
- **Inhibitor Switch (automatic transaxle)**—is located under the selector level console.
- **Injector Resistor**—is located at the rear of the engine compartment on the firewall.
- **Inner Vent Solenoid Valve**—is located under the air cleaner assembly.
- **Intake Air Temperature (TA) Sensor**—is located in the intake runner or in the air cleaner housing.
- **Integrated Control Unit**—is located under the center of the dash, under the heater unit.
- **Interior Light Timer**—is located behind the left side of the dash.
- **Interlock Control Unit**—is located under the center of the dash in front of the console, next to the radio panel bracket.
- **Intermittent Wiper Relay**—is located behind the instrument cluster.
- **Key Switch**—is located at the ignition key cylinder in the steering column.
- **Left Headlight Retractor Relay**—is located behind the left headlight.
- **Lighting Relay**—is located in the underhood relay box.
- **Low Fuel Thermistor**—is located in the fuel tank on the fuel gauge sending unit.
- **Main Air Jet Solenoid Valve**—is located on the bottom of the air cleaner housing.
- **Manifold Absolute Pressure (MAP) Sensor**—is located inside the control box at the left rear of the engine compartment.
- **Oil Pressure Alarm Unit**—is located below the left side of the dash.
- **Oil Pressure Sending Unit**—is located on the top of the oil filter adapter.
- **Oxygen Sensor (O_2)**—is located in the exhaust manifold or exhaust downpipe.
- **Parking Brake Switch**—is located under the rear of the parking brake lever.
- **PGM-CARB Control Unit (carbureted)**—is located at the passenger side floor under the carpet.
- **PGM-FI Electronic Control Unit**—is located on the right front passenger floor, under the carpet.
- **PGM-FI Relay**—is located under the left side of the dash, near the kick panel.

• **Power Door Lock Control Unit**—is located in the middle of the passenger's side door.
• **Power Steering Oil Pressure Switch**—is located on the timing belt side of the engine.
• **Power Valve Control Solenoid Valve**—is located at the right rear of the engine compartment, near the fresh air duct.
• **Power Window Control Unit**—is located in the middle of the driver's side door.
• **Power Window Relay**—is located in the fuse box under left side of the dash.
• **Primary Slow Fuel Cut-Off Solenoid**—is located on the fuel inlet side of the carburetor.
• **Purge Cut Off Solenoid Valve**—is located inside the control box at the left rear of the engine compartment.
• **Radiator Cooling Fan Motor**—is located on the back of the radiator.
• **Radiator Cooling Fan Relay**—is located in the underhood relay box.
• **Rear Window Defogger Relay**—is located in the fuse box under left side of the dash.
• **Recirculation Solenoids**—is located under the right side of the dash.
• **Relay Box**—is located at the right rear of the engine compartment.
• **Retractable Headlight Control Unit**—is located under the right side of the dash.
• **Right Headlight Retractor Relay**—is located behind the right headlight.
• **Seat Belt Retractors (w/solenoid sensor and solenoid)**—are located in the door, behind the door panel.
• **Seat Belt/Key Timer**—is located near the fuse box under the left side of dash.
• **Side Marker Relay**—is located under the left side of the dash.
• **Solenoid Control Valve Unit**—is located under the right side of the dash.
• **Speed Sensor Amplifier**—is located on the back of the speedometer.
• **Speed Sensor**—is located in the speedometer gear housing.
• **Starter Relay**—is located in the fuse box under the left side of the dash.
• **Sunroof Close Relay**—is located in the fuse box, located under the left hand side of the dash.
• **Sunroof Open Relay**—is located in the fuse box, located under the left hand side of the dash.
• **TDC/Crank Sensor**—is located inside the distributor.
• **Throttle Angle Sensor**—is located in the throttle body.
• **Trunk Latch Switch**—is located at the rear of the trunk, behind the trim panel.
• **Turn Signal/Hazard Flasher Relay**—is located in the fuse box, located under the left hand side of the dash.
• **Underhood Relay Box**—is located on the right hand front inner fender panel.
• **Vacuum Piston Control Solenoid Valve**—is located inside the control box at the left rear of the engine compartment.
• **Vacuum Piston Control Valve**—is located next to the master cylinder on the firewall.
• **Vacuum Switch**—is located inside the control box at the left rear of the engine compartment.

HYUNDAI

Circuit Breakers

The fuse box is located low on the left side of the dashboard behind a cover, or at the left side kick panel, behind a cover.

Fusible Links

Fusible links are located in a holder next to the battery.

Relay, Sensors And Computer Locations

1989 EXCEL

• **A/C Capacitor**—is located at the right rear of the engine compartment.
• **A/C Condenser Fan Relay**—is located at the left front of the engine compartment.
• **A/C Diode**—is located under the right side of the dash.
• **A/C Dual Pressure Switch**—is located on the side of the receiver drier.
• **A/C Fast Idle Control Device (carbureted)**—is located under the air cleaner at the base of the carburetor.
• **A/C Relay**—is located under the right side of the dash.
• **Air Control Solenoid Valve**—is located at the top of the engine on the transaxle side.
• **Back-Up Light Switch**—is located at the front of the transaxle, near the radiator.
• **Bowl Vent Valve**—is located on the top of the carburetor, on float chamber cover.
• **Brake Fluid Sensor**—is located in the master cylinder reservoir.
• **Brake/Stoplight Switch is located above the brake pedal.**
• **Chime Bell**—is located under the center of the dash.
• **Cold Advance Solenoid Valve**—is located at the top of the engine on the transaxle side.
• **Cold Heater**—is located at the right rear of the engine compartment, near the wiring harness grommet on the firewall.
• **Coolant Temperature Switch**—is located on the intake manifold coolant passage.
• **Deceleration Solenoid**—is located on the float chamber of the carburetor.
• **Distributor Advance Solenoid Valve**—is located at the top of the engine on the transaxle side.
• **Door Warning Lamp Diode**—is located under the center of the dash.
• **Electric Choke Relay**—is located at the right rear of the engine compartment, on the firewall.
• **Enrichment Solenoid**—is located on the float chamber of the carburetor.
• **Feed Back Carburetor (FBC) Unit**—is located under the center of the dash.
• **Feedback Solenoid Valve**—is located at the carburetor.
• **Flasher Relay**—is located in the relay box under the left side of the dash.
• **Fuse Box**—is located at the lower left of the dash.
• **Fusible Link Box**—is located next to the battery.
• **Headlight Relay**—is located in the relay box under the left side of the dash.
• **Horn Relay**—is located in the relay box under the left side of the dash.

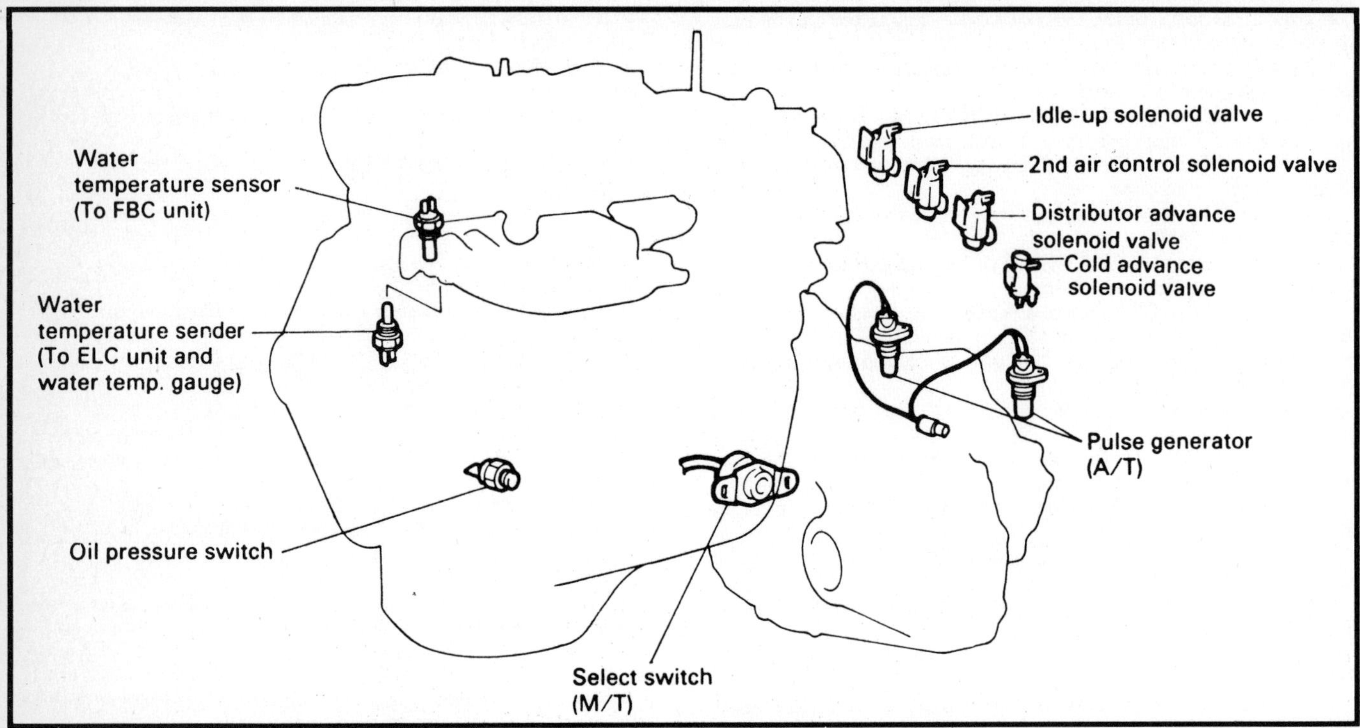

Under hood components—1989 Excel

- **Idle-Up Relay**—is located in the relay box under the left side of the dash.
- **Idle-Up Solenoid**—is located at the top of the engine on the transaxle side.
- **In Manifold Heater Relay**—is located at the right rear of the engine compartment, on the firewall.
- **Inhibitor Switch (automatic transaxle)**—is located on the top of the transaxle, linked to the control cable.
- **Intermittent Wiper Relay**—is located under the dash, to the right of the steering column.
- **Jet Mixture Solenoid**—is located on the float chamber of the carburetor.
- **Lock-Up Control Unit**—is located under the right side of the dash, at the kick panel.
- **Lock-Up Solenoid (automatic transaxle)**—is located at the top of the transaxle.
- **Neutral Switch (manual transaxle)**—is located in the right side of the transaxle.
- **Oil Pressure Switch**—is located at the back of the block near the firewall, on the distributor side of the engine.
- **Oxygen Sensor Checker**—is located on the center right side of the engine compartment.
- **Parking Brake Switch**—is located in the center console at the base of the parking brake.
- **Power Steering Pump Switch**—is located at the left front of the engine compartment.
- **Pulse Generator**—is located at the top of the transaxle.
- **Radiator Thermo Switch**—is located at the bottom of the radiator.
- **Rear Defogger Timer**—is located under the left side of the dash.
- **Relay Box**—is located under the left side of the dash.
- **Seat Belt Switch**—is located at the base of driver's seat belt buckle.
- **Seat Belt Timer**—is located under the center of the dash.
- **Select Switch (manual transaxle)**—is located at the back of the block near the firewall, on the transaxle side of the engine.
- **Slow Cut Solenoid Valve**—is located at the carburetor.
- **Starter Solenoid**—is located on the rear bottom of the engine compartment.
- **Taillight Relay**—is located in the relay box under the left side of the dash.
- **Throttle Position Sensor**—is located at the base of the carburetor.
- **Vacuum Switch**—is located at the left rear of the engine compartment, on the firewall.
- **Water Temperature Sender**—is located at the top of the block on the distributor side.
- **Water Temperature Sensor**—is located on the intake manifold.

1990–91 EXCEL

- **A/C Diode**—is located under the right side of the dash.
- **A/C Dual Pressure Switch**—is located in the receiver drier.
- **A/C Relay**—is located at the right front of the engine compartment.
- **Accelerator Switch**—is located on the accelerator pedal bracket.
- **Air Flow Sensor**—is located in the air cleaner.
- **Automatic Transaxle Control Unit (TACU)**—is located under the left front seat.
- **Automatic Transaxle Solenoid Valve**—is located at the radiator side of the transaxle.
- **Back-Up Light Switch**—is located on top of the transaxle.
- **Bowl Vent Valve (carburetor)**—is located on the top of the carburetor, on float chamber cover.
- **Brake Fluid Sensor**—is located in the master cylinder.
- Cold Mixture Heater (carburetor)—is located under the carburetor.
- **Condenser Fan Relay**—is located at the left front of the engine compartment.

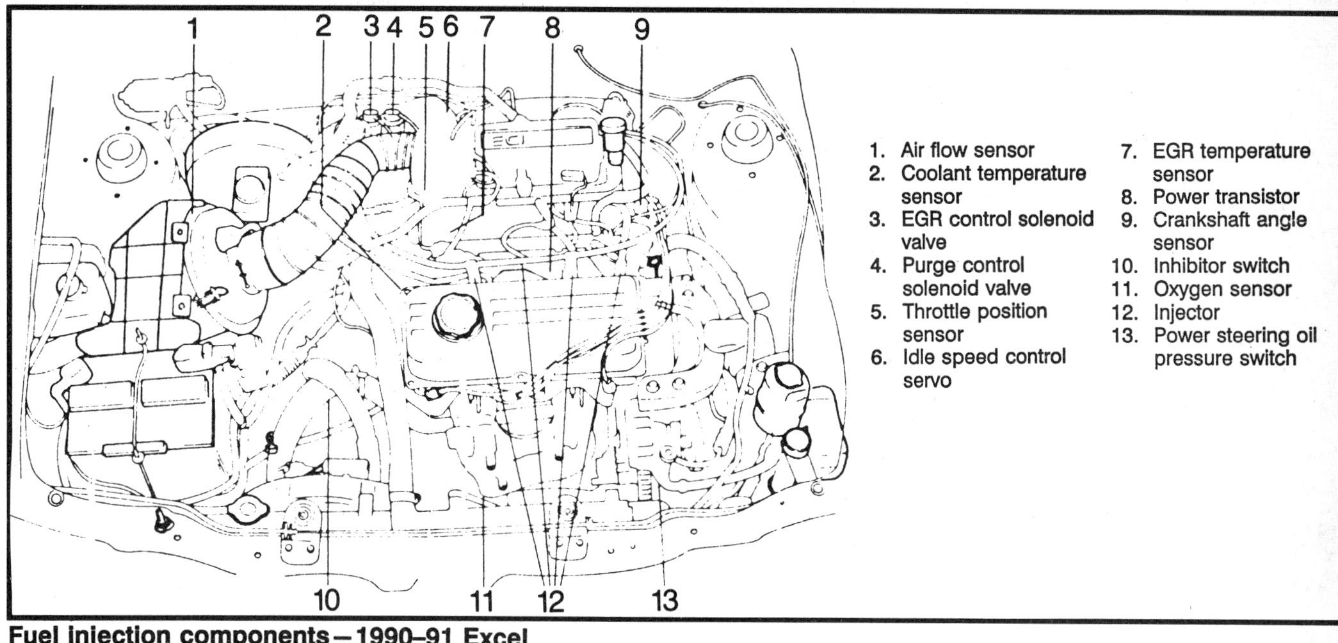

Fuel injection components—1990–91 Excel

• **Coolant Temperature Sensor**—is located in the rear of the engine under the fresh air duct.

• **Crankshaft Angle Sensor**—is located in the distributor.

• **Daytime Running Light Unit (Canada)**—is located at the right front of the engine compartment.

• **Door Warning Switch**—is located at the ignition switch.

• **EGR Control Solenoid Valve (California)**—is located on the firewall in the engine compartment.

• **EGR Temperature Sensor (California)**—is located on the EGR valve.

• **Electronic Control Unit (ECU)**—is located under the dash on the left side.

• **Exhaust Gas Recirculation (EGR) Valve**—is located near the fuel injection unit mounted to the engine block.

• **Feedback Solenoid Valve (carbureted)**—is located at the carburetor.

• **Fuel Injection**—see Multi-Point Injection (MPI).

• **Fuse Box Relay (red)**—is located in the fusible link box, at the battery.

• **Fuse Box**—is located in the left kick panel.

• **Hazard Flasher**—is located in the relay box under the left side of the dash.

• **Headlight Relay (pink)**—is located in the fusible link box, at the battery.

• **Idle Speed Control Sensor**—is located on the fuel injection unit near the firewall.

• **Ignition Lock Switch (manual transaxle)**—is located on the clutch pedal bracket.

• **Ignition Relay (pink)**—is located in the fusible link box, at the battery.

• **Inhibitor Switch**—is located on the top of the transaxle.

• **Intake Air Temperature Sensor**—is located in the air cleaner.

• **Kick Down Switch**—is located is located on the radiator side of the transaxle.

• **Main Fuse Box**—is located on the side of the battery.

• **Main-Fusible Link Box**—is located at the battery.

• **MPI Diagnostic Connector**—is located at the left kick panel.

• **MPI Relay (blue)**—is located in the fusible link box, at the battery.

• **Multi-Point Injection (MPI) Control Unit**—is located to the left of the center console under the dash.

• **Noise Filter**—is located at the left front of the engine compartment.

• **Oil Pressure Switch**—is located behind the alternator.

• **Oil Temperature Sensor**—is located is located on the radiator side of the transaxle.

• **Oxygen Sensor**—is located in the exhaust manifold.

• **Oxygen Sensor Checker**—is located on the center right side of the engine compartment.

• **PCV Valve**—is located on the back of the valve cover, near the spark plug wires.

• **Power Steering Oil Pressure Switch**—is located on the power steering pump.

• **Power Transistor**—is located on the back of the valve cover near the injectors.

• **Power/Economy Switch**—is located in the transaxle shift lever on the console.

• **Pulse Generator**—is located on the top of the transaxle.

• **Purge Control Solenoid Valve**—is located on the firewall in the engine compartment.

• **Radiator Fan Motor Relay**—is located at the left front of the engine compartment.

• **Radiator Fan Resistor**—is located near the thermostat switch.

• **Relay Box**—is located under the left side of the dash.

• **Self Diagnosis Check Connector**—is located in the left kick panel.

• **Slow Cut Solenoid Valve (carbureted)**—is located at the carburetor.

• **Starter Relay**—is located in the relay box under the left side of the dash.

• **Sub-Fusible Link Box**—is located at the left front of the engine compartment.

• **Taillight Relay**—is located in the relay box under the left side of the dash.

• **Thermo Valve**—is located at the rear of the engine on the battery side.

• **Thermostat Switch**—is located at the injector side of the engine near the firewall.

• **Throttle Position Sensor**—is located on the front of the fuel injection unit, or on the carburetor.

• **Transaxle Control Unit (TCU)**—is located under the right front seat.

• **Two Way Valve**—is located in the fuel tank.

- **Vehicle Speed Sensor**—is located in the speedometer.

SCOUPE

- **Accelerator Switch**—is located at the accelerator pedal bracket.
- **A/C Condenser Fan Relay**—is located at the right front of the engine compartment.
- **A/C Dual Pressure Switch**—is located in the receiver drier.
- **A/C Relay**—is located at the right front of the engine compartment in the sub-fusible link box.
- Air Flow Sensor—is located inside the air filter.
- **ASC Actuator**—is located at the right rear of the engine compartment, above the master cylinder.
- **ASC Control Unit**—is located under the left side of the dash.
- **Automatic Transaxle Control Unit**—is located under the left front seat.
- **Automatic Transaxle Solenoid Valve Connector**—is located on the front of the transaxle, near the dipstick.
- **Brake Fluid Switch**—is located in the master cylinder.
- **Clutch Switch**—is located on the clutch pedal bracket.
- **Control Relay**—is located under the left side of the dash, next to the relay box.
- **Coolant Temperature Sensor**—is located under the fresh air duct on the engine block.
- **Cooling System Resistor With Diode**—is located on the firewall.
- **Crank Angle Sensor**—is located inside the distributor.
- **Cruise Control**—see Automatic Speed Control (ASC).
- **Daytime Running Light Control Unit (Canada)**—is located at the right front of the engine compartment.
- **Diagnosis Terminal**—is located in the left kick panel.
- **EGR Control Solenoid Valve**—is located next to the purge control solenoid valve on the firewall.
- **EGR Temperature Sensor**—is located on the EGR valve.
- **Electronic Control Unit (ECU)**—is located under the left side of the dash.
- **Electronic Time and Alarm Control System**—see ETACS.
- **ETACS Control Unit**—is located under the left side of the dash.
- **Exhaust Gas Recirculation (EGR) Valve**—is located next to the throttle body at the top of the engine.
- **Fuel Injection**—see Multi Point Injection (MPI).
- **Fuse Box**—is located at the left side kick panel.
- **Idle Speed Control (ISC) Servo**—is located at the throttle body.
- **Inhibitor Switch**—is located at the top of the transaxle.
- **Key Lock Control Unit**—is located at the left quarter panel, behind the trim panel.
- **Key Lock Solenoid**—is located at the ignition key in the steering column.
- **Kickdown Switch**—is located at the back of the transaxle, near the right inner fender well.
- **Main Fusible Link Box**—is located next to the battery.
- **MPI Control Relay**—is located under the left side of the dash.
- **MPI Control Unit**—is located at the right side kick panel.
- **Oil Temperature Sensor**—is located is located at the front of the transaxle, near the dipstick.
- **Oxygen Sensor**—is located in the exhaust manifold near the alternator.
- **PCV Valve**—is located on the valve cover.
- **Power Steering Oil Pressure Switch**—is located on the power steering pump.
- **Power Transistor**—is located at the valve cover near the injectors.
- **Pulse Generator**—is located at the top of the transaxle.

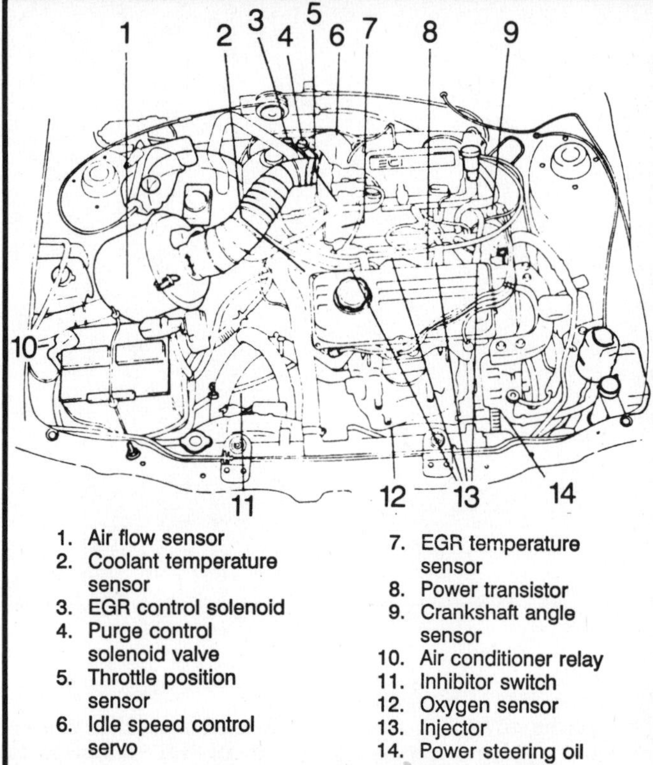

Under hood components—Scoupe

- **Purge Control Solenoid Valve**—is located on the firewall in the engine compartment.
- **Relay Box (engine compartment)**—is located at the left front of the engine compartment.
- **Relay Box (passenger compartment)**—is located under the left side of the dash.
- **Stop Light Switch**—is located on the brake pedal bracket.
- **Thermo Valve**—is located on the right side of the engine next to the fresh air duct.
- **Throttle Position Sensor (TPS)**—is located at the throttle body.
- **Transaxle Control Unit**—is located under the right front seat.
- **Two Way Valve**—is located at the fuel tank.
- **Vehicle Speed Sensor**—is located in the speedometer.

SONATA

- **Accelerator Switch**—is located at the accelerator pedal bracket.
- **A/C Relay**—is located at the right front of the engine compartment in the sub-fusible link box.
- **A/C Pressure Switches**—are located at the left front of the engine compartment and at the center of the firewall.
- **Air Flow Sensor**—is located inside the air filter.
- **ASC Actuator**—is located at the right rear of the engine compartment, above the master cylinder.
- **ASC Control Unit**—is located under the left side of the dash.
- **Automatic Transaxle Solenoid Valve Connector**—is located on the front of the transaxle, near the dipstick.
- **Blower Relay**—is located at the right front of the engine compartment.
- **Clutch Switch**—is located on the clutch pedal bracket.

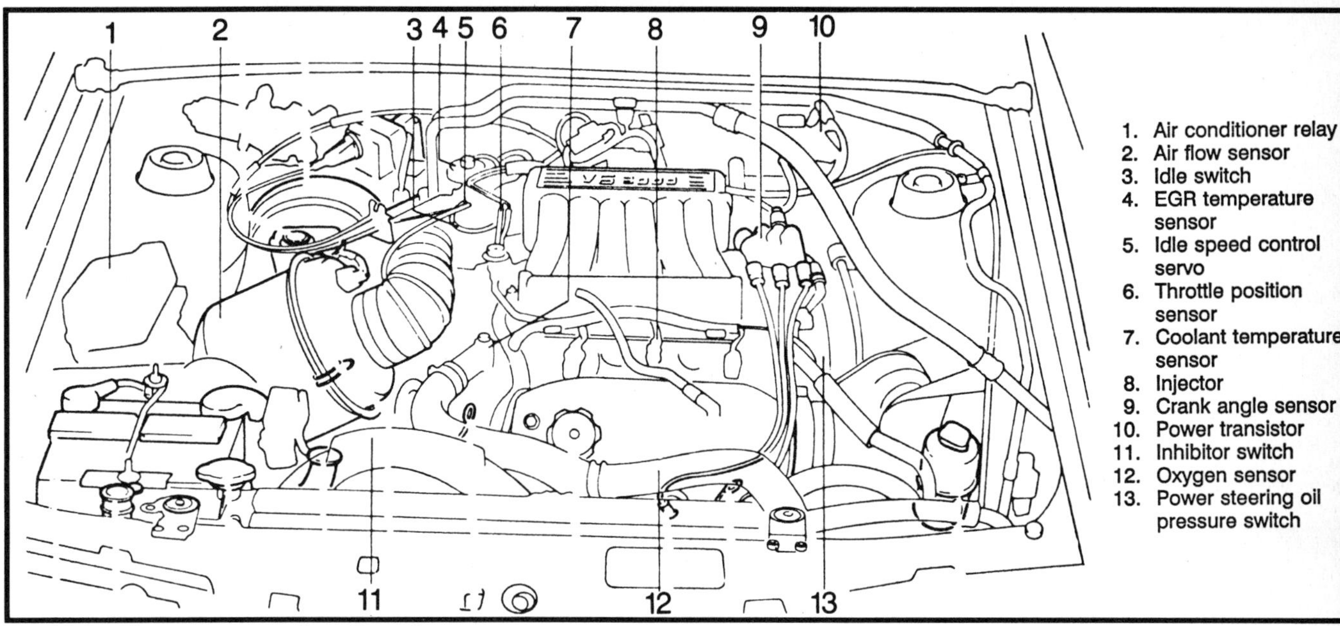

Fuel injection components—Sonata

- **Condenser Fan Relay**—is located at the left front of the engine compartment.
- **Control Relay**—is located under the left side of the dash, next to the relay box.
- **Control Relay**—is located under the right side of the dash, at the kick panel.
- **Coolant Temperature Sensor (except V6)**—is located next to the intake manifold on the engine block.
- **Coolant Temperature Sensor (V6)**—is located at the right front of the engine, next to the engine lifting tab.
- **Coolant Temperature Sensor**—is located at the front of the engine, near the radiator.
- **Cooling System Resistor With Diode**—is located on the firewall.
- **Crank Angle Sensor**—is located inside the distributor.
- **Cruise Control**—see Automatic Speed Control (ASC).
- **Daytime Running Light Control Unit (Canada)**—is located at the right front of the engine compartment.
- **Dedicated Fuse**—is located in the sub-fusible link box.
- **Diagnosis Terminal**—is located under the left side of the dash.
- **EGR Temperature Sensor**—is located on the EGR valve.
- **Electronic Time and Alarm Control System**—see ETACS.
- **ETACS Control Unit**—is located under the left side of the dash.
- **Exhaust Gas Recirculation (EGR) Valve**—is located next to the throttle body at the top of the engine.
- **Fuel Injection**—see Multi Point Injection (MPI).
- **Fuse Box**—is located at the left side of the dash, near the hood release latch or at the kick panel.
- **Idle Speed Control (ISC) Servo**—is located at the throttle body.
- **Inhibitor Switch**—is located at the top of the transaxle.
- **Key Lock Control Unit**—is located under the center of the dash, at the console.
- **Key Lock Solenoid (automatic transaxle)**—is located in the shift lever assembly.
- **Kickdown Switch**—is located at the back of the transaxle, near the right inner fender well.
- **Main Fusible Link Box**—is located next to the battery.
- **MPI Control Relay**—is located at the right kick panel.
- **MPI Control Unit**—is located at the right side kick panel.
- **Oil Temperature Sensor**—is located is located at the front of the transaxle, near the dipstick.
- **Oil Temperature Sensor**—is located is located at the front of the transaxle, near the dipstick.
- **Oxygen Sensor**—is located in the exhaust manifold.
- **Park Position Switch**—is located in the shift lever assembly.
- **Positive Crankcase Ventilation (PCV) Valve**—is located on the valve cover.
- **Power Transistor (except 3.0L**—is located at the left rear of the engine compartment, on the firewall.
- **Power Transistor (3.0L)**—is located at the rear of the engine, near the injectors.
- **Pulse Generator**—is located at the top of the transaxle.
- **Purge Control Solenoid Valve**—is located at the right rear corner of the engine compartment.
- **Relay Box**—is located under the left side of the dash.
- **Stop Light Switch**—is located on the brake pedal bracket.
- **Sub-Fusible Link Box**—is located at the right front of the engine compartment.
- **Sunroof Relays**—are located at the sunroof motor.
- **Thermo Valve (except V6)**—is located on the right side of the engine next to the fresh air duct.
- **Thermo Valve (V6)**—is located near the throttle body at the front of the engine.
- **Throttle Position Sensor (TPS)**—is located at the throttle body.
- **Two Way Valve**—is located at the fuel tank.
- **Vehicle Speed Sensor**—is located in the speedometer.

INFINITI

Circuit Breakers

G20

Fuses are located at the left side of the engine compartment in the fuse and fusible link box or under the left side of the dash in the fuse block. Two main fuses are located under the left side of the dash.

M30

Fuses are located at the right side of the engine compartment near the battery. A main fuse is located under the left side of the dash.

Q45

Fuses are located in the fuse, fusible link and relay box at the right front of the engine compartment, near the battery. Other fuses are located under the left side of the dash.

Fusible Links

G20

Fusible links are located in the fuse and fusible link box at the left front of the engine compartment.

M30

Fusible links are located in the fuse and fusible link box at the right front of the engine compartment.

Q45

Fusible links are located in the fuse and fusible link box at the right front of the engine compartment.

Relays, Sensors, Modules and Computer Locations

G20

- **A/C Dual Pressure Switch**—is located at the receiver drier.
- **A/C Relay**—is located in the right relay box.
- **A/C Resistor**—is located next to the blower motor.
- **ABS Acutator**—is located at the right front of the engine compartment.
- **ABS Control Unit**—is located at the right side kick panel.
- **Accessory Relay 1**—is located under the left side of the dash.
- **Accessory Relay 2**—is located under the left side of the dash.

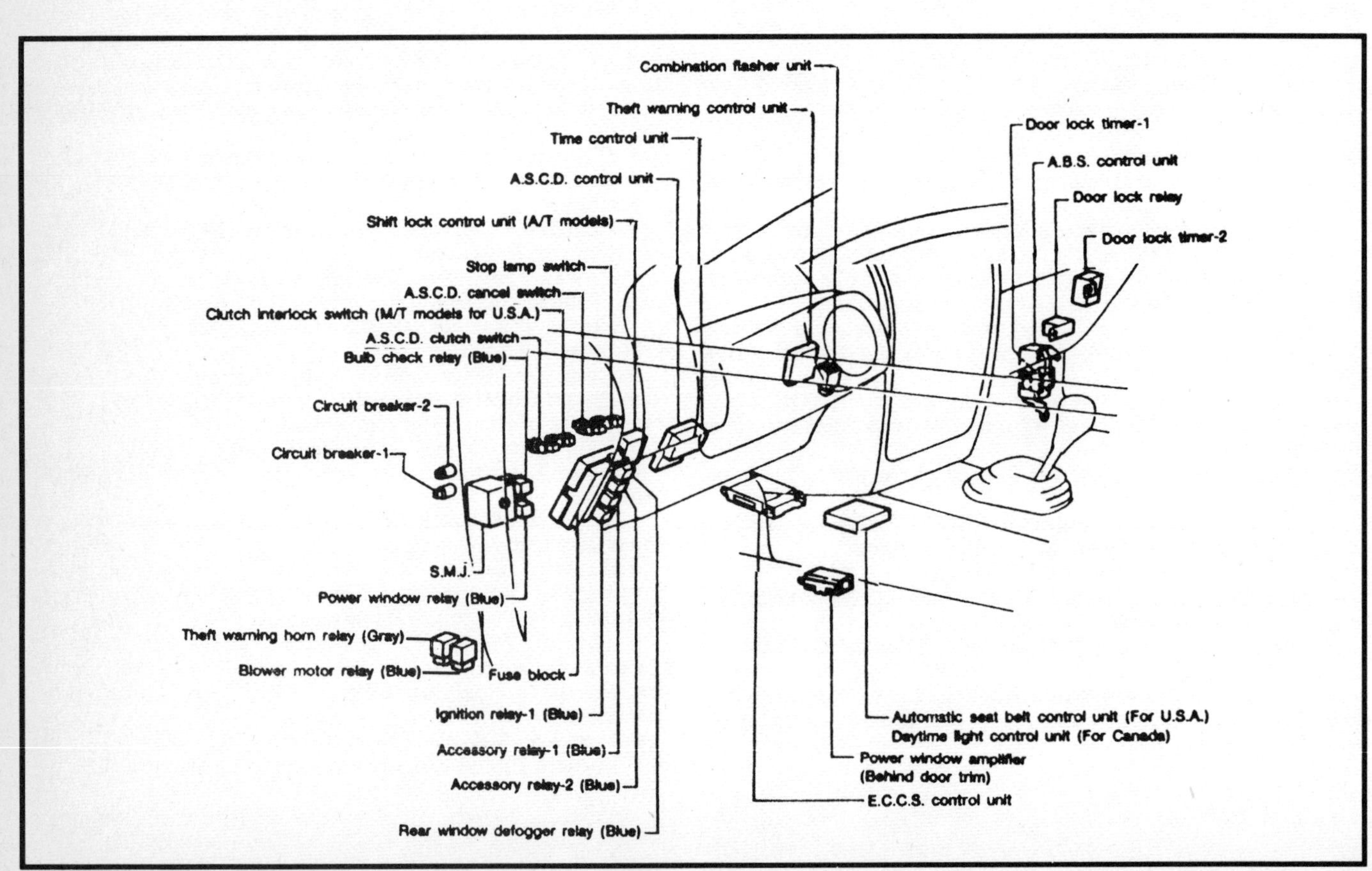

Passenger compartment component locations—G20

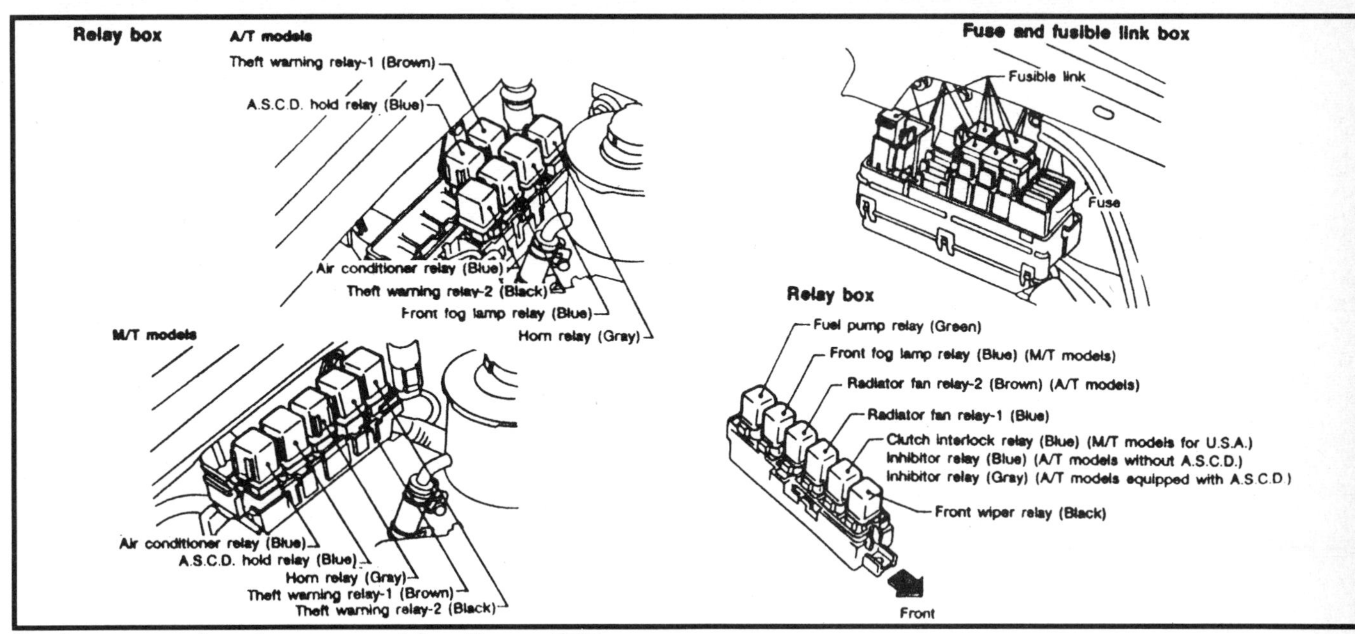

Engine compartment component locations—G20

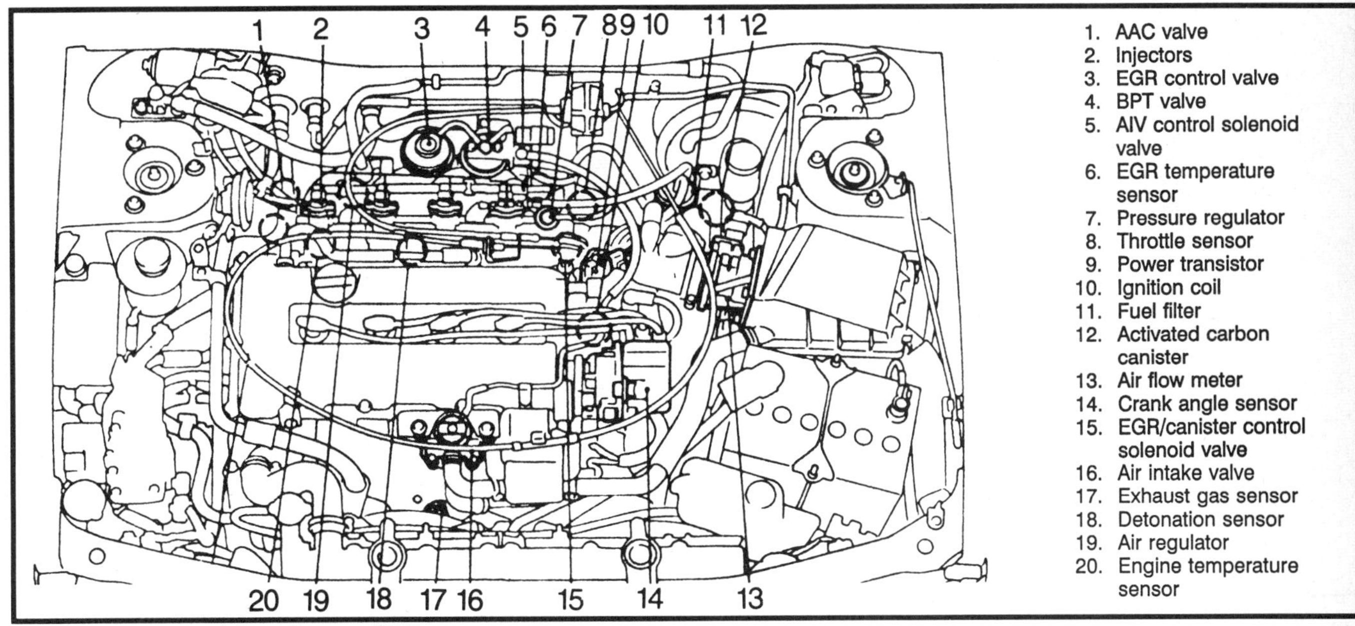

ECCS component locations—G20

• **Air Flow Meter**—is located near the air cleaner in the air intake tract.

• **Air Induction Valve (AIV) Solenoid Valve**—is located at the center of the firewall.

• **Air Induction Valve**—is located at the front of the engine near the radiator.

• **Air Regulator**—is located near the right side of the firewall.

• **Anti-Lock Brakes**—see Anti-Lock Brake System (ABS).

• **ASCD Actuator**—is located at the rear center of the engine compartment.

• **ASCD Cancel Switch**—is located at the clutch mounting bracket.

• **ASCD Clutch Switch**—is located at the clutch mounting bracket.

• **ASCD Control Unit**—is located under the dash to the left of the steering column.

• **ASCD Hold Relay**—is located in the right relay box.

• **ASCD Pump**—is located at the left rear of the engine compartment.

• **Automatic Seat Belt Control Unit**—is located under the console.

• **Auxiliary Air Control Valve**—is located at the right rear of the engine compartment.

• **Blower Motor Relay**—is located at the left side kick panel.

• **Brake Fluid Level Switch**—is located at the master cylinder.

• **Bulb Check Relay**—is located under the left side of the dash.

• **Circuit Breaker 1**—is located under the left side of the dash.

• **Circuit Breaker 2**—is located under the left side of the dash.

• **Clutch Interlock Relay (manual transmission)**—is located in the left relay box.

• **Clutch interlock Switch (manual transmission)**—is located under the left side of the dash.

• **Combination Flasher Unit**—is located under the dash to the right of the steering column.

• **Crank Angle Sensor**—is located inside the distributor.

• **Cruise Control**—see Automatic Speed Control Device (ASCD).

• **Detention Switch**—is located at the shifter lever.

• **Detonation Sensor**—is located at the center of the engine block on the firewall side.

• **Diagnostic Connector**—is located at the fuse block.

• **Door Lock Relay**—is located at the right side kick panel.

• **Door Lock Timers**—are located at the right side kick panel.

• **ECCS Control Unit**—is located under the front of the console.

• **EGR BPT Valve**—is located —is located at the center of the firewall.

• **EGR Control Valve**—is located at the center of the firewall.

• **EGR/Canister Control Solenoid Valve**—is located at the rear of the engine on the distributor side.

• **Electronic Control Unit (ECU)**—see Electronic Concentrated Control System (ECCS) Unit.

• **Engine Temperature Sensor**—is located near the oil filter.

• **Exhaust Gas Sensor**—is located in the exhaust manifold.

• **Exhaust Gas Temperature Sensor**—is located at the rear of the engine near the EGR valve.

• **Front Fog Lamp Relay**—is located in the right relay box (automatic transmission) or the left relay box (manual transmission).

• **Front Wiper Relay**—is located in the left relay box.

• **Fuel Pump Relay**—is located in the left relay box.

• **Fuse Block**—is located under the left side of the dash.

• **Fusible Link/Fuse Box**—is located at the left front of the engine compartment.

• **Horn Relay**—is located in the right relay box.

• **Idle Speed Control FICD Solenoid Valve**—is located at the right rear of the engine compartment.

• **Ignition relay**—is located under the left side of the dash.

• **Inhibitor relay (automatic transmission)Relay**—is located in the left relay box.

• **Inhibitor Switch**—is located on the left side of the transmission.

• **Junction Box**—see Super Multiple Junction (SMJ).

• **Lock-Up Cancel Solenoid**—is located at the transmission valve body.

• **Oil Pressure Switch**—is located in the engine block at the right side of the engine compartment.

• **Overdrive Cancel Solenoid**—is located at the transmission valve body.

• **Overdrive Control Switch**—is located on the shifter lever.

• **Oxygen Sensor**—is located in the exhaust manifold.

• **Power Antenna Timer**—is located at the right quarter panel inside the trunk.

• **Power Transistor**—is located at the rear of the engine near the accelerator cables.

• **Power Window Amplifier**—is located in the left door behind the door trim panel.

• **Power Window Relay**—is located under the left side of the dash.

• **Radiator Fan Relay**—is located in the left relay box.

• **Rear Window Defogger Relay**—is located under the left side of the dash.

• **Relay Box (left)**—is located at the front of the engine compartment, to the left of the engine.

• **Relay Box (right)**—is located at the right of the engine compartment, on the fender.

• **Shift Lock Control Unit (automatic transmission)**—is located under the left side of the dash.

• **Shift Lock Solenoid**—is located at the shifter lever.

• **Sun Roof Relay**—is located at the sunroof motor.

• **Theft Warning Control Unit**—is located under the dash to the right of the steering column.

• **Theft Warning Horn Relay**—is located at the left side kick panel.

• **Theft Warning Relay**—is located in the right relay box.

• **Throttle Sensor**—is located at the throttle body.

• **Time Control Unit**—is located under the dash to the left of the steering column.

• **Washer Level Switch**—is located at the washer bottle.

M30

• **A/C Ambient Sensor**—is located mounted on the hood lock bracket.

• **A/C Aspirator Motor**—is located in front of the cooling unit.

• **A/C Cooling Unit**—is located under the right side of the dash.

• **A/C Dual Pressure Switch**—is located on the receiver drier.

• **A/C In Vehicle Sensor**—is located at the control panel.

• **A/C Intake Sensor**—is located at the cooling unit.

• **ABS Actuator**—is located at the left rear of the engine compartment.

• **ABS Control Unit**—is located at the front of the trunk.

• **ABS Motor Relay**—is located inside the actuator.

• **ABS Solenoid Valve Relay**—is located inside the actuator.

• **Accessory Relays**—are located under the dash to the left of the steering column.

• **Air Bags**—see Supplemental Restraint System (SRS).

• **Air Conditioner Relay**—is located is located in the fuse, fusible link and relay box.

• **Air Flow Meter**—is located at the left front of the engine compartment inside the fresh air duct.

• **Air Regulator**—is located at the middle of the intake manifold on the right side.

• **Anti-Lock Brakes**—see Anti-Lock Brake System (ABS).

• **ASCD Actuator**—is located at the right side of the engine compartment, near the shock tower.

• **ASCD Cancel Switch**—is located at the brake pedal mounting bracket.

• **ASCD Control Unit**—is located at the left side quarter panel behind the trim panel.

• **ASCD Pump**—is located at the right side of the engine compartment, near the shock tower.

• **Automatic Air Conditioner Valve**—is located at the left rear of the engine, near the firewall.

• **Automatic Transmission Control Unit**—is located at the left side kick panel.

• **Automatic Transmission Dropping Resistor**—is located at the right front of the engine compartment.

• **Auxiliary Air Control Valve**—is located at the left center of the intake manifold.

• **Blower Relays**—are located behind the center of the dash.

• **Combination Flasher Unit**—is located under the dash to the left of the steering column.

• **Crankshaft Angle Sensor**—is located inside the distributor.

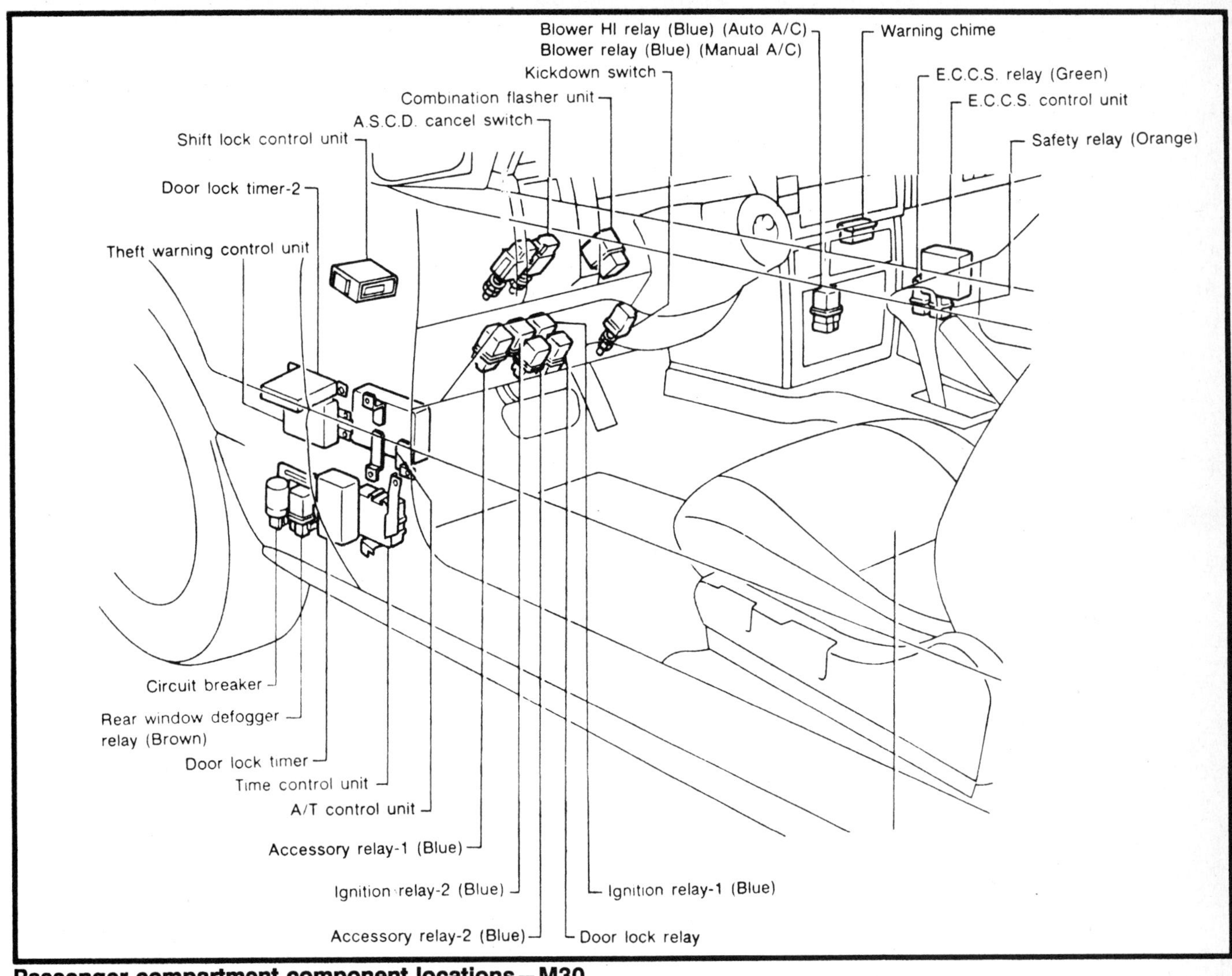

Passenger compartment component locations—M30

- **Cruise Control**—see Automatic Speed Control Device (ASCD).
- **Detention Switch**—is located at the gear shift lever.
- **Door Lock Relay**—is located under the dash to the left of the steering column.
- **Door Lock Timers**—are located at the left side kick panel.
- **Door Unlock Sensors**—are located at the rear of the doors inside the door lock actuators.
- **ECCS Control Unit**—is located at the right side kick panel.
- **ECCS Relay**—is located at the right side kick panel.
- **EGR Control Solenoid Valve**—is located next to the EGR control valve.
- **EGR Control Valve**—is located at the right rear of the engine.
- **Electronic Control Unit (ECU)**—see Electronic Concentrated Control System (ECCS) Unit.
- **Engine Temperature Sensor**—is located at the front of the engine block.
- **Exhaust Gas Temperature Sensor**—is located at the right rear of the intake manifold.
- **Fan Control Amplifier**—is located at the cooling unit.
- **Fuel Filler Lid Opener Relay**—is located the rear of the trunk.
- **Fuel Pump Relay**—is located at the rear of the trunk.
- **Fuel Temperature Sensor**—is located inside the pressure regulator at the front of the engine.
- **Fuse, Fusible Link and Relay Box**—is located at the right front of the engine compartment.
- **Horn Relay**—is located is located in the fuse, fusible link and relay box.
- **Idle Speed Control FICD Solenoid Valve**—is located next to the throttle body on the intake manifold.
- **Ignition Relays**—are located under the dash to the left of the steering column.
- **Inhibitor Relay**—is located is located in the fuse, fusible link and relay box.
- **Inhibitor Switch**—is located at the transmission.
- **Kickdown Switch**—is located at the accelerator pedal.
- **Main Circuit Breaker**—is located at the left side kick panel.
- **Oil Pressure Switch**—is located near the oil filter.
- **Overdrive Switch**—is located at the gear shift lever.
- **Power Transistor**—is located at the ignition coil.
- **Power Window Amplifier**—is located under the left seat or under the console.
- **Pressure Regulator Control Solenoid Valve**—is located at the right front of the engine on the intake manifold.

- **Radiator Fan Relay**—is located is located in the fuse, fusible link and relay box.
- **Rear Window Defogger Relay**—is located at the left side kick panel.
- **Relay Box**—is located at the right front of the engine compartment.
- **Revolution Sensor**—is located at the transmission.
- **Safety Relay**—is located at the right side kick panel.
- **Shift Lock Control Unit**—is located under the dash to the left of the steering column.
- **Shift Lock Solenoid**—is located at the gear shift lever.
- **Shock Absorber Actuators**—are located at the top of each shock absorber.
- **Sonar Road Surface Sensor**—is located at the right side of the vehicle behind the bumper cover.
- **Sonar Suspension Control Unit**—is located at the left quarter panel behind the trim panel.
- **Sonar Suspension Control Unit**—is located at the left side quarter panel behind the trim panel.
- **Speed Sensor**—is located on the extension housing of the transmission.
- **SRS Center Crash Zone Sensor**—is located at the hood latch.
- **SRS Control Unit**—is located under the console.
- **SRS Left Crash Zone Sensor**—is located at the left side of the vehicle behind the bumper cover.
- **SRS Right Crash Zone Sensor**—is located at the right side of the vehicle behind the bumper cover.
- **SRS Safing Sensor**—is located under the console.
- **SRS Tunnel Sensor**—is located under the console.
- **Starter Relay**—is located in front of the battery.
- **Steering Angle Sensor**—is located at the steering column behind the steering wheel.
- **Sunroof Relay**—is located at the sunroof motor.
- **Sunload Sensor**—is located on the right defroster grille.
- **Switching Relay**—is located in the relay box.
- **Theft Warning Control Unit**—is located at the left side kick panel.
- **Theft Warning Horn Relay**—is located in the relay box.
- **Theft Warning Relays**—are located in the relay box.
- **Thermo Switch**—is located at the bottom of the radiator.
- **Throttle Sensor**—is located below the distributor.
- **Throttle Valve Switch**—is located below the distributor.
- **Time Control Unit**—is located at the left side kick panel.
- **Transmission Fluid Temperature Sensor**—is located at the lower valve body.
- **Trunk Lid Opener Relay**—is located at the rear of the trunk.
- **Vehicle Speed Sensor**—is located at the speedometer.
- **Warning Chime**—is located under the center of the dash.
- **Warning Lamp Diode**—is located at the warning lamp behind the instrument panel.
- **Wiper Relay**—is located is located in the fuse, fusible link and relay box.

Q45

- **A/C Ambient Sensor**—is located at the left side condenser.
- **A/C Condenser Fan Relay**—is located in the fuse, fusible link and relay box.
- **A/C Cooling Unit**—is located under the right side of the dash.
- **A/C Dual Pressure Switch**—is located at the receiver drier.
- **A/C Intake Sensor**—is located on the cooling unit.
- **A/C Relay**—is located in the fuse, fusible link and relay box.
- **A/C Sunload Sensor**—is located on the right defroster grille.

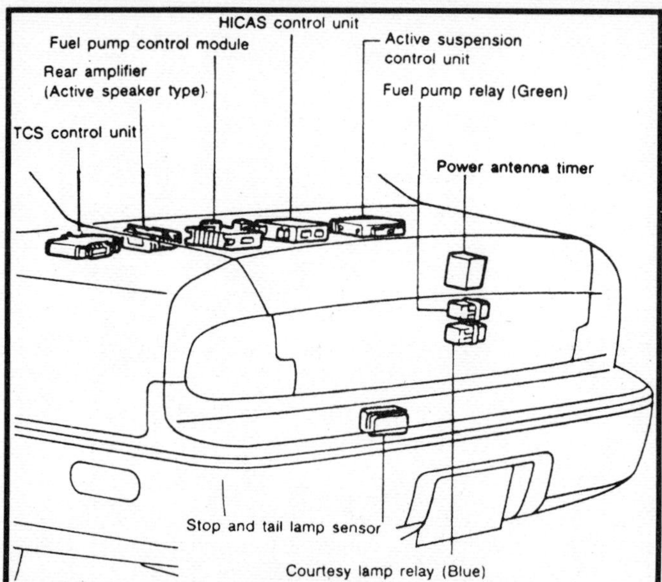

Luggage compartment component locations—Q45

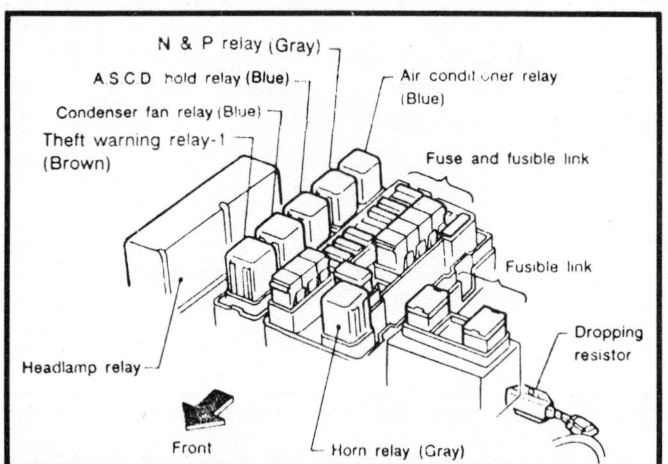

Engine compartment component locations—Q45

- **ABS Actuator**—is located at the right rear of the engine compartment next to the wiper motor.
- **ABS Control Unit**—is located under the right side of the dash.
- **Accessory Relays**—are located under the dash to the left of the steering column.
- **Active Suspension Control Unit**—is located at the front of the trunk.
- **Automatic Drive Positioner**—see ADP
- **ADP Control Unit**—is located under the dash to the left of the steering column.
- **ADP Reclining Motor (limit switches and sensor)**—is located in the left front seat back.
- **ADP Slide Motor and Sensor**—are located under the left front seat.
- **ADP Sliding Limit Switch**—is located under the left front seat.
- **ADP Telescopic Motor and Sensor**—are located in the steering column.
- **ADP Tilt Motor and Sensor**—are located in the steering column.
- **Air Bag Control Unit**—is located under the console.

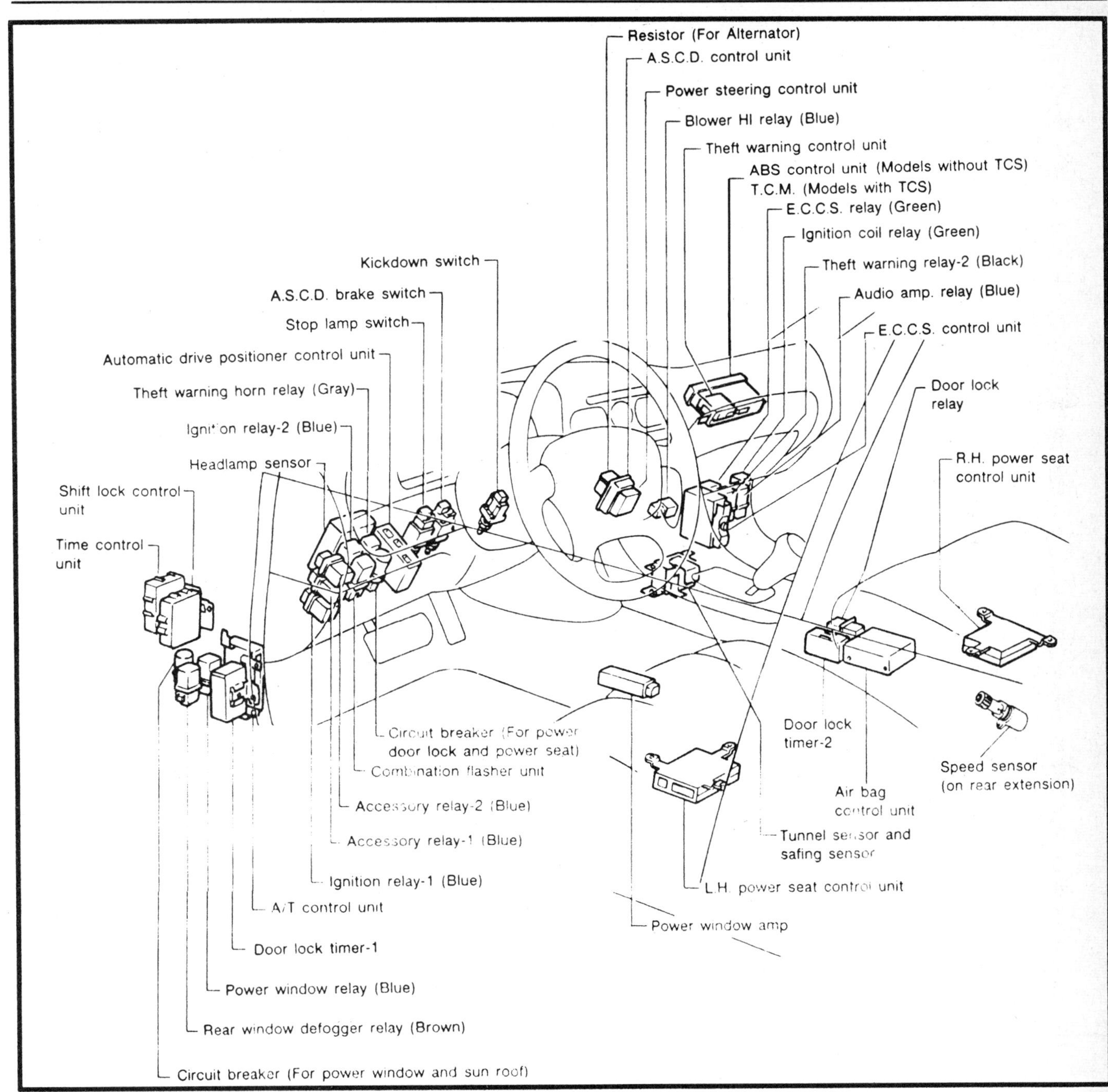

Passenger compartment component locations – Q45

- **Air Bags** – see Supplemental Restraint System (SRS).
- **Alternator Resistor** – is located under the center of the dash.
- **Anti-Lock Brakes** – see Anti-Lock Brake System (ABS).
- **ASCD Actuator** – is located at the left rear of the engine compartment.
- **ASCD Control Unit** – is located under the center of the dash.
- **ASCD Pump** – is located at the left rear of the engine compartment.
- **ASCD Relay** – is located in the fuse, fusible link and relay box.
- **Audio Lamp Relay** – is located at the right side kick panel.
- **Automatic Transmission Control Unit** – is located at the left kick panel.
- **Automatic Transmission Control Unit** – is located at the left side kick panel.
- **Automatic Transmission Range Switch** – is located at the gear selector lever in the console.
- **Blower Relay** – is located under the right side of the dash.
- **Canister Control Solenoid Valve** – is located near the throttle body.
- **Chime** – is located behind the instrument panel.
- **Combination Flasher Unit** – is located under the dash to the left of the steering column.
- **Courtesy Lamp Relay** – is located at the right side quarter panel inside the trunk.

• **Cruise Control**—see Automatic Speed Control Device (ASCD).

• **Detention Switch**—is located in the console at the gear selection lever.

• **Detonation Sensors**—are located at the top rear of the intake manifold.

• **Diagnostic Connector**—is located at the fuse block on the left side of the dash.

• **Door Lock Timer**—is located at the left side kick panel.

• **Dropping Resistor**—is located behind the battery.

• **ECCS Control Unit**—is located at the right side kick panel.

• **ECCS Relay**—is located at the right side kick panel.

• **EGR BPT Valve**—is located at the throttle body.

• **EGR Control Valve** —is located next to the throttle body.

• **EGR Solenoid Control Valve**—is located at the engine left camshaft cover.

• **Electronic Control Unit (ECU)**—see Electronic Concentrated Control System (ECCS) Unit.

• **Engine Temperature Sensor**—is located at the top front of the intake manifold.

• **Exhaust Gas Sensors**—are located in the side exhaust manifolds.

• **FAS Active Suspension Control Unit**—is located at the right rear suspension assembly.

• **FAS Actuators**—are located at the shock absorbers.

• **FAS Fore and AFT G-Sensor**—is located under the console.

• **FAS Front Lateral G-Sensor 1**—is located under the console.

• **FAS Front Lateral G-Sensor 2**—is located under the console.

• **FAS Front Main Accumulator**—is located under the vehicle at the center front.

• **FAS Front Pressure Control Unit**—is located at the right front of the vehicle.

• **FAS Front Vertical G-Sensor**—is located under the vehicle at the left front foot well.

• **FAS Left Rear Vertical G-Sensor**—is located the left rear suspension assembly.

• **FAS Multi-Valve Unit**—is located at the left front of the vehicle.

• **FAS Oil Cooler**—is located at the left front of the vehicle.

• **FAS Pump**—is located at the left front of the vehicle.

• **FAS Rear Main Accumulator**—is located at the right rear suspension assembly.

• **FAS Rear Pressure Control Unit**—is located at the right rear suspension assembly.

• **FAS Reservoir Tank**—is located at the left front of the vehicle.

• **FAS Right Rear Vertical G-Sensor**—is located at the right rear suspension assembly.

• **FAS Vehicle Height Sensor**—is located at the left rear A-arm.

• **Fuel Damper**—is located at the throttle body.

• **Fuel Pump Control Module**—is located above the fuel tank.

• **Fuel Pump Relay**—is located at the right side quarter panel inside the trunk.

• **Fuse, Fusible Link and Relay Box**—is located behind the battery.

• **Headlamp Relay**—is located behind the battery.

• **Headlight Relay**—is located next to the fuse, fusible link and relay box.

• **Headlight Sensor**—is located under the dash to the left of the steering column.

• **Heating Unit**—is located under the right side of the dash.

• **HICAS Control Unit**—is located at the top right front of the trunk.

• **HICAS Fail Safe Valve**—is located under the left side of the body at the oil tubes.

• **HICAS Oil Pump**—is located at the left front of the engine.

• **HICAS Power Cylinder**—is located at the rear differential.

• **HICAS Power Steering Solenoid**—is located at the front suspension.

• **HICAS Reservoir Tank**—is located at the left front of the engine compartment.

• **HICAS Solenoid**—is located near the master cylinder.

• **HICAS Steering Angle Sensor**—is located inside the steering column.

• **High Captivity Actively Controlled Steering**—see HICAS.

• **Ignition Coil Relay**—is located in the right side kick panel.

• **Ignition Relays**—are located under the dash to the left of the steering column.

• **Inhibitor Switch**—is located at the right side of the transmission case.

• **Kickdown Switch**—is located at the accelerator pedal mounting bracket.

• **Oil Pressure Switch**—is located on the left side of the engine under the exhaust manifold.

• **Power Antenna Timer**—is located at the right side quarter panel inside the trunk.

• **Power Door Lock Circuit Breaker**—is located under the dash to the left of the steering column.

• **Power Seat Circuit Breaker**—is located under the dash to the left of the steering column.

• **Power Seat Control Unit**—is located under the seat.

• **Power Seats**—see Automatic Drive Positioner (ADP).

• **Power Steering Control Unit**—is located under the center of the dash.

• **Power Steering Oil Pressure Switch**—is located in the power steering high pressure line.

• **Power Transistor**—is located at the engine left camshaft cover.

• **Power Window Amplifier**—is located under the console or under the left seat.

• **Power Window Circuit Breaker**—is located at the left side kick panel.

• **Power Window Relay**—is located at the left side kick panel.

• **Rear Window Defogger Relay**—is located at the left side kick panel.

• **Revolution Sensor**—is located at left side of the transmission case.

• **Safing Sensor**—is located under the console.

• **Secondary Throttle Sensor**—is located at the throttle body.

• **Shift Lock Control Unit**—is located at the left side kick panel.

• **Shift Lock Solenoid**—is located in the console at the gear selection lever.

• **Speed Sensor**—is located on the transmission extension housing.

• **SRS Center Crash Zone Sensor**—is located at the hood latch assembly.

• **SRS Left Crash Zone Sensor**—is located at the left front of the vehicle behind the bumper cover.

• **SRS Right Crash Zone Sensor**—is located at the right front of the vehicle behind the bumper cover.

• **Starter Relay**—is located at the right rear of the engine compartment.

• **Stop/Taillight Sensor**—is located at the rear of the trunk.

• **Sunroof Circuit Breaker**—is located at the left side kick panel.

• **Suspension**—see Full-Active Suspension (FAS).

• **Tail/Stop Light Sensor**—is located at the rear of the trunk.

• **TCS Actuator**—is located near the battery.
• **TCS Control Unit**—is located at the right front of the trunk.
• **TCS Fluid Reservoir**—is located at the TCS actuator.
• **TCS Pump**—is located in front of the right front wheel well.
• **TCS Rear Wheel Sensors**—arc located at the differential housing.
• **TCS Secondary Throttle Sensor**—is located at the throttle body.
• **TCS Throttle Control Module**—is located at the front right steering member.
• **TCS Throttle Motor**—is located at the throttle body.
• **Theft Warning Control Unit**—is located under the right side of the dash.
• **Theft Warning Horn Relay**—is located under the dash to the left of the steering column.
• **Theft Warning Relay 1**—is located in the fuse, fusible link and relay box.
• **Theft Warning Relay 2**—is located in the right side kick panel.
• **Theft Warning System Tamper Switch**—is located at the door key cylinder assembly.
• **Thermo-Switch**—is located at the bottom of the radiator.
• **Time Control Unit**—is located at the left side kick panel.
• **Traction Control System**—see TCS.
• **Tunnel Sensor**—is located under the console.
• **Turbine Revolution Sensor**—is located at the left side of the transmission case.
• **Valve Timing Control Solenoid Valve**—is located at the front of the intake camshafts.
• **Vehicle Speed Sensor**—is located at the speedometer.
• **Warning Light/Chime Diode**—is located built into the instrument panel.
• **Water Temperature Sensor**—is located the heating unit.
• **Wiper Amplifier**—is located at the right rear of the engine compartment.

ISUZU

Circuit Breakers

I-MARK

This vehicle does not incorporate circuit breakers.

IMPULSE

A 20 amp circuit breaker is used to protect the power window or sunroof circuit, and is located in the Junction Block.

STYLUS

A 30 amp circuit breaker is used to protect the power window or sunroof circuit, and is located in the Junction Block.

Fusible Links

The fusible links or maxi-fuses are located in the relay and fuse block locations and can be identified by there large size and amperage rating.

Relays, Sensors, Modules and Computer Locations

I-MARK

• **Accelerator Switch**—is located under left side of dash, right of the steering column.
• **A/C Compressor Relay**—is located in right front corner of engine compartment.
• **A/C Dual Pressure Switch**—is located in the right front of the engine compartment, near the A/C condenser.
• **A/C Heater Relay**—is located under left side of dash, at kick panel.
• **A/C Pressure Cycling Switch**—is located on top front of radiator.
• **A/C Pressure Switch**—is located under the instrument panel near the evaporator.
• **A/C Thermostatic Switch**—is located on the top of the evaporator housing.
• **A.I.R. Vacuum Switching Valve**—is located on the right hand side of the firewall.
• **Anti-Dieseling Solenoid**—is located on the rear of the carburetor.

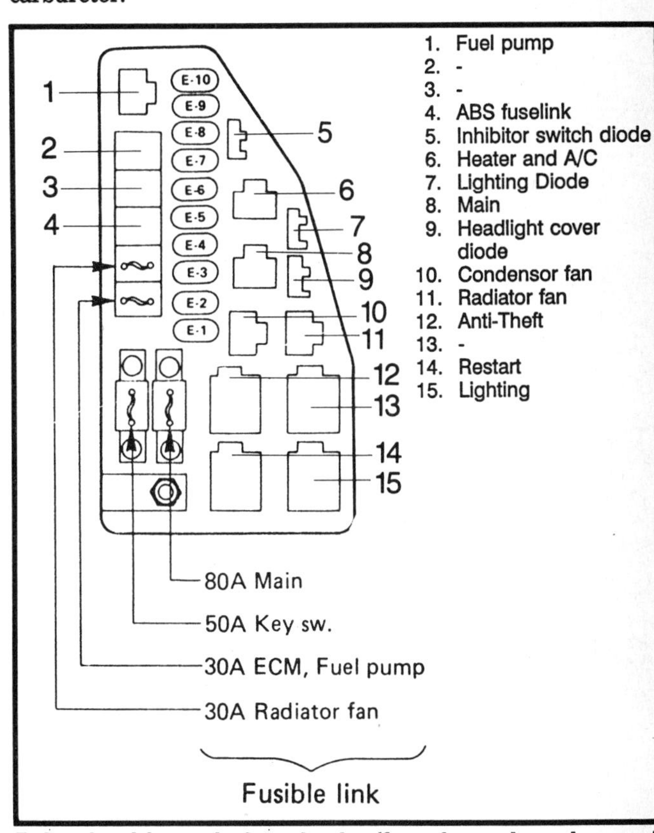

Driver's side underhood relay/fuse box—Impulse and Stylus

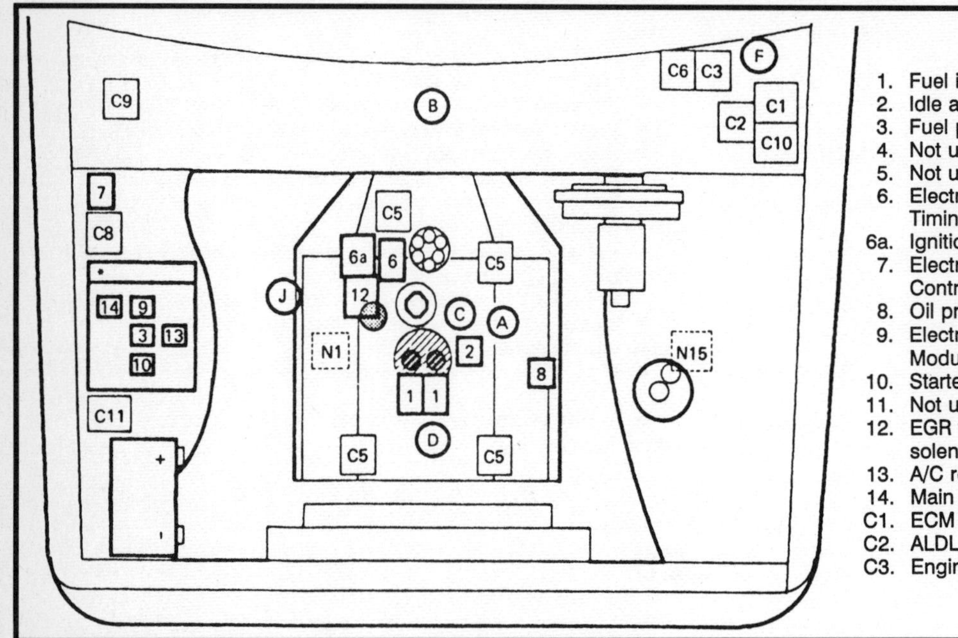

Components location—Light trucks with 3.1L engine

• **A/C Sub-Relay (turbocharged)**—is located in right rear corner of the engine compartment.

• **A/C Sub-Relay (except turbocharged)**—is located rear of the engine compartment, on the left side of firewall.

• **A/C Sub-Relay Condenser**—is located in the lower right rear of engine compartment, on shock tower.

• **A/C Vacuum Switching Valve (turbocharged)**—is located in the right rear corner of the engine compartment.

• **A/C Vacuum Switching Valve (except turbocharged)**—is located in the right rear corner of the engine compartment.

• **Air/Fuel Mixture Solenoid**—is located in the right rear corner of engine compartment.

• **Air/Fuel Mixture Solenoid Resistor**—is located in right rear of engine compartment, on the air/fuel mixture solenoid.

• **Air Vacuum Switching Valve (fuel injected and turbocharged)**

• **Altitude Switch**—is located in right rear corner of engine, behind bracket, near shock tower.

• **Assembly Line Diagnostic Link (ALDL) Connector**—is located under right side of dash, at kick panel.

• **Automatic Choke Relay**—is located near the starter relay or under the left side of the instrument panel.

• **Back-Up Light Switch**—is located on top of the transaxle.

• **Brake Fluid Level Switch**—is located in left rear corner of engine compartment, on brake fluid reservoir.

• **Brake Light Switch**—is located under left side of dash, on brake pedal bracket.

• **Canister Vacuum Switching Valve (turbocharged)**—is located in the right rear corner of the engine compartment.

• **Canister Vacuum Switching Valve (except turbocharged)**—is located in the right rear of engine compartment, on right side of firewall.

• **Canvas Top Relay**—is located under left side of dash, on clutch pedal bracket.

• **Chime Control Unit**—is located under left side of dash, right of the steering column.

• **Choke Heater Relay**—is located right rear corner of engine compartment

• **Clutch Interrupt Switch**—is located under left side of dash, on clutch pedal bracket.

• **Clutch Start Switch**—is located under the left side of dash, on clutch pedal bracket.

• **Control Unit (Turbo)**—is located under the right hand side of the instrument panel, under the glove box.

• **Coolant Temperature Gauge Sender (turbocharged or carburated)**—is located top left front of engine, on the coolant outlet.

• **Coolant Temperature Gauge Sender (fuel injected, except turbocharged)**—is located left front corner of engine, below the distributor assembly.

• **Coolant Temperature Switch (fuel injected)**—is located on the right side of the radiator.

• **Coolant Temperature Sensor (except Fuel injected)**—is located on the rear of engine, below the carburetor.

• **Cooling Fan Diode**—is located underside of left front wheelwell, above panel.

• **Cooling Fan Relay**—is located in left front corner of engine compartment, next to battery.

• **Cooling Fan Test Connector**—is located in the left rear corner of the engine compartment, next to brake level fluid switch.

• **Condenser Fan Relay**—is located in the right front corner of engine compartment.

• **Cruise Control Module**—is located behind center of dash.

• **Dash Fuse Box**—is located on the left side of dash, behind panel.

• **Detonation Sensor**—is located on the lower rear of engine.

• **Diode Box A**—is located under the right side, above the kick panel.

• **Diode Box B and C**—are located under the left side of dash, at kick panel.

• **Dome Light Diode**—is located under the left side of dash, at the kick panel.

• **Door Ajar Buzzer Relay**—is located under the right side of the instrument panel, early vehicles when equipped.

• **Dual Pressure Switch**—is located in the right front of the engine compartment, near the A/C condenser.

• **Duty Monitor**—is located in the lower right rear corner of engine compartment.

• **Duty Solenoid**—is located on the top center of the engine, on the carburetor.

• **EFE Heater Relay**—is located on the right rear corner of the engine compartment.

• **Electronic Control Unit (ECM)**—is located under right side of dash, at kick panel.

• **Evaporator Temperature Switch**—is located behind the glove box, on evaporator.

• **Exhaust Gas Recirculation (EGR) Vacuum Switching Valve (turbocharged)**—is located in the right rear corner of the engine compartment.

• **Exhaust Gas Recirculation (EGR) Vacuum Switching Valve (except turbocharged)**—is located in rear of engine compartment, on left side firewall.

• **Fast Idle Control Diaphragm (FICD) Relay**—is located in the right rear corner of the engine compartment, next to choke heater relay.

• **Fast Idle Control Diaphragm Relay Condenser A and B**—are located in the lower right rear of the engine compartment, taped to harness.

• **Fast Idle Control Vacuum Switching Valve (fuel injected and turbocharged)**—is located in the rear of the engine compartment, on left side of firewall.

• **Fog Light Relay**—is located at the left front corner of the engine compartment, next to battery and cooling fan relay.

• **Fuel Cut-Off Solenoid**—is located on the rear of engine, on left side of carburetor.

• **Fuel Pump Relay (fuel injected and turbocharged)**—is located in the right rear of engine compartment.

• **Fuel Pump Relay (fuel injected, except turbocharged)**—is located in the rear of the engine compartment, on left side of firewall.

• **Fuel Pump Fuse (Turbo)**—30 amp slow blow fuse is located in the slow blow fuse box, if equipped.

• **Fuel Tank Pressure Control Vacuum Switching Valve**—is located in rear of engine compartment, on center of firewall, next to canister.

• **Flasher Unit**—is located under left side of dash, at kick panel.

• **Fusible Link D**—is located at the lower left side of engine compartment, below rear of battery.

• **Heater Relay**—is located under the left side of the instrument panel, if equipped.

• **Idle Air Control Valve (fuel injected and turbocharged)**—is located on top rear of engine, on the left side of throttle body.

• **Idle-Up Solenoid**—is located on the rear of engine, on right side of carburetor.

• **Idle Switch**—is incorporated into the TPS on the throttle linkage.

• **In-Line Capacitors**—is located left rear corner of engine compartment, at the front windshield wiper motor.

• **In-Line Circuit Breaker**—is located in the left rear corner of engine compartment, at front of the windshield wiper motor.

• **Inlet Air Temperature Switch**—is located on top of engine, in the air cleaner.

• **Intake Air Vacuum Switching Valve**—is located on rear of engine, below the air intake.

• **Kickdown Solenoid**—is located on the lower front of transaxle.

• **Kickdown Switch**—is located under the left side of dash, on accelerator bracket.

• **Kickdown Switch Diode**—is located under the left side of dash, above accelerator bracket.

• **Light Driver Module**—is located under the right side of dash, above the kick panel.

• **Lights/Wiper Control Unit**—is located under the left side of dash, at kick panel.

• **Main Fuse Box (fuel injected)**—is located on left side of engine compartment.

• **Main Fuse Box (except fuel injected)**—is located on the left side of the engine compartment, behind the battery.

• **Main Relay**—is located under the left side of dash, at kick panel.

• **Manifold Absolute Pressure (MAP) Sensor (fuel injected and turbocharged)**—is located in the right rear corner of the engine compartment, near the turbocharger boost sender.

• **Manifold Absolute Temperature (MAT) Sensor (fuel injected and turbocharged)**—is located on the top rear of engine, on left side of throttle body.

• **Mixture Bypass Solenoid**—is located rear of engine, on the left side of the carburetor.

• **Neutral Safety Switch**—is located on top of the transaxle.

• **Oil Pressure Sending Unit**—is located on the lower right rear of engine, near oil filter.

• **Oil Pressure Switch**—is located on the lower right rear of engine, near the oil filter.

• **Oxygen Sensor**—is located in the exhaust manifold.

• **Parking Brake Switch**—is located below rear corner of console, on the parking brake shaft

• **Power Steering Pressure Switch**—is located on right side of engine compartment, next to valve cover.

• **Rear Window Defogger Relay**—is located under the left side of dash, at kick panel.

• **Restart Relay**—is located under the left side of dash, at kick panel.

• **Super Heat Switch**—is located behind the glove box.

• **Super Heat Switch Control Unit**—is under the left side of dash, right of steering column.

• **Supplementary Distributor Vacuum Switching Valve**—is located on the left side of the engine compartment, behind the battery.

• **Throttle Position (TPS) Sensor (fuel injected and turbocharged)**—is located on the top rear of engine, on left side of throttle body.

• **Throttle Vacuum Switching Valve**—is located in the rear of the engine compartment, on right side of firewall.

• **Seat Belt Buzzer Relay**—is located behind the left side of the instrument cluster, if equipped.

• **Shift Reminder Relay**—is located under the right side of the instrument panel, if equipped.

• **Timer Relay**—is located under the left side of dash, right of the steering column.

• **Turbocharger Boost Sender**—is located in the right rear corner of the engine compartment, next to the fuel pump relay.

• **Upshift Relay**—is located under the left side of dash, at kick panel.

• **Vent Switch Valve**—is located rear of engine, on right side of the carburetor.

• **Waste Gate Vacuum Switching Valve**—is located in top left rear of engine.

1989 IMPULSE

• **A/C Actuator Relay**—is located under the right hand side of the instrument panel, near the kick panel.

• **A/C Blower Controller**—is located in the left hand rear corner of the engine compartment.

• **A/C Blower Relay**—is located under the right hand side of the instrument panel, near the kick panel.

• **A/C Charge Relay**—is located in the fuse/relay box in the front of the battery.

• **A/C Cut-Out Relay**—is located in the left hand front corner of the engine compartment.
• **A/C-Heater Blower Motor Relay**—is located in the right side switch module.
• **A/C-Heater Blower Motor Resistor**—is located on the heater box.
• **A/C Pressure Switch**—is located in the A/C high pressure hose near the firewall.
• **A/C Relay**—is located in the fuse/relay box in the front of the battery.
• **A/C Timer (4ZC1)**—is located under the right hand side of the instrument panel, near the kick panel.
• **A/C Thermostatic Switch**—is located on the evaporator upper case.
• **Air Relay (Turbo)**—is located in the air cleaner.
• **Airflow Sensor**—is located at the left front corner of the engine compartment.
• **Anti–Theft Controller**—is located behind the center of the tailgate panel.
• **Automatic A/C Computer**—is located in the right side switch module.
• **Automatic A/C Mixture Door Actuator**—is located on the evaporator housing.
• **Automatic A/C Sensors**—is located on the evaporator unit.
• **Automatic Seatbelt Controller**—is located under the center of the instrument panel.
• **Back-Up Light Switch**—is located on the top left of the transmission.
• **Blower Motor Relay**—is located in the relay block on the right inner fender panel.
• **Boost Sensor**—is located on the right inner fender near relay block, if so equipped.
• **Brake/Stoplight Switch**—is located on the brake pedal bracket.
• **Charge Warning Relay**—is located in the relay block on the right inner fender panel.
• **Clutch/Safety Switch**—is located on the clutch pedal bracket.
• **Cooling Fan Relay**—is located in the fuse/relay box in the front of the battery.
• **Crank Angle Sensor**—is located inside the distributor.
• **Cruise Control Servo**—is located at the left front corner of the engine compartment.
• **Cruise Control Unit**—is located in the right or left hand side kick panel.
• **Detonation (Knock) Sensor**—is located on the right side of the engine block.
• **Diagnostic Connector**—is located under the left side of the instrument panel near the MCU.
• **Dimmer Relay**—is located in the fuse/relay box in the front of the battery.
• **Door Ajar Buzzer**—is located behind the right side of the instrument panel.
• **Door Lock Control Unit**—is located behind the left side of the instrument panel or under the driver's seat.
• **Fan Relay**—is located on the right inner fender panel.
• **Fast Idle Solenoid**—is located near the throttle housing or near the relay block, if so equipped.
• **Fast Idle Relay**—is located in the left hand front corner of the engine compartment.
• Front Washer Motor—is located in the bottom of the washer fluid reservoir.
• **Fuel Gauge Sending Unit**—is located on the top of the fuel tank.
• **Fuel Pump**—is located under the rear seat.
• **Fuel Pump Relay**—is located in the relay block on the right inner fender panel.
• **Fuse Block**—is located under the left side of the instrument panel.
• **Fuse/Relay Box**—is located in front the of battery, in the engine compartment.
• **Headlight Cover Motor**—is located behind the center of the grille.
• **Headlight Cover Relay**—is located in the fuse/relay box on the front of the battery.
• **Heater Control Unit**—is located on the heater box.
• **Horn Relay**—is located on the right inner fender panel.
• **Idle Stepper Motor (Turbo)**—is located on the left inner fender panel.
• **Inhibitor Switch (automatic transmission)**—is located on the shift lever mounting bracket.
• **Injector Blower Control Unit**—is located on the left hand side kick panel.
• **Lighting Relay**—is located in the fuse/relay box in front of the battery.
• **Light Reminder Buzzer**—is located under the left hand side of the instrument panel.
• **Main Relay**—is located in the relay block on the right inner fender panel.
• **Microcomputer Control Unit (MCU)**—is located under the left side of the instrument panel.
• **Multi-Display Unit**—is located in the center of the instrument panel console.
• **Neutral Switch**—is located in the transmission quadrant box cover.
• **O/D Controller (4ZC1)**—is located under the right hand side of the instrument panel, on the kick panel.
• **O/D Relay (4ZD1 Engine)**—is located under the left hand side of the instrument panel, near the kick panel.
• **O/D Switch Relay (4ZD1 Engine)**—is located under the left hand side of the instrument panel, near the kick panel.
• **Oil Pressure Sending Unit**—is located in the lower right side of the engine block near the oil filter.
• **Oil Pressure Switch**—is located on the right rear of the engine near the starter.
• **Overdrive Relay (Turbo)**—is located under the left side of the instrument panel.
• **Oxygen Sensor**—is located on the exhaust manifold.
• **Parking Brake Switch**—is located inside the rear of the center console.
• **Power Door Lock Relay**—is located under the left hand side of the instrument panel.
• **Power Window Relay**—is located under the left hand side of the instrument panel.
• **Power One Touch Window Relay (4ZC1 Engine)**—is located under the left hand side of the instrument panel, near the kick panel.
• **Rear Washer Motor**—is located in the bottom of the washer fluid reservoir.
• **Rear Wiper Motor**—is located in the center of the liftgate.
• **Relay Block**—is located on the right inner fender panel.
• **Seat Belt Buzzer**—is located behind the center of the instrument panel.
• **Speed Sensor**—is located on the back of the speedometer assembly.
• **Taillight Relay**—is located in the fuse/relay box in front of the battery.
• **Throttle Valve Switch**—is located on the throttle body housing.
• **Vacuum Switching Solenoid Valve**—is located on the right inner fender panel.
• **Vapor Relay**—is located under the left hand side of the instrument panel.
• **Water Temperature Sensor**—is located on the bottom of the intake manifold.
• **Wiper Relays (2)**—are located on the front inner fender panel.

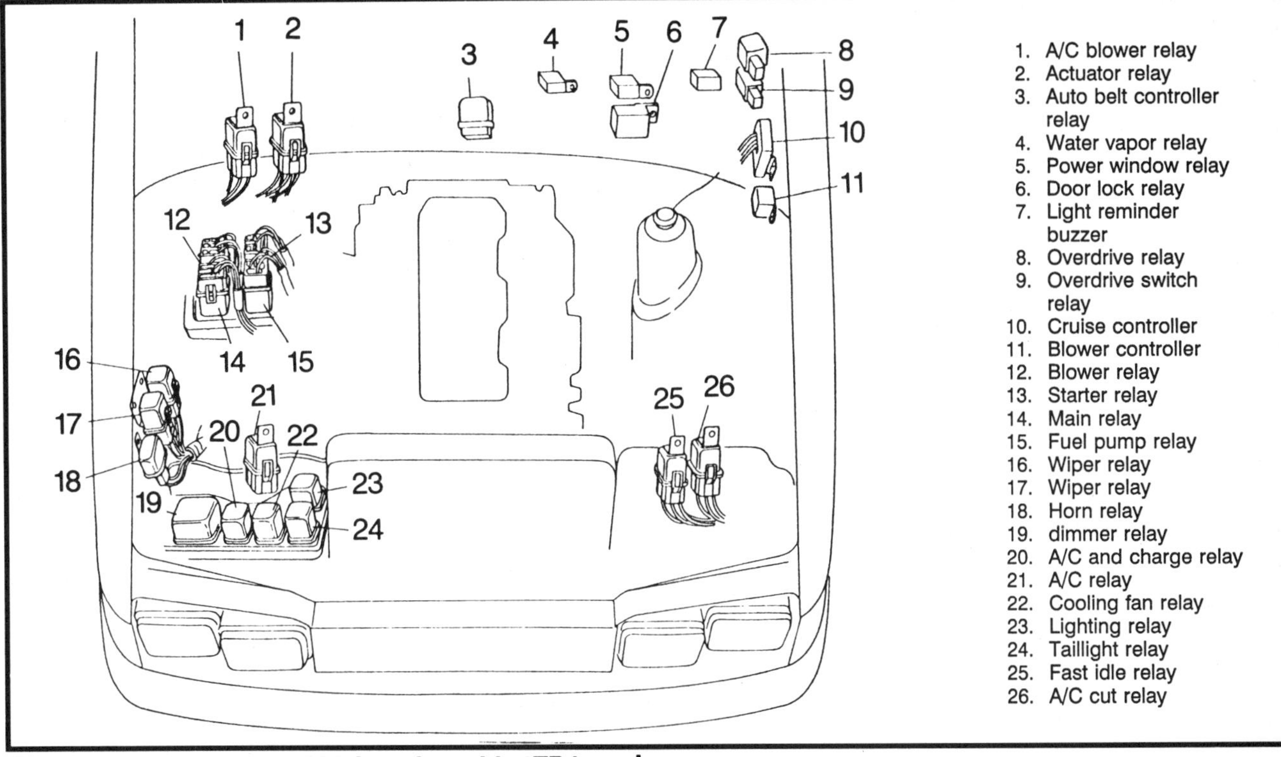

Components location—1989 Impulse with 4ZD1 engine

1990–91 IMPULSE

- **A/C and Heater Relay**—is located on the left side of engine compartment, in fuse/relay box.
- **A/C Compressor Relay**—is located on the right side of engine compartment, in the relay box.
- **A/C Cut-Control Unit**—is located behind behind the right side of instrument panel, below glove box.
- **A/C Triple Pressure Switch**—is located right of condenser, on receiver/drier.
- **Assembly Line Diagnostic Link (ALDL) Connector C-405 (3-White)**—is located at right kick panel, behind trim panel.
- **Air Bag**—see Supplement Inflatable Restraint (SIR).
- **Assembly Line Diagnostic Link Connector C434 (3-Red)**—is located at right kick panel, behind trim panel.
- **Automatic Door Lock Control Unit**—is located in rear of driver's door, behind the trim panel.
- **Condenser Fan Relay**—is located on the left side of engine compartment, in fuse/relay box.
- **Back-Up Lights Switch**—is located in lower left side of engine compartment, on top of transaxle.
- **Brake Diodes**—is located below the driver's seat, under carpet.
- **Brake Fluid Level Switch**—is located in left rear corner of engine compartment, in bottom of brake fluid reservoir.
- **Brake Light Switch**—is located behind the left side of instrument panel, on brake pedal support.
- **Clutch Interrupt Switch**—is located behind left side of instrument panel, on clutch pedal bracket.
- **Clutch Start Switch**—is located behind left side of instrument panel, on clutch pedal bracket.
- **Condenser Fan Relay**—is located on the left side of engine compartment, in fuse/relay box.
- **Coolant Temperature Gauge Sender**—is located in left front corner of engine, below distributor assembly.
- **Coolant Temperature Sensor (CTS)**—is located on the top left side of engine, in coolant outlet.
- **Coolant Temperature Switch**—is located on the lower left rear of radiator.
- **Cruise Control Module**—is located at the right kick panel, behind the trim panel.
- **Diagnostic Energy Reserve Module (DERM)**—is located behind front console panel.
- **Diagnostic Energy Reserve Module (ALDL-DERM) Connector C434 (3-Red)**—is located at right kick panel, behind trim panel.
- **Diode Box 1**—is located on the left side of engine compartment, in fuse/relay box.
- **Diode Box 3**—is located on the right side of engine compartment, in relay box.
- **Dropping Resistor**—is located in left rear of engine compartment, below brake fluid reservoir.
- **Electro Thermo Unit**—is located on the right side of instrument, behind the glove box.
- **Electronic Control Module (ECM)**—is located behind the left side of instrument panel
- **Exhaust Gas Recirculation (EGR) Vacuum Switching Valve**—is located on top left side of engine, behind the distributor assembly.
- **Flasher Unit**—is located behind the left side of instrument panel, on bracket.
- **Fog Light Relay**—is located on the right side of engine compartment, in relay box.
- **Forward Discriminating Sensor**—is located behind the center of front bumper.
- **Fuel Pump Relay**—is located on the left side of engine compartment, in fuse/relay box.
- **Fuse/Relay Box**—is located on the left side of engine compartment, next to strut tower.
- **Horn Relay**—is located on the right side of engine compartment, in relay box.

• **Idle Air Control Valve**—is located on top left rear of engine, on throttle valve assembly.
• **Inhibitor Switch**—is located in lower left side of engine compartment, on top of transaxle.
• **Intake Air Vacuum Switching Valve**—is located in left rear of engine, below the common chamber.
• **Junction Block**is located at left kick panel, behind the trim panel.
• **Main Relay**—is located on the left side of engine compartment, in fuse/relay box.
• **Manifold Absolute Pressure (MAP) Sensor**—is located in the left rear of engine compartment.
• **Manifold Air Temperature (MAT) Sensor**—is located in top left rear corner of engine, in rear of common chamber.
• **Neutral Relay**—is located in the right side of engine compartment, in relay box.
• **Neutral Switch**—is located in the lower left side of engine compartment, on top of transaxle.
• **Oil Pressure Switch**—is located in lower center rear of engine, near oil filter.
• **Oxygen Sensor**—is located in lower front of engine, in exhaust manifold.
• **Park Switch**—is located under floor console, under the shifter control.
• **Parking Brake Switch**—is located under rear of floor console, on parking brake shaft.
• **Passenger Compartment Discriminating Sensor**—is located behind front console, under diagnostic energy reserve module (DERM).
• **Power Steering Pressure Switch**—is located in right front corner of engine, in power steering oil pump
• **Power Window Relay**—is located behind left side of instrument panel, on bracket.
• **Radiator Fan Relay**—is located on the left side of engine compartment, in fuse/relay box.
• **Radiator Fan Test Connector C539 (1-CLR)**—is located in left rear of engine compartment, taped to harness.
• **Rear Defogger Relay**—is located behind left side of instrument panel, on bracket.
• **Relay Box**—is located on the right side of engine compartment.
• **Resistor Block**—is located behind right side of instrument panel, on heater unit.
• **Restart Relay**—is located on the left side of engine compartment, in fuse/relay box.
• **Rise-Up/Intermittent Relay**—is located behind the left side of instrument panel, on bracket.
• **Shift Lock Control Unit**—is located under floor console, under the shifter console.
• **Shift Lock Solenoid**—is located under floor console, in front of shifter control
• **SIR Arming Sensor**—is located behind center of instrument panel.
• **SIR Forward Discriminating Sensor**—is located behind the center of front bumper.
• **SIR Passenger Compartment Discriminating Sensor**—is located behind front console, under diagnostic energy reserve module (DERM).
• **SIR Resistor Module**—is located behind left side of instrument panel, on top of steering column.
• **Thermo Switch**—is located on top left side of engine, in coolant outlet.
• **Thermo Switch Relay**—is located on the right side of engine compartment, in relay box.
• **Throttle Position Sensor (TPS)**—is located in top left rear corner of engine, on throttle valve assembly.
• **Transmission Control Module (TCM)**—is located behind the left side of instrument panel.
• **Transmission Control Module (TCM) Diagnostic Connector C406 (5-GRN)**—is located at the right kick panel, behind trim panel.
• **Triple Pressure Switch**—is located right of condenser, on receiver/drier.

STYLUS

• **A/C and Heater Relay**—is located on the left side of engine compartment, in fuse/relay box.
• **A/C Compressor Relay**—is located on the right side of engine compartment, in the relay box.
• **A/C Cut-Control Unit**—is located behind behind the right side of instrument panel, below glove box.
• **A/C Triple Pressure Switch**—is located right of condenser, on receiver/drier.
• **Assembly Line Diagnostic Link (ALDL) Connector C-405 (3-White)**—is located at right kick panel, behind trim panel.
• **Air Bag**—see Supplement Inflatable Restraint (SIR).
• **Assembly Line Diagnostic Link: Diagnostic Energy Reserve Module (ALDL-DERM) Connector C434 (3-Red)**—is located at right kick panel, behind trim panel.
• **Automatic Door Lock Control Unit**—is located in rear of driver's door, behind the trim panel.
• **Condenser Fan Relay**—is located on the left side of engine compartment, in fuse/relay box.
• **Back-Up Lights Switch**—is located in lower left side of engine compartment, on top of transaxle.
• **Brake Diodes**—is located below the driver's seat, under carpet.
• **Brake Fluid Level Switch**—is located in left rear corner of engine compartment, in bottom of brake fluid reservoir.
• **Brake Light Switch**—is located behind the left side of instrument panel, on brake pedal support.
• **Clutch Interrupt Switch**—is located behind left side of instrument panel, on clutch pedal bracket.
• **Clutch Start Switch**—is located behind left side of instrument panel, on clutch pedal bracket.
• **Condenser Fan Relay**—is located on the left side of engine compartment, in fuse/relay box.
• **Coolant Temperature Gauge Sender**—is located in left front corner of engine, below distributor assembly.
• **Coolant Temperature Sensor (CTS)**—is located on the top left side of engine, in coolant outlet.
• **Coolant Temperature Switch**—is located on the lower left rear of radiator.
• **Cruise Control Module**—is located at the right kick panel, behind the trim panel.
• **Diagnostic Energy Reserve Module (DERM)**—is located behind front console panel.
• **Diode Box 1**—is located on the left side of engine compartment, in fuse/relay box.
• **Diode Box 3**—is located on the right side of engine compartment, in relay box.
• **Dropping Resistor**—is located in left rear of engine compartment, below brake fluid reservoir.
• **Electro Thermo Unit**—is located on the right side of instrument, behind the glove box.
• **Electronic Control Module (ECM)**—is located behind the left side of instrument panel
• **Exhaust Gas Recirculation (EGR) Vacuum Switching Valve**—is located on top left side of engine, behind the distributor assembly.
• **Flasher Unit**—is located behind the left side of instrument panel, on bracket.
• **Fog Light Relay**—is located on the right side of engine compartment, in relay box.
• **Forward Discriminating Sensor**—is located behind the center of front bumper.
• **Fuel Pump Relay**—is located on the left side of engine compartment, in fuse/relay box.

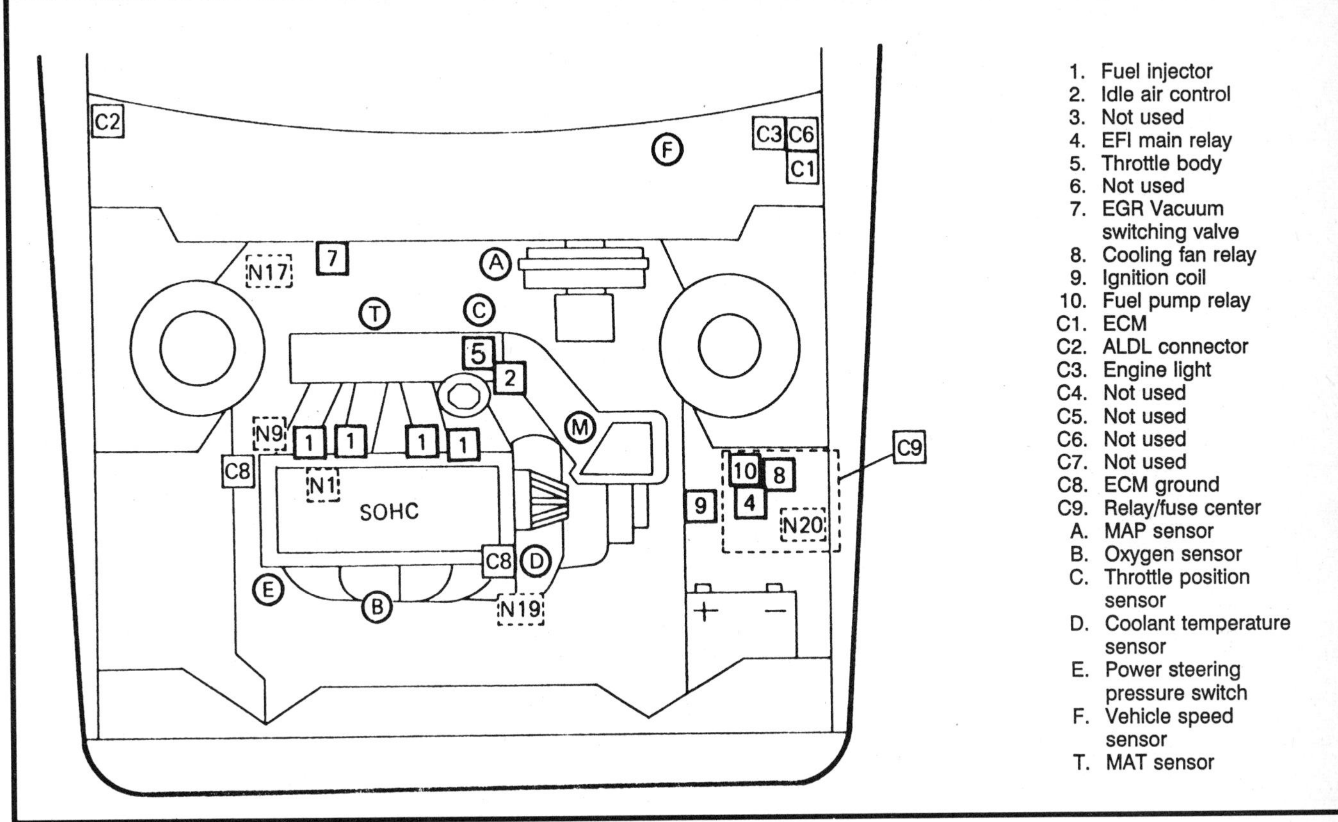

Components location—Stylus with SOHC

- **Fuse/Relay Box**—is located on the left side of engine compartment, next to strut tower.
- **Horn Relay**—is located on the right side of engine compartment, in relay box.
- **Idle Air Control Valve**—is located on top left rear of engine, on throttle valve assembly.
- **Inhibitor Switch**—is located in lower left side of engine compartment, on top of transaxle.
- **Intake Air Vacuum Switching Valve**—is located in left rear of engine, below the common chamber.
- **Junction Block**—is located at left kick panel, behind the trim panel.
- **Main Relay**—is located on the left side of engine compartment, in fuse/relay box.
- **Manifold Absolute Pressure (MAP) Sensor**—is located in the left rear of engine compartment.
- **Manifold Air Temperature (MAT) Sensor**—is located in top left rear corner of engine, in rear of common chamber.
- **Neutral Relay**—is located in the right side of engine compartment, in relay box.
- **Neutral Switch**—is located in the lower left side of engine compartment, on top of transaxle.
- **Oil Pressure Switch**—is located in lower center rear of engine, near oil filter.
- **Oxygen Sensor**—is located in lower front of engine, in exhaust manifold.
- **Park Switch**—is located under floor console, under the shifter control.
- **Parking Brake Switch**—is located under rear of floor console, on parking brake shaft.
- **Passenger Compartment Discriminating Sensor**—is located behind front console, under diagnostic energy reserve module (DERM).
- **Power Steering Pressure Switch**—is located in right front corner of engine, in power steering oil pump
- **Power Window Relay**—is located behind left side of instrument panel, on bracket.
- **Radiator Fan Relay**—is located on the left side of engine compartment, in fuse/relay box.
- **Radiator Fan Test Connector C539 (1-CLR)**—is located in left rear of engine compartment, taped to harness.
- **Rear Defogger Relay**—is located behind left side of instrument panel, on bracket.
- **Relay Box**—is located on the right side of engine compartment.
- **Resistor Block**—is located behind right side of instrument panel, on heater unit.
- **Restart Relay**—is located on the left side of engine compartment, in fuse/relay box.
- **Rise-Up/Intermittent Relay**—is located behind the left side of instrument panel, on bracket.
- **Shift Lock Control Unit**—is located under floor console, under the shifter console.
- **Shift Lock Solenoid**—is located under floor console, in front of shifter control
- **SIR Arming Sensor**—is located behind center of instrument panel.
- **SIR Forward Discriminating Sensor**—is located behind the center of front bumper.
- **SIR Passenger Compartment Discriminating Sensor**—is located behind front console, under diagnostic energy reserve module (DERM).
- **SIR Resistor Module**—is located behind left side of instrument panel, on top of steering column.
- **Thermo Switch**—is located on top left side of engine, in coolant outlet.

• **Thermo Switch Relay**—is located on the right side of engine compartment, in relay box.

• **Throttle Position Sensor (TPS)**—is located in top left rear corner of engine, on throttle valve assembly.

• **Transmission Control Module (TCM)**—is located behind the left side of instrument panel.

• **Transmission Control Module (TCM) Diagnostic Connector C406 (5-GRN)**—is located at the right kick panel, behind trim panel.

• **Triple Pressure Switch**—is located right of condenser, on receiver/drier.

ISUZU TRUCKS

Circuit Breakers

AMIGO

A 20 amp circuit breaker is used to protect the power window circuit, and is located in the dash fuse box.

PICK-UP

A 20 amp circuit breaker is used to protect the power window circuit, and is located in the dash fuse box.

RODEO

A 20 amp circuit breaker is used to protect the power window circuit, and is located in the dash fuse box.

TROOPER AND TROOPER II

This vehicle does not incorporate circuit breakers.

Fusible Links

In addition to circuit breakers and fuses, some circuits use fusible links to protect the wiring. Like fuses, the fusible links are ONE TIME protection devices that will melt and create an open circuit.

The fusible links used on the newer vehicles may also be called main fuses or maxi-fuses. They are large plug-in type protection devices. These fusible links are inspected and replace in the same manner as fuses.

The fusible links or maxi-fuses are located in the relay and fuse block locations and can be identified by there large size and amperage rating.

Relays, Sensors, Modules and Computer Locations

AMIGO

• **A/C Heater Relay**—is located on the right side of the engine compartment, in the fuse/relay box.

• **Air Control Vacuum Switching Valve**—is located in the left front of engine compartment

• **Air Flow Sensor**—is located left front of engine compartment, on the air flow assembly.

• **Air Injection Reactor Vacuum Switching Valve**—is located on the left side of the engine compartment, on inner fender panel.

• **Air Injector Vacuum Switching Valve**—is located on the left side of engine compartment, on the inner fender

• **Assembly Line Diagnostic Link (ALDL) Connector**—is located below the left side of dash, at kick panel.

• **Back-Up Light Switch**—is located on the left side the transmission.

• **Brake Fluid Level Switch**—is located in the left rear of engine compartment, in brake fluid reservoir.

• **Brake Light Switch**—is located behind the left side of dash, on brake pedal support.

• **Canister Vacuum Switching Valve**—is located on the right side of the engine compartment, on the inner fender panel, next to ignition vacuum switching valve.

• **Canister Purge Control Vacuum Switching Valve**—is located on the right side of the engine compartment, on the inner fender panel.

• **Charge Relay**—is located on the right side of engine compartment, in the fuse/relay box.

• **Chime Control Unit**—is located behind right side of dash, at kick panel.

• **Clutch Start Switch**—is located behind left side of dash, on clutch pedal support.

• **Combination Switch**—is located on the top left side of the steering column.

• **Coolant Temperature Gauge Sender**—is located on the right side of engine in the intake manifold.

• **Coolant Temperature Sensor**—is located on the right side of engine, in the intake manifold.

• **Crank Angle Sensor**—is located in the right rear of engine, in bottom of the distributor assembly.

• **Dash Fuse Box**—is located on the left side of dash, behind panel.

• **Diagnostic Start Terminals C104 and C516**—are located below the left side of dash, at kick panel.

• **Diode Box A and B**—are located on the right side of the engine compartment, in the fuse/relay box.

• **Duty Solenoid (2.3L engine)**—is located on top center of the engine, in front of carburetor.

• **Duty Solenoid (2.6L engine)**—is located on top rear center of engine, on the valve cover.

• **EFE Heater Relay**—is located in the right side of the engine compartment, in fuse/relay box.

• **Electronic Control Module**—is located below the left side of dash, at kick panel.

• **Electronic Control Module (ECM) Relay**—is located in the right side of the engine compartment, in the fuse/relay box.

• **Exhaust Gas Recirculation (EGR) Sensor**—is located top rear center of engine, on intake manifold.

• **Exhaust Gas Recirculation Vacuum Switching Valve**—is located top rear center of engine, on the valve cover.

• **Exhaust Gas Temperature Sensor**—is located on lower right side of engine, below the intake manifold.

• **Fast Idle Solenoid Valve (2.6L engine)**—is located on the right side of the engine compartment, on inner fender panel, near fuse/relay box.

• **Flasher Unit**—is located on the left side of dash, above the kick panel.

• **Four Wheel Drive (4WD) Indicator Light**—is located on the right side of transmission.

• **Fuel Pump Relay**—is located on the right side of the engine compartment, in the fuse/relay box.

• **Fuse/Relay Box**—is located on the right side of the engine compartment, on the inner fender panel.

• **Headlight Relay**—is located on the right side of the engine compartment, in the fuse/relay box.

• **Idle Vacuum Switch**—is located on the right side of engine , on inner fender panel, near fuse/relay box.

• **Ignition Vacuum Switching Valve**—is located on the right side of engine compartment.

• **Main Fuse 1**—is located on the right side of the engine compartment, in the fuse/relay box.

• **Main Fuse 2**—is located on the right side of the engine compartment, in the fuse/relay box.

• **Manifold Absolute Pressure Vacuum Switching Valve**—is located on the right side of engine compartment, on inner fender panel, next to the fuse/relay box.

• **Oil Pressure Sending Unit**—is located on the lower right front of engine, near the oil filter.

• **Oil Pressure Switch**—is located in the lower right,rear of engine, above oil pan.

• **Oxygen Sensor**—is located on lower left side of engine, in the exhaust manifold.

• **Parking Brake Switch**—is located behind left side of dash, above the kick panel.

• **Pressure Regulator Control Vacuum Switching Valve**—is located on the right side of engine compartment, on the inner fender panel, next to the fuse/relay box.

• **Rear Wheel Anti-Lock Brake Controller**—is located behind right side of dash, above kick panel.

• **Rear Wheel Anti-Lock Brake Valve**—is located under right side of vehicle, on inside frame rail.

• **Slow Cut Solenoid**—is located on top center of engine, on rear of carburetor.

• **Throttle Valve Switch**—is located on the top rear center of engine, on throttle assembly.

• **Wiper Relay**—is located on the right side of the engine compartment, in the fuse/relay box.

PICK-UP

• **A/C Diode**—is located on the right side of dash, behind the glove box.

• **A/C Dual Pressure Switch**—is located behind the left side of radiator grille.

• **A/C Heater Relay**—is located on the right side of engine compartment, in fuse/relay box.

• **Air Flow Sensor**—is located in left front of engine compartment, on air flow assembly.

• **Air Injection Reactor Vacuum Switching Valve**—is located on the left side of engine compartment, on inner fender panel.

• **Air Regulator**—is located on the lower right rear of engine, below the intake manifold.

• **Altitude Switch**—is located behind the right side of dash, above the kick panel.

• **Assembly Line Diagnostic Link**—is located below the left side of dash, at kick panel.

• **Back-Up Light Switch (manual transmission)**—is located on the left side of transmission.

• **Back-Up Light Switch (automatic transmission)**—is located on the right side of transmission.

• **Brake Fluid Level Switch**—is located left rear of engine compartment, in brake fluid reservoir.

• **Brake Light Switch**—is located behind left side of dash, on clutch pedal support.

• **Canister Purge Control Vacuum Switching Valve**—is located on the right side of engine compartment, on fender inner panel.

• **Canister Vacuum Switching Valve**—is located on the right side of engine compartment, on inner fender panel

• **Charge Relay**—is located on the right side of engine compartment, in fuse/relay box.

• **Chime Control Unit**—is located behind the right side of dash, above the kick panel.

• **Clutch Interrupt Switch**—is located behind the left side of dash, on clutch pedal support.

• **Clutch Start Switch**—is behind the left side of dash, on the clutch pedal support.

• **Coolant Temperature Gauge Sender**—is located on the right side of engine, below the intake manifold.

• **Coolant Temperature Sensor (CTS)**—is located on the right side of engine, below the intake manifold.

• **Crank Angle Sensor**—is located on the right rear of engine, in bottom of distributor assembly.

• **Cruise Control Module**—is located below right side of dash, at kick panel.

• **Dash Fuse Box**—s located on the left side of dash, behind panel.

• **Diagnostic Start Terminals C104, C516 and 517**—are located below the left side of dash, at kick panel.

• **Diode Box A and B**—is located on the right side of engine compartment, in fuse/relay box.

• **Diode Box C, D and E**—is located behind left side of dash, taped to harness.

• **Dual Pressure Switch**—is located behind the left side of radiator grille.

• **Duty Solenoid (2.3L engine)**—is located on the top center of engine, in front of carburetor

• **EFE Heater Relay**—is located on the right side of engine compartment, in fuse/relay box.

• **Electronic Control Module (ECM)**—is located below the left side of dash, at kick panel.

• **Electronic Control Module (ECM) Relay**—is located on the right side of engine compartment, in fuse/relay box.

• **Evaporator Temperature Switch**—is located on the right side of dash, behind glove box.

• **Exhaust Gas Recirculation (EGR) Sensor**—is located on top rear center of engine, on valve cover.

• **Exhaust Gas Temperature Sensor**—is located on lower right engine, below the intake manifold.

• **Fast Idle Solenoid Valve (2.3L engine)**—is located on the right rear of engine.

• **Fast Idle Solenoid Valve (2.6L engine)**—is located on the right side of engine compartment, on inner fender panel, near fuse/relay box.

• **Flasher Unit**—is located behind the left side of dash, above the kick panel.

• **Four Wheel Drive Indicator Light**—is located on the right side of transmission.

• **Fuel Pump Relay**—is located on the right side of engine compartment, in fuse/relay box.

• **Fuse/Relay Box**—is located on the right side of engine compartment, on inner fender panel.

• **Headlight Relay**—is located on the right side of engine compartment, in fuse/relay box.

• **Idle Position Switch**—is located on the right side of engine compartment, on inner fender panel.

• **Idle Vacuum Switch**—is located on the right side of engine compartment, on inner fender panel, next to WOT position switch.

• **Ignition Vacuum Switching Valve**—is located on the right side of engine compartment, on inner fender panel.

• **Inhibitor Switch**—is located on the left side of transmission.

• **Inlet Air Temperature Switch**—is located on the top center of engine, in air cleaner.

• **Manifold Absolute Pressure Vacuum Switching Valve**—is located on the right side of engine compartment, on inner fender panel.

• **Neutral Safety Switch**—is located on the right side of transmission.

• **Oil Pressure Sending Unit**—is located on the lower right front of engine, near the oil filter.

- **Oil Pressure Switch**—is located on the lower right rear of engine, above the oil pan.
- **Overdrive Off Relay**—is located on the right side of engine compartment, in fuse/relay box.
- **Overdrive Off Solenoid**—is located on left side of transmission.
- **Oxygen Sensor**—is located on the lower left side of engine, in the exhaust manifold.
- **Parking Brake Switch**—is located behind the left side of dash, on parking brake lever.
- **Power Window Relay**—is located behind right side of dash, above kick panel.
- **Pressure Differential Switch**—is located in left rear of engine compartment, in brake fluid valve.
- **Rear Wheel Anti-Lock Brake Controller**—is located under the right front seat.
- **Rear Wheel Anti-Lock Brake Valve**—Under right side of vehicle, on inside frame rail.
- **Slow-Cut Solenoid**—is located on the top center of engine, on rear of carburetor.
- **Starter Relay**—is located on the right side of engine compartment, in fuse/relay box.
- **Tachometer Test Connector**—is located on the right side of engine compartment, behind the fuse/relay box.
- **Throttle Position Sensor (TPS)**—is located on top rear center of engine, on throttle assembly.
- **Throttle Valve Switch**—is located on top rear center of engine, on throttle assembly.
- **Vent Switch Valve**—is located on top center of engine, on front of carburetor.
- **Wiper Relay**—is located on the right side of engine compartment, in fuse box relay.
- **WOT Position Switch**—is located on the right side of engine compartment, on inner fender panel.

RODEO

- **A/C Diode**—is located on the right side of dash, behind the glove box.
- **A/C Dual Pressure Switch**—is located behind the left side of radiator grille.
- **A/C Heater Relay**—is located on the right side of engine compartment, in fuse/relay box.
- **Air Flow Sensor**—is located in left front of engine compartment, on air flow assembly.
- **Air Injection Reactor Vacuum Switching Valve**—is located on the left side of engine compartment, on inner fender panel.
- **Air Regulator**—is located on the lower right rear of engine, below the intake manifold.
- **Altitude Switch**—is located behind the right side of dash, above the kick panel.
- **Assembly Line Diagnostic Link**—is located below the left side of dash, at kick panel.
- **Back-Up Light Switch (manual transmission)**—is located on the left side of transmission.
- **Back-Up Light Switch (automatic transmission)**—is located on the right side of transmission.
- **Brake Fluid Level Switch**—is located left rear of engine compartment, in brake fluid reservoir.
- **Brake Light Switch**—is located behind left side of dash, on clutch pedal support.
- **Canister Purge Control Vacuum Switching Valve**—is located on the right side of engine compartment, on fender inner panel.
- **Canister Vacuum Switching Valve**—is located on the right side of engine compartment, on inner fender panel
- **Charge Relay**—is located on the right side of engine compartment, in fuse/relay box.
- **Chime Control Unit**—is located behind the right side of dash, above the kick panel.
- **Clutch Interrupt Switch**—is located behind the left side of dash, on clutch pedal support.
- **Clutch Start Switch**—is behind the left side of dash, on the clutch pedal support.
- **Coolant Temperature Gauge Sender**—is located on the right side of engine, below the intake manifold.
- **Coolant Temperature Sensor (CTS)**—is located on the right side of engine, below the intake manifold.
- **Crank Angle Sensor**—is located on the right rear of engine, in bottom of distributor assembly.
- **Cruise Control Module**—is located below right side of dash, at kick panel.
- **Dash Fuse Box**—s located on the left side of dash, behind panel.
- **Diagnostic Start Terminals C104, C516 and 517**—are located below the left side of dash, at kick panel.
- **Diode Box A and B**—is located on the right side of engine compartment, in fuse/relay box.
- **Diode Box C, D and E**—is located behind left side of dash, taped to harness.
- **Dual Pressure Switch**—is located behind the left side of radiator grille.
- **Duty Solenoid (2.3L engine)**—is located on the top center of engine, in front of carburetor
- **EFE Heater Relay**—is located on the right side of engine compartment, in fuse/relay box.
- **Electronic Control Module (ECM)**—is located below the left side of dash, at kick panel.
- **Electronic Control Module (ECM) Relay**—is located on the right side of engine compartment, in fuse/relay box.
- **Evaporator Temperature Switch**—is located on the right side of dash, behind glove box.
- **Exhaust Gas Recirculation (EGR) Sensor**—is located on top rear center of engine, on valve cover.
- **Exhaust Gas Temperature Sensor**—is located on lower right engine, below the intake manifold.
- **Fast Idle Solenoid Valve (2.3L engine)**—is located on the right rear of engine.
- **Fast Idle Solenoid Valve (2.6L engine)**—is located on the right side of engine compartment, on inner fender panel, near fuse/relay box.
- **Flasher Unit**—is located behind the left side of dash, above the kick panel.
- **Four Wheel Drive Indicator Light**—is located on the right side of transmission.
- **Fuel Pump Relay**—is located on the right side of engine compartment, in fuse/relay box.
- **Fuse/Relay Box**—is located on the right side of engine compartment, on inner fender panel.
- **Headlight Relay**—is located on the right side of engine compartment, in fuse/relay box.
- **Idle Position Switch**—is located on the right side of engine compartment, on inner fender panel.
- **Idle Vacuum Switch**—is located on the right side of engine compartment, on inner fender panel, next to WOT position switch.
- **Ignition Vacuum Switching Valve**—is located on the right side of engine compartment, on inner fender panel.
- **Inhibitor Switch**—is located on the left side of transmission.
- **Inlet Air Temperature Switch**—is located on the top center of engine, in air cleaner.
- **Manifold Absolute Pressure Vacuum Switching Valve**—is located on the right side of engine compartment, on inner fender panel.
- **Neutral Safety Switch**—is located on the right side of transmission.
- **Oil Pressure Sending Unit**—is located on the lower right front of engine, near the oil filter.
- **Oil Pressure Switch**—is located on the lower right rear of engine, above the oil pan.

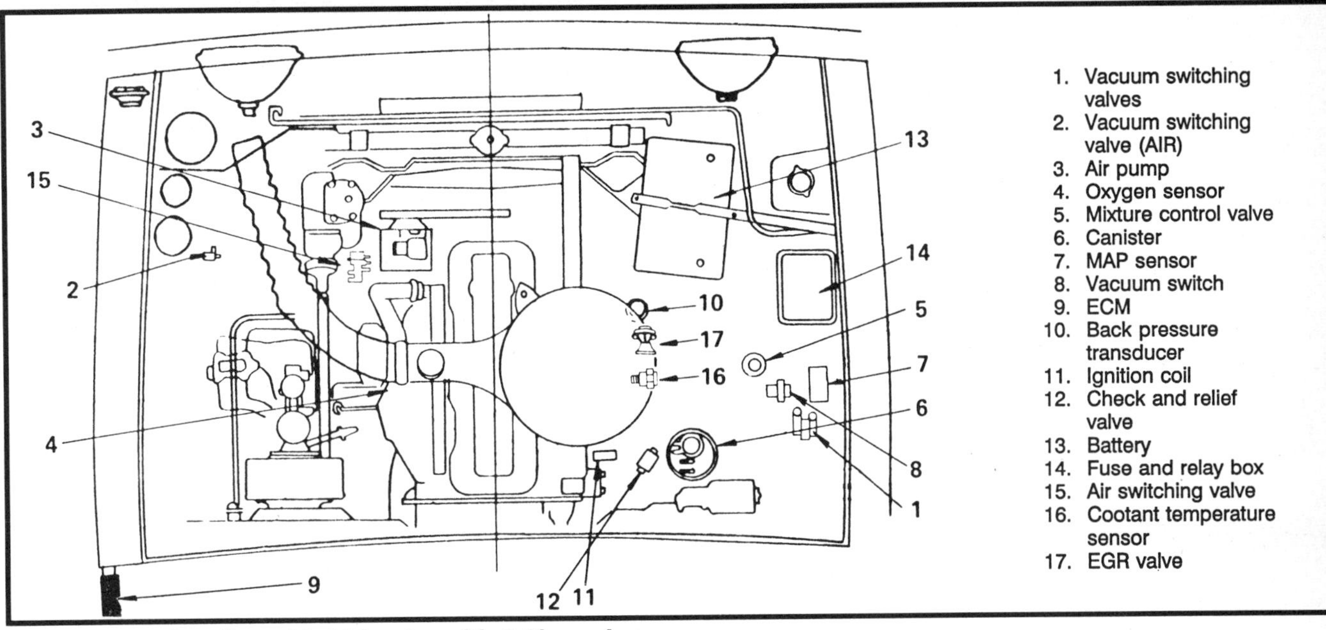

Components location—Light trucks with 2.3L engine

• **Overdrive Off Relay**—is located on the right side of engine compartment, in fuse/relay box.
• **Overdrive Off Solenoid**—is located on left side of transmission.
• **Oxygen Sensor**—is located on the lower left side of engine, in the exhaust manifold.
• **Parking Brake Switch**—is located behind the left side of dash, on parking brake lever.
• **Power Window Relay**—is located behind right side of dash, above kick panel.
• **Pressure Differential Switch**—is located in left rear of engine compartment, in brake fluid valve.
• **Rear Wheel Anti-Lock Brake Controller**—is located under the right front seat.
• **Rear Wheel Anti-Lock Brake Valve**—Under right side of vehicle, on inside frame rail.
• **Slow-Cut Solenoid**—is located on the top center of engine, on rear of carburetor.
• **Starter Relay**—is located on the right side of engine compartment, in fuse/relay box.
• **Tachometer Test Connector**—is located on the right side of engine compartment, behind the fuse/relay box.
• **Throttle Position Sensor (TPS)**—is located on top rear center of engine, on throttle assembly.
• **Throttle Valve Switch**—is located on top rear center of engine, on throttle assembly.
• **Vent Switch Valve**—is located on top center of engine, on front of carburetor.
• **Wiper Relay**—is located on the right side of engine compartment, in fuse box relay.
• **WOT Position Switch**—is located on the right side of engine compartment, on inner fender panel.

TROOPER AND TROOPER II

• **A/C Blower In-Line Fuse**—is located behind left side of instrument panel, on the steering column.
• **A/C Blower Relay**—is located on left front corner of engine compartment.
• **A/C Compressor Cut-Out Relay No. 2**—is located on right side of engine compartment, behind the relay bracket.
• **A/C Defrost Solenoid**—is located below right side of instrument panel.
• **A/C Dual Pressure Switch**—is located in left front of engine compartment, on A/C reservoir tank.
• **AIR Control Solenoid**—is located on the left side of engine compartment, below fuse block.
• **Air Flow Sensor**—is located on left front side of engine compartment, on air intake duct.
• **AIR Regulator Solenoid**—is located on lower right side of engine compartment, ahead of starter assembly.
• **AIR Vacuum Switching Valve**—is located on lower right front of engine.
• **ALCL Connector**—is located on left side of engine compartment, below fuse block.
• **Assembly Line Diagnostic Link (ALDL) Connector**—is located on center of floor, below the console.
• **Blower Cut-Out Relay**—is located below left side of instrument panel, on heater plenum housing.
• **Brake Fluid Level Switch**—is located in left rear of engine compartment, in brake fluid reservoir.
• **Brake Switch**—is located below left side of instrument panel, on brake pedal support.
• **Chime Control Module**—is located behind the right side of instrument panel, near kick panel.
• **Clutch/Start Switch**—iss located below left side of instrument panel, on clutch pedal support.
• **Coolant Temperature Sensor (2.6L engine)**—is located on lower right side of engine, below intake manifold.
• **Coolant Temperature Sensor (2.8L engine)**—is located on top center of engine, near coolant outlet.
• **Coolant Temperature Switch**—is located on the right side of engine, below intake manifold, next to coolant temperature sensor.
• **Cruise Control Module**—is located on the right side of instrument panel, behind glove box.
• **Detonation Sensor**—is located on lower right side of engine.
• **Diagnostic Test Connector**—is located on center of floor, below console.
• **Diode Box A**—is located behind left side of instrument panel, near the kick panel.

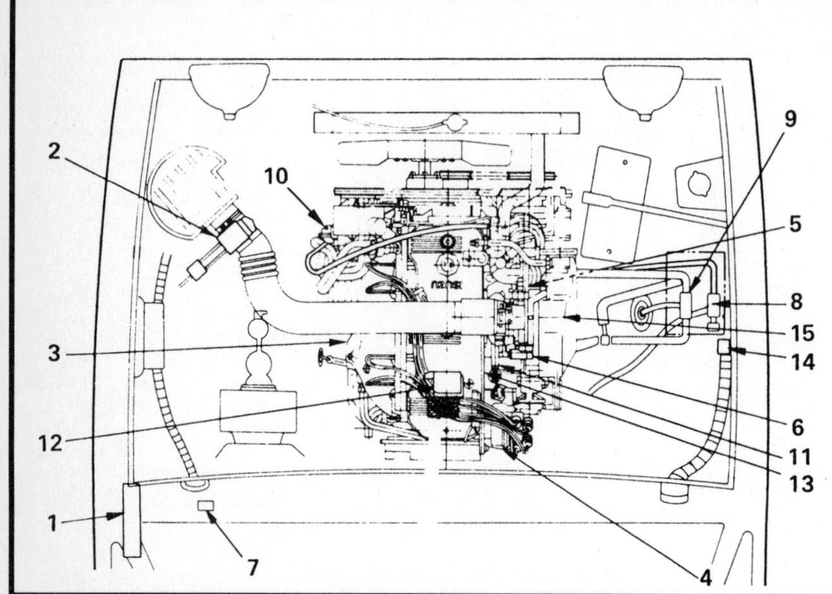

1. ECM
2. Air flow sensor
3. Oxygen sensor
4. Crank angle sensor
5. Coolant Temperature Sensor
6. Throttle valve switch
7. Speed sensor (in speedometer)
8. Purge control vacuum switching valve
9. Pressure regulator vacuum switching valve
10. AIR management valve
11. Fuel injector
12. Ignition coil
13. Power switch
14. MAP gas temperature sensor (California only)
15. Air regulator

Components location—Light trucks with 2.6L engine

- **Dropping Resistor Assembly**—is located in right rear of engine compartment, on bracket.
- **EGR Sensor**—is located on top right rear of engine.
- **Electronic Control Module**—is located on center of floor, below console.
- **Electronic Spark Control Module**—is located on the right side of engine compartment, on inner fender panel.
- **Electronic Transmission Controller (ETC)**—is located behind left side of instrument panel, near kick panel.
- **Exhaust Gas Recirculation Control Module**—is located in right rear corner of engine.
- **Fast Idle Solenoid**—is located on the right side of engine compartment.
- **Fuel Pump Relay Diodes**—is located below left side of instrument panel, above kick panel.
- **Fuse Block**—is located on the left side of engine compartment.
- **Fusible Link Box**—is located on right front corner of engine compartment.
- **Hazard Relay**—is located below left side of instrument panel, on brake pedal support.
- **Heater High Speed Blower Relay**—is located below left side of instrument panel, on heater plenum housing.
- **High Beam Headlight Relay**—is located on right side of engine compartment, behind wiper/washer reservoir.
- **Idle Air Control Valve**—is located on top center of engine.
- **In-Line Diode A**—is located below left side of instrument panel, above kick panel.
- **In-Line Diode B**—is located on right side of instrument panel, behind glove box.
- **In-Line Resistor**—is located behind left side of instrument panel, above the kick panel.
- **Knock (Detonation) Sensor**—is located on lower right side of engine.
- **Low Beam Headlight Relay**—is located on right side of engine compartment, behind wiper/washer reservoir.
- **Main Relay**—is located on the right side of engine compartment, on bracket.
- **Manifold Absolute Pressure (MAP) Sensor**—is located on top center of engine, on left side of air cleaner.
- **Neutral Switch**—is located under vehicle, on top of transmission.
- **Oil Pressure Switch (2.8L engine)**—is located on lower left side of engine, near starter assembly.
- **Oxygen Sensor (2.6L engine)**—is located on left side of engine, in exhaust manifold.
- **Oxygen Sensor (2.8L engine)**—is located under left side of vehicle, in front of catalytic converter.
- **Park Brake Switch**—is located below left side of instrument panel, on park brake shaft
- **Pressure Regulator Control Solenoid**—is located on right side of engine compartment, on bracket.
- **Purge Control Solenoid**—is located on right side of engine compartment, on bracket.
- **Rear Defogger In-Line Fuse**—is located behind left side of instrument panel, right of steering column.
- **Rear Defogger Relay**—is located on right side of engine compartment, on bracket.
- **Recirculating/Outside Air Solenoid**—is located below right side of instrument panel, behind glove box.
- **Refrigerant Temperature Switch**—is located on the right side of engine compartment, behind glove box.
- **Starter Relay**—is located on the right side of engine compartment, on relay bracket.
- **Temperature Sending Unit Resistor**—is located on the right side of engine, below intake manifold.
- **Throttle Position Sensor**—is located on top center of engine, behind throttle assembly.
- **Throttle Valve Switch**—is located on top center of engine, behind throttle assembly.
- **Transfer Case Oil Temperature Sensor**—is located on left rear side of transmission.
- **Transfer Position Switch (automatic transmission)**—is located on left side of transmission.
- **Transmission Diagnostic Connector**—is located under the left side of instrument panel, near the ECT.
- **Transmission Oil Temperature Sensor**—is located on the right side of transmission.
- **Transmission Position Switch**—is located under vehicle, on right side of transmission.

• **Turn Signal and Hazard Relay**—is located below left side of instrument panel, on brake pedal support.
• **Vehicle Speed Sensor No. 2 (2.6L engine)**—is located under vehicle, on left side of transmission.
• **Vehicle Speed Sensor No. 2 (2.8L engine)**—is located below left side of instrument panel, at kick panel.

LEXUS

Circuit Breakers

ES 250

Fuses are located in junction/relay boxes located at the left kick panel, left front of the engine compartment, and the right kick panel.

ES 400

Fuses are located in the junction/relay boxes located at the left side of the steering column, left side of the engine compartment and under the left headlight.

Fusible Links

ES 250

Fusible Links are located in the junction/relay box at the left side of the engine compartment or at the battery positive terminal.

ES 400

Fusible Links are located in the junction/relay box at the left side of the engine compartment.

Relays, Sensors, Modules and Computer Locations

ES 250

• **A/C Amplifier**—is located—is located under the right side of the dash.
• **A/C Compressor Control Amplifier**—is located—is located under the right side of the dash.
• **A/C Compressor Sensor**—is located at the front of the engine near the radiator.
• **A/C Condenser Fan Control Amplifier**—is located—is located under the right side of the dash.
• **A/C Dual Pressure Switch**—is located at the receiver drier.

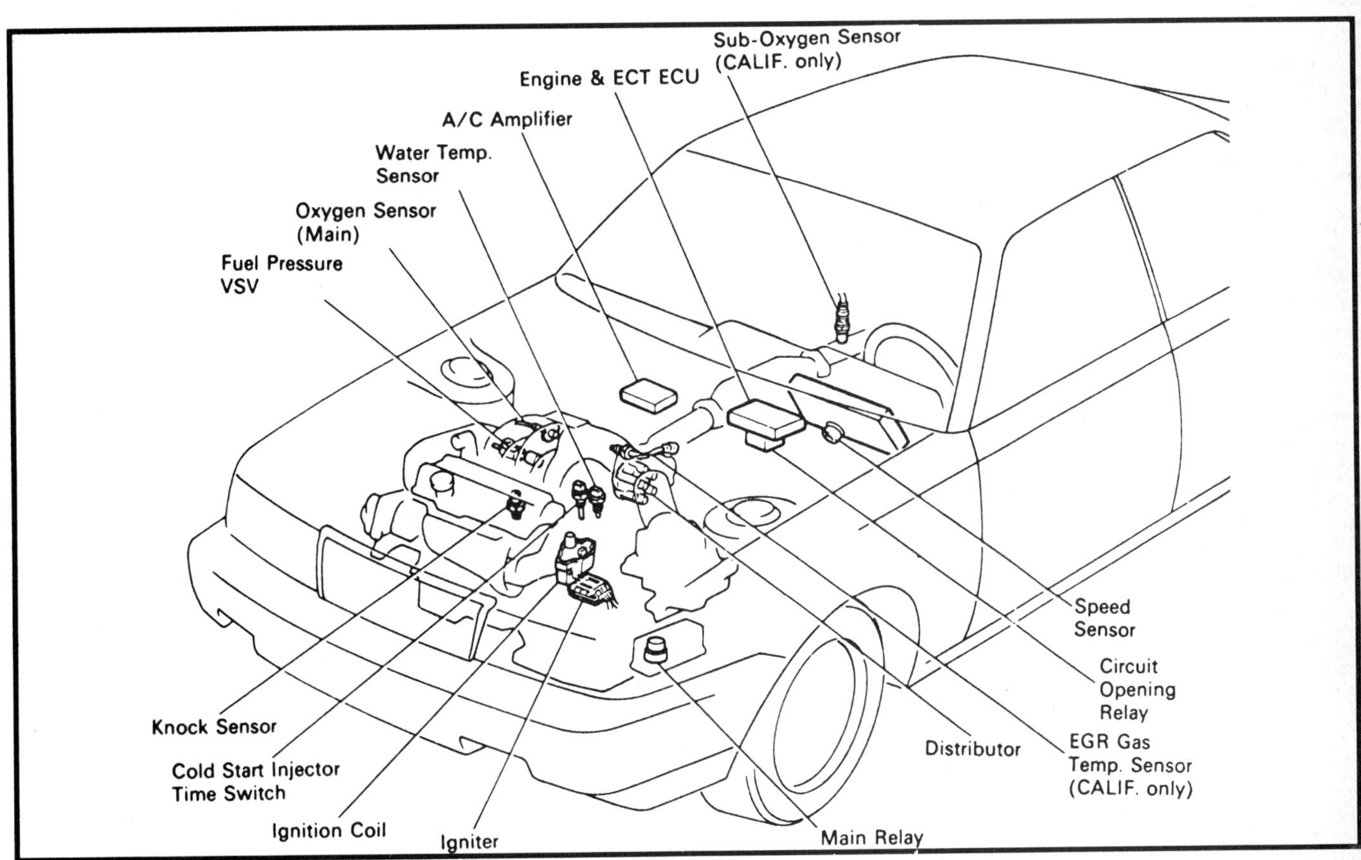

Electronic control systems—ES250

- **A/C Fan Relay 2**—is located in the junction/relay box on the left side of the engine compartment.
- **A/C Fan Relay 3**—is located in the junction/relay box on the left side of the engine compartment.
- **A/C High Pressure Switch (radiator fan)**—is located at the receiver drier.
- **A/C Magnet Clutch Relay**—is located at the left rear of the engine compartment.
- **A/C System Amplifier**—is located—is located under the right side of the dash.
- **ABS Actuator**—is located at the right front of the engine compartment.
- **ABS Electronic Control Unit**—is located at the center front of the trunk.
- **Air Bags**—see ABS.
- **Air Flow Meter**—is located at the air cleaner assembly.
- **Air Inlet Control Relay**—is located at the left rear of the engine compartment.
- **Airbag System**—see Supplemental Restraint System (SRS).
- **Anti-Lock Brake System**—see ABS.
- **Auto Antenna Control Relay**—is located at the left quarter panel inside the trunk.
- **Backup Light Switch (manual transmission)**‹m-dash›is located at the transmission case.
- **Blower Control Relay**—is located—is located under the right side of the dash.
- **Blower Resistor**—is located—is located under the right side of the dash.
- **Brake Fluid Level Switch**—is located in the master cylinder.
- **Canister Vacuum Sensing Valve**—is located near the fuel rail.
- **Check Connector**—is located at the left shock tower.
- **Circuit Opening Relay**—is located—is located under the center console.
- **Coolant Temperature Sensor**—is located on the distributor side of the engine.
- **Cooling Fan ECU**—is located at the center of the firewall.
- **Cooling Fan Relays**—is located the junction/relay box on the left side of the engine compartment.
- **Cruise Control Actuator**—is located on the right side of the engine compartment.
- **Cruise Control ECU**—is located—is located at the right kick panel.
- **Cruise Control Vacuum Pump**—is located on the right side of the engine compartment.
- **Daytime Running Light Relay (Canada)**—is located—is located under the center console.
- **Defogger Relay**—is located in the junction/relay box at the left kick panel.
- **Door Lock/Theft Deterrent**—is located‹m-dash›is located under the right side of the dash.
- **ECT Solenoid**—is located at the transaxle case.
- **EFI Fuel Pressure Vacuum Sensing Valve**—is located at the top of the intake manifold on the alternator side of the engine.
- **EFI Injector Time Switch (cold start)**—is located next to the coolant temperature sensor.
- **EFI Main Relay**—is located in the junction/relay box on the left side of the engine compartment.
- **EGR Temperature Sensor (California)**—is located at the EGR valve.
- **EGR Vacuum Modulator**—is located near the EGR valve.
- **EGR Vacuum Sensing Valve**—is located near the fuel rail.
- **EGR Valve**—is located near the throttle body.
- **Engine and ECT ECU**—is located—is located under the center console.
- **Engine Main Relay**—is located in the junction/relay box on the left side of the engine compartment.
- **Fog Light Relay**—is located under the center of the dash.
- **Fuel Injection**—see Electronic Fuel Injection (EFI).
- **Head Light Relay**—is located in the junction/relay box on the left side of the engine compartment.
- **Heater Relay**—is located in the junction/relay box at the right kick panel.
- **Horn Relay**—is located in the junction/relay box at the right kick panel..
- **Idle Speed Control Valve**—is located at the throttle body.
- **Integration Relay**—is located at the left kick panel.
- **Integration Relay**—is located in the junction/relay box at the left kick panel.
- **Junction/Relay Box 1**—is located at the left kick panel.
- **Junction/Relay Box 2**—is located at the front left of the engine compartment.
- **Junction/Relay Box 4**—is located at the right kick panel.
- **Knock Sensor**—is located in the engine block near the front camshaft cover.
- **Light Failure Sensor**—is located at the right quarter panel inside the trunk.
- **Mirror Heater Relay**—is located—is located under the center console.
- **Moon Roof Control Relay**—is located at the moon roof.
- **Neutral Start Switch (automatic transmission)**‹—is located at the transaxle case.
- **Oxygen Sensor (sub-oxygen sensor)**—is located rearward of the catalytic converter in the exhaust system.
- **Oxygen Sensor**—is located at the front of the engine near the upper radiator hose.
- **PCV Valve**—is located in the rear camshaft cover.
- **Power Main Relay**—is located in the junction/relay box at the left kick panel.
- **Power Seat Front Vertical Motor**—is located under the seat.
- **Power Seat Rear Vertical Motor**—is located under the seat.
- **Power Seat Slide Motor**—is located under the seat.
- **Power Steering Oil Reservoir**—is located on the right side of the engine compartment.
- **Power Steering**—see Progressive Power Steering (PPS).
- **PPS Control Unit**—is located under the right side of the dash.
- **PPS Solenoid**—is located near the master cylinder.
- **Radiator Fan Relay 1**—is located in the junction/relay box on the left side of the engine compartment.
- **Seat Belt Warning Relay**—is located under the center of the dash.
- **Shift Lock Control Computer**—is located under the console.
- **Shift Lock Control Switch**—is located under the console.
- **Shift Lock ECU**—is located—is located under the center console.
- **Shift Lock Solenoid**—is located under the console.
- **Speed Sensor**—is located at the speedometer.
- **SRS Center Sensor Assembly**—is located‹m-dash›is located under the center console.
- **SRS Left Sensor**—is located at the left front of the engine compartment.
- **SRS Right Sensor**—is located at the right front of the engine compartment.
- **Starter Relay**—is located in the junction/relay box at the left kick panel.
- **Taillight Relay**—is located in the junction/relay box at the left kick panel.
- **Theft Deterrent/Door Lock Control Unit**—is located under the right side of the dash.

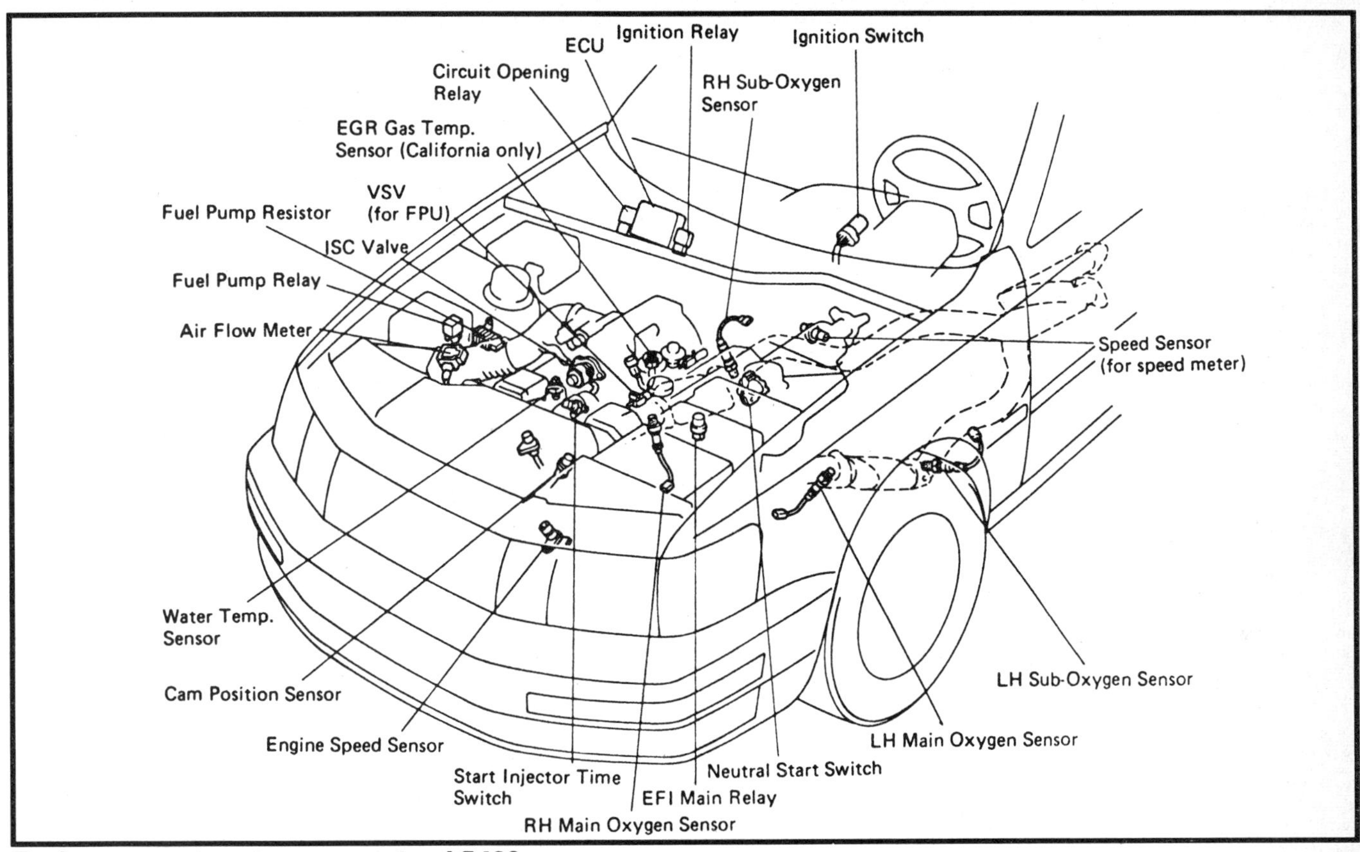

Engine compartment components—LS400

• **Throttle Position Sensor**—is located at the throttle body.
• **Transmission**—see Electronically Controlled Transmission (ECT).
• **Turn Signal Flasher**—is located in the junction/relay box at the left kick panel.

LS 400

• **A/C Ambient Temperature Sensor**—is located behind the front bumper.
• **A/C Clutch Magnet Relay**—is located in the junction/relay box under the left side of the dash.
• **A/C Power Transistor**—is located in the cooling box under the right side of the dash.
• **A/C Pressure Switch**—is located at the receiver drier.
• **A/C Room Temperature Sensor**—is located to the right of the steering column.
• **A/C Solar Sensor**—is located at the right side defogger grille.
• **ABS Actuator**—is located at the right front of the engine compartment.
• **ABS ECU**—is located under the right side of the dash.
• **ABS Relay**—is located at the right front of the engine compartment.
• **Air Bags**—see Supplemental Restraint System (SRS)
Air Flow Meter—is located in the air duct near the air cleaner.
• **Air Suspension ECU**—is located at the right quarter panel inside the trunk.
• **Anti-Lock Brakes**—see Anti-Lock Brake System (ABS).
• **Auto Antenna Relay**—is located at the left quarter panel inside the trunk.
• **Blower Motor Resistor**—is located next to the blower motor.
• **Blower Relay (extra high speed)**—is located under the right side of the dash.
• **Brake Fluid Level Switch**—is located in the master cylinder.
• **Cam Position Sensor**—is located at the front of the camshaft cover.
• **Charcoal Canister Vacuum Sensing Valve**—is located at the left front of the intake manifold.
• **Circuit Opening Relay**—is located under the right side of the dash.
• **Coolant Level Switch**—is located in the overflow bottle.
• **Coolant Level Warning ECU**—is located under the left side of the dash.
• **Coolant Temperature Sender**—is located at the right front of the intake manifold.
• **Cooling Fan Relay 1**—is located in the junction/relay box under the left headlight.
• **Cooling Fan Relay 2**—is located in the junction/relay box under the left headlight.
• **Cooling Fan Relay 3**—is located in the junction/relay box under the left headlight.
• **Cruise Control Actuator**—is located at the firewall.
• **Cruise Control ECU**—is located under the left side of the dash.
• **Dash Pot**—is located at the throttle body.
• **Daytime Running Light Relay**—is located to the right of the steering column.
• **Defogger Relay**—is located in the junction/relay box under the left side of the dash.
• **Dimmer Relay (Canada)**—is located in the junction/relay box under the left side of the dash.

• **Door Lock/Theft Deterrent ECU**—is located under the left side of the dash.
• **ECU Pattern Select Switch**—is located under the console.
• **EFI Main Relay**—is located in the junction/relay box under the left side of the dash.
• **EFI Start Injector Time Switch**—is located the front of the intake manifold.
• **EGR Gas Temperature Sensor**—is located near the EGR valve.
• **EGR Vacuum Sensing Valve**—is located next to the EGR valve.
• **EGR Valve Modulator**—is located forward of the EGR valve.
• **EGR Valve**—is located at the left side of the plenum.
• **Engine and ECT ECU**—is located under the right side of the dash.
• **Engine Main Relay**—is located in the junction/relay box under the left side of the dash.
• **Engine Oil Level Warning Switch**—is located near the oil pan on the right front of the engine.
• **Engine Speed Sensor**—is located at the lower front of the engine.
• **Fog Light Relay**—is located in the junction/relay box under the left side of the dash.
• **Fuel Injection**—see Electronic Fuel Injection (EFI).
• **Fuel Pump Control Relay**—is located at the right front of the engine compartment.
• **Fuel Pump Relay**—is located at the right shock tower.
• **Fuel Pump Resistor**—is located at the right shock tower.
• **Headlight Cleaner Relay**—is located below the left headlight.
• **Headlight Relay**—is located in the junction/relay box at the left side of the engine compartment.
• **Heater Relay**—is located in the junction/relay box under the left side of the dash.
• **Height Control Relay 2**—is located at the right quarter panel inside the trunk.
• **Height Control Relay**—is located in the junction/relay box under the left headlight.
• **Height Control Sensors**—are located at the wheel assemblies.
• **Height Control Valve 1**—is located at the right front of the vehicle.
• **Height Control Valve 2**—is located at the right rear of the vehicle.
• **Horn Relay**—is located in the junction/relay box under the left side of the dash.
• **Ignition Main Relay**—is located under the right side of the dash.
• **Integration Relay**—is located in the junction/relay box under the left side of the dash.
• **Integration Relay**—is located under the left side of the dash.
• **Light Control Rheostat**—is located under the right side of the dash.
• **Light Failure Sensor**—is located at the left front of the trunk.
• **Moonroof Control Relay**—is located at the moonroof.
• **Neutral Start Switch**—is located at the gear selector lever.
• **Oil Pressure Switch**—is located at the left front of the engine.
• **Oil Pressure Switch**—is located at the oil filter.
• **Oxygen Sensor (sub-oxygen sensor)**—is located in the exhaust pipe.
• **Oxygen Sensor**—is located in the exhaust manifold.
• **PCV Valve**—is located in the left camshaft cover.
• **Power Main Relay**—is located in the junction/relay box under the left side of the dash.
• **Power Seat Belt Relay**—is located under the right side of the dash.
• **Power Seat ECU**—is located under the left seat.
• **Power Steering**—see Progressive Power Steering (PPS).
• **PPS ECU**—is located under the left side of the dash.
• **Remote Control Mirror ECU**—is located under the right side of the dash.
• **Seat Belt Warning Relay**—is located to the right of the steering column.
• **Seat Heater Relay**—is located under the right seat.
• **Speed Sensor 1**—is located under the console.
• **Speed Sensor 2**—is located at the transmission case.
• **SRS Center Sensor**—is located under the console at the center of the dash.
• **SRS Left Sensor**—is located at the left front of the engine compartment.
• **SRS Right Sensor**—is located at the right front of the engine compartment.
• **Starter Relay**—is located in the junction/relay box under the left side of the dash.
• **Suspension Control Actuators**—are located at the top of the shock absorbers.
• **Suspension Steering Sensor**—is located in the steering column.
• **Taillight Relay**—is located in the junction/relay box under the left side of the dash.
• **Theft Deterrent/Door Lock ECU**—is located under the left side of the dash.
• **Tilt/Telescopic ECU**—is located under the dash near the steering column.
• **Tilt/Telescopic Motor**—is located inside the steering column.
• **Tilt/Telescopic Position Sensor**—is located inside the steering column.
• **Tilt/Telescopic Switch**—is located inside the steering column.
• **TRAC Brake Main Relay**—is located at the left front of the engine compartment.
• **TRAC Control Motor Relay**—is located at the left rear of the engine compartment.
• **TRAC ECU**—is located under the right side of the dash.
• **TRAC Pump**—is located at the left rear of the engine compartment.
• **TRAC Throttle Relay**—is located under the right side of the dash.
• **Traction Control System**—see TRAC.
• **Turn Signal Flasher**—is located in the junction/relay box on the left side of the steering column.
• **Twin Trip Switch**—is located under the dash to the right of the instrument cluster.
• **Water Temperature Sensor**—is located in the heater box under the center of the dash.
• **Water Temperature Switch**—is located at the bottom of the radiator.
• **Wiper Control Relay**—is located under the left side of the dash.
• **Wireless Door Lock ECU**—is located at the left quarter panel inside the trunk.

MAZDA

Circuit Breakers

323 AND PROTEGE

Fuses are located at the fuse box under the left side of the dash. A circuit breaker is also located above this box.

626 AND MX6

Fuses are located in the fuse box at the left kick panel. A circuit breaker is also located at this box.

929

Fuses are located in the fuse box at the left kick panel.

MIATA

Fuses are located in the fuse box under the left side of the dash. A circuit breaker is located at the fuse box also.

RX7

Fuses are located in the fuse box at the left kick panel. A circuit breaker is also located at this box.

Fusible Links

323 AND PROTEGE

Fusible links are located in the main fuse box at the left side of the engine compartment. The fusible links are of the maxi-fuse type.

626 AND MX6

Fusbile links are located in the main fuse box at the left front of the engine compartment. The fusible links are of the maxi-fuse type.

929

Fusbile links are located in the main fuse box behind the battery. The fusible links are of the maxi-fuse type.

MIATA

Fusible links are located in the main fuse box at the right rear of the engine compartment. The fusible links are of the maxi-fuse type.

RX7

Fusbile links are located in the main fuse box at the left front of the engine compartment. The fusible links are of the maxi-fuse type.

Relays, Sensors, Modules and Computer Locations

323 AND PROTEGE

- **4 Wheel Drive Control Unit**—is located under the left front seat.

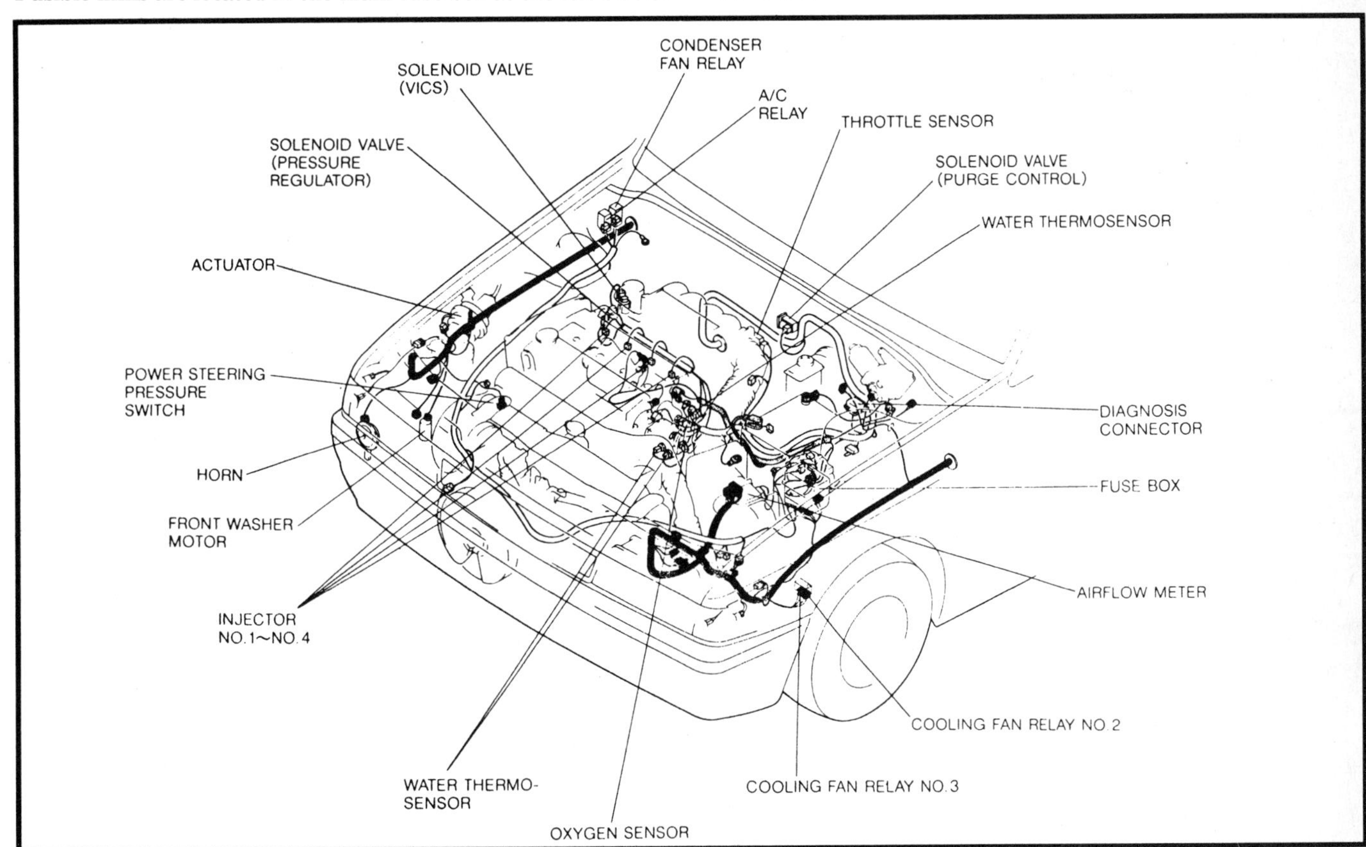

Engine compartment component locations—323 and Protege

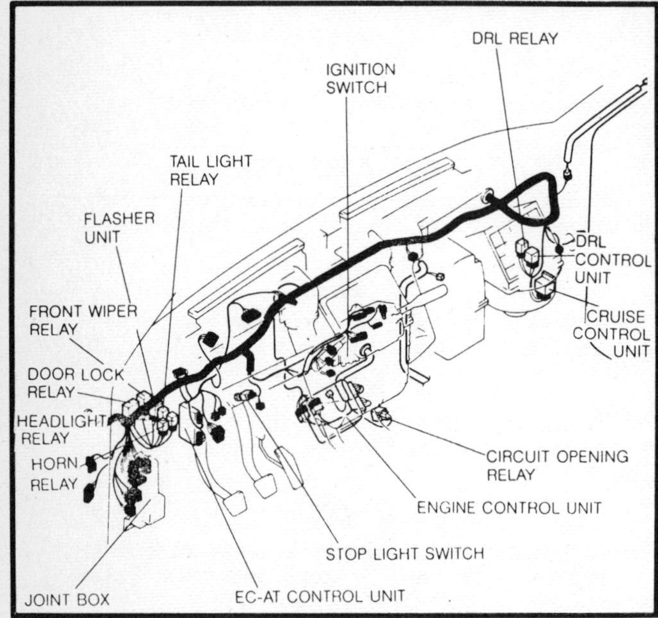

Under-dash component locations—323 and Protege

- **4 Wheel Drive Differential Lock Motor Switch**—is located at the top of the transmission.
- **4 Wheel Drive Differential Lock Sensor**—is located at the top of the transmission.
- **4 Wheel Drive Differential Lock Switch**—is located under the left side of the dash.
- **A/C Condenser Fan Relay**—is located at the right rear of the engine compartment.
- **A/C Diode**—is located —is located at the left front of the engine compartment.
- **A/C Pressure Switch**—is located at the left front of the engine compartment.
- **A/C Relay**—is located at the right rear of the engine compartment.
- **Air Flow Meter**—is located at the left front of the engine.
- **Automatic Transmission Control Unit**—is located under the left side of the dash.
- **Backup Light Switch**—is located at the left side of the engine compartment on the transmission.
- **Blower Resistor**—is located under the right side of the dash.
- **Circuit Opening Relay**—is located under the center of the dash.
- **Coolant Thermosensor**—is located at the front of the engine.
- **Coolant Thermoswitch**—is located at the radiator.
- **Cooling Fan Relay 2 and 3**—are located at the left front fender.
- **Cruise Control Actuator**—is located at the right front of the engine compartment.
- **Cruise Control Unit**—is located under the right side of the dash.
- **Daytime Running Light Control Unit**—is located under the right side of the dash.
- **Daytime Running Light Relay**—is located under the right side of the dash.
- **Diagnosis Connector**—is located at the left rear of the engine compartment.
- **Door Lock Relay**—is located under the left side of the dash.
- **Engine Control Unit (ECU)**—is located under the center of the dash.
- **Flasher Unit**—is located under the left side of the dash.
- **Front Wiper Relay**—is located under the left side of the dash.
- **Fuse Box**—is located at the left front fender.
- **Headlight Relay**—is located under the left side of the dash.
- **Horn Relay**—is located under the left side of the dash.
- **Idle Speed Control Valve**—is located at the throttle body.
- **Inhibitor Switch (and solenoid valve)**—is located at the transmission on the left side of the engine compartment.
- **Interlock Switch**—is located under the left side of the dash.
- **Main Fuse**—is located on the left side of the engine compartment.
- **Neutral Switch**—is located —is located at the transmission on the left side of the engine compartment.
- **Oxygen Sensor**—is located at the front left of the engine.
- **Passive Shoulder Belt Control Unit**—is located under the left front seat.
- **Passive Shoulder Belt Limit Switch**—is located at the windsheild pillar.
- **PCV Valve**—is located at the cylinder head cover.
- **Power Steering Pressure Switch**—is located at the right front of the engine compartment.
- **Pressure Regulator Solenoid Valve**—is located at the top right rear of the engine.
- **Pulse Generator**—is located at the top of the transmission.
- **Purge Control Valve**—is located at the firewall.
- **Radiator Thermoswitch**—is located at the radiator or at the left side of the engine block.
- **Shift Lock Unit**—is located at the gear shift lever.
- **Sunroof Relay**—is located at the sunroof.
- **Taillight Relay**—is located under the left side of the dash.
- **Throttle Sensor**—is located at the rear of the engine.
- **Variable Inertia Charging System**—see VICS.
- **Vehicle Speed Sensor**—is located at the speedometer.
- **VICS Shutter Valve Actuator**—is located at the dynamic chamber on top of the engine.
- **VICS Solenoid Valve**—is located at the top right rear of the engine.
- **Washer Level Sensor**—is located at the washer reservoir bottle.

626 AND MX6

- **A/C Diode**—is located at the receiver drier.
- **A/C Dual Pressure Switch**—is located at the receiver drier.
- **A/C Relay**—is located to the rear of the receiver drier.
- **A/C Resistor**—is located on the cooling unit under the dash.
- **A/C Thermoswitch**—is located on the cooling unit under the dash.
- **AAS Actuators**—are located at the shock absorbers.
- **AAS Check Connector**—is located at the left rear of the engine compartment.
- **AAS Control Unit**—is located under the right front seat.
- **ABS Check Connector**—is located at the ABS control unit.
- **ABS Control Unit**—is located under the left front seat.
- **ABS Motor**—is located at the left front of the engine compartment.
- **ABS Relay**—is located at the hydraulic unit.
- **Air Bypass Valve (turbo)**—is located forward of the distributor.
- **Air Flow Meter**—is located at the air cleaner.
- **Anti-Lock Brakes**—see ABS.
- **Automatic Transaxle Control Unit**—is located to the right of the steering column under the dash.

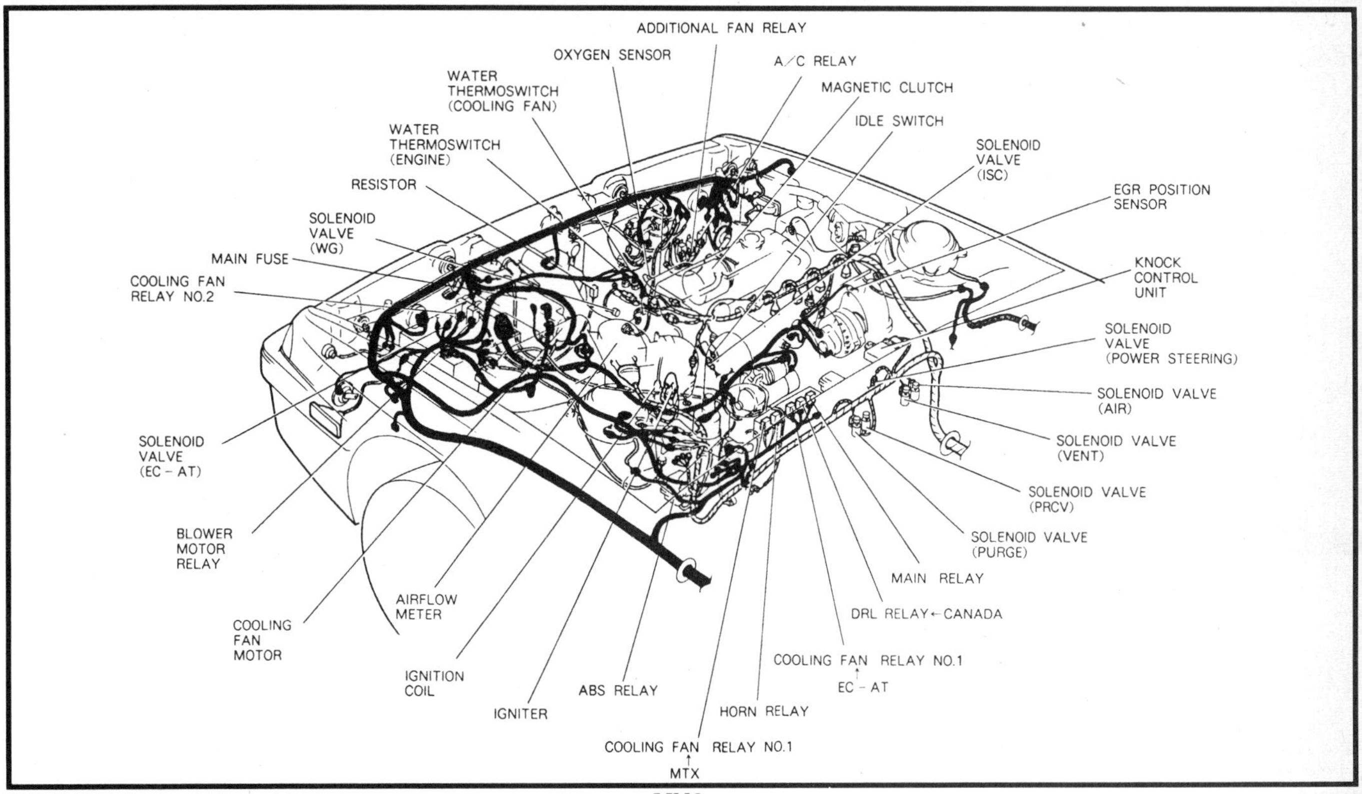

Engine compartment component locations—626 and MX6

• **Backup Light Switch (manual transaxle)**—is located at the front of the transaxle near the radiator.
• **Blower Motor Relay**—is located at the radiator support.
• **Brake Fluid Level Sensor**—is located at the master cylinder.
• **Circuit Opening Relay**—is located at the relay box under the left side of the dash.
• **Coolant Thermosensor**—is located to the right of the distributor.
• **Coolant Thermoswitch**—is located at the thermostat housing on the right side of the engine.
• **Cooling Fan Relay**—is located at the relay box on the firewall.
• **Cruise Control Actuator**—is located at the right side of the engine conpartment.
• **Daytime Running Light Relay**—is located at the relay box on the firewall.
• **Defroster Relay**—is located at the relay box under the left side of the dash.
• **EGI BAC Valve**—is located at the throttle body.
• **EGI Idle Speed Control Valve**—is located at the throttle body.
• **EGI Idle Switch**—is located at the throttle body.
• **EGI Main Fuse**—is located above the distributor.
• **EGI Main Relay**—is located at the firewall.
• **EGI Test Connector**—is located under the wiper motor.
• **EGR Control Valve**—is located at the EGR valve.
• **EGR Modulator Valve**—is located near the injectors on the top of the engine.
• **EGR Position Sensor (California)**—is located at the EGR valve.
• **EGR Solenoid Valve**—is located at the firewall.
• **EGR Valve**—is located at the right front of the intake manifold.

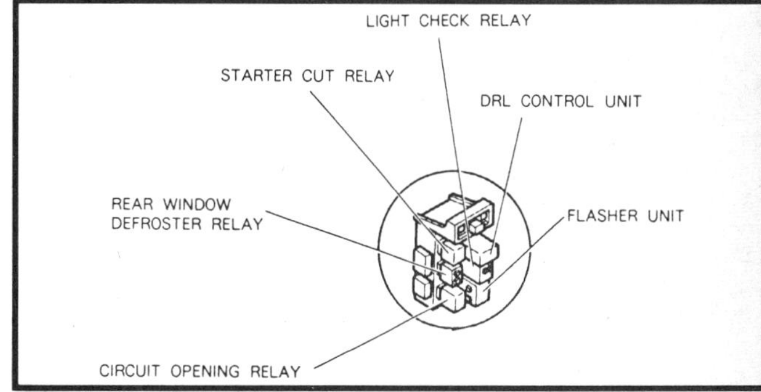

Under-dash component locations—626 and MX6

• **Engine Control Unit**—is located under the center of the dash.
• **Flasher Unit**—is located at the relay box under the left side of the dash.
• **Fuel Injection**—see EGI.
• **Horn Relay**—is located at the relay box on the firewall.
• **Inhibitor Switch (automatic transaxle)**—is located at the top of the transaxle.
• **Inhibitor Switch**—is located at the top of the transaxle.
• **Intake Air Thermosensor**—is located inside the air flow meter.
• **Interlock Switch**—is located at the pedal mounting bracket under the left side of the dash.
• **Knock Sensor**—is located next to the oil filter.
• **Main Fuse Block**—is located near the battery.
• **Main Relay** —is located at the relay box on the firewall.
• **Neutral Switch (manual transaxle)**—is located at the top of the transaxle.

• **Neutral Switch**—is located at the rear of the transaxle near the firewall.

• **Oil Pressure Switch**—is located at the front of the engine.

• **Oxygen Sensor**—is located at the front of the engine.

• **Passive Shoulder Belt Control Unit**—is located under the right front seat.

• **PCV Valve**—is located at the right side of the valve cover.

• **Power Steering Control Unit**—is located under the left front seat.

• **Power Steering Pressure Switch**—is located at the steering unit.

• **Power Steering Solenoid Valve**—is located at the firewall.

• **Pressure Regulator Solenoid Valve**—is located at the firewall.

• **Pulse Generator**—is located at the top of the transaxle.

• **Purge Control Valve**—is located at the firewall.

• **Shift Lock Actuator**—is located at the gear shift lever.

• **Starter Cut Relay**—is located at the relay box under the left side of the dash.

• **Sunroof Relay**—is located at the sunroof motor.

• **Suspension**—see AAS.

• **Taillight Checker**—is located at the relay box under the left side of the dash.

• **Theft Deterrent Control Unit**—is located in the engine control unit.

• **Throttle Sensor**—is located at the throttle body.

• **Transaxle Test Connnector**—is located at the left rear of the engine compartment.

• **Transmission Fluid Thermoswitch**—is located at the top of the transaxle.

• **Under Dash Fuse Box**—is located under the left side of the dash at the kick panel.

• **Vehicle Speed Sensor**—is located at the speedometer.

929

• **A/C Refrigerant Pressure Switch**—is located at the receiver drier.

• **AAS Actuators**—are located at the top of the shock absorbers.

• **AAS Control Unit**—is located at the front of the trunk.

• **ABS Control Unit**—is located at the right kick panel.

• **ABS Hydraulic Unit**—is located at the right rear of the engine compartment.

• **ABS Relay**—is located at the right kick panel.

• **Air Flow Meter**—is located in the air duct near the air cleaner.

• **ATP Sensor**—is located at the right kick panel.

• **Automatic Transmission Check Connector**—is located at the right rear of the engine compartment.

• **Automatic Transmission Control Unit**—is located under the right side of the dash.

• **Automatic Transmission Turbine Sensor**—is located at the transmission bell housing.

• **BAC Valve (DOHC)**—is located at the front of the intake manifold.

• **BAC Valve (SOHC)**—is located at the left rear of the engine.

• **Brake Fluid Level Switch**—is located at the master cylinder.

• **Brake Fluid Pressure Switch**—is located at the master cylinder.

• **Circuit Opening Relay**—is located at the left kick panel.

• **Coolant Thermosensor**—is located at the right front side of the engine.

• **Crank Angle Sensor**—is located at the distributor.

• **Cruise Control Unit**—is located at the left kick panel.

• **Daytime Running Light Control Unit (Canada)**—is located behind the rear seat.

• **Defroster Relay**—is located at the front of the trunk.

• **Door Lock Relay**—is located in the relay box.

• **EGR Control Valve (DOHC)**—is located at the rear of the intake manifold.

• **EGR Control Valve (SOHC)**—is located at the throttle body.

• **EGR Position Sensor**—is located at the top right rear of the engine.

• **EGR Solenoid Valve (DOHC)**—is located at the left rear of the engine compartment.

• **EGR Solenoid Valve (SOHC)**—is located at the top right side of the engine.

• **Emissions Control Unit**—is located at the left kick panel.

• **Engine Control Unit**—is located under the right side of the dash.

• **Flasher/Hazard Relay**—is located in the relay box.

• **Fuel Pressure Test Connector**—is located on the left side of the engine compartment.

• **Fuel Pump Relay**—is located at the left kick panel.

• **Fuse Box**—is located at the left kick panel.

• **Horn Relay**—is located in the relay box.

• **Idle Speed Control Solenoid Valve**—is located at the throttle body.

• **Inhibitor Switch**—is located at the transmission case.

• **Intake Air Thermosensor**—is located at the left side of the intake manifold.

• **Knock Control Unit**—is located at the left side of the engine compartment.

• **Knock Sensors**—are located at the left front and right rear of the engine.

• **Light Checker Relay**—is located in the relay box.

• **Main Fuse**—is located at the right front of the engine compartment.

• **Main Relay**—is located at the left side of the engine compartment.

• **Oil Pressure Switch (DOHC)**—is located top left front of the engine.

• **Oil Pressure Switch (SOHC)**—is located at the oil filter.

• **Oxygen Sensor Relay (DOHC)**—is located at the left front of the engine compartment.

• **Oxygen Sensor**—is located in the exhaust manifold.

• **Passive Shoulder Belt Control Unit**—is located at the front of the trunk.

• **Passive Shoulder Belt Control Unit**—is located behind the rear seat.

• **PCV Valve (DOHC)**—is located at the right rear of the engine compartment.

• **PCV Valve (SOHC)**—is located at the right rear of the engine on the intake manifold.

• **Power Seat Relay**—is located in the relay box.

• **Power Steering Switch**—is located at the front center of the engine compartment.

• **PRC Solenoid Valve (DOHC)**—is located at the right front of the intake manifold.

• **PRC Solenoid Valve (SOHC)**—is located near the pressure regulator on the intake manifold.

• **PRCV Solenoid Valve**—is located at the top right rear of the engine.

• **Pressure Regulator Control System**—see PRC.

• **Purge Solenoid Valve**—is located at the right rear of the engine compartment.

• **Rear Window Defroster Relay**—is located at the front of the trunk.

• **Self Diagnosis Check Connector**—is located at the left front of the engine compartment.

• **Shutter Valve Actuator (DOHC)**—is located at the rear of the intake manifold.

• **Shutter Valve Actuator (SOHC)**—is located at the right front of the engine.

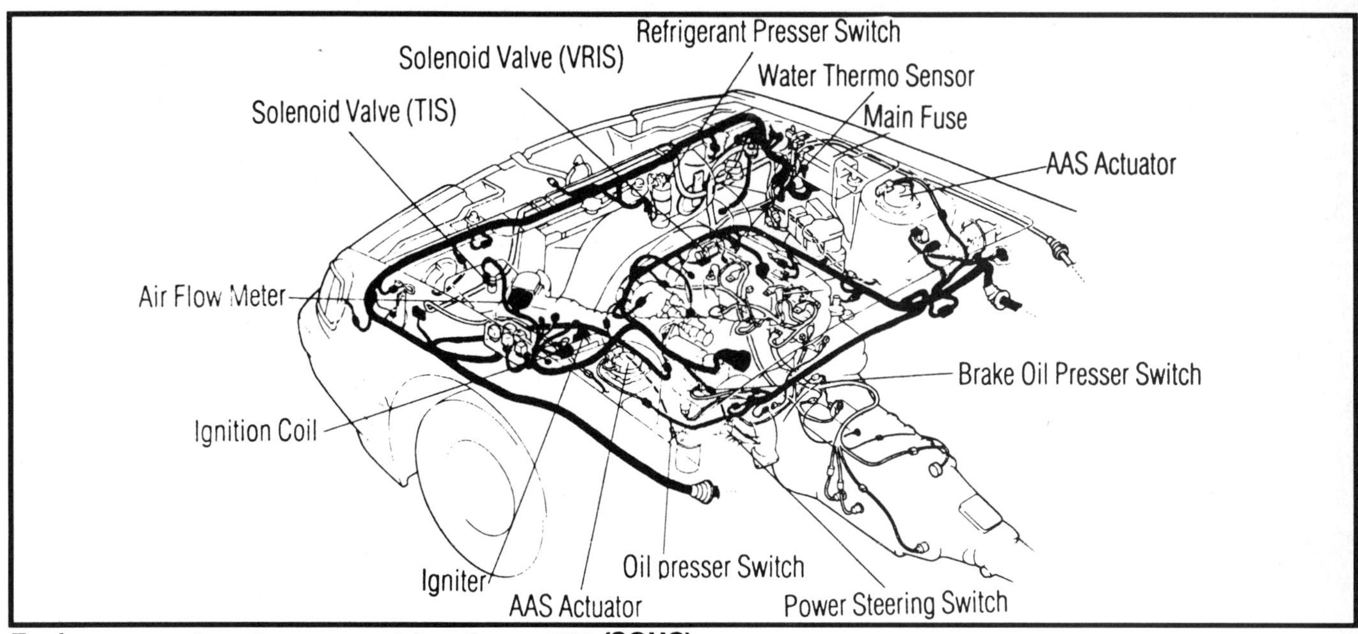

Engine compartment component locations—929 (SOHC)

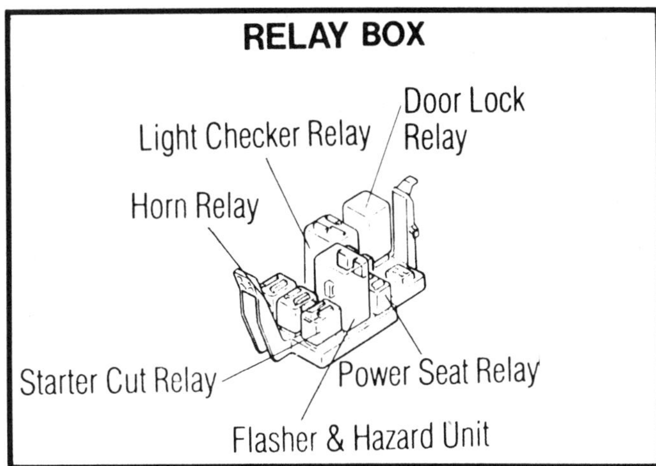

Relay Box—929

- **Speed Sensor (DOHC)**—is located at the left side of the transmission.
- **Speed Sensor**—is located at the transmission case.
- **Starter Cut Relay**—is located in the relay box.
- **Sunroof Relay**—is located at the sunroof motor.
- **Swirl Control Valve Actuator**—is located at the front of the intake manifold.
- **Throttle Sensor**—is located at the throttle body.
- **TIS Solenoid Valve**—is located at the left front of the engine compartment.
- **Variable Resonance Induction System**—see VRIS.
- **Vehicle Speed Sensor**—is located inside the speedometer.
- **VRIS Solenoid Valve**—is located at the right front of the engine.
- **Wiper Relay**—is located at the left kick panel.

MIATA

- **A/C Relay**—is located at the right front of the engine compartment.
- **ABS Hydraulic Unit**—is located at the right rear of the engine compartment.
- **Air Bag Backup Battery**—is located on the air bag unit.
- **Air Bag Crash Sensor (center)**—is located at the radiator support.
- **Air Bag Crash Sensor (left)**—is located in the left front fender.
- **Air Bag Crash Sensor (rear)**—is located under the dash at the center of the windsheild.
- **Air Bag Crash Sensor (right)**—is located in the right front fender.
- **Air Bag Module**—is located under the center of the dash.
- **Air Bag Unit**—is located under the left side of the dash.
- **Air Flow Meter**—is located at the air cleaner.
- **Automatic Transmission Control Unit**—is located under the left side of the dash.
- **Automatic Transmission Oil Pressure Switch**—is located at the transmission case.
- **Backup Light Switch**—is located at the transmission case.
- **Blower Motor Relay**—is located at the left rear of the engine compartment.
- **Brake Fluid Level Sensor**—is located inside the master cylinder.
- **Circuit Opening Relay**—is located under the left side of the dash.
- **Coolant Thermosensor**—is located at the top of the intake manifold and at the front of the engine.
- **Coolant Thermoswitch**—is located to the left of the blower motor.
- **Cooling Fan Relay**—is located in the main relay box.
- **Crank Angle Sensor**—is located inside the distributor.
- **Cruise Control Actuator**—is located at the left front of the engine compartment.
- **Cruise Control Unit**—is located under the left side of the dash.
- **Daytime Running Light Control Unit**—is located under the left side of the dash.
- **Diagnosis Connector**—is located at the left side of the engine compartment.
- **Engine Control Unit**—is located under the right side of the dash.

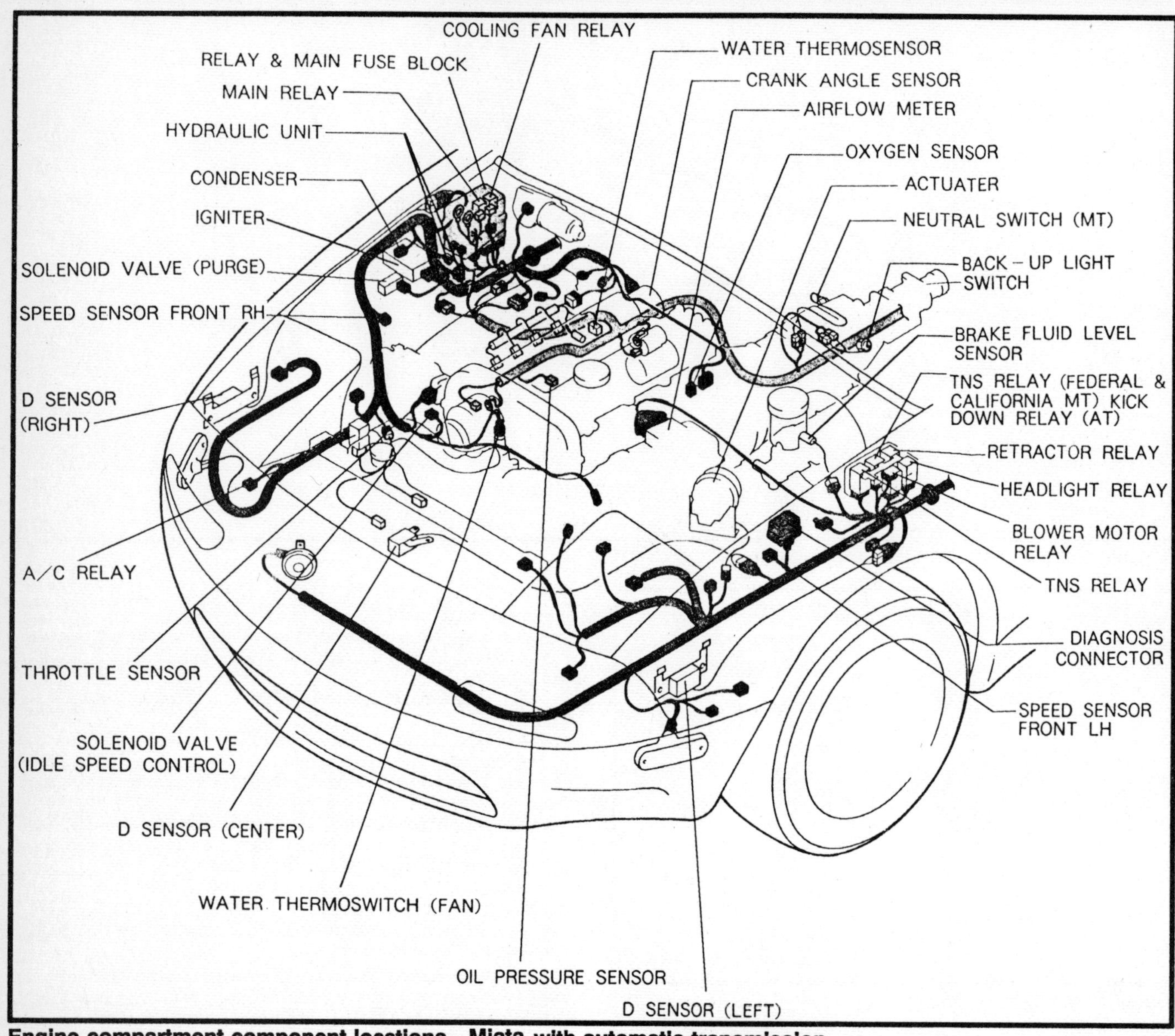

Engine compartment component locations—Miata with automatic transmission

- **Headlight Relay**—is located at the left rear of the engine compartment.
- **Horn Relay**—is located under the left side of the dash.
- **Inhibitor Switch (automatic transmission)**—is located at the transmission case.
- **Kickdown Switch**—is located under the center of the dash.
- **Lockup Solenoid**—is located at the transmission.
- **Main Fuse Box**—is located at the right rear of the engine compartment.
- **Neutral Switch**—is located at the transmission case.
- **Oil Pressure Sensor**—is located at the top of the engine near the injectors.
- **Overdrive Off Switch**—is located at the console.
- **Overdrive Switch**—is located at the transmission.
- **Oxygen Sensor**—is located in the exhaust manifold.
- **Power Connector**—is located at the left side of the engine compartment.
- **Power Steering Pressure Switch**—is located at the lower left of the engine on the power steering pump.
- **Purge Solenoid Valve**—is located at the right rear of the engine compartment.
- **Refrigerant Pressure Switch**—is located at the front of the engine compartment.
- **Relay Box**—is located at the right rear of the engine compartment.
- **Retractor Relay**—is located at the left rear of the engine compartment.
- **Shift Lock Actuator**—is located at the console.
- **Starter Interlock Switch**—is located at the clutch pedal.
- **Throttle Sensor**—is located at the right front of the engine.
- **TNS Relay**—is located at the left rear of the engine compartment.
- **Turn Signal/Hazard Flasher Unit**—is located under the left side of the dash.
- **Warning Chime**—is located under the left side of the dash.
- **Washer Level Sensor**—is located inside the washer reservoir bottle.

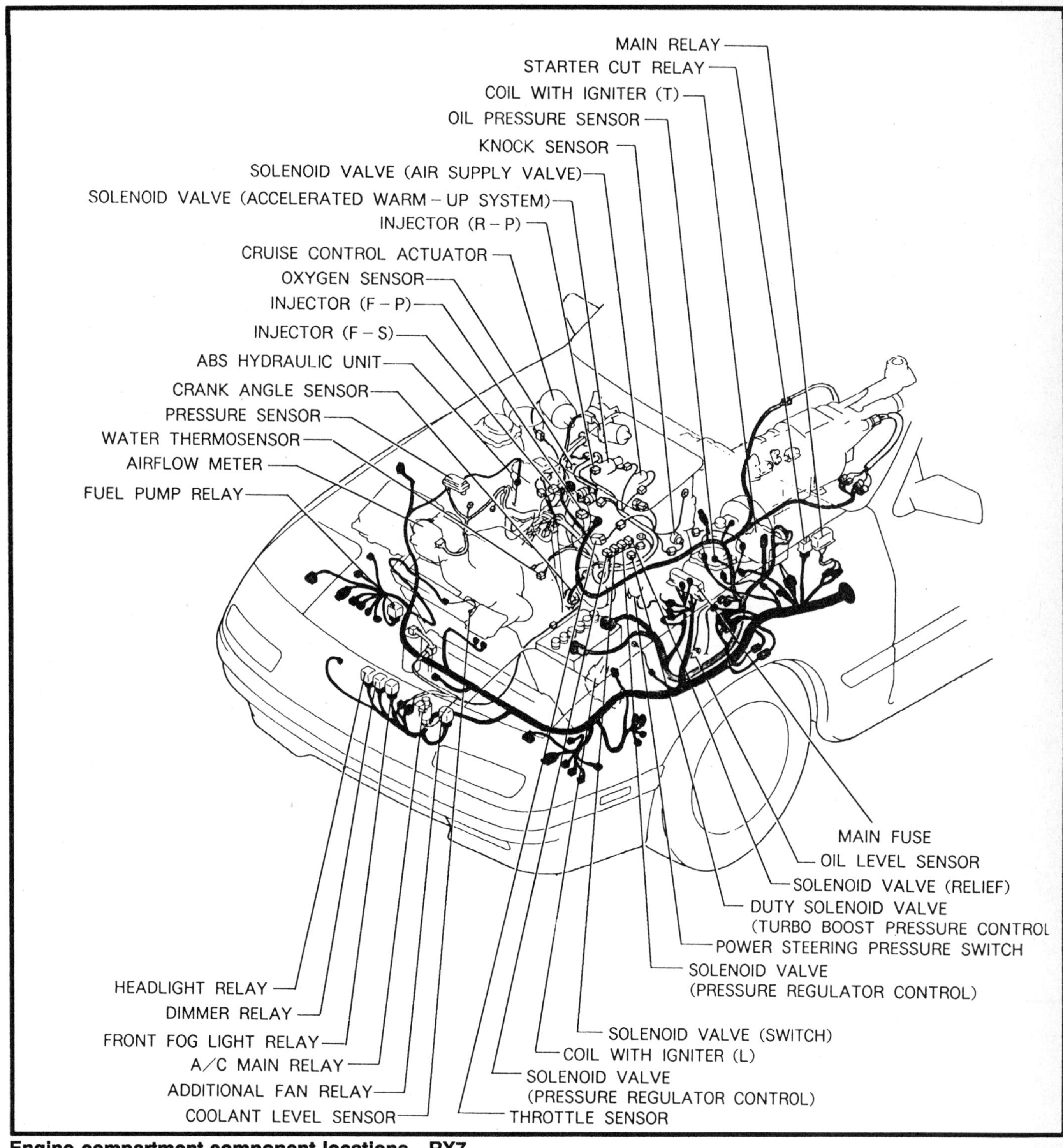

Engine compartment component locations – RX7

RX7

• **A/C Main Relay** – is located on the front center of the engine compartment, on the radiator support.

• **A/C Mode Control Motor** – is located on the right side of the heater unit.

• **A/C Thermostat** – is located on the right side of the instrument panel, behind the glove box, inside the cooling unit.

• **A/C-Heater Blower Motor Power Transistor** – is located on the right side of the instrument panel, on top of the blower motor housing.

• **A/C-Heater Blower Motor Resistor** – is located on the right side of the instrument panel, below the blower motor housing.

• **A/C-Heater Blower Motor** – is located on the right side of the instrument panel, on bottom of the blower motor housing.

• **A/C Refrigerant Pressure Switch**—is located on the front center of the engine compartment.

• **Automatic transmission Control Unit**—is located behind the right side of the instrument panel.

• **Automatic transmission Relay**—is located in the front of the vehicle, center of the radiator support.

• **AAS Actuators**—is located at the shock absorbers.

• **AAS Control Module**—is located at the right rear of the trunk.

• **AAS Steering Angle Sensor**—is located inside the steering column.

• **ABS Control Unit**—is located under the right hand side of the instrument panel.

• **ABS Hydraulic Unit**—is located at the right rear side of the engine compartment.

• **ABS Main Relay**—is located under the right hand side of the instrument panel.

• **ABS Motor Relay**—is located on the hydraulic unit, on the right hand rear of the engine compartment.

• **ABS Valve Relay**—is located on the hydraulic unit, on the right hand rear of the engine compartment.

• **ABS Wheel Sensors**—are located at each respective wheel spindle.

• **Accelerated Warm Up Solenoid Valve**—is located at the top right rear of the engine.

• **Air Bypass Relay**—is located on the front right side of the engine compartment, near airflow meter.

• **Air Bypass Solenoid Valve**—is located on the left side of the engine, near the oil filter.

• **Air Mix Control Motor**—is located on the left side of the heater unit.

• **Air Supply Valve**—is located on the right hand rear side of the engine compartment.

• **Airbag Backup Battery**—is located under the left side of the dash.

• **Airbag Diagnostic Module**—is located under the left side of the dash.

• **Airbag Front Crash Sensor**—is located at the center of the radiator support.

• **Airbag Intermediate Crash Sensor**—is located under the center of the dash on the firewall.

• **Airbag Left Crash Sensor**—is located at the left front of the vehicle behind the bumper cover.

• **Airbag Right Crash Sensor**—is located at the right front of the vehicle behind the bumper cover.

• **Airflow Meter**—is located on the front right side of the engine compartment, under the the air cleaner.

• **Anti-Lock Brakes**—see ABS

Atmospheric Pressure Sensor—is located behind the right side of the instrument panel.

• **Auto Adjust Suspension Accelerator Switch**—is located on the accelerator pedal.

• **Auto Adjust Suspension Actuators (4)**—are located on the top of each shock tower.

• **Auto Adjust Suspension Control Unit**—is located on the rear of the vehicle, to the right of license plate.

• **Auto Adjust Suspension Switch**—is located in the center the console.

• **Automatic Adjustable Suspension**—see AAS.

• **Back-Up Light Switch**—is located on the left side of the transmission case.

• **Boost Sensor**—is located on the front right corner of the engine compartment, behind air cleaner.

• **Brake Fluid Level Sensor**—is located in the brake fluid reservoir.

• **Brake Fluid Pressure Switch**—is located on the bottom of master cylinder brake assembly.

• **Brake/Stoplight Switch**—is located on the top of the brake pedal bracket.

• **Bypass Air Control Valve**—is located on the top left side of the engine, near alternator.

• **Central Processing Unit**—is located behind the left kick panel, near the fuse box.

• **Check Connectors (3)**—is located on the front right & left corners of the engine compartment.

• **Circuit Opening Relay (EGI)**—is located behind the instrument panel.

• **Clutch Switch (manual transmission)**—is located on the top of the clutch pedal bracket.

• **Coolant Level Sensor**—is located on the top of the radiator.

• **Coolant Temperature Sending Unit**—is located on the rear left side of the engine block, near the oil filter.

• **Coolant Temperature Switch**—is located on the bottom left corner of the radiator.

• **Coolant Thermo Sensor**—is located in the water pump.

• **Coolant Thermosenser**—is located at the left front of the engine.

• **Crank Angle Sensor**—is located on the front left side of the engine.

• **Cruise Control Actuator**—is located on the rear right corner of the engine compartment.

• **Cruise Control Unit**—is located under the left side of the instrument panel, near the central processing unit.

• **Dimmer Relay**—is located at the front of the vehicle on the radiator support.

• **EGI Main Fuse**—is located in the main fuse box.

• **EGI Main Relays**—is located on the left fender apron, behind the front left shock tower.

• **EGR Solenoid Valve**—is located on the left side of the engine, behind the alternator in the solenoid cluster.

• **Electric Fan Control Unit (automatic transmission)**—is located behind the right side of the instrument panel.

• **Electric Fan Motor (automatic transmission)**—is located on the front of vehicle, behind the radiator.

• **Electric Fan Relay (automatic transmission)**—is located on the front of the vehicle, center of the radiator support.

• **Electric Fan Sub Relay (automatic transmission)**—is located on the front of vehicle, center of the radiator support.

• **Electric Fan Temperature Switch (automatic transmission)**—is located on the top of the coolant intake.

• **Emission Control Solenoid Resistor**—is located behind the right headlight, on the right fender apron.

• **Emission Control Unit**—is located below the right side of the instrument panel.

• **Fog Light Relay**—is located at the front of the vehicle on the radiator support.

• **Front Speaker/Amplifier**—is located behind the right side of the instrument panel.

• **Fuel Gauge Sending Unit**—is located in the left side of the fuel tank.

• **Fuel Pump Relay/Resistor**—is located on the front right hand corner of the engine compartment.

• **Fuel Pump**—is located inside the fuel tank, on the right side.

• **Fuse Box**—is located below the left hand side kick panel.

• **Headlight Cleaner Motor (2)**—are located on the front corners of the engine compartment, near each headlight.

• **Headlight Dimmer Relay**—is located on the front of the vehicle, center of the radiator support.

• **Headlight Relay**—is located on the front of vehicle, center of the radiator support.

• **Headlight Retractor Motor (2)**—are located behind each headlight assembly.

• **Headlight Retractor Relays (2)**—are incorporated into the headlight retractor motor assembly.

• **Heat Hazard Sensor**—is located under the front right side seat.

• **Heater Relay**—is located behind the glove box, on the left side of the blower motor housing.

• **Inhibitor Switch (automatic transmission)**—is located on the right side of the transmission case.

- **Intake Air Temperature Sensor**—is located on the left side of the throttle body.
- **Kickdown Solenoid**—is located on the rear left side of the transmission.
- **Kickdown Switch (automatic transmission)**—is located on the accelerator pedal bracket.
- **Knock Control Unit (Turbo)**—is located in the right hand side kick panel.
- **Knock Sensor**—is located on the rear of the engine, in the engine block.
- **Lock-Up Control Solenoid**—is located on the bottom left side of the transmission.
- **Lock-Up Relay**—is located on the front of the vehicle, center of the radiator support.
- **Main Fuse Box**—is located in front of the front left strut tower.
- **Main Relay**—is located at the left rear of the engine compartment under the fender.
- **Neutral Switch (manual transmission)**—is located on the right side of transmission.
- **Oil Level Sensor**—is located on the left side of the oil pan.
- **Oil Pressure Sending Unit**—is located on the rear left side the of block, below the oil filter.
- **Over Top Switch (manual transmission)**—is located on the left side of the transmission, near starter motor.
- **Overdrive (5th) Switch**—is located on the left side of the transmission.
- **Overdrive Cancel Solenoid (automatic transmission)**—is located on the left side of the transmission.
- **Overdrive Oil Pressure Switch (automatic transmission)**—is located on the left side of the transmission.
- **Oxygen Sensor**—is located on the right side of the engine, in the exhaust manifold.
- **Parking Brake Switch**—is located on the bottom of the parking brake lever.
- **Port Air Solenoid Valve**—is located on the right side of the engine, on the secondary air injection assembly.
- **Power Antenna Motor**—is located on the rear left corner of the engine compartment.
- **Power Antenna Relay**—is located on the rear left corner of the luggage compartment, on the antenna motor.
- **Power Steering Control Unit**—is located under the steering column.
- **Power Steering Relay**—is located on the front of the engine, near the power steering pump.
- **Power Steering Switch**—is located on the front left corner of the engine, near the power steering pump.
- **Pressure Control Solenoid Valve**—is located on the left side of the engine, behind the alternator in the solenoid cluster.
- **Pressure Sensor**—is located on the right hand strut tower, in the engine compartment.
- **Rear Washer Motor**—is located on the rear of the vehicle, to the left of the license plate.
- **Rear Window Defogger Relay**—is located on the rear left corner of the luggage compartment.
- **Rear Wiper Motor**—is located on the bottom right side of the rear hatch.
- **Recirculation Select Motor**—is located on the right side of the instrument panel, behind the glove box.
- **Refrigerant Pressure Switch**—is located on the front center of the engine compartment.
- **Relief Solenoid Valve (Blue)**—is located on the left side of the engine, behind the alternator in the solenoid cluster.
- **Seat Belt Switch**—is located in the driver's seat belt buckle.
- **Speed Sensor**—is incorporated into the combination meter inside the instrument panel.
- **Split Air Solenoid Valve**—is located on the right side of engine, on the secondary air injection assembly.
- **Starter Cut Relay**—is located at the left rear of the engine compartment under the fender.
- **Starter Cut Relay**—is located on the left fender, behind the front left shock tower.
- **Stop Light Warning Relay**—is located on the left kick panel, on the bottom of the CPU.
- **Sub Zero Motor**—is located on the rear right corner of the engine compartment, near the wiper motor.
- **Sub Zero Sensor**—is located on the rear left side of the engine.
- **Sunroof Motor**—is located on the rear center of the sunroof opening.
- **Sunroof Relay No. 1**—is located in the front of the sunroof opening, left side.
- **Sunroof Relay No. 2**—is located in the front of the sunroof opening, right side.
- **Switching Solenoid Valve (Gray)**—is located on the left side of the engine, behind the alternator in the solenoid cluster.
- **Theft Deterrent Control Unit**—is located below the right side of the instrument panel, behind the glove box.
- **Theft Deterrent Door Lock Switch**—is located inside each door, near the door handle.
- **Theft Deterrent Horn**—is located on the front center of the vehicle, below the hood release switch.
- **Throttle Sensor**—is located at the throttle body.
- **Turbo Boost Pressure Control Valve**—is located at the left side of the engine.
- **Turn Cancel & Angle Sensor**—is located in the steering column.
- **Turn Signal/Hazard Flasher**—is located in the left kick panel, on the bottom of the CPU.
- **Twin Scroll Turbocharged Solenoid Valve**—is located ion the left side of the engine, behind the alternator in the solenoid cluster.
- **Vacuum Variable Resistor**—is located on the front right corner of the engine compartment, behind the air cleaner.
- **Variable Dynamic Effect Intake System**—see VDI

VDI Actuator—is located at the intake manifold.

- **VDI Solenoid Valve**—is located at the intake manifold.
- **Vehicle Speed Sensor**—is located in the speedometer.
- **Washer Fluid Level Sensor**—is located on the bottom of the washer fluid reservoir.
- **Windshield Washer Motor**—is located under the left side of the cowl, in the washer reservoir.

MAZDA TRUCKS

Circuit Breakers

2200 AND 2600

Fuses are located in the fuse box under the left side of the dash.

MPV

Fuses are located in the fuse box at the left kick panel. A circuit breaker is located at the fuse box also.

NAVAJO

Fuses are located under the left side of the dash at the fuse box. The tail gate wiper fuse is located above the glove box.

Fusible Links

2200 AND 2600

Fusbile links are located in the main fuse box at the left front of the engine compartment. The fusible links are of the maxi-fuse type.

MPV

Fusible links are located at the main fuse box on the right side of the engine compartment. The fusible links are of the maxi-fuse type.

2200 AND 2600

- **A/C Thermoswitch**—is located on the cooling unit under the dash.
- **Air Control Valve(2.2L carbureted engine)**—is located at the air filter.
- **Air Vent Solenoid Valve (2.2L carbureted engine)**—is located at the carburetor.
- **Air/Fuel Solenoid Valve (2.2L carbureted engine)**—is located at the carburetor.
- **Airflow Sensor (2.2L and 2.6L EGI)**—is located at the air cleaner.
- **Atmospheric Pressure Sensor (2.2L carbureted engine)**—is located at the right side of the engine compartment.
- **Automatic Transmission Control Unit**—is located under the left side of the dash.
- **BAC Valve (2.2L and 2.6L EGI)**—is located at the throttle body.
- **Backup Light Switch**—is located at the side of the transmission case.
- **Carburetor ACV Solenoid**—is located at the left side of the engine comapartment.
- **Circuit Open Relay (2.2L and 2.6L EGI)**—is located at the left kick panel.
- **Coasting Richer Solenoid (2.2L carbureted engine)**—is located at the carburetor.
- **Coolant Temperature Switch (2.2L carbureted engine)**—is located at the radiator.
- **Coolant Thermosensor (2.2L and 2.6L EGI)**—is located at the front of the engine block.
- **Coolant Thermosensor (2.2L carbureted engine)**—is located at the front of the intake manifold.
- **Coolant Thermovalve (2.2L carbureted engine)**—is located at the front of the intake manifold.

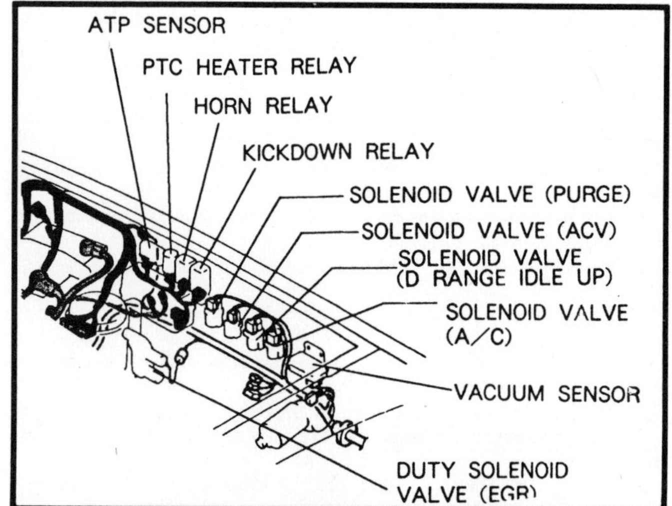

Engine compartment component locations—2.2L engine (except fuel injection)

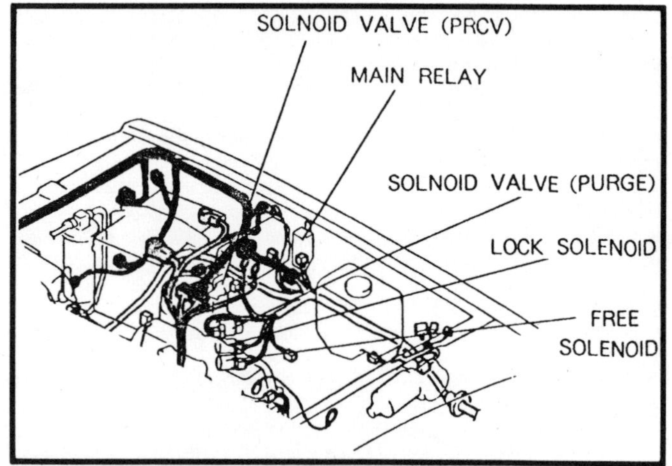

Engine compartment component locations—2.6L engine

- **Cruise Control Actuator (2.2L engine)**—is located at the left side of the engine compartment.
- **Cruise Control Actuator (2.6L engine)**—is located at the right side of the engine compartment.
- **Cruise Control Unit**—is located under the left side of the dash.
- **Daytime Running Light Control Unit**—is located under the dash to the right of the steering column.
- **Duty Solenoid Valve (2.2L carbureted engine)**—is located at the right front of the engine compartment.
- **EGI Main Relay**—is located at the right front of the engine compartment.
- **EGR Control Valve (2.2L carbureted engine)**—is located below the carburetor.
- **EGR Position Sensor (2.2L carbureted engine)**—is located below the carburetor.
- **Engine Control Unit (2.2L EGI and 2.6L engine)**—is located at the right kick panel.
- **Engine Control Unit**—is located at the right kick panel.

• **Feedback Carburetor Control Unit (2.2L carbureted engine)**—is located at the right kick panel.

• **Flasher Unit**—is located under the left side of the dash.

• **Four Wheel Drive Indicator Switch**—is located at the transmission tail shaft.

• **Fuel Box**—is located under the dash to the left of the steering column.

• **Fuel Cut Relay**—is located under the left side of the dash.

• **Fuel Injection**—see EGI.

• **HAT Control Unit**—is located under the left side of the dash.

• **High Altitude Compensator (2.2L carbureted engine)**—is located at the right side of the engine compartment.

• **Idle Compensator (2.2L carbureted engine)**—is located inside the air cleaner.

• **Idle Switch (2.2L and 2.6L EGI)**—is located at the throttle body.

• **Idle Switch (2.2L carbureted engine)**—is located at the carburetor.

• **Inhibitor Switch**—is located at the top of the transmission.

• **Intake Air Thermosensor (2.2L and 2.6L EGI)**—is located at the front of the intake manifold.

• **Intake Air Thermosensor (2.2L carbureted engine)**—is located inside the air cleaner.

• **Mixture Control Valve (2.2L carbureted engine)**—is located at the right front of the engine.

• **Neutral Switch (manual transmission)**—is located at the transmission case.

• **Oxygen Sensor (2.2L and 2.6L EGI)**—is located at the left side exhaust manifold.

• **Oxygen Sensor**—is located in the exhaust manifold.

• **PCV Valve (2.2L and 2.6L EGI)**—is located at the front of the camshaft cover.

• **PCV Valve (2.2L carbureted engine)**—is located at the front of the valve cover.

• **Power Steering Pressure Switch**—is located at the power steering pump.

• **PRC Solenoid Valve (2.2L and 2.6L EGI)**—is located at the charcoal canister.

• **PTC Heater (2.2L carbureted engine)**—is located under the carburetor.

• **Purge Control Solenoid Valve (2.2L and 2.6L EGI)**—is located at the charcoal canister.

• **Purge Control Valve(2.2L carbureted engine)**—is located at the charcoal canister.

• **Purge Solenoid Valve (2.2L carbureted engine)**—is located at the right side of the engine compartment.

• **Rear Wheel ABS Check Connector**—is located under the master cylinder.

• **Rear Wheel ABS Control Unit**—is located under the dash to the right of the steering column.

• **Rear Wheel ABS Differential Switch**—is located at the master cylinder.

• **Rear Wheel ABS Hydraulic Unit**—is located at the right rear wheel assembly.

• **Rear Wheel ABS Speed Sensor**—is located at the rear drive axle.

• **Reed Valve Switch (2.2L carbureted engine)**—is located at the air cleaner.

• **Refrigerant Pressure Swtich**—is located at the receiver drier.

• **Remote Free Wheel**—see RFW
RFW Actuator—is located at the transmission.

• **RFW Control Unit**—is located under the left side of the dash.

• **RFW Solenoid Valves**—are located at the right side of the engine compartment.

• **RFW Switch**—is located at the side of the transmission.

• **RFW Vacuum Reservoir**—is located under the vehicle near the front drive axle.

• **Slow Cut Fuel Solenoid (2.2L carbureted engine)**—is located at the carburetor.

• **Throttle Sensor (2.2L and 2.6L EGI)**—is located at the throttle body.

• **Vacuum Control Valve (2.2L carbureted engine)**—is located at the charcoal canister.

• **Vacuum Sensor (2.2L carbureted engine)**—is located at the right rear of the engine compartment.

• **Vacuum Solenoid Valve (2.2L carbureted engine)**—is located at the front of the intake manifold.

• **Warning Buzzer Unit**—is located under the left side of the dash.

MPV

• **A/C Condenser Fan Relay**—is located at the right side of the engine compartment.

• **A/C Rear Cooler Relays**—are located at the rear cooler unit on the left side of the rear passenger compartment.

• **A/C Relay**—is located at the right side of the engine compartment.

• **A/C thermoswitch**—is located at the cooling unit under the dash.

• **AFW Actuator**—is located at the left side of the front differential.

• **AFW Solenoids**—are located at the left rear of the engine compartment.

• **AFW Switch**—is located at the left side of the front differential.

• **AFW Unit**—is located at the front differential.

• **AFW Vacuum Reservoir**—is located at the firewall.

• **ALL Compressor Assembly**—is located at the right front of the engine comaprtment.

• **ALL Compressor Relay**—is located at the left side of the engine compartment.

• **ALL Control Unit**—is located —is located at the rear of the passenger compartment behind the left trim panel.

• **ALL Height Sensor**—is located at the rear differential.

• **ALL Relay**—is located at the relay box on the left side of the engine compartment.

• **Atmospheric Pressure Sensor (3.0L engine)**—is located inside the engine control unit.

• **Atmospheric Pressure Switch**—is located inside the engine control unit.

• **Automatic Freewheel**—see AFW.

• **Automatic Load Leveling**—see ALL.

• **Automatic Transmission Control Unit**—is located at the left kick panel.

• **Automatic Transmission Thermosensor**—is located at the transmission valve body.

• **BAC Valve**—is located at the throttle body.

• **Blower Motor Relay**—is located at the relay box on the left side of the engine compartment.

• **Central Procesing Unit**—is located at the left kick panel.

• **Circuit Opening Relay**—is located at the side of the engine control unit.

• **Coolant Thermosensor (3.0L engine)**—is located at the front of the engine.

• **Cruise Control Unit**—is located at the right side kick panel.

• **Dip-Dim Relay (Canada)**—is located at the relay box on the left side of the engine compartment.

• **Engine Control Unit**—is located under the center of the dash.

• **Engine RPM Sensor**—is located inside the coil.

• **Horn Relay**—is located at the relay box on the left side of the engine compartment.

• **Inhibitor Switch (automatic transmission)**—is located at the top of the transmission.

• **Intake Air Thermosensor**—is located at the side of the plenum.

• **ir Flow Meter**—is located at the air cleaner.

• **Main Relay**—is located at the left side of the engine compartment.

• **Mileage Sensor**—is located at the speedometer.

• **Neutral Switch (manual transmission)**—is located at the transmission tail shaft.

• **Oil Pressure Switch**—at the oil filter or at the side of the block near the oil filter.

• **Oxygen Sensor**—is located at the exhaust manifold.

• **PCV Valve (2.6L engine)**—is located at the right side of the engine.

• **PCV Valve (3.0L engine)**—is located at the rear of the engine compartment behind the engine.

• **Power Door Lock Timer**—is located near the blower unit.

• **Power Steering Pressure Switch**—is located at the power steering pump.

• **PRC Solenoid Valve**—is located at the right side of the engine compartment.

• **Purge Control Solenoid Valve (3.0L engine)**—is located at the right front of the engine compartment.

• **Rear Heater Blower Motor Relay**—is located at the rear heater unit on the left side of the rear passenger compartment.

• **Rear Wheel ABS Check Connector**—is located under the master cylinder.

• **Rear Wheel ABS Control Unit**—is located at the rear of the passenger compartment behind the left trim panel.

• **Rear Wheel ABS Hydraulic Unit**—is located at the right rear wheel assembly.

• **Rear Wheel ABS Pressure Differential Switch**—is located at the left front of the engine compartment.

• **Rear Wheel ABS Relay**—is located at the left rear of the engine compartment.

• **Rear Wheel ABS Relay**—is located at the relay box on the left side of the engine compartment.

• **Rear Wheel ABS Sensor**—is located at the rear differential.

• **Rear Window Defroster Relay**—is located at the relay box on the left side of the engine compartment.

• **Relay Box**—is located on the left side of the engine compartment.

• **Shutter Valve Acutator (3.0L engine)**—is located at the front of the intake manifold.

• **Speed Sensor**—is located at the speedometer.

• **Starter Interlock Switch**—is located at the left rear of the engine compartment.

• **Throttle Sensor**—is located at the throttle body.

• **Transfer Case Change Motor Relay**—is located at the firewall.

• **Transmission Dropping Resistor**—is located at the top of the transmission.

• **Turn And Flasher Unit**—is located at the left kick panel.

• **Vacuum Chamber (3.0L engine)**—is located at the rear of the engine.

• **VRIS Solenoid Valve (3.0L engine)**—is located at the front of the intake manifold.

NAVAJO

• **A/C Clutch Cycling Pressure Switch**—is located at the right rear of the engine compartment.

• **A/C Compressor Clutch Solenoid**—is located at the compressor.

• **Air Charge Temperature Sensor**—is located at the left rear of the engine.

• **Air Charge Temperature Sensor**—is located in a cylinder runner on the intake manifold.

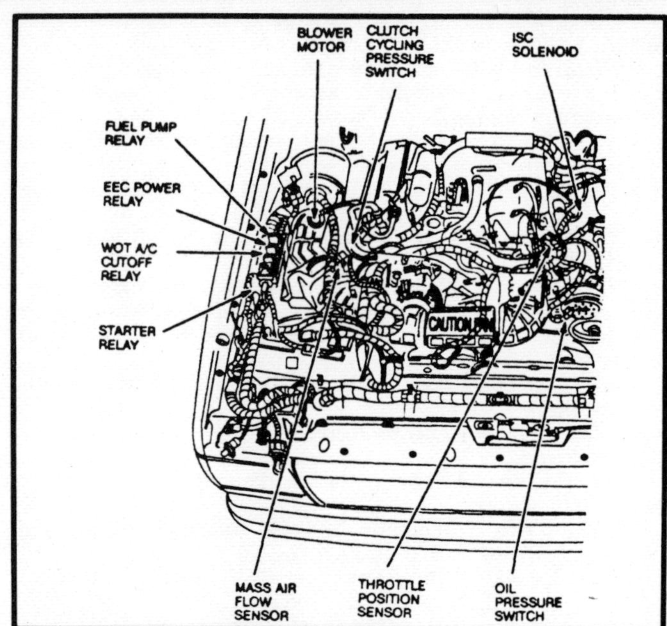

Component Locations—Navajo

• **Air Cleaner Cold Weather Modulator**—is located at the air cleaner.

• **Air Cleaner Temperature Sensor**—is located at the air cleaner.

• **Barometric Pressure Sensor**—is located at the firewall.

• **Blower Motor Resistor**—is located at the blower motor in the engine compartment.

• **Brake Fulid Level Warning Switch**—is located at the master cylinder.

• **Cannister Purge Solenoid**—is located at the left front of the engine compartment.

• **Coolant Temperature Sensor**—is located at the top center of the intake manifold.

• **Daytime Running Light Jumper**—is located at the left front headlight.

• **Diagnostic Self Test Connector**—is located at the right rear of the engine compartment.

• **Diode Resistor Network**—is located at the left side of the engine compartment.

• **EEC Power Relay**—is located at the right side of the engine compartment.

• **EEC Relay Assembly**—is located at the ignition switch.

• **Electronic DIS Module**—is located at the right front of the engine compartment.

• **Electronic Engine Control (EEC) Module**—is located at the right kick panel.

• **Electronic Shift Control Module**—is located at the floor in the rear passenger compartment.

• **Fuel Pump Inertia Switch**—is located under the center of the dash.

• **Fuel Pump Relay**—is located at the right side of the engine compartment.

• **Fuse Box**—is located at under the left side of the dash.

• **Idle Air Bypass Motor**—is located at the top of the throttle body.

• **Idle Speed Solenoid**—is located at the throttle body.

• **Interval Wiper Module**—is located under the center of the dash.

• **Low Oil Level Relay**—is located at the right kick panel.

• **Mass Air Flow Sensor**—is located at the right rear of the engine compartment.

- **Oil Level Switch**—is located at the top center of the intake manifold.
- **Oil Pressure Switch**—is located at the left front of the engine.
- **Oxygen Sensor**—is located at the right of the engine.
- **PCV Valve**—is located at the rear of the valve cover.
- **Power Distribution Box**—is located at the right side of the engine compartment.
- **RABS Differential Sensor**—is located at the rear differential.
- **RABS Proportioning Valve Switch Assembly**—is located at the left kick panel.
- **Rear Anti Lock Brake System**—see RABS.
- **Speed Control Servo**—is located at the left rear of the engine compartment.
- **Starter Relay**—is located at the right side of the engine compartment.
- **Stop/Turn Signal Relay**—is located at the left quarter panel in the rear passenger compartment.
- **Tachometer Test Connector**—is located at the right rear of the engine compartment.
- **Taillight Relay**—is located at the left quarter panel in the rear passenger compartment.
- **Throttle Position Sensor**—is located at the left rear of the engine on the throttle body.
- **Transmission Solenoid Valve**—is located at the transmission.
- **Variable Reluctance Sensor**—is located at the front of the engine.
- **Vehicle Speed Sensor**—is located at the transmission.
- **Warning Buzzer Module**—is located under the center of the dash.
- **WOT A/C Cutoff Relay**—is located at the right side of the engine compartment.

MITSUBISHI

Circuit Breakers

3000GT

Fuses are located at the right front of the engine compartment, at the left side of the engine compartment and under the left side of the dash.

ECLIPSE

Fuses are located at the right front of the engine compartment, the left rear of the engine compartment and under the left side of the dash.

GALANT

Fuses are located at the right front of the engine compartment and under the left side of the dash.

MIRAGE

Fuses are located under the left side of the dash. Dedicated fuses for the air conditioner are located at the left front of the engine compartment. Other dedicated fuses are located at the right front of the engine compartment.

PRECIS

Fuses are located in the fuse box at the left kick panel and the relay box under the left side of the dash.

SIGMA

Fuses are located under the left side of the dash and at the right side of the engine compartment.

STARION

Fuses are located at the left side of the dash.

Fusible Links

3000GT

Fusible links (maxi-fuses) are located at the right front of the engine compartment.

ECLIPSE

Fusible links are located at the battery. Sub-fusible links are located at the right front of the engine compartment.

GALANT

Fusible links are located at the battery and at the right side of the engine compartment.

MIGHTY MAX

Fusible links are located at the battery and the left rear of the engine compartment.

MIRAGE

Fusible links are located at the right front of the engine compartment.

PRECIS

Fusible links are located in a holder next to the battery or in a holder at the left front of the engine compartment.

SIGMA

Fusible links are located at the battery and at the right side of the engine compartment.

STARION

Fusible links are located at the left front of the engine compartment near the battery.

Relays, Sensors and Computer Locations

3000GT

- **4WS Fluid Level Warning Diode**—is located under the right side of the dash.
- **A/C Air Inlet Sensor**—is located at the top of the air box.
- **A/C Control Unit**—is located under the center of the dash.
- **A/C Interior Temperature Sensor**—is located at the headliner.
- **A/C Photo Sensor**—is located at the right side defogger grille.
- **A/C Relay Box**—is located at the left front of the engine compartment.
- **A/C Revolution Sensor**—is located on the compressor.
- **A/C Thermosensor**—is located at the evaporator.
- **A/C Thermostat**—is located on the compressor.
- **ABS Control Unit**—is located next to the rear seat at the right quarter panel.
- **ABS Diode**—is located at the right side of the engine compartment on the fender.
- **ABS G-Sensor**—is located under the console.
- **ABS Motor Relay**—is located at the right front of the engine compartment.
- **ABS Relay**— Relay—is located in the relay box at the right side of the engine compartment.
- **ABS Valve Relay**—is located at the right front of the engine compartment.
- **Active Aero Control Unit**—is located at the left quarter panel inside the trunk compartment.
- **Active Exhaust Control Unit**—is located at the left rear of the trunk compartment.
- **Air Flow Sensor**—is located at the air cleaner.
- **Airbags**—see Supplemental Restraint System (SRS) Alternator Relay—is located in the relay box at the right side of the engine compartment.
- **Anti-Lock Brakes—see ABS**

Automatic Transmission Control Unit—at the front of the console under the dash.

- **Automatic Transmission Fluid Temperature Sensor**—is located at the front of the transmission near the radiator.
- **Automatic Transmission Kickdown Servo Switch**—is located next to the fluid temperature sensor.
- **Barometric Pressure Sensor**—is located in the air flow sensor.
- **Condenser Fan Motor**—is located in the A/C relay box at the left front of the engine compartment.
- **Control Relay**—is located at the right front of the console.
- **Coolant Temperature Sensor**—is located on the battery side of the engine.
- **Crank Angle Sensor/TDC Sensor**—is located at the right side of the engine near the battery.
- **Defogger Relay**—is located in the interior relay box under the left side of the dash.
- **Detonation Sensor**—is located at the top of the intake manifold between the intake runners.
- **Door Lock Relay**—is located in the interior relay box under the left side of the dash.
- **ECS Control Unit**—is located at the right quarter panel behind the right rear wheel.
- **ECS Steering Wheel Angle Sensor**—is located in the steering column.
- **EGR Control Solenoid Valve (California)**—is located at the firewall.
- **EGR Temperature Sensor (California)**—is located at the EGR valve.
- **Electronic Time and Control System**—see ETACS.
- **Engine ECU**—is located under the front of the console.
- **Engine Speed Detection Sensor**—is located at the right rear of the engine compartment.
- **ETACS Unit**—is located under the left side of the dash.
- **Fog Light Diode**—is located under the left side of the dash.
- **Fog Light Relay Relay**—is located in the relay box at the right side of the engine compartment.
- **Fuel Injection**—see Multi Point Injection (MPI).
- **Fuel Pump Check Connector**—is located at the right rear of the engine compartment.
- **Hazard Flasher/Turn Signal Unit**—is located at the left kick panel.
- **Headlight Relay**—is located in the relay box at the right side of the engine compartment.
- **Horn Relay**—is located in the relay box at the right side of the engine compartment.
- **Ignition Timing Adjustment Connector**—›is located at the right rear of the engine compartment.
- **Inhibitor Switch**—is located at the transmission.
- **Intake Air Temperature Sensor**—is located in the air flow sensor.
- **Interior Relay Box**—is located under the left side of the dash.
- **Magnetic Clutch Relay**—is located in the A/C relay box at the left front of the engine compartment.
- **MPI Diode**—is located at the left kick panel.
- **MPI Fuel Pressure Control Valve (turbo)**—is located at the firewall.
- **MPI Idle Speed Control Servo**—is located at the rear of the engine near the battery.
- **MPI Variable Induction Motor (non-turbo)**—is located at the left side of the engine.
- **Oil Pressure Sensor**—is located at the bottom of the engine near the front suspension.
- **PCV Valve**—is located at the camshaft cover.
- **Pop-Up Motor Relay**—is located in the relay box at the right side of the engine compartment.
- **Power Steering Oil Pressure Switch**—is located at the power steering pump.
- **Power Window Relay**—is located in the interior relay box under the left side of the dash.
- **Pulse Generators**—are located at the top of the transmission.
- **Purge Control Solenoid Valve**—is located at the firewall.
- **Radiator Fan Motor Control Relay**—is located in the A/C relay box at the left front of the engine compartment.
- **Radiator Fan Motor Relay**—is located in the relay box at the right side of the engine compartment.
- **Rear Intermittent Wiper Relay**—is located next to the rear seat at the left quarter panel.
- **Relay Box**—is located at the right side of the engine compartment.
- **Seat Belt Diode**—is located behind the instrument cluster.
- **Self-Diagnosis Check Connector**—is located under the left side of the dash at the fuse box.
- **SRS Diagnosis Unit**—is located under the console.
- **SRS Front Impact Sensors**—are located at the front of the engine compartment behind the headlights.
- **Starter Relay**—is located in the relay box at the right side of the engine compartment.
- **Suspension—see Electronic Control Suspension (ECS).**
- **Taillight Relay**—is located in the relay box at the right side of the engine compartment.
- **TDC Sensor/Crank Angle Sensor**—is located at the right side of the engine near the battery.
- **Theft Alarm Diode**—is located behind the instrument cluster.

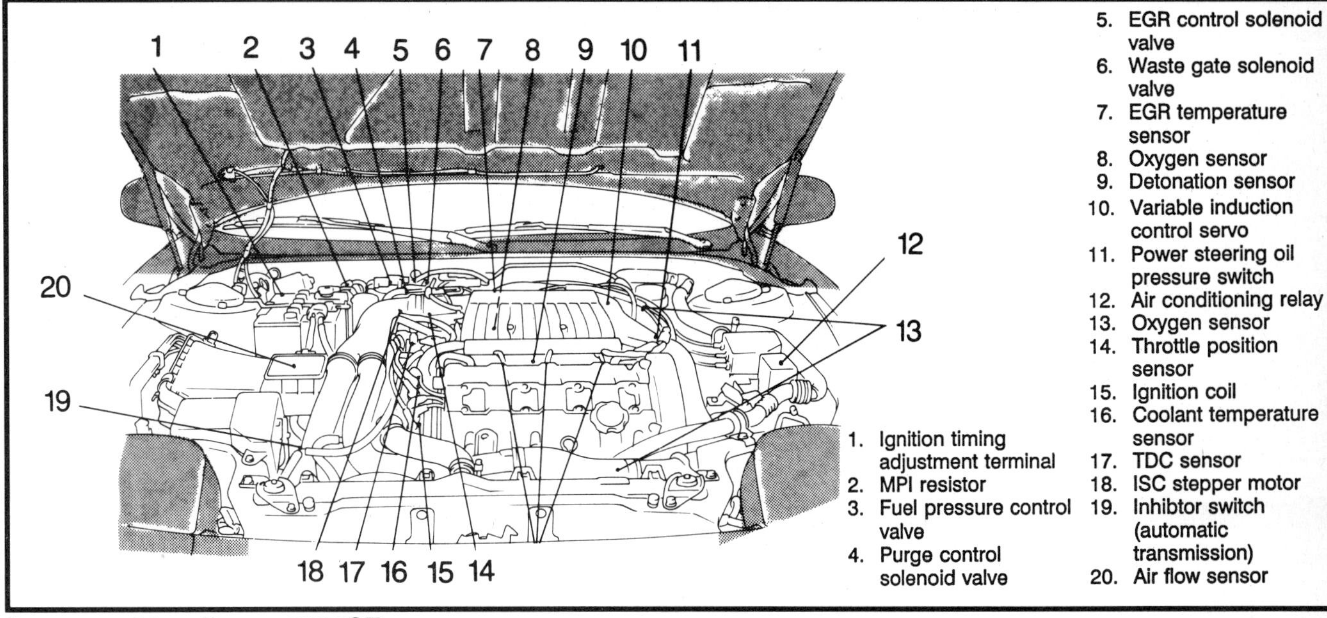

Component locations—3000GT

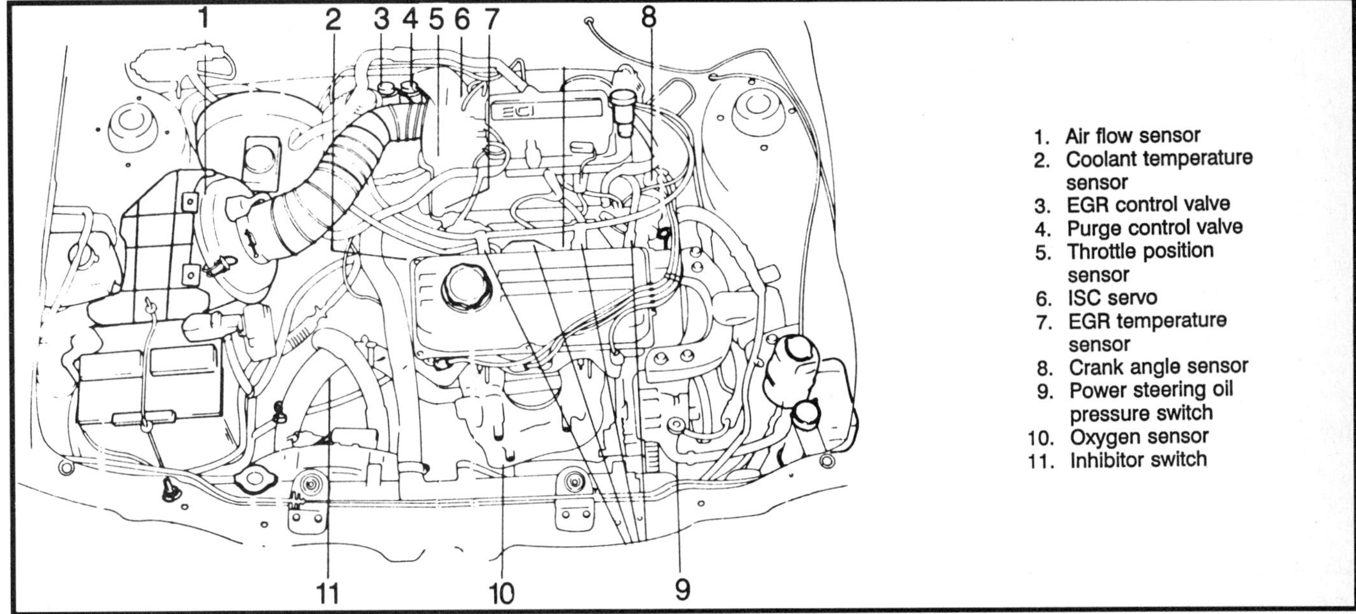

Component locations—Precis

• **Theft Alarm Starter Relay**—is located at the left front of the console.

• **Throttle Position Sensor**—is located at the right rear of the engie near the battery.

• **Turbocharger Resistor**—is located at the right side of the firewall.

• **Turn Signal/Hazard Flasher Unit**—is located at the left kick panel.

• **Vehicle Speed Sensor**—is located at the speedometer.

• **Waste Gate Solenoid Valve**—is located at the firewall.

ECLIPSE

• **A/C Control Unit**—is located under the right side of the dash near the A/C unit.

• **A/C Dedicated Fuse**—is located at the left rear of the engine compartment.

• **A/C Dual Pressure Switch**—is located at the right side of the engine compartment on the refrigerant line.

• **A/C Inlet Sensor**—is located at the A/C unit under the right side of the dash.

• **ABS Control Unit**—is located behind the rear seat.

• **ABS Diode**—is located at the right side quarter panel behind the trim panel.

• **ABS Diode**—is located behind the rear seat.

• **ABS G-Sensor (AWD)**—is located between the seat belt buckles at the front seats.

• **ABS Motor Relay**—is located the right side of the engine compartment.

• **ABS Power Relay**—is located behind the rear seat.

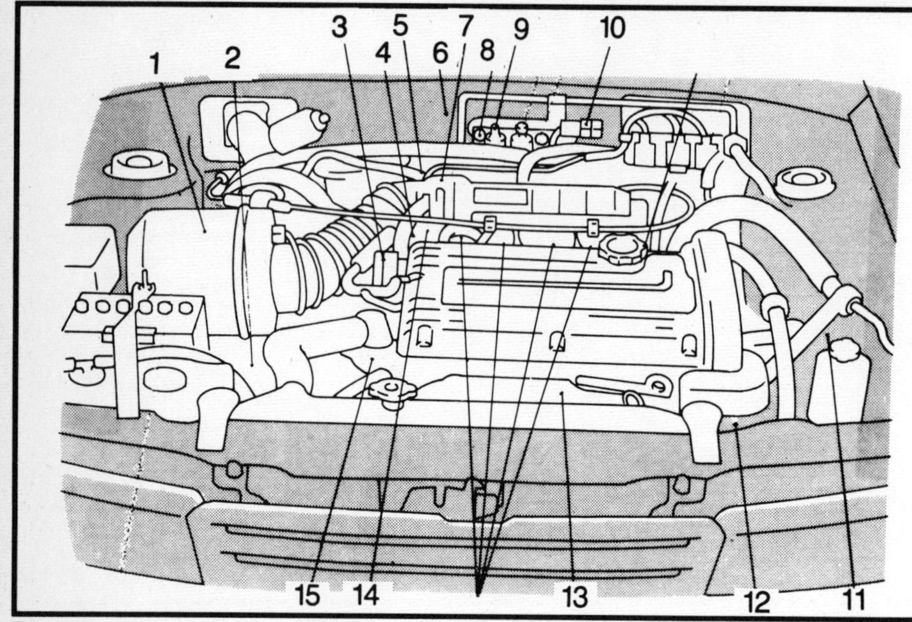

1. Air flow sensor
2. Inhibitor switch
3. Crank angle sensor
4. Idle speed sensor
5. Idle position switch
6. Ignition timing adjustment terminal
7. EGR temperature sensor
8. Fuel pump check terminal
9. EGR control solenoid valve
10. Purge control solenoid valve
11. Air conditioning relay
12. Power steering oil pressure switch
13. Oxygen sensor
14. Throttle position sensor
15. Coolant temperature sensor

Component locations—Mirage

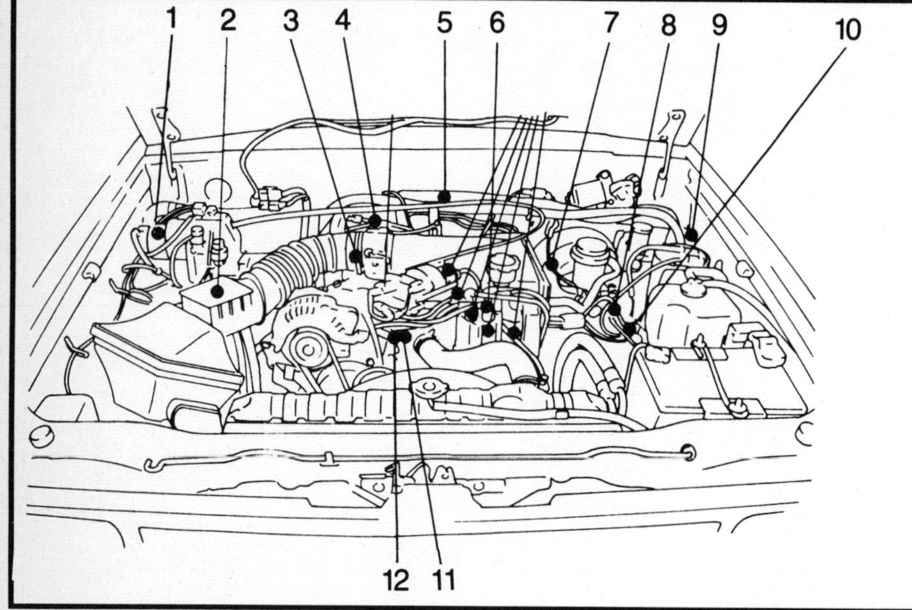

1. Ignition timing adjustment terminal
2. Air flow sensor
3. Idle speed control servo
4. Throttle position sensor
5. Oxygen sensor
6. Crank angle sensor
7. EGR temperature sensor
8. Purge control solenoid valve
9. Air conditioner compressor power relay
10. EGR control solenoid valve
11. Engine coolant temperature sensor
12. Air conditioner temperature sensor

Component locations—Mighty Max

• **ABS Self Diagnosis Connector**—is located under the left side of the dash.

• **ABS Valve Relay**—is located the right side of the engine compartment.

• **Air Flow Sensor**—is located at the air cleaner.

• **Air Thermosensor**—is located at the A/C unit under the right side of the dash.

• **Alternator Relay**—is located at the relay box on the right side of the engine compartment.

• **Automatic Seat Belt Control Unit**—is located at the left quarter panel behind the left seat.

• **Automatic Seat Belt Motor Relay**—is located at the left quarter panel behind the left seat.

• **Automatic Transaxle Control Unit (2.0L engine)**—is located at the front of the console under the dash.

• **Automatic Transaxle Diagnosis Connector (2.0L engine)**—is located under the left side of the dash.

• **Barometric Pressure Sensor**—is located inside the air flow sensor.

• **Condenser Fan Motor Changeover Relay**—is located at the relay box on the left side of the engine compartment.

• **Condenser Fan Motor Relay**—is located at the relay box on the left side of the engine compartment.

• **Coolant Temperature Sensor**—is located at the thermostat housing.

• **Crankshaft Angle Sensor (1.8L engine)**—is located inside the distributor.

• **Crankshaft Angle Sensor (2.0L engine and turbo)**—is located at the cam cover near the thermostat housing.

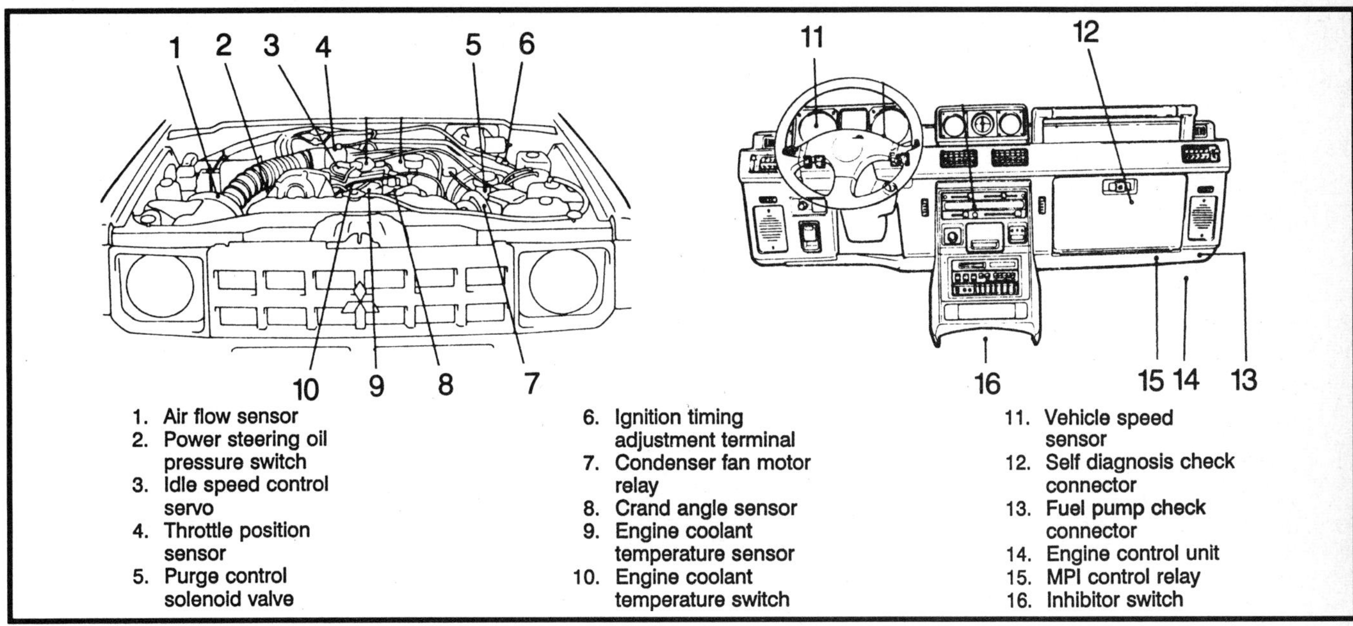

Component locations—Montero

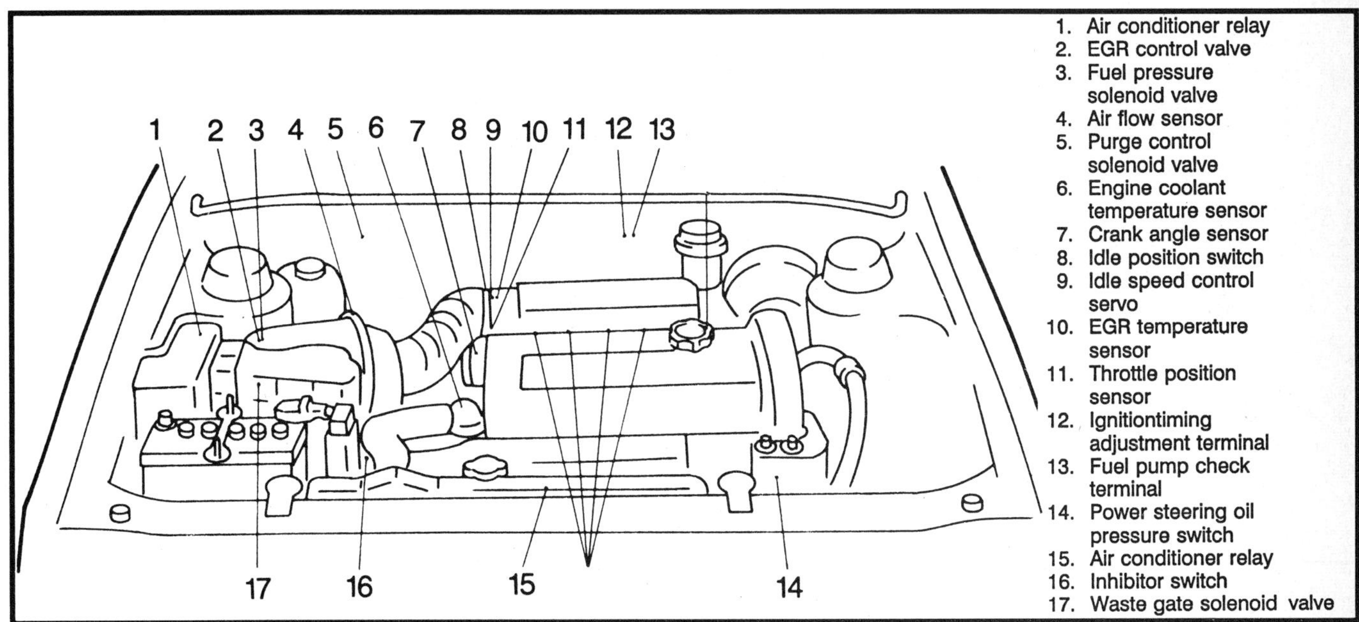

Component locations—Galant

• **Cruise Control Actuator**—is located at the left shock tower in the engine compartment.

• **Cruise Control Unit**—is located under the left side of the dash.

• **Cruise Control Vacuum Pump**—is located at the firewall.

• **Defogger Timer**—is located at the relay box under the left side of the dash.

• **Detonation Sensor (turbo)**—is located at the rear of the engine block near the injectors.

• **Door Ajar Warning Diode**—is located at the left door.

• **Door Lock Control Unit**—is located at the right kick panel.

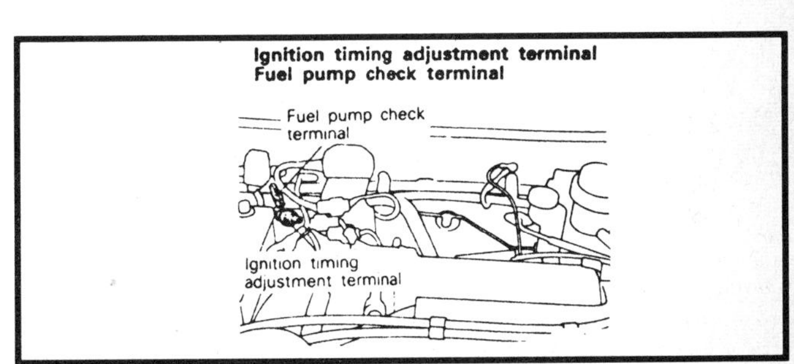

Component locations—Eclipse

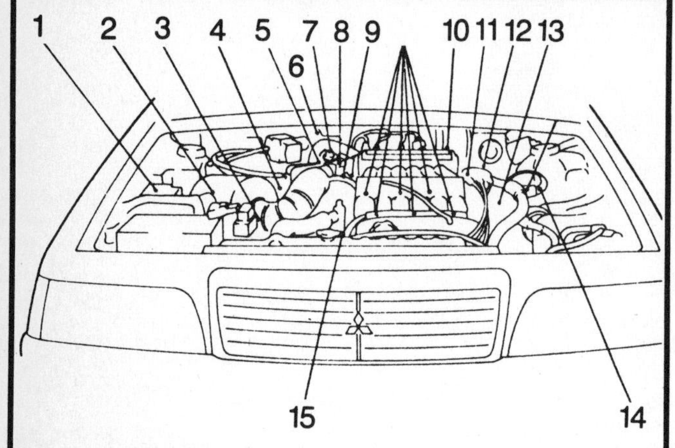

Component locations—Sigma

- **Door Lock Relay**—is located at the relay box under the left side of the dash.
- **EGR Control Solenoid Valve (California)**—is located at the firewall.
- **EGR Temperature Sensor (California)**—is located at the EGR valve.
- **EGR Thermo Valve (2.0L engine)**—is located at the thermostat housing.
- **EGR Valve**—is located at the right side of the engine.
- **Engine Control Unit (2.0L engine)**—is located at the front of the console under the dash.
- **Engine Speed Connector (2.0L engine)**—is located at the rear of the engine near the firewall.
- **Fog Light Relay**—is located at the relay box on the right side of the engine compartment.
- **Fuel Pump Check Connector**—is located at the right rear of the engine compartment.
- **Headlight Relay**—is located at the relay box on the right side of the engine compartment.
- **Heater Relay**—is located under the left side of the dash.
- **Idle Position Switch**—is located inside the idle speed control servo.
- **Idle Speed Control Servo**—is located at the throttle body.
- **Ignition Timing Adjustment Connector**—is located at the right rear of the engine compartment.
- **Inhibitor Switch**—is located at the transmission.
- **Intake Air Temperature Sensor**—is located inside the air flow sensor.
- **Intermittent Front Wiper Relay**—is located inside the steering column.
- **Intermittent Rear Wiper Relay**—is located at the left quarter panel behind the left seat.
- **Magnet Clutch Relay**—is located at the left rear of the engine compartment.
- **Oxygen Sensor Check Connector (2.0L engine)**—is located under the right side of the dash.
- **Oxygen Sensor**—is located at the exhaust manifold.
- **PCV Valve**—is located at the rear of the cam cover.
- **Pop Up Diode**—is located under the right side of the dash.
- **Pop Up Relay**—is located at the relay box on the right side of the engine compartment.
- **Power Steering Fluid Pressure Switch**—is located at the power steering pump.
- **Power Window Relay**—is located at the relay box on the right side of the engine compartment.
- **Pulse Generators**—are located at the transmission.
- **Purge Control Solenoid Valve**—is located at the firewall.
- **Radiator Fan Motor Relay**—is located at the relay box on the right side of the engine compartment.
- **Self-Diagnosis Connector**—is located under the left side of the dash.
- **Starter Relay**—is located at the relay box under the left side of the dash.
- **Taillight Relay**—is located at the relay box on the right side of the engine compartment.
- **TDC Sensor (1.8L engine)**—is located inside the distributor.
- **TDC Sensor (2.0L engine and turbo**—is located at the cam cover near the thermostat housing.
- **Theft Alarm Control Unit**—is located at the right kick panel.
- **Theft Alarm Diode**—is located under the left side of the dash.
- **Theft Alarm Relay**—is located at the relay box under the left side of the dash.
- **Theft Alarm Starter Relay (automatic transmission)**—is located under the left side of the dash.
- **Theft Alarm Starter Relay (manual transmission)**—is located under the front of the console.
- **Throttle Position Sensor**—is located at the throttle body.
- **Transmission Oil Temperature Sensor**—is located at the transmission.
- **Vehicle Speed Sensor (2.0L engine)**—is located at the speedometer.
- **Warning Buzzer**—is located under the dash at the steering column.
- **Waste Gate Control Valve (turbo)**—is located at the right front of the engine compartment near the air filter.

GALANT

- **4 Wheel Steering Diode (1991)**—is located behind the instrument panel.
- **A/C Air Inlet Sensor**—is located inside the evaporator housing.
- **A/C Air Thermo Sensor**—is located inside the evaporator housing.
- **A/C Compressor Control Unit**—is located under the dash near the glove box.
- **A/C Compressor Relay**—is located in the relay box at the right side of the engine comartment.
- **ABS Brake Fluid Pressure Switch (AWD)**—is located at the ABS hydraulic unit.
- **ABS Control Unit**—is located at the left side of the trunk.
- **ABS Diode (1989–90)**—is located at the left kick panel.
- **ABS Diode**—is located at the left kick panel.
- **ABS G-Sensors**—are located under the console and forward of the spare tire.
- **ABS Hydraulic Unit**—is located at the left front of the engie compartment.
- **ABS Motor Relay**—is located at the ABS hydraulic unit.
- **ABS Power Relay**—is located at the left kick panel.

• **ABS Valve Relay**—is located at the ABS hydraulic unit.
• **Active-ECS Diode (1991)**—is located under the left side of the dash.
• **Air Conditioner Relay**—is located in the relay box at the right side of the engine compartment.
• **Air Flow Sensor**—is located at the right side of the engine compartment in the air cleaner.
• **Alternator Relay**—is located in the relay box at the right side of the engine comartment.
• **Automatic Seat Belt Control Unit**—is located under the rear of the console.
• **Automatic Seat Belt Motor Relay**—is located at the left side door pillar near the floor.
• **Automatic Transaxle Control Unit**—is located under the left side of the dash.
• **Automatic transaxle Fluid Temperature Diode**—is located behind the instrument panel.
• **Automatic Transaxle Oil Temperature Sensor**—is located at the front of the transaxle.
• **Automatic Transmission Check Connector**—is located under the left side of the dash.
• **Barometric Pressure Sensor**—is located inside the air flow meter.
• **Coolant Temperature Sensor**—is located at the thermostat housing.
• **Crank Angle Sensor/TDC Sensor (DOHC)**—is located at the right side of the cam cover near the air cleaner.
• **Crank Angle Sensor/TDC Sensor (SOHC)**—is located at the distributor.
• **Cruise Control Actuator (sohc or dohc/vacuum)**—is located at the right rear of the engine compartment.
• **Cruise Control Actuator (sohc/electrical)**—is located at the right rear of the engine compartment.
• **Cruise Control Diode (1989–90)**—is located behind the instrument panel.
• **Cruise Control Diode**—is located behind the instrument panel.
• **Cruise Control Unit**—is located under the left side of the dash.
• **Cruise Control Vacuum Pump (SOHC or DOHC/vacuum)**—is located at the right rear of the engine compartment.
• **Defogger Relay**—is located at the relay box under the left side of the dash.
• **Door Lock Control Unit**—is located inside the ETACS control unit.
• **Door Lock Relay**—is located at the relay box under the left side of the dash.
• **ECS Actuators**—are located at the shock absorbers.
• **ECS Air Compressor Relay**—is located at the right side of the engine compartment.
• **ECS Air Compressor**—is located at the right side of the engine compartment.
• **ECS Control Unit**—is located at the right side of the trunk.
• **ECS Exhaust Solenoid Valve**—is located above the front height sensor on the front suspension assembly.
• **ECS G-Sensor**—is located under the front of the vehicle at the centermember.
• **ECS Height Sensors**—are located at the front right and left rear suspension assemblies.
• **ECS High/Low Pressure Switch**—is located at the right front of the engin compartment.
• **ECS Power Relay**—is located at the left kick panel.
• **ECS Relay**—is located in the relay box at the right side of the engine comartment.
• **ECS Reserve Tank**—is located inside the return pump at the right front of the vehicle.
• **ECS Return Pump Relay**—is located at the right side of the engine compartment.
• **ECS Self Diagnosis Connector**—is located at the left kick panel.
• **ECS Solenoid Valve Power Relay**—is located at the relay box on the right side of the engine compartment.
• **ECS Solenoid Valves**—are located at the firewall and at the right side of the trunk.
• **ECS Steering Wheel Angular Velocity Sensor**—is located at the steering wheel.
• **EGR Control Solenoid Valve (California)**—is located at the right rear of the engine compartment.
• **EGR Temperature Sensor (California)**—is located at the EGR valve.
• **Electronic Timer and Control System Control Unit**—is located under the left side of the dash.
• **Engine Control Unit**—is located under the right side of the dash.
• **Engine Speed Detection Connector**—is located at the rear side of the valve cover.
• **EPS Control Unit**—is located under the center of the dash at the front of the console.
• **EPS Self Diagnosis Check Connector**—is located under the right side of the dash.
• **Fluid Level Warning Light Diode (1991)**—is located behind the instrument panel.
• **Fog Light Relay**—is located in the relay box at the right side of the engine comartment.
• **Fuel Pump Check Connector**—is located at the firweall.
• **Headlight Relay**—is located in the relay box at the right side of the engine comartment.
• **Heater Relay**—is located under the left side of the dash.
• **Idle Speed Control Servo**—is located at the throttle body.
• **Ignition Timing Adjustment Connector**—is located at the firweall.
• **Inhibitor Switch (automatic transaxle)**—is located at the top of the transaxle.
• **Intake Air Temperature Sensor**—is located inside the air flow meter.
• **MPI Control Relay**—is located under the right side of the dash.
• **Oxygen Sensor Check Connector**—is located at the right kick panel.
• **Oxygen Sensor**—is located in the exhaust manifold at the front of the engine.
• **Power Steering Oil Pressure Switch**—is located at the power steering pump.
• **Power Steering**—see Electronic Control Power Steering (EPS).
• **Power Window Relay**—is located at the relay box under the left side of the dash.
• **Pulse Generator**—is located at the top of the transaxle.
• **Purge Control Solenoid Valve**—is located at the firewall.
• **Radiator Fan Motor Relay**—is located in the relay box at the right side of the engine comartment.
• **Seat Belt Timer**—is located at the relay box under the left side of the dash.
• **Self Diagnosis Connector**—is located under the left side of the dash.
• **Sunroof Diode (1991)**—is located under the left side of the dash.
• **Sunroof Relay**—is located at the sunroof motor in the headliner.
• **Suspension**—see Electronic Control Suspension (ECS).
• **Taillight Relay**—is located in the relay box at the right side of the engine comartment.
• **TDC Sensor/Crank Angle Sensor (DOHC)**—is located at the right side of the cam cover near the air cleaner.
• **TDC Sensor/Crank Angle Sensor (SOHC)**—is located at the distributor.

• **Theft Alarm Diode 3 (1991)**—is located behind the instrument panel.
• **Theft Alarm Headlight Relay**—is located at the right front of the engine compartment.
• **Theft Alarm Horn Relay**—is located at the left rear of the engine compartment.
• **Theft Alarm Starter Relay**—is located at the relay box under the left side of the dash.
• **Theft Alarm System Diode 1 and 2 (1991)**—is located behind the instrument panel.
• **Throttle Position Sensor**—is located at the throttle body.
• **Vehicle Speed Sensor**—is located at the speedometer.
• **Waste Gate Control (DOHC)**—is located at the right side of the engine compartment near the air cleaner.
• **Wiper Relay**—is located next to the wiper motor.

MIRAGE

• **A/C Air Inlet Sensor**—is located at the evaporator under the center of the dash.
• **A/C Air Thermo Sensor**—is located at the evaporator under the center of the dash.
• **A/C Compressor Control Unit**—is located above the evaporator under the center of the dash.
• **A/C Compressor Relay 1**—is located at the left side of the engine compartment.
• **A/C Compressor Relay 2**—is located at the relay box on the right side of the engine compartment.
• **A/C Refrigerant Temperature Sensor**—is located at the rear of the compressor.
• **Air Flow Sensor**—is located at the air cleaner.
• **Alternator Relay**—is located at the relay box on the right side of the engine compartment.
• **Automatic Seat Belt Control Unit**—is located under the console near the parking brake lever.
• **Automatic Seat Belt Motor Relay**—is located at the left side door pilar.
• **Automatic Transmission Control Unit**—is located under the center of the dash.
• **Automatic Transmission Inspection Connector**—is located under the left side of the dash.
• **Automatic Transmission Oil Temeprature Sensor (4 speed)**—is located at the front of the transmission.
• **Barometric Pressure Sensor**—is located inside the air flow sensor.
• **Condenser Fan Motor Control Relay**—is located at the relay box on the right side of the engine compartment.
• **Condenser Fan Motor**—is located at the relay box on the right side of the engine compartment.
• **Coolant Temperature Sensor (1.5L engine)**—is located at the right side of the engine below the camshaft cover on the cylinder head.
• **Coolant Temperature Sensor (1.6L engine)**—is located at the thermostat housing.
• **Crank Angle Sensor**—is located at the cylinder head above the thermostat housing.
• **Cruise Control Acutator**—is located at the firewall.
• **Cruise Control Unit**—is located under the left side of the dash.
• **Cruise Control Vacuum Pump**—is located at the right side of the engine compartment.
• **Damper Clutch Control Solenoid Valve (DCCSV) (3 speed)**—is located at the valve body.
• **Door Lock Control Unit**—is located at the left kick panel.
• **Door Lock Relay**—is located at the left kick panel.
• **EGR Control Solenoid Valve**—is located at the firewall.
• **EGR Temperature Sensor**—is located at the EGR valve.
• **Engine Speed Detection Connector (1.6L engine)**—is located at the left side of the engine.
• **Fuel Injection—see Multi Point Injection (MPI).**
• **Fuel Pump Check Connector**—is located at the firewall.
• **Headlight Relay**—is located at the relay box on the right side of the engine compartment.
• **Heater Relay**—is located at the left kick panel.
• **Idle Position Switch**—is located at the throttle body.
• **Ignition Timing Adjustment Connector**—is located at the firewall.
• **Inhibitor Switch**—is located under the battery at the transmission.
• **Intake Air Temperature Sensor**—is located inside the air flow sensor.
• **Intermittent Wiper Relay**—is located inside the steering column.
• **Motor Position Switch**—is located at the throttle body.
• **MPI Control Relay**—is located under the console at the center of the dash.
• **MPI Control Unit (1.5L engine)**—is located next to the blower motor under the dash.
• **MPI Control Unit (1.6L engine)**—is located at the right kick panel.
• **Oil Pressure Switch**—is located at the right rear of the engine.
• **Oxygen Sensor Check Connector (1.6L engine)**—is located next to the blower motor under the right side of the dash.
• **Oxygen Sensor**—is located at the exhaust manifold.
• **Power Steering Oil Pressure Switch**—is located at the power steering pump.
• **Power Window Relay**—is located at the relay box on the right side of the engine compartment.
• **Pulse Generator**—is located at the top of the transmission.
• **Purge Control Solenoid Valve**—is located at the firewall.
• **Radiator Fan Motor Relay**—is located at the relay box on the right side of the engine compartment.
• **Self Diagnosis Connector**—is located under the left side of the dash.
• **Self Diagnosis Terminal**—is located under the left side of the dash.
• **Throttle Position Sensor**—is located at the throttle body.
• **Vehicle Speed Sensor**—is located at the speedometer.

PRECIS

• **A/C Diode**—is located under the right side of the dash.
• **A/C Dual Pressure Switch**—is located in the receiver drier.
• **A/C Relay**—is located under the left side of the dash.
• **Accelerator Switch**—is located on the accelerator pedal bracket.
• **Air Flow Sensor**—is located in the air cleaner.
• **Automatic transaxle Control Unit (TACU)**—is located under the left front seat.
• **Automatic transaxle Solenoid Valve**—is located at the radiator side of the transaxle.
• **Back-Up Light Switch**—is located on top of the transaxle.
• **Blower Relay**—is located under the left side of the dash.
• **Bowl Vent Valve (carburetor)**—is located on the top of the carburetor, on float chamber cover.
• **Brake Fluid Sensor**—is located in the master cylinder.
• **Cold Mixture Heater (carburetor)**—is located under the carburetor.
• **Condenser Fan Relay**—is located at the left front of the engine compartment.
• **Condenser**—is located at the left front of the engine compartment.

- **Coolant Temperature Sensor**—is located in the rear of the engine under the fresh air duct.
- **Crankshaft Angle Sensor**—is located in the distributor.
- **Daytime Running Light Unit (Canada)**—is located at the right front of the engine compartment.
- **Door Warning Switch**—is located at the ignition switch.
- **EGR Control Solenoid Valve (California)**—is located on the firewall in the engine compartment.
- **EGR Temperature Sensor (California)**—is located on the EGR valve.
- **Electronic Control Unit (ECU)**—is located under the dash on the left side.
- **Exhaust Gas Recirculation (EGR) Valve**—is located near the fuel injection unit mounted to the engine block.
- **Feedback Solenoid Valve (carbureted)**—is located at the carburetor.
- **Fuel Injection**—see Multi-Point Injection (MPI).
- **Fuse Box Relay (red)**—is located in the fusible link box, at the battery.
- **Fuse Box**—is located in the left kick panel.
- **Hazard Flasher**—is located in the relay box under the left side of the dash.
- **Headlight Relay**—is located in the fusible link box, at the battery.
- **Idle Speed Control Sensor**—is located on the fuel injection unit near the firewall.
- **Ignition Lock Switch (manual transaxle)**—is located on the clutch pedal bracket.
- **Ignition Relay**—is located in the fusible link box, at the battery.
- **Inhibitor Switch**—is located on the top of the transaxle.
- **Intake Air Temperature Sensor**—is located in the air cleaner.
- **Kick Down Switch**—is located is located on the radiator side of the transaxle.
- **Main Fuse Box**—is located on the side of the battery.
- **Main-Fusible Link Box**—is located at the battery.
- **MPI Diagnostic Connector**—is located at the left kick panel.
- **MPI Relay**—is located under the left side of the dash.
- **Multi-Point Injection (MPI) Control Unit**—is located to the left of the center console under the dash.
- **Noise Filter**—is located at the left front of the engine compartment.
- **Oil Pressure Switch**—is located behind the alternator.
- **Oil Temperature Sensor**—is located is located on the radiator side of the transaxle.
- **Oxygen Sensor**—is located in the exhaust manifold.
- **Oxygen Sensor Checker**—is located on the center right side of the engine compartment.
- **PCV Valve**—is located on the back of the valve cover, near the spark plug wires.
- **Power Steering Oil Pressure Switch**—is located on the power steering pump.
- **Power Transistor**—is located on the back of the valve cover near the injectors.
- **Power/Economy Switch**—is located in the transaxle shift lever on the console.
- **Pulse Generator**—is located on the top of the transaxle.
- **Purge Control Solenoid Valve**—is located on the firewall in the engine compartment.
- **Radiator Fan Motor Relay**—is located at the left front of the engine compartment.
- **Radiator Fan Resistor**—is located near the thermostat switch.
- **Relay Box**—is located under the left side of the dash.
- **Self Diagnosis Check Connector**—is located in the left kick panel.
- **Slow Cut Solenoid Valve (carbureted)**—is located at the carburetor.
- **Starter Relay**—is located in the relay box under the left side of the dash.
- **Sub-Fusible Link Box**—is located at the left front of the engine compartment.
- **Taillight Relay**—is located in the relay box under the left side of the dash.
- **Thermo Valve**—is located at the rear of the engine on the battery side.
- **Thermostat Switch**—is located at the injector side of the engine near the firewall.
- **Throttle Position Sensor**—is located on the front of the fuel injection unit, or on the carburetor.
- **Transaxle Control Unit (TCU)**—is located under the right front seat.
- **Two Way Valve**—is located in the fuel tank.
- **Vehicle Speed Sensor**—is located in the speedometer.

SIGMA

- **A/C Air Flow Sensor**—is located inside the cooling unit.
- **A/C Condenser Fan Motor Relay**—is located at the left front of the engine compartment.
- **A/C Control Unit**—is located under the center of the dash.
- **A/C Coolant Temperature Switch**—is located at the thermostat housing.
- **A/C Dual Pressure Switch**—is located at the receiver drier.
- **A/C Outside Temperature Sensor**—is located at the grille.
- **A/C Passenger Compartment Temperature Sensor**—is located at the headliner.
- **A/C Photo Sensor**—is located in the defroster grille.
- **A/C Power Relay**—is located under the center of the dash.
- **A/C Pressure Switch**—is located at the refrigerant line on the left side of the engine compartment.
- **A/C Relay**—is located at the right side of the engine compartment in the relay box.
- **A/C Thermoswitch**—is located at the thermostat housing.
- **ABS Diode**—is located under dash at the steering column.
- **ABS Motor Relay**—is located at the hydraulic unit.
- **ABS Relay**—is located at under the left side of the dash in the relay box.
- **ABS Relay**—is located under the left side of the dash.
- **ABS Valve Relay**—is located at the hydraulic unit.
- **Airbag Diagnosis Unit**—is located at the center of the dash under the heater controls.
- **Airbag Front G-Sensor**—is located at the left and right side front wheel well.
- **Alternator Relay**—is located at the right front of the engine compartment.
- **Anti-Lock Brakes**—see ABS.
- **Coolant Temperature Sensor**—is located next to the engine lifting tab at the front of the engine.
- **Crank Angle Sensor**—is located inside the distributor.
- **Cruise Control Actuator**—is located at the right side of the engine compartment.
- **Cruise Control Diode**—is located to the left of the steering wheel.
- **Cruise Control Unit**—is located under the left side of the dash, near the ETACS unit.
- **Defogger Relay**—is located at under the left side of the dash in the relay box.
- **Door Lock Control Relay**—is located at the left kick panel.
- **ECS Air Compressor**—is located at the right side of the engine compartment.
- **ECS Compressor Relay**—is located at the right front of the engine compartment.

• **ECS Control Unit**—is located at the right side of the trunk.

• **ECS Front Solenoid Valve**—is located at the right rear of the engine compartment.

• **ECS Height Sensors**—are located at the right front and left rear suspension assemblies.

• **ECS Rear Solenoid Valve**—is located at the right side of the trunk.

• **ECS Reserve Tank**—is located next to the battery.

• **ECS Steering Wheel Angular Velocity Sensor**—is located inside the steering column.

• **EGR Control Solenoid Valve**—is located at the firewall.

• **EGR Temperature Sensor**—is located at the EGR valve.

• **EGR Valve**—is located at the right rear of the engine near the firewall.

• **Electronic Control Suspension**—see ECS.

• **Electronic Control Unit**—is located at the left quarter panel in the trunk.

• **Electronic Timer and Alarm Control System (ETACS) Control Unit**—is located under the left side of the dash.

• **Engine Control Unit (ECU)**—is located next to the blower motor.

• **Fuel Pump Drive Connector**—is located the left side of the firewall next to the wiper motor.

• **Headlight Relay**—is located at the right side of the engine compartment in the relay box.

• **Heater Relay**—is located at under the left side of the dash in the relay box.

• **Ignition Timing Adjustment Connector**—is located at the left side of the engine compartment.

• **Inhibitor Switch**—is located at the top of the transmission.

• **Magnetic Clutch Relay**—is located at the right side of the engine compartment in the relay box.

• **MPI Air Flow Sensor**—is located in the fresh air duct near the air filter.

• **MPI Control Relay**—is located next to the blower motor.

• **MPI Idle Position Switch**—is located at the throttle body.

• **MPI Idle Speed Control Servo**—is located at the throttle body.

• **MPI Purge Control Valve**—is located at the right side of the engine compartment.

• **MPI Throttle Position Sensor**—is located at the throttle body.

• **Multi Point Injection**—see MPI.

• **Oxygen Sensor**—is located at the exhaust manifold.

• **Power Steering Pressure Switch**—is located at the power steering pump.

• **Power Window Relay**—is located at the right side of the engine compartment in the relay box.

• **Pulse Generator**—is located at the top of the transmission.

• **Radiator Fan Relay**—is located at the right side of the engine compartment in the relay box.

• **Self Diagnosis Check Connector**—is located inside the glove box.

• **Start Inhibitor Relay**—is located next to the battery.

• **Sunroof Relay**—is located at the right kick panel.

• **Taillight Relay**—is located at the right side of the engine compartment in the relay box.

• **Theft Alarm Diode**—is located under the right side of the dash.

• **Transaxle Control Unit**—is located under the center of the dash.

• **Transaxle Oil Cooler Fan Motor Relay**—is located at the right front of the engine compartment.

• **Transaxle Oil Temperature Sensor**—is located at the transmission valve body.

• **Turn Signal/Hazard Flasher Unit**—is located at under the left side of the dash in the relay box.

• **Vehicle Speed Sensor**—is located at the speedometer.

• **Warning Buzzer Diode (seat belt and door ajar)**—is located under the right side of the dash.

• **Wiper Control Relay**—is located at the right front of the engine compartment.

STARION

• **A/C Compressor Clutch Relay**—is located on the relay block on the left front inner fender panel.

• **A/C Dual Pressure Switch**—is located in the A/C line next to the receiver.

• **A/C Heater Blower Motor Relay**—is located on the blower motor housing.

• **A/C-Heater Blower Motor Resistor**—is located on the blower motor housing.

• **A/C Power Relay**—is located on the evaporator housing.

• **A/C Pressure Switch (W/Intercooler)**—is located on the A/C line next to the receiver.

• **A/C Thermister**—is located on the A/C evaporator housing.

• **Airflow Sensor**—is located inside the air cleaner housing.

• **Automatic A/C Control Unit**—is located behind the automatic A/C panel.

• **Automatic A/C Evaporator Temperature Sensor**—is located on the A/C evaporator fins.

• **Automatic A/C In-Car Photo Sensor**—is located on the instrument panel.

• **Automatic A/C In-Car Temperature Sensor**—is located on the right lower outlet vent.

• **Automatic A/C In-Car Temperature Sensor**—is located on the rear part of roll bar trim.

• **Automatic A/C Power Transistor**—is located on the blower unit air outlet.

• **Automatic A/C Temperature Controller**—is located on the evaporator housing.

• **Automatic A/C Vacuum Solenoid Valves**—is located on the A/C evaporator housing.

• **Automatic Seat Belt Control Unit**—is located in the center console, in the passenger's compartment.

• **Automatic Transmission Diode**—is located above the left hand side kick panel.

• **Back-Up Light Switch**—is located on the right side of the transmission.

• **Brake/Stoplight Switch**—is located above the brake pedal.

• **Blower Motor High Speed Relay**—is located under the right hand side of the instrument panel.

• **Blower Motor Relay**—is located under the left hand side of the instrument panel, to the right of the steering column.

• **Blower Motor Starter Cut-Out Relay**—is located under the right hand side of the instrument panel.

• **Chassis Diode**—is located below the left side of the instrument panel.

• **Condenser Fan Relay**—is located on the left hand inner fender panel in the engine compartment.

• **Coolant Temperature Sensor**—is located in the front of the intake manifold.

• **Cooling Fan Relays**—are located on the right front corner of the engine compartment.

• **Detonation (Knock) Sensor**—is located on the right front of the engine.

• **Diagnostic Connector**—is located under the right side of the instrument panel.

• **Downshift Solenoid**—is located on the side of the transmission.

• **ECI Control Relay**—is located behind the right hand side kick panel.

• **ECI Control Unit**—is located behind the right hand side kick panel.

• **ECI & Oxygen Sensor Test Connector**—is located near the right shock tower.

• **ECU Control Relay**—is located above the ECU on the right side kick panel.

• **EGR Control Solenoid**—is located on the left inner fender.

• **Electric Controlled Injection (ECI) Resistors**—are located on the right headlight support.

• **Electric Controlled Injection (ECI) Diodes**—one is located behind the right hand side kick panel, one is located under the left of the instrument panel.

• **Electronic Control Unit (ECU)**—is located on the right hand side kick panel.

• **Electronic Time & Alarm Control System (ETACS) Unit**—is located under the driver's seat.

• **Engine Spark Control (ESC) Ignitor**—is located on the left inner fender panel.

• **Engine Speed Sensor**—is located on the back of the speedometer.

• **Fog Light Diodes**—one is located behind the instrument panel, one is located on the center of the instrument panel to the right of the console.

• **Fog Light Relay**—is located near the right headlight door.

• **Foot Area Temperature Sensor**—is located under the right hand side of the instrument panel.

• **Fuel Gauge Sending Unit**—is located in the top of the fuel tank.

• **Fuel Pump**—is located in the top of the fuel tank.

• **Fuel Pump Test Connector**—is located near the right shock tower.

• **G-Sensor**—is located on the rear floor crossmember.

• **Hazard Flasher**—is located under the left hand side instrument panel.

• **Headlight Lighting Relay**—is located on the front relay panel.

• **Ignition Timing Adjusting Terminal**—is located near the right shock tower.

• **Inhibitor Switch**—is located on the right side of the transmission.

• **Instrument Panel Lighting Control**—is located on the A/C evaporator housing.

• **Interior Temperature Sensor**—is located on the front center of the roof headliner.

• **Left Headlight Pop-Up Relay**—is located on the front relay panel.

• **Intake Air Temperature Sensor**—is located inside the air cleaner.

• **Manifold Pressure Sensor**—is located on the left corner of the engine compartment.

• **Oil Pressure Sender**—is located on the side of the engine near the oil filter.

• **Oil Pressure Switch**—is located on the front of the engine block.

• **Overdrive Relay**—is located under the left side of the instrument panel.

• **Parking Brake Switch**—is located at the base of the parking brake lever.

• **Passing Control Relay**—is located under the right side of the instrument panel near radio.

• **Passing Control Relay (w/Theft Alarm System)**—is located on the left hand side of the firewall.

• **Pop-Up Relay**—is located on the left hand front corner of the engine compartment.

• **Power Antenna Relay**—is located in the front of the left hand side rear taillight.

• **Power Door Lock Relay**—is located under the left hand side of the instrument panel.

• **Power Door Un-Lock Relay**—is located under the left hand side of the instrument panel.

• **Power Window Relay**—is located on the front relay panel, in the left hand front corner of the engine compartment.

• **Pulse Generator**—is located on the transmission extension housing.

• **Radiator A/C Fan Relay**—is located on the front relay panel, in the left hand inner fender panel in the engine compartment.

• **Radiator Fan Relay**—is located on the right hand front corner of the engine compartment.

• **Rear Brake Lock-Up Control Modulator**—is located on the right rear corner of the engine compartment.

• **Rear Brake Lock-Up Control Relay**—is located under the left hand side of the instrument panel.

• **Rear Brake Lock-Up Control Unit**—is located under the right hand rear luggage compartment panel.

• **Rear Brake Lock-Up Diode**—is located above the left hand side kick panel.

• **Rear Brake Lock-Up Resistor**—is located above the left hand side kick panel.

• **Rear Brake Lock-Up Solenoid Valve**—is located on the rear brake lock-up modulator.

• **Rear Defroster Relay**—is located on the left hand front corner in the engine compartment.

• **Relay Panels**—are located on the left hand side kick panel and the front of the engine compartment.

• **Right Headlight Pop-Up Relay**—is located on the front relay panel.

• **Self Test Connector**—is located in the top center of the glove box.

• **Speed Control Unit**—is located behind the trim panel on the rear of the luggage compartment.

• **Speed Control Vacuum Pump Relay**—is located on the right rear of the engine compartment.

• **Speed Control Vacuum Switch**—is located on the right rear corner of the engine compartment.

• **Starter Inhibitor Relay**—is located on the left hand front corner in the engine compartment.

• **TAC Unit**—is located on the top of the driver's front door pillar.

• **Taillight Lighting Relay**—is located on the front relay panel.

• **Thermo Sensor Number One**—is located on the front of the radiator support.

• **Thermo Sensor Number Two**—is located on the bottom of the radiator.

• **Throttle Position Sensor**—is located on the throttle body assembly.

• **Turn Signal Flasher**—is located under the left hand side of the instrument panel.

• **Vacuum Pump Relay**—is located on the right hand rear corner of the engine compartment.

• **Wiper Power Relay**—is located on the front relay panel, on the left front inner fender panel.

• **Wiper Low & High Relay**—is located on the front relay panel, on the left front inner fender panel.

MITSUBISHI TRUCKS

Circuit Breakers

MIGHTY MAX

Fuses are located at the fuse block under the left side of the dash.

MONTERO

Montero uses In-line, dedicated fuses inplace of circuit breakers. Fuses are located at the left side of the dash. They are located as follows:
A/C Fuse—is located above the evaporator.
Center Locking Door Fuse—is located to the right of the blower assembly.
Dual A/C Fuse—is located at the blower assembly.
Headlight Fuse—is located at the right front of the engine compartment.
Sunroof Fuse—is located to the right of the blower assembly.

Fusible Links

MIGHTY MAX

Fusible links are located at the battery and the left rear of the engine compartment.

MONTERO

Fusible links are located as follows:
Defogger Fusible Link (3.0L engine)—is located at the firewall.
Defogger Fusible Link (2.6L engine)—is located at the right side of the engine compartment.
3.0L Engine Fusible Link—is located at the right rear of the engine compartment.
2.6L Engine Fusible Link—is located at the left rear of the engine compartment.

Relays, Sensors, Modules and Computer Locations

MIGHTY MAX

- **A/C Power Relay**—is located at the left rear of the engine compartment.
- **A/C Temperature Sensor (3.0L engine)**—is located behind the alternator on the intake manifold.
- **Air Flow Sensor**—is located at the air cleaner.
- **Anti Lock Brakes—see Rear Wheel Anti Lock Brakes (RWAL).**
- **Automatic Free Wheeling Hub Control Unit**—is located at the right kick panel.
- **Automatic Transmission Indicator Diode**—is located under the left side of the dash.
- **Barometric Pressure Sensor**—is located inside the air flow sensor.
- **Central Locking Control Relay**—is located at the right door behind the trim panel.
- **Coolant Temperature Sensor**—is located at the front of the engine.
- **Crank Angle Sensor**—is located at the distributor.
- **Cruise Control Unit**—is located under the left side of the dash.
- **Cruise Control Vacuum Pump Relay**—is located at the right rear of the engine compartment.
- **EGR Control Solenoid Valve**—is located at the left front of the engine compartment.
- **EGR Temperature Sensor (California)**—is located at the EGR valve.
- **Engine Control Relay**—is located under the right side of the dash.
- **Engine Control Unit (ECU)**—is located under the right side of the dash.
- **Fuel Pump Check Terminal**—is located at the right rear of the engine compartment.
- **Idle Speed Control Servo**—is located at the throttle body.
- **Ignition Timing Adjustment Terminal**—is located at the right rear of the engine compartment.
- **Intake Air Temperature Sensor**—is located inside the air flow sensor.
- **Oil Pressure Switch**—is located at the oil filter.
- **Oxygen Sensor Check Terminal**—is located at the right rear of the engine compartment.
- **Oxygen Sensor**—is located at the exhaust manifold.
- **Power Window Control Relay**—is located at the left door behind the trim panel.
- **Power Window Relay**—is located in the relay box.
- **Purge Control Solenoid Valve**—is located on the left side of the engine compartment.
- **Rear Wheel Anti Lock Brakes—see RWAL.**
- **Relay Box**—is located under the left side of the dash.
- **RWAL Control Unit**—is located under the center of the dash.
- **RWAL G-Sensor**—is located under the center of the dash.
- **RWAL Modulator**—is located forward of the righ rear wheel.
- **RWAL Self Diagnosis Connector**—is located at the fuse block.
- **Seat Belt Warning Timer Relay**—is located in the relay box.
- **Self-Diagnosis Terminal**—is located at the fuse block under the left side of the dash.
- **Speed Sensor**—is located at the rear differential.
- **TDC Sensor (2.4L engine)**—is located at the distributor.
- **Throttle Position Sensor**—is located at the throttle body.
- **Turn Signal/Hazard Flasher Unit**—is located in the relay box.
- **Vehicle Speed Sensor**—is located at the speedometer.

MONTERO

- **A/C Condenser Fan Relay (dual air)**—is located below the master cylinder.
- **A/C Condenser Fan Relay (single air)**—is located next to the ignition coil.
- **A/C Coolant Temperature Switch**—is located at the thermostat housing.
- **A/C Magnetic Valve (rear evaporator)**—is located at the rear evaporator on the right side of the rear passenger compartment.
- **A/C Pressure Switch**—is located next to the right headlight.
- **A/C Relay (dual air)**—is located in a storage compartment behind the rear seat.
- **A/C Relay**—is located at the evaporator.
- **A/C Thermoswitch (rear evaporator)**—is located at the rear evaporator on the right side of the rear passenger compartment.

• **A/C Thermoswitch (single air)**—is located above the evaporator.
• **A/C Vacuum Solenoid Valve (single air)**—is located next to the wiper motor.
• **Air Flow Sensor**—is located at the air cleaner.
• **Auto Choke Relay**—is located in the device box on the left side of the engine compartment.
• **Automatic Transmission Oil Temperature Warning Light Diode (3.0L engine)**—is located above the master cylinder reservoir.
• **Condenser Fan Motor Relay**—is located under the master cylinder.
• **Coolant Temperature Sensor**—is located at the thermostat housing.
• **Cruise Control Actuator**—is located at the left side of the engine compartment.
• **Cruise Control Unit**—is located under the left side of the dash.
• **Door Lock Control Unit**—is located under the console.
• **Engine Control Unit**—is located under the right side of the dash.
• **Feedback Carburetor Control Unit**—is located under the right side of the dash.
• **Feedback Carburetor Solenoid Valve**—is located at the carburetor.
• **Fuel Injection—see Multi Point Injection (MPI).**
• **Fuel Pump Drive Terminal (3.0L engine)**—is located under the right side of the dash.
• **Headlight Washer Relay**—is located at the left kick panel.
• **Heater Relay**—is located to the left of the evaporator under the dash.
• **Idle Up Solenoid**—is located on the firewall.
• **Inhibitor Switch (automatic transmission)**—is located at the gear selector lever.
• **Inhibitor Switch (automatic transmission)**—is located at the gear selector lever.
• **Intermittent Wiper Relay (front)**—is located under the left side of the dash.
• **Intermittent Wiper Relay (rear)**—is located under the right side of the dash.
• **Maintenance Warning Light Diode**—is located under the dash above the steering column.
• **MPI Control Motor Relay**—is located at the right kick panel.
• **MPI Coolant Temperature Switch**—is located at the thermostat facing upward.
• **MPI Crank Angle Sensor/TDC Sensor**—is located inside the distributor.
• **MPI Idle Speed Control Servo**—is located at the throttle body.
• **MPI Idle Switch**—is located inside the throttle position sensor.
• **MPI Throttle Position Sensor**—is located at the throttle body.
• **Overdrive Control Relay**—is located under the right side of the dash.
• **Oxygen Sensor**—is located at the right side exhaust manifold.
• **Oxygen Sensor**—is located forward of the catalytic converter in the exhaust pipe.
• **Power Steering Oil Pressure Switch**—is located at the power steering pump.
• **Power Window Control Relay**—is located inside the left front door.
• **Power Window Relay**—is located at the left kick panel.
• **Purge Control Valve**—is located at the firewall.
• **Seat Belt Warning Timer**—is located at the left kick panel.
• **Secondary Air Control Valve**—is located at the device box on the left side of the engine compartment.
• **Self Diagnosis Check Connector (2.6L engine)**—is located at the right rear of the engine compartment.
• **Self Diagnosis Check Connector (3.0L engine)**—is located above the blower assembly.
• **Slow Cut Solenoid Valve**—is located at the carburetor.
• **Spark Timing Adjuster Connector (3.0L engine)**—is located at the left rear of the engine compartment.
• **Sunroof Relay**—is located at the sunroof motor.
• **Throttle Position Sensor (carbureted)**—is located at the carburetor.
• **Vacuum Switch**—is located at the device box on the left side of the engine compartment.
• **Vehicle Speed Sensor**—is located at the speedometer.
• **Vehicle Speed Sensor**—is located at the speedometer.

NISSAN

Circuit Breakers

240SX

Headlamp Retractor Motor—circuit breaker is located within the motor assembly.
Power Window—circuit breaker is located in the fusebox below the left dash.

SENTRA AND NX/COUPE

Power Door Lock—circuit breakers are contained within each actuator motor.
Power Window—circuit breakers are contained within each motor.
Power Window System—circuit breaker is located beside the steering column bracket under the dash.
Automatic Seat Belt—circuit breakers are located in each seat belt motor.
Automatic Seat Belt System—circuit breaker is located beside the steering column bracket under the dash.

AXXESS

Power Window/Sunroof—circuit breaker is located on the fuse block under the left dashboard.

300ZX

Power Window—circuit breaker is located under left side dash, just above fusebox. It is the left-most component in the row of relays.

MAXIMA

Circuit breakers No. 1 and 2 are located under the left dash, behind the fusebox. No.1 is on top of the SMJ and No. 2 is below the SMJ.

Circuit breakers for the automatic seatbelt motors are contained within each motor assembly.

STANZA

Circuit breakers No.s 1 and 2 for the power windows and power door locks are located under the left dash to the right of the fuse block.
Individual thermal circuit breakers for each power window, power lock motor and automatic seat belt motor are contained within the motor assembly.

Fusible Links

240SX

The fusible links are located in fusebox **A** on the right front side of the engine compartment.

SENTRA

The fusible links (1989–90) are located on the left fender apron, just ahead of the shock tower. Fusible links on 1991 vehicles are in the fuse, fusible link and relay box located at the left front of the engine, between the battery and bodywork.

AXXESS

Fusible links are located at the underhood fuse and relay panel.

PULSAR

Fusible links are located on the left front shock tower, to rear of the battery.

300ZX

The fusible link holder is located on the right fender apron to rear of the shock tower.

MAXIMA

The fusible link holder is located on the forward edge of the left fender apron, between the battery and the bodywork.

STANZA

Fusible links are contained in a holder mounted near the battery on the left front fender apron.

Relays, Sensors, Modules and Computers

240SX

- **A/C Thermo-Control Amplifier**—is located under right dash at evaporator case.
- **A/C Dual Pressure Switch**—is located on the receiver dryer.
- **A/C Condensor Fan Relay (1991)**—is located in relay box B.
- **A/C Fusible Plug**—is located on receiver dryer.
- **A/C Relay**—is located in relay box B.
- **ABS control unit**—is located behind the left rear trim panel in the passenger compartment.
- **Accessory Relay No. 1**—is located in the underdash fuse box, left side of dash.
- **Accessory Relay No. 2**—is located in relay box B.
- **Air Flow Meter**—is located is located at the exit port of the air filter housing.
- **Antenna Timer (1990-91, with power antenna)**—is located in the left rear luggage compartment, at the base of the antenna.
- **Anti-lock Brakes**—see ABS
- **ASCD Cancel Switch**—is located behind dash to left of steering wheel.
- **ASCD Control Module**—is located behind right side kick panel.
- **ASCD Hold Relay (1989–90)**—is located in relay box B.
- **ASCD Hold Relay (1991)**—is located behind the right side kick panel.
- **Automatic Seat Belt Control Module**—is located under the center console, immediately behind the parking brake lever.
- **Automatic Transmission Control Module**—is located behind right dashboard, above glove box.
- **Backup Lamp Switch**—see Reverse lamp switch
- **Bulb check Relay**—is located on the SMJ behind upper left dash.
- **Check Connector**—is located beside the fusebox, under left side dashboard.
- **Chime Unit**—is located behind left front kick panel.
- **Clutch Interlock Switch**—is located on the clutch pedal bracket.
- **Clutch Switch**—is located on the clutch pedal bracket
- **Combination Flasher Unit**—is located behind dash to left of steering wheel
- **Crank Angle Sensor**—is built into the bottom of the distributor.
- **Daytime running light module**—is located on right front fender apron.
- **Door Lock Timer**—is located behind right side kick panel.
- **Door Mirror Actuator Motors**—are located within the mirror housings.
- **ECCS Control Module**—is located behind right side kick panel.
- **ECCS Relay**—is located in fusebox A.
- **EGR Valve**—is located at the rear of the intake manifold.
- **Engine Temperature Sensor**—is located at the front of the intake manifold.
- **Exhaust Temperature Sensor**—is located in exhaust manifold.
- **FICD Solenoid Valve**—is located at right rear of engine at rear of air collector.
- **Fifth Gear Switch (manual transmission)**—is located on top of the transmission case.
- **Flasher Unit**—see Combination flasher unit
- **Fog Lamp Relay**—is located in relay box B.
- **Front Limit Switch (automatic seat belts)**—is located at the front of the upper belt track.
- **Front Wiper Amplifier**—may be located at either front fender on the firewall.
- **Fuel Pressure Regulator**—is located at the rear of the engine on the intake side.
- **Fuel Pump Relay**—is located in fusebox A.
- **Fuel Pump**—is located in the fuel tank.
- **Fuse and Relay Box A**—is located at right front of engine compartment near the battery.
- **Fuse Block**—is located is behind lower left dashboard.
- **Headlamp Retractor Relay No. 4**—is located in fusebox A.
- **Headlamp Retractor Relays No. 1, 2 and 3**—are located in relay box B.
- **Headlamp Timer**—is located behind left front kick panel.
- **Horn Relay**—is located in relay box B.
- **Ignition Coil and Power Transisitor**—is located at the left side of the engine compartment, just forward of the shock tower.

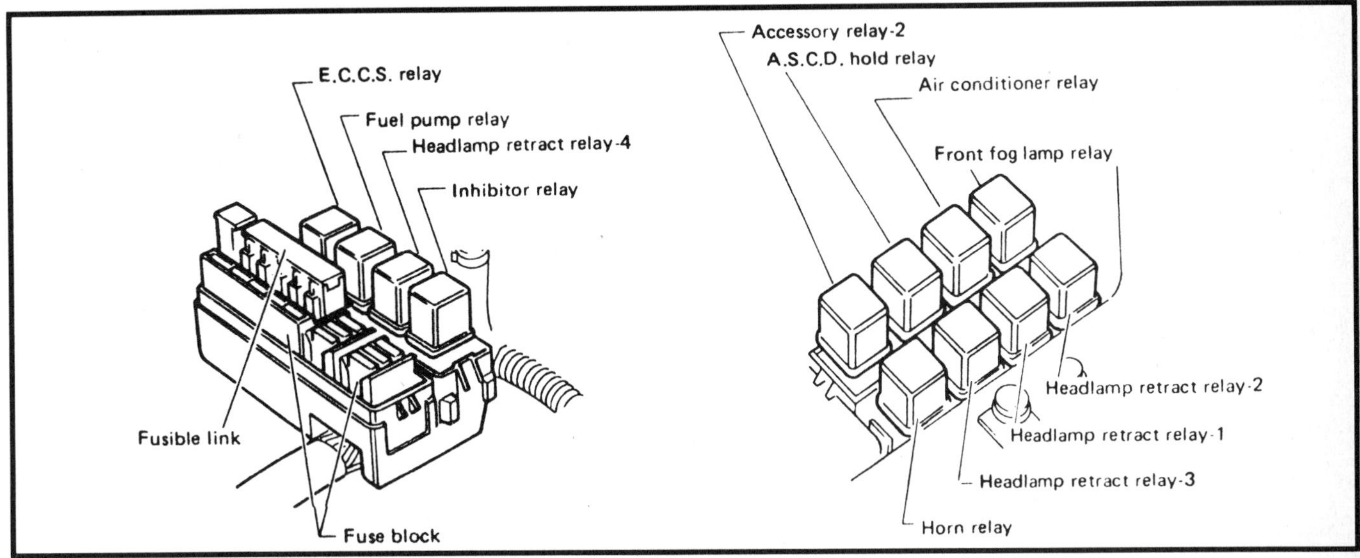

Engine compartment relays—240SX

- **Ignition Relay**—is located in the underdash fuse box, left side of dash.
- **Inhibitor Relay (1989–90)**—is located in fusebox **A**.
- **Inhibitor Relay (1991)**—is located in relay box B.
- **Interlock Relay**—is located on right front fender apron.
- **Key Lock Solenoid**—is located on the ignition key lock assembly.
- **Lap Belt Switch (Left—automatic seat belts)**—is located within the seat belt buckle.
- **Neutral Switch**—is located on the right side of the transmission case.
- **Oil Pressure Switch**—is located on the bottom of the oil filter housing.
- **Overdrive Switch**—is located on the right side of the transmission case.
- **Oxygen Sensor**—is located in exhaust manifold.
- **PCV Valve**—is located on the side of the air collector.
- **Pressure Regulator Control Solenoid Valve**—is located at the rear of the engine, between the valve cover and the firewall.
- **Rear Defogger Relay**—is located behind upper left dash at SMJ.
- **Rear Wiper Amplifier**—is located at center of rear panel, near hatch release mechanism.
- **Relay Box B**—is located at left front of engine compartment behind left headlight.
- **Reverse Lamp Switch**—is located on the right side of the transmission case.
- **Seat Belt Rear Limit Switch**—is located at the rear of the upper seat belt track.
- **Shift Lock Control Module (automatic transmission)**—is located behind dash to left of the steering wheel.
- **SMJ (Super Multiple Junction)**—is located behing upper left dash.
- **Speed Sensor**—is located on tailshaft of transmission housing.
- **Sunroof Close Relay**—is located forward of the sunroof, within the headliner.
- **Sunroof Limit Switch**—is located forward of the sunroof, within the headliner.
- **Sunroof Motor**—is located forward of the sunroof, within the headliner.
- **Sunroof Open Relay**—is located forward of the sunroof, within the headliner.
- **Sunroof Safety Relay**—is located forward of the sunroof, within the headliner.
- **SUPER HICAS Control Unit**—is located behind right rear trim panel in the passenger compartment.
- **Swirl Control Valve (SCV) control solenoid valve**—is located at the rear of the engine, between the valve cover and the firewall.
- **Throttle Valve Sensor**—is located on the the throttle chamber at the end of the air collector.
- **Time Control Unit**—is located behind left front kick panel.

1989–91 SENTRA AND 1991 SENTRA/NX COUPE

- **A/C Condenser Fan Relay (1989–90)**—is located at left firewall, behind shock tower
- **A/C Dual Ppressure Switch**—is located on the receiver/dryer.
- **A/C Relay (1991)**—is located in the relay box.
- **A/C Relay (1989–90)**—is located at left firewall, behind shock tower.
- **A/C Thermal Protector**—is located in the body of the air conditioning compressor.
- **AAC Valve (1991)**—is located to left of oil filter.
- **Accessory Relay (1989–90)**—is located in the underdash fusebox.
- **Accessory Relay (1991)**—is located in the underdash fusebox.
- **Air Bag Control Module (1991)**—is located behind the center console.
- **Air Flow Meter (1989–90)**—is located on the throttle body.
- **Air Flow Meter (1991)**—is located at the exit port of the air cleaner housing.
- **Air Intake Valve (AIV) (1989–90)**—is located on the left rear side of the head.
- **Air Intake Valve (AIV) (1991)**—is located above exhaust manifold.
- **Anti-lock Brake System Control Module (1991)**—is located behind the right front kick panel.
- **ASCD Hold Relay (1991)**—is located behind the left front kick panel.

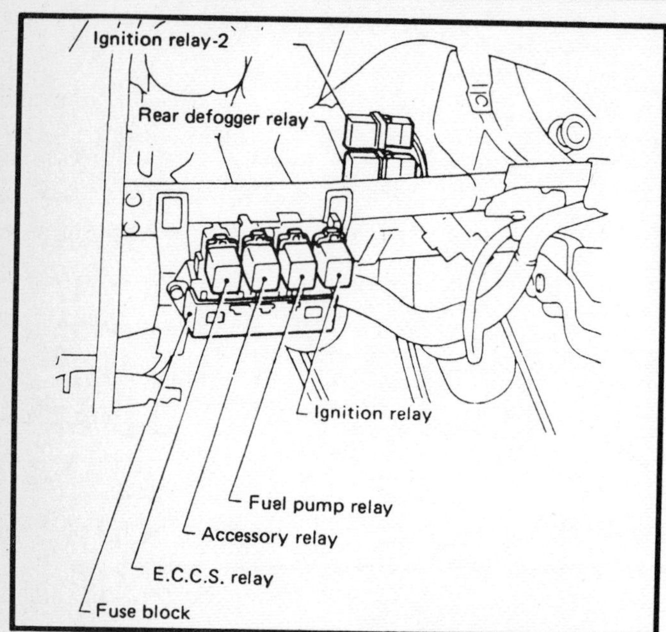

Passenger compartment relays—1989–90 Sentra

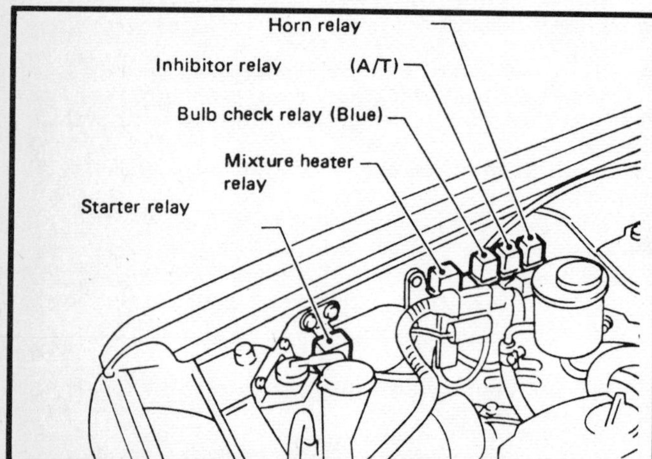

Engine compartment relays—1989–90 Sentra

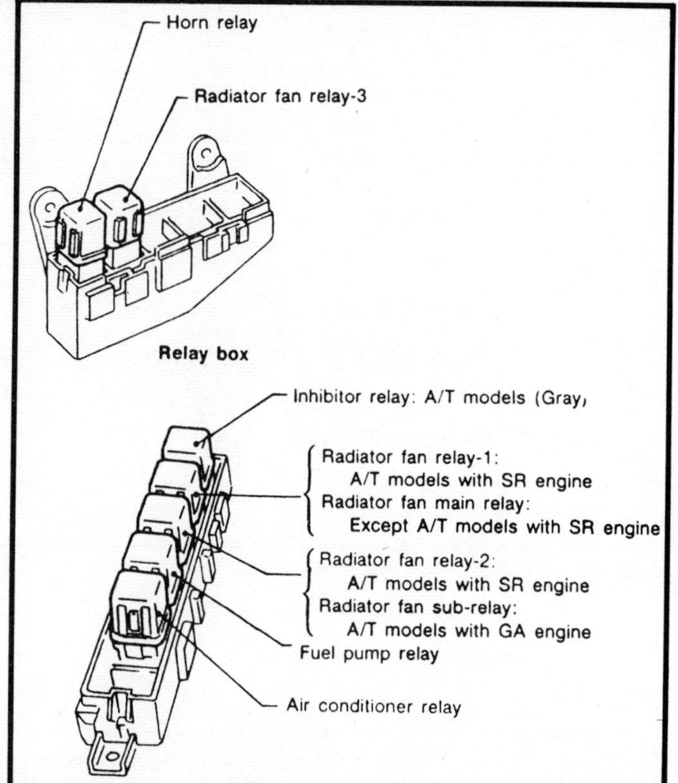

Relay locations—1991 Sentra

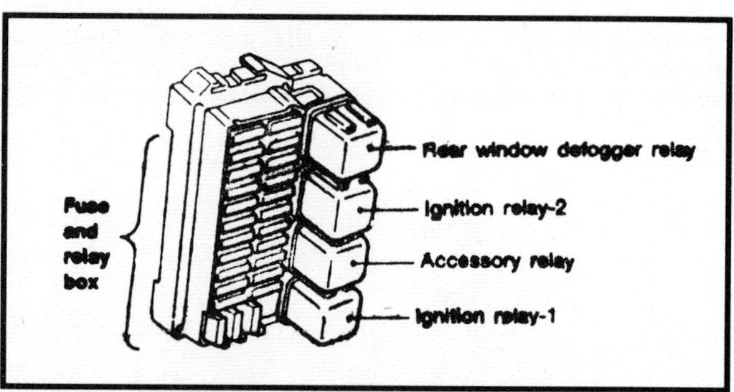

Passenger compartment relays—1991 Sentra

• **Automatic Seat Belt Control Module (1991)**—is located behind the center console, ahead of the shifter.

• **Auxilairy Air Control (AAC) Valve (1989–90)**—is located on the throttle body.

• **BPT Valve (1991)**—is located next to the EGR valve.

• **Bulb Check Relay (1989–90)**—is located on the underhood relay board.

• **Clutch Interlock Switch**—is located on the pedal bracket.

• **Combination Flasher Module (1991)**—is located behind the left dash.

• **Combination Flasher Unit (1989–90)**—is located on small bracket attached to pedal support at firewall under dash.

• **Cooling Fan Relays 1,2, 3 and sub-relays (1991)**—are located in the relay box.

• **Crank Angle Sensor (1989–90)**—is located in the base of the distributor.

• **Crank Angle Sensor (1991)**—is located in the bottom of the distributor.

• **Daytime Lighting Control Module (Canadian, 1989–90)**—is located on the left firewall.

• **Daytime Lighting Control Module (Canadian, 1991)**—is located with the ASCD unit behind the left front kick panel.

• **Detonation Sensor (1991)**—is located approximately in the center of the intake manifold.

• **Diagnostic Connector for CONSULT Tester (1991)**—is located behind fuse box cover under left dash.

• **Door Latch Switch**—is located in each door latch.

• **Door Lock Actuators**—are located within each door.

• **Door Mirror Electric Motors (1991)**—are located within each mirror housing.

• **Dropping Resistor (1989–90)**—is located on the left firewall, to right of brake booster.

• **ECCS Control Module (1991)**—is located behind center console, mounted on floor hump.

• **ECCS Control Module, 2WD (1989–90)**—is located under the right front seat.

• **ECCS Control Module, 4WD (1989–90)**—is located under the driver's seat.

• **ECCS Relay (1989–90)**—is located in the underdash fusebox.

• **ECCS Relay (1991)**—is located on at the ECCS control module.

• **EGR Temperature Sensor (1989–90 Califorina)**—is located below the intake manifold.

• **EGR Valve (1989–90)**—is located on the left side of the intake manifold.

• **EGR Valve (1991)**—is located just behind intake manifold.

• **Engine Temperature Sensor (1991)**—is located at right side of intake manifold, just above the oil filter.

• **FICD Solenoid Control Valve (1991)**—is located to the left of the oil filter.

• **FICD Solenoid Valve (1989–90)**—is located on the throttle body.

• **Flasher**—see Combination Flasher Unit

• **Fog Lamp Relay (1991 Coupe)**—is located in the relay box.

• **Front Limit Switch**—is located at the leading edge of each automatic seat belt rail.

• **Fuel Injector (1989–90)**—is located in the throttle body.

• **Fuel pressure regulator (1989–90)**—is located on a bracket on the throttle body.

• **Fuel Pressure Regulator (1991)**—is located at the fuel rail on left side.

• **Fuel Pump Relay (1989–90)**—is located in the underdash fusebox.

• **Fuel Pump Relay (1991)**—is located in the relay box.

• **Fuel Pump**—is located in the fuel tank.

• **Fuse and Relay Box (1991)**—is located under the left side dash.

• **Fuse Block (1989–90)**—is located under left dashboard.

• **Fuse, Fusible Link and Relay Box (1991)**—is located at left front of engine compartment, between the battery and bodywork.

• **Horn Relay (1989–90)**—is located on underhood relay board.

• **Horn Relay (1991)**—is located in the fusible link and relay box (GA engines) or relay box (SR engines).

• **Idle Switch (1989–90)—see Throttle Sensor**

• **Ignition Coil (1991)**—is located just behind the distributor.

• **Ignition Coil and Power Transisitor (1989–90)**—is located at left side of engine compartment, just behind battery.

• **Ignition Relay No. 1 (1989–90)**—is located in underdash fusebox.

• **Ignition Relay No. 2 (1989–90)**—is located above and to the right of the underdash fusebox.

• **Ignition Relays No. 1 and 2 (1991)**—are located in the underdash fusebox.

• **Inhibitor Relay (1991 auto. trans.)**—is located in the relay box.

• **Inhibitor Relay (1989–90)**—is located on underhood relay board.

• **Key Lock Solenoid (1989–90)**—is located on the ignition key switch.

• **Lap Belt Switch**—is located in the lap belt latch.

• **Mixture Heater (1989–90)**—is located under the throttle body

• **Mixture Heater Relay (1989–90)**—is located on the underhood relay board.

• **Oil Pressure Switch (1989–90)**—is located in engine block to the right of filter.

• **Oxygen Sensor**—is located in the exhaust manifold.

• **Power Transistor (1991)**—is located at the left side of the intake manifold.

• **Radiator Fan Relay (1989–90)**—is located at left front of engine compartment, between battery and bodywork.

• **Rear Defogger Relay (1989–90)**—is located above and to the right of the underdash fusebox.

• **Rear Limit Switch**—is located at the rear of each automatic seat belt rail.

• **Rear Window Defogger Relay (1991)**—is located in the underdash fusebox.

• **Relay Box (1991)**—is located either at the right side of the engine compartment on SR series engines or between the battery and the engine on the left side of the engine compartment on GA series engines.

• **Reverse Lamp Switch (manual trans.)**—is located in the transmission case.

• **Seat Belt Control Module (1989–90)**—is located in the center console, ahead of shifter assembly.

• **Seat Belt Timer (1989–90)**—is located behind the dashboard to the right of the steering column.

• **Shift Lock Control Module (1989–90)**—is located on firewall under dashboard, to left of brake pushrod.

• **Shift Lock Control Module (1991)**—is located behind the left dash.

• **Shoulder Belt Switch**—is located in the shoulder belt latch.

• **SMJ (Super Multiple Junction) (1989–90)**—is located behind left dash.

• **Starter Relay (manual transmission) (1989–90)**—is located on right fender apron, just ahead of underhood relay board.

• **Thermoswitch (1989–90)**—is located in the thermostat housing.

• **Throttle Body (1989–90)**—is located on the intake manifold, rear of engine

• **Throttle Sensor/Idle Switch (1989–90)**—is located on the throttle body.

• **Timer Control Module (1991)**—is located behind left dash.

• **Underhood Relay Board (1989–90)**—is located at right side of engine compartment, just ahead of shock tower.

• **Wiper Amplifier (1989–90)**—is located at left firewall, behind shock tower.

• **Wiper Amplifier (1991)**—is located within the combination switch.

AXXESS

• **A/C Dual Pressure Switch—is located on the receiver/dryer.**

• **A/C Relay**—is located in the underhood fuse and relay case.

• **Accessory Relay**—is located on the fuse block.

• **Air Flow Meter**—is located at the exit port of the air cleaner housing.

• **Air intake valve (AIV)**—is located below air intake duct, next to battery.

• **ASCD Control Module**—is located behind left front kick panel.

• **ASCD Relay**—is located behind SMJ

• **Automatic Seat Belt Front Limit Switch**—is located at the leading edge of each seat belt rail.

• **Automatic Seat Belt Rear Limit Switch**—is located at the rear of each seat belt rail.

• **Automatic Seatbelt Control Module**—is located behind fuse block.

• **Bulb Check Relay**—is located on the fuse block

• **Daytime Lighting Control Module (Canada)**—is located at the left front of the engine compartment, ahead of the fuse and relay box.

• **Door Lock Timer**—is located behind right front kick panel.

• **ECCS Control Module**—is located under the dashboard behind center console.

• **EGR temperature sensor**—is located in the intake manifold.

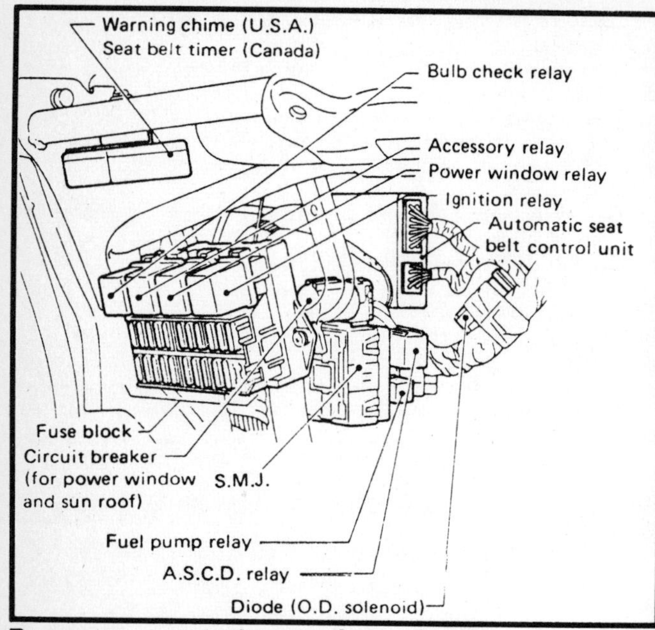

Passenger compartment relays—Axxess

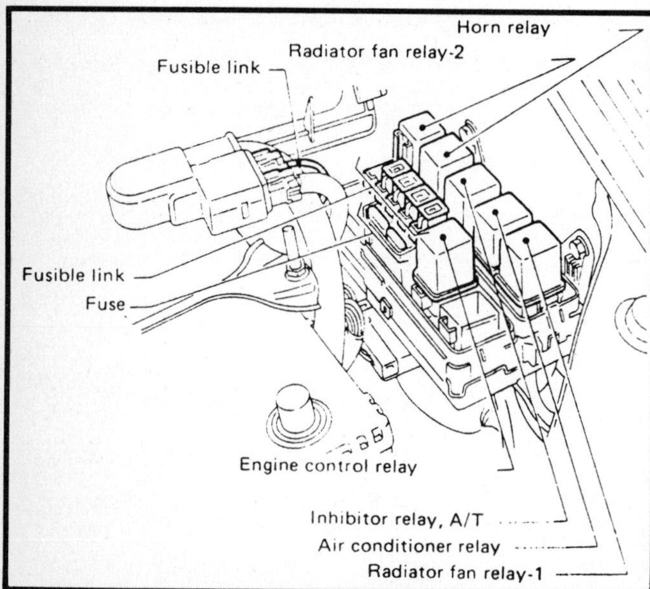

Engine compartment relays—Axxess

- **EGR Valve**—is located on side of intake manifold.
- **Engine Control Relay**—is located in the underhood fuse and relay case.
- **Engine Temperature Sensors**—are located on the intake manifold.
- **Flasher Unit**—is located under dashboard, just to right of brake pedal.
- **Fuel Lid Buzzer**—is located just above left taillight assembly.
- **Fuel Pump Relay**—is located behind SMJ
- **Fuse block**—is located under left side dashboard.
- **Horn Relay**—is located in the underhood fuse and relay case.
- **Ignition Relay**—is located on the fuse block.
- **Inhibitor Relay**—is located in the underhood fuse and relay case.
- **Inhibitor Switch (automatic transmission)**—is located on the side of the transmission case.
- **Lap Belt Switch**—is located within the lap belt latch.
- **Manual Transmission Shifter Position Switch**—is located in the transmission case.
- **Neutral Switch**—see Inhibitor Switch.
- **Oil Pressure Switch**—is located on the oil filter housing
- **Overdrive Solenoid Diode**—is taped onto the wire harness behind SMJ
- **Oxygen Sensor**—is located in exhaust pipe just below exhaust manifold.
- **Power Window Amplifier**—is located within the left front door.
- **Power Window Relay**—is located on the fuse block.
- **Radiator Fan Relays Nos. 1 and 2**—are located in the underhood fuse and relay case.
- **Rear Wiper Amplifier**—is located in right rear quarter panel.
- **Rear Wiper Relay**—is located behind center dash, above left side of glove box.
- **Seatbelt Timer**—is located above fuse block.
- **Shift Lock Control Module (Auto. trans)**—is located under dashboard to left of steering column.
- **SMJ (Super Multiple Junction)**—is located behind fuse block.
- **Sunroof Close/Up Relay**—is located behind the headliner in the roof.
- **Sunroof Open/Down Relay**—is located behind the headliner in the roof.
- **Transfer Switch**—is located on the transfer case.
- **Underhood fuse and relay box**—is located at left front of engine compartment, behind left headlamp
- **Vehicle Speed Sensor**—is located on the transfer case.
- **Warning Chime**—is located above fuse block.
- **Wiper Amplifier**—is located at the left side of firewall

PULSAR

- **A/C Condenser Fan Relay (1989–1.8L engine)**—is located at the right rear of engine compartment on the firewall.
- **A/C Condenser Fan Relay (1.6L engine)**—is located at the left rear of the engine compartment on the firewall.
- **A/C Relay (1989 1.8L engine)**—is located at the right rear of engine compartment on the firewall.
- **A/C Relay (1.6L engine)**—is located at the left rear of the engine compartment on the firewall.
- **A/C Thermal Protector**—is located on the compressor
- **AAC Valve**—is located at the left side of the cylinder head.
- **Accessory Relay**—is located in the underdash fuse block.
- **Air Bag Control Module (1990)**—is located at the bottom of center console, just forward of shifter console.
- **Air Flow Meter (1.8L engine)**—is located at the outlet port of the air cleaner housing.
- **Bulb Check Relay**—is located under left side dash above the fuse block.
- **Clutch Switch**—is located on the clutch pedal bracket.
- **Combination Flasher Module**—is located behind brake pedal bracket.
- **Crank Angle Sensor**—is located at the timing belt end of the exhaust camshaft.
- **Daytime Lighting Control Module (1990)**—is located under dash, behind center console
- **ECCS Control Module**—is located between front seats under console.
- **ECCS Relay**—is located in the underdash fuse block.
- **EGR Temperature Sensor (California only)**—is located in the passage cover at the rear of cylinder head.
- **EGR Valve (1.6L engine)**—is located at the left side of the intake manifold.
- **FICD Solenoid Valve**—is located at the left side of the cylinder head.

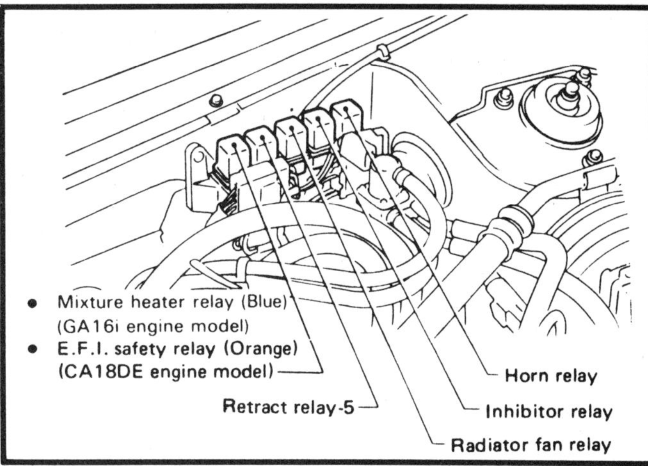

Engine compartment relays—Pulsar

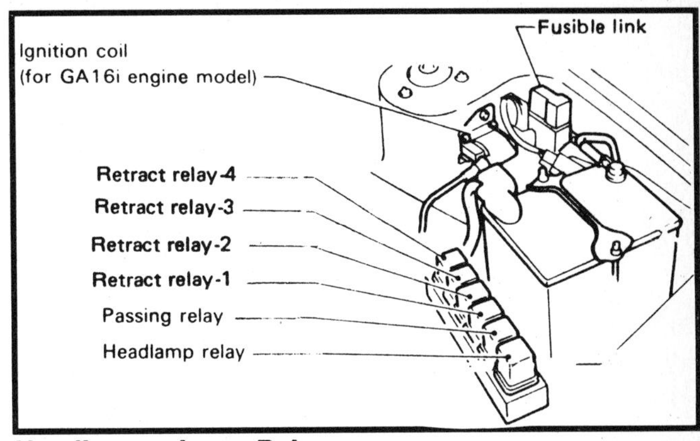

Headlamp relays—Pulsar

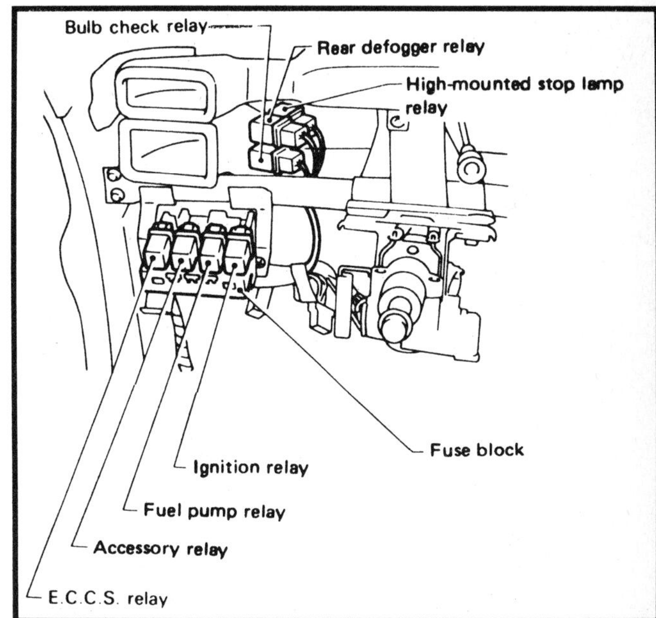

Passenger compartment relays—Pulsar

- **Fuel Injection Safety Relay (1989–1.8L engine)**—is located on right side of engine compartment.
- **Fuel Pump Relay**—is located in the underdash fuse block.
- **Fuse Block**—is located under left side dash.
- **Headlamp Relay**—is located next to battery at the left front of the engine compartment.
- **Headlight Retract Relay No. 5**—is located on right side of engine compartment.
- **Headlight Retract Relays Nos. 1–4**—are located next to battery at the left front of the engine compartment.
- **High Mounted Stop Lamp Relay**—is located under left side dash above the fuse block.
- **Horn Relay**—is located on right side of engine compartment.
- **Ignition Coil (1.6L engine)**—is located on the left front shock tower.
- **Ignition Relay**—is located in the underdash fuse block.
- **Inhibitor Relay**—is located on right side of engine compartment.
- **Interlock Relay (US manual transaxle)**—is located on the radiator support behind the right headlight.
- **Mixture Heater (1.6L engine)**—is located just below the throttle body.
- **Mixture Heater Relay**—is located on the right fender apron, just ahead of the shock tower.
- **Oil Pressure Switch**—is located to the right of, or below, the oil filter.
- **Oxygen Sensor**—is located in the exhaust manifold.
- **Passing Relay**—is located next to battery at the left front of the engine compartment.
- **Passing Switch**—is located behind right front kick panel.
- **Position Switch (manual transaxle)**—is located in the transmission case.
- **Power Transisitor Relay (1989–1.8L engine)**—is located at the left rear of the engine compartment on the firewall.
- **Power Transistor (1.8L engine)**—is located at the upper left side of engine.
- **Power Valve Actuator (1.8L engine)**—is located at the side of the intake manifold.
- **Radiator fan relay**—is located on right side of engine compartment
- **Rear Defogger Relay**—is located under left side dash above the fuse block.
- **Seat Belt Timer**—is located under the center dash, behind center console.
- **Stop Lamp Switch**—is located on the brake pedal bracket.
- **Throttle Body (1.6L engine)**—is located on the intake manifold.
- **Throttle Chamber (1.8L engine)—is located on the intake manifold.**
- **Throttle Sensor/Idle Switch (1.6L engine)**—is located on the side of the throttle body.
- **Windshield Wiper Amplifier**—is located to the left of the wiper motor on the firewall.
- **Wiper Amplifier**—is located on the firewall in the engine compartment.

300ZX

- **A/C Ambient Temperature Sensor (1989)**—is located at the left side of grille at the front of the vehicle.
- **A/C Condenser Fan Relay (1989)**—is located on the right fender apron to rear of the shock tower.
- **A/C Duct Temperature Sensor (automatic air conditioning—1989)**—is located in the respective ducting, i.e., floor, defroster, etc.
- **A/C Fan Control Amplifier and Transisitor (automatic a/c—1989)**—is located on the blower motor housing.
- **A/C Low Pressure Switch**—is located on the receiver/dryer.

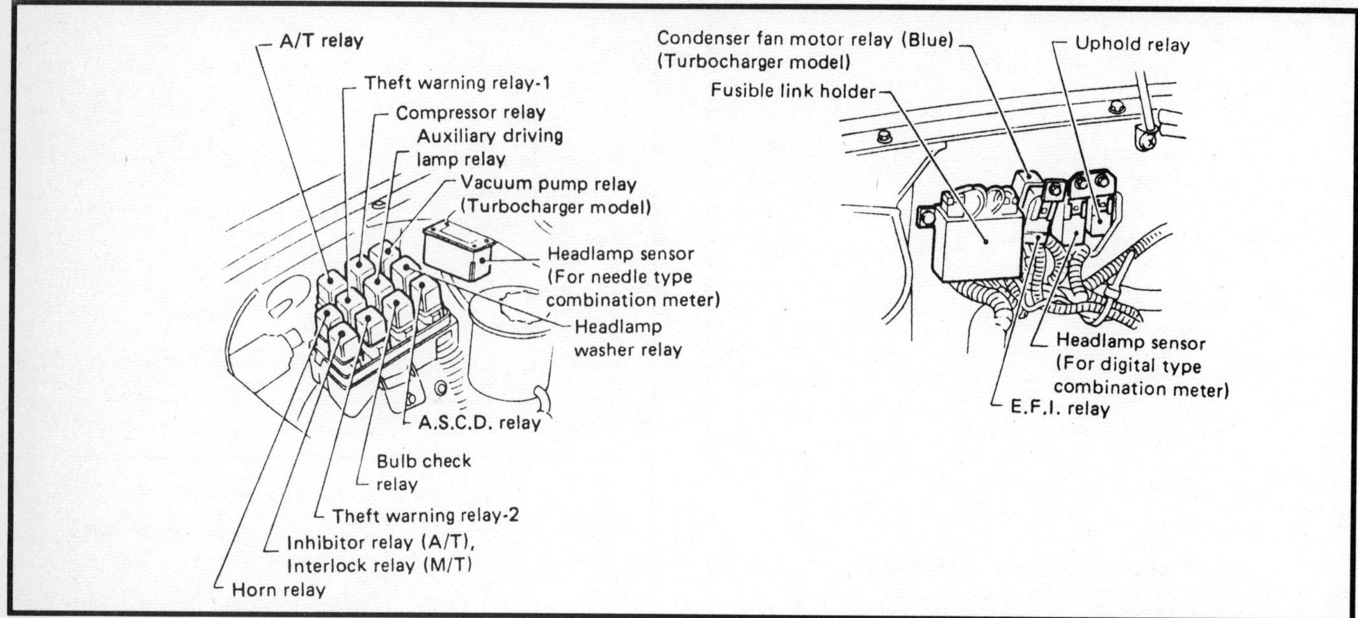

Relay locations – 1989 300ZX

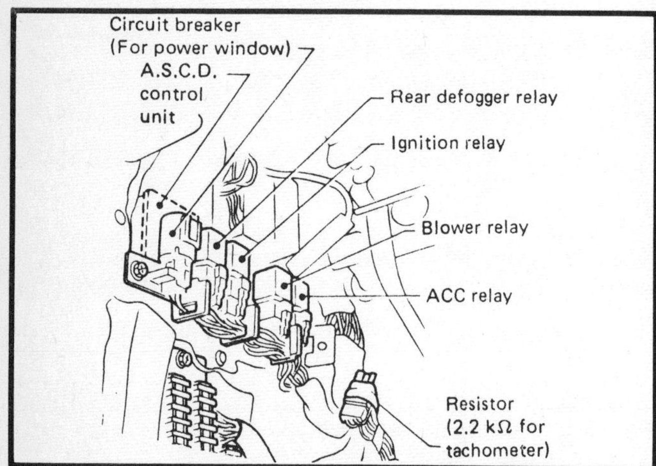

Passenger compartment relays – 1989 300ZX

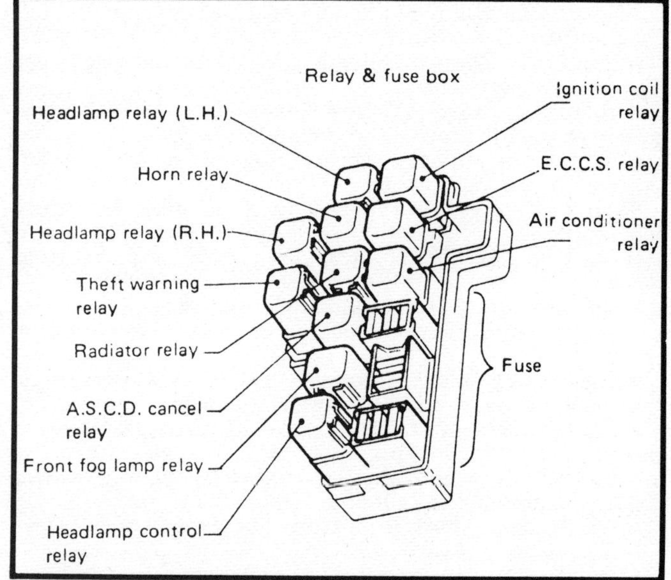

Engine compartment relays – 300ZX

- **A/C Relay (1990–91)** – is located in the underhood relay and fuse box.
- **A/C Sunload Sensor (1989)** – is located at the bottom of the windshield in the defroster grille.
- **A/C Sunload Sensor (1990–91)** – is located in right defroster grille at base of windshield.
- **A/C Temperature In-Vehicle Sensor** – is located in the headliner at the front center of the windshield.
- **A/C Ignition Relay (1991)** – is located in right dash, behind glove box.
- **ABS** – see Anti-lock Brake
- **Accessory Relay (1989)** – is located under left side dash, above fuse box.
- **Accessory Relay (1990–91)** – is located on fuse block under left dash.
- **Adjustable Shock Absorber Control Unit (1989)** – is located at the rear of vehicle, behind spare tire.
- **Air Bag Control Module (1991)** – is located behind left side dashboard.
- **Air Flow Meter (1989)** – is located at the outlet port of the air cleaner assembly.
- **Air Flow Meter (1990–91)** – is located at center of grille.
- **AIV Control Solenoid Valve (1990–91)** – is located at right rear of engine compartment, near battery.
- **Ambient Temperature Sensor (automatic air conditioning-1989)** – is located at the left side of grille at the front of the vehicle.
- **Antenna Amplifier (1990–91)** – is located in right quarter panel.
- **Anti-lock Brake Actuator (1990–91)** – is located in right quarter panel.
- **Anti-lock Brake Control Module (1990–91)** – is located in right quarter panel.
- **Anti-lock Brake Rear Wheel Speed Sensors (1990–91)** – are located on either side of the differential housing.
- **ASCD Cancel Relay (1990)** – is located in the underhood relay and fuse box.

- **ASCD Control Module (1990–91)** – is located in right front footwell.
- **ASCD Control Unit (1989)** – is located under left side dash, behind row of relays above the fusebox.
- **ASCD Relay (1989)** – is located on the underhood relay board.
- **ASCD Relay (1990–91)** – is located behind right dashboard.
- **Audio Relay (1991 Bose system)** – is located behind right front kick panel.
- **Automatic Transmission Control Module (1989)** – is located in the right rear quarter panel.
- **Automatic Transmission Control Module (1990–91)** – is located in right front footwell.
- **Automatic Transmission Interlock Control Module (1989)** – is located under left dash, to left of brake pedal.
- **Automatic Transmission Lock-up Control Unit (1989)** – is located at rear of vehicle, behind spare tire.
- **Automatic Transmission Relay (1989)** – is located on the underhood relay board.
- **Auxiliary Driving Lamp Relay (1989)** – is located on the underhood relay board.
- **Backup Switch (1990–91–manual transaxle)** – is located on the right side of the transmission case.
- **Blower Motor Relay (1990–91)** – is located on fuse block under left dash.
- **Blower Motor Relays Nos. 2 and 3 (1990–91) – are located behind right front kick panel.**
- **Blower Relay (1989)** – is located under left side dash, above fuse box.
- **Blower Relay No.1 (1990)** – is located under right dash, with blower assembly.
- **Blower Resistor (1990–91)** – is located under right dash, with blower assembly.
- **Boost Sensor (1989)** – is located on bracket at left front of engine compartment.
- **Boost Sensor (1991 Turbo)** – is located on left fender apron at the firewall.
- **Bulb Check Relay (1989)** – is located on the underhood relay board.
- **Bulb Check Relay (1990–91)** – is located on fuse block under left dash.
- **Chime Assembly (1990–91)** – is located in dashboard behind instrument cluster.
- **Clutch Interlock Relay (1990 – manual transaxle)** – is located on the firewall at the left fender.
- **Combination Flasher Module (1990–91)** – is located behind dash, to right of steering column.
- **Compressor Relay (1989)** – is located on the underhood relay board.
- **Condenser (1989)** – see radio noise suppressor.
- **Consult Diagnostic Connector (1990–91)** – is located under left side dashboard, near hood release handle.
- **Coolant Temperature Sensor (1990–91)** – is located in upper radiator tube.
- **Crank Angle Sensor (1990–91)** – is located on front of left camshaft housing.
- **Crank angle sensor** – is located in bottom of distributor.
- **Cylinder Head Teperature Sensor (1989)** – is located at forward end of left head.
- **Daytime Running Lamp Control Module (Canada) (1990–91)** – is located on the right front fender apron near the firewall.
- **Detonation Sensor** – is located on right rear of engine block.
- **Downshift Solenoid (1989)** – is located on the transmission case.
- **ECCS Control Module (1989)** – is located behind right front kick panel.
- **ECCS Control Module (1990–91)** – is located in right front footwell.
- **ECCS Relay (1990–91)** – is located in the underhood relay and fuse box.
- **EFI Relay (1989)** – is located on the right fender apron to rear of the shock tower.
- **EGR Control Solenoid Valve (1989)** – is located at right rear of engine near EGR.
- **EGR Control Valve (1990–91)** – is located at rear of intake manifold.
- **EGR Temperature Sensor (California – 1990–91)** – is located at the EGR valve.
- **EGR Valve (1989)** – is located at right rear of engine on intake manifold.
- **Exhaust Gas Temperature Sensor** – is located at the EGR valve.
- **Fan Control Amplifier and Transisitor (automatic air conditioning – 1989)** – is located on the blower motor housing.
- **FICD (1989)** – is located at left center of intake manifold.
- **Flasher** – see combination flasher
- **Front Fog Lamp Relay (1990–91)** – is located in the underhood relay and fuse box.
- **Fuel Pump (1990–91)** – is located in the fuel tank.
- **Fuel Pump Control Module (1990 and 1991 2+2)** – is located in left quarter panel.
- **Fuel Pump Control Module (1991 2 seat)** – is located behind driver's seat on floor.
- **Fuel Pump Relay (1989)** – is located in the right rear quarter panel.
- **Fuel Pump Relay (1990–91)** – is located behind left kick panel.
- **Fuel Pump** – is located in the fuel tank.
- **Fuel Temperature Sensor (1989)** – is located in the fuel pressure regulator.
- **Fuel Temperature Sensor (1990–91)** – is located in left fuel rail.
- **Fuse Block (1990–91)** – is located under left side dash, at kick panel.
- **Fuse Box** – is located under left side dashboard.
- **Headlamp Control (Dimmer) Relay (1990–91)** – is located in the underhood relay and fuse box.
- **Headlamp Relay (1989)** – is located on the left fender apron at the firewall.
- **Headlamp Relay, left lamp (1990–91)** – is located in the underhood relay and fuse box.
- **Headlamp Relay, right lamp (1990–91)** – is located in the underhood relay and fuse box.
- **Headlamp Sensor (Analog gauges-1989)** – is located on the underhood relay board.
- **Headlamp Sensor (Digital gauges-1989)** – is located on the right fender apron to rear of the shock tower.
- **Headlamp Timer (1989)** – is located on the left fender apron at the firewall.
- **Headlamp Washer relay (1989)** – is located on the underhood relay board.
- **Headlamp Washer Relay (1990–91)** – is located on the right front fender apron near the firewall.
- **Heater Control Amplifier (1990–91)** – is located in left side of console, to right of steering column.
- **HICAS Control Module (1991 Turbo)** – is located in right front footwell.
- **HICAS solenoid valve (1991 Turbo)** – is located on the right front fender apron.
- **Horn Relay (1989)** – is located on the underhood relay board.
- **Horn Relay (1990–91)** – is located in the underhood relay and fuse box.
- **IAA unit (1990–91)** – is located at rear of left intake manifold.
- **Idle-up Solenoid (Non-turbo, 1989)** – is located with FICD unit at left center of intake manifold.

- **Ignition Coil (1989)**—is located at left front of engine compartment.
- **Ignition Control Relay (1990–91)**—is located in the underhood relay and fuse box.
- **Ignition Relay (1989)**—is located under left side dash, above fuse box.
- **Ignition Relay (1990–91)**—is located on fuse block under left dash.
- **Inhibitor Relay (1989)**—is located on the underhood relay board.
- **Inhibitor Switch (1990–91)**—is located on right side of transmission case.
- **Interlock Relay (1989)**—is located on the underhood relay board.
- **Kickdown Switch (1990–91)**—is located above accelerator pedal, on the same bracket.
- **Kickdown Switch (1989)**—is located on firewall just above accelerator pedal.
- **Lock-up Solenoid (1989)**—is located on the left side of the transmission case.
- **Neutral Switch (manual transaxle)**—is located on the right side of the transmission case.
- **Oil Pressure Switch (1989)**—is located on right side of engine block, to left (behind) oil filter.
- **Oil Pressure Switch (1990–91)**—is located on right side of engine, immediately above oil filter.
- **Overdrive Cancel Solenoid (1989)**—is located on the left side of the transmission case.
- **Oxygen Sensor**—is located in the exhaust pipe, ahead of the catlytic converter.
- **Oxygen Sensors (1990–91)**—are located in each exhaust manifold.
- **Passing Relay (1989)**—is located on the left fender apron at the firewall.
- **Power Antenna Timer (1989)**—is located in left rear quarter, at antenna motor.
- **Power Door Lock Switch and Actuator**—is located in respective door.
- **Power Module (Digital gauges-1989)**—is located behind center of dashboard, to right of steering column.
- **Power Steering Control Module (1990-91 non turbo)**—is located in right front footwell.
- **Power Steering Oil Pressure Switch (Non-turbo, 1989)**—is located on the power steering pump.
- **Power Transistor (1989)**—is located at left front of engine compartment.
- **Power Transistor Module (1990–91)**—is located on right side of timing belt cover at front of engine.
- **Power Window/Power Seat Relay (1990)**—is located on fuse block under left dash.
- **Pressure Regulator Control Valve (1989)**—is located at left front of engine compartment.
- **Radiator Fan Relay (1990–91)**—is located in the underhood relay and fuse box.
- **Radiator Fan Sub-relay (1991 turbo)**—is located in the underhood fuse and relay board.
- **Radio Noise Suppress (1989)**—is located at left front of engine compartment, near coil.
- **Rear Defogger Relay (1989)**—is located under left side dash, above fuse box.
- **Rear Defogger Relay (1990–91)**—is located on fuse block under left dash.
- **Reverse Lamp Switch (1989—manual transaxle)**—is located on the right side of the transmission case.
- **Revolution Sensor (1990–91)**—is located on right side of transmission case.
- **Room Lamp (Interior) Relay**—is located with fuel pump control module.
- **Shift Lock Control Unit (1990–91)**—is located behind left side dashboard.
- **Shift Switch/Low Temperature Sensor (1989)**—is located on the transmission case.
- **Shock Absorber Control Module (1991—turbocharged**—is located on floor behind driver's seat on 2 seater models or is in the left quarter panel, ahead of wheel on the 2+2 with a rear seat.
- **Speed Sensor (analog gauges—1989)**—is located on the transmission case.
- **Starter Relay (1990–91)**—is located on the firewall at the left fender.
- **Stop and Taillamp Sensor (1990–91)**—is located in left quarter panel at left side.
- **Sunload Sensor (1989)**—is located at the bottom of the windshield in the defroster grille.
- **Sunload Sensor (1990–91)**—is located in right defroster grille at base of windshield.
- **Tachometer Resistor (1989)**—is located under left side dash, taped into wire harness near relays.
- **Temperature Sensor In-Vehicle (automatic air conditioning-1989)**—is located in the headliner at the front center of the windshield.
- **Theft Warning Control Module (1989)**—is located on right front floor, under right front seat.
- **Theft Warning Control Module (1990–91)**—is located in right front footwell.
- **Theft Warning Relay (1990–91)**—is located in the underhood relay and fuse box.
- **Theft Warning Relays (1989)**—are located on the underhood relay board.
- **Throttle Sensor and Throttle Valve Switch (1990–91)**—is located on front of left intake manifold at throttle chamber.
- **Throttle Valve Switch (1989)**—is located on the throttle body at the intake manifold.
- **Time Control Module (1990–91)**—is located behind left kick panel.
- **Timer Control Module (1989)**—is located behind right front kick panel, above ECCS control module.
- **Underhood Relay and Fuse Box (1990–91)**—is located at left side of engine compartment.
- **Underhood Relay Board**—is located on right front fender apron, ahead of the shock tower.
- **Uphold Relay (1989)**—is located on the right fender apron to rear of the shock tower.
- **Vacuum Pump Relay (Turbocharged only-1989)**—is located on the underhood relay board.
- **Warning Chime (1989)**—is located behind center of dashboard, to right of steering column.
- **Wiper Amplifier (1990–91)**—is located on the left fender apron, behind the shock tower.
- **Wiper Relay (1989)**—is located on left fender apron at the firewall.

MAXIMA

- **A/C HI Blower Relay (automatic air condiionig)**—is located behind right front kick panel.
- **A/C Fan Control Amplifier (automatic air conditioning)**—is located under right dash in heater/AC unit.
- **A/C Relay**—is located in the underhood relay box.
- **A/C Sunload Sensor**—is located in defroster grille, extreme right side of windshield.
- **Anti-lock Brake System Actuator**—is located at right front of engine compartment.
- **AAC Valve/Step Motor**—is located on left side of upper intake manifold collector.
- **ABS**—see Anti-lock Brakes
- **Accessory Relay No.s 1 and 2— are located on underdash fuse block.**
- **Air Flow Meter**—is located at outlet port of air cleaner assembly.

● **Anti-lock Brake Control Module**—is located in trunk, below rear window shelf.

● **ASCD Actuator**—is located on right fender apron, ahead of shock tower.

Inhibitor relay (A/T model)
Radiator fan relay-3
Fog lamp relay (SE model)
Radiator fan relay-2
A.S.C.D. hold relay
Radiator fan relay-1
Air conditioner relay
Bulb check relay
Horn relay
Wiper relay

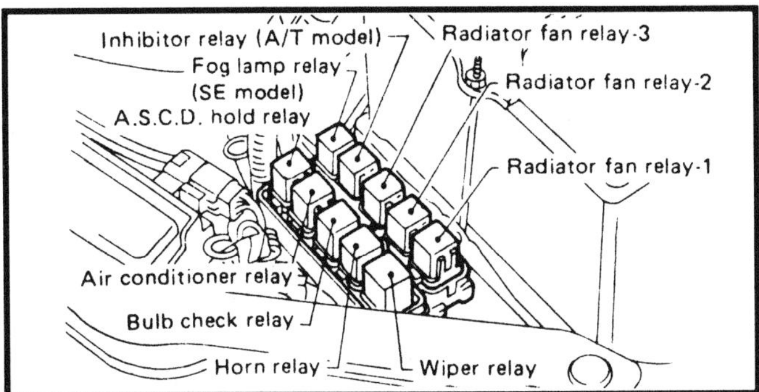

Engine compartment relays—Maxima

Trunk lid opener relay
Fuel pump relay
Safety relay
Trunk lid opener solenoid

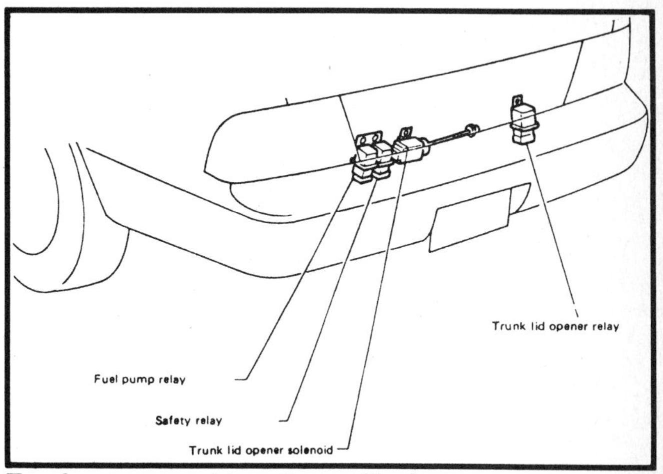

Trunk component locations—Maxima

Stop lamp switch
A.S.C.D. control unit
A.S.C.D. cancel switch
Combination flasher unit
Theft warning control unit (For U.S.A.)
Daytime light control unit (For Canada)
A/T control unit (A/T model)
E.C.C.S. control unit
Time control unit
Digital touch entry control unit
Circuit breaker-1
Interrupt relay
Blower HI relay (Auto A/C)
S.M.J.
Shift lock control unit (A/T model)
Circuit breaker-2
Rear window defogger relay
Accessory relay-2
Sonar suspension control unit (For sonar suspension system)
Accessory relay-1
Automatic seat belt control unit (For U.S.A.)
Theft warning control unit (For Canada)
Cornering lamp unit
Ignition relay
Switching relay (BOSE type)
Ignition relay-2
Fuse block

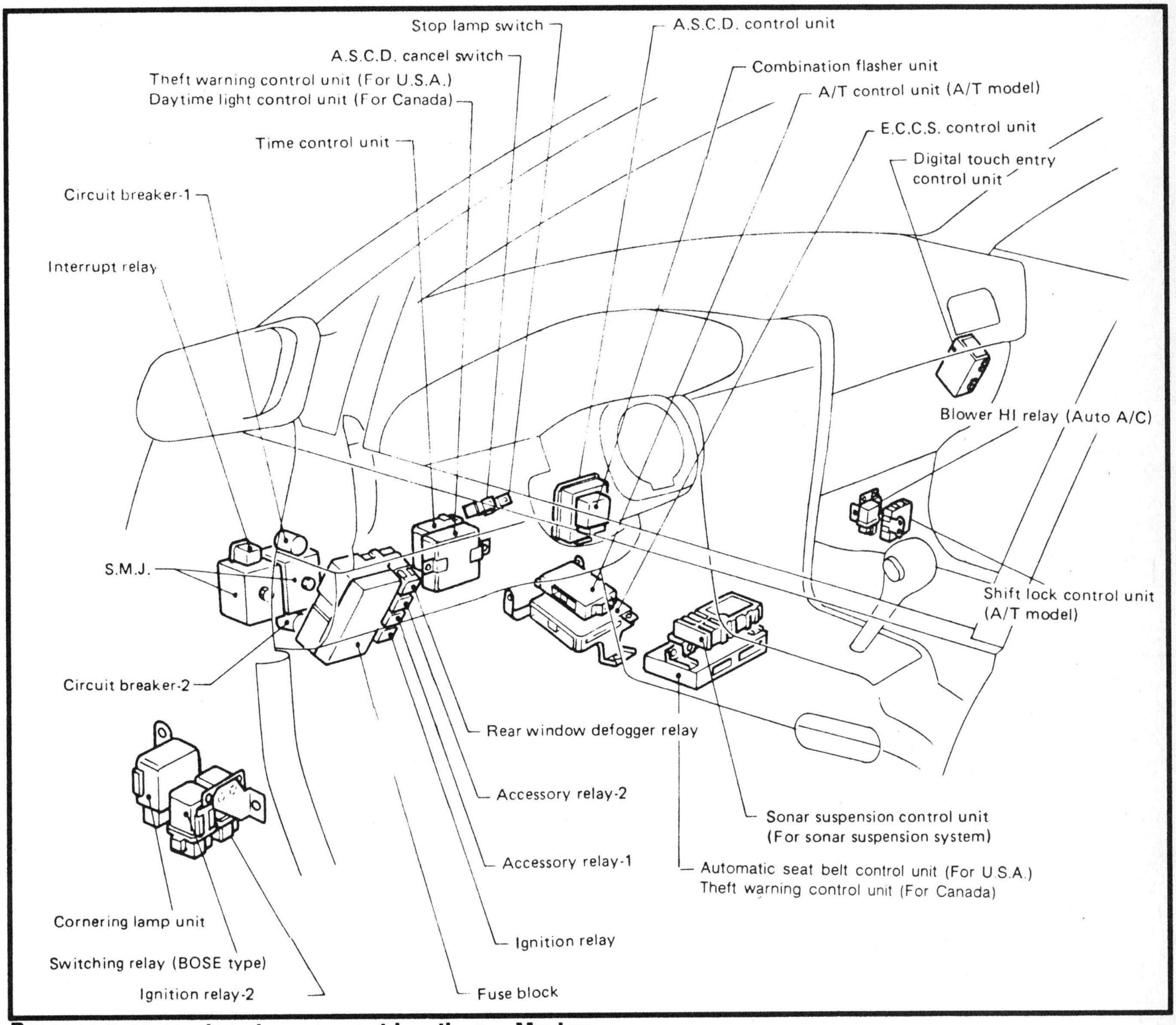

Passenger compartment component locations—Maxima

- **ASCD Control Module**—is located behind the left dash, to right of steering column.
- **ASCD Hold Relay**—is located in the underhood relay box.
- **Automatic Seat Belt Control Module (US)**—is located under center console, just forward of shift selector.
- **Automatic Transmission Control Module**—is located on floor hump behind center console; it is on top of the ECCS module.
- **Blower HI Relay (automatic air conditioning)**—is located behind right front kick panel.
- **Bulb Check Relay**—is located in the underhood relay box.
- **Combination Flasher Module**—is located behind the left dash, to right of steering column.
- **Cornering Lamp Module**—is located behind left front kick panel.
- **Crank Angle Sensor**—is located within distributor.
- **Daytime Lighting Control Module (Canada)**—is located behind left dash, in front of time control unit.
- **Diagnostic Connector for ECCS Checker**—is located below left dash, above hood release lever.
- **Digital Touch Entry Control Module**—is located at extreme right of dash, to right of glovebox.
- **Dropping Resistor (automatic transaxle)**—is located on left fender apron, adjacent to the fuse and relay box.
- **ECCS Control Module**—is located on floor hump behind center console.
- **ECCS Relay**—is located in the fuse and relay board near the battery.
- **EGR Valve**—is located on rear of upper intake manifold collector.
- **Engine Temperature Sensor**—is located at right rear of engine.
- **Flasher**—see Combination Flasher
- **Fog Lamp Relay**—is located in the underhood relay box.
- **Front Limit Switch (automatic seat belts)**—is located at the leading edge of the seat belt rail.
- **Fuel Pump Relay**—is located in rear panel at rear of trunk.
- **Fuse Block**—is located under the left dash.
- **Fuse, Relay and Fusible Link Box**—is located on left fender apron, between battery and bodywork.
- **Hood Switch**—is located on right fender apron, ahead of shock tower.
- **Horn Relay**—is located in the underhood relay box.
- **Ignition Relay No. 2**—is located behind left front kick panel.
- **Ignition Relay**—is located on underdash fuse block.
- **Inhibitor Relay (automatic transaxle)**—is located in the underhood relay box.
- **Inhibitor Switch (automatic transaxle)**—is located on the transmission case.
- **Interior Temperature Sensor (automatic air conditioning)**—is located in center console.
- **Interlock Relay (US—manual transaxle)**—is located on left shock tower.
- **Interrupt Relay**—is located on top of SMJ under left side dash.
- **Oil Pressure Switch**—is located below oil filter.
- **Power Steering Oil Pressure Switch**—is located at right rear of engine compartment, behind shock tower.
- **Power Transistor**—is located on right front of engine.
- **Radiator Fan Relay No.s 1, 2 and 3—are located in the underhood relay box.**
- **Rear Amplifier (active speaker system)**—is located in trunk, below rear window shelf.
- **Rear Limit Switch (automatic seat belts)**—is located at the rear of the seat belt rail.
- **Rear Window Defogger Relay**—is located on underdash fuse block.
- **Relay Box**—is located behind left headlamp
- **Safety Relay**—is located in rear panel at rear of trunk.
- **Shift Lock Control Module (automatic transaxle)**—is located behind right front kick panel.
- **Shock Absorber Actuator (sonar suspension)**—is located on top of each strut assembly.
- **SMJ (Super Multiple Junctions)—are located under left dash, behind fuse block.**
- **Sonar Road Surface Monitor**—is located behind front bumper below the left headlamp.
- **Sonar Suspension Control Module**—is located under center console, just forward of shift selector.
- **Speed Sensor** —is located in transmission case.
- **Steering Angle Sensor (sonar suspension)**—is located at the top of the steering column, under the column covers.
- **Sunload Sensor (automatic air conditioning)**—is located in defroster grille, extreme right side of windshield.
- **Sunroof Close/Up Relay**—is located above front headliner.
- **Sunroof Open/Down Relay**—is located above front headliner.
- **Switching Relay**—is located behind left front kick panel.
- **Theft Warning Control Module (Canada)**—is located under center console, just forward of shift selector.
- **Theft Warning Control Module (US)**—is located behind left dash, in front of time control unit.
- **Theft Warning Relay**—is located in the fuse and relay board near the battery.
- **Throttle Sensor and Idle Switch**—is located on dual throttle chamber, center front of engine.
- **Time Control Module**—is located behind left dash, to left of steering column.
- **Trunk Opener Relay**—is located in rear panel at rear of trunk.
- **Water Cock Solenoid**—is located at the center of firewall.
- **Wiper Relay**—is located in the underhood relay box.

STANZA

- **A/C Relay**—is located in underhood relay box.
- **AAC Valve**—is located at right rear of engine, on upper air intake chamber.
- **Accessory Relay (1989) or Acc. Relays No. 1 and 2 (1990–91)**—are located in underdash fuse block.
- **Air Flow Meter**—is located at the exit port of the air cleaner assembly.
- **Anti-lock Brake Control Unit**—is located in trunk, mounted below rear window shelf.
- **ASCD Control Module (1989)**—is located under center console, forward of the shift selector.
- **ASCD Control Module (1990–91)**—is located under left dash, to right of steering column.
- **ASCD Hold Relay (1989)**—is located in underhood relay box.
- **ASCD Main Relay**—is located in underhood relay box.
- **Automatic Seat Belt Control Module (1990–91)**—is located under center console, forward of shift selector.
- **Automatic Transmission Control Module (1990–91)**—is located under center console, forward of the shift selector.
- **Battery Relay Board**—is located at left front of engine compartment, adjacent to the battery.
- **Blower Relay (1990–91)**—is located on the battery relay board.
- **Bulb Check Relay (1990–91)**—is located on the battery relay board.
- **Clutch Relay (1989)**—is located in underhood relay box.
- **Clutch Relay (1990–91)**—is located on the battery relay board.
- **Combination Flasher Unit**—is located under left dash to right of steering column.

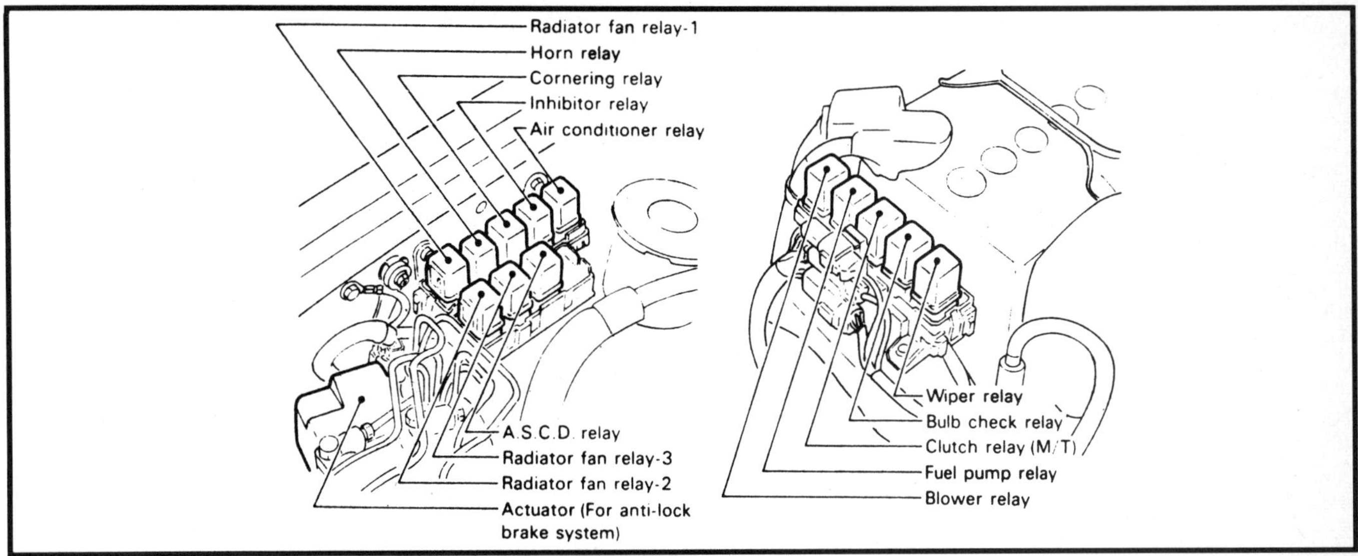

Engine compartment component locations—1990–91 Stanza

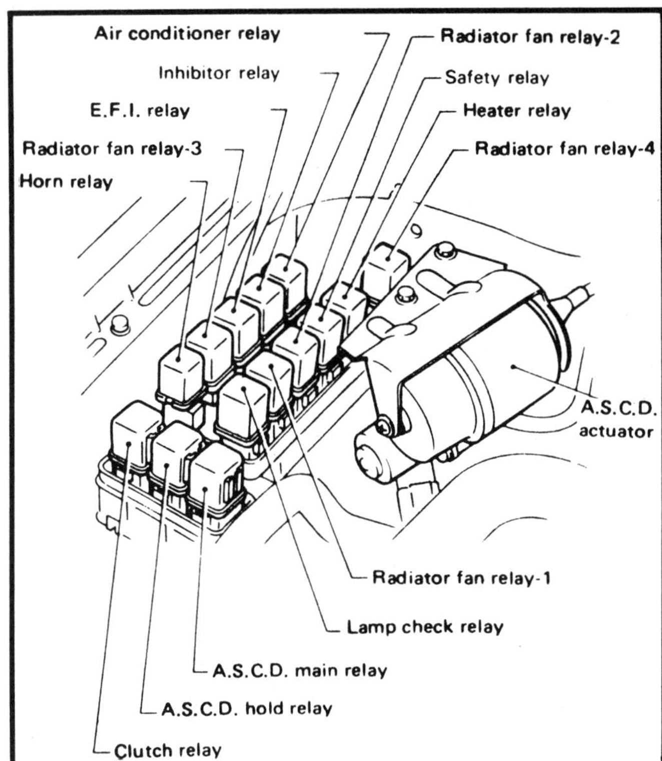

Engine compartment relays—1989 Stanza

- **CONSULT Diagnostic Connector (1990–91)**—is located below dash to right of steering wheel.
- **Coolant Temperature Sensor (1989)**—is located in the water outlet housing (thermostat housing)
- **Coolant Temperature Sensor (1990–91)**—is located at right rear of engine.
- **Cornering Lamps Relay (1990–91)**—is located in underhood relay box.
- **Crank Angle Sensor**—is located in the base of the distributor.
- **Daytime Lighting Control Module (Canada, 1990–91)**—is located under left dash, to right of fuse block.

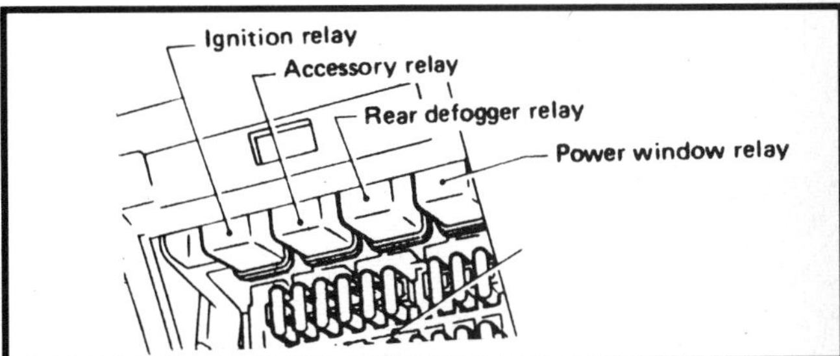

Passenger compartment relays—1989 Stanza

- **Door Lock Timer (1989)**—is located behind time control unit in left front kick panel.
- **Door Lock Timer (1990–91)**—is located behind right front kick panel.
- **Dropping Resistor (1990–91—automatic transaxle)**—is located in the engine compartment below the air cleaner assembly.
- **ECCS Control Module (1989)**—is located under front passenger seat.
- **ECCS Control Module (1990–91)**—is located under center console, forward of shift selector.
- **ECCS Relay (1990–91)**—is located on the left fender apron at the fusible link holder.
- **EFI Relay (1989)**—is located in underhood relay box.
- **FICD**—is located at right rear of engine, on upper air intake chamber.
- **Flasher**—see Combination Flasher.
- **Fuel Pump Relay (1990–91)**—is located on the battery relay board.
- **Fuel Pump**—is located in the fuel tank.
- **Fuse Block**—is located under left dashboard.
- **Heater Relay (1989)**—is located in underhood relay box.
- **Horn Relay**—is located in underhood relay box.
- **IAA Unit**—is located at right rear of engine, on upper air intake chamber.
- **Ignition Relay**—is located in underdash fuse block.
- **Inhibitor Relay**—is located in underhood relay box.
- **Inhibitor Relay**—is located in underhood relay box.
- **Inhibitor Switch (automatic transaxle)**—is located on side of the transmission case.
- **Interlock Relay (1989)**—is located behind left headlight.

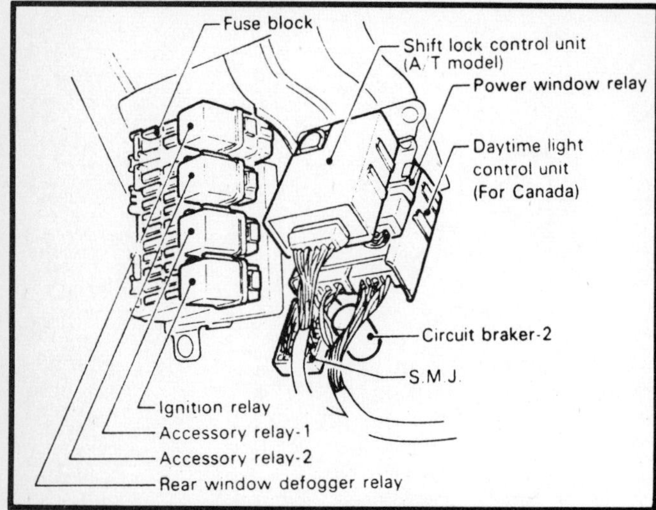

Passenger component relays—1990–91 Stanza

- **Lamp Check Relay (1989)**—is located in underhood relay box.
- **Oil Pressure Switch**—is located at oil filter mounting; 1989 is below the filter, 1990–91 is above it.
- **Oxygen Sensor**—is located in the exhaust manifold.
- **Power Antenna Timer (1989)**—is located under center console, forward of shift selector.
- **Power Antenna Timer (1990–91)**—is located at the antenna in the trunk.
- **Power Steering Oil Pressure Switch (1990–91)**—is located in the fluid line near the steering gear.
- **Power Transistor**—is located at the ignition coil.
- **Power Window Relay (1989)**—is located in underdash fuse block.
- **Power Window Relay (1990–91)**—is located under left dash, to right of fuse block.
- **Radiator Fan Relays No.s 1–4 (1989) or 1–3 (1990–91)**—are located in underhood relay box.
- **Rear Defogger Relay**—is located in underdash fuse block.
- **Safety Relay (1989)**—is located in underhood relay box.
- **Shift Lock Control Module (1990–91—automatic transaxle**—is located under left dash, to right of fuse block.
- **Shifter Position Switch (manual transaxle.)**—is located on the transmission case.
- **SMJ (Super Multiple Junction, 1990–91)**—is located below and behind fuse block.
- **Stop and Tail Lamp Sensor (1989)**—is located near antenna in right side trunk panel.
- **Sunroof Close/Up Relay**—is located in front roof, above headliner.
- **Sunroof Open/Down Relay**—is located in front roof, above headliner.
- **Throttle Sensor/Throttle Valve Switches**—are located on the side of the throttle chamber on the upper air intake chamber.
- **Time Control Module**—is located behind left front kick panel.
- **Transmission RPM Sensor (1990–91) automatic transaxle)**—is located in the lower transmission case.
- **Underhood Relay Board**——is located on right fender apron ahead of shock tower.
- **Wiper Relay (1989)**—is located on right firewall near wiper motor.
- **Wiper Relay (1990–91)**—is located on the battery relay board.

NISSAN TRUCKS

Circuit Breakers

Fuses are located under the left side of the dash. Circuit breakers are located in the fuse box, the relay box or at the component.

Fusbile Links

Fusible Links are located at the fuse box, the relay box or along the circuit wiring.

Relays, Sensors, Modules and Computer Locations

TRUCK AND PATHFINDER

- **4WD Sensor Switch**—is located in transfer case.
- **A/C Sunload Sensor (1990–91)**—is located in defroster grille at base of windshield.
- **A/C Relay (1990–91)**—is located in underhood relay holder.
- **A/C Relay**—is located on left fender apron, just to rear of air intake duct.
- **AAC Valve (1990–91—3.0L engine)**—is located on intake manifold at rear of engine.
- **Accessory Relay (1989)**—is located above fuse box.
- **Air Flow Meter (1990–91—2.4L engine)**—is located on side of throttle chamber.
- **Air Temperature Sensor (1989)**—is located in bottom of air cleaner.
- **Ambient Temperature Sensor (automatic Air Conditioning, 1990–91)**—is located behind grille at front of vehicle.
- **ASCD Control Module (Pathfinder)**—is located in left quarter panel, over the wheel wheel.
- **ASCD Control Module (Truck)**—is located under driver's seat.
- **ASCD Hold Relay (1990–91—3.0L engine)**—is located on right fender apron.
- **ASCD Relay (1989)**—is located on left fender apron, behind canister bracket.
- **Auto Amplifier Relay (1990–91—3.0L engine)**—is located on right fender apron, near battery.
- **Automatic Transmission Control Module (Pathfinder)**—is located in right quarter panel, over the wheel wheel.
- **Automatic Transmission Control Module (Truck)**—is located under front passenger seat.
- **Automatic Transmission Indicator Relay (1989)**—is located on left fender apron, behind canister bracket.
- **Automatic Transmission Indicator Relay (1990–91)**—is located on left fender apron, behind canister bracket.
- **Automatic Transmission Revolution Sensor (RE4R01A trans., 1989)**—is located at top rear of transmission case.

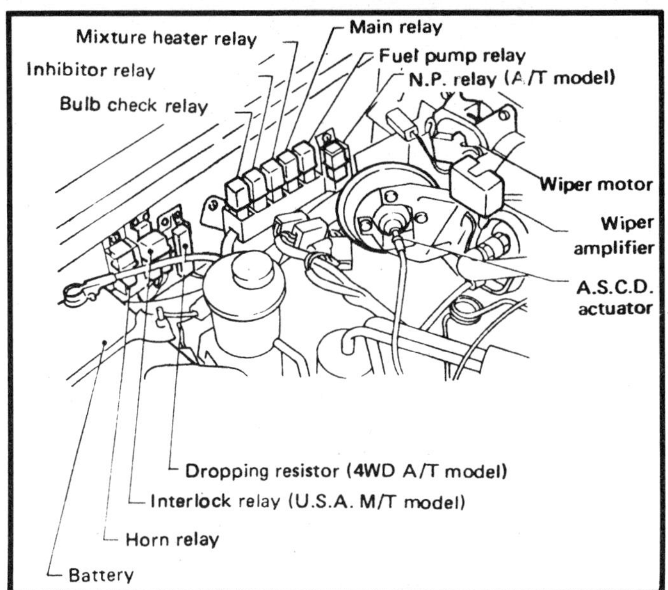

Engine compartment relays—1989 Truck and Pathfinder

- **Blower Relay (1990–91)**—is located in underhood relay holder.
- **Blower Signal Relay (1989)**—is located on left fender apron, behind canister bracket.
- **Bulb Check Relay**—is located in underhood relay holder.
- **Combination Flasher Module**—is located under left dash, to left of brake pedal shaft.
- **Crank Angle Sensor**—is located in bottom of distributor.
- **Daytime Lighting Control Module (1990–91—3.0L engine)**—is located on right fender apron, between battery and bodywork.
- **Diagnostic Connector for ECCS Checker (1990–91)**—is located under left dash, near hood release lever.
- **Diode Box (manual transmission)**—is located under left dash, above left kick panel.
- **Door Lock Timer (Pathfinder)**—is located in left quarter panel, to rear of driver's door.
- **Door Lock Timer (Truck)**—is located under driver's seat.
- **Dropping Resistor (4WD with automatic transmission)**—is located on right fender apron, between relay holder and battery.
- **ECCS Control Module**—is located under front passenger seat.
- **ECCS Relay (1990–91)**—is located in underhood relay holder.
- **EGR Valve (2.4L engine)**—is located on intake manifold at right rear of engine.
- **EGR Valve (3.0L engine)**—is located on left side of intake manifold.
- **Engine Temperature Sensor (1990–91—3.0L engine)**—is located in right front of intake manifold.
- **Flasher**—see Combination Flasher.
- **Fuel Pump Relay**—is located in underhood relay holder.
- **Fuse Box**—is located below left dash.
- **Horn Relay**—is located on right fender apron.
- **Hot Air Intake Valve (1989)**—is located at right front of engine compartment.
- **Idle-up Solenoid Valve (1989)**—is located in the side of the injector body.
- **Ignition Coil/Power Transistor (1990–91)—2.4L engine**—is located on left fender apron, behind air cleaner assembly.

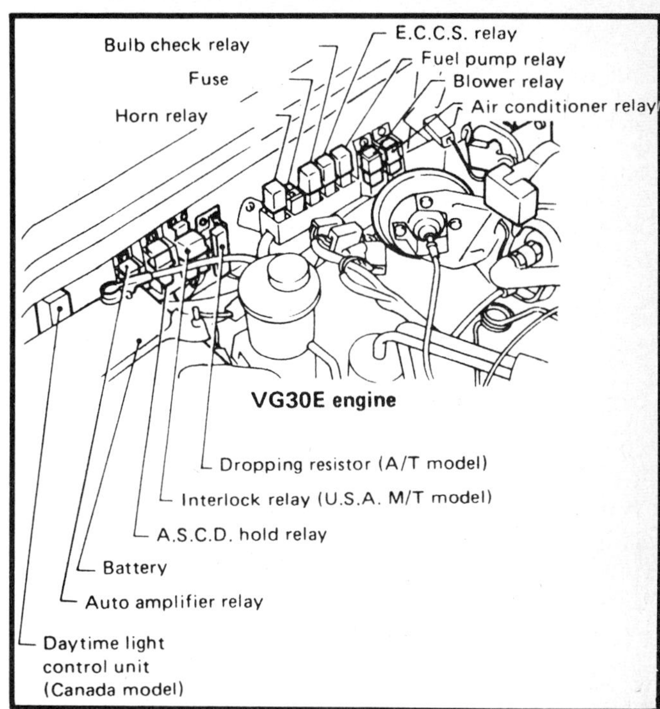

Engine compartment relays—1990 and 1991 Truck and Pathfinder

- **Ignition Relay (1989) or Ignition Relays No. 1 and 2 (1990–91)**—is/are located above fuse box.
- **Inhibitor Relay (1989)**—is located in underhood relay holder.
- **Inhibitor Relay (1990–91)**—is located on left fender apron behind canister bracket.
- **Interlock Emergency Relay (1990–91—4WD manual transmission)**—is located on left fender apron, behind canister bracket.
- **Interlock Emergency Relay (1989—4WD with manual transmission)**—is located to rear of underhood relay holder.
- **Interlock Relay (manual transmission)**—is located on right fender apron, to rear of battery.
- **Main Relay (1989)**—is located in underhood relay holder.
- **Mixture Heater (1989—3.0L engine)**—is located under the injection unit on the intake manifold.
- **Mixture Heater Relay (1989)**—is located in underhood relay holder.
- **Neutral Switch (manual transmission)**—is located on side of transmission case.
- **NP Relay (1990–91)**—is located on left fender apron, behind canister bracket.
- **NP Relay (1989)**—is located to rear of underhood relay holder.
- **Oil Pressure Switch (1989)**—is located to left of oil filter.
- **Oxygen Sensor (1989)**—is located in exhaust pipe, ahead of catalytic converter.
- **Oxygen Sensor (1990–91—2.4L engine)**—is located in exhaust manifold, left side of engine.
- **Power Transisitor (1990–91—3.0L engine)**—is located right side of engine at ignition coil.
- **Power Window Amplifier (1990–91)**—is located behind right front kick panel.
- **Rear Anti-lock Brake Actuator (1990–91)**—is located on right frame rail under vehicle.

• **Rear Anti-lock Brake Control Module (1990–91)**—is located under center console.
• **Rear Defogger Relay (Pathfinder)**—is located in left quarter panel, at rear of cargo compartment.
• **Rear Defogger Timer (Pathfinder)**—is located in left quarter panel, at rear of cargo compartment.
• **Rear Wiper Amplifier (Pathfinder)**—is located in left quarter panel, to rear of driver's door.
• **Rear Wiper Relay (Pathfinder)**—is located in left quarter panel, at rear of cargo compartment.
• **Reverse Lamp Switch (manual transmission)**—is located on side of transmission case.
• **Safety Relay (1989)**—is located in right front kick panel.
• **Seat Belt Timer (1989)**—is located behind left front kick panel.
• **Speed Sensor (RE4R01A transmission)**—is located in combination meter in the dashboard.
• **Sunload Sensor (automatic air conditioning, 1990–91)**—is located in defroster grille at base of windshield.
• **Underhood Relay Holder**—is located on right fender apron, near firewall.
• **Warning Chime**—is located behind left front kick panel.
• **Wiper Amplifier**—is located at wiper motor on right firewall.

SUBARU

Fusible Links

LEGACY

The main fusible link is located in the underhood fuse box.

LOYALE

The fusible links are located in a box on the left fender apron, ahead of the shock tower.

JUSTY

The 30 and 60 amp main fuses are located in a holder on the left front shock tower, near the brake master cylinder.

XT

The fusible links are located in a box at the left side of the engine compartment, near the battery.

Circuit Breakers

The power window circuit breakers are located under the front seat.

Relays, Sensors, Modules and Computers

LEGACY

• **A/C Cut Relay**—is located on evaporator case behind upper right dash.
• **A/C Fuse**—is located in the main fuse box.
• **A/C Main Fan Relay**—is located in the main fuse box.
• **A/C Pressure Switch**—is located on receiver/dryer at right rear of engine compartment.
• **A/C Relay**—is located in the main fuse box.
• **A/C Sub-fan Relay**—is located in the main fuse box.
• **A/C Sub-fan Water Temperature Relay**—is located in the main fuse box.
• **Air Suspension Charge Solenoid**—is located in left front fender near battery.
• **Air Suspension Compressor Relay**—is located at left rear of engine compartment, at firewall.
• **Air Suspension Compressor**—is located in left front fender, near battery.
• **Air Suspension Control Module**—is located under the driver's seat.
• **Air Suspension Pressure Switch**—is located in left front fender near battery.
• **Anti-lock Brake Control Module**—is located under front passenger seat.
• **Anti-lock Brake G-Sensor**—is located on frame rail at right shock tower.
• **Automatic Shoulder Belt Control Module (sedan)**—is located in left side of trunk, near left trunk lid hinge mount.
• **Automatic Shoulder Belt Control Module (wagon)**—is located on left rear shock tower, just below rear speaker.
• **Automatic Transmission Control Module**—is located under left dash, immediately to left of steering column.
• **Blower Relay**—is located behind upper left dash.
• **Camshaft Angle Sensor**—is located at front of left camshaft.
• **Check Connector (Black)**—is located behind left side of center console, under dashboard.
• **Clutch Relay (manual transaxle)**—is located under right dash, to right of glove box.
• **Crank Angle Sensor**—is located on the oil pump at the front center of the engine.
• **Cruise Control Module**—is located under right dash, to right of glove box.
• **Cruise Control Pump**—is located low on right shock tower, near frame rail.
• **Daytime Running Light Control Module (Canada)**—is located under right dash, above right kick panel.
• **Daytime Running Light High Beam Relay (Canada)**—is located under right dash, above right kick panel.
• **Daytime Running Light Relay (Canada)**—is located under right dash, above right kick panel.
• **Daytime Running Light Resistor**—is located on right shock tower.
• **Diagnosis Connector**—is located behind left side of center console, under dashboard.
• **Diagnostic Connector (ground)**—is single connector taped to Diagnostic Connector harness.
• **Dropping Resistor**—is located on right shock tower.
• **ECU**—is located under left dash, to left of steering column.
• **Fuel Injection Control Module**—see MPFI.
• **Fuel Pump Relay**—is located behind upper left dash.
• **Fuel Pump**—is located in the fuel tank.
• **Fuse Box**—is located under left side of instrument panel.
• **FWD Switch**—is located at right front shock tower in the engine compartment.
• **Headlight Relay (left)**—is located in the main fuse box.
• **Headlight Relay (right)**—is located in the main fuse box.
• **Horn Relay**—is located behind fuse box under left dash.

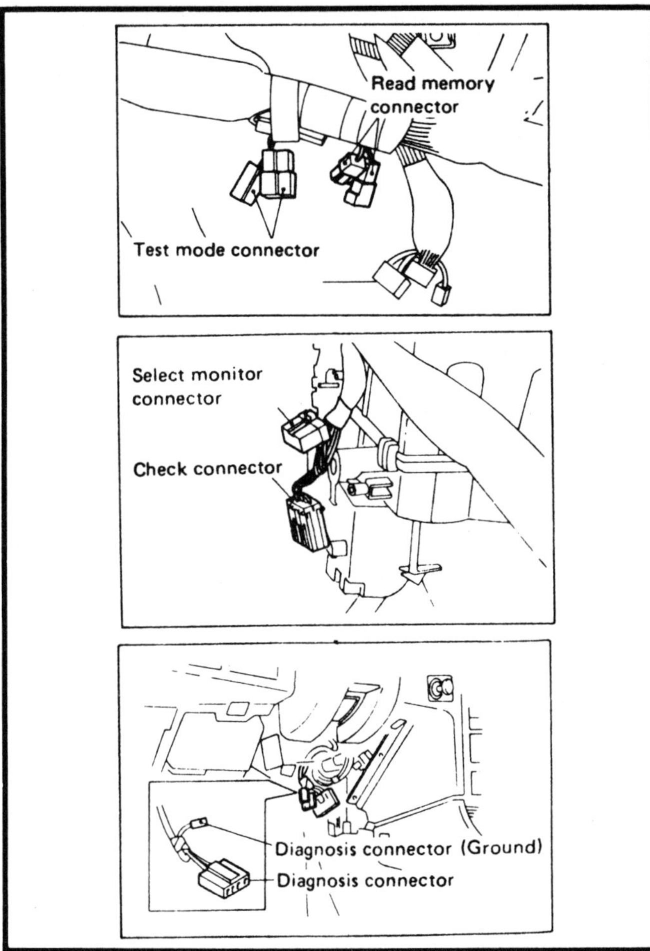

Test connectors—Legacy

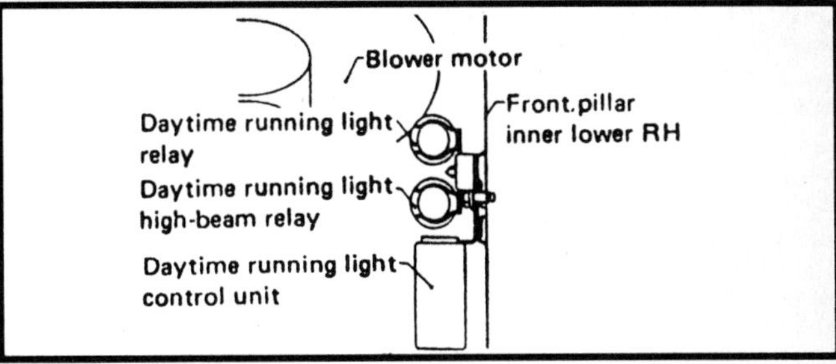

Daytime running light controller—typical Subaru

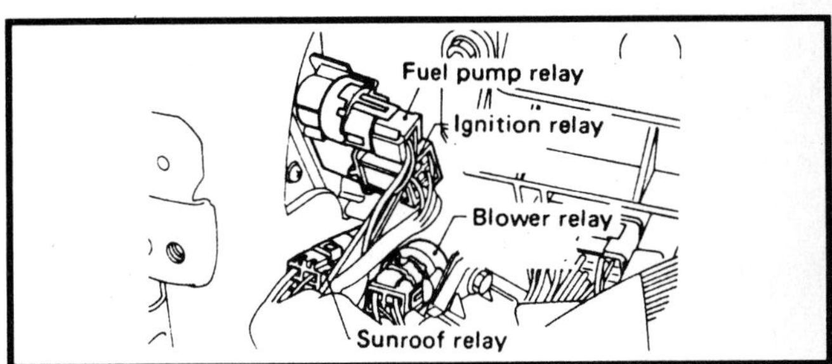

Under dashboard relays—Legacy

- **Igniter**—is located on center of firewall in engine compartment.
- **Ignition Relay**—is located behind upper left dash.
- **Illumination Control Unit**—is located behind center dashboard, to left of glovebox.
- **Inhibitor Relay (automatic transaxle)**— —is located under right dash, to right of glove box.
- **Inhibitor Switch (automatic transaxle)**—is located on the right side of the transmission case.
- **Knock Sensor (1991)**—is located at left rear of engine.
- **Main Fan Relay**—is located on fuse box under dash.
- **Main Fuse Box**—is located at the rear of the battery.
- **Main Relay**—is located under right dash, to right of glove box.
- **MPFI Control Module**—is located behind left dash, above fuse box.
- **Neutral Switch (manual transaxle—4WD)**—is located on the left side of the transfer case.
- **Neutral Switch (manual transaxle—FWD)**—is located on the left side of the transmission rear case.
- **Oil Pressure Switch**—is located on upper right area of engine.
- **Oxygen Sensor (except turbocharged)**—is located in Y-pipe of exhaust system in catalytic converter.
- **Oxygen Sensor (turbocharged, 1991)**—is located is exhaust exit pipe below turbocharger.
- **PCV Valve**—is located in intake manifold.
- **Power Window Relay**—is located under the driver's seat.
- **Purge Control Solenoid Valve**—is located at front of intake manifold.
- **Read Memory Connector (black)**—is located below right side of steering column.
- **Rear Defogger Relay**—is located on fuse box under dash.
- **Rear Wiper Relay**—is located on rear of right rear shock tower, behind and below right rear speaker.
- **Reverse Light Switch (manual transaxle—4WD)**—is located on the left side of the transfer case.
- **Reverse Light Switch (manual transaxle—FWD)**—is located on the left side of the transmission rear case.
- **Seat Belt Timer**—is located behind center dashboard, to left of glove box.
- **SELECT Monitor Connector (yellow)**—is located behind left side of center console, under dashboard.
- **Shift Lock Control Module**—is located under left center dash, behind left side of center console.
- **Starter Interlock Relay**—is located on brake pedal bracket.
- **Sunroof Control Module**—is located in roof, at rear of sunroof.
- **Sunroof Relay**—is located behind upper left dash.
- **Tail and Illumination Relay**—is located on fuse box under dash.
- **Test Mode Connector (green)**—is located is located below right side of steering column.
- **Throttle Position Sensor/Idle Switch**—is located on the on the throttle body.
- **Turn Signal/Flasher Module**—is located behind center dashboard, to left of glove box.
- **Wastegate Valve and Controller (1991)** —is located at exhaust side of turbocharger.
- **Water Temperature Sensor**—is located at right rear of engine block.

LOYALE

- **A/C Amplifier**—is located on evaporator unit under right dash.
- **A/C Cut Relay**—is located on evaporator unit under right dash.

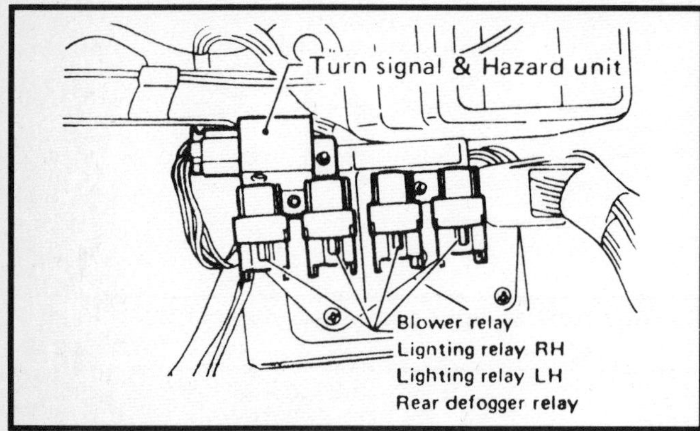

Relay locations—Loyale

- **A Fuse**—is located on right shock tower.
- **A Relay**—is located on right shock tower.
- **Air Control Valve (SPFI)**—is located on throttle chamber.
- **Air Flow Meter**—is located on right fender apron.
- **Automatic Transmission Control Module (4 speed)**—is located in left quarter panel.
- **Auxiliary Air Valve (MPFI)**—is located on intake manifold.
- **Blower Relay**—is located on relay board under left dash.
- **Chime Unit**—is located behind center dash, at right side of center console.
- **Crank Angle Sensor**—is located within the distributor.
- **FICD Solenoid**—is located on throttle body at intake manifold.
- **Fuel Pump Relay**—is located behind left dash.
- **Fuel Pump**—is located at right rear of vehicle, below floorpan.
- **FWD Switch**—is located on left front shock tower.
- **FWD/4WD Solenoid Valve**—is located on left front shock tower.
- **Igniter (SPFI)**—is located under ignition coil.
- **Ignition Relay**—is located behind left dash.
- **Inhibitor Switch (3 spd. automatic transaxle)**—is located at the base of the shift selector.
- **Inhibitor Switch (4 spd. automatic transaxle)**—is located on the transmission case.
- **Knock Sensor**—is located at the rear of the engine.
- **Lighting Relays**—both left and right relays are located on relay board under left dash.
- **MPFI Module**—is located under left dash, directly below the steering column.
- **MPFI Resistor**—is located on the right front shock tower.
- **Oil Pressure Switch**—is located in the oil pump.
- **Oxygen Sensor**—is located in the exhaust pipe.
- **Power Window Control Module**—is located under the front passenger seat.
- **Power Window Relay**—is located under the front passenger seat.
- **Radiator Fan Relay**—is located on the right front shock tower.
- **Rear Defogger Relay**—is located on relay board under left dash.
- **Rear Defogger Timer (3 door)**—is located near taillamp assemblies in rear skirt.
- **Reverse Lamp Switch**—is located on transmission case.
- **Seat Belt Timer**—is located behind upper right center dash, near clock.
- **Speed Sensor**—is located in combination meter.
- **Throttle Position Sensor**—is located on throttle body.
- **Transmission Resistor (4 speed automatic transaxle)**—is located on the rear of the right front shock tower.
- **Turn Signal/Hazard Flasher Module**—is located behind lower left dash, to left of steering column.

JUSTY

- **4WD Indicator Light Switch**—is located in transfer case.
- **Accelerator Switch**—is located on accelerator pedal bracket.
- **Air Temperature Sensor**—is located on air cleaner assembly.
- **Automatic Seat Belt Module**—is located behind right front kick panel.
- **Automatic Seat Belt Warning System Diode**—is located in wiring harness near control module.
- **Check Connector (under dash)**—is located under left side dashboard.
- **Check Connectors (ECVT)**—are located in ECVT module harness at the control module.
- **Check Connectors (underhood)**—are located in wire harness at left front shock tower.
- **Chime Unit**—is located behind instrument panel to right of steering wheel.
- **Condenser**—is taped to wire harness just below ignition coil.
- **CPC Solenoid**—is located on right fender apron, ahead of shock tower.
- **Daytime Running Lamp Control Module (Canada)**—is located behind right front kick panel.
- **Daytime Running Light Relay (Canada)**—is located on left front fender apron, forward of battery.
- **Daytime Running Light Resistor (Canada)**—is located on left front fender apron, forward of battery.
- **ECVT Module**—is located under left dash, above hood release.
- **EFC Control Module**—See Fuel Control Module
- **EGR Solenoid**—is located on bracket at center of firewall.
- **FCV Solenoid**—is located on right side of firewall in engine compartment.
- **Front Wiper Intermittent Control Module**—is located behind the fusebox.
- **Fuel Control Module (EFC or MPFI)**—is located under left dash, near hood release.
- **Fuel Pump Relay**—is located under left dash, to right of fuel injection module.
- **Fuse Box**—is located under the left side of the dashboard.
- **FWD/4WD Solenoid**—is located on right side of firewall in engine compartment.
- **HAC Solenoid**—is located on right side firewall in engine compartment.
- **Headlight relays**—are located behind the fuse box.
- **Idle-up Solenoid**—is located on bracket at center of firewall.
- **Ignition Coil**—is located at center of firewall in engine compartment.
- **Illumination Control Module**—is located on brake pedal bracket.
- **Inhibitor Switch**—is located at the base of the shifter assembly.
- **ISC Solenoid**—is located under air cleaner assembly.
- **Key Lock Solenoid**—is located at bottom of ignition key switch.
- **MPFI Control Module**—See Fuel Control Module
- **Oil Pressure Switch**—is located on the side of the engine block, above the alternator.
- **Oxygen Sensor**—is located in exhaust manifold.
- **Radiator Fan Relay**—is located with fuel injection relay under left dash.
- **Read Memory Connector**—is located under left dashboard.

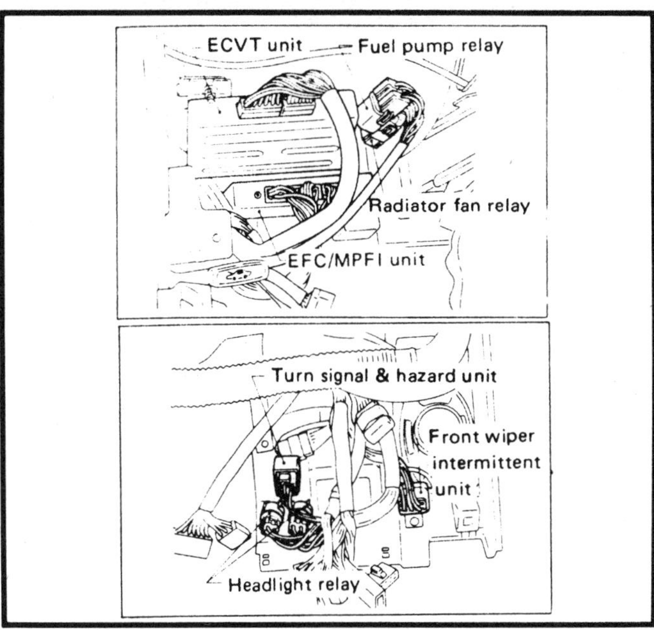

Dashboard component locations—Justy

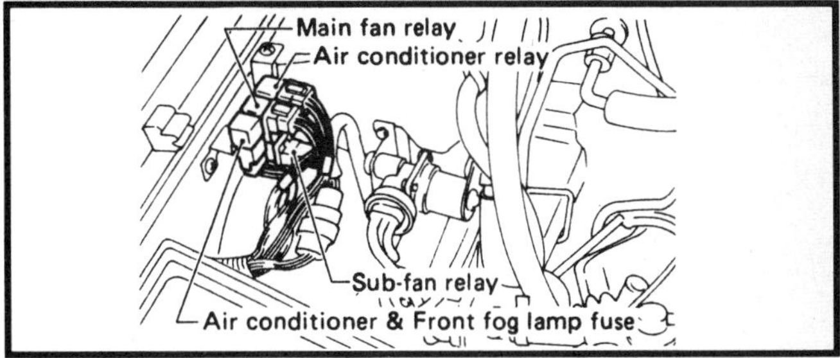

Underhood relays—XT

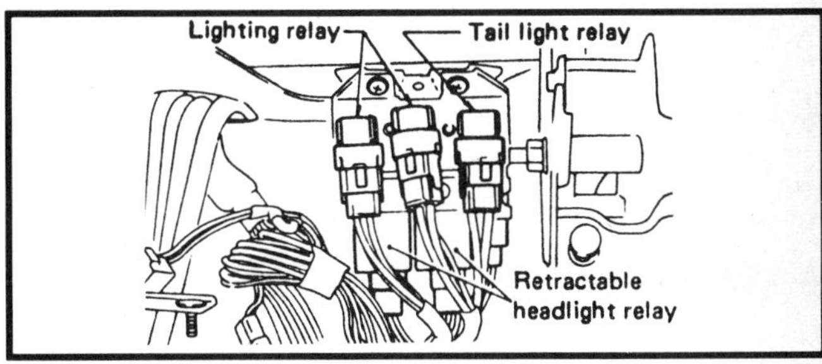

Under dash relays—XT

- **Rear Wiper Relay**—is located behind right dash, above kick panel.
- **Reverse Lamp Switch**—is located on transmission case.
- **SELECT Diagnostic Connector**—is located in wire harness, just below ignition coil on firewall.
- **Shift Lock Module**—is located on brake pedal bracket.
- **Shift Lock Solenoid**—is located at the base of the shifter assembly.
- **Throttle Position Switch**—is located on accelerator pedal bracket.
- **Turn Signal/Hazard Flasher**—is located behind fuse box.
- **VLC Solenoid**—is located on right fender apron, ahead of shock tower.
- **Water Temperature Sensor (EFC)**—is located at flywheel end of engine, below and to right of distributor.
- **Water Temperature Sensor (MPFI)**—is located in intake manifold, below throttle body.

XT

- **A/C Amplifier**—is located on evaporator case, above and to left of blower motor.
- **A Cut Relay**—is located in right quarter panel, behind right door.
- **A Fuse**—is located on right fender apron, ahead of shock tower.
- **A Relay**—is located on right fender apron, ahead of shock tower.
- **A/Front Fog Lamps Fuse (2.7L engine)**—is located on right fender apron, ahead of shock tower.
- **Air Flow Meter**—is located at exit port of air cleaner assembly.
- **Automatic Seat Belt Control Module**—is located in right quarter panel, behind right door.
- **Automatic Transmission Control Module**—is located in left quarter panel, behind left door.
- **Blower Relay**—is located in center of dash, behind center console.
- **Check Connectors (underhood, 17-pin and 11-pin)**—are located in wire harness at left side of firewall.
- **Chime Unit**—is located at the rear of the instrument cluster.
- **Cruise Control Module**—is located in right side dash, above glove box light assembly.
- **Differential Lock Solenoid**—is located at the center of the firewall.
- **FICD Solenoid**—is located on throttle body.
- **Fog Lamp Fuse (2.7L engine)**—see Air Conditioner
- **Fuel Pump Relay**—is located in center of dash, behind center of console.
- **Fuel Pump**—is located under floor of trunk.
- **Fuse Box**—is located in lower left dashboard.
- **FWD Switch Fuse Holder**—is located on bracket at ignition coil.
- **FWD/4WD Solenoid**—is located at the center of the firewall.
- **Headlamp Washer Module**—is located in right quarter panel, behind right door.
- **Headlight Washer Pump**—is located inside right front fender.
- **Igniter**—is located under ignition coil on left fender apron.
- **Ignition Coil**—is located on left fender apron at shock tower.
- **Ignition Relay**—is located in center of dash, behind center console.
- **Illumination Control Module**—is located on top of steering column, under upper column cover.
- **Inhibitor Switch**—is located on the side of transmission case.
- **Intermittent Wiper Module**—is located in center console, just ahead of shifter assembly.
- **Knock Sensor**—is located at right rear of engine.
- **Lighting Relays**—are located behind left dashboard, to left of steering column.
- **Main Fan Relay**—is located on right fender apron, ahead of shock tower.
- **Mode Control Module**—is located under left center dash, behind center console.
- **MPFI Control Module**—is located in front of trunk, mounted to underside of rear window shelf.
- **MPS Controller**—is located in left quarter panel, to rear of automatic seat belt motor.
- **Oil Pressure Sensor**—is located in oil filter housing.

• **Oxygen Sensor**—is located in catalytic converter.

• **Pneumatic Suspension Air Charge Solenoid Valve**—is located inside left front fender.

• **Pneumatic Suspension Compressor**—is located inside left front fender.

• **Pneumatic Suspension Control Module**—is located under the driver's seat.

• **Pneumatic Suspension Dryer**—is located inside left front fender.

• **Pneumatic Suspension Relay**—is located on left side firewall at fender apron.

• **Pneumatic Suspension Solenoid Valve**—is located on left side firewall at fender apron.

• **Power Window Control Module**—is located under front passenger seat.

• **Power Window Relay**—is located under front passenger seat.

• **Read Memory Connector**—is located in wiring harness at front of trunk, under rear window shelf. The connectors are black.

• **Rear Defogger Relay**—is located in center of dash, behind center console.

• **Retractable Headlight Relays (left and right)**—are located behind left dash, to left of steering column.

• **Retractable Headlight Timer**—is located on bracket above lighting relays, under left dash.

• **Speed Sensor**—is located within the instrument cluster.

• **Steering Sensor**—is located on steering column at floor.

• **Stop Lamp Checker**—is located within right tail lamp assembly.

• **Sub-fan Relay (2.7L engine)**—is located on right fender apron, ahead of shock tower.

• **Tail Lamp Relay**—is located behind left dashboard, to left of steering column.

• **Test Mode Connectors**—are located in front of trunk, under rear window shelf. The 2 connectors are green.

• **Throttle Sensor**—is located on the throttle body.

• **Trip Computer Module**—is located in center dashboard, to right of steering column.

• **Windshield Washer Pump**—is located inside right front fender.

SUZUKI

Fusible Links

SAMURAI

Battery Fusible Link—is located at the battery positive terminal.

SWIFT

Main Fusible Link—is located at the battery positive terminal.

Relays, Sensors, Modules and Computer Locations

SAMURAI

• **Bi-metal Vacuum Switching Valve**—is located in the intake manifold water passages, has 2 vacuum hoses.

• **Cancel Switch**—is located under the steering column, used to cancel emission maintenance intervals.

• **Check Relay**—is located at the right kick panel.

• **Clutch Switch**—is located at the clutch pedal.

• **Delay Valve (Orifice)**—is located inline to the choke piston vacuum hose.

• **Diagnostic (Duty Check) Terminal**—is located in the main harness, at the firewall.

• **EGR Modulator**—is located near the carburetor.

• **Electronic Control Module (ECM)**—is located behind the glove compartment.

• **Fifth Gear Switch**—is located at the transmission, 2 wires.

• **Fuel Cut Solenoid**—is threaded into the carburetor, 2 wires.

• **Hazard Flasher**—is the same as the turn signal flasher.

• **High Altitude Compensator (HAC)**—is located at the firewall, under the thermal engine room switch.

• **Horn Relay**—is located behind the instrument panel, near the left kick panel.

• **Hot Idle Compensator (HIC)**—is located air intake assembly.

• **Idle Micro Switch**—is located at the carburetor.

• **Ignition Condenser**—is located at the ignition coil mounting bracket.

• **Mileage Sensor**—is located in the speedometer assembly.

• **Mixture Control Solenoid Valve (MCSV)**—is located at the carburetor, long shape with a O-ring at the bottom.

• **Mixture Control Valve (MCV)**—is located near the thermostat housing.

• **Oxygen Sensor**—is located at the exhaust manifold.

• **Radio Noise Suppressor**—is located at the main harness, near the ignition coil.

• **Thermal Engine Room Switch**—is located at the firewall, near the battery.

• **Thermal Switch**—is located at the thermostat housing, hexagon shape.

• **Three-way Solenoid Valve (TWSV)**—is located near the thermostat housing.

• **Turn Signal Flasher**—is located near the left kick panel.

• **Vacuum Transmitting Valve (Thermostatic Air Cleaner)**—is located in the air cleaner housing.

• **Vent Solenoid Valve**—is located at the carburetor float bowl.

• **Water Temperature Sender**—is located at the thermostat housing.

• **Wide-Open Micro Switch**—is located at the carburetor.

SIDEKICK

• **4WD Switch**—is located on top of the transfer case.

• **4WD Low Switch**—is located on the side of the transfer case.

• **Air Temperature Sensor**—is located behind the water temperature sensor.

• **Automatic Transmission Shift Switch**—is located at the transmission linkage attachment.

• **Backup Light Switch**—is located at the transmission, forward most switch.

• **Blower Resistor**—is located is located at the blower housing, right side.

• **Brake Fluid Level Switch**—is located at the master cylinder.

• **Check Engine Cancel Switch**—is located next to the steering column.

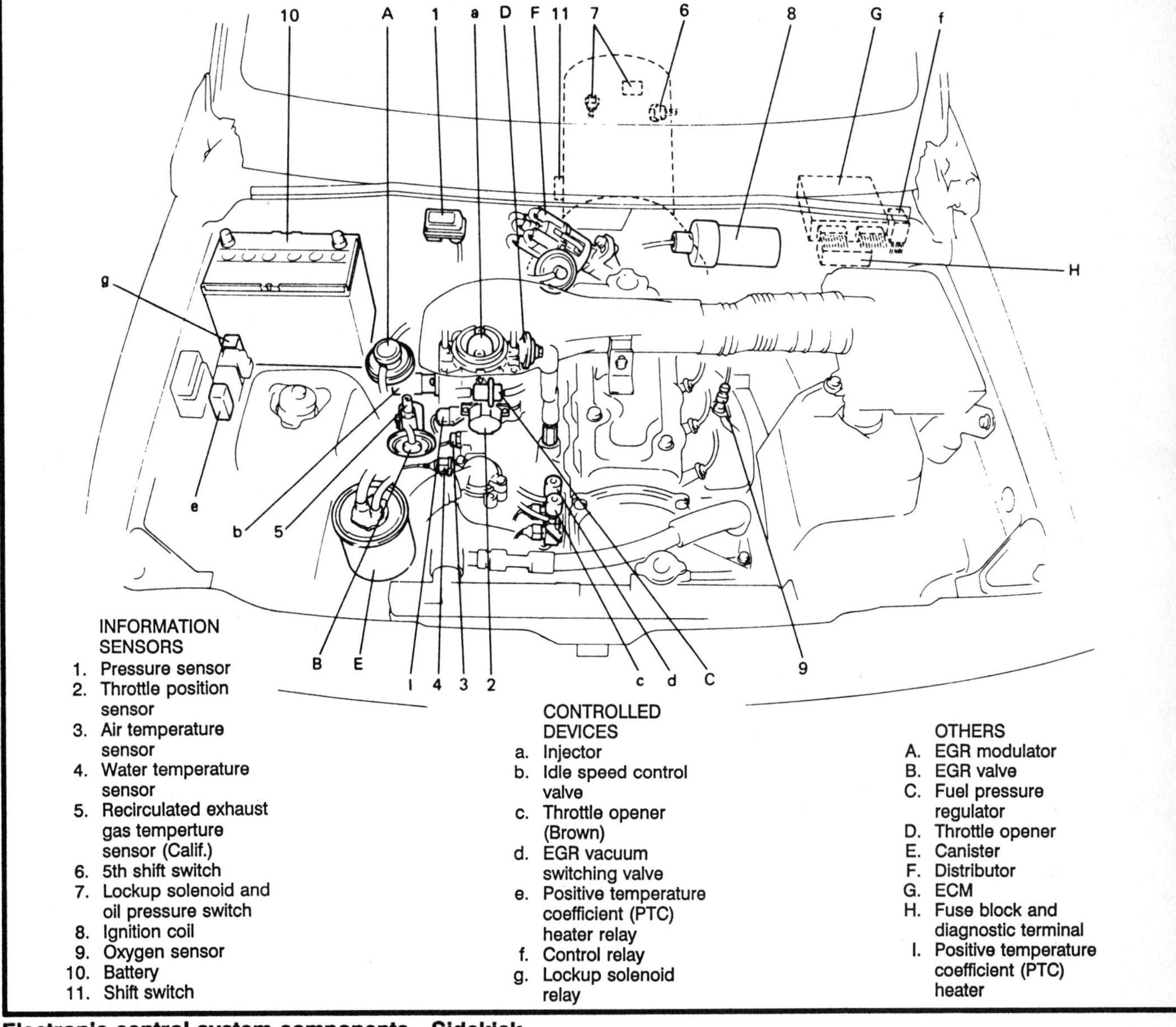

Electronic control system components—Sidekick

- **Clutch Start Switch**—is located at the clutch pedal.
- **Condenser**—is located at the ignition coil mounting bracket.
- **Control Relay**—is located next to the ECM, left kick panel.
- **Cruise Control Unit**—is located behind the instrument cluster.
- **Diagnostic Check Terminal**—is located at the ECM.
- **Door Lock Controller**—is located next the cruise control unit.
- **EGR Modulator**—is located to the left of the battery.
- **EGR Temperature Sensor (California)**—is located at the EGR valve assembly.
- **EGR Vacuum Switching Valve (blue)**—is located behind the throttle opener.
- **Electronic Control Module (ECM)**—is located at the left kick panel.
- **Fifth Gear Switch**—is located at the transmission.
- **Fuse Box**—is located behind the ECM, left kick panel.
- **Hazard Flasher**—is the same as the turn signal flasher.
- **Horn Relay**—is located behind the ECM, left kick panel.
- **Idle Speed Control Valve**—is located at the throttle body, under the EGR modulator.
- **Lockup Solenoid and Oil Pressure Switch**—is located inside the transmission.
- **Main Fuse Block**—is located at the right inner fender.
- **Main Switch**—is located next to the steering column.
- **Noise Suppressor**—is located at the main harness, under the wiper motor.
- **Oxygen Sensor**—is located at the exhaust manifold.
- **Positive Temperature Coefficient (PTC) Heater**—is located under the throttle body.
- **Positive Temperature Coefficient (PTC) Relay**—is located at the main fuse block, right inner fender, forward position.
- **Throttle Opener (brown)**—is located at the right side of the timing belt cover.
- **Transmission Lockup Relay**—is located at the main fuse block, right inner fender, rearward position.

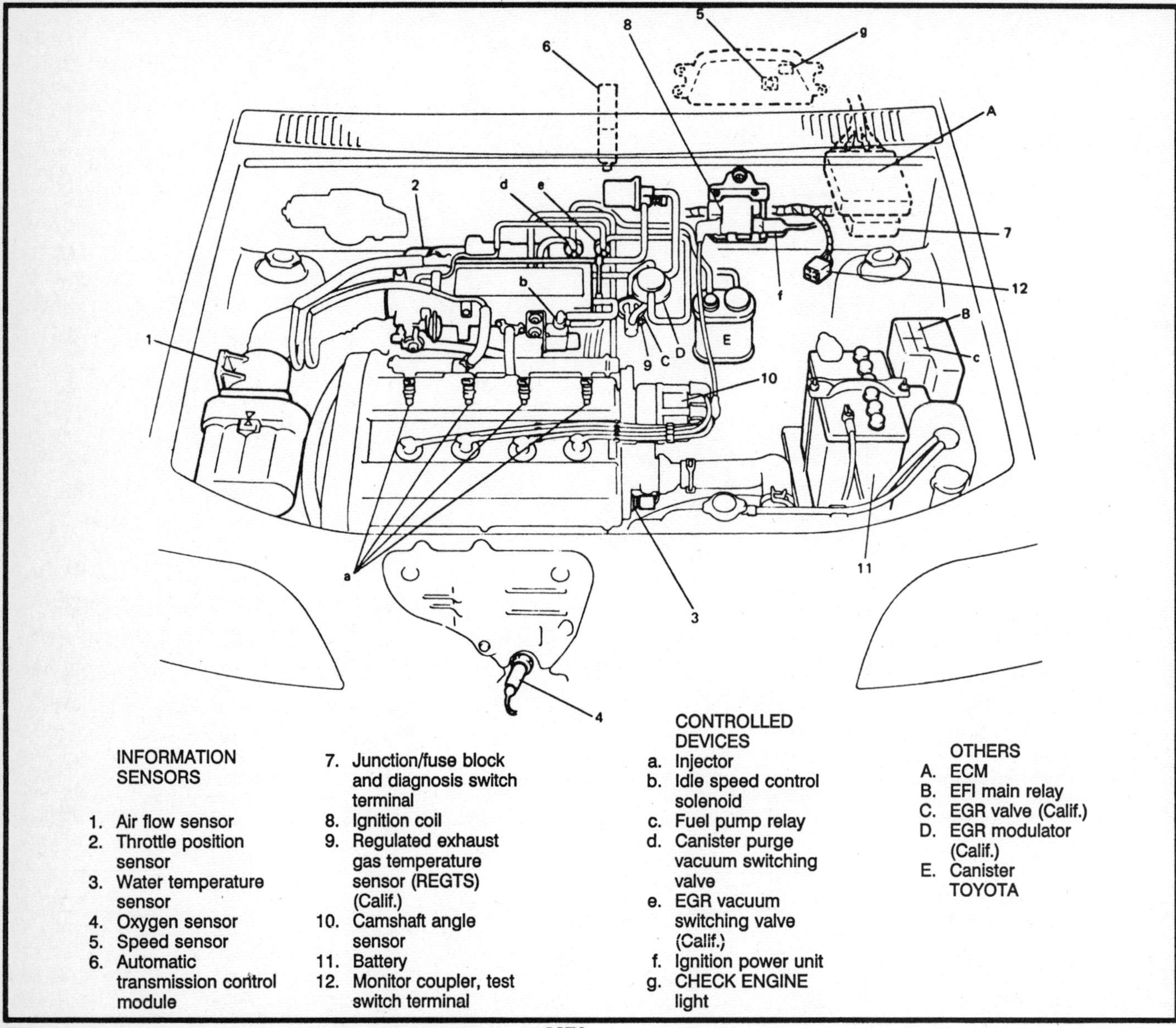

Electronic control system components—Swift 1.3L MPI

- **Turn Signal Flasher**—is located behind the ECM.
- **Warning Buzzer**—is located to the left of the instrument cluster.
- **Water Temperature Sensor**—is located behind the thermostat housing.

SWIFT

- **Air Flow Sensor (AFS) (MPI engine)**—is located at the air cleaner assembly.
- **Air Temperature Sensor (ATS) (TBI engine)**—is located at the air cleaner assembly.
- **Automatic Control Module**—is located behind the instrument panel, in the middle.
- **Automatic Seat Belt Control Module**—is located near the engine ECM, left kick panel.
- **Automatic Shift Solenoid**—is located at the bottom of the transmission case.
- **Automatic Transmission Control Unit Monitor Terminal**—is located behind the instrument panel, left kick panel.
- **Automatic Transmission Shift Lever Switch**—is located at the shift control linkage.
- **Backup Light Switch**—is located at the top of the transmission.
- **Brake Fluid Level Switch**—is located at the master cylinder.
- **Camshaft Angle Sensor (CAS) (MPI engine)**—is located in the distributor.
- **Canister Purge Vacuum Switching Valve (MPI engine)**—is located next to the EGR VSV, intake manifold.
- **Clutch Start Switch**—is located at the clutch pedal.
- **Condenser**—is located under the ignition coil.
- **Diagnostic Check Terminal**—is located above the master cylinder.
- **Diagnostic Switch Terminal**—is located near the ECM, left kick panel.
- **Door Switch Diodes**—is located in the main harness, left kick panel.
- **EGR Modulator (California)**—is located next to the EGR valve, vacuum hoses attached.

• **EGR Temperature Sensor (REGTS) (MPI engine, California)**—is located at the EGR valve.

• **EGR Vacuum Switching Valve (California)**—is located at the intake manifold, rear section (MPI engine), near the distributor assembly, at the intake manifold (TBI engine).

• **Engine Electronic Control Module (ECM)**—is located behind the instrument panel, on the left side.

• **Fuel Injector Resistor (TBI engine)**—is located to the right of the ignition coil.

• **Fuel Pump Relay**—is located forward the left strut tower, in the relay block.

• **Hazard Flasher**—is the same as the turn signal flasher.

• **Horn Relay**—is located at the left inner fender, forward the strut tower.

• **Idle Speed Control (ISC) Solenoid Valve (MPI engine)**—is located at the air intake assembly, vacuum hoses attached.

• **Idle Speed Control (ISC) Valve (TBI engine)**—is located at the throttle body assembly.

• **Main Power Relay**—is located next the fuel pump relay, in the relay block, left strut tower.

• **Noise Suppressor**—is located attached to the left strut tower.

• **Oil Pressure Switch**—is located near the oil filter mounting.

• **Oxygen Sensor**—is located at the exhaust manifold.

• **Pressure Sensor (TBI engine)**—is located near the wiper motor.

• **Speed Sensor**—is located inside the speedometer assembly.

• **Speedometer Speed Sensor**—is located at the transmission.

• **Throttle Position Sensor**—is located at the throttle body.

• **Turn Signal Flasher**—is located in the junction/fuse block.

• **Water Temperature Sensor (WTS)**—is located at the rear portion of the intake manifold (TBI engine), near the distributor (MPI engine).

TOYOTA

Circuit Breakers

CAMRY

Power 30 amp Circuit Breaker—is located in the junction block No. 1, at the left side kick panel, 2 wires.
Automatic Shoulder Belt 30 amp Circuit Breaker—is located in the junction block No. 1, under the power circuit breaker. It has 2 wires connected to it.
Heater 40 amp Circuit Breaker—is located in the relay block No. 4, at the right side kick panel. It has 2 wires connected to it.
Defogger 30 amp Circuit Breaker—is located in the junction block No. 1, on the left side, in the middle. It has 2 wires connected to it.

CELICA

Power 30 amp Circuit Breaker—is located in the relay block No. 1, below the starter relay, 2 wires.
Door Lock 30 amp Circuit Breaker—is located in the relay block No. 1, above the starter relay, 2 wires.
Defogger 30 amp Circuit Breaker—is located in the junction block No. 1, on the left side, upper section, 2 wires.
Heater 30 amp Circuit Breaker—is located in the relay block No. 4, at the right side kick panel, 2 wires.

COROLLA

Heater 30 amp Circuit Breaker—is located in the relay block No. 4, right kick panel, below the heater relay, 2 wires.
Defogger 30 amp Circuit Breaker—is located in the junction block No. 1, left kick panel.
Power 30 amp Circuit Breaker—is located in the junction block No. 1, left kick panel.

CRESSIDA

Heater 40 amp Circuit Breaker—is located in the relay block No. 4, right kick panel, 2 wires.
Defogger 30 amp Circuit Breaker—is located in the junction block No. 1, left kick panel.
Power 30 amp Circuit Breaker—is located in the junction block No. 1, left kick panel.
Automatic Shoulder Belt 30 amp Circuit Breaker—is located in the relay block No. 3, left kick panel, in the middle of the block.
Door Lock 20 amp Circuit Breaker—is located in the relay block No. 3, left kick panel, bottom of the block.

MR2

Door Lock 14 amp Circuit Breaker—is located in the relay block No. 1, left kick panel, upper section, 2 wires.

SUPRA

Defogger 30 amp Circuit Breaker—is located in the junction block No. 1, left kick panel, 2 wires.
Power 30 amp Circuit Breaker—is located in the relay block No. 5, left kick panel, 2 wires.
Heater 40 amp Circuit Breaker—is located in the relay block No. 4, right kick panel, 2 wires.

TERCEL

Defogger 30 amp Circuit Breaker—is located in the junction block No. 1, left kick panel.

Fusible Links

CAMRY

Condenser Fan 30 amp Fusible Link—is located in the relay block No. 2, in the upper left side, next to 2 15A headlight fuses.
Radiator Fan 30 amp Fusible Link—is located in the relay block No. 2, in the lower right side, next to the engine main relay.
Ignition 30 amp Fusible Link—is located in the fusible link box near the battery.
Headlight and Dimmer 40 amp Fusible Link—is located in the fusible link box near the battery.
Dimmer 40 amp Fusible Link—refer to headlight fusible link.

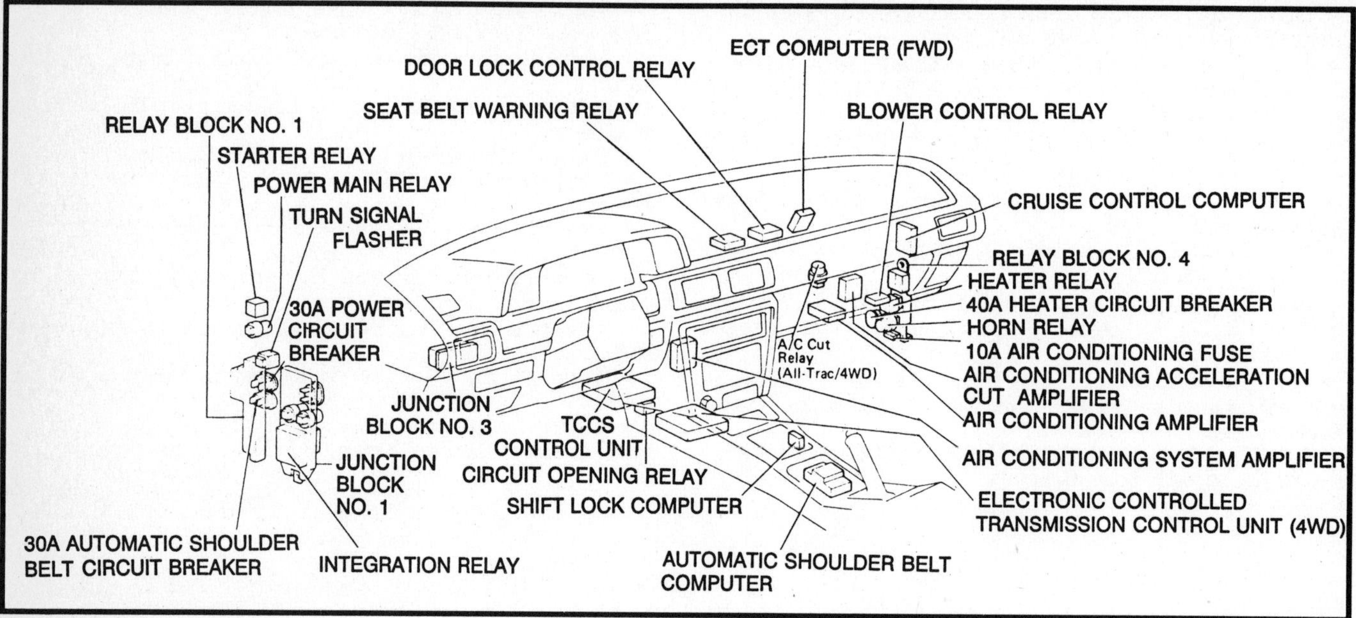

Component location—Camry

Alternator 80 amp Fusible Link—is located in the fusible link box near the battery.
Auto Seat Belt, Starter Relay and Voltage Regulator 0.5 amp Fusible Link—is located near the battery, green.
Anti-lock Brake System 1.0 amp Fusible Link—is located near the battery, yellow.
Diagnostic Connector—is located near the master cylinder.

1989 CELICA

Condenser Fan 30 amp Fusible Link—is located in the relay block No. 5, right side of radiator.
Radiator Fan 30 amp Fusible Link—is located in the junction block No. 2, left inner fender, next to the engine main relay.
Ignition System 40 amp Fusible Link 2—is located in the fusible link box near the battery.
Starter and Alternator 30 amp Fusible Link 1—is located in the fusible link box near the battery.
Alternator 100 amp Fusible Link—is located in the fusible link box near the battery.
Anti-lock Brake System 60 amp Fusible Link—is located in the fusible link box near the battery.
Fog Lights, Anti-lock Brake System 15 amp Fuse—is located in the lower portion of the junction block No. 1, left kick panel.
A/C 10 amp Fuse—is located in the relay block No. 4, right kick panel, below the horn relay.

1990-91 CELICA

Condenser Fan 30 amp Fusible Link—is located in the relay block No. 5, right side of radiator.
Radiator Fan 30 amp Fusible Link—is located in the junction block No. 2, left inner fender, next to the engine main relay.
Ignition System 40 amp Fusible Link 2—is located in the fusible link box near the battery.
Starter and Alternator 30 amp Fusible Link 1—is located in the fusible link box near the battery.
Alternator 100 amp Fusible Link—is located in the fusible link box near the battery.
Anti-lock Brake System 60 amp Fusible Link—is located in the fusible link box near the battery.
Radiator Fan 30 amp Fuse—is located in junction block No. 2, near the battery.
Condenser Fan 30 amp Fuse—is located in junction block No. 2, near the battery.

COROLLA

Condenser Fan 30 amp Fusible Link—is located in the relay block No. 5, left side inner fender, block with angled side.
Radiator Fan 30 amp Fusible Link—is located in the junction block No. 2, left side inner fender, square shape.
A/C 7.5 amp Fuse—is located in the bottom of the relay block No. 4, right kick panel.

CRESSIDA

Condenser Fan 30 amp Fusible Link—is located in the junction block No. 2, near the battery.
Ignition Switch 30 amp Fusible Link—is located in the middle of junction block No. 2. near the battery.
Ignition Switch 40 amp Fusible Link—is located in the middle of junction block No. 2. near the battery.
Anti-lock Brake System (ABS) 60 amp Fusible Link—is located in the junction block No. 2, near the battery.
Alternator 100 amp Fusible Link—is located in the junction block No. 2, near the battery, in the middle.
A/C 10 amp Fuse—is located in the relay block No. 4, right kick panel.

1989 MR2

Heater 40 amp Fusible Link—is located in the relay block No. 2, left engine compartment.
Ignition Switch 50 amp Fusible Link—is located in the relay block No. 2, left side engine compartment.
Headlight 50 amp Fusible Link—is located in the relay block No. 2, left side engine compartment.
A/C 10 amp Fuse—is located in the relay block No. 4, right kick panel.
Heater 30 amp Fuse—is located in the relay block No. 4, right kick panel.

1990-91 MR2

Ignition Switch 50 amp Fusible Link—is located in the relay block No. 5, right side luggage compartment, first link.
Heater 40 amp Fusible Link—is located in the relay block No. 5, right side luggage compartment, second link.
Anti-lock Brake System (ABS) 80 amp Fusible Link—is located in the relay block No. 5, right side luggage compartment, third link.
Alternator 120 amp Fusible Link—is located in the relay block No. 5, right side luggage compartment, fourth link.
Ignition Switch 40 amp Fusible Link—is located in the relay block No. 5, right side luggage compartment, fifth link.

SUPRA

Fog Light 15 amp Fuse—is located in the fuse block on the left kick panel.
Seat Heater 15 amp Fuse—is located in the fuse block on the left kick panel.
ECU-Battery 15 amp Fuse—is located in the fuse block on the left kick panel.
Ignition Switch 30 amp Fusible Link—is located in the junction block No. 2, left fender, next to the 15A hazard/horn fuse.
Ignition Switch 40 amp Fusible Link—is located in the junction block No. 2, left fender, next to the headlight relay.
Condenser Fan 40 amp Fusible Link—is located in the junction block No. 2, left fender, next to the 60A ABS fusible link.
Anti-lock Brake System (ABS) 60 amp Fusible Link—is located in the junction block No. 2, left fender, next to the 40A condenser fan fusible link.
Alternator 100 amp Fusible Link—is located in the junction block No. 2, left fender, at the top of the block.

1989-90 TERCEL

Condenser Fan 30 amp Fusible Link—is located in the relay block No. 2, left inner fender.
Radiator Fan 30 amp Fusible Link—is located in the relay block No. 2, left inner fender.
Heater 30 amp Fuse—is located in the relay block No. 4, right kick panel.
A/C 10 amp Fuse—is located in the relay block No. 4, right kick panel.

1991 TERCEL

Defogger 30 amp Fusible Link—is located in the relay block No. 6, left kick panel.
Heater 30 amp Fusible Link—is located in the relay block No. 4, right kick panel.
Ignition Switch 50 amp Fusible Link—is located in the relay block No. 2, left inner fender.
Alternator 100 amp Fusible Link—is located in the relay block No. 2, left inner fender.
A/C 10 amp Fuse—is located in the relay block No. 4, right kick panel.

Relays, Sensors, Modules and Computer Location

CAMRY

- **A/C Amplifier**—is located behind the radio.
- **A/C Compressor Sensor**—is located at the compresseor.
- **A/C Dual Pressure Switch**—is located at the left inner fender, next to the A/C high pressure switch.
- **A/C Fan Relay No. 1**—is located in the relay block No. 2, in the upper right side of the relay block, 4 wires, on the left side inner fender.
- **A/C Fan Relay No. 2**—is located in the relay block No. 2, to the left of the EFI main relay, 6 wires.
- **A/C Fan Relay No. 3**—is located in the relay block No. 2, to right of the condenser fan fusible link, 4 wires.
- **A/C Magnet Clutch Relay (Canada)**—is located on the left strut tower.
- **A/C Magnet Clutch Relay (US), Dimmer Relay (Canada)**—is located in the relay block No. 2, in the lower left side of the relay block, 4 wires.
- **A/C unit Relay**—is located behind the instrument panel, towards the right side, next to the air conditioning amplifier (All-Trac).
- **Air Flow Meter**—is located on the air cleaner assembly.
- **Air Intake Temperature Sensor**—is located at the air cleaner assembly.
- **Anti-lock Brake System Control Unit**—is located on the right side rear compartment, under the trim panel.
- **Anti-lock Brake System Check Connector**—is located at the right inner fender, forward of strut tower.
- **Auto Antenna Control Relay**—is on the left side, in the trunk, behind the trim panel.
- **Automatic Shoulder Belt Control Unit**—is located under the console, in from of the emergency brake handle.
- **Blower Control Relay**—is located in the relay block No. 4, on the right side kick panel. The relay is above the heater relay.
- **Circuit Opening Relay**—is located next to the engine ECU, behind the radio.
- **Cold Start Injector**—is located at the air intake plenum.
- **Coolant Temperature Sensor**—is located in the thermostat housing, to the right of the start injector time switch.
- **Cruise Control Unit**—is located above the relay block No. 4, on the right side.
- **Diagnostic Check Connector**—is located near the master cylinder.
- **Door Lock Control Relay**—is located to the left of the electronic controlled transmission (ECT) control unit, behind the instrument panel.
- **EFI Main Relay**—is located in the relay block No. 2, a round relay with 4 wires.
- **EFI Water Temperature Sensor**—is located at the intake manifold, near the driver's side.
- **EGR Gas Temperature Sensor**—is located on the lower portion of the intake plenum.
- **Electrical Idle-up Diode**—is located in the main harness, left side instrument panel.
- **Electronic Controlled Transmission (ECT) Control Unit (4WD)**—is located behind the console, on the right.
- **Electronic Controlled Transmission (ECT) Control Unit (FWD)**—is located behind the instrument panel, to the right of the door lock control relay.
- **Engine Electronic Control Unit (ECU)**—is located behind the radio, on the floor.
- **Engine Main Relay**—is located to the left of the radiator fan fusible line in the relay block No. 2, 5 wires.
- **Fuel Pump Relay**—refer to the circuit opening relay.
- **Hazard Flasher**—is located within the turn signal flasher.
- **Headlight Relay**—is located in the relay block No.2, right of the A/C or dimmer relay, 5 wires.
- **Heater Relay**—is located in the relay block No. 4. It has a 5 wire connector.
- **Horn Relay**—is located in the relay block No. 4, on the right side kick panel. It is to the right of the heater circuit breaker.
- **Idle Speed Control Valve**—is located at the intake air plenum, near the throttle body.

• **Integration Relay (auto light turn OFF and interior light fade)**—is located in the junction block No. 1 on the left side kick panel.
• **Interior Light and Door Lock Diode**—is located above the relay block on the right side.
• **Key Interlock Solenoid**—is located near the ignition switch.
• **Knock Sensor**—is threaded into the cylinder block, under the intake manifold.
• **Light Failure Sensor**—is located in the rear trunk compartment, on the left side, behind the trim panel.
• **Overdrive Diode**—is located in the main harness, behind the glove compartment.
• **Oxygen Sensor (main)**—is located in the exhaust pipe, before the catalytic converter.
• **Oxygen Sensor (sub)**—is located in the exhaust pipe, after the catalytic converter.
• **Moonroof Control Relay**—is located at the switch, under the switch bezel.
• **Neutral Start Switch**—is located at the transmission.
• **Power Main Relay**—is located in the relay block No. 1, left kick panel, the lower right relay.
• **Seat Belt Warning Relay (Canada)**—is located behind the instrument panel, in the center, to the left of the door lock control relay.
• **Shift Lock Control Unit**—is located under the console, in front of the automatic shoulder belt control unit.
• **Start Injector Time Switch**—is located in the thermostat housing, to the left of the coolant temperature sensor.
• **Starter Relay**—is located in the relay block No. 1, left kick panel, the upper relay.
• **Taillight Relay**—is located in the junction block No. 1, left kick panel, to the right of the defogger relay, 4 wires.
• **Throttle Position Sensor**—is located on the throttle body.
• **Turn Signal Flasher**—is located in the relay block No. 1, left kick panel, upper section, 3 wires.
• **Vehicle Speed Sensor**—is located inside the speedometer head.
• **Windshield Wiper Diode**—is located in the main harness, left side instrument panel.
• **Wiper (rear) Diode**—is located in the main harness behind the instrument cluster.

1989 CELICA

• **A/C Ambient Sensor**—is located at the radiator, in the middle.
• **A/C Compressor Sensor**—is located at the compresseor.
• **A/C Dual and High Pressure Switches**—is located at the right inner fender, in the rear corner.
• **A/C Amplifier**—is located behind the relay block No. 4, right side kick panel.
• **A/C Clutch Relay**—is located in the relay block No. 5, right beside radiator, 3 wires.
• **A/C Fan Relay 2**—is located in the relay block No. 5, right beside radiator, 5 wires.
• **A/C Fan Relay 3**—is located in the relay block No. 5, right beside radiator, 4 wires.
• **Air Flow Meter**—is located on the air cleaner assembly.
• **Air Intake Temperature Sensor**—is located at the air cleaner assembly.
• **Anti-lock Brake System Check Connector**—is located at the right inner fender, forward of strut tower.
• **Anti-lock Brake System (ABS) Relay**—is located beside the left strut tower.
• **Anti-lock Brake System Computer (All Trac)**—is located in the rear seat area, right side.
• **Anti-lock Brake System Computer (FWD)**—is located on top of the ECU, behind the console.

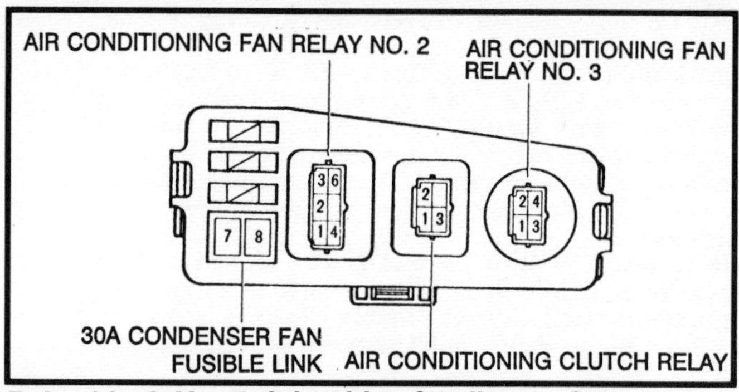

Relay block No. 5 right side of radiator—Celica

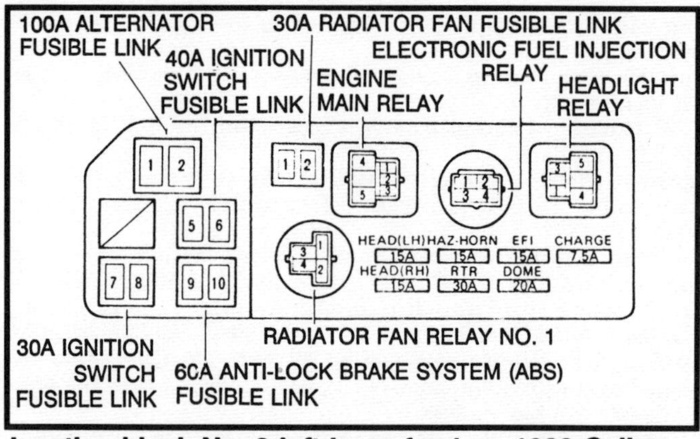

Junction block No. 2 left inner fender—1989 Celica

• **Auto Antenna Control Relay**—is located behind the rear left trim panel, behind the wheelhouse.
• **Blower Relay**—is located behind the relay block No. 4, right side kick panel.
• **Circuit Opening Relay**—is located next to the ECU, behind the console.
• **Cold Start Injector**—is located at the air intake plenum.
• **Coolant Temperature Sensor**—is located in the thermostat housing, to the right of the start injector time switch.
• **Cruise Control Computer**—is located just above the relay block No. 4, right side kick panel.
• **Cruise Control Diode**—is located on the left side, behind the instrument panel.
• **Defogger Relay**—is located in the junction block No. 1, left kick panel, left relay.
• **Diagnostic Check Connector**—is located rearward of the left strut tower.
• **Door Lock Control Relay**—is located in the left door.
• **EFI Resistor**—is located rearward of the EGR valve.
• **EFI Water Temperature Sensor**—is located at the intake manifold, near the driver's side.
• **EGR Gas Temperature Sensor**—is located on the lower portion of the intake plenum.
• **Electrical Idle-up Diode**—is located in the main harness, left side instrument panel.
• **Electronic Controlled Transmission (ECT) Control Unit**—is located under console, in front of shifter.
• **Engine Electronic Control Unit (ECU)**—is located under the radio, behind the console.
• **Fuel Pump Resistor**—is located under the left strut tower reinforcement.
• **Fog Light Relay**—is located above the relay block No. 4, right side kick panel.
• **Fuel Pump Control Relay**—is located in engine compartment, center of firewall.

• **Hazard Flasher**—is located within the turn signal flasher.

• **Headlight Retract Relay**—refer to the integration relay.

• **Heater Relay**—is located in the relay block No. 4, right side kick panel, 5 wires.

• **Horn Relay**—is located in the relay block No. 4, right side kick panel, 4 wires.

• **Idle Speed Control Valve**—is located at the intake air plenum, near the throttle body.

• **Ignitor**—is located in the center of the firewall, near the intake manifold.

• **Integration Relay 1 (interior light fade out, seat belt warning)**—is located in the junction block No. 1, left kick panel.

• **Integration Relay 2 (light retract, light retainer)**—is located in front of the ECU, behind console.

• **Intercooler Computer**—is located under the instrument panel, right side kick panel.

• **Intercooler Pump Check Connector**—is located next to the left headlight.

• **Interior Light and Door Lock Diode**—is located below the junction block on the left side.

• **Knock Sensor**—is threaded into the cylinder block, under the intake manifold.

• **Light Failure Sensor**—is located in the rear seat area, left side.

• **Oil Pressure Switch**—is located at the transmission side of the engine.

• **Overdrive Diode**—is located in the main harness, behind the radio.

• **Oxygen Sensor (main)**—is located in the exhaust pipe, before the catalytic converter.

• **Oxygen Sensor (sub)**—is located in the exhaust pipe, after the catalytic converter.

• **Neutral Start Switch**—is located at the transmission.

• **Rear Wiper Relay**—is located in rear hatch.

• **Start Injector Time Switch**—is located in the thermostat housing, to the left of the coolant temperature sensor.

• **Starter Relay**—is located in the relay block No. 1, below the door lock circuit breaker.

• **Sunroof Control Computer**—is located in the roof near the control switch.

• **System Amplifier (radio)**—is located behind the radio.

• **Taillight Relay**—is located in the junction block No. 1, left kick panel, right relay.

• **Throttle Position Sensor**—is located on the throttle body.

• **Turbo Charger Pressure Sensor**—is located at the right side firewall.

• **Turn Signal Flasher**—is located in the relay block No. 1, upper position.

• **Vehicle Speed Sensor**—is located inside the speedometer head.

• **Water Temperature Sender**—is located on the left side of the engine cylinder head.

1990-91 CELICA

• **A/C Ambient Temperature Sensor**—is located at the top center of the radiator.

• **A/C Amplifier**—is located behind the relay block No. 4, right kick panel.

• **A/C Pressure Switch**—is located at the compressor, on the right side of the engine.

• **A/C System Amplifier**—is located behind the engine ECU, is a small unit.

• **Air Flow Meter**—is located on the air cleaner assembly.

• **Air Intake Temperature Sensor**—is located at the air cleaner assembly.

• **Anti-lock Brake System (ABS) Relay**—is located on the right side of the radiator, next to the relay block No. 5.

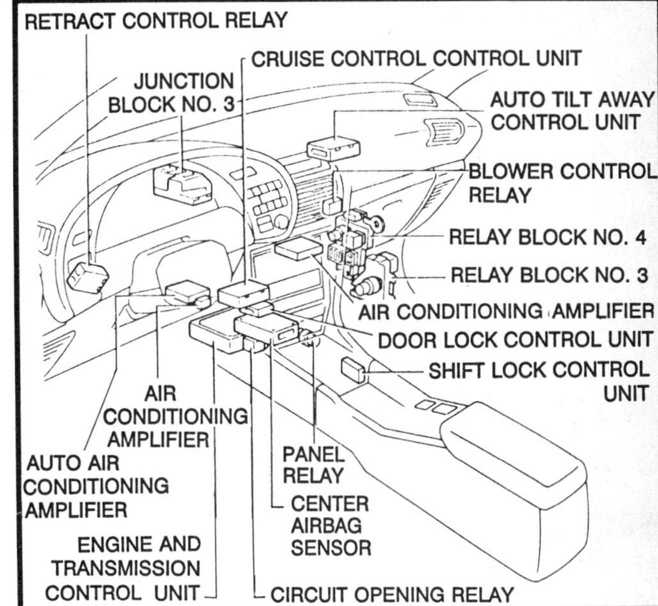

Component location—1990-91 Celica

• **Anti-lock Brake System Check Connector**—is located at the right side of the radiator.

• **Anti-lock Brake System Computer**—is located in the rear seat area, right side.

• **Anti-lock Brake System Deceleration Sensor (All-Trac)**—is located under the left side trim panel, next to the rear seat.

• **Auto Antenna Control Relay**—is located behind the rear left trim panel, behind the wheelhouse.

• **Auto Tilt Away Control Unit**—is located above the relay block No. 4, right kick panel.

• **Automatic A/C System Amplifier**—is located behind the engine ECU.

• **Blower Control Relay**—is located at the blower housing.

• **Center Air Bag Sensor**—is located on top of the engine ECU.

• **Circuit Cutting Relay**—is located in front of the ECU, behind the console.

• **Cold Start Injector**—is located at the air intake plenum.

• **Coolant Temperature Sensor**—is located in the thermostat housing, to the right of the start injector time switch.

• **Cruise Control Unit**—is located above the engine ECU.

• **Cruise Control Diode**—is located on the left side, behind the instrument panel.

• **Daytime Running Light System Diode**—is located behind the instrument panel on the left side.

• **Diagnostic Check Connector**—is located rearward of the left strut tower.

• **Door Lock Control Unit**—is located between the cruise control unit and air bag sensor, behind console.

• **EFI Water Temperature Sensor**—is located at the left side of the cylinder head, above the transmission.

• **EFI and Fuel Pump Resistors**—is located near the junction block No. 2.

• **EGR Gas Temperature Sensor**—is located on the lower portion of the intake plenum.

• **Electronic Fuel Injection (EFI) Relay**—is located in the junction block No. 2, near the battery, round shape, 4 wires.

• **Engine Control Unit (ECU)**—is located behind the console, on the floor.

• **Engine Main Relay**—is located in the junction block No.

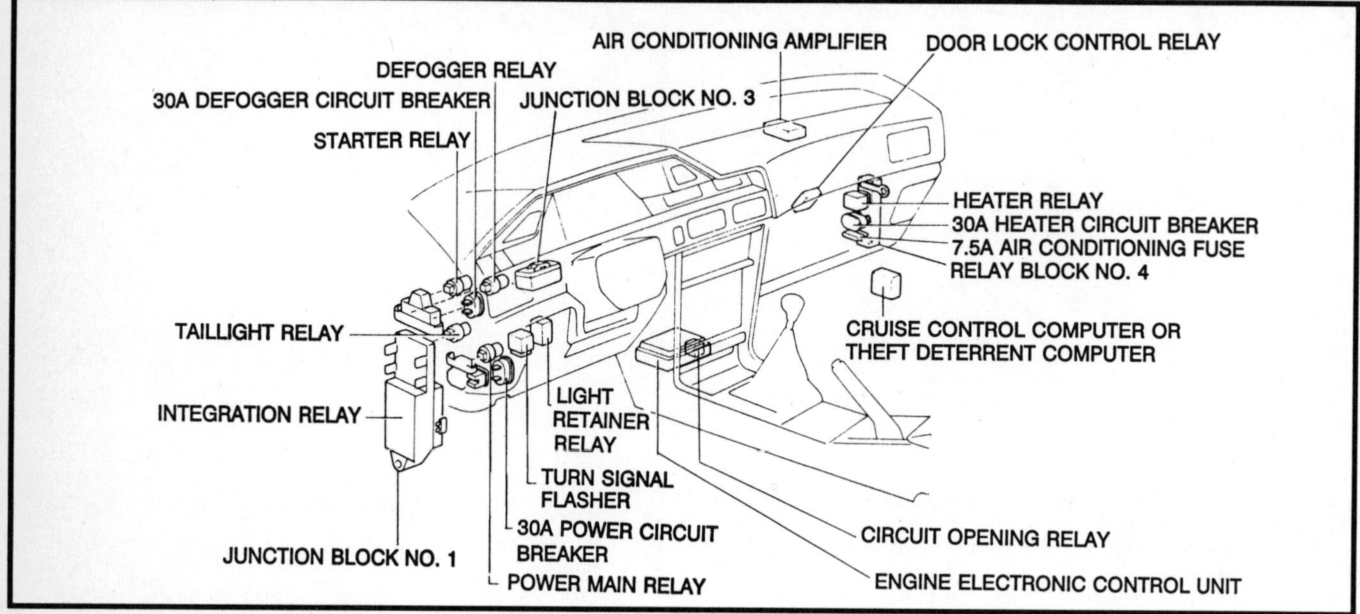

Component location—Corolla

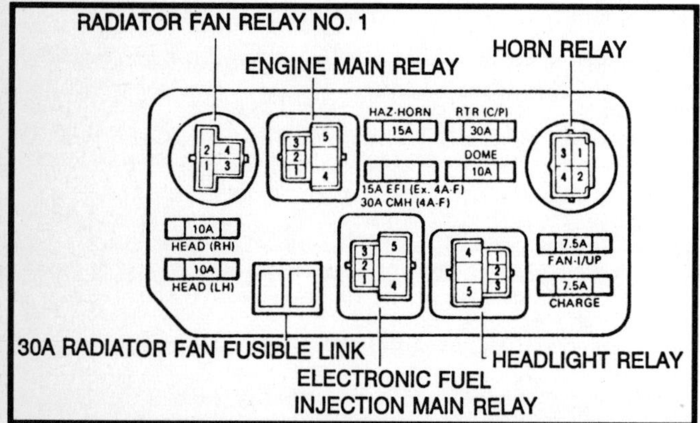

Junction block No. 2 left inner fender—Corolla

2, near the battery, between the headlight and engine main relays, 5 wires.

- **Fan Check Connector**—is located at the connector near the master cylinder.
- **Fuel Pump Relay**—refer to the circuit opening relay.
- **Headlight Relay**—is located in the junction block No. 2, near the battery, 4 wires.
- **Idle Speed Control Valve**—is located at the intake air plenum, near the throttle body.
- **Ignitor**—is located at the firewall, above the master cylinder.
- **Key Off Diode**—is located to the left of the daytime running light diode, left side instrument panel.
- **Knock Sensor**—is threaded into the cylinder block, under the intake manifold.
- **Oil Pressure Switch**—is located at the driver's side of the engine.
- **Overdrive Diode**—is located in the main harness, behind the radio.
- **Oxygen Sensor (main)**—is located in the exhaust pipe, before the catalytic converter.
- **Oxygen Sensor (sub)**—is located in the exhaust pipe, after the catalytic converter.
- **Neutral Start Switch**—is located at the transmission.
- **Panel Relay**—is located near the ECU, behind the console.
- **Radiator Fan Relay**—is located in the junction block No. 2, near the battery, 4 wires.
- **Rear Wiper Relay**—is located in rear hatch.
- **Retract Control Relay**—is located behind the instrument cluster.
- **Shift Lock Control Unit**—is located under the console, in front of emergence brake handle.
- **Start Injector Time Switch**—is located in the thermostat housing, to the left of the coolant temperature sensor.
- **Sunroof Relay**—is located in the roof, near the control switch.
- **Throttle Position Sensor**—is located on the throttle body.
- **Turbo Charger Pressure Sensor**—is located at the driver's side of the engine, towards the rear.
- **Vehicle Speed Sensor**—is located inside the speedometer head.
- **Water Temperature Sender**—is located at the driver's side of the engine.

COROLLA

- **A/C Amplifier**—is located behind the relay block No. 4, right kick panel.
- **A/C Dual and High Pressure Switch**—is located near the right strut tower.
- **A/C Clutch Relay**—is located in the relay block No. 5, left inner fender, 6 wires.
- **A/C Fan Relay No. 2**—is located in the relay block No. 5, left inner fender, square shape, 4 wires.
- **A/C Fan Relay No. 3**—is located in the relay block No. 5, left inner fender, round shape, 4 wires.
- **Air Flow Meter**—is located on the air cleaner assembly.
- **Air Intae Temperature Sensor**—is located at the air cleaner assembly.
- **Circuit Opening Relay**—is located next to the engine ECU.
- **Cold Start Injector**—is located at the air intake plenum.
- **Coolant Temperature Sensor**—is located in the thermostat housing, to the right of the start injector time switch.

• **Cruise Control or Theft Deterrent Control Unit**—is located under the relay block No. 4, right kick panel.

• **Cruise Control Diode**—is located on the left side, behind the instrument panel.

• **Defogger Relay**—is located in the junction block No. 1, left kick panel.

• **Diagnostic Check Connector**—is located rearward of the left strut tower.

• **Door Lock Relay**—is located behind the relay block No. 4, right kick panel.

• **EGR Gas Temperature Sensor**—is located on the lower portion of the intake plenum.

• **EFI Water Temperature Sensor**—is located at the left side of the cylinder head, above the transmission.

• **Electronic Fuel Injection (EFI) Relay**—is located in the junction block No. 2, left inner fender.

• **EGR Gas Temperature Sensor (California)**—is located near the air cleaner assembly.

• **Engine Electronic Control Unit (ECU)**—is located behind the radio, on the floor.

• **Engine Main Relay**—is located in the junction block No. 2, left inner fender.

• **Fuel Pump Relay**refer to the circuit opening relay.

• **Headlight Relay**—is located in the junction block No. 2, left inner fender.

• **Heater Relay**—is located in the upper portion of the relay block No. 4, right kick panel.

• **Horn Relay**—is located in the junction block No. 2, left inner fender.

• **Idle Speed Control Valve**—is located at the intake air plenum, near the throttle body.

• **Idle-up System Diode**—is located above the left kick panel.

• **Integration Relay (lighting system)**—is located in the lower part of the junction block No. 1, left kick panel, large box.

• **Interior Light or Theft Deterrent Diode**—is located above the left kick panel.

• **Knock Sensor**—is threaded into the cylinder block, under the intake manifold.

• **Light Retainer Relay**—is located next to the turn signal flasher.

• **Oil Pressure Switch**—is located at the front of the engine, near the distributor.

• **Overdrive Diode**—is located in the main harness, behind the radio (stationwagon) and at the left kick panel (sedan).

• **Oxygen Sensor (main)**—is located in the exhaust pipe, before the catalytic converter.

• **Oxygen Sensor (sub)**—is located in the exhaust pipe, after the catalytic converter.

• **Neutral Start Switch**—is located at the transmission.

• **Power Main Relay**—is located in the upper part of the junction block No. 1, left kick panel.

• **Radiator Fan Relay No. 1**—is located in the junction block No. 2, left inner fender.

• **Rear Wiper Relay**—is located in the rear hatch.

• **Start Injector Time Switch**—is located in the thermostat housing, to the left of the coolant temperature sensor.

• **Starter Relay (Manual Trans) or Theft Deterrent System Relay**—is located above the junction block No. 1, left kick panel.

• **Sunroof Relay**—is located in the roof, near the switch.

• **Taillight Relay**—is located in the junction block No. 1, left kick panel.

• **Throttle Position Sensor**—is located on the throttle body.

• **Turn Signal Flasher**—is located to the right of the junction block No. 1, under the instrument panel.

• **Hazard Flasher**—is located within the turn signal flasher.

• **Vehicle Speed Sensor**—is located inside the speedometer head.

• **Water Temperature Sender (4A-GE engine)**—is located at the right side of the intake manifold.

• **Windshield Wiper Diode**—is located above the left kick panel.

CRESSIDA

• **A/C Amplifier**—is located behind the radio.

• **A/C Ambient Temperature Sensor**—is located at the top center of the radiator.

• **A/C Pressure Switch**—is located at the compressor, on the right side of the engine.

• **Air Flow Meter**—is located on the air cleaner assembly.

• **Air Intake Temperature Sensor**—is located at the air cleaner assembly.

• **A/C Thermistor**—is located behind the radio or glove compartment.

• **Anti-lock Brake System (ABS) Control Unit**—is located behind the trunk trim panel, on the right side.

• **Anti-lock Brake System (ABS) Relay**—is located in the engine compartment, behind right headlight.

• **Auto Antenna Relay**—is located behind the right rear trim panel in the trunk.

• **Automatic Shoulder Belt ECU**—is located behind the instrument panel, on the left side, next to the door lock control relay (Canada).

• **Blower Control Relay**—is located above the relay block No. 4, right kick panel.

• **Circuit Opening Relay**—is located in the relay block No. 4, right kick panel, 6 wires.

• **Cold Start Injector**—is located at the air intake plenum.

• **Condenser Fan Relay**—is located at the left strut tower.

• **Coolant Temperature Sensor**—is located in the thermostat housing, to the right of the start injector time switch.

• **Cruise Control Unit**—is located behind the instrument panel, left side, next to the theft deterrent control unit.

• **Daytime Running Light Relay (Canada)**—is located behind the instrument panel, on the left side, next to the door lock control relay (Canada).

• **Defogger Relay**—is located in the junction block No. 1, left kick panel, on the right side of the block, 2 wires.

• **Diagnostic Check Connector**—is located rearward of the left strut tower.

• **Dimmer Relay**—is located in the relay block No. 7, left inner fender (Canada).

• **Door Lock Control Relay**—is located behind the instrument panel, on the left side, next to the wiper relay.

• **EFI Water Temperature Sensor**—is located at the right side of the cylinder head, towards the front of the vehicle, near the air cleaner.

• **EGR Gas Temperature Sensor**—is located on the lower portion of the intake plenum.

• **Electronic Controlled Transmission (ECT) Solenoid**—is located to the right of the power brake booster.

• **Engine and Transmission Control Unit**—is located behind the glove compartment.

• **Engine Control System Diode**—is located in the relay block No. 3, left kick panel, upper diode, 3 wires.

• **Extra High Speed Relay**—is located above the relay block No. 4, right kick panel.

• **Fuel Pump Relay**—is located in the relay block No. 4, right kick panel, 4 wires.

• **Fuel Pump Resistor**—is located at the right strut tower.

• **Hazard Flasher**—is located within the turn signal flasher.

• **Headlight Cleaner Relay**—is located forward of the junction block No. 2, left inner fender.

• **Headlight Relay**—is located in the relay block No. 7, left inner fender (Canada), middle of block.

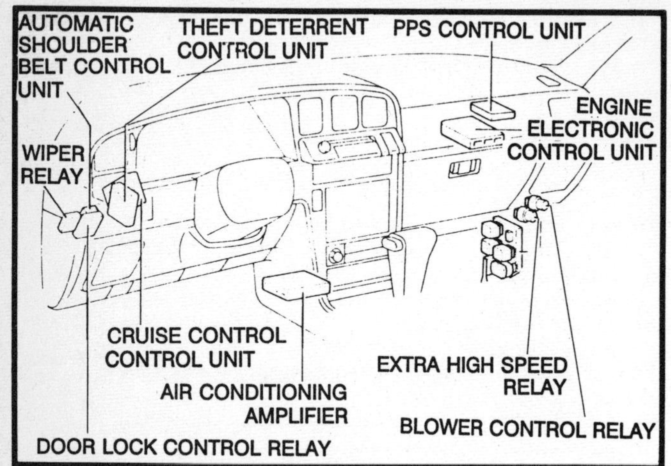

Component location – Cressida

- **Heater Relay** – is located in the relay block No. 4, right kick panel, 5 wires.
- **Idle Speed Control Valve** – is located at the intake air plenum, near the throttle body.
- **Ignitor** – is located at the right inner fender, behind the headlight.
- **Integration Relay** – is located in junction block No. 1, left kick panel, large unit at the bottom.
- **Interior Lights/Theft Deterrent System Diode** – is located in the relay block No. 3, left kick panel, lower diode, 4 wires.
- **Key Interlock Solenoid** – is located near the ignition switch.
- **Knock Sensor** – is threaded into the cylinder block, under the intake manifold.
- **Light Failure Sensor** – is located behind the trunk trim panel, on the right side.
- **Oil Pressure Switch** – is located at the right side of the engine, towards the front.
- **Overdrive Main Switch** – is located under the center console, near the shifter.
- **Oxygen Sensor (main)** – is located in the exhaust pipe, before the catalytic converter.
- **Oxygen Sensor (sub)** – is located in the exhaust pipe, after the catalytic converter.
- **Moonroof Control Unit** – is located in the roof, near the control switch.
- **Neutral Start Switch** – is located at the transmission.
- **Noise Filter** – is located in the junction block No. 1, left kick panel, next to the 7.5A gauge fuse.
- **Power Main Relay** – is located in the relay block No. 3, left kick panel, bottom of the block, square shape.
- **Power Window Master Switch** – is located in the left driver door.
- **PPS Control Unit** – is located behind the glove compartment, on the right side.
- **Seat Heater Relay (Canada)** – is located in the relay block No. 3, left kick panel, middle of the block.
- **Shift Lock Control Unit** – is located under the console, behind the shifter.
- **Start Injector Time Switch** – is located in the thermostat housing, to the left of the coolant temperature sensor.
- **Starter Relay (US)** – is located in the relay block No. 3, left kick panel, middle of the block.
- **Taillight Relay** – is located in the junction block No. 1, left kick panel, on the left side of the block, 2 wires.
- **Theft Deterrent Control Unit (US)** – is located behind the instrument panel, left side of the cruise control unit.
- **Theft Deterrent System Diode** – is located in the relay block No. 3, left kick panel, middle diode, 4 wires.
- **Throttle Position Sensor** – is located on the throttle body.
- **Toyota Diagnostic Communication Link (TDCL)** – is located the the left of the steering column, behind the instrument panel.
- **Turn Signal Flasher** – is located in the relay block No. 3, left kick panel, top of the block.
- **Vehicle Speed Sensor** – is located inside the speedometer head.
- **Water Temperature Sender** – is located at the right side of the engine, towards the front.
- **Wiper Relay** – is located behind the instrument panel, on the left side, next to the door lock control relay.

1989 MR2

- **A/C Amplifier** – is located behind the radio, on the right side.
- **A/C Fan Relay 2** – is located in the relay block No. 5, front luggage compartment, upper left corner.
- **A/C Fan Relay 3** – is located in the relay block No. 5, front luggage compartment, square shape, 6 wires.
- **A/C Idle-up System Diode** – is located at the left kick panel.
- **A/C Thermostor** – is located.is located to the right of the center instrument panel.
- **Air Flow Meter** – is located on the air cleaner assembly.
- **Air Intake Temperature Sensor** – is located at the air cleaner assembly.
- **Auto Antenna Relay** – is located in the engine compartment, behind the trim panel.
- **Blower Resistor** – is located behind the instrument panel, in the center.
- **Circuit Cut Relay** – is located in the engine compartment, next to the engine ECU.
- **Cold Start Injector** – is located at the air intake plenum.
- **Compressor Sensor** – is located at the compressor.
- **Coolant Temperature Sensor** – is located in the thermostat housing, to the right of the start injector time switch.
- **Cooling Fan Computer** – is located on the left side of firewall.
- **Cooling Fan Temperature Sensor** – is located behind the engine, on the left side.
- **Cruise Control Diode** – is located on the left side, behind the instrument panel.
- **Cruise Control Unit** – is located on the right side of firewall, in back of the electronic controlled transmission (ECT) control unit.
- **Diagnostic Check Connector** – is located at the firewall.
- **Door Lock Control Relay** – is under the instrument panel, on the right side.
- **EFI Water Temperature Sensor** – is located at the cylinder head, left side.
- **EGR Gas Temperature Sensor (California)** – is located in the front of the cylinder head, on the left side.
- **EGR Gas Temperature Sensor** – is located on the lower portion of the intake plenum.
- **Electronic Controlled Transmission (ECT) Solenoid** – is located under the air cleaner assembly.
- **Electronic Controlled Transmission (ECT)** – is located on the right side of firewall, next to the cruise control unit.
- **Electronic Idle-up Cut Relay** – is located behind the glove compartment, to the right.
- **Engine Electronic Control Unit (ECU)** – is located on center of the firewall, between the circuit and super charger relays.
- **Fan Main Relay** – is located in the relay block No. 5, front luggage compartment, next to 30A RTR MTR fuse.

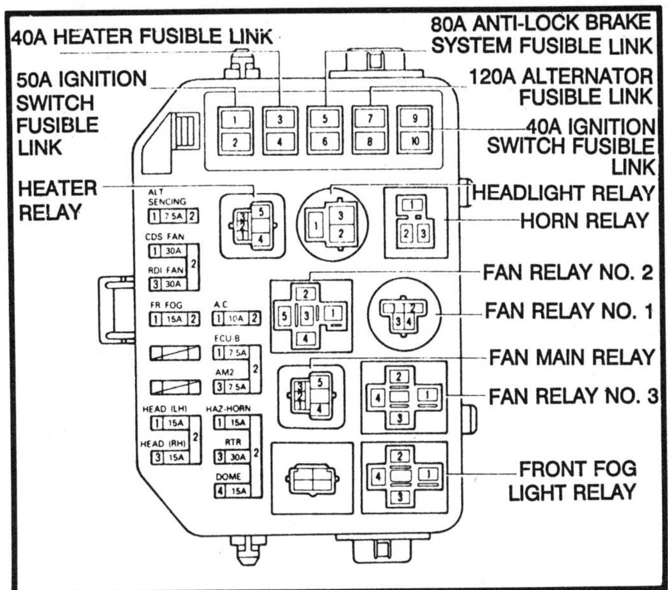

Engine compartment component location—1989 MR2

- **Fuel Pump Relay**refer to the circuit opening relay.
- **Hazard Flasher**—is located within the turn signal flasher.
- **Headlight Relay**—is located in the relay block No. 5, front luggage compartment, next to air conditioning relay 2, 5 wires.
- **Heater Relay**—is located in the relay block No. 4, right kick panel, upper portion.
- **Heater Servo Motor Amplifier**—is located behind the radio, on the left side.
- **Idle Speed Control Valve**—is located at the intake air plenum, near the throttle body.
- **Idle-up System Diode**—is located at the center of the engine compartment, rear section or at the left kick panel.
- **Interior Light or Theft Deterrent Diode**—is located above the left kick panel.
- **Knock Sensor**—is threaded into the cylinder block, front of engine, to the left.
- **Light Retainer Relay**—is located in the luggage compartment, on the left side.
- **Oil Pressure Switch**—is located at the rear of the engine, on the right side.
- **Oxygen Sensor (main)**—is located in the exhaust pipe, before the catalytic converter.
- **Oxygen Sensor (sub)**—is located in the exhaust pipe, after the catalytic converter.
- **Neutral Start Switch**—is located at the transmission.
- **Power Window Control Relay**—is located in the driver door.
- **Radiator Fan Relay**—is located in the relay block No. 5, front luggage compartment, next to air conditioning relay 3.
- **Rear Window Idle-up System Diode**—is located at the left kick panel.
- **Retract Control Relay**—is located in the luggage compartment, on the right side.
- **Seat Belt Warning Relay**—is located behind the left quarter panel trim panel.
- **Start Injector Time Switch**—is located in the thermostat housing, to the left of the coolant temperature sensor.
- **Super Charger Relay**—is located in the engine compartment, next to the engine ECU, on the other side of the circuit cut relay.
- **Taillight Relay**—is located in the relay block No. 1, left kick panel.
- **Throttle Position Sensor**—is located on the throttle body.
- **Turn Signal Flasher**—is located behind the instrument panel, on the left side, near the relay block No. 1.
- **Vehicle Speed Sensor**—is located inside the speedometer head.
- **Water Temperature Sender**—is located at the right side of the intake manifold.

1990-91 MR2

- **A/C Amplifier**—is located behind the console, on the right side.
- **A/C Clutch Relay**—is located behind the instrument panel, on the right side.
- **A/C Dual Pressure Switch**—is located behind the glove compartment.
- **A/C System Diode**—is located at the right side of the instrument panel, behind the glove compartment.
- **A/C Thermistor**—is located behind the glove compartment.
- **Air Flow Meter**—is located on the air cleaner assembly.
- **Air Intake Temperature Sensor**—is located at the air cleaner assembly.
- **Air Temperature Sensor**—is located at the left strut tower.
- **Anti-lock Brake System (ABS) Control Unit**—is located under the instrument panel, on the far right.
- **Auto Antenna Motor and Relay**—is located on the right side, behind the rear trim panel.
- **Blower Resistor**—is located behind the instrument panel, near the glove compartment.
- **Center Air Bag Sensor**—is located under the radio.
- **Circuit Opening Relay**—is located in the relay block No. 2, left side engine compartment, rectangular shape.
- **Fuel Pump Relay**refer to the circuit opening relay.
- **Cold Start Injector**—is located at the air intake plenum.
- **Coolant Temperature Sensor**—is located in the thermostat housing, to the right of the start injector time switch.
- **Cooling Fan Control Unit**—is located on the center of the firewall.
- **Cooling Fan Relay**—is located in the relay block No. 2, left side engine compartment, round shape.
- **Cruise Control Unit**—is located on the right kick panel.
- **Defogger Relay**—is located in the relay block No. 1, left kick panel, to the left of the taillight relay.
- **Diagnostic Check Connector**—is located at the rear firewall, on the left side.
- **Door Lock Control Unit**—is located near the relay block No. 1, left kick panel.
- **EFI Resistor**—is located at the rear firewall, on the left side.
- **EFI Water Temperature Sensor**—is located at the cylinder head, left side.
- **EGR Gas Temperature Sensor (California)**—is located in the front of the cylinder head, on the left side.
- **Electronic Controlled Transmission (ECT) Solenoid**—is located under the air cleaner assembly.
- **Electronic Fuel Injection (EFI) Relay**—is located in the relay block No. 2, left side engine compartment, round shape.
- **Engine Electronic Control Unit (ECU)**—is located on the firewall, towards the right side.
- **Engine Oil Level Control Unit**—is located behind the right rear trim panel.
- **Fan Main Relay**—is located in the relay block No. 5, right luggage compartment.
- **Fan Relay No. 1**—is located in the relay block No. 5, right luggage compartment.
- **Fan Relay No. 2**—is located in the relay block No. 5, right luggage compartment.

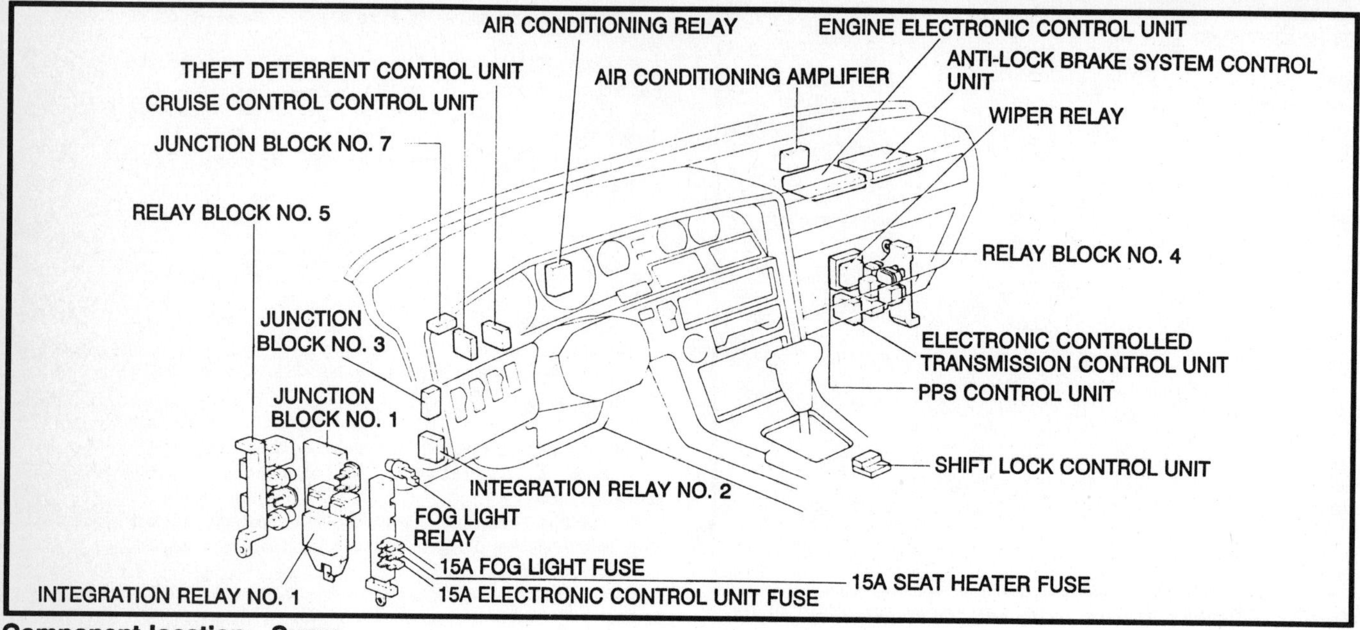

Component location—Supra

- **Fan Relay No. 3**—is located in the relay block No. 5, right luggage compartment.
- **Front Fog Light Relay**—is located in the relay block No. 5, right luggage compartment.
- **Fuel Pump Resistor**—is located at the rear firewall, on the left side.
- **Hazard Flasher**—is located within the turn signal flasher.
- **Headlight Relay**—is located in the relay block No. 5, right luggage compartment.
- **Heater Relay**—is located in the relay block No. 5, right luggage compartment.
- **Horn Relay**—is located in the relay block No. 5, right luggage compartment.
- **Idle Speed Control Valve**—is located at the intake air plenum, near the throttle body.
- **Idle-up System Diode**—is located at the left side, above the junction block No. 1, behind the glove compartment.
- **Ignition Main Relay**—is located in the relay block No. 2, left side engine compartment, square shape.
- **Interior Light Control Relay**—is located above the relay block No. 1, left kick panel.
- **Knock Sensor**—is threaded into the cylinder block, under the intake manifold.
- **Oil Pressure Switch**—is located at the rear of the engine, on the left side.
- **Oxygen Sensor (main)**—is located in the exhaust pipe, before the catalytic converter.
- **Oxygen Sensor (sub)**—is located in the exhaust pipe, after the catalytic converter.
- **Neutral Start Switch**—is located at the transmission.
- **Power Main Relay**—is located above the relay block No. 1, left kick panel.
- **Power Steering Control Unit**—is located on the right side of the luggage compartment, near the relay block No. 5.
- **Power Steering Driver**—is located next to the power steering control unit, right side luggage compartment.
- **Power Steering Relay**—is located next to the power steering control unit, right side luggage compartment.
- **Power Window Diode**—is located at the left side, above the junction block No. 1.
- **Rear Woofer Amplifier**—is located behind the left rear trim panel.
- **Retract Control Relay**—is located on the left side of the luggage compartment.
- **Seat Belt Warning Relay**—is located behind the console, on the left side.
- **Shift Lock Control Unit**—is located under the console.
- **Start Injector Time Switch**—is located in the thermostat housing, to the left of the coolant temperature sensor.
- **Starter Relay**—is located on the rear firewall, next to the engine ECU.
- **Stereo Amplifier**—is located behind the left rear trim panel.
- **Taillight Relay**—is located in the relay block No. 1, left kick panel, to the right of the defogger relay.
- **Theft Deterrent Control Unit**—is located behind the right rear trim panel.
- **Theft Deterrent Diode**—is located on the left side, behind the instrument panel.
- **Throttle Position Sensor**—is located on the throttle body.
- **Turbo Charger Pressure Sensor**—is located at the right side of the engine.
- **Turn Signal Flasher**—is located in the relay block No. 1, left kick panel, at the top.
- **Vacuum Sensor**—is located at the right side of the engine, towards the front.
- **Vehicle Speed Sensor**—is located inside the speedometer head.
- **Water Temperature Sender**—is located at the left side of the intake manifold.

SUPRA

- **A/C Ambient Temperature Sensor**—is located in the center of the radiator support.
- **A/C Amplifier**—is located next to the engine ECU.
- **A/C Condenser Fan Relay No. 1**—is located next to the junction block No. 2, left inner fender.
- **A/C Condenser Fan Relay No. 2**—is located next to the right headlight, right inner fender.

• **A/C Condenser Fan Relay No. 3**—is located next to the right headlight, right inner fender.
• **A/C Dual Pressure Switch**—is located at the right strut tower.
• **A/C High Pressure Switch**—is located at the right strut tower.
• **A/C In-car Sensor**—is located behine the glove compartment.
• **A/C Relay**—is located behind the instrument cluster.
• **A/C Solar Sensor**—is located at the right side of the instrument panel.
• **A/C Thermistor**—is located behind the glove compartment.
• **A/C Water Temperature Switch**—is located at the right side of the cylinder head.
• **Air Flow Meter**—is located on the air cleaner assembly.
• **Air Intake Temperature Sensor**—is located at the air cleaner assembly.
• **Anti-lock Brake System (ABS) Control Unit**—is located behind the glove compartment, next to the ECU.
• **Auto Antenna Relay**—is located behind the right rear trim panel.
• **Automatic Transmission Diode**—is located above the junction block No. 1, left kick panel.
• **Blower Resistor**—is located near the relay block, right kick panel.
• **Cam Position Sensor**—is located at the distributor location.
• **Center Air Bag Sensor**—is located under the center console compartment.
• **Circuit Opening Relay**—is located in the relay block No. 4, right kick panel, above the starter relay.
• **Cold Start Injector**—is located at the air intake plenum.
• **Coolant Temperature Sensor**—is located in the thermostat housing, to the right of the start injector time switch.
• **Cruise Control Unit**—is located behind the instrument panel on the left side.
• **Defogger Relay**—is located in junction block No. 1, left kick panel, left side of the block.
• **Diagnostic Check Connector**—is located at the left strut tower.
• **Door Lock Relay**—is located in the driver door.
• **EFI Resistor**—is located at the left strut tower.
• **EFI Water Temperature Sensor**—is located under the upper radiator hose.
• **EFI Resistor**—is located next to the left strut tower.
• **EGR Gas Temperature Sensor (California)**—is located at the intake manifold, near the center.
• **EGR Gas Temperature Sensor**—is located on the lower portion of the intake plenum.
• **Electronic Controlled Transmission (ECT) Solenoid**—is located above the air cleaner assembly.
• **Electronic Controlled Transmission (ECT) Control Unit**—is located next to the relay block No. 4, right kick panel.
• **Electronic Fuel Injection (EFI) Relay**—is located in the junction block No. 2, left fender, 4 wires.
• **Engine Electronic Control Unit (ECU)**—is located behind the glove compartment, on the right side.
• **Fog Light Relay**—is located behind the instrument panel on the left side.
• **Front Airbag Sensors**—is located on each side of the inner fender.
• **Fuel Pump Relay**—is located at the right strut tower.
• **Fuel Pump Resistor**—is located at the right strut tower.
• **Headlight Cleaner Relay**—is located at the left strut tower.
• **Headlight Relay**—is located in the junction block No. 2, left fender, 5 wires.
• **Heater Relay**—is located in the relay block No. 4, right kick panel, above the panel relay.
• **Horn Relay**—is located in the relay block No. 5, left kick panel, bottom of the block.
• **Idle Speed Control Valve**—is located at the intake air plenum, near the throttle body.
• **Illumination Diode**—is locatedis located above the junction block No. 1, left kick panel.
• **Integration Relay No. 1**—is located in junction block No. 1, left kick panel.
• **Integration Relay No. 2**—is located behind the instrument panel on the left side.
• **Knock Sensor**—is threaded into the cylinder block, under the intake manifold.
• **Light Failure Sensor**—is located next to the left rear taillight assembly.
• **Oil Pressure Switch**—is located at the right of the engine, near the throttle body.
• **Oxygen Sensor (main)**—is located in the exhaust pipe, before the catalytic converter.
• **Neutral Start Switch**—is located at the transmission.
• **Panel Relay (Canada)**—is located in the relay block No. 4, right kick panel, lower right of the block.
• **Power Main Relay**—is located in the relay block No. 5, left kick panel, second from the top.
• **Rear Wiper Relay**—is located in the rear hatch.
• **Reclining Seat Relay**—is located under the driver seat.
• **Shift Lock Control Unit**—is located under the center console, behind the shifter.
• **Start Injector Time Switch**—is located in the thermostat housing, to the left of the coolant temperature sensor.
• **Starter Relay**—is located in the relay block No. 4, right kick panel, lower left of the block.
• **Oxygen Sensor (sub)**—is located in the exhaust pipe, after the catalytic converter.
• **Sunroof Control Relay**—is located in the roof, near the control switch.
• **Taillight Relay**—is located in junction block No. 1, left kick panel, right side of the block.
• **Theft Deterrent Control Unit**—is located behind the instrument panel on the left side.
• **Throttle Position Sensor**—is located on the throttle body.
• **Turbo Charger Pressure Sensor**—is located at the left strut tower.
• **Turn Signal Relay**—is located in the relay block No. 5, left kick panel, top of the block.
• **Hazard Flasher**—is located within the turn signal flasher.
• **Vacuum Sensor**—is located at the right side of the engine, towards the front.
• **Vehicle Speed Sensor**—is located inside the speedometer head.
• **Water Temperature Sender**—is located at the right side of the intake manifold.
• **Wiper Relay**—is located next to the relay block No. 4, right kick panel.

1989-90 TERCEL

• **A/C Acceleration Cut Relay**—is located behind the radio.
• **A/C Amplifier**—is located behind the instrument panel, on the right side.
• **A/C Dual Pressure Switch**—is located at the right strut tower.
• **A/C Clutch Relay**—is located in the relay block No. 2, left inner fender.
• **A/C Condenser Fan Relay No. 2**—is located behind the left front headlight.
• **A/C Condenser Fan Relay No. 3**—is located in the relay block No. 2, left inner fender, small block near the relay block.

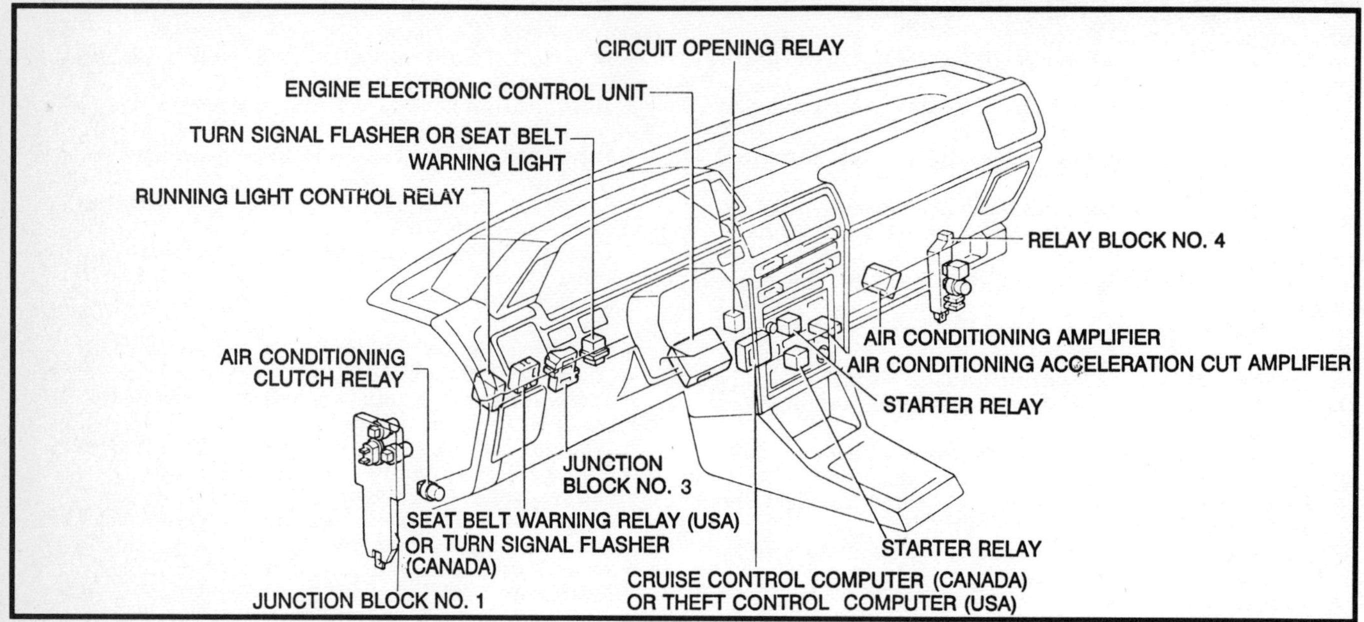

Component location—1989-90 Tercel

- **A/C Thermistor**—is located behind the glove compartment.
- **Blower Resistor**—is located behind the instrument panel.
- **Circuit Opening Relay**—is located behind the radio.
- **Cruise Control Computer (Canada) or Theft Deterent Computer (US)**—is located behind the radio.
- **Cruise Control Diode**—is located above the junction block No. 1, left kick panel.
- **Diagnostic Check Connector**—is located at the left strut tower.
- **Defogger Relay**—is located in junction block No. 1, left kick panel, right side of block.
- **EGR Gas Temperature Sensor (California)**—is located at the intake manifold, near the right.
- **Engine Electronic Control Unit (ECU)**—is located behind the radio.
- **Engine Main Power Relay**—is located in the relay block No. 2, left inner fender.
- **Fuel Cut Solenoid Valve**—is located at the carburetor, upper housing, 3 wire connector.
- **Fuel Heater**—is located at the bottom of the carburetor.
- **Hazard Flasher**—is located within the turn signal flasher.
- **Headlight Relay**—is located in the relay block No. 2, left inner fender.
- **Heater Relay**—is located in the relay block No. 4, right kick panel, square shape, 5 wires.
- **Horn Relay**—is located in the relay block No. 4, right kick panel, round shape.
- **Interior Light Diode**—is located next to the junction block No. 1, left kick panel.
- **Oil Pressure Switch**—is located at the front of the engine.
- **Radiator Fan Relay No. 1**—is located in the relay block No. 2, left inner fender.
- **Running Light Control Relay (Canada)**—is located behind the instrument panel, on the left side.
- **Starter Relay**—is located behind the radio.
- **Taillight Relay**—is located in junction block No. 1, left kick panel, left side of block.
- **Thermostatic Air Cleaner Vacuum Valve**—is located in the air cleaner housing.
- **Throttle Position Switch**—is located at the carburetor, a plunger with a 3 terminal connector.
- **Throttle Solenoid Actuator**—is located at the throttle cable connection.
- **Turn Signal Flasher (US) or Seat Belt Warning Relay (Canada)**—is located behind the instrument panel, on the left side.
- **Vacuum Sensor**—is located at the center of the firewall.
- **Water Temperature Sensor (emission control)**—is located at the thermostat housing.

1991 TERCEL

- **A/C Amplifier**—is located behind the glove compartment.
- **A/C Dual Pressure Switch**—is located behind the glove compartment.
- **A/C High Pressure Switch**—is located at the receiver/drier.
- **A/C Thermistor**—is located behind the glove compartment.
- **A/C Clutch Relay**—is located above the glove compartment.
- **A/C Condenser Fan Relay No. 2**—is located in the relay block No. 2, left inner fender.
- **A/C Condenser Fan Relay No. 3**—is located in the relay block No. 2, left inner fender.
- **Air Flow Meter**—is located on the air cleaner assembly.
- **Air Intake Temperature Sensor**—is located at the air cleaner assembly.
- **Blower Resistor**—is located near the relay block, right kick panel.
- **Circuit Opening Relay**—Is located behind the radio.
- **Cold Start Injector**—is located at the air intake plenum.
- **Coolant Temperature Sensor**—is located in the thermostat housing, to the right of the start injector time switch.
- **Daytime Running Light Relay**—Is located behind the radio.
- **Defogger Relay**—is located in the relay block No. 6, left kick panel, 4 wires.

• **Diagnostic Check Connector**—is located at the left strut tower.

• **EGR Gas Temperature Sensor (California)**—is located to the right of the intake manifold.

• **Electronic Fuel Injection (EFI) Relay**—is located in the relay block No. 2, left inner fender.

• **Engine Electronic Control Unit (ECU)**—Is located behind the radio, on the floor.

• **Engine Main Relay**—is located in the relay block No. 2, left inner fender.

• **Fuel Pump Relay**refer to the circuit opening relay.

• **Hazard Flasher**—is located within the turn signal flasher.

• **Headlight Diode**—is located at the left kick panel, in main harness.

• **Headlight Relay**—Is located behind the radio.

• **Heater Relay**—is located in the relay block No. 4, right kick panel, 5 wires.

• **Horn Relay**—is located in the relay block No. 2, left inner fender.

• **Idle Speed Control Valve**—is located at the intake air plenum, near the throttle body.

• **Interior Light Diode**—is located in junction block No. 1, left kick panel.

• **Knock Sensor**—is threaded into the cylinder block, under the intake manifold.

• **Oil Pressure Switch**—is located at the front of the engine, near the upper radiator hose.

• **Oxygen Sensor (main)**—is located in the exhaust pipe, before the catalytic converter.

• **Neutral Start Switch**—is located at the transmission.

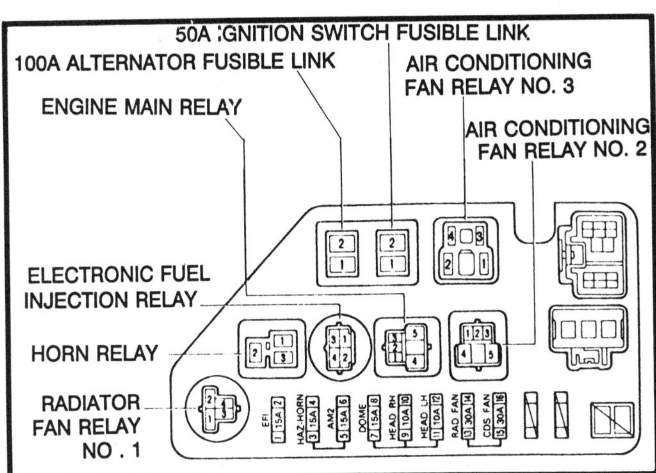

Relay block No. 2 left inner fender—1991 Tercel

• **Radiator Fan Relay No. 1**—is located in the relay block No. 2, left inner fender.

• **Seat Belt Warning Relay**—is located behind the instrument cluster.

• **Shift Lock Control Unit**—Is located under the radio.

• **Start Injector Time Switch**—is located in the thermostat housing, to the left of the coolant temperature sensor.

• **Starter Relay**—Is located behind the radio.

• **Oxygen Sensor (sub)**—is located in the exhaust pipe, after the catalytic converter.

• **Taillight Relay**—Is located behind the radio.

• **Theft Deterrent Diode**—is located behind the heater control.

• **Throttle Position Sensor**—is located on the throttle body.

• **Turn Signal Flasher**—is located behind the instrument panel on the left side.

• **Vacuum Sensor**—is located at the center of the firewall.

• **Vehicle Speed Sensor**—is located inside the speedometer head.

• **Water Temperature Sender**—is located at the thermostat housing.

• **Water Temperature Sensor (EFI)**—is located at the thermostat housing.

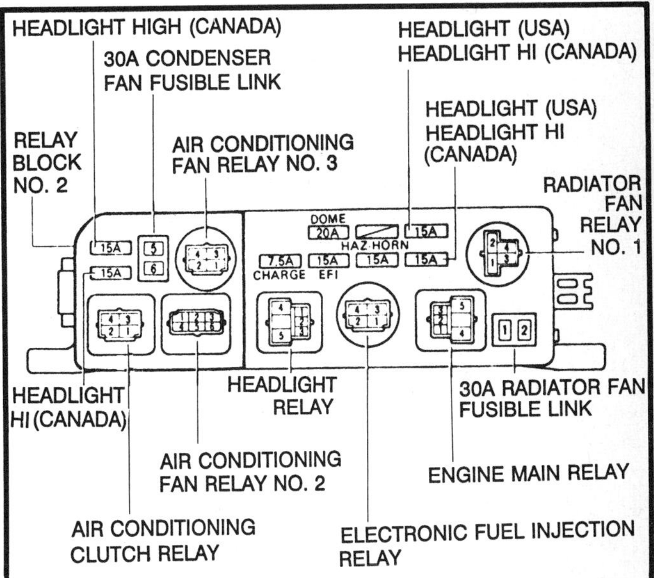

Relay block No. 2 left inner fender—Camry and typical Celica

TOYOTA TRUCK

Circuit Breakers

1989-90 4RUNNER

Power, Door Lock and Power Window Circuit Breakers—is located in junction block No. 1, at the left side kick panel, inside the passenger compartment.

1991 4RUNNER

Power 30 amp Circuit Breaker—is located in the junction block No. 1, at the left side kick panel. It has 2 wires connected to it.

PICKUP

Power 30 amp Circuit Breaker—is located in the junction block No. 1, left kick panel, 2 wires.

LAND CRUISER

The Land Cruiser uses large 50–100 amp fuses, located in the fuse box or at the battery main links in place of circuit breakers.

PREVIA

Heater 40 amp Circuit Breaker—is located in the junction/relay block No. 1, center of instrument panel.

VAN

Power 20 amp Circuit Breaker—is located near the air conditioning amplifier.
Heater 30 amp Circuit Breaker—is located in the junction block No. 1, left side of glove compartment.
Rear Heater 30 amp Circuit Breaker—is located near the air conditioning amplifier.
Condenser Fan 30 amp Circuit Breaker—is located near the air conditioning amplifier.

Fusible Links

4RUNNER

Ignition Switch 30 amp Fusible Link—is located in the relay block No. 2, right inner fender.
Ignition Switch 40 amp Fusible Link—is located in the relay block No. 2, right inner fender.
Alternator 80 amp (manual trans), 100 amp (auto trans) Fusible Link—is located in the relay block No. 2, right inner fender.
Condenser Fan 30 amp Fusible Link—is located in the relay block No. 4, right inner fender.
A/C 10 amp Fuse—is located in the relay block No. 3, right kick panel.
Heater 20 amp Fuse—is located in the relay block No. 3, right kick panel.

LAND CRUISER

Ignition Switch 50 amp Fuse—is located in the relay block No. 2, left inner fender.
Heater 30 amp Fuse—is located in the fuse block, instrument panel left.
Power 30 amp Fuse—is located in the fuse block, to the right of the heater fuse.

PICKUP

Ignition Switch 30 amp Fusible Link—is located in the relay block No. 2, right inner fender.
Ignition Switch 40 amp Fusible Link—is located in the relay block No. 2, right inner fender.
Alternator 80 amp Fusible Link—is located in the relay block No. 2, right inner fender.
Heater 30 amp Fuse—is located in the relay block No. 3, right kick panel.
A/C 10 amp Fuse—is located in the relay block No. 3, right kick panel.

PREVIA

Power 30 amp Fuse—is located in the junction/relay block No. 1, center instrument panel, next to power main relay.
Door 30 amp Fuse—is located in the junction/relay block No. 1, center instrument panel, next to power fuse.

VAN

Ignition Switch 30 amp Fusible Link—is located near the battery.
Alternator 100 amp Fusible Link—is located near the battery.
Headlight 40 amp Fusible Link—is located in the fusible link box in the engine compartment.
Ignition Switch 60 amp Fusible Link—is located in the fusible link box in the engine compartment.
Ignition Switch 30 amp Fusible Link—is located in the fusible link box in the engine compartment.
Electronic Fuel Injection 30 amp Fusible Link—is located in the fusible link box in the engine compartment.

Relays, Sensors, Modules and Computer Location

4RUNNER

- **A/C Amplifier**—is located behind the glove compartment.
- **A/C Cut Relay**—is located behind the glove compartment.
- **A/C Dual Pressure Switch and Thermistor**—is located behind the glove compartment.
- **A/C High Pressure Switch**—is located at the receiver/drier.
- **A/C Fan Relay No. 1**—is located in the relay block No. 4, beside the relay block No. 2, right inner fender.
- **A/C Fan Relay No. 2**—is located in the relay block No. 4, beside the relay block No. 2, right inner fender.
- **ADD Control Relay**—is located behind the instrument cluster.
- **ADD Diode**—is located at the right kick panel.
- **Air Flow Meter**—is located on the air cleaner assembly.
- **Air Intake Temperature Sensor**—is located at the air cleaner assembly.
- **Anti-lock Check Connector**—is located next to the wiper motor.
- **Auto Antenna Relay**—is located behind the instrument cluster.
- **Blower Resistor**—is located near the relay block, right kick panel.
- **Circuit Opening Relay**—is located below the relay block No. 3, right kick panel.
- **Fuel Pump Relay**refer to the circuit opening relay.
- **Cold Start Injector**—is located at the air intake plenum.
- **Coolant Temperature Sensor**—is located in the thermostat housing, to the right of the start injector time switch.
- **Cruise Control Computer**—is located behind the instrument panel, on the left side, near the junction block No. 1.
- **Cruise Control Main Relay**—is located behind the instrument panel, on the left side, near the junction block No. 1.
- **Daytime Running Light Relay**—is located behind the radio.
- **Defogger Relay**—is located in the junction block No. 1, left kick panel.
- **Diagnostic Check Connector**—is located at the relay block No. 2, right inner fender.
- **Dimmer Relay (Canada)**—is located in the relay block No. 2, right inner fender.
- **Door Control Relay**—is located behind the instrument panel, on the left side, near the junction block No. 1.
- **EFI Water Temperature Sensor**—is located at the thermostat housing (4 cyl.) and at the rear portion of the intake manifold (6 cyl.).
- **EGR Gas Temperature Sensor (California)**—is located near the EGR valve.
- **EGR Gas Temperature Sensor**—is located on the lower portion of the intake plenum.

• **Electronic Controlled Transmission (ECT)**—is located on the right side of the engine, near the firewall.

• **Electronic Fuel Injection (EFI) Relay**—is located in the relay block No. 2, right inner fender, next to the headlight relay.

• **Engine Electronic Control Unit (ECU)**—is located at the right kick panel.

• **Front Heater Relay**—is located in the relay block No. 3, right kick panel, right side of block.

• **Hazard Flasher**—is located within the turn signal flasher.

• **Headlight Relay**—is located in the relay block No. 2, right inner fender, next to the ignition switch fusible links.

• **Integration Relay**—is located in the junction block No. 1, left kick panel, large square box.

• **Knock Sensor**—is threaded into the intake manifold (6 cyl.) and under the intake manifold (4 cyl.).

• **Light Reminder Relay**—is located behind the radio.

• **Oil Pressure Switch**—is located at the front of the engine, near the upper radiator hose.

• **Oxygen Sensor (main)**—is located in the exhaust pipe, before the catalytic converter.

• **Oxygen Sensor (sub)**—is located in the exhaust pipe, after the catalytic converter.

• **Overdrive Relay**—is located behind the instrument cluster.

• **Power Window Diode**—is located in the main harness, in the center of the instrument panel.

• **Neutral Start Switch**—is located at the transmission.

• **Rear Heater Relay**—is located in the relay block No. 3, right kick panel, left side of block.

• **Rear Power Window and Rear Wiper Control Relay**—is located behind the left rear trim panel.

• **Shift Lock Control Unit**—is located under the center console.

• **Start Injector Time Switch**—is located in the thermostat housing, to the left of the coolant temperature sensor.

• **Starter Relay**—is located in the junction block No. 1, left kick panel.

• **Sunroof Relay**—is located in the junction block No. 1, left kick panel.

• **Taillight Relay**—is located in the junction block No. 1, left kick panel.

• **Throttle Position Sensor**—is located on the throttle body.

• **Transfer Fluid Temperature Sensor**—is located on the right side of the engine, near the firewall.

• **Turn Signal Flasher**—is located behind the instrument cluster.

• **Vehicle Speed Sensor**—is located inside the speedometer head.

• **Water Temperature Sender**—is located at the intake manifold.

LAND CRUISER

• **A/C Amplifier**—is located below the engine ECU, right kick panel.

• **A/C Cut Relay**—is located next to the engine ECU, behind glove compartment.

• **A/C Fan Relay**—is located in the relay block No. 2, left inner fender, round shape, 4 wires.

• **A/C Thermistor**—is located behind the glove compartment.

• **Air Flow Meter**—is located on the air cleaner assembly.

• **Air Intake Temperature Sensor**—is located at the air cleaner assembly.

• **Blower High Relay**—is located above the relay block No. 1, left kick panel, on the right side.

• **Blower Resistor**—is located near the relay block, right kick panel.

• **Center Differential Lock Control Relay**—is located above the relay block No. 1, left kick panel.

• **Charge Light Relay**—is located in the relay block No. 2, left inner fender, square shape, 4 wires, next to EFI main relay.

• **Circuit Opening Relay**—is located below the relay block No. 1, left kick panel.

• **Cold Start Injector**—is located at the air intake plenum.

• **Coolant Temperature Sensor**—is located in the thermostat housing, to the right of the start injector time switch.

• **Cooling Fan Control Unit**—is located at the right kick panel.

• **Cooling Fan Relay**—is located above the relay block No. 1, left kick panel, on the left side.

• **Cruise Control Unit**—is located behind the instrument cluster.

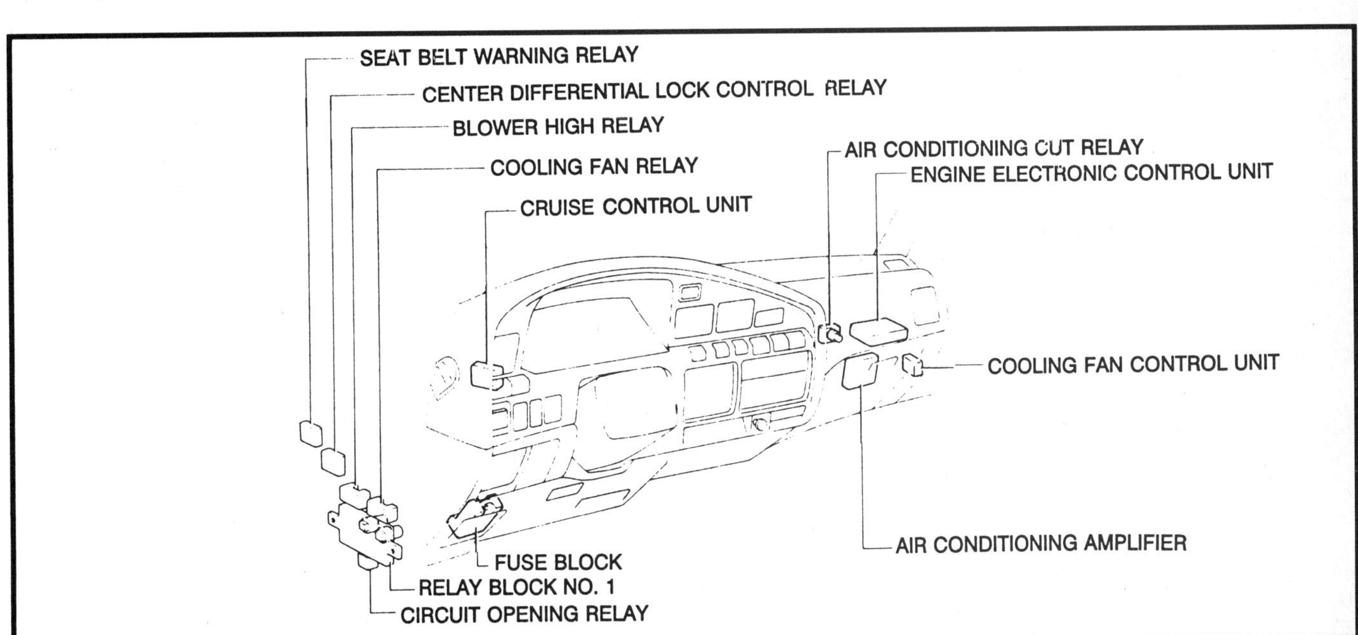

Component location—Land Cruiser

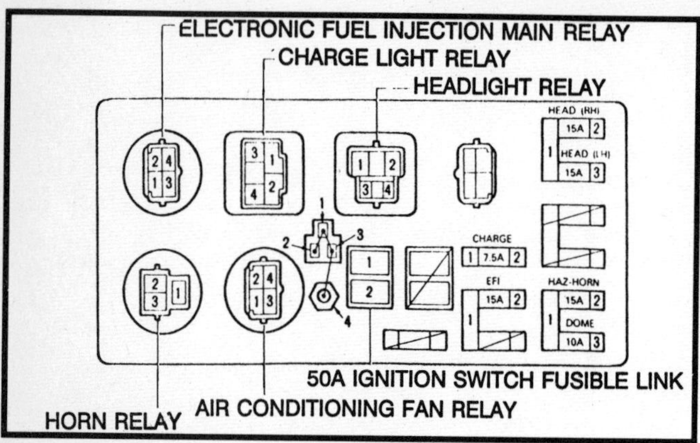

Relay block No. 2—Land Cruiser

- **Defogger Relay**—is located in the relay block No. 1, left kick panel, upper left corner.
- **Diagnostic Check Connector**—is located at the right inner fender, towards the rear.
- **EGR Gas Temperature Sensor (California)**—is located near the EGR valve.
- **Diodes**—is located behind the instrument panel on the left side.
- **Door Lock Control Relay**—is located in the driver door.
- **EGR Gas Temperature Sensor**—is located on the lower portion of the intake plenum.
- **Electronic Fuel Injection (EFI) Main Relay**—is located in the relay block No. 2, left inner fender, round shape, 4 wires.
- **Engine Electronic Control Unit (ECU)**—is located behind the glove compartment, to the right.
- **Fuel Pump Relay**refer to the circuit opening relay.
- **Hazard Flasher**—is located within the turn signal flasher.
- **Headlight Cleaner Relay**—is located at the right side of the firewall.
- **Headlight Relay**—is located in the relay block No. 2, left inner fender, round square shape, 4 wires.
- **Heater Relay**—is located in the relay block No. 1, left kick panel, lower left corner.
- **Horn Relay**—is located in the relay block No. 2, left inner fender, round shape, 3 wires.
- **Oxygen Sensor (main)**—is located in the exhaust pipe, before the catalytic converter.
- **Oxygen Sensor (sub)**—is located in the exhaust pipe, after the catalytic converter.
- **Moonroof Control Relay**—is located in the roof, near the control switch.
- **Neutral Start Switch**—is located at the transmission.
- **Pressure Switch**—is located behind the at the reciever/drier.
- **Power Main Relay**—is located in the relay block No. 1, left kick panel, upper, center.
- **Rear Heater Relay**—is located near rear heater assembly.
- **Rear Wiper Control Relay**—is located in the rear hatch.
- **Seat Belt Warning Relay**—is located above the relay block No. 1, left kick panel.
- **Shift Lock Control Unit**—is located near driver door post.
- **Start Injector Time Switch**—is located in the thermostat housing, to the left of the coolant temperature sensor.
- **Oil Pressure Switch**—is located at the front of the engine, right side.
- **Taillight Relay**—is located in the relay block No. 1, left kick panel, lower, center.
- **Throttle Position Sensor**—is located on the throttle body.
- **Turn Signal Flasher**—is located in the relay block No. 1, left kick panel, upper right corner.
- **Vehicle Speed Sensor**—is located inside the speedometer head.
- **Water Temperature Sender**—is located near the thermostat housing.

PICK UP

- **A/C Amplifier**—is located to the right of the glove compartment.
- **ADD Control Relay**—is located behind the instrument cluster.
- **A/C Dual Pressure Switch and Thermistor**—is located behind the glove compartment.
- **A/C High Pressure Switch**—is located at the receiver/drier.
- **ADD Diode**—is located at the right kick panel.
- **Air Flow Meter**—is located on the air cleaner assembly.
- **Air Intake Temperature Sensor**—is located at the air cleaner assembly.
- **Anti-lock Check Connector**—is located next to the wiper motor.
- **Auto Antenna Relay**—is located behind the instrument cluster.
- **Blower Resistor**—is located near the relay block, right kick panel.
- **Circuit Opening Relay**—is located above the right kick panel.
- **CMH Relay**—is located in the relay block No. 2, right inner fender.
- **Cold Start Injector**—is located at the air intake plenum.
- **Coolant Temperature Sensor**—is located in the thermostat housing, to the right of the start injector time switch.
- **Cruise Control Computer**—is located next the cruise control relay.
- **Cruise Control Main Relay**—is located behind the instrument panel, on the left side.
- **Defogger Relay**—is located in the junction block No. 1, left kick panel, middle part, 4 wires.
- **Defogger Relay**—is located in the junction block No. 1, left kick panel, lower part, 4 wires.
- **Diagnostic Check Connector**—is located at the relay block No. 2, right inner fender.
- **Door Control Relay**—is located behind the instrument cluster.
- **EGR Gas Temperature Sensor**—is located on the lower portion of the intake plenum.
- **EGR Gas Temperature Sensor (California)**—is located near the EGR valve.
- **Electronic Fuel Injection (EFI) Relay**—is located in the relay block No. 2, right inner fender.
- **Electronic Controlled Transmission (ECT)**—is located on the right side of the engine, near the firewall.
- **Engine Electronic Control Unit (ECU)**—is located at the right kick panel.
- **Fuel Pump Relay**refer to the circuit opening relay.
- **Hazard Flasher**—is located within the turn signal flasher.
- **Headlight Relay**—is located in the relay block No. 2, right inner fender.
- **Heater Relay**—is located in the relay block No. 3, right kick panel.
- **Knock Sensor**—is threaded into the intake manifold (6 cyl.) and under the intake manifold (4 cyl.).
- **Light Reminder Relay**—is located behind the ash tray.
- **Oil Pressure Switch**—is located at the front of the engine, near the upper radiator hose.

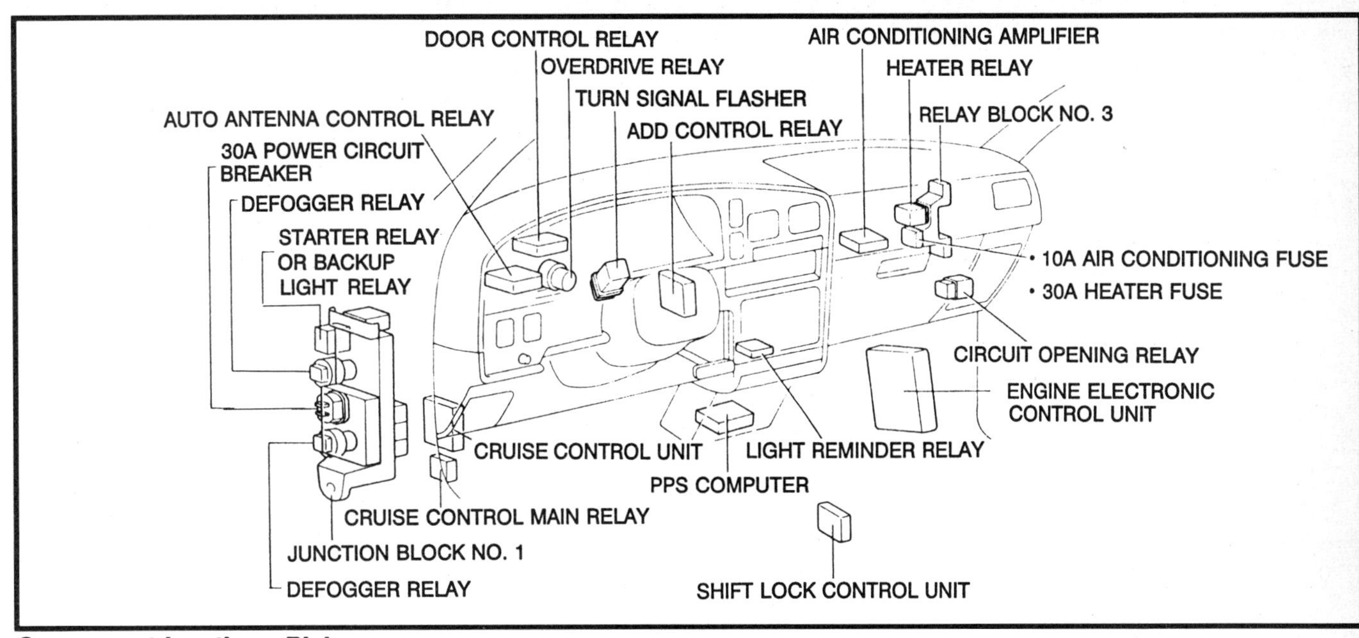

Component location—Pickup

• **Oxygen Sensor (main)**—is located in the exhaust pipe, before the catalytic converter.

• **Oxygen Sensor (sub)**—is located in the exhaust pipe, after the catalytic converter.

• **Overdrive Relay**—is located behind the instrument cluster.

• **Power Window Diode**—is located in the main harness, in the center of the instrument panel.

• **PPS Control Unit**—is located behind the radio.

• **Neutral Start Switch**—is located at the transmission.

• **Shift Lock Control Computer**—is located at the center hump, near the driver seat.

• **Start Injector Time Switch**—is located in the thermostat housing, to the left of the coolant temperature sensor.

• **Starter or Backup Light Relay**—is located in the junction block No. 1, left kick panel, upper part, 4 wires.

• **Taillight Relay**—is located in the junction block No. 1, left kick panel, upper part, 3 wires.

• **Throttle Position Sensor**—is located on the throttle body.

• **Transfer Fluid Temperature Sensor**—is located on the right side of the engine, near the firewall.

• **Turn Signal Flasher**—is located behind the instrument cluster.

• **Vehicle Speed Sensor**—is located inside the speedometer head.

• **Water Temperature Sensor (EFI)**—is located at the thermostat housing (4 cyl.) and at the rear portion of the intake manifold (6 cyl.).

• **Water Temperature Sender**—is located at the intake manifold.

PREVIA

• **A/C Amplifier**—is located to the right side of the center instrument panel.

• **A/C Clutch Relay**—is located to the right side of the center instrument panel.

• **A/C Cut Relay**—is located to the right side of the center instrument panel.

• **A/C High Pressure Switch**—is located at the receiver/drier.

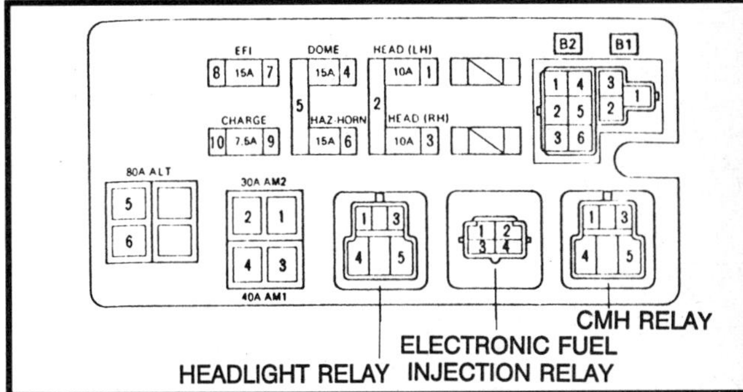

Relay block No. 2 right inner fender—Pickup

• **Air Flow Meter**—is located on the air cleaner assembly.

• **Air Intake Temperature Sensor**—is located at the air cleaner assembly.

• **Anti-lock Brake System (ABS) Control Unit**—is located to the right side of the center instrument panel.

• **Automatic Transmission Temperature Switch (4WD)**—is located at the transmission.

• **Circuit Opening Relay**—is located in the junction/relay block No. 1, center instrument panel.

• **Fuel Pump Relay**refer to the circuit opening relay.

• **Cold Start Injector**—is located at the air intake plenum.

• **Coolant Temperature Sensor**—is located in the thermostat housing, to the right of the start injector time switch.

• **Cruise Control Unit**—is located behind instrument panel, to the left of the steering column.

• **Daytime Running Light Relay (auto trans)**—is located behind instrument panel, to the left of the steering column.

• **Daytime Running Light Relay (manual trans)**—is located behind instrument panel, to the left of the steering column.

• **Deceleration Relay**—is located to the right side of the center instrument panel.

• **Defogger Relay**—is located behind instrument panel, to the left of the steering column.

• **Diagnostic Check Connector**—is located under the left front seat.

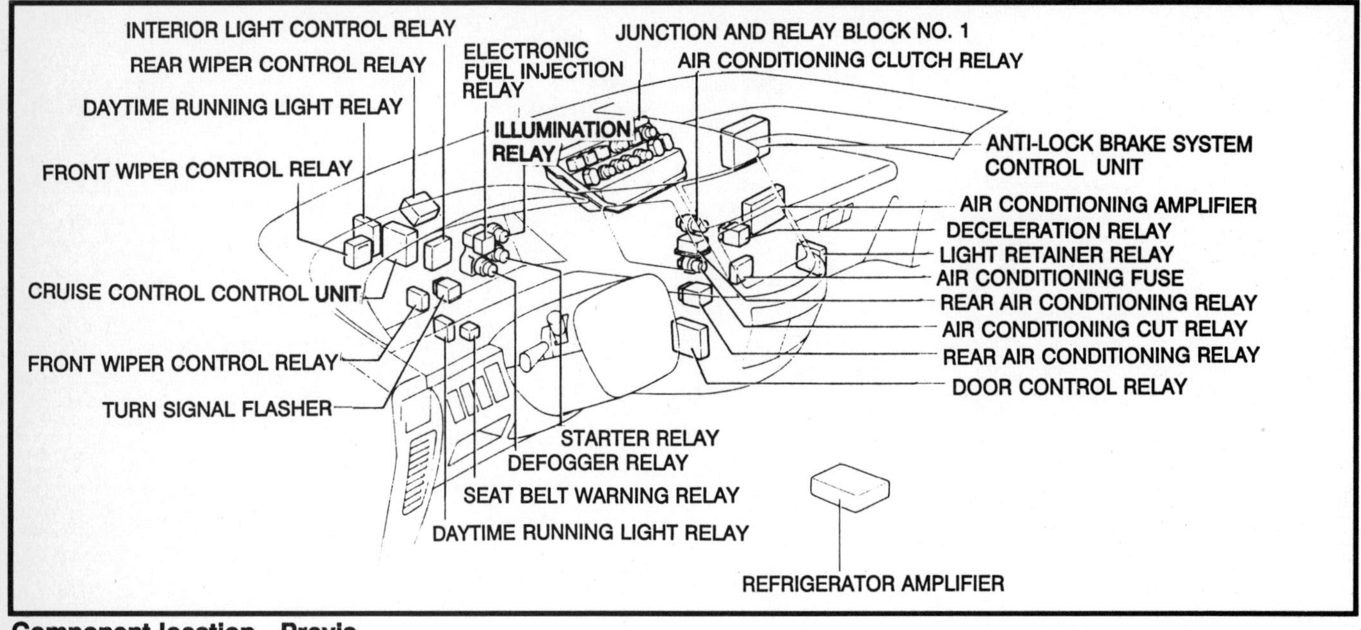

Component location—Previa

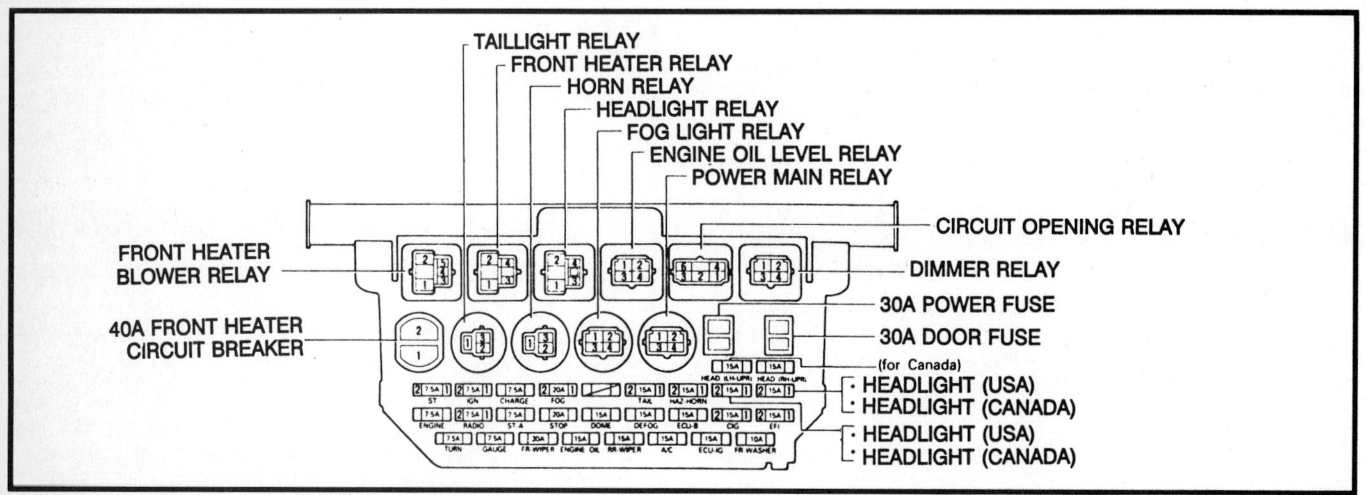

Junction and relay block No. 1—Previa

- **Dimmer Relay**—is located in the junction/relay block No. 1, center instrument panel.
- **Door Control Relay**—is located to the right side of the center instrument panel.
- **EFI Water Temperature Sensor**—is located at the right side of the engine, in the front.
- **EGR Gas Temperature Sensor (California)**—is located under the throttle body.
- **EGR Gas Temperature Sensor**—is located on the lower portion of the intake plenum.
- **Electronic Fuel Injection (EFI) Relay**—is located behind instrument panel, to the left of the steering column.
- **Engine and Transmission (ECT) Electronic Control Unit (ECU)**—is located under the driver seat.
- **Engine Oil Level Relay**—is located in the junction/relay block No. 1, center instrument panel.
- **Fog Light Relay**—is located in the junction/relay block No. 1, center instrument panel.
- **Front Heater Blower Relay**—is located in the junction/relay block No. 1, center instrument panel.
- **Front Heater Hi Blower Relay**—is located in the junction/relay block No. 1, center instrument panel.
- **Front Wiper Control Relay (auto trans)**—is located behind instrument panel, to the left of the steering column.
- **Front Wiper Control Relay**—is located behind instrument panel, to the left of the steering column.
- **Hazard Flasher**—is located within the turn signal flasher.
- **Headlight Relay**—is located in the junction/relay block No. 1, center instrument panel.
- **Horn Relay**—is located in the junction/relay block No. 1, center instrument panel.
- **Idle Speed Control Valve**—is located at the intake air plenum, near the throttle body.
- **Illumination Diode**—is located behind the instrument panel, near the steering column.
- **Illumination Relay**—is located behind instrument panel, to the left of the steering column.
- **Interior Light Control Relay**—is located behind instrument panel, to the left of the steering column.

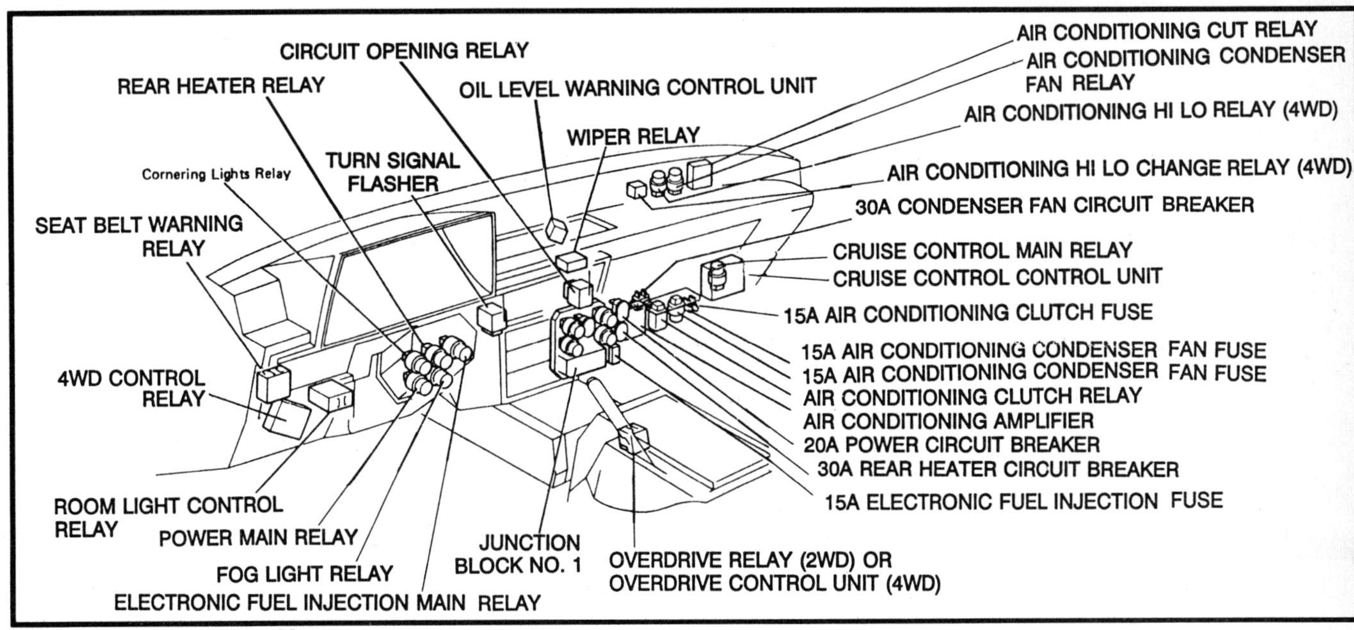

Component location—Van

- **Interior Light Diode**—is located at the left kick panel.
- **Knock Sensor**—is threaded into the intake manifold.
- **Light Retainer Relay**—is located to the right side of the center instrument panel.
- **Moonroof Control Relay**—is located in the roof, near the control switch.
- **Neutral Start Switch**—is located at the transmission.
- **Oil Pressure Switch**—is located at the front of the engine, near the upper radiator hose.
- **Oxygen Sensor (main)**—is located in the exhaust pipe, before the catalytic converter.
- **Oxygen Sensor (sub)**—is located in the exhaust pipe, after the catalytic converter.
- **Power Main Relay**—is located in the junction/relay block No. 1, center instrument panel.
- **Power Window Diode**—is located in the main harness, in the center of the instrument panel.
- **Rear A/C Fuse**—is located to the right side of the center instrument panel.
- **Rear A/C Relay**—is located to the right side of the center instrument panel.
- **Rear Wiper Control Relay**—is located behind instrument panel, to the left of the steering column.
- **Refrigerator**—is located next to the refrigerator.
- **Refrigerator Amplifier**—is located near the refrigerator harness.
- **Refrigerator Thermistor**—is located near the refrigerator harness.
- **Seat Belt Warning Relay**—is located behind instrument panel, to the left of the steering column.
- **Start Injector Time Switch**—is located in the thermostat housing, to the left of the coolant temperature sensor.
- **Starter Relay**—is located behind instrument panel, to the left of the steering column.
- **Taillight Relay**—is located in the junction/relay block No. 1, center instrument panel.
- **Throttle Position Sensor**—is located on the throttle body.
- **Turn Signal Flasher**—is located behind instrument panel, to the left of the steering column.
- **Vehicle Speed Sensor**—is located inside the speedometer head.
- **Water Temperature Sender**—is located at the intake manifold, in front.

VAN

- **4WD Control Relay**—is located behind the instrument panel, on the left side.
- **A/C Amplifier**—is located behind the glove compartment, to the right.
- **A/C Clutch Relay**—is located to the right of the junction block No. 1.
- **A/C Condenser Fan Relay**—is located at the upper right hand corner of the instrument panel.
- **A/C Cut Relay**—is located at the upper right hand corner of the instrument panel.
- **A/C Dual Pressure Switch**—is located at the receiver/drier.
- **A/C High Pressure Switch**—is the same as the dual pressure switch.
- **A/C High/Low Relay**—is located at the upper right hand corner of the instrument panel.
- **A/C ST Cut Relay**—is located to the right of the junction block No. 1.
- **A/C Thermistor**—is located behind the glove compartment.
- **A/C Volume Switch**—is located behind the glove compartment, to the left.
- **Air Flow Meter**—is located on the air cleaner assembly.
- **Air Intake Temperature Sensor**—is located at the air cleaner assembly.
- **Automatic Transmission Fluid Temperature Sensor (4WD)**—is located at the transmission.
- **Automatic Transmission Diode (4WD)**—is located behind the center of the instrument panel.
- **Blower Resistor**—is located near the relay block, right kick panel.
- **Circuit Opening Relay**—is located behind the heater controls, to the right.
- **Cold Start Injector**—is located at the air intake plenum.
- **Coolant Temperature Sensor**—is located in the thermostat housing, to the right of the start injector time switch.

• **Cornering Light Relay**—is located under the instrument cluster.

• **Cruise Control Computer**—is located at the right kick panel.

• **Cruise Control Diode**—is located behind the instrument cluster.

• **Cruise Control Main Relay**—is located at the right kick panel.

• **Diagnostic Check Connector for the Engine**—is located at the left inner fender, near the firewall.

• **Diagnostic Check Connector for the Fuel Pump**—is located at the left inner fender.

• **Diagnostic Check Connector for the Torque Converter Clutch**—is located at the left inner fender, near the firewall.

• **Diagnostic Check Connector for the Oxygen Sensor**—is located at the left inner fender.

• **EGR Gas Temperature Sensor (California)**—is located near the EGR valve.

• **Electronic Fuel Injection (EFI) Relay**—is located under the instrument cluster.

• **Engine Main Relay**—is located in the junction block No. 1, left side glove compartment, 4 wires.

• **Fog Light Relay**—is located under the instrument cluster.

• **Fuel Pump Relay**refer to the circuit opening relay.

• **Hazard Flasher**—is located within the turn signal flasher.

• **Headlight Diode**—is located behind the radio.

• **Headlight Relay**—is located in the junction block No. 1, left side glove compartment, 3 wires.

• **Heater Relay**—is located in the junction block No. 1, left side glove compartment, 4 wires.

• **Idle Speed Control Valve**—is located at the intake air plenum, near the throttle body.

• **Interior Light Diode**—is located behind the radio.

• **Knock Sensor**—is threaded into the cylinder block.

• **Neutral Start Switch**—is located at the transmission.

• **Oxygen Sensor (main)**—is located in the exhaust pipe, before the catalytic converter.

• **Oxygen Sensor (sub)**—is located in the exhaust pipe, after the catalytic converter.

• **Oil Level Switch**—is located at the front left of the engine.

• **Oil Level Warning Computer**—is located behind the heater controls, to the right.

• **Oil Pressure Switch**—is located at the right side of the engine.

• **Overdrive Relay (2WD) or Overdrive Computer (4WD)**—is located under the center console.

• **Power Main Relay**—is located under the instrument cluster.

• **Rear Heater Relay**—is located under the instrument cluster.

• **Room Light Control Relay**—is located behind the instrument panel, on the left side.

• **Seat Belt Warning Relay**—is located behind the instrument panel, on the left side.

• **Start Injector Time Switch**—is located in the thermostat housing, to the left of the coolant temperature sensor.

• **Taillight Relay**—is located in the junction block No. 1, left side glove compartment, 3 wires.

• **Throttle Position Sensor**—is located on the throttle body.

• **Turn Signal Flasher**—is located to the left of the heater controls.

• **Vehicle Speed Sensor**—is located inside the speedometer head.

• **Water Temperature Sensor (EFI)**—is located at the front of the engine, in the middle.

• **Water Temperature Switch**—is located at the front of the engine, towards the center.

• **Wiper Relay**—is located behind the heater controls, to the right.

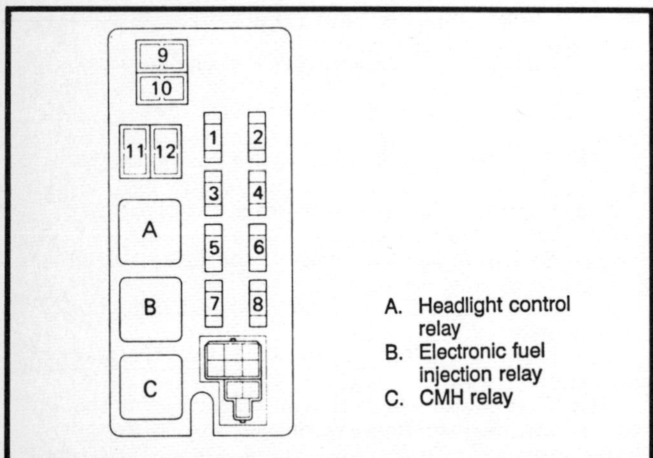

Relay block No. 2—1989 4Runner

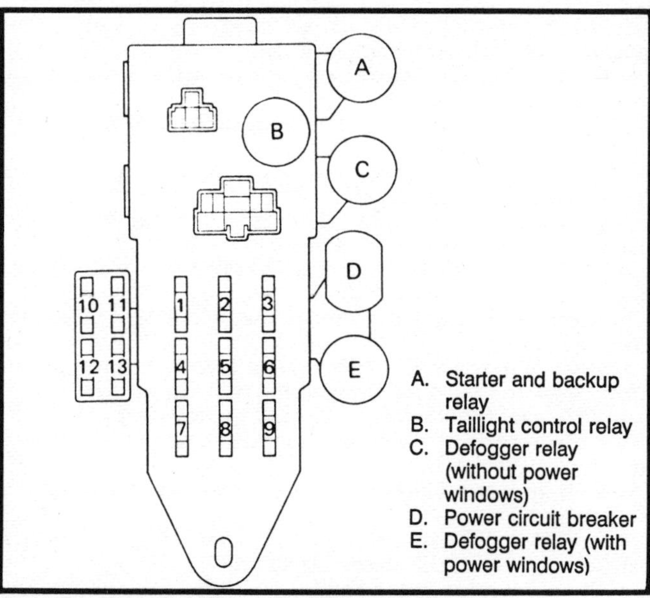

Junction block No. 1—1989-90 4Runner

Component Locator

SECTION 3

ALFA ROMEO

Circuit Breakers and Fuses

SPIDER, SPIDER VELOCE AND GRADUATE

The central fusebox is located in a special drawer on the instrument panel to the left of the steering column. On some models, inline fuses are inserted in the electrical system for special loads.

On models with knee padding, the centralized fuse box is located under the dashboard on the driver's side. It can be reached by pulling out a catch. A protective cover is over the fuses.

MILANO

The central fusebox is located in a special drawer on the instrument panel to thc left of the steering column. Access is by a pull-down cover. On some models, inline fuses are inserted in the electrical system for special loads. Note that on the Milano, relays are located in the fusebox and also on brackets in the left and right front corners of the engine compartment.

164L AND 164S

The central fusebox is located behind the dashboard knee padding left of the steering column. A swing-down door covers the fusebox.

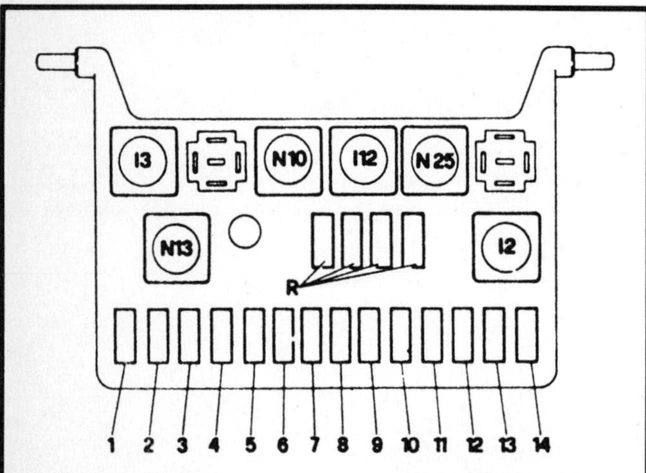

Fuse box is located to the driver's left—typical Spider

Additional fuses and relay assemblies are located is various spots around the vehicle. Note that many fuses are mounted on the relay they protect. Many relays are mounted in locations difficult to reach. By opening the glove box, removing the square plastic plugs in the back panel and removing the screws under the plugs, the bracket holding the dome light relay, seat belt buzzer and ABS relay can be removed. Another bank of relays if located behind the instrument cluster which must be removed to access the relays.

A flat piece in the back of the engine compartment known as the utilities bay cover is removed for access to several components and sensors.

Relays, Sensors, Modules and Computer Locations

SPIDER, SPIDER VELOCE, GRADUATE

- **A/C Control Unit**—is located on the rear face of the cooler unit.
- **A/C Expansion Valve**—is located at the top of the blower housing.
- **A/C Pressure Switch**—is located on the drier.
- **A/C Temperature Knob**—is located in the center console, lower left corner.
- **A/C Thermistor Probe**—is located inside the cooler case, next to the evaporator.
- **A/C Three Speed Fan Control Knob**—is located in the center console, lower left corner.
- **Air Bag Control Unit**—is mounted on the floor behind the driver's seat under the floor unpholstery.
- **Air Bag Sensors (Accelerometers)**—are 3 in number, 2 are located on the right and left sides of the engine compartment and 1 is located on the control unit.
- **Air Flow Sensor**—is located between the air filter cover and the rubber intake duct.
- **Back-Up Lamps and Neutral Safety Switch, automatic transmission**—is located on the side of the transmission case near the cooling hose connections.
- **Back-Up Lamp Switch, manual transmission**—is located on the gearbox case.
- **Brake Fluid Level Sensor**—is located in the brake fluid reservoir.
- **Combination Switch**—including the turn signals, windshield wiper and washer switch and headlight/parking light switch is on the steering column, accessed by removing the steering wheel and column casings.
- **Motronic Ignition and Fuel Injection Control Unit**—is located under the rear shelf.
- **Coolant Temperature Sensor**—is located in the cylinder head near the fuel injectors.
- **Cooling Fan Radiator Switch**—is located at the corner of the bottom radiator tank.
- **Crankshaft Position Sensor**—is located in the engine compartment on the left side, next to the crankshaft mounted trigger wheel.
- **Evaporative Emission Canister Purge Solenoid**—is located on a bracket near the vapor canister which is mounted behind the right front inner fender.
- **Fuel Level Sensor**—is built into the fuel gauge sender/submerged fuel pump assembly and is located at the left side of the luggage compartment floor under the lining.
- **Fuel Pressure Regulator**—is located in line with the fuel feed, on the fuel rail, connected to a vacuum line.
- **Fuel Pump (primary)**—is located under the vehicle next to the fuel filter.

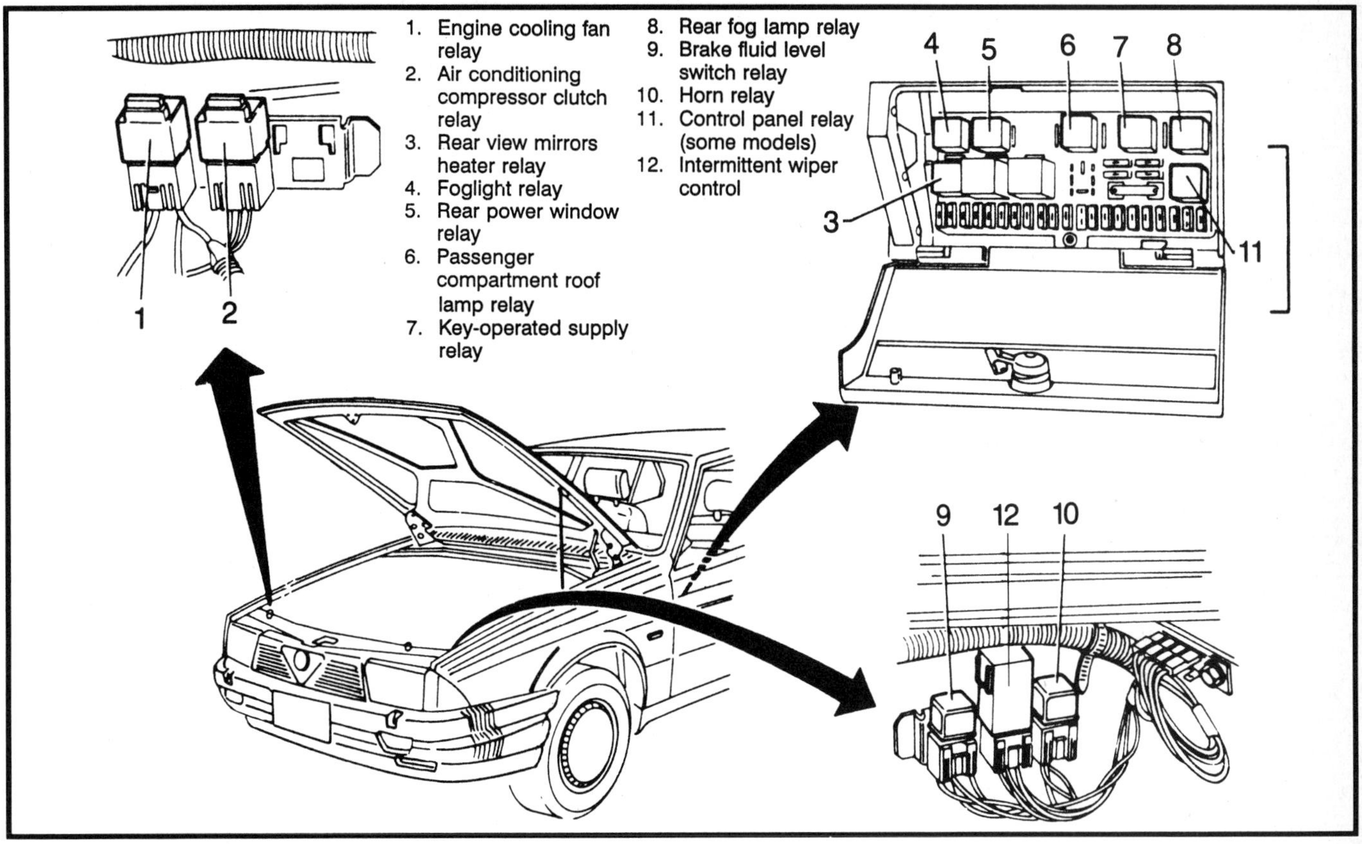

1. Engine cooling fan relay
2. Air conditioning compressor clutch relay
3. Rear view mirrors heater relay
4. Foglight relay
5. Rear power window relay
6. Passenger compartment roof lamp relay
7. Key-operated supply relay
8. Rear fog lamp relay
9. Brake fluid level switch relay
10. Horn relay
11. Control panel relay (some models)
12. Intermittent wiper control

Relay locations—Milano

- **Fuel Pump (secondary)**—is located inside the fuel tank.
- **Hazard Flasher**—is located in the fuse box.
- **Hazard Flasher Switch**—is located on the rear console facing.
- **Headlight Switch**—is built into the Combination Switch.
- **Heated Rear Window Relay**—is located in the fuse box.
- **Horn Relay**—is located in the fuse box.
- **Idle Speed Actuator**—is located in line with the by-pass hose.
- **Ignition and Fuel Injection Control Unit**—is located under the rear shelf.
- **Intake Air Temperature Sensor**—is located in the air filter housing.
- **Intermittent Windshield Wiper Controller**—is located under the dashboard on the left valence panel.
- **Instrument Cluster Rheostat**—is located in the instrument panel beneath the instrument cluster.
- **Motronic Ignition and Fuel Injection Control Unit**—is located under the rear shelf.
- **Neutral Safety and Back-Up Lamp Switch (automatic transmission)**—is located on the side of the transmission case near the cooling hose connections.
- **Oxygen Sensor (lambda sensor)**—is located in the exhaust just in front of the catalytic converter.
- **Parking Brake On Warning Switch**—is attached to a bracket on the parking brake support, accessed by removing the rear console.
- **Power Window Relay**—is located in the fuse box.
- **Rear Fog Light Relay**—is located in the fuse box.
- **Seat Belt and Door Ajar Warning Buzzer**—is located under the dashboard on the left valence panel, accessed by removing the knee padding.

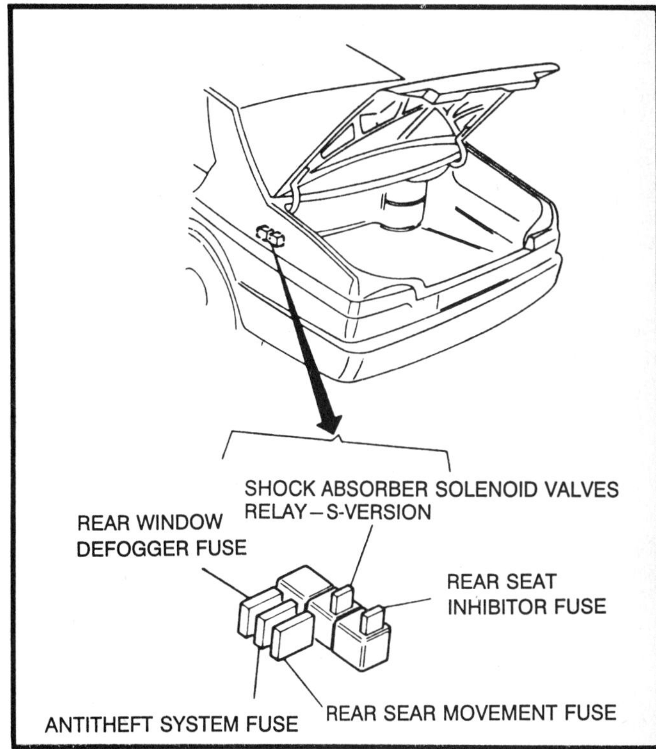

Trunk compartment fuses—164 Series

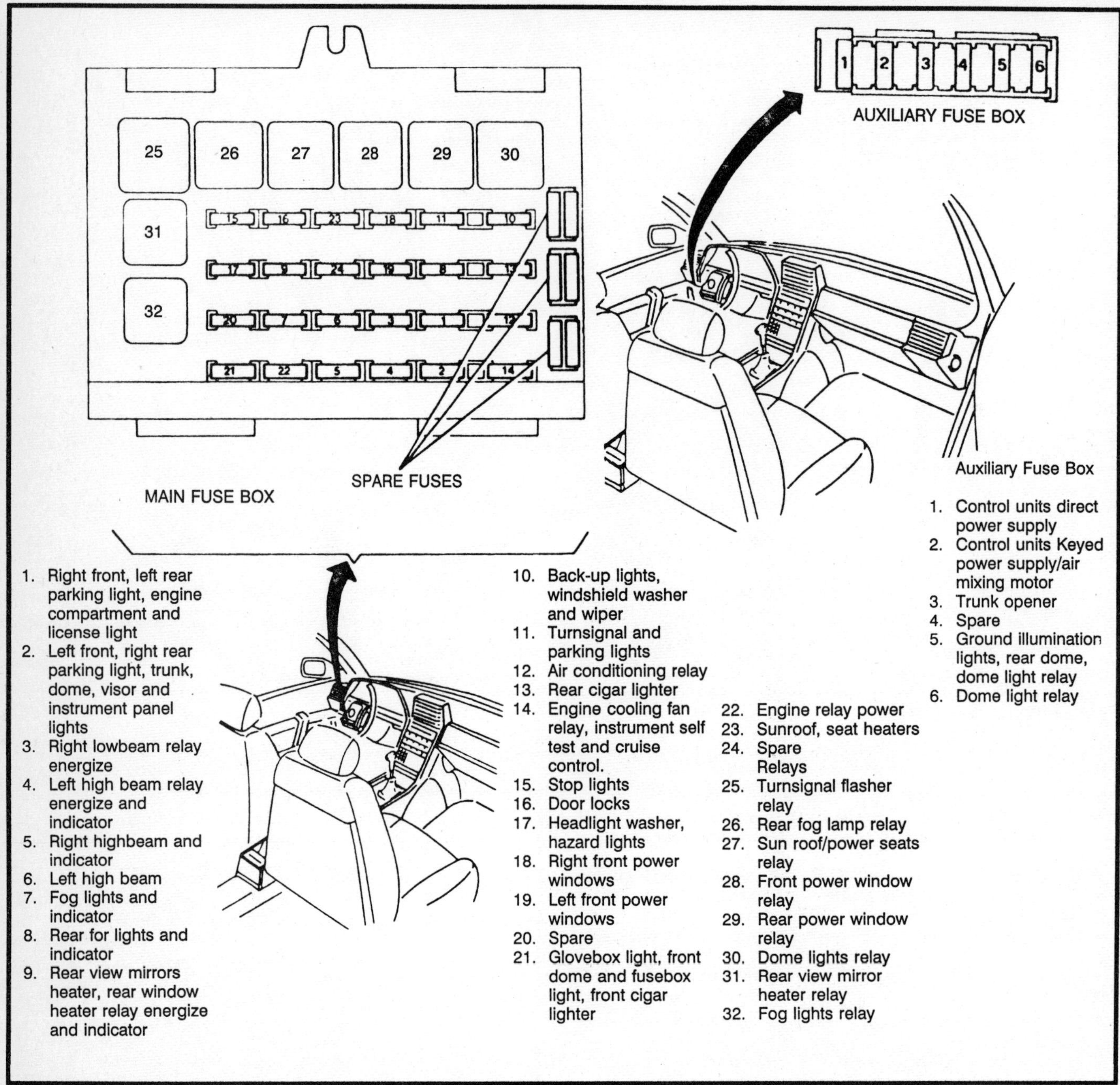

Main and auxiliary fuse box inside vehicle—164 Series

• **Self-Diagnostic Pushbutton**—is located under the rear upholstery close to the electronic control unit.

• **Speedometer Sensor**—is located on the side of the transmission tailshaft housing, just forward of the driveshaft flex joint.

• **Stop Light Switch**—is located on a bracket below the steering column, working against the brake pedal lever.

• **Throttle Position Sensor**—is located on the side of the throttle body.

• **Turn Signal Flasher**—is located in the fuse box.

• **Turn Signal Switch**—is built into the combination switch.

• **Ventilating Fan Switch**—is located in the center console.

• **Windshield Washer Motor**—is built into the washer fluid reservoir located in the front left hand side of the vehicle.

• **Windshield Washer Switch**—is built into the combination switch.

• **Windshield Wiper Motor**—is mounted below the wiper transmission accessed by removing the air intake grill and engine compartment-to-hood seal.

• **Windshield Wiper Switch**—is built into the combination switch.

MILANO

• **A/C Clutch Relay**—is mounted on a bracket on the right front corner of the engine compartment.

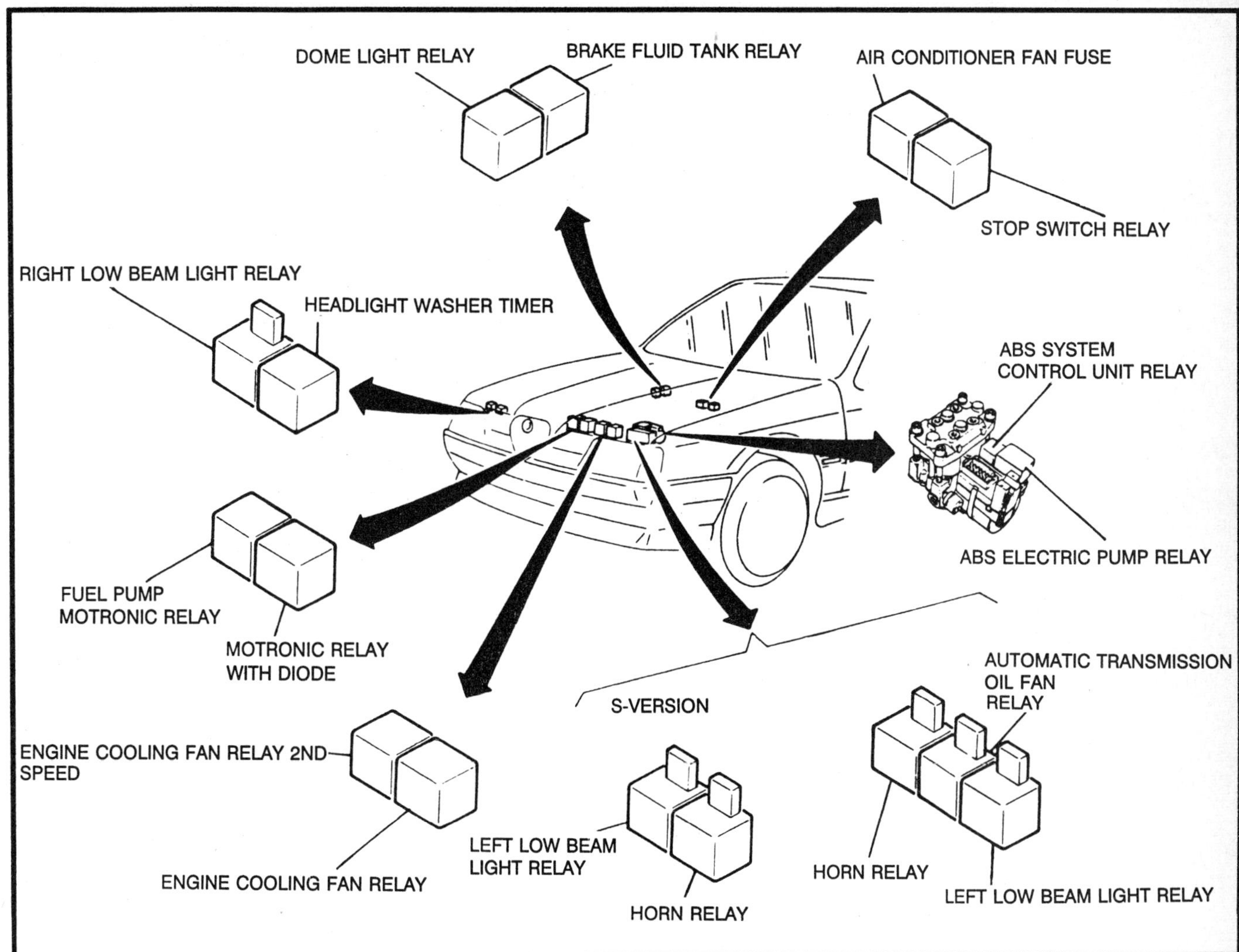

Underhood relays – 164 Series

• **A/C Control Unit** – is located on the rear face of the cooler unit.

• **A/C Expansion Valve** – is located at the top of the blower housing at the evaporator inlet.

• **A/C Pressure Switch** – is located on the drier. Some models may use 2 switches.

• **A/C Temperature Knob** – is located at the right side of the air conditioner control cluster.

• **A/C Thermistor Probe** – is located inside the cooler case, next to the evaporator.

• **A/C Three Speed Fan Control Knob** – is located at the right side of the air conditioner control cluster.

• **ABS System Wheel Sensors** – are located next to the trigger wheel mounted at each wheel, inboard of the wheel hub.

• **ABS Master Cylinder** – is built into the ABS electrovalve unit

• **ABS Electrovalve Unit** – is built into the ABS master cylinder

• **ABS Pump and Accumulator** – are built into 1 unit and mounted on the driver's side forward of the windshield washer container.

• **ABS Electronic Control Unit** – is located in the luggage compartment.

• **Air Flow Sensor** – is located in the air intake system between the air filter and the corrugated hose feeding air to the intake manifold.

• **Altitude Compensation Device** – is located on the relay bracket inside the engine compartment at the back on the right.

• **Auxiliary Air Device** – is located near or just under the corrugated intake air hose.

• **Back-Up Lamp Switch** – is mounted on the right side of the gearbox differential case.

• **Brake Fluid Level Sensor** – is located in the brake and clutch fluid reservoir.

• **Brake Fluid Level Switch Relay** – is located on a bracket on the left front corner of the engine compartment.

• **Brake Light Switch** – is located on a bracket on the steering column rear support.

• **Combination Switch** – including the turn signals, windshield wiper and washer switch and headlight/parking light switch is on the steering column, accessed by removing the steering wheel and column casings.

• **Cold Start Fuel Injector** – is located on the intake air box attached with 2 screws.

• **Cold Start Thermal Switch** – is located on the thermostat body.

• **Cooling Fan Radiator Switch** – is located at the corner of the bottom radiator tank.

• **Coolant Level Sensor** – is located in the coolant header or overflow tank.

• **Coolant Temperature Gauge Sender (lamp)** – is located on the thermostat body.

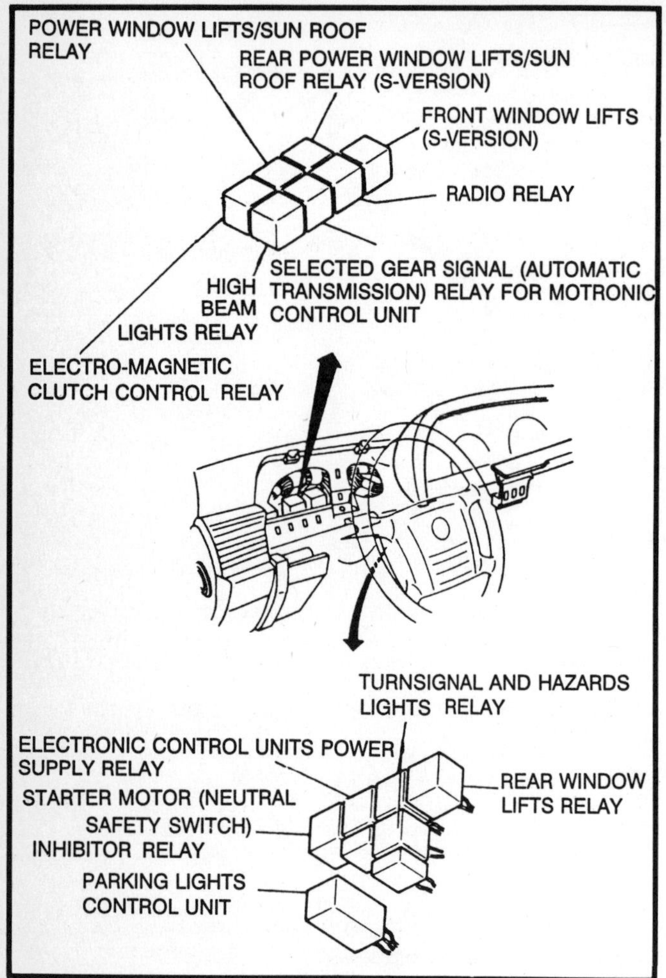

Inside vehicle relays—164 Series

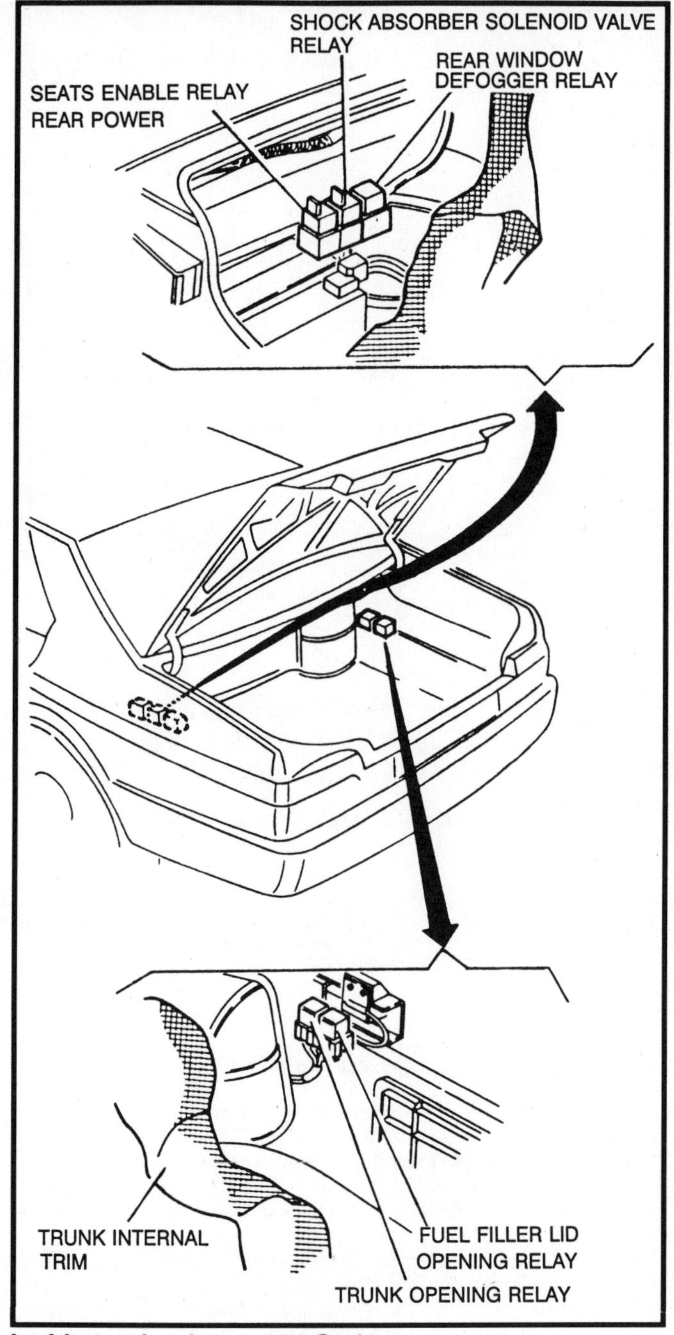

Inside trunk relays—164 Series

- **Coolant Temperature Sender**—is located on the thermostat body.
- **Engine Cooling Fan Relay**—is mounted on a bracket on the right front corner of the engine compartment.
- **Engine Temperature Sensor**—for the ignition advance ECU is located on the front right side of the thermostat body.
- **Fog Light Relay**—is mounted in the fusebox, top left.
- **Fog Light Switch**—is located on the right side of the instrument cluster.
- **Fuel Filter**—is located under the vehicle downstream of the fuel pump attached to the underbody by a bracket.
- **Fuel Injection Electronic Control Unit**—is located in a special compartment in the front of the vehicle floor.
- **Fuel Injection Relay Set**—is located on a relay holder bracket inside the engine compartment at the back, on the right, near the altitude compensation device.
- **Fuel Pressure Regulator**—is located near the air intake, attached to the supply lines to the fuel injectors.
- **Fuel Pump**—is located under the vehicle close to the fuel tank just upstream of the fuel filter.
- **Hazard Light Switch**—is located on the instrument cluster, left side.
- **Headlight Switch**—is built into the Combination Switch.
- **Headlight Wiper Intermittent Timer**—is located on a bracket on the left front corner of the engine compartment.
- **Heated Rear Window Relay**—is mounted in the fusebox, bottom left.
- **Heated Rear Window Switch**—is mounted on the left side of the instrument cluster.
- **High Beam Switch**—is built into the Combination Switch.
- **Horn Relay**—is located on a bracket on the left front corner of the engine compartment.
- **Ignition Advance Control Unit**—is located at the front right side of the passenger compartment, under the dashboard.
- **Instrument Cluster Dimmer Rheostat**—is located on the left side of the instrument cluster.
- **Intermittent Windshield Wiper Relay**—is mounted in the fusebox, bottom row, center.
- **Key-Operated Supply Relay**—is mounted in the fusebox, top row, next to the rear fog light relay.

• **Oxygen Sensor**—is located in the headpipe built onto the catalytic converter.

• **Parking Brake On Switch**—is located on the parking brake handle assembly inside the trim cover.

• **Power Door Lock Control Unit**—is located on a bracket inside the dashboard, above the central fusebox.

• **Power Seat Switches**—are located next to the cigar lighter in the panel in the central console.

• **Power Window Relay**—is mounted in the fusebox, top row, next to the foglight relay.

• **Power Window Switches**—are located in the roof front panel. The 2 switches for the rear power power windows are located in the rear part of the center console.

• **Power Window Inhibitor (safety) Switch**—is located in the roof front panel.

• **Rear Fog Light Relay**—is mounted in the fusebox, top right.

• **Rear Fog Light Switch**—is located on the right side of the instrument cluster.

• **Roof Lamp Relay**—is mounted in the fusebox, top row, center.

• **Roof Lamp Switch**—is located on the roof front panel.

• **Roof Mounted Central Spot Light Switch**—is located on the roof front panel.

• **Seat Back Inclination Switches**—are located in the central console panel near the cigar lighter.

• **Seat Belt Control Unit**—is located inside the dashboard on the lid above the right glove box, accessed by removing the glove box.

• **Speedometer Pulse Generator**—is inserted in the clutch/gearbox casing.

• **Stop Light Switch**—is located on a bracket on the steering column rear support.

• **Thermo-Time Switch for the Injection System**—is located on the right side of the thermostat body.

• **Throttle Position Sensor**—is located on the side of the throttle body, secured by 2 screws.

• **Turn Signal/Hazard Lights Relay**—is mounted in the fusebox, bottom row, next to the heated rear window relay.

• **Turn Signal Switch**—is built into the Combination Switch.

• **Voltage Regulator**—is built into the alternator as part of the brush holder assembly.

• **Warning Lamp Panel (control display)**—is located on the instrument panel on the cluster right side.

• **Warning Lamp Panel Control Unit**—is located inside the dashboard on the lid above the right glove box.

• **Windshield Washer Switch**—is built into the Combination Switch.

• **Windshield Wiper Motor**—is mounted below the wiper transmission.

• **Windshield Wiper Switch**—is built into the Combination Switch.

164L AND 164S

• **A/C Anti-frost Thermostat**—is located inside the cooler case, next to the evaporator.

• **A/C Automatic Control Unit**is located in the center console.

• **A/C Cabin Air Temperature Sensor**—is located in the overhead panel housing the dome light next to the rear view mirror.

• **A/C Computer Controller (automatic)**—is located in the dashboard accessed after removing the thin vertical trim piece from the face of the controller.

• **A/C Disengage Switch**—is located on the control panel, upper left corner.

• **A/C Drier/Filter Assembly**is located at the top of the air conditioner evaporator unit.

• **A/C Expansion Valve**—is located at the top of the blower housing, next to the drier.

• **A/C Fan Fuse**—is located in the engine compartment on the fire wall next to the engine cooling fan fuse.

• **A/C Fan Speed Manual Selector Switch**—is located on the control panel, top row.

• **A/C Pressure Switch**—is located on the drier.

• **A/C Speed Variator Heat Dissipator**—is located next to drier.

• **A/C System ON/OFF Switch**—is located on the control panel, top row, far right.

• **A/C Temperature Setting Switch**—is located on the control panel, top row, just to the right of the disengage switch.

• **ABS Computer Control Unit**—is located in the center tunnel along with the fuel injection control unit, air bag control unit and cruise control unit.

• **ABS Electro-Hydraulic Unit Main Relay**—is located inside the vehicle behind a small trim panel in the dashboard to the right of the glove box.

• **ABS Electro-Hydraulic Unit System Relays**—are located under the cover of the electro-hydraulic unit, accessed by removing 1 screw and the cover.

• **ABS Sensors**—are located in brackets close to the wheel hub toothed wheels on the spindles.

• **Air Bag Control Unit**—is located in the center tunnel along with the fuel injection control unit, ABS control unit and cruise control unit, accessed by removing the right side tunnel trim panel.

• **Air Bag Sensors (Accelerometers)**—are located in the front left and front right corners of the engine compartment.

• **Anti-theft System Alarm**—is located inside the trunk behind the right side trim panel.

• **Anti-theft System Computer Control Unit**—is located inside the trunk behind the left side trim panel.

• **Anti-theft System Fuse**—is located in the trunk on a relay bracket on the driver's side inner fenderwell near the left side trunk hinge.

• **Automatic Transmission Fan Fuse**—is located on its relay on a small bracket in the engine compartment, driver's side front.

• **Automatic Transmission Lock Control Unit**—is located to the left of the steering column accessed by opening the fusebox door.

• **Automatic Transmission Lock Solenoid**—is located at the rear of the shift lever bracket requiring removal of gear shift lever knob and selector panel.

• **Automatic Transmission Oil Temperature Sensors**—are located in a fitting connecting a cooling line near the automatic transmission oil reservoir, accessed by removing the air cleaner and related supports.

• **Auxiliary Fuse Box**—is located just above the main fuse box, also on the left side of the steering column.

• **Back-Up Lights Switch, Automatic Transmission**—is located inside the floor shift assembly requiring removal of gear shift lever knob and selector panel.

• **Back-Up Lights Switch, Manual Transmission**—is located on the transaxle case near the gearshift assembly.

• **Brake Fluid Level Warning Light Switch**—is built into the brake fluid reservoir cap.

• **Brake Light Switch**—is located on a bracket just above the brake pedal arm.

• **Brake Light Switch for Cruise Control**—is located on a bracket just above the brake pedal arm to the right of the service brake light switch.

• **Brake Pad Wear Indicator**—is built into the front caliper inner brake pad.

• **Charcoal Canister for Evaporative Emission System**—is located inside the left front fender housing accessed by removing the left front wheel and front inner fender.

• **Charcoal Canister Purge Solenoid**—is located on top of the charcoal canister.

• **Clutch Switch for Cruise Control**—is located on a bracket just above the clutch pedal arm.

• **Combination Switch**—is located on the steering column access requires removing the steering wheel and column shrouds.

• **Controlled Dampening Suspension System Accelerometer (Vertical Acceleration Sensor) (S-model)**—is located in the trunk along the passenger side inner fender.

• **Controlled Dampening Suspension System Braking Sensor (S-model)**—is installed vertically on the brake master cylinder front end.

• **Controlled Dampening Suspension System Computer Control Unit (S-model)**—is located in the trunk on the passenger's side inner fenderwell under the trim panel.

• **Controlled Dampening Suspension System Engine Throttle Sensor (S-model)**—is a microswitch located on the throttle body.

• **Controlled Dampening Suspension System Gearbox Sensor (S-model)**—signals that 1st or 2nd gear has been selected and threads into the top of the gearbox housing.

• **Controlled Dampening Suspension System Relay Fuse (S-model)**—is located in the trunk on a relay bracket on the driver's side inner fenderwell near the left side trunk hinge.

• **Controlled Dampening Suspension System Shock Absorber Solenoid Valve Control Relay (S-model)**—is located on the relay bracket mounted on the driver's side trunk inside fender.

• **Controlled Dampening Suspension System Speedometer Sensor (S-model)**—is located on the gearbox.

• **Controlled Dampening Suspension System Steering Angle and Rotation Speed Sensor (S-model)**—is fixed to the steering column near the universal joint connecting the upper and lower sections.

• **Crankshaft Position Sensor**—is located on the front of the engine, down by a crankshaft pulley mounted trigger wheel.

• **Cruise Control Computer Control Unit**—is located in the center tunnel along with the air bag control unit, ABS control unit and fuel injection control unit, accessed by removing the right side tunnel trim panel.

• **Cruise Control Lever**—is mounted on the steering column accessed by removing the 2-piece column shroud around it.

• **Cruise Control Vacuum Tank**—is located inside the left front fender housing next to the charcoal canister and is accessed by removing the left front wheel and front inner fender.

• **Diagnostic Pushbutton**—is located on the steering column, accessed by removing the column shrouds.

• **Door Lock Sensors, Front and Rear**—are built into the door lock together with the locking motors; replacement requires replacing the entire unit.

• **Engine Coolant Level Sensor**—is located in the overflow header tank.

• **Engine Coolant Temperature Sensor**—is located on the water pump body.

• **Engine Cooling Fan Fuse**—is located in the engine compartment on the fire wall next to the air conditioning fan fuse.

• **Fuel Filler Door Motor**—is located inside the trunk, passenger side, behind the trim panel.

• **Fuel Filter**—is located under the car, downstream from the pump, near the rear axle assembly.

• **Fuel Injection Control Unit**—is located in the center tunnel along with the air bag control unit, ABS control unit and cruise control unit, accessed by removing the right side tunnel trim panel.

• **Fuel Pressure Regulator**—is located on the feed end of the fuel injection fuel rail.

• **Fuel Pump**—is located in the fuel tank.

• **Gearbox Sensor (S-model)**—is located on the manual transaxle next to the back-up light switch.

• **Headlight Washer Pump**—is located in the washer reservoir tank.

• **Horn Fuse**—is located on its relay on a small bracket in the engine compartment, driver's side front.

• **Idle Speed Actuator**—is located in-line with the by-pass hose, secured by a bracket to the intake manifold.

• **Ignition Coil**—is located on a bracket near the radiator.

• **Ignition Switch**—is located on the steering column accessed by removing the column shrouds and disconnecting the wiring by working through the fuse holder opening.

• **Mixed Air Temperature Sensor**—is located behind the small trim panel on the left side of the glovebox.

• **Neutral Safety Switch (automatic transmission)**—is located inside the floor shift assembly requiring removal of gear shift lever knob and selector panel.

• **Odometer Sensor**—is located above the right side inner CV joint.

• **Oil Level Warning Light Sensor**—is located on the side of the block near the dipstick tube.

• **Oil Pressure Gauge Sender**—is located on the side of the block, near the bellhousing. It screws in vertically.

• **Oil Pressure Light Sender**—is located on the side of the block, near the bellhousing. It screws in horizontally.

• **Outside Air Temperature Sensor**—is located under the utilities bay cover in the engine compartment.

• **Oxygen Sensor (lambda probe)**—is located in the front top of the catalytic converter.

• **Parking Brake ON Light Switch**—is located at the base of the parking brake handle, accessed by removing the rear console.

• **Power Door Lock Button**—is located in a central panel on the center console.

• **Power Seat Heating Pads, Front and Rear**—are located in the seat backrest as well as the seat cushion and accessed after the seat is removed from the vehicle.

• **Power Seat Motors, Front and Rear**—are located in the seat and are accessed after the seat is removed from the vehicle.

• **Power Seat Switches, Front**—are located in a narrow panel to the left of the seat, near the floor.

• **Power Seat Switches, Rear**—are located in the rear console.

• **Power Window Switches**—are located in a central panel on the center console.

• **Radiator Cooling Fan Sensor**—is located in the, upper portion of the left side radiator tank.

• **Radiator Cooling Fan Sensor Resistor**—is located near the sensor on the fan shroud and gives a second speed to the fan.

• **Rear Light Control Unit**—is located under the dashboard on the passenger side, secured by 2 screws.

• **Rear Power Seat Fuse**—is located in the trunk on a relay bracket on the driver's side inner fenderwell near the left side trunk hinge.

• **Rear Power Seat Inhibitor System Fuse**—is located in the trunk on a relay bracket on the driver's side inner fenderwell near the left side trunk hinge.

• **Rear Power Seat Inhibitor System Switch**—is located in a central panel on the center console.

• **Rear Window Defogger Fuse**—is located in the trunk on a relay bracket on the driver's side inner fenderwell near the left side trunk hinge.

• **Rear View Mirror (external) Power Motors**—are located inside the mirror heads and repair requires replacing the entire unit.

• **Rear View Mirror (external) Power Switches**—are located in the door trim panels and after trim removal, unclip for removal.

• **RPM and Stroke Sensor**—is located next to the crankshaft trigger wheel behind the front pulley.

• **Seat Belt Sensor**—is built into the seat belt buckle, replacement requires replacing the whole buckle assembly.

• **Speedometer Pulse Generator**—is located in the transaxle case near the final drive ring gear.

• **Sunroof Opening Motor**—is located in the overhead panel housing the dome light which is removed for access.

• **Throttle Position Sensor**—is located on the Motronic Fuel Injection System throttle body.

• **Trunk Opening Motor**—is located inside the trunk lid next to the trunk light pushbutton.

• **Voltage Regulator**—is built into the back of the alternator and includes the brush holder.

• **Windshield Washer Fluid Level Sensor**—is located in the washer reservoir tank mounted inside right front fender assembly and can be accessed by removing the right headlight and working through the headlamp opening.

• **Windshield Washer Pump**—is located in the washer reservoir tank mounted inside right front fender assembly, and may be removed without removing the reservoir by removing the right headlamp and working through the headlamp opening.

• **Windshield Wiper Motor**—is located under the utilities bay cover and is removed after removing the wiper linkage assembly.

AUDI

Circuit Breaker and Fuses

80 AND 90 SERIES

• **Power Seat**—circuit breaker is located at position 18 in the auxiliary relay panel.

• **Power Window/Sunroof**—circuit breaker is located at position 18 in the auxiliary relay panel.

100 AND 200 SERIES

• **Power Window/Sunroof**—circuit breaker is located at position 14 in the auxiliary relay panel.

V8 QUATTRO

• **Power Seat/Windows**—circuit breaker is located at position 13 in the main fuse/relay panel.

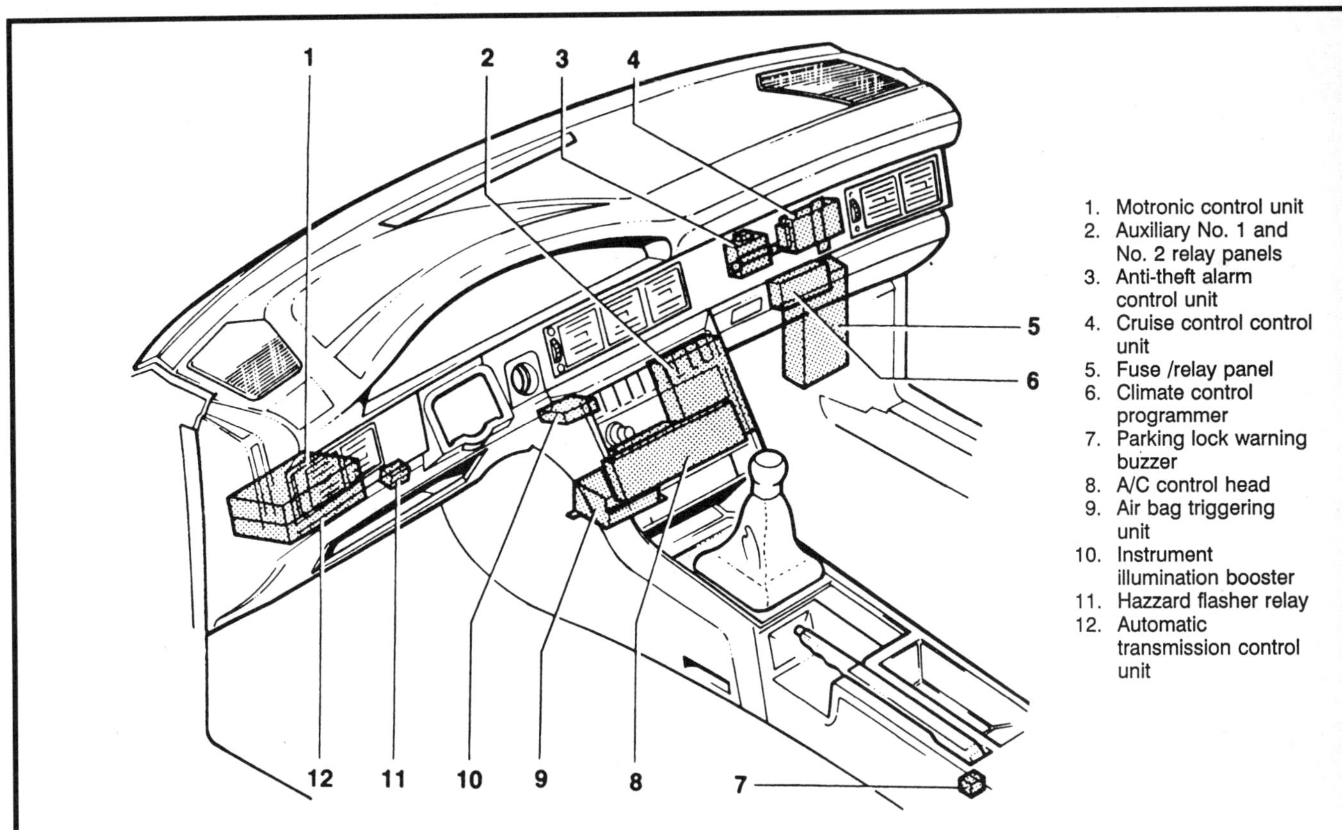

Component locations—V8 Quattro

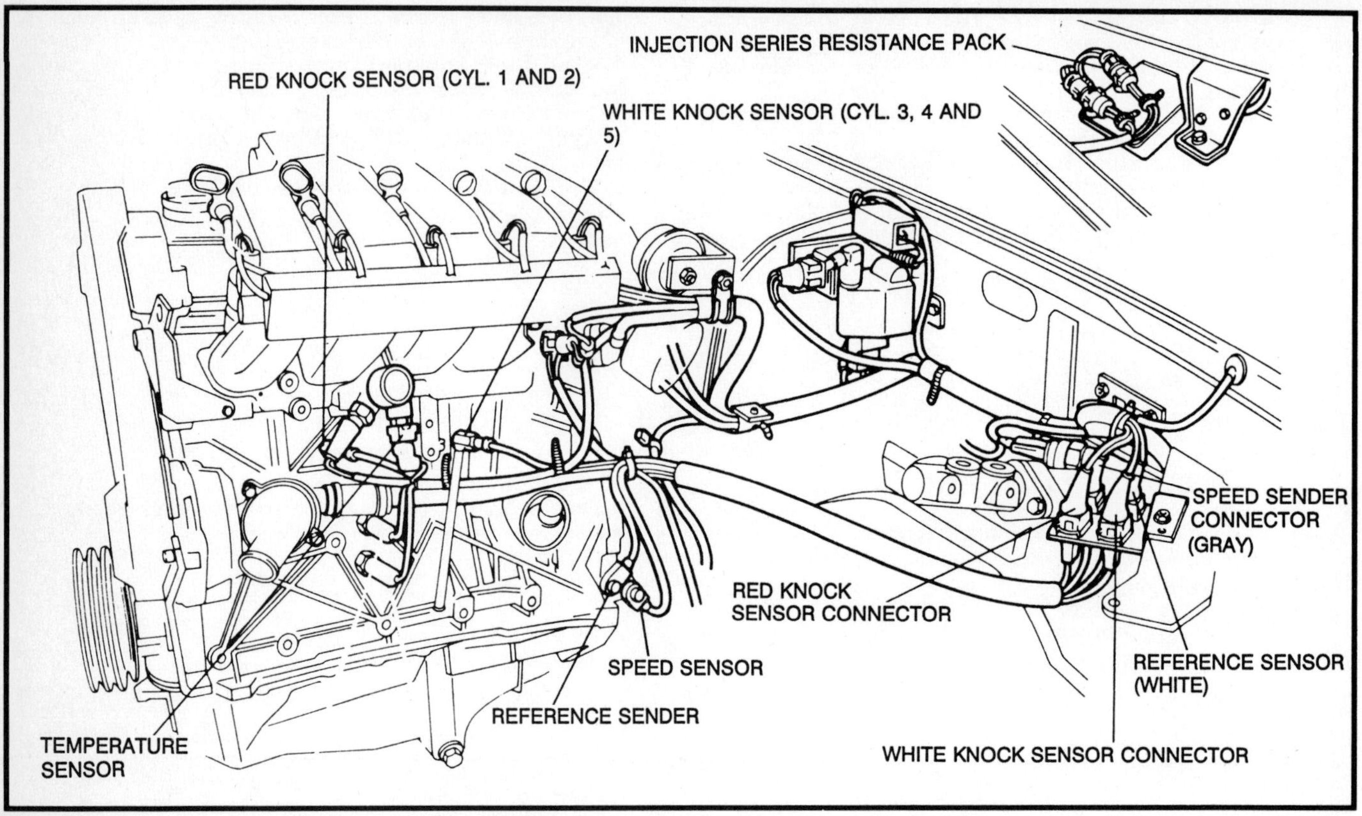

INJECTION SERIES RESISTANCE PACK
RED KNOCK SENSOR (CYL. 1 AND 2)
WHITE KNOCK SENSOR (CYL. 3, 4 AND 5)
SPEED SENDER CONNECTOR (GRAY)
RED KNOCK SENSOR CONNECTOR
SPEED SENSOR
REFERENCE SENSOR (WHITE)
REFERENCE SENDER
TEMPERATURE SENSOR
WHITE KNOCK SENSOR CONNECTOR

Component locations—80, 90 and 100, 200 Series

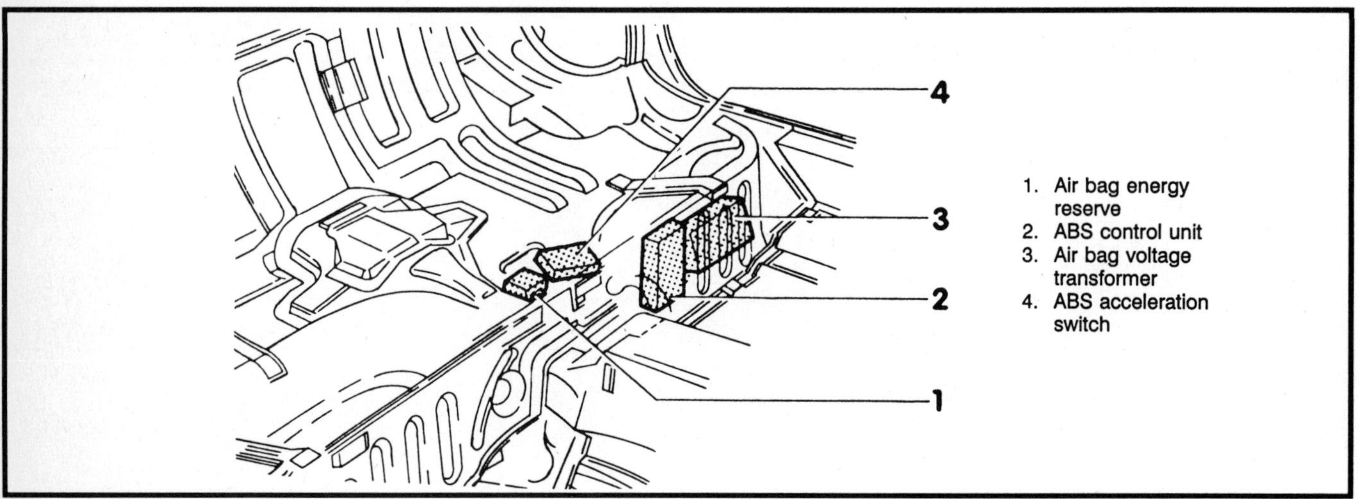

4
3
2
1
1. Air bag energy reserve
2. ABS control unit
3. Air bag voltage transformer
4. ABS acceleration switch

Component locations—V8 Quattro

Fusible Links

No major fusible links are used on these vehicles.

Relays, Sensors, Modules and Computer Locations

80 AND 90 SERIES

- **A/C Control Unit Relay (manual climate control)**—is located at position 4 in the auxiliary relay panel.
- **A/C Control Unit Relay (digital climate control)**—is located at position 4 in the auxiliary relay panel.
- **A/C High Pressure Switch (radiator fan)**—is located in condenser outlet hose.
- **A/C High Pressure Switch (compressor clutch-4 cylinder engine)**—is located in condenser inlet hose upper right area.
- **A/C High Pressure Switch (compressor clutch-5 cylinder engine)**—is located in condenser outlet hose front area.
- **A/C Low Pressure Switch**—is located right side of passenger compartment between evaporator housing and firewall. Access by removing glove compartment and fuel injection control unit.

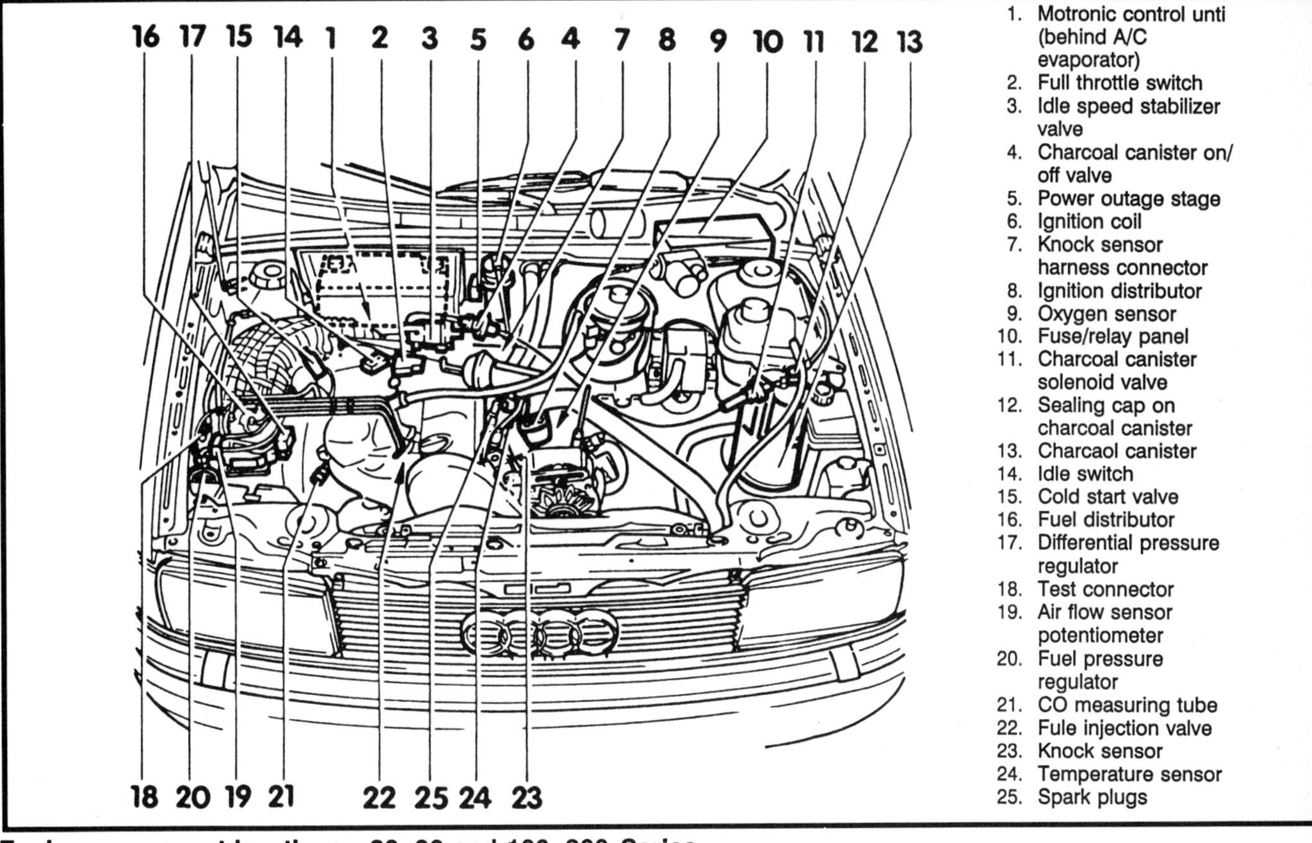

Engine component locations—80, 90 and 100, 200 Series

- **A/C Programmer (digital climate control)**—is located behind the glove compartment assembly.
- **A/C Relay (manual climate control)**—is located at position 6 in the main fuse/relay panel.
- **A/C Inside Temperature No. 1 Sensor (digital climate control)**—is located near blower motor behind glove box.
- **A/C Inside Temperature No. 2 Sensor (digital climate control)**—is located in the dome light assembly.
- **A/C Outside Temperature Sensor (digital climate control)**—is located near front grille assembly.
- **A/C Outside Temperature Switch**—is located in blower motor or fresh air fan intake plenum.
- **ABS Anti-lock Brake System Accelerator Switch**—is located beneath rear seat assembly on the left side.
- **ABS Combination Relay**—is located at position 1 in the auxiliary relay panel.
- **ABS Control Unit**—is located beneath the rear seat assembly on the left side.
- **ABS Return Flow Pump Relay**—is located in the engine compartment (larger of two relays) beside the master cylinder.
- **ABS Solenoid Relay**—is located in the engine compartment (smaller of two relays) beside the master cylinder.
- **Anti-theft Alarm Light Warning Relay**—is located at position 17 in the auxiliary relay panel.
- **Anti-theft Alarm Control Unit**—is located in the left rear luggage compartment area.
- **Anti-theft Alarm Warning Horn**—is located in the left rear luggage compartment area.
- **Air Bag Energy Reserve**—is located under the rear bench seat assembly.
- **Air Bag Ground Point**—is located behind the instrument panel.
- **Air Bag Triggering Unit**—is located behind center console assembly.
- **Air Bag Voltage Supply Connector (red single-point)**—is located under the instrument panel.
- **Air Bag Voltage Transformer**—is located under the rear bench seat assembly.
- **Altitude Sensor**—is located behind the lower right kick panel of the vehicle.
- **Automatic Transmission Relay**—is located at position 8 in the main fuse/relay panel.
- **Auxiliary Relay Panel**—is located under the dash, on the left side. Access can be gained by removing the lower dash trim panel.
- **Back-Up Light Switch/Neutral Safety (automatic transmission)**—is located to the left of the shifter assembly.
- **Back-Up Light Switch (manual transmission)**—is located in the transmission assembly.
- **Blower Motor**—is located behind glove box assembly.
- **Brake Fluid Level Switch**—is located in the brake fluid reservoir.
- **Central Lock System Motor (bi-pressure pump)**—is located behind the right side luggage compartment trim.
- **Charcoal Canister Solenoid Valve**—is located near the accelerator linkage connection on the top of the engine.
- **Coolant Low Level Switch**—is located in the coolant overflow bottle.
- **Coolant Temperature Sender**—is located in the lower portion of the thermostat housing.
- **Cruise Control Unit**—is located under instrument panel behind the glovebox assembly.
- **Daytime Driving Lights Relay**—is located at position 12 in the auxiliary relay panel.
- **Differential lock Control Unit**—is located under the rear seat.
- **Driver Heated Seat Control Unit**—is located at position 13 in the auxiliary relay panel.

• **Electronic Thermoswitch (5 cylinder)**—is located in engine coolant connection on cylinder head.

• **Emergency Flasher Relay**—is located under the dash above the brake pedal assembly to the right of the auxiliary relay panel.

• **Engine Reference Sensor**—is located at the bottom of the engine block on the flywheel side, above engine speed sensor.

• **Engine Speed Sensor**—is located at the bottom of the engine block on the flywheel side, above oil pan.

• **Fog Light Relay**—is located at position 1 in the main fuse/relay panel.

• **Front Lamp Control Unit**—is located at position 6 in the auxiliary relay panel.

• **Fuel Injection Control Unit**—is located behind the air conditioner evaporator assembly.

• **Fuel Pump Relay**—is located at position 10 in the main fuse/relay panel.

• **Gear Selector Warning Buzzer**—is located in the parking brake assembly.

• **Headlight Washer System Relay**—is located at position 4 in the main fuse/relay panel.

• **Heated Lock Control Unit**—is located in the door assembly.

• **Horn Relay**—is located at position 7 in the main fuse/relay panel.

• **Ignition Control Unit**—is located behind the lower right kick panel of the vehicle.

• **Injector Series Resistance Pack**—is located in the plenum chamber near wiper motor.

• **Instrument Panel Light Booster**—is located under the instrument panel to the right of the steering wheel.

• **Interior Light Delay Control Unit**—is located at position 6 in the auxiliary relay panel.

• **Main Fuse/Relay Panel**—is located under the hood, on the left side in the water drain tray. The fuses are protected by a cover.

• **Knock Sensor (red-cylinders 1 and 2)**—is located in

• **Knock Sensor (white-cylinders 3, 4 and 5)**—is located in the engine block assembly below cylinder 3.

• **Load Reduction Relay**—is located at position 5 in the main fuse/relay panel.

• **Lock Cylinder Heating Element**—is located in the door assembly.

• **Neutral Safety/Back-Up Light Switch (automatic)**—is located to the left of the shifter assembly.

• **Park/Neutral Shift Lock Control Unit**—is located at position 9 in the auxiliary relay panel.

• **Park/Neutral Shift Lock Solenoid**—is located to the right of the gear shift selector assembly.

• **Passenger Heated Seat Control Unit**—is located at position 14 in the auxiliary relay panel.

• **Power Seat Control Unit**—is located under the seat assembly.

• **Main Fuse And Relay Panel Ground Connection**—is a bolted connection to the chassis ground behind the left side of the instrument panel.

• **Motronic Control Unit Fuse (1989-90)**—is located at position 27 in the main fuse/relay panel.

• **Multipoint Injection Control Unit**—is located behind the A/C evaporator assembly.

• **Oil Pressure Control Unit Relay**—is located at position 6 in the auxiliary relay panel.

• **Oil Pressure Sender Unit (4 cylinder engine)**—is located on the top of the oil filter housing.

• **Oil Pressure Sender Unit (5 cylinder engine)**—is located on the lower side of the engine block.

• **Oil Pressure Switch (0.3 brown bar switch)**—is located on the bottom of the oil filter mounting bracket.

• **Oil Pressure Switch (1.8 white bar switch)**—is located on the top oil filter mounting bracket.

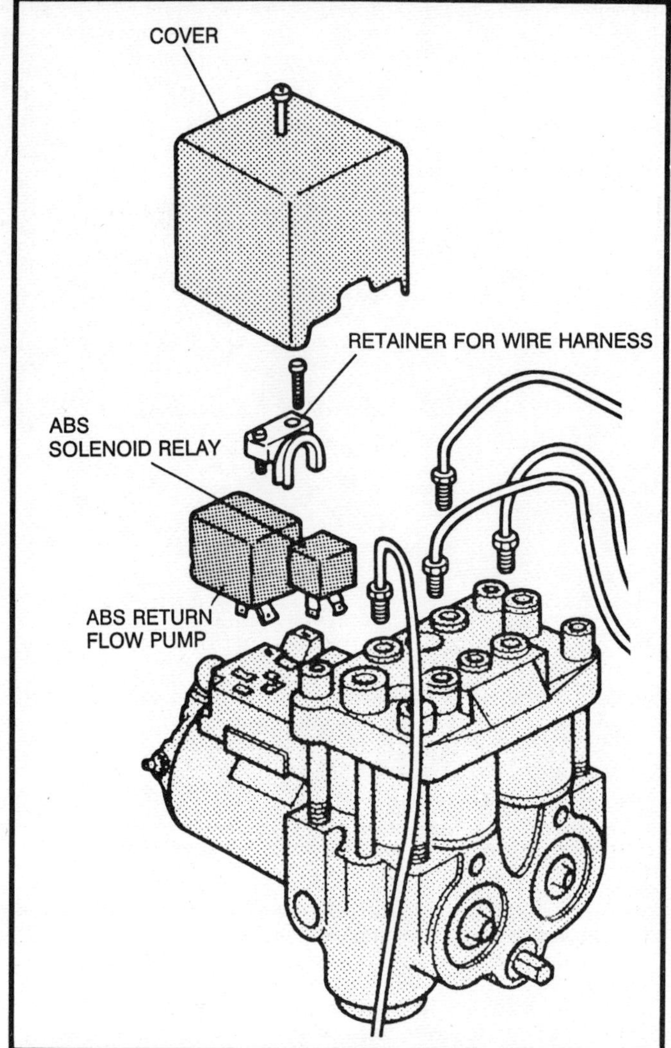

ABS hydraulic Unit—80, 90 and 100, 200 Series

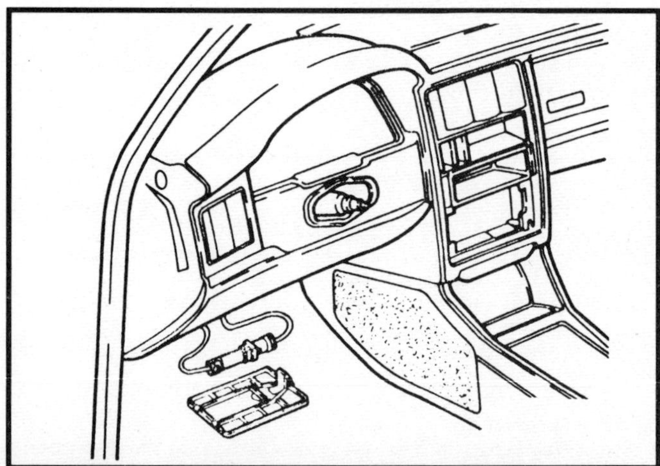

Air bag voltage supply connector—80, 90 and 100, 200 Series

1. Open
2. Radiator coolant fan relay 2nd stage
3. Radiator coolant fan after run control unit
4. Open
5. Load reduction relay
6. Open
7. Horn relay
8. Automatic transmission relay
9. Wash/wipe delay relay
10. Fuel pump relay
11. A/C relay

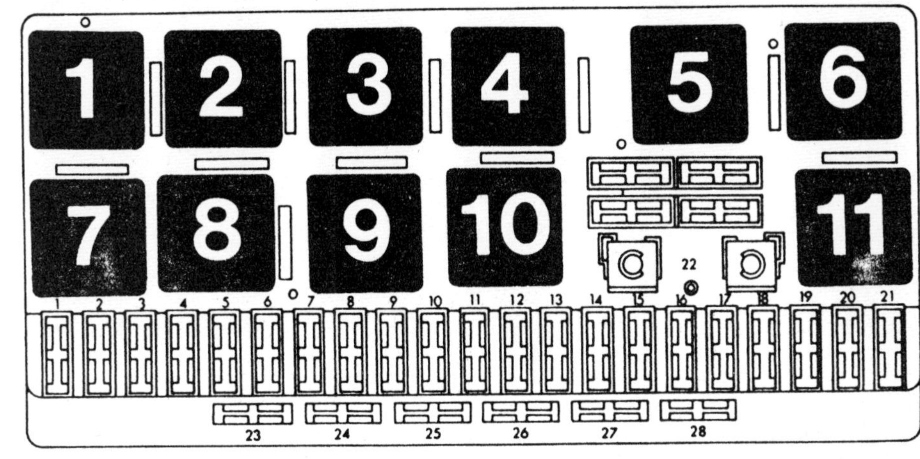

Fuse/relay panel

- **Oil Temperature Sensor (4 cylinder engine)**—is located in the side oil filter housing.
- **Oil Temperature Sensor (5 cylinder engine)**—is located on front right side of the engine assembly.
- **Power Window/Sunroof Control Unit**—is located at position 15 and 16 in the auxiliary relay panel.
- **Radiator Cooling Fan Relay (low speed)**—is located at position 11 in the main fuse/relay panel.
- **Radiator Cooling Fan Relay (high speed-manual climate control)**—is located at position 2 in the main fuse/relay panel.
- **Radiator Cooling Fan Relay (high speed-digital climate control)**—is located at position 6 in the main fuse/relay panel.
- **Radiator Cooling Fan Relay (after run control)**—is located at position 3 in the main fuse/relay panel.
- **Radiator Cooling Fan After Run Thermoswitch**—is located in the cylinder head assembly near the back of the valve cover.
- **Radiator Cooling Fan Thermoswitch**—is located at the lower end of the radiator assembly.
- **Radio Front Amplifier**—is located on the right front A pillar.
- **Radio Rear Amplifier**—is located on the left rear D pillar.
- **Rear Lamp Control Unit (Coupe Quattro)**—is located in the left rear luggage compartment area above the anti-theft alarm control unit.
- **Rear Lamp Control Unit (80 and 90 Series)**—is located in the left rear luggage compartment area.
- **Rear Window Wiper/Washer Relay (Coupe Quattro)**—is located at position 5 in the auxiliary relay panel.
- **Seat Belt Warning Control Unit**—is located at position 2 in the auxiliary relay panel.
- **Speedometer Sender**—is located near the left side of the transaxle near the driveshaft flange.
- **Temperature Sensor**—is located in the cylinder head assembly between cylinders 2 and 3.
- **Turn Signal Flasher Relay**—is located under the dash above the brake pedal assembly to the right of the auxiliary relay panel.
- **Wiper/Washer Intermittent Relay**—is located at position 9 in the main fuse/relay panel.

100 AND 200 SERIES

- **A/C Control Unit Relay**—is located at position 11 in the main fuse/relay panel.
- **A/C Control Unit Relay (digital climate control)**—is located at position 4 in the auxiliary relay panel.
- **A/C High Pressure Switch (radiator fan)**—is located in condenser outlet hose.
- **A/C Low Pressure Switch**—is located right side of passenger compartment between evaporator housing and firewall. Access by removing glove compartment and fuel injection control unit.
- **A/C Programmer (digital climate control)**—is located behind the glove compartment assembly.
- **A/C Relay (manual climate control)**—is located at position 6 in the main fuse/relay panel.
- **A/C Inside Temperature No. 1 Sensor (digital climate control)**—is located near blower motor behind glove box.
- **A/C Inside Temperature No. 2 Sensor (digital climate control)**—is located in the dome light assembly.
- **A/C Outside Temperature Sensor (digital climate control)**—is located near front grille assembly.
- **A/C Outside Temperature Switch**—is located in blower motor or fresh air fan intake plenum.

- **ABS Anti-lock Brake System Accelerator Switch**—is located beneath rear seat assembly on the left side.
- **ABS Combination Relay**—is located at position 8 in the auxiliary relay panel.
- **ABS Control Unit**—is located beneath the rear seat assembly on the left side.
- **ABS Return Flow Pump Relay**—is located in the engine compartment (larger of two relays) beside the master cylinder.
- **ABS Solenoid Relay**—is located in the engine compartment (smaller of two relays) beside the master cylinder.
- **Anti-lock Brakes**—see ABS section.
- **Anti-theft Relay**—is located at position 8 in the main fuse/relay panel.
- **Anti-theft Alarm Control Unit**—is located behind the glove box on the right lower dash panel.
- **Anti-theft Alarm Warning Horn**—is located in the left rear luggage compartment area.

- **Air Bag Energy Reserve**—is located under the rear bench seat assembly.
- **Air Bag Ground Point**—is located behind the instrument panel.
- **Air Bag Triggering Unit**—is located behind center console assembly.
- **Air Bag Voltage Supply Connector (red single-point)**—is located under the instrument panel.
- **Air Bag Voltage Transformer**—is located under the rear bench seat assembly.

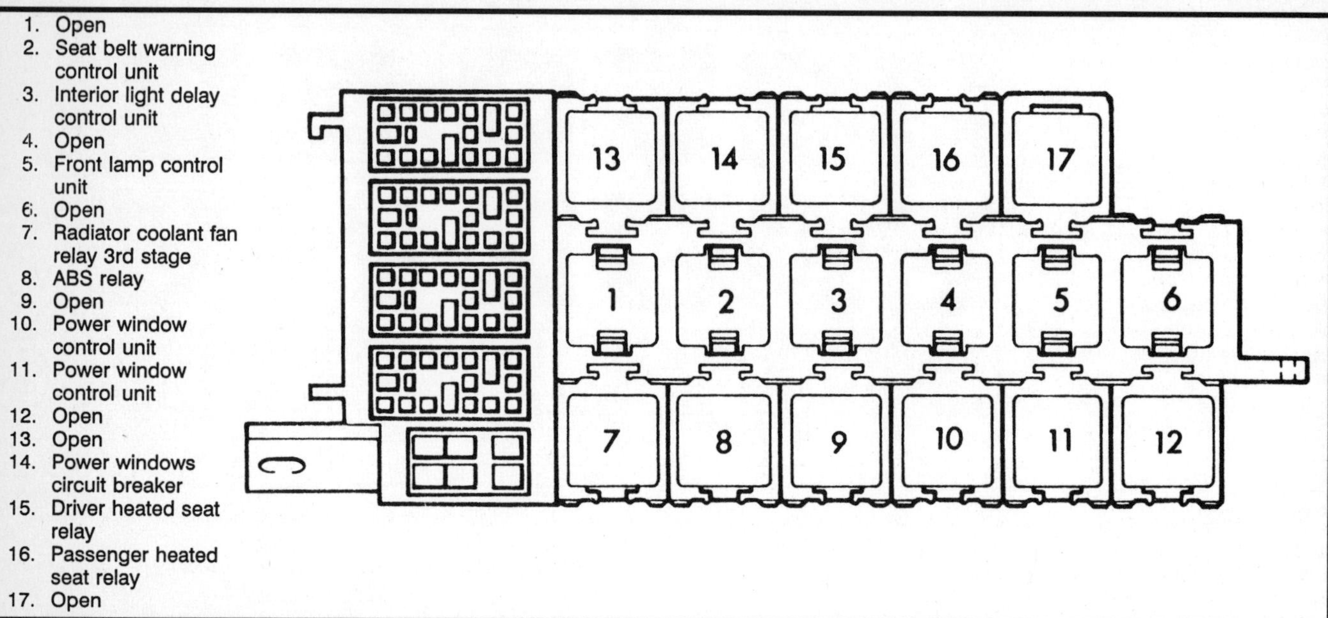

Auxiliary relay panel

- **Altitude Sensor (100 Series)**—is located behind the lower left kick panel of the vehicle.
- **Automatic Transmission Shift Lock/Warning Buzzer**—is located in the front area of emergency brake assembly.
- **Auxiliary Relay Panel**—is located under the dash, on the left side. Access can be gained by removing the lower dash trim panel.
- **Back-Up Light Switch/Neutral Safety (automatic transmission)**—is located to the left of the shifter assembly.
- **Back-Up Light Switch (manual transmission)**—is located in the transmission assembly.
- **Blower Motor**—is located behind glove box assembly.
- **Brake Fluid Level Switch**—is located in the brake fluid reservoir.
- **Central Lock System Motor (bi-pressure pump)**—is located behind the right side luggage compartment trim.
- **Charcoal Canister Solenoid Valve**—is located near the accelerator linkage connection on the top of the engine.
- **Coolant Low Level Switch**—is located in the coolant overflow bottle.
- **Coolant Temperature Sender**—is located in the lower portion of the thermostat housing.
- **Cruise Control Unit**—is located under instrument panel behind the glovebox assembly.
- **Differential lock Control Unit**—is located driveshaft tunnel under the rear seat.
- **Driver Heated Seat Control Unit**—is located at position 15 in the auxiliary relay panel.
- **Emergency Flasher Relay**—is located under the center area of the dash.
- **Engine Control Unit (200 Series)**—is located behind the right side kick panel area.
- **Engine Reference Sensor**—is located at the bottom of the engine block on the flywheel side, above engine speed sensor.
- **Engine Speed Sensor**—is located at the bottom of the engine block on the flywheel side, above oil pan.
- **Fog Light Relay**—is located at position 1 in the main fuse/relay panel.
- **Front Lamp Control Unit**—is located at position 5 in the auxiliary relay panel.
- **Fuel Injection Control Unit (100 Series)**—is located behind the right side kick panel area.
- **Fuel Deceleration/Idle Stabilizer Control Unit (200 Series)**—is located behind the left lower kick panel.
- **Fuel Pump Relay**—is located at position 10 in the main fuse/relay panel.
- **Gear Selector Warning Buzzer**—is located in the parking brake assembly.
- **Headlight Washer System Relay**—is located at position 4 in the main fuse/relay panel.
- **Heated Lock Control Unit**—is located in the door assembly.
- **Horn Relay**—is located at position 7 in the main fuse/relay panel.
- **Idle Stabilizer/Fuel Deceleration Control Unit (200 Series)**—is located behind the left lower kick panel.
- **Ignition Control Unit (100 Series)**—is located behind the lower left kick panel of the vehicle.
- **Injector Series Resistance Pack**—is located in the plenum chamber near wiper motor.
- **Instrument Panel Light Booster**—is located under the instrument panel to the right of the steering wheel.
- **Interior Light Delay Control Unit**—is located at position 3 in the auxiliary relay panel.
- **Intensive Washer Relay (200 Series)**—is located at position 9 in the auxiliary relay panel.
- **Main Fuse/Relay Panel**—is located under the hood, on the left side in the water drain tray. The fuses are protected by a cover.
- **Load Reduction Relay**—is located at position 5 in the main fuse/relay panel.
- **Lock Cylinder Heating Element**—is located in the door assembly.
- **Neutral Safety/Back-Up Light Switch (automatic)**—is located to the left of the shifter assembly.
- **Park/Neutral Shift Lock Solenoid**—is located to the right of the gear shift selector assembly.
- **Passenger Heated Seat Control Unit**—is located at position 16 in the auxiliary relay panel.
- **Power Seat Control Unit**—is located under the seat assembly.
- **Power Window/Sunroof Control Unit**—is located at position 10 in the auxiliary relay panel.
- **Power Window/Sunroof Control Unit**—is located at position 11 in the auxiliary relay panel.

• **Main Fuse And Relay Panel Ground Connection**—is a bolted connection to the chassis ground behind the left side of the instrument panel.

• **Oil Pressure Control Unit Relay**—is located at position 6 in the auxiliary relay panel.

• **Radiator Cooling Fan Relay (2nd stage)**—is located at position 2 in the main fuse/relay panel.

• **Radiator Cooling Fan Relay (200 Series-3rd stage)**—is located at position 7 in the auxiliary relay panel.

• **Radiator Cooling Fan Relay (100 Series-after run control)**—is located at position 3 in the main fuse/relay panel.

• **Radiator Cooling Fan Relay (200 Series)**—is located at position 3 in the main fuse/relay panel.

• **Radiator Cooling Fan Relay (200 Series-after run control)**—is located behind the lower left kick panel area.

• **Radiator Cooling Fan Thermoswitch**—is located at the lower end of the radiator assembly.

• **Radio Front Amplifier**—is located on the right front A pillar.

• **Radio Rear Amplifier**—is located on the left rear D pillar.

• **Rear Window Wiper/Washer Relay**—is located at position 12 in the auxiliary relay panel.

• **Seat Belt Warning Control Unit**—is located at position 2 in the auxiliary relay panel.

• **Speedometer Sender**—is located near the left side of the transaxle near the driveshaft flange.

• **Sunroof/Power Window Control Unit**—is located at position 10 in the auxiliary relay panel.

• **Sunroof/Power Window Control Unit**—is located at position 11 in the auxiliary relay panel.

• **Turbocharger Secondary Coolant Pump (200 Series)**—is located behind the lower left kick panel area.

• **Turn Signal Flasher Relay**—is located under the center area of dash.

• **Wiper/Washer Intermittent Relay**—is located at position 9 in the main fuse/relay panel.

V8 QUATTRO

• **A/C Control Unit Relay**—is located at position 10 in the auxiliary No. 1 relay panel.

• **A/C Programmer**—is located behind the glove compartment assembly.

• **ABS Anti-lock Brake System Accelerator Switch**—is located beneath rear seat assembly on the left side.

• **ABS Combination Relay**—is located at position 2 in the auxiliary No. 1 relay panel.

• **ABS Control Unit**—is located beneath the rear seat assembly on the left side.

• **ABS Return Flow Pump Relay**—is located in the engine compartment (larger of two relays) beside the master cylinder.

• **ABS Solenoid Relay**—is located in the engine compartment (smaller of two relays) beside the master cylinder.

• **Anti-theft Alarm Light Warning Relay**—is located at position 18 in the auxiliary No. 2 relay panel.

• **Anti-theft Alarm Control Unit**—is located behind the glove box on the right lower dash panel.

• **Anti-theft Alarm Warning Horn**—is located in the left rear luggage compartment area.

• **Air Bag Energy Reserve**—is located under the rear bench seat assembly.

• **Air Bag Ground Point**—is located behind the instrument panel.

• **Air Bag Triggering Unit**—is located behind center console assembly.

• **Air Bag Voltage Supply Connector (red single-point)**—is located under the instrument panel.

• **Air Bag Voltage Transformer**—is located under the rear bench seat assembly.

• **Automatic Transmission Relay**—is located at position 8 in the main fuse/relay panel.

• **Automatic Transmission Control Unit**—is located under the dash to the far left area.

• **Auxiliary No.1 Relay Panel**—is located behind the right side trim in the front passenger footwell attached to main fuse/relay panel. For access, unscrew both knurled screws, remove the floor mat and detach side trim panel.

• **Auxiliary No.2 Relay Panel**—is located behind the right side trim in the front passenger footwell attached to main fuse/relay panel. For access, unscrew both knurled screws, remove the floor mat and detach side trim panel.

• **Back-Up Light Switch/Neutral Safety (automatic transmission)**—is located to the left of the shifter assembly.

• **Back-Up Light Relay**—is located in position 14 in the auxiliary No. 2 relay panel.

• **Blower Motor**—is located behind glove box assembly.

• **Brake Fluid Level Switch**—is located in the brake fluid reservoir.

• **Catalytic Converter Control Unit**—is located in position 9 in the auxiliary No. 1 relay panel.

• **Coolant Low Level Switch**—is located in the coolant overflow bottle.

• **Cruise Control Unit**—is located under instrument panel behind the glovebox assembly.

• **Daytime Driving Light Relay (Canada)**—is located at position 20 in the auxiliary No. 2 relay panel.

• **Driver Heated Seat Control Unit**—is located at position 17 in the auxiliary No. 2 relay panel.

• **Emergency Flasher Relay**—is located under the dash to the left of the steering wheel.

• **Fog Light Relay**—is located at position 1 in the main fuse/relay panel.

• **Front Lamp Control Unit**—is located at position 7 in the auxiliary No. 1 relay panel.

• **Fuel Pump Relay**—is located at position 10 in the main fuse/relay panel.

• **Gear Selector Warning Buzzer**—is located in the parking brake assembly.

• **Heated Lock Control Unit**—is located in the door assembly.

• **Horn Relay**—is located at position 7 in the main fuse/relay panel.

• **Instrument Panel Light Booster**—is located under the instrument panel to the right of the steering wheel.

• **Intensive Washer Relay**—is located at position 13 in the auxiliary No. 2 relay panel.

• **Main Fuse/Relay Panel**—is located behind the right side trim in the front passenger footwell. For access, unscrew both knurled screws, remove the floor mat and detach side trim panel.

• **Memory Seat Control**—is located under seat assembly.

• **Motronic Control Unit**—is located under the dash in the lower left area.

• **Load Reduction Relay**—is located at position 5 in the main fuse/relay panel.

• **Lock Cylinder Heating Element**—is located in the door assembly.

• **Neutral Safety/Back-Up Light Switch (automatic transmission)**—is located to the left of the shifter assembly.

• **Park Lock Warning Buzzer**—is located in the parking brake assembly.

• **Passenger Heated Seat Control Unit**—is located at position 16 in the auxiliary No. 2 relay panel.

• **Power Seat Control Unit**—is located under the seat assembly.

• **Power Window/Sunroof Control Unit**—is located at position 1 and 6 in the auxiliary No. 1 relay panel.

• **Main Fuse And Relay Panel Ground Connection**—is a bolted connection to the chassis ground behind the left side of the instrument panel.

• **Radiator Cooling Fan Relay (low speed)**—is located at position 2 in the main fuse/relay panel.
• **Radiator Cooling Fan Relay (2nd stage)**—is located at position 6 in the mian fuse/relay panel.
• **Radiator Cooling Fan Relay (3rd stage)**—is located at position 12 in the mian fuse/relay panel.
• **Radio Front Amplifier**—is located on the right front A pillar.
• **Radio Rear Amplifier**—is located on the left rear D pillar.
• **Radio Speaker Relay**—is located at position 19 in the auxiliary No. 2 relay panel.
• **Rear Heated Seat Control Unit (right)**—is located at position 11 in the auxiliary No. 2 relay panel.
• **Rear Heated Seat Control Unit (left)**—is located at position 12 in the auxiliary No. 2 relay panel.
• **Shift lock Control Unit**—is located at position 15 in the auxiliary No. 2 relay panel.
• **Turn Signal Flasher Relay**—is located under the dash to the left of the steering wheel.
• **Wiper/Washer Intermittent Relay**—is located at position 9 in the main fuse/relay panel.

BMW

Circuit Breakers and Fuses

318 AND 325 SERIES

There is a power window circuit breaker located on the center console, near the gear shift lever.

635 SERIES

There is a power window/sunroof circuit breaker located on the left hand side of the dash panel.

Fusible Links

318 AND 325 SERIES

Fusible link A—is located on the right hand rear corner of the engine compartment, at the battery.

525i AND 535i SERIES

Fusible link 80A—is located on the right hand side of the engine compartment.
Fusible link 50A—is located below the right hand side of the rear seat.

735 AND 750 SERIES

Fusible links A and B—are located below the right hand side of the seat, to the right of the battery.
Fusible links 50A and 80A—are located below the right hand side of the seat, near the B+ terminal on the battery.
Fusible link 10A is—located in the right hand corner of the luggage compartment.

850 SERIES

Fusible links 50A and 50A—are located on the battery harness.
Fusible link 80A—is located in the rear power distribution box, in the left hand corner of the luggage compartment.

Relays, Sensors, Modules and Computer Locations

318, 325 AND M3 SERIES

• **A/C Compressor Clutch Diode**—is located in the lower right hand front side of the engine on the air conditioner compressor.
• **A/C Evaporative Temperature Regulator**—is located on the left hand side of the evaporator housing.
• **A/C Evaporative Temperature Sensor**—is located on the left hand side of the evaporator housing.
• **A/C In-Line Fuse**—is located on the left hand rear side of the evaporator housing.
• **A/C Low Pressure Cut-Out Switch**—is located on the receiver dryer, behind the right hand headlight.
• **Air Bag**—see SRS supplemental restraint system.
• **ABS Clutch Switch**—is located behind the left hand side of the dash, on the clutch pedal support.
• **ABS Electronic Control Unit**—is located behind the left hand side of the dash panel, above the hood release handle.
• **ABS Hydraulic Unit**—is located in the left hand front corner of the engine compartment.
• **ABS Neutral Input Relay**—is located behind the left hand side of the dash panel, on the accessory connector bracket.
• **Active Check Control Unit**—is located above the rear view mirror.
• **Air Flow Meter**—is located in the left hand front side of the engine compartment, behind air cleaner.
• **Amplifier**—is located in the left hand front corner of the trunk compartment.
• **Auxiliary Fan Normal Speed Blower Resistor**—is located in the front of the radiator on the right hand side of the auxiliary fan.
• **Auxiliary Fuse**—is located in the left hand rear of the engine compartment, above the brake fluid reservoir.
• **Back-Up Light Switch**—is located on the top right hand side of the transmission.
• **Battery Junction Block**—is located in the right hand rear corner of the engine compartment, on the battery.
• **Blower Motor**—is located inside the fresh air intake cowl.
• **Blower Resistors**—is located on the blower motor.
• **Board Computer Horn**—is located behind the left hand corner of the front bumper.
• **Brake Fluid Level Switch**—is located on the brake fluid reservoir.
• **Brake Switch**—is located behind the left hand side of the dash, on the brake pedal support.
• **Brake Wear Sensors**—is located on the left hand front and right hand rear brake calipers.
• **Central Locking Control Unit**-inside the left hand kick panel, below left hand front speaker.
• **Chime Module**-is mounted on the left hand dash hush panel.
• **Clutch Switch**—is located behind the left hand side of the dash, on the clutch pedal support.
• **Convertible Top Position Switch**—is located on the left hand side of the soft top stowage compartment.
• **Coolant Level Switch**—is located in the left hand front wheel well, in the coolant reservoir.

• **Coolant Temperature Sender**—is located on the top of the engine, on top of the thermostat housing.

• **Coolant Temperature Sensor**—is located on the top of the engine, on top of the thermostat housing.

• **Cruise Control Actuator**—left hand front of the engine compartment.

• **Cruise Control Unit**—is located behind the right hand side of the dash, above the glove box.

• **Cylinder Identification Sensor**—is located on top right hand side of the engine, near the distributor.

• **Deceleration Sensor**—is located behind the left hand front shock tower.

• **Diagnostic Connector**—is located on the top left hand front side of the engine.

• **Dual Temperature Switch**—is located on the top right hand side of the radiator.

• **Engine Speed Sensor**—is located on the lower right hand front of the engine.

• **Evaporative Purge Valve**—is located below the left hand side of the throttle body.

• **Filter Capacitor**—is located on the lower left hand front of the engine, on the alternator.

• **Flasher**—is located on the upper part of the steering column.

• **Fog Light Relay**—is located in the power distribution box.

• **Fresh/Recirculating Air Flap Door Motors**—is located behind the air conditioner face plate, on either side of the evaporator housing.

• **Fresh/Recirculating Air Relays**—is located behind the air conditioner face plate.

• **Fuel Pump Relay**—is located on the front of the left hand front shock tower, on the bracket.

• **Tank Fuel Sender (left)**—is located below the left hand side of the rear seat.

F44• **Gas Filler Lock Motor**—is located on the right hand side of the trunk, behind the right hand wheel well.

• **High Beam Relay**—is located in the power distribution box.

• **High Pressure Cut-Out Switch**—is located on the receiver dryer, located behind the right hand headlight.

• **High Speed Relay**—is located in the power distribution box.

• **Horns**—are located behind the left hand corner of the front bumper.

• **Horn Relay**—is located in the power distribution box.

• **Hot Water Cut-Off Switch**—is located behind the center of the dash panel, near the rotary temperature control.

• **Idle Speed Actuator**—is located on the top left hand side of the engine.

• **Interior Light Timer Control**—is located inside the left hand kick panel, below the left hand front speaker.

• **Low Beam Check Relay**—is located in the power distribution box.

• **Low Beam Relay**—is located in the power distribution box.

• **Main Fuel Pump**—is located below the right hand side of the rear seat, in the fuel tank.

• **Main Relay**—is located on the front of the left hand shock tower, on the bracket.

• **Motronic Control Unit**—is located behind the right hand side of the dash, above the glove box.

• **Normal Speed Relay**—is located in the power distribution box.

• **Oil Level Sensor**—is located on the top left hand side of the oil pan.

• **Oil Pressure Switch**—is located on the lower right hand front of the engine, below oil filter.

• **On-Board Computer Module**—is located in the center of the dash panel, on the right hand side of the digital radio.

• **On-Board Computer Relay Box**—is located behind the left hand side of the dash, near the ABS electronic control unit.

• **Outside Temperature Sensor**—is located behind the left hand corner of the front bumper, on the splash guard.

• **Outside Temperature Sensor (325iX)**—is located inside the air intake, near the left hand fog light.

• **Over Voltage Protection Relay**—is located behind the left hand side of the dash panel, near the ABS electronic control unit.

• **Oxygen Sensor**—is located on the lower right hand rear of the engine compartment, on the exhaust manifold.

• **Oxygen Sensor Heater Relay**—is located on the front of the left hand front shock tower, on the bracket.

• **Power Antenna**—is located on the left hand side of the trunk, behind the left hand wheel well.

• **Power Distribution Box**—is located on the left hand rear corner of the engine compartment.

• **Power Window Circuit Breaker**—is located on the center console, near the gear shift lever.

• **Pulse Wheels**—is located on the respective wheels in the brake housing.

• **Rear Lights Check Relay**—is located in the front of the rear quarter panel behind the trim panel.

• **Rear Window Blower**—is located behind the center of the rear seat back.

• **Rear Window Blower Relay**—is located behind the center of the rear seat back, on the rear window.

• **Seatbelt Warning Timer**—is located behind the left hand side of the dash, on the electrical bracket.

• **Speed Detectors**—are located on the wheels in the brake housing.

• **Speedometer Sender**—is located on the rear of the differential.

• **Supplemental Restraint System (SRS) Connector 240**—is located behind the left hand side of the dash panel, on the right hand side of the accessory connector.

• **Start Relay**—is located behind the left hand side of the dash panel. on the accessory connector bracket.

• **Throttle Switch**—is located below the left hand side of the throttle body.

• **Un-Loader Speed Relay**—is located in the power distribution box.

• **Unlock Inhibit Switch**—in the top rear of the left hand door.

• **Water Shut-Off Solenoid**—is located on the left hand side of the evaporator housing.

• **Wiper Control Unit**—is located in the power distribution box.

• **Wiper Motor**—is located inside the left hand side of the fresh air intake cowl.

525i, 535i AND M5 SERIES

• **A/C Evaporator Temperature Sensor**—is located behind the left hand side of the dash, on the lower left hand side of the IHKR plenum.

• **A/C Integrated Climate Regulation Control Unit (IHKR)**—is located behind the center of the dash panel, ahead of the IHKR plenum.

• **A/C Low Pressure Switch**—is located on the right hand front side of the engine compartment, below the washer reservoir.

• **A/C Relay**—is located on the left hand side of the engine compartment, in the auxiliary relay box.

• **Air Bag**—see SRS supplemental restraint system.

• **ABS Electronic Control Unit**—is located in the E-Box, behind the right hand front shock tower.

• **ABS Hydraulic Unit**—is located in the left hand center of the engine compartment, near the shock tower.

F44• **Air Circulating Flap Motor**—is located behind the left hand side of the dash panel, on the left hand side of the IHKR plenum.
• **Air Flow Meter (M20 engine)**—is located on the left hand side of the engine.
• **Air Flow Meter (M30 engine)**—is located on the top center of the engine, ahead of the oil fill cap.
• **Antenna Amplifier**—is located in the left hand C pillar.
• **Audible Turn Signal Relay**—is located below the steering column.
• **Auxiliary Relay Box**—is located on the left hand side of the engine compartment, ahead of the shock tower.
• **Back-Up Switch**—is located on the top right hand side of the transmission.
• **Battery (M20 engine)**—is located in the right hand front of the engine compartment.
• **Battery (M30 engine)**—is located below the right hand rear seat.
• **Battery Switch**—is located under the right hand side of the rear seat, near the battery.
• **Blower Motor**—is located behind the center of the cowl.
• **Blower Relay**—is located in the left hand rear side of the engine compartment, in the front power distribution box.
• **Brake Fluid Level Switch**—is located on the top of the brake reservoir.
• **Charging Plug**—is located in the left hand side of the glove box.
• **Check Control Module**—is located in the left hand rear side of the engine compartment, in the front power distribution box.
• **Chime Module**—is located behind the left hand side of the dash panel, mounted in the hush panel.
• **Compressor Control Unit**—is located in the left hand kick panel.
• **Coolant Level Switch**—is located on the top of the coolant reservoir.
• **Coolant Temperature Sender**—is located on the coolant inlet, near the valve cover.
• **Coolant Temperature Sensor**—is located on the coolant inlet, near the valve cover.
• **Crash Control Unit**—is located in the left hand rear of the engine compartment, in the front power distribution box.
• **Cruise Control Actuator (Tempomat)**—is located in the left center of the engine compartment, ahead of the shock tower.
• **Cruise Control Module (Tempomat)**—is located in the E-Box, behind the right hand front shock tower.
• **Cylinder Identification Sensor**—is located on the front of the engine, near the distributor.
• **Defogger Control Unit (Canada)**—is located behind the center of the dash panel, on the right side of the IHKR plenum.
• **Defogger Coupler**—is located in the right hand C pillar.
• **Defroster Flap Motor**—is located behind the left hand side of the dash panel, on the left hand side of the IHKR plenum.
• **Diagnostic Connector**—is located in the left hand rear of the engine compartment, on the right hand side shock tower.
• **Diode**—is located behind the center of the dash panel.
• **Door Lock Heater**—is located in the door, at the key lock assembly.
• **Driver's Seat Heater**—is located in the driver's seat.
• **Driver's Seatback Heater**—is located in the back of the driver's seat.
• **E-Box Fan**—is located in the E-Box, below modules.
• **E-Box**—is located on the right hand side of the engine, behind the right hand front shock tower.
• **Electric Power Protection Relay**—is located below the left hand side of the rear seat, on the rear power distribution box.
• **Electro-Hydraulic Converter (Servotronic)**—is located on the lower left hand front side of the engine compartment, behind the left hand front wheel.
• **Electronic Transmission Control Unit**—is located inside the right hand kick panel.
• **Engine Speed/Reference Point Sensor**—is located on the front of the engine, below the distributor.
• **Final Stage Unit**—is located behind the left hand side of the right hand footwell, ahead of the IHKR plenum.
• **Footwell Flap Motor (left)**—is located behind the left hand side of the dash panel, on the left hand side of the IHKR plenum.
• **Footwell Flap Motor (right)**—is located behind the right hand side of the dash panel, on the right hand side of the IHKR plenum.
• **Fresh Air Flap Motor**—is located behind the left hand side of the dash panel, on the left hand side of the IHKR plenum.
• **Front Brake Pad Sensor (left)**—is located behind the left hand front wheel, on the caliper.
• **Front Brake Pad Sensor (right)**—is located behind the right hand front wheel, on the caliper.
• **Front Crash Sensor (left)**—is located in front of the left hand shock tower.
• **Front Crash Sensor (right)**—is located in front of the right hand shock tower.
• **Front Power Distribution Box**—is located in the left hand rear of the engine compartment.
• **Front Speed Sensor (left)**—is located behind the left hand front wheel.
• **Front Speed Sensor (right)**—is located behind the right hand front wheel.
• **Fuel Air Valve (M20 engine)**—is located on the left hand rear of the engine.
• **Fuel Air Valve (M30 engine)**—is located on the left hand side of the engine, on the right side of the oil filter.
• **Fuel Pump Relay**—is located in the E-Box, behind the right hand front shock tower.
• **Fuel Pump**—is located below the luggage compartment, on the right hand side of the spare tire.
• **Fuel Tank Sensor**—is located below the luggage compartment, through the right hand access panel, on the right hand spare tire.
• **Gas Filler Motor**—is located in the luggage compartment, behind the right wheel well.
• **General Module**—is located below the left hand side of the rear seat in the rear power distribution box.
• **Hazard Flasher Relay**—is located in the left hand rear side of the engine compartment, in the front power distribution box.
• **Heat Exchanger Temperature Sensor (left)**—is located behind the left hand side of the dash, in the left side of the IHKR plenum.
• **Heat Exchanger Temperature Sensor (right)**—is located behind the right hand side of the dash, in the right side of the IHKR plenum.
• **Hifi Amplifier**—is located in left hand side of the luggage compartment, on the brace.
• **High Pressure Switch**—is located on the right hand front side of the engine compartment, below the washer reservoir.
• **High Speed Relay**—is located on the left hand side of the engine compartment, in the auxiliary relay box.
• **Horn Relay**—is located in the left hand rear side of the engine compartment, in the front power distribution box.
• **Idle Speed Actuator**—is located on the center rear portion of the throttle body.
• **Intensive Washer Pump**—is located on the right hand front of the engine compartment, on the washer fluid reservoir.
• **Intermediate Pressure Switch**—is located on the right hand front side of the engine compartment, below the washer reservoir.
• **Inertia Switch**—is located below the center of the rear seat, on the right hand side of the rear power distribution box.

- **Jumper Plug**—is located in the left hand rear of the engine compartment, in the front power distribution box.
- **Junction Posts For Front Power Distribution Box**—is located behind the left hand side of the dash, under the carpet. Also there are 2 more located in the left hand rear side of the engine compartment, in front of the power distribution box.
- **Lamp Control Module**—is located in the left hand rear side of the engine compartment, in the front power distribution box.
- **Main Relay**—is located in the E-Box, behind the right hand front shock tower.
- **Mixing Flap Motor (right)**—is located behind the center of the dash panel, on the right side of the radio.
- **Motronic Control Unit (DME)**—is located in the E-Box, behind the right hand front shock tower.
- **Normal Speed Relay**—is located on the left hand side of the engine compartment, in the auxiliary relay box.
- **Oil Level Sensor**—is located on the bottom of the oil pan.
- **Oil Pressure Switch (M20 engine)**—is located on the lower left hand front of the engine.
- **Oil Pressure Switch (M30 engine)**—is located on the top rear of the engine, on the rear on the cylinder head.
- **On-Board Computer Anti-theft Horn**—is located behind the center of the cowl.
- **On-Board Computer Horn Relay**—is located below the left hand side of the rear seat, on the rear power distribution box.
- **On-Board Computer Temperature Sensor**—is located under the left hand side of the front bumper.
- **On-Board Computer**—is located behind the center of the dash panel, on the right side of the radio.
- **Outside Temperature Sensor**—is located behind the center cowl, on the right hand side of the blower motor.
- **Oxygen Sensor (M20 Engine)**—is located on the lower right hand side of the engine compartment.
- **Oxygen Sensor (M30 Engine)**—is located in the top of the catalyst, near the transmission.
- **Oxygen Sensor Relay**—is located in the E-Box, behind the right hand front shock tower.
- **Passenger's Seat Heater**—is located in the passenger's seat.
- **Passenger's Seatback Heater**—is located in the back of the passenger's seat.
- **Rear Defogger Relay**—is located below the left hand side of the rear seat, on the rear power distribution box.
- **Rear Speed Sensor (left)**—is located behind the left hand rear wheel, on the axle.
- **Rear Speed Sensor (right)**—is located behind the right hand rear wheel, on the axle.
- **Rear Power Distribution Box**—is located below the left hand side of the rear seat.
- **Rear Vent Flap Switch**—is located in the rear of the console, on the rear vent flap.
- **Relay Module**—is located below the left hand side of the rear seat in the rear power distribution box.
- **Safety Switch**—is located on the left hand side of the engine compartment, near the left front crash sensor.
- **Servotronic Control Unit**—is located in the left hand kick panel.
- **Starter Relay**—is located in the left hand rear side of the engine compartment, in the front power distribution box.
- **Sunroof Motor**—is located in the center of the windshield header, near the rear view mirror.
- **Supplemental Restraint System (SRS) Diagnostic Module**—is located behind the left hand side of the dash panel, on the left hand side of the steering column.
- **SRS Driver's Air Bag Generator**—is located inside the steering wheel.
- **SRS Front Crash Sensor (left)**—is located in front of the left hand shock tower.
- **SRS Front Crash Sensor (right)**—is located in front of the right hand shock tower.
- **Temperature Distribution Potentiometer**—is located behind the center of the dash, above radio.
- **Temperature Switch-in the E-Box, behind the right hand front shock tower.**
- **Temperature Switch**—is located on the right hand top side of the radiator.
- **Throttle Switch (M20 engine)**—is located on the left hand rear side of the engine.
- **Throttle Switch (M30 engine)**—is located on the throttle body.
- **Transmission Kickdown Switch**—is located behind the left hand side of the dash panel, underneath the acceleration pedal.
- **UnLoader Relay KL-15**—is located in the left hand rear side of the engine compartment, in the front power distribution box.
- **UnLoader Relay KLR**—is located in the left hand rear side of the engine compartment, in the front power distribution box.
- **Vehicle Speed Sensor**—is located on the rear of the vehicle, on the differential.
- **Washer Fluid Level Switch**—is located of the right hand side of the washer fluid reservoir.
- **Washer Jet Heater (left)**—is located under the cover, on the engine hood.
- **Washer Jet Heater (right)**—is located under the cover, on the engine hood.
- **Washer Pump Relay**—is located in the left hand rear side of the engine compartment, in the front power distribution box.
- **Washer Pump**—is located on the right hand front of the engine compartment, on the washer fluid reservoir.
- **Water Relay**—is located in the left hand rear side of the engine compartment, in the front power distribution box.
- **Water Valve Assembly**—is located on the left hand rear side of the engine compartment, on the engine bulkhead.
- **Wiper Motor**—is located behind the left hand side of the fresh air cowl.

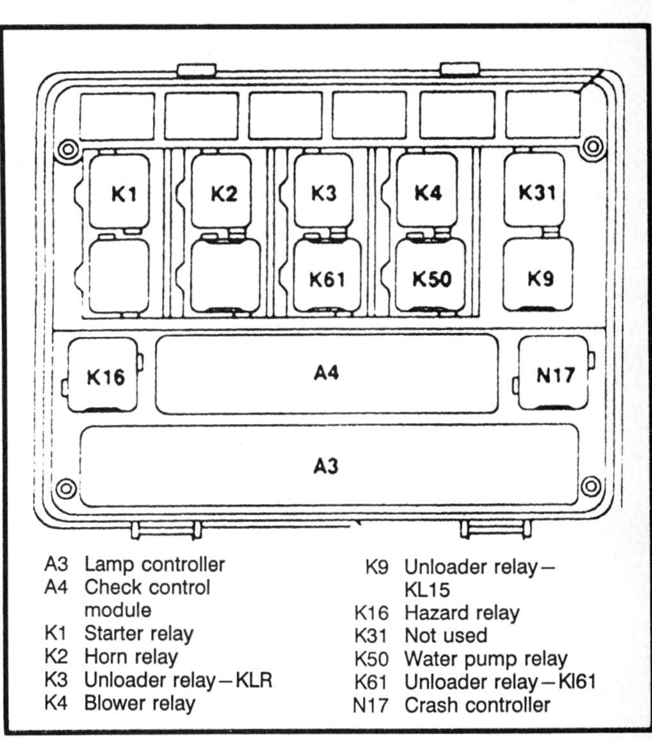

Typical power distribution box—5 and 7 Series

• **Wiper Pressure Control (ADV) Relay**—is located below the left hand side of the rear seat, on the rear power distribution box.

• **Wiper Pressure Control Motor (ADV)**—is located behind the left hand side of the fresh air cowl.

• **Wiper Relay**—is located below the left hand side of the rear seat, on the rear power distribution box.

635CSi SERIES

• **A/C Compressor Clutch Diode**—is located on the lower front side of the engine compartment, on the right hand side of the engine compressor.

• **A/C Compressor Oil Temperature Switch**—is located on the lower right hand front side of the engine compartment, on the air conditioner compressor.

• **A/C Evaporative Temperature Regulator**—is located on the left hand side of the heater-air conditioner unit.

• **A/C Evaporative Temperature Sensor**—is located in the center console, below the back of the radio.

• **A/C Rear Auxiliary Refrigerant Valve**—is located under the right hand rear seat.

• **A/C Rear Evaporator Temperature Sensor**—is located under rear console, in front of the rear evaporator.

• **ABS Electronic Control Unit**—is located below the right hand side of the windshield, behind the shock tower.

• **ABS Hydraulic Unit**—is located on the left hand side of the engine compartment.

• **Accessory Fuse Box**—is located on the left hand side of the engine compartment, near the coolant reservoir.

• **Active Control Checker**—is located in the dash panel, to the left of the steering column.

• **Air Bag**—see SRS supplemental restraint system.

• **Air Flow Meter**—is located on the top right hand side of the engine.

• **Amplifier**—is located on the right hand side of the trunk.

• **Auxiliary Fan Blocking Diode**—is located inside the power distribution box.

• **Auxiliary Fuel Pump**—is located in the right hand side of the trunk floor, below the access panel.

• **Back-Up Light Switch**—is located on the left hand side of the manual transmission.

• **Blower Select Relay**—is located under the dash panel, to the left of the glove box.

• **Board Computer Horn**—is located under the left hand side of the fresh air intake cowl.

• **Brake Accumulator Pressure Switch**—is located in the left hand rear side of the engine compartment, near the brake fluid reservoir.

• **Brake Fluid Level Switch**—is located in the left hand rear side of the engine compartment, on the brake fluid reservoir.

• **Brake Switch**—is located, above the brake pedal.

• **Brake Wear Sensor**—is located near each brake caliper, connected to the brake pad.

• **Central locking Control Unit**—is located under the dash panel, to the left of the glove box.

• **Chime Module**—is located under the left hand side of the dash panel, on the hush panel.

• **Clutch Switch**—is located, above the clutch pedal.

• **Coolant Level Switch**—is located on the top of the coolant reservoir.

• **Coolant Temperature Sender/Switch**—is located on the front of the engine, on the thermostat housing.

• **Coolant Temperature Sensor**—is located on the front of the engine, on the thermostat housing.

• **Coolant Temperature Switch**—is located on the top right hand side of the radiator.

• **Cruise Control Actuator**—is located on the left hand side of the engine compartment.

• **Cruise Control Unit**—is located under the left hand side of the dash panel, above the speaker.

• **Cylinder Head Identification Sensor**—is located on the right hand front side of the engine.

• **Diagnostic Connector**—is located on the right hand side of the power distribution box.

• **Dual Coolant Temperature Switch**—is located on the top right hand side of the radiator.

• **Electro-Hydraulic Converter**—is located on the lower left hand side of the engine compartment, on the steering assembly.

• **Engine Speed Sensor**—is located in the right hand front side of the engine, above the air conditioner compressor.

• **Evaporative Purge Valve**—is located on the top center of the engine, below the throttle body.

• **Filter Capacitor**—is located in the left hand front of the engine, on the back of the alternator.

• **Fog Light Relay**—is located in the power distribution box.

• **Footwell Flap Motor (left)**—is located below the left hand side of the dash panel, on the left hand side of the IHKA/HR plenum.

• **Footwell Flap Motor (right)**—is located below the right hand side of the dash panel, on the right hand side of the IHKA/HR plenum.

• **Footwell Temperature Sensor (left)**—is located below the left hand side of the dash panel, above the kick panel.

• **Footwell Temperature Sensor (right)**—is located below the right hand side of the dash panel, above the kick panel.

• **Fresh Air Door Control Potentiometer**—is located behind the center of the dash panel.

• **Fresh Air Door Control Unit**—is located on the left hand side of the heater-air conditioner unit.

• **Front Brake Pad Sensor (left)**—is located behind the left hand front wheel on the caliper.

• **Front Brake Pad Sensor (right)**—is located behind the right hand front wheel on the caliper.

• **Front Crash Sensor (left)**—is located in front of the left hand shock tower.

• **Front Crash Sensor (right)**—is located in front of the right hand shock tower.

• **Front Speed Detectors**—is located on the back of the front wheels, on the dust shields.

• **Front Speed Sensor (left)**—is located behind the left hand front wheel.

• **Front Speed Sensor (right)**—is located behind the right hand front wheel.

• **Fuel Pump Relay**—is located in the power distribution box.

• **Fuel Tank Sender Switch**—is located on the right hand side of the trunk floor, below the access panel.

• **Gas Filler Lock Motor**—is located in the trunk, behind the right hand rear wheel well.

• **Heat Exchanger Temperature Sensor (left)**—is located behind the left hand side of the dash, in the left side of the IHKA/HR plenum.

• **Heat Exchanger Temperature Sensor (right)**—is located behind the right hand side of the dash, in the right side of the IHKA/HR plenum.

• **Heater Regulator**—is located behind the temperature select control.

• **Heater Temperature Sensor**—is located on the left hand side of the heater-air conditioner unit.

• **Horn Diode**—is located under the left hand side of the fresh air intake cowl, near the board computer horn.

• **Horn Relay**—is located in the power distribution box.

• **High Pressure Cut-Out Switch**—is located in the right hand front corner of the engine compartment, on the receiver/drier.

• **High Beam Relay**—is located in the power distribution box.

• **High Speed Relay**—is located in the power distribution box.

• **Hydraulic Height Level Control System**—is located in the trunk, under the spar tire.

• **Hydraulic Low Pressure Switch**—is located under the left hand side of the vehicle, in front of the rear axle.

• **Hydraulic Pressure Switch**—is located in the left hand rear side of the engine compartment, near the brake fluid reservoir.

• **Idle Speed Actuator**—is located on the top center of the engine.

• **Intensive Washer Pump**—is located behind the right hand front wheel well, in the reservoir.

• **Interior Light Timer Control**—is located under the left hand side of the dash, on the body electrical bracket.

• **Interior Temperature Sensor**—is located under the left hand side of the dash , on the hush panel.

• **Jet Heaters**—are located on the washer jet nozzles.

• **Level Control Unit**—is located under the left hand side of the vehicle, in front of the rear axle.

• **Low Beam Relay**—is located in the power distribution box.

• **Main Fuel Pump**—is located under the vehicle, above the right rear axle.

• **Main Relay**—is located on the power distribution box.

• **Memory Seat Control Module**—is located under the left hand front seat.

• **Mixing Flap Motor (right)**—is located in the center of the dash, to the right of the radio.

• **Motronic Control Unit**—is located under the right hand side of the dash panel, above the glove box.

• **Normal Speed Blower Resistor**—is located ahead of the radiator, on the auxiliary fan shield.

• **Normal Speed Relay**—is located in the power distribution box.

• **Normal Washer Pump**—is located in front of the right hand front wheelwell, in the reservoir.

• **Oil Level Sensor**—is located in the bottom of the oil pan.

• **Oil Pressure Switch**—is located in the left rear end of the cylinder head.

• **On Board Computer Module**—is located in the center of the dash panel, to the right of the radio face.

• **On Board Computer Relay Box**—is located under the left hand side of the dash panel, above the speaker.

• **Outside Temperature Sensor**—is located under the left hand front side of the bumper.

• **Oxygen Sensor**—is located underneath the vehicle, in the catalytic converter.

• **Power Antenna**—is located in the right hand side of the trunk, near the hinge.

• **Power Distribution Box**—is located on the top front of the left hand front wheel well.

• **Power Window Relay**—is located in the power distribution box.

• **Pulse Wheels**—is located in the inner sides of the rotors.

• **Rear Blower Motor**—is located under rear console, in front of the rear evaporator.

• **Rear Lights Check Relay**—is located in the trunk, on the left rear panel center support.

• **Rear Seat Heating/Position Relays (right)**—is located in under the left hand side of the rear seat, on the rear power distribution box.

• **Rear Seat Movement Motor (left)**—is located underneath the right hand rear seat.

• **Rear Seat Movement Motor (right)**—is located underneath the right hand rear seat.

• **Rear Speed Detectors**—is located on the back of the rear wheels, near the brake assembly.

• **Rear Speed Sensor (left)**—is located behind the left hand rear wheel, on the axle.

• **Rear Speed Sensor (right)**—is located behind the right hand rear wheel, on the axle.

• **Seatbelt Warning Timer**—is located under the left hand side of the dash panel, on the body electrical bracket.

• **Servotronic Control Unit**—is located behind the right hand side of the dash panel.

• **Speedometer Sender**—is located in the rear of the differential.

• **Supplemental Restraint System (SRS) Diagnostic Module**—is located under the right hand side of the dash panel.

• **SRS Air Bag Gas Generator**—is located in the center of the steering wheel.

• **SRS Front Crash Sensor (left)**—is located in front of the left hand shock tower.

• **SRS Front Crash Sensor (right)**—is located in front of the right hand shock tower.

• **Starter Relay**—is located under the left hand side of the dash panel, on the body electrical bracket.

• **Stepping Motor**—is located under the dash panel, to the left of the glove box.

• **Sunroof Motor**—is located above the headliner, above the rear view mirror.

• **Sunroof Motor Relay**—is located above the headliner, above the rear view mirror.

• **Throttle Position Sensor**—is located on the top center of the engine, behind the rubber boot.

• **Throttle Switch**—is located on the top center of the engine, behind the rubber boot.

• **Transmission Control Unit**—is located under the left hand side of the dash panel, above the speaker.

• **Transmission Kickdown Switch**—is located in the passenger compartment, under the acceleration pedal.

• **Unloader Speed Relays**—is located in the power distribution box.

• **Unlock Inhibit Switch**—is located in the driver's door at the lock cylinder.

• **Ventilation Flap Motor (left)**—is located below the left

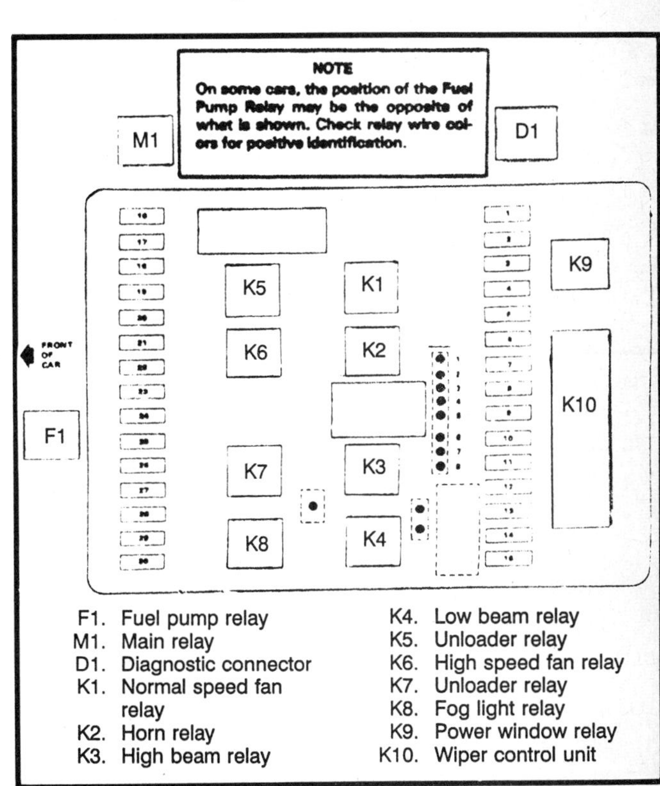

F1. Fuel pump relay
M1. Main relay
D1. Diagnostic connector
K1. Normal speed fan relay
K2. Horn relay
K3. High beam relay
K4. Low beam relay
K5. Unloader relay
K6. High speed fan relay
K7. Unloader relay
K8. Fog light relay
K9. Power window relay
K10. Wiper control unit

Typical power distribution box—3 and 6 Series

hand side of the dash panel, on the left hand side of the IHKA/HR plenum.

• **Ventilation Flap Motor (right)** – is located below the right hand side of the dash panel, on the right hand side of the IHKA/HR plenum.

• **Washer Fluid Level Switch** – is located in front of the right hand front wheelwell, in the reservoir.

• **Washer Jet Heater (left)** – is located under the cover, on the engine hood.

• **Washer Jet Heater (right)** – is located under the cover, on the engine hood.

• **Water Shut-Off Valve** – is located in the left hand rear of the engine compartment.

• **Wiper Control Wiper** – is located in the power distribution box.

735i, 735iL and 750iL SERIES

• **Air Circulation Flap Motor** – is located below the left hand side of the dash panel, on the left hand side of the IHKA/HR plenum.

• **Air Conditioning Motronic Relay** – is located on the left hand of the engine compartment, in the relay box, in front of the shock tower.

• **A/C Compressor Control Relay** – is located is located by the driver's footrest, behind the speaker (IHKA).

• **A/C Evaporative Temperature Sensor** – is located behind the left hand side of the dash, in the left side of the IHKA/HR plenum.

• **ABS Electronic Control Unit** – is located in the E-Box, behind the right hand front shock tower.

• **ABS Hydraulic Unit (735 Series)** – is located in the left hand center of the engine compartment, near the shock tower.

• **ABS Hydraulic Unit (750 Series)** – is located in the left hand front of the engine compartment, behind headlight.

• **ABS Overvoltage Protection Relay** – is located in the front distribution box.

• **ABS/ASC Electronic Control Unit** – is located in the E-Box, behind the right hand front shock tower.

• **Air Bag** – see SRS supplemental restraint system.

• **Air Flow Meter** – is located on the top center of the engine, ahead of oil fill cap.

• **Air Mass Meter 1 (cylinders 1–6)** – is located in the left hand front side of the engine.

• **Air Mass Meter 2 (cylinder 7–12)** – is located in the right hand front side of the engine.

• **Antenna Amplifier** – is located in the left hand C pillar.

• **Anti-theft Horn (DWA)** – is located below the right hand fresh air cowl.

• **Anti-theft Module (DWA)** – is located under the left hand side of the rear seat, ahead of the rear power distribution box.

• **Audible Turn Signal Relay** – is located under the right hand side of the steering column.

• **Automatic Heating And A/C Control Unit (IHKA)** – is located between the front footwells, ahead of the HR plenum.

• **Auxiliary Battery Relay** – is located in the right hand corner of the luggage compartment.

• **Auxiliary Battery** – is located in the right hand corner of the luggage compartment.

• **Auxiliary Fan Motor** – is located in the center front of the engine compartment, behind the front bumper.

• **Auxiliary Relay Box** – is located on the left hand side of the engine compartment, in front of the shock tower.

• **Back-Up Switch** – is located on the top of the right hand side of the transmission.

• **Blower Motor** – is located below the center cowl, behind the coolant expansion tank support panel.

• **Blower Relay** – is located in the front distribution box.

• **Booster Amplifier** – is located in the upper right hand corner of the luggage compartment.

• **Brake Fluid Level Switch** – is located on top of the brake fluid reservoir.

• **Brake Pressure Regulating Switch** – is located on the left hand side of the engine compartment, to the right of the shock tower.

• **Brake Pressure Switch** – is located on the left hand side of the engine compartment, to the right of the shock tower.

• **Catalyst Temperature Switching Unit (Japan)** – is located on the rear power distribution box.

• **Catalyst Thermocouple Left** – is located on the catalytic converter.

• **Catalyst Thermocouple Right** – is located on the catalytic converter.

• **Check Control Module** – is located in the front distribution box.

• **Cigar Lighter Relay Jumper** – is located in the front power distribution box.

• **Cigar Lighter Relay** – is located in the front power distribution box.

• **Coolant Level Switch** – is located on top of the coolant reservoir.

• **Coolant Temperature Sender (735 Series)** – is located on the coolant inlet near the valve cover.

• **Coolant Temperature Sender (750 Series)** – is located on the right hand rear side of the engine, near the E-Box.

• **Coolant Temperature Sensor** – is located on the coolant inlet, near the valve cover.

• **Crash Control Unit** – is located in the front power distribution box.

• **Cruise Control Actuator (Tempomat)** – is located in the left center of the engine compartment, ahead of the shock tower.

• **Cruise Control Module (Tempomat)** – is located in the E-Box, behind the right hand front shock tower.

• **Cylinder Identification Sensor 1** – is located on the spark plug wire 12, under the left hand distributor cover.

• **Cylinder Identification Sensor 2** – is located on the spark plug wire 6, under the right hand distributor cover.

• **Cylinder Identification Sensor** – is located on the right hand front of the engine, on the distributor.

• **Defroster Flap Motor** – is located below the left hand side of the dash panel, on the left hand side of the IHKA/HR plenum.

• **Diagnostic Connector (735 Series)** – is located in the right hand rear of the engine compartment, ahead of the shock tower.

• **Diagnostic Connector (750 Series)** – is located in the left hand rear of the engine compartment, ahead of the shock tower.

• **Driver's Air Bag Generator** – is located in the center of the steering wheel.

• **Driver's Day Light Coding Diode** – is located in front of dash, near light switch.

• **E-Box Fan** – is located in the E-Box below the modules.

• **E-Box** – is located on the right hand side of the engine, behind the right hand front shock tower.

• **EDC Electronic Control Unit** – is located under the right hand side of the rear seat, near the battery.

• **EDC Right Front Shock Absorber** – is located on the top right hand front shock tower.

• **Electric Power Protection Relay** – is located in under the left hand side of the rear seat, on the rear power distribution box.

• **Electro-Hydraulic Converter (Servotronic)** – is located below the left hand front of the vehicle, behind the left hand front wheel.

• **Electronic Heater Control Unit** – is located between the front footwells, ahead of the HR plenum.

• **Electronic Throttle Control Unit** – is located in the E-Box, behind the right hand front shock tower.

• **Electronic Transmission Control Unit (AEGS)**—is located behind the right hand kick panel.

• **EML Electronic Control Unit**—is located in the E-Box, behind the right hand front shock tower.

• **Engine Intake Air Temperature Sensor 1 (cylinders 1–6)**—is located in the right hand rear side of the engine, near the E-Box.

• **Engine Intake Air Temperature Sensor 2 (cylinders 7–12)**—is located in the left hand rear side of the engine compartment, to the right of the front power distribution box.

• **Engine Speed Sensors**—is located on the lower front of the engine.

• **Engine Speed/Reference Point Sensor**—is located on the front of the engine, below the distributor.

• **Evaporative Purge Valve 1 (cylinders 1–6)**—is located in the left hand front side of the engine compartment.

• **Evaporative Purge Valve 2 (cylinders 7–12)**—is located in the right hand front side of the engine compartment.

• **Evaporative Purge Valve**—is located in the left hand side of the engine, to the right of the oil filter.

• **Final Stage Unit**—is located on the left side of the right hand footwell, ahead of the IHKA/HR plenum.

• **Fog Light Washer Pump**—is located left hand front of the engine compartment, on the washer fluid reservoir.

• **Footwell Flap Motor (left)**—is located below the left hand side of the dash panel, on the left hand side of the IHKA/HR plenum.

• **Footwell Flap Motor (right)**—is located below the right hand side of the dash panel, on the right hand side of the IHKA/HR plenum.

• **Footwell Temperature Sensor (left)**—is located below the left hand side of the dash panel, above the kick panel.

• **Footwell Temperature Sensor (right)**—is located below the right hand side of the dash panel, above the kick panel.

• **Fresh Air Flap Motor**—is located below the left hand side of the dash panel, on the left hand side of the IHKA/HR plenum.

• **Front Brake Pad Sensor (left)**—is located behind the left hand front wheel on the caliper.

• **Front Brake Pad Sensor (right)**—is located behind the right hand front wheel on the caliper.

• **Front Crash Sensor (left)**—is located in front of the left hand shock tower.

• **Front Crash Sensor (right)**—is located in front of the right hand shock tower.

• **Front Defogger/Water Pump Relay**—is located in the front distribution box.

• **Front Power Distribution Box**—is located in the left rear side of the engine compartment.

• **Front Speed Detectors**—is located on the back of the front wheels, on the dust shields.

• **Front Speed Sensor (left)**—is located behind the left hand front wheel.

• **Front Speed Sensor (right)**—is located behind the right hand front wheel.

• **Fuel Pump 2**—is located below the luggage compartment, to the right of the spare tire.

• **Fuel Pump Relay 1 (cylinders 1–6)**—is located in the auxiliary relay box, front of the right hand shock tower.

• **Fuel Pump Relay 2 (cylinders 7–12)**—is located in the auxiliary relay box, front of the right hand shock tower.

• **Fuel Pump Relay**—is located in the E-Box, behind the right hand shock tower.

• **Fuel Pump**—is located below the luggage compartment, to the right of the spare tire.

• **Fuel Tank Sensor**—is located below the luggage compartment, thru the right hand access panel, to the right of the spare tire.

• **Gas Filler Lock Motor**—is located in the luggage compartment, behind the right wheel well.

• **General Module**—is located under the left hand side of the rear seat, in the rear power distribution box.

• **Hazard Flasher Relay**—is located in the front power distribution box.

• **Headlight Washer Pump**—is located left hand front of the engine compartment, on the washer fluid reservoir.

• **Headlight/Front Fog Light Module (SRA)**—is located on the left hand side of the engine compartment, in the relay box.

• **Heat Exchanger Temperature Sensor (left)**—is located behind the left hand side of the dash, in the left side of the IHKA/HR plenum.

• **Heat Exchanger Temperature Sensor (right)**—is located behind the right hand side of the dash, in the right side of the IHKA/HR plenum.

• **Hifi Amplifier**—is located behind the luggage compartment left hand trim panel, on a brace.

• **High Speed Relay**—is located on the left hand side of the engine compartment, in the relay box, on the front of the shock tower.

• **Horn Relay**—is located in the front distribution box.

• **Hydraulic Height Level Control System**—is located in the rear of the vehicle, in the spare tire housing.

• **Idle Speed Actuator**—is located on the center rear portion of the throttle body.

• **Inertia Switch**—is located under the center rear seat, to the right of the distribution box.

• **Infra-Red Locking Control Unit**—is located below the left hand side of the rear seat.

• **Infra-Red Receiver**—is located in the center of the windshield header, near the rear view mirror.

• **Intensive Washer Pump**—is located on the washer fluid reservoir.

• **Jumper Plug**—is located in the front power distribution box.

• **Junction Posts**—are located in the left hand rear corner of the engine compartment.

• **Kick-Down Prevent Relay**—is located behind the right hand kick panel.

• **KSA Relay**—is located under the left hand side of the rear seat, on the rear distribution box.

• **Lamp Control Module**—is located in the front distribution box.

• **Left And Right Rear Seat Heater Relay**—is located under the left hand side of the rear seat.

• **Level Control Unit**—is located below the vehicle, left on the differential.

• **Lock Sensor Control Unit**—is located behind the kick panel, in the driver's side footwell.

• **Main Relay 1 (cylinders 1–6)**—is located in the auxiliary relay box, front of the right hand shock tower.

• **Main Relay 2 (cylinders 7–12)**—is located in the auxiliary relay box, front of the right hand shock tower.

• **Main Relay**—is located in the E-Box, behind the right hand shock tower.

• **Memory Seat/Mirrors Control Unit**—is located under the driver's seat.

• **Mixing Flap Motor (right)**—is located in the center of the dash, to the right of the radio.

• **Motronic Control Unit 1 (DME)**—is located in the E-Box, behind the right hand front shock tower.

• **Motronic Control Unit (DME)**—is located in the E-Box, behind the right hand front shock tower.

• **Motronic Control Unit 2 (DME)**—is located in the E-Box, behind the right hand front shock tower.

• **Normal Speed Relay**—is located on the left hand side of the engine compartment, in the relay box, on the front of the shock tower.

• **Oil Level Sensor**—is located on the bottom of the oil pan.

• **Oil Pressure Switch (735 Series)**—is located on the top rear of the engine, in the rear of the cylinder head.

• **Oil Pressure Switch (750 Series)**—is located on the left hand side of the engine, near the wheel well.

• **On Board Computer Temperature Sensor**—is located under the front bumper, on the right side.

• **On-Board Computer Horn Relay**—is located under the left hand side of the rear seat, in front of the rear power distribution box.

• **On-Board Computer**—is located in the center of the dash panel, to the right of the radio.

• **Outside Temperature Sensor**—is located behind the coolant expansion tank support panel, on the right of the M30 blower motor.

• **Oxygen Sensor Relay**—is located in the auxiliary relay box, front of the right hand shock tower.

• **Oxygen Sensor**—is located in the top of the catalyst, near the rear of the transmission.

• **Oxygen Sensors**—is located underneath the vehicle, in the top of the catalytic converter.

• **Park Heating Metering Pump**—is located below the rear of the car, near the right hand rear wheel.

• **Park Heating Unit**—is located on the right hand side of the engine compartment.

• **Park Heating/Ventilation Control Unit**—is located under the right hand rear seat, behind the battery.

• **Park Heating/Ventilation Relay Box**—is located behind the right hand side of the dash panel, above the glove box.

• **Parking Light Monitor Relay**—is located in the front distribution box.

• **Pedal Position Sensor**—is located under the left hand side of the dash panel, on the right hand side of the brake pedal.

• **Phone Alert Relay (735 Series)**—is located in the front power distribution box.

• **Phone Alert Relay (750 Series)**—is located under the left hand side of the dash panel.

• **Power Steering Fluid Level Switch**—is located on the power steering reservoir.

• **Rear Defogger Relay**—is located in under the left hand side of the rear seat, on the rear power distribution box.

• **Rear Headrest Control Unit**—is located on the rear power distribution box.

• **Rear Power Distribution Box**—is located below the left hand side of the rear seat.

• **Rear Seat Heating Relay**—is located in under the left hand side of the rear seat, on the rear power distribution box.

• **Rear Seat Heating/Position Relays (right)**—is located in under the left hand side of the rear seat, on the rear power distribution box.

• **Rear Seat Movement Motor (left)**—is located underneath the right hand rear seat.

• **Rear Seat Movement Motor (right)**—is located underneath the right hand rear seat.

• **Rear Speed Sensor (left)**—is located behind the left hand rear wheel, on the axle.

• **Rear Speed Sensor (right)**—is located behind the right hand rear wheel, on the axle.

• **Rear Vent Flap Switch**—is located in the rear console, on the rear vent flap.

• **Relay Module**—is located under the left hand side of the rear seat, in the rear power distribution box.

• **Safety Switch**—is located in front of the left hand shock tower.

• **Servotronic Control Unit**—is located by the driver's footrest, behind the speaker.

• **Solenoid Valves 1 and 2**—is located on the left hand side of the engine, near the oil filter.

• **Starter Relay**—is located in the front distribution box.

• **Sunroof Motor**—is located in the center of the windshield header, near the rear view mirror.

• **Sunroof Position Switch**—is located in the center of the windshield header, near the rear view mirror.

• **Supplemental Restraint System (SRS) Diagnostic Module**—is located below the left hand side of the dash panel, to the left of the steering column.

• **SRS Driver's Air Bag Generator**—is located in the center of the steering wheel.

• **Temperature Distribution Potentiometer**—is located above the radio, in the dash center IHKA/HR outlets.

• **Temperature Switch**—is located in the E-Box, behind right hand front shock tower.

• **Temperature Switch**—is located on the right hand top of the radiator.

• **Throttle Position Meter 1 (cylinders 1–6)**—is located in the left hand front side of the engine compartment.

• **Throttle Position Module 2 (cylinders 7–12)**—is located in the right hand front side of the engine compartment.

• **Throttle Position Motor**—is located on top of the engine, on the throttle body.

• **Throttle Switch**—is located on the top of the engine, on the throttle body.

• **Trailer Module (AHM)**—is located in the left hand rear corner of the luggage compartment, on the rear panel.

• **Unloader Relay**—is located in the front power distribution box.

• **Unloader Relays**—is located in the front distribution box.

• **Vehicle Speed Sensor**—is located of the rear of the vehicle, on the differential.

• **Ventilation Flap Motor (left)**—is located below the left hand side of the dash panel, on the left hand side of the IHKA/HR plenum.

• **Ventilation Flap Motor (right)**—is located below the right hand side of the dash panel, on the right hand side of the IHKA/HR plenum.

• **Washer Fluid Level Switch**—is located on top of the washer fluid reservoir.

• **Washer Jet Heater (left)**—is located under the cover, on the engine hood.

• **Washer Jet Heater (right)**—is located under the cover, on the engine hood.

• **Washer Pump**—is located on the washer fluid reservoir.

• **Washer Pump Relay**—is located in the front distribution box.

• **Water Pump**—is located on the left hand rear side of the engine compartment, on the engine bulkhead.

• **Water Temperature Sensor (735 Series)**—is located on the coolant inlet near the valve cover.

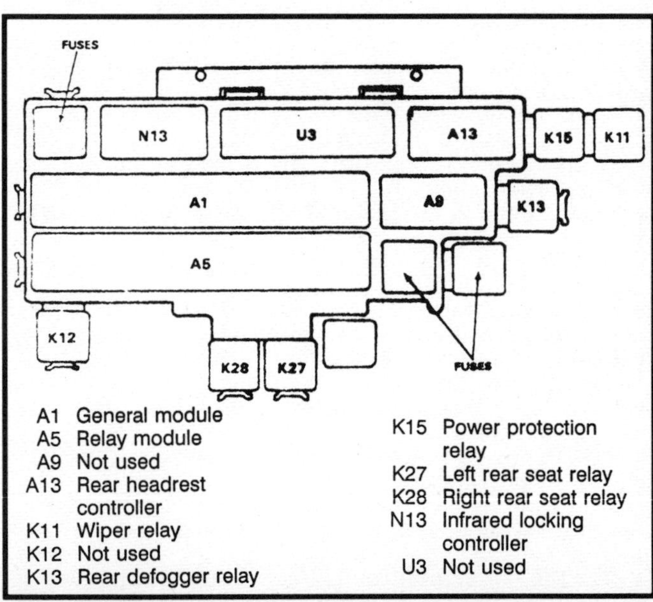

Typical view of the rear power distribution box—5 and 7 Series

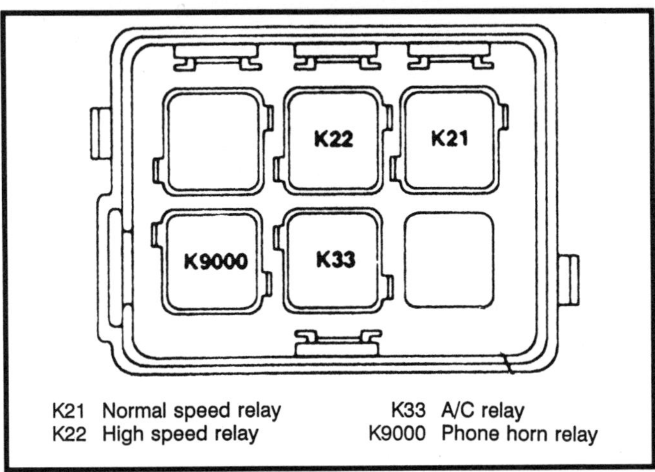

Typical auxiliary relay box—5, 7 and 8 Series

- **Water Temperature Sensor (750 Series)**—is located on the right hand rear side of the engine, near the E-Box.
- **Water Temperature Sensor (DME)**—is located in the right hand rear of the engine, near filter.
- **Water Valve Assembly**—is located in the left hand rear side of the engine compartment, on the engine bulkhead.
- **Wheel Camber Control Unit**—is located below the vehicle, above the right hand side halfshaft.
- **Wiper Motor**—is located behind left hand fresh air cowl.
- **Wiper Pressure Control Motor (ADV)**—is located below the left hand side of the fresh air cowl.
- **Wiper Pressure Control Relay (ADV)**—is located in under the left hand side of the rear seat, on the rear power distribution box.
- **Wiper Relay**—is located in under the left hand side of the rear seat, on the rear power distribution box.

850i

- **A/C Compressor Control Relay**—is located in the front power distribution box.
- **A/C Compressor Cut-Off Relay**—is located in the front power distribution box.
- **A/C Evaporator Temperature Sensor**—is located on the right hand side of the left hand footwell, on the left hand side of the IHKA plenum.
- **A/C Relay**—is located in the front power distribution box.
- **ABS Relay**—is located in the front power distribution box.
- **ABS/ASC + T Control Unit**—is located behind left hand side of the left hand footwell.
- **ABS/ASC Electronic Control Unit**—is located behind left hand side of the left hand footwell.
- **Acoustic Device**—is located below the right hand side of the dash.
- **Air Bag**—see SRS supplemental restraint system.
- **Air Mass Meter 1**—is located on the front left hand side of the engine compartment.
- **Air Mass Meter 2**—is located on the front right hand side of the engine compartment.
- **Antenna Amplifier**—is located in the upper left hand C-pillar.
- **Anti-theft Module (DWA)**—is located inside the box on the interior side of the right hand door sill.
- **ASC Switch**—is located in the center console.
- **Automatic Heating And A/C Control Unit (IHKA)**—is located between the front footwells, in front of the IHKA plenum.
- **Auxiliary Anti-theft Module (DWA)**—is located inside the box on the interior side of the right hand door sill.
- **Auxiliary Fuse Box**—is located in the left hand side of the engine compartment.
- **Auxiliary Water Pump Relay**—is located in the front power distribution box.
- **Back-Up Switch**—is located on the right hand side of the transmission.
- **Battery 1 Left**—is located in the left hand rear side of the luggage compartment.
- **Battery 2 Right**—is located in the right hand rear side of the luggage compartment.
- **Blower Motor**—is located behind the center of the cowl, behind coolant expansion tank support panel.
- **Blower Relay**—is located in the front power distribution box.

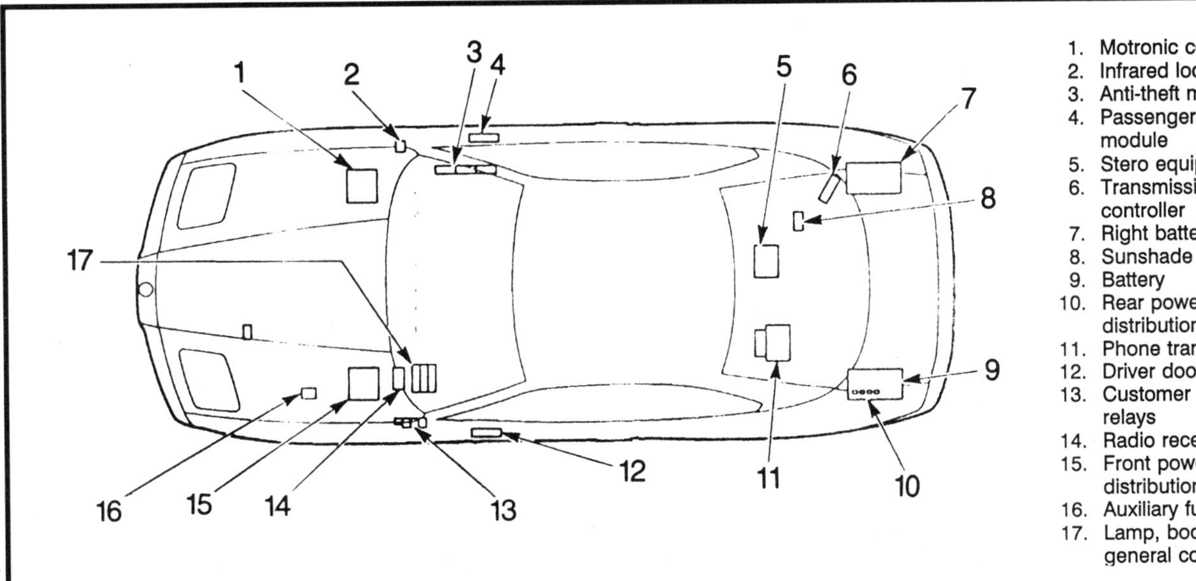

Exploded view of the component locations—850i Series

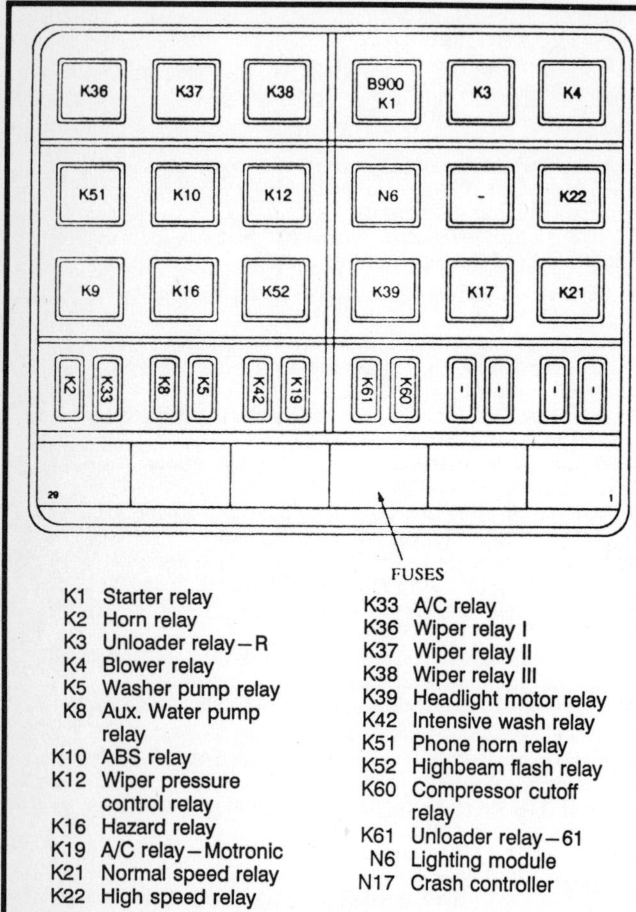

Exploded view of the front power distribution box—850i Series

- **Brake Fluid Level Switch**—is located on the rear left hand side of the engine compartment.
- **Brake Light Switch**—is located below the left hand side of the dash panel, on the brake pedal.
- **Brake Pressure Regulating Switch**—is located on the rear left hand side of the engine compartment.
- **Brake Pressure Switch**—is located on the rear left hand side of the engine compartment.
- **CD Changer**—is located in luggage compartment.
- **Central Locking Trunk Lid Motor Relay**—is located in the rear power distribution box, in the left hand side of the luggage compartment.
- **Concealing Headlights Relay**—is located in the front power distribution box.
- **Consumer Cut-Off Relay 1**—is located in the rear power distribution box, in the left hand side of the luggage compartment.
- **Consumer Cut-Off Relay 2**—is located in the rear power distribution box, in the left hand side of the luggage compartment.
- **Coolant Level Switch**—is located in the front right hand side of the engine compartment.
- **Coolant Temperature Sender**—is located on the coolant inlet.
- **Crash Control Unit**—is located in the front power distribution box.
- **Cylinder Identification Sensor 1**—is located front of the engine compartment.

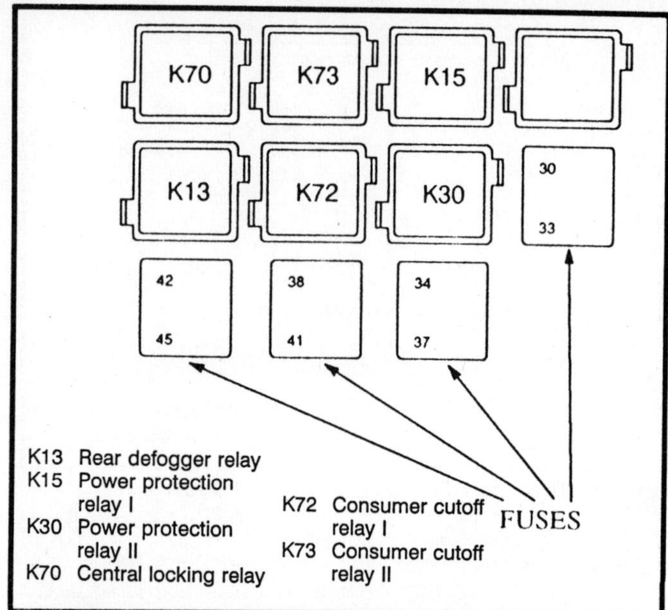

Exploded view of the rear power distribution box—850i Series

- **Cylinder Identification Sensor 2**—is located front of the engine compartment.
- **Cylinder Identification Sensor**—is located near the distributor.
- **Dash Vent Mixing Flap Motor**—is located below the center of the dash, to the right of the radio.
- **Dash Vent Mixing Flap Motor**—is located below the left hand side of the glove box.
- **Defroster Flap Motor**—is located below the left hand side of the dash, on the left hand side of the IHKA plenum.
- **Diagnostic Connector**—is located on the front right hand side of the engine compartment.
- **Driver's Backrest/Lumbar Relay 1**—is located under the left hand front seat.
- **Driver's Backrest/Lumbar Relay 2**—is located under the left hand front seat.
- **Driver's Door Module**—is located in the lower left hand front door.
- **Driver's Power Window Motor/Increment Sensor**—is located in the lower left hand front door.
- **E-Box Fan**—is located in the E-Box, under the control units.
- **E-Box**—is located in the rear right hand side of the engine compartment.
- **EDC Control Unit**—is located in the left hand rear side of the luggage compartment.
- **EDC Relay**—is located in the left hand rear side of the luggage compartment.
- **Electric Power Protection Relay 2**—is located in the rear power distribution box, in the left hand side of the luggage compartment.
- **Electric Power Protection Relay**—is located in the rear power distribution box, in the left hand side of the luggage compartment.
- **Electronic Body Module**—is located below left hand side of the dash panel.
- **Electronic Transmission Control Unit (EGS)**—is located in the right hand side of the luggage compartment.
- **EML (1.2) Electronic Control Unit**—is located in the rear right hand side of the engine compartment, in the E-Box.
- **Engine Intake Air Temperature Sensor 1**—is located on the coolant inlet.

• **Engine Intake Air Temperature Sensor 2**—is located on the rear of the engine.

• **Engine Speed Sensor 1**—is located front of the engine compartment.

• **Engine Speed Sensor 2**—is located front of the engine compartment.

• **Final Stage Unit**—is located in the left hand side of the right hand footwell, in front ahead of the IHKA plenum.

• **Footwell Flap Motor (left)**—is located below the left hand side of the dash, on the left hand side of the IHKA plenum.

• **Footwell Flap Motor (right)**—is located below the left hand side of the right hand footwell.

• **Fresh Air Flap Motor**—is located below the left hand side of the dash, on the left hand side of the IHKA plenum.

• **Front Brake Pad Sensor (left)**—is located on the left hand front wheel, above the brake caliper.

• **Front Brake Pad Sensor (right)**—is located on the left hand front wheel, above the brake caliper.

• **Front Crash Sensor (left)**—is located ahead of the left hand side shock tower.

• **Front Crash Sensor (right)**—is located ahead of the right hand side shock tower.

• **Front Power Distribution Box Junction Post**—is located in the left hand footwell, under the footrest.

• **Front Power Distribution Box**—is located in the rear left hand side of the engine compartment.

• **Fuel Level Sensor 1**—is located under the right hand rear seat.

• **Fuel Level Sensor 2**—is located under the left hand rear seat.

• **Fuel Pump Relay 1**—is located in the right hand side of the engine compartment in the E-Box.

• **Fuel Pump Relay 2**—is located in the right hand side of the engine compartment in the E-Box.

• **Gas Filler Lock Motor**—is located in the right hand rear side of the luggage compartment.

• **General Module**—is located below the left hand side of the instrument panel.

• **Gradient Monitor (DWA)**—is located in the left hand side of the luggage compartment.

• **Hazard Flasher Relay**—is located in the front power distribution box.

• **Headlight/Front Fog Light Module (SRA)**—is located in the front power distribution box.

• **Heat Exchanger Temperature Sensor (left)**—is located below side of the dash panel, on the left hand side of the IHKA plenum.

• **Heat Exchanger Temperature Sensor (right)**—is located in the left side of the right hand footwell.

• **HIFI Amplifier**—is located in the luggage compartment.

• **High Beam/Flasher Light Relay**—is located in the front power distribution box.

• **High Speed Relay**—is located in the front power distribution box.

• **Horn Relay**—is located in the front power distribution box.

• **Infrared Locking Control Unit**—is located behind the right hand footwell kickpanel.

• **Infrared Receiver**—is located in the center of the windshield header.

• **Intensive Wash Relay**—is located in the front power distribution box.

• **Intensive Washer Pump**—is located on the front right hand side of the engine compartment, near the windshield washer reservoir.

• **Interior Light Relay**—is located behind left hand footwell speaker grill.

• **IR/DWA LED**—is located in the center of the dash panel.

• **Jet Washer Heater (left)**—is located on the underside of the engine hood.

• **Jet Washer Heater (right)**—is located on the underside of the engine hood.

• **Jumper for Horn (Telephone)**—is located in the front power distribution box.

• **Jumper Plug**—is located in the front power distribution box.

• **Lamp Control Module**—is located below the left hand side of the instrument panel.

• **Lock-Sensor Control Unit**—is located behind left hand footwell speaker grill.

• **Main Relay 1**—is located in the right hand side of the engine compartment in the E-Box.

• **Main Relay 2**—is located in the right hand side of the engine compartment in the E-Box.

• **Memory Seat/Mirrors Control Unit**—is located in the left hand front seat.

• **Memory Steering Column Control Unit**—is located below left hand side of the dash panel.

• **Mixing Flap Motor**—is located below the center of the dash, to the left of the radio.

• **Motronic Control Unit 1 (DME)**—is located in the rear right hand side of the engine compartment, in the E-Box.

• **Motronic Control Unit 2 (DME)**—is located in the rear right hand side of the engine compartment, in the E-Box.

• **Normal Speed Relay**—is located in the front power distribution box.

• **Oil Pressure Switch**—is located on the left hand side of the engine compartment.

• **On-Board Computer Horn Relay**—is located inside the box on the interior side of the right hand door sill.

• **Oxygen Sensor 1**—is located on the catalytic converter.

• **Oxygen Sensor 2**—is located on the catalytic converter.

• **Oxygen Sensor Relay** —is located in the right hand side of the engine compartment in the E-Box.

• **Passenger's Backrest/Lumbar Relay 2**—is located under the right hand front seat.

• **Passenger's Door Module**—is located in the lower right hand front door.

• **Passenger's Power Window Motor/Increment Sensor**—is located in the lower right hand front door.

• **Passenger's Seatback/Lumbar Relay 1**—is located under the right hand front seat.

• **Passenger's Side Rear Entrance Assist Relay**—is located under the right hand front seat.

• **Pedal Position Sensor**—is located below the left hand side of the dash panel, near the brake pedal.

• **Power Sun Shade Electronic Control Unit**—is located under the rear window shelf.

• **Radio Receiver**—is located in luggage compartment.

• **Rear Defogger Relay**—is located in the rear power distribution box, in the left hand side of the luggage compartment.

• **Rear Power Distribution Box**—is located in the left hand side of the luggage compartment.

• **Rear Brake Pad Sensor (right)**—is located behind the right hand rear wheel, on the caliper.

• **Starter Relay**—is located in the front power distribution box.

• **Steering Angle Sender**—is located in left hand footwell, which is under the footrest.

• **Sunroof Module**—is located in the center of the windshield header.

• **Sunroof Motor**—is located in the center of the windshield header.

• **Supplement Restraint System (SRS) Diagnostic Module**—is located below the left hand side of the instrument panel.

• **Temperature Sensor**—is located in the front left hand side of the engine compartment.

• **Temperature Switch**—is located in the front right hand side of the engine compartment.

• **Temperature Switch**—is located in the rear right hand side of the engine compartment, in the E-Box.
• **Throttle Position Motor 1 (EML)**—is located on the front left hand side of the engine compartment.
• **Throttle Position Motor 2 (EML)**—is located on the front right hand side of the engine compartment.
• **Unloader Relay KL15**—is located in the front power distribution box.
• **Unloader Relay KL61**—is located in the front power distribution box.
• **Unloader Relay KLR**—is located in the front power distribution box.
• **Ventilating Flap Motor**—is located below the left hand side of the dash panel.
• **Washer Fluid Level**—is located in the front right hand side of the engine compartment.
• **Washer Pump Relay**—is located in the front power distribution box.
• **Washer Pump**—is located on the right hand side of the engine compartment.
• **Water Temperature Sensor (DME)**—is located front of the engine compartment.
• **Water Temperature Sensor**—is located on the coolant inlet.
• **Wiper Motor**—is located behind the left hand fresh air cowl.
• **Wiper Pressure Control (ADV) Relay**—is located in the front power distribution box.
• **Wiper Relay 1**—is located in the front power distribution box.
• **Wiper Relay 2**—is located in the front power distribution box.
• **Wiper Relay 3**—is located in the front power distribution box.

JAGUAR

Circuit Breakers and Fuses

XJ6

Fuses boxes are located at the right rear of the engine compartment, near the battery; under the right side of the dash; under the center console between the seats and at the left rear quarter panel inside the trunk (accessory fuse box).

XJS

Window lift thermal circuit breaker is located at the left kick panel.
Fuses are located at the auxiliary fuse box under the right side of the dash, the main fuse box, under the left side of the dash.

Fusible Links

Fusible links, if used, may be located in the engine compartment at the battery, starter or alternator.

Sensors, Relays, Modules and Computer Locations

XJ6

• **A/C Ambient Air Temperature Sensor**—is located under the right side of the dash.
• **A/C Clutch Relay**—is located at the left front of the trunk.
• **A/C Control Unit**—is located at the air box under the center of the dash.
• **A/C Evaporator Temperature Sensor**—is located at the air box under the center of the dash.
• **A/C Feedback Potentiometer (upper and lower)**—are located on the air box under the center of the dash.
• **A/C thermistor**—is located at the under the right side of the dash.
• **ABS Control Unit Relay**—is located at the left side of the dash near the steering column.
• **ABS Control Unit**—is located at the left rear of the trunk.
• **ABS Diagnostic Connector**—is located at the left rear of the trunk.
• **ABS Inline Fuse**—is located under the right side of the dash behind the fuse box.
• **ABS Main Relay**—is located next to the ABS control unit relay.
• **ABS Motor Relay**—is located at the dash near the steering column.
• **ABS Pump Test Connector**—is located at the left rear of the engine compartment.
• **ABS Pump**—is located at the left rear of the engine compartment.
• **Accessory Fuse Box Relay**—is located at the left rear quarter panel inside the trunk.
• **Air Flow Meter**—is located at the air cleaner.
• **Air Pump Relay**—is located at the left front of the engine compartment.
• **Air Pump Solenoid Valve**—is located at the left front of the engine.
• **Air Pump**—is located at the left front of the engine.
• **Antenna Relay**—is located at the right front of the trunk.
• **Anti-lock Brakes**—see ABS.
• **Automatic Transmission Decoder Module**—is located under the right side of the dash.
• **Automatic Transmission ECU**—is located under the right side of the dash.
• **Battery Cut Out Relay**—is located near the battery on the right side of the engine compartment.
• **Battery Posts**—are located at the left rear and right rear of the engine compartment.
• **Bulb Failure Module**—is located at the left rear quarter panel inside the trunk.
• **Buzzer**—is located under the right side of the dash.
• **Catalyst Relay**—is located at the right front of the engine compartment.
• **Catalyst Switch Module**—is located at the left front of the engine compartment.
• **Central Door Lock Inertia Switch**—is located under the left side of the dash.
• **Central Door Lock Infra Red Receiver**—is located under the center console.
• **Central Door Lock Security Connector**—is located under the left side of the dash.
• **Coolant Level Sensor**—is located at the left rear of the engine.
• **Coolant Temperature Sensor**—is located at the left front of the engine.

• **Crank Sensor**—is located at the front of the engine near the camshaft cover.
• **Cruise Control ECU**—is located behind the instrument panel or under the right side of the dash.
• **Cruise Control Relay**—is located under the left side of the dash.
• **EGR Control Valve**—is located at the left rear of the engine compartment on the firewall.
• **Electronic Control Unit (ECU)**—see microprocessor.
• **EMS (high power board)**—is located under the right side of the dash.
• **EMS (low power board)**—is located under the right side of the dash.
• **EMS Diagnostic Connector**—is located at the left rear of the engine compartment.
• **Engine Management System**—see EMS.
• **Fail Module (headlight)**—is located behind the headlight at the front of the engine compartment.
• **Fail Module (tail light)**—is located at the rear quarter panel inside the trunk.
• **Fog Lamp Relay**—is located at the right front of the engine compartment.
• **Fuel Fail Reset**—is located at the center front of the engine compartment.
• **Fuel Tank Level Sensor**—is located at the left and right rear of the engine compartment.
• **Fuse Failure Circuit**—is located inside the center fuse box.
• **Headlight Relay**—is located at the right front fo the engine compartment.
• **Headlight Washer Relay**—is located at the right front of the engine compartment.
• **High Level Stoplight Relay**—is located at the right rear of the trunk.
• **Idle Speed Control (ISC)**—between the injectors on the left side of the engine.
• **Ignition On Relay**—is located under the right side of the dash.
• **Inertia Switch**—is located at left and right rear of the engine compartment on the fenders.
• **Instrument Pack Diagnostic Connector**—is located under the right side of the dash.
• **Lighting Logic Module**—is located under the left side of the dash.
• **Lights On Warning Module**—is located under the left side of the dash at the steering column.
• **Load Dump Module**—is located at the left front of the engine.
• **Microprocessor**—is located under the right side of the dash.
• **Oil Pressure Sensor**—is located at the left front of the engine.
• **Oxygen Sensor**—is located at the right rear of the engine on the exhaust manifold.
• **Passive Restraint Module**—is located at the steering column.
• **Passive Restraint Relay**—is located behind the instrument panel.
• **PI Main Relay**—is located under the right side of the dash.
• **Power Window Relays**—are located inside the doors.
• **Puddle Lamp Relay**—is located under the right side of the dash.
• **Purge Control Valve**—is located at the left rear of the engine compartment on the firewall.
• **Rear Window Defogger Relay**—is located at the right front of the trunk.
• **Rear Window Defogger Timer**—is located under the right side of the dash.
• **Reverse Switch**—is located under the console near the dash.
• **Ride Level Circuit**—is located at the right front of the trunk.
• **Ride Level Control Unit**—is located at the right front of the trunk.
• **Ride Level Rectifier Units**—are located at the right front of the engine compartment.
• **Ride Level Relay**—is located at the right front of the trunk.
• **Ride Level Solenoids**—are located at the right front of the engine compartment.
• **Seat Entry Switch Relay**—is located under the right side of the dash.
• **Seat Entry/Exit Switch**—is located under the seat.
• **Seat Heater Thermostat**—is located inside the seat cushion.
• **Seat Heaters**—are located under the front seats.
• **Seat Motors**—are located under the seat.
• **Seat Relay**—is located under the center console.
• **Seat Switch Relay**—is located under the seat.
• **Sidelight Relay**—is located under the right side of the dash.
• **Speed Audible Warning Module**—is located under the right side of the dash.
• **Speed Control Relay**—is located under the right side of the dash.
• **Speed Input Module**—is located under the right side of the dash.
• **Speed Sensor**—is located at the center console.
• **Start Inhibitor Switch**—is located at gearshift lever.
• **Starter Relay**—is located under the center console between the seats.
• **Sunroof Relay**—is located at the sunroof.
• **Throttle Position Sensor**—is located at the left rear of the engine on the throttle body.
• **Trailer Towing Module**—is located at the right rear of the trunk.
• **Washer Fluid Level Sensor**—is located at the right front of the engine compartment.
• **Windsheild Washer Relay**—is located at the right front of the engine compartment.
• **Windsheild Wiper Logic Module**—is located under the right side of the dash next to the microprocessor.

XJS

• **A/C Compressor Relay**—is located at the right rear of the engine compartment, first in the row.
• **ABS Control Unit**—is located at the left front of the trunk.
• **ABS Main Relay**—is located at the left front of the trunk.
• **main fuse box.**
• **ABS Pump Relay**—is located under the right side of the dash to the right of the fuse box.
• **Anti-stall Relays**—are located at the front center of the engine compartment.
• **Auxiliary Fuse Box**—is located under the right side of the dash.
• **Bulb Failure Unit**—is located at the left kick panel.
• **Convertible Top Relay**—is located under the right side of the rear compartment.
• **Coolant Temperature Sender**—is located at the right front of the engine.
• **Cooling Fan Diode Pack**—is located at the left front of the engine compartment at the front of the relay rack.
• **Cooling Fan Relay**—is located at the left front of the engine compartment, third from the front.
• **Door Lock Control Unit**—is located inside the right door.
• **Feedback Inhibit Relay**—is located at the right rear of the engine compartment, second from the front.

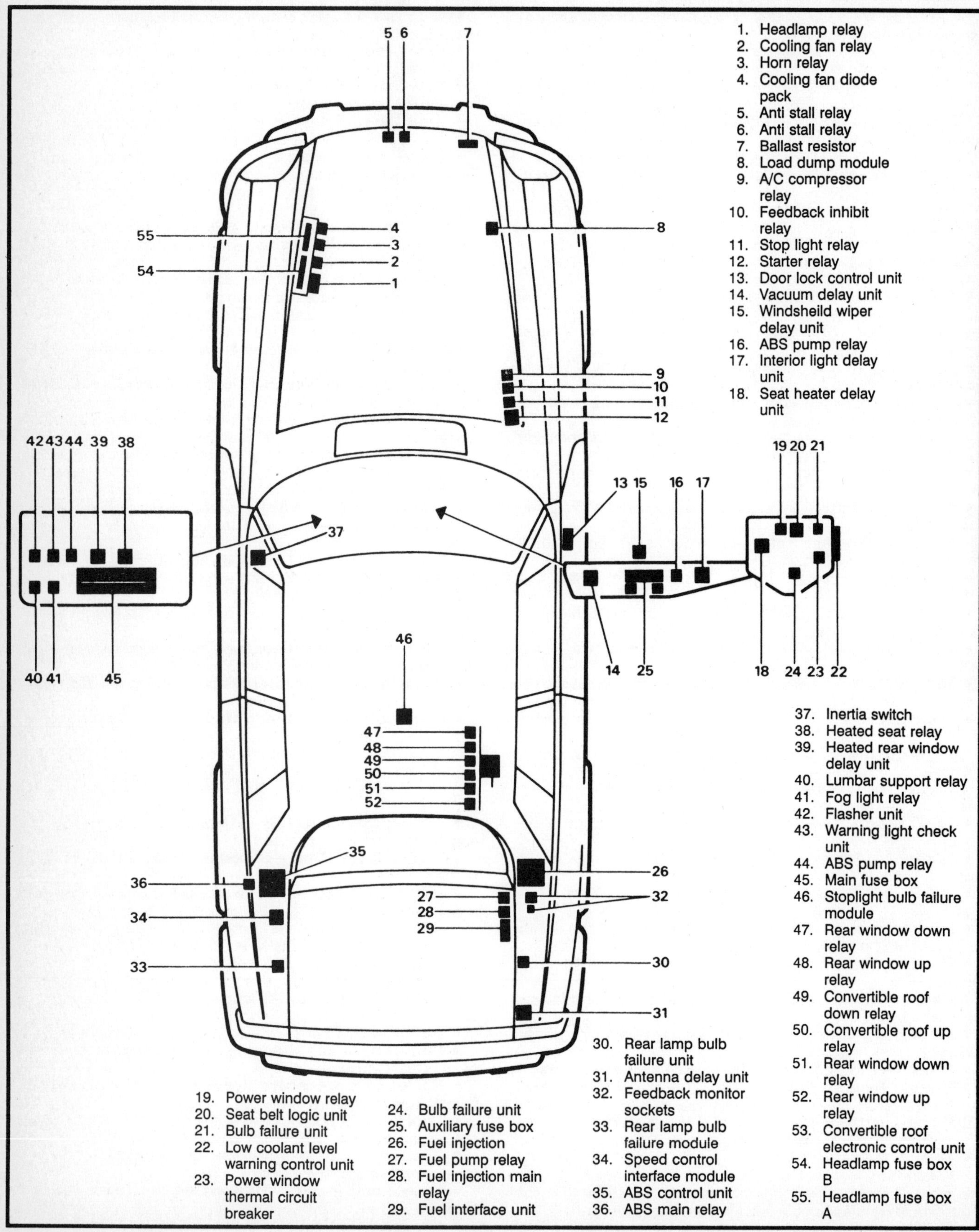

Component locations—XJS

• **Flasher Unit**—is located under the left side of the dash next to the main fuse box.

• **Fog Light Relay**—is located under the left side of the dash next to the main fuse box.

• **Fuel Injection Electronic Control Unit**—is located at the right rear quarter panel inside the trunk.

• **Fuel Injection Main Relay**—is located at the right rear quarter panel inside the trunk.

• **Fuel Interface Unit**—is located at the right rear quarter panel inside the trunk.

• **Fuel Pump Relay**—is located at the right rear quarter panel inside the trunk.

• **Headlight Fuse Box A**—is located at the left side of the engine compartment.

• **Headlight Fuse Box B**—is located at the left side of the engine compartment.

• **Heated Rear Window Delay Unit**—is located under the left side of the dash next to the main fuse box.

• **Heated Seat Relay**—is located under the left side of the dash next to the main fuse box.

• **Horn Relay**—is located at the left front of the engine compartment, second from the front.

• **Inertia Switch**—is located at the left kick panel.

• **Interior Light Delay Unit**—is located under the right side of the dash to the right of the fuse box.

• **Load Dump Module**—is located at the right front of the engine compartment.

• **Low Coolant Warning Control Unit**—is located at the left kick panel.

• **Lumbar Support Relay**—is located under the left side of the dash next to the main fuse box.

• **Main Fuse Box**—is located under the left side of the dash.

• **Oil Pressure Sender**—is located at the rear of the engine near the firewall.

• **Oil Pressure Switch**—is located at the rear of the engine near the firewall.

• **Rear Bulb Failure Module**—is located at the left quarter panel inside the trunk.

• **Rear Window Relay**—is located under the right side of the rear seat.

• **Seat Belt Logic Unit**—is located at the left kick panel.

• **Seat Heater Delay Unit**—is located at the left kick panel.

• **Speed Control Interface Module**—is located at the left quarter panel inside the trunk.

• **Starter Relay**—is located at the right rear of the engine compartment, closest to the firewall.

• **Stop Light Relay**—is located at the right rear of the engine compartment, third from the front.

• **Stoplight Bulb Failure Module**—is located at the left or right quarter panel in the trunk.

• **Vacuum Delay Unit**—is located under the right side of the dash to the left of the fuse box.

• **Warning Light Check Unit**—is located under the left side of the dash next to the main fuse box.

• **Window Lift Relay**—is located at the left kick panel.

• **Windsheild Delay Wiper Unit**—is located under the right side of the dash to the left of the fuse box.

MERCEDES-BENZ

Circuit Breaker and Fuses

The fuse/relay box is located on the left side of engine compartment. Some vehicles may be equipped with circuit breakers which are located in the fuse/relay box.

Fusible Links

No major fusible links are used on these vehicles.

Relays, Sensors, Modules and Computer Locations

190 SERIES

• **A/C Compressor Control Unit**—is located right side of engine compartment, behind battery.

• **A/C RPM Sensor**—is located in at the rear of the compressor.

• **ABS Control Unit**—is located at right side of engine compartment, behind battery.

• **ABS Hydraulic Unit**—is located in the left front corner of engine compartment.

• **ABS Left Front Wheel Speed Sensor**—is located in the left side steering knuckle.

• **ABS Right Front Wheel Speed Sensor**—is located in the right side steering knuckle.

• **ABS Rear Axle Speed Sensor**—is located in the rear differential housing.

• **Altitude Correction Capsule**—is located right side of engine compartment, behind battery.

• **Air Bag**—see Supplement Restraint System (SRS).

• **Air Flow Sensor Position Indicator**—is located on the left side of mixture control unit.

• **Anti-lock Brake (ABS)**—see ABS.

• **Anti-theft Alarm Control Unit**—is located right front of passenger compartment, underside of footrest.

• **Anti-theft Alarm Horn**—is located at the left front corner of the engine compartment.

• **Anti-towing Sensor**—is located below left side of rear seat assembly.

• **Automatic Locking Differential (ASD) Control Unit**—is located in the right front engine compartment area.

• **Auxiliary Coolant Pump**—is located behind right headlamp unit.

• **Auxiliary Fan Relay**—is located in auxiliary relay box at code C.

• **Auxiliary Fan Pre-Resistor**—is located in lower left front corner of the engine compartment.

• **Auxiliary Fan/Magnetic Clutch Engine Fan Relay (double contact)**—is located in fuse box (electrical center) at code R3.

• **Auxiliary Fuse Box**—is located on the left side of engine compartment below main fuse box.

• **Blower Motor Auxiliary Fuse Holder**—is located left side of engine compartment.

• **Brake Fluid Level Switch**—is located on the left side of the engine compartment at the top of the brake fluid reservoir.

• **CIS-E Control Unit**—is located right side of engine compartment, behind the battery.

• **Coolant Level Switch**—is located at the bottom of the coolant reservoir.

• **Coolant Temperature Gauge Sensor**—is located front of engine, behind the thermostat housing.

• **Coolant Temperature Sensor**—is located on the top of engine assembly.

• **Coolant Temperature Switch**—is located on the top front of engine.

• **Crankshaft Position Sensor**—is located lower left of engine assembly.

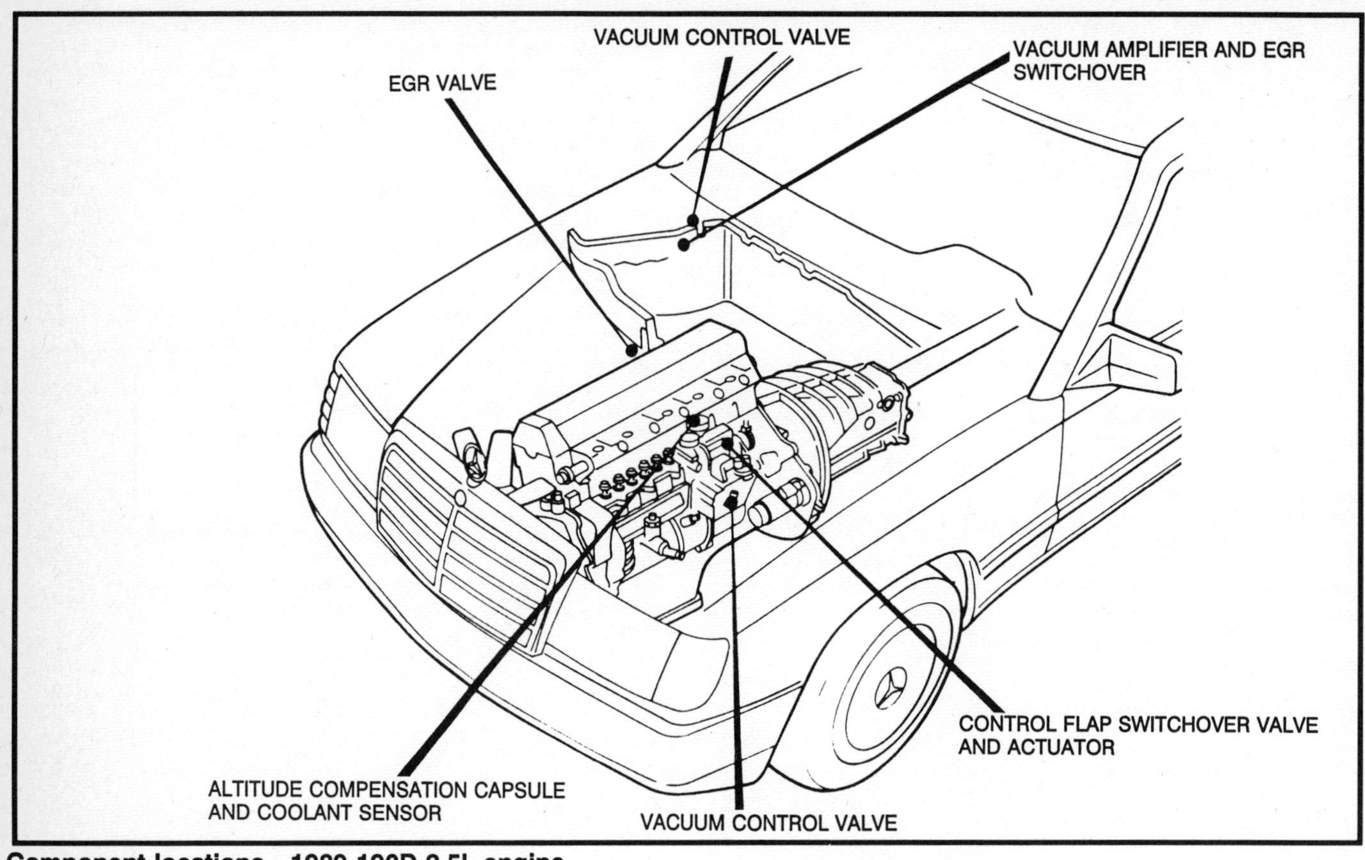

Component locations—1989 190D 2.5L engine

- **Cruise Control Actuator**—is located right side of the engine compartment.
- **Cruise Control Amplifier**—is located underside of the right front footrest.
- **Deceleration Shut-Off Microswitch**—is located on top of engine assembly, rear side of throttle body.
- **Diagnostic Connection LED (California)**—is located on the left side of the engine compartment.
- **Diagnostic Connection/Terminal Block**—is located on the left side of the engine compartment.
- **Electrical Center (fuse box)**—is located on the left side of engine compartment.
- **Electronic Ignition Control Unit**—is located on the left side of engine compartment.
- **Electro-Hydraulic Actuator**—is located at the top of the engine, rear of mixture control unit.
- **Engine Ground**—is located lower left front corner of engine compartment.
- **Feedback Potentiometer**—is located behind dash panel at top center of the plenum area.
- **Front Seat Memory Control Unit**—is located on the underside of the left front seat.
- **Fuel Level Sensor**—Is located front of truck at the top of fuel tank area.
- **Fuel Pump**—is located under left rear of the vehicle, forward of rear axle.
- **Fuel Pump Relay**—is located at right side of engine compartment, behind battery.
- **Fuse Box**—is located on the left side of engine compartment.
- **Hall Effect Speed Sensor**—is located on the rear of the instrument cluster.
- **Headlamp Washer Pump**—is located right front of engine compartment, front of washer fluid reservoir.
- **Head Restraint Adjustment Relay**—is located on the underside of the seat assembly.
- **Hood Switch**—is located right side of engine compartment.
- **Idle Speed Air Valve**—is located at the left side of the engine, behind mixture control unit.
- **In-Car Temperature Sensor**—is located on center of windshield header.
- **Instrument Illumination Control Unit**—is located below instrument cluster, left side of steering column.
- **Intake Air Temperature Sensor**—is located in rear of air cleaner.
- **Key Warning Switch**—is part of ignition switch assembly.
- **Magnetic Clutch Engine Fan/Auxiliary Fan (double contact relay)**—is located in fuse box (electrical center) at code R3.
- **Oil Level Switch**—is located on the side of the oil pan.
- **Oil Pressure Sensor**—is located on oil filter housing.
- **Oil Temperature Sensor**—is located lower left rear of the engine.
- **Outside Temperature Sensor**—is located at front of the vehicle below the bumper assembly.
- **Overvoltage Protection Relay**—is located on the right side of engine compartment, behind the battery.
- **Oxygen Sensor (heated)**—is mounted in exhaust pipe to the rear of the transmission assembly.
- **Power Seat Adjustment Relay**—is located in the fuse/relay box at relay code A.
- **Radio Amplifier Control Unit**—is located in the trunk on the right rear of the wheelwell.
- **Seat Heater Relay**—is located below carpeting, forward of the front seat assembly.
- **Speed Sensor**—is located on the transmission assembly.

• **Supplement Restraint System Control Unit (SRS)**—is located below front footrest area.

• **SRS Energy Accumulator**—is located below footrest in right front footwell area.

• **SRS Voltage Converter**—is located behind the right kick panel.

• **Supply Pump**—is located below right side of rear seat assembly.

• **Temperature Switch (100°C)**—is located on the top front of engine assembly.

• **Temperature Switch (100/110°C)**—is located on the top left front of engine assembly.

• **Throttle Valve Switch**—is located left side of engine, below the throttle body.

• **Trunk Lid lock Actuator**—is located near center of end panel in trunk area.

• **Warning Buzzer Switch**—is part of the ignition switch assembly.

• **Warning Module**—is located behind the left kick panel in the passenger compartment.

• **Windshield Washer Fluid Level Switch**—is located at the top of the washer reservoir.

• **Windshield Washer Pump**—is located right front of engine compartment, front of washer fluid reservoir.

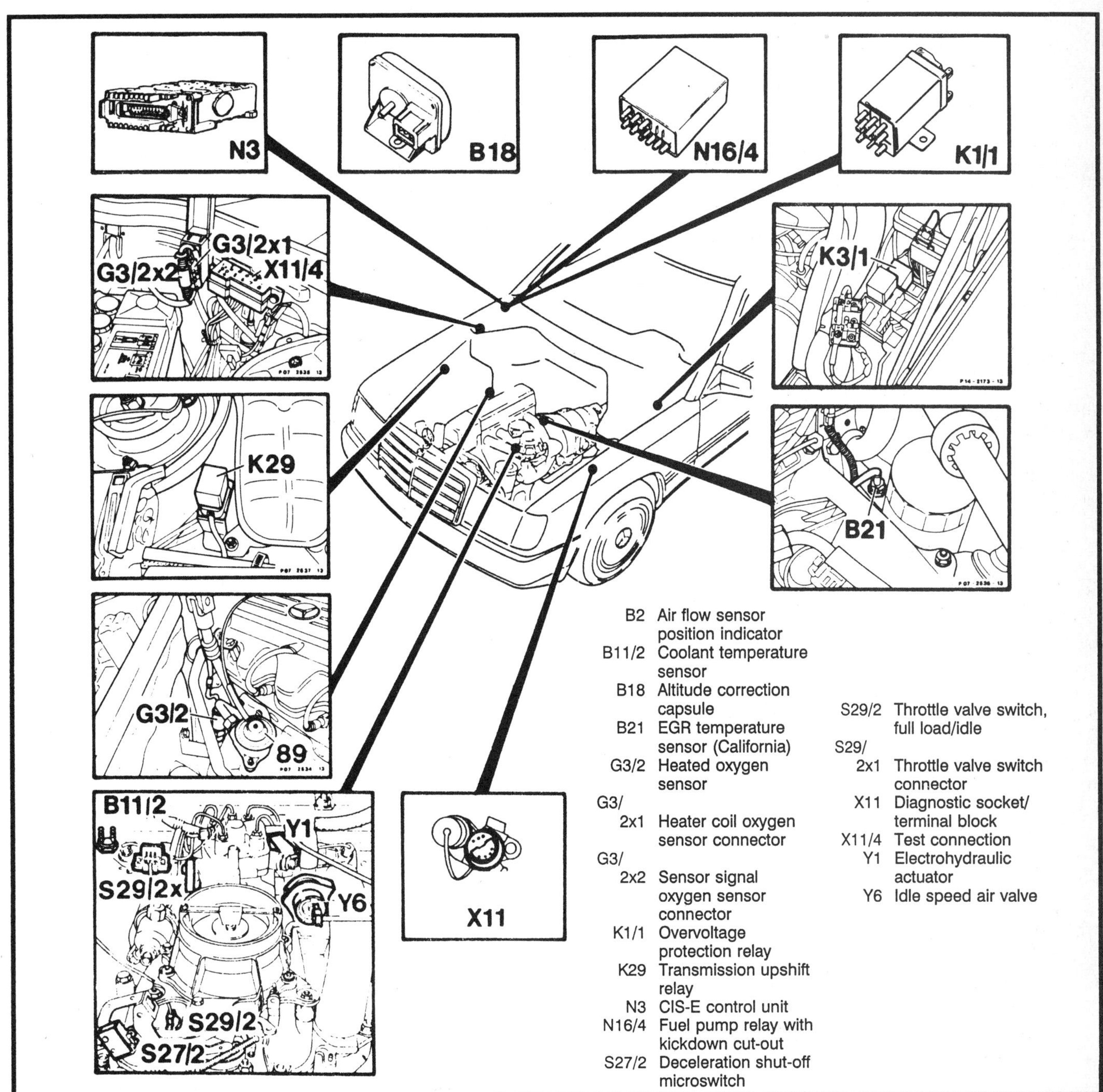

Component locations—1991 190E 2.3L engine

300 SERIES

• **A/C Compressor Control Unit**—is located right side of engine compartment, behind battery.
• **A/C Compressor Cut-Out Switch (diesel)**—is located lower left side of engine.
• **A/C Compressor Speed Sensor**—is located on the rear of the compressor unit.
• **A/C High Pressure Switch**—is located lower left front of engine compartment, at accumulator.
• **A/C High Pressure Switch (diesel)**—is located lower left front of engine compartment, under hydraulic suspension reservoir.
• **ABS Control Unit**—is located at right side of engine compartment, behind battery.
• **ABS Hydraulic Unit**—is located in the left front corner of engine compartment.
• **ABS Left Front Wheel Speed Sensor**—is located in the left side wheel.
• **ABS Right Front Wheel Speed Sensor**—is located in the right side wheel.
• **ABS Rear Axle Speed Sensor**—is located in the right side rear housing.
• **Air Bag**—see Supplement Restraint System (SRS).
• **Air Flow Sensor (diesel)**—is located left front of engine compartment, behind left of headlamp unit.
• **Altitude Correction Capsule**—is located right side of engine compartment, behind battery.
• **Altitude Correction Capsule (diesel)**—is located right side of engine compartment, on front of cowl.
• **Anti-lock Brake (ABS)**—see ABS.
• **Anti-theft Alarm Control Unit**—is located right front of passenger compartment, underside of footrest.
• **Anti-theft Alarm Horn**—is located at the left front corner of the engine compartment.
• **Anti-towing Sensor**—is located below left side of rear seat assembly.
• **Automatic Locking Differential (ASD) Control Unit**—is located in the right front engine compartment area.
• **Auxiliary Fuse Holder (blower motor)**—is located left side of engine compartment.
• **Auxiliary Fuse Box**—is located in the engine compartment in the left side area.
• **Auxiliary Fuse Box**—is located in the right side trunk area.
• **Backup Lamp Switch/Starter Lock-Out**—is located on the left side of the transmission assembly.
• **Brake Fluid Level Switch**—is located on the left side of the engine compartment at the top of the brake fluid reservoir.
• **CIS-E Control Unit**—is located right side of engine compartment, behind the battery.
• **Coolant Level Switch**—is located right side of engine compartment, at the bottom of the coolant reservoir.
• **Coolant Pump**—is located lower right side of the engine compartment.
• **Coolant Temperature Gauge Sensor**—is located top rear of engine, right of air cleaner.
• **Coolant Temperature Gauge Sensor (diesel)**—is located at the left side of the engine, below intake manifold.
• **Coolant Temperature Sensor**—is located on the top center of engine assembly.
• **Coolant Temperature Sensor (diesel)**—is located on the top left side of engine assembly.
• **Crankshaft Position Sensor**—is located on the top of bellhousing, behind oil filter.
• **Cruise Control Actuator**—is located lower left side of the engine assembly.
• **Cruise Control Amplifier**—is located behind left side of dash, right of steering column.
• **Deceleration Shut-Off Microswitch**—is located on the top left rear of engine, on bracket above intake manifold.
• **Diagnostic Connection/Terminal Block**—is located on the left side of the engine compartment.
• **Electrical Center (fuse box)**—is located on the left side of engine compartment.
• **Electronic Ignition Control Unit**—is located on the left side of engine compartment.
• **Electronic Diesel Control Unit (diesel)**—is located on right side of engine compartment, rear of the battery.
• **Electro-Hydraulic Actuator**—is located left side of engine, rear of the throttle body.
• **Glow Plugs (diesel)**—are located at top of engine, at each cylinder intake.
• **Ground (engine)**—is located on the air conditioning compressor assembly.
• **Ground (battery)**—is located on the right side of engine compartment, on rear of shock tower.
• **Heater Core Temperature Sensor**—Is located behind center of dash panel on plenum.
• **In-Car Temperature Sensor**—is located center of windshields header, in front dome lamp unit.
• **Front Seat Memory Control Unit**—is located on the underside of the left front seat.
• **Fuel Level Sensor**—Is located front of truck at the top of fuel tank area.
• **Fuel Pump**—is located under left rear of the vehicle, forward of rear axle.
• **Fuel Pump Relay**—is located at right side of engine compartment, behind battery.
• **Fuel Rack Position Sensor (diesel)**—is located lower left side of engine assembly.
• **Fuse/Relay Box**—is located on the left side of engine compartment.
• **Hall Effect Speed Sensor**—is located on the rear of the instrument cluster.
• **Headlamp Washer Pump**—is located right front of engine compartment, front of washer fluid reservoir.
• **Head Restraint Adjustment Relay (front)**—is located on the underside of the seat assembly.
• **Head Restraint Release Valve (rear/with shut-off delay)**—is below the left side of the rear seat.
• **Idle Speed Air Valve**—is located at the left side of the engine, left of oil dipstick.
• **Instrument Illumination Control Unit**—is located below instrument cluster on steering column.
• **Kick-Down Solenoid**—is located right rear corner of the transmission.
• **Oil Level Switch**—is located on the left side of the oil pan.
• **Oil Pressure Sensor**—is located lower left rear of engine, at base of oil filter.
• **Outside Temperature Sensor**—is located the left front corner of bumper assembly.
• **Overload Protection Switch (diesel)**—is located at the top left side of the engine assembly.
• **Overvoltage Protection Relay**—is located on the right side of engine compartment, behind the battery.
• **Oxygen Sensor (heated)**—is mounted in exhaust pipe to the rear of the transmission assembly.
• **Preglow Relay (diesel)**—is located on left side of engine compartment, on wheel well.
• **Rear Window Sun Shade Motor**—is located under the hat shelf in the trunk area.
• **Rear Window Washer Pump**—is located behind right rear quarter panel.
• **Rear Window Wiper Interval Relay**—Is located left corner of tailgate behind panel.
• **Rear Window Wiper Motor**—is located in center of tailgate, behind panel.
• **Resistance Trimming Plug (diesel)**—is located on left side of engine compartment, right of brake fluid reservoir.
• **Ring Gear Speed Sensor (diesel)**—is located lower left side of bell housing.

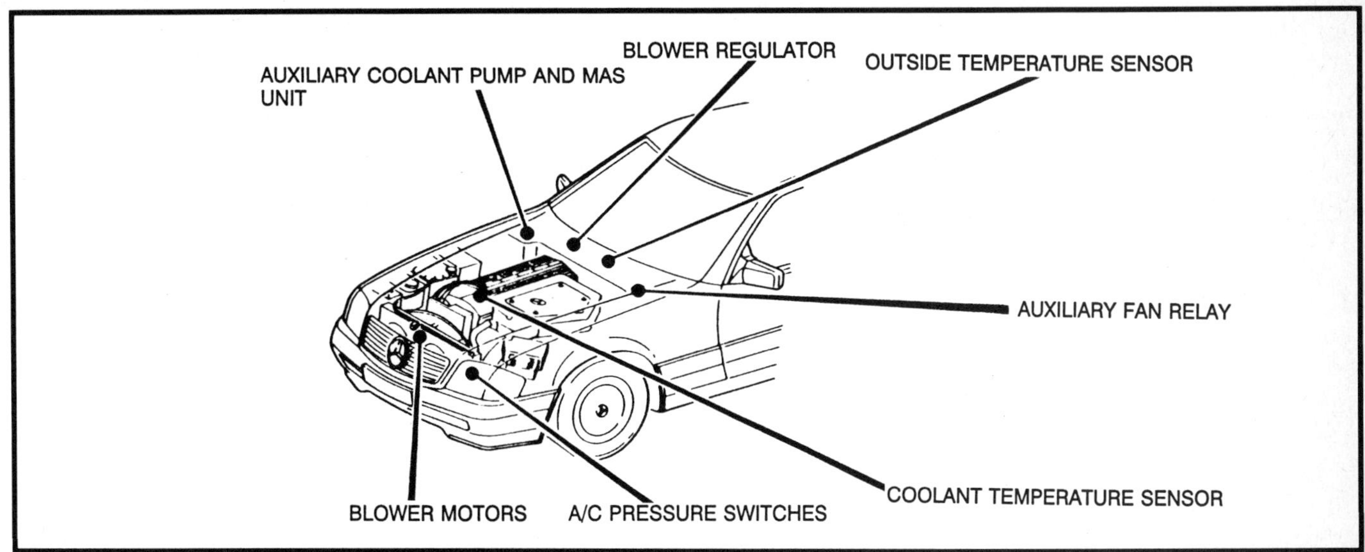

Component locations—1990 300 and 500SL series

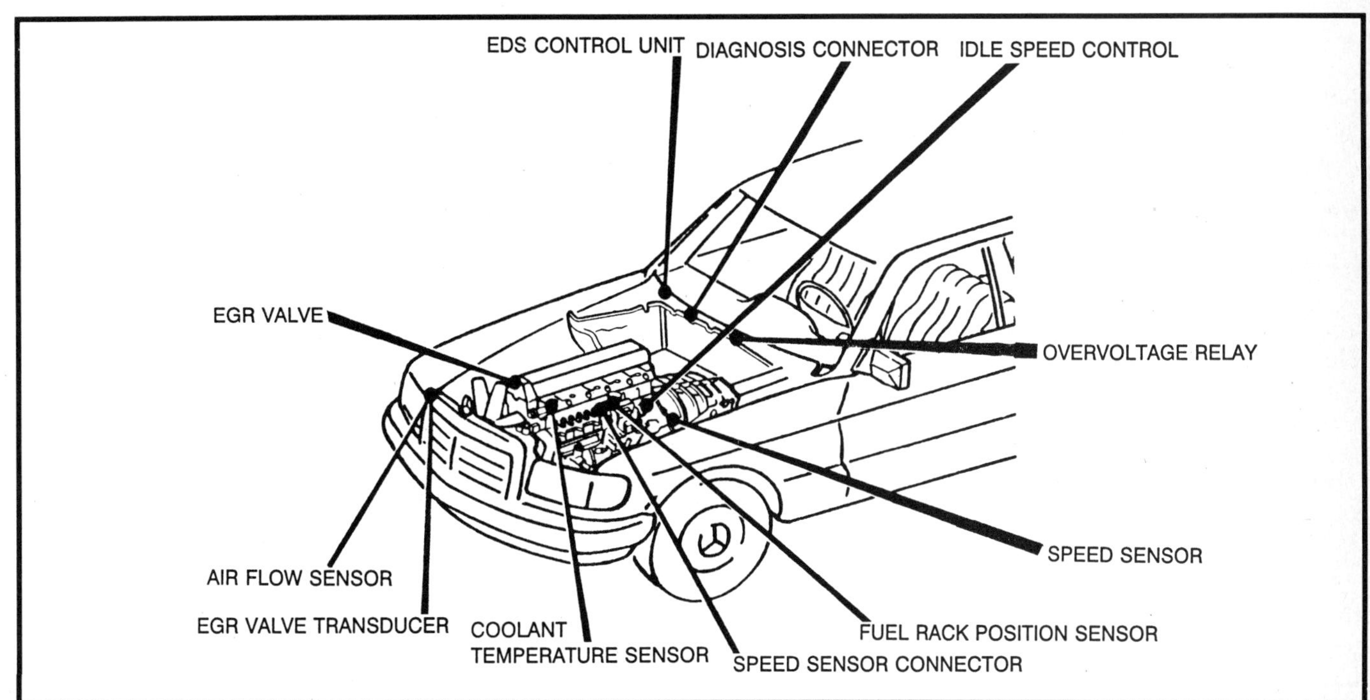

Component locations—1990 350D 2.5 turbocharged engine

- **Safety Switch (rear power windows)**—is located below rear of the console.
- **Seat Backrest Locking Valve**—is located behind left side of dash panel.
- **Seat Belt Warning Relay**—is located left side of front footwell.
- **Seat Heater Relay**—is located below carpeting, forward of the front seat assembly.
- **Starting Valve**—is located top center of engine, right of air cleaner.
- **Starter Lock-Out/Backup Lamp Switch**—is located on the left side of the transmission assembly.
- **SRS Energy Accumulator**—is located below footrest in right front footwell area.
- **Supplement Restraint System Control Unit (SRS)**—is located behind front of console, below radio.
- **SRS Voltage Converter**—is located behind the right kick panel.
- **Supply Pump**—is located below right side of rear seat assembly.
- **TDC Sensor**—is located front of the engine assembly.
- **Telescopic Steering Column Motor**—is located on the left side of steering column.
- **Temperature Switch (105/115°C)**—is located on the top center of cylinder head, next to air cleaner.
- **Temperature Switch (105/115°C diesel)**—is located on the top left side of the engine assembly.

- **Temperature Switch (50°C diesel)**—is located lower right side of engine assembly.
- **Throttle Valve Switch**—is located left side of engine, lower left of the throttle body.
- **Warning Buzzer Switch**—is part of the glow/starter switch assembly.
- **Warning Module**—is located behind right side of the instrument cluster assembly.
- **Window Safety Switch (rear windows)**—is located below rear of the console.
- **Windshield Washer Fluid Level Switch**—is located at right side of engine compartment at the top of the washer reservoir.
- **Windshield Washer Pump**—is located right front of engine compartment, front of washer fluid reservoir.

420 AND 500 SERIES

- **A/C Compressor Control Unit**—is located in the engine compartment, right of the brake reservoir.
- **A/C Compressor Speed Sensor**—is located on the compressor unit.
- **A/C High Pressure Switch**—is located lower left front of engine compartment, at accumulator.
- **ABS Control Unit**—is located center of engine compartment.
- **ABS Hydraulic Unit**—is located in the left front corner of engine compartment.
- **ABS Left Front Wheel Speed Sensor**—is located in the left side wheel.
- **ABS Right Front Wheel Speed Sensor**—is located in the right side wheel.
- **ABS Rear Axle Speed Sensor**—is located in the rear differential.
- **Air Bag**—see Supplement Restraint System (SRS).
- **Air Flow Sensor Position Indicator**—is located on the right side of mixture control unit.
- **Air Injection Relay**—is located in fuse/relay box at location E.
- **Air Pump Vacuum Valve**—is located right front corner of engine compartment.
- **Altitude Correction Capsule**—is located below the right front footrest.
- **Anti-lock Brake System (ABS)**—see ABS.
- **Anti-theft Alarm Control Unit**—is located right front of passenger compartment, underside of footrest.
- **Anti-theft Alarm Horn**—is located at right side of engine compartment.
- **Anti-towing Sensor**—is located at left front corner of trunk.
- **Automatic Locking Differential (ASD) Control Unit**—is located in the right front engine compartment area.
- **Auxiliary Coolant Pump**—is located right side of engine compartment.
- **Auxiliary Fuse Box**—is located in the engine compartment in the left side area.
- **Auxiliary Fuse Box**—is located in the right side trunk area.
- **Auxiliary Fuse Holder (blower motor)**—is located left side of engine compartment.
- **Backup Lamp Switch/Starter Lock-Out**—is located on the left side of the transmission assembly.
- **Brake Fluid Level Switch**—is located on the left side of the engine compartment at the top of the brake fluid reservoir.
- **CIS-E Control Unit**—is located behind right kick panel.
- **Coolant Level Switch**—is located right side of engine compartment, at the bottom of the coolant reservoir.
- **Coolant Temperature Gauge Sensor**—is located top front of engine assembly.
- **Coolant Temperature Sensor**—is located on the top left front of engine assembly.
- **Crankshaft Position Sensor**—is located on the top of bellhousing.
- **Cruise Control Actuator**—is located right front of the engine assembly.
- **Cruise Control Amplifier**—is located behind left side of dash, left of steering column.
- **Diagnostic Connection/Terminal Block**—is located on the left side of the engine compartment.
- **Dome Lamp Timer Relay**—is located at center of windshield header.
- **EGR Temperature Sensor**—is located at top left rear of engine.
- **Electrical Center (fuse box)**—is located on the left side of engine compartment.
- **Electronic Ignition Control Unit**—is located on the lower left side of engine compartment.
- **Electro-Hydraulic Actuator**—is located at top left rear of engine assembly.
- **Ground (engine)**—is located at ABS hydraulic unit.
- **Ground (battery)**—is located on the right side of engine compartment.
- **Fuel Level Sensor**—Is located front of truck at the top of fuel tank area.
- **Fuel Pumps**—are located right of rear differential.
- **Fuel Pump Relay**—is located in engine compartment, right of brake fluid reservoir.
- **Fuse/Relay Box**—is located on the left side of engine compartment.
- **Hall Effect Speed Sensor**—is located on the rear of the instrument cluster.
- **Headlamp Washer Pump**—is located right front of engine compartment, front of washer fluid reservoir.
- **Heater Core Temperature Sensor**—is located in the air conditioning module, behind console.
- **Idle Speed Control Unit**—is located in right front footwell area.
- **Idle Speed Air Valve**—is located at the top of the engine, at mixture control unit.
- **In-Car Temperature**—is located on the left side of air conditioning module, above the accelerator pedal.
- **Instrument Illumination Control Unit**—is located behind instrument cluster.
- **Oil Pressure Sensor**—is located at oil filter.
- **Outside Temperature Sensor**—is located on front corner on rear of license plate bracket.
- **Overvoltage Protection Relay**—is located on the right side of brake booster assembly.
- **Oxygen Sensor (heated)**—is mounted in catalytic converter.
- **Rear Window Sun Shade Motor**—is located under the center of hat shelf in the trunk area.
- **Resistance Trimming Plug (CIS-E)**—is located at right kick panel.
- **Roll Bar Control Unit**—is located in the center of the rear floor area.
- **Safety Switch (rear power windows)**—is located below rear of the console.
- **Seat Backrest Locking Valve**—is located behind left side of dash panel.
- **Seat Belt Warning Relay**—is located left side of front footwell.
- **Seat Heater Relay**—is located below carpeting, forward of the front seat assembly on air duct.
- **Soft Top Power Control Unit**—is located in the center of the rear floor area, next to roll bar control unit.
- **Soft Top Power Hydraulic Unit**—Is located under the spare tire in the spare tire well.
- **Speaker Amplifier (left)**—is located behind the left side of the rear seat backrest.
- **Speaker Amplifier (right)**—is located behind the right side of the rear seat backrest.

- **Starting Valve** – is located top center of engine assembly.
- **Starter Lock-Out/Backup Lamp Switch** – is located on the left side of the transmission assembly.
- **Supplement Restraint System Control Unit (SRS)** – is located behind front of console, below radio.
- **SRS Energy Accumulator** – is located below footrest in right front footwell area.
- **SRS Voltage Converter** – is located behind the right kick panel.
- **Supply Pump** – is located in spare tire well.
- **TDC Sensor** – is located front of the engine assembly.
- **Temperature Switch (105/115°C)** – is located on the top front of the engine assembly.
- **Throttle Valve Switch (full load/idle)** – is located at the throttle body.
- **Warning Buzzer Switch** – is part of the ignition/starter switch assembly.
- **Warning Module** – is located behind dash panel, left of steering column.
- **Window Safety Switch (rear windows)** – is located below rear of the console.
- **Windshield Washer Fluid Level Switch** – is located at right side of engine compartment at the top of the washer reservoir.
- **Windshield Washer Pump** – is located right front of engine compartment, front of washer fluid reservoir.

MERKUR

Circuit Breakers and Fuses

SCORPIO

The circuit breakers and fuses are located in either the main fuse/relay panel or in the auxiliary fuse panel. They are identified in number value, measured in amperes. The fuses can also be identified by color code.

XR4Ti

Fuses are located at the left rear corner of the engine compartment in the fuse panel. An in-line fuse for the fuel computer is located behind the instrument panel.

Fusible Links

SCORPIO

Fusible links are located at the battery, attached to the positive post.

XR4Ti

Fusible links may be located at the battery, alternator or starter.

Relays, Sensors, Modules and Computer Locations

SCORPIO

- **A/C Condenser Cooling Fan Temperature Switch** – Located on the right side of the radiator.
- **A/C Condenser Cooling Fan Temperature Relay** – Located in the main fuse/relay panel.
- **A/C De-Icing Switch** – is located inside the evaporator case.
- **ABS Electronic Control Module** – On the right instrument panel.
- **ABS Indicator Diode** – is located under the dash, on the right instrument panel.
- **ABS Relay Diode** – is located on the left side of the auxiliary warning module.
- **ABS Power Relay** – is located on the auxiliary fuse panel.
- **ABS Pressure Control Switch** – is located on the forward side of the hydraulic actuation assembly.

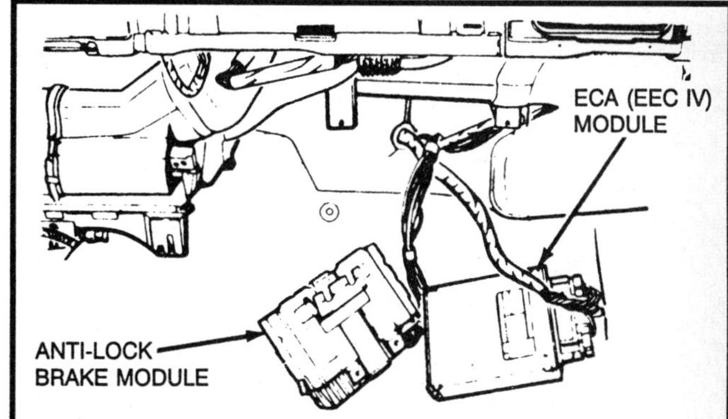

Location of the Anti-lock brake and Electronic Control Assembly (ECA) modules – Scorpio

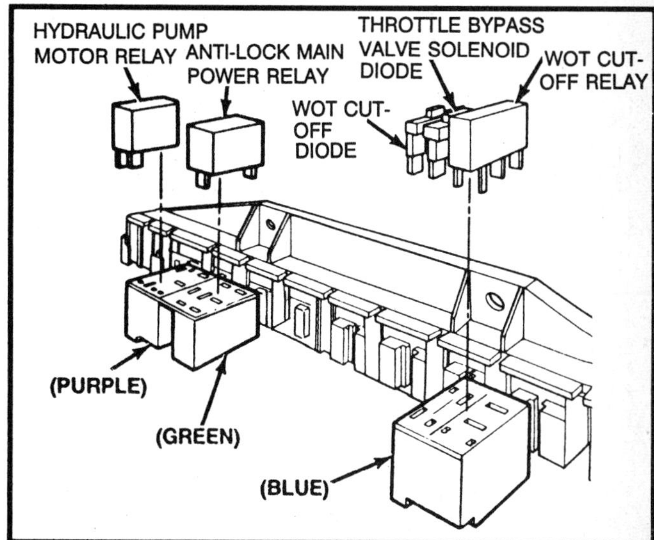

View of the auxiliary relay panel – Scorpio

- **Ambient Temperature Sensor** – is located on the center of the cowl, in the engine compartment.
- **Antenna Module** – is located on the liftgate lower back panel.
- **Air Charge Temperature Sensor (ACT)** – is located on the right side of the intake manifold.

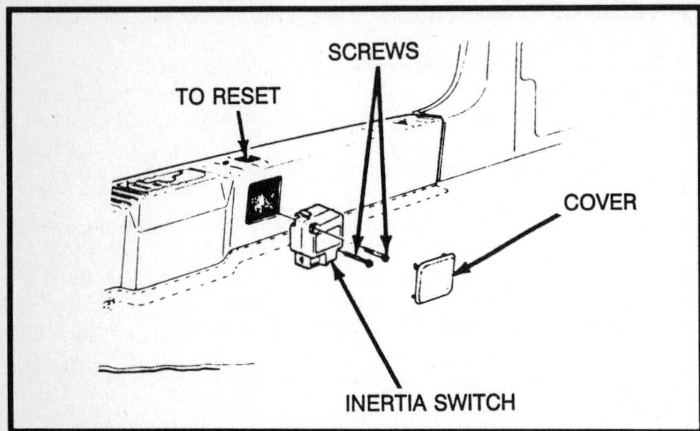

Location of the inertia switch—Scorpio

- **Auxiliary fuse panel**—is located in the glove box.
- **Auxiliary Warning Module**—is located on the right side of the instrument panel.
- **Backup Lamp Switch**—is located on the left side of the transmission.
- **Brake Hydraulic Motor Diode**—is located in the harness on the left fender apron.
- **Canister Purge Solenoid**—is located above the right frame rail.
- **Circuit Breakers 23 and 24**—are located in the main fuse/relay panel.
- **Circuit Breaker 36**—is located in the auxiliary fuse panel, inside the glove box.
- **Coolant Temperature Sensor**—is located on the thermostat housing.
- **EATC Control Module**—is located in the center of the instrument panel, behind the dash pad.

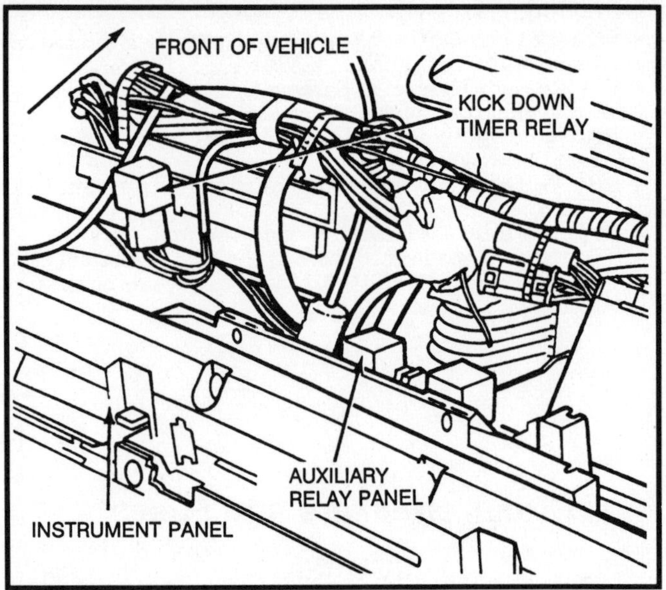

Location of the transmission kickdown timer relay—Scorpio

- **ECC Power Relay**—is located in the Main fuse/Relay panel.
- **Electronic Control Assembly (ECA)**—is located at the lower right instrument panel.
- **Engine Coolant Temperature Sensor (ECTS)**—Located on the thermostat housing.
- **Fuel Pump Relay**—is located in the main fuse/relay panel.

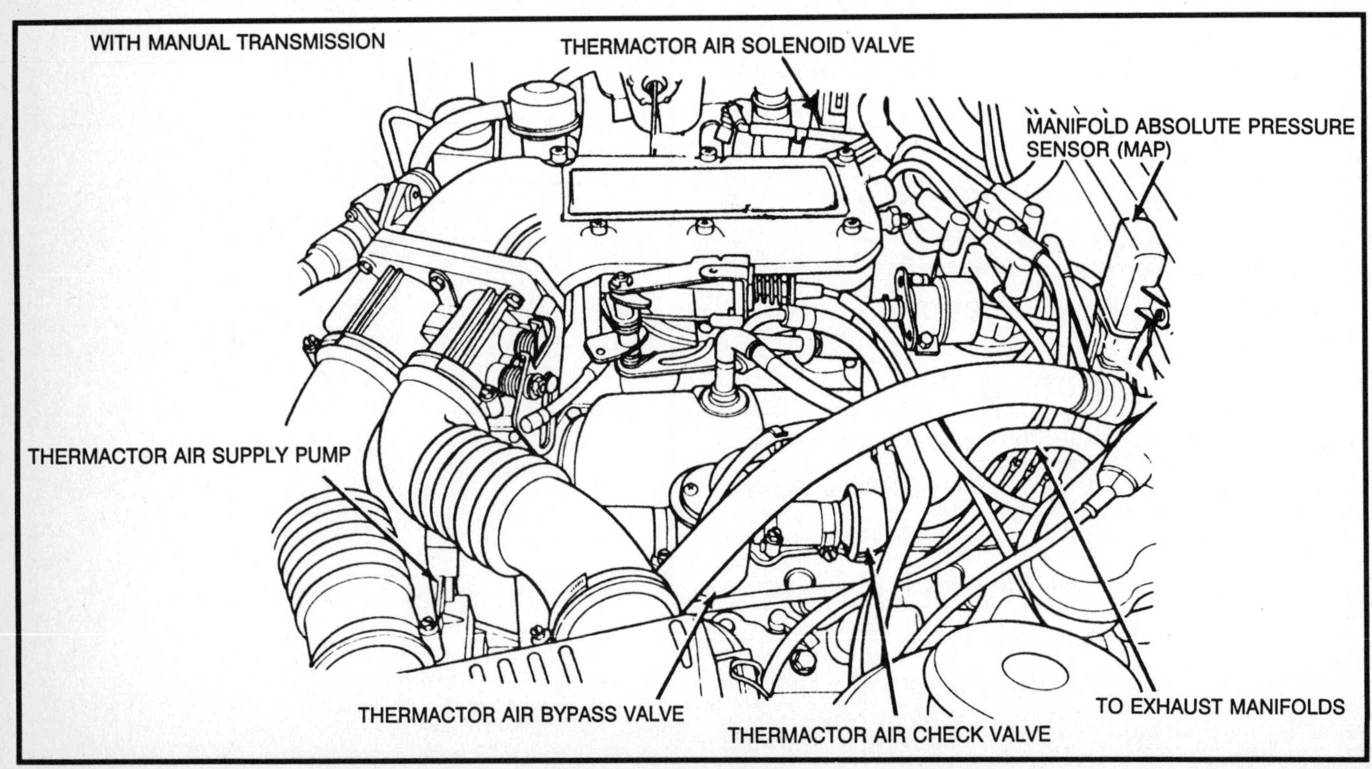

Location of the thermactor and related components— Scorpio

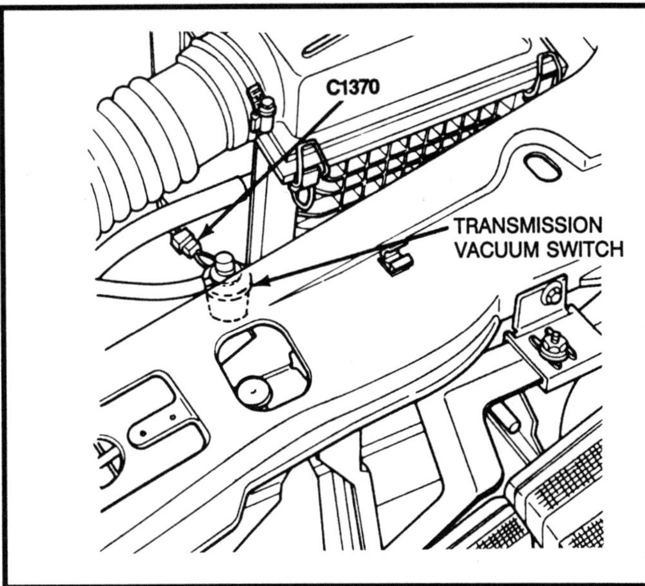

Location of the transmission vacuum switch—Scorpio

• **Fuse 31**—is located under right side dash, taped around the wiring harness leading to fuse 37.
• **Fuse 32, 33**—are located in the auxiliary fuse panel.
• **Fuses 33 and 34**—are located in the auxiliary fuse panel, inside the glove compartment.
• **Fuse 37**—is located in the auxiliary fuse panel.
• **Fusible links A and B**—are located at the battery, attached to the positive post.
• **Fuel Computer**—is located on the left side of the instrument panel.
• **Fuel Filler Door Relay**—is located in the Main fuse/Relay panel.
• **Graphic Display Module**—Mounted in the instrument cluster.
• **Heated Exhaust Gas Oxygen Sensor (HEGO)**—Threaded into the left Y-pipe near the manifold junction.
• **Head lamp Courtesy Delay Relay**—is located in the Main fuse/Relay panel
• **High Beam Relay**—is located in the main fuse/relay panel.
• **Heated Seat Relay**—is located in the main fuse/relay panel.
• **Heated Seat Resistors**—is located inside the seat cushions and backs.
• **Ice Warning Sensor**—is located on the lower radiator support.

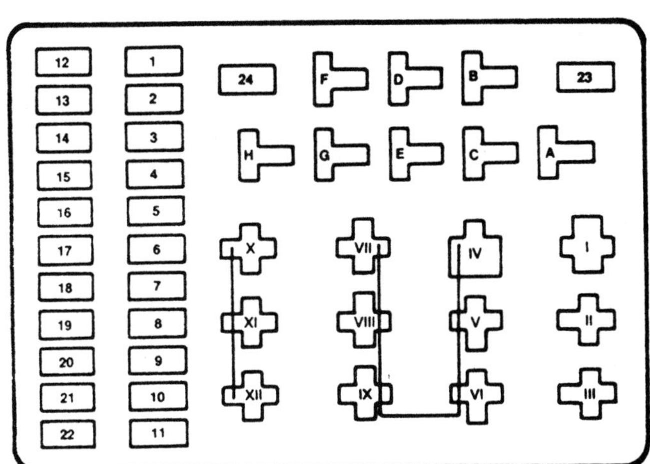

MAIN FUSE/RELAY PANEL

1 Left head light-high beam
2 Right head light-high beam
3 Left head light-low beam
4 Right head light-low beam
5 Left parking lamps, front side marker lamps, rear side marker lamps and license lamp
6 Right parking lamps, front side marker lamps, rear side marker lamps and engine compartment lamp
7 Instrument illumination, Ash receptacle lamp
8 Automatic Transmission Shift Control, Air conditioning cooling fan
9 Fuel filler door release, Tailgate release
10 Courtesy lamps, Power door locks, Power Mirror, Vanity Mirror, EATC, Fuel Computer, Clock, Radio, Luggage Compartment lamp, Liftgate Ajar Sensor
11 Air conditioning Cooling Fan Motor, Parking lamp
12 Hazard Flasher
13 Cigar lighters, Heated Seats
14 Horn
15 Liftgate Wiper/ Washer, Front Wiper/ Washer
16 Rear Window Defrost, Heated Mirrors
17 Fog lamps
18 EATC Module, Blower Motor
19 Not used
20 Automatic Transmission Shift Control, Back-up lamps, Turn Signal Lamps
21 Brake lamps, Auxiliary Warning
22 Speedometer, Instrument Cluster, Speed Control, Fuel Computer, Lamp-Out Module, Warning Chime, Clock, Auxiliary Warning, Graphic Display, Tachometer
23 Front Power Windows, Power Sun Roof, Rear Seat Cut-off
24 Rear Power Windows, Rear Power Seats

Relay Position	Circuit
A	Fuel Pump Relay
B	Heated Mirror Relay
C	Horn Relay
D	Liftgate Lock Relay
E	Fuel Filler Door Release Relay
F	A/C WOT Cutoff Relay
G	Heated Seats
H	Fog Lamp Relay

Relay Position	Circuit
I	Ignition Switch Relay
II	Parking Lamp Relay
III	A/C Condenser Cooling Fan Relay
IV	Headlamp Delay Relay (45 seconds)
V	Interval Wiper Relay
VI	Rear Wiper Reverse Relay
VII	EEC Power Relay
VIII	Interior Lamp/Delay Relay
IX	Rear Compartment Cut-off Relay
X	High Beam Relay
XI	Engine Run Relay
XII	Start Relay

Fuse and relay positions in the main fuse/relay and auxiliary panels—Scorpio

• **Ignition Module**—Thick Film Ignition (TFI) module is mounted on the side of the distributor.

• **Interior Lamp Courtesy Delay Relay**—is located in main fuse panel.

• **Interior Lamp Delay Relay**—is located in the main fuse/relay panel.

• **Inertia Switch**—is located in luggage compartment, in the lower back panel.

• **Interval Wiper Relay**—is located in the main fuse/relay panel.

• **In Vehicle Temperature Sensor**—is located on the left side of the roof console.

• **Kickdown Actuator Solenoid**—is located on the left side of the transmission.

• **Kickdown Time Delay Relay**—is located behind the instrument panel at the center of the dash panel.

• **Lamp Out Relay Module**—Mounted on back of the lower right instrument trim panel.

• **Liftgate Release Solenoid**—is located at the liftgate latch.

• **Liftgate Ajar Sensor**—is located at the liftgate latch.

• **Low Engine Coolant Warning Sensor**—is located in the coolant reservoir

• **Manifold Absolute Pressure (MAP) Sensor**—is located on the firewall just above the engine.

• **Multi-function Switch**—is located on the left side of the steering column.

• **Main Fuse/Relay Panel**—is located in the left rear corner of the engine compartment.

• **Neutral Safety Switch**—is located on the side of the transmission case.

• **Outlet Air Temperature Sensor**—is located in the center vent duct next to the heater core.

• **Pressure Feedback EGR Sensor (PFE)**—is located on the air cleaner housing.

• **Parking lamp relay**—is located in the main/relay panel.

• **Power Sunroof Micro Switch**—Integral with the motor assembly.

• **Rear Seat Power Relay**—is located in the main fuse/relay panel.

• **Rear Seat Cut-off Switch**—is located on the center console front panel.

• **Rear Defroster Relay**—is located in the main fuse/relay panel.

• **Recir/Outside Air Solenoid**—is located on the left right fender apron near the battery.

• **Recir/Outside Solenoid Diode**—Taped to wiring harness, above the battery.

• **Speed Control Module**—is located in the passenger compartment on the right side below the dash pad.

• **Speed Sensor**—is located on the left side of the transmission tail housing.

• **Starter Relay**—is located in the main fuse/relay panel.

• **Vacuum Servo**—is located on the left fender apron behind the shock tower.

• **TFI Ignition Module**—Mounted on the side of the distributor.

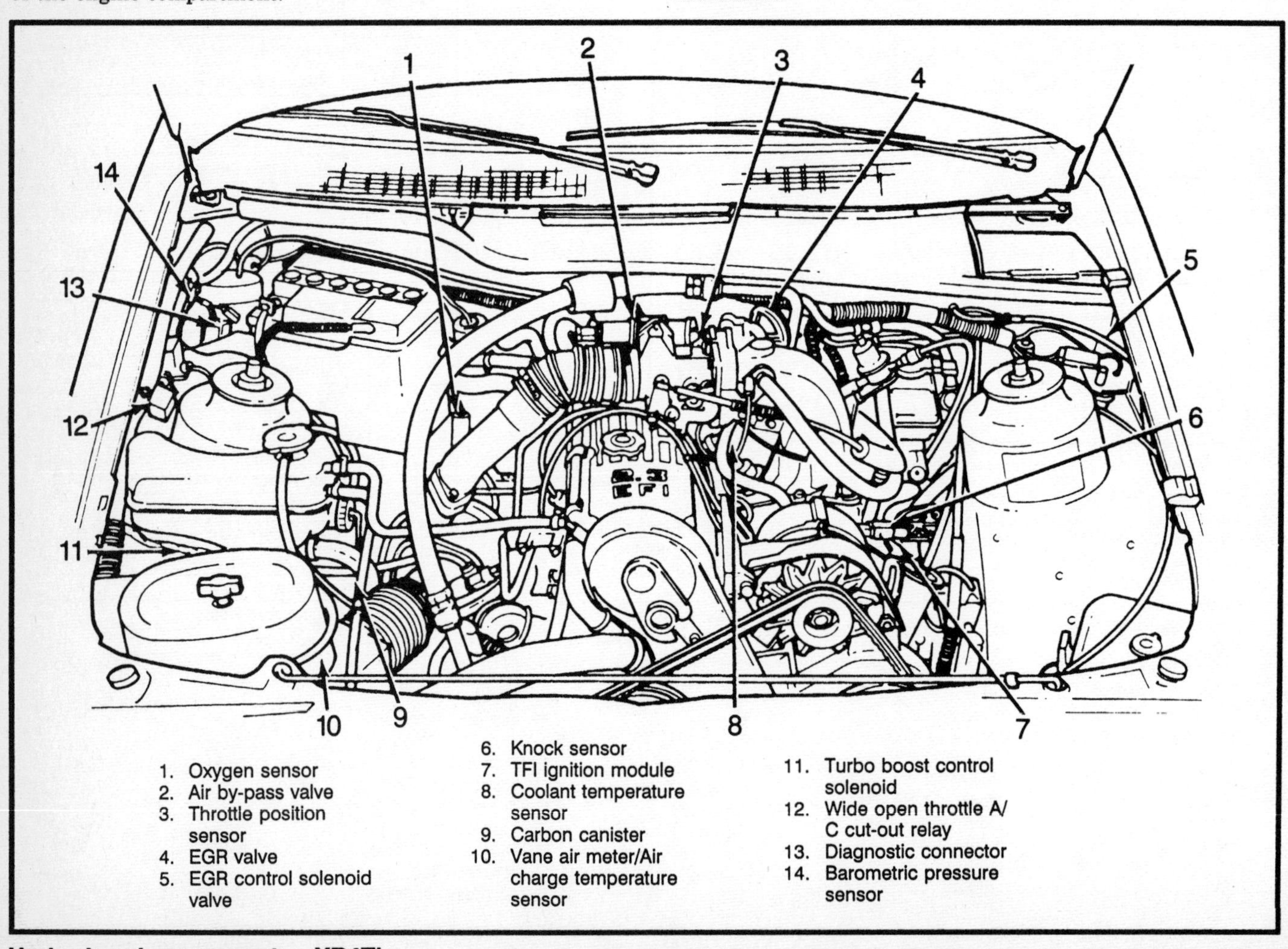

Under hood components—XR4Ti

• **Thermactor Air Solenoid**—is located on the right fender apron.
• **Throttle Air Bypass Valve Solenoid**—is located on the throttle body.
• **Throttle Position Sensor**—is located on the throttle body.
• **Transmission Vacuum Switch**—is located on the left frame rail below the air cleaner.
• **Three-Way Pressure Switch**—Attached to the receiver/drier.
• **Turnsignal/Hazard Flasher**—Attached to the multifunction switch.
• **Vacuum Regulator Solenoid (EVR)**—is located on the right fender apron.
• **Wide Open Throttle Cut-off Relay**—is located in the auxiliary relay panel.
• **Warning Chime Module**—is located behind the instrument panel pad, center of the dash panel.

XR4Ti

• **A/C Clutch Wide Open Throttle Relay**—is located in the underhood fuse panel.
• **A/C Fan Relay**—is located under the instrument panel.
• **A/C Pressure Switch**—is located at the receiver drier.
• **A/C Solenoid**—is located at the right rear of the engine compartment.
• **A/C Temperature Switch Relay**—is located in the underhood fuse panel.

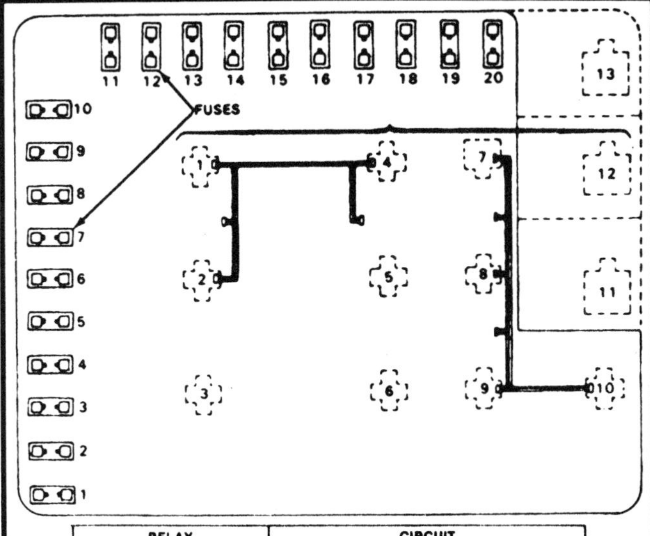

RELAY POSITION	CIRCUIT PROTECTED
1	A/C Temp. Switch
2	Horn
3	A/C Clutch W.O.T.
4	Fuel Pump
5	Fog Lamps
6	(Blank)
7	Interval Windshield Wipers
8	Stop Lamp
9	Seat Belt Reminder
10	Ignition Switch
11	Rear Wipers
12	Interior Lamp Delay
13	Heated Backlite

Fuse box schematic—XR4Ti

• **Air Charge Temperature Sensor/Air Vane Meter**—is located at the right front of the engine compartment.
• **Air Vane Meter**—is located at the right front of the engine compartment.
• **Auxiliary Warning Module**—is located under the right side of the dash on the electronic control assembly.
• **Backup Light Switch (manual transmission)**—is located at the right rear of the transmission case.
• **Backup Light/Neutral Start Switch (automatic transmission)**—is located at the left side of the transmission case.
• **Barometric Pressure Sensor**—is located at the right rear of the engine compartment.
• **Brake Pad Wear Sensor**—is located at the brake caliper.
• **Brakelight Relay**—is located in the underhood fuse panel.
• **Bulb Test Control Relay**—is located under the instrument panel.
• **Central Door Locking Relay**—is located under the instrument panel.
• **Coolant Temperature Sender**—is located above the TFI module.
• **Coolant Temperature Sensor**—is located at the top left side of the engine.
• **Cooling Fan Temperature Switch**—is located at the intake manifold near the upper radiator hose.
• **Diagnostic Test Connector**—is located near the battery and right strut tower.
• **Dual Brake Warning Switch**—is located at the master cylinder.
• **EEC Power Relay**—is located under the instrument panel.
• **EGR Solenoid**—is located at the left rear of the engine compartment.
• **Electric Fan Switch**—is located at the left rear of the engine.
• **Electronic Control Assembly**—is located under the right side of the dash.
• **Electronic Engine Control**—see EEC.
• **Engine Fan Relay**—is located under the instrument panel.
• **Fog Lamp Relay**—is located in the underhood fuse panel.
• **Fuel Pump Relay**—is located under the instrument panel or in the underhood fuse panel.
• **Hazard Flasher/Warning Light Relay**—is located on the brake pedal support bracket.
• **Heated Front Seat Relay**—is located on the brake pedal support bracket.
• **Horn Relay**—is located in the underhood fuse panel.
• **Ignition Switch Relay**—is located in the underhood fuse panel.
• **Ignition Module**—Thick Film Ignition (TFI) module is located at the distributor.
• **Inertia Switch**—is located in the spare tire well.
• **Interior Lamp Delay Relay**—is located in the underhood fuse panel.
• **Interval Windsheild Wiper Relay**—is located in the underhood fuse panel.
• **Knock Sensor**—is located next to the distributor.
• **Lamp Module**—is located under the right side of the dash on the electronic control assembly.
• **Low Coolant Sensor**—is located at the right front of the engine compartment, on the coolant overflow bottle.
• **Low Oil Level Switch**—is located at the left rear of the engine.
• **Low Windsheild Washer Fluid Switch**—is located at the windsheild washer reservoir.
• **Neutral Start Switch (manual transmission)**—is located at the right front of the transmission case.
• **Oil Pressure Switch**—is located at the top left rear of the engine.

• **Oxygen Sensor**—is located at the right rear of the engine on the turbo boost outlet.

• **Power Antenna Relay**—is located on the brake pedal support bracket.

• **Power Window Relay**—is located on the brake pedal support bracket.

• **PVC Valve**—is located above the distributor.

• **Rear Window Defogger Relay**—is located in the underhood fuse panel.

• **Seat Belt Reminder Relay**—is located in the underhood fuse panel.

• **Speed Control Amplifier**—is located at the left rear of the engine compartment.

• **Speed Control Modulating Valve**—is located at the left front of the engine compartment.

• **Speed Control Servo**—is located at the left front of the engine compartment.

• **Speed Sensor**—is located at the speedometer cable.

• **Temperature Switch Relay**—is located under the instrument panel.

• **TFI Module**—is located at the distributor.

• **Throttle Air Bypass Valve Solenoid**—is located at the throttle body.

• **Throttle Position Sensor**—is located at the throttle body.

• **Turbo Boost Pressure Switch**—is located at the elft rear of the engine compartment.

• **Turbo Boost Solenoid**—is located at the right front of the engine compartment.

• **Warning Light Relay**—is located under the instrument panel.

• **Windsheild Wiper Relay**—is located in the underhood fuse panel.

PEUGEOT

Circuit Breakers and Fuses

405 SERIES

The Peugeot 405 Series has a main fuse box located under the dashboard to the left of the steering column. Several relays and the flasher are located in this fuse box.

A relay box is mounted under the hood on the right side inner fender wall ahead of the strut tower. This relay box contains both relays and some fuses.

505 SERIES

The Peugeot 505 Series has a main fuse box located at the left rear corner of the engine compartment. In addition, an accessory power board containing more fuses is located above the top of the glove box. Additional fuses can be found underhood at the right shock tower and several more fuses are behind the ashtray.

A relay bracket is mounted under the hood at the left rear corner of the engine compartment. Relays can also be found at various places throughout the vehicle, often near the electrical device they serve.

Relays, Sensors, Modules and Computer Locations

405 SERIES

• **A/C Compressor Cut-Out Relay**—is located on the relay bank mounted on a bracket on the right side of the engine compartment just forward of the strut tower.

• **A/C Evaporator Temperature Sensor**—is located behind the left side of the dashboard at the evaporator.

• **A/C Pressure Switch**—is located on the drier at the left front of the engine compartment.

• **ABS ECU**—is located at the left rear of the engine compartment.

• **ABS Electro Pump Assembly**—is located at the right front of the engine compartment.

• **ABS Electro-Valve Assembly**—is located at the left side rear corner of the engine compartment.

• **ABS Indicator Relay**—is located behind the right side of the dashboard above the glove box.

• **ABS Test Connector**—is located on the right side of the engine compartment in the relay box.

• **ABS Tooth Sensor Rings**—are located at each respective wheel, on the inner side.

• **ABS Wheel Sensors**—are located down by the wheel spindles next to the toothed wheel hubs.

• **Air Flow Sensor**—is located in the air intake duct at the front left corner of the engine compartment just after the air filter housing.

• **Air Mix Door Control Motor**—is located behind the right side of the dashboard.

• **Anti-lock Brake System**—see components listed under ABS.

• **Automatic Transmission Input Relay**—is located on the relay bank mounted on a bracket on the right side of the engine compartment just forward of the strut tower.

• **Auxiliary Air Device**—is located at the left side of the engine below the distributor.

• **Back-Up Light/Neutral Safety Switch**—is located at the left side front of the transaxle.

• **Blower Motor**—is located behind the center of the dashboard.

• **Brake Fluid Level Switch**—is located in the brake fluid reservoir at the left rear corner of the engine compartment.

• **Brake Light Switch**—is located on a bracket just above the brake pedal arm.

• **Brake Wear Indicator Sensors**—are located in the inboard front caliper brake pads.

• **Centralized Power Door Lock Remote Control Receiver**—is located in the center of the windshield header. The transmitter is to be carried on the vehicle's key ring.

• **Charcoal Canister Purge Solenoid Valve**—is located at the left side front corner of the engine compartment behind the radiator.

• **Chime, Lights/Key Warning**—is located behind the left side of the dashboard, left of the steering column.

• **Climate Control Module**—is located behind the front of the console.

• **Climate Control ECU**—is located behind the right side of the dashboard above the glove box.

• **Clutch Switch for Cruise Control**—is located on a bracket just above the clutch pedal arm.

• **Combination Switch**—including headlight, turn signal and horn switch is attached to the left side of the steering column.

• **Coolant Level Sender**—is located at the bottom right side of the radiator.

• **Coolant Temperature Sender**—feeds a signal to the coolant temperature dashboard gauge is located on the end of the head just opposite of the battery.

• **Cooling Fan Relay A**—is located in the front of the engine compartment at the left side of the radiator shroud.

• **Cooling Fan Relay B**—is located in the front of the engine compartment at the center of the radiator shroud.

• **Courtesy Light Delay Off Module**—is located behind the right side of the dashboard above the glove box.

• **Courtesy Light Door Jam Switch**—is located in each respective door jam.

• **Crankshaft Position Sensor**—is located next to the trigger wheel mounted on the crankshaft behind the front pulley.

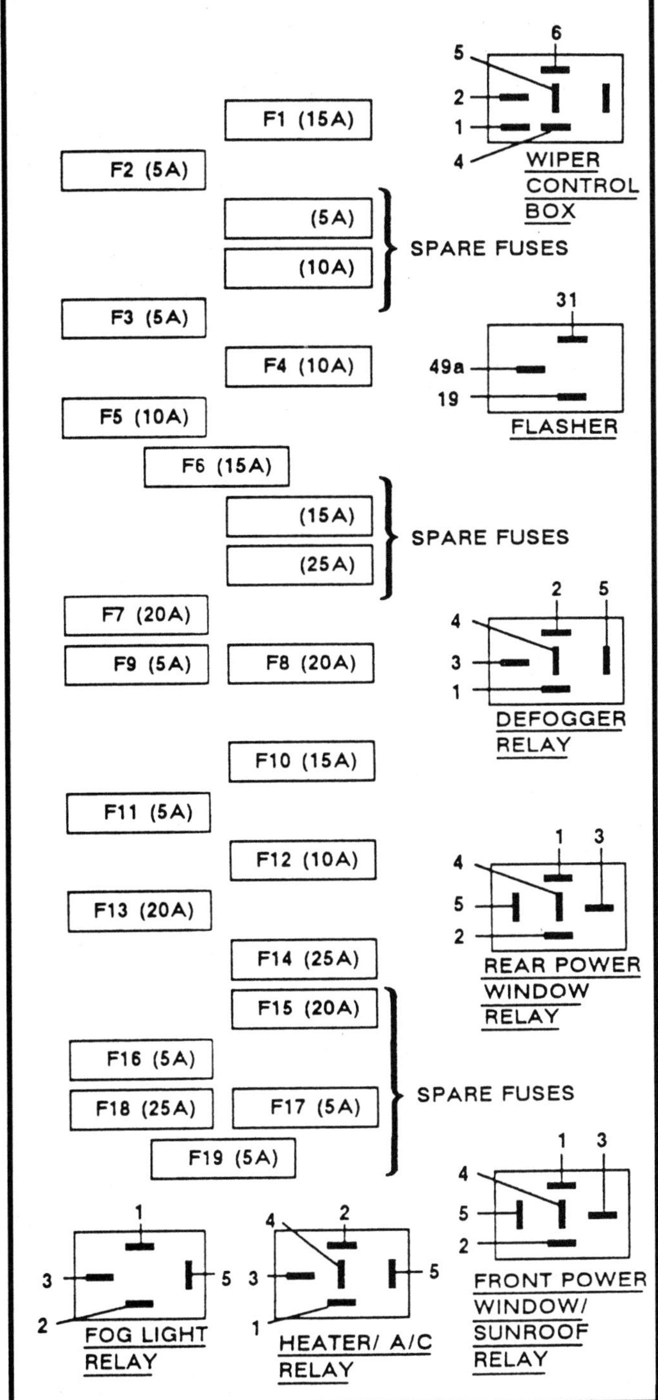

Fuse box—405 Series

Fuse Name and Letter	Size	Circuits Protected
ABS Main Relay Power "G"	30A	Antilock Brake System
ABS Pump Relay Power "F"	30A	Antilock Brake System

Fuses located on right side shock tower

Fuse Name and Letter	Size/Color	Circuits Protected
Antilock Indicator "B"	7.5A (BROWN)	Antilock Brake System
Antilock Brake Controller "C"	7.5A (BROWN)	
Lambda Sensor Heater "E"	15A or 10A (BLUE)	Fuel Injection (N9TEA) (N9TE) (ZDJL) (ZN3J)
Fuel Pump "D"	15A (BLUE)	Fuel Injection (N9TEA) (N9TE) (ZDJL) (ZN3J)

Fuses located behind ashtray

• **Cruise Control ECU**—is located behind the right side of the dashboard above the glove box.

• **Coolant Thermocontact**—feeds a signal to the coolant temperature warning indicator (red light) and is located on the left side of the engine.

• **Cooling Fan A**—is located at the front left side of the radiator.

• **Cooling Fan B**—is located at the front right side of the radiator.

• **Cooling Fan In-Line Fuses**—are located at the left side of the engine compartment, at the positive battery junction connector.

• **Cooling Fan Low Speed Relay**—is located in the front of the engine compartment on the right side of the radiator shroud.

• **Cruise Control Safety Relay**—is located behind the left side of the dashboard above the shroud, near the starter relay and engine A/C compressor cut-out relay.

• **Cruise Control Throttle Actuator**—is located on the top of the intake manifold, on XU9J2 1.9L SOHC engines and on the top front of the engine on XU9J4 1.9L DOHC engines.

• **Cruise Control Vacuum Dump Electro-Valve**—is located at the right side front of the engine compartment.

• **Cruise Control Vacuum Pump/Vent Valve**—is located at the right side front of the engine compartment.

• **Cruise Control Vehicle Speed Transducer**—is located under the left side of the dashboard mounted on the speedometer cable.

• **Defogger Relay**—is located in the fuse box

• **Delay Off Module**—is located behind the right side of the dashboard above the glove box.

• **Detonation (Knock) Sensor**—is located at the front lower right side of the engine next to the oil filter on XU9J4 1.9L DOHC.

• **Diagnostic Plug**—is located in the relay box mounted on a bracket on the right side of the engine compartment just forward of the strut tower.

• **Distributor**—is located at the top left side rear of the engine.

• **Door Jamb Switches**—are located in their respective doors.

• **Door Lock Motors**—are located in their respective doors.

• **Electronic Control Unit Fuse**—is located on the relay bank mounted on a bracket on the right side of the engine compartment just forward of the strut tower.

• **Engine A/C Compressor Cut-Out Relay**—is located behind the left side of the dashboard above the shroud.

• **Engine Speed Sensor**—is located at the left side of the engine, on the transaxle.

• **Engine Temperature Sensor**—is located at the left side rear of the engine block, above the coolant outlet.

• **Flasher (turn signal)**—is located in the fuse box, behind the left side of the dash panel.

• **Foglight Relay**—is located in the fuse box, behind the left side of the dashboard.

• **Fuel Feed Pump**—is located under the rear of the vehicle near the spare tire.

• **Fuel Filler Door Locking Motor**—is located in the trunk on the right side inner fender, under the trim.

• **Fuel Filter**—is located under the vehicle on the delivery side of the pump.

• **Fuel Injection ECU**—is located at the left side rear of the engine compartment.

• **Fuel Injection ECU Fuse**—is located at the right side front of the engine compartment in the relay box.

• **Fuel Injection Motronic Computer Control Unit**—is located under the hood just behind the strut tower on the driver's side.

• **Fuel Injection Pressure Regulator**—is located on the fuel feed end of the injector for rail.

• **Fuel Injection Relay**—is located at the right side front corner of the engine compartment in the relay box.

• **Fuel Injection System Main Relay**—is located on the relay bank mounted on a bracket on the right side of the engine compartment just forward of the strut tower.

• **Fuel Pump, Auxiliary (Primer)**—is located on top of the fuel tank under the rear seat.

• **Fuel Pump, Main**—is located under the vehicle just upstream of the fuel filter.

• **Fuel Pump Fuse**—is located on the relay bank mounted on a bracket on the right side of the engine compartment just forward of the strut tower.

• **Fuel Pump Relay**—is located on the relay bank mounted on a bracket on the right side of the engine compartment just forward of the strut tower.

• **Fuel Tank Sending Unit**—is located on top of the fuel tank under the rear seat.

• **Fuse Block**—is located behind the left side of the dashboard.

• **Hazard Flasher Indicator**—is located in the fuse box, behind the left side of the dash panel.

• **Horn Relay**—is located at the left side rear corner of the engine compartment on a relay bank next to the brake fluid reservoir.

• **Hot Wire Air Mass Sensor**—is located in-line with air intake system.

• **Idle Compensating Electrovalve (A/C equipped)**—is located in the throttle body just behind the throttle cable cam.

• **Ignition Amplifier Module**—is located at the left side of the engine compartment to the right of the battery.

• **Ignition Coil (XU9J2–1.9L SOHC engine)**—is located under the air intake manifold.

• **Ignition Coil (XU9J4–1.9L DOHC engine)**—is located at the top left side of the air intake manifold.

• **Ignition Switch**—is located on the right side of the steering column.

• **Inside Air Temperature Sensor**—is located at the top right side of the dashboard.

• **Instrument Panel Lights Dimmer Switch**—is located on the underside of the steering column panel.

• **Intake Air Temperature Sensor**—is located on the throttle body just under the throttle position sensor.

• **Junction Block A**—is located behind the left side of the dashboard, taped in the dash harness.

• **Junction Block B**—is located behind the left side of the dashboard, taped in the dash harness.

• **Noise Suppressor**—is located under the front of the intake manifold.

• **Neutral Safety/Back-Up Light Switch**—is located at the left side front of the transaxle.

• **Oil Level Sensor**—is located at the bottom rear center of the engine near the halfshaft.

• **Oil Pressure Switch**—is located at the lower right side front of the engine.

• **Oil Temperature Sensor**—is located at the bottom rear of the engine oil pan, just above the oil drain plug.

• **Outside Air Temperature Sensor**—is located in a square opening in the plenum intake under the cowl cover.

• **Oxygen Sensor (lambda sensor)**—is located in the exhaust head pipe between the manifold and the catalytic converter.

• **Oxygen Sensor (lambda sensor) Heater Fuse**—is located in the relay box at the right side front of the engine compartment just forward of the strut tower.

• **Park/Neutral Relay**—is located behind the left side of the dashboard above the shroud.

• **Parking Brake ON Switch**—is located at the base of the parking brake lever.

• **Positive Battery Junction Block Connector**—is located at the left side of the engine compartment forward of the strut tower.

• **Power Antenna Motor**—is located in the trunk on the left side of the inner fender under the trim panel.

• **Power Door Lock Control Module**—is located behind the right side of the dashboard, above the glove box.

• **Power Door Lock Motors**—are located in their respective doors.

• **Power Door Lock Remote Control Receiver**—is located in the center of the windshield header. The transmitter is to be carried on the vehicle's key ring.

• **Power Seat Motors**—are located under the seats.

• **Power Side View Mirror Motors**—are located in their respective mirror assemblies.

• **Power Window Motors**—are located in their respective doors.

• **Power Window Relay (front)**—also powers the sunroof and is located in the fuse box.

• **Power Window Relay (rear)**—is located in the fuse box.

• **Pulsation Damper**—is installed in the fuel line near the battery.

• **Radio Fuse**—is located in-line at the radio, behind the center console panel.

• **Relay Box**—is located on the right side front of the engine compartment just forward of the strut tower.

• **Seatbelt Contact Switches**—are in the track around the front doors.

• **Seatbelt ECU (driver's)**—is located under the driver's seat behind a panel.

• **Seatbelt ECU (passenger's)**—is located under the passenger's seat behind a panel.

• **Seatbelt Motor (driver's)**—is located at the base of the left side door pillar, under the trim panel.

• **Seatbelt Motor (passenger's)**—is located at the base of the right side door pillar, under the trim panel.

• **Seatbelt Warning Chime Module**—is located behind the left side of the dashboard right of the steering column.

• **Starter Motor**—is located at the front of the engine under the air intake manifold.

• **Starter Relay**—is located under the left side of the dashboard above the shroud.

• **Stop Light Switch**—is located on a bracket just above the brake pedal arm.

• **Sunroof Motor**—is located in the center of the windshield header panel.

• **Sunroof Relay**—also powers the front power windows and is located in the fuse box. An additional sunroof relay is located in the front windshield header panel next to the sunroof motor.

• **Temperature Electronic Control Unit**—is located behind the center console, below the blower motor.

• **Thermo-Contact Switch (coolant temperature input to ECU)**—is located left side of the engine.

• **Throttle Position Sensor**—is located on the throttle body at the left side.

• **Throttle Switch Unit (idle/WOT Switch)**—is located at the front of the engine, rear of the air intake manifold.

• **Trunk Light Switch**—is located at the right side front of the trunk.

• **Trunk Locking Motor**—is located in the center of the end panel.

• **Turn Signal Flasher**—is located in the fuse box, behind the left side of the dash panel.

• **Windshield Washer Pump**—is located on the lower front of the washer reservoir which is mounted at the right side rear of the engine compartment.

• **Windshield Wiper Motor**—is located between the engine partition and the firewall, next to the brake fluid reservoir.

505 SERIES

• **A/C Cutout Relay**—is located at the left front corner of the engine compartment on a covered relay bracket.

• **A/C Diode A**—is located near the blower motor.

• **A/C Diode B**—is located at the left front corner of the engine compartment in the box.

• **A/C ECU**—is located behind the right side of the dashboard behind the glove box.

• **A/C Evaporator Temperature Sensor**—is located at the evaporator behind the center of the dashboard.

• **A/C Idle Solenoid**—is located at the top of the intake manifold at the throttle.

• **ABS Controller**—is located at the right front of the passenger compartment under the footrest.

• **ABS Controller Fuse**—is located in the front of the console behind the ashtray.

• **ABS Diode**—is located at the right front of the passenger compartment under the footrest.

• **ABS Front Wheel Sensors**—are located at the front wheel hubs next to the toothed wheels.

• **ABS Indicator Fuse**—is located in the front of the console behind the ashtray.

• **ABS Main Electrovalve**—is located at the left rear corner of the engine compartment.

• **ABS Main Relay**—is located at the right rear corner of the engine compartment.

• **ABS Main Relay Power Fuse**—is located in-line at the wiring running at the right rear of the engine compartment along the right shock tower.

• **ABS Pressure Switch**—is located at the left rear corner of the engine compartment.

• **ABS Pump Motor**—is located at the left rear corner of the engine compartment.

• **ABS Pump Relay**—is located in-line at the wiring running at the right rear of the engine compartment along the right shock tower.

• **ABS Pump Relay Diode**—is located in-line at the wiring running at the right rear of the engine compartment along the right shock tower.

• **ABS Pump Relay Fuse**—is located in-line at the wiring running at the right rear of the engine compartment along the right shock tower.

• **ABS Rear Wheel Sensors**—are located at the inboard ends of the rear axle shafts next to the center section gear carrier.

• **ABS Right Front Wheel Speed Sensor Connector**—is located in-line at the wiring running at the right rear of the engine compartment along the right shock tower.

• **Accessory Power Board**—is located behind the right side of the dashboard above the top or to the left of the glove box.

• **Air Flow Sensor**—is located in the air intake duct in the engine compartment.

• **Air Flow Temperature Sensor**—is located behind the right side of the dashboard behind the glove box.

• **Alternator**—is located at the lower left front of the engine except the ZN3J—2.8L engine where the alternator is at the lower right.

• **Altitude Sensor**—is located at the front of the right side shock tower.

• **Anti-lock Brakes System**—see components listed under ABS.

• **Automatic Transmission Temperature Switch**—is located on the left side of the transmission.

• **Auxiliary Air Device**—is located at the top left front of the engine (ZDJL—2.2L engine), or at the top rear of the engine (N9TEA—2.1L engine).

• **Auxiliary Cooling Fan Low Speed Relay**—is located on the left side inner fender panel next to the battery.

• **Back-Up Lights/Starter Lockout Switch**—is located at the left front of the transmission.

• **Blower Control Module**—is located at the right rear corner of the right side front fender behind the engine cowl insulation pad.

• **Blower Motor**—is located at the right side of the engine cowl.

• **Blower Motor Relay**—is attached to the blower control module.

• **Brake Fluid Level Switch**—is located on the side of the brake fluid reservior.

• **Brake Light Switch**—is located on a bracket just above the brake pedal arm.

• **Brake Pad Wear Indicator**—is located on the respective brake pad.

• **Centralized Power Door Lock Remote Control Receiver**—is located in the center of the windshield header. The transmitter is to be carried on the vehicle's key ring.

• **Cargo Light Switch**—is located at the tailgate.

• **Charcoal Canister Solenoid Valve**—is located at the right front corner of the engine compartment.

• **Climate Control Module**—is located behind the right side of the dashboard at the shroud.

• **Cold Start Injector (N9TEA—2.1L engine)**—is located at the lower left side of the engine.

• **Combination Switch**—containing the headlight, turn signal and horn switch is attached to the left side of the steering column.

• **Coolant Low Level Module**—is located on the left side of the engine compartment in front of the shock tower.

• **Coolant Low Level Switch**—is located on the top right

side of the radiator, except ZN3J – 2.8L engine which on the top left side.

• **Cooling Fan Low Speed Relay**—is located at the left front corner of the engine compartment on a covered relay bracket.

• **Cooling Fan High Speed Relay**—is located at the left front corner of the engine compartment on a covered relay bracket.

• **Cruise Control Clutch Switch**—is located on a bracket next to the clutch arm.

• **Cruise Control ECU**—is located behind the right side of the dashboard at the shroud.

• **Cruise Control Throttle Actuator**—is located at the top rear of the engine.

• **Cruise Control Vacuum Dump Electrovalve**—is located at the left rear corner of the engine compartment.

• **Cruise Control Vacuum Pump/Vent Valve**—is located below the battery tray.

• **Cruise Control Vehicle Speed Transducer**—is mounted on the speedometer cable.

• **Delay Off Module**—is located under the dashboard near the steering column.

• **Detonation (Knock) Sensor**—is located at the lower left side of inline engines and lower left and lower right side of V6 engine.

• **Diode C**—is located at the left front corner of engine compartment in box.

• **Diode D**—is located at the side of the right shock tower.

• **Distributor (N9TEA – 2.1L engine)**—is located at the top front of the engine.

• **Distributor (ZDJL – 2.2L engine)**—is located at the lower left side of the engine.

• **Distributor (ZN3J – 2.8L engine)**—is located at the top left front of the engine.

• **Door Jamb Switches**—are located in their respective door jambs.

• **Door Lock Control Module**—is located under the left side of the dashboard, attached to the steering column support brace.

• **Engine Speed Sensor (ZN3J – 2.8L engine)**—is located at the rear of the engine at the top of the bellhousing.

• **Engine Temperature Sender**—is located on the front left of the engine just behind the power steering pump.

• **Engine Temperature Sender (ZN3J – 2.8L engine)**—is located on the front of the engine on the left side of the coolant outlet.

• **Flasher, Turn Signal**—is located under the left side of the dashboard, near the steering column.

• **Fog Light Relay**—is located in front of the windshield washer reservoir.

• **Fuel Feed Pump**—is located under the left side of the vehicle near the rear axle.

• **Fuel Filler Door Locking Motor**—is located behind the right side trunk trim panel (sedan) or the left panel of the cargo compartment (station wagon).

• **Fuel Injection Diode**—is located at the left rear corner of the engine compartment taped to the emissions-injection harness.

• **Fuel Injection ECU**—is located behind the right side of the dashboard behind the glove box.

• **Fuel Injection Factory Assembly Test Connector**—is located at the left rear of the engine compartment behind the cowl.

• **Fuel Injection Relay**—is located at the left rear corner of the engine compartment on the relay bracket.

• **Fuel Pump Fuse**—is located in the front of the console behind the ashtray.

• **Fuel Pump Relay**—is located at the left rear corner of the engine compartment on the relay bracket.

• **Fuel Pump Tachymetric Relay**—is located behind the left side of the dashboard left of the steering column.

• **Fuel Vapor Electrovalve**—is located at the left side of the engine compartment.

• **Fuse Block**—is located at the left rear corner of the engine compartment.

• **Headlight/Turn Signal/Horn Switch**—is attached to the left side of the steering column.

• **Heater Electrovalve**—is located at the lower right rear of the engine compartment except on ZN3J – 2.8L engine on which the valve is located at the lower right front of the engine compartment.

• **Idle Regulation Electrovalve (ZN3J – 2.8L engine)**—is located at the top right rear of the engine.

• **Idle Richness Test Connector (ZN3J – 2.8L engine)**—is located at the right front corner of the engine compartment.

• **Ignition Amplifier Module**—is located on the left side of the engine compartment below the ignition coil.

• **Ignition Coil**—is located on the left side of the engine compartment at the rear of the battery.

• **Ignition Diode**—is located at the left rear corner of the engine compartment behind the relay bracket.

• **Ignition ECU**—is located in the right front of the passenger's compartment under the footrest.

• **Ignition ECU Relay**—is located at the left rear corner of the engine compartment on the relay bracket.

• **Ignition Switch**—is located at the right side of the steering column.

• **Inside Air Temperature Sensor**—is located at the top right of the dashboard.

• **Instrument Panel Illumination Dimmer**—is located at the underside of panel on the left side of the dashboard.

• **Neutral Safety/Back-Up Light Switch**—is located at the left side front of the transmission.

• **No. 1 Cylinder Position Sensor**—is located at the top left front of the engine on No. 1 cylinder spark plug cable.

• **Noise Suppressor**—is located near the ignition coil.

• **Oil Level Sensor**—is located on the left side of the oil pan.

• **Oil Pressure Switch (ZN3J – 2.8L engine)**—is located at the lower right front of the engine, near the oil filter, close to the alternator.

• **Oil Temperature Sender (ZN3J – 2.8L engine)**—is located at the lower right front of the engine, near the oil filter, close to the alternator.

• **Outside Air Temperature Sensor**—is located at the outside air inlet.

• **Overboost Pressure Switch**—is located at the top left front of the engine.

• **Oxygen Sensor (lambda sensor)**—is located either in the exhaust manifold or below the rear of the engine in the exhaust head pipe upstream of the catalytic converter.

• **Oxygen Sensor (lambda sensor) Heater Fuse**—is located in the front of the console behind the ashtray.

• **Park Brake Switch**—is located at the base of the parking brake lever.

• **Passive Seat Belt Relay**—is located behind the left side of the dashboard, near the ignition switch and steering column.

• **Positive Battery Junction Connector**—is located at the left side of the engine compartment near the battery.

• **Power Steering ECU (variable ratio PS)**—is located behind the right side of the dashboard above the top of the glove box.

• **Power Steering Test Connector**—is located at the left side of the engine compartment.

• **Power Window Motors**—are located inside their respective doors.

• **Primer Fuel Pump**—is located in the top of the fuel tank.

• **Radio Fuse**—is located in-line at the radio, behind the center console panel.

• **Radio Power Antenna**—is located behind the right panel of the trunk (sedan) or left side quarter panel/cargo compartment (station wagon).

• **Resistor A**—is located at the left side of the engine compartment at the shock tower.
• **Seat Heaters**—are located in their respective seats.
• **Starter Motor**—is located at the lower left rear of the engine.
• **Starter Relay**—is located at the left rear corner of the engine compartment on the relay bracket.
• **Stop Light Switch**—is located on a bracket just above the brake pedal arm.
• **Sunroof Motor**—is located in the left side of the trunk, behind the trim panel.
• **Test Connector**—is located at the right side fender usually taped to the injection harness.
• **Thermocontact Switch**—is located at the top front of the engine.
• **Thermotime Switch**—is located at the left front of the engine block.
• **Throttle Position Sensor**—is located on the top left side of the engine on the throttle body.
• **Throttle Switch (ZN3J–2.8L engine)**—is located above the rear of the engine on the air intake.
• **Trunk Light Switch**—is located in left side of trunk near the hinge.
• **Turbocharger Boost Indicator Sender**—is located at the lower right front corner of the engine compartment.
• **Turbocharger Wastegate**—also called the regulator electro-valve, is located at the right side of the engine compartment next to the right side shock tower.
• **Two-Tone Chime**—is located under the left side side of the dashboard near the steering column.
• **Washer Pump (tailgate)**—is located behind the left panel of the cargo compartment.
• **Window Motors**—are located in their respective doors.
• **Wiper Motor (tailgate)**—is located inside the tailgate, toward the center.
• **Wiper Motor (windshield)**—is attached to the frame under the windshield wiper cowling.
• **Wiper Motor Control Box (windshield)**—is located under the left side of the dashboard near the steering column.
• **Wiper Motor Intermittent Relay (tailgate)**—is located inside the tailgate.
• **Wiper Motor Relay (tailgate)**—is located inside the tailgate, on the right side.

PORSCHE

Circuit Breaker and Fuses

Some vehicles may be equipped with circuit breakers which are located in the fuse/relay panel.

Fusible Links

No major fusible links are used on these vehicles.

Relay, Sensors And Computer Locations

911 SERIES

• **A/C Relay**—is located on front fuse/relay panel.
• **A/C Sight Glass**—is located on the drier assembly in the left front wheel house area.
• **Air Bag Control Unit**—is located beneath the glove box area.

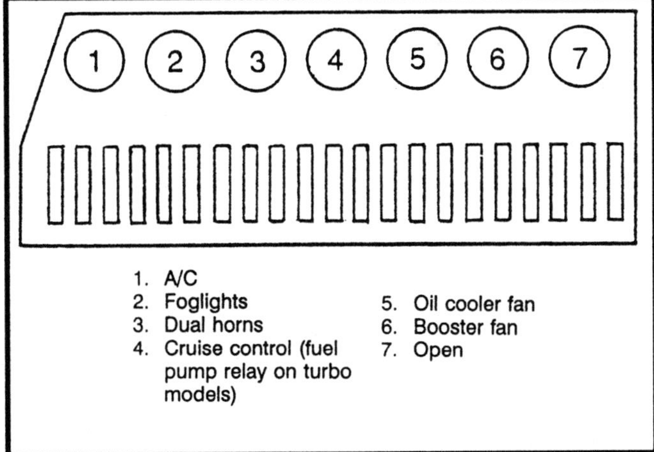

Fuse/relay panel (front)—911

• **Air Bag Front Impact Sensors**—are located in the luggage compartment area.
• **Air Conditioner/Heater Control Unit**—is located under center area of dashboard.
• **Anti-lock Brake System (ABS) Control Unit**—is located in the luggage compartment area.
• **ABS Hydraulic Unit**—is located in the luggage compartment area.
• **Anti-theft Alarm Control Unit**—is located beneath the right hand seat area.

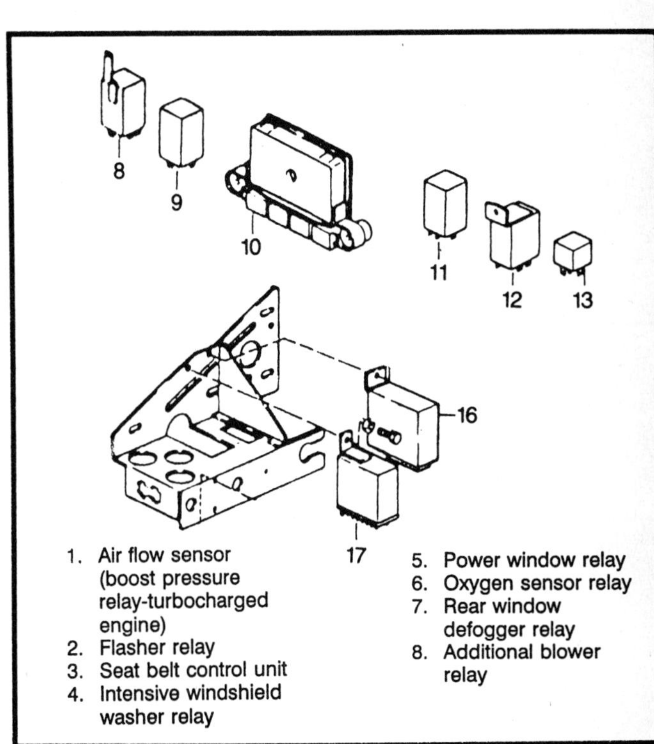

Fuse/relay panel (rear)—911

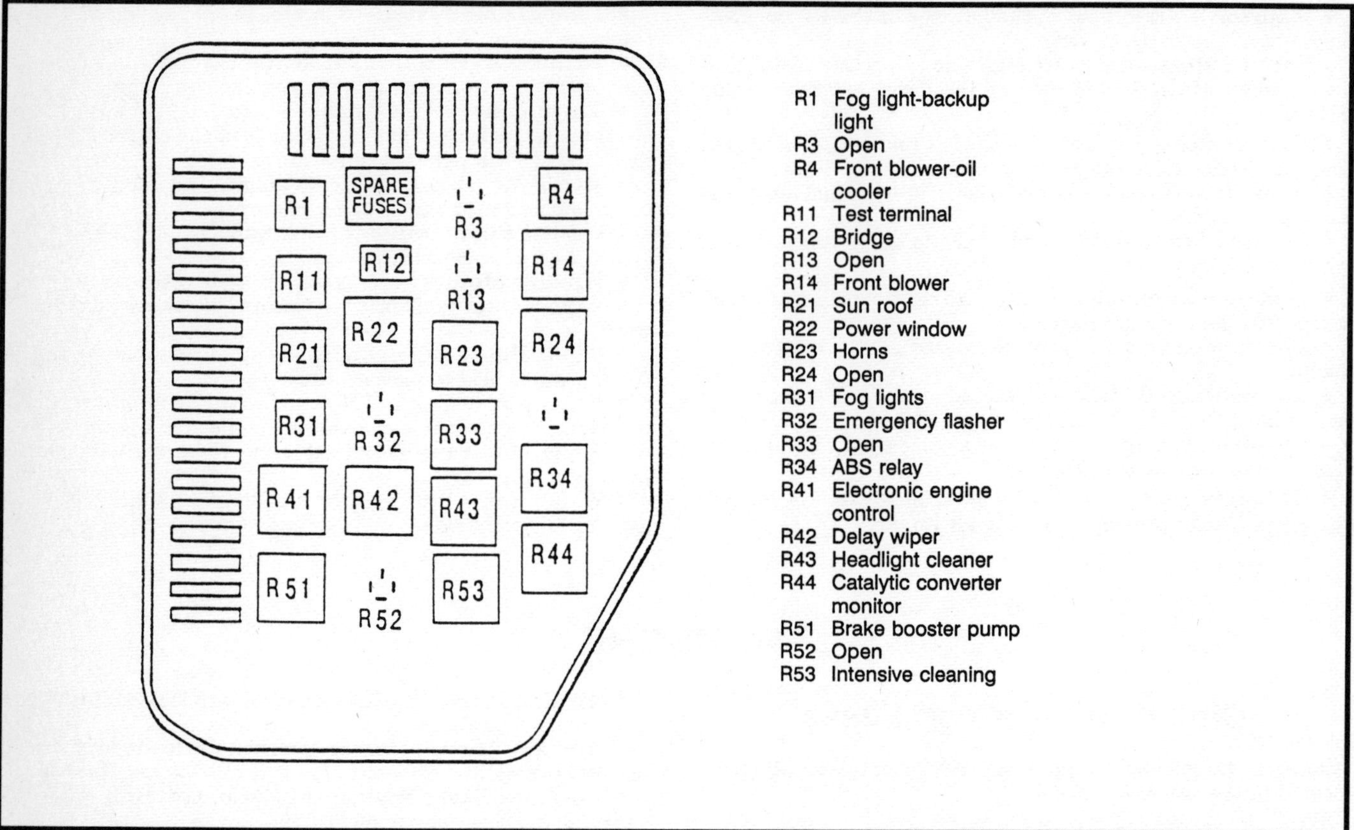

Fuse/relay panel—911 Carrera 2/4

- **Anti-theft Alarm Relay**—is located on the left rear side of the luggage compartment area.
- **Air Sensor Boost Relay (turbo)**—is located on rear fuse/relay panel.
- **Auxiliary Blower Motor Relay**—is located on the front fuse/relay panel.
- **Axial Acceleration Sensor**—is located on sheet metal console on the tunnel underneath the center console.
- **Brake Booster Pump**—is located in the luggage compartment area.
- **Central Informer Unit**—is located underneath the dashboard on the left side area.
- **Central Lock Control Unit**—is located under the dashboard right side area.
- **Cooling Fan Relay**—is located on the front fuse/relay panel.
- **Cruise Control Drive Motor**—is located on the crankcase at the rear left area.
- **Cruise Control Unit**—is located underneath the right seat assembly.
- **Diagnostic Plug Connection**—is located in the engine compartment area.
- **Digital Motor Electronics Control (DME) Unit**—is located underneath left seat area.
- **Fog Light Relay**—is located on the front fuse/relay panel.
- **Fuel Pump Relays**—are located on the front fuse/relay panel.
- **Fuse/Relay Panel (front)**—is located in the luggage compartment area.
- **Fuse/Relay Panel (rear)**—is located in the engine compartment area.
- **Hazard/Turn Signal Flasher Relay**—is located on the left rear corner of the luggage compartment area.
- **Heater Blower Relay**—is located on the rear fuse/relay panel.
- **Heater/Air Conditioner Control Unit**—is located under center area of dashboard.
- **Horn Relay**—is located on the front fuse/relay panel.
- **Instrument Light Control Unit**—is located in the luggage compartment left side area.
- **Intermittent Wiper Relay**—is located on cowl area in rear center of luggage compartment.
- **Lateral Acceleration Sensor**—is located on sheet metal console on the tunnel underneath the center console.
- **Oil Cooler Fan Relay**—is located on the front fuse/relay panel.
- **Oxygen Sensor Heated Relay**—is located on the rear fuse/relay panel.
- **Radio Booster**—is located underneath the right seat assembly.
- **Rear Spoiler Control Unit**—is located underneath right seat area.
- **Rear Window Defogger Relay**—is located on the rear fuse/relay panel.
- **Time Delay Relay**—is located on the rear fuse/relay panel.
- **Turn Signal/Hazard Flasher Relay**—is located on the left rear corner of the luggage compartment area.

928 SERIES

- **A/C Compressor (speed limiter) Relay**—is located in the central fuse/relay panel.
- **Anti-lock Brake System (ABS) Control Unit**—is located above the hood release handle on the driver's side of the car above the fuse/relay panel.

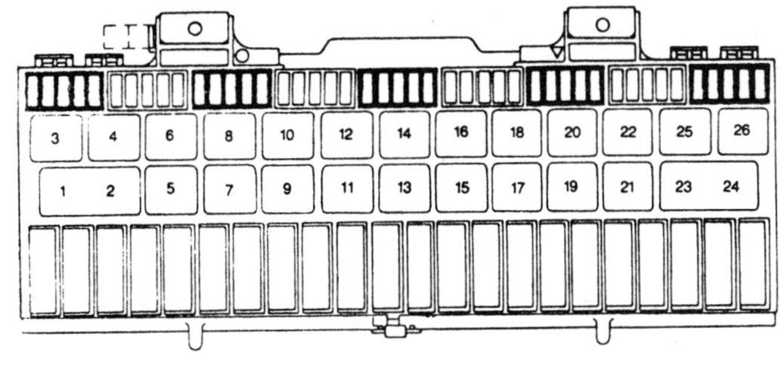

1. Rear window defroster
2. Rear window defroster
3. Open
4. Ignition relay
5. Flasher indicator
6. Power window
7. Wiper delay timer
8. Defrost
9. Supplementary cleaning system
10. Fresh air blower
11. Interference suppressor
12. Twin tone horn
13. Foglights
14. Starter
15. Kick-down
16. Electronic ignition
17. Anti-lock brake system
18. Cooling air flap adjustment
19. Headlamp washing system
20. Fuel pump
21. Interior lights
22. Reverse lights
23. Headlight system
24. Headlight system
25. LH- Jetronic
26. Open

Fuse/relay panel—928

- **ABS Valve Relay**—is located on the hydraulic control unit.
- **ABS Pump Motor Relay**—is located on the hydraulic control unit.
- **ABS Hydraulic Unit**—is located in the back area of the left front wheel house.
- **Anti-theft Alarm Control Unit**—is located on the glove box area.
- **Blower Motor Relay**—is located in the central fuse/relay panel.
- **Cruise Control Unit**—is located at right side of center console area.
- **Defroster Fan Relay**—is located in the central fuse/relay panel.
- **Emission Counter Switch**—is located to the right of the passenger's seat area.
- **Engine Speed Sensor**—is located at the top of the bellhousing area.
- **Fog Light Relay**—is located in the central fuse/relay panel.
- **Fuel Pump Relay**—is located in the central fuse/relay panel.
- **Fuel Gauge Sending Unit**—is located in the fuel tank assembly.
- **Fuse/Relay Panel**—is located in the footwell of the front passenger's side area.
- **Headlight Beam Power Supply Relay**—is located in the central fuse/relay panel.
- **Headlight High/Low Beam Relay**—is located in the central fuse/relay panel.
- **Headlight Main Power Supply Relay**—is located in the central fuse/relay panel.
- **Headlight Motor Relay**—is located in the central fuse/relay panel.
- **Headlight Washer Pump Relay**—is located in the central fuse/relay panel.
- **Horn Relay**—is located in the central fuse/relay panel.
- **Intensive Cleaner Pump Relay**—is located in the central fuse/relay panel.

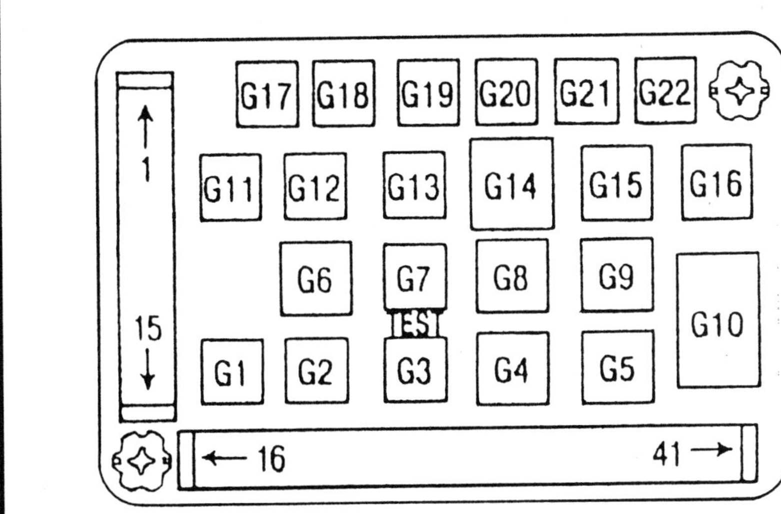

G1 Fresh air blower
G2 Ignition relay
G3 Rear window
G4 Flasher indicator
G5 DME relay
G6 Open
G7 Power window
G8 Warning buzzer
G9 Wiper delay
G10 Cooling fan
G11 Foglight
G12 Driving light
G13 Horn
G14 Ignition relay X
G15 Headlamp washinh system
G16 Catalytic converter warning
G17 A/C compressor
G18 Alarm system
G19 Open
G20 ABS system
G21 Sun roof
G22 Water pump turbocharged engine

Fuse/relay panel—944

• **Intermittent Wiper Relay**—is located in the central fuse/relay panel.
• **Power Seat Relay**—is located underneath the seat on the adjusting frame.
• **Power Window Relay**—is located in the central fuse/relay panel.
• **Radiator Fan Relay**—is located in the central fuse/relay panel.
• **Rear Window Defogger Relay**—is located in the central fuse/relay panel.
• **Relay Panel/Fuse**—is located in the footwell of the front passenger's side area.
• **Seat Belts Time Relay**—is located in the central fuse/relay panel.
• **Starter Cut-Out Relay (automatic transmission) Relay**—is located in the central fuse/relay panel.
• **Turn Signal Flasher Relay**—is located in the central fuse/relay panel.

944 SERIES

• **A/C Compressor Relay**—is located in the main fuse/relay panel.
• **A/C Low Pressure Switch**—is located in engine compartment on the the drier assembly.
• **A/C High Pressure Switch**—is located in the engine compartment on the the air conditioning condenser assembly.
• **Anti-lock Brake System (ABS) Relay**—is located in the main fuse/relay panel.
• **ABS Valve Relay**—is located on the hydraulic control unit.
• **ABS Pump Motor Relay**—is located on the hydraulic control unit.
• **ABS Control Unit**—is located in right side upper area below dashboard.
• **ABS Hydraulic Unit**—is located in the back area of the right front wheel house.
• **Air bag Control Unit**—is located on the right side area of the engine compartment.
• **Anti-theft Alarm Control Unit**—is located in right side upper area below dashboard.
• **Anti-theft Alarm Relay**—is located in the main fuse/relay panel.
• **Blower Motor Relay**—is located in the main fuse/relay panel.
• **Brake Fluid Level Switch**—is located in the brake fluid reservoir cap.
• **Brake Pressure Regulator**—is located in the line connection at the rear axle assembly.
• **Catalytic Converter Warning/Chime Relay**—is located in the main fuse/relay panel.
• **Central Locking System Relay**—is located in the main fuse/relay panel.
• **Central Warning System Control Unit**—is located underneath the footrest on the driver's side area.
• **Cooling Fan Relay**—is located in the main fuse/relay panel.
• **Cooling Fan Temperature Switch**—is located at the bottom of the radiator assembly.
• **Cruise Control Unit**—is located in right side upper area below dashboard.
• **Diagnostic Connector**—is located on the left side of the engine compartment area.
• **Digital Motor Electronics (DME) Relay**—is located in the main fuse/relay panel.
• **Door Lock Control Unit**—is located under left side of dash area.
• **Fog Light Relay**—is located in the main fuse/relay panel.
• **Fuel Gauge Sending Unit**—is located in the fuel tank assembly.
• **Fuse/Relay Panel**—is located in the engine compartment area.
• **Hazard/Turn Signal Flasher Relay**—is located in the main fuse/relay panel.
• **Headlight Relay**—is located in the main fuse/relay panel.
• **Headlight Washer Relay**—is located in the main fuse/relay panel.
• **Horn Relay**—is located in the main fuse/relay panel.
• **Ignition Booster**—is located in the left fron wheel house wall area.
• **Ignition Relay**—is located in the main fuse/relay panel.
• **Ignition Timing Sensor**is located on the top center of the engine bellhousing.
• **Interior Temperature Sensor**—is located under the right side of the dash area.
• **Knock Sensors**—are located on the engine block between cylinders No. 1 and No. 2 and No. 3 and No. 4 cylinders.
• **Oxygen Sensor**—is located in the exhaust pipe.
• **Power Window Relay**—is located in the main fuse/relay panel.
• **Radio Relay**—is located under left side of dash, near center console area.
• **Rear Window Defogger Relay**—is located in the main fuse/relay panel.
• **Relay/Fuse Panel**—is located in the engine compartment area.
• **Sunroof Relay**—is located in the main fuse/relay panel.
• **Turbocharger Cooling Pump Relay**—is located in the main fuse/relay panel.
• **Turn Signal/Hazard Flasher Relay**—is located in the main fuse/relay panel.
• **Warning Buzzer Relay**—is located in the main fuse/relay panel.
• **Windshield Wiper Delay Relay**—is located in the main fuse/relay panel.
• **Windshield Wiper Motor**—is located under the middle of the cowl vent area.

SAAB

Circuit Breakers and Fuses

900

Fuses are located in the electrical distribution box on the left hand wheel housing under the hood. The oxygen sensor fuse is located on the right side of the engine compartment at the fresh air intake. The convertible top fuse is located in the engine compartment at the right side distribution block. Passive seat belt fuses are located under the left rear seat.

9000

Fuses are located in a fuse box and can be reached through an

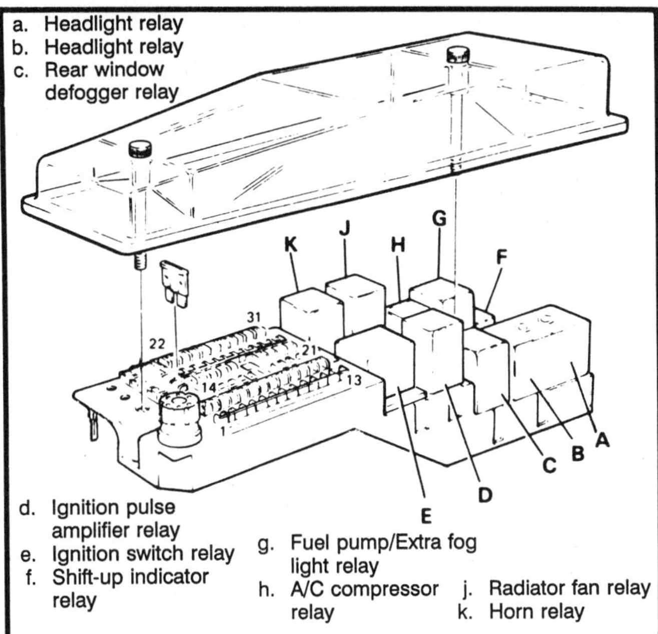

Electrical distribution box—900

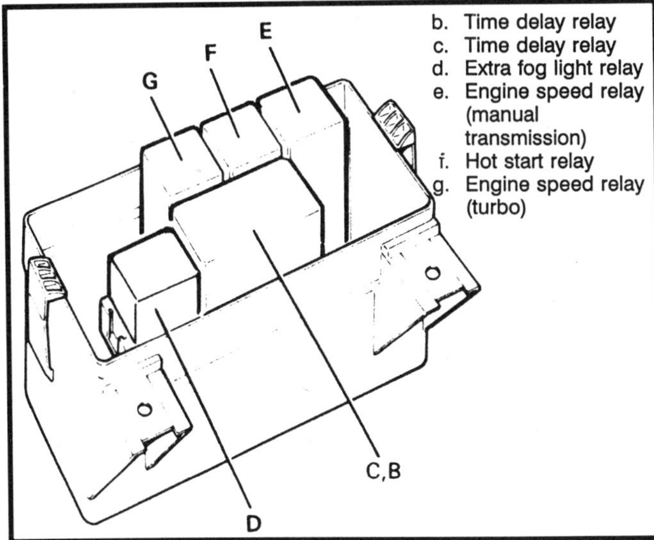

Emissions relay box—900

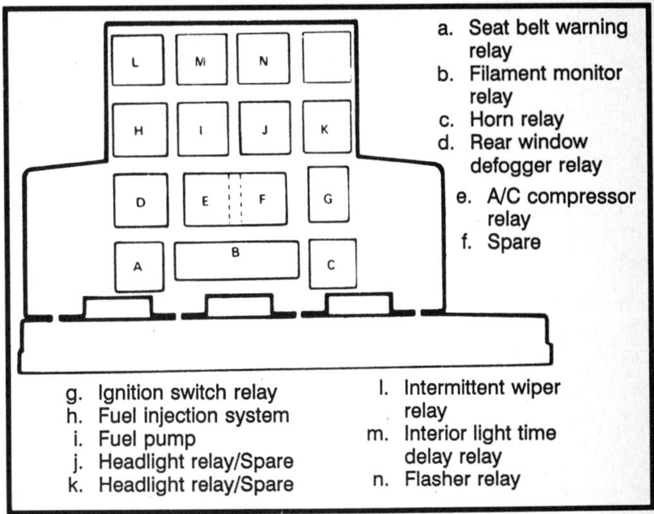

Electrical distribution box—9000

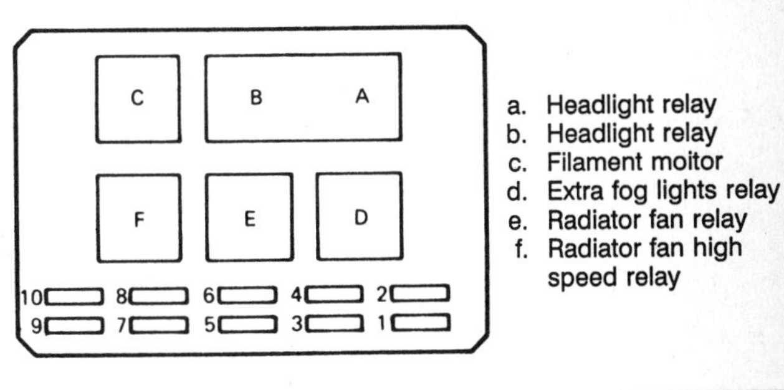

Glove compartment relay box—9000

access panel in the glove compartment. Fuses are also located in the electrical distribution box near the left headlight. ABS fuses are located in the engine compartment behind the firewall partition on the ABS relay and fuse board.

Fusible Links

Fusible links may be located at the battery, starter or alternator.

Relays, Sensors, Modules and Computer Locations

900

- **A/C Compressor Diode**—is located in the harness at the rear of the valve cover.
- **A/C Compressor Relay**—is located at the electrical distribution box on the left hand wheel housing in the engine compartment.
- **A/C Coolant Temperature Switch**—is located on the radiator hose inlet near the distributor.
- **A/C Coolant Thermostat**—is located on the right side of the air conditioner housing.
- **A/C Pressure Switch**—is located on the receiver drier.
- **A/C Recirculation Valve**—is located above the right side wheel housing in the engine compartment.
- **APC Control Unit**—is located in the engine compartment forward of the left wheel housing.
- **APC Knock Sensor**—is located on the engine between the two center intake ports.
- **APC Pressure Sensor**—is located under the dash to the left of the steering column.
- **APC Solenoid Valve**—is located on the radiator fan shroud.
- **APC Vacuum Switch**—is located in the engine compartment at the left side wheel housing.
- **Automatic Performance Control System**—see APC.
- **Backup Light Switch**—is located at the gear selector lever in the center console.
- **Boost Pressure Switch (turbo)**—is located under the dash to the left of the steering column, behind the flasher relay holder.
- **Brake Fluid Level Warning Switch**—is located in the master cylinder reservoir.
- **Brake Light Testing Diode**—is located in the instrument panel.
- **Central Door Lock Control Unit**—is located under the right side of the dash.

• **Convertible Top Diode**—is located under the right rear seat in the cable harness running to the relays.

• **Convertible Top Relays**—are located under the right side rear seat.

• **Coolant Temperature Sensor**—is located on the right side of the thermostat.

• **Coolant Temperature Warning Buzzer**—is located under the dash to the left of the steering column.

• **Coolant Temperature Warning Switch**—is located on the radiator hose.

• **Cruise Control Solenoid Valve**—is located above the radiator fan.

• **Cruise Control Speed Sensor**—is located in the instrument panel.

• **Cruise Control Unit**—is located under the left side of the dash.

• **Cruise Control Vacuum Pump**—is located forward of the left side wheel housing.

• **Cruise Control Vacuum Switch**—is located forward of the left side wheel housing.

• **EGR Selector**—is located under the dash to the left of the steering column.

• **Emission Control Unit**—is located under the right rear seat.

• **Emission System Diode**—is located at the right side kick panel.

• **Emission System Temperature Switches**—are located on the intake manifold and in the thermostat housing.

• **Emission Timing Valve**—is located in the engine compartment on the inside of the left wheel housing.

• **Emissions Time Delay Relay**—is located at the emissions relay box on the inner side of the left front fender.

• **Engine Speed Relay (turbo)**—is located at the emissions relay box on the inner side of the left front fender.

• **Engine Speed Relay**—is located at the emissions relay box on the inner side of the left front fender or forward of the right front door behind the trim panel.

• **Engine Temperature Sensor**—is located on the intake manifold between cylinders 2 and 3.

• **Flasher Relay**—is located under the left side of the dash.

• **Fog Light Relay**—is located at the emissions relay box or the electrical distribution box on the left side of the engine compartment.

• **Fuel Injection Air Mass Meter (LH)**—is located on the air hose at the air cleaner.

• **Fuel Injection Air Valve**—is located at the front of the engine beside the thermostat housing.

• **Fuel Injection Control Pressure Valve**—is located at the front of the engine on the thermostat housing.

• **Fuel Injection Control Unit**—is located under the right side of the dash.

• **Fuel Injection Idle Speed Adjustment Motor (LH)**—is located at the left front of the cylinder head.

• **Fuel Injection Relay (LH)**—is located at the right side kick panel.

• **Fuel Injection Start Valve**—is located at the top of the engine throttle housing.

• **Fuel Injection Temperature Time Switch**—is located at the front of the thermostat housing.

• **Fuel Injection Test Connector**—is located in the engine compartment behind the right side wheel housing.

• **Fuel Injection Throttle Angle Sensor**—is located on the throttle housing.

• **Fuel Injection Vacuum Switch**—is located on the inside of the left wheel housing at the fuel filter.

• **Fuel Pump Relay (CI)**—is located at the electrical distribution box on the left hand wheel housing in the engine compartment.

• **Fuel Pump Relay (LH)**—is located at the fuel injection control unit.

• **Fuel System Shut-off Valve**—is located on a rubber hose above the engine air cleaner.

• **Headlight High Beam Relay**—is located at the electrical distribution box on the left hand wheel housing in the engine compartment.

• **Headlight Low Beam Relay**—is located at the electrical distribution box on the left hand wheel housing in the engine compartment.

• **Horn Relay**—is located at the electrical distribution box on the left hand wheel housing in the engine compartment.

• **Hot Start Relay**—is located at the emissions relay box on the inner side of the left front fender.

• **Idle Up Solenoid Valve (automatic transmission)**—is located at the engine throttle hosing in the air valve hose.

• **Idle Up Switch (automatic transmission)**—is located under the center console at the gear selector lever.

• **Ignition Pulse Amplifier Relay**—is located at the electrical distribution box on the left hand wheel housing in the engine compartment.

• **Ignition Switch Relay**—is located at the electrical distribution box on the left hand wheel housing in the engine compartment.

• **Ignition System Control Unit**—is located in the engine compartment forward of the left hand wheel housing.

• **Ignition System Diagnostic Terminal**—is located on the left side wheel housing forward of the electrical distribution box.

• **Interior Lighting Time Delay Relay**—is located under the right rear seat.

• **Intermittent Wiper Relay**—is located under the dash to the left side of the steering column.

• **Oil Pressure Sensor**—is located on the left side of the engine near the oil filter.

• **Oxygen Sensor Pre-Heater**—is located at the oxygen sensor.

• **Oxygen Sensor**—is located at the exhaust manifold.

• **Passive Seat Belt G-Sensor**—is located under the left rear seat.

• **Passive Seat Belt Logic Unit**—is located under the left rear seat.

• **Passive Seat Belt Motor Relay**—is located at the electrical distribution box on the left hand wheel housing in the engine compartment.

• **Passive Seat Belt Relays**—are located under the left rear seat.

• **Power Window Relay**—is located under the left rear seat.

• **Radiator Fan Relay**—is located at the electrical distribution box on the left hand wheel housing in the engine compartment.

• **Radiator Fan Temperature Switch**—is located at the left side of the radiator.

• **Radiator Fan Time Delay**—is located at the front of the left side wheel housing.

• **Rear Defogger Mercury Switch**—is located on the left side of the convertible top mounting frame.

• **Rear Window Defogger Relay**—is located at the electrical distribution box on the left hand wheel housing in the engine compartment.

• **Shift Indicator Engine Speed Relay**—is located at the emissions relay box on the inner side of the left front fender.

• **Shift Indicator Switch (manual transmission)**—is located in the front side cover of the gearbox.

• **Shift Indicator Time Delay Relay**—is located at the emissions relay box on the inner side of the left front fender.

• **Shift Up Indicator Relay**—is located at the electrical distribution box on the left hand wheel housing in the engine compartment.

• **SRS Control Unit**—is located under the left side of the dash.

• **SRS Impact Sensors**—are located at the left and right front of the engine compartment.

• **Start Inhibitor Switch**—is located at the gear selector lever.

• **Supplemental Restraint System**—see SRS.

• **Timing Service Adjustment Socket**—is located at the electrical distribution box on the left wheel housing.

• **Ventilation Fan Resistor**—is located under the left speaker grille.

9000

• **A/C Compressor Relay**—is located in the electrical distribution box behind the glove box.

• **A/C Coolant Thermostat**—is located on the evaporator housing.

• **A/C Pressure Switch**—is located at the receiver drier.

• **ABS Control Unit**—is located in the engine compartment behind the firewall partition above the ignition system control unit.

• **ABS Main Relay**—is located in the engine compartment behind the firewall partition on the ABS relay and fuse board.

• **ABS Pump Relay**—is located in the engine compartment behind the firewall partition on the ABS relay and fuse board.

• **ACC Air Mixture Sensor**—is located in the air distribution housing under the center of the dash.

• **ACC Diagnostic Socket**—is located at the left kick panel.

• **ACC Fan Speed Control**—is located on the evaporator housing behind the firewall.

• **ACC Interior Temperature Sensor**—is located in the panel between the steering wheel and the center console.

• **ACC Outdoor Temperature Sensor**—is located on the left hand side behind the front spoiler.

• **ACC Sun Transmitter**—is located under the right front speaker grille or at the center of the dash.

• **Air Bag Control Unit**—is located under the right side of the dash.

• **Air Bag Diagnostic Connector**—is located in the center console under the dash.

• **Air Bag Electronic Control Unit**—is located under the right side of the dash.

• **Air Bag Electronic Control Unit**—is located under the right side of the dash.

• **Air Bag Sensors**—are located below the electrical distribution box at the left front of the engine compartment and on a mounting plate at the right front fender.

• **Anti-lock Brakes**—see ABS.

• **Automatic Climate Control**—see ACC.

• **Brake Fluid Level Sensor**—is located inside the master cylinder fluid reservoir.

• **Bulb Filament Monitor**—is located in the electrical distribution box behind the glove box.

• **Bulb Filament Monitor**—is located in the electrical distribution box near the left headlight.

• **Burglar Alarm Electronic Control Unit**—is located under the right side of the dash.

• **Burglar Alarm Electronic Control Unit**—is located under the right side of the dash.

• **Burglar Alarm Siren**—is located near the washer fluid reservoir in the right front fender.

• **Coolant Temperature Sensor**—is located on the intake manifold between cylinders 2 and 3.

• **Cooling Fan Temperature Switch**—is located on the left side of the radiator.

• **Crankshaft Sensor**—is located on the oil pump casing.

• **Cruise Control Unit**—is located under the dash to the left of the steering column.

• **Cruise Control Vacuum Pump**—is located on the right side of the engine compartment.

• **Daytime Driving Lights Relay (Canada)**—is located in the electrical distribution box behind the glove box.

• **DI-APC Control Unit**—is located under the left front seat.

• **DI-APC Pressure Sensor**—is located on a bracket below the left side of the dash.

• **Direct Ignition/Automatic Performance Control**—see DI-APC.

• **Door Fan Resistor**—is located under the left front seat.

• **Electronic Ignition Amplifier**—is located near the battery.

• **Flasher Relay**—is located in the electrical distribution box behind the glove box.

• **Foglight Relay**—is located in the electrical distribution box near the left headlight.

• **Fuel Injection Air Mass Meter (LH)**—is located at the air cleaner.

• **Fuel Injection Cold Start Coding Socket (LH)**—is located on the firewall at the fuel injection control unit.

• **Fuel Injection Cold Start Valve (LH)**—is located on the intake manifold.

• **Fuel Injection Control Unit (LH)**—is located at the left side of the firewall.

• **Fuel Injection Diagnostic Connector (LH)**—is located at the left side of the firewall or under the left front seat.

• **Fuel Injection Engine Idle Speed Control (LH)**—is located at the center of the intake manifold.

• **Fuel Injection Idle Up Switch (LH)**—is located at the gear selector lever in the console.

• **Fuel Injection Pressure Switch**—is located to the left of the steering column.

• **Fuel Injection System Relay**—is located in the electrical distribution box behind the glove box.

• **Fuel Injection Throttle Angle Sensor (LH)**—is located at the throttle housing.

• **Fuel Pump Relay**—is located in the electrical distribution box behind the glove box.

• **Headlight High Relay**—is located in the electrical distribution box near the left headlight.

• **Headlight Low Beam Resistor**—is located at the left front of the engine compartment.

• **Headlight Low Relay**—is located in the electrical distribution box near the left headlight.

• **Horn Relay**—is located in the electrical distribution box behind the glove box.

• **Ignition Switch Relay**—is located in the electrical distribution box behind the glove box.

• **Ignition System Diagnostic Socket (EZK)**—is located at the left side of the firewall.

• **Ignition System Knock Sensor**—is located below the intake manifold.

• **Ignition System Solenoid Valve**—is located on the radiator fan casing.

• **Ignition System Vacuum Switch**—is located under the dash to the left of the steering column.

• **Instrument Light Electronic Unit**—is located under the right hand side of the dash.

• **Interior Light Delay Relay**—is located in the electrical distribution box behind the glove box.

• **Interlock Switch**—is located at the gear selector lever in the console.

• **Intermittent Windshield Wiper Relay**—is located in the electrical distribution box behind the glove box.

• **Oil Pressure Sensor**—is located at the top of the oil filter housing.

• **Oxygen Sensor**—is located at the exhaust manifold.

• **Radiator Fan Relay**—is located in the electrical distribution box near the left headlight.

• **Radiator Fan High Speed Relay**—is located in the electrical distribution box near the left headlight.

• **Rear Window Defogger Relay**—is located in the electrical distribution box behind the glove box.

• **Seat Belt Tensioner Electronic Control Unit**—is located at the front of the center console.
• **Seat Belt Warning Relay**—is located in the electrical distribution box behind the glove box.
• **Speed Sensor**—is located in the speedometer.
• **Speed Warning Buzzer**—is located at the bottom of the storage compartment in the center console.
• **Timing Service Socket**—is located on the left side of the engine compartment at the firewall.
• **Trailer Wiring Connector**—is located at the left side of the trunk on the lighting cluster.
• **Ventilation Fan Resistor**—is located in the frame edging of the fan housing at the cable connection.

STERLING

Circuit Breakers and Fuses

Circuit breakers are located in the underhood fuse box on the left side of the engine compartment. Fuses are located in the under hood fuse box on the left side of the engine compartment and the passenger compartment fuse box located under the left side of the dash.

Fusible Links

Fusible links are located in the under hood fuse box on the left side of the engine compartment.

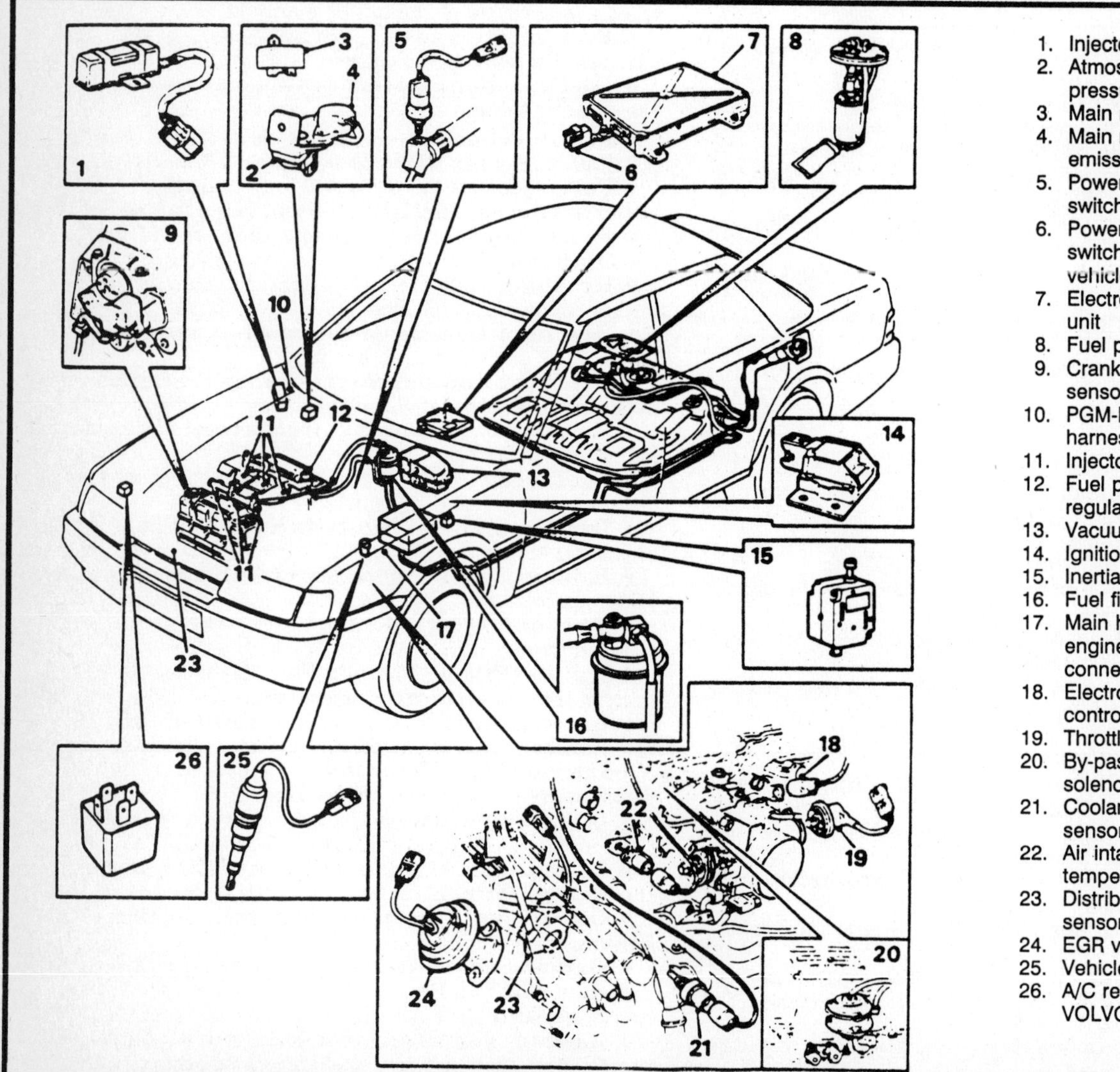

1. Injector resistor pack
2. Atmospheric pressure sensor
3. Main relay
4. Main relay (non-emission vehicles)
5. Power steering switch
6. Power steering switch (non-emission vehicles)
7. Electronic control unit
8. Fuel pump
9. Crankshaft angle sensor
10. PGM-FI firewall harness connectors
11. Injectors
12. Fuel pressure regulator
13. Vacuum control box
14. Ignition igniter unit
15. Inertia switch
16. Fuel filter
17. Main harness-to-engine harness connector
18. Electronic idle control valve
19. Throttle angle sensor
20. By-pass control solenoid
21. Coolant temperature sensor
22. Air intake temperature sensor
23. Distributor TDC sensor
24. EGR valve
25. Vehicle speed pulser
26. A/C relay

VOLVO

Vehicle component locations

Relays, Sensors, Modules and Computer Locations

827

• **A/C Compressor Clutch Relay**—is located in the engine compartment fusebox.

• **A/C Condenser Fan Relay**—is located behind the battery.

• **A/C Coolant Temperature Sensor**—is located at the left front of the engine compartment.

• **A/C Diode Resistor Pack**—is located on the cooling box under the center of the dash.

• **A/C Dual Pressure Switch**—is located at the right front of the engine compartment.

• **A/C Evaporator Sensor**—is located behind the glove box.

• **A/C Fan Speed Interface**—is located on the cooling box under the center of the dash.

• **A/C High Pressure Switch**—is located at the right front of the engine compartment.

• **A/C Relay**—is located on the cooling box under the center of the dash.

• **ABS Control Unit**—is located at the left side of the trunk behind a trim panel.

• **ABS Modulator Relay**—is located in the engine compartment fusebox.

• **ABS Modulator**—is located bear the battery and engine compartment fuse box.

• **ABS Over Voltage Relay**—is located at the left side of the trunk.

• **ABS Relay**—is located in the engine compartment fusebox.

• **Air Intake Temperature Sensor**—is located near the throttle body.

• **Air Reservoir**—is located inside the control box.

• **Air Suction Control Valve**—is located inside the control box.

• **Anti-theft Alarm**—is located at the left rear of the engine compartment.

• **Anti-theft Control Unit**—is located under the front of the center console.

• **Atmospheric Pressure Sensor**—is located at the right rear of the engine compartment.

• **Automatic Transmission Control Unit**—is located under the left front seat.

• **Backup Light Switch**—is located at the front of the transmission.

• **Blower Motor Relay**—is located under the right side of the dash.

• **Brake Fluid Level Switch**—is located at the master cylinder.

• **Bypass Control Diaphram**—is located behind the throttle body.

• **Bypass Control Solenoid (A and B)**—is located inside the control box.

• **Central Door Locking Control Unit**—is located under the left side of the dash.

• **Cigar Lighter Relay**—is located in the relay tower.

• **Constant Vacuum Control Valve**—is located inside the control box.

• **Control Box**—is located at the firewall.

• **Coolant Fan Switch**—is located at the right front of the engine compartment.

• **Coolant Level Switch**—is located near the cruise control actuator.

• **Coolant Temperature Sensor**—is located near the distributor.

• **Coolant Temperature Sensor**—is located next to the distributor.

• **Cooling Fan Changeover Relay**—is located in the engine compartment fusebox.

• **Cooling Fan Relay**—is located in the engine compartment fusebox.

• **Crankshaft Angle Sensor**—is located on the timing belt side of the engine.

• **Cruise Control Actuator**—is located at the right front of the engine compartment.

• **Cruise Control Unit**—is located—is located under the left side of the dash.

• **Dash Fuse Box**—is located under the left side of the dash.

• **Diagnostic Connector**—is located under the front of the center console.

• **EGR Control Solenoid Valve**—is located inside the control box.

• **EGR Valve Lift Sensor**—is located under the distributor.

• **EGR Valve**—is located near the distributor.

• **Electronic Control Unit**—is located under the right front seat.

• **Electronic Idle Control Valve (EICV)**—is located near the distributor.

• **Emission Control Box**—is located at the left rear of the engine compartment.

• **Engine Overheat Electronic Control Unit**—is located at the right front of the engine compartment, under the washer fluid reservoir.

• **Fan Speed Interface Unit**—is located at the center of the dash.

• **Flasher Unit**—is located under the left side of the dash.

• **Front Wiper Control Unit**—is located—is located under the left side of the dash.

• **Fuel Electronic Control Unit**—is located under the right front seat.

• **Fuel Low Interface Unit**—is located under the left front seat.

• **Headlight Changeover Unit**—is located in the relay tower.

• **Headlight Delay Unit**—is located on the relay tower.

• **Headlight Monitor (left)**—is located at the left front of the engine compartment.

• **Headlight Monitor (right)**—is located at the left front of the engine compartment.

• **High Speed Blower Relay**—is located under the right side of the dash.

• **Hot Restart Control Unit**—is located under the right front seat.

• **Ignition Timing Sensor**—is located inside the control box.

• **In-line Diodes**—are located at the battery and running along the left side of the passenger compartment under the carpet.

• **Inertia Switch**—is located under the front of the center console.

• **Injector Resistors**—are located at the right rear of the engine compartment.

• **Intake Air Temperature Sensor**—is located near the distributor.

• **Integrated Control Unit**—is located to the right of the steering column.

• **Interior Light Delay Unit**—is located on the relay tower.

• **Lockup Control Solenoid Valve**—is located at the front of the transmission.

• **Low Oil Level Switch**—is located at the bottom of the engine on the alternator side.

• **Main Fuel Relay**—is located in the engine compartment fusebox.

• **MAP Sensor**—is located inside the control box.

• **Memory Seat/Memory Mirror Control Unit**—is located under the drivers seat.

• **Oil Pressure Sensor (Switch)**—is located on the timing belt side of the engine at the lower rear.

- **Oil Temperature Switch**—is located near the alternator.
- **Outside Air Temperature Sensor**—is located behind the left front fender.
- **Oxygen Sensor (rear)**—is located at the exhaust manifold near the firewall.
- **Oxygen Sensor (front)**—is located at the exhaust manifold on the radiator side of the engine.
- **Passive Restraint Control Module**—is located in the left hand center post, between the front and rear doors.
- **Passive Restraint Control Unit**—is located in the right hand center post, between the front and rear doors.
- **Passive Restraint Emergency Switch**—is located in the center post, between the front and rear doors.
- **Power Steering Switch**—is located near the firewall on the power steering pump.
- **Power Window Relay (front)**—is located on the relay tower.
- **Power Window Relay (rear)**—is located on the relay tower.
- **Power Window Relays**—are located in the doors.
- **Pressure Regulator Control Cut-Off Solenoid Valve**—is located inside the control box.
- **Rear Defogger Time Relay**—is located in the engine compartment fusebox.
- **Rear Defogger/Timer Relay**—is located on the relay tower.
- **Rear Seat Relays**—are located under the rear seats.
- **Relay Tower**—is located under the left side of the dash.
- **Seat Relay Boxes**—are located under the front seats.
- **Side Light Relay**—is located in the relay tower.
- **TDC Sensor**—is located inside the distributor.
- **Throttle Angle Sensor**—is located near the distributor.
- **Throttle Dashpot Air Filter**—is located inside the control box.
- **Vacuum Control Box**—is located at the firewall.
- **Vehicle Monitor Unit**—is located under the left front seat.
- **Vehicle Speed Pulser**—is located at the transmission.
- **Wiper Control Unit (rear)**—is located in the relay tower.
- **Wiper Motor Relay**—is located in the relay tower.

VOLKSWAGEN

Circuit Breaker and Fuses

Some vehicles may be equipped with circuit breakers which are located in the fuse/relay panel.

Fusible Links

No major fusible links are used on these vehicles.

Relay, Sensors And Computer Locations

CABRIOLET AND SCIROCCO

- **A/C Ambient Temperature Sensor**—is located on the left side of the radiator.
- **A/C Relay**—is located on the fuse/relay panel.
- **A/C Thermo Fuse (Cabriolet)**—is located on the fuse/relay panel.
- **Air Flow Sensor (16 valve engine)**—is located on the fuel distribution head.
- **Altitude Sensor (16 valve engine)**—is located in the tray area at the rear of the engine compartment.
- **Back-Up Light Switch (manual transaxle)**—is located on the transaxle.
- **Brake Fluid Level Sensor**—is located in the brake fluid reservoir cap.
- **Brake/Stoplight Switch**—is located on the master cylinder.
- **Coil Control Unit (16 valve engine)**—is located in the tray area at the rear of the engine compartment.
- **Cold Start Valve**—is located on the front of the intake manifold area.
- **Control Pressure Regulator**—is located at the front of the engine compartment.
- **Coolant Level Relay (Scirocco)**—is located on the fuse/relay panel.
- **Coolant Level Sensor**—is located in the coolant reservoir tank.
- **Coolant Temperature Sending Unit**—is located in the water outlet, at the end of the cylinder head.
- **Cooling Fan Thermoswitch**—is located in the left radiator tank.
- **CIS-E Control Unit (16 valve engine)**—is located at the left rear of the engine compartment in the tray area.
- **Cruise Control Brake Vent Switch**—is located on the hanger, over the brake pedal.
- **Cruise Control Speed Sensor**—is located on the rear of the instrument panel.
- **Cruise Control Unit**—is located under the right side of the instrument panel.
- **Dual Horn Relay**—is located on the fuse/relay panel.
- **Dynamic Oil Pressure Control Unit**—is located on the back of the speedometer.
- **Dynamic Low Pressure Switch**—is located at the rear of the cylinder head.
- **Dynamic Low Pressure Switch (16 valve engine)**—is located on the oil filter bracket.
- **Dynamic High Pressure Switch**—is located on the oil filter bracket.

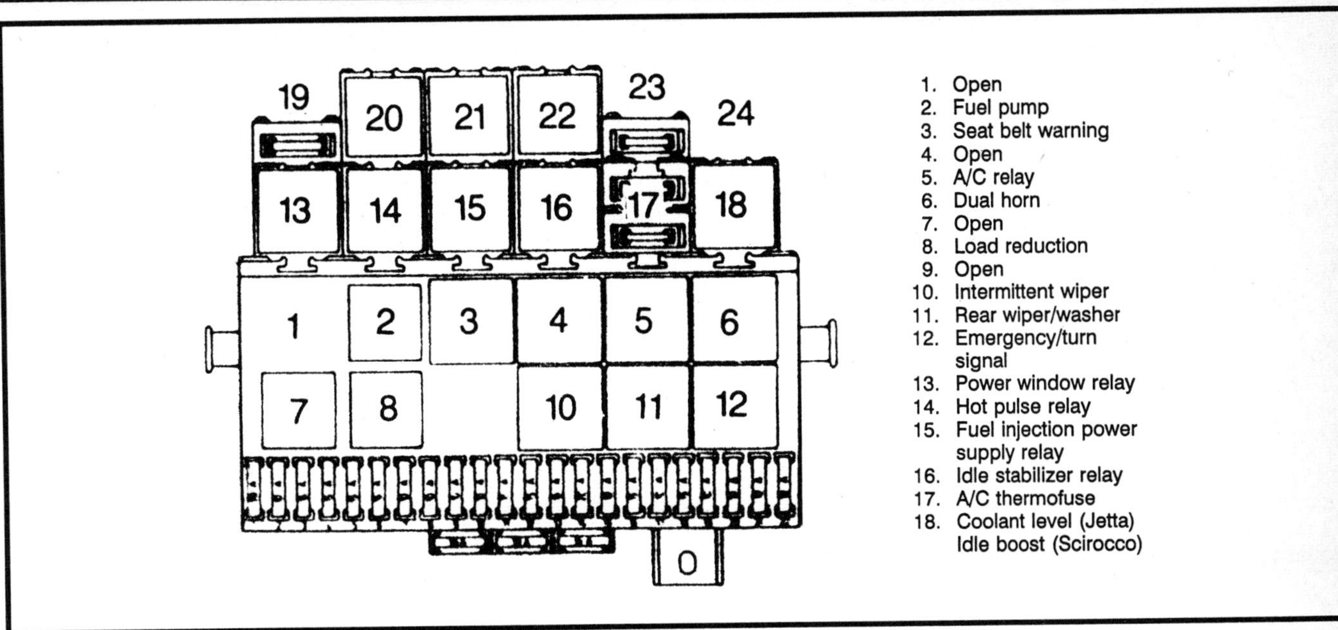

Typical fuse/relay panel—Cabriolet, Jetta and Scirocco

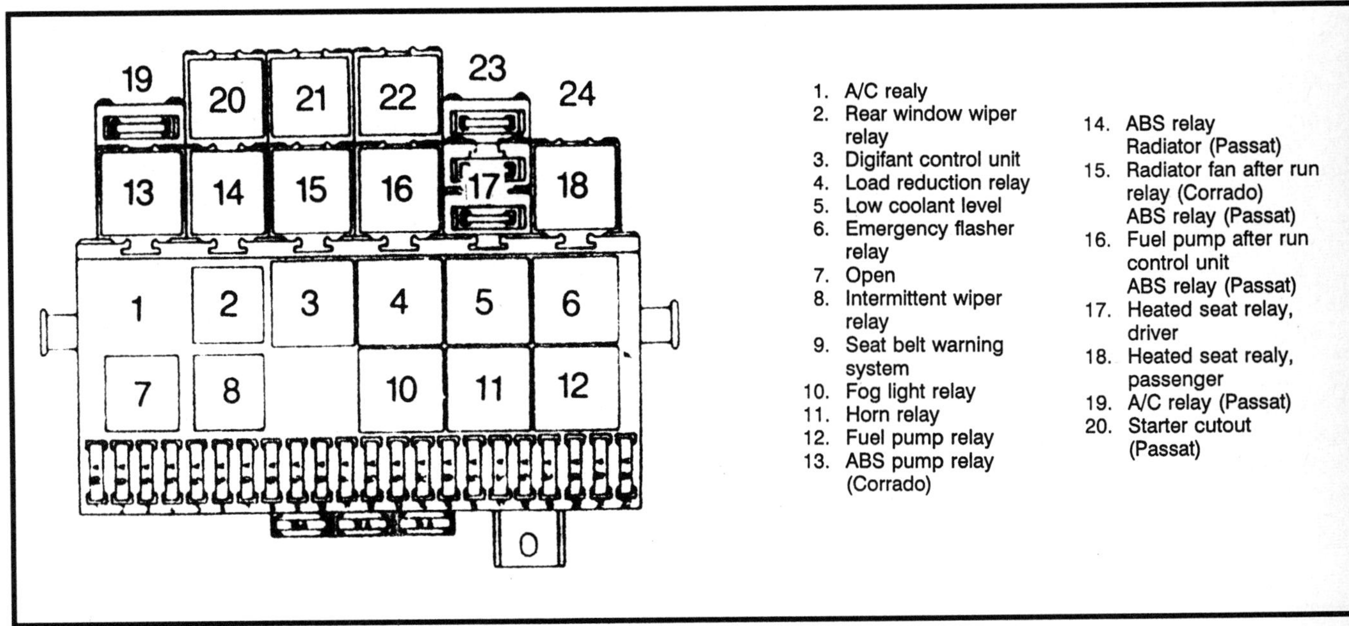

Typical fuse/relay panel—Corrado and Passat

- **Front Washer Motor**—is located near the washer fluid reservoir.
- **Front Wiper Motor**—is located in the tray area at the rear of the engine compartment.
- **Fuel Differential Pressure Regulator**—is located on the fuel distribution head.
- **Fuel Gauge Sending Unit**—is located in the top center of fuel tank (under the rear seat).
- **Fuel Injection Control Unit (8 valve engine)**—is located behind the glove box trim panel.
- **Fuel Injection Power Relay (Cabriolet)**—is located on the fuse/relay panel.
- **Fuel Pump**—is located under the right side of vehicle, at the frame.
- **Fuel Pump (transfer pump)**—is mounted in tank with the fuel gauge sending unit.
- **Fuel Pump Relay**—is located on the fuse/relay panel.
- **Fuse/Relay Panel**—is located under the left side of the instrument panel.
- **Horn Relay**—is located on the fuse/relay panel.
- **Hot Pulse Relay (Cabriolet)**—is located on the fuse/relay panel.
- **Idle Shut-Off Valve**—is located at the base of the carburetor.
- **Idle Speed Boost Relay (Scirocco)**—is located on the fuse/relay panel.
- **Idle Stabilizer Control Unit**—is located in the tray area at the left rear of the engine compartment.
- **Idle Stabilizer Relay (Cabriolet)**—is located on the fuse/relay panel.
- **Idle Switch**—is located on the throttle linkage.

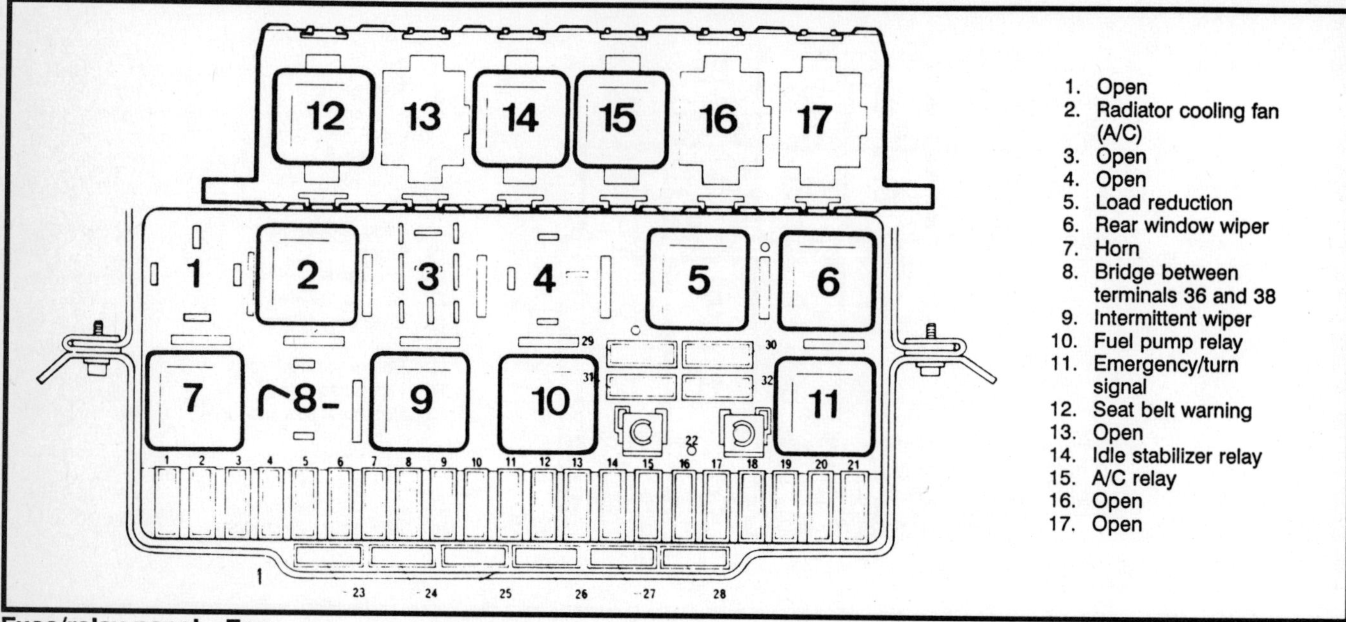

Fuse/relay panel—Fox

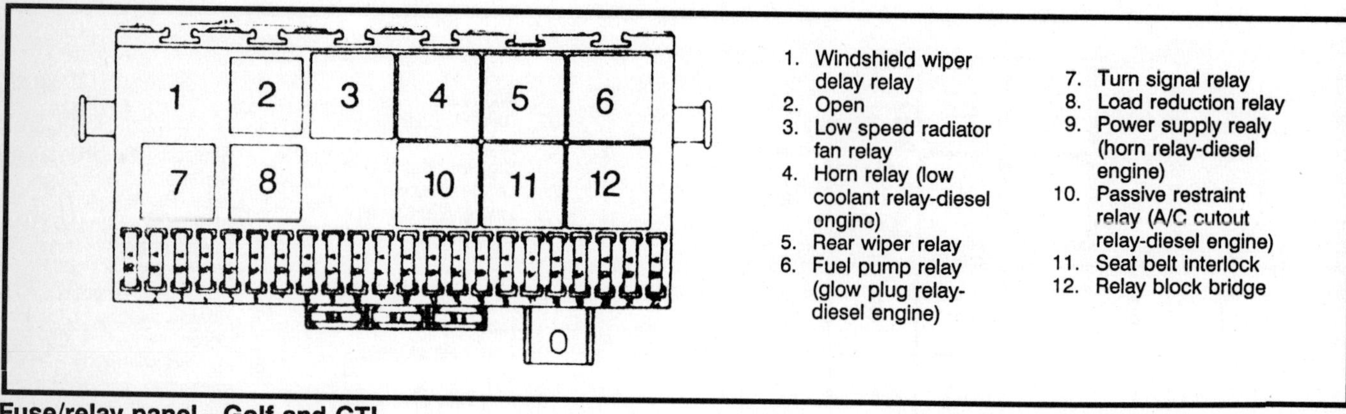

Fuse/relay panel—Golf and GTI

- **Ignition Control Unit**—is located in the tray area at the left rear of the engine compartment.
- **Intermittent Wiper Relay**—is located on the fuse/relay panel.
- **Knock Sensor**—is located on the block, under the intake manifold.
- **Knock Sensor Control Unit (16 valve engine)**—is located on the engine block.
- **Load Reduction Relay**—is located on the fuse/relay panel.
- **Neutral Start Switch (automatic transxale)**—is located under the console, at the bottom of the selector lever.
- **Oil Temperature Sensor**—is located on the oil filter bracket.
- **Overheat Temperature Sensor**—is located in the water outlet, at the end of the cylinder head.
- **Oxygen Sensor**—is located in the exhaust manifold.
- **Oxygen Sensor Control Unit**—is located at the right side of the glove box.
- **Oxygen Sensor Control Unit (16 valve engine)**—is located in the tray area at the rear of the engine compartment.
- **Oxygen Sensor Mileage Counter**—is located in the tray area at the left rear of the engine compartment.
- **Parking Brake Switch**—is located at the rear of the parking brake lever.
- **Power Lock Motor**—is located in the right trunk side panel.
- **Power Supply Relay (Scirocco)**—is located at the rear of the engine compartment.
- **Power Window Relay (Cabriolet)**—is located on the fuse/relay panel.
- **Rear Washer Motor**—is located on the washer reservoir inside the right panel.
- **Rear Wiper Motor**—is located inside the bottom of the liftgate.
- **Rear Wiper Relay**—is located on the fuse/relay panel.
- **Seat Belt Warning Relay**—is located on the fuse/relay panel.
- **TDC Sensor (16 valve engine)**—is located in the transmission bell housing.
- **Thermo Time Switch**—is located in the coolant supply flange, between the No. 1 and No. 2 cylinders.
- **Thermo Time Switch (16 valve engine)**—is located on the block, below the heater outlet housing.
- **Turn Signal/Hazard Flasher**—is located on the fuse/relay panel.
- **Upshift Indicator Control Unit**—is located on the fuse/relay panel.
- **Upshift Indicator Pressure Switch**—is located in the vacuum line to the distributor vacuum chamber.

• **Wide Open Throttle Switch**—is located on the throttle linkage.

CORRADO

• **A/C Compressor Relay**—is located in the engine compartment on the top left side of the radiator shroud.
• **A/C Control Relay**—is located at position 1 in the fuse/relay panel.
• **A/C Pressure Switch**—is located on the left side of the engine compartment, next to the radiator and condenser.
• **A/C Sight Glass**—is located in the high pressure tube between the high pressure service valve and receiver drier.
• **Anti-lock Brake System Control (ABS) Unit**—is located left front kick panel area.
• **ABS Relay**—is located at position 14 in the fuse/relay panel.
• **ABS Hydraulic Modulator**—is located in the right side area of the engine compartment.
• **ABS Hydraulic Pump Relay**—is located at position 13 in the fuse/relay panel.
• **ABS Pressure Warning Switch**—is located on the top of the hydraulic modulator assembly.
• **Brake Fluid Level Sensor**—is located inside the brake fluid reservoir.
• **Carbon Canister Control Valve**—is located on the right side of the engine compartment near the air filter assembly.
• **Coolant Fan After Run Switch**—is located next to the fuel pressure regulator.
• **Coolant Temperature Switch**—is located on the top of the engine area between No. 3 and No. 4 cylinders.
• **CO Potentiometer**—is located on the air intake duct before the throttle body assembly.
• **Cruise Control Unit**—is located to the right area of the instrument cluster.
• **Digifant Electronic Control Unit**—is located in the top center area of the engine compartment.
• **Digifant Electronic Control Unit Relay**—is located at position 3 in the fuse/relay panel.
• **Emergency/Turn Signal Flasher Relay**—is located at position 6 in the fuse/relay panel.
• **Fog Light Relay**—is located at position 10 in the fuse/relay panel.
• **Fuel Pressure Switch**—is located on the left side of the intake manifold in front of the throttle body.
• **Fuel Pump**—is located in the fuel tank assembly.
• **Fuel Pump After Run Control Unit Relay**—is located at position 16 in the fuse/relay panel.
• **Fuel Pump Relay**—is located at position 12 in the fuse/relay panel.
• **Fuse/Relay Panel**—is located underneath the left side of the instrument panel.
• **Horn Relay**—is located at position 11 in the fuse/relay panel.
• **Idle Switch**—is located on the top of the engine near the throttle valve housing.
• **Intercooler Assembly**—is located at the left front engine compartment area below the left headlight.
• **Intermittent Wiper Relay**—is located at position 8 in the fuse/relay panel.
• **Knock Sensor**—is located to the left of the oil dipstick area near No. 2 cylinder.
• **Load Reduction Relay**—is located at position 4 in the fuse/relay panel.
• **Low Coolant Level**—is located at position 5 in the fuse/relay panel.
• **Manifold Pressure Sensor**—is located inside the Digifant ECU assembly.
• **Power Window Control Unit**—is located in the left rear quarter panel area.

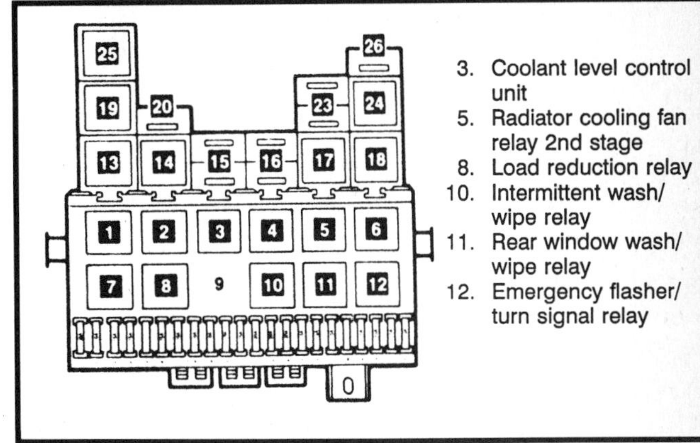

Fuse/relay panel—Vanagon

• **Radiator Cooling Fan (2nd stage)**—is located in the engine compartment on the top left side of the radiator shroud.
• **Radiator Cooling Fan After Run Relay**—is located at position 15 in the fuse/relay panel.
• **Radiator Thermoswitch**—is located on the left side of the radiator assembly.
• **Rear Window Relay**—is located at position 2 in the fuse/relay panel.
• **Relay/Fuse Panel**—is located underneath the left side of the instrument panel.
• **Seat Belt Warning System Relay**—is located at position 9 in the fuse/relay panel.
• **Seat Heater Control Relays**—are located on the right rear quarter panel area.
• **Speaker Amplifiers**—are located in the door panels.
• **Turn Signal/Hazard Flasher Relay**—is located at position 6 in the fuse/relay panel.
• **Voltage Stabilizer**—is located on the instrument cluster housing above the fuel gauge.
• **Windshield Washer Pump**—is located on fluid washer reservoir bottle.

FOX

• **A/C Pressure Switch (low)**—is located on the middle area of the receiver-drier assembly.
• **A/C Pressure Switch (high)**—is located on the upper area of the receiver-drier assembly.
• **A/C Relay**—is located on the fuse/relay panel.
• **A/C Radiator Cooling Fan Relay**—is located on the fuse/relay panel.
• **Air Sensor Potentiometer**—is located on the side area of the air cleaner housing.
• **Brake Fluid Low Warning Switch**—is located in the brake fluid reservoir cap assembly.
• **Cold Start Valve**—is located on upper front of intake manifold assembly.
• **CIS-E Control Unit**—is located on the right side of the glove box area.
• **Fuel Pump Relay**—is located on the fuse/relay panel.
• **Fuse/Relay Panel**—is located under the lft side dash area.
• **Horn Relay**—is located on the fuse/relay panel.
• **Idle Speed Boost Solenoid Valve**—is located on the engine, near the throttle cable retainer bracket.
• **Idle Stabilizer Control Unit**—is located on the fuse/relay panel.
• **Ignition Control Unit**—is located on the top of engine, between ignition coil and distributor assembly.
• **Intermittent Wiper Relay**—is located on the fuse/relay panel.

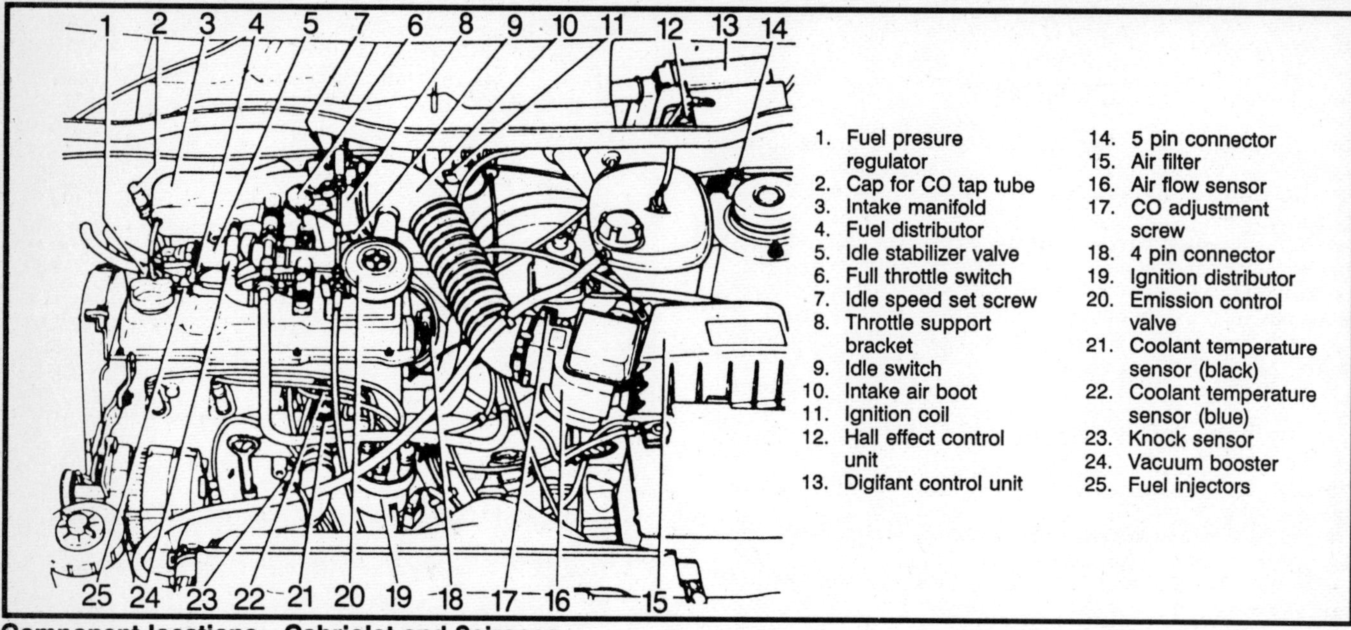

Component locations—Cabriolet and Scirocco

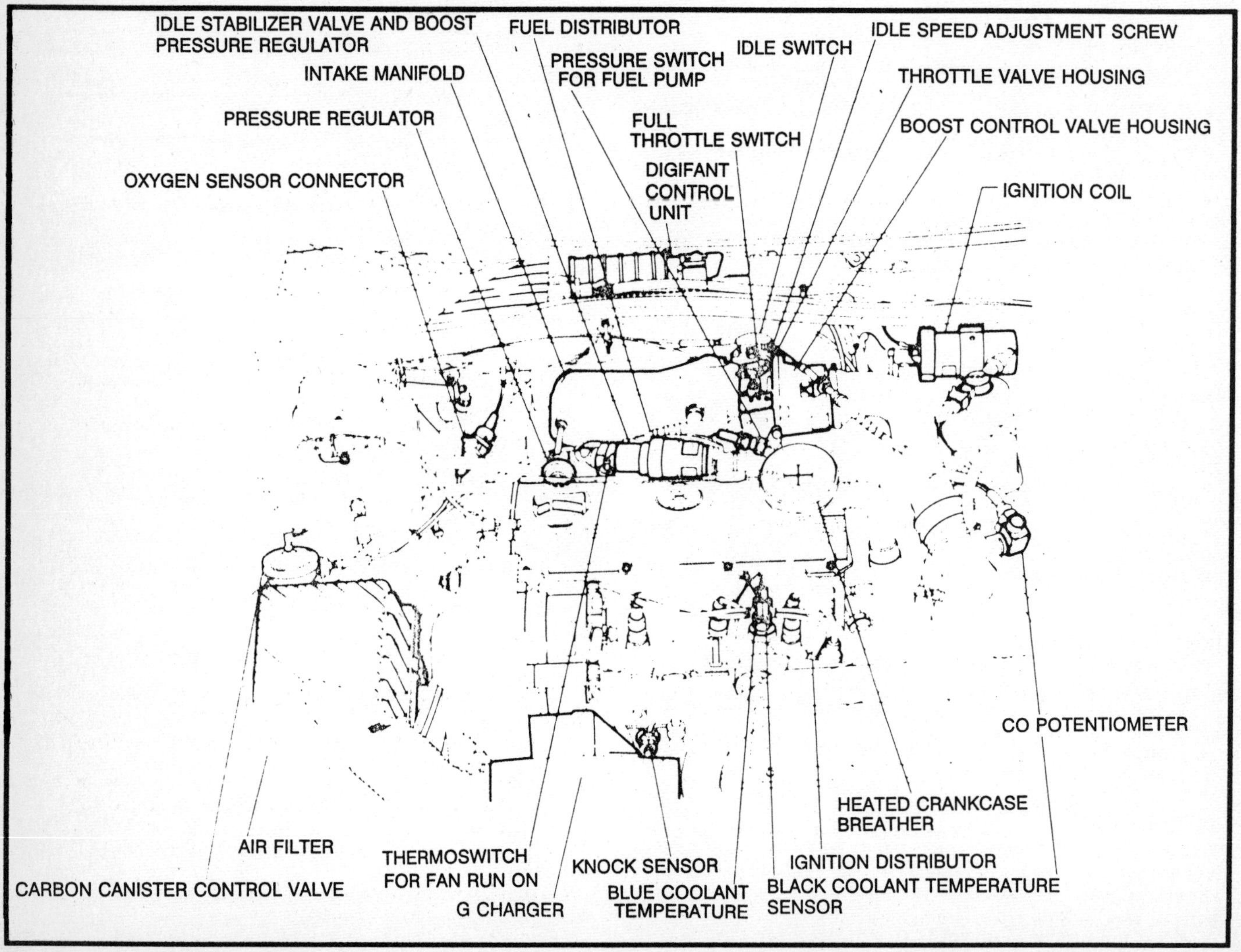

IDLE STABILIZER VALVE AND BOOST PRESSURE REGULATOR
FUEL DISTRIBUTOR
IDLE SPEED ADJUSTMENT SCREW
INTAKE MANIFOLD
PRESSURE SWITCH FOR FUEL PUMP
IDLE SWITCH
THROTTLE VALVE HOUSING
PRESSURE REGULATOR
FULL THROTTLE SWITCH
BOOST CONTROL VALVE HOUSING
OXYGEN SENSOR CONNECTOR
DIGIFANT CONTROL UNIT
IGNITION COIL
CO POTENTIOMETER
HEATED CRANKCASE BREATHER
AIR FILTER
THERMOSWITCH FOR FAN RUN ON
KNOCK SENSOR
IGNITION DISTRIBUTOR
CARBON CANISTER CONTROL VALVE
G CHARGER
BLUE COOLANT TEMPERATURE
BLACK COOLANT TEMPERATURE SENSOR

Component locations—Corrado

- **Load Reduction Circuit Relay**—is located on the fuse/relay panel.
- **Oxygen Sensor**—is located in the exhaust manifold.
- **Rear Wiper Relay**—is located on the fuse/relay panel.
- **Relay/Fuse Panel**—is located under the lft side dash area.
- **Seat Belt Warning Relay**—is located on the fuse/relay panel.
- **Temperature Sensor**—is located on coolant flange, near the distributor assembly.
- **Thermo Time Switch**—is located in the coolant flange assembly.
- **Turn Signal/Hazard Flasher**—is located on the fuse/relay panel.
- **Upshift Indicator Vacuum Switch**—is located in distributor vacuum advance line.

GOLF AND GTI

- **A/C High/Low Pressure Switch**—is located at the top area of the receiver-drier assembly.
- **A/C Hi-Speed Fan Relay**—is located on the fuse/relay panel.
- **Anti-Lock Brake Control Unit (ABS)**—is located in the rear seat area.
- **ABS Brake Fluid Warning Switch**—is located in the brake fluid reservoir cap.
- **Airflow Sensor**—is located on the fuel distribution head.
- **Altitude Sensor**—is located on the left plenum panel.
- **Back-Up/Upshift Indicator Light Switch**—is located on the top center of the transaxle.
- **Brake Failure Switch**—is located in the brake line proportioning valve.
- **Brake/Stoplight Switch**—is located on the bracket above the brake pedal.
- **Central Lock Vacuum Motor**—is located in the left trunk panel.
- **Cold Start Valve**—is located on the rear of the intake manifold.
- **Coolant Level Sensor**—is located in the coolant reservoir tank.
- **Coolant Temperature Sensor**—is located in the upper hose flange, on the left side of the engine.
- **Cooling Fan Series Resistor**—is attached to the fan motor housing.
- **Cooling Fan Thermoswitch**—is located in the lower left corner of the radiator.
- **Control Pressure Regulator (CIS-E)**—is located on the fuel distribution head.
- **Cruise Control Brake Switch**—is located on the brake pedal bracket.
- **Cruise Control Clutch Switch**—is located on the clutch pedal bracket.
- **Cruise Control Unit**—is located under the radio in the center console.
- **Differential Pressure Regulator**—is located in the fuel distribution head.
- **ECU Upshift Relay**—is located on the fuse/relay panel.
- **EFI Coolant Thermoswitch**—is located in the upper hose flange, on the left side of the engine.
- **EFI Temperature Sensor**—is located on the left side of the engine block.
- **Front Washer Motor**—is located in the fluid reservoir.
- **Front Wiper Motor**—is located on the plenum panel.
- **Fuel Gauge Sending Unit**—is located in the top of fuel tank.
- **Fuel Pump**—is located under the right side of the vehicle on the frame.
- **Fuel Pump Relay**—is located on the fuse/relay panel.
- **Fuse/Relay Panel**—is located under the left hand side of the instrument panel.
- **High Speed Cooling Fan Relay**—is attached to the upper left corner of the fan shroud.
- **Horn Relay**—is located on the fuse/relay panel.
- **Idle Speed Boost Valve**—is located on the inner fender panel, at the front of the right shock tower.
- **Idle Speed Control Relay (Golf)**—is located on the fuse/relay panel.
- **Idle Speed Stabilizer Valve**—is located in the air bypass hose.
- **Idle Switch (CIS-E)**—is located on the throttle linkage.
- **Ignition Control Unit**—is located on the plenum panel, near the wiper motor.
- **Instrument Voltage Stabilizer**—is located on the rear of the instrument panel, above the speedometer.
- **Intermittent Wiper Relay**—is located on the fuse/relay panel.
- **Knock Sensor**—is located on the lower left corner of the block.
- **Knock Sensor Control Unit**—is located on the rear of the engine compartment.
- **Load Reduction Relay**—is located on the fuse/relay panel.
- **Low Speed Cooling Fan Relay**—is located on the fuse/relay panel.
- **Oil Pressure Consumption Switch (automatic transaxle)**—is located on the right side of transaxle.
- **Oil Low Pressure Switch**—is located at the rear of the cylinder head.
- **Oil High Pressure Switch**—is located on the oil filter bracket.
- **Oil Temperature Sending Unit**—is located on the oil filter bracket.
- **Oxygen Sensor**—is located in the exhaust manifold.
- **Parking Brake Switch**—is located at the base of the parking brake lever.
- **Pulse Wiper System Relay (Golf)**—is located on the fuse/relay panel.
- **Rear Washer Motor**—is located on the washer fluid reservoir.
- **Rear Wiper Motor**—is located on the rear hatch.
- **Rear Wiper Relay**—is located on the fuse/relay panel.
- **Seat Belt Warning Relay**—is located on the fuse/relay panel.
- **Time Warning Interlock Relay (Golf)**—is located on the fuse/relay panel.
- **Turn Signal/Hazard Flasher**—is located on the lower left corner of the fuse/relay panel.
- **Upshift Relay**—is located in the fuse/relay panel.
- **Vacuum Switch**—is located in the vacuum line, near the distributor.
- **Wide Open Throttle Switch**—is located on the throttle linkage.

JETTA

- **A/C Pressure Switch**—is located in the A/C line, near the condenser assembly.
- **A/C Relay**—is located on the fuse/relay panel.
- **A/C Thermofuse**—is located on the fuse/relay panel.
- **A/C Thermoswitch**—is located in the coolant flange on the front left corner of the engine.
- **Airflow Sensor**—is located in the fuel distribution head.
- **Anti-Lock Brake Control Unit (ABS)**—is located in the rear seat area.
- **ABS Brake Fluid Warning Switch**—is located in the brake fluid reservoir cap.
- **Back-Up/Consumption Indicator Switch**—is located on the top center of the transaxle.
- **Brake Failure Switch**—is located in the brake line proportioning valve.

• **Brake/Stoplight Switch**—is located on the bracket above the brake pedal.

• **Coolant Level Indicator Relay**—is located on the fuse/relay panel.

• **Coolant Level Sensor (diesel)**—is located in the coolant reservoir tank.

• **Coolant Temperature Sending Unit (diesel)**—is located in the coolant flange, on the rear of the engine.

• **Coolant Temperature Sensor (diesel)**—is located in the coolant flange, on the front left corner of the engine.

• **Coolant Temperature Sensor (8 valve engine)**—is located in the coolant flange, on the left of the cylinder head.

• **Coolant Temperature Sensor (16 valve engine)**—is located under the colant flange, under the distributor assembly.

• **Coolant Temperature Switches (diesel)**—is located in the coolant flange, on the rear of the engine.

• **Cooling Fan Series Resistor**—is attached to the fan motor housing.

• **Cooling Fan Thermoswitch**—is located on the lower left corner of the radiator.

• **Cruise Control Brake Switch**—is located on the brake pedal bracket.

• **Cruise Control Clutch Switch**—is located on the clutch pedal bracket.

• **Cruise Control Unit**—is located under the radio in the center console.

• **Differential Pressure Regulator**—is located on the fuel distribution head.

• **EFI Coolant Thermoswitch**—is located in the coolant flange, on the left rear corner of the engine.

• **Fuel Cut-off Solenoid (diesel)**—is located on the rear of the diesel injection pump.

• **Fuel Gauge Sending Unit**—is located in the top of the fuel tank.

• **Fuel Injection Temperature Sender**—is located in the coolant flange, on the left rear corner of the engine.

• **Fuel Pump**—is located under the right side of the vehicle at the frame.

• **Fuel Pump Relay**—is located on the fuse/relay panel.

• **Fuse/Relay Panel**—is located under the left side of the instrument panel.

• **Glow Plug Fuse (diesel)**—is located on the fuse/relay panel.

• **Glow Plug Relay (diesel)**—is located on the fuse/relay panel.

• **Heated Seat Relays**—are located on the fuse/relay panel.

• **High Oil Pressure Switch No. 1**—is located on the oil filter bracket.

• **High Oil Pressure Switch No. 2**—is located on the right side of cylinder head.

• **High Speed Cooling Fan Relay**—is attached to the upper left corner of the fan shroud.

• **Horn Relay (dual)**—is located on the fuse/relay panel.

• **Idle Speed Boost Valve**—is located on the inner fender panel, at the front of the right shock tower.

• **Idle Speed Stabilizer Valve**—is located on the rear of the instrument panel, above the speedometer.

• **Idle Stabilizer Relay**—is located on the fuse/relay panel.

• **Idle Switch**—is located on the throttle linkage.

• **Intermittent Wiper Relay**—is located on the fuse/relay panel.

• **Knock Sensor**—is located on the lower left corner of the engine block.

• **Knock Sensor Control Unit**—is located on the left rear corner of the engine compartment.

• **Load Reduction Circuit Relay**—is located on the fuse/relay panel.

• **Low Oil Pressure Switch No. 1**—is located on the right side of cylinder head.

• **Low Oil Pressure Switch No. 2**—is located in the rear of the cylinder head.

• **Oil Pressure Consumption Switch (automatic transaxle)**—is located on the right side of transaxle.

• **Oil Pressure Sending Unit**—is located in the oil filter bracket.

• **Oil Temperature Sending Unit**—is located on the oil filter bracket.

• **Oxygen Sensor**—is located in the exhaust manifold.

• **Oxygen Sensor Control Unit**—is located on the plenum panel at the rear of the engine compartment.

• **Parking Brake Switch**—is located at the base of the parking brake lever.

• **Power Window Relay**—is located on the fuse/relay panel.

• **Rear Washer Motor**—is located on the washer fluid reservoir.

• **Rear Wiper Motor**—is located on the rear hatch.

• **Rear Wiper/Washer Relay**—is located on the fuse/relay panel.

• **Seat Belt Warning System Relay**—is located on the fuse/relay panel.

• **TCI-H (Ignition) Control Unit**—is located on the plenum panel, near the wiper motor.

• **Turn Signal/Hazard Flasher**—is located on the fuse/relay panel.

• **Upshift Indicator Idle Switch (diesel)**—is located on the opposite sprocket end of the injection pump.

• **Upshift Indicator Relay**—is located on the fuse/relay panel.

• **Vacuum Switch**—is located in the vacuum hose, near the distributor.

• **Wide Open Throttle Switch (diesel)**—is located on the sprocket end of the injection pump.

• **Wide Open Throttle Switch (gas)**—is located on the throttle linkage.

PASSAT

• **A/C Compressor Clutch Cut-Off Relay (automatic transaxle)**—is located behind the center console area.

• **A/C Pressure Switch**—is located on the right rear area of the engine compartment.

• **A/C Relay**—is located at position 1 in the fuse/relay panel with production control No. 13 stamped on relay housing.

• **A/C Time Delay Relay (manual transaxle)**—is located behind the center console area.

• **Ambient Temperature Switch**—is located on the lower right rear area of the engine compartment.

• **Anti-lock Brake System (ABS) Hydraulic Pump Relay**—is located at position 15 in the fuse/relay panel with production control No. 78 stamped on relay housing.

• **ABS Relay**—is located at position 16 in the fuse/relay panel with production control No. 79 stamped on relay housing.

• **CIS-E Motronic Control Unit**—is located at the firewall area below the windshiels wipers.

• **Emergency/Turn Signal Flasher Relay**—is located at position 6 in the fuse/relay panel with production control No. 21 stamped on relay housing.

• **Fuel Pump Relay**—is located at position 12 in the fuse/relay panel with production control No. 67 or 80 stamped on relay housing.

• **Horn Relay**—is located at position 11 in the fuse/relay panel with production control No. 53 stamped on relay housing.

• **Intermittent Washer/Wiper Relay**—is located at position 8 in the fuse/relay panel with production control No. 19 stamped on relay housing.

• **Load Reduction Relay**—is located at position 4 in the fuse/relay panel with production control No. 18 stamped on relay housing.

• **Low Coolant Level Control Unit**—is located at position 5 in the fuse/relay panel with production control No. 43 stamped on relay housing.

• **Oxygen Sensor Harness Connector**—is located on the right engine mount.

• **Radiator Cooling Fan After Run Control Unit**—is located at position 14 in the fuse/relay panel with production control No. 31 stamped on relay housing.

• **Rear Window Wash/Wiper Relay (wagon)**—is located at position 2 in the fuse/relay panel with production control No. 72 stamped on relay housing.

• **Seat Belt Warning System Control Unit**—is located at position 9 in the fuse/relay panel with production control No. 27 or 74 stamped on relay housing.

• **Turn Signal/Hazard Flasher Relay**—is located at position 6 in the fuse/relay panel with production control No. 21 stamped on relay housing.

• **Voltage Stabilizer**—is located on the instrument panel, behind the tachometer.

• **Windshield Washer Pump**—is located in the windshield washer fluid reservoir.

VANAGON

• **A/C Service Valve**—is located under the left rear evaporator panel area.

• **Brake Warning Switch**—is located in the master cylinder reservoir housing.

• **Cruise Control Unit**—is located behind right side of the instrument panel area.

• **Emergency/Turn Signal Flasher Relay**—is located at position 12 in the fuse/relay panel with production control No. 21 stamped on relay housing.

• **EFI/Ignition Control Unit**—is located on truck floor, behind the rear seat area.

• **Fuel Pump**—is located under the vehicle, front of the tank area.

• **Idle Stabilization Control Unit**—is located on the right side of the engine compartment.

• **Ignition Control/EFI Unit**—is located on truck floor, behind the rear seat area.

• **Intermittent Washer/Wiper Relay**—is located at position 10 in the fuse/relay panel with production control No. 19 stamped on relay housing.

• **Load Reduction Relay**—is located at position 8 in the fuse/relay panel with production control No. 18 stamped on relay housing.

• **Low Coolant Level Control Unit**—is located at position 3 in the fuse/relay panel with production control No. 43 stamped on relay housing.

• **Oil Pressure Switch (0.3 bar)**—is located under the left side valve cover on engine assembly.

• **Oil Pressure Switch (0.9 bar)**—is located in the lower center rear area of the engine assembly.

• **Oxygen Sensor**—is located in the exhaust system in front of the catalytic converter.

• **Radiator Cooling Fan (2nd stage)**—is located at position 5 in the fuse/relay panel with production control No. 53 stamped on relay housing.

• **Rear Window Wash/Wiper Relay**—is located at position 11 in the fuse/relay panel with production control No. 72 stamped on relay housing.

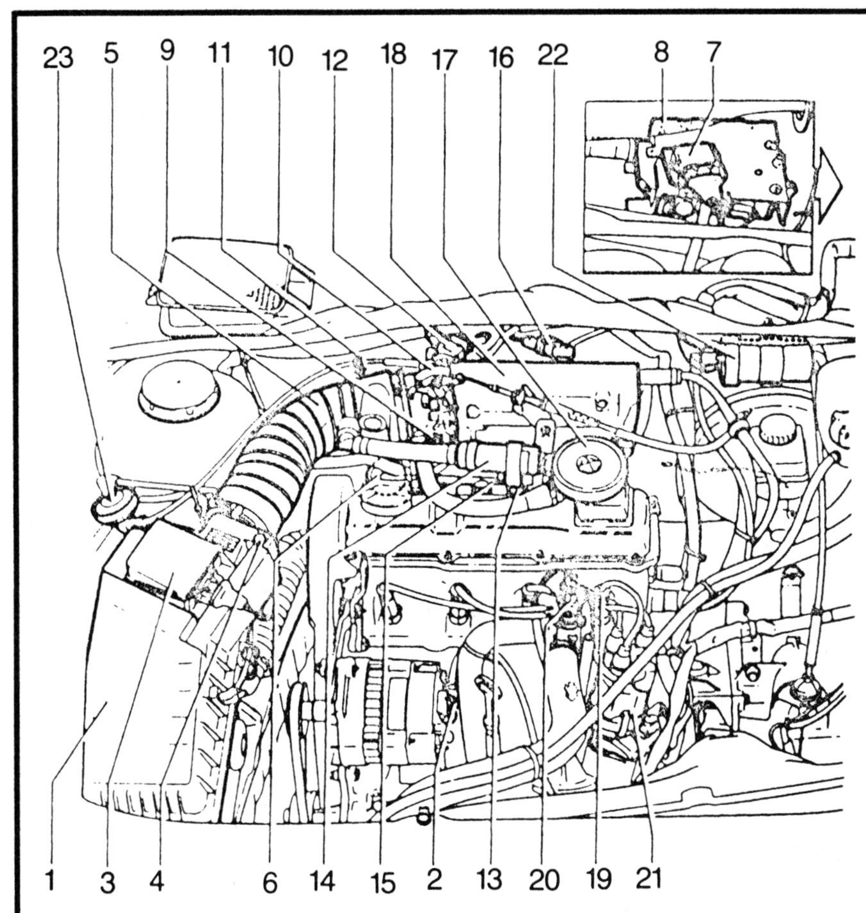

1. Air filter
2. Knock sensor
3. Air flow sensor
4. CO adjusting screw
5. Intake hose
6. Fuel pressure regulator
7. Hall effect control unit
8. Digifant control unit
9. Idle speed adjusting screw
10. Throttle valve housing
11. Idle switch
12. Full throttle switch
13. Fuel injectors
14. Idle stabilizer valve
15. Fuel rail
16. Oxygen sensor harness connector
17. Emission control valve
18. Intake manifold
19. Coolant temperature Sensor (black)
20. Coolant temperature Sensor (blue)
21. Ignition distributor
22. Ignition coil
23. Carbon canister shut-off solenoid

Component locations—Golf, GTI and Jetta

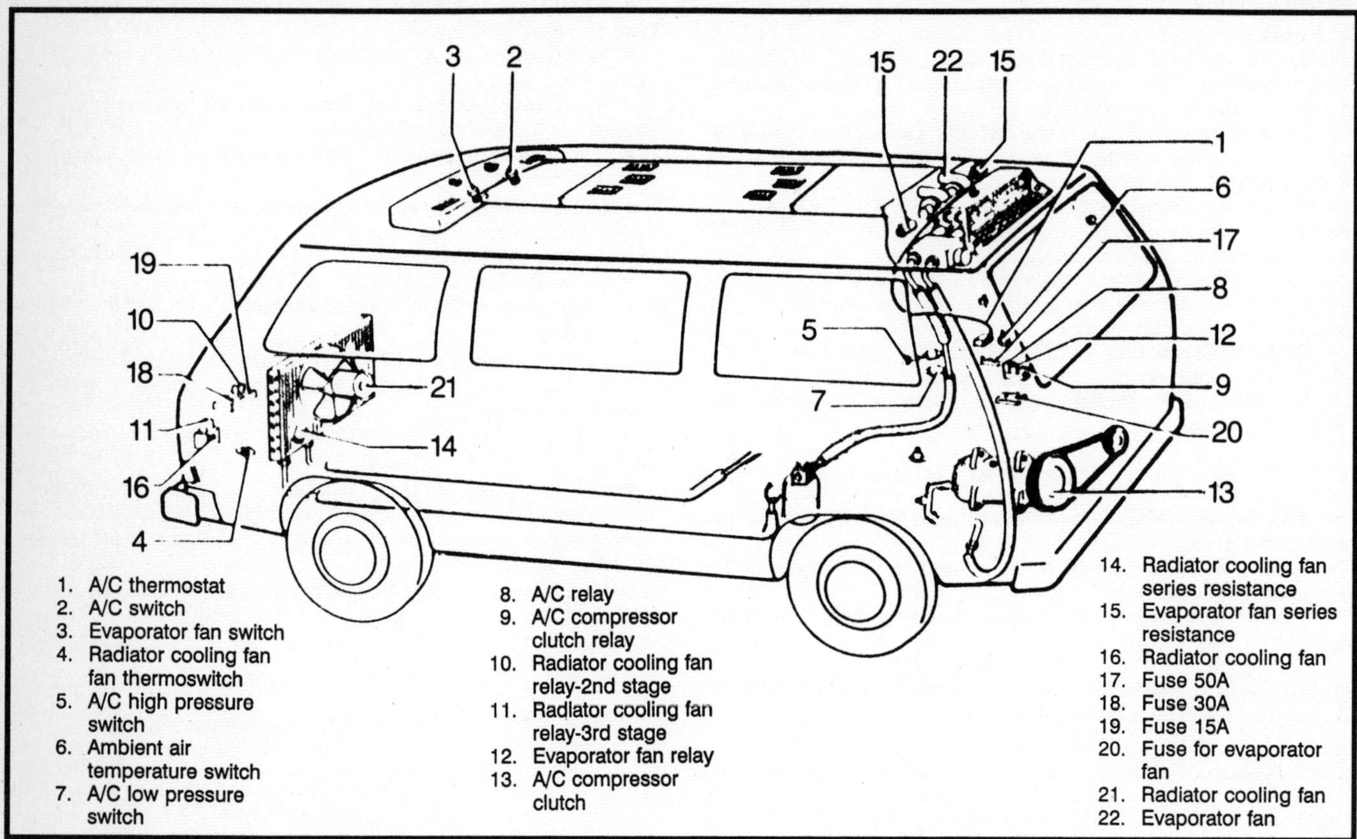

Component locations—Vanagon

- **Seat Belt Warning System Control Unit**—is located at position 19 in the fuse/relay panel.
- **TDC Sensor**—is located on the top of the bellhousing area.
- **Turn Signal/Hazard Flasher Relay**—is located at position 12 in the fuse/relay panel with production control No. 21 stamped on relay housing.
- **Voltage Stabilizer**—is located behind the instrument panel.

VOLVO

Circuit Breakers and Fuses

200 SERIES

Fuses are located at the left side kick panel. An in-line fuse serving the Jetronic fuel injection system is located on the left hand wheel housing by the ignition coil. An in-line fuse serving the EZ-116-K ignition system is located at the left hand wheel housing by the ignition coil.

940 AND 700 SERIES

Fuses are located under the center of the dash attached to the side of the relay box or at the left kick panel.

Fusible Links

Fusible links may be located at the battery, starter or alternator.

Sensors, Relays, Modules and Computer Locations

200 SERIES

- **ABS Control Unit**—is located under the left side of the dash.
- **ABS Hydraulic Unit**—is located at the right front of the engine compartment.
- **A/C Pressure Sensor**—is located at the receiver drier.
- **A/C Relay**—is located under the center of the dash behind the switch panel.
- **Anti-lock Brakes**—see ABS.
- **Bulb Failure Warning Sensor**—is located under the left side of the dash.
- **Bulb Failure Warning Sensor**—is located under the left side of the dash.
- **Central Door Lock Relays**—are located under the center of the dash above the switch panel.

• **Chime**—is located under the left side of the dash.

• **Coolant Temperature Sensor**—is located at the right front of the engine or at the center rear of the engine (diesel).

• **Cruise Control Unit**—is located above the steering column under the left side of the dash.

• **Cruise Control Unit**—is located at the steering column under the left side of the dash.

• **Cruise Control Vacuum Pump**—is located at the left rear of the engine compartment.

• **Cruise Control Vacuum Pump**—is located at the left rear of the engine compartment.

• **Cruise Control Vacuum Servo**—is located at the accelerator pedal.

• **Cruise Control Vacuum Valves**—are located at the brake and clutch pedal brackets.

• **Delayed Courtesy Light Relay**—is located under the left side of the dash near the steering column.

• **Dwell Meter Connector**—is located at the left side of the engine compartment near the shock tower.

• **Fuel Injection Air Mass Meter (LH)**—is located at the left front of the engine compartment.

• **Fuel Injection Auxiliary Air Valve (CI)**—is located at the top of the engine next to the valve cover.

• **Fuel Injection Contact Breaker (LH)**—is located on the engine near the master cylinder.

• **Fuel Injection Control Pressure Regulator (CI)**—is located next to the distributor.

• **Fuel Injection Control Unit**—is located at the right side kick panel under the dash.

• **Fuel Injection Diagnostic Unit**—is located at the left rear of the engine compartment.

• **Fuel Injection Idle Valve (LH)**—is located at the left front of the engine.

• **Fuel Injection Thermal Time Switch (CI)**—is located at the rear of the engine near the valve cover.

• **Fuel Pump Relay**—is located under the left side of the dash.

• **Fuel Shut-off**—is located at the throttle body.

• **Glow Plug Relay (diesel)**—is located at the left side of the engine compartment near the shock tower.

• **Headlight Relay**—is located at the left side kick panel.

• **Headlight Step Relay**—is located on the left front fender near the battery.

• **Hot Start Valve Relay**—is located near the battery on the left side of the engine compartment.

• **Idle Speed Switch**—is located at the throttle body.

• **Ignition System Control Unit**—is located at the left front of the engine compartment under the battery.

• **Ignition System Control Unit**—is located at the right side kick panel next to the fuel injection control unit.

• **Ignition System Control Unit**—is located under the right side of the dash above the glove box.

• **Ignition System Diagnostic Unit**—is located at the left rear of the engine compartment.

• **Impulse Sender**—is located at the top of the transmission bell housing.

• **Intermittent Wiper Relay (front)**—is located at the left side kick panel.

• **Intermittent Wiper Relay (rear)**—is located at the left side kick panel.

• **Knock Sensor**—is located at the top of the engine next to the valve cover.

• **Overdrive Relay**—is located under the center of the dash.

• **Oxygen Sensor Control Unit**—is located at the right side kick panel.

• **Oxygen Sensor Frequency Valve**—is located at the left rear of the engine.

• **Oxygen Sensor Relay**—is located at the left fender in the engine compartment.

• **Oxygen Sensor Relay**—is located under the right side of the dash near the glove box.

• **Oxygen Sensor**—is located at the right side of the engine in the exhaust manifold.

• **Power Window Relay**—is located under the center of the dash.

• **Pre-Heater Control Unit (diesel)**—is located at the left side of the engine compartment.

• **Pressure Transducer**—is located at the left side shock tower.

• **PTC Heater (carburetor)**—is located at the base of the carburetor.

• **Rear Window Defogger Relay**—is located under the left side of the dash near the steering column.

• **Solenoid Valve (carburetor)**—is located at the base of the carburetor.

• **SRS Crash Sensor**—is located under the center of the dash.

• **SRS Diagnostic Socket**—is located under the left side of the dash.

• **Start Inhibitor Switch**—is located at the gear selection lever.

• **Supplemental Restraint System**—see SRS.

• **Throttle Switch**—is located at the throttle body.

• **Transmission Overdrive Relay**—is located under the right side of the dash.

• **Transmission Overdrive Solenoid**—is located inside the tailshaft of the transmission.

• **Turn Signal Relay**—is located under the center of the dash behind the switch panel.

940 AND 700 SERIES

• **A/C Compressor Delay Relay**—is located under the right side of the dash above the glovebox.

• **A/C Cutout Relay**—is located on the left side of the engine compartment at the shock tower.

• **A/C Dual Pressure Switch**—is located at the receiver drier.

• **ABS Control Unit**—is located at the left side kick panel.

• **ABS Hydraulic Unit**—is located at either the left or right side fender in the engine compartment.

• **ABS Surge Protector**—is located next to the ABS control unit.

• **Air Control Valve (LH)**—is located at the intake manifold near the alternator.

• **Air Intake Temperature Sensor**—is located at the air cleaner.

• **Air Mass Meter (LH)**—is located at the left front of the engine compartment near the air cleaner.

• **Air Valve (CI)**—is located at the top of the engine near the valve cover.

• **Backup Light Switch (automatic transmission)**—is located at the gear selector lever.

• **Backup Light Switch (manual transmission)**—is located at the top of the transmission case.

• **Blower Relay**—is located under the right side of the dash above the glovebox.

• **Brake Fluid Level Sensor**—is located at the master cylinder.

• **Bulb Failure Warning Sensor**—is located at the fuse box under the center of the dash.

• **Central Lock Relay**—is located at the fuse box under the center of the dash.

• **Cold Start Valve (LH)**—is located at the front of the intake manifold.

• **Control Pressure Regulator (CI)**—is located at the left front of the engine.

• **Coolant Temperature Sensor (LH)**—is located at the left rear of the engine block near the oil pan rail.

• **Coolant Temperature Sensor**—is located at the left rear of the engine block near the oil pan rail.

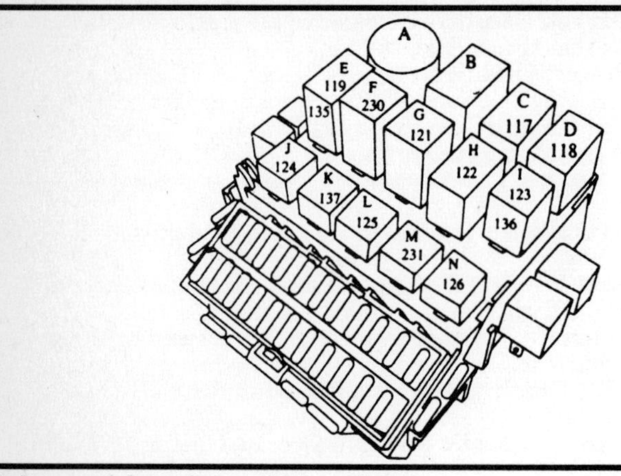

a. Bulb failure warning sensor
b. Seat belt reminder
c. Windshield wiper intermittent relay
d. Tailgate wiper intermittent relay
e. Fuel injection relay
f. Foglight relay
g. Flasher
h. Not used
i. Overdrive relay
j. Power window/Seat heater relay
k. Headlight relay
l. Central lock relay
m. Rear fog light relay
n. Supplementary high beam relay

Relay and fuse box—200 series

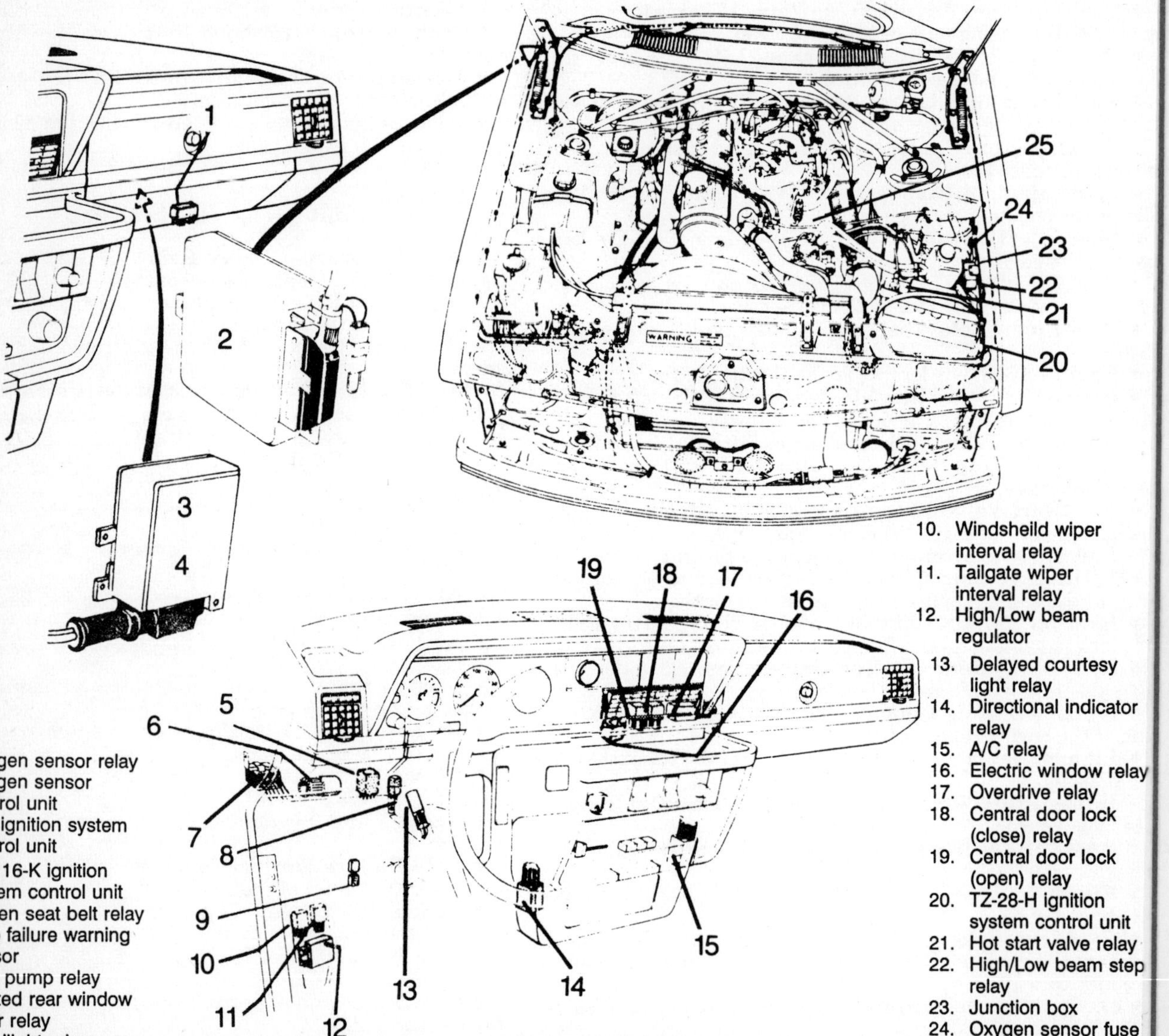

1. Oxygen sensor relay
2. Oxygen sensor control unit
3. Rex ignition system control unit
4. EZ-116-K ignition system control unit
5. Fasten seat belt relay
6. Bulb failure warning sensor
7. Fuel pump relay
8. Heated rear window timer relay
9. Headlight relay
10. Windsheild wiper interval relay
11. Tailgate wiper interval relay
12. High/Low beam regulator
13. Delayed courtesy light relay
14. Directional indicator relay
15. A/C relay
16. Electric window relay
17. Overdrive relay
18. Central door lock (close) relay
19. Central door lock (open) relay
20. TZ-28-H ignition system control unit
21. Hot start valve relay
22. High/Low beam step relay
23. Junction box
24. Oxygen sensor fuse
25. Glow plug relay Volkswagen

Relay locations—700 series and 940

• **Cooling Fan Relay**—is located on the right side of the engine compartment at the shock tower.

• **Cruise Control Unit**—is located at the left side kick panel.

• **Cruise Control Vacuum Pump**—is located at the left side shock tower in the engine compartment.

• **EGR Converter (California)**—is located at the right side of the engine compartment.

• **EGR Relay**—is located at the fuse box under the center of the dash.

• **EGR Temperature Sensor (California)**—is located at the rear of the engine near the firewall.

• **Electric Cooling Fan Pressure Sensor**—is located at the right side of the firewall.

• **Electric Cooling Fan Relay**—is located at the right side shock tower.

• **Electric Cooling Fan Thermal Switch**—is located at the right front of the engine compartment.

• **Engine Temperature Sensor (diesel)**—is located at the rear of the engine near the firewall.

• **Flasher**—is located at the fuse box under the center of the dash.

• **Foglight Relay**—is located at the fuse box under the center of the dash.

• **Fuel Injection Ballast Resistor (LH)**—is located at the left front of the engine compartment.

• **Fuel Injection Control Unit (LH)**—is located under the right side of the dash.

• **Fuel Injection Diagnostic Socket (LH)**—is located at the left side of the engine compartment behind the shock tower.

• **Fuel Injection Relay**—is located at the fuse box under the center of the dash.

• **Fuel Injection Service Socket (CI)**—is located at the left fender in the engine compartment.

• **Fuel Injection Test Socket (LH)**—is located at the left fender in the engine compartment.

• **Fuel Injector Relay**—is located at either the left or right side of the engine compartment on the shock tower.

• **Fuel Valve (diesel)**—is located at the left rear of the engine.

• **Glow Plug Relay (diesel)**—is located at the right side of the engine compartment near the shock tower.

• **Glow Plug Relay (diesel)**—is located on the left side of the engine compartment at the shock tower.

• **Headlight Relay**—is located at the fuse box under the center of the dash.

• **Heater Fan Resistor**—is located under the left side of the dash.

• **ICS Idle Compensation Relay**—is located at the left side shock tower.

• **ICS Idle Compensation Solenoid Valve**—is located on the under side of the intake manifold.

• **ICS Service Socket**—is located at the left side of the engine compartment near the shock tower.

• **Idle Control System (automatic transmission)**—see ICS.

• **Idling Compensation Relay**—is located on the left side of the engine compartment at the shock tower.

• **Ignition System Control Unit**—is located under the left side of the dash near the accelerator pedal.

• **Impulse Sensor**—is located at the transmission bell housing.

• **Inhibitor Switch**—is located at the gear selection lever.

• **Intermittent Wiper Relay (front)**—is located at the fuse box under the center of the dash.

• **Intermittent Wiper Relay (rear)**—is located at the fuse box under the center of the dash.

• **Knock Sensor**—is located at the left front of the engine block near the oil pan rail.

• **Manifold Inlet Pressure Sensor (Regina)**—is located to the left of the master cylinder.

• **Overdrive Contact**—is located at the transmission case.

• **Overdrive Relay**—is located at the fuse box under the center of the dash.

• **Overdrive Solenoid**—is located at the transmission case.

• **Overload Protection Solenoid Valve (turbo)**—is located at the left rear of the engine compartment.

• **Oxygen Sensor (LH)**—is located at the catalytic converter.

• **Power Driver Seat Motors**—are located under the seat.

• **Power Window/Seat Heater Relay**—is located at the fuse box under the center of the dash.

• **Pressure Sensor (turbo)**—is located at the left rear of the engine compartment.

• **PTC Heater (carburetor)**—is located at the base of the carburetor.

• **PTC Heater Relay**—is located on the left side of the engine compartment at the shock tower.

• **PTC Thermostat**—is located in the intake manifold near the PTC heater.

• **Radio Interference Supression Relay**—is located at the right fender in the engine compartment near the shock tower.

• **Rear Defogger Relay**—is located at the fuse box under the center of the dash.

• **Seat Belt Reminder**—is located at the fuse box under the center of the dash.

• **Seat Heater/Power Window Relay**—is located at the fuse box under the center of the dash.

• **Speedometer Relay**—is located at the rear differential.

• **SRS Crash Sensor**—is located under the left front seat.

• **SRS Diagnostic Connector**—is located under the center of the dash at the console.

• **SRS Standby Power Unit**—is located under the left front seat.

• **Supplemental Restraint System**—see SRS.

• **Thermal Time Switch (CI)**—is located at the left rear of the engine block.

• **Thermal Vent Switch**—is located on top of the engine in the intake manifold.

• **Three Port Vacuum Valve**—is located on the carburetor.

• **Throttle Switch (LH)**—is located at the rear of the intake manifold.

• **Throttle Kicker**—is located next to the carburetor.

• **Turn Flasher Relay**—is located on the fuse/relay panel, on the right hand inner fender panel.

• **Water Temperature Sending Unit**—is located on the center of the engine block, below the cylinder head.

• **Windshield Wiper Motor**—is located on the left rear engine compartment, in the engine cowl.

YUGO

Circuit Breaker and Fuses

Some vehicles may be equipped with circuit breakers which are located in the fuse/relay panel.

Fusible Links

No major fusible links are used on these vehicles.

Relay, Sensors And Computer Locations

YUGO

- **Air Temperature Switch**—is located in the air cleaner.
- **Back-Up Light Switch**—is located on the front of the transaxle.
- **Brake Light Switch**—is attached to the brake pedal bracket.
- **Component Relays**—are located in the fuse/relay panel, on the right hand inner fender panel.
- **Coolant Fan 8 Amp Fuse**—is located on the coolant fan motor.
- **Coolant Fan Thermal Switch**—is located on the bottom of the radiator.
- **Engine Cooling Fan Motor**—is located in the front of the engine compartment, next to the radiator.
- **Float Bowl Solenoid**—is located on the carburetor.
- **Four Port Vacuum Valve**—is located on the carburetor.
- **Fuel Tank Sending Unit**—is attached to the fuel tank.
- **Hazard Flasher Relay**—is located on the fuse/relay panel, on the right hand inner fender panel.
- **Heater Blower Motor**—is located on the right rear engine compartment, near the firewall.
- **High Altitude Compensator**—is located on the carburetor.
- **Oil Pressure Sending Unit**—is located on the center of the engine block, below the cylinder head.
- **Parking Brake Switch**—is attached to the parking brake lever bracket.
- **Rear Wiper Motor**—is located on the left side, of the hatch back.
- **Starter Motor Solenoid**—is located on the starter motor.